Life

The Essentials of Human Development

Gabriela **Martorell**

Mc Graw Hill Education

LIFE

Published by McGraw-Hill Education, 2 Penn Plaza, New York, NY 10121. Copyright © 2019 by McGraw-Hill Education. All rights reserved. Printed in the United States of America. No part of this publication may be reproduced or distributed in any form or by any means, or stored in a database or retrieval system, without the prior written consent of McGraw-Hill Education, including, but not limited to, in any network or other electronic storage or transmission, or broadcast for distance learning.

Some ancillaries, including electronic and print components, may not be available to customers outside the United States.

This book is printed on acid-free paper.

1 2 3 4 5 6 7 8 9 LWI 21 20 19 18

ISBN 978-1-260-09225-7
MHID 1-260-09225-9

Cover Credit: ©pinstock/E+/Getty Images, ©elenaleonova/iStock/Getty Images Plus

connect McGraw-Hill Education Psychology APA Documentation Style Guide

contents

③ part Early Childhood

Middle Childhood

part

chapter 9

Physical and Cognitive Development in Middle Childhood *210*

chapter 10

Psychosocial Development in Middle Childhood *239*

⑨ The End of Life

connect McGraw-Hill Education
Psychology APA
Documentation Style Guide

Life: The Essentials of Human Development is designed to be a brief but thorough account of human development from conception to death, exposing students to culture and diversity, and immersing them in practical application. Written from a developmental framework and borrowing from multiple traditions and theoretical perspectives, *Life: The Essentials of Human Development* also addresses the major periods of development and focuses on the important biological, psychological, and social forces driving change, highlighting theoretical distinctions, research findings, and new directions in the field. *Life: The Essentials of Human Development* will engage your students intellectually and encourage the application of psychological concepts to everyday life.

Paired with McGraw-Hill Education Connect, a digital assignment and assessment platform that strengthens the link between faculty, students, and course work, instructors and students accomplish more in less time. Connect for Lifespan Development includes assignable and assessable videos, quizzes, exercises, and interactivities, all associated with learning objectives. Interactive assignments and videos allow students to experience and apply their understanding of psychology to the world with fun and stimulating activities.

Diversity

In response to requests from faculty, substantial space has been devoted to addressing issues of diversity. When relevant, each chapter includes current U.S. statistics drawn from census data and national governmental databases, including not just major population trends but also demographic and statistical information on ethnic and racial minorities. Moreover, in many cases, information on global statistics, trends, and cultural differences has been included as well.

Additionally, each chapter includes a **Window on the World** feature. In this feature, a cross-cultural issue of interest is addressed from a global perspective. These features address a wide variety of topics, including, for example, cultural differences in children's books, wedding traditions, or funeral ceremonies along with research-based features on topics such as malnutrition, prenatal care, or autism. Each feature ends with What's Your View—a series of questions that can be used as springboards for class discussion or writing prompts. A complete listing of Window on the World can be found on pages xviii.

Other forms of diversity have also been included. For example, information is included on different family systems, including gay and lesbian parents, stepparents, divorced parents, and those families in which adults remain single by choice.

Current Research

Life: The Essentials of Human Development draws a current picture of the state of the field. In well-established areas of psychology, there is an emphasis on the inclusion of review articles and meta-analyses in order to capture the major trends found through decades of psychological research. In research areas with less information available, the emphasis is on the inclusion of the newest research available in that area. Additionally, topical areas that have arisen in the public consciousness in recent years have been included. For example, new information has been included on, among other areas, the influence of technology on young children, the opioid epidemic, and the development of transgender children.

Each chapter in *Life: The Essentials of Human Development* includes a **Research in Action** feature, in which a closer look is taken at an issue or area relevant to the chapter. The Research in Action features are designed to stimulate critical thinking about a wide variety of engaging topics, and they include such topics as Barbie dolls, terrorism, the impact of technology on development, and intimate partner violence. As with Window on the World features, each Research in Action feature ends with What's Your View question prompts. A complete listing of Research in Action can be found on page xviii.

Real People, Real World, Real Life

At the higher end of Bloom's taxonomy, the **McGraw-Hill Education Milestones video series** offers an observational tool that allows students to experience life as it unfolds, from infancy to late adulthood. This ground-breaking, longitudinal video series tracks the development of real children as they progress through the early stages of physical, social, and emotional development in their first few weeks, months, and years of life. Assignable and assessable within Connect for Lifespan Development, Milestones also includes interviews with adolescents and adults to reflect development throughout the entire life span.

Power of Process for

PSYCHOLOGY

Mc Graw Hill Education **connect**®

Preparing Students for Higher-Level Thinking

Also at the higher end of Bloom's, **Power of Process** for Lifespan Development helps students improve critical-thinking skills and allows instructors to assess these skills efficiently and effectively in an online environment. Available through Connect, pre-loaded journal articles are available for instructors to assign. Using a scaffolded framework such as understanding, synthesizing, and analyzing, Power of Process moves students toward higher-level thinking and analysis.

Inform and Engage on Psychological Concepts

At the lower end of Bloom's taxonomy, students are introduced to **Concept Clips**—the dynamic, colorful graphics and stimulating animations that break down some of psychology's most difficult concepts in a step-by-step manner, engaging students and aiding in retention. They are assignable and assessable in Connect or can be used as a jumping-off point in class. Complete with audio narration, Concept Clips focus on topics such as object permanence and conservation, as well as theories and theorists such as Bandura's social cognitive theory, Vygotsky's sociocultural theory, Buss's evolutionary theory, and Kuhl's language development theory.

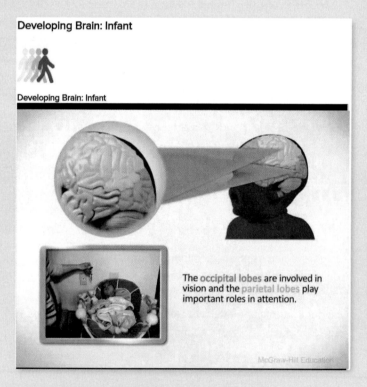

Developing Brain: Infant

Developing Brain: Infant

The occipital lobes are involved in vision and the parietal lobes play important roles in attention.

McGraw-Hill Education

Provide a Smarter Text and Better Value

Available within Connect, **SmartBook**® makes study time as productive and efficient as possible by identifying and closing knowledge gaps. SmartBook is powered by the proven **LearnSmart**® engine, which identifies what an individual student knows and doesn't know based on the student's confidence level, responses to questions, and other factors.

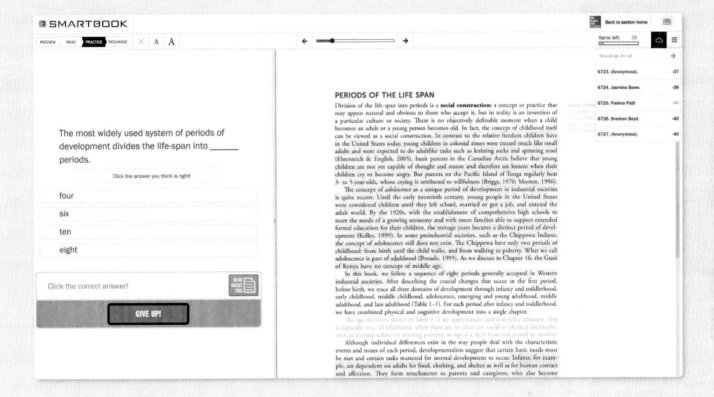

SmartBook builds an optimal, personalized learning path for each student, so students spend less time on concepts they already understand and more time on those they don't. As a student engages with SmartBook, the reading experience continuously adapts by highlighting the most impactful content a student needs to learn at that moment in time. This ensures that every minute spent with SmartBook is returned to the student as the most value-added minute possible. The result? More confidence, better grades, and greater success.

Powerful Reporting

Whether a class is face-to-face, hybrid, or entirely online, Connect for Lifespan Development provides tools and analytics to reduce the amount of time instructors need to administer their courses. Easy-to-use course management tools allow instructors to spend less time administering and more time teaching, while easy-to-use reporting features allow students to monitor their progress and optimize their study time.

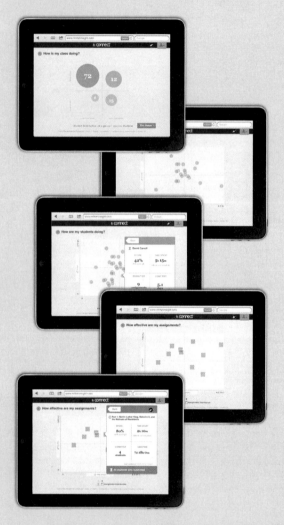

The **At-Risk Student Report** provides instructors with one-click access to a dashboard that identifies students who are at risk of dropping out of the course due to low engagement levels.

The **Category Analysis Report** details student performance relative to specific learning objectives and goals, including APA outcomes and levels of Bloom's taxonomy.

Connect Insight is a one-of-a-kind visual analytics dashboard—now available for both instructors and students—that provides at-a-glance information regarding student performance.

The **LearnSmart Reports** allow instructors and students to easily monitor progress and pinpoint areas of weakness, giving each student a personalized study plan to achieve success.

Online Instructor Resources

The resources listed here accompany *Life: The Essentials of Human Development*. Please contact your McGraw-Hill representative for details concerning the availability of these and other valuable materials that can help you design and enhance your course.

Instructor's Manual Broken down by chapter, this resource provides chapter outlines, suggested lecture topics, classroom activities and demonstrations, suggested student research projects, essay questions, and critical-thinking questions.

Test Bank and Computerized Test Bank This comprehensive Test Bank includes more than 1,500 multiple-choice and approximately 75 essay questions. Organized by chapter, the questions are designed to test factual, applied, and conceptual understanding. All test questions are available within TestGen™ software.

PowerPoint Slides The PowerPoint presentations, now WCAG compliant, highlight the key points of the chapter and include supporting visuals. All of the slides can be modified to meet individual needs.

Acknowledgments

A special thank you to Rebecca Howell, Forsyth Technical Community College, and Dr. Khia Thomas, Broward College, for their important cultural and research contributions to Window on the World and Research in Action.

Many thanks to those faculty instructors whose insight and feedback contributed to the development of
Life: The Essentials of Human Development:

Phaer Bonner, Jefferson State Community College

Virginia Cashion, Liberty University

Kimberly DuVall, James Madison University

Lisa Fozio-Thielk, Waubonsee Community College

Erin Holloway, University of Alabama

Samuel Jones, Jefferson State Community College, Birmingham

James Jordan, Lorain County Community College

Susan LaCascio, Calhoun Community College

Tammie Lukefahr, Mineral Area College

Claire Lyons, James Madison University

Yvonne Malone, Tennessee Tech University

Tesia Marshik, University of Wisconsin, La Crosse

Robert Martinez, University of the Incarnate Word

Daniel McConnell, University of Central Florida

Valerie McCoy, Mineral Area College

Joe Moon, Houston Community College

Jill Ramet, Metropolitan Community College

Patricia Riely, Moberly Area Community College

Ronald Sabatelli, University of Connecticut

Edie Sample, Metropolitan Community College, South Omaha Campus

Jason Scofield, University of Alabama

Melissa Sudduth, University of Alabama, Tuscaloosa

Rachelle Tannenbaum, Anne Arundel Community College

Kay Walsh, James Madison University

Kelly Welch, Kansas State University

From Gabi Martorell: To Daphne Bugental, my graduate advisor. Thanks for all the things I realized you were teaching me at the time you taught them to me, and for all the things I didn't realize you were teaching me until years later.

Gabriela Martorell

Research in Action

Window on the World

The Study of Human Development

©Rachel Weill 2006/UpperCut Images/age fotostock

learning objectives

Describe human development and how its study has evolved.

Describe the domains and periods of human development.

Give examples of the influences that make one person different from another.

Discuss the principles of the life-span perspective.

In this chapter we describe how the field of human development evolved. We identify aspects of development and show how they interrelate. We summarize major developments during each period of life. We look at influences on development and the contexts in which each occurs.

Human Development:
An Ever-Evolving Field

From the moment of conception, human beings begin a lifelong process of change. A single cell develops into a living, breathing, walking, talking person who moves through an ever-changing world, both being influenced by and influencing it. Although we all follow our own unique trajectory, we also share a species heritage, many common experiences, and broad patterns of development. These patterns of development are explored throughout this book.

The field of **human development** focuses on the scientific study of the systematic processes of change and stability in people. Developmental scientists investigate the ways in which people change or stay the same from conception to death. The work of developmentalists can have a dramatic impact on people's lives. Research findings often have applications to child rearing, education, health, and social policy.

human development
Scientific study of processes of change and stability throughout the human life span.

STUDYING THE LIFE SPAN

When the field of developmental psychology emerged as a scientific discipline, most researchers focused their energies on infant and child development. Growth and development are more obvious during these times given the rapid pace of change. As the field matured, however, it became clear that developmental science should include more than infancy and childhood. Now researchers consider **life-span development** to be from "womb to tomb," comprising the entire human life span from conception to death. Moreover, they acknowledge that development can be either positive (e.g., becoming toilet trained or enrolling in a college course after retirement) or negative (e.g., once again wetting the bed after a traumatic event or isolating yourself after retirement).

life-span development
Concept of human development as a lifelong process which can be studied scientifically.

HUMAN DEVELOPMENT TODAY

As the field of human development itself developed, its goals came to include description, explanation, prediction, and intervention. For example, to *describe* when most children say their first word or how large their vocabulary is at a certain age, developmental scientists observe large groups of children and establish norms, or averages, for behavior at various ages. They then attempt to *explain* how children acquire language and why some children learn to speak later than usual. This knowledge may make it possible to *predict* future behavior, such as the likelihood that a child will have serious speech problems. Finally, an understanding of how language develops may be used to *intervene* in development, for example, by giving a child speech therapy.

The scientific study of human development is ever evolving. The questions that developmental scientists try to answer, the methods they use, and the explanations they propose reflect progress in understanding as new investigations build on or challenge those that went before. They also reflect advances in technology. Scientists now have access to instruments that measure eye movement, heart rate, and muscle tension. They are able to use digital technology that allows them to analyze how mothers and babies communicate. Advances in brain imaging make it possible to probe the mysteries of temperament or to compare a normally aging brain with the brain of a person with dementia.

Development is messy. It's complex and multifaceted and shaped by interacting arcs of influence. Thus development is best understood with input from a variety of theoretical and research orientations. Students of human development draw from a wide range of disciplines, including psychology, psychiatry, sociology, anthropology, biology, genetics, family science, education, history, and medicine. This book includes findings from research in all these fields.

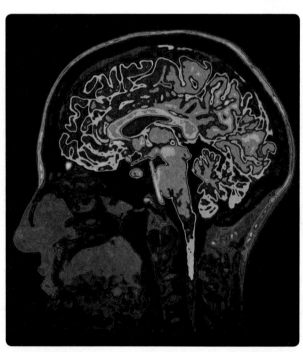

Brain imaging techniques are used to map out where certain thought processes take place within the structure of the brain. ©SpeedKingz/Shutterstock

The Study of Human Development: Basic Concepts

Developmentalists study processes of change and stability in all domains, or aspects, of development throughout all periods of the life span.

DOMAINS OF DEVELOPMENT

Developmental scientists study three major *domains,* or aspects, of development: physical, cognitive, and psychosocial. Growth of the body and brain, sensory capacities, motor skills, and health are parts of **physical development.** Learning, attention, memory, language, thinking, reasoning, and creativity make up **cognitive development.** Emotions, personality, and social relationships are aspects of **psychosocial development.**

Although in this book we talk separately about physical, cognitive, and psychosocial development, these domains are interrelated: Each aspect of development affects the others. For example, physical development affects cognitive and psychosocial development. A child with frequent ear infections may develop language more slowly than a child without this physical problem. In late adulthood, physical changes in the brains of some adults may lead to intellectual and personality deterioration.

Similarly, cognitive advances and declines are related to physical and psychosocial development. A child who is precocious in language development may bring about positive reactions in others and thus gain in self-worth. Memory development reflects gains or losses in physical connections in the brain. An adult who has trouble remembering people's names may feel shy in social situations.

And finally, psychosocial development can affect cognitive and physical functioning. Without meaningful social connections, physical and mental health suffers. Motivation and self-confidence are important contributors to school success, whereas negative emotions such as anxiety can impair performance. Researchers have even identified links between a conscientious personality and length of life.

PERIODS OF THE LIFE SPAN

Division of the life span into periods is a **social construction:** a concept or practice that is an invention of a particular culture or society. There is no objectively definable moment when a child becomes an adult or a young person becomes old. Because the concept of childhood is a social construction, the form it takes varies across cultures. In contrast to the relative freedom children have in the United States today, young children in colonial times were expected to do adultlike tasks such as knitting socks and spinning wool (Ehrenreich & English, 2005). Inuit parents in the Canadian Arctic believe that young children are not yet capable of thought and reason and therefore are lenient when their children cry or become angry (Briggs, 1970). And Maniq parents in Southern Thailand regularly allow their toddlers to play with knives, and by 4 years of age most children can easily gut small animals (Lancy, 2016).

A similar construction involves *adolescence,* which is a recent concept that emerged as society became more industrialized. Until the early twentieth century, young people in the United States were considered adults once they left school, married, or got a job. By the 1920s, with the establishment of comprehensive high schools to meet the needs of a growing economy and with more families able to support extended formal education for their children, the teenage years became a distinct period of development (Keller, 1999). In some preindustrial societies, such as the Chippewa Indians, the concept of adolescence still does not exist. The Chippewa have only two periods of childhood: from birth

physical development
Development of the body and brain, including patterns of change in sensory capacities, motor skills, and health.

cognitive development
Pattern of change in mental abilities, such as learning, attention, memory, language, thinking, reasoning, and creativity.

psychosocial development
(1) Pattern of change in emotions, personality, and social relationships.

social construction
A concept or practice that may appear natural and obvious to those who accept it, but that in reality is an invention of a particular culture or society.

These children are engaging in all three domains of development: sensory perception (physical development), learning (cognitive development), and social relationships building (psychosocial development). ©Ariel Skelley/Blend Images

until the child walks, and from walking to puberty. What we call adolescence is part of adulthood (Broude, 1995).

In this book, we follow a sequence of eight periods generally accepted in Western industrial societies. After describing the crucial changes that occur in the first period, before birth, we trace all three domains of development through infancy and toddlerhood, early childhood, middle childhood, adolescence, emerging and young adulthood, middle adulthood, and late adulthood (Table 1.1). For each period after infancy and toddlerhood, we have combined physical and cognitive development into a single chapter.

TABLE 1.1 Typical Major Developments in Eight Periods of Human Development

Age Period	Physical Developments	Cognitive Developments	Psychosocial Developments
Prenatal Period (conception to birth)	Conception occurs. Genes interact with environmental influences. Basic body structures and organs form; brain growth spurt begins. Physical growth is the most rapid in the life span. Vulnerability to environmental influences is great.	Abilities to learn and remember and to respond to sensory stimuli are developing.	Fetus responds to mother's voice and develops a preference for it.
Infancy and Toddlerhood (birth to age 3)	All senses and body systems operate at birth to varying degrees. The brain grows in complexity and is highly sensitive to environmental influence. Physical growth and development of motor skills are rapid.	Abilities to learn and remember are present, even in early weeks. Use of symbols and ability to solve problems develop by end of second year. Comprehension and use of language develop rapidly.	Attachments to parents and others form. Self-awareness develops. Shift from dependence toward autonomy occurs. Interest in other children increases.
Early Childhood (ages 3 to 6)	Growth is steady; appearance becomes more slender and proportions more adultlike. Appetite diminishes, and sleep problems are common. Handedness appears; fine and gross motor skills and strength improve.	Understanding of other people's perspectives grows. Cognitive immaturity results in some illogical ideas about the world. Memory and language improve. Intelligence becomes more predictable. Preschool experience is common, and kindergarten experience is more so.	Self-concept and understanding of emotions become more complex; self-esteem is global. Independence, initiative, and self-control increase. Gender identity develops. Play becomes more imaginative, elaborate, and social. Altruism, aggression, and fearfulness are common. Family is still the focus of social life, but other children become more important.
Middle Childhood (ages 6 to 11)	Growth slows. Strength and athletic skills improve. Respiratory illnesses are common, but health is generally better than at any other time in the life span.	Egocentrism diminishes. Children begin to think logically but concretely. Memory and language skills increase. Some children show special educational needs and strengths.	Self-concept becomes more complex, affecting self-esteem. Coregulation reflects gradual shift in control from parents to child. Peers assume central importance.

The age divisions shown in Table 1.1 are approximate and arbitrary. This is especially true of adulthood, when there are no clear-cut social or physical landmarks, such as starting school or entering puberty, to signal a shift from one period to another. Although individual differences exist in the way people deal with the characteristic events and issues of each period, developmentalists suggest that certain basic needs must be met and certain tasks mastered for normal development to occur.

TABLE 1.1 Typical Major Developments in Eight Periods of Human Development

Age Period	Physical Developments	Cognitive Developments	Psychosocial Developments
Adolescence (ages 11 to about 20)	Physical growth and other changes are rapid and profound. Reproductive maturity occurs. Major health risks arise from behavioral issues, such as eating disorders and drug abuse.	Ability to think abstractly and use scientific reasoning develops. Immature thinking persists in some attitudes and behaviors. Education focuses on preparation for college or vocation.	Search for identity, including sexual identity, becomes central. Relationships with parents are generally good. Peer group may exert a positive or negative influence.
Emerging and Young Adulthood (ages 20 to 40)	Physical condition peaks, then declines slightly. Lifestyle choices influence health.	Thought and moral judgments become more complex. Educational and occupational choices are made, sometimes after period of exploration.	Personality traits and styles become relatively stable. Intimate relationships and personal lifestyles are established but may not be lasting. Most people marry, and most become parents.
Middle Adulthood (ages 40 to 65)	Slow deterioration of sensory abilities, health, stamina, and strength may begin, but individual differences are wide. Women experience menopause.	Mental abilities peak; expertise and practical problem-solving skills are high. Creative output may decline but improve in quality. Career success and earning powers may peak; or burnout or career change may occur.	Sense of identity continues to develop; midlife transition may occur. Dual responsibilities of caring for children and parents may cause stress. Launching of children leaves empty nest.
Late Adulthood (age 65 and over)	Most people are healthy and active, although health and physical abilities generally decline. Slowing of reaction time affects some aspects of functioning.	Most people are mentally alert. Although intelligence and memory may deteriorate in some areas, most people find ways to compensate.	Retirement from workforce may occur. People develop more flexible strategies to cope with personal losses and impending death. Relationships with family and close friends can provide important support. Search for meaning in life assumes central importance.

Influences on Development

individual differences
Differences in characteristics, influences, or developmental outcomes.

Although students of development are interested in the universal processes of development experienced by all typical human beings, they also study **individual differences** in characteristics, influences, and developmental outcomes. People differ in gender, height, weight, and body build; in health and energy level; in intelligence; and in temperament, personality, and emotional reactions. The contexts of their lives differ too: the homes, communities, and societies they live in; the relationships they have; the schools they attend (or whether they go to school at all); and how they spend their free time. Every person has a unique developmental trajectory. Developmental psychology aims to identify the universal influences on development, and then apply those to understanding individual differences in developmental trajectories.

HEREDITY, ENVIRONMENT, AND MATURATION

heredity
Inborn traits or characteristics inherited from the biological parents.

environment
Totality of nonhereditary, or experiential, influences on development.

Some influences on development originate primarily with **heredity:** inborn traits or characteristics inherited from the biological parents. Other influences come largely from the **environment:** the world outside the self, beginning in the womb, and the learning that comes from experience. Which of these two factors has more impact on development? The issue of the relative importance of *nature* (heredity) and *nurture* (environmental influences both before and after birth) historically generated intense debate.

Today scientists have found ways to more precisely measure the roles of heredity and environment in the development of specific traits within a population. Research with regard to almost all characteristics points to a blend of inheritance and experience. For example, even though intelligence is strongly influenced by heredity, parental stimulation, education, peer influence, and other variables also affect it. Contemporary theorists and researchers are more interested in finding ways to explain how nature and nurture work together than in arguing about which factor is more important.

maturation
Unfolding of a natural sequence of physical and behavioral changes.

Many typical changes of infancy and early childhood, such as the abilities to walk and talk, are tied to **maturation** of the body and brain—the unfolding of a natural sequence of physical changes and behavior patterns. As children grow into adolescents and then into adults, individual differences in innate characteristics and life experience play a greater role. Throughout life, however, maturation continues to influence certain biological processes, such as brain development.

Even in processes that all people undergo, rates and timing of development vary. Throughout this book, we talk about average ages for the occurrence of certain events: the first word, the first menstruation or nocturnal emission, the development of logical thought, and menopause. But there is wide variation among people with respect to these norms. Only when deviation from the average is extreme should we consider development exceptionally advanced or delayed.

To understand development, then, we need to look at the *inherited* characteristics that give each person a start in life. We also need to consider the many *environmental* factors that affect development, especially such major contexts as family, neighborhood, socioeconomic status, race/ethnicity, and culture. We need to consider how heredity and environment interact. We need to understand which aspects of development are primarily maturational and which are not. We need to look at influences that affect many or most people at a certain age or a certain time in history and also at those that affect only certain individuals. Finally, we need to look at how timing can accentuate the impact of certain influences.

CONTEXTS OF DEVELOPMENT

Human beings are social beings. From the beginning they develop within a social and historical context. For an infant, the immediate context normally is the family, but the family in turn is subject to the wider and ever-changing influences of neighborhood, community, and society.

Family The **nuclear family** is a household unit consisting of one or two parents and their children, whether biological, adopted, or stepchildren. Historically, the two-parent nuclear family has been the normative family unit in the United States and other Western societies. However, instead of the large, rural family in which parents and children worked side by side on the family farm, we now see smaller, urban families in which both parents work outside the home and children spend much of their time in school or child care. The increased incidence of divorce also has affected the nuclear family. Children of divorced parents may live with one or the other parent or may move back and forth between them. The household may include a stepparent and stepsiblings or a parent's live-in partner. There are increasing numbers of single and childless adults, unmarried parents, and gay and lesbian households (Dye, 2010; Brown, Manning & Stykes, 2015; Umberson, Thomeer, Kroeger, Lodge & Xu, 2015).

In many societies in Asia, Africa, and Latin America and among some U.S. families that trace their lineage to those countries, the **extended family**—a multigenerational network of grandparents, aunts, uncles, cousins, and more distant relatives—is the traditional family form. Many people live in *extended-family households*, where they have daily contact with kin. Adults often share breadwinning and child-raising responsibilities, and older children are responsible for younger brothers and sisters.

Today the extended-family household is becoming slightly less typical in many developing countries (Bradbury, Peterson & Liu, 2014) in part due to industrialization and migration to urban centers (Kinsella & Phillips, 2005). Meanwhile, in the United States, economic pressures, housing shortages, immigration patterns, out-of-wedlock childbearing and an increase in life expectancy have helped to fuel a trend toward three- and even four-generational family households. In 2014, about 19 percent of households could be characterized as multigenerational (Cohn & Passel, 2016).

Socioeconomic Status and Neighborhood A family's **socioeconomic status (SES)** is based on family income and the educational and occupational levels of the adults in the household. SES is related to developmental processes (such as mothers' verbal interactions with their children) and to developmental outcomes (such as health and cognitive performance). SES affects these processes and outcomes indirectly, through such related factors as the kinds of homes and neighborhoods people live in and the quality of nutrition, medical care, and schooling available to them.

nuclear family
Two-generational kinship, economic, and household unit consisting of one or two parents and their biological children, adopted children, or stepchildren.

extended family
Multigenerational kinship network of parents, children, and other relatives, sometimes living together in an extended-family household.

socioeconomic status (SES)
Combination of economic and social factors describing an individual or family, including income, education, and occupation.

An extended-family household might include grandparents, aunts, and cousins. ©Blend Images/Alamy Stock Photo

FIGURE 1.1

Number of Extreme Poor, 1990–2013

Source: World Bank. *Poverty and Shared Prosperity 2016: Taking on Inequality.* Washington, DC: World Bank, 2016.

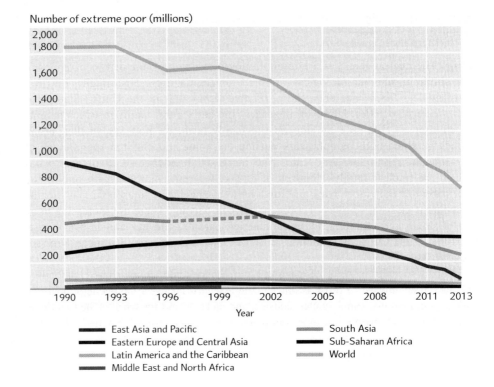

Number of extreme poor (millions)

Year

East Asia and Pacific
Eastern Europe and Central Asia
Latin America and the Caribbean
Middle East and North Africa
South Asia
Sub-Saharan Africa
World

More than 767 million people lived on less than $1.90 a day in 2013. Although this represents a large number of people, it has fallen by almost 1.1. billion people since 1990. (Figure 1.1; World Bank, 2016). The expanding global economy is one of the major factors contributing to the overall decrease in poverty (United Nations, 2009). While China, Indonesia, and India have made significant gains, sub-Saharan Africa still struggles greatly with poverty (World Bank, 2016).

In the United States, 15 million children—approximately 20 percent of all children under age 18—live in poverty, and over 40 percent of those children are in extreme poverty (Children's Defense Fund, 2017). Children from middle- and lower-income families, even if above the poverty line, also suffer the negative effects of employment insecurity and income inequality (Foundation for Child Development, 2015). The number of children living in poor or low income families has been on the rise since the recession of 2008 (Jiang, Ekono & Skinner, 2015).

Poverty, especially if it is long-lasting, can be harmful to the physical, cognitive, and psychosocial well-being of children and families. Poor children are more likely than other children to have emotional or behavioral problems (Yoshikawa, Aber & Beardsley, 2012), and their cognitive potential and school performance suffer more (Luby, 2015). The harm done by poverty may be indirect, through its impact on parents' emotional state and parenting practices and on the home environment they create. Threats to well-being multiply if, as often happens, several **risk factors**—conditions that increase the likelihood of a negative outcome—are present. However, a number of strengths can still be found within the family context. Parents in poor families report being just as close to their children, they attend church with their families just as often, and they eat meals together as a family more often than wealthier families. It may be that the scientific community has not paid enough attention to the strengths and resilience found in lower SES homes (Valladares & Moore, 2009).

Affluence doesn't necessarily protect children from risk. Some children in affluent families face pressure to achieve and are often left on their own by busy parents. Such children may be at increased risk for substance abuse, anxiety, and depression (Luthar & Latendresse, 2005).

Culture and Race/Ethnicity Culture refers to a society's or group's total way of life, including its customs, traditions, laws, knowledge, beliefs, values, language, and physical

risk factors

Conditions that increase the likelihood of a negative developmental outcome.

culture

A society's or group's total way of life, including customs, traditions, beliefs, values, language, and physical products— all learned behavior, passed on from parents to children.

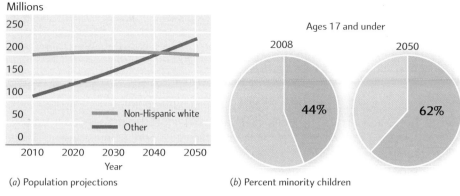

Millions

(a) Population projections — Non-Hispanic white / Other — 2010 2020 2030 2040 2050 Year

Ages 17 and under

2008 — 44%

2050 — 62%

(b) Percent minority children

(a and b): Source: U.S. Census Bureau. Population profile of the United States. 2008. Retrieved from www.census.gov/population/www/pop-profile/profiledynamic.html

FIGURE 1.2

Population Projections for Non-Hispanic White and Minority Groups, 2010–2050

(a) According to Census Bureau projections, racial/ethnic minorities will reach 54 percent of the U.S. population, exceeding the proportion of non-Hispanic white people by 2050. (b) Also by 2050, "minority" children under age 18 are expected to make up 62 percent of the child population.

products, from tools to artworks—all of the behavior and attitudes that are learned, shared, and transmitted among members of a social group. Culture is constantly changing, often through contact with other cultures. Today cultural contact has been enhanced by computers and telecommunications.

An **ethnic group** consists of people united by a distinctive culture, ancestry, religion, language, or national origin, all of which contribute to a sense of shared identity and shared attitudes, beliefs, and values. By 2044 ethnic minorities in the United States are expected to become the majority. This benchmark has already been reached by minority children, who comprised some 56 percent of all children in the United States in 2014 (Colby & Ortman, 2014). It is predicted that by 2050, 62 percent of the nation's children will be members of what are now minority groups, and the proportion of Hispanic or Latino/a children—39 percent—will surpass the 38 percent who will be non-Hispanic white (U.S. Census Bureau, 2008a; Figure 1.2). Already, nearly one-fourth of U.S. kindergarteners and one-fifth of all kindergarten through 12th grade students are Hispanic (U.S. Census Bureau, 2009a, 2009b).

The United States has always been a nation of immigrants and ethnic groups, but the primary ethnic origins of the immigrant population have shifted from Europe and Canada to Asia and Latin America (Hernandez, 2004). In 2007, more than 20 percent of the population were immigrants or children of immigrants (see Window on the World). More immigrants came from Mexico, 40 percent, than from any other country, and the remaining 60 percent came from nations in the Caribbean, East and West Asia, Australia, Central and South America, Indochina, the former Soviet Union, and Africa. It is important to remember that wide diversity exists within broad ethnic groups. Given this diversity within groups, a term such as *black* or *Hispanic* can be an ethnic gloss—an overgeneralization that obscures or blurs such variations.

The term *race,* historically and popularly viewed as an identifiable biological category, is best defined as a social construct. There is no clear scientific consensus on its definition, and it is impossible to measure reliably (Helms, Jernigan & Mascher, 2005). Human genetic variation occurs along a broad continuum, and 90 percent of such variation occurs *within* rather than among socially defined races (Bonham, Warshauer-Baker & Collins, 2005; Ossorio & Duster, 2005). Nevertheless, race as a social category remains a factor in

ethnic group
A group united by ancestry, race, religion, language, or national origins, which contribute to a sense of shared identity.

The existence of Marcia and Millie Biggs, who as fraternal twins share approximately 50 percent of their genes, calls into question the concept of race as a biological construct. ©SWNS.com

window on the world

IMMIGRANT FAMILIES

The United States is a nation of immigrants, known for its cultural diversity and appeals to those seeking refuge, freedom, financial security, or a second chance. As of October 2016, the Census Bureau estimates that 42.4 million immigrants—13 percent of the population—now live in the United States (Children in U.S. Immigrant Families, 2015).

The ethnic origins of the immigrant population have shifted significantly over the past 100 years. In 1910, most U.S. immigrants came from Europe and Canada. By 2010, the largest numbers of immigrants were from Mexico, Asia, and the Caribbean. Since that time, the largest percentage increases have occurred in immigration from Southern Asia, the Middle East, and Northern Africa. However, more immigrants come from Mexico (25 percent) than from any other country (Camarota & Zeigler, 2016).

One-fourth (25.5 percent) of U.S. children lived in immigrant families in 2015, and 88 percent of these children were born in the United States, making them U.S. citizens (Children in U.S. Immigrant Families, 2015). Immigrant children are the fastest growing group of children in the United States. While earlier waves of immigrants were predominately Caucasian with Christian beliefs, this new wave of immigrants is far more diverse.

Immigrant families must navigate a different culture, religion, and language, and often different ethics and values. Immigrants may arrive with little education and are often undocumented. Thus, although there are few differences in rates of work between immigrants and U.S. natives, immigrants are more likely to work at low-paying jobs requiring manual labor. Not surprisingly, 21 percent of immigrant families live in poverty. In 2014, it was reported that 42 percent of immigrant families used at least one welfare program compared to 27 percent of U.S. natives, a number driven largely by the presence of U.S.-born children (Camarota & Zeigler, 2016). Though most of these families qualify legally for services and pay taxes into the system, 18 percent of immigrant families lack health insurance and access to proper health care.

Many immigrants live in fear of interrogation or deportation and face bigotry and discrimination. In 2012 the deferred action for childhood arrivals (DACA) program was started. It can gain children of immigrants, often brought to the United States as babies or young children, more time to work out documentation, but qualifying can be tricky and its future is uncertain (Consideration of Deferred Action for Childhood Arrivals (DACA), 2016). Though immigration can be difficult, the longer immigrants are in the United States, the more progress they make. The same struggles are not as pronounced in second- and third-generation immigrant families as they become acculturated to the nation.

Immigrants bring racial, cultural, and ethnic diversity to the country. This allows Americans to experience different ways of life, languages, religions, and foods. Immigrants also bring innovative ideas and economic benefits. One-fourth of all U.S. engineering and technology companies founded between 1995 and 2005 had at least one immigrant founder (The Effects of Immigration on the United States' Economy, 2016). More than half of all patent grants in 2014 were to foreign-born individuals (Grenier, 2014). Immigrants often work in farming, food service, maintenance, construction, and manufacturing industries. Many of these industries would collapse without immigrant labor (Jacobi, 2012). It is sometimes easy to forget the United States was founded by immigrants and what role our ancestors played in that process. Immigration will continue to bring a depth and richness to the nation and its culture.

what's your view

How do you see immigration influencing the United States? How do you imagine life may be different for immigrants 40 years from now?

---

research because it makes a difference in "how individuals are treated, where they live, their employment opportunities, the quality of their health care, and whether [they] can fully participate" in their society (Smedley & Smedley, 2005, p. 23).

The Historical Context At one time developmentalists paid little attention to the historical context—the time in which people live. Then, as early longitudinal studies of childhood extended into the adult years, investigators began to focus on how certain experiences, tied to time and place, affect the course of people's lives. Today, the historical context is an important part of the study of development.

NORMATIVE AND NONNORMATIVE INFLUENCES

To understand similarities and differences in development, we need to look at two types of **normative** influences: biological or environmental events that affect many or most people in a society in similar ways and events that touch only certain individuals (Baltes & Smith, 2004).

Normative age-graded influences are highly similar for people in a particular age group. The timing of biological events is fairly predictable within a normal range. For example, people don't experience puberty at age 35 or menopause at 12.

Normative history-graded influences are significant events (such as the Great Depression or World War II) that shape the behavior and attitudes of a **historical generation:** a group of people who experience the event at a formative time in their lives. For example, the generations that came of age during the Depression and World War II tend to show a strong sense of social interdependence and trust that has declined among more recent generations (Rogler, 2002). Depending on when and where they live, entire generations may feel the impact of famines, nuclear explosions, or terrorist attacks.

A historical generation is not the same as an age **cohort:** a group of people born at about the same time. A historical generation may contain more than one cohort, but cohorts are part of a historical generation only if they experience major, shaping historical events at a formative point in their lives (Rogler, 2002).

Nonnormative influences are unusual events that have a major impact on *individual* lives because they disturb the expected sequence of the life cycle. They are either typical events that happen at an atypical time of life (such as the death of a parent when a child is young) or atypical events (such as surviving a plane crash). Some of these influences are largely beyond a person's control and may present rare opportunities or severe challenges that the person perceives as turning points. On the other hand, people sometimes help create their own nonnormative life events—say, by deciding to have a baby in their midfifties or taking up a risky hobby such as skydiving—and thus participate actively in their own development. Taken together, the three types of influences—normative age-graded, normative history-graded, and nonnormative—contribute to the complexity of human development.

TIMING OF INFLUENCES: CRITICAL OR SENSITIVE PERIODS

In a well-known study, Konrad Lorenz (1957), an Austrian ethologist, showed that newly hatched ducklings will instinctively follow the first moving object they see. This phenomenon is called **imprinting.** Usually, this automatic and irreversible bond is with the mother. When the natural course of events is disturbed, however, other attachments, or none at all, can form. Imprinting, said Lorenz, is the result of a *predisposition toward learning:* the readiness of an organism's nervous system to acquire certain information during a brief *critical period* in early life.

A **critical period** is a specific time when a given event, or its absence, has a specific impact on development. If a necessary event does not occur during a critical period of maturation, normal development will not occur; and the resulting abnormal patterns may be irreversible (Kuhl, Conboy, Padden, Nelson & Pruitt, 2005).

Do human beings experience critical periods, as ducklings do? If a woman receives X-rays, takes certain drugs, or contracts certain diseases at certain times during pregnancy, the fetus may show specific ill effects, depending on the nature of the insult, its timing, and characteristics of the fetus itself. If a muscle problem interfering with the ability to focus both eyes on the same object is not corrected within a critical period early in childhood, depth perception probably will not develop (Bushnell & Boudreau, 1993).

However, the concept of critical periods in humans is controversial. Because many aspects of development, even in the physical domain, have been found to show **plasticity,** or modifiability of performance, it may be more useful to think about **sensitive periods,** when a developing person is particularly responsive to certain kinds of experiences (Bruer, 2001).

normative
Characteristic of an event that occurs in a similar way for most people in a group.

historical generation
A group of people strongly influenced by a major historical event during their formative period.

cohort
A group of people born at about the same time.

nonnormative
Characteristic of an unusual event that happens to a particular person or a typical event that happens at an unusual time of life.

imprinting
Instinctive form of learning in which, during a critical period in early development, a young animal forms an attachment to the first moving object it sees, usually the mother.

critical period
Specific time when a given event or its absence has a specific impact on development.

plasticity
(1) Range of modifiability of performance. (2) Modifiability, or "molding," of the brain through experience.

sensitive periods
Times in development when a person is particularly open to certain kinds of experiences.

Newborn ducklings followed and became attached to the first moving object they saw, which happened to be ethologist Konrad Lorenz. Lorenz called this behavior imprinting. ©Nina Leen/TimePix/Getty Images

There is growing evidence that plasticity is not just a general characteristic of development that applies to all members of a species, but that there are individual differences in plasticity of responses to environmental events as well. It appears as if some children—especially those with difficult temperaments, those who are highly reactive, and those with particular gene variants—may be more profoundly affected by childhood experiences, whether positive or negative, than other children (Belsky & Pluess, 2009). This new research also suggests that characteristics generally assumed to be negative—such as a difficult or reactive temperament—can be adaptive (positive) when the environment is supportive of development. For example, one study found that children who were highly reactive to environmental events showed, as expected, negative responses such as aggression and behavior problems when faced with stressors such as marital conflict in their families. Surprisingly, however, when the levels of family adversity were low, highly reactive children showed even more adaptive profiles than children low in reactivity. These highly reactive children were more prosocial, more engaged in school, and showed lower levels of externalizing symptoms (Obradovic et al., 2010). Research such as this clearly points to a need to reconceptualize the nature of plasticity in early development with an eye toward examining issues of resilience as well as risk. Research in Action discusses how the concepts of critical and sensitive periods apply to language development.

The Life-Span Developmental Approach

Paul B. Baltes (1936–2006) and his colleagues (1987; Baltes & Smith, 2004; Baltes, Lindenberger & Staudinger, 1998; Staudinger & Bluck, 2001) have identified seven key principles of a life-span developmental approach that sum up many of the concepts discussed in this chapter.

1. *Development is lifelong.* Development is a lifelong process of change. Each period of the life span is affected by what happened before and will affect what is to come. No period is more or less important than any other.

2. *Development is multidimensional.* It occurs along multiple interacting dimensions—biological, psychological, and social—each of which may develop at varying rates.

3. *Development is multidirectional.* Although we generally think of development as proceeding in a positive direction, people can show gains or losses at any point in the life span.

4. *Relative influences of biology and culture shift over the life span.* The process of development is influenced by both biology and culture, but the balance between these influences changes. Biological abilities, such as sensory acuity and muscular strength and coordination, weaken with age, but cultural supports, such as education, relationships, and technologically age-friendly environments, may help compensate.

CROSS-CULTURAL LANGUAGE DIFFERENCES ("BABY TALK")

Imagine you're cradling a baby in your arms. She displays a toothless grin as you begin to speak. Do you notice a difference in your speech patterns? Are your words simpler? Do you make silly sounds to attract her attention?

Cross-cultural research helps us to tease out what aspects of our behavior are universal—or common to humans everywhere—or culturally specific, the product of our upbringing. One area of cross-cultural research involves this "baby talk," or distinctive speech patterns with preverbal infants. Infant-directed (ID) speech includes simplified grammar, slower tempo, pitch variations, exaggerated sound intonation, and repetition of key words and phrases (Estes & Hurley, 2013; Ma, Golinkoff, Houston & Hirsh-Pasek, 2011). Neither gender is exempt, as both women and men use ID speech patterns (Pegg, Werker & McLeod, 1992; Soderstrom, 2007). Infants find ID speech highly engaging, and it draws their attention to spoken language. Adults speak in this fashion even to newborns (Johnson, Caskey, Rand, Tucker & Vohr, 2014), and infants as young as 7 weeks display ID speech preferences. In fact, babies pay special attention to ID speech even in languages other than their own. Pegg, Werker, and McLeod (1992) found exaggerated intonation of ID speech (the rise and fall of the voice) attractive to infants, whether presented in their native English language or Cantonese (Chinese).

American English is the most studied language with respect to ID speech, but there is evidence of ID speech patterns cross-culturally (e.g., French, Spanish, Hebrew, Japanese, Fijian, and the Luo of Kenya and Tanzania). Similarities are also found in prosody (stressed syllables and intonation) across different languages (Broesch & Bryant, 2015; Soderstrom, 2007). A study of mother-infant vocalization across 11 countries suggests that ID speech engages infants in the social function of language. Baby talk captures attention and elicits vocalization in a conversational, turn-taking manner (Bornstein, Putnick, Cote, Haynes & Suwalsky, 2015).

ID speech may also help convey cultural norms. Fernald and Morikawa (1993) found that American mothers use noun-labeling more frequently ("Look at the car.... Those are wheels."). Japanese mothers use ID speech to emphasize social interactions ("Car goes 'vrooom'.... I give to you.... You give back"). Japanese mothers also emphasized cultural

norms of empathy and politeness within ID speech, promoting cultural values of interdependence, connectedness, and harmony (Fernald & Morikawa, 1993). Mastin and Vogt (2016) drew a similar conclusion from a study of Mozambican infants. Rural Mozambicans used more words related to kinship, emphasizing collectivist values even more so than those in urban areas.

Some cultures discourage ID speech. The Gusii of Kenya do not believe it is useful or necessary to speak to infants (Richman, Miller & LeVine, 2010). The Ifaluk of Micronesia see no point in baby talk, as it is believed infants lack understanding (Le, 2000), and remote Senegalese villagers express fears that evil spirits will possess babies who are spoken to (Weber, Fernald & Diop, 2017; Zeitlin, 2011). As a result, little to no effort is made to speak to infants in these cultures, despite near constant contact with caregivers.

ID speech has been associated with numerous benefits, including association of sounds of words with meanings (Estes & Hurley, 2013; Ma, Golinkoff, Houston & Hirsch-Pasek, 2011; Bergelson & Swingley, 2012), increase in long-term word recognition (Singh, Nestor, Parikh & Yull, 2009), and increased neural activity when words are spoken in ID speech (Zangl & Mills, 2007). The attention-grabbing features orient babies to spoken language, and the simplified and repetitive nature of ID speech is a supportive framework for language acquisition. ID speech is not the sole source of language input, however, perhaps representing as little as 15 percent of total language. Children also listen to the language adults direct toward each other or to other siblings and learn from that as well (Soderstrom, 2007). ID speech preference begins to decline as early as 9 to 12 months, as infants become more linguistically sophisticated (Soderstrom, 2007). Interestingly, whether ID speech is used or not, infants achieve language fluency along roughly the same timetable worldwide.

 **what's your view** Is baby talk a common practice in your culture? What about singing lullabies, reading books, or bedtime stories to preverbal infants? How would you continue to stimulate language development once infants begin to respond using babbles or first words?

5. *Development involves changing resource allocations.* Individuals choose to invest their resources of time, energy, talent, money, and social support in varying ways. The allocation of resources to these three functions changes throughout life as the total available pool of resources decreases. In childhood and young adulthood, the bulk of resources typically goes to growth; in old age, to regulation of loss. In midlife, the allocation is more evenly balanced among the three functions.

6. *Development shows plasticity.* Many abilities, such as memory, strength, and endurance, can be improved significantly with training and practice, even late in life. One of the tasks of developmental research is to discover to what extent particular kinds of development can be modified at various ages.

7. *Development is influenced by the historical and cultural context.* Each person develops within multiple contexts—circumstances or conditions defined in part by maturation and in part by time and place. Human beings not only influence but also are influenced by their historical-cultural context.

summary and key terms

Human Development: An Ever-Evolving Field

- Human development is the scientific study of processes of change and stability and has important real-world applications.
- Life-span development has become a field of study.
- The study of human development seeks to describe, explain, predict, and, when appropriate, intervene in development.
- Students of human development draw on multiple disciplines.
- Methods of studying human development are still evolving, making use of advanced technologies.
  human development, life-span development

The Study of Human Development: Basic Concepts

- Developmental scientists study change and stability in all domains of development throughout the life span.
- The three major domains of development are physical, cognitive, and psychosocial. Each affects the others.
- The concept of periods of development is a social construction.
  physical development, cognitive development, psychosocial development, social construction

Influences on Development

- Influences on development come from both heredity and environment. Many typical changes during childhood are related to maturation. Individual differences tend to increase with age.

- In some societies, the nuclear family predominates; in others, the extended family.
- Socioeconomic status (SES) affects developmental processes and outcomes through the quality of home and neighborhood environments, nutrition, medical care, and schooling. Multiple risk factors increase the likelihood of poor outcomes.
- Important environmental influences stem from culture, race/ethnicity, and historical context. Race is a social construction.
- Influences may be normative (age-graded or history-graded) or nonnormative.
- There is evidence of critical or sensitive periods for certain kinds of early development.
  individual differences, heredity, environment, maturation, nuclear family, extended family, socioeconomic status (SES), risk factors, culture, ethnic group, normative, historical generation, cohort, nonnormative, imprinting, critical period, plasticity, sensitive periods

The Life-Span Developmental Approach

- The principles of the life-span developmental approach include the propositions that (1) development is lifelong, (2) development is multidimensional, (3) development is multidirectional, (4) the relative influences of biology and culture shift over the life span, (5) development involves changing resource allocations, (6) development shows plasticity, and (7) development is influenced by the historical and cultural context.

Theory and Research

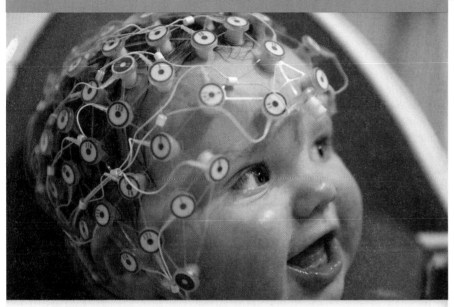

chapter 2

©Oli Scarff/Getty Images

learning objectives

Describe the purpose of theories in research and two theoretical issues on which developmental scientists differ.

Summarize the main theories of human development.

Describe the methods developmental researchers use to collect data and the advantages and disadvantages of each.

Explain ethical guidelines for researchers who study people.

In this chapter we present an overview of the major theories of human development and of the research methods used to study it. We explore important issues and theoretical perspectives that underlie much research in human development, and we look at how researchers gather and assess information. Ethical issues that may arise in research on humans are also addressed.

Basic Theoretical Issues

theory
Coherent set of logically related concepts that seeks to organize, explain, and predict data.

A scientific **theory** of development is a set of logically related concepts or statements that seek to describe and explain development and to predict the kinds of behavior that might occur under certain conditions. Theories organize and explain *data,* the information gathered by research. As painstaking research adds, bit by bit, to the body of knowledge, theoretical concepts help us make sense of, and see connections between, isolated pieces of data.

Theory and research are interwoven strands in the fabric of scientific study. Theories inspire further research and predict its results. They do this by generating **hypotheses,** explanations or predictions that can be tested by further research. Research can indicate whether a theory is accurate in its predictions but cannot conclusively show a theory to be true. Science is built upon falsifiability, and no theory is *ever* proven. However, theories can be *disproved*. Sometimes research supports a hypothesis and the theory on which it was based. At other times, scientists must modify their theories to account for unexpected data. This flexibility is one of the greatest strengths of science.

hypotheses
Possible explanations for phenomena, used to predict the outcome of research.

The way theorists explain development depends in part on their assumptions about two basic issues: (1) whether people are active or reactive in their own development, and (2) whether development is continuous or occurs in stages. A third issue is whether development is more influenced by heredity or by environment.

ISSUE 1: IS DEVELOPMENT ACTIVE OR REACTIVE?

Psychology is an outgrowth of philosophy in many ways, and philosophers have frequently grappled with questions of psychology and development.

There have been a variety of perspectives. For example, the eighteenth-century English philosopher John Locke held that a young child is a *tabula rasa*—a "blank slate"—upon which society writes. How the child developed, in either positive or negative ways, depended entirely on experiences. In contrast, the French philosopher Jean Jacques Rousseau believed that children are born "noble savages" who develop according to their own positive natural tendencies if not corrupted by society. This debate remains important today, although in modern terms we speak of heredity and environmental influences.

Additional philosophical debates about development, and the same basic issues philosophers argued about, are reflected in the psychological theories of today. In this section we address the debate about active and reactive development. Psychologists who believe in reactive development conceptualize the developing child as a hungry sponge that soaks up experiences and is shaped by this input over time. Psychologists who believe in active development argue that people create experiences for themselves and are motivated to learn about the world around them. Things aren't just happening to them; they are involved in making their world what it is.

mechanistic model
Model that views human development as a series of predictable responses to stimuli.

Mechanistic Model Locke's view was the forerunner of the **mechanistic model.** In this model, people are like machines that react to environmental input (Pepper, 1942, 1961).

Machines do not operate of their own will; they react automatically to physical forces or inputs. Fill a car with gas, turn the ignition key, press the accelerator, and the car will move. In the mechanistic view, human behavior is much the same: It results from the operation of biological parts in response to external or internal stimuli. If we know enough about how the human "machine" is put together and about the forces acting on it, we can predict what the person will do.

Mechanistic researchers want to identify the factors that make people behave as they do. For example, to explain why some college students drink too much alcohol, a mechanistic theorist might look for environmental influences, such as advertising and whether the student's friends are heavy drinkers.

organismic model
Model that views human development as internally initiated by an active organism and as occurring in a sequence of qualitatively different stages.

Organismic Model Rousseau was the precursor of the **organismic model.** This model sees people as active, growing organisms that set their own development in motion (Pepper, 1942,

Continuity

(a)

Stage theory
(Discontinuity)

(b)

FIGURE 2.1

Quantitative and Qualitative Change

A major difference among developmental theories is (a) whether it proceeds continuously, as learning theorists and information-processing theorists propose, or (b) whether development occurs in distinct stages, as Freud, Erikson, and Piaget maintained.

1961). The driving force for change is internal. Environmental influences do not *cause* development, though they can speed or slow it. Development is believed to have an underlying, orderly structure, though it may not be obvious from moment to moment.

Because human behavior is viewed as an organic whole, it cannot be predicted by breaking it down into simple responses to environmental stimulation. An organismic theorist, in studying why some students drink too much, looks at what kinds of situations they choose to participate in, and with whom. Do they choose friends who prefer to party or to study?

ISSUE 2: IS DEVELOPMENT CONTINUOUS OR DISCONTINUOUS?

The mechanistic and organismic models also differ on the second issue: Is development *continuous,* that is, gradual and incremental, or *discontinuous,* that is, abrupt or uneven? Mechanist theorists see development as continuous: as occurring in small incremental stages (Figure 2.1a). Development is always governed by the same processes and involves the gradual refinement and extension of early skills into later abilities, allowing one to make predictions about future characteristics on the basis of past performance. This type of change is known as **quantitative change**—a change in number or amount, such as in height, weight, or vocabulary size.

Organismic theorists see development as discontinuous; as marked by the emergence of new phenomena that could not be easily predicted on the basis of past functioning. Development at different points in the life span is, in this view, fundamentally different in nature. It is a change in kind, structure, or organization, not just in number. This type of change is known as **qualitative change.**

Organismic theorists are proponents of *stage theories* in which development is seen as occurring in a series of distinct stages, like stairsteps (Figure 2.1b). At each stage, what is going on is fundamentally different from previous stages. Moreover, stages build upon each other. Stages cannot be skipped, and development only proceeds in a positive direction. It is believed that these processes are universal and account for the development of all humans everywhere, although the particular timing may vary a bit.

Theoretical Perspectives

Five major perspectives underlie much influential theory and research on human development: (1) psychoanalytic, which focuses on unconscious emotions and drives; (2) learning, which studies observable behavior; (3) cognitive, which analyzes thought processes; (4) contextual, which emphasizes the impact of the historical, social, and cultural context; and (5) evolutionary/sociobiological, which considers evolutionary and biological underpinnings of behavior. Following is a general overview of each of these perspectives. These are summarized in Table 2.1.

quantitative change
Changes in number or amount, such as in height, weight, size of vocabulary, or frequency of communication.

qualitative change
Discontinuous changes in kind, structure, or organization.

TABLE 2.1 Five Perspectives on Human Development

Perspective	Important Theories	Basic Propositions	Stage-Oriented	Causal Emphasis	Active/Reactive Individual
Psycho-analytic	Freud's psychosexual theory	Behavior is controlled by powerful unconscious urges.	Yes	Innate factors modified by experience	Reactive
	Erikson's psychosocial theory	Personality is influenced by society and develops through a series of crises.	Yes	Interaction of innate and experiential factors	Active
Learning	Behaviorism, or traditional learning theory (Pavlov, Skinner, Watson)	People are responders; the environment controls behavior.	No	Experience	Reactive
	Social learning (social cognitive) theory (Bandura)	Children learn by observing and imitating models; they are active contributors to learning.	No	Experience modified by innate factors	Active and reactive
Cognitive	Piaget's cognitive stage theory	Qualitative changes in thought occur between infancy and adolescence. Children are active initiators of development.	Yes	Interaction of innate and experiential factors	Active
	Vygotsky's sociocultural theory	Social interaction is central to cognitive development.	No for general stages; yes for concept formation.	Experience	Active
	Information-processing theory	Human beings are processors of symbols.	No	Interaction of innate and experiential factors	Active
Contextual	Bronfenbrenner's bioecological theory	Development occurs through interaction between a developing person and five surrounding, interlocking contextual systems of influences.	No	Interaction of innate and experiential factors	Active
Evolutionary/ sociobiological	Evolutionary psychology; Bowlby's attachment theory	Human beings are the product of adaptive processes; there are evolutionary and biological bases for behavior and learning.	No	Interaction of innate and experiential factors	Active and reactive (theorists vary)

PERSPECTIVE 1: PSYCHOANALYTIC

Sigmund Freud (1856–1939) was a Viennese physician who was the originator of the **psychoanalytic perspective.** He believed in reactive development, and qualitative change. Freud proposed that humans were born with a series of innate, biologically based drives such as hunger, sex, and aggression. He thought people were motivated to satisfy these drives, and that much of development involved learning how to do so in

psychoanalytic perspective
View of human development as shaped by unconscious forces that motivate human behavior.

socially acceptable ways. In addition, Freud believed that early experiences shaped later functioning. Freud also promoted the idea that what we consciously know about and experience is only the small tip of the iceberg of who we are. Following is a summary of Freud's theory. Other theorists, including Erik H. Erikson, have expanded and modified Freud's theory.

Sigmund Freud: Psychosexual Development Freud (1953, 1964a, 1964b) believed that people are born with biological drives that must be redirected to make it possible to live in society. He proposed three hypothetical parts of the personality: the *id*, the *ego*, and the *superego*. Newborns are governed by the *id*, which operates under the *pleasure principle*—the drive to seek immediate satisfaction of their needs and desires. When gratification is delayed, as it is when infants have to wait to be fed, they begin to see themselves as separate from the outside world. The *ego*, which represents reason, develops gradually during the first year or so of life and operates under the *reality principle*. The ego's aim is to find realistic ways to gratify the id that are acceptable to the *superego*, which develops at about age 5 or 6. The *superego* includes the conscience and incorporates socially approved "shoulds" and "should nots" into the child's value system. The superego is highly demanding; if its standards are not met, a child may feel guilty and anxious. The ego mediates between the impulses of the id and the demands of the superego.

Freud proposed that personality forms through unconscious childhood conflicts between the inborn urges of the id and the requirements of civilized life. These conflicts occur in a sequence of five stages of **psychosexual development** (Table 2.2), in which sensual pleasure shifts from one body zone to another—from the mouth to the anus and then to the genitals. At each stage, the behavior that is the chief source of gratification (or frustration) changes.

According to Freud, if children receive too little or too much gratification in the first three stages, they are at risk of *fixation,* an arrest in development that can show up in adult personality. Babies whose needs are not met during the *oral stage,* when feeding is the main source of pleasure, may grow up to become nail-biters or smokers. A person who, as a toddler, had too-strict toilet training may be fixated at the *anal stage,* and be obsessively clean, rigidly tied to schedules and routines, or defiantly messy.

According to Freud, a key event in psychosexual development occurs in the *phallic stage* of early childhood. Boys develop sexual attachment to their mothers, and girls to their fathers, and they have aggressive urges toward the same-sex parent, whom they regard as a rival. Freud called these developments the *Oedipus* and *Electra complexes.*

Children eventually resolve their anxiety over these feelings by identifying with the same-sex parent and move into the *latency stage* of middle childhood, a period of relative emotional calm and intellectual and social exploration.

The *genital stage,* the final stage, lasts throughout adulthood. The sexual urges repressed during latency now resurface to flow in socially approved channels, which Freud defined as heterosexual relations with persons outside the family of origin.

Freud's theory made historic contributions; however, many of Freud's ideas now are widely considered obsolete or are impossible to investigate scientifically. Nevertheless, several of his central themes have stood the test of time. Freud made us aware of the importance of unconscious thoughts, feelings, and motivations; the role of childhood experiences in forming personality; the ambivalence of emotional responses, the role of mental representations of the self and others in the establishment of intimate relationships; and the path of normal development from an immature, dependent state to a mature, interdependent state. In all these ways, Freud left an indelible mark on psychoanalysis and developmental psychology (Gedo, 2001; Westen, 1998).

We need to remember that Freud based his theories about normal development on a clientele of Victorian upper-middle-class adults, mostly women, in therapy. His concentration on the influences of sexual urges and early experience did not take into account other, and later, influences on personality—including the influences of society and culture, which many heirs to the Freudian tradition, such as Erik Erikson, stress.

psychosexual development
In Freudian theory, an unvarying sequence of stages of childhood personality development in which gratification shifts from the mouth to the anus and then to the genitals.

TABLE 2.2 Developmental Stages According to Various Theories

Psychosexual Stages (Freud)	Psychosocial Stages (Erikson)	Cognitive Stages (Piaget)
Oral (birth to 12–18 months). Baby's chief source of pleasure involves mouth-oriented activities (sucking and feeding).	*Basic trust versus mistrust (birth to 12–18 months).* Baby develops sense of whether world is a good and safe place. Virtue: hope.	*Sensorimotor (birth to 2 years).* Infant learns about the environment through sensory and motor activity.
Anal (12–18 months to 3 years). Child derives pleasure from withholding and expelling feces. Zone of gratification is anal region, and toilet training is important activity.	*Autonomy versus shame and doubt (12–18 months to 3 years).* Child develops a balance of independence and self-sufficiency over shame and doubt. Virtue: will.	*Preoperational (2 to 7 years).* Child develops a representational system and uses symbols to represent people, places, and events. Language and imaginative play are important manifestations of this stage. Thinking is still not logical.
Phallic (3 to 6 years). Child becomes attached to parent of the other sex leading to identification with same-sex parent. Superego develops. Zone of gratification shifts to genitals.	*Initiative versus guilt (3 to 6 years).* Child develops initiative when trying out new activities and is not overwhelmed by guilt. Virtue: purpose.	
Latency (6 years to puberty). Time of relative calm between more turbulent stages.	*Industry versus inferiority (6 years to puberty).* Child must learn skills of the culture or face feelings of incompetence. Virtue: skill.	*Concrete operations (7 to 11 years).* Child can solve problems logically if they are focused on the here and now but cannot think abstractly.
Genital (puberty through adulthood). Reemergence of sexual impulses of phallic stage, channeled into mature adult sexuality.	*Identity versus identity confusion (puberty to young adulthood).* Adolescent must determine sense of self or experience role confusion. Virtue: fidelity. *Intimacy versus isolation (young adulthood).* Person makes commitments to others or may suffer from isolation and self-absorption. Virtue: love. *Generativity versus stagnation (middle adulthood).* Mature adult contributes to the next generation or risks personal impoverishment. Virtue: care. *Integrity versus despair (late adulthood).* Older adult achieves acceptance of death, or else despairs over inability to relive life. Virtue: wisdom.	*Formal operations (11 years through adulthood).* Person can think abstractly, deal with hypothetical situations, and think about possibilities.

Note: All ages are approximate.

psychosocial development
In Erikson's eight-stage theory, the socially and culturally influenced process of development of the ego, or self.

Erik Erikson: Psychosocial Development Erik Erikson (1902-1994) modified and extended Freudian theory and was a pioneer in taking a life-span perspective. Note that both theorists, as they proposed stage theories, believed in qualitative change.

Erikson's (1950, 1982; Erikson, Erikson & Kivnick, 1986) theory of **psychosocial development** covers eight stages across the life span (refer to Table 2.2). Each stage involves what Erikson originally called a *crisis* in personality*—a major psychosocial challenge that is particularly important at that time. These issues must be satisfactorily resolved for healthy ego development.

Each stage requires balancing a positive and a negative tendency. The positive quality should dominate, but some degree of the negative quality is needed as well. The critical theme of infancy, for example, is *basic trust versus basic mistrust.* People need to

*Erikson broadened the concept of "crisis" and later referred instead to conflicting or competing tendencies.

trust the world and the people in it. However, they also need some mistrust to protect themselves from danger. The successful outcome of each stage is the development of a particular *virtue,* or strength—in this case, the virtue of *hope.*

Successful resolution of each crisis puts the person in a particularly good position to address the next crisis, a process that occurs iteratively across the life span. So, for example, a child who successfully develops a sense of trust in infancy would be well prepared for the development of a sense of autonomy—the second psychosocial challenge—in toddlerhood. After all, if you feel that others have your back, you are more likely to try to develop your skills knowing that they will be there to comfort you if you fail.

Erikson's theory is important because of its emphasis on social and cultural influences and on development beyond adolescence.

PERSPECTIVE 2: LEARNING

The **learning perspective** maintains that development results from *learning,* a long-lasting change in behavior based on experience or adaptation to the environment. Learning theorists see development as continuous. Their terms are defined precisely, and their focus on observable behaviors means that theories can be tested in the laboratory. Two important learning theories are *behaviorism* and *social learning theory.*

learning perspective
View of human development that holds that changes in behavior result from experience or from adaptation to the environment.

Behaviorism **Behaviorism** is a mechanistic theory that describes observed behavior as a predictable response to experience. Behaviorists consider development as reactive and continuous. Behavioral research focuses on *associative learning,* in which a mental link is formed between two events. Two kinds of associative learning are *classical conditioning* and *operant conditioning.*

behaviorism
Learning theory that emphasizes the predictable role of environment in causing observable behavior.

Classical Conditioning The Russian physiologist Ivan Pavlov (1849–1936) devised experiments in which dogs learned to salivate at the sound of a bell that rang at feeding time. These experiments were the foundation for **classical conditioning,** in which a response (in this case, salivation) to a stimulus (the bell) is evoked after repeated association with a stimulus that normally elicits the response (food).

classical conditioning
Learning based on associating a stimulus that does not ordinarily elicit a response with another stimulus that does elicit the response.

The American behaviorist John B. Watson (1878–1958) applied such stimulus-response theories to children, claiming that he could mold any infant in any way he chose. In one of the earliest and most famous demonstrations of classical conditioning in human beings (Watson & Rayner, 1920), he taught an 11-month-old baby known as "Little Albert" to fear furry white objects. In this study, Albert was exposed to a loud noise that frightened him whenever he reached for a rat. After repeated pairings of the rat with the loud noise, Albert whimpered with fear when he saw the rat. Albert also started showing fear responses to white rabbits and cats, and the beards of elderly men. The study, although unethical, demonstrated that fear could be conditioned.

Classical conditioning occurs throughout life. Fear responses to objects like a car or a dog may be the result of a bad experience. Much advertising is based upon attempts to condition associations between products (like a car) and positive stimuli (like an attractive person).

Operant Conditioning Angel lies in his crib. When he starts to babble, his mother smiles and repeats the syllables. Angel learns that his behavior (babbling) can produce a desirable consequence (loving attention from a parent), and so he keeps babbling to attract his mother's attention. An originally accidental behavior (babbling) has become a conditioned response.

This type of learning is called **operant conditioning** because the individual learns from the consequences of "operating" on the environment. Unlike classical conditioning, operant conditioning involves voluntary behavior, such as Angel's babbling and involves the consequences rather than the predictors of behavior.

operant conditioning
(1) Learning based on association of behavior with its consequences.
(2) Learning based on reinforcement or punishment.

The American psychologist B. F. Skinner (1904–1990) argued that an organism—animal or human—will tend to repeat a response that has been reinforced by desirable consequences

reinforcement
The process by which a behavior is strengthened, increasing the likelihood that the behavior will be repeated.

punishment
The process by which a behavior is weakened, decreasing the likelihood of repetition.

and will suppress a response that has been punished. Thus **reinforcement** is the process by which a behavior is strengthened, *increasing* the likelihood that the behavior will be repeated. In Angel's case, his mother's attention reinforces his babbling. **Punishment** is the process by which a behavior is weakened, *decreasing* the likelihood of repetition. If Angel's mother frowned when he babbled, he would be less likely to babble again.

Reinforcement is most effective when it immediately follows a behavior. If a response is no longer reinforced, it will eventually be *extinguished,* that is, return to its original (baseline) level. If, after a while, no one repeats Angel's babbling, he may babble less often than if his babbles still brought reinforcement.

While Skinnerian psychology has been useful in helping us understand how to eliminate undesirable behaviors or instill desirable behaviors, it is limited in application. It does not adequately address individual differences, cultural and social influences, or biologically influenced behavioral patterns.

social learning theory
Theory that behaviors are learned by observing and imitating models. Also called *social cognitive theory.*

reciprocal determinism
Bandura's term for bidirectional forces that affect development.

observational learning
Learning through watching the behavior of others.

Social Learning (Social Cognitive) Theory The American psychologist Albert Bandura (b. 1925) developed many of the principles of **social learning theory.** Whereas behaviorists see the environment as the chief impetus for development, Bandura (1977, 1989; Bandura & Walters, 1963) suggests that the impetus for development is bidirectional. Bandura called this concept **reciprocal determinism**—the person acts on the world as the world acts on the person.

Classic social learning theory maintains that people learn appropriate social behavior chiefly by observing and imitating models—that is, by watching other people. This process is called **observational learning,** or *modeling.* Note that this is an active process, and that it can occur even if a person does not imitate the observed behavior.

Bandura's (1989) updated version of social learning theory is *social cognitive theory.* The change of name reflects a greater emphasis on cognitive processes as central to development. Cognitive processes are at work as people observe models, learn *chunks* of behavior, and mentally put the chunks together into complex new behavior patterns. Rita, for example, imitates the toes-out walk of her dance teacher but models her dance steps after those of Carmen, a slightly more advanced student. Even so, she develops her own style of dancing by putting her observations together into a new pattern.

self-efficacy
Sense of one's capability to master challenges and achieve goals.

Through feedback on their behavior, children gradually form standards for judging their actions and become more selective in choosing models who demonstrate those standards. They also begin to develop a sense of **self-efficacy,** the confidence that they have what it takes to succeed.

PERSPECTIVE 3: COGNITIVE

cognitive perspective
View that thought processes are central to development.

The **cognitive perspective** focuses on thought processes and the behavior that reflects those processes. This perspective encompasses both organismic and mechanistically influenced theories. It includes the cognitive-stage theory of Piaget and Vygotsky's sociocultural theory of cognitive development. It also includes the information-processing approach and neo-Piagetian theories.

cognitive-stage theory
Piaget's theory that children's cognitive development advances in a series of four stages involving qualitatively distinct types of mental operations.

Jean Piaget's Cognitive-Stage Theory Our understanding of how children think owes a great deal to the work of the Swiss theoretician Jean Piaget (1896–1980). Piaget's **cognitive-stage theory** emphasized mental processes. Piaget viewed development organismically, as the product of children's efforts to understand and act on their world. He also believed that development was discontinuous, so his theory describes development as occurring in stages.

Piaget's *clinical method* combined observation with flexible questioning. In the process of asking children questions, he realized that children of the same ages made similar types of logical errors. So, for example, he discovered that a typical 4-year-old believed that pennies or flowers were more numerous when arranged in a line than when heaped or piled up. From his observations, Piaget created a comprehensive theory of cognitive development.

Piaget suggested that cognitive development begins with an inborn ability to adapt to the environment. This cognitive growth occurs through three interrelated processes: *organization, adaptation,* and *equilibration.*

Organization is the tendency to create categories, such as birds, by observing the characteristics that individual members of a category, such as sparrows and cardinals, have in common. According to Piaget, people create increasingly complex cognitive structures called **schemes,** ways of organizing information about the world that govern the way the child thinks and behaves in a particular situation. As children acquire more information, their schemes become more and more complex. Take sucking, for example. A newborn infant has a simple scheme for sucking but soon develops varied schemes for how to suck at the breast, a bottle, or a thumb. The infant may have to open her mouth wider, or turn her head to the side, or suck with varying

Jean Piaget studied children's cognitive development by observing and talking with them in many settings, asking questions to find out how their minds worked.
©Bill Anderson/Science Source

strength. Schemes are originally concrete in nature (e.g., how to suck on objects) and become increasingly abstract over time (e.g., what a dog is).

Adaptation is Piaget's term for how children handle new information in light of what they already know. Adaptation occurs through two complementary processes: (1) **assimilation,** taking in new information and incorporating it into existing cognitive structures, and (2) **accommodation,** adjusting one's cognitive structures to fit the new information.

How does the shift from assimilation to accommodation occur? Piaget argued that children strive for **equilibration** between their cognitive structures and new experiences. Children want what they understand of the world to match what they observe around them. When children's understanding of the world does not match what they are experiencing, they find themselves in a state of disequilibrium. Disequilibrium can be thought of as an uncomfortable motivational state, and it pushes children into accommodation. For example, a child knows what birds are and sees a plane for the first time. The child labels the plane a "bird" (assimilation). Over time the child notes differences between planes and birds, which makes her somewhat uneasy (disequilibrium) and motivates her to change her understanding (accommodation) and provide a new label for the plane. She then is at equilibrium. Thus assimilation and accommodation work together to produce equilibrium. Throughout life, the quest for equilibrium is the driving force behind cognitive growth.

Piaget described cognitive development as occurring in four universal, qualitatively different stages (listed in Table 2.2). From infancy through adolescence, mental operations evolve from learning based on simple sensory and motor activity to logical, abstract thought.

Piaget's observations have yielded much information and some surprising insights. Piaget has shown us that children's minds are not miniature adult minds. Knowing how children think makes it easier for parents and teachers to understand and teach them. However, Piaget seems to have seriously underestimated the abilities of infants and children. Some contemporary psychologists also question his distinct stages, pointing instead to evidence that cognitive development is more gradual and continuous (Courage & Howe, 2002). Further, cross-cultural research indicates that performance on formal reasoning tasks is as much a function of culture as it is of development; people from industrialized societies who have participated in a formal educational system show better performance on those tasks (Buck-Morss, 1975). Last, research on adults suggests that

According to Lev Vygotsky, children learn through social interaction.
©Sovfoto/UIG/Getty Images

sociocultural theory
Vygotsky's theory of how contextual factors affect children's development.

zone of proximal development (ZPD)
Vygotsky's term for the difference between what a child can do alone and what the child can do with help.

scaffolding
Temporary support to help a child master a task.

information-processing approach
Approach to the study of cognitive development that analyzes processes involved in perceiving and handling information.

Piaget's focus on formal logic as the climax of cognitive development is too narrow. It does not account for the emergence of such mature abilities as practical problem solving, wisdom, and the capacity to deal with ambiguous situations.

Lev Vygotsky's Sociocultural Theory The Russian psychologist Lev Semenovich Vygotsky (1896–1934) focused on the social and cultural processes that guide children's cognitive development. Vygotsky's (1978) **sociocultural theory,** like Piaget's theory, stresses children's active engagement with their environment. Vygotsky saw cognitive growth as a *collaborative* process. People, said Vygotsky, learn through social interaction. They acquire cognitive skills as part of their induction into a way of life. Shared activities help children internalize their society's modes of thinking and behaving. Vygotsky placed special emphasis on *language,* not merely as an expression of knowledge and thought but as an essential tool for learning and thinking about the world.

According to Vygotsky, adults or more advanced peers must help direct and organize a child's learning before the child can master and internalize it. This guidance is most effective in helping children cross the **zone of proximal development (ZPD),** the gap between what they are already able to do by themselves and what they can accomplish with assistance. Sensitive and effective instruction, then, should be aimed at the ZPD and increase in complexity as the child's abilities improve. Responsibility for directing learning gradually shifts to the child, such as when an adult teaches a child to float: The adult first supports the child in the water and then lets go gradually as the child learns to relax into a horizontal position.

Some followers of Vygotsky (Wood, 1980; Wood, Bruner & Ross, 1976) have applied the metaphor of *scaffolds*—the temporary platforms on which construction workers stand—to this way of teaching. **Scaffolding** is the support that parents, teachers, or others give a child in doing a task until the child can do it alone and it helps children work at the high end of their ZPD.

Vygotsky's theory has important implications for education and for cognitive testing. Tests that focus on a child's potential for learning provide a valuable alternative to standard intelligence tests; and many children may benefit from the sort of expert guidance Vygotsky prescribes. Moreover, Vygotsky's ideas have successfully been implemented in preschool children's curricula and show great promise for promoting the development of self-regulation, which affects later academic achievement (Barnett et al., 2008).

The Information-Processing Approach The **information-processing approach** seeks to explain cognitive development by analyzing the processes involved in making sense of incoming information and performing tasks effectively: such processes as attention, memory, planning strategies, decision making, and goal setting. The information-processing approach is not a single theory but a framework that supports a wide range of theories and research.

Some information-processing theorists compare the brain to a computer: There are certain inputs (such as sensory impressions) and certain outputs (such as behaviors). Information-processing theorists are interested in what happens in the middle. Why does the same input sometimes result in different outputs? In large part, information-processing researchers use observational data to *infer* what goes on between a stimulus and a response. For example, they may ask a person to recall a list of words and then observe any difference in performance if the person repeats the list over and over before being asked to recall the words or is kept from doing so. Through such studies, some information-processing researchers have developed *computational models* or flowcharts that analyze the specific steps people go through in gathering, storing, retrieving, and using information.

Like Piaget, information-processing theorists see people as active thinkers about their world. Unlike Piaget, they view development as continuous and incremental rather than as occurring in stages. They note age-related increases in the speed, complexity, and efficiency of mental processing and in the amount and variety of material that can be stored in memory.

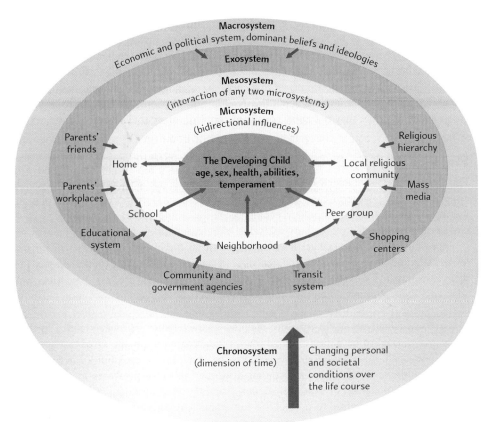

FIGURE 2.2
Bronfenbrenner's Bioecological Theory

Concentric circles show five levels of environmental influence on the individual, from the most intimate environment (the microsystem) to the broadest (the chronosystem)—all within the perpendicular dimension of time.

PERSPECTIVE 4: CONTEXTUAL

According to the **contextual perspective,** development can be understood only in its social context. Contextualists see the individual not as a separate entity interacting with the environment, but as an inseparable part of it. (Vygotsky's sociocultural theory, which we discussed as part of the cognitive perspective, also can be classified as contextual.)

The American psychologist Urie Bronfenbrenner's (1917–2005) **bioecological theory** (1979, 1986, 1994; Bronfenbrenner & Morris, 1998) identifies five levels of environmental influence, ranging from very intimate to very broad: *microsystem, mesosystem, exosystem, macrosystem,* and *chronosystem* (Figure 2.2). To understand the complexity of influences on development, we must see a person within the context of these multiple environments.

A *microsystem* is the everyday environment of home, school, work, or neighborhood, including face-to-face relationships with spouse, children, parents, friends, classmates, teachers, employers, or colleagues.

The *mesosystem* is the interlocking of various microsystems. For example, a parent's bad day at work might affect interactions with a child later that evening in a negative way. Despite never having actually gone to the workplace, the child is still affected by it.

The mesosystem focuses on interactions between microsystems, but the *exosystem* consists of interactions between a microsystem and an outside system or institution. For example, different countries have policies on what type, if any, of maternal or paternal leave accommodations are available for new parents. Thus governmental policies trickle down and can affect a child's day-to-day experiences.

The *macrosystem* consists of overarching cultural patterns, such as dominant beliefs, ideologies, and economic and political systems. How is an individual affected by living in a capitalist or socialist society?

Finally, the *chronosystem* adds the dimension of time: change or constancy in the person and the environment. Time marches on, and, as it does, changes occur. These can include changes in family composition, place of residence, or parents' employment, as well as larger events such as wars, ideology, political system, and economic cycles.

contextual perspective
View of human development that sees the individual as inseparable from the social context.

bioecological theory
Bronfenbrenner's approach to understanding processes and contexts of human development that identifies five levels of environmental influence.

According to Bronfenbrenner, a person is not merely an outcome of development but is also a shaper of it. People affect their development through their biological and psychological characteristics, talents and skills, disabilities, and temperament.

By looking at systems that affect individuals in and beyond the family, this bioecological approach helps us to see the variety of influences on development. The contextual perspective also reminds us that findings about the development of people in one culture or in one group within a culture may not apply equally to people in other societies or cultural groups.

PERSPECTIVE 5: EVOLUTIONARY/SOCIOBIOLOGICAL

The **evolutionary/sociobiological perspective** proposed by E. O. Wilson (1975) focuses on evolutionary and biological bases of behavior. Influenced by Darwin's theory of evolution, it draws on findings of anthropology, ecology, genetics, ethology, and evolutionary psychology to explain the adaptive, or survival, value of behavior for an individual or species.

According to Darwin, species have developed through the related processes of *survival of the fittest* and *natural selection*. Individuals with heritable traits *fitted* (better adapted) to their environments survive and reproduce more than those that are less fitted (less well adapted). Thus, through differential reproduction success, individuals with more adaptive characteristics pass on their traits to future generations at higher levels than individuals who are less adaptively fit. In this way, adaptive characteristics, ultimately coded in their genes, are selected to be passed on, and the less adapted ones die out. Over vast spans of time, these small, incremental changes add up and result in the evolution of new species.

Evolved mechanisms are behaviors that developed to solve problems in adapting to an earlier environment. For example, sudden aversion to certain foods during pregnancy may originally have evolved to protect the vulnerable fetus from toxic substances (Profet, 1992). Such evolved mechanisms may survive even though they no longer serve a useful purpose (Bjorklund & Pellegrini, 2002), or they may evolve further in response to changing environmental conditions.

Ethology is the study of the adaptive behaviors of animal species in natural contexts. The assumption is that such behaviors evolved through natural selection. Ethologists generally compare animals of different species and seek to identify which behaviors are universal and which are specific to a particular species or modifiable by experience.

For example, one widespread characteristic throughout the animal kingdom is called *proximity-seeking*, or, more casually, "staying close to mommy." This was first studied by Konrad Lorenz in newborn ducklings, who imprint on and follow the first moving object they see. Many other animals also engage in similar behaviors. The reason for this is that those baby animals that did not stay close to their mothers tended not to survive, and therefore did not reproduce later in life.

But why discuss animal research in a human development text? The answer is humans have also been subject to the forces of evolution and thus are likely to also have innate adaptive behaviors. In fact, one of the most important theories in developmental psychology was strongly influenced by the ethological approach. The British psychologist John Bowlby (1969) drew upon his knowledge of proximity-seeking behavior in animals of different species as he formed his ideas about attachment in humans.

A related extension of the ethological approach can be found in **evolutionary psychology.** Ethologists focus on cross-species comparisons, whereas evolutionary psychologists focus on humans and apply Darwinian principles to human behavior. Evolutionary psychologists believe that just as we have a heart specialized as a pump, lungs specialized for air exchange, and thumbs specialized for grasping, we also have aspects of our human psychology specialized for solving adaptive problems. According to this theory, people unconsciously strive to perpetuate their genetic legacy. They do so by seeking to maximize their chances of having offspring who will survive to reproduce and pass down their characteristics.

It is important to note that an evolutionary perspective does not reduce human behavior to the effects of genes seeking to reproduce themselves despite arguing that ultimately the transmission of genes is what drives many evolved behaviors. Evolutionary psychologists place great weight on the environment to which humans must adapt and the flexibility of the human mind.

A SHIFTING BALANCE

One of the strengths of the scientific method is that as new data emerges and as our understanding evolves, theories shift and change. Most of the early pioneers in the field, including Freud, Erikson, and Piaget, favored organismic, or stage, approaches. The mechanistic view gained support during the 1960s with the popularity of learning theories. Today much attention is focused on the biological and evolutionary bases of behavior.

Moreover, instead of looking for broad stages, developmental scientists seek to discover what specific kinds of behavior show continuity and what processes are involved in each. For example, most infants do not learn to walk overnight, but rather by a series of tentative movements that gradually become more self-assured. And even when observable behavior seems to change suddenly, the biological or neurological processes that underlie that behavioral change may be continuous (Courage & Howe, 2002).

Instead of debating active versus reactive development, investigators often find that influences are *bidirectional:* people change their world even as it changes them. A baby girl born with a cheerful disposition is likely to get positive responses from adults, which strengthen her trust that her smiles will be rewarded and motivate her to smile more.

Theories of human development grow out of, and are tested by, research. Research questions and methods often reflect a researcher's particular theoretical orientation. For example, in trying to understand how a child develops a sense of right and wrong, a behaviorist would examine the way the parents respond to the child's behavior: what kinds of behavior they punish or praise. A social learning theorist would focus on imitation of moral examples, possibly in stories or in movies. An information-processing researcher might do a task analysis to identify the steps a child goes through in determining the range of moral options available and then in deciding which option to pursue. An evolutionary psychologist might be interested in universal aspects of moral development that serve adaptive purposes and in how they affect social behavior.

With the vital connection between theory and research in mind, let's look at the methods developmental researchers use.

Research Methods

Researchers in human development work within two methodological traditions: quantitative and qualitative. Each of these traditions has different goals and different ways of seeing and interpreting reality and emphasizes different means of collecting and analyzing data.

QUANTITATIVE AND QUALITATIVE RESEARCH

Generally, when most people think of scientific research, they are thinking of what is called *quantitative research.* **Quantitative research** deals with objectively measurable, numerical data that can answer questions such as "how much?" or "how many?" and that is amenable to statistical analysis. For example, quantitative researchers might study the fear and anxiety children feel before surgery by asking them to answer questions, using a numerical scale, about how fearful or anxious they are. These data could then be compared to data for children not facing surgery to determine whether a statistically significant difference exists between the two groups.

Quantitative research on human development is based on the **scientific method,** which has traditionally characterized most scientific inquiry. Its usual steps are:

1. *Identification of a problem* to be studied, often on the basis of a theory or of previous research.

2. *Formulation of hypotheses* to be tested by research.

3. *Collection of data.*

quantitative research
Research that deals with objectively measurable data.

scientific method
System of established principles and processes of scientific inquiry, which includes identifying a problem to be studied, formulating a hypothesis to be tested by research, collecting data, analyzing the data, forming tentative conclusions, and disseminating findings.

4. *Statistical analysis of the data* to determine whether they support the hypothesis.

5. *Formation of tentative conclusions.*

6. *Dissemination of findings* so other observers can check, learn from, analyze, repeat, and build on the results.

qualitative research
Research that focuses on nonnumerical data, such as subjective experiences, feelings, or beliefs.

Qualitative research, in contrast, focuses on the how and why of behavior. It more commonly involves nonnumerical (verbal or pictorial) descriptions of participants' subjective understanding, feelings, or beliefs about their experiences. Qualitative researchers might study the same subject areas as quantitative researchers, but their perspective informs both how they collect data and how they interpret it. For example, if qualitative researchers were to study children's emotional state prior to surgery, they might do so with unstructured interviews or by asking children to draw their perceptions of the upcoming event. Whereas the goal in quantitative research is to generate hypotheses from previous research and empirically test them, the goal in qualitative research is to understand the "story" of the event.

The selection of quantitative or qualitative methods may depend on the purpose of the study, how much is already known about the topic, and the researcher's theoretical orientation. Quantitative research often is done in controlled laboratory settings; qualitative research typically is conducted in everyday settings, such as the home or school.

SAMPLING

sample
Group of participants chosen to represent the entire population under study.

Because studying an entire *population* (a group to whom the findings may apply) is usually too costly and time-consuming, investigators select a **sample,** a smaller group within the population. To be sure that the results of quantitative research are true generally, the sample should adequately represent the population under study—that is, it should show relevant characteristics in the same proportions as in the entire population. Otherwise the results cannot properly be *generalized,* or applied to the population as a whole.

random selection
Selection of a sample in such a way that each person in a population has an equal and independent chance of being chosen.

Often quantitative researchers seek to achieve representativeness through **random selection,** in which each person in a population has an equal and independent chance of being chosen. The result of random selection is a *random sample.* A random sample, especially a large one, is likely to represent the population well. Unfortunately, a random sample of a large population is often difficult to obtain. Instead, many studies use samples selected for convenience or accessibility (for example, children born in a particular hospital). The findings of such studies may not apply to the population as a whole.

In qualitative research, samples tend to be focused rather than random. Participants may be chosen for their ability to communicate the nature of a certain experience, such as how it feels to go through puberty or menopause. A carefully selected qualitative sample may have a fair degree of generalizability.

FORMS OF DATA COLLECTION

Common ways of gathering data (Table 2.3) include *self-reports* (verbal or visual reports by study participants), *observation* of participants in laboratory or natural settings, and *behavioral* or *performance measures.* Researchers may use one or more of these data collection techniques in any research design. Qualitative research tends to rely on self-reports, often in the form of in-depth, open-ended interviews or visual techniques and on observation in natural settings. Quantitative research typically uses standardized, structured methods involving numerical measurements of behavior or performance.

Let's look more closely at several common methods of data collection.

Self-Reports: Diaries, Visual Techniques, Interviews, and Questionnaires The simplest form of self-report is a *diary* or log. Adolescents may be asked, for example, to record what they eat each day or the times when they feel depressed. In studying young children, *parental self-reports*—diaries, journals, interviews, or questionnaires—are commonly used, often together with other methods, such as videotaping or recording.

TABLE 2.3 Major Methods of Data Collection

Type	Main Characteristics	Advantages	Disadvantages
Self-report: diary, visual reports, interview, or questionnaire	Participants are asked about some aspect of their lives; questioning may be highly structured or more flexible; self-report may be verbal or visual.	Can provide firsthand information about a person. Visual techniques (e.g., drawing, mapping, graphing) avoid need for verbal skills.	Participant may not remember information accurately or distort responses in a socially desirable way; how question is asked or by whom may affect answer.
Naturalistic observation	People are observed in their normal setting, with no attempt to manipulate behavior.	Provides good description of behavior; does not subject people to unnatural settings that may distort behavior.	Lack of control; observer bias.
Laboratory observation	Participants are observed in the laboratory, with no attempt to manipulate behavior.	Provides good descriptions; greater control than naturalistic observation because all participants are observed under same conditions.	Observer bias; controlled situation can be artificial.
Behavioral and performance measures	Participants are tested on abilities, skills, knowledge, competencies, or physical responses.	Provides objectively measurable information; avoids subjective distortions.	Cannot measure attitudes or other nonbehavioral phenomena; results may be affected by extraneous factors.

In a face-to-face or telephone *interview*, researchers ask questions about attitudes, opinions, or behavior. In a *structured* interview, each participant is asked the same set of questions. An *open-ended* interview is more flexible; the interviewer can vary the topics and order of questions and can ask follow-up questions based on the responses. To reach more people and to protect their privacy, researchers sometimes distribute a printed or online *questionnaire,* which participants fill out and return.

By questioning a large number of people, investigators can get a broad picture—at least of what the respondents *say* they believe or do or did. However, people willing to participate in interviews or fill out questionnaires may not accurately represent the population as a whole. Furthermore, heavy reliance on self-reports may be unwise because people may not have thought about what they feel and think or honestly may not know. They may forget when and how events took place or may consciously or unconsciously distort their replies to fit what is considered socially desirable.

Naturalistic and Laboratory Observation Observation takes two forms: *naturalistic observation* and *laboratory observation*. In **naturalistic observation,** researchers look at people in real-life settings. The researchers do not try to alter behavior or the environment; they simply record what they see. In **laboratory observation,** researchers observe and record behavior in a controlled environment, such as a laboratory.

Both kinds of observation can provide valuable descriptions of behavior, but they have limitations. For one, they do not explain *why* people behave as they do, though the observers may suggest interpretations. Then, too, an observer's presence can alter behavior. When people know they are being watched, they may act differently. Finally, there is a risk of *observer bias:* the researcher's tendency to interpret data to fit expectations or to emphasize some aspects and minimize others.

Behavioral and Performance Measures For quantitative research, investigators typically use more objective measures of behavior or performance instead of, or in addition to, self-reports or observation. Tests and other behavioral and neuropsychological

naturalistic observation
Research method in which behavior is studied in natural settings without intervention or manipulation.

laboratory observation
Research method in which all participants are observed under the same controlled conditions.

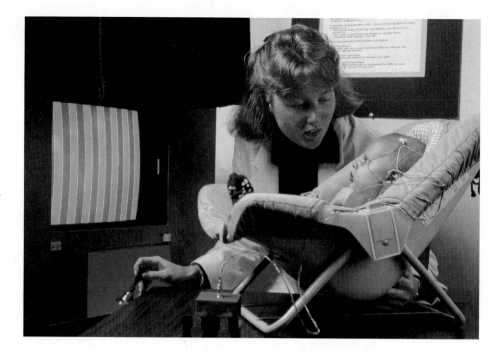

A baby under laboratory observation may or may not behave the same way as in a naturalistic setting, such as at home, but both kinds of observation can provide valuable information.
©Lawrence Migdale/Science Source

operational definition
Definition stated solely in terms of the operations or procedures used to produce or measure a phenomenon.

cognitive neuroscience
Study of links between neural processes and cognitive abilities.

measures may be used to assess abilities, skills, knowledge, competencies, or physiological responses, such as heart rate and brain activity.

Some written tests, such as intelligence tests, compare performance with that of other test-takers. Such tests can be meaningful and useful only if they are both *valid* (the tests measure the abilities they claim to measure) and *reliable* (the results are reasonably consistent from one time to another). To avoid bias, tests must be *standardized,* that is, given and scored by the same methods and criteria for all test-takers.

When measuring a characteristic such as intelligence, it is important to define exactly what is to be measured in a way that other researchers will understand so they can repeat the experiment and comment on the results. For this purpose, researchers use an **operational definition**—a definition stated solely in terms of the operations used to measure a phenomenon. Intelligence, for example, can be defined as the ability to achieve a certain score on a test covering logical relationships, memory, and vocabulary recognition. Some people may disagree with this definition, but no one can reasonably claim that it is not clear.

For most of the history of psychology, theorists and researchers studied cognitive processes apart from the physical structures of the brain in which these processes occur. Now, sophisticated imaging instruments, such as functional magnetic resonance imaging (fMRI) and positron emission tomography (PET), make it possible to see the brain in action, and the new field of **cognitive neuroscience** is linking our understanding of cognitive functioning with what happens in the brain.

EVALUATING QUANTITATIVE AND QUALITATIVE RESEARCH

Qualitative research has both strengths and limitations. On the positive side, findings of qualitative research can be a rich source of insights into attitudes and behavior. The interactive relationship between investigators and participants can humanize the research process and reveal information that would not emerge under the more impersonal conditions of quantitative research. On the other hand, qualitative research tends to be less rigorous and more subject to bias than quantitative research. Because samples are often small and usually not random, results are less generalizable and replicable than the results of quantitative research. The large volume of data makes analysis and interpretation time-consuming, and the quality of the findings and conclusions depends greatly on the skills of the researcher (Mathie & Carnozzi, 2005).

Yet the line between these methodologies is not necessarily clear-cut. Qualitative data may be analyzed quantitatively—for example, by statistical analysis of interview transcripts or videotaped observations to see how many times certain themes or behaviors occur. Conversely, quantitative data may be illuminated by qualitative research—for example, by interviews designed to examine the motivations and attitudes of children who make high scores on achievement tests (Yoshikawa, Weisner, Kalil & Way, 2008).

BASIC RESEARCH DESIGNS

A research design is a plan for conducting a scientific investigation: what questions are to be answered, how participants are to be selected, how data are to be collected and interpreted, and how valid conclusions can be drawn. Four basic designs used in developmental research are *case studies, ethnographic studies, correlational studies,* and *experiments.* The first two designs are qualitative; the last two are quantitative. Each design has advantages and drawbacks, and each is appropriate for certain kinds of research problems (Table 2.4).

Case Studies A **case study** is a study of an individual. Some theories, such as Freud's, grew out of clinical case studies, which included careful observation and interpretation of what patients said and did. Case studies also may use behavioral or physiological measures and biographical, autobiographical, or documentary materials. Case studies are particularly useful when studying something relatively rare, when it simply is not possible to find a large enough group of people with the characteristic in question to conduct a traditional laboratory study. They can explore sources of behavior and can test treatments, and they suggest directions for further research.

Case studies do have shortcomings, however. Using case studies, we can learn much about the development of a single person, but not how the information applies to people

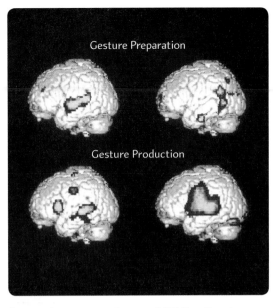

Researchers can analyze an fMRI (functional magnetic resonance imaging) brain scan taken during an activity or task to observe the link between cognitive activity and what happens in the brain. The regions shown in red are activated when thinking about making a gesture (preparation) and then in performing it (production). ©WDCN/University College London/Science Source

case study
Study of a single subject, such as an individual or family.

TABLE 2.4 Basic Research Designs

Type	Main Characteristics	Advantages	Disadvantages
Case study	In-depth study of single individual.	Flexibility; provides detailed picture of one person's behavior and development; can generate hypotheses.	May not generalize to others; conclusions not directly testable; cannot establish cause and effect.
Ethnographic study	In-depth study of a culture or subculture.	Can help overcome culturally based biases in theory and research; can test universality of phenomena.	Subject to observer bias.
Correlational study	Attempt to find positive or negative relationship between variables.	Enables prediction of one variable on basis of another; can suggest hypotheses about causal relationships.	Cannot establish cause and effect.
Experiment	Controlled procedure in which an experimenter controls the independent variable to determine its effect on the dependent variable; may be conducted in the laboratory or field.	Establishes cause-and-effect relationships; highest degree of control, and can be repeated by another investigator.	Findings, especially when derived from laboratory experiments, may not generalize to situations outside the laboratory.

in general. Furthermore, case studies cannot explain behavior with certainty or make strong causal statements because there is no way to test their conclusions.

Ethnographic Studies An **ethnographic study** seeks to describe the pattern of relationships, customs, beliefs, technology, arts, and traditions that make up a society's way of life. In a way, it is like a case study of a culture. Ethnographic research can be qualitative, quantitative, or both. It uses a combination of methods, including informal, unstructured interviewing and **participant observation.** Participant observation is a form of naturalistic observation in which researchers live or participate in the societies or smaller groups they observe, as anthropologists often do for long periods of time.

Because of ethnographers' involvement in the events or societies they are observing, their findings are especially open to observer bias. On the positive side, ethnographic research can help overcome cultural biases in theory and research (Window on the World). Ethnography demonstrates the error of assuming that principles developed from research in Western cultures are universally applicable.

Correlational Studies A **correlational study** seeks to determine whether a *correlation,* or statistical relationship, exists between *variables,* phenomena that change or vary among people or can be varied for purposes of research. Correlations are expressed in terms of direction (positive or negative) and magnitude (degree). Two variables that are correlated *positively* increase or decrease together. Studies show a positive, or direct, correlation between televised violence and aggression. That is, children who watch more violent television tend to fight more than children who watch less violent television. Two variables have a *negative,* or inverse, correlation if, as one increases, the other decreases. Studies show a negative correlation between amount of schooling and the risk of developing dementia (mental deterioration) due to Alzheimer's disease in old age. In other words, the less education, the more dementia (Katzman, 1993).

Correlations are reported as numbers ranging from -1.0 (a perfect negative relationship) to $+1.0$ (a perfect positive relationship). The closer a correlation comes to $+1.0$ or -1.0, the stronger the relationship, either positive or negative. A correlation of zero means that the variables have no relationship.

Correlations enable us to predict one variable in relation to another. On the basis of the positive correlation between watching televised violence and aggression, we can predict that children who watch violent shows are more likely to get into fights than children who do *not* watch such shows. The greater the magnitude of the correlation between the two variables, the greater the ability to predict one from the other.

Although strong correlations suggest possible cause-and-effect relationships, these are merely hypotheses. We cannot be sure from a positive correlation between televised violence and aggressiveness that watching televised violence *causes* aggression; we can conclude only that the two variables are related. It is possible that the causation goes the other way: Aggressive behavior may lead children to watch more violent programs. Or a third variable—perhaps an inborn predisposition toward aggressiveness—may cause a child *both* to watch violent programs and to act aggressively. The only way to show with certainty that one variable causes another is through experimentation.

Experiments An **experiment** is a controlled procedure in which the experimenter manipulates variables to learn how one affects another. Scientific experiments must be conducted and reported in such a way that another experimenter can *replicate* them, that is, repeat them in exactly the same way with different participants to verify the results and conclusions.

Groups and Variables A common way to conduct an experiment is to divide the participants into two kinds of groups. An **experimental group** consists of people who are to be exposed to the experimental manipulation or *treatment*—the phenomenon the researcher wants to study. Afterward, the effect of the treatment will be measured one or more times

Sidebar definitions

ethnographic study
In-depth study of a culture, which uses a combination of methods including participant observation.

participant observation
Research method in which the observer lives with the people or participates in the activity being observed.

correlational study
Research design intended to discover whether a statistical relationship between variables exists.

experiment
Rigorously controlled, replicable procedure in which the researcher manipulates variables to assess the effect of one on the other.

experimental group
In an experiment, the group receiving the treatment under study.

window on the world

PURPOSES OF CROSS-CULTURAL RESEARCH

When David, a European American child, was asked to identify the missing detail in a picture of a face with no mouth, he said, "The mouth." Ari, an Asian immigrant child in Israel, said the body was missing. As art in his culture did not typically present a head as a complete picture, he thought the absence of a body was more important than the omission of "a mere detail like the mouth" (Anastasi, 1988, p. 360). One might wonder if perception of art is culturally influenced, or tends to be similar across all children. By looking at children from different cultural groups, researchers can learn in what ways development is universal and in what ways it is culturally determined. This is the value of cross-cultural research.

For example, research has shown us children everywhere learn to speak in the same sequence, advancing from cooing and babbling to single words and then to simple combinations of words. The words vary from culture to culture, but toddlers around the world put them together in the same ways to form sentences. These findings suggest that the capacity for learning language is universal and innate.

Research has also shown us culture seems to exert an influence on early motor development. African babies, whose parents often prop them in a sitting position and bounce them on their feet, tend to sit and walk earlier than U.S. babies (Rogoff & Morelli, 1989). The society in which children grow up also influences the skills they learn. In the United States, children learn to read, write, and, increasingly, to operate computers. In rural Nepal, they learn how to drive water buffalo and find their way along mountain paths.

A majority of the research in child development has focused on Western industrialized societies. Typical development in these societies is often interpreted as the norm, or standard of behavior, for all societies. Measuring against this Westernized norm can lead to incorrect ideas about development in other cultures and beliefs that children are not developing appropriately if they deviate from these norms (Rogoff & Morelli, 1989).

Barriers exist to our understanding of cultural differences. As with David and Ari in our opening example, a question or task may have different conceptual meanings for different cultural groups. Sometimes the barriers are linguistic. In a study of children's understanding of kinship relations among the Zinacanta people of Chiapas, Mexico (Greenfield & Childs, 1978), instead of asking, "How many brothers do you have?" the researchers, knowing that the Zinacantas have separate terms for older and younger siblings, asked, "What is the name of your older brother?" Using the same question across cultures might have obscured, rather than revealed, cultural differences and similarities (Parke, 2004b). As seen in this example, it is important for researchers to understand the cultures they are researching before drawing conclusions.

Researchers also need to account for their own perspective when they are observing other cultures. In one study, European American observers noted more conflict and restrictiveness in African American mother-daughter relationships than African American observers noted (Gonzales, Cauce & Mason, 1996). As seen in this example, results can be influenced by the culture of the researchers.

Research has shown that there are cultural differences in gender roles, abstract thinking, moral reasoning, motor development, skill development as well as social and emotional development. It is important to understand how closely many components of development tie to society and culture. As learners, we need to keep in mind that development is different across many cultures and take the time to understand and embrace these differences.

what's your view

Can you think of a situation in which you made an incorrect assumption about a person because you were unfamiliar with her or his cultural background? Do you think it is possible for people to be truly objective when they view others' behavior?

---

to find out what changes, if any, it caused. A **control group** consists of people who are similar to the experimental group but do not receive the experimental treatment or may receive a different treatment. An experiment may include one or more of each type of group. If the experimenter wants to compare the effects of different treatments (say, of two methods of teaching), the overall sample may be divided into *treatment groups,* each

control group
In an experiment, a group of people, similar to those in the experimental group, who do not receive the treatment under study.

of which receives one of the treatments under study. To ensure objectivity, some experiments, particularly in medical research, use *double-blind* procedures, in which neither participants nor experimenters know who is receiving the treatment and who is instead receiving an inert *placebo*.

One team of researchers wanted to find out if 11-month-old infants could be trained to focus their attention (Wass, Porayska-Pomsta & Johnson, 2011). The researchers brought 42 infants to their laboratory and had them participate in a variety of tasks. Half of the infants were given about an hour of attentional training. This training required babies to use sustained gaze to make a fun event happen on a computer. For example, if babies fixated on an elephant, the elephant became animated. If the babies looked away, the elephant stopped moving. The other group of children were shown television clips and animations, but were not trained. At the end of 2 weeks, the babies were tested on a series of cognitive tasks. Babies who underwent the training performed better on the tasks than did the babies who were not trained. It is reasonable to conclude, then, that the attentional training improved the babies' performance on the tasks as it was the only thing varied between the two groups.

In this experiment, the type of activity (training versus watching television) was the *independent variable,* and the children's test performance the *dependent variable.* An **independent variable** is something over which the experimenter has direct control. A **dependent variable** is something that may or may not change as a result of changes in the independent variable; in other words, it *depends* on the independent variable. In an experiment, a researcher manipulates the independent variable to see how changes in it will affect the dependent variable. The hypothesis for a study states how a researcher thinks the independent variable affects the dependent variable.

Random Assignment If an experiment finds a significant difference in the performance of the experimental and control groups, how do we know that the cause was the independent variable? For example, in the attentional training experiment, how can we be sure that the training and not some other factor (such as intelligence) caused the difference in test performance of the two groups? The best way to control for effects of such extraneous factors is **random assignment:** assigning the participants to groups in such a way that each person has an equal chance of being placed in any group.

If assignment is random and the sample is large enough, differences in such factors as age, gender, and ethnicity will be evenly distributed so that the groups initially are as alike as possible in every respect except for the variable to be tested. Otherwise, unintended differences between the groups might *confound,* or contaminate, the results, and any conclusions drawn from the experiment would have to be viewed with suspicion. To control for confounds, the experimenter must make sure that everything except the independent variable is held constant during the course of the experiment.

Of course, with respect to some variables we might want to study, such as age, gender, and race/ethnicity, random assignment is not possible. We cannot assign Terry to be 5 years old and Brett to be 10, or one to be a boy and the other a girl. When studying such a variable researchers can strengthen the validity of their conclusions by randomly selecting participants and by trying to make sure that they are statistically equivalent in other ways that might make a difference in the study.

Laboratory, Field, and Natural Experiments There are various ways to conduct research, and one essential distinction is between laboratory, field, and natural experiments. A laboratory experiment is best for determining cause and effect. It generally consists of asking participants to visit a laboratory where they are subject to conditions manipulated by the experimenter. The tight control of a laboratory study allows researchers to be more certain that their independent variable caused change in their dependent variable; however, because of the artificiality of the laboratory experience, the results may be less generalizable to real life.

A field experiment is a controlled study conducted in an everyday setting, such as a home or school. Variables can still be manipulated, so causal claims can still be investigated. Because the experiments occur in the real world, there is more confidence that

independent variable
In an experiment, the condition over which the experimenter has direct control.

dependent variable
In an experiment, the condition that may or may not change as a result of changes in the independent variable.

random assignment
Assignment of participants in an experiment to groups in such a way that each person has an equal chance of being placed in any group.

the behaviors that are seen are generalizable to natural behaviors. However, researchers have less control over events that may occur—the real world is often messy, and things do not always go as planned.

When, for practical or ethical reasons, it is impossible to conduct a true experiment, a *natural experiment,* also called a *quasi-experiment,* may provide a way of studying certain events. A natural experiment compares people who have been accidentally "assigned" to separate groups by circumstances of life—one group who were exposed, say, to famine or HIV or superior education, and another group who were not. A natural experiment, despite its name, is actually a correlational study because controlled manipulation of variables and random assignment to treatment groups are not possible.

Controlled experiments have two important advantages over other research designs: They can establish cause-and-effect relationships, and they permit replication. However, such experiments can be too artificial and too narrowly focused. In recent decades, many researchers have concentrated less on laboratory experimentation or have supplemented it with a wider array of methods.

DEVELOPMENTAL RESEARCH DESIGNS

One of the primary goals of developmental research is to study change over time, and developmental psychologists have developed a variety of methods to do so. The two most common research strategies are *cross-sectional* and *longitudinal studies* (Figure 2.3). A **cross-sectional study** most clearly illustrates similarities or differences among people of different ages; a **longitudinal study** tracks people over time and focuses on individual change with age. Both designs have pros and cons. A third type of study, a **sequential study,** combines the two approaches to minimize the drawbacks of the separate approaches.

Cross-Sectional, Longitudinal, and Sequential Studies In a cross-sectional study, children of different ages are assessed at one point in time. For example, in one cross-sectional study, researchers asked children from 7 months to 5 years to pick one of two objects, which were identical with the exception that one object was always pink, and the other was either green, blue, yellow, or orange. The researchers found that girls showed no preference for pink objects until age 2, when they began to reach for the pink object more frequently. The girls increasingly preferred the pink object as they aged. Boys, however, showed a different pattern. Like girls, they initially showed no preference for pink over the other colors. Starting at about 2 years of age, however, they became less and less likely to choose the pink object. The researchers concluded that girls' preference for the color pink was learned over time, and they theorized that it was related to the acquisition of knowledge about gender (LoBue & DeLoache, 2011).

Can we draw this conclusion with certainty? The problem with cross-sectional studies is that we cannot know whether the 5-year-olds' preference for certain colors when they were under the age of 2 years was the same as that of the current babies in the study. We cannot be certain that this is a developmental change rather than merely a difference in formative experiences for the two age groups. For example, if a popular television program that targets children over the age of 2 and that strongly promotes gender stereotypes had been introduced in the year previous to the study, the older children might show color preferences as a result of watching the show and not because of an increased understanding of gender. Although it may appear to be a change related to age, it might instead be the result of television programming.

The only way to know whether change occurs with age is to conduct a longitudinal study of a particular person or group. In a longitudinal study, researchers study the same person or group of people over time, sometimes years apart.

cross-sectional study
Study designed to assess age-related differences, in which people of different ages are assessed on one occasion.

longitudinal study
Study designed to assess age changes in a sample over time.

sequential study
Study design that combines cross-sectional and longitudinal techniques.

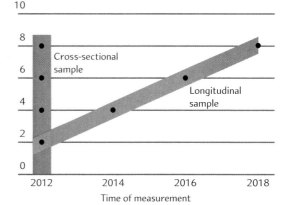

FIGURE 2.3
Developmental Research Designs

In the cross-sectional study, groups of 2-, 4-, 6-, and 8-year-olds were tested in 2012 to obtain data about age-related differences. In the longitudinal study, a sample of children were first measured in 2012, when they were 2 years old; follow-up testing is done when the children are 4, 6, and 8, to measure age-related changes. Note: Dots indicate times of measurement.

TABLE 2.5 Cross-Sectional, Longitudinal, and Sequential Research: Pros and Cons

Type of Study	Procedure	Advantages	Disadvantages
Cross-sectional	Data are collected on people of different ages at the same time.	Can show similarities and differences among age groups; speedy, economical; no attrition or repeated testing.	Cannot establish age effects; masks individual differences; can be confounded by cohort effects.
Longitudinal	Data are collected on same person or persons over a period of time.	Can show age-related change or continuity; avoids confounding age with cohort effects.	Is time-consuming, expensive; presents problems of attrition, bias in sample, and effects of repeated testing; results may be valid only for cohort tested or sample studied.
Sequential	Data are collected on successive cross-sectional or longitudinal samples.	Can avoid drawbacks of both cross-sectional and longitudinal designs.	Requires large amount of time and effort and analysis of very complex data.

One large longitudinal study examined the Internet habits of 754 people and the relationship their Internet usage had with loneliness. Researchers found that over the course of a year, more web browsing was associated with an increase in a global loneliness measure (Stepanikova, Nie & He, 2010). Just as with cross-sectional designs, there is a caveat. Because individual people are studied over time, researchers have access to each person's specific individual trajectory. However, the results from one cohort might not apply to a study of a different cohort. The study used data collected from 2004 to 2005, and the link between browsing history and loneliness might differ now.

In attempting to determine the best research design, neither cross-sectional nor longitudinal design is superior. Rather, both designs have strengths and weaknesses (Table 2.5). For example, cross-sectional design is fast—we don't have to wait 30 years for results. This also makes it a more economical choice. Moreover, because participants are assessed only once, we don't have to consider attrition (people dropping out of the study) or repeated testing (which can produce practice effects). But cross-sectional design uses group averages, so individual differences and trajectories may be obscured. More important, the results can be affected by the differing experiences of people born at different times, as previously explained.

Longitudinal research shows a different and complementary set of strengths and weaknesses. Because the same people are studied over time, researchers can track individual patterns of continuity and change. This is more time-consuming and expensive than cross-sectional studies. In addition, repeated testing of participants can result in practice effects. For example, your performance on an intelligence test might get better over time from practice rather than from any increase in intelligence. Attrition can be problematic in longitudinal research as well because it tends to be nonrandom, which can introduce a positive bias to the study. Those who stay with the study tend to be above average in intelligence and socioeconomic status, and those who drop out tend to have more chaotic lives and worse overall outcomes. Moreover, practical issues, such as turnover in research personnel, loss of funding, or the development of new measures or methodologies, can introduce potential problems with data collection.

Researchers are attempting to overcome the drawbacks of longitudinal and cross-sectional design with the design of sequential studies. Sequential designs track people of different ages (like cross-sectional designs) over time (like longitudinal designs). The combination of cross-sectional and longitudinal designs (as shown in Figure 2.4) allows researchers to separate age-related changes from cohort effects, and provides a more complete picture of development than would be possible with either design alone. The

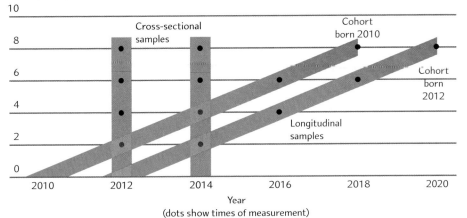

Age of participants (years)

FIGURE 2.4

A Sequential Design

Two successive cross-sectional groups of 2-, 4-, 6-, and 8-year-olds were tested in 2012 and 2014. Also, a longitudinal study of a group of children first measured in 2012, when they were 2 years old, is followed by a similar longitudinal study of another group of children who were 2 years old in 2014.

major drawbacks of sequential studies relate to time, effort, and complexity. Sequential designs require large numbers of participants and collection and analysis of huge amounts of data over a period of years. Interpreting these findings and conclusions can demand a high degree of sophistication.

Ethics of Research

Should research that might harm its participants ever be undertaken? How can we balance the possible benefits against the risk of mental, emotional, or physical injury to individuals?

Institutional review boards at colleges, universities, and other institutions review proposed research from an ethical standpoint. Guidelines of the American Psychological Association (APA, 2002) cover such issues as *informed consent* (consent freely given with full knowledge of what the research entails), *avoidance of deception,* protection of participants from *harm and loss of dignity,* guarantees of *privacy and confidentiality,* the *right to decline or withdraw* from an experiment at any time, and the responsibility of investigators to *correct any undesirable effects,* such as anxiety or shame.

In resolving ethical dilemmas, researchers should be guided by three principles. The first is *beneficence,* which is the obligation to maximize potential benefits to participants and to minimize potential harm. For example, suppose you are a researcher studying the effect of failure on self-esteem. If you are going to deceive some of your participants by telling them they failed on a laboratory task, what steps will you take to mitigate any potential harm you might cause them? The second principle is *respect* for participants' autonomy and protection of those who are unable to exercise their own judgment. For example, if you are conducting research with toddlers, and a 2-year-old refuses to participate, should you force the child to participate? What is the appropriate action in this case? The third principle is *justice,* which, in this case, is the inclusion of diverse groups together with sensitivity to any special impact the research may have on them. For example, it may be important that your study includes an appropriate and representative selection of diverse people. If this is the case, have you developed culturally appropriate materials and methods to use?

Developmental psychologists must be particularly careful as their research frequently involves vulnerable individuals, such as infants or children. In response, the Society for Research in Child Development (2007) has developed standards for age-appropriate treatment of children in research, covering such principles as avoidance of physical or psychological harm, obtaining the child's assent as well as a parent's or guardian's informed consent, and responsibility to follow up on any information that could jeopardize the child's well-being.

research in action

PRENATAL ALCOHOL RESEARCH

What would you think if you saw a pregnant women sitting down to dinner with a glass of wine? Is the woman being selfish and endangering her fetus? Should she be prevented from drinking alcohol?

In 2016, New York City enacted a law prohibiting bartenders from refusing to serve pregnant women (McPhate, 2016). On one side, proponents argued it is the woman's choice whether to drink alcohol or abstain, and furthermore, the risk of drinking small amounts of alcohol is minimal. On the other side, critics argue that any alcohol is an unacceptable risk and that fetuses need to be protected. Tennessee, Alabama, and South Carolina have even gone so far as to prosecute women who use drugs—alcohol included—while pregnant (Miranda, Dixon & Reyes, 2015).

Why does this ambiguity exist regarding the effects of alcohol in pregnant women? Why can't scientists determine what, if any, is a safe level of alcohol for a developing fetus, and base legal action around that?

The answer to this question lies in experimental ethics. The gold standard in experimental research of this nature is a randomized, double-blind design, where, for example, half of pregnant women would be assigned to drink alcohol and half would be asked to abstain. They could be offered the same level of prenatal care, and also matched for factors such as race, age, or socioeconomic status. Then, the effects of alcohol could be studied more definitively. By doing this across multiple studies with differing levels of alcohol exposure, we could theoretically determine what a "safe" amount might be. But this type of study would violate the principle of beneficence—that researchers do no harm to their participants. A study such as the one outlined above would expose the pregnancies to unacceptable risk.

Conducting research is a balancing act between what critical thinking and theoretical concerns would lead us to do in an ideal world in order to best answer a question, and the ethical and pragmatic concerns of the real world. Given this, what options for research are left?

One option is the use of animal models. However, concerns about the use of alcohol in pregnancy are centered on the brain. While other animals might tell us about basic processes, they cannot tell us how alcohol would ultimately affect a human brain. This is particularly true if we are talking about subtle forms of brain damage or variations in executive control.

Another option is correlational designs, where women are surveyed about their alcohol usage during pregnancy and their babies are assessed. While this can answer many questions for us—for example, we know that heavy drinking is associated with fetal alcohol syndrome—the messiness of the real world does not allow us to tease out a detailed understanding. For instance, a woman may use multiple substances throughout pregnancy, including legal and illegal drugs (Forray & Foster, 2015), and thus the identification of negative effects often involves disentangling multiple drug interactions. Researchers also have difficulty distinguishing the effects of prenatal drug exposure from other risk factors, such as poor nutrition, lack of prenatal care, and chaotic social environment (Forray & Foster, 2015). Last, it is reasonable to suspect that women who continue to drink throughout their pregnancy might differ in other ways from women who abstain.

All these factors serve to muddle the conclusions that can be reached on the basis of correlational research. Thus, the best we can do now is to definitively state that high alcohol consumption is dangerous to a pregnancy, and that there is no "safe" limit known.

what's your view

What do you think about the impact of universal drug-screening policies or stiff criminal penalties on pregnant women with substance use disorders and their unborn babies? Do you think the same ethical questions exist for research into the use of illegal drugs, such as heroin or methamphetamine?

summary and key terms

Basic Theoretical Issues

- A theory is used to organize and explain data and generate testable hypotheses.
- Developmental theories differ on two basic issues: the active or reactive character of development and the existence of continuity or discontinuity in development.
- Two contrasting models of human development are the mechanistic model and the organismic model.

  theory, hypotheses, mechanistic model, organismic model, quantitative change, qualitative change

Theoretical Perspectives

- The psychoanalytic perspective sees development as motivated by unconscious emotional drives or conflicts. Leading examples are Freud's and Erikson's theories.

  psychoanalytic perspective, psychosexual development, psychosocial development

- The learning perspective views development as a result of learning based on experience. Leading examples are Watson's and Skinner's behaviorism and Bandura's social learning (social cognitive) theory.

  learning perspective, behaviorism, classical conditioning, operant conditioning, reinforcement, punishment, social learning theory, reciprocal determinism, observational learning, self-efficacy

- The cognitive perspective is concerned with thought processes. Leading examples are Piaget's cognitive-stage theory, Vygotsky's sociocultural theory, and the information-processing approach.

  cognitive perspective, cognitive-stage theory, organization, schemes, adaptation, assimilation, accommodation, equilibration, sociocultural theory, zone of proximal development (ZPD), scaffolding, information-processing approach

- The contextual perspective focuses on the individual in a social context. A leading example is Bronfenbrenner's bioecological theory.

  contextual perspective, bioecological theory

- The evolutionary/sociobiological perspective, influenced by Darwin's theory of evolution, focuses on the adaptiveness of behavior. A leading example is Bowlby's attachment theory.

  evolutionary/sociobiological perspective, ethology, evolutionary psychology

Research Methods

- Research can be either quantitative or qualitative, or both.
- To arrive at sound conclusions, quantitative researchers use the scientific method.
- Random selection of a research sample can ensure generalizability.
- Three forms of data collection are self-reports, observation, and behavioral and performance measures.

  quantitative research, scientific method, qualitative research, sample, random selection, naturalistic observation, laboratory observation, operational definition, cognitive neuroscience

- A design is a plan for conducting research. Two qualitative designs used in developmental research are the case study and the ethnographic study. Cross-cultural research can indicate whether certain aspects of development are universal or culturally influenced.
- Two quantitative designs are the correlational study and the experiment. Only experiments can firmly establish causal relationships.
- Experiments must be rigorously controlled to be valid and replicable. Random assignment of participants can help ensure validity.
- Laboratory experiments are easiest to control and replicate, but findings of field experiments may be more generalizable. Natural experiments may be useful in situations in which true experiments would be impractical or unethical.
- The two most common designs used to study age-related development are cross-sectional and longitudinal. Cross-sectional studies assess age differences; longitudinal studies describe continuity or change in the same participants. The sequential study is intended to overcome the weaknesses of the other two designs.

  case study, ethnographic study, participant observation, correlational study, experiment, experimental group, control group, independent variable, dependent variable, random assignment, cross-sectional study, longitudinal study, sequential study

Ethics of Research

- Researchers seek to resolve ethical issues on the basis of principles of beneficence, respect, and justice.
- Ethical issues in research include the rights of participants to informed consent, avoidance of deception, protection from harm and loss of dignity and self-esteem, and guarantees of privacy and confidentiality.
- There are special standards for protection of children used in research.

chapter 3

Forming a New Life

learning objectives

Explain how conception occurs and what causes multiple births.

Describe the mechanisms of heredity in normal and abnormal human development.

Explain how heredity and environment interact in human development.

Describe prenatal development, including environmental influences.

Discuss the importance of high-quality prenatal care.

©Flashon Studio/Shutterstock

We describe how conception normally occurs, how the mechanisms of heredity operate, and how biological inheritance interacts with environmental influences within and outside the womb. We trace the course of prenatal development, describe influences on it, and discuss ways to monitor it.

Conceiving New Life

Most people think of development as beginning on the day of birth, when the new child—squalling and thrashing—is introduced to the world. However, development starts at conception, as sperm and egg meet and an entirely new individual is created. Development continues as the fertilized egg grows and differentiates and edges closer to independent life outside the womb. And it persists in the dance between nature and nurture that shapes the unique individual that is the product of these processes. This chapter is about that story.

HOW FERTILIZATION TAKES PLACE

Fertilization, or *conception,* is the process by which sperm and ovum—the male and female *gametes,* or sex cells—combine to create a single cell called a **zygote,** which then duplicates itself again and again by cell division to produce all the cells that make up a baby.

At birth, a girl is believed to have about 2 million immature ova in her two ovaries, each ovum in its own *follicle,* or small sac. In a sexually mature woman, *ovulation*—rupture of a mature follicle in either ovary and expulsion of its ovum—occurs about once every 28 days until menopause. The ovum is swept along through one of the fallopian tubes by the *cilia,* tiny hair cells, toward the uterus, or womb.

Sperm are produced in the testicles (testes), or reproductive glands, of a mature male at a rate of several hundred million a day and are ejaculated in the semen at sexual climax. Deposited in the vagina, they try to swim through the *cervix,* the opening of the uterus, and into the fallopian tubes; but only a tiny fraction make it that far. Fertilization normally occurs while the ovum is passing through the fallopian tube.

WHAT CAUSES MULTIPLE BIRTHS?

Multiple births happen in two ways. Although twins are the most common variation, triplets, quadruplets, and other multiple births are possible.

Dizygotic twins, or fraternal twins, are the result of two separate eggs being fertilized by two different sperm to form two unique individuals. Genetically, they are like siblings who inhabit the same womb at the same time, and they can be the same or different sex. Dizygotic twins tend to run in families and are the result of multiple eggs being released at one time. This tendency may have a genetic basis and seems to be passed down from a woman's mother (Martin & Montgomery, 2002; National Center for Health Statistics [NCHS], 1999). When dizygotic twins skip generations, it is normally because a mother of dizygotic twins has only sons to whom she cannot pass on the tendency (NCHS, 1999).

Monozygotic twins result from the cleaving of one fertilized egg and are generally genetically identical. They can still differ outwardly, however, because people are the result of the interaction between genes and environmental influences. For example, in one condition that affects only monozygotic twins (twin-to-twin transfusion syndrome), the blood vessels of the placenta form abnormally, and the placenta is shared unequally between the twins. One twin receives a smaller share of nutrients than does the other. Mortality is high, but if both twins survive, one twin will be significantly larger than the other at birth despite being genetically identical.

Moreover, environmental differences add up over time. The differences between identical twins generally magnify as twins grow older. So, for example, 3-year-old monozygotic twins appear more similar than 30-year-old monozygotic twins. These differences may result from chemical modifications in a person's genome shortly after conception or may be due to later experiences or environmental factors, such as exposure to smoke or other pollutants (Bell & Saffery, 2012; Fraga et al., 2005). This process, known as *epigenesis*, is discussed later in this chapter.

fertilization
Union of sperm and ovum to produce a zygote; also called *conception*.

zygote
One-celled organism resulting from fertilization.

dizygotic twins
Twins conceived by the union of two different ova with two different sperm cells; also called *fraternal twins*; they are no more alike genetically than any other siblings.

monozygotic twins
Twins resulting from the division of a single zygote after fertilization; also called *identical twins*; they are genetically similar.

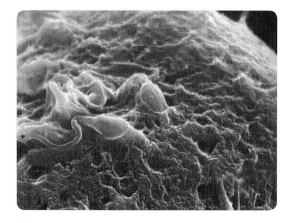

This color-enhanced scanning electron micrograph (SEM) shows two sperm (orange) attracted to an ovum's blue surface. A sperm's long tail enables it to swim through the cervix and up the fallopian tube. The sperm's rounded head releases enzymes that help it penetrate the ovum's thick surface and fertilize the ovum by fusing with its nucleus.
©Pascal Goetgheluck/Science Source

The rate of monozygotic twins (slightly under 4 per 1,000 live births) appears to be constant at all times and places, but the rate of dizygotic twins, the more common type, varies (Smits & Monden, 2011). The incidence of multiple births in the United States has grown rapidly since 1980. By 2009 the twin birthrate had risen by 76 percent, from 18.9 to 33.3 twins per 1,000 live births (Martin, Hamilton & Osterman, 2012). Two related factors in the rise in multiple births are (1) the trend toward delayed childbearing and (2) the increased use of fertility drugs, which spur ovulation, and of assisted reproductive techniques such as in vitro fertilization, which tend to be used by older women (Martin, Kirmeyer, Osterman & Shepherd, 2009).

The explosion of multiple births, especially triplets and higher multiples, is of concern because such births, which often result from assisted reproduction, are associated with increased risks: pregnancy complications, premature delivery, low-birth-weight infants, and disability or death of the infant. Perhaps because of such concerns, the proportion of assisted reproduction procedures involving three or more embryos has declined, and the birthrate for triplets and higher multiples, which had quadrupled during the 1980s and 1990s, has since taken a downturn (Martin, Hamilton, Osterman, Driscoll & Mathews, 2017).

Mechanisms of Heredity

The science of genetics is the study of *heredity:* the genetic transmission of heritable characteristics from parents to offspring. When ovum and sperm unite, they endow the baby-to-be with a genetic makeup that influences a wide range of characteristics from color of eyes and hair to health, intellect, and personality.

THE GENETIC CODE

The genetic code is transmitted via a molecule called **deoxyribonucleic acid (DNA).** The double-helix structure of a DNA molecule resembles a long, spiraling ladder whose steps are made of pairs of chemical units called *bases* (Figure 3.1). The bases—adenine (A), thymine (T), cytosine (C), and guanine (G)—are the "letters" of the **genetic code,** which cellular machinery "reads."

Chromosomes are coils of DNA that consist of smaller segments called **genes,** the functional units of heredity. Each gene is located in a definite position on its chromosome and contains thousands of bases. The sequence of bases in a gene tells the cell how to make the proteins that enable it to carry out specific functions. The complete sequence of genes in the human body constitutes the **human genome.** Of course, every human has a unique genome. The human genome is not meant to be a recipe for making a particular human. Rather, the human genome is a reference point, or representative genome, that shows the location of all human genes.

A useful analogy is to consider the DNA of an individual as a series of books in a library. Until those books are "read" by an enzyme called RNA polymerase and transcribed into a readable copy of messenger RNA (m-RNA), the knowledge contained within the books is not actualized. And what books will be pulled down from the shelf and read is in part determined by environmental factors that turn genes on and off at different points in development (Champagne & Mashoodh, 2009).

Every cell in the normal human body except the sex cells (sperm and ova) has 23 pairs of chromosomes—46 chromosomes in all. Through a type of cell division called *meiosis,* which the sex cells undergo when they are developing, each sex cell ends up with only 23 chromosomes—one from each pair. When sperm and ovum fuse at conception, they produce a zygote with 46 chromosomes, 23 from the father and 23 from the mother (Figure 3.2).

At conception, then, the single-celled zygote has all the biological information needed to guide its development into a unique individual. Through *mitosis,*

deoxyribonucleic acid (DNA)
Chemical that carries inherited instructions for the development of all cellular forms of life.

genetic code
Sequence of bases within the DNA molecule; governs the formation of proteins that determine the structure and functions of living cells.

chromosomes
Coils of DNA that consist of genes.

genes
Small segments of DNA located in definite positions on particular chromosomes; functional units of heredity.

human genome
Complete sequence of genes in the human body.

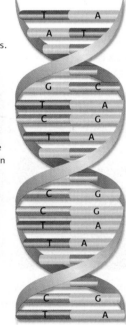

DNA is the genetic material in all living cells. It consists of four chemical units, called bases. These bases are the letters of the DNA alphabet. A (adenine) pairs with T (thymine) and C (cytosine) pairs with G (guanine). There are 3 billion base pairs in human DNA.

T = Thymine
A = Adenine
G = Guanine
C = Cytosine

FIGURE 3.1
DNA: The Genetic Code

Source: Adapted from Ritter, J. "Scientists close in on DNA code." *Chicago Sun-Times,* November 23, 1999, p. 7.

a process by which the non-sex cells divide in half over and over again, the DNA replicates itself, so that each newly formed cell has the same DNA structure as all the others. Each cell division creates a genetic duplicate of the original cell, with the same hereditary information. As the cells divide, they differentiate, specializing in a variety of complex bodily functions that enable the child to grow and develop. Sometimes a mistake in copying is made, and a **mutation** may result. Mutations are permanent alterations in genetic material, most of which are harmful.

Genes spring into action when conditions call for the information they can provide. Sometimes this may be triggered by internal processes such as hormones. Other times they are affected by such environmental conditions as nutrition and stress. Thus, from the start, heredity and environment are interrelated.

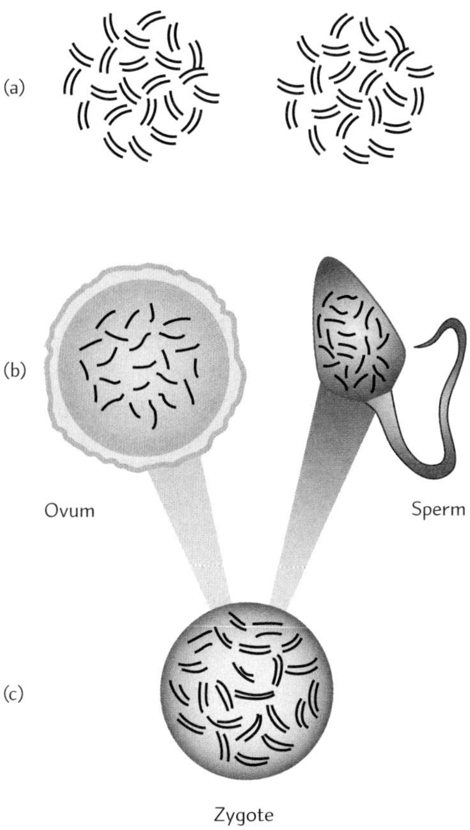

(a)

(b)

Ovum   Sperm

(c)

Zygote

Source: Adapted from Babu & Hirschhorn, 1992; March of Dimes Birth Defects Foundation, 1987.

FIGURE 3.2
Hereditary Composition of the Zygote

(a) Body cells of women and men contain 23 pairs of chromosomes, which carry the genes, the basic units of inheritance. (b) Each sex cell (ovum and sperm) has only 23 single chromosomes because of a special kind of cell division (meiosis). (c) At fertilization, the 23 chromosomes from the sperm join the 23 from the ovum so that the zygote receives 46 chromosomes, or 23 pairs.

WHAT DETERMINES SEX?

At the moment of conception, the 23 chromosomes from the sperm and the 23 from the ovum form 23 pairs. Twenty-two pairs are **autosomes,** chromosomes that are not related to sexual expression. The twenty-third pair are **sex chromosomes**—one from the father and one from the mother—that govern the baby's sex.

Sex chromosomes are either *X chromosomes* or *Y chromosomes*. Genetic females are XX, genetic males are XY. Thus, mothers pass on only X chromosomes, but a father's sperm may contain either an X or a Y chromosome. When an ovum (X) is fertilized by an X-carrying sperm, the zygote formed is XX, a genetic female. When an ovum (X) is fertilized by a Y-carrying sperm, the resulting zygote is XY, a genetic male (Figure 3.3). Thus, it is the father's sperm that genetically determines a child's sex.

Initially, the embryo's rudimentary reproductive system appears almost identical in males and in females. However, on the Y chromosome is a gene called the *SRY* gene. Research with mice has found that once hormones signal the *SRY* gene to turn on, cell differentiation and formation of the testes is triggered. At 6 to 8 weeks after conception, the testes start to produce the male hormone testosterone. Exposure of a genetically male embryo to steady, high levels of testosterone ordinarily results in the development of a male body with male sexual organs (Kashimada & Koopman, 2010; Hughes, 2004). Without this hormonal influence, a genetically male mouse will develop genitals that appear female rather than male. Thus, male development for a genetically male fetus is not automatic. It is likely that a similar mechanism occurs in human males.

The development of the female reproductive system is equally complex and depends on a number of genetic variants. These variants promote ovarian development and inhibit testicular development (Ono & Harley, 2013). For example, one of these is the signaling molecule called *Wnt-4*, a variant form of which can masculinize a genetically female fetus (Biason-Lauber, Konrad, Navratil & Schoenle, 2004).

Further complexities arise from the fact that women have two X chromosomes, whereas men have only one. For many years researchers believed that the duplicate genes on one of a woman's two X chromosomes are inactive, or turned off. However, researchers discovered

mutation
Permanent alteration in genes or chromosomes that may produce harmful characteristics.

autosomes
In humans, the 22 pairs of chromosomes not related to sexual expression.

sex chromosomes
Pair of chromosomes that determines sex: XX in the normal human female, XY in the normal human male.

Mechanisms of Heredity | LIFE: THE ESSENTIALS OF HUMAN DEVELOPMENT | **43**

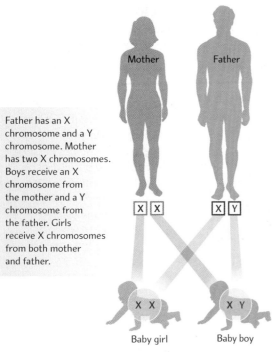

Father has an X chromosome and a Y chromosome. Mother has two X chromosomes. Boys receive an X chromosome from the mother and a Y chromosome from the father. Girls receive X chromosomes from both mother and father.

Mother   Father

X X   X Y

X X   X Y
Baby girl   Baby boy

FIGURE 3.3

Genetic Determination of Sex

Because all babies receive an X chromosome from the mother, sex is determined by whether an X or a Y chromosome is received from the father.

alleles
Two or more alternative forms of a gene that occupy the same position on paired chromosomes and affect the same trait.

homozygous
Possessing two identical alleles for a trait.

heterozygous
Possessing differing alleles for a trait.

dominant inheritance
Pattern of inheritance in which, when a child receives different alleles, only the dominant one is expressed.

recessive inheritance
Pattern of inheritance in which a child receives identical recessive alleles, resulting in expression of a nondominant trait.

polygenic inheritance
Pattern of inheritance in which multiple genes at different sites on chromosomes affect a complex trait.

that only 75 percent of the genes on the extra X chromosome are inactive. About 15 percent remain active, and 10 percent are active in some women but not in others (Carrel & Willard, 2005). This variability in gene activity could help explain gender differences linked to the X chromosome, which are discussed later in this chapter. The extra X chromosome also may help explain why women are generally healthier and longer lived than men: Harmful changes in a gene on one X chromosome may be offset by a backup copy on the other X chromosome (Migeon, 2006).

PATTERNS OF GENETIC TRANSMISSION

During the 1860s, Gregor Mendel, an Austrian monk, crossbred pea plants that produced only yellow seeds with pea plants that produced only green seeds. The resulting hybrid plants produced only yellow seeds, meaning, he said, that yellow was *dominant* over green. Yet when he bred the yellow-seeded hybrids with each other, only 75 percent of their offspring had yellow seeds, and the other 25 percent had green seeds. This showed, Mendel said, that a hereditary characteristic (in this case, the color green) can be *recessive;* that is, be carried by an organism that does not express, or show, it. By breeding for two traits at once, such as both color and shape, Mendel also found that color and shape were independent of each other and transmitted separately.

Mendel's groundbreaking work laid the foundations for our modern understanding of genetics. Although some human traits, such as the presence of facial dimples, are inherited via simple dominant transmission, most human traits fall along a continuous spectrum and result from the actions of many genes in concert.

Dominant and Recessive Inheritance Genes that can produce alternative expressions of a characteristic are called **alleles.** Alleles are alternate versions of the same gene. Every person receives one maternal and one paternal allele for any given trait. When both alleles are the same, the person is **homozygous** for the characteristic; when they are different, the person is **heterozygous.** In **dominant inheritance,** the dominant allele is always expressed, or shows up as a trait in that person. The person will look the same whether or not he or she is heterozygous or homozygous for the characteristic because the recessive allele doesn't show. For the trait to be expressed in **recessive inheritance,** the person must have two recessive alleles, one from each parent. If a recessive trait is expressed, that person cannot have a dominant allele.

Let's take red hair as an example. Because red hair is a recessive trait, you must receive two recessive copies (r) of the gene—one from each parent—in order to express red hair. Having hair that is not red (R; brown in this example) is a dominant trait, so you will have brown hair if you receive at least one copy (R) from either parent (Rr or RR) (Figure 3.4). If you receive one copy of the red hair allele (r) and one copy of an allele for brown hair (R), you are heterozygous (Rr); if you have two copies of the allele for brown hair, you are homozygous dominant (RR). In both of these cases, you will have brown hair. If you inherited one allele for red hair from each parent, you are homozygous recessive for this trait (rr) and will have red hair. Thus the only situation in which you would have red hair is if you received two recessive copies (r), one from each parent.

Relatively few traits are determined in this simple fashion. Most traits result from **polygenic inheritance,** the interaction of many genes. For example, there is not an "intelligence" gene that determines whether or not you are smart. Rather, a large number of genes work in concert to determine your intellectual potential. Although single genes often determine abnormal traits, there is no single gene that by itself significantly accounts for individual differences in any complex normal behavior.

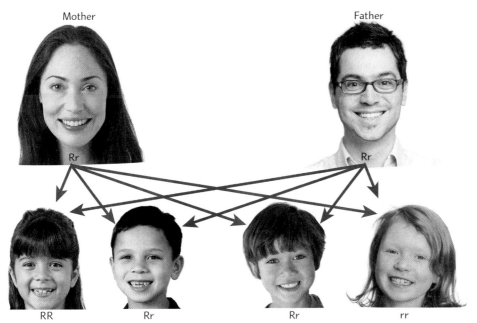

Mother   Father

Rr   Rr

RR   Rr   Rr   rr

(mother): ©Dougal Waters/Getty Images; (father): ©Ioannis Pantzi/Shutterstock; (girl RR): ©McGraw-Hill Education/
Ed-Imaging, photographer; (boy Rr): ©McGraw-Hill Education/Ed-Imaging, photographer; (boy Rr): ©BDLM/Getty
Images; (girl rr): ©Pete Panham/Shutterstock

FIGURE 3.4
Dominant and Recessive Inheritance

Because of dominant inheritance, the same observable phenotype (in this case, brown hair) can result from two different genotypes (RR and Rr). A phenotype expressing a recessive characteristic (such as red hair) must have a homozygous recessive genotype (rr).

Genotypes and Phenotypes: Multifactorial Transmission If you have red hair, that is part of your **phenotype,** the observable characteristics through which your **genotype,** or underlying genetic makeup, is expressed. The phenotype is the product of the genotype and any relevant environmental influences. The difference between genotype and phenotype helps explain why a clone (a genetic copy of an individual) or even an identical twin can never be an exact duplicate of another person.

As Figure 3.4 illustrates, people with different genotypes may exhibit the same phenotype. For example, a child who is homozygous dominant for brown hair (RR) will have brown hair, but so will a child who is heterozygous (Rr) for that same allele.

Furthermore, the recessive alleles can float around undetected for generations. For example, if you are heterozygous for red hair, and you find a mate who is also heterozygous for red hair, approximately one-fourth of your children should have red hair. Each child has a 25 percent chance to inherit both of the recessive alleles, and thus express the recessive trait (red hair). Because the dominant trait is always expressed, all that you would know, upon seeing a child with brown hair, is that the child had to have at least one brown hair allele.

Red hair has a strong genetic base, but experience modifies the expression of the genotype for most traits—a phenomenon called **multifactorial transmission.** Multifactorial transmission illustrates the action of nature and nurture and how they mutually and reciprocally affect outcomes. Imagine that Steven has inherited musical talent. If his family nurtures his talent and he practices regularly, he may become a skilled musician. However, if he is not encouraged and not motivated to play music, his genotype for musical ability may not be expressed (or may be expressed to a lesser extent) in his phenotype. Some physical characteristics (including height and weight) and most psychological characteristics (such as intelligence and musical ability) are products of multifactorial transmission. Many disorders arise when an inherited predisposition (an abnormal variant of a normal gene) interacts with an environmental factor, either before or after birth. Attention-deficit/hyperactivity disorder (ADHD) is one of several behavioral disorders thought to be transmitted multifactorially (Yang et al., 2013).

Epigenesis: Environmental Influence on Gene Expression Who you are is not just a function of your genes. It is also a function of which of your genes are expressed at any particular moment. Genes are turned off or on as they are needed by the developing body or when triggered by the environment. This phenomenon is called **epigenesis,** or *epigenetics.*

phenotype
Observable characteristics of a person.

genotype
Genetic makeup of a person, containing both expressed and unexpressed characteristics.

multifactorial transmission
Combination of genetic and environmental factors to produce certain complex traits.

epigenesis
Mechanism that turns genes on or off and determines functions of body cells.

Rainbow, on the left, nuzzles her clone, Cc, on the right. They are genetically identical, but have different appearances and personalities. ©Pat Sullivan/AP Images

Far from being fixed once and for all, epigenetic activity is affected by a continual bidirectional interplay with nongenetic influences (Mazzio & Soliman, 2012).

Epigenesis (meaning "on, or above, the genome") refers to chemical molecules (or "tags") attached to a gene that alter the way a cell "reads" the gene's DNA. If we think of the human genome as a piano keyboard, the epigenetic framework can be visualized as the particular tune being played at that time (Stelmach & Merlich, 2015). Different situations call for different melodies. Thus, while every cell in the body inherits the same DNA sequence, the chemical tags differentiate various types of body cells, such as brain cells, skin cells, and liver cells.

Epigenetic changes can occur throughout life in response to environmental factors such as nutrition, smoking, sleep habits, stress, and physical activity (Wong et al., 2014). Epigenetics may contribute to such common ailments as cancer, diabetes, and heart disease (Dawson & Kouzarides, 2012; Slomko, Heo & Einstein, 2012; Webster, Yan & Marsden, 2013). It may explain why one monozygotic twin is susceptible to a disease such as schizophrenia whereas the other twin is not, and why some twins get the same disease but at different ages (Fraga et al., 2005; Wong, Gottesman & Petronis, 2005). Environmental influences can also be social in nature. For example, social isolation can lead to a variety of health vulnerabilities including cardiovascular disease, decreased immune responses, and an increased risk of inflammation-related diseases (Cole, 2009).

Cells are particularly susceptible to epigenetic modification during critical periods such as puberty and pregnancy (Mayo Foundation for Medical Education and Research, 2009; Rakyan & Beck, 2006). Furthermore, epigenetic modifications, especially those that occur early in life, may be heritable. Studies of human sperm cells found age-related epigenetic variations capable of being passed on to future generations (Rakyan & Beck, 2006).

One example of epigenesis is *genome,* or *genetic, imprinting.* Imprinting is the differential expression of certain genetic traits, depending on whether the trait has been inherited from the mother or the father. In imprinted gene pairs, genetic information inherited from the parent of one sex is activated, but genetic information from the other parent is suppressed. Imprinted genes play an important role in regulating fetal growth and development. When a normal pattern of imprinting is disrupted, abnormal fetal growth or congenital growth disorders may result (Lee & Bartolemei, 2013).

An example of genomic imprinting can be found in Prader-Willi syndrome, a genetic disease that leads to feeding disturbances, behavioral problems, and intellectual disabilities. The most common form of the disorder occurs from the deletion of a gene segment on paternal chromosome 15, while the genes on the maternal chromosome 15 are turned off (Ishida & Moore, 2013).

Problems in genome imprinting may explain why a child with an asthmatic mother is more likely to develop asthma than a child with an asthmatic father.
©bubutu/Shutterstock

GENETIC AND CHROMOSOMAL ABNORMALITIES

Most birth disorders are fairly rare (Table 3.1), affecting only about 3 percent of live births (Waknine, 2006). Nevertheless, they are the leading cause of infant death in the United States, accounting for 20 percent of all deaths in the first year in 2013 (Mathews, MacDorman & Thorma, 2015). The most prevalent defects are Down syndrome, followed by cleft lip or cleft palate. Other serious malformations involve the eye, the face, the mouth, or the circulatory, gastronomical, or musculoskeletal systems (Parker et al., 2010).

It is in genetic defects and diseases that we see most clearly the operation of dominant and recessive transmission, and also of a variation, *sex-linked inheritance,* discussed in a subsequent section.

Dominant or Recessive Inheritance of Defects Most of the time, "good" genes are dominant over those carrying abnormal traits, but sometimes the gene for an abnormal trait is dominant. When one parent has one dominant abnormal gene and one recessive "good" gene and the other parent has two recessive "good" genes, each of their children has a 50-50 chance of inheriting the abnormal gene. Among the 1,800 disorders known

TABLE 3.1 Some Birth Defects

Problem	Characteristics of Condition	Who Is at Risk	What Can Be Done
Alpha thalassemia	Severe anemia that reduces ability of the blood to carry oxygen; most affected infants are stillborn or die soon after birth.	Primarily families of Malaysian, African, and Southeast Asian descent	Frequent blood transfusions.
Beta thalassemia (Cooley's anemia)	Severe anemia resulting in weakness, fatigue, and frequent illness; usually fatal by young adulthood.	Primarily families of Mediterranean descent	Frequent blood transfusions.
Cystic fibrosis	Overproduction of mucus, which collects in the lung and digestive tract; breathing and digestive difficulty, most die by 30.	1 in 2,000 white births	Chest physical therapy, exercise, antibiotics digestive enzymes.
Duchenne muscular dystrophy	Fatal usually in males, muscle weakness; minor mental retardation; respiratory failure, death usually occurs in young adulthood.	1 in 3,000 to, 5,000 male births	No treatment.
Hemophilia	Clotting disorder, usually males; in its most severe form can lead to crippling arthritis in adulthood.	1 in 10,000 families with a history of hemophilia	Frequent transfusions of blood with clotting factors.
Anencephaly	Absence of brain tissues; infants are stillborn or die soon after birth.	1 in 1,000	No treatment.
Spina bifida	Incompletely closed spinal canal resulting in muscle weakness or paralysis and loss of bladder and bowel control; can co-occur with mental retardation.	1 in 1,000	Surgery to close spinal canal prevents further injury; shunt placed in brain drains excess fluid.
Phenylketonuria (PKU)	Metabolic disorder resulting in mental retardation.	1 in 15,000 births	Special diet begun in first few weeks of life can prevent mental retardation.
Polycystic kidney disease	*Infantile form:* enlarged kidneys, respiratory problems, and congestive heart failure. *Adult form:* kidney pain, kidney stones, and hypertension resulting in chronic kidney failure.	1 in 1,000	Kidney transplants.
Sickle-cell anemia	Deformed red blood cells clog the blood vessels, depriving the body of oxygen; symptoms include severe pain, stunted growth, frequent infections, leg ulcers, gallstones, susceptibility to pneumonia, and stroke.	1 in 500 African Americans	Painkillers, transfusions for anemia and to prevent stroke, antibiotics for infections.
Tay-Sachs disease	Degenerative disease of the brain and nerve cells, resulting in death before age 5.	Historically found mainly in Eastern European Jews	No treatment.

Source: Adapted from AAP Committee on Genetics, 1996; NIH Consensus Development Panel, 2001; Tisdale, 1988, pp. 68–69.

to be transmitted by dominant inheritance are achondroplasia (a type of dwarfism) and Huntington's disease. Defects transmitted by dominant inheritance are less likely to be lethal at an early age than those transmitted by recessive inheritance because any affected children would be likely to die before reproducing. Therefore, that gene would not be passed on to the next generation and would soon disappear from the population.

Recessive defects are expressed only if the child is homozygous for that gene; in other words, a child must inherit a copy of the recessive gene from each parent. Defects transmitted by recessive genes tend to be lethal at an earlier age, in contrast to those transmitted by dominant genes, because recessive genes can be transmitted by heterozygous carriers who do not themselves have the disorder. Thus they are able to reproduce and pass the genes down to the next generation.

FIGURE 3.5
Sex-Linked Inheritance

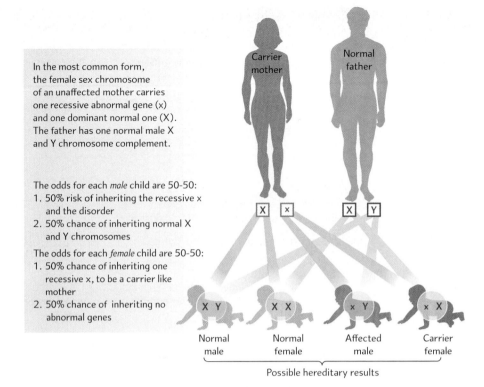

In the most common form, the female sex chromosome of an unaffected mother carries one recessive abnormal gene (x) and one dominant normal one (X). The father has one normal male X and Y chromosome complement.

The odds for each *male* child are 50-50:
1. 50% risk of inheriting the recessive x and the disorder
2. 50% chance of inheriting normal X and Y chromosomes

The odds for each *female* child are 50-50:
1. 50% chance of inheriting one recessive x, to be a carrier like mother
2. 50% chance of inheriting no abnormal genes

Carrier mother

Normal father

Normal male — X Y

Normal female — X X

Affected male — x Y

Carrier female — x X

Possible hereditary results

incomplete dominance
Pattern of inheritance in which a child receives two different alleles, resulting in partial expression of a trait.

sex-linked inheritance
Pattern of inheritance in which certain characteristics carried on the X chromosome inherited from the mother are transmitted differently to her male and female offspring.

In **incomplete dominance,** a trait is not fully expressed. Normally the presence of a dominant/recessive gene pair results in the full expression of the dominant gene and the masking of the recessive gene. In incomplete dominance, the resulting phenotype is a combination of both genes. For example, people with only one sickle-cell allele and one normal allele do not have sickle-cell anemia with its distinctive, abnormally shaped blood cells. Their blood cells are not the typical round shape either. They are an intermediate shape, which shows that the sickle-cell gene for these people is incompletely dominant.

Sex-Linked Inheritance of Defects In **sex-linked inheritance** (Figure 3.5), certain recessive disorders affect male and female children differently. This is due to the fact that males are XY and females are XX. In humans, the Y chromosome is smaller and carries far fewer genes than the X chromosome. One outcome of this is that males receive only one copy of any gene that happens to be carried on the sex chromosomes, whereas females receive two copies. So, if a woman has a "bad" copy of a particular gene, she has a backup copy. However, if a male has a "bad" copy of a particular gene, that gene will be expressed.

Heterozygote females who carry one "bad" copy of a recessive gene and one "good" one are called carriers. If such a woman has children with an unaffected male (a man who has a "good" copy of the gene), she has a 50 percent chance of passing the disorder on to any sons they might have. If they have a son (who is XY by virtue of being male), the father contributed a Y chromosome, and the mother contributed the X chromosome. Because she has one "good" copy and one "bad" copy, either outcome is equally likely. Daughters (who are XX by virtue of being female) may be protected because the father will pass on his "good" copy to daughters, so the girls have a 50 percent chance either of being completely unaffected or of carrying a hidden recessive copy of the gene.

Sex-linked recessive disorders are more common in males than in females. For example, red-green color blindness, hemophilia (a disorder in which blood does not clot properly), and Duchenne muscular dystrophy (a disorder that results in muscle degeneration and eventually death) are all more common in males, and all result from genes located on the X chromosome. Occasionally, a female does inherit a sex-linked condition. For this to happen, the father must have a "bad" copy, and the mother must also be a carrier or herself have the condition.

TABLE 3.2 Sex Chromosome Abnormalities

Pattern/Name	Typical Characteristics*	Incidence	Treatment
XYY	Male; tall stature; tendency toward low IQ, especially verbal.	1 in 1,000 male births	No special treatment.
XXX (triple X)	Female; normal appearance, menstrual irregularities, learning disorders, mental retardation.	1 in 1,000 female births	Special education.
XXY (Klinefelter)	Male; sterility, underdeveloped secondary sex characteristics, small testes, learning disorders.	1 in 1,000 male births	Hormone therapy, special education.
XO (Turner)	Female; short stature, webbed neck, impaired spatial abilities, no menstruation, infertility, underdeveloped sex organs, incomplete development of secondary sex characteristics.	1 in 1,500 to 2,500 female births	Hormone therapy, special education.
Fragile X	Minor-to-severe mental retardation; symptoms, which are more severe in males, include delayed speech, motor development, and hyperactivity.	1 in 1,200 male births; 1 in 2,000 female births	Educational and behavioral therapies when needed.

*Not every affected person has every characteristic.

Chromosomal Abnormalities Chromosomal abnormalities typically occur because of errors in cell division, resulting in an extra or missing chromosome. For example, Klinefelter syndrome is caused by an extra female sex chromosome (shown by the pattern XXY). Turner syndrome results from a missing sex chromosome (XO). The likelihood of errors increase in offspring of women age 35 or older. Characteristics of the most common sex chromosome disorders are shown in Table 3.2.

Down syndrome, the most common chromosomal abnormality, accounts for about 40 percent of all cases of moderate-to-severe mental retardation (Pennington, Moon, Edgin, Stedron & Nadel, 2003). The condition is also called *trisomy-21* because it is characterized in more than 90 percent of cases by an extra 21st chromosome.

Approximately 1 in every 700 babies born alive has Down syndrome. Although the risk of having a child with Down syndrome rises with age (Society for Neuroscience, 2008), because of the higher birthrates of younger women, more young mothers have children with Down syndrome (National Institute of Child Health and Development, 2008).

The brains of children with Down syndrome appear nearly normal at birth but shrink in volume by young adulthood, particularly in the hippocampal area and prefrontal cortex, resulting in cognitive dysfunction, and in the cerebellum, leading to problems with motor coordination and balance (Davis, 2008; Pennington et al., 2003). With early intervention the prognosis for these children is brighter than was once thought. Children with Down syndrome, like other children with disabilities, tend to benefit cognitively, socially, and emotionally when placed in regular classrooms rather than in special schools (Davis, 2008) and when provided with regular, intensive therapies designed to help them achieve important skills. As adults, many live in small group homes and support themselves; they tend to do well in structured job situations. More than 70 percent of people with Down syndrome live into their 60s, but they are at elevated risk of early death from various causes, including leukemia, cancer, Alzheimer's disease, and cardiovascular disease (Bittles, Bower, Hussain & Glasson, 2006; Hill et al., 2003).

Down syndrome
Chromosomal disorder characterized by moderate-to-severe mental retardation and by such physical signs as a downward-sloping skin fold at the inner corners of the eyes. Also called *trisomy-21*.

genetic counseling
Clinical service that advises prospective parents of their probable risk of having children with hereditary defects.

Although Down syndrome is a major cause of mental retardation, people with this chromosomal abnormality can live productive lives. ©Stoked/George Doyle/Media Bakery

GENETIC COUNSELING AND TESTING

Genetic counseling can help prospective parents assess their risk of bearing children with genetic or chromosomal defects. People who have already had a child with a genetic defect, who have a family history of

FIGURE 3.6
Karyotype of a Female with Down Syndrome

A karyotype is a photograph that shows the chromosomes when they are separated and aligned for cell division. We know that this is a karyotype of a person with Down syndrome because there are three chromosomes instead of the usual two on pair 21. Because pair 23 consists of two Xs, we know that this is the karyotype of a female.

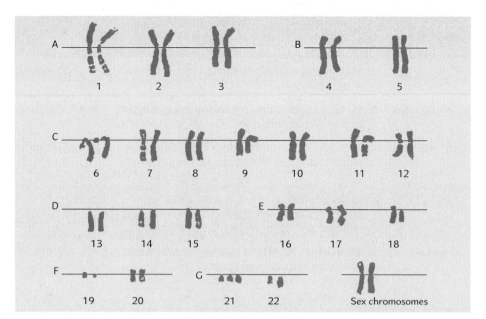

Source: Adapted from Babu & Hirschhorn, 1992; March of Dimes Birth Defects Foundation, 1987.

hereditary illness, who suffer from conditions known or suspected to be inherited, or who come from ethnic groups at higher-than-average risk of passing on genes for certain diseases can get information about their likelihood of producing affected children.

Geneticists have made great contributions to avoidance of birth defects. For example, genetic testing has virtually eliminated Tay-Sachs disease in the Jewish population (Cao, Rosatelli, Monni & Galanello, 2002). Similarly, screening and counseling of women of childbearing age from Mediterranean countries, where beta thalassemia (refer to Table 3.1) is common, has brought a decline in births of affected babies and greater knowledge of the risks of being a carrier (Cao & Kan, 2013).

A genetic counselor takes a family history and gives the prospective parents and any biological children physical examinations. Chromosomes from body tissues may be analyzed and photographed, and the photographs enlarged and arranged according to size and structure on a chart called a *karyotype*. This chart can show chromosomal abnormalities and can indicate whether a person who appears unaffected might transmit genetic defects to a child (Figure 3.6). The counselor tries to help clients understand the mathematical risk of a particular condition, explains its implications, and presents information about alternative courses of action.

Today researchers are rapidly identifying genes that contribute to many serious diseases and disorders, as well as those that influence normal traits. Their work is likely to lead to widespread genetic testing to reveal genetic profiles—a prospect that involves dangers as well as benefits (Research in Action).

Nature and Nurture: Influences of Heredity and Environment

Phenotypes for most traits, such as intelligence and personality, are subject to a complex array of hereditary and environmental forces. Let's see how scientists study and explain the influences of heredity and environment and how these two forces work together.

STUDYING HEREDITY AND ENVIRONMENT

behavioral genetics
Quantitative study of relative hereditary and environmental influences on behavior.

One approach to the study of heredity and environment is quantitative: It seeks to measure *how much* heredity and environment influence particular traits and determine the relative influence of each. This is the traditional goal of the science of **behavioral genetics.**

research *in action*

EPIGENETICS: IDENTICAL TWINS THAT AREN'T IDENTICAL

Have you ever known a pair of identical twins? Were you able to tell them apart? Have you ever wondered why identical twins—who share 100 percent of their genetic code—look and act slightly different?

Epigenetic variation can help explain this. The field of epigenetics includes the study of biochemical modifications of genetic expression "above the genome"—without altering DNA sequence (van Ijzendoorn, Bakermans-Kranenburg & Ebstein, 2011). Epigenetics explains why a skin cell and a heart cell look different, even though both carry the entire genetic code. The differences arise as certain genes are turned on or off depending on need and environmental influences. These changes augment, dampen, or mute genetic expression entirely (Wong et al., 2010).

Previous researchers have theorized that there should be a high degree of epigenetic change in the embryonic period, when cells are highly susceptible to maternal factors such as diet, nutrition, and stress (Champagne, 2014). What environmental factors might influence identical twins in this scenario? One likely factor is whether twins are monochorionic (share a placenta) and thus are subject to similar environmental influences or are dichorionic (have separate placentas) and are therefore exposed to somewhat different placental environments. Gordon and others (2011) examined twins' epigenetic changes in the womb by analyzing amniotic tissue samples at birth. In this study, monochorionic twins showed greater epigenetic similarity at birth; gene expression was more "alike" than dichorionic twins with separate womb environments. Twin pairs also varied in level of epigenetic difference across samples, such that genetic expression was similar in certain tissues more than others.

These epigenetic differences continue after birth. The Peri/Post-natal Epigenetic Twins Study is a longitudinal study of twins from birth to 5 years (Saffrey et al., 2012). This study also found a wide range of epigenetic difference between newborn twins. Similar to the Gordon (2011) study, monochorionic identicals were more similar in genetic expression than

dichorionic identicals. A followup study of the twin pairs revealed that one-third of the epigenome changes "significantly" between birth and 18 months (Loke, Novaknovic, Ollikainen & Wallace, 2013)—a phenomenal change for twins sharing postnatal environment.

As twins age, even when identical, and even when raised in the same family, they will have somewhat different experiences and be exposed to varied environmental influences. Over time, and particularly in adulthood where most twins will follow different life paths, these differences add up. The accumulated differences result in what has been termed "epigenetic drift." The older the twins, the more different their epigenome becomes (Bell & Spector, 2011; Fraga et al., 2005; Martino et al., 2013; Wong et al., 2010). Epigenetic drift is often associated with adoption of differing lifestyles and less shared time together. By old age, lifestyle choices may result in very different developmental pathways. Martin (2005) describes identical twins varying in age of onset of Alzheimer's disease—one in their 60s, the other in their 80s. Another longitudinal study of elderly identical twins noted specific epigenetic biomarkers influencing disease or longevity over the span of 10 years (Tan et al., 2016).

Epigenetic studies create a strong case that identical twins are indeed *not* the same, even at birth and even given an identical genetic code. Epigenetic studies may confirm what many identical twins have asserted all along: They are truly individuals and have always been so.

what's **your** view

As epigenetic drift results in increasingly different identical twins, how might other people's responses to these increasing differences further shape the process? How might the concept of epigenetics explain differences in nonidentical siblings who share only roughly 50 percent of their genetic code?

Measuring Heritability Behavioral geneticists have developed a means of estimating how much of a trait is due to genetics and how much is the result of environmental influences by using a concept known as **heritability.** Every trait is a consequence of genes and environment. By looking at groups of people with known genetic relationships, and assessing whether or not they are **concordant,** meaning *the same,* on a given trait, behavioral geneticists can estimate the relative influence of genes and environment.

heritability
Statistical estimate of contribution of heredity to individual differences in a specific trait within a given population.

concordant
Term describing tendency of twins to share the same trait or disorder.

For example, we may wish to know what the relative influences of genes and environment are for homosexuality. One way to estimate this is to look at large groups of monozygotic and dizygotic twins and calculate how concordant they are on the trait. In other words, if one twin is homosexual, what are the chances the other twin is as well? Remember that monozygotic twins generally share 100 percent of their genes, whereas dizygotic twins share approximately 50 percent. If genes are implicated in homosexuality, the concordance rates for monozygotic twins should be higher than that of those for dizygotic twins because they share more genes. If genes don't matter, the concordance rate should be the same for both types of twins. By the same token, if the environment exerts a large influence on a trait, people who live together should be more similar on traits than people who do not live together, and those who live apart should be less similar. By comparing concordance rates of family members of known genetic relatedness and in either the same or different environments, we can determine the relative influences of genes versus environment. Twin and adoption studies support a moderate to high hereditary basis for many normal and abnormal characteristics (Polderman et al., 2015).

There are multiple variations of this basic approach. For example, immediate family members might be compared to more distant relatives, adopted children might be compared to their biological and adopted parents, or twins adopted by two different families might be compared to twins raised in the same family—but the essential logic is the same. If we know, on average, how many genes people share by virtue of knowing their genetic relationship, and whether or not they are raised together or apart, we can measure how similar they are on traits and work backward to determine the relative environmental influence.

Heritability is expressed as a percentage ranging from 0.0 to 1.0: The higher the number, the greater the heritability of a trait. A heritability estimate of 1.0 indicates that genes are 100 percent responsible for variances in the trait within the population. A heritability estimate of 0.0 percent would indicate the environment shaped a trait exclusively. Note that heritability does not refer to the influences that shaped any one particular person because those influences are virtually impossible to separate. Nor does heritability tell us how traits develop. It merely indicates the statistical extent to which genes contribute to a trait at a certain time within a given population.

Behavioral geneticists recognize that even in a trait strongly influenced by heredity, the environment can have substantial impact. In fact, environmental interventions sometimes can overcome genetically "determined" conditions. For example, a special diet begun soon after birth often can prevent mental retardation in children with the genetic disease phenylketonuria (PKU) (Widaman, 2009; refer to Table 3.1).

Monozygotic twins separated at birth are sought by researchers who want to study the impact of genes on personality. These twins, adopted by different families and not reunited until age 31, both became firefighters. Was this a coincidence, or did it reflect the influence of heredity? ©Thomas Wanstall/The Image Works

HOW HEREDITY AND ENVIRONMENT WORK TOGETHER

Today many developmental scientists have come to regard a solely quantitative approach to the study of heredity and environment as simplistic. They see these two forces as fundamentally intertwined. Instead of looking at genes and experience as operating directly on an organism, they see both as part of a complex *developmental system* (Gottlieb, 1991, 1997; Lickliter & Honeycutt, 2003). From conception on, throughout life, a combination of constitutional factors (related to biological and psychological makeup) and social, economic, and cultural factors help shape development.

Let's consider several ways in which inheritance and experience work together.

Reaction Range Many characteristics vary, within limits, under varying hereditary or environmental conditions. The concept of *reaction range* can help us visualize how this happens.

Reaction range refers to a range of potential expressions of a hereditary trait. Body size, for example, depends largely on biological processes, which are genetically regulated. Tall people have tall children, and short people have short children. Even so, a range of sizes is possible. In societies in which nutrition has dramatically improved, an entire generation has grown up to tower over the generation before. The better-fed children share their parents' genes but have responded to a healthier world. And ultimately, height has genetic limits; we don't see people who are only 1 foot tall or who are 10 feet tall.

Heredity can influence whether a reaction range is wide or narrow. For example, a child born with a defect producing mild cognitive limitations is more able to respond to a favorable environment than a child born with more severe limitations. Likewise, a child with greater native intelligence is likely to benefit more from an enriched home and school environment than a child with normal intelligence (Figure 3.7).

Canalization Some traits have an extremely narrow range of reaction. The metaphor of **canalization** illustrates how heredity restricts the range of development for some traits. After a heavy storm, the rainwater has to go somewhere. If the street has potholes, the water will fill them. If deep canals have been dug along the edges of the street, the water will flow into the canals. Highly canalized traits, such as eye color, are analogous to the deep canals. They are strongly programmed by genes, and there is little opportunity for variance in their expression. Because of the deep, genetically dug channel, it would take an extreme change in environment to alter their course.

Many highly canalized traits tend to be those necessary for survival. In the case of very important traits such as these, natural selection has designed them to develop in a predictable and reliable way within a variety of environments and a multitude of influences. They are too important to be left to chance. Thus, typical babies follow a predictable sequence of motor development: crawling, walking, and running, in that order, at certain approximate ages. This sequence is said to be canalized, in that children will follow this same blueprint irrespective of many variations in the environment.

Other traits are more subject to variations in experience: the kinds of families children grow up in, the schools they attend, and the people they encounter. Consider reading. Environment plays a large part in reading skills development. Parents who play letter and word games and who read to their children are likely to have children who learn to read earlier than if these skills are not encouraged or reinforced. And children who are not taught to read do not learn to do so spontaneously.

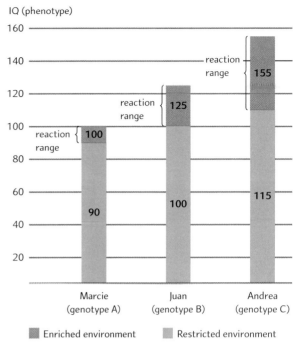

FIGURE 3.7

Intelligence and Reaction Range

Children with different genotypes for intelligence will show varying reaction ranges when exposed to a restricted (blue portion of bar) or enriched (entire bar) environment.

reaction range
Potential variability, depending on environmental conditions, in the expression of a hereditary trait.

canalization
Limitation on variance of expression of certain inherited characteristics.

genotype-environment interaction
The portion of phenotypic variation that results from the reactions of genetically different individuals to similar environmental conditions.

Genotype-Environment Interaction **Genotype-environment interaction** usually refers to the effects of similar environmental conditions on genetically different individuals, and a discussion of these interactions is a way to conceptualize and talk about the different ways nature and nurture interact. To take a familiar example, many children are exposed to pollen and dust, but those with a genetic predisposition are more likely to develop allergic reactions. Interactions can work the other way as well. Genetically similar children can develop differently depending on their home environments. A child born with a difficult temperament may develop adjustment problems in one family and thrive in another, depending largely on parental handling. Thus it is the interaction of hereditary and environmental factors, not just one or the other, that produces certain outcomes.

genotype-environment correlation
Tendency of certain genetic and environmental influences to reinforce each other; may be passive, reactive (evocative), or active. Also called *genotype-environment covariance*.

Genotype-Environment Correlation Because genes influence a person's exposure to particular environments, the environment often reinforces genetic differences (Rutter, 2012). This is called **genotype-environment correlation,** or *genotype-environment covariance,* and it works in three ways to strengthen the phenotypic expression of a genotypic tendency (Bergeman & Plomin, 1989; Scarr, 1992; Scarr & McCartney, 1983). The first two ways are common among younger children, the third among older children, adolescents, and adults.

- *Passive correlations:* Biological parents, who provide genes that might predispose a child toward a trait, might also provide an environment that encourages the development of that same trait. For example, a musical parent is likely to create a home environment in which music is heard regularly, to give a child music lessons, and to take the child to musical events. If the child inherited the parent's musical genes, then by virtue of that inheritance, the child will be uniquely well-suited to respond to those particular environmental influences. This type of correlation is called *passive* because the child does not control it. Passive correlations are most applicable to young children, whose parents have a great deal of control over their early experiences. Additionally, passive correlations function only when a child is living with a biologically related parent.

- *Reactive, or evocative, correlations:* Children with differing genetic makeups evoke different reactions from others. For example, parents who are not musically inclined may make a special effort to provide musical experiences for a child who shows genuine interest and ability in music. This response, in turn, strengthens the child's genetic inclination toward music. This type of correlation is called *reactive* because the other people react to the child's genetic makeup.

niche-picking
Tendency of a person, especially after early childhood, to seek out environments compatible with his or her genotype.

- *Active correlations:* As children get older and have more freedom to choose their own activities and environments, they *actively* select or create experiences consistent with their genetic tendencies. An adolescent with a talent for music will probably seek out musical friends, take music classes, and go to concerts if such opportunities are available. This tendency to seek out environments compatible with one's genotype is called **niche-picking;** it helps explain why identical twins reared apart tend to have similar characteristics.

What Makes Siblings So Different? The Nonshared Environment Although two children in the same family may bear a striking physical resemblance, siblings can differ greatly in intellect and especially in personality (Plomin & Daniels, 2011). One reason may be genetic differences, which lead children to need different kinds of stimulation or to respond differently to a similar home environment. For example, one child may be more affected by family discord than another (Horowitz et al., 2010). In addition, studies in behavioral genetics suggest that the influence of the family environment varies for different children in a family (McGuffin, Riley & Plomin, 2001; Plomin & Daniels, 1987; Plomin & DeFries, 1999). Children may live in the same family, but that does not imply that their experiences are identical.

nonshared environmental effects
The unique environment in which each child grows up, consisting of distinctive influences or influences that affect one child differently than another.

These **nonshared environmental effects** result from the unique environment in which each child in a family grows up. Children in a family have a shared environment—the home they live in, the people in it, and the activities family members jointly engage in—but they also, even if they are twins, have experiences that are not shared by their brothers and sisters. Parents and siblings may treat each child differently. Certain events, such as illnesses and accidents, and experiences outside the home affect one child and not another. For example, if you are the oldest child in a family, one of your early influences was the ability to have your parents' undivided attention. Later siblings must share their parents' attention. Therefore, despite being in the same family, the influences are not identical. Indeed, some behavioral geneticists have concluded that although heredity accounts for most of the similarity between siblings, the nonshared environment accounts for much of the difference (Heatherington, Reiss & Plomin, 2013).

Children also mold their environments by the choices they make—what they do and with whom—and their genetic makeup influences these choices. These differences tend to be accentuated as children grow older and have more experiences outside the family (Plomin, 1996; Scarr, 1992).

The nature-nurture puzzle will never be fully resolved. Nevertheless, a variety of research designs can continue to augment and refine our understanding of the forces affecting development.

An adolescent with musical abilities may seek out musical friends and might even start a band. This is an example of niche-picking. ©Fuse/Getty Images

SOME CHARACTERISTICS INFLUENCED BY HEREDITY AND ENVIRONMENT

Obesity **Obesity** is measured by body mass index, or BMI (comparison of weight to height). Children between the 85th and 95th percentiles are classified as overweight, and those above the 95 percentile as obese (Ogden, Carroll, Curtin, Lamb, & Flegal, 2010). Another criterion, used primarily for adults, is percentage of body fat: 25 percent or more for men and 30 percent or more for women. Obesity is a multifactorial condition; twin studies, adoption studies, and other research suggest that 40 to 70 percent of the risk is genetic, but environmental influences also contribute to it (Willyard, 2014). More than 430 genes or chromosome regions are associated with obesity (Nirmala, Reddy, & Reddy, 2008; Snyder et al., 2004). There are also small subsets of obese people who have a genetic profile making them particularly prone to obesity; for instance, one such subset includes obese adults suffering from a deletion of approximately 30 genes (Bochukova et al., 2009).

The risk of obesity is 2 to 3 times higher for a child with a family history of obesity, especially severe obesity (Nirmala et al., 2008). However, this increased risk is not solely genetic. The kind and amount of food eaten in a particular home and the amount of exercise that is encouraged can increase or decrease the likelihood that a child will become overweight. And the wider social context is at play as well. Obesity rates rise in countries with rapid socioeconomic growth and increases in gross domestic product (Min, Chiu & Wang, 2013). In Western countries, obesity likely stems from the interaction of a genetic predisposition with overeating, supersized portions, and inadequate exercise (Arner, 2000).

obesity
Extreme overweight in relation to age, sex, height, and body type as defined by having a body mass index at or above the 95th percentile.

Intelligence Heredity exerts a strong influence on general intelligence (as measured by intelligence tests) and, to a lesser extent, on specific abilities such as memory, verbal ability, and spatial ability. Intelligence is a polygenic trait; it is influenced by the additive effects of large numbers of genes working together. In support of this assertion, adopted children's IQs are consistently closer to the IQs of their biological mothers than to those of their adoptive parents and siblings, and monozygotic twins are more alike in intelligence than dizygotic twins (Petrill et al., 2004). Experience counts too; as Figure 3.7 shows, an enriched or impoverished environment can substantially affect the development and expression of innate ability (Neisser et al., 1996). Environmental influence is greater, and heritability lower, among poor families than among more economically privileged families (Nisbett et al., 2012).

The influence of genes increases with age. This increase is probably a result of niche-picking. The shared family environment has a strong influence on young children but little influence on adolescents, who are more apt to find their own niche by actively selecting environments compatible with their hereditary abilities and related interests (Bouchard, 2013).

This shy 3-year-old boy may "just be in a phase," or his shyness may be an inborn aspect of his temperament. ©Digital Vision/Photodisc/Getty Images

temperament
Characteristic disposition, or style of approaching and reacting to situations.

gestation
Period of development between conception and birth.

gestational age
Age of an unborn baby, usually dated from the first day of an expectant mother's last menstrual cycle.

germinal stage
First 2 weeks of prenatal development, characterized by rapid cell division, blastocyst formation, and implantation in the wall of the uterus.

implantation
The attachment of the blastocyst to the uterine wall, occurring at about day 6.

Personality Personality is also affected by a combination of nature and nurture influences. Scientists have identified genes directly linked with specific aspects of personality such as neuroticism and extraversion (Vinkhuyzen et al., 2012). Overall, the heritability of personality traits appears to be around 40 percent (Vukasovic & Bratko, 2015), and there is little evidence of shared environmental influence (Plomin, 2011). As with intelligence, genetic influences appear to become more important with age (Briley & Tucker-Drob, 2014).

Temperament is an infant's characteristic way of approaching and reacting to situations. It is believed to underlie eventual personality. Temperament appears to be largely inborn and is relatively consistent over the years, though it may respond to special experiences or parental handling (Thomas & Chess, 1984; Thomas, Chess, & Birch, 1968). Siblings—both twins and nontwins—tend to be similar in temperament on such traits as positive affect, activity level (Saudino & Micalizzi, 2015), and behavior regulation (Gagne & Saudino, 2010).

Prenatal Development

For many women, the first clear (though not necessarily reliable) sign of pregnancy is a missed menstrual period. But even before that first missed period, a pregnant woman's body undergoes subtle but noticeable changes and many women may suspect a pregnancy.

During **gestation,** the period between conception and birth, an unborn child undergoes dramatic processes of development. The normal range of gestation is between 37 and 41 weeks (Martin et al., 2009). **Gestational age** is usually dated from the first day of an expectant mother's last menstrual cycle.

In this section we trace the course of gestation, or prenatal development, and discuss environmental factors that can affect the developing person-to-be. In the next section, we assess techniques for determining whether development is proceeding normally and explain the importance of prenatal care.

STAGES OF PRENATAL DEVELOPMENT

Prenatal development takes place in three stages: *germinal, embryonic,* and *fetal.* (Table 3.3 gives a month-by-month description.) During these three stages of gestation, the original single-celled zygote grows into an *embryo* and then a *fetus.*

Both before and after birth, development proceeds according to two fundamental principles: Growth and motor development occur from the top down and from the center of the body outward. The embryo's head and trunk develop before the limbs, and the arms and legs before the fingers and toes.

Germinal Stage (Fertilization to 2 Weeks) During the **germinal stage,** from fertilization to about 2 weeks of gestational age, the zygote divides, becomes more complex, and is implanted in the wall of the uterus.

Within 36 hours after fertilization, the zygote enters a period of rapid cell division and duplication (mitosis). It continues this rapid pace of growth throughout the germinal stage. While the fertilized ovum is dividing, it is also making its way through the fallopian tube to the uterus, a journey of 3 or 4 days. Its form changes into a *blastocyst,* a fluid-filled sphere, which floats freely in the uterus until the sixth day after fertilization, when it begins to implant itself in the uterine wall. Only about 10 to 20 percent of fertilized ova complete the task of **implantation** and continue to develop. Where the egg implants will determine the placement of the placenta.

Before implantation, as cell differentiation begins, some cells around the edge of the blastocyst cluster on one side to form the *embryonic disk,* a thickened cell mass from which the embryo begins to develop. This mass will differentiate into three layers. The *ectoderm,* the upper layer, will become the outer layer of skin, the nails, hair, teeth, sensory organs, and the nervous system, including the brain and spinal cord. The *endoderm,* the

TABLE 3.3 Prenatal Development

Month	Description

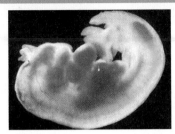

1 month
©Petit Format/Nestle/Science Source

During the first month, growth is more rapid than at any other time during life; the embryo reaches a size 10,000 times greater than the zygote. By the end of the first month, it measures about ½ inch in length. Blood flows through its veins and arteries. It has a minuscule heart, beating 65 times a minute. It has the beginning of a brain, kidneys, liver, and digestive tract. The umbilical cord is working. By looking closely through a microscope, it is possible to see the swellings on the head that will eventually become eyes, ears, mouth, and nose. Its sex cannot yet be detected.

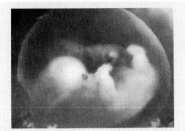

7 weeks
©Petit Format/Nestle/Science Source

By the end of the second month, the embryo becomes a fetus. It is less than 1 inch long and weighs only ⅓ ounce. Its head is half its total body length. Facial parts are developed, with tongue and teeth buds. The arms have hands, fingers, and thumbs, and the legs have knees, ankles, feet, and toes. The fetus has a thin covering of skin. Bone cells appear at about 8 weeks. Sex organs are developing; the heartbeat is steady. The stomach produces digestive juices; the liver, blood cells. The kidneys remove uric acid from the blood. The skin is now sensitive enough to react to tactile stimulation.

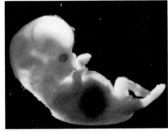

3 months
©Science Pictures Ltd./Science Source

By the end of the third month, the fetus weighs about 1 ounce and measures about 3 inches in length. It has fingernails, toenails, eyelids (still closed), vocal cords, lips, and a nose. Its head is still large—about one-third its total length—and its forehead is high. Sex is detectable. The organ systems are functioning but not at full capacity. Its ribs and vertebrae have turned into cartilage. The fetus can now move its legs, feet, thumbs, and head; its mouth can open and close and it can swallow. If its palm is touched, it makes a partial fist; if its lip is touched, it will suck; and if the sole of the foot is stroked, the toes will fan out. These reflexes will be present at birth but will disappear during the first months.

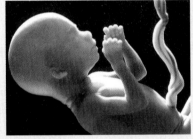

4 months
©Tissuepix/Science Source

The head is now only one-fourth the total body length, the same proportion it will be at birth. The fetus measures 8 to 10 inches and weighs about 6 ounces. The placenta is now fully developed. The mother may be able to feel the fetus kicking, a movement known as *quickening*. The reflex activities that appeared in the third month are now brisker because of increased muscular development.

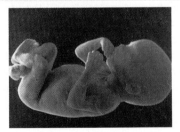

5 months
©James Stevenson/Science Source

The fetus, now weighing about 12 ounces to 1 pound and measuring about 1 foot, now has definite sleep-wake patterns, a favorite position in the uterus (called its *lie*), and becomes more active—kicking, stretching, squirming, and even hiccuping. The sweat and sebaceous glands are functioning. The respiratory system is not yet adequate to sustain life outside the womb; a baby born at this time does not usually survive. Coarse hair has begun to grow for eyebrows and eyelashes, fine hair is on the head, and a woolly hair called *lanugo* covers the body.

(*continued*)

TABLE 3.3 Prenatal Development (*continued*)

Month	Description
 *6 months* ©Anatomical Travelogue/Science Source	The rate of fetal growth has slowed a little—by the end of the sixth month, the fetus is about 14 inches long and weighs 1 ¼ pounds. It has fat pads under the skin; the eyes can open, close, and look in all directions. It can hear, and it can make a fist with a strong grip. A fetus born early in the sixth month has only a slight chance of survival because the lungs have not matured.
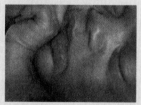 *7 months* ©Petit Format/Nestle/Science Source	By the end of the seventh month, the fetus, about 16 inches long and weighing 3 to 5 pounds, has fully developed reflex patterns. It cries, breathes, and swallows, and it may suck its thumb. The lanugo may disappear, or it may remain until shortly after birth. Head hair may continue to grow. The chances that a fetus weighing at least 3½ pounds will survive are good, providing it receives intensive medical attention.
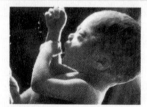 *8 months* ©Petit Format/Nestle/Science Source	The 8-month-old fetus is 18 to 20 inches long and weighs between 5 and 7 pounds. Its living quarters are becoming cramped, and so its movements are curtailed. During the next two months a layer of fat develops, which will help the fetus to adjust to varying temperatures outside the womb.
 *9 months–newborn* ©Luke Schmidt/Shutterstock	About a week before birth, the fetus stops growing, having reached an average weight of about 7½ pounds and a length of about 20 inches, with boys tending to be slightly larger. Fat pads continue to form, the organ systems are operating more efficiently, the heart rate increases, and more wastes are expelled through the umbilical cord. The reddish color of the skin is fading. At birth, the fetus will have been in the womb for about 266 days, though gestational age is usually estimated at 280 days because most doctors date the pregnancy from the mother's last menstrual period.

Note: Even in these early stages, individuals differ. The figures and descriptions given here represent averages.

inner layer, will become the digestive system, liver, pancreas, salivary glands, and respiratory system. The *mesoderm,* the middle layer, will develop and differentiate into the inner layer of skin, muscles, skeleton, and excretory and circulatory systems.

Other parts of the blastocyst begin to develop into organs that will nurture and protect development in the womb: the *amniotic cavity,* or *amniotic sac,* with its outer layers, the *amnion* and *chorion;* the *placenta;* and the *umbilical cord.* The *amniotic sac* is a fluid-filled membrane that encases the developing embryo, protecting it and giving it room to move and grow. The *placenta* is a life support system that allows oxygen, nourishment, and wastes to pass between mother and embryo. It is connected to the embryo by the *umbilical cord.* Nutrients from the mother pass from her blood to the embryonic blood vessels, which carry them, via the umbilical cord, to the embryo. In turn, embryonic blood vessels in the umbilical cord carry embryonic wastes to the placenta, where they can be eliminated by maternal blood vessels. The placenta also helps to combat internal infection and gives the

FIGURE 3.8

When Birth Defects Occur

Body parts and systems are most vulnerable during organogenesis, when they are developing most rapidly, generally within the first trimester of pregnancy.

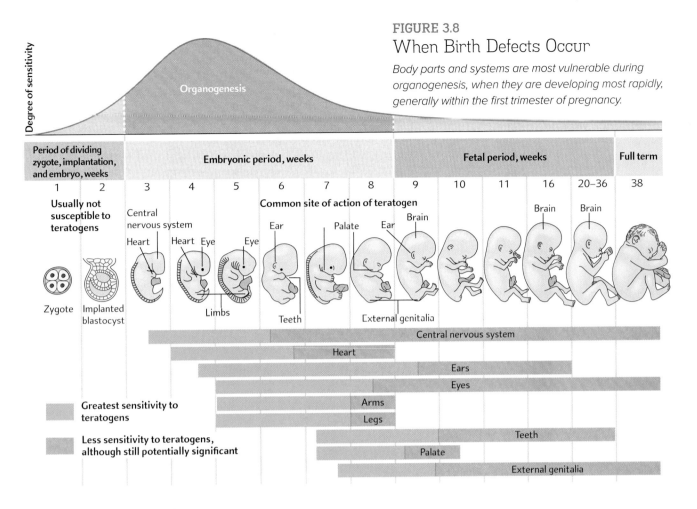

Note: Intervals of time are not all equal.

Source: Adapted from E. Brody, 1995; data from March of Dimes.

unborn child immunity to various diseases. It produces the hormones that support pregnancy, prepare the mother's breasts for lactation, and eventually stimulate the uterine contractions that will expel the baby from the mother's body.

Embryonic Stage (2 to 8 Weeks) During the **embryonic stage,** from about 2 to 8 weeks, the organs and major body systems—respiratory, digestive, and nervous—develop rapidly. This process is known as *organogenesis.* This is a critical period, when the embryo is most vulnerable to destructive influences in the prenatal environment (Figure 3.8). Any organ system or structure that is still developing at the time of exposure is most likely to be affected. Because of this, defects that occur later in pregnancy are likely to be less serious as the major organ systems and physical structures of the body are complete. Brain growth and development begins during the embryonic stage and continues after birth and beyond.

The most severely defective embryos usually do not survive beyond the first *trimester,* or 3-month period, of pregnancy. A **spontaneous abortion,** commonly called a *miscarriage,* is the expulsion from the uterus of an embryo or fetus that is unable to survive outside the womb. A miscarriage that occurs after 20 weeks of gestation is generally characterized as a stillbirth. As many as 1 in 4 recognized pregnancies end in miscarriage, and the actual figure may be as high as 1 in 2 because many spontaneous abortions take place before the woman realizes she is pregnant. Estimates are that this results in approximately 1 million fetal deaths each year in the United States alone (MacDorman & Kirmeyer, 2009). Most miscarriages occur during the first trimester (American College of Obstetricians and Gynecologists, 2015). Most miscarriages result from abnormal pregnancies; about 50 to 70 percent involve chromosomal

embryonic stage
Second stage of gestation (2 to 8 weeks), characterized by rapid growth and development of major body systems and organs.

spontaneous abortion
Natural expulsion from the uterus of an embryo that cannot survive outside the womb; also called *miscarriage*.

abnormalities (Hogge, 2003). Smoking, drinking alcohol, and drug use increase the risks of miscarriage. Miscarriages are more common in African American, Native American, and Alaskan native women, in both young and older (greater than 35 years of age) mothers, and are more likely to occur in pregnancies involving twins or higher order multiples (MacDorman & Kirmeyer, 2009).

Males are more likely than females to be spontaneously aborted or to be *stillborn* (dead at or after the 20th week of gestation). Thus, although about 125 males are conceived for every 100 females—a fact that has been attributed to the greater mobility of sperm carrying the smaller Y chromosome—only about 105 boys are born for every 100 girls. Males' greater vulnerability continues after birth: More die early in life, and at every age they are more susceptible to many disorders. As a result, there are only about 96 males for every 100 females in the United States (Martin et al., 2009; Spraggins, 2003).

fetal stage
Final stage of gestation (from 8 weeks to birth), characterized by increased differentiation of body parts and greatly enlarged body size.

Fetal Stage (8 Weeks to Birth) The appearance of the first bone cells at about 8 weeks signals the beginning of the **fetal stage,** the final stage of gestation. During this period, the fetus grows rapidly to about 20 times its previous length, and organs and body systems become more complex. Right up to birth, "finishing touches" such as fingernails, toenails, and eyelids continue to develop.

Fetuses are not passive passengers in their mothers' wombs. They breathe, kick, turn, flex their bodies, do somersaults, squint, swallow, make fists, hiccup, and suck their thumbs. The flexible membranes of the uterine walls and amniotic sac, which surround the protective buffer of amniotic fluid, permit and stimulate limited movement. Fetuses also can feel pain, but it is highly unlikely that they do so before the third trimester (Bellieni & Buonocore, 2012).

Scientists can observe fetal movement through **ultrasound,** the use of high-frequency sound waves to detect the outline of the fetus. Other instruments can monitor heart rate, changes in activity level, states of sleep and wakefulness, and cardiac reactivity.

The movements and activity level of fetuses show marked individual differences, and their heart rates vary in regularity and speed. Male fetuses, regardless of size,

ultrasound
Prenatal medical procedure using high-frequency sound waves to detect the outline of a fetus and its movements, so as to determine whether a pregnancy is progressing normally.

are more active and tend to move more vigorously than female fetuses throughout gestation (Almli, Ball & Wheeler, 2001). Thus infant boys' tendency to be more active than girls may be inborn (DiPietro et al., 2002).

Beginning at about the 12th week of gestation, the fetus swallows and inhales some of the amniotic fluid in which it floats. Because the amniotic fluid contains substances that cross the placenta from the mother's bloodstream, swallowing it may stimulate the budding senses of taste and smell (Mennella & Beauchamp, 1996). Mature taste cells appear at about 14 weeks of gestation. The olfactory system, which controls the sense of smell, also is well developed before birth (Savage, Fisher & Birch, 2007).

Fetuses respond to the mother's voice and heartbeat and the vibrations of her body, suggesting that they can hear and feel. Responses to sound and vibration seem to begin at 26 weeks of gestation, increase, and then reach a plateau at about 32 weeks (Kisilevsky & Haines, 2010; Kisilevsky, Muir & Low, 1992). In addition, fetuses nearing full term recognize the voice of their mother (Voegtline, Costigan, Pater & DiPietro, 2013) and prefer it to that of their father (Lee & Kisilevsky, 2014).

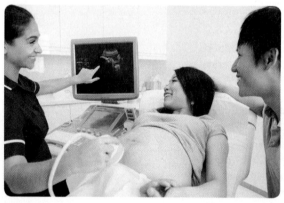

Ultrasound, the procedure this woman is undergoing, is a diagnostic tool that presents an image of the fetus in the womb. High-frequency sound waves directed at the woman's abdomen reveal the fetus's outline and movements. Ultrasound is widely used to monitor fetal development and to detect abnormalities. ©Monkey Business Images/Shutterstock

ENVIRONMENTAL INFLUENCES: MATERNAL FACTORS

Because the prenatal environment is the mother's body, virtually everything that influences her well-being, from her diet to her moods, may alter her unborn child's environment and affect its growth.

A **teratogen** is an environmental agent, such as a virus, a drug, or radiation, that can interfere with normal prenatal development. However, not all environmental hazards are equally risky for all fetuses. An event, substance, or process may be teratogenic for some fetuses but have little or no effect on others. Sometimes vulnerability may depend on a gene either in the fetus or in the mother. The timing of exposure, dose, duration, and interaction with other teratogenic factors also may make a difference.

Nutrition and Maternal Weight Pregnant women typically need 300 to 500 additional calories a day, including extra protein. Women of normal weight and body build who gain 16 to 40 pounds are less likely to have birth complications or to bear babies whose weight at birth is dangerously low or overly high. Yet about one-third of U.S. mothers gain more or less than the recommended amount (Martin et al., 2009). Either too much or too little weight gain can be risky. If a woman does not gain enough, her baby may suffer growth retardation in the womb, be born prematurely, experience distress during labor and delivery, or die at or near birth. Additionally, some research has shown that maternal calorie restriction during pregnancy might put children at risk for later obesity, perhaps by setting their metabolism to be thrifty (Caballero, 2006). A woman who gains too much weight risks having a large baby that needs to be delivered by induced labor or cesarean section (Chu et al., 2008; Martin et al., 2009).

Desirable weight gain depends on body mass index (BMI) before pregnancy. Women who are overweight or obese before becoming pregnant or in the early months of pregnancy tend to have longer deliveries, need more health care services (Chu et al., 2008), and be more likely to bear infants with birth defects (Gilboa et al., 2009; Stothard, Tennant, Bell & Rankin, 2009). Obesity also increases the risk of other complications of pregnancy, including miscarriage, difficulty inducing labor, and a greater likelihood of cesarean delivery (Brousseau, 2006; Chu et al., 2008). Current recommendations are that women who are underweight should gain 28 to 40 pounds, normal weight women should gain 25 to 35 pounds, overweight women should gain 15 to 25 pounds, and obese women should gain only 11 to 20 pounds (American College of Obstetrics and Gynecology, 2013).

Folic acid, or folate (a B vitamin), is critical in a pregnant woman's diet. A lack of folic acid can result in anencephaly and spina bifida. Addition of folic acid to enriched grain products has been mandatory in the United States since 1998, reducing the incidence of these defects (Honein, Paulozzi, Mathews, Erickson & Wong, 2001). It is estimated that if all women took 5 milligrams of folic acid each day before pregnancy and during the first trimester, an estimated 85 percent of neural-tube defects could be prevented (Wald, 2004). Milder folic acid deficiencies in pregnant mothers can result in less severe, but still troubling problems. For example, low folate levels during pregnancy have been associated with later attention-deficit/hyperactivity in 7- to 9-year-old children (Schlotz et al., 2009).

Malnutrition Prenatal malnutrition may have long-range effects. In rural Gambia, in western Africa, people born during the *hungry season*, when foods from the previous harvest are depleted, are 10 times more likely to die in early adulthood than people born during other parts of the year (Moore et al., 1997), and there are suggestions that these effects may persist across generations (Rickard et al., 2012). In studies done in the United Kingdom, children whose mothers had low vitamin D levels late in pregnancy had low bone mineral content at age 9, potentially increasing their risk of osteoporosis in later life (Javaid et al., 2006). And, several studies have revealed a link between fetal undernutrition and schizophrenia.

It is important to identify malnutrition early in pregnancy so it can be treated. Malnourished women who take dietary supplements while pregnant tend to have bigger, healthier infants (Imdad & Bhutta, 2011; Haider & Bhutta, 2012); and women with low zinc levels who take daily zinc supplements are less likely to have babies with low birth weight and small head circumference (Hess & King, 2009).

Physical Activity and Strenuous Work Moderate exercise any time during pregnancy does not seem to endanger the fetuses of healthy women (Committee on Obstetric Practice,

2002; Riemann & Kanstrup Hansen, 2000). Regular exercise prevents constipation and improves respiration, circulation, muscle tone, and skin elasticity, all of which contribute to a more comfortable pregnancy and an easier, safer delivery (Committee on Obstetric Practice, 2002). Employment during pregnancy generally entails no special hazards. However, strenuous working conditions, occupational fatigue, and long working hours may be associated with a greater risk of premature birth (Bell, Zimmerman & Diehr, 2008).

The American College of Obstetricians and Gynecologists (2016) recommends that women in low-risk pregnancies be guided by their own abilities and stamina. The safest course seems to be for pregnant women to exercise moderately, not pushing themselves, and to stay well hydrated.

Drug Intake Almost everything an expectant mother takes in makes its way to the uterus. Drugs may cross the placenta, just as oxygen, carbon dioxide, and water do. Vulnerability is greatest in the first few months of gestation, when development is most rapid.

Medical Drugs In the early 1960s a tranquilizer called *thalidomide* was banned after it was found to have caused stunted or missing limbs, severe facial deformities, and defective organs in some 12,000 babies. The thalidomide disaster sensitized medical professionals and the public to the potential dangers of taking drugs while pregnant.

The American Academy of Pediatrics (AAP) Committee on Drugs (2001) recommends that no medication be taken by a pregnant or breast-feeding woman unless it is essential for her health or her child's (Koren, Pastuszak & Ito, 1998). Among the medical drugs that may be harmful during pregnancy are the antibiotic tetracycline; certain barbiturates, opiates, and other central nervous system depressants; several hormones, including diethylstilbestrol (DES) and androgens; certain anticancer drugs, such as methotrexate; Accutane, a drug often prescribed for severe acne; drugs used to treat epilepsy; and several antipsychotic drugs (Briggs, Freeman & Yaffe, 2012; Einarson & Boskovic, 2009; Koren et al., 1998). Angiotensin-converting enzyme (ACE) inhibitors and nonsteroidal anti-inflammatory drugs (NSAIDs), such as naproxen and ibuprofen, have been linked to birth defects when taken anytime from the first trimester on (Cooper et al., 2006; Ofori, Oraichi, Blais, Rey & Berard, 2006). In addition, certain antipsychotic drugs used to manage severe psychiatric disorders may have serious potential effects on the fetus, including withdrawal symptoms at birth (Hudak & Tan, 2012).

Opiods In recent years, the number of pregnant women abusing legal and illegal opioids has risen (Martin, Longinaker & Terplan, 2015; Kocherlakota, 2014). While opioid use has not been implicated in birth defects, it is associated with small babies, fetal death, preterm labor, and aspiration of meconium (Center for Substance Abuse Treatment, 2008). Moreover, babies born to drug-addicted mothers are often addicted themselves and go through withdrawal once they are born and no longer receiving the drug. This results in neonate abstinence syndrome, a condition in which newborns may show sleep disturbances, tremors, difficulty regulating their bodies, irritability and crying, diarrhea, fever, and feeding difficulties (Jansson & Velez, 2012). Long-term effects include deficiencies in growth as well as attentional, memory, and perceptual problems. However, studies on cognitive outcomes are conflicting, and results may be due to other variables (such as socioeconomic status or other drug use) that are correlated with opiate use (Behnke & Smith, 2013). To date, punitive measures such as jailing pregnant women who use these drugs have been shown to be ineffective. This has led to calls to address the opioid crisis in pregnant women as a public health problem rather than a law enforcement issue (Patrick & Schiff, 2017).

Alcohol Prenatal alcohol exposure is the most common cause of mental retardation and the leading preventable cause of birth defects in the United States. **Fetal alcohol syndrome (FAS)** is characterized by a combination of retarded growth, face and body malformations, and disorders of the central nervous system. FAS and other less severe alcohol-related conditions are estimated to occur in nearly 1 in every 20 births (Sacks, Gonzalez, Bouchery, Tomedy & Brewer, 2015).

fetal alcohol syndrome (FAS)
Combination of mental, motor, and developmental abnormalities affecting the offspring of some women who drink heavily during pregnancy.

A mother who drinks during pregnancy risks having a child born with fetal alcohol syndrome.
©PhotoMediaGroup/Shutterstock

Even small amounts of social drinking may harm a fetus (Sokol, Delaney-Black & Nordstrom, 2003), and the more the mother drinks, the greater the effect. Moderate or heavy drinking during pregnancy seems to disturb an infant's neurological and behavioral functioning, and this may affect early social interaction with the mother, which is vital to emotional development (Hannigan & Armant, 2000). Heavy drinkers who continue to drink after becoming pregnant are likely to have babies with reduced skull and brain growth as compared with babies of nondrinking women or expectant mothers who stop drinking (Handmaker et al., 2006).

FAS-related problems can include, in infancy, reduced responsiveness to stimuli, slow reaction time, and reduced visual acuity (sharpness of vision) (Carter et al., 2005; Sokol et al., 2003) and, throughout childhood, short attention span, distractibility, restlessness, hyperactivity, learning disabilities, memory deficits, and mood disorders (Sokol et al., 2003) as well as aggressiveness and problem behavior (Sood et al., 2001). Prenatal alcohol exposure is a risk factor for development of drinking problems and alcohol disorders in young adulthood (Alati et al., 2006; Baer, Sampson, Barr, Connor & Streissguth, 2003).

Some FAS problems recede after birth; but others, such as retardation, behavioral and learning problems, and hyperactivity, tend to persist. Enriching these children's education or general environment does not always enhance their cognitive development (Kerns, Don, Mateer & Streissguth, 1997; Spohr, Willms & Steinhausen, 1993; Strömland & Hellström, 1996), but recent interventions targeted at cognitive skills in children with FAS are showing promise (Paley & O'Connor, 2011). Children with FAS may be less likely to develop behavioral and mental health problems if they are diagnosed early and are reared in stable, nurturing environments (Streissguth et al., 2004).

Nicotine Maternal smoking during pregnancy has been identified as the single most important factor in low birth weight in developed countries (DiFranza, Aligne & Weitzman, 2004). Women who smoke during pregnancy are more than 1½ times as likely as nonsmokers to bear low-birth-weight babies (weighing less than 5½ pounds at birth). While even light smoking (fewer than five cigarettes a day) is associated with a greater risk of low birth weight (Martin et al., 2005; Shankaran et al., 2004) the effect is dose dependent. Thus, those mothers who smoke more than 20 cigarettes a day have the smallest babies (Ko et al., 2014).

Tobacco use during pregnancy also brings increased risks of miscarriage, growth retardation, stillbirth, small head circumference, sudden infant death, colic (uncontrollable, extended crying for no apparent reason) in early infancy, hyperkinetic disorder (excessive movement), and long-term respiratory, neurological, cognitive, attentional, and behavioral problems (AAP Committee on Substance Abuse, 2001; DiFranza, Aligne & Weitzman, 2004; Froehlich et al., 2009; Hoyert, Mathews, Menacker, Strobino & Guyer, 2006; Linnet et al., 2005; Martin et al., 2007; Shah, Sullivan & Carter, 2006; Smith et al., 2006). The effects of prenatal exposure to secondhand smoke on development tend to be worse when children also experience socioeconomic hardship during the first 2 years of life (Rauh et al., 2004), when they are exposed to additional teratogens such as lead (Froehlich et al., 2009), or deprived of necessary nutrients such as folic acid (Mook-Kanamori et al., 2010) at the same time. However, not all fetuses respond in the same way. Some are more robust than others by virtue of their genotype and seem to be less affected by moderate maternal smoking (Price, Grosser, Plomin & Jaffee, 2010).

Caffeine Can the caffeine a pregnant woman consumes in coffee, tea, cola, or chocolate cause trouble for her fetus? For the most part, results have been mixed. It does seem clear that caffeine is *not* a teratogen for human babies (Christian & Brent, 2001). However, studies have found a slightly increased risk of miscarriage, still birth, and low birth weight in mothers who consume caffeine while pregnant (Greenwood et al., 2014) and there are suggestions that risk may increase with dosage (Chen et al., 2014). Thus, while results are unclear, current recommendations on limiting caffeine to 200 milligrams or less (about one cup of coffee) are still in place.

Marijuana Marijuana is the most commonly used illegal drug during pregnancy, and rates of women who report using marijuana while pregnant have risen sharply in the last 10 years (Martin, Longinaker, Mark, Chisholm & Terplan, 2015), perhaps as a result of more liberal usage laws in many states. Research on marijuana is difficult. For example, many pregnant women who smoke marijuana also smoke cigarettes or consume alcohol, and socioeconomic factors also seem to be important (Metz & Stickrath, 2015). However, research does show that while marijuana exposure is not associated with low birth weight, preterm delivery (Mark, Desai & Terplan, 2016), or decreases in general intelligence (Behnke & Smith, 2013), it has been been implicated in subtle deficits in problem-solving skills (Fried, 2002), and learning and memory problems (Richardson, Ryan, Willford, Day & Goldschmidt, 2002). This may explain why marijuana exposure during the prenatal period is also associated with decreases in academic achievement (Goldschmidt, Richardson, Cornelius & Day, 2004).

Cocaine Cocaine use during pregnancy has been associated with spontaneous abortion, delayed growth, premature labor, low birth weight, small head size, birth defects, and impaired neurological development (Chiriboga, Brust, Bateman, & Hauser, 1999; March of Dimes Birth Defects Foundation, 2004a; Shankaran et al., 2004). In some studies, cocaine-exposed newborns show acute withdrawal symptoms and sleep disturbances (O'Brien & Jeffery, 2002). It appears that cocaine may preferentially affect areas of the brain involved in attention and executive functioning (Behnke & Smith, 2013). Other studies, however, have found no specific connection between prenatal cocaine exposure and physical, motor, cognitive, emotional, or behavioral deficits that could not also be attributed to other risk factors, such as low birth weight; exposure to tobacco, alcohol, or marijuana; or a poor home environment (Frank, Augustyn, Knight, Pell & Zuckerman, 2001; Messinger et al., 2004; Singer et al., 2004).

Methamphetamine Prenatal methamphetamine exposure is associated with fetal growth restriction (Smith et al., 2006). Additionally, prenatal exposure to methamphetamines has been implicated in fetal brain damage to areas of the brain involved in learning, memory, and control (Roussotte et al., 2011). Methamphetamine-exposed children also have less white matter in their brains, a finding that has implications for the developmental delays commonly found in such children (Cloak, Ernst, Fujii, Hedemark & Chang, 2009).

acquired immune deficiency syndrome (AIDS)
Viral disease that undermines effective functioning of the immune system.

Maternal Illnesses **Acquired immune deficiency syndrome (AIDS)** is a disease caused by the human immunodeficiency virus (HIV), which undermines functioning of the immune system. If an expectant mother has the virus in her blood, *perinatal transmission* may occur: The virus may cross over to the fetus's bloodstream through the placenta during pregnancy, labor, or delivery or, after birth, through breast milk.

The biggest risk factor for perinatal HIV transmission is a mother who is unaware she has HIV. In the United States, new pediatric AIDS cases have declined steadily since 1992 due to routine testing and treatment of pregnant women and newborn babies and to advances in the prevention, detection, and treatment of HIV infection in infants. As a result, the estimated rate of perinatal HIV infection is now less than 2 percent. The risk of transmission also can be reduced by choosing cesarean delivery, especially when a woman has not received antiretroviral therapy, and by promotion of alternatives to breast-feeding among high-risk women (CDC, 2006a).

Rubella (German measles), if contracted by a woman before her 11th week of pregnancy, is almost certain to cause deafness and heart defects in her baby. Chances of catching rubella during pregnancy have been greatly reduced in Europe and the United States since the late 1960s, when a vaccine was developed that is now routinely administered to infants and children. Efforts in less developed countries to provide rubella vaccinations resulted in a decrease of reported rubella cases of more than 80 percent from 2000 to 2009 (Reef et al., 2011). Recent outbreaks in the United States most likely stem from importation of the disease from international travel. Most of the people who were infected were not vaccinated (Clemmons, Gastanaduy, Fiebelkorn, Redd & Wallace, 2015).

An infection called *toxoplasmosis,* caused by a parasite harbored in the bodies of cattle, sheep, and pigs and in the intestinal tracts of cats, typically produces either no symptoms or symptoms like those of the common cold. In an expectant woman, however, especially in the second and third trimesters of pregnancy, it can cause fetal brain damage, severely impaired eyesight or blindness, seizures, miscarriage, stillbirth, or death of the baby. If the baby survives, there may be later problems, including eye infections, hearing loss, and learning disabilities. Treatment with antiparasitic drugs during the first year of life can reduce brain and eye damage (McLeod et al., 2006). To avoid infection, expectant mothers should not eat raw or very rare meat, should wash hands and all work surfaces after touching raw meat, should peel or thoroughly wash raw fruits and vegetables, and should not dig in a garden where cat feces may be buried. Women who have a cat should have it checked for the disease, should not feed it raw meat, and, if possible, should have someone else empty the litter box (March of Dimes Foundation, 2012).

Offspring of mothers with diabetes are 3 to 4 times more likely than offspring of other women to develop a wide range of birth defects (Correa et al., 2008). Women with diabetes need to be sure their blood glucose levels are under control *before* becoming pregnant (Li, Chase, Jung, Smith & Loeken, 2005). Use of multivitamin supplements during the 3 months before conception and the first 3 months of pregnancy can help reduce the risk of diabetes-associated birth defects (Correa, Botto, Liu, Mulinare & Erickson, 2003).

Maternal Anxiety, Stress, and Depression Some tension and worry during pregnancy are normal and do not necessarily increase risks of birth complications (Littleton, Breitkopf & Berenson, 2006).

Maternal self-reported **stress** and anxiety during pregnancy has been associated with more active and irritable temperament in newborns (DiPietro et al., 2010), inattentiveness during a developmental assessment in 8-month-olds (Huizink, Robles de Medina, Mulder, Visser & Buitelaar, 2002), and negative emotionality or behavioral disorders in early childhood (Martin, Noyes, Wisenbaker & Huttunen, 2000; O'Connor, Heron, Golding, Beveridge & Glover, 2002). Additionally, chronic stress can result in preterm delivery, perhaps through the action of elevated levels of stress hormones (which are implicated in the onset of labor) or the resulting dampened immune functioning, which makes women more vulnerable to inflammatory diseases and infection that can also trigger labor (Schetter, 2009).

Depression may have also have negative effects on development. Children of mothers who were depressed during pregnancy were more likely to be born premature (Grigoriadis et al., 2013), be developmentally delayed as toddlers (Deave, Heron, Evans & Emond, 2008), and show elevated levels of violent and antisocial behaviors in adolescence, (Hay, Pawlby, Waters, Perra & Sharp, 2010).

Maternal Age Birthrates of U.S. women in their 30s and 40s are at their highest levels since the 1960s, in part due to fertility treatments—an example of a history-graded influence (Figure 3.9) (Martin et al., 2010). From 2000 to 2014, there was a 23 percent increase in first births for women over the age of 35 years, for all ethnic and racial groups, and in all states (Mathews & Hamilton, 2016).

The chance of miscarriage or stillbirth rises with maternal age and reaches 90 percent for women age 45 or older. Women 30 to 35 are more

stress
Physical or psychological demands on a person or organism.

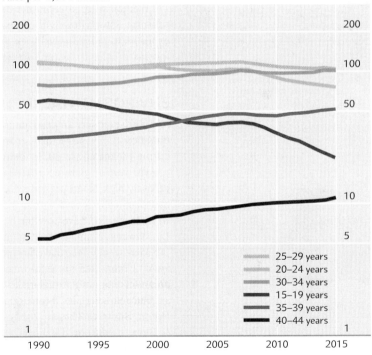

FIGURE 3.9

U.S. Birthrates, by Age of Mother, 1990–2015

Source: Martin, J. A.; Hamilton, B. E.; Osterman, M. J.; Driscoll, A. K.; & Mathews, T. J. "Births: Final Data for 2015." National vital statistics reports: from the Centers for Disease Control and Prevention, National Center for Health Statistics, National Vital Statistics System, 66(1), 1, 2017.

likely to suffer complications due to diabetes, high blood pressure, or severe bleeding. There is also higher risk of premature delivery, retarded fetal growth, birth defects, and chromosomal abnormalities, such as Down syndrome (Heffner, 2004).

Adolescent mothers tend to have premature or underweight babies—perhaps because a young girl's still-growing body consumes vital nutrients the fetus needs (Martin et al., 2007) or because of inadequate or missing prenatal care (Malabarey, Balayla, Klam, Shrim & Abenhaim, 2012). These newborns are at heightened risk of death in the first month, disabilities, or health problems. While rates of teen pregnancy in the United States have been in a steady, long-term decline, they are still among the highest of industrialized nations (Hamilton & Ventura, 2012).

Outside Environmental Hazards Air pollution, chemicals, radiation, extremes of heat and humidity, and other environmental hazards can affect prenatal development. Pregnant women who regularly breathe air that contains high levels of fine combustion-related particles are more likely to bear infants who are premature or undersized (Parker, Woodruff, Basu & Schoendorf, 2005; Pederson et al., 2013) or have chromosomal abnormalities (Bocskay et al., 2005). Exposure to high concentrations of disinfection by-products is associated with low birth weight and congenital abnormalities (Nieuwenhuijsen, Dadvand, Grellier, Martinez & Vrijheid, 2013). Two insecticides, chlorpyrifos and diazinon, are associated with stunted prenatal growth (Whyatt et al., 2004).

Fetal exposure to low levels of environmental toxins, such as lead, mercury, and dioxin, as well as nicotine and ethanol, may help explain the sharp rise in asthma, allergies, and autoimmune disorders such as lupus (Dietert, 2005). Both maternal exposure to the hydrocarbons and the children's asthma symptoms were associated with epigenetic changes in the gene ACSL3, which affects the lungs (Perera et al., 2009). Childhood cancers, including leukemia, have been linked to pregnant mothers' drinking chemically contaminated groundwater (Boyles, 2002) and use of home pesticides (Menegaux et al., 2006). Infants exposed prenatally even to low levels of lead, especially during the third trimester, tend to show IQ deficits during childhood (Schnaas et al., 2006).

Women who have routine dental X-rays during pregnancy triple their risk of having full-term, low-birth-weight babies (Hujoel, Bollen, Noonan & del Aguila, 2004). In utero exposure to radiation has been linked to miscarriage, mental retardation, small head size, increased cancer risk, and lowered IQ (Groen, Bay & Lim, 2012).

ENVIRONMENTAL INFLUENCES: PATERNAL FACTORS

A man's exposure to lead, marijuana or tobacco smoke, large amounts of alcohol or radiation, DES, pesticides, or high ozone levels may result in abnormal or poor-quality sperm (Sokol et al., 2006; Swan et al., 2003). Offspring of men stationed on military vessels were at elevated risk of infant mortality and their mothers were at risk for dangerously high blood pressure during pregnancy (Baste et al., 2014). Babies whose fathers had diagnostic X-rays within the year prior to conception or had high lead exposure at work tended to have low birth weight and slowed fetal growth (Chen & Wang, 2006; Lin, Hwang, Marshall & Marion, 1998; Shea, Little & the ALSPAC Study Team, 1997).

Men who smoke have an increased likelihood of transmitting genetic abnormalities (AAP Committee on Substance Abuse, 2001) and heart defects (Deng et al., 2013). A pregnant woman's exposure to the father's secondhand smoke has been linked with asthma (Simons, To, Moneiddin, Stieb & Dell, 2014), attentional problems (Langley, Heron, Smith & Thapar, 2012), low birth weight (Rubin, Krasilnikoff, Leventhal, Weile & Berget, 1986), and cancer in childhood and adulthood (Ji et al., 1997).

Older fathers may be a significant source of birth defects due to damaged or deteriorated sperm. Birthrates for fathers ages 30 to 49 have risen substantially since 1980 (Martin et al., 2009). Advancing paternal age is associated with increases in the risk of several rare conditions, including dwarfism (Wyrobek et al., 2006). Advanced age of the father also may be a factor in a disproportionate number of cases of schizophrenia (Byrne et al., 2003; Malaspina et al., 2001), bipolar disorder (Frans et al., 2008), and autism and related disorders (Reichenberg et al., 2006; Tsuchiya et al., 2008).

Monitoring and Promoting Prenatal Development

Historically, once a baby was conceived, parents were in the dark regarding the characteristics and health of the baby. Now scientists have developed an array of tools to assess an unborn baby's progress and well-being and even to intervene to correct some abnormal conditions (Table 3.4).

TABLE 3.4 Prenatal Assessment Techniques

Technique	Description	Uses and Advantages	Risks and Notes
Amniocentesis	Sample of amniotic fluid is withdrawn under guidance of ultrasound and analyzed. Most commonly used procedure to obtain fetal cells for testing.	Can detect chromosomal disorders and many genetic defects; more than 99 percent accuracy rate. Usually performed in women ages 35 and over; recommended if prospective parents are known carriers of genetic diseases. Can help diagnose sex-linked disorders.	Performed after 15 weeks' gestation. Results usually take 1 to 2 weeks. Small (0.5–1%) added risk of fetal loss or injury. Can be used for sex-screening of unborn babies.
Chorionic villus sampling (CVS)	Tissues from hairlike chorionic villi (projections of membrane surrounding fetus) are removed from placenta and analyzed.	Early diagnosis of birth defects and disorders. Can be performed between 10 and 12 weeks' gestation; yields highly accurate results within a week.	Should not be performed before 10 weeks' gestation. Some studies suggest 1–4% more risk of fetal loss than with amniocentesis.
Embryoscopy, fetoscopy	Tiny viewing scope is inserted in woman's abdomen to view embryo or fetus. Can assist in diagnosis of nonchromosomal genetic disorders.	Can guide fetal blood transfusions and bone marrow transplants.	Riskier than other prenatal diagnostic procedures.
Maternal blood test	A sample of the prospective mother's blood is tested for hormone levels associated with fetal abnormalities.	May indicate defects in formation of brain or spinal cord; also can predict Down syndrome and other abnormalities. Permits monitoring of at-risk pregnancies.	No known risks, but false negatives are possible. Ultrasound and/or amniocentesis needed to confirm suspected conditions.
Preimplantation genetic diagnosis	After in vitro fertilization, a sample cell is removed from the blastocyst and analyzed.	Can avoid transmission of genetic defects or predispositions known to run in the family; a defective blastocyst is *not* implanted in uterus.	No known risks.
Ultrasound (sonogram), sonoembryology	High-frequency sound waves produce a picture of fetus in uterus. Sonoembryology uses high-frequency transvaginal probes and digital image processing to produce a picture of embryo in uterus.	Monitor fetal growth, movement, position, and form; assess amniotic fluid volume; judge gestational age; detect multiple pregnancies. Detect major abnormalities or death of a fetus. Guide amniocentesis and chorionic villus sampling.	Done routinely in many places. Can be used for sex-screening of unborn babies.
Umbilical cord sampling (cordocentesis, or fetal blood sampling)	Needle guided by ultrasound is inserted into blood vessels of umbilical cord.	Allows direct access to fetal DNA for diagnostic measures, allows therapeutic measures such as blood transfusions.	Fetal loss or miscarriage is reported in 1–2% of cases; increases risk of bleeding from umbilical cord and fetal distress.

Sources: Chodirker et al.; 2001; Cicero, Curcio, Papageorghiou, Sonek, & Nicolaides, 2001; Cunniff & the Committee on Genetics, 2004; Kurjak, Kupesic, Matijevic, Kos, & Marton, 1999; Verlinsky et al.; 2002

PRENATAL CARE AROUND THE WORLD

UNICEF (United Nations International Children's Emergency Fund) estimates that approximately 130 million babies are born worldwide each year (UNICEF, 2005). About 830 women die each day from childbirth-related complications, with 99 percent of these deaths occurring in low-resource areas (World Health Organization, 2016c). Hemorrhage, hypertensive disorders, and infection are responsible for more than half of all maternal deaths; most of these deaths could have been prevented with proper education and prenatal care (UNICEF Millennium Development Goals, 2015).

Proper prenatal care is vital to the survival of pregnant women and their babies. The World Health Organization (WHO) recommends a minimum of four, and preferably eight, prenatal visits to a skilled health care provider. At the minimum, prenatal services should include education about proper nutrition, activity levels, and substance use. Additionally, medical services should include a tetanus vaccination and vitamin supplements of at least folic acid and iron (March of Dimes, 2014).

Standards of prenatal care are not equal worldwide. In developed countries, pregnant women receive this standard of care routinely. In low-income/developing countries, only 40 percent of women receive the minimum WHO standard of four visits (World Health Organization, 2016, November 7). Poverty often limits both access and availability of services. Women living in remote areas have limited access to health care, sometimes the distance to facilities is too great, or there are not enough skilled workers to serve the population. Skilled care at birth leads to a 54 percent reduction of maternal mortality (World Health Organization, 2016c).

Nearly half of all births worldwide happen at home. In developing countries many of these births are either unattended, or attended by a family member or traditional birth attendant (TBA). Many TBAs have little formal training. TBAs are often older women who learned their skills through experience. TBAs often give advice on what to eat, herbal remedies for pain, abdominal massages, support and assistance with the delivery of the baby. TBAs' limited access to equipment or medical facilities put mother and child at higher risk if complications occur (Garces, et al., 2011).

The most common risks of not having proper prenatal care are low birth weight, birth defects, infections, premature birth, and placental concerns. These factors can lead to long-term health problems or death for the mother and/or newborn (March of Dimes, 2014).

The maternal/infant mortality rate has been declining over the past 20 years, but is still too high. An estimated 5 million babies died or were stillborn during 2015 (UNICEF, 2014). Childbirth is still the leading cause of death among adolescent girls in developing countries (Patton, et al., 2009). Globalized efforts by the WHO, the CDC (Centers for Disease Control), Save the Children, Doctors without Borders, Care, UNICEF, and many others are helping to make a difference. All women need access to prenatal care, education, family planning, and support during pregnancy and the weeks following childbirth.

what's your view

How important is prenatal care during pregnancy? What can you do to help promote healthy pregnancies around the world? The United States has one of the worst maternal mortality rates of the developed countries. In 2015 it was 14 deaths per 100,000 live births (Central Intelligence Agency, 2015). What factors do you see contributing to this?

Progress is being made in the use of noninvasive procedures, such as ultrasound and blood tests, to detect chromosomal abnormalities. In one study, a combination of three noninvasive tests conducted at 11 weeks of gestation predicted the presence of Down syndrome with 87 percent accuracy. When the 11-week tests were followed by further noninvasive testing early in the second trimester, accuracy reached 96 percent (Malone et al., 2005). Contrary to previous findings, amniocentesis and chorionic villus sampling, which can be used earlier in pregnancy, carry only a slightly higher miscarriage risk than these noninvasive procedures (Caughey, Hopkins & Norton, 2006; Eddleman et al., 2006).

Screening for defects and diseases is only one important reason for early prenatal care. Early, high-quality prenatal care, which includes educational, social, and nutritional services, can help prevent maternal or infant death and other birth complications. It can provide first-time mothers with information about pregnancy, childbirth, and infant care. The amount of prenatal care received by a woman is related linearly to positive outcomes (Partridge, Balayla, Holcroft & Abenhaim, 2012).

DISPARITIES IN PRENATAL CARE

In the United States prenatal care is widespread, but not universal as in many European countries; and it lacks uniform national standards and guaranteed financial coverage. Use of early prenatal care (during the first 3 months of pregnancy) rose modestly between 1990 and 2003 but then plateaued and declined slightly in 2006, possibly due to changes in welfare and Medicaid policies (Martin et al., 2010). In 2014, 6 percent of expectant mothers received late or no prenatal care during their pregnancies (Child Trends Databank, 2015).

Historically, rates of low birth weight and premature birth continue to rise. Why? One answer is the increasing number of multiple births, which often are early births, with heightened risk of death within the first year. However, new data suggest that this increase may have finally peaked, as rates of premature delivery have decreased, particularly for triplets and higher order multiples (Martin, Hamilton, Osterman, Driscoll & Mathews, 2017).

A second answer is that the benefits of prenatal care are not evenly distributed. Although usage of prenatal care has grown, especially among ethnic groups that have tended not to receive early care, the women most at risk of bearing low-birth-weight babies—teenage and unmarried women, those with little education, and some minority women—are still least likely to receive it (Partridge, Balayla, Holcroft & Abelhaim, 2012; Martin et al., 2006).

A related concern is an ethnic disparity in fetal and postbirth mortality. After adjusting for such risk factors as SES, overweight, smoking, hypertension, and diabetes, the chances of perinatal death (death between 20 weeks' gestation and 1 week after birth) remain 3.4 times higher for blacks, 1.5 times higher for Hispanics, and 1.9 times higher for other minorities than for whites (Healy et al., 2006).

THE NEED FOR PRECONCEPTION CARE

A more fundamental answer is that even early prenatal care is insufficient. Care should begin *before* pregnancy to identify preventable risks. The CDC (2017p) has comprehensive, research-based guidelines for *preconception care* for all women of childbearing age. Such care should include the following:

- *Physical examinations* and the taking of medical and family histories.
- *Vaccinations* for rubella and hepatitis B.
- *Risk screening* for genetic disorders and infectious diseases such as STDs.
- *Counseling* women to avoid smoking and alcohol, maintain a healthy body weight, and take folic acid supplements.

Good preconception and prenatal care can give every child the best possible chance for entering the world in good condition to meet the challenges of life outside the womb.

summary and key terms

Conceiving New Life

- Fertilization, the union of an ovum and a sperm, results in the formation of a one-celled zygote, which then duplicates itself by cell division.
- Multiple births can occur either by the fertilization of two ova or by the splitting of one fertilized ovum. Higher multiple births result from either one of these processes or a combination of the two.
- Dizygotic (fraternal) twins have different genetic makeups and may be of different sexes. Although monozygotic (identical) twins typically have the same genetic makeup, they may have phenotypic differences.

fertilization, zygote, dizygotic twins, monozygotic twins

Mechanisms of Heredity

- The basic functional units of heredity are the genes, which are made of deoxyribonucleic acid (DNA). DNA carries the genetic code. Each gene is located by function in a definite position on a particular chromosome. The complete sequence of genes in the human body is called the *human genome*.

   deoxyribonucleic acid (DNA), genetic code, chromosomes, genes, human genome, mutation

- At conception, each normal human being receives 23 chromosomes from the mother and 23 from the father. These form 23 pairs of chromosomes—22 pairs of autosomes and 1 pair of sex chromosomes. A child who receives an X chromosome from each parent is genetically female. A child who receives a Y chromosome from the father is genetically male.

- The simplest patterns of genetic transmission are dominant and recessive inheritance. When a pair of alleles are the same, a person is homozygous for the trait; when they are different, the person is heterozygous.

   autosomes, sex chromosomes, alleles, homozygous, heterozygous, dominant inheritance, recessive inheritance

- Most normal human characteristics are the result of polygenic or multifactorial transmission. Dominant inheritance and multifactorial transmission explain why a person's phenotype does not always express the underlying genotype.

- The epigenetic framework controls the functions of particular genes; it can be affected by environmental factors.

   polygenic inheritance, phenotype, genotype, multifactorial transmission, epigenesis

- Birth defects and diseases may result from simple dominant, recessive, or sex-linked inheritance, from mutations, or from genome imprinting.

- Through genetic counseling, prospective parents can receive information about the mathematical odds of bearing children with certain defects.

- Genetic testing involves risks as well as benefits.

   incomplete dominance, sex-linked inheritance, Down syndrome, genetic counseling

Nature and Nurture: Influences of Heredity and Environment

- Research in behavioral genetics is based on the assumption that the relative influences of heredity and environment within a population can be measured statistically. If heredity is an important influence on a trait, genetically closer persons will be more similar in that trait. Family studies, adoption studies, and studies of twins enable researchers to measure the heritability of specific traits.

- The concepts of reaction range, canalization, genotype-environment interaction, genotype-environment correlation, and niche-picking describe ways in which heredity and environment work together.

- Siblings tend to be more different than alike in intelligence and personality. According to some behavioral geneticists, heredity accounts for most of the similarity, and nonshared environmental effects account for most of the difference.

   behavioral genetics, heritability, concordant, reaction range, canalization, genotype-environment interaction, genotype-environment correlation, niche-picking, nonshared environmental effects

- Obesity, longevity, intelligence, temperament, and other aspects of personality are influenced by both heredity and environment.

   obesity, temperament

Prenatal Development

- Prenatal development occurs in three stages of gestation: the germinal, embryonic, and fetal stages.

- As fetuses grow, they move less, but more vigorously. Swallowing amniotic fluid, which contains substances from the mother's body, stimulates taste and smell. Fetuses seem able to hear, exercise sensory discrimination, learn, and remember.

   gestation, gestational age, germinal stage, implantation, embryonic stage, spontaneous abortion, fetal stage, ultrasound

- The developing organism can be greatly affected by its prenatal environment. The likelihood of a birth defect may depend on the timing and intensity of an environmental event and its interaction with genetic factors.

- Important environmental influences involving the mother include nutrition, smoking, intake of alcohol or other drugs, transmission of maternal illnesses or infections, maternal stress, anxiety, depression, maternal age and physical activity, and external environmental hazards, such as chemicals and radiation. External influences also may affect the father's sperm.

   teratogen, fetal alcohol syndrome (FAS), acquired immune deficiency syndrome (AIDS), stress

Monitoring and Promoting Prenatal Development

- Ultrasound, sonoembryology, amniocentesis, chorionic villus sampling, fetoscopy, preimplantation genetic diagnosis, umbilical cord sampling, and maternal blood tests can be used to determine whether an unborn baby is developing normally.

- Early, high-quality prenatal care is essential for healthy development. It can lead to detection of defects and disorders and may help reduce maternal and infant death, low birth weight, and other birth complications.

- Racial/ethnic disparities in prenatal care may be a factor in disparities in low birth weight and perinatal death.

- Preconception care for every woman of childbearing age would reduce unintended pregnancies and increase the chances of good pregnancy outcomes.

Birth and Physical Development during the First Three Years

chapter 4

©Wave Royalty Free/Design Pics Inc /Alamy Stock Photo

In this chapter we describe how babies come into the world, how newborn babies look, and how their body systems work. We discuss ways to safeguard their life and health and observe their rapid early physical development. We see how infants become busy, active toddlers and how caregivers can foster healthy growth and development.

learning objectives

Specify how childbirth has changed in developed countries.

Describe the birth process.

Describe the adjustment of a healthy newborn and the techniques for assessing its health.

Explain potential complications of childbirth and the prospects for infants with complicated births.

Identify factors affecting infants' chances for survival and health.

Discuss the patterns of physical growth and development in infancy.

Describe infants' motor development.

Childbirth and Culture: How Birthing Has Changed

Prior to the twentieth century, childbirth in Europe and in the United States was a female social ritual.* The woman sat up in her bed or perhaps in the stable. She might stand, walk around, or squat over a birth stool. The midwife who presided over the event had no formal training; she offered "advice, massages, potions, irrigations, and talismans" (Fontanel & d'Harcourt, 1997, p. 28). After the baby emerged, the midwife cut and tied the umbilical cord and cleaned and examined the newborn. Within a few hours or days, a peasant mother would be back at work in the fields; a more affluent woman could rest for several weeks. Childbirth in those times was "a struggle with death" for both mother and baby (Fontanel & d'Harcourt, 1997, p. 34). In seventeenth- and eighteenth-century France, a woman had a 1 in 10 chance of dying while or shortly after giving birth. Thousands of babies were stillborn, and 1 out of 4 who were born alive died during their first year.

Childbirth is still a dangerous endeavor in some developing countries in sub-Saharan Africa and South Asia. There, 60 million women deliver at home each year without the benefit of skilled care, and until recently more than 500,000 women and 4 million newborns died in or shortly after childbirth (Sines, Syed, Wall & Worley, 2007). There are promising trends in maternal mortality though. Estimates suggest that maternal mortality dropped to approximately 289,000 in 2013, representing a 45 percent decline from 1990 (World Health Organization, 2014).

At the start of the twentieth century, childbirth began to be professionalized in the United States, at least in urban settings. The growing use of maternity hospitals led to safer, more antiseptic conditions for childbirth, which reduced mortality for women. In 1900, only 5 percent of U.S. deliveries occurred in hospitals; by 1920, in some cities 65 percent did (Scholten, 1985). A similar trend took place in Europe. Most recently, in the United States 98.7 percent of babies are born in hospitals, and 86.1 percent of births are attended by physicians (Martin, Hamilton, Ventura, Osterman & Mathews, 2013).

The dramatic reductions in risks surrounding pregnancy and childbirth in industrialized countries are largely due to the availability of antibiotics, blood transfusions, safe anesthesia, improved hygiene, and drugs for inducing labor. In addition, improvements in prenatal assessment and care make it far more likely that a baby will be born healthy. Mortality rates for both mothers and children have decreased dramatically as noted in Figures 4.1 and 4.2.

Today a small but growing percentage of women in developed countries are going back to the intimate, personal experience of home birth (MacDorman, Menacker & Declercq, 2010). Home births usually are attended by a trained nurse-midwife, with the resources of medical science close at hand. Arrangements may be made with a physician and a nearby hospital in case an emergency arises. Some studies suggest that planned home births with speedy transfer to a hospital available in case of need can be as safe as hospital births for low-risk deliveries attended by skilled, certified midwives or nurse-midwives (American College of Nurse-Midwives, 2016). However, the American College of Obstetricians and Gynecologists (ACOG, 2017) and the American Medical Association (AMA House of Delegates, 2008) point out that

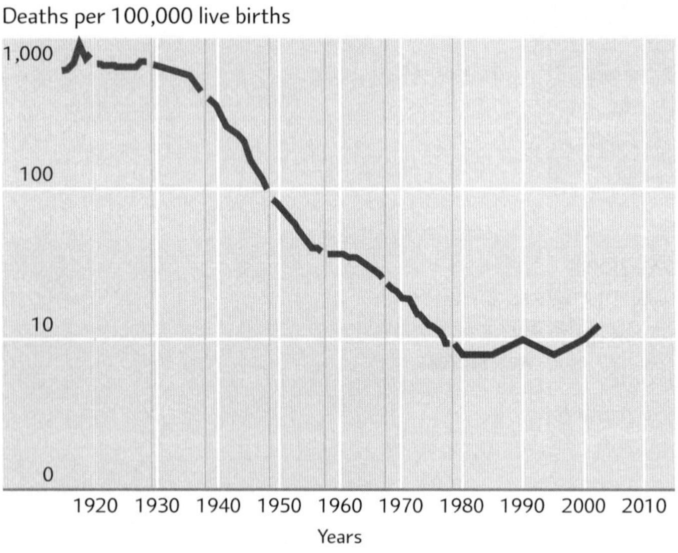

Deaths per 100,000 live births

FIGURE 4.1
U.S. Maternal Mortality Rates, 1915–2003

Since 1915 the maternal mortality rate in the United States has dropped from 607.9 deaths per 100,000 live births for the birth registration area to 12.1 deaths per 100,000 live births in 2003.

Before 1933, data for birth registration states only. Line breaks are shown between successive *International Classification of Diseases* revisions.

Sources: National Center for Health Statistics, 2007; S. L. Clark, 2012.

*This discussion is based on Eccles (1982), Fontanel and d'Harcourt (1997), Gélis (1991), and Scholten (1985).

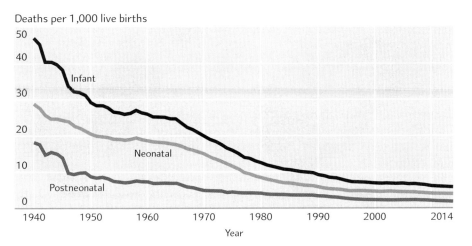

Deaths per 1,000 live births

Source: Kochanek, K. D., Murphy, S. L., Xu, J. Q., Tejada-Vera, B. "Deaths: Final data for 2014." *National Vital Statistics Reports,* 65(4). Hyattsville, MD: *National Center for Health Statistics,* 2016.

FIGURE 4.2

U.S. Infant Mortality Rates, 1940–2014

The U.S. infant mortality rate has decreased from 47.0 infant deaths per 1,000 live births in 1940 to 5.8 in 2014. During the same period, the neonatal rate decreased from 28.8 to 3.94 deaths per 1,000 live births, and the postneonatal rate decreased from 18.3 to 1.88 deaths per 1,000 live births.

complications can arise suddenly, even in low-risk pregnancies, and hospitals or accredited birthing centers are best equipped to respond to such emergencies.

Today hospitals are finding ways to humanize childbirth. Labor and delivery may take place in a comfortable birthing room, under soft lights, with the father or partner present as a coach and older siblings invited to visit after the birth. Rooming-in policies allow a baby to stay in the mother's room much or all of the time. These changes allow hospitals to allay concerns about an overly medicalized experience while still providing a safe environment in the event of complications.

The Birth Process

Labor is brought on by a series of uterine, cervical, and other changes called **parturition.** Parturition is the act or process of giving birth, and it typically begins about 2 weeks before delivery, when sharply rising estrogen levels stimulate the uterus to contract and the cervix to become more flexible.

The uterine contractions that expel the fetus begin—typically about 266 days after conception—as a tightening of the uterus. A woman may have felt false contractions (known as *Braxton-Hicks contractions*) at times during the final months of pregnancy, or even as early as the second trimester, when the muscles of the uterus tighten for up to 2 minutes. In comparison with the relatively mild and irregular Braxton-Hicks contractions, real labor contractions are more frequent, rhythmic, and painful, and they increase in frequency and intensity.

parturition
The act or process of giving birth.

STAGES OF CHILDBIRTH

Labor takes place in three overlapping stages (Figure 4.3).

Stage 1: Dilation of the Cervix The first stage, dilation of the cervix, is the longest, typically lasting 12 to 14 hours for a woman having her first child. In subsequent births, the first stage tends to be shorter. During this stage, regular and increasingly frequent uterine contractions—15 to 20 minutes apart at first—cause the cervix to shorten and dilate, or widen, in preparation for delivery. Toward the end of the first stage, contractions occur every 2 to 5 minutes. This stage lasts until the cervix is fully open (10 centimeters, or about 4 inches) so the baby can descend into the birth canal.

Stage 2: Descent and Emergence of the Baby The second stage, descent and emergence of the baby, typically lasts up to an hour or two. It begins when the baby's head begins to move through the cervix into the vaginal canal, and it ends when the baby

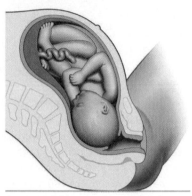

Stage one: Baby positions itself

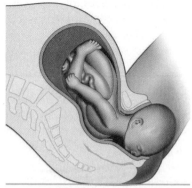

Stage two: Baby begins to emerge

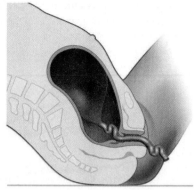

Stage three: Placenta is expelled

FIGURE 4.3

The Three Stages of Childbirth

(a) During the first stage of labor, a series of increasingly stronger contractions dilates the cervix, the opening to the mother's womb. (b) During the second stage, the baby's head moves down the birth canal and emerges from the vagina. (c) During the brief third stage, the placenta and umbilical cord are expelled from the womb. Then the cord is cut.

emerges completely from the mother's body. If this stage lasts longer than 2 hours, signaling that the baby may need help, a doctor may use vacuum extraction with a suction cup to pull the baby out of the mother's body. The use of forceps—an instrument shaped like a large pair of salad tongs—is increasingly rare, occurring at less than 1 percent of births (Martin, Hamilton, Osterman, Driscoll & Mathews, 2017). At the end of this stage, the baby is born but is still attached to the placenta in the mother's body by the umbilical cord, which must be cut and clamped.

Stage 3: Expulsion of the Placenta The third stage, expulsion of the placenta, lasts between 10 minutes and 1 hour. During this stage, the placenta and the remainder of the umbilical cord are expelled from the mother.

ELECTRONIC FETAL MONITORING

electronic fetal monitoring
Mechanical monitoring of fetal heartbeat during labor and delivery.

Most births have a happy outcome, but labor and delivery are nonetheless risky. To lessen these risks, technologies have been developed to monitor the fetus prior to delivery. **Electronic fetal monitoring** can be used to track the fetus's heartbeat during labor and delivery and to indicate how the fetal heart is responding to the stress of uterine contractions. Monitoring is most commonly done with the use of sensors attached to the woman's midsection and held in place with an electric belt. The procedure was used in 89 percent of live births in the United States in 2004 (Chen, Chauhan, Ananth, Vintzileos & Abuhamad, 2013).

Electronic fetal monitoring can provide valuable information in high-risk deliveries. However, monitoring can have drawbacks if it is used routinely in low-risk pregnancies. It is costly; it restricts the mother's movements during labor; and, most important, it has an extremely high false-positive rate, suggesting that fetuses are in trouble when they are not. Such warnings may prompt doctors to deliver by the riskier cesarean method rather than vaginally (Banta & Thacker, 2001).

VAGINAL VERSUS CESAREAN DELIVERY

cesarean delivery
Delivery of a baby by surgical removal from the uterus.

The usual method of childbirth, previously described, is *vaginal delivery*. Alternatively, **cesarean delivery** can be used to surgically remove the baby from the uterus through an incision in the mother's abdomen. The cesarean birth rate peaked in 2009 at 32.9 percent. Although still high, the rate in 2015 is now at 32 percent, and has declined for the third year in a row (Martin et al., 2017).

The operation is commonly performed when labor progresses too slowly, when the fetus seems to be in trouble, or when the mother is bleeding vaginally. Often a cesarean is needed when the fetus is in the breech position (feet or buttocks first) or in the transverse position (lying crosswise in the uterus) or when the head is too big to pass through the mother's pelvis.

The increase in cesarean rates is attributed largely to rising proportions of older first-time mothers, who tend to have multiple births, and of very premature infants (Martin, Hamilton, et al., 2010) for whom cesarean delivery significantly reduces the risk of dying during the 1st month of life (Malloy, 2008). Physicians' fear of malpractice suits and women's preferences also may play a part in the choice of cesarean deliveries (Ecker & Frigoletto, 2007; Martin, Hamilton, et al., 2009), as may the increased revenue hospitals generate when a woman has a cesarean rather than a vaginal birth.

Cesarean deliveries carry risks of serious complications for the mother, such as bleeding, infection, damage to pelvic organs, and postoperative pain, and heighten risks of problems in future pregnancies (Ecker & Frigoletto, 2007). Cesarean delivery also may negatively affect breast-feeding, which can influence bonding (Zanardo et al., 2010). Vaginal delivery also stimulates the release of oxytocin, a hormone involved in uterine contractions that stimulates maternal behavior in animals. There are indications that oxytocin may have similar effects in humans (Swain et al., 2008).

Many physicians warn that a vaginal birth after cesarean (VBAC) should be attempted only with caution. VBACs have been associated with greater (though still low) risks of uterine rupture and brain damage (Landon et al., 2004) as well as infant death (Smith, Pell, Cameron & Dobbie, 2002). However, other research shows that there are also risks associated with repeat cesarean deliveries, including postpartum endometriosis (a painful condition in which uterine cells are found outside of the uterus), complications related to the use of anesthesia, or hysterectomy (Fong et al., 2016). Today, if a woman has had a cesarean delivery and attempts a vaginal birth, chances of a successful VBAC are about 12 percent (National Center for Health Statistics, 2015).

Because the risks of a VBAC are still quite low and repeat cesarean deliveries also carry risk, a recent NIH (2010b) Consensus Development Conference has concluded that a trial of labor is a reasonable option for women who have had a previous low transverse uterine incision. In addition, in 2010 the American Congress of Obstetricians and Gynecologists issued new guidelines with the goal of expanding the pool of women eligible for VBAC. For example, a trial of labor is now recommended for twin pregnancies, as well as for women who have had more than one cesarean (Grady, 2010).

MEDICATED VERSUS NONMEDICATED DELIVERY

For centuries, pain was considered an unavoidable part of giving birth. Then, in the mid-nineteenth century, sedation with ether or chloroform became common practice as more births took place in hospitals (Fontanel & d'Harcourt, 1997).

During the twentieth century, several alternative methods of **natural childbirth** or **prepared childbirth** were developed. These methods minimize or eliminate the use of drugs that may pose risks for babies and enable both parents to participate fully in a natural, empowering experience.

The Lamaze method, introduced by the French obstetrician Fernand Lamaze in the late 1950s, acknowledges that labor is painful and teaches an expectant mother to relax her muscles through controlled breathing. Using the LeBoyer method a woman gives birth in a quiet room under low lights to reduce stress, and the newborn is gently massaged to ease crying. Another technique, developed by the French physician Michael Odent, is submersion of the laboring mother in a soothing pool of water. Other methods use mental imagery, massage, gentle pushing, and deep breathing. Perhaps most extreme is the Bradley method, which rejects all obstetrical procedures and other medical interventions.

Today, improvements in medicated delivery have led many mothers to choose pain relief, sometimes along with natural methods. A woman may be given local (vaginal) anesthesia, also called a *pudendal block,* usually during the second stage of labor. Or she

natural childbirth
Method of childbirth that seeks to prevent pain by eliminating the mother's fear through education about the physiology of reproduction and training in breathing and relaxation during delivery.

prepared childbirth
Method of childbirth that uses instruction, breathing exercises, and social support to induce controlled physical responses to uterine contractions and reduce fear and pain.

A doula, or experienced helper, stays at a woman's bedside throughout labor and provides emotional support. Research has found that women attended by doulas tend to have shorter labor and easier deliveries. ©Anderson Ross/Photoplay/Media Bakery

doula
An experienced mentor who furnishes emotional support and information for a woman during labor.

can receive an *analgesic* (painkiller), which reduces the perception of pain by depressing the activity of the central nervous system. However, analgesics may slow labor, cause maternal complications, and make the baby less alert after birth.

Among women who give birth vaginally to a singleton, 61 percent have regional (*epidural or spinal*) injections (Osterman & Martin, 2011). Regional anesthesia, which is injected into a space in the spinal cord between the vertebrae in the lumbar (lower) region, blocks the nerve pathways that would carry the sensation of pain to the brain. Epidurals given early can shorten labor with no added risk of needing cesarean delivery (C. A. Wong et al., 2005).

With any of these forms of anesthesia, a woman can see and participate in the birth process and can hold her newborn immediately afterward. All of these drugs, however, pass through the placenta and enter the fetal blood supply and tissues and thus may pose some danger to the baby.

In many traditional cultures, childbearing women are attended by a **doula,** an experienced mentor, coach, and helper who can furnish emotional support and information and can stay at a woman's bedside throughout labor. In 11 randomized, controlled studies, women attended by doulas had shorter labor, less anesthesia, and fewer cesarean deliveries than women not attended by doulas (Hodnett, Gates, Hofmeyr & Sakala, 2005).

The Newborn Baby

The **neonatal period,** the first 4 weeks of life, is a time of transition from the uterus, where a fetus is supported entirely by the mother, to an independent existence. What are the physical characteristics of newborn babies, and how are they equipped for this crucial transition?

SIZE AND APPEARANCE

An average **neonate,** or newborn, in the United States is about 20 inches long and weighs about 7½ pounds. Boys tend to be slightly longer and heavier than girls. In their first few days, neonates lose as much as 10 percent of their body weight. They begin to gain weight again at about the 5th day and are generally back to birth weight by the 10th to the 14th day.

New babies have a large head (one-fourth the body length) and a receding chin (which makes it easier to nurse). Newborn infants also have soft spots on their heads known as *fontanels* where the bones of the skull do not meet. Fontanels are covered by a tough membrane that allows for flexibility in shape, which eases the passage of the neonate through the vaginal canal. In the first 18 months of life, the plates of the skull gradually fuse together.

Newborns have skin so thin that it barely covers the capillaries through which blood flows. Often they are hairy because the *lanugo,* a fuzzy prenatal hair, has not yet fallen off. Most new babies are covered with *vernix caseosa* ("cheesy varnish"), an oily protection against infection that dries within the first few days.

"Witch's milk," a secretion that sometimes leaks from the swollen breasts of newborn boys and girls around the 3rd day of life, was believed during the Middle Ages to have special healing powers. Like the whitish or blood-tinged vaginal discharge of some newborn girls, this fluid emission results from high levels of the hormone estrogen, which is secreted by the placenta just before birth and goes away within a few days or weeks. A newborn, especially if premature, also may have swollen genitals.

BODY SYSTEMS

Before birth, blood circulation, respiration, nourishment, elimination of waste, and temperature regulation are accomplished through the mother's body. All these systems, with the exception of the lungs, are functioning to some degree by the time a full-term birth occurs, but the fetus is not yet an independent entity. After birth, all of the baby's systems and functions must operate on their own.

During pregnancy, the fetus gets oxygen through the umbilical cord, which carries used blood to the placenta and returns a fresh supply. Once born, a neonate must take over this function fully. Most babies start to breathe as soon as they are exposed to air. If a neonate does not begin breathing within about 5 minutes, the baby may suffer permanent brain injury caused by **anoxia,** lack of oxygen, or *hypoxia,* a reduced oxygen supply. This form of *birth trauma* can leave permanent brain damage, causing intellectual disability, behavior problems, or even death.

In the uterus, the fetus relies on the umbilical cord to bring food from the mother and to carry fetal body wastes away. At birth, babies instinctively suck to take in milk, and their own gastrointestinal secretions digest it. During the first few days infants secrete *meconium,* a stringy, greenish-black waste matter formed in the fetal intestinal tract.

The layers of fat that develop during the last 2 months of fetal life help healthy full-term infants to keep their body temperature constant after birth despite changes in air temperature. Newborn babies also maintain body temperature by increasing their activity when air temperature drops.

Three or four days after birth, about half of all babies (and a larger proportion of babies born prematurely) develop **neonatal jaundice:** Their skin and eyeballs look yellow. This kind of jaundice is caused by the immaturity of the liver. Usually it is not serious, does not need treatment, and has no long-term effects. However, severe jaundice that is not monitored and treated promptly may result in brain damage.

neonatal period
First 4 weeks of life, a time of transition from intrauterine dependency to independent existence.

neonate
Newborn baby, up to 4 weeks old.

anoxia
Lack of oxygen, which may cause brain damage.

neonatal jaundice
Condition, in many newborn babies, caused by immaturity of liver and evidenced by yellowish appearance; can cause brain damage if not treated promptly.

TABLE 4.1 Apgar Scale			
Sign*	0	1	2
Appearance (color)	Blue, pale	Body pink, extremities blue	Entirely pink
Pulse (heart rate)	Absent	Slow (below 100)	Rapid (over 100)
Grimace (reflex irritability)	No response	Grimace	Coughing, sneezing, crying
Activity (muscle tone)	Limp	Weak, inactive	Strong, active
Respiration (breathing)	Absent	Irregular, slow	Good, crying

*Each sign is rated in terms of absence or presence from 0 to 2; highest overall score is 10.

Source: Apgar, V. "A proposal for a new method of evaluation of the newborn infant." *Current Researches in Anesthesia and Analgesia*, 32(4), 1953, 260–267.

MEDICAL AND BEHAVIORAL ASSESSMENT

The first few minutes, days, and weeks after birth are crucial for development. It is important to know as soon as possible whether a baby has any problem that needs special care.

The Apgar Scale One minute after delivery, and then again 5 minutes after birth, most babies are assessed using the **Apgar scale** (Table 4.1). Its name, after its developer, Dr. Virginia Apgar (1953), helps us remember its five subtests: *a*ppearance (color), *p*ulse (heart rate), *g*rimace (reflex irritability), *a*ctivity (muscle tone), and *r*espiration (breathing). The newborn is rated 0, 1, or 2 on each measure, for a maximum score of 10. A 5-minute score of 7 to 10–achieved by 98.4 percent of babies born in the United States— indicates that the baby is in good to excellent condition (Martin, Hamilton et al., 2009). A score below 5–7 means the baby needs help to establish breathing; a score below 4 means the baby needs immediate lifesaving treatment.

Neonatal Screening for Medical Conditions Children who inherit the enzyme disorder phenylketonuria, or PKU, will develop intellectual disability unless they are fed a special diet beginning in the first 3 to 6 weeks of life (National Institute of Child Health and Human Development, 2017). Screening tests administered soon after birth often can discover this and other correctable defects.

Routine screening of all newborn babies for such rare conditions as PKU (1 case in 15,000 births), congenital hypothyroidism (1 in 3,600 to 5,000), galactosemia (1 in 60,000 to 80,000), and other, even rarer, disorders is expensive. Yet the cost of testing thousands of newborns to detect one case of a rare disease may be less than the cost of caring for one intellectually disabled person for a lifetime. The Recommended Uniform Screening Panel, developed by the U.S. government in conjunction with professionals in the field, includes 34 core conditions and 26 secondary conditions for which it recommends screening all newborns. However, states vary with respect to which conditions they include (United States Department of Health and Human Services, 2017).

STATES OF AROUSAL

Babies have an internal clock that regulates their daily cycles of eating, sleeping, and elimination. These periodic cycles of wakefulness, sleep, and activity, which govern an infant's **state of arousal,** or degree of alertness (Table 4.2), seem to be inborn and highly individual. Changes in state are coordinated by multiple areas of the brain (Tokariev, Videman, Palva & Vanhatalo, 2016) and are accompanied by changes in the functioning of virtually all body systems (Scher, Epstein & Tirosh, 2004).

Youngest babies sleep the most and wake up the most frequently. Parents report that from 0 to 2 months of age, infants sleep about 14.5 hours a day and wake 1.7 times per night. However, by a year of age, that number has dropped to 12.6 hours of sleep per night and 0.7 times night wakings each evening. Likewise, their longest sleep period rises

Apgar scale
Standard measurement of a newborn's condition; it assesses appearance, pulse, grimace, activity, and respiration.

state of arousal
An infant's physiological and behavioral status at a given moment in the periodic daily cycle of wakefulness, sleep, and activity.

TABLE 4.2 States of Arousal in Infancy

State	Eyes	Breathing	Movements	Responsiveness
Regular sleep	Closed; no eye movement	Regular and slow	None, except for sudden startles	Not aroused by mild stimuli.
Irregular sleep	Closed; occasional rapid eye movements	Irregular	Muscles twitch, but no major movements	Sounds or light bring smiles or grimaces in sleep.
Drowsiness	Open or closed	Irregular	Somewhat active	May smile, startle, suck, or have erections in response to stimuli.
Quiet alert	Open	Even	Quiet; some body movement	An interesting environment may initiate or maintain this state.
Waking activity and crying	Open	Irregular	Much activity	External stimuli cause more activity, often starting slowly and turning into crying or kicking.

Sources: Prechtl & Beintema, 1964; P. H. Wolff, 1966.

from 5.7 hours at 2 months of age to 8.3 hours at 6 to 24 months of age. With respect to daytime napping, a similar developmental trend emerges. At 0 to 5 months, the typical child will nap about 3 hours every day. By 1 to 2 years of age, most children are napping only about an hour (Galland, Taylor, Elder & Herbison, 2012).

Newborns' sleep alternates between quiet (regular) and active (irregular) sleep. Active sleep is the equivalent of rapid eye movement (REM) sleep, which in adults is associated with dreaming. Active sleep appears rhythmically in cycles of about 1 hour and accounts for up to 50 percent of a newborn's total sleep time. The amount of REM sleep declines to less than 30 percent of daily sleep time by age 3 and continues to decrease steadily throughout life (Hoban, 2004).

Babies' sleep rhythms and schedules vary across cultures. Among the Micronesian Truk and the Canadian Hare peoples, babies and children have no regular sleep schedules; they fall asleep whenever they feel tired. Mothers in rural Kenya allow their babies to nurse as they please, and their 4-month-olds continue to sleep only 4 hours at a stretch (Broude, 1995). In many predominantly Asian countries, bedtimes are later and total sleep time is shorter than in predominantly Caucasian countries (Mindell et al., 2010).

Complications of Childbirth

Although the great majority of births result in healthy babies, some, sadly, do not. Let's look at these potential complications of birth and how they can be avoided or treated to maximize the chances of favorable outcomes.

LOW BIRTH WEIGHT

Low-birth-weight babies (LBW) are those neonates born weighing less than 2,500 grams (5½ pounds) at birth. There are two types of LBW babies: those born early and those born small. Typical gestation is 40 weeks, and babies born before the 37th week of gestation are known as **preterm (premature) infants.** After declining from 2007 to 2014, the preterm birthrate rose slightly in 2015 to 9.63 percent (Martin, Hamilton, Osterman, Driscoll & Mathews, 2017). More than 43 percent of preterm infants are of low birth weight, as compared with only about 3 percent of full-term infants (Martin et al., 2009) (Figure 4.4). Some babies, known as **small-for-date (small-for-gestational-age) infants,** are

low-birth-weight babies
Weight of less than 5½ pounds (2,500 grams) at birth because of prematurity or being small for date.

preterm (premature) infants
Infants born before completing the 37th week of gestation.

small-for-date (small-for-gestational-age) infants
Infants whose birth weight is less than that of 90 percent of babies of the same gestational age, as a result of slow fetal growth.

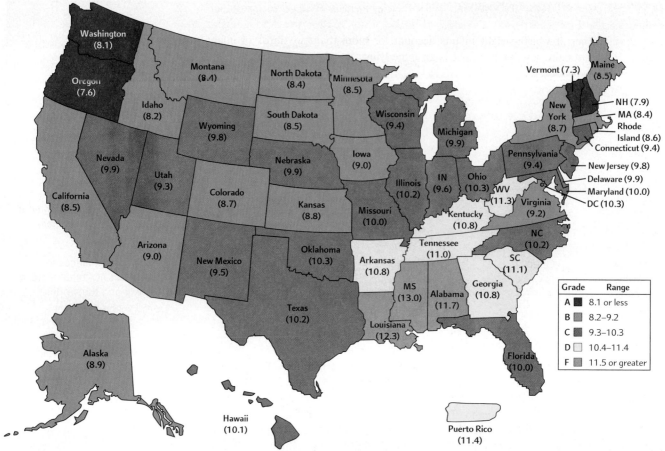

FIGURE 4.4
Preterm birthrates
and grades by state

Source: March of Dimes. *Premature Birth
Report Card.* 2016.

born at or around their due dates, but are smaller than would be expected. These babies weigh less than 90 percent of babies of the same gestational age. They are small, not because they were born early and did not have a chance to finish putting on weight, but for other reasons, most commonly inadequate prenatal nutrition, which slows fetal growth.

An estimated 15 percent of all infants worldwide are born with low birth weight, and the percentages are far greater in less economically developed countries. The true extent of low birth weight may be much higher because nearly half of the newborns in the developing world are not weighed at birth (UNICEF, 2013b). Low birth weight in developing regions stems primarily from the mother's poor health and nutrition. In the industrialized world, smoking during pregnancy is the leading factor in low birth weight (UNICEF & WHO, 2004).

In the United States, 8.1 percent of infants born in 2015 were low-birth-weight babies—a number that has remained more or less unchanged since 2012. In the same year, 9.6 percent of U.S. infants were preterm. Much of the incidence of low-birth-weight and preterm births is due to delayed childbearing, multiple births, and use of fertility drugs and induced and cesarean deliveries. The risk of both preterm delivery and low birth weight increases rapidly with the number of babies being carried, approaching 100 percent for quadruplets (Martin et al., 2017).

In 2015, the late preterm birthrate rose slightly to 6.9 percent after declining each year from 2007 to 2014 (Martin et al., 2017). Late preterm infants, delivered between 34 and 36 weeks' gestation, tend to weigh more and to fare better than those born earlier in gestation; but in comparison with full-term babies, they too are at greater risk of early death or adverse effects (Martin, Hamilton, et al., 2009) such as respiratory distress, hospitalization, and brain injuries.

Birth weight and length of gestation are the two most important predictors of an infant's survival and health (Mathews & MacDorman, 2008). Together they constitute the second leading cause of death in infancy in the United States after birth defects

(Kochanek, Murphy, Xu & Tejada-Vera, 2016). Preterm birth is involved in nearly half of neurological birth defects, such as cerebral palsy, and more than one-third of infant deaths; altogether, low-birth-weight infants account for more than two-thirds of infant deaths. Internationally, low birth weight is an underlying factor in 60 to 80 percent of neonatal deaths worldwide (UNICEF, 2008b).

The United States has been more successful than any other country in saving low-birth-weight babies, but the rate of such births to U.S. women remains higher than in some European and Asian nations (MacDorman & Mathews, 2009). Preventing preterm births would greatly increase the number of babies who survive the first year of life. In the last decade, some countries have halved deaths attributed to preterm delivery, most notably with training and the provision of equipment and supplies. For example, even low-tech changes such as ensuring appropriate warmth, support for breast-feeding, and training in basic care for infections and breathing problems can reduce mortality rates.

Who Is Likely to Have a Low-Birth-Weight Baby? Factors increasing the likelihood that a woman will have an underweight baby include (1) *demographic and socioeconomic factors,* such as being African American, under age 17 or over 40, poor, unmarried, or undereducated, and being born in certain regions, such as the Southern and Plains states (Thompson, Goodman, Chang & Stukel, 2005); (2) *medical factors predating the pregnancy,* such as having no children or more than four, being short or thin, having had previous low-birth-weight infants or multiple miscarriages, having had low birth weight oneself, having particular genetic variants associated with higher risk (National Institutes of Health, 2010a), or having genital or urinary abnormalities or chronic hypertension; (3) *prenatal behavioral and environmental factors,* such as poor nutrition, inadequate prenatal care, smoking, use of alcohol or other drugs, or exposure to stress, high altitude, or toxic substances; and (4) *medical conditions associated with the pregnancy,* such as vaginal bleeding, infections, high or low blood pressure, anemia, depression, and too little weight gain (Arias, MacDorman, Strobino & Guyer, 2003; Chomitz, Cheung & Lieberman, 1995; Nathanielsz, 1995; Shiono & Behrman, 1995), and having last given birth fewer than 6 months or more than 5 years before (Conde-Agudelo, Rosas-Bermúdez & Kafury-Goeta, 2006).

The high proportion of low-birth-weight newborns—13.35 percent (Martin, Hamilton, Osterman, Driscoll & Mathews, 2017)—is a major factor in the high mortality rates of black babies. Reasons for the greater prevalence of low birth weight, preterm births, and infant mortality among African American babies include (1) health behaviors and socio-economic status (SES); (2) higher levels of stress in African American women; (3) greater susceptibility to stress; (4) the impact of racism, which may contribute to or exacerbate stress; and (5) ethnic differences in stress-related body processes, such as blood pressure and immune reactions (Giscombé & Lobel, 2005).

kangaroo care
Method of skin-to-skin contact in which a newborn is laid face down between the mother's breasts for an hour or so at a time after birth.

Immediate Treatment and Outcomes The most pressing fear regarding very small babies is that they will die in infancy. A low-birth-weight or at-risk preterm baby may be placed in an *isolette* (an antiseptic, temperature-controlled crib) and fed through tubes. These infants' nervous systems may be too immature for them to perform functions basic to survival, such as sucking, so they may need to be fed intravenously (through the veins). Moreover, because they do not have enough fat to insulate them and to generate heat, it is hard for them to stay warm. Preterm babies are especially at risk for slowed growth and developmental delays (Scharf, Stroustrup, Conaway & DeBoer, 2016). Gentle massage seems to foster growth, weight gain, motor activity, alertness, and behavioral organization (Field, Diego & Hernandez-Reif, 2007). Girls tend to be hardier than boys (Glass, Costarino, Stayer, Brett, Cladis & Davis, 2015).

Kangaroo care, a method of skin-to-skin contact in which a newborn is laid face down between the mother's breasts for an

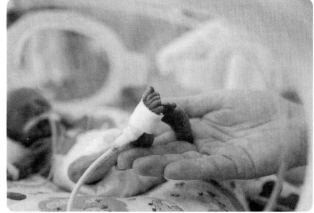

The antiseptic, temperature-controlled crib, or isolette, in which this premature baby lies has holes through which the infant can be examined, touched, and massaged. Frequent human contact helps low-birth-weight infants thrive.
©Kristina Bessolova/Shutterstock

hour or so at a time after birth, can help preemies—and full-term infants—make the adjustment from fetal life to the outside world. This soothing maternal contact seems to reduce stress on the central nervous system and help with self-regulation of sleep and activity (Ferber & Makhoul, 2004).

Respiratory distress syndrome is common in preterm babies who lack an adequate amount of an essential lung-coating substance called *surfactant*, which keeps air sacs from collapsing. These babies may breathe irregularly or stop breathing altogether. Administering surfactant to high-risk preterm newborns has dramatically increased survival rates since the late 1990s (Glass et al., 2015) as well as neurological and developmental status at 18 to 22 months (Vohr, Wright, Poole & McDonald for the NICHD Neonatal Research Network Follow-up Study, 2005). Since 2000 the percentage of *extremely-low-birth-weight* infants (about 1 to 2 pounds at birth) who survived without neurological impairment has increased further (Wilson-Costello et al., 2007).

Long-Term Outcomes Even if low-birth-weight babies survive the dangerous early days, their future is in question. For example, both preterm and small-for-gestational-age infants may be at increased risk of adult-onset diabetes, and small-for-gestational-age infants appear to be at increased risk of cardiovascular disease (Hofman et al., 2004; Sperling, 2004). Moreover, preterm birth leads to heightened risk of death throughout childhood, diminished reproductive rates in adulthood, and, for women, increased risk of bearing preterm infants themselves (Swamy, Ostbye & Skjaerven, 2008). In addition, the shorter the period of gestation, the greater the likelihood of cerebral palsy, mental retardation, autistic disorders, and low educational and job-related income levels (Moster, Lie & Markestad, 2008).

In longitudinal studies of extremely low-birth-weight infants (about 1 to 2 pounds at birth) and infants born before 26 weeks of gestation, the survivors tend to be smaller than full-term children and more likely to have neurological, sensory, cognitive, educational, and behavioral problems (Hutchinson, DeLuca, Doyle, Roberts, Anderson & Victorian Infant Collaborative Study Group, 2013; Samara, Marlow & Wolke for the EPICure Study Group, 2008). The smaller the baby, the greater the risk. The less low-birth-weight children weigh at birth, the lower their IQs and achievement test scores tend to be and the more likely they are to require special education or to repeat a grade (Saigal, Hoult, Streiner, Stoskopf & Rosenbaum, 2000). Cognitive deficits have been noted among very-low-birth-weight babies (2 to 3½ pounds at birth) by age 5 or 6 months, continuing through childhood (Rose, Feldman & Jankowski, 2002), adolescence (Litt, Gerry Taylor, Margevicius, Schluter, Andreias & Hack, 2012) and into adulthood (Ergigit Madzwamuse, Buamann, Jaekel, Bartmann & Wolke, 2015; Fearon et al., 2004). Very-low-birth-weight children and adolescents also tend to have more behavioral and mental health problems than those born at normal weight (Hack et al., 2004) as well as impaired motor development both in the 1st year of life and throughout childhood and adolescence (de Kieviet, Piek, Aarnousde-Moens & Oosterlaan, 2009). However, birth weight alone does not necessarily determine the outcome. Factors such as maternal education, family structure, and SES also help determine outcomes (Voss, Jungmann, Wachtendorf & Neubauer, 2012; Saigal et al., 2006), and given supportive postnatal environments, a significant proportion of low-birth-weight babies can become well-functioning adults. Environmental factors make a difference, as we discuss in the following section.

Thanks to their own resilience, many children who live in less than ideal circumstances, such as this child in war-torn Afghanistan, can develop into self-confident, successful adults. ©U.S. Air Force photo by Staff Sgt. Marcus McDonald

POSTMATURITY

When people think about birth complications, they generally think about issues related to being born too early or too small. However, babies can also be negatively affected by staying too long in the womb. In fact, approximately 7 percent of pregnant women in the United States have not gone into labor after 42 or more weeks' gestation (Galal, Symonds, Murray, Petraglia & Smith, 2012). At that point, a baby is considered **postmature.** Postmature babies tend to be long and thin because they have kept growing in the womb but have had an insufficient blood supply toward the end of gestation. Possibly because the placenta has aged and become less efficient, it may provide less oxygen. The baby's greater size also complicates labor; the mother has to deliver a baby the size of a normal

postmature
A fetus not yet born as of 2 weeks after the due date or 42 weeks after the mother's last menstrual period.

1-month-old. Because postmature fetuses are at risk of brain damage or even death, doctors sometimes must induce labor or perform cesarean deliveries.

STILLBIRTH

Stillbirth, the sudden death of a fetus at or after the 20th week of gestation, is a tragic union of opposites–birth and death. Sometimes fetal death is diagnosed prenatally; in other cases, the baby's death is discovered during labor or delivery.

Worldwide, about 3.2 million fetuses are stillborn annually (Lawn et al., 2010). In 2013, there were almost 24,000 stillbirths in the United States, a number representing 5.96 fetal deaths for every 1,000 live births. Boys are more likely to be stillborn than girls, non-Hispanic black fetuses are more likely to be stillborn than fetuses of other racial/ethnic groups, and twins and higher multiples are more likely to be stillborn than singletons (MacDorman & Gregory, 2015).

Although the cause of stillbirth is often not clear, many stillborn fetuses are small for gestational age, indicating malnourishment in the womb (MacDorman & Gregory, 2015). Fetuses believed to have problems can have prenatal surgery in the womb to correct congenital problems or be delivered prematurely (Goldenberg, Kirby & Culhane, 2004). Interventions such as these could prevent a large proportion of stillbirths (Bhutta et al., 2011).

stillbirth
Death of a fetus at or after the 20th week of gestation.

Survival and Health

Infancy and toddlerhood are risky times of life. How many babies die during the first year, and why? What can be done to prevent dangerous or debilitating childhood diseases? How can we ensure that infants and toddlers live, grow, and develop as they should?

REDUCING INFANT MORTALITY

Great strides have been made in protecting the lives of new babies, but these advances are not evenly distributed. In 2015, there were 5.9 million worldwide deaths of children 5 years of age and younger (World Health Organization, 2015b). Of those deaths, 2.7 million were infants 28 days or younger in age (UNICEF, 2015e). The vast majority of these early deaths are in developing countries, especially in South Asia and West and Central Africa (World Health Organization, 2013; Figure 4.5).

FIGURE 4.5
Under-5 Mortality Rate, 2015

Most neonatal deaths occur in sub-Saharan Africa and Asia.

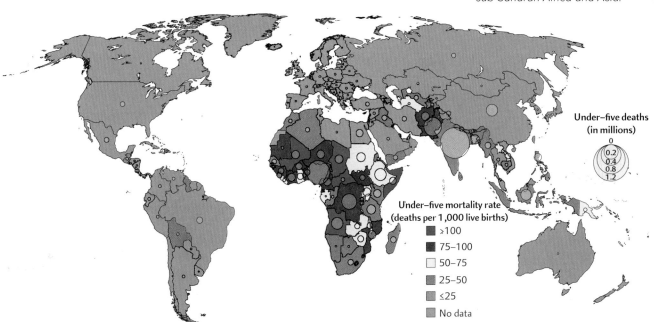

Source: UNICEF. *Committing to Child Survival: A Promise Renewed, Progress Report 2015.* New York: UNICEF, 2016.

The chief causes of neonatal death worldwide are preterm birth complications (35 percent), childbirth complications (24 percent), and sepsis (15 percent). Many of these deaths are preventable, resulting from a combination of poverty, poor maternal health and nutrition, infection, and inadequate medical care (UNICEF, 2015e). Although maternal mortality declined 44 percent from 1990 to 2015, the number of women and girls who die in childbirth is still about 303,000 a year. Most of these deaths (27 percent) are due to hemorrhage, with preexisting medical conditions, eclampsia, embolisms, and complications of unsafe abortions also playing a role (UNICEF, 2015d). About two-thirds of maternal deaths occur during the immediate postnatal period, and infants whose mothers have died are more likely to die than infants whose mothers remain alive (Sines, Syed, Wall & Worley, 2007). As with neonatal deaths, many of these deaths are preventable.

In the United States, the **infant mortality rate**—the proportion of babies who die within the 1st year—has fallen almost continuously since the beginning of the twentieth century, when 100 infants died for every 1,000 born alive. In 2014, the rate fell to a record low of 5.82 infant deaths per 1,000 live births (Kochanak, Murphy, Xu & Tejada-Vera, 2016). More than half of U.S. infant deaths take place in the first week of life, and about two-thirds occur during the neonatal period (Heron et al., 2009).

Birth defects and genetic abnormalities are the leading cause of infant deaths in the United States, followed by disorders related to prematurity or low birth weight, maternal complications of pregnancy, sudden infant death syndrome (SIDS), accidents, and complications of the placenta, umbilical cord, and membranes (Kochanak, Murphy, Xu & Tejada-Vera, 2016). In 2005, more than two-thirds of all deaths in infancy were of preterm babies, and more than half were of very preterm infants (Mathews & MacDorman, 2008).

The overall improvement in U.S. infant mortality rates since 1990 is attributable largely to prevention of SIDS (discussed in the next section) as well as to effective treatment for respiratory distress and medical advances in keeping very small babies alive (Arias et al., 2003). Still, mainly because of the prevalence of preterm births and low birth weight, U.S. babies have less chance of reaching their 1st birthday than do babies in many other developed countries (MacDorman & Mathews, 2009). The U.S. infant mortality rate in 2008 was higher than in 44 countries worldwide (Kaiser Family Foundation, 2017; Figure 4.6).

Racial/Ethnic Disparities in Infant Mortality Although infant mortality has declined for all races and ethnic groups in the United States, large disparities remain. Black babies are

infant mortality rate
Proportion of babies born alive who die within the 1st year.

FIGURE 4.6
Infant Mortality Rates in Comparable Countries

Despite dramatic improvements, the United States has a higher infant mortality rate than that of comparable nations.

Source: Kaiser Family Foundation analysis of data from OECD, "OECD Health Data: Health status: Health status indicators", OECD Health Statistics database, 2017.

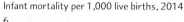
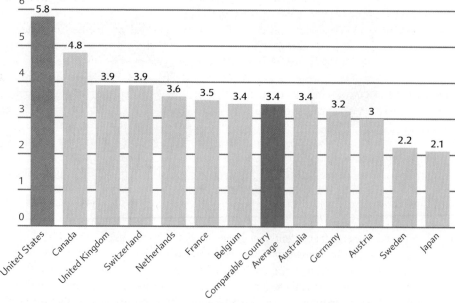

Infant mortality per 1,000 live births, 2014

United States 5.8; Canada 4.8; United Kingdom 3.9; Switzerland 3.9; Netherlands 3.6; France 3.5; Belgium 3.4; Comparable Country Average 3.4; Australia 3.4; Germany 3.2; Austria 3; Sweden 2.2; Japan 2.1

Countries are defined as those with above median GDP and above median GDP per capita in at least one of the past 10 years. Canada data estimated from 2012.

nearly 2½ times as likely to die in their 1st year as white and Hispanic babies (Figure 4.7). This disparity largely reflects the greater prevalence of low birth weight and SIDS among African Americans. Infant mortality among American Indians and Alaska Natives is about 1½ times that among white babies, mainly due to SIDS and fetal alcohol syndrome (American Public Health Association, 2004; Mathews & MacDorman, 2008).

Racial or ethnic disparities in access to and quality of health care for minority children (National Center for Health Statistics, 2016) may help account for differences in infant mortality, but behavioral factors such as obesity, smoking, and alcohol consumption also play a part. Because causes and risk factors for infant mortality vary among ethnic groups, efforts to further reduce infant deaths need to focus on factors specific to each ethnic group (Hesso & Fuentes, 2005).

Sudden Infant Death Syndrome (SIDS) **Sudden infant death syndrome (SIDS)** is the sudden death of an infant under age 1 in which the cause of death remains unexplained after a thorough investigation that includes an autopsy. SIDS accounts for 7 percent of infant mortality rates (Mathews, MacDorman & Thoma, 2015). It peaks between 2 and 3 months and is most common among African American and American Indian/Alaska Native babies, boy babies, those born preterm, and those whose mothers are young and received late or no prenatal care (AAP Task Force on Sudden Infant Death Syndrome, 2005).

SIDS most likely results from a combination of factors. An underlying biological defect may make some infants vulnerable during a critical period to certain contributing or triggering experiences, such as prenatal exposure to smoke—one of the major identified risk factors. There may be genetic mutations affecting the heart that predispose children to SIDS as well (Arnestad et al., 2007; Wang et al., 2007). In the absence of any risk factors, SIDS is rare. Babies who die from SIDS frequently have multiple risk factors (Ostfeld, Esposity, Perl & Hegyl, 2010).

An important clue has emerged from the discovery of defects in the brain stem, which regulates breathing, heartbeat, body temperature, and arousal (Machaalani & Waters, 2014). These defects may prevent SIDS babies who are sleeping face down or on their sides from waking or turning their heads when they breathe stale air containing carbon dioxide trapped under their blankets (Panigrahy et al., 2000). Similarly, babies who have low levels of serotonin may not awaken under conditions of oxygen deprivation and carbon dioxide buildup and are thus at greater risk as well (Duncan et al., 2010).

Research strongly supports a relationship between SIDS and sleeping on the stomach. SIDS rates declined in the United States by 53 percent between 1992 and 2001 (AAP Task Force on Sudden Infant Death Syndrome, 2005) and in some other countries by as much as 70 percent following recommendations that healthy babies be laid down to sleep on their backs (Dwyer, Ponsonby, Blizzard, Newman & Cochrane, 1995; Hunt, 1996; Skadberg, Morild & Markestad, 1998; Willinger, Hoffman & Hartford, 1994).

Doctors recommend that infants *not* sleep on soft surfaces, such as pillows, quilts, or sheepskin, or under loose covers, which, especially when the infant is face down, may increase the risk of overheating or rebreathing (breathing the infant's own exhaled carbon dioxide). Current recommendations for risk reduction also include sleeping in the parent's room, but on a separate surface, breast-feeding, immunizations, and the use of a pacifier (AAP Task Force on Sudden Infant Death Syndrome, 2005).

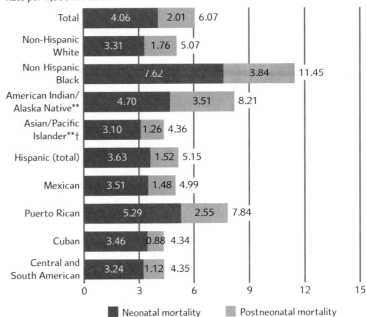

Rate per 1,000 live births

	Neonatal	Postneonatal	Total
Total	4.06	2.01	6.07
Non-Hispanic White	3.31	1.76	5.07
Non Hispanic Black	7.62	3.84	11.45
American Indian/ Alaska Native**	4.70	3.51	8.21
Asian/Pacific Islander**†	3.10	1.26	4.36
Hispanic (total)	3.63	1.52	5.15
Mexican	3.51	1.48	4.99
Puerto Rican	5.29	2.55	7.84
Cuban	3.46	0.88	4.34
Central and South American	3.24	1.12	4.35

■ Neonatal mortality ■ Postneonatal mortality

*Infant deaths are of those less than 1 year old; neonatal deaths are of those less than 28 days old; postneonatal deaths are of those at least 28 days old and less than 1 year old. **May include Hispanics. †Separate data for Asians, native Hawaiians, and other Pacific Islanders are not available.*

FIGURE 4.7

Infant Mortality Rates by Maternal Race/ Ethnicity, United States

Ethnicity influences mortality, and African American babies have the highest death rates.

Source: U.S. Department of Health and Human Services (USDHHS), Health Resources and Services Administration, Maternal and Child Health Bureau. *Child health USA 2014.* Rockville, MD: U.S. Department of Health and Human Services, 2011.

sudden infant death syndrome (SIDS) Sudden and unexplained death of an apparently healthy infant.

Deaths from Injuries Unintentional injuries are the fifth leading cause of death in infancy in the United States (Kochanek, Murphy, Xu & Tejada-Vera, 2016). Infants have the second highest death rate from unintentional injuries among children and adolescents, exceeded only by 15- to 19-year-olds. About 90 percent of all injury deaths in infancy are due to one of four causes: suffocation, motor vehicle traffic, drowning, and residential burns or fires (Pressley et al., 2007). About two-thirds of injury deaths in the 1st year of life are by suffocation. Among children ages 1 to 4, traffic accidents are the leading cause of unintentional injury deaths, followed by drowning and burns. Falls are by far the major cause of nonfatal injuries in both infancy (52 percent) and toddlerhood (43 percent). Boys of all ages are more likely to be injured and to die from their injuries than girls (Borse et al., 2008). African American infants are 2½ times as likely to die of injuries as white infants and more than 3 times as likely to be victims of homicide (Tomashek, Hsia & Iyasu, 2003).

IMMUNIZATION FOR BETTER HEALTH

Such once-familiar and sometimes fatal childhood illnesses as measles, pertussis (whooping cough), and polio are now largely preventable, thanks to the development of vaccines that mobilize the body's natural defenses. Unfortunately, many children still are not adequately protected.

Worldwide, more than 86 percent of children received routine vaccinations during their 1st year in 2016 (UNICEF, 2017). A Global Immunization Vision Strategy for 2006–2015 seeks to extend routine vaccinations to every eligible person (Department of Immunization, Vaccines, and Biologicals, WHO; United Nations Children's Fund; Global Immunization Division, National Center for Immunization and Respiratory Diseases; & McMorrow, 2006).

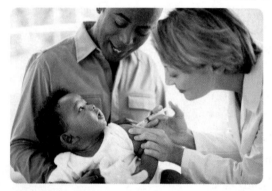

In the United States, thanks to a nationwide immunization initiative, over 90 percent of 19- to 35-month-olds had completed a recommended series of childhood vaccinations, including measles, mumps, rubella, hepatitis B, and chicken pox. Still, many children, especially poor or African American children, lack one or more of the required shots and there are regional differences in coverage (Centers for Disease Control and Prevention, 2014a).

Some parents hesitate to immunize their children because of speculation that certain vaccines—particularly the diphtheria-pertussis-tetanus (DPT) and measles-mumps-rubella (MMR) vaccines—may cause autism or other neurodevelopmental disorders. However, there is no empirical evidence that this link exists. A recent meta-analysis representing data from over 1.26 million children showed no link between autism, autism-spectrum disorders, mental retardation, and vaccines (Taylor, Swerdfeger & Eslick, 2014). Despite this data, however, many parents elect not to vaccinate their children, or vaccinate them incompletely or on a delayed schedule. This, as well as imported disease from international travel, has resulted in a resurgence of some diseases (Ventola, 2016). For example, with nearly 8 percent of children who are eligible for vaccination left unprotected against measles, recent outbreaks of the disease have occurred in certain communities (Darling et al., 2008). Currently, exemptions for religious or philosophical reasons are allowed in many states, and in some areas, the exemption rate is as high as 20 percent (Ventola, 2016).

The rates of infectious diseases have plummeted in the United States thanks to widespread immunization, but many children in low-income urban areas are not properly immunized.
©Ian Hooton/Science Source

Another parental worry is that infants receive too many vaccines for their immune system to handle safely. Actually, the opposite is true. Multiple vaccines fortify the immune system against a variety of bacteria and viruses and reduce related infections (Offit et al., 2002).

Early Physical Development

Fortunately, most infants survive, develop normally, and grow up healthy. What principles govern their development? What are the typical growth patterns of body and brain? How do babies' needs change? How do their abilities develop?

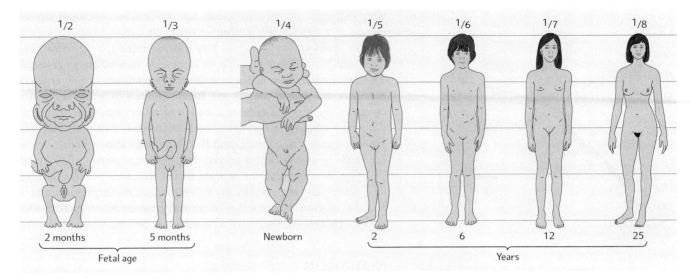

| 1/2 | 1/3 | 1/4 | 1/5 | 1/6 | 1/7 | 1/8 |

| 2 months | 5 months | Newborn | 2 | 6 | 12 | 25 |

Fetal age — Years

FIGURE 4.8

Changes in Proportions of the Human Body during Growth

The most striking change is that the head becomes smaller relative to the rest of the body. The fractions indicate head size as a proportion of total body length at several ages. More subtle is the stability of the trunk proportion (from neck to crotch). The increasing leg proportion is almost exactly the reverse of the decreasing head proportion.

PRINCIPLES OF DEVELOPMENT

As before birth, physical growth and development follow the *cephalocaudal principle* and the *proximodistal principle*.

According to the **cephalocaudal principle,** growth occurs from the top down. Because the brain grows rapidly before birth, a newborn baby's head is disproportionately large. The head becomes proportionately smaller as the child grows in height and the lower parts of the body develop (Figure 4.8). Sensory and motor development proceed according to the same principle: Infants learn to use the upper parts of the body before the lower parts. So, for example, a baby learns to use her arms for grasping prior to learning to use her legs for walking, and holds her head up before she can sit unaided.

According to the **proximodistal principle** (inner to outer), growth and motor development proceed from the center of the body outward. In the womb, the head and trunk develop before the arms and legs, then the hands and feet, and then the fingers and toes. During infancy and early childhood, the limbs continue to grow faster than the hands and feet. Babies learn to use the parts of their bodies closest to the center of their body before they learn to use the outermost parts. For example, babies first learn to control their arms when reaching, then use their hands in a scooping motion, then finally learn to use their thumb and pointer finger in a pincer grip.

cephalocaudal principle
Principle that development proceeds in a head-to-tail direction, that is, that upper parts of the body develop before lower parts of the trunk.

proximodistal principle
Principle that development proceeds from within to without, that is, that parts of the body near the center develop before the extremities.

GROWTH PATTERNS

Children grow faster during the first 3 years, especially during the first few months, than they ever will again (Figure 4.9). By 5 months, the average U.S. baby boy's birth weight has doubled to nearly 16 pounds, and, by 1 year, has more than tripled to exceed 25 pounds. This rapid growth rate tapers off during the 2nd and 3rd years. A boy typically gains about 5½ pounds by his second birthday and 3 more pounds by his third, when he tips the scales at almost 34 pounds. A boy's height typically increases by 10 inches during the 1st year (making the average 1-year-old boy about 30 inches tall), by 5 inches during the 2nd year (so that the average 2-year-old boy is about 3 feet tall), and by 2½ inches during the 3rd year (to approach 39 inches). Girls follow a similar pattern but are slightly smaller at most ages (Kuczmarski et al., 2000; McDowell et al., 2008). As a baby grows into a toddler,

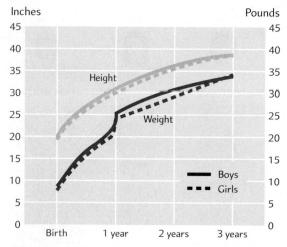

Inches · Pounds

FIGURE 4.9

Growth in Height and Weight during Infancy and Toddlerhood

Babies grow most rapidly in both height and weight during the first few months of life and then taper off somewhat by age 3. Baby boys are slightly larger, on average, than baby girls.

Note: Curves shown are for the 50th percentiles for each sex.

body shape and proportions change too; a 3-year-old typically is slender compared with a chubby, potbellied 1-year-old.

The genes an infant inherits have a strong influence on whether the child will be tall or short, thin or stocky, or somewhere in between. This genetic influence interacts with such environmental influences as nutrition and living conditions. Today children in many developed countries are growing taller and maturing at an earlier age than children did a century ago, probably because of better nutrition, improved sanitation and medical care, and the decrease in child labor.

Teething usually begins around 3 or 4 months, when infants begin grabbing almost everything in sight to put into their mouths; but the first tooth may not actually arrive until sometime between 5 and 9 months, or even later. By the 1st birthday, babies generally have 6 to 8 teeth; by age 2½, they have a mouthful of 20.

NUTRITION

Proper nutrition is essential to healthy growth. Feeding needs change rapidly during the first 3 years of life.

Breast or Bottle? Nutritionally speaking, breast-feeding is almost always best for infants—and mothers (Table 4.3). The American Academy of Pediatrics Section on Breastfeeding recommends that babies be *exclusively* breast-fed for 6 months. Breast-feeding should begin immediately after birth and should continue for at least 1 year, longer if mother and baby wish (Eidelman et al., 2012). A recent study on the benefits of breast-feeding has determined that if 90 percent of U.S. mothers complied with the AAP's recommendation to breast-feed for 6 months, it could potentially prevent 911 infant deaths and save the United States $13 billion annually (Bartick & Reinhold, 2010). The only acceptable alternative to breast milk is an iron-fortified formula that is based on either cow's milk or soy protein and contains supplemental vitamins and minerals. Infants weaned during the 1st year should receive iron-fortified formula. At 1 year, babies can switch to cow's milk.

TABLE 4.3 Benefits of Breast-Feeding over Formula-Feeding

BREAST-FED BABIES . . .

- Are less likely to contract infectious illnesses such as diarrhea, respiratory infections, otitis media (an infection of the middle ear), and staphylococcal, bacterial, and urinary tract infections.
- Have a lower risk of SIDS and of postneonatal death.
- Have less risk of inflammatory bowel disease.
- Have better visual acuity, neurological development, and long-term cardiovascular health, including cholesterol levels.
- Are less likely to develop obesity, asthma, eczema, diabetes, lymphoma, childhood leukemia, and Hodgkin's disease.
- Are less likely to show language and motor delays.
- Score higher on cognitive tests at school age and into young adulthood.
- Have fewer cavities and are less likely to need braces.

BREAST-FEEDING MOTHERS . . .

- Enjoy quicker recovery from childbirth with less risk of postpartum bleeding.
- Are more likely to return to their prepregnancy weight and less likely to develop long-term obesity.
- Have reduced risk of anemia and almost no risk of repeat pregnancy while breast-feeding.
- Report feeling more confident and less anxious.
- Are less likely to develop osteoporosis or ovarian and premenopausal breast cancer.

Sources: AAP Section on Breastfeeding, 2005; Black, Morris, & Bryce, 2003; Chen & Rogan, 2004; Dee, Li, Lee, & Grummer-Strawn, 2007; Kramer et al.; 2008; Lanting, Fidler, Huisman, Touwen, & Boersma, 1994; Mortensen, Michaelson, Sanders, & Reinisch, 2002; Owen, Whincup, Odoki, Gilg, & Cook, 2002; Singhal, Cole, Fewtrell, & Lucas, 2004; United States Breastfeeding Committee, 2002.

Increases in breast-feeding in the United States are most notable in socioeconomic groups that historically have been less likely to breast-feed: black women, teenage women, poor women, working women, and those with no more than high school education. Postpartum maternity leave, flexible scheduling, the ability to take relatively frequent and extended breaks at work to pump milk, privacy for nursing mothers at work and at school, as well as education about the benefits of breast-feeding, and availability of breast pumping facilities might increase its prevalence in these groups (Guendelman et al., 2009; Ryan, Wenjun & Acosta, 2002; Taveras et al., 2003).

Contraindications for breast-feeding are rare. Breast-feeding is inadvisable if a mother is infected with the AIDS virus or any other infectious illness, if she has untreated active tuberculosis, if she has been exposed to radiation, or if she is taking any drug that would not be safe for the baby (AAP Section on Breastfeeding, 2005).

Breast milk can be called the "ultimate health food" because it offers so many benefits to babies—physical, cognitive, and emotional.
©Westend61/Getty Images

The risk of transmitting HIV infection to an infant continues as long as an infected mother breast-feeds (Breastfeeding and HIV International Transmission Study Group, 2004). However, medication can significantly reduce this risk (Kumwenda et al., 2008).

Other Nutritional Concerns Healthy babies should consume *nothing* but breast milk or iron-fortified formula for the first 6 months. Pediatric experts recommend that iron-enriched solid foods—usually beginning with cereals—be introduced gradually during the second half of the 1st year. Water may be introduced at this time (AAP Section on Breastfeeding, 2005). Unfortunately, many parents do not follow these guidelines. According to random telephone interviews with parents and caregivers of more than 3,000 U.S. infants and toddlers, 29 percent of infants are given solid food before 4 months, 17 percent drink juice before 6 months, and 20 percent drink cow's milk before 12 months. Furthermore, many infants and toddlers eat too much and the wrong kinds of food. From 7 to 24 months, the median food intake is 20 to 30 percent above normal daily requirements (Fox, Pac, Devaney & Jankowski, 2004). By 19 to 24 months, French fries become the most commonly consumed vegetable. More than 30 percent of children this age eat no fruit, but 60 percent eat baked desserts, 20 percent candy, and 44 percent sweetened beverages each day (American Heart Association [AHA] et al., 2006).

In many low-income communities around the world, malnutrition in early life is widespread—and often fatal. Malnutrition is implicated in more than half of deaths of children globally, and many children are irreversibly damaged by age 2 (UNICEF, 2015c). Undernourished children are at high risk for stunted growth and poor health and functioning throughout life (Martorell, 2010), although intervention programs that provide nutrition supplements, nutrition education, health care, and financial assistance for the family can result in better growth and lower rates of anemia for enrolled infants (Rivera et al., 2004).

Being overweight has increased in infancy as in all age groups in the United States. In 2000–2001, 5.9 percent of U.S. infants up to 6 months old were obese, meaning that their weight for height was in the 95th percentile for age and gender, up from 3.4 percent in 1980. An additional 11.1 percent were overweight (in the 85th percentile), up from 7 percent in 1980 (Kim, McHale, Osgood & Crouter, 2006). Rapid weight gain during the first 4 to 6 months is associated with future risk of overweight (AHA et al., 2006).

An important factor that influences the chances that an overweight child will become an obese adult is whether the child has an obese parent. Having one obese parent increases the odds of obesity in adulthood by 3 to 1, and if both parents are obese, the odds increase to more than 10 to 1 (AAP Committee on Nutrition, 2003). Other risk

on the world

MALNUTRITION: THE FIRST YEARS

Chronic malnutrition is caused by factors such as poverty, low-quality foods, poor dietary patterns, contaminated water, unsanitary conditions, insufficient hygiene, inadequate health care, and diarrheal diseases and other infections. Approximately 3.1 million children around the world die each year from chronic malnutrition, accounting for 45 percent of all deaths of children under 5 (UNICEF, 2017). Worldwide, 25 percent of children under 5 are malnourished; most of these children live in West/Central Africa, Southeast Asia, Latin America, and the Caribbean (Lake, 2015). Malnutrition is not confined to developing countries. In North America, 13.1 million children in the United States, 1.1 million in Canada, and 2.5 million in Mexico are undernourished (Patterson, 2017).

Conducting research on malnutrition is a challenging proposition, given both ethical and practical considerations. However, the Institute of Nutrition of Central America and Panama (INCAP) successfully conducted a longitudinal quasi-experiment to address this issue. In this study, two large (900 people) and two small (500 people) Guatemalan villages were identified. The villages were matched on variables known to be important to development, such as overall health and socioeconomic status. Children under the age of 7 in both villages were given a vitamin and mineral supplement twice a day and closely monitored. In one of each village size, the supplement also contained additional protein.

This research showed that early protein supplementation resulted in substantial improvements in cognitive skills, physical development, and economic productivity. A number of follow-up studies conducted over the course of three decades illustrated results. The children who received the protein supplementation were taller, had better performance on a wide variety of cognitive tasks, and had greater fat-free mass. As adults, they were at lower risk of living in poverty and (in men) showed greater work capacity. Currently, additional follow-up work on susceptibility to chronic diseases of adulthood is being conducted on these children, who are now 39 to 53 years of age. Early results indicate that the supplementation had a positive result here as well (Martorell, 2016).

There is a caveat here, however. The positive effects of supplementation occurred only for those children who participated in the study before the age of 3 years. Supplementation did not have the same effect for older children. Why would this be?

The author of the study argues that the first 1,000 days are a critical time period for healthy physical and cognitive development. First, this is a time of exceedingly rapid physical growth and brain development. Thus, any deficiencies encountered during this time period are likely to have a stronger effect. This rapid growth also implies increased caloric requirements relative to body size, making younger children even more vulnerable to deprivation. Second, young children have greater susceptibility to infections, such as diarrheal diseases, that can impact their ability to successfully digest nutrients. Last, younger children are more dependent upon others to take care of their needs and thus are less able to take compensatory action (Martorell, 2016).

This research along with numerous other lines of inquiry has led the United Nations International Children's Emergency Fund (UNICEF) to implement initiatives designed to assess the nutritional and health needs of affected people, educate and support breastfeeding women, provide essential vitamins and nutrients, and provide food and clean water for malnourished children (UNICEF, 2015a). Dozens of other organizations have joined in the fight to decrease world hunger. The World Hunger Education Service reports that there was a 42 percent decrease in the prevalence of malnourished people in developing nations between 1990 and 2014, and 13.5 percent of the overall population in developing nations remains chronically undernourished, down from 23.4 percent in 1990 (Hunger Notes, 2016). Progress is being made in the fight against world hunger, but it cannot be solved overnight.

what's
your
view

What do you think some of the ethical considerations are when conducting research with malnourished children? What responsibility do wealthy nations have toward developing nations?

factors in infancy include high birth weight, rapid weight gain in the first year, maternal smoking during pregnancy, and early introduction of solid foods (Weng, Redsell, Swift, Yang & Glazebrook, 2012).

THE BRAIN AND REFLEX BEHAVIOR

The **central nervous system** includes the brain and *spinal cord* (a bundle of nerves running through the backbone) and the peripheral network of nerves extending to every part of the body. Through this network, sensory messages travel to the brain, and motor commands travel back.

central nervous system
Brain and spinal cord.

Building the Brain The growth of the brain is a lifelong process fundamental to physical, cognitive, and emotional development. The brain at birth is only about one-fourth to one-third of its eventual adult volume (Toga, Thompson & Sowell, 2006). By age 6, it is almost adult size, but specific parts of the brain continue to grow and develop functionally into adulthood. The brain's growth occurs in fits and starts called *brain growth spurts*. Different parts of the brain grow more rapidly at different times.

Major Parts of the Brain Beginning about 3 weeks after conception, the brain gradually develops from a long hollow tube into a spherical mass of cells (Figure 4.10). By birth, the growth spurt of the spinal cord and *brain stem* (the part of the brain responsible for such basic bodily functions as breathing, heart rate, body temperature, and the sleep-wake cycle) has nearly run its course. The *cerebellum* (the part of the brain that maintains balance and motor coordination) grows fastest during the 1st year of life (Knickmeyer et al., 2008).

The *cerebrum,* the largest part of the brain, is divided into right and left halves, or hemispheres, each with specialized functions. This specialization of the hemispheres is called **lateralization.** The left hemisphere is mainly concerned with language and logical thinking, the right hemisphere with visual and spatial functions such as map reading and drawing. Joining the two hemispheres is a tough band of tissue called the *corpus callosum,* which allows them to share information and coordinate commands. The corpus callosum grows dramatically during childhood, reaching adult size by about age 10. Each cerebral hemisphere has four lobes or sections, which control different functions. They include the *occipital,*

lateralization
Tendency of each of the brain's hemispheres to have specialized functions.

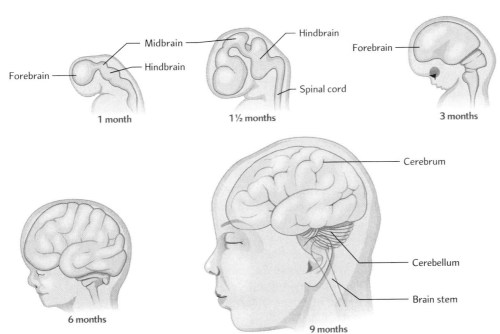

FIGURE 4.10
Brain Development during Gestation

Fetal nervous system development begins at about 3 weeks. At 1 month, major regions of the brain appear: the forebrain, midbrain, and hindbrain. As the brain grows, the front part expands to form the cerebrum, the seat of conscious brain activity. The cerebellum grows most rapidly during the 1st year of life.

Source: Cowan, W. M. "The development of the brain." *Scientific American,* 241(3), 1979, 113–133.

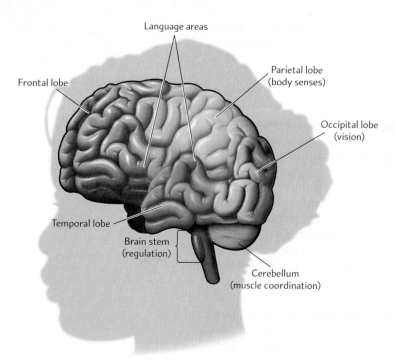

Language areas

Frontal lobe

Parietal lobe
(body senses)

Occipital lobe
(vision)

Temporal lobe

Brain stem
(regulation)

Cerebellum
(muscle coordination)

FIGURE 4.11

The Human Brain

neurons
Nerve cells.

parietal, temporal, and *frontal lobes* (Figure 4.11). The occipital lobe is the smallest of the four lobes and is primarily concerned with visual processing. The parietal lobe is involved with integrating sensory information from the body. It helps us move our bodies through space and manipulate objects in our world. The temporal lobe helps us interpret smells and sounds and is involved in memory. The frontal lobes, the newest region of the brain, are involved with a variety of higher-order processes, such as goal setting, inhibition, reasoning, planning, and problem solving. The regions of the *cerebral cortex* (the outer surface of the cerebrum) that govern vision, hearing, and other sensory information grow rapidly in the first few months after birth and are mature by age 6 months, but the areas of the frontal cortex responsible for abstract thought, mental associations, remembering, and deliberate motor responses grow very little during this period and remain immature for several years (Gilmore et al., 2007).

The brain growth spurt that begins at about the third trimester of gestation and continues until at least the 4th year of life is important to the development of neurological functioning. Smiling, babbling, crawling, walking, and talking—all the major sensory, motor, and cognitive milestones of infancy and toddlerhood—reflect the rapid development of the brain, particularly the cerebral cortex. (Research in Action discusses autism, a disorder related to abnormal brain growth.)

Brain Cells The brain is composed of *neurons* and *glial cells*. **Neurons,** or nerve cells, send and receive information. *Glia,* or glial cells, nourish and protect the neurons. They are the support system for our neurons.

Beginning in the 2nd month of gestation, an estimated 250,000 immature neurons are produced every minute through cell division (mitosis). At birth, most of the more than 100 billion neurons in a mature brain are already formed but are not yet fully developed. The number of neurons increases most rapidly between the 25th week of gestation and the first few months after birth. This cell proliferation is accompanied by a dramatic growth in cell size.

Originally the neurons are simply cell bodies with a nucleus, or center, composed of deoxyribonucleic acid (DNA), which contains the cell's genetic programming. As the brain grows, these rudimentary cells migrate to various parts of the brain (Bystron, Rakic, Molnar & Blakemore, 2006). Most of the neurons in the cortex are in place by 20 weeks of gestation, and its structure becomes fairly well defined during the next 12 weeks.

Once in place, the neurons sprout *axons* and *dendrites*—narrow, branching, fiberlike extensions. Axons send signals to other neurons, and dendrites receive incoming messages from them, through *synapses,* tiny gaps, which are bridged with the help of chemicals called *neurotransmitters* that are released by the neurons. Eventually, a particular neuron may have anywhere from 5,000 to 100,000 synaptic connections.

The multiplication of dendrites and synaptic connections, especially during the last 2½ months of gestation and the first 6 months to 2 years of life, accounts for much of the brain's growth and permits the emergence of new perceptual, cognitive, and motor abilities. As the neurons multiply, migrate to their assigned locations, and develop connections, they undergo the complementary processes of *integration* and *differentiation.* Through **integration,** the neurons that control various groups of muscles coordinate their activities. Through **differentiation,** each neuron takes on a specific, specialized structure and function.

At first the brain produces many more neurons and synapses than it needs. The large number of excess neurons provided by this early proliferation give the brain flexibility—

integration
Process by which neurons coordinate the activities of muscle groups.

differentiation
Process by which cells acquire specialized structures and functions.

AUTISM

Autism spectrum disorders (ASD) are characterized by deficits in social communication and language, difficulties with social interaction, and restrictive, repetitive patterns of behavior, interests, or activities (American Psychiatric Association, 2013). Recent figures show 1 in 68 children diagnosed with ASD (CDC, 2016e), an apparent increase from previous years. To what might we attribute this increase, and what can research tell us about what is going on?

One of the factors that has been theorized to be important centers on the diagnostic criteria. The DSM-5 now collapses several disorders into the single diagnosis of ASD. Severe *autistic disorder* as well as *Asperger syndrome* are now classified as falling on the autism spectrum (Zylstra, Prater, Walthour & Aponte, 2014), where they were not before. Thus, many children and adults who were not previously diagnosed as having ASD now qualify as such. Changes in ASD rates can also be explained by increased public awareness, referrals by doctors and schools, and more sensitive diagnostic tools (Zylstra et al., 2014). However, the rise in rates cannot be fully explained by changes in diagnosis (Hansen, Schendel & Parner, 2015).

Research has indicated that ASD has a strong genetic basis (Ozonoff et al., 2011; Sandin et al., 2014). Siblings of children with ASD are at increased risk (Ozonoff et al., 2011), and behavioral genetics studies confirm that increased risk is associated with genetic relatedness (Sandin et al., 2014). However, genes are not fully deterministic, and proposed key genetic variations are also found in individuals without ASD (Nardone & Elliott, 2016). Moreover, the rise in prevalence rates is unlikely to be attributable solely to genetics, as it has occurred too rapidly to reflect significant genomic change.

What other factors have been investigated? Ng and others (2017) conducted a meta-analysis of 315 international studies, noting a "vast literature riddled with inconsistent findings." Nevertheless, several key factors emerged. These include physiological factors such as advanced parental age, preterm birth, low birth weight, and clustering of pregnancy complications. Other culprits include pesticides, leads, heavy metals, traffic-related air pollutants, chemicals found in everyday household products (Boggess et al., 2016; Wong et al, 2015), and other substances that might be able to cross the placental barrier and affect brain development (Kalkbrenner, Schmidt & Penlesky, 2014; Nardone & Elliott, 2016). No conclusive evidence has been found yet.

The environmental factor that has received the most attention is the purported link between vaccines and autism. Anti-vaccine activists have argued that vaccines trigger autism in certain individuals. This theory has been repeatedly debunked (Taylor, Swerdfeger & Eslick, 2014). However, anti-vaccination attitudes proliferate and are spread via websites, forums, and social media (Basch, Zybert, Reeves & Basch, 2017; Venkatraman, Garg & Kumar, 2015). Thimerosal, an antibacterial preservative composed of a mercury compound, has at times been the center of controversy, despite being "much less toxic" than mercury found in fish or other sources (Roy, Aggarwal, Dhangar & Aneja, 2016). Meta-analyses have failed to substantiate claims of links between thimerosal and ASD (Ng et al., 2017; Roy et al., 2016). Nonetheless, it has been largely removed from vaccines in response to the public debate. Vaccines are safe for almost all children and far less risky than failing to immunize against potentially life-threatening diseases (Roy et al., 2016).

More research is needed to lay claim to definitive causes of ASD. A complex interplay of genetics and environmental factors is responsible for brain and behavioral changes associated with ASD. The relevant research questions to explore are daunting, in consideration of critical windows of exposure, ASD subtypes, gender variations, and individual genetic susceptibility (Kalkbrenner et al., 2014). Science can give us answers, but not all of them, and not right away.

 what's your view Do you support the view that autism rates are indeed on the rise? Given what you know today, how would you respond to claims that vaccinations are linked to autism?

with more connections available than will ever be needed, many potential paths are open for the growing brain. As early experience shapes the brain, the paths are selected, and unused paths are pruned away. This process involves **cell death,** which may sound negative but is a way to calibrate the developing brain to the local environment. This process begins during the prenatal period and continues after birth.

cell death
In brain development, normal elimination of excess brain cells to achieve more efficient functioning.

Only about half the neurons originally produced survive and function in adulthood (Society for Neuroscience, 2008). Yet, even as unneeded neurons die, others may continue to form during adult life (Deng, Aimone & Gage, 2010; Gould, Reeves, Graziano & Gross, 1999). Meanwhile, connections among cortical cells continue to strengthen and to become more reliable and precise, enabling more flexible and more advanced motor and cognitive functioning (Society for Neuroscience, 2008).

Myelination Much of the credit for efficiency of neural communication goes to the glia that coat the neural pathways with a fatty substance called *myelin*. This process of **myelination** enables signals to travel faster and more smoothly.

Myelination begins about halfway through gestation in some parts of the brain and continues into adulthood in others. The pathways related to the sense of touch—the first sense to develop—are myelinated by birth. Myelination of visual pathways, which are slower to mature, begins at birth and continues during the first 5 months of life. Pathways related to hearing may begin to be myelinated as early as the 5th month of gestation, but the process is not complete until about age 4. The parts of the cortex that control attention and memory are not fully myelinated until young adulthood. Myelination of the *hippocampus,* a structure deep in the temporal lobe that plays a key role in memory, continues to increase until at least age 70 (Benes, Turtle, Khan & Farol, 1994).

Myelination of sensory and motor pathways before birth in the spinal cord and after birth in the cerebral cortex may account for the appearance and disappearance of early reflexes, a sign of neurological organization and health.

Early Reflexes When your pupils contract as you turn toward a bright light, they are acting involuntarily. Such an automatic, innate response to stimulation is called a **reflex behavior.** Reflex behaviors are controlled by the lower brain centers that govern other involuntary processes, such as breathing and heart rate.

Human infants have an estimated 27 major reflexes, many of which are present at birth or soon after (Noble & Boyd, 2012; Table 4.4). *Primitive reflexes,* such as sucking, rooting for the nipple, and the Moro reflex (a response to being startled or beginning to fall), are related to instinctive needs for survival and protection or may support the early connection to the caregiver. Some primitive reflexes may be part of humanity's evolutionary legacy. One example is the grasping reflex, which enables infant monkeys to hold on to their mothers' fur. Human infants show a similar reflex wherein they tightly grasp any object placed in their palm, a holdover from our ancestral past.

As the higher brain centers become active during the first 2 to 4 months, infants begin to show *postural reflexes:* reactions to changes in position or balance. For example, infants who are tilted downward extend their arms in the parachute reflex, an instinctive attempt to break a fall. *Locomotor reflexes,* such as the walking and swimming reflexes, resemble voluntary movements that do not appear until months after the reflexes have disappeared.

Most of the early reflexes disappear during the first 6 to 12 months. Reflexes that continue to serve protective functions—such as blinking, yawning, coughing, gagging, sneezing, shivering, and dilation of the pupils in the dark—remain. Disappearance of unneeded reflexes on schedule is a sign that motor pathways in the cortex have been partially myelinated, enabling a shift to voluntary behavior. Thus we can evaluate a baby's neurological development by seeing whether certain reflexes are present or absent.

Molding the Brain: The Role of Experience Although the brain's early development is genetically directed, it is continually modified by environmental experience. The physical architecture of our brain is a reflection of the experiences we have had throughout our life. Our brains are not static; rather, they are living, changeable organs that respond to environmental influences. The technical term for this malleability of the brain is **plasticity.** Plasticity may be an evolutionary mechanism to enable adaptation to environmental change (Gomez-Robles, Hopkins & Sherwood, 2013; Toga et al., 2006).

Plasticity enables learning. Individual differences in intelligence may reflect differences in the brain's ability to develop neural connections in response to experience

myelination
Process of coating neural pathways with a fatty substance called myelin, which enables faster communication between cells.

reflex behaviors
Automatic, involuntary, innate responses to stimulation.

plasticity
(1) Range of modifiability of performance. (2) Modifiability, or "molding," of the brain through experience.

TABLE 4.4 Early Human Reflexes

Reflex	Stimulation	Baby's Behavior	Typical Age of Appearance	Typical Age of Disappearance
Moro	Baby is dropped or hears loud noise.	Extends legs, arms, and fingers, arches back, draws back head.	7th month of gestation	3 months
Darwinian (grasping)	Palm of baby's hand is stroked.	Makes strong fist; can be raised to standing position if both fists are closed around a stick.	7th month of gestation	4 months
Tonic neck	Baby is laid down on back.	Turns head to one side, assumes fencer position, extends arm and leg on preferred side, flexes opposite limbs.	7th month of gestation	5 months
Babkin	Both of baby's palms are stroked at once.	Mouth opens, eyes close, neck flexes, head tilts forward.	Birth	3 months
Babinski	Sole of baby's foot is stroked.	Toes fan out; foot twists in.	Birth	4 months
Rooting	Baby's cheek or lower lip is stroked with finger or nipple.	Head turns; mouth opens; sucking movements begin.	Birth	9 months
Walking	Baby is held under arms, with bare feet touching flat surface.	Makes steplike motions that look like well-coordinated walking.	1 month	4 months
Swimming	Baby is put into water face down.	Makes well-coordinated swimming movements.	1 month	4 months

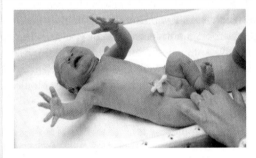

Moro reflex
©Picture Partners/Alamy Stock Photo

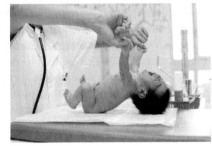

Darwinian reflex
©Phanie/Alamy Stock Photo

Tonic neck reflex
©Custom Medical Stock Photo/Alamy Stock Photo

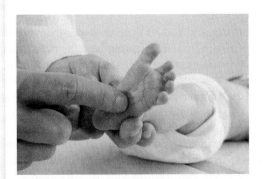

Babinski reflex
©Custom Medical Stock Photo/Alamy Stock Photo

Rooting reflex
©Science Photo Library/Shutterstock

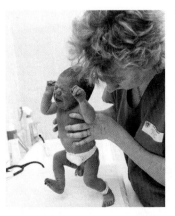

Walking reflex
©BSIP/Universal Images Group/Getty Images

(Garlick, 2003). Early experience can have lasting effects on the capacity of the central nervous system to learn and store information (Society for Neuroscience, 2008).

Enriched experience can spur brain development. Animals raised in toy-filled cages sprout more axons, dendrites, and synapses than animals raised in bare cages (Society for Neuroscience, 2008). Plasticity continues throughout life as neurons change in size and shape in response to environmental experience (Rutter, 2002).

But there are two sides to every coin. Just as plasticity allows learning in response to appropriate environmental input, it can also lead to damage in the case of harmful input. During the formative period of early life when the brain is most plastic, the brain is especially vulnerable. Exposure to hazardous drugs, environmental toxins, or maternal stress before or after birth can threaten the developing brain, and malnutrition can interfere with normal cognitive growth. Early abuse or sensory impoverishment can leave an imprint on the brain as it adapts to the environment in which the developing child must live, delaying neural development or affecting brain structure (AAP, Stirling, and the Committee on Child Abuse and Neglect and Section on Adoption and Foster Care; American Academy of Child and Adolescent Psychiatry, Amaya-Jackson; & National Center for Child Traumatic Stress, Amaya-Jackson, 2008).

Ethical constraints prevent controlled experiments on the effects of environmental deprivation on human infants. However, the discovery of thousands of infants and young children raised in overcrowded Romanian orphanages offered a natural experiment (Becket et al., 2006). These abandoned children had spent much of their time lying quietly in their cribs or beds with nothing to look at. Most of the 2- and 3-year-olds did not walk or talk, and the older children played aimlessly. PET scans of their brains showed extreme inactivity in the temporal lobes, which regulate emotion and receive sensory input.

Some of these children were placed in adoptive homes in Canada or the United Kingdom. In one longitudinal study, Romanian children who had been removed from institutions *before* age 6 months and adopted by English families showed no cognitive impairment by age 11 as compared with a control group of English children adopted within the United Kingdom. By contrast, the average IQs of Romanian children adopted into English families *after* age 6 months were 15 points lower. At ages 6 and 11, the latest-placed adoptees were the most cognitively impaired (Beckett et al., 2006). These findings suggest that high-quality foster care may partly overcome the adverse effects of early institutionalization on the processing of socio-emotional information (Moulson, Fox, Zeanah & Nelson, 2009).

EARLY SENSORY CAPACITIES

The rearward regions of the developing brain, which control sensory information, grow rapidly during the first few months of life, enabling newborn infants to make fairly good sense of what they touch, see, smell, taste, and hear (Gilmore et al., 2007).

Touch and Pain Touch is the first sense to develop, and for the first several months it is the most mature sensory system. When a newborn's cheek is stroked near the mouth, the baby responds by trying to find a nipple, an evolved survival mechanism (Rakison, 2005).

In the past, physicians performing surgery (such as circumcision) on newborn babies often used no anesthesia because of a mistaken belief that neonates cannot feel pain or feel it only briefly. Actually, there is evidence that the capacity for pain perception may emerge during the third trimester of pregnancy (Belliene & Buonocore, 2012; Lee, Ralston, Drey, Partridge & Rosen, 2005). Newborns can and do feel pain, and they become more sensitive to it during the next few days. The American Academy of Pediatrics (2006) maintains that prolonged or severe pain can do long-term harm to newborns and that pain relief during surgery is essential.

Smell and Taste The senses of smell and taste also begin to develop in the womb. A preference for certain tastes and smells can be learned in utero and during the first few days after birth, and the odors transmitted through the mother's breast milk may further contribute to this learning (Ventura & Worobey, 2013). Exposure to the flavors of healthy foods through breast-feeding may improve acceptance of healthy foods after weaning and later in life (AHA et al., 2006).

Certain taste preferences seem to be largely innate. Newborns much prefer sweet tastes to sour, bitter, or salty taste (Mennella, 2014). An inborn sweet tooth may help a baby adapt to life outside the womb, as breast milk is quite sweet (Ventura & Mennella, 2011). Newborns' rejection of bitter tastes is probably another survival mechanism, as many bitter substances are toxic (Beauchamp & Mennella, 2011). The taste preferences developed in infancy may last into early childhood; children offered different flavors in early infancy later have less restricted food preferences (Trabulsi & Mennella, 2012).

Hearing Hearing, too, is functional before birth; fetuses respond to sounds and seem to learn to recognize them. From an evolutionary perspective, early recognition of voices and language heard in the womb may lay the foundation for the relationship with the mother, which is critical to early survival (Rakison, 2005).

Auditory discrimination develops rapidly after birth. Even in the womb, fetuses can tell new speech sounds from those they have heard before (Partanen, Kujala, Naatanen, Liitola, Sambeth & Huotilainen, 2013). In addition, infants as young as 2 days old were able to recognize a word they heard up to a day earlier (Swain, Zelano & Clifton, 1993). At 1 month, babies can distinguish sounds as close as *ba* and *pa* (Eimas, Siqueland, Jusczyk & Vigorito, 1971). There are even indications that infants can recognize music that is typical of their culture from a young age (Virtala, Huotinainen, Partanen, Fellman & Tervaniemi, 2013).

Because hearing is a key to language development, hearing impairments should be identified as early as possible. Hearing loss occurs in 1 to 3 of 1,000 live births (Gaffney, Gamble, Costa, Holstrum & Boyle, 2003).

Sight Vision is the least developed sense at birth, perhaps because there is so little to see in the womb. From an evolutionary developmental perspective, the other senses, as we have pointed out, are more directly related to a newborn's survival. Visual perception and the ability to use visual information—identifying caregivers, finding food, and avoiding dangers—become more important as infants become more alert and active (Rakison, 2005).

The eyes of newborns are smaller than those of adults, the retinal structures are incomplete, and the optic nerve is underdeveloped. A neonate's eyes focus best from about 1 foot away—just about the typical distance from the face of a person holding a newborn. Newborns blink at bright lights. Their field of peripheral vision is very narrow; it more than doubles between 2 and 10 weeks and is well developed by 3 months (Maurer & Lewis, 1979; Tronick, 1972). The ability to follow a moving target also develops rapidly in the first months, as does color perception (Haith, 1986). The development of these abilities is tied closely to cortical maturation (Braddick & Atkinson, 2011).

Visual acuity at birth is approximately 20/400 but improves rapidly, reaching the 20/20 level by about 8 months (Kellman & Arterberry, 1998). *Binocular vision*—the use of both eyes to focus, enabling perception of depth and distance—usually does not develop until 4 or 5 months (Bushnell & Boudreau, 1993). Early screening is essential to detect any problems that may interfere with vision (AAP Committee on Practice and Ambulatory Medicine and Section on Ophthalmology, 2002).

Motor Development

Babies do not have to be taught such basic motor skills as grasping, crawling, and walking. They just need room to move and freedom to see what they can do. When the baby is ready and the environment offers the right opportunities, babies will develop new abilities spontaneously.

TABLE 4.5 Milestones of Motor Development

Skill	50 Percent	90 Percent
Rolling over	3.2 months	5.4 months
Grasping rattle	3.3 months	3.9 months
Sitting without support	5.9 months	6.8 months
Standing while holding on	7.2 months	8.5 months
Grasping with thumb and finger	8.2 months	10.2 months
Standing alone well	11.5 months	13.7 months
Walking well	12.3 months	14.9 months
Building tower of two cubes	14.8 months	20.6 months
Walking up steps	16.6 months	21.6 months
Jumping in place	23.8 months	2.4 years
Copying circle	3.4 years	4.0 years

Note: This table shows the approximate ages when 50 percent and 90 percent of children can perform each skill, according to the Denver Training Manual II.

Source: Frankenburg, W. K.; Dodds, J.; Archer, P.; Bresnick, B.; Maschka, P.; Edelman, N.; & Shapiro, H. *Denver II training manual.* Denver: Denver Developmental Materials, 1992.

MILESTONES OF MOTOR DEVELOPMENT

Motor development is marked by a series of milestones: achievements that develop systematically, each newly mastered ability preparing a baby to tackle the next. Babies first learn simple skills and then combine them into increasingly complex **systems of action,** which permit a wider or more precise range of movement and more effective control of the environment. In developing the precision grip, for example, an infant first tries to rake things up with the whole hand, fingers closing against the palm. Later the baby masters the *pincer grasp,* in which thumb and index finger meet at the tips to form a circle, making it possible to pick up tiny objects.

The **Denver Developmental Screening Test** (Frankenburg, Dodds, Fandal, Kazuk & Cohrs, 1975) is used to chart progress between ages 1 month and 6 years and to identify children who are not developing normally. The test measures **gross motor skills** (those using large muscles), such as rolling over and catching a ball, and **fine motor skills** (using small muscles), such as grasping a rattle and copying a circle. It also assesses language development (for example, knowing the definitions of words) and personality and social development (such as smiling spontaneously and dressing without help). The newest edition, the Denver II Scale (Frankenburg et al., 1992), includes revised norms. Table 4.5 provides some examples.

When we talk about what the "average" baby can do, we refer to the 50 percent Denver norms, but normality covers a wide range: About half of babies master these skills before the ages given, and about half afterward.

Head Control At birth, most infants can turn their heads from side to side while lying on their backs. When lying chest down, many can lift their heads enough to turn them. Within the first 2 to 3 months, they lift their heads higher and higher—sometimes to the point where they lose their balance and roll over on their backs. By 4 months, almost all infants can keep their heads erect while being held or supported in a sitting position.

Hand Control Babies are born with a grasping reflex. If the palm of an infant's hand is stroked, the hand closes tightly. At about 3½ months, most infants can grasp an object of moderate size, such as a rattle, but have trouble holding a small object. Next, they begin to grasp objects with one hand and transfer them to the other, and then to hold

---

systems of action
Increasingly complex combinations of motor skills, which permit a wider or more precise range of movement and more control of the environment.

Denver Developmental Screening Test
Screening test given to children 1 month to 6 years old to determine whether they are developing normally.

gross motor skills
Physical skills that involve the large muscles.

fine motor skills
Physical skills that involve the small muscles and eye–hand coordination.

Lifting and holding up the head from a prone position, crawling along the floor to reach something enticing, such as a colorful toy, and walking well enough to push a wagon full of blocks are important early milestones of motor development.

©Yu Zhang/Shutterstock

©PhotoAlto/Alamy Stock Photo

©OJO Images Ltd/Alamy Stock Photo

(but not pick up) small objects. Sometime between 7 and 11 months, their hands become coordinated enough to pick up a tiny object, such as a pea, using the pincer grasp. By 15 months, the average baby can build a tower of two cubes. A few months after the 3rd birthday, the average toddler can copy a circle fairly well.

Locomotion After 3 months, the average infant begins to roll over deliberately—first from front to back and then from back to front. The average baby can sit without support by 6 months and can assume a sitting position without help by about 8½ months.

Between 6 and 10 months, most babies begin to get around under their own power by means of creeping or crawling. This new achievement of *self-locomotion* has striking cognitive and psychosocial ramifications (Bertenthal, Campos & Kermoian, 1994; Karasik, Tamis-LeMonda & Adolph, 2011). Crawling infants become more sensitive to where objects are, how big they are, whether they can be moved, and how they look. Crawling helps babies learn to judge distances and perceive depth. They learn to look to caregivers for clues as to whether a situation is secure or frightening—a skill known as *social referencing* (Campos, Sorce, Emde & Svejda, 2013).

By holding onto a helping hand or a piece of furniture, the average baby can stand at a little past age 7 months. The average baby can let go and stand alone well at about 11½ months.

All these developments lead up to the major motor achievement of infancy: walking. For some months before they can stand without support, babies practice cruising while holding onto furniture. Soon after they can stand alone well most infants take their first unaided steps. Within a few weeks, shortly after the first birthday, the average child is walking fairly well and thus achieves the status of toddler.

During the 2nd year, children begin to climb stairs one at a time, putting one foot after another on the same step; later they will alternate feet. Walking down stairs comes later. Also in their 2nd year, toddlers run and jump. By age 3½, most children can balance briefly on one foot and begin to hop.

MOTOR DEVELOPMENT AND PERCEPTION

Sensory perception enables infants to learn about themselves and their environment so they can make better judgments about how to navigate in it. Motor experience, together with awareness of their changing bodies, sharpens and modifies their perceptual understanding of what is likely to happen if they move in a certain way. This bidirectional connection between perception and action, mediated by the developing brain, gives infants much useful information about themselves and their world (Adolph & Eppler, 2002).

Sensory and motor activity seem fairly well coordinated from birth (von Hofsten, 2004). Infants begin reaching for and grasping objects at about 4 to 5 months; by 5½ months they can adapt their reach to moving or spinning objects (Wentworth, Benson & Haith, 2000). Piaget and other researchers long maintained that reaching depended on **visual guidance:** the use of the eyes to guide the movement of the hands (or other parts of the body). However, more recent research suggests that children 6 months of age and younger do not use visually directed reaching, and in fact, reach objects more rapidly in the dark than the light. However, by a year of age, infants reach for objects more quickly when they are able to use their vision (Berthier & Carrico, 2010).

visual guidance
Use of the eyes to guide movements of the hands or other parts of the body.

depth perception
Ability to perceive objects and surfaces three-dimensionally.

Depth perception, the ability to perceive objects and surfaces in three dimensions, depends on several kinds of cues that affect the image of an object on the retina of the eye. These cues involve not only binocular coordination but also motor control (Bushnell & Boudreau, 1993). *Kinetic cues* are produced by movement of the object or the observer, or both. To find out whether an object is moving, a baby might hold his or her head still for a moment, an ability that is well established by about 3 months.

Sometime between 5 and 7 months, after babies can reach for and grasp objects, they develop **haptic perception,** the ability to acquire information through touch, for example, by handling objects rather than by simply looking at them. Haptic perception enables babies to respond to such cues as relative size and differences in texture and shading (Bushnell & Boudreau, 1993).

haptic perception
Ability to acquire information about properties of objects, such as size, weight, and texture, by handling them.

ELEANOR AND JAMES GIBSON'S ECOLOGICAL THEORY OF PERCEPTION

visual cliff
Apparatus designed to give an illusion of depth and used to assess depth perception in infants.

ecological theory of perception
Theory developed by Eleanor and James Gibson, which describes developing motor and perceptual abilities as interdependent parts of a functional system that guides behavior in varying contexts.

Depth perception has implications when it comes to the development of self-propelled motion, which for most children involves learning how to crawl. In a classic experiment by Richard Walk and Eleanor Gibson (1961), 6-month-old babies were seated on a plexiglass tabletop laid over two ledges. From the far side of the table, the infants' mothers beckoned their children. To the babies, it appeared that their mothers were asking them to crawl over a **visual cliff**—a steep drop down to the floor. Walk and Gibson wanted to know if babies would willingly crawl over the deep end of the visual cliff when urged to do so by their mothers.

Experiments such as these were pivotal in the development of Eleanor Gibson and James J. Gibson's **ecological theory of perception** (E. J. Gibson, 1969; J. J. Gibson, 1979; Gibson & Pick, 2000). In this approach, locomotor development depends on infants' increasing sensitivity to the interaction between their changing physical characteristics and new and varied characteristics of their environment. Babies' bodies continually change with age—their weight, center of gravity, muscular strength, and abilities. And each new environment provides a new challenge for babies to master. For example, sometimes a baby might have to make her way down a slight incline, and other times might have to navigate stairs. Instead of relying on solutions that previously worked, babies must learn to continually gauge their abilities and adjust their movements to meet the demands of their current environment.

No matter how enticing a mother's arms are, this baby is staying away from them. As young as she is, she can perceive depth and wants to avoid falling off what looks like a cliff.
©Mark Richards/PhotoEdit

This process of "learning to learn" (Adolph, 2008, p. 214) is an outcome of both perception and action. It involves visual and manual exploration, testing alternatives, and flexible problem solving. What worked at one time may not work now, and what worked in one environment may not work well in another. For example, when faced with steep downward slopes, infants who have just begun to crawl or walk seem unaware of the limits of their abilities and are more likely to plunge recklessly down steep slopes. Infants who have been crawling for some time are better at judging slopes and know how far they can push their limits without losing their balance (Adolph, 2008; Adolph, Vereijken, & Shrout, 2003). For example, they may gauge the steepness with their hands first, or turn around to go down backward as if they are going down stairs.

In this approach, the baby is somewhat like a small scientist testing new ideas in each situation. According to Gibson, "Each problem space has its own set of information-generating behaviors and its own learning curve" (Adolph, 2008, p. 214). So, for example, babies who learn how far they can reach for a toy across a gap while in a sitting position without tumbling over must acquire this knowledge anew for situations involving crawling. Likewise, when crawling babies who have mastered slopes begin to walk, they have to learn to cope with slopes all over again (Adolph & Eppler, 2002).

HOW MOTOR DEVELOPMENT OCCURS: THELEN'S DYNAMIC SYSTEMS THEORY

Traditionally, motor development was thought to be genetically determined and largely automatic. Presumably, the maturing brain would produce a predetermined set of motor abilities at the appropriate point in development. Today many developmental psychologists consider this view too simplistic. Instead, motor development is considered to be a continuous process of interaction between the baby and the environment (Thelen, 1995; Smith & Thelen, 2003).

Esther Thelen, in her influential **dynamic systems theory (DST),** argued that "behavior emerges in the moment from the self-organization of multiple components" (Spencer et al., 2006, p. 1523). Infant and environment form an interconnected, dynamic system. Opportunities and constraints presented by the infant's physical characteristics, motivation, energy level, motor strength, and position in the environment at a particular moment in time affect whether and how an infant achieves a goal. Ultimately, a solution emerges as the baby explores various combinations of movements and assembles those that most efficiently contribute to that end. Furthermore, the solution must be flexible and subject to modification in changing circumstances. Rather than being solely in charge of it, the maturing brain is but one component of a dynamic process. Indeed, no one factor determines the pace of development, and no predetermined timetable specifies when a particular skill will emerge. Rather, normal babies tend to develop the same skills in the same order because they are built approximately the same way and have similar challenges and needs. However, because these factors can vary from baby to baby, this approach also allows for variability in the timeline of individual development.

Thelen used the walking reflex to illustrate her approach. When neonates are held upright with their feet touching a surface, they spontaneously make coordinated stepping movements. This behavior usually disappears by the 4th month. Not until the latter part of the 1st year, when a baby is getting ready to walk, do the movements appear again. The traditional explanation focused on cortical control, and the belief was that an older baby's deliberate walking was a new skill masterminded by the developing brain. However, this explanation did not make sense to Thelen. She wondered why the stepping reflex—which used the same series of movements that would become walking—should stop, particularly as other early behaviors, such as kicking, persisted. The answer, she suggested, might be found by considering other relevant variables that could affect movement. For example, babies' legs become thicker and heavier during the early months of life, but the large leg muscles used to control movements are not yet strong enough to handle the increased weight (Thelen & Fisher, 1982, 1983). In support of this hypothesis, when infants who had stopped stepping were held in warm water, stepping reappeared. Presumably, the water helped support their legs and lessened the pull of gravity on their muscles, allowing them to once again demonstrate the skill. Their ability to produce the movement had not changed—only the physical and environmental conditions that inhibited or promoted it. Maturation alone cannot explain such an observation, said Thelen. These same systems of dynamic influences affect all motor movements, from reaching for a rattle to sitting independently to learning to walk.

dynamic systems theory (DST)
Esther Thelen's theory, which holds that motor development is a dynamic process of active coordination of multiple systems within the infant in relation to the environment.

CULTURAL INFLUENCES ON MOTOR DEVELOPMENT

Although motor development follows a virtually universal sequence, its *pace* does respond to certain cultural factors. According to some research, African babies tend to be more advanced than U.S. and European infants in sitting, walking, and running. In Uganda, for example, babies typically walk at 10 months, as compared with 12 months in the United States and 15 months in France. Brazilian children, who are encouraged to play physically active and expressive games, outperform British children in running and walking (Victora, Victora & Barros, 1990). Such differences may, in part, be related to ethnic differences in temperament (H. Kaplan & Dove, 1987) or may reflect a culture's child-rearing practices (Venetsanou & Kambas, 2010).

Some cultures actively encourage early development of motor skills. In many African and West Indian cultures in which infants show advanced motor development, adults use special *handling routines,* such as bouncing and stepping exercises, to strengthen babies' muscles. In one study, Jamaican infants, whose mothers used such handling routines daily, sat, crawled, and walked earlier than English infants, whose mothers gave them no such special handling (Hopkins & Westra, 1988, 1990). In Western countries, motor intervention programs that encourage locomotor skills in young children have been shown to accelerate some forms of motor development, such as horizontal jumping or skipping (Deli, Bakle & Zachopoulou, 2006).

On the other hand, some cultures discourage early motor development. Children of the Ache in eastern Paraguay do not begin to walk until age 18 to 20 months (H. Kaplan & Dove, 1987). Ache mothers pull their babies back to their laps when the infants begin to crawl away. Yet, as 8- to 10-year-olds, Ache children climb tall trees, chop branches, and play in ways that enhance their motor skills (H. Kaplan & Dove, 1987). Normal development, then, need not follow the same timetable to reach the same destination.

summary and key terms

Childbirth and Culture: How Birthing Has Changed

- In Europe and the United States, childbirth before the twentieth century was not much different from childbirth in some developing countries today. Birth was a female ritual that occurred at home and was attended by a midwife. Pain relief was minimal, and risks for mother and baby were high.
- The development of the science of obstetrics professionalized childbirth. Births took place in hospitals and were attended by physicians. Medical advances dramatically improved safety.
- Today, delivery at home or in birth centers attended by midwives can be a relatively safe alternative to physician-attended hospital delivery for women with normal, low-risk pregnancies.

The Birth Process

- Birth normally occurs after a preparatory period of parturition.
- The birth process consists of three stages: (1) dilation of the cervix, (2) descent and emergence of the baby, and (3) expulsion of the umbilical cord and the placenta.

- Electronic fetal monitoring can detect signs of fetal distress.
- About 32 percent of births in the United States are by cesarean delivery.
- Alternative methods of childbirth can minimize the need for painkilling drugs and maximize parents' active involvement.
- Modern epidurals can give effective pain relief with smaller doses of medication than in the past.
- The presence of a doula can provide physical benefits as well as emotional support.

  parturition, electronic fetal monitoring, cesarean delivery, natural childbirth, prepared childbirth, doula

The Newborn Baby

- The neonatal period is a time of transition from intrauterine to extrauterine life.
- At birth, the circulatory, respiratory, digestive, elimination, and temperature regulation systems become independent of the mother's. If a newborn cannot start breathing within about 5 minutes, brain injury may occur.
- Newborns have a strong sucking reflex and secrete meconium from the intestinal tract. They are commonly subject to neonatal jaundice due to immaturity of the liver.

- At 1 minute and 5 minutes after birth, a neonate's Apgar score can indicate how well he or she is adjusting to extrauterine life. The Brazelton Neonatal Behavioral Assessment Scale can predict future development.
- Neonatal screening is done for certain rare conditions, such as PKU and congenital hypothyroidism.
- A newborn's state of arousal is governed by periodic cycles of wakefulness, sleep, and activity. Sleep takes up the major, but a diminishing, amount of a neonate's time.
- Cultural customs affect sleep patterns.

neonatal period, neonate, anoxia, neonatal jaundice, Apgar scale, Brazelton Neonatal Behavioral Assessment Scale (NBAS), state of arousal

Complications of Childbirth

- Complications of childbirth include low birth weight, postmature birth, and stillbirth.
- Low-birth-weight babies may be either preterm (premature) or small for gestational age. Low birth weight is a major factor in infant mortality and can cause long-term physical and cognitive problems.
- A supportive postnatal environment and other protective factors often can improve the outcome for babies suffering from birth complications.

low-birth-weight babies, preterm (premature) infants, small-for-date (small-for-gestational-age) infants, kangaroo care, protective factors, postmature, stillbirth

Survival and Health

- The vast majority of infant deaths occur in developing countries. Postnatal care can reduce infant mortality.
- Although infant mortality has diminished in the United States, it is still disturbingly high, especially among African American babies. Birth defects are the leading cause of death in infancy.
- Sudden infant death syndrome (SIDS) is a leading cause of postneonatal death in the United States. SIDS rates have declined markedly following recommendations to lay babies on their backs to sleep.
- Vaccine-preventable diseases have declined as immunization rates have improved, but many preschoolers are not fully protected.

infant mortality rate, sudden infant death syndrome (SIDS)

Early Physical Development

- Normal physical growth and sensory and motor development proceed according to the cephalocaudal and proximodistal principles.
- A child's body grows most dramatically during the 1st year of life; growth proceeds at a rapid but diminishing rate throughout the first 3 years.

- Breast-feeding offers many health advantages and sensory and cognitive benefits.
- Babies are at risk of becoming obese adults if they have obese parents or grow very quickly in the first year.
- The central nervous system controls sensorimotor activity. Lateralization enables each hemisphere of the brain to specialize in different functions.
- The brain grows most rapidly during the months before and immediately after birth as neurons migrate to their assigned locations, form synaptic connections, and undergo integration and differentiation. Cell death and myelination improve the efficiency of the nervous system.
- Reflex behaviors—primitive, locomotor, and postural—are indications of neurological status. Most early reflexes drop out during the 1st year as voluntary, cortical control develops.
- Especially during the early period of rapid growth, environmental experiences can influence brain development positively or negatively.
- Sensory capacities, present from birth and even in the womb, develop rapidly in the first months of life. Very young infants show pronounced abilities to discriminate between stimuli.
- Touch is the first sense to develop and mature. Smell, taste, and hearing begin to develop in the womb. Newborns are sensitive to pain.
- Vision is the least well-developed sense at birth.

cephalocaudal principle, proximodistal principle, central nervous system, lateralization, neurons, integration, differentiation, cell death, myelination, reflex behaviors, plasticity

Motor Development

- Motor skills develop in a certain sequence, which may depend on maturation, context, experience, and motivation. Simple skills combine into increasingly complex systems.
- Self-locomotion brings about changes in all domains of development.
- Perception is intimately related to motor development. Depth perception and haptic perception develop in the first half of the 1st year.
- According to Gibson's ecological theory, sensory perception and motor activity are coordinated from birth, helping infants figure out how to navigate in their environment.
- Thelen's dynamic systems theory holds that infants develop motor skills, not by maturation alone but by active coordination of multiple systems of action within a changing environment.
- Cultural practices may influence the pace of early motor development.

systems of action, Denver Developmental Screening Test, gross motor skills, fine motor skills, visual guidance, depth perception, haptic perception, visual cliff, ecological theory of perception, dynamic systems theory (DST)

5

Cognitive Development during the First Three Years

learning objectives

Identify six approaches to the study of cognitive development.

Describe how infants learn and remember.

Discuss infant assessment measures and how intelligence is predicted.

Summarize and evaluate Piaget's theory of cognitive development.

Explain how infants process information and begin to understand the characteristics of the physical world.

Describe language development in infancy.

©UpperCut Images/Superstock

In this chapter we look at infants' and toddlers' cognitive abilities from a variety of perspectives: behaviorist, psychometric, Piagetian, information processing, cognitive neuroscientific, and social-contextual. We trace the early development of language.

Studying Cognitive Development: Six Approaches

How do babies learn to solve problems? When does memory develop? What accounts for individual differences in cognitive abilities? These questions have long intrigued developmental scientists, many of whom have taken one of six approaches to their study:

- The **behaviorist approach** studies the basic *mechanics* of learning. Behaviorists are concerned with how behavior changes in response to experience.
- The **psychometric approach** measures *quantitative differences* in abilities that make up intelligence by using tests that indicate or predict these abilities.
- The **Piagetian approach** looks at changes, or stages, in the *quality* of cognitive functioning. It is concerned with how the mind structures its activities and adapts to the environment.
- The **information-processing approach** focuses on the nuts and bolts of cognition—perception, learning, memory, and problem solving. It aims to discover how children process information.
- The **cognitive neuroscience approach** seeks to identify what brain structures are involved in specific aspects of cognition.
- The **social-contextual approach** examines the effects of environmental aspects of the learning process, particularly the role of parents and other caregivers.

behaviorist approach
Approach to the study of cognitive development that is concerned with basic mechanics of learning.

psychometric approach
Approach to the study of cognitive development that seeks to measure intelligence quantitatively.

Piagetian approach
Approach to the study of cognitive development that describes qualitative stages in cognitive functioning.

information-processing approach
Approach to the study of cognitive development by observing and analyzing the mental processes involved in perceiving and handling information.

cognitive neuroscience approach
Approach to the study of cognitive development that links brain processes with cognitive ones.

social-contextual approach
Approach to the study of cognitive development that focuses on environmental influences, particularly parents and other caregivers.

Behaviorist Approach: Basic Mechanics of Learning

Babies are born with the ability to see, hear, smell, taste, and touch, and they have some ability to remember what they learn. Learning theorists are interested in mechanisms of learning.

CLASSICAL AND OPERANT CONDITIONING

Eager to capture Ella's growth, her father took many pictures. Whenever the flash went off, Ella blinked. One evening Ella saw her father hold the camera up to his eye—and she blinked *before* the flash. She had learned to associate the camera with the bright light, so that the sight of the camera alone activated her blinking reflex.

This is an example of **classical conditioning,** in which a person learns to make a response (in this case, blinking) to a stimulus (the camera) that originally did not bring about the response. Classical conditioning enables infants to anticipate an event before it happens. Classically conditioned learning will become *extinct,* or fade, if it is not reinforced by repeated association. Thus, if Ella frequently saw the camera without the flash, she would eventually stop blinking at the sight of the camera alone.

If classical conditioning is the before—the prediction of events to come—operant conditioning is the after—the consequences of a behavior. **Operant conditioning** focuses on how the consequences of a behavior affect the likelihood of that behavior occurring again. Specifically, behaviors may be reinforced and become more likely to occur, or they may be punished and become less likely to occur. For example, a baby may learn that when she babbles her parents respond with smiles and attention, and she may increase this behavior to receive even more smiles and attention. In other words, she has been reinforced for her babbling. By contrast, a baby may see that when she throws her food her parents tend to frown and speak sharply to her. To avoid this punishment, she might learn not to throw her food.

classical conditioning
Learning based on associating a stimulus that does not ordinarily elicit a response with another stimulus that does elicit the response.

operant conditioning
(1) Learning based on association of behavior with its consequences. (2) Learning based on reinforcement or punishment.

INFANT MEMORY

Can you remember anything that happened to you before you were about 2 years old? Chances are you can't. Why do we experience infantile amnesia? Part of the reason is that early procedural knowledge (e.g., how to hold a pencil) and perceptual knowledge (e.g., what an apple tastes like) are not the same as the later explicit, language-based memories used by adults (e.g., what you did last Sunday).

Luckily, we can use operant conditioning techniques to "ask" infants questions about what they remember. For example, Carolyn Rovee-Collier (1999) and her associates (1996) brought 2- to 6-month-old infants to their laboratory and attached a string between one of their ankles and a mobile. The babies soon learned that when they kicked their leg, the mobile moved. As this was reinforcing to them, the number of kicks increased. When they were later brought back they kicked more than other infants who had not been conditioned in this fashion, even if their ankles were no longer attached. This demonstrated that the recognition of the mobiles triggered a memory of their initial experience with them. Similar research has been conducted with older infants and toddlers, and in this way researchers have been able to determine that the length of time a conditioned response lasts increases with age. At 2 months of age, the typical infant can remember a conditioned response for 2 days; 18-month-olds can remember it for 13 weeks (Hartshorn et al., 1998; Rovee-Collier, 1999; Rovee-Collier, 1996).

Young infants do have the capacity to remember events, but this memory is less robust than for older children. Infant memory appears to be linked specifically to the original cues encoded during conditioning. For example, 2- to 6-month-olds trained to press a lever to make a train go around a track repeated the learned behavior *only* when they saw the original train. By 9 to 12 months, infants and toddlers could generalize their memory and press the lever to make a different train move if no more than 2 weeks had gone by since the conditioning (Rovee-Collier, 1999).

Research using operant conditioning techniques has illustrated that infants' memory processes may not differ fundamentally from those of older children and adults except that their retention time is shorter and memory is more dependent on encoding cues. Moreover, studies have found that just as with adults, memory can be aided by reminders. Brief, nonverbal exposure to the original stimulus can sustain a memory from early infancy through age 1½ to 2 years (Rovee-Collier, 1999).

Researchers have creatively used everyday objects such as infant mobiles to "ask" babies what they know and remember about their world. ©Lifebrary/Shutterstock

Psychometric Approach: Developmental and Intelligence Testing

Although there is no clear scientific consensus on a definition of intelligence, most professionals agree on some basic criteria. Intelligence enables people to acquire, remember, and use knowledge; to understand concepts and relationships; and to solve everyday problems. Moreover, **intelligent behavior** is presumed to be goal oriented and adaptive.

The goals of psychometric testing are to quantitatively measure the factors that are thought to make up intelligence (such as comprehension and reasoning) and, from the results of that measurement, to predict future performance (such as school achievement). **IQ (intelligence quotient) tests** consist of questions or tasks that show how much of the measured abilities a person has by comparing that person's performance with norms established by a large group of test-takers.

For school-age children, intelligence test scores can predict academic performance fairly accurately and reliably. Testing infants and toddlers is another matter. Because babies cannot tell us what they know and how they think, the most obvious way to gauge their intelligence is by assessing what they can do. But if they do not grasp a rattle, is it because they do not know how, do not feel like doing it, do not realize what is expected of them, or have simply lost interest?

TESTING INFANTS AND TODDLERS

Although it is virtually impossible to measure infants' intelligence, we can still test their functioning by assessing their behavior on tasks and comparing their performance with established norms. So, for example, if a child is unable to perform a task that the "average baby" can do by a particular age, that child may be delayed in that area. By contrast, a baby can also be ahead of the curve by performing better than her same-age peers.

The **Bayley Scales of Infant and Toddler Development** (Bayley, 1969, 1993, 2005) is a developmental test designed to assess children from 1 month to 3½ years. Scores on the Bayley-III indicate a child's competencies in each of five developmental areas: *cognitive, language, motor, social-emotional,* and *adaptive behavior.* An optional *behavior rating scale* can be completed by the examiner, in part on the basis of information from the child's caregiver. Separate scores, called *developmental quotients* (DQs), are calculated for each scale. DQs are most commonly used for early detection of emotional disturbances and sensory, neurological, and environmental deficits and can help parents and professionals plan for a child's needs.

ASSESSING THE IMPACT OF THE EARLY HOME ENVIRONMENT

Using the **Home Observation for Measurement of the Environment (HOME)** (R. H. Bradley, 1989; Caldwell & Bradley, 1984), trained observers interview the primary caregiver and rate on a yes-or-no checklist the intellectual stimulation and support observed in a child's home. HOME scores are significantly correlated with measures of cognitive development (Totsika & Sylva, 2004).

Research has identified a number of variables important to cognitive development. These include the number of books in the home, the presence of playthings that encourage the development of concepts, parents' involvement in children's play, and overall parental responsiveness, including kissing and caressing the child during the interview (Bradley, Corwyn, Burchinal, McAdoo & Coll, 2001). Additionally, researchers have identified seven aspects of the early home environment that help prepare children for school. These seven conditions are (1) encouraging exploration of the environment; (2) mentoring in basic cognitive and social skills; (3) celebrating developmental advances; (4) guidance in practicing and extending skills; (5) protection from inappropriate disapproval, teasing, and punishment; (6) communicating richly and responsively; and (7) guiding and limiting behavior (Ramey & Ramey, 2003, p. 4).

Some HOME items may be less culturally relevant in non-Western than in Western families (Bradley, Corwyn, McAdoo & Coll, 2001). Also, we cannot be sure on the basis

intelligent behavior
Behavior that is goal oriented and adaptive to circumstances and conditions of life.

IQ (intelligence quotient) tests
Psychometric tests that seek to measure intelligence by comparing a test-taker's performance with standardized norms.

Bayley Scales of Infant and Toddler Development
Standardized test of infants' and toddlers' mental and motor development.

Home Observation for Measurement of the Environment (HOME)
Instrument to measure the influence of the home environment on children's cognitive growth.

HOME gives positive ratings to parents who praise their children and are attentive to their questions.
©Thanasis Zovoilis/Moment/Getty Images

of correlational findings that parental responsiveness or an enriched home environment increases a child's intelligence. All we can say is that these factors are associated with high intelligence. Intelligent, well-educated parents may be more likely to provide a positive, stimulating home environment as well as genes for high intelligence.

EARLY INTERVENTION

Early intervention is a systematic process of planning and providing therapeutic and educational services for families that need help in meeting young children's developmental needs.

A number of research programs, such as Project CARE (Wasik, Ramey, Bryant & Sparling, 1990) and the Abcedarian (ABC) Project (Campbell, Ramey, Pungello, Sparling & Miller-Johnson, 2002) have sought to determine the effectiveness of their programs. In each project, an at-risk experimental group was enrolled in Partners for Learning, a full-day, year-round early childhood education program at a university child development center. Control groups received pediatric and social work services, but they were not enrolled in Partners for Learning (Ramey & Ramey, 2003). The children who received the early intervention showed a widening advantage over the control groups in developmental test scores between 12 and 18 months, and performed equal to or better than the average for the general population. By age 3, the average IQ in the Abcedarian experimental group was 101 and in the CASE experimental group it was 105. By contrast, the control groups had average IQs of 84 and 93, respectively (Ramey & Ramey, 1998b).

These findings and others like them (Camilli, Vargas, Ryan & Barnett, 2010) show that early educational interventions can help offset environmental risks. The most effective early interventions are those that (1) start early and continue throughout the preschool years; (2) are highly time-intensive; (3) are center-based, providing direct educational experiences, not just parental training; (4) take a comprehensive approach, including health, family counseling, and social services; and (5) are tailored to individual differences and needs. As occurred in the two North Carolina projects, initial striking gains tend to diminish without sufficient ongoing environmental support (Brooks-Gunn, 2003; Ramey & Ramey, 1998a).

Piagetian Approach: The Sensorimotor Stage

The first of Piaget's four stages of cognitive development is the **sensorimotor stage.** During this stage (birth to approximately age 2), infants learn about themselves and their world through their developing sensory and motor activity. Babies change from creatures who respond primarily through reflexes and random behavior into goal-oriented toddlers.

SUBSTAGES OF THE SENSORIMOTOR STAGE

The sensorimotor stage consists of six substages (Table 5.1) that flow from one to another as a baby's **schemes,** organized patterns of thought and behavior, become more elaborate. During the first five substages, babies learn to coordinate input from their senses and organize their activities in relation to their environment. During the sixth substage, they progress to using symbols and concepts to solve simple problems.

Much of this early cognitive growth comes about through **circular reactions,** in which an infant learns to reproduce events originally discovered by chance. Initially, an activity such as sucking produces an enjoyable sensation that the baby wants to repeat. The repetition produces pleasure, which motivates the baby to do it yet again (Figure 5.1). The originally chance behavior has been consolidated into a new scheme. These are called circular reactions because they stimulate their own repetition.

In the *first substage* (birth to about 1 month), neonates practice their reflexes. For example, newborns suck reflexively when their lips are touched. But they soon learn to find the nipple even when they are not touched, and they suck at times when they are not hungry. Infants thus modify and extend the scheme for sucking.

In the *second substage* (about 1 to 4 months), babies learn to purposely repeat pleasant actions first achieved by chance (as shown in Figure 5.1a). Also, they begin to turn

schemes
Piaget's term for organized patterns of thought and behavior used in particular situations.

circular reactions
Piaget's term for processes by which an infant learns to reproduce desired occurrences originally discovered by chance.

TABLE 5.1 Substages of Piaget's Sensorimotor Stage of Cognitive Development*

Substage	Ages	Description	Behavior
1. Use of reflexes	Birth to 1 month	Infants exercise their inborn reflexes and gain some control over them. They do not coordinate information from their senses.	Dorri begins sucking when her mother's breast is in her mouth.
2. Primary circular reactions	1 to 4 months	Infants repeat pleasurable behaviors that first occur by chance (such as thumb sucking). Activities focus on the infant's body rather than on the environment. Infants make first acquired adaptations (such as sucking different objects differently). They begin to coordinate sensory information.	When given a bottle, Dylan, who is usually breast-fed, is able to adjust his sucking to the rubber nipple.
3. Secondary circular reactions	4 to 8 months	Infants become more interested in the environment; they repeat actions that bring interesting results (such as shaking a rattle). Actions are intentional but not initially goal directed.	Ro pushes cereal over the edge of her high chair one piece at a time and watches each piece as it falls.
4. Coordination of secondary schemes	8 to 12 months	Behavior is more deliberate and purposeful as infants coordinate previously learned schemes (such as looking at and grasping a rattle) and use previously learned behaviors to attain their goals (such as crawling across the room to get a toy). They can anticipate events.	Anica pushes the button on her musical nursery rhyme book, and "ABCD" plays. She pushes this button over and over again.
5. Tertiary circular reactions	12 to 18 months	Toddlers show curiosity and experimentation; they purposefully vary their actions to test results (for example, by shaking different rattles to hear their sounds). They actively explore their world to determine what is novel about an object, event, or situation. They try new activities and use trial and error in solving problems.	When Bjorn's big sister holds his favorite book up to his crib, he reaches for it. The book is too wide to pull in lengthwise, so he turns it sideways, pulls it in, and hugs it.
6. Mental combinations	18 to 24 months	The emerging capacity for mental representation allows toddlers to think about events and anticipate their consequences without always resorting to action. Toddlers begin to demonstrate insight. They can use symbols, such as gestures and words, and can pretend.	Jenny plays with her shape box, searching carefully for the right hole for each shape before trying—and succeeding.

*Infants show enormous cognitive growth during Piaget's sensorimotor stage, as they learn about the world through their senses and their motor activities. Note their progress in problem solving and the coordination of sensory information. All ages are approximate.

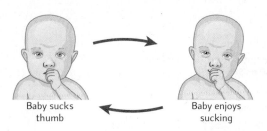

(a) Primary circular reaction: Action and response both involve infant's own body (1 to 4 months).

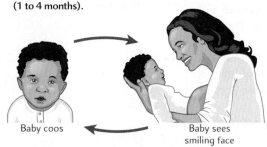

(b) Secondary circular reaction: Action gets a response from another person or object, leading to baby's repeating original action (4 to 8 months).

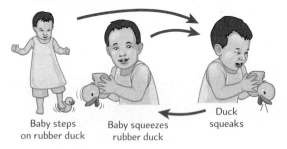

(c) Tertiary circular reaction: Action gets one pleasing result, leading baby to perform similar actions to get similar results (12 to 18 months).

FIGURE 5.1
Primary, Secondary, and Tertiary Circular Reactions

representational ability
Piaget's term for capacity to store mental images or symbols of objects and events.

visible imitation
Imitation with parts of one's body that one can see.

invisible imitation
Imitation with parts of one's body that one cannot see.

deferred imitation
Piaget's term for reproduction of an observed behavior after the passage of time by calling up a stored symbol of it.

toward sounds, showing the ability to coordinate different kinds of sensory information (vision and hearing).

In the *third substage* (about 4 to 8 months) babies intentionally repeat an action not merely for its own sake, as in the second substage, but to get results *beyond the infant's own body* (as shown in Figure 5.1b). For example, a baby this age might repeatedly shake a rattle to hear the noise.

By the time infants reach the *fourth substage* (about 8 to 12 months), they have learned to generalize from past experience to solve new problems. They modify and coordinate previous schemes, such as the schemes for crawling, pushing, and grabbing, to find one that works. This substage marks the development of complex, goal-directed behavior.

In the *fifth substage* (about 12 to 18 months), babies begin to experiment to see what will happen. They now vary a behavior to see what might happen. For example, a toddler may squeeze a rubber duck that squeaked when stepped on, to see whether it will squeak again (as shown in Figure 5.1c). By trial and error, they try behaviors until they find the best way to attain a goal.

The *sixth substage* (about 18 months to 2 years) is a transition to the preoperational stage of early childhood. **Representational ability**—the ability to mentally represent objects and actions in memory, largely through symbols such as words, numbers, and mental pictures—frees toddlers from immediate experience. They can pretend, and their representational ability affects the sophistication of their pretending (Bornstein, Haynes, O'Reilly & Painter, 1996). They can think about actions before taking them and try out solutions in their mind.

During these six substages, infants develop the ability to think and remember, and develop knowledge about the physical world. Researchers have found that some of these developments conform fairly closely to Piaget's observations, but others may occur earlier than Piaget claimed. (Table 5.2 compares Piaget's views on these and other topics with more current findings.)

DO IMITATIVE ABILITIES DEVELOP EARLIER THAN PIAGET THOUGHT?

One-year-old Clara watches as her older sister brushes her hair. When her sister puts the brush down, Clara picks it up and tries to brush her hair too.

Imitation becomes increasingly valuable late in the first year of life as babies try new skills (Nelson, 2005). Piaget noted this behavior in his own observations, and maintained that **visible imitation**—imitation that uses body parts such as hands or feet that babies can see—develops first and is then followed by **invisible imitation**—imitation that involves parts of the body that babies cannot see—at 9 months.

Piaget believed that children under 18 months could not engage in **deferred imitation.** Deferred imitation is the reproduction of an observed behavior after the passage of time. As the behavior is no longer happening, deferred imitation requires that a stored representation of the action be recalled. Piaget argued that young children could not engage in deferred imitation because they lacked the ability to retain mental representations. However, deferred imitation of novel or complex events seems to begin by about 6 to 9 months (Bauer, 2002). For example, in one study 6-month-old German and Cameroonian infants were able to imitate how an adult interacted with a doll after a 10-minute delay (Goertz et al., 2011). The ability to hold material in memory over a longer time span increases with age. Note that the findings on deferred imitation agree with those on operant conditioning (Rovee-Collier, 1999).

TABLE 5.2 Key Developments of the Sensorimotor Stage

Concept or Skill	Piaget's View	More Recent Findings
Imitation	Invisible imitation develops around 9 months; deferred imitation begins with mental representations at 18 to 24 months.	Controversial studies have found invisible imitation of facial expressions in newborns and deferred imitation as early as 6 weeks. Deferred imitation of complex activities seems to exist as early as 6 months.
Object permanence	Develops gradually between the third and sixth substage.	Infants as young as 3½ months seem to show object knowledge, although findings are controversial.
Symbolic development	Develops at 18 to 24 months with representational thinking.	Understanding that pictures stand for something else occurs at about 19 months. Children under 3 have difficulty interpreting scale models.
Categorization	Develops at 18 to 24 months with representational thinking.	Infants as young as 3 months recognize perceptual categories; by the end of the first year they categorize by function.
Causality	Develops between 4 to 6 months and 1 year, based on an infant's discovery, first of effects of own actions and then of effects of outside forces.	Some evidence suggests early awareness of specific causal events in the physical world, but general understanding of causality may be slower to develop.
Number	Develops at 18 to 24 months with the use of symbols.	Infants as young as 5 months recognize and mentally manipulate small numbers; interpretation of findings is controversial.

In **elicited imitation,** infants and toddlers are induced to imitate a specific series of actions they have seen, but not done before. For example, more than 40 percent of 9-month-olds can reproduce two steps, such as dropping a toy car down a vertical chute and then pushing a car with a rod to make it roll to the end of a ramp and turn on a light. Moreover, they can do this after a delay of 1 month (Bauer, 2002; Bauer, Wiebe, Carver, Waters & Nelson, 2003). Four factors seem to determine young children's long-term recall: (1) the number of times a sequence of events has been experienced, (2) whether the child actively participates or merely observes, (3) whether the child is given verbal reminders of the experience, and (4) whether the sequence of events occurs in a logical, causal order (Bauer, Wenner, Dropik & Wewerka, 2000).

elicited imitation
Research method in which infants or toddlers are induced to imitate a specific series of actions they have seen but not necessarily done before.

object permanence
Piaget's term for the understanding that a person or object still exists when out of sight.

DEVELOPMENT OF KNOWLEDGE ABOUT OBJECTS AND SYMBOLS

The *object concept*—the idea that objects have their own independent existence, characteristics, and locations in space—is a later *cognitive* development fundamental to an orderly view of physical reality. The object concept is the basis for children's awareness that they themselves exist apart from objects and other people.

When Does Object Permanence Develop? One aspect of the object concept is **object permanence,** the realization that an object or person continues to exist when out of sight.

Piaget believed object permanence develops gradually during the sensorimotor stage. At first, infants appear to have no such concept. At about 4 months, they will look for something they have dropped, but if they cannot see it, they act as if it no longer exists.

Some research suggests that babies may fail to physically search for hidden objects because they cannot yet carry out a two-step sequence of actions, such as lifting the cover of a box and then grasping the object. Methods based only on infants' looking behavior eliminate the need for coordination with

This little girl seems to be showing some concept of object permanence by searching for an object that is partially hidden.
©Doug Goodman/Science Source

motor activity and thus can be used at very early ages. With this technique, we can get a better assessment of what babies really know.

Over the next few months, this ability continues to develop. For example, infants will continue to look for an object in the place where they first found it after seeing it hidden, even if they were later shown the object being moved to a new location (the A-not-B error). Somewhere between 5 and 8 months they start *looking* at the correct location where the object was moved, but do not reach for it. At about 9 to 10 months, infants will start looking and reaching for the object in the correct location (Cuevas & Bell, 2010). At 12 to 18 months, most infants will reliably search for an object in the last place they saw it hidden. However, they will not search for it in a place where they did *not* see it hidden. At 18 to 24 months, object permanence is fully achieved; toddlers will look for an object even if they did not see it hidden.

As we discuss later in this chapter, research using information-processing methodology suggests that infants as young as 3 or 4 months seem not only to have a sense of object permanence but also to understand causality and categorization, to have a rudimentary concept of number, and to know other principles governing the physical world.

Symbolic Development, Pictorial Competence, and Understanding of Scale Much of the knowledge people acquire about their world is gained through *symbols,* intentional representations of reality. Learning to interpret symbols is an essential task of childhood. One aspect of symbolic development is the growth of *pictorial competence,* the ability to understand the nature of pictures (DeLoache, Pierroutsakos & Uttal, 2003). For example, consider how suns are represented in children's books. Generally they are drawn as a yellow circle with radiating spires. A child who understands that this graphic stands in for the ball of light in the sky has attained some degree of pictorial competence.

Until about 15 months, infants use their hands to explore pictures as if they were objects—rubbing, patting, or attempting to lift a depicted object off the page. By about 19 months children are able to point at a picture of an object while saying its name, demonstrating an understanding that a picture is a symbol of something else (DeLoache, Pierroutsakos & Uttal, 2003). By age 2, children understand that a picture is *both* an object and a symbol (Preissler & Bloom, 2007).

Although toddlers may spend a good deal of time watching television, at first they seem unaware that what they are seeing is a representation of reality (Troseth, Saylor & Archer, 2006). In one series of experiments, 2- and 2½-year-olds watched a video of an adult hiding an object in an adjoining room. When taken to the room, the 2½-year-olds found the hidden object easily, but 2-year-olds could not. Yet the younger children were able to find the object if they watched through a window as it was hidden (Troseth & DeLoache, 1998). Apparently, what the 2-year-olds lacked was representational understanding of screen images.

Have you ever seen toddlers try to put on a hat that is too small for their head, or sit in a chair much too tiny to hold them? This is known as a *scale error*—a momentary misperception of the relative sizes of objects (DeLoache, LoBue, Vanderborght & Chiong, 2013). In one study, 18- to 36-month-olds were first allowed to interact with play objects that fit their body size, such as a toy car to ride in or a plastic slide to slide down. Then the life-size objects were replaced with miniature replicas. The children tried to slide down the tiny slides and squeeze their bodies into the miniature cars. Why would they still treat the objects as if they were full size?

The researchers suggested that these actions might in part be based on a lack of impulse control—the children wanted to play with the objects so badly that they ignored perceptual information about size. However, toddlers might also be exhibiting faulty communication between immature brain systems. One brain system enables the child to recognize and categorize an object ("That's a chair") and to plan what to do with it ("I'm going to sit in it"). A separate system may be involved in perceiving the size of the object and using visual information to control actions pertaining to it ("It's big enough to sit in"). When communication between these areas breaks down, children momentarily, and amusingly, treat the objects as if they were full size (DeLoache, Uttal & Rosengren, 2004).

The **dual representation hypothesis** offers yet another proposed explanation for scale errors. An object such as a toy chair has two potential representations. The chair is both an object in its own right, as well as a symbol for a class of things ("chairs"). According to this hypothesis, it is difficult for toddlers to simultaneously mentally represent both the actual object and the symbolic nature of what it stands for. In other words, they can either focus on the particular chair they are faced with ("This is a miniature chair") or the symbol and what it represents ("Chairs are for sitting in"), and so they may confuse the two (DeLoache, 2011).

dual representation hypothesis
Proposal that children under age 3 have difficulty grasping spatial relationships because of the need to keep more than one mental representation in mind at the same time.

EVALUATING PIAGET'S SENSORIMOTOR STAGE

According to Piaget, the journey from reflex behavior to the beginnings of thought is a long, slow one. For a year and a half or so, babies learn only from their senses and movements; not until the last half of the 2nd year do they make the breakthrough to conceptual thought. However, research using simplified tasks and modern tools suggests that limitations Piaget saw in infants' early cognitive abilities may instead have reflected immature linguistic and motor skills. The answers that Piaget received were as much a function of the ways in which he asked the questions as they were a reflection of the actual abilities of young children.

In terms of describing what children do under certain circumstances, and the basic progression of skills, Piaget was correct. However, infants and toddlers are more cognitively competent than Piaget imagined. This does not mean that infants come into the world with minds fully formed. As Piaget observed, immature forms of cognition precede more mature forms. However, Piaget may have been mistaken in his emphasis on motor experience as the primary engine of cognitive growth. Infants' perceptions are far ahead of their motor abilities, and today's methods enable researchers to make observations and inferences about those perceptions, as we discuss it in the next section.

Information-Processing Approach: Perceptions and Representations

Information-processing researchers analyze the separate parts of a complex task to figure out what abilities are necessary for each part of the task and at what age these abilities develop.

HABITUATION

At about 6 weeks, Stefan lies peacefully in his crib near a window, sucking a pacifier. It is a cloudy day, but suddenly the sun breaks through, and an angular shaft of light appears on the end of the crib. Stefan stops sucking for a few moments, staring at the pattern of light and shade. Then he looks away and starts sucking again.

We cannot directly observe what was going on in Stefan's mind when he saw the shaft of light, but we can tell by his sucking and looking behavior at what point he began paying attention and when he stopped. Much information-processing research with infants is based on **habituation,** a type of learning in which repeated or continuous exposure to a stimulus, such as the shaft of light, reduces attention to that stimulus. In other words, familiarity breeds loss of interest.

habituation
Type of learning in which familiarity with a stimulus reduces, slows, or stops a response.

When doing research with babies, researchers need to figure out how to ask questions in ways that babies can answer. Habituation is a type of learning in which repeated or continuous exposure to a stimulus (such as a shaft of light) reduces attention to that stimulus (such as looking away). It can be compared to boredom, and the rate of habituation (how quickly infants look away) can be used to "ask" infants how interesting they think various objects are.

Researchers study habituation in newborns by presenting a stimulus such as a sound or visual pattern, and then monitoring responses such as sucking or eye movements. A baby who has been sucking typically stops or sucks less vigorously when a stimulus is first presented in order to pay attention to the stimulus. After the stimulus loses its novelty, the infant generally resumes sucking vigorously. This indicates that habituation has occurred. If a new sight or sound is presented, the baby's attention is generally captured once again, and the baby will reorient toward the interesting stimulus and once again sucking slows. This response to a new stimulus is called **dishabituation.**

Researchers gauge the efficiency of infants' information processing by measuring how quickly babies habituate to familiar stimuli, how fast their attention recovers when they are exposed to new stimuli, and how much time they spend looking at new or old stimuli. Liking to look at new things and habituating to them quickly correlates with later signs of cognitive development, such as a preference for complexity, rapid exploration of the environment, sophisticated play, quick problem solving, and the ability to match pictures. In fact, as we will see, speed of habituation and other information-processing abilities show promise as predictors of intelligence (Rose, Feldman, Jankowski & VanRossem, 2012; Fagan, Holland & Wheeler, 2007).

VISUAL AND AUDITORY PERCEPTUAL AND PROCESSING ABILITIES

Babies tend to spend more time looking at some visual objects than others. This tendency is presumed to indicate their preferences. This tendency has been exploited by scientists in a visual paradigm known as **visual preference.** For example, if babies given a choice between looking at a curved or straight line spend more time focused on the curved line, the implication is that babies like curved lines more than straight lines. With this technique, researchers have determined that babies less than 2 days old prefer curved lines to straight lines, complex patterns to simple patterns, three-dimensional objects to two-dimensional objects, pictures of faces or facelike configurations to pictures of other things, and new sights to familiar sights (Fantz, 1963, 1964, 1965; Fantz, Fagen & Miranda, 1975; Fantz & Nevis, 1967; Turati, Simion, Milani & Umilta, 2002). The tendency to prefer new sights to familiar ones is called *novelty preference.*

The realization that babies like to look at new things afforded researchers with yet another tool with which to ask them questions. Babies can be shown a stimulus and be allowed to habituate to it. Then they can be concurrently presented with the familiar stimulus, as well as an additional novel stimulus. If the baby spends longer looking at the novel stimulus, that suggests that the baby recognizes the familiar stimulus. In other words, because the novel stimulus is new and babies like new things, it is more interesting and thus warrants a better look than the previously seen, more boring, stimulus. This behavior demonstrates **visual recognition memory,** an ability that depends on the capacity to form and refer to mental representations (P. R. Zelazo, Kearsley & Stack, 1995).

Contrary to Piaget's view, such studies suggest that a rudimentary representational ability exists at birth or very soon after and quickly becomes more efficient. Individual differences in efficiency of information processing reflect the speed with which infants form and refer to such mental images. When shown two sights at the same time, infants who quickly shift attention from one to another tend to have better recognition memory and stronger novelty preference than infants who take longer looks at a single sight (Jankowski, Rose & Feldman, 2001).

Speed of processing increases rapidly during infants' 1st year. It continues to increase during the 2nd and 3rd years, as toddlers become better able to distinguish new information from information they have already processed (Rose, Feldman & Jankowski, 2002; P. R. Zelazo et al., 1995).

Auditory discrimination studies also are based on attentional preference. Such studies have found that newborns can tell sounds they have already heard from those they have not. In one study, infants who heard a certain speech sound one day after birth remembered that sound 24 hours later, as shown by a reduced tendency to turn their heads toward the sound and even a tendency to turn away (Swain, Zelazo & Clifton, 1993).

Piaget held that the senses are unconnected at birth and are only gradually integrated through experience. However, this integration begins almost immediately. The fact that

dishabituation
Increase in responsiveness after presentation of a new stimulus.

visual preference
Tendency of infants to spend more time looking at one sight than another.

visual recognition memory
Ability to distinguish a familiar visual stimulus from an unfamiliar one when shown both at the same time.

neonates will look at a source of sound shows that at the very least they associate hearing and sight. A more sophisticated ability is **cross-modal transfer,** the ability to use information gained from one sense to guide another—as when a person negotiates a dark room by feeling for the location of familiar objects. In one study, 1-month-olds showed that they could transfer information gained from sucking (touch) to vision. When the infants saw a rigid object (a hard plastic cylinder) and a flexible one (a wet sponge) being manipulated by a pair of hands, the infants looked longer at the object they had just sucked (Gibson & Walker, 1984).

cross-modal transfer
Ability to use information gained by one sense to guide another.

Researchers also study how attention itself develops. From birth to about 2 months, the amount of time infants typically gaze at a new sight increases (Colombo, 2002). Between about 4 to 8 months, looking time shortens, with the fastest decline seen at 4 to 6 months (Colombo, Shaddy, Anderson, Gibson, Blaga & Kannass, 2010). Presumably, this is because infants learn to scan objects more efficiently and thus shift attention more rapidly. Indeed, those infants who look for less time at novel stimuli show better memory for it later (Reynolds, Guy & Zhang, 2011). Later in the 1st year and into the 2nd, when sustaining attention becomes more voluntary and task-oriented, looking time plateaus or increases (Colombo et al., 2004).

The capacity for *joint attention*—which is of fundamental importance to social interaction, language acquisition, and the understanding of others' intentions and mental states—develops between 10 and 12 months, when babies follow an adults' gaze by looking or pointing in the same direction (Behne, Liszkowski, Carpenter & Tomasello, 2012). Young children who follow an adults' gaze at 10 or 11 months have a larger vocabulary at 18 months and 2 years than those who do not, especially if they spontaneously point at the object as well (Brooks & Meltzoff, 2005, 2008).

INFORMATION PROCESSING AS A PREDICTOR OF INTELLIGENCE

Because of a weak correlation between infants' scores on developmental tests such as the Bayley Scales and their later IQ (Bjorkland & Causey, 2017), many psychologists assumed that the cognitive functioning of infants had little in common with that of older children and adults. However, when cognitive functioning is examined more closely, some aspects of mental development do seem to be fairly continuous from birth (Courage & Howe, 2002).

Four core cognitive domains appear to be associated with later IQ: attention, processing speed, memory and representational competence (as indexed by cross-modal transfer and the ability to anticipate future events). In one study, performance on these tasks in infancy (7 and 12 months) was related to performance on the same tasks in toddlerhood (24 and 36 months) as well as to performance on IQ tests at 11 years of age (Rose, Feldman, Jankowski & VanRossem, 2012). Similar relationships to school performance have been found for the ability to shift attention rapidly (Hitzert, Van Braeckel, Bos, Hunnius & Geuze, 2014) and the ability to inhibit attention toward irrelevant stimuli (Markant & Amso, 2014). This provides evidence for the continuity of cognitive processes. Essentially, children who, from the start, are efficient at attending to, taking in, and interpreting sensory information score well on later intelligence tests.

INFORMATION PROCESSING AND THE DEVELOPMENT OF PIAGETIAN ABILITIES

Here we consider categorization, causality, object permanence, and number, all of which depend on formation of mental representations (refer to Table 5.2).

Categorization Adults can understand that plants and animals are both living things but a television is not. Furthermore, they can understand that some animals are pets, that among those pets are cats and dogs, and that a chihuahua is a type of dog. These nested relationships are known as *categories.* Dividing the world into meaningful categories is vital to thinking about objects or concepts and their relationships. It is the foundation of language, reasoning, problem solving, and memory.

research in action

INFANTS, TODDLERS, AND TV

Eighteen-month-old Caitlin picks up her LeapPad tablet and presses an icon. Cheerful music plays and she giggles as colorful images flash across the screen. Her mother is preparing dinner and content to let her child play an educational game.

About 90 percent of parents report their children under 2 using electronic media (AAP, 2011). Media technology geared toward young children is expansive, including TV, DVDs, tablets, apps, and streaming video (AAP, 2013). TV outranks other media in consumption (Vittrup, Snider, Rose & Rippy, 2016), with near constant access possible through the proliferation of mobile media devices (AAP, 2013; Northwestern University Center on Human Development, 2014).

"Baby media" geared toward infants and toddlers directly or indirectly implies early education benefits, and parents perceive its educational value as a jump start to learning. Unlike preschool programming, there is no conclusive evidence that baby media positively impact learning (Wartella, Richert & Robb, 2010). Attention is drawn toward sights and sounds, but age-related constraints in memory, cognition, and brain development place limitations on early learning. Researchers believe that infants and toddlers are unable to comprehend the meanings of what they are viewing. TV, DVDs, and other educational videos are believed to have little value until about 24 months of age (Courage & Howe, 2010).

The American Academy of Pediatrics (AAP) has renewed recommendations that children under age 2 be discouraged from watching TV (AAP, 2013). The committee echoes expert advice that children learn best through hands-on play and recommends that young children engage in interpersonal activities, such as talking, reading, or playing with toys. Nevertheless, few parents enforce TV viewing limitations with infants (Barr, Danziger, Hilliar, Andolina & Ruskis, 2010). As children display interest and become more competent,

parents tend to encourage media use (Lauricella, Wartella & Rideout, 2015). Positive attitudes toward "baby media" use are maintained in spite of cautionary messages. Experts question whether parents are unfamiliar with or outright disagree with AAP recommendations (Vittrup et al., 2016).

More research is necessary to determine the long-term effects of early media use. TV and media use results in the displacement effect, whereby time spent, even with educational programming, takes precious time away from more beneficial activities (Christakis, 2014). Preliminary studies have explored background TV use, suggesting near constant TV noise interferes with children's cognitive functioning and social play (Lapierre et al., 2012). Other studies link heavy media use with poor self-regulation in early childhood (Radesky et al., 2014). Others question the impact of trends of increasingly private use through mobile media devices (Lauricella et al., 2015), and whether early social interactions are altered in terms of quality communication and time spent with family members (Vittrup et al., 2016).

Parents represent the most influential social partner in their children's lives, modeling media use from birth (Vittrup et al., 2016). Increasingly, it is understood that change in infant and toddler media use requires a family effort, as parents' media use is mirrored in children's use across media types (Lauricella et al., 2015; Northwestern University Center on Human Development, 2014).

what's your view What restrictions, if any, would you place on infant or toddler TV, video, or mobile media use? Do you believe that there are negative consequences as a result of young children's media use?

According to Piaget, the ability to group things into categories does not appear until around 18 months. Yet, by looking longer at items in a new category, even 3-month-olds seem to know, for example, that a dog is not a cat (French, Mareschal, Mermillod & Quinn, 2004). Indeed, brain imaging has found that basic components of the neural structures needed to support categorization are functional within the first 6 months of life (Quinn, Westerlund & Nelson, 2006). Infants at first seem to categorize on the basis of *perceptual* features, such as shape, color, and pattern, but by 12 to 14 months their categories become *conceptual,* based on real-world knowledge, particularly of function (Mandler, 1998, 2007). In one series of experiments, 10- and 11-month-olds recognized that chairs with zebra-striped upholstery belong in the category of furniture, not animals

(Pauen, 2002). As time goes on, these broad concepts become more specific. For example, 2-year-olds recognize particular categories, such as "car" and "airplane," within the overall category of "vehicles" (Mandler, 2007).

Categorization is not limited to visual stimuli. There is evidence that 3-month-old babies categorize words differently than tones (Ferry, Hespos & Waxman, 2010) and can even categorize musical chords into dissonant versus consonant and major versus minor dimensions (Virtala, Huotilainen, Partanen, Fellman & Tervaniemi, 2013). Furthermore, in the 2nd year, language becomes a factor in the ability to categorize. In one study, 14-month-olds who understood more words were more flexible in their categorizing than those with smaller understood vocabularies (Ellis & Oakes, 2006).

Causality Eight-month-old Aviva accidentally squeezes her toy duck and it quacks. Startled, she drops it, and then, staring at it intently, she squeezes it again. Aviva is beginning to understand causality—the principle that one event (squeezing) causes another (quacking). Piaget maintained that this understanding develops slowly during infants' 1st year.

However, information-processing studies suggest that an understanding of causality emerges earlier. In one study, infants as young as 4½ months were able to understand simple causality (a ball knocking another ball out of position). However, only those infants who had practiced playing with a Velcro-covered ball and Velcro mittens—allowing them to easily manipulate the ball and therefore practice performing causal actions—were able to do so (Rakison & Krogh, 2012). By 6 months of age, this ability is more robust and does not require training (Leslie, 1995). Moreover, by 8 months of age, infants make causal attributions for simple events even when they cannot see the actual moment of contact between the two objects (Muentener & Carey, 2010). And, by 10 to 12 months old, the types of inferences made by infants become even more sophisticated. For example, 10- to 12-month-old infants looked longer when a hand emerged from the opposite side of a stage onto which a beanbag had been thrown than when the hand emerged from the same side as the beanbag, suggesting the infants understood that the hand had probably thrown the beanbag. The infants did *not* have the same reaction when a toy train rather than a hand appeared or when the thrown object was a self-propelled puppet (Saxe, Tenebaum & Carey, 2005).

It may be that, with age, infants accumulate more information about how objects behave, thus they are better able to see causality as a general principle operating in a variety of situations (Cohen & Amsel, 1998; Cohen, Chaput & Cashon, 2002). Increasing experience with the environment may also be a factor. For example, 7-month-olds who had begun to crawl recognized self-propulsion of objects, but noncrawling 7-month-olds did not. This finding suggests that infants' ability to identify self-propelled motion is linked to the development of self-locomotion, which gives them new ways of understanding objects in their world (Cicchino & Rakison, 2008).

Object Permanence When Piaget investigated object permanence, he used infants' motor responses to gauge whether or not infants understood that a hidden object still existed. Their failure to reach for the hidden object was interpreted to mean they did not. However, it was possible that infants understood object permanence but could not demonstrate this knowledge with motor activity. At that time, infant development research methodologies were more limited. Researchers needed to ask babies the question in a different way, using what has since become known as the violation-of-expectations paradigm.

Violation of expectations begins with a familiarization phase in which infants see an event happen normally. After the infant becomes bored and has habituated to this procedure (most commonly as indexed by looking away), the event is changed in a way that conflicts with—or violates—normal expectations. If the baby looks longer at this changed event, researchers assume the additional interest shown by the baby implies that the baby is surprised.

For example, in one experiment, infants as young as 3½ months were first shown an animation of a carrot moving back and forth behind a screen (Hespos & Baillargeon, 2008). The center of the screen was notched, and a tall carrot should have shown momentarily as it moved in front of the notch, as shown in Figure 5.2. In the "possible" event, the short carrot, as expected, could not be seen as it passed in front of the notch. In the

Seven-month-old babies appear to understand that an object incapable of self-motion, such as a beanbag or a tennis ball, must be set in motion by a causal agent, such as a hand.
©Pixelbliss/Shutterstock

violation of expectations
Research method in which dishabituation to a stimulus that conflicts with experience is taken as evidence that an infant recognizes the new stimulus as surprising.

FIGURE 5.2

How Early Do Infants Show Object Permanence?

In this experiment, 3½-month-olds watched a short carrot and then a tall carrot slide along a track, disappear behind a screen, and then reappear. After they became accustomed to seeing these events, the opaque screen was replaced by a screen with a large notch at the top. The short carrot did not appear in the notch when passing behind the screen; the tall carrot, which should have appeared in the notch, also did not. The babies looked longer at the tall than at the short carrot event, suggesting that they were surprised that the tall carrot did not appear in the notch.

Habituation Events

Test Events

Possible event   Impossible event

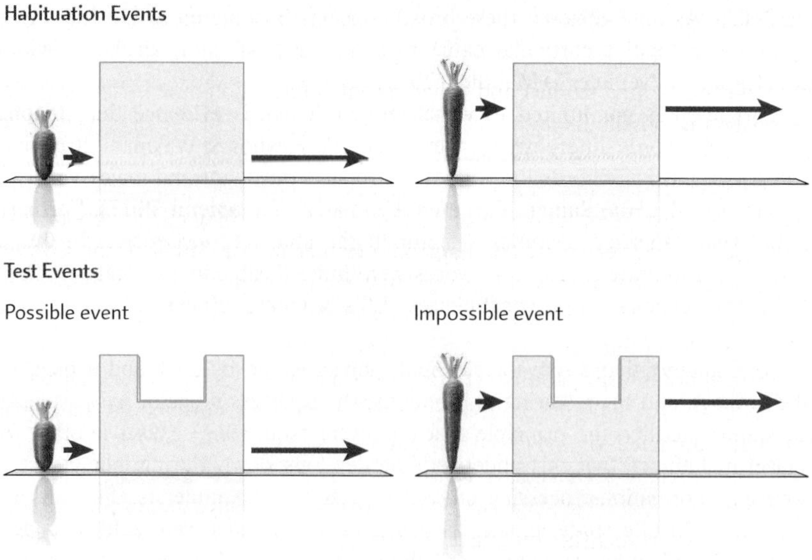

Source: Adapted from Baillargeon, R.; & DeVos, J. "Object permanence in young infants: Further evidence." *Child Development*, 62, 1991, 1227–1246.

"impossible" event, the tall carrot would appear at one side, never show in the middle, and then emerge out the other side. Infants showed surprise by looking longer at the "impossible" event, indicating that the "impossible" event violated their expectations.

This procedure was important to the study of object permanence because for babies to be surprised by the carrot's failure to show, they needed to be able to remember that the carrot continued to exist. Thus, it provides evidence for the development of this ability at much younger ages than Piaget thought possible.

Number The violation-of-expectations paradigm can also be used to ask babies questions about their understanding of numbers. Karen Wynn (1992b) tested whether 5-month-old babies can add and subtract small numbers of objects. The infants watched as Mickey Mouse dolls were placed behind a screen, and a doll was either added or taken away. The screen then was lifted to reveal either the number of dolls that should have been there or a different number of dolls. Babies looked longer at surprising "wrong" answers than at expected "right" ones, suggesting that they had mentally computed the right answers. This understanding of number seems to begin long before Piaget's sixth substage.

Wynn interpreted this research as suggesting that numerical concepts are inborn. However, critics argued the infants might simply have been responding *perceptually* to the puzzling presence or the absence of the doll behind the screen (Cohen & Marks, 2002; Haith, 1998). Other researchers suggest that, although infants do seem to discriminate visually between sets of, say, two and three objects, they may merely notice differences in the overall contours, area, or collective mass of sets of objects rather than compare the number of objects in the sets (Mix, Huttenlocher & Levine, 2002).

In response to such criticisms, McCrink and Wynn (2004) designed an experiment to find out whether 9-month-olds can add and subtract numbers too large for mere perceptual discrimination. The infants saw five abstract objects go behind an opaque square. Five more objects then appeared and went behind the square. The infants looked longer when the screen dropped to reveal five objects than when it revealed 10. The authors concluded that "humans possess an early system that supports numerical combination and manipulation" (p. 780). Moreover, the ability, in preschool, to estimate approximate numbers is related to later mathematical achievement, and this relationship is particularly true for lower achieving students (Bonny & Lourenco, 2013).

EVALUATING INFORMATION-PROCESSING RESEARCH ON INFANTS

Violation-of-expectations studies and other recent information-processing research with infants raises the possibility that at least rudimentary forms of categorization, causal reasoning, object permanence, and number sense may be present in the early months of life. One proposal is that infants are born with reasoning abilities—*innate learning mechanisms* that help them make sense of the information they encounter—or that they acquire these abilities very early (Baillargeon, Gertner & Wu, 2011). Some investigators go further, suggesting that infants at birth may already have intuitive *core knowledge* of basic physical principles in the form of specialized brain modules that help infants organize their perceptions and experience (Spelke, 2017).

However, these interpretations are controversial. Theorists argue whether an infant's visual interest in an impossible condition reveals a *perceptual* awareness that something unusual has happened or a *conceptual* understanding of the way things work. For instance, if an infant looks longer at one scene than another, it may be because the two scenes look different from each other rather than because of any conceptual processes. Alternatively, it's possible that an infant, in becoming accustomed to a habituation event, has developed an expectation about what should happen that is then violated by the surprising event (Goubet & Clifton, 1998; Haith, 1998; Haith & Benson, 1998; Munakata, McClelland, Johnson & Siegler, 1997). Defenders of violation-of-expectations research insist that a conceptual interpretation best accounts for the findings (Baillargeon, 1999; Spelke, 1998).

Cognitive Neuroscience Approach: The Brain's Cognitive Structures

Current brain research bears out Piaget's assumption that neurological maturation is a major factor in cognitive development. Brain growth spurts (periods of rapid growth and development) do indeed coincide with changes in cognitive behavior (Fischer, 2008).

Some researchers have used brain scans to determine which brain structures are tied to cognitive functions and to chart developmental changes. These brain scans provide physical evidence of the location of two separate long-term memory systems—*implicit* and *explicit*—that acquire and store different kinds of information and mature at different rates (Bauer, DeBoer & Lukowski, 2007). **Implicit memory** refers to remembering that occurs without effort or even conscious awareness, for example, knowing how to tie your shoe or throw a ball. It most commonly pertains to habits and skills. Implicit memory seems to develop early and is demonstrated by such actions as an infant's kicking on seeing a familiar mobile (Nelson, 2005). **Explicit memory,** also called *declarative memory,* is conscious or intentional recollection, usually of facts, names, events, or other things that can be stated or declared. Delayed imitation of complex behaviors is evidence that declarative memory has developed. This is because delayed imitation requires a representation of a behavior to be stored in memory. While infants cannot yet speak, and thus the memory cannot technically be "declared," this is nonetheless a demonstration of symbolic representation (Bauer, DeBoer & Lukowski, 2007).

In early infancy, when the structures responsible for memory storage are not fully formed, memories are relatively fleeting. The maturing of the *hippocampus,* a structure deep in the temporal lobes, along with the development of cortical structures coordinated by the hippocampal formation make longer-lasting memories possible (Lavenex & Lavenex, 2013; Bauer et al., 2003).

The *prefrontal cortex* (the large portion of the frontal lobe directly behind the forehead) is believed to control many aspects of cognition. This part of the brain develops more slowly than any other (Diamond, 2002), making it more sensitive to environmental disruption (Kolb, Mychasiuk, Muhammad, Li, Frost & Gibb, 2012). During the second half of the 1st year, the prefrontal cortex and associated circuitry develop the

implicit memory
Unconscious recall, generally of habits and skills; sometimes called *procedural memory.*

explicit memory
Intentional and conscious memory, generally of facts, names, and events.

working memory
Short-term storage of information being actively processed.

capacity for **working memory** (Pelphrey et al., 2004). Working memory is short-term storage of information the brain is actively processing, or working on. For example, when you try to estimate how much an item on sale will cost, you are using working memory to make the calculations. Working memory can be overwhelmed, as when someone speaks to you while you try to calculate the sale price.

Working memory appears relatively late in development and may be responsible for the slow development of object permanence, which seems to be seated in a rearward area of the prefrontal cortex (Bell, 2012; Nelson, 1995). By 12 months, this region may be developed enough to permit an infant to avoid the A-not-B error by controlling the impulse to search in a place where the object previously was found (Bell & Fox, 1992; Diamond, 1991).

Although memory systems continue to develop beyond infancy, the early emergence of the brain's memory structures underlines the importance of environmental stimulation from the first months of life. Social-contextual theorists and researchers pay particular attention to the impact of environmental influences.

Social-Contextual Approach: Learning from Interactions with Caregivers

guided participation
Adult's participation in a child's activity that helps to structure it and bring the child's understanding of it closer to the adult's.

Researchers influenced by Vygotsky's sociocultural theory study how cultural context affects early social interactions that may promote cognitive competence. **Guided participation** refers to mutual interactions with adults that help structure children's activities and bridge the gap between a child's understanding and an adult's. This concept was inspired by Vygotsky's view of learning as a collaborative process. Guided participation often occurs in shared play and in ordinary, everyday activities in which children informally learn the skills, knowledge, and values important in their culture.

In a series of cross-cultural studies (Göncü, Mistry, & Mosier, 2000; Rogoff, Mistry, Göncü & Mosier, 1993), researchers visited the homes of 1- to 2-year-old children in four culturally different places: a Mayan town in Guatemala, a tribal village in India, and middle-class urban neighborhoods in Salt Lake City and Turkey. The investigators interviewed caregivers about their child-rearing practices and watched them help the toddlers learn to dress themselves and to play with unfamiliar toys.

Cultural differences affected the types of guided participation the researchers observed. In the Guatemalan town and the Indian village, the children customarily played while the mother worked nearby. When children needed to be shown how to do something, such as tie their shoes, the mothers tended to provide an initial demonstration and instruction, and then allow the children to take over while they remained available to help if needed. The instruction was primarily nonverbal. The U.S. toddlers, who had full-time caregivers, interacted with adults in the context of child's play rather than work or social worlds. Caregivers managed and motivated children's learning with praise and excitement. Their instruction was highly verbal in nature, often consisting of "lessons." Turkish families, who were in transition from a rural to an urban way of life, showed a pattern somewhere in between.

The cultural context influences the way caregivers contribute to cognitive development. Direct adult involvement in children's play and learning may be better adapted to a middle-class urban community, in which parents or caregivers have more time, greater verbal skills, and possibly more interest in children's play and learning, than to a rural community in a developing country, in which children frequently observe and participate in adults' work activities (Rogoff et al., 1993).

Language Development

language
Communication system based on words and grammar.

Language is a communication system based on words and grammar. Once children know words, they can use them to represent objects and actions. They can reflect on people, places, and things; and they can communicate their needs, feelings, and ideas.

In this section, we look first at a typical sequence of milestones in language development (Table 5.3) and at some characteristics of early speech. Then we consider how babies acquire language, how brain growth is linked to language development, and how parents and other caregivers contribute to it.

SEQUENCE OF EARLY LANGUAGE DEVELOPMENT

Before babies can use words, they make their needs and feelings known through sounds that progress from crying to cooing and babbling, then to accidental imitation, and then deliberate imitation. These sounds are known as **prelinguistic speech.** Infants also grow in the ability to recognize and understand speech sounds and to use meaningful gestures. Babies typically say their first word around the end of the 1st year, and toddlers begin speaking in sentences about 8 months to a year later.

prelinguistic speech
Forerunner of linguistic speech; utterance of sounds that are not words. Includes crying, cooing, babbling, and accidental and deliberate imitation of sounds without understanding their meaning.

TABLE 5.3 Language Milestones from Birth to 3 Years	
Age in Months	**Development**
Birth	Can perceive speech, cry, make some response to sound.
1½ to 3	Coos and laughs.
3	Plays with speech sounds.
5 to 6	Recognizes frequently heard sound patterns.
6 to 7	Recognizes all phonemes of native language.
6 to 10	Babbles in strings of consonants and vowels.
9	Uses gestures to communicate and plays gesture games.
9 to 10	Intentionally imitates sounds.
9 to 12	Uses a few social gestures.
10 to 12	No longer can discriminate sounds not in own language.
10 to 14	Says first word (usually a label for something).
10 to 18	Says single words.
12 to 13	Understands symbolic function of naming; passive vocabulary grows.
13	Uses more elaborate gestures.
14	Uses symbolic gesturing.
16 to 24	Learns many new words, expanding expressive vocabulary rapidly from about 50 words to as many as 400; uses verbs and adjectives.
18 to 24	Says first sentence (two words).
20	Uses fewer gestures; names more things.
20 to 22	Has comprehension spurt.
24	Uses many two-word phrases; no longer babbles; wants to talk.
30	Learns new words almost every day; speaks in combinations of three or more words; makes grammatical mistakes.
36	Says up to 1,000 words, 80 percent intelligible; makes some mistakes in syntax.

Sources: Bates, O'Connell, & Shore, 1987; Capute, Shapiro, & Palmer, 1987; Kuhl, 2004; Lalonde & Werker, 1995; Lenneberg, 1969. Newman, 2005.

Early Vocalization *Crying* is a newborn's first means of communication. Different pitches, patterns, and intensities signal hunger, sleepiness, or anger (Lester & Boukydis, 1985). Adults find crying aversive for a reason—it motivates them to find the source of the problem and fix it (Leerkes, Weaver & O'Brien, 2012). Thus crying has great adaptive value.

Between 6 weeks and 3 months, babies start *cooing* when they are happy—squealing, gurgling, and making vowel sounds like "ahhh." *Babbling*—repeating consonant-vowel strings, such as "da-da-da-da"—occurs between ages 6 and 10 months and is often mistaken for a baby's first word. Babbling, although initially nonsensical, becomes more wordlike over time.

Imitation is key to early language development. First, infants accidentally imitate language sounds. Generally, they are reinforced by their parents' positive responses, and thus encouraged to produce such sounds more and more over time. Then, at about 9 to 10 months, infants deliberately imitate sounds without understanding them. Once they have a repertoire of sounds, they string them together in prelinguistic speech patterns that sound like language but appear to have no meaning. Finally, after infants become familiar with the sounds of words and phrases, they begin to attach meanings to them (Fernald, Perfors & Marchman, 2006; Jusczyk & Hohne, 1997).

Perceiving Language Sounds and Structure Imitation of language sounds requires the ability to perceive subtle differences between sounds. Infants' brains seem to be preset to discriminate basic linguistic units, perceive linguistic patterns, and categorize them as similar or different (Kuhl, 2010).

This process of sound discrimination apparently begins in the womb. In one experiment, 35-week-old fetuses showed slowed heart rate to a tape recording of a rhyme the mother had spoken frequently, but not for a different rhyme spoken by another woman. There are also indications that hearing the "mother tongue" before birth may pretune an infant's ears to pick up its sounds (DeCasper, Lecanuet, Busnel, Granier-Deferre & Maugeais, 1994). In fact, newborn babies even cry with an "accent" as a result of early experiences with sound. In French, words tend to have a pattern of rising intonation, whereas in German the converse is true. Newborn French and German babies show this same pattern in their cries, presumably as a consequence of hearing language in the womb (Mampe, Friederici, Christophe & Wemke, 2009). This process continues in the 1st year of life as infants become rapidly sensitized to their native language.

Phonemes are the smallest units of sound in speech. For example, the word *dog* has three phonemes: the *d,* the *o,* and the *g* sound. Every language has its own unique phonology, or system of sounds, that are used in the production of speech. At first, infants can discriminate the sounds of any language. In time, however, exposure to a native language commits the brain's neural networks to further learning of the patterns of the infant's native language and constrains future learning of nonnative language patterns (Kuhl & Rivera-Gaxiola, 2008). This exposure can either occur prenatally or postnatally. If a mother speaks two languages regularly during pregnancy, her newborn baby will recognize both languages and be more interested in listening to speakers in the languages he or she was previously exposed to. Even more important, the baby will show differential responses to both languages, suggesting that even newborns have some understanding that two language systems are involved, and that they are sensitive not just to the overall sounds but to the patterns and rhythms that distinguish the two languages (Byers-Heinlein, Burns & Werker, 2010). By 6 to 7 months, hearing babies have learned to recognize the phonemes used in their native language (Kuhl, Williams, Lacerda, Stevens & Lindblom, 1992), and by 8 months they begin to lose sensitivity to phonemes that are not used in their native language (Gervain & Mehler, 2010). By the end of the 1st year, babies lose their sensitivity to sounds that are not part of the language or languages they usually hear spoken. This process begins earlier for vowels, and later for consonants (Kulh & Rivera-Gaxiola, 2008). The ability to discriminate native-language sounds at this age predicts individual differences in language abilities during the 2nd year (Tsao, Liu & Kuhl, 2004), whereas nonnative sound discrimination does not (Kuhl et al., 2005). The increased sensitivity to native sounds helps the child more efficiently acquire language. Interestingly, analogous processes occur in deaf children with gestures (Kulh & Rivera-Gaxiola, 2008).

How does this change occur? One hypothesis is that infants mentally compute the relative frequency of particular phonetic sequences in their language and learn to ignore sequences they infrequently hear (Werker, Yeung & Yoshida, 2012; Kuhl, 2004). Another hypothesis is that early language experience modifies neural structures, facilitating detection of word patterns in the native language while suppressing attention to nonnative patterns that would slow native language learning. In support of this, toddlers who at 7½ months had shown better neural discrimination of native phonemes were more advanced in word production and sentence complexity at 24 months and at 30 months than toddlers who, at 7½ months, had been better able to discriminate phonetic contrasts in nonnative languages (Kuhl & Rivera-Gaxiola, 2008).

In addition to learning what the phonemes in their language are, babies also learn the rules for how they fit together. For example, in English, the sound combination in "kib" is acceptable, although "kib" is not a word. However, the nonsense word "bnik" breaks the phonological rules in English as a "b" and an "n" are not typically found next to each other within the same word. Between 6 and 12 months, babies begin to become aware of the phonological rules of their language. Research with infants supports this, and suggests that they may have a mechanism for discerning abstract rules of sentence structure (Saffran, Pollak, Seibel & Shkolnik, 2007).

This toddler is communicating with his father by pointing at something that catches his eye. Gesturing seems to come naturally to young children and may be an important part of language learning. ©Photodisc/Getty Images

Gestures Before babies can speak, they point (Liszkowski, Carpenter & Tomasello, 2008). Pointing is important to language acquisition, and indeed pointing and later language development are correlated (Colonnesi, Stams, Koster & Noom, 2010) and serve several functions.

By 12 months, most babies have learned some *conventional social gestures;* for example, waving bye-bye, nodding the head for "yes," and shaking the head for "no." By about 13 months, they use more elaborate *representational gestures;* for example, holding an empty cup to the mouth to indicate thirst.

Symbolic gestures, such as blowing to mean "hot" or sniffing to mean "flower," often emerge around the same time that babies say their first words. Girls show a developmental advantage and use gestures at a slightly earlier age than do boys (Ozcaliskan & Goldin-Meadow, 2010). Both hearing and deaf babies use such gestures in much the same ways (Goldin-Meadow, 2007). By using gestures, babies show an understanding that symbols refer to specific objects, events, desires, and conditions. Gestures usually appear before children have a vocabulary of 25 words and drop out when children learn the word for the idea they were gesturing and can say it instead (Lock, Young, Service & Chandler, 1990).

Toddlers often combine gestures with words. Gesture-word combinations serve as a signal that a child is about to begin using multiword sentences (Goldin-Meadow, 2007).

First Words The average baby says a first word sometime between 10 and 14 months, initiating **linguistic speech**—verbal expression that conveys meaning. At first, an infant's total verbal repertoire is likely to be "mama" or "dada." Or it may be a simple syllable that has more than one meaning depending on the context in which the child utters it. "Da" may mean "I want that," "I want to go out," or "Where's Daddy?" A word like this, in which an entire sentence is expressed with one word, is called a **holophrase**.

Long before infants can connect sounds to meanings, they learn to recognize sound patterns they hear frequently, such as their name. Infants 5 months old listen longer to their name than to other names (Newman, 2005). Infants at 8 months or younger start discerning perceptual cues such as syllables that usually occur together (such as *ba* and *by*) and store these possible word forms in memory. They also notice pronunciation,

linguistic speech
Verbal expression designed to convey meaning.

holophrase
Single word that conveys a complete thought.

stress placed on syllables, and changes in pitch. This early auditory learning lays the foundation for vocabulary growth (Swingley, 2008).

Babies understand many words before they can use them. Six-month-olds look longer at a video of their mothers when they hear the word "mommy" and of their fathers when they hear "daddy" (Tincoff & Jusczyk, 1999). By 13 months, most children understand that a word stands for a specific thing or event, and they can quickly learn the meaning of a new word (Woodward, Markman & Fitzsimmons, 1994).

Between 10 months and 2 years, there is a shift from simple associations to following social cues. At 10 months, infants tend to assume a new word they hear refers to whatever object they find most interesting, whether or not the name is correct for that object. At 12 months, they begin to pay attention to cues from adults, such as looking or pointing at an object while saying its name. However, they still learn words only for interesting objects and ignore uninteresting ones. By 18 to 24 months, children follow social cues in learning words, regardless of the intrinsic interest of the objects (Golinkoff & Hirsh-Pasek, 2006; Pruden, Hirsh-Pasek, Golinkoff & Hennon, 2006). At 24 months, children quickly recognize names of familiar objects in the absence of visual cues (Swingley & Fernald, 2002).

Receptive vocabulary—what infants understand—continues to grow as verbal comprehension gradually becomes faster and more accurate and efficient (Fernald et al., 2006). Generally, infants have a far greater receptive vocabulary than an expressive—or spoken—vocabulary. By 18 months, 3 out of 4 children can understand 150 words and can say 50 of them (Kuhl, 2004). Children with larger vocabularies and quicker reaction times can recognize spoken words from just the first part of the word. For example, when they hear "daw" or "ki," they will point to a picture of a dog or kitten (Fernald, Swingley & Pinto, 2001). This early language learning is closely related to later cognitive development. In a longitudinal study, children's speed of recognition of spoken words and vocabulary size at 25 months predicted linguistic and cognitive skills at 8 years (Marchman & Fernald, 2008).

Addition of new words to the *expressive* (spoken) *vocabulary* is slow at first. Then, sometime between 16 and 24 months, a "naming explosion" may occur (Ganger & Brent, 2004). Within a few months, many toddlers go from saying about 50 words to saying several hundred (Courage & Howe, 2002). Rapid gains in spoken vocabulary reflect increases in speed and accuracy of word recognition during the 2nd year (Fernald et al., 2006) as well as an understanding that things belong in categories (Courage & Howe, 2002).

Nouns seem to be the easiest type of word to learn. In a cross-cultural study, Spanish, Dutch, French, Hebrew, Italian, Korean, and U.S. parents all reported that their 20-month-old children knew more nouns than any other class of words (Bornstein et al., 2004). At 24 to 36 months, children can figure out the meaning of unfamiliar adjectives from context or from the nouns they modify (Mintz, 2005).

First Sentences The next important linguistic breakthrough comes when a toddler puts two words together to express one idea ("Dolly fall"). Generally, children do this between 18 and 24 months. However, this age range varies greatly.

A child's first sentences typically deal with everyday events, things, people, or activities (Braine, 1976; Rice, 1989). Children typically use **telegraphic speech,** consisting of only a few essential words. When Rita says, "Damma deep," she means, "Grandma is sweeping the floor." Children's use of telegraphic speech, and the form it takes, varies, depending on the language being learned (Braine, 1976; Slobin, 1983).

Sometime between 20 and 30 months, children show increasing competence in **syntax,** the fundamental rules for putting sentences together in their language. Syntax is why a sentence like "man bites dog" differs from "dog bites man," and it allows us to understand and produce an infinite number of utterances. At this age, children become more comfortable with articles (*a, the*), prepositions (*in, on*), conjunctions (*and, but*), plurals, verb forms, and forms of the verb *to be* (*am, are, is*). They also become increasingly aware of the communicative purpose of speech and of whether their words are being understood (Dunham, Dunham & O'Keefe, 2000; Shwe & Markman, 1997)—a sign of growing sensitivity to the mental lives of others. By age 3, speech is fluent, longer, and more complex.

telegraphic speech
Early form of sentence use consisting of only a few essential words.

syntax
Rules for forming sentences in a particular language.

CHARACTERISTICS OF EARLY SPEECH

Early speech has a character all its own, no matter what language a child is speaking (Slobin, 1990). As we have seen, young children *simplify*. They use telegraphic speech to say just enough to get their meaning across ("No drink milk!").

Young children *understand grammatical relationships they cannot yet express.* For example, Nina understands that a dog is chasing a cat but does not yet produce multiple-word sentences easily, so her sentence comes out as "Puppy chase" rather than "The puppy is chasing the kitty." The order of the words shows she understand the underlying syntactic rules: She does not say "Kitty chase."

Children also make mistakes with respect to what category a word describes by either underextending or overextending word meaning. When they *underextend word meanings,* they use words in too narrow of a category. For example, Lisa knows their family pet is a "doggy." However, she shakes her head no when her mother points out other dogs outside their home. To her, her dog, and *only* her dog, is a "doggy." Lisa is underextending the word *doggy* by restricting it to only her pet.

Alternatively, children also *overextend word meanings* by using words in too broad of a category. At 14 months, Amir jumped in excitement at the sight of a gray-haired man on the television screen and shouted, "Gampa!" Amir was overgeneralizing, or overextending, a word. He thought that because his grandfather had gray hair, all gray-haired men could be called "Grandpa."

Young children also *overregularize rules.* Overregularization is a language error, but it nonetheless illustrates children's growing knowledge of syntax. It occurs when children inappropriately apply a syntactical rule. For instance, when children say sentences such as "Daddy goed to the store" or "I drawed that," they are applying the English language rule "add *-ed* to a verb to make it past tense." It takes a while for children to learn the rule as well as the exceptions to it. For example, children commonly use the exceptions to the rule first. They generally learn these by rote for phrases they commonly hear ("Daddy went to the store"). Then they learn the rule and use that to fill in the blanks when they can't recall the exception ("Daddy goed to the store"). By early school age, as they become more proficient in language, they memorize the exceptions and begin to apply them, once again saying the phrase correctly ("Daddy went to the store").

LANGUAGE DEVELOPMENT IN DEAF CHILDREN

Deaf babies seem to learn sign language in much the same fashion and in the same sequence as hearing infants learn speech, providing they are raised in a language-rich environment (Lederberg, Schick & Spencer, 2013). Just as hearing babies of hearing parents imitate vocal utterances, deaf babies of deaf parents seem to imitate the sign language they see their parents using, first stringing together meaningless motions and then repeating them over and over in what has been called hand-babbling. As parents reinforce these gestures, the babies attach meaning to them (Petitto & Marentette, 1991; Petitto, Holowka, Sergio & Ostry, 2001).

Deaf babies begin hand-babbling between ages 7 and 10 months, about the age when hearing infants begin voice-babbling (Petitto et al., 2001). Deaf babies also begin to use sentences in sign language at about the same time that hearing babies begin to speak in sentences (Meier, 1991). These observations suggest that an inborn language capacity may underlie the acquisition of both spoken and signed language and that advances in both kinds of language are tied to brain maturation, a point germane to the following discussion.

CLASSIC THEORIES OF LANGUAGE ACQUISITION: THE NATURE-NURTURE DEBATE

Is linguistic ability learned or inborn? In the 1950s, a debate raged between two schools of thought: one led by B. F. Skinner, the foremost proponent of learning theory, the other by the linguist Noam Chomsky.

Skinner (1957) maintained that language learning, like other learning, is based on experience and learned associations. According to classic learning theory, children learn language through the processes of operant conditioning. At first, babies utter sounds at random. Caregivers reinforce the sounds that happen to resemble adult speech. Infants then repeat these reinforced sounds, and language is gradually shaped. Social learning theorists extended this early model to account for imitation. According to social learning theory, babies imitate the sounds they hear adults make and, again, are reinforced for doing so.

For example, Lila, while babbling, inadvertently says "da." Her parents hear her and provide her with smiles and praise. Lila is thus reinforced and continues to say "da." Eventually, her parents no longer provide as much reinforcement. But then Lila happens to say "dada," perhaps by imitating her parents. Now her parents once again reward her lavishly. Again, their praise eventually tapers off, and now the word is only reinforced when her father is present. Over time, her parents' selective reinforcement of closer and closer approximations to speech in the right context results in the shaping of language.

Observation, imitation, and reinforcement do contribute to language development, but, as Chomsky (1957) persuasively argued, they cannot fully explain it. For one thing, word combinations and nuances are so numerous and so complex that they cannot all be acquired by specific imitation and reinforcement. In addition, caregivers often reinforce utterances that are not strictly grammatical, as long as they make sense ("Gampa go bye-bye"). Adult speech itself is an unreliable model to imitate, as it is often ungrammatical and contains false starts, unfinished sentences, and slips of the tongue. Also, learning theory does not account for children's imaginative ways of saying things they have never heard, such as when 2-year-old Clara insisted "I *am* hayve" after being told she needed to behave.

Chomsky's view is called **nativism.** Unlike Skinner's learning theory, nativism emphasizes the active role of the learner. Chomsky (1957, 1972, 1995) proposed that the human brain has an innate capacity for acquiring language. He suggested that an inborn **language acquisition device (LAD)** programs children's brains to analyze the language they hear and to figure out its rules.

Support for the nativist position comes from newborns' ability to differentiate phonemes easily, suggesting that they are born with perceptual "tuning rods" that pick up characteristics of speech. Nativists point out that almost all children master their native language in the same age-related sequence without formal teaching. Furthermore, our brains have structures that have been shown to be directly implicated in language use (Friederici, 2011), which is what would be predicted on the basis of the nativist position. Still, the nativist approach does not tell us why some children acquire language more rapidly and efficiently than others, why children differ in linguistic skill and fluency, or why (as we'll see) speech development appears to depend on having someone to talk with, not merely on hearing spoken language.

Most developmental scientists today maintain that language acquisition, like most other aspects of development, depends on an intertwining of nature and nurture. Children have an inborn capacity to acquire language, which may be activated or constrained by experience.

INFLUENCES ON EARLY LANGUAGE DEVELOPMENT

What determines how quickly and how well children learn to understand and use language? Research has focused on both neurological and environmental influences.

Brain Development The tremendous brain growth during the early months and years is closely linked with language development. A newborn's cries are controlled by the *brain stem* and *pons,* the most primitive parts of the brain and the earliest to

nativism
Theory that human beings have an inborn capacity for language acquisition.

language acquisition device (LAD)
In Chomsky's terminology, an inborn mechanism that enables children to infer linguistic rules from the language they hear.

Is linguistic ability learned or inborn? Though inborn language capacity may underlie this baby's ability to speak, when this mother repeats the sounds her baby makes, she is reinforcing the likelihood the baby will repeat those sounds—highlighting the influences of both nature and nurture. ©Jani Bryson/Getty Images

develop. Repetitive babbling may emerge with the maturation of parts of the *motor cortex,* which control movements of the face and larynx. A link exists between the brain's phonetic perception and motor systems as early as 6 months—a connection that strengthens by 6 to 12 months (Imada et al., 2006). The development of language actively affects brain networks, committing them to the recognition of native language sounds only (Kuhl, Conboy, Padden, Nelson & Pruitt, 2005). In other words, language exposure helps shape the developing brain, and then the developing brain helps the infant learn language.

Brain scans confirm the sequence of vocabulary development outlined earlier in this chapter. In toddlers with large vocabularies, brain activation focuses on the left temporal and parietal lobes, whereas in toddlers with smaller vocabularies, brain activation is more scattered (Kuhl & Rivera-Gaxiola, 2008). Cortical regions associated with language continue to develop until at least the late preschool years or beyond—some even until adulthood. In about 98 percent of people, the left hemisphere is dominant for language, though the right hemisphere participates as well (Knecht et al., 2000).

Social Interaction: The Role of Parents and Caregivers Language is a social act. It requires interaction. Language takes not only the necessary biological machinery and cognitive capacity but also interaction with a live communicative partner. Children who grow up without normal social contact do not develop language normally. Neither do children who are exposed to language only through television. For example, in one experiment, 9-month-old English-speaking infants learned and retained Mandarin when they played and interacted with adults speaking Mandarin, but not when they merely watched television in Mandarin (Kuhl & Rivera-Gaxiola, 2008). As Bronfenbrenner's bioecological model would predict, the age of caregivers, the way they interact with an infant, child care experience, and, later, schooling, peers, and television exposure all affect the course of language acquisition. The milestones of language development described in this chapter are typical of Western, middle-class children who are spoken to directly. They are not necessarily typical in all cultures, nor at all socioeconomic levels (Hoff, 2006).

Prelinguistic Period At the babbling stage, adults help an infant advance toward true speech by repeating the sounds the baby makes and rewarding her efforts. The baby finds this imitation engaging and soon joins in the game, repeating the sounds back. Parents' imitation of babies' sounds affects the amount of infant vocalization (Goldstein, King & West, 2003) and the pace of language learning (Schmitt, Simpson & Friend, 2011). It also helps babies experience the social aspect of speech (Kuhl, 2004).

Vocabulary Development When babies begin to talk, parents or caregivers can boost vocabulary development by repeating their first words and pronouncing them correctly. Joint attention leads to more rapid vocabulary development (Hoff, 2006). In one longitudinal study, mothers' responsiveness to 9-month-olds' and, even more so, to 13-month-olds' vocalization and play predicted the timing of language milestones (Tamis-LeMonda, Bornstein & Baumwell, 2001). This is not surprising; a shared understanding and focus on an event or object coupled with maternal labeling is an extremely supportive framework for language acquisition.

A strong relationship exists between the frequency of specific words in mothers' speech and the order in which children learn these words (Brent & Siskind, 2001) as well as between mothers' talkativeness and the size of toddlers' vocabularies (Schmitt, Simpson & Friend, 2011). Mothers with higher socioeconomic status tend to use richer vocabularies and longer utterances, and their 2-year-olds have larger spoken vocabularies (Hoff, 2003; C. T. Ramey & Ramey, 2003). By age 3, vocabularies of low-income children vary greatly, depending in large part on the diversity of word types they have heard their mothers use (Pan, Rowe, Singer & Snow, 2005). Parental sensitivity and responsiveness can act as a buffer, however. Specifically, low-income parents' sensitivity, positive regard for the child, and cognitive stimulation provided during play predicted their child's receptive vocabulary and cognitive development at ages 2 and 3 (Tamis-LeMonda, Shannon, Cabrera & Lamb, 2004).

window on the world

CHILDREN'S BOOKS: WHAT DO THEY TEACH US?

Children develop much of their capacity for learning in the first three years of life. Reading to children improves their language skills and cognitive abilities, encourages creativity, and promotes social, emotional and moral development (Crippen, 2017). As parents, talk, sing, and read aloud to children, their children's brains are stimulated and strengthened. Research shows that we need to hear about 1,000 stories out loud before we can begin to read for ourselves. (Raising Readers: The Tremendous Potential of Families, 1999). Reading at a young age helps to create a nurturing bond with caregivers and begins a lifelong love of reading (O'Keefe, 2014).

Children's books change our lives and shape us into who we become, nurturing the development of personality and social skills. Children's stories teach us about morals, values, justice, social skills, and friendships. They teach us how to laugh, love, and use our imagination. They give us information, let us raise questions, and teach us to use reason and analyze our world. Stories communicate self-acceptance and model coping strategies for children who are learning to deal with their emotions (Bradbery, 2012). Stories can help us consider the feelings and viewpoints of others, allowing us to accept other people and their differences (Norton, 2010).

Children around the world are taught by stories. Before the written word, stories were shared orally by storytellers. Books and stories are the main way we transmit our heritage from one generation to the next (Norton, 2010). Reading is encouraged in most countries around the world, but access to books and ability to read and write can be deterrents. Nearly 250 million children worldwide are unable to read and write (All Children Reading: A Grand Challenge for Development, 2017). In 2015, Finland was listed with the highest literacy rates, nearly 100 percent and South Sudan at the bottom with 27 percent (CIA, 2015). Regardless of the way they are transmitted, stories are important in children's educational and social worlds.

Here are a few popular 2017 titles from around the world:

- *Our Nana Was a Nutcase,* by Ranjit Lal (India). A story that talks about love, heartbreak, truths about aging and family bonding (Varma, 2017).
- *The Storyteller,* by Evan Turk (Morocco). A story of a boy who came to the square for a drink and found something that quenched his thirst even more—a storyteller (25th Annual Children's Africana Book Awards, 2017).
- *Chinese Year,* by Cao Cong (China). A story of Chinese family life and traditions (Koetse, 2017).

what's your view

What was your favorite children's book? What lessons did you learn from reading this book? Here are a few favorite quotes from some well-known children's stories (Staff, 2016). What lesson do you think each is trying to teach?

- "No act of kindness, no matter how small, is ever wasted." —"The Lion and the Mouse," *Aesop's Fables* (Greece)
- "It is only with the heart that one can see rightly. What is essential is invisible to the eye." —Antoine de Saint Exupéry, *The Little Prince* (France)
- "We can't take any credit for our talents. It's how we use them that counts." —Madeleine L'Engle, *A Wrinkle in Time* (America)
- "You're Braver than you believe, Stronger than you seem, and Smarter than you think." —A. A. Milne, *Winnie-the-Pooh* (United Kingdom)

code mixing
Use of elements of two languages, sometimes in the same utterance, by young children in households where both languages are spoken.

In households where more than one language is spoken, babies achieve similar milestones in each language on the same schedule as children who hear only one language (Petitto & Kovelman, 2003). However, children learning two languages tend to have smaller vocabularies in each language than children learning only one language (Hoff, 2006). Bilingual children often use elements of both languages, sometimes in the same utterance—a phenomenon called **code mixing** (Petitto & Kovelman, 2003).

In Montreal, children as young as 2 in dual-language households differentiate between the two languages, using French with a French-speaking parent and English with a English-speaking parent (Genesee, Nicoladis & Paradis, 1995). This ability to shift from one language to another is called **code switching.**

Child-Directed Speech If, when you talk to an infant or toddler, you speak slowly in a sing-song, high-pitched voice with exaggerated ups and downs, simplify your speech, exaggerate vowel sounds, and use short words and sentences and repetition, you are engaging in **child-directed speech (CDS),** sometimes called *parentese, motherese,* or *baby talk.* Most adults and even children do it naturally, and other babyish stimuli, such as puppies or kittens, also can elicit it. Such baby talk has been documented in many languages and cultures, suggesting it is universal in nature and serves a function.

Many researchers believe that CDS helps infants learn their native language or at least pick it up faster by exaggerating and directing attention to the distinguishing features of speech sounds (Kuhl et al., 2005). Moreover, infants are "captured" attentionally by the sound and find it highly engaging, resulting in more rapid learning (Golinkoff, Can, Soderstrom & Hirsh-Pasek, 2015). Infants, even before a month of age, clearly prefer to hear CDS (Cooper & Aslin, 1990; Kuhl et al., 1997).

PREPARING FOR LITERACY: THE BENEFITS OF READING ALOUD

Most babies love to be read to. The frequency with which caregivers read to them can influence how well children speak and eventually how well and how soon they develop **literacy**—the ability to read and write. Children's emerging language abilities have repercussions for school readiness and later academic achievement, and those who develop language earlier are better prepared to enter school. Moreover, early language ability is affected strongly by home environment, suggesting that intervention programs targeting home variables (like reading to children) might be highly effective (Forget-Dubois et al., 2009). For example, in one study, children from low-income families who had been read to daily had better cognitive and language skills at age 3 than those who had not been read to (Raikes et al., 2006).

code switching
Changing one's speech to match the situation, as in people who are bilingual.

child-directed speech (CDS)
Form of speech often used in talking to babies or toddlers; includes slow, simplified speech, a high-pitched tone, exaggerated vowel sounds, short words and sentences, and much repetition; also called *parentese* or *motherese.*

literacy
(1) Ability to read and write. (2) In an adult, ability to use printed and written information to function in society, achieve goals, and develop knowledge and potential.

By reading aloud to their young children and asking questions about the pictures in the book, parents help their children build language skills and learn how letters look and sound. ©Keith Brofsky/ Blend Images

summary and key terms

Studying Cognitive Development: Six Approaches

- Six approaches to the study of cognitive development are behaviorist, psychometric, Piagetian, information-processing, cognitive neuroscience, and social-contextual.
- All of these approaches can shed light on how early cognition develops.

behaviorist approach, psychometric approach, Piagetian approach, information-processing approach, cognitive neuroscience approach, social-contextual approach

Behaviorist Approach: Basic Mechanics of Learning

- Two simple types of learning that behaviorists study are classical conditioning and operant conditioning.
- Rovee-Collier's research suggests that infants' memory processes are much like those of adults, though this conclusion has been questioned.

classical conditioning, operant conditioning

Psychometric Approach: Developmental and Intelligence Testing

- Psychometric tests measure factors presumed to make up intelligence.
- Developmental tests, such as the Bayley Scales of Infant and Toddler Development, can indicate current functioning but are generally poor predictors of later intelligence.
- The home environment may affect measured intelligence.
- If the home environment does not promote cognitive competence, early intervention may be needed.

  intelligent behavior, IQ (intelligence quotient) tests, Bayley Scales of Infant and Toddler Development, Home Observation for Measurement of the Environment (HOME), early intervention

Piagetian Approach: The Sensorimotor Stage

- During Piaget's sensorimotor stage, infants' schemes become more elaborate. They progress from primary to secondary to tertiary circular reactions and finally to the development of representational ability, which makes possible deferred imitation, pretending, and problem solving.
- Object permanence develops gradually, according to Piaget, and is not fully operational until 18 to 24 months.
- Research suggests that a number of abilities, including imitation and object permanence, develop earlier than Piaget described.

  sensorimotor stage, schemes, circular reactions, representational ability, visible imitation, invisible imitation, deferred imitation, elicited imitation, object permanence, dual representation hypothesis

Information-Processing Approach: Perceptions and Representations

- Information-processing researchers measure mental processes through habituation and other signs of visual and perceptual abilities.
- Indicators of the efficiency of infants' information processing, such as speed of habituation, tend to predict later intelligence.
- Information-processing research techniques such as habituation, novelty preference, and the violation-of-expectations method have yielded evidence that infants as young as 3 to 6 months may have a rudimentary grasp of such Piagetian abilities as categorization, causality, object permanence, a sense of number, and an ability to reason about characteristics of the physical world.
- Some researchers suggest that infants may have innate learning mechanisms for acquiring such knowledge. However, the meaning of these findings is in dispute.

  habituation, dishabituation, visual preference, visual recognition memory, cross-modal transfer, violation of expectations

Cognitive Neuroscience Approach: The Brain's Cognitive Structures

- Explicit memory and implicit memory are located in different brain structures.
- Working memory emerges between 6 and 12 months of age.
- Neurological developments help explain the emergence of Piagetian skills and memory abilities.

  implicit memory, explicit memory, working memory

Social-Contextual Approach: Learning from Interactions with Caregivers

- Social interactions with adults contribute to cognitive competence through shared activities that help children learn skills, knowledge, and values important in their culture.

  guided participation

Language Development

- The acquisition of language is an important aspect of cognitive development.
- Prelinguistic speech includes crying, cooing, babbling, and imitating language sounds. By 6 months, babies have learned the basic sounds of their language and have begun to link sound with meaning. Perception of categories of sounds in the native language may commit the neural circuitry to further learning in that language only.
- Before they say their first word, babies use gestures.
- The first word typically comes sometime between 10 and 14 months. For many toddlers, a naming explosion occurs sometime between 16 and 24 months.
- The first brief sentences generally come between 18 and 24 months. By age 3, syntax and communicative abilities are fairly well developed.
- Early speech is characterized by oversimplification, underextending and overextending word meanings, and overregularizing rules.
- Two classic theoretical views about how children acquire language are learning theory and nativism. Today, most developmental scientists hold that an inborn capacity to learn language may be activated or constrained by experience.
- Influences on language development include neural maturation and social interaction.
- Family characteristics, such as socioeconomic status, adult language use, and maternal responsiveness affect a child's vocabulary development.
- Child-directed speech (CDS) seems to have cognitive, emotional, and social benefits, and infants show a preference for it.
- Reading aloud to a child from an early age helps pave the way for literacy.

  language, prelinguistic speech, linguistic speech, holophrase, telegraphic speech, syntax, nativism, language acquisition device (LAD), code mixing, code switching, child-directed speech (CDS), literacy

Psychosocial Development during the First Three Years

chapter 6

©Bob Lewine/Tetra Images/Corbis

learning objectives

Discuss the development of emotions and personality in infancy.

Describe infants' social relationships with caregivers, including attachment.

Discuss the emerging sense of self, autonomy, and moral development in toddlerhood.

Explain how social contexts influence early development.

Explain child maltreatment and its effects.

In this chapter, we examine foundations of psychosocial development and consider Erikson's views about the development of trust and autonomy. We look at relationships with caregivers, the emerging sense of self, and the foundations of conscience. We explore relationships with siblings and other children and consider the impact of parental employment and early child care. Finally, we discuss child maltreatment and what can be done to protect children from harm.

Foundations of Psychosocial Development

Although babies share common patterns of development, each, from the start, shows a distinct set of behavioral tendencies, known as temperament. One baby may usually be cheerful; another easily upset. One toddler plays happily with other children; another prefers to play alone. Eventually, temperament becomes what we think of as **personality:** the relatively consistent blend of emotions, thought, and behavior that makes each person unique. From infancy on, personality development is intertwined with social relationships; this combination is called *psychosocial development*. See Table 6.1 for highlights of psychosocial development during the first 3 years.

In our exploration of psychosocial development, we first look at emotions, which shape responses to the world. Then we focus on temperament, an early building block of personality. Finally, we discuss an infant's earliest social experiences in the family.

EMOTIONS

Emotions, such as fear, anger, or joy, are subjective reactions to experience that are associated with physiological and behavioral changes. For example, the subjective feeling of fear is associated with changes in heart rate, breathing, and startle response. A person's characteristic pattern of emotional reactions begins to develop during infancy and is a basic element of personality. People differ in how often and how strongly they feel a particular emotion, in the kinds of events that may produce it, in the physical manifestations they show, and in how they act as a result. Culture, too, influences the way people feel about a situation and the way they show their emotions. Newborns clearly feel emotions, and they emerge over development in a predictable sequence.

Crying Crying is the earliest and most powerful way infants can communicate their needs. There are four patterns of crying (Wolff, 1969): the basic *hunger cry* (a rhythmic cry, which is not always associated with hunger); the *angry cry* (a variation of the rhythmic cry, in which excess air is forced through the vocal cords); the *pain cry* (a sudden onset of loud crying without preliminary moaning, sometimes followed by holding the breath); and the *frustration cry* (two or three drawn-out cries, with no prolonged breath-holding) (Wood & Gustafson, 2001). As children age, they begin to realize that crying serves a communicative function. By 5 months of age, babies have learned to monitor their caregivers' expressions, and if ignored will first cry harder in an attempt to get attention, and then stop crying if their attempt is unsuccessful (Goldstein, Schwade & Bornstein, 2009).

Some parents worry that picking up a crying baby will spoil the infant. However, this is not the case, especially when levels of distress are high. For example, if parents

Side notes

personality
The relatively consistent blend of emotions, temperament, thought, and behavior that makes a person unique.

emotions
Subjective reactions to experience that are associated with physiological and behavioral changes.

TABLE 6.1 Highlights of Infants' and Toddlers' Psychosocial Development, Birth to 36 Months

Approximate Age, Months	Characteristics
0–3	Infants are open to stimulation. They show interest and curiosity, and they smile readily at people.
3–6	Infants can anticipate what is about to happen and may become angry or act warily when disappointed. They smile, coo, and laugh. Reciprocal exchanges between the baby and the caregiver begin.
6–9	Infants play social games and elicit responses from people. They talk to and touch other babies to get them to respond. They show joy, fear, anger, and surprise.
9–12	Infants become attached to their primary caregiver and may become afraid of strangers and new situations. By 1 year, they communicate emotions more clearly, showing moods, ambivalence, and gradations of feeling.
12–18	Toddlers explore their environment, using attachment figures as a secure base. As they master the environment, they become more confident and eager to assert themselves.
18–36	Toddlers sometimes become anxious at longer separations from their caregivers. They work out their awareness of their limitations in fantasy and in play and by identifying with adults.

Source: Sroufe, L. A. "Socioemotional development." In J. Osofsky (Ed.), *Handbook of infant development* (pp. 462–516). New York: Wiley, 1979.

wait it may become more difficult to soothe the baby; and such a pattern, if experienced repeatedly, may interfere with an infant's developing ability to regulate his or her own emotional state (R. A. Thompson, 2011). Indeed, mothers' rapid and sensitive response to crying is associated with later social competence and positive adjustment, regardless of whether or not babies cry frequently or rarely (Leerkes, Blankson & O'Brien, 2009).

Smiling and Laughing The earliest faint smiles occur spontaneously soon after birth, apparently as a result of subcortical nervous system activity. These involuntary smiles frequently appear during periods of REM sleep. Through 1 month of age, smiles are often elicited by high-pitched tones when an infant is drowsy. During the 2nd month, as visual recognition develops, babies smile more at visual stimuli, such as faces they know (Sroufe, 1997).

Social smiling, when newborn infants gaze at their parents and smile at them, develops during the 2nd month of life. Social smiling signals the infant's active, positive participation in the relationship. Laughter is a smile-linked vocalization that becomes more common between 4 and 12 months (Salkind, 2005).

As babies grow older, they become more actively engaged in mirthful exchanges. A 6-month-old may giggle in response to the mother making unusual sounds or appearing with a towel over her face; a 10-month-old may laughingly try to put the towel back on her face when it falls off. This change reflects cognitive development: By laughing at the unexpected, babies show that they know what to expect; by turning the tables, they show awareness that they can make things happen (Sroufe, 1997).

Anticipatory smiling—in which infants smile at an object and then gaze at an adult while continuing to smile—rises sharply between 8 and 10 months and seems to be among the first types of communication in which the infant refers to an object or experience. By 12 to 15 months, infants are intentionally communicating to the partner about objects.

When Do Emotions Appear? Emotional development is an orderly process; complex emotions unfold from simpler ones. According to one model (Lewis, 1997; Figure 6.1),

Crying is the most powerful way, and sometimes the only way, that babies can communicate their needs. Parents learn to recognize whether their baby is crying because of hunger, anger, frustration, or pain.
©Irina Rogova/Shutterstock

social smiling
Beginning in the 2nd month, newborn infants gaze at their parents and smile at them, signaling positive participation in the relationship.

anticipatory smiling
Infant smiles at an object and then gazes at an adult while still smiling.

FIGURE 6.1

Differentiation of Emotions during the First 3 Years

The primary, or basic, emotions emerge during the first 6 months or so; the self-conscious emotions develop beginning in the 2nd year, as a result of the emergence of self-awareness together with accumulation of knowledge about societal standards.

Source: Lewis, M. (1997). "The self in self-conscious emotions." In S. G. Snodgrass & R. L. Thompson (Eds.), *The self across psychology: Self-recognition, self-awareness, and the self-concept: Vol. 818*. New York: New York Academy of Sciences.

(infant): ©Frare/Davis Photography/Brand X/ Corbis; (Asian toddler): ©Amos Morgan/Getty Images; (Caucasian toddler): ©file404/ Shutterstock

Children who do not live up to behavioral standards may feel guilty and try to make amends by cleaning up after they've spilled. Guilt is thought to develop between ages 2½ and 3.
©enterphoto/Shutterstock

self-conscious emotions
Emotions, such as embarrassment, empathy, and envy, that depend on self-awareness.

self-awareness
Realization that one's existence and functioning are separate from those of other people and things.

self-evaluative emotions
Emotions, such as pride, shame, and guilt, that depend on both self-awareness and knowledge of socially accepted standards of behavior.

altruistic behavior
Activity intended to help another person with no expectation of reward.

babies show signs of contentment, interest, and distress soon after birth. These are diffuse, reflexive, mostly physiological responses to sensory stimulation or internal processes. During the next 6 months or so, these early emotional states differentiate into true emotions: joy, surprise, sadness, disgust, and then anger and fear—reactions to events that have meaning for the infant. As we discuss in a subsequent section, the emergence of these basic, or primary, emotions is related to neurological maturation.

Self-conscious emotions, such as embarrassment, empathy, and envy, arise only after children have developed **self-awareness:** the cognitive understanding that they have an identity that is separate and different from others. This consciousness of self emerges between 15 and 24 months. Self-awareness is necessary before children can be aware of being the focus of attention, identify with what other "selves" are feeling, or wish they had what someone else has.

By about age 3, having acquired self-awareness plus knowledge about their society's accepted standards, rules, and goals, children become better able to evaluate their own thoughts, plans, desires, and behavior against what is considered socially appropriate. Only then can they demonstrate the **self-evaluative emotions** of pride, guilt, and shame (Lewis, 1995, 1997, 1998, 2007).

Brain Growth and Emotional Development The development of the brain after birth is closely connected with changes in emotional life: Emotional experiences are affected by brain development and can have long-lasting effects on the structure of the brain (Davidson, Jackson & Kalin, 2000).

Four major shifts in brain organization roughly correspond to changes in emotional processing (Schore, 1994; Sroufe, 1997). During the first 3 months, differentiation of basic emotions begins as the *cerebral cortex* becomes functional, bringing cognitive perceptions into play. REM sleep and reflexive behavior, including the spontaneous neonatal smile, diminish.

The second shift occurs around 9 or 10 months, when the *frontal lobes* begin to interact with the *limbic system,* a seat of emotional reactions. At the same time, limbic structures such as the *hippocampus* become larger and more adultlike. Connections between the frontal cortex and the *hypothalamus* and limbic system, which process sensory information, may facilitate the relationship between the cognitive and emotional spheres.

The third shift takes place during the 2nd year, when infants develop self-awareness, self-conscious emotions, and a greater capacity for regulating their emotions and activities. These changes, which coincide with greater physical mobility and exploratory behavior, may be related to myelination of the frontal lobes.

The fourth shift occurs around age 3, when hormonal changes in the autonomic (involuntary) nervous system coincide with the emergence of evaluative emotions. Underlying the development of such emotions as shame may be a shift away from dominance by the *sympathetic system,* the part of the autonomic system that prepares the body for action, as the *parasympathetic system,* the part of the autonomic system that is involved in excretion and sexual excitation, matures.

Altruistic Helping, Empathy, and Social Cognition A guest of 18-month-old Alex's father dropped his pen on the floor, and it rolled under a cabinet. Alex crawled under the cabinet, retrieved the pen, and gave it to the guest. By acting out of concern for a stranger with no expectation of reward, Alex showed **altruistic behavior** (Warneken & Tomasello, 2006).

Altruistic behavior seems to come naturally to toddlers. In one study, infants at 12 months of age spontaneously helped an adult reach or find a toy that had fallen out of reach. By 15 months of age, infants also seemed to have expectations about fairness, as illustrated by their tendency to stare longer at an unfair distribution of goods than to an equal distribution. Moreover, those infants who looked the longest at the unequal sharing were also more likely to themselves share toys later (Sommerville, Schmidt, Yun & Burns, 2013). Other research has also documented that well before the 2nd birthday, children are likely to help others, share belongings and food, and offer comfort at the distress of others (Dunfield,

Kuhlmeier, O'Connell & Kelley, 2011; Warneken & Tomasello, 2008). Interestingly, the tendency to share, to help, and to comfort seem to be unrelated to each other, presumably reflecting separate developmental trajectories. In other words, a baby who shares may not necessarily tend to comfort or help (Dunfield & Kuhlmeier, 2013). Nonetheless, Zahn-Waxler and colleagues (1992) have concluded that such behavior may collectively reflect **empathy,** the ability to imagine how another person might feel in a particular situation.

Research in neurobiology has identified special brain cells called *mirror neurons,* which may underlie empathy and altruism. **Mirror neurons** fire when a person does something but also when he or she observes someone else doing the same thing. By "mirroring" the activities and motivations of others, they may help a person to see the world from someone else's point of view (Iacoboni, 2008; Iacoboni & Mazziotta, 2007; Oberman & Ramachandran, 2007). Interestingly, infants also show similar sympathetic nervous system arousal when they help someone directly *and* when they see a third party doing the helping. They do not show the same pattern of arousal if the person is not helped (Hepach, Vaish & Tomasello, 2012).

Some theorist doubt the conclusions that have been reached about mirror neurons. They point out, for example, that people sometimes feel empathy for others even without the action of mirror neurons. Moreover, this theory, while intriguing, lacks direct empirical support (Lamm & Majdandzic, 2015).

Empathy also depends on **social cognition,** the ways in which we process information about other people. Part of social cognition involves the understanding that others have mental states, feelings, and intentions different than our own. Research suggests that social cognition begins in the 1st year of life. In one study, 9-month-olds (but not 6-month-olds) reacted differently to a person who was unwilling to give them a toy than to a person who tried to give them a toy but accidentally dropped it. This finding suggests that the older infants had gained some understanding of another person's intentions (Behne, Carpenter, Call & Tomasello, 2005).

TEMPERAMENT

From the very first day of life, all babies are unique. Some babies are fussy; others are happy and placid. Some are active; others lay calmly. Some babies like meeting new people; some shrink from contact.

Psychologists call these early individual differences **temperament.** Temperament can be defined as an early-appearing, biologically based tendency to respond to the environment in predictable ways. Temperament affects how children approach and react to the outside world, as well as how they regulate their mental, emotional, and behavioral functioning (Rueda & Rothbart, 2009). Temperament is closely linked to emotional responses to the environment, and many responses, such as smiles or cries, are emotional in nature. However, unlike emotions such as fear, excitement, and boredom, which come and go, temperament is relatively consistent and enduring. Individual differences in temperament, which are thought to derive from a person's basic biological makeup, form the core of the developing personality.

Studying Temperamental Patterns: The New York Longitudinal Study In this pioneering study on temperament, researchers followed 133 infants into adulthood. The researchers looked at how active the children were; how regular their hunger, sleep, and bowel habits were; how readily they accepted new people and situations; how they adapted to changes in routine; how sensitive they were to sensory stimuli; whether their mood tended to be joyful or unhappy; and whether they persisted at tasks (A. Thomas, Chess & Birch, 1968). Over time, it became clear to the researchers that for the most part, children could be placed into one of three temperamental categories.

- Forty percent were **"easy" children**: Easy children are generally happy and accepting of frustration. They tolerate novelty well, are adaptable, and usually smile at and are friendly with strangers. They are rhythmic in biological functioning, sleep, eat and eliminate at the same times each day, and are easy to put on a schedule. They are as they sound—easy babies to parent.

empathy
Ability to put oneself in another person's place and feel what the other person feels.

mirror neurons
Neurons that fire when a person does something or observes someone else doing the same thing.

social cognition
The ability to understand that others have mental states and to gauge their feelings and actions.

temperament
Characteristic disposition, or style of approaching and reacting to situations.

"easy" children
Children with a generally happy temperament, regular biological rhythms, and a readiness to accept new experiences.

- Ten percent were what the researchers called **"difficult" children**: Difficult children are irritable and harder to please. They tend to display intense and frequently negative moods, and are intolerant of frustration and changes in their schedule. They adjust slowly to new routines, and are irregular in their biological rhythms, They tend to be active, and are suspicious of strangers and new situations.

- Fifteen percent were **"slow-to-warm-up" children**: These babies are mildly negative about new situations and change but, if given support and time, generally warm up and adapt. They sleep and eat less regularly than easy babies, but more regularly than difficult babies. In most aspects, they are somewhat in the middle of easy and difficult babies (A. Thomas & Chess, 1977, 1984).

Some children (including 35 percent of the NYLS sample) do not fit neatly into any of these three categories. A baby may eat and sleep regularly but be afraid of strangers. Another child may warm up slowly to new foods but adapt quickly to new babysitters (A. Thomas & Chess, 1984). A child may laugh intensely but not show intense frustration, and a child with rhythmic toilet habits may show irregular sleeping patterns (Rothbart et al., 2000). All these variations are normal.

How Stable Is Temperament? From the beginning, babies show different patterns of sleeping, fussing, and activity, and these differences tend to persist to some degree (Bornstein, Putnick, Gartstein, Hahn, Auestad & O'Connor, 2015). Studies using the Infant Behavior Questionnaire (IBQ), a parental report instrument, have found strong links between infant temperament and childhood personality at age 7 (Rothbart, Ahadi, Hershey & Fisher, 2001). Other researchers, using temperament types similar to those of the NYLS, have found that temperament at age 3 closely predicts aspects of personality at ages 18 and 21 (Caspi, 2000; Newman, Caspi, Moffitt & Silva, 1997).

Temperament is generally conceptualized as being inborn, and influenced by genetics (Braungart, Plomin, DeFries & Fulker, 1992; Emde et al., 1992; Schmitz, Saudino, Plomin, Fulker & DeFries, 1996; Thomas & Chess, 1984). That does not mean, however, that temperament is fully formed at birth, or that the environment does not matter. Temperament develops as various emotions and self-regulatory capacities appear (Rothbart et al., 2000) and can change in response to parental treatment and other life experiences (Belsky, Fish & Isabella, 1991; Kagan & Snidman, 2004). Current conceptions of temperament view it as being strongly influenced by genetics early in life, with greater influence wielded by the environment over time (Shiner, Buss, McClowry, Putnam, Saudino & Zentner, 2012).

Temperament and Adjustment: Goodness of Fit According to the NYLS, the key to healthy adjustment is **goodness of fit**—the match between a child's temperament and the environmental demands and constraints the child must deal with. If a very active child is expected to sit still for long periods, if a slow-to-warm-up child is constantly pushed into new situations, or if a persistent child is constantly taken away from absorbing projects, tensions may occur. Infants with difficult temperaments may be more susceptible to the quality of parenting than infants with easy or slow-to-warm-up temperaments and may need more emotional support (Belsky, 2005; Stright, Gallagher & Kelley, 2008). Caregivers who recognize that a child acts in a certain way, not out of willfulness, laziness, or spite but because of inborn temperament, may be less likely to feel guilty, anxious, or hostile. They can anticipate the child's reactions and help the child adapt—for example, by giving early warnings of the need to stop an activity or by gradually introducing a child to new situations.

Shyness and Boldness: Influences of Biology and Culture Temperament has a biological basis. One biologically based individual difference that has

Charlotte's habit of smiling at strangers and playing happily in a shopping cart during trips to the grocery store are signs of her easy temperament.
©Ipatov/Shutterstock

been identified is *behavioral inhibition*. Behavioral inhibition has to do with how boldly or cautiously a child approaches unfamiliar objects and situations, and it is associated with certain biological characteristics (Kagan, Reznick, Clarke, Snidman & Garcia-Coll, 1984).

Behavioral inhibition is most clearly seen when babies are presented with novel stimuli. When babies high in behavioral inhibition are presented with a new stimulus, they became physiologically aroused, pumping their arms and legs vigorously and sometimes arching their backs. This feeling of being overaroused is unpleasant for them, and most start to fuss and cry. Approximately 20 percent of babies respond in this way. Babies low in behavioral inhibition, however, respond quite differently. When presented with a new stimulus, these babies are relaxed. They show little distress or motor activity, and often calmly stare at new stimuli, sometimes smiling at it. About 40 percent of babies respond in this manner. These differences between babies are theorized to be the result of an underlying difference in physiology: Inhibited children may be born with an unusually excitable amygdala. The amygdala detects and reacts to unfamiliar events, and, in the case of behaviorally inhibited children, responds vigorously and easily to most novel events (Kagan & Snidman, 2004).

If behavioral inhibition is indeed due to an underlying physiological arousal pattern, then we should expect some consistency in patterns of behavior over time. This is the case. Infants who are identified as inhibited or uninhibited seemed to maintain these patterns over time (Kagan, 1997; Kagan & Snidman, 2004). Many highly inhibited infants remain so through the first two years of age (Fox, Henderson, Rubin, Calkins & Schmidt, 2001), inhibited toddlers are then likely to turn into shy 7-year-olds (Kagen, Reznick, Snidman, Gibbons & Johnson, 1988), and behaviorally inhibited 8- to 12-year-old children are less likely as young adults to have a positive, active social life and more likely to live close to their family of origin in adulthood (Gest, 1997).

However, experience can moderate or accentuate early tendencies. Toddler boys who were inclined to be fearful and shy were more likely to outgrow their inhibition if parents did not completely shield them from new situations and instead supported them during anxiety-provoking situations (Park, Belsky, Putnam & Crnic, 1997). In other research, when mothers responded neutrally to infants who were behaviorally inhibited, the inhibition tended to remain stable or increase (Fox, Hane & Pine, 2007). Other environmental influences, such as birth order, race/ethnicity, culture, relationships with teachers and peers, and unpredictable events also can reinforce or soften a child's original temperament bias (Kagan & Snidman, 2004).

EARLIEST SOCIAL EXPERIENCES: THE INFANT IN THE FAMILY

Infant care practices and patterns of interaction vary greatly around the world. In Bali, infants are believed to be ancestors or gods brought to life in human form and thus must be treated with utmost dignity and respect. The Beng of West Africa think young babies can understand all languages, whereas people in the Micronesian atoll of Ifaluk believe babies cannot understand language at all, and therefore adults do not speak to them (DeLoache & Gottlieb, 2000).

Among the Efe people of central Africa, infants typically receive care from multiple caregivers and are routinely breast-fed by other women and the mother (Tronick, Morelli & Ivey, 1992). In cultures where infant mortality is high, such as the Gusii in western Kenya (LeVine, 1994), and who are nomadic, such as the Aka hunter-gatherers in central Africa (Hewlett, Lamb, Shannon, Leyendecker & Scholmerich, 1998), parents keep their infants close to them, respond quickly when they cry, and feed them on demand. However, Ngandu farmers, who tend to live far apart and to stay in one place for long periods of time, are more likely to leave their infants alone and to let them fuss or cry, smile, vocalize, or play (Hewlett, et al., 1998).

Many of the patterns of adult-infant interaction are culture-based. There is wide diversity in family systems, even within the United States, where the number of nontraditional families, such as those headed by single parents and gay and lesbian couples, has increased in recent years. Let's look first at the roles of the mother and father—how they care for and play with their babies, and how they shape personality differences between boys and

When infant monkeys could choose whether to go to a wire "mother" or a warm, soft, terry-cloth "mother," they spent more time clinging to the cloth mother, even if their food came from the wire mother.
©Harlow Primate Laboratory, University of Wisconsin-Madison

girls. Later in this chapter, we look more deeply at relationships with parents and then at interactions with siblings.

The Mother's Role In a series of pioneering experiments by Harry Harlow and his colleagues, rhesus monkeys were separated from their mothers 6 to 12 hours after birth. The infant monkeys were put into cages with one of two kinds of surrogate "mothers": a plain cylindrical wire-mesh form or a form covered with terry cloth. Some monkeys were fed from bottles connected to the wire mothers; others were fed by the warm, cuddly cloth mothers. When the monkeys were allowed to spend time with either kind of mother, they all spent more time clinging to the cloth surrogates, even if they were being fed only by the wire surrogates.

None of the monkeys in either group grew up normally (Harlow & Harlow, 1962), and none were effectively able to nurture their own offspring (Suomi & Harlow, 1972). It is hardly surprising that a dummy mother would not provide the same kinds of stimulation and opportunities for positive development as a live mother. However, what is striking and important about these experiments was that they brought about a conceptual shift in the understanding of mothers. They showed that the previous model of mothering—that attachment resulted from an association with food—was incorrect. Feeding is not the only, or even the most important, thing babies get from their mothers. Mothering includes the comfort of close bodily contact and, at least in monkeys, the satisfaction of an innate need to cling.

Human infants also have needs that must be satisfied if they are to grow up typically. One of these needs is for a mother who responds warmly and promptly to the infant. Later in this chapter we discuss how responsiveness contributes to the mutual attachment between infants and mothers that develops during infancy, with far-reaching effects on psychosocial and cognitive development.

The Father's Role The fathering role is in many ways a social construction (Doherty, Kouneski & Erickson, 1998), having different meanings in different cultures. The role may be taken or shared by someone other than the biological father: the mother's brother, as in Botswana; or a grandfather, as in Vietnam (Engle & Breaux, 1998; Richardson, 1995; Townsend, 1997). In some societies fathers are more involved in their young children's lives—economically, emotionally, and in time spent—than in others.

Among the Huhot of Inner Mongolia, fathers traditionally are responsible for economic support and discipline and mothers for nurturing (Jankowiak, 1992). Men almost never hold infants. Fathers interact more with toddlers but perform child care duties only if the mother is absent. However, urbanization and maternal employment are changing these attitudes. Fathers—especially college-educated fathers—now seek more intimate relationships with children, especially sons (Engle & Breaux, 1998). Among the Aka of central Africa, in contrast with the Huhot, "fathers provide more direct infant care than fathers in any other known society" (Hewlett, 1992, p. 169). In Aka families, husbands and wives frequently cooperate in subsistence tasks and other activities (Hewlett, 1992).

In the United States, fathers' involvement in caregiving has greatly increased as more mothers have begun to work outside the home and as concepts of fathering have changed (Cabrera, Tamis-LeMonda, Bradley, Hofferth & Lamb, 2000). A father's frequent and positive involvement with his child, from infancy on, is directly related to the child's well-being and physical, cognitive, and social development (Kelley, Smith, Green, Berndt, & Rogers, 1998; Shannon, Tamis-LeMonda, London & Cabrera, 2002).

GENDER: HOW DIFFERENT ARE BABY BOYS AND GIRLS?

Identifying as male or female affects how people look, how they move their bodies, and how they work, dress, and play. All these characteristics—and more—are included in the word **gender:** what it means to be male or female.

gender
Significance of being male or female.

Gender Differences in Infants and Toddlers Differences between baby boys and baby girls are few, at least in U.S. samples. Boys are a bit longer and heavier and may be slightly stronger. However, boys are more physically vulnerable from conception on, while girls are less reactive to stress and more likely to survive infancy. Beginning prenatally, boys are more active than girls (Davis & Emory, 1995). Boys' brains at birth are about 10 percent larger than girls' brains, a difference that continues into adulthood (Gilmore et al., 2007). On the other hand, the two sexes are equally sensitive to touch and tend to teethe, sit up, and walk at about the same ages (Maccoby, 1980). They also achieve other motor milestones of infancy at about the same times.

One of the earliest *behavioral* differences between boys and girls, appearing between ages 1 and 2, is in preferences for toys and play activities and for playmates of the same sex (Campbell, Shirley, Heywood & Crook, 2000; Serbin, Poulin-Dubois, Colburne, Sen & Eichstedt, 2001). Toddler boys tend to play more aggressively and actively than girls, while girls show better self-control and inhibitory processes (Baillargeon et al., 2007; Else-Quest, Hyde, Goldsmith & VanHulle, 2006). Between ages 2 and 3, boys and girls tend to say more words pertaining to their own sex (such as "tractor" versus "necklace") than to the other sex (Stennes, Burch, Sen & Bauer, 2005). Girls are also more likely to use affiliative speech—speech used to forge or enhance social connections—while boys are more likely to use assertive speech (Leaper & Smith, 2004).

Infants can perceive differences between males and females long before their behavior is gender-differentiated and even before they can talk. Habituation studies have found that 6-month-olds respond differently to male and female voices. By 9 to 12 months, infants can tell the difference between male and female faces, apparently on the basis of hair and clothing. At approximately 19 months, children start to use gender labels such as "mommies" and "daddies" to describe other people (Zosuls et al., 2009). During the 2nd year, infants begin to associate toys as being either for boys or for girls (Martin, Ruble & Szkrybalo, 2002).

How Parents Shape Gender Differences Parents in the United States tend to *think* baby boys and girls are more different than they actually are. For example, despite identical performance, mothers of 11-month-old infants expect sons to crawl more effectively than daughters (Mondschein, Adolph & Tamis-LeMonda, 2000).

U.S. parents begin to influence boys' and girls' personalities very early. Children from single-mother families, for example, tend to hold less stereotypical views about male-female roles (Hupp, Smith, Coleman & Brunell, 2010). Fathers, especially, promote **gender-typing,** the process by which children learn behavior that their culture considers appropriate for each sex (Bronstein, 1988). Fathers treat boys and girls more differently than mothers do, even during the 1st year (M. E. Snow, Jacklin & Maccoby, 1983). During the 2nd year, fathers talk more and spend more time with sons than with daughters (Lamb, 1981). Mothers talk more, and more supportively, to daughters than to sons (Leaper, Anderson & Sanders, 1998), and girls at this age tend to be more talkative than boys (Leaper & Smith, 2004). Fathers of toddlers play more roughly with sons and show more sensitivity to daughters (Leavell, Tamis-LeMonda, Ruble, Zosuls & Cabrera, 2012; Kelley, Smith, Green, Berndt & Rogers, 1998).

However, a highly physical style of play, characteristic of many fathers in the United States, is not typical of fathers in all cultures. Swedish and German fathers usually do not play with their babies this way (Lamb, Frodi, Frodi & Hwang, 1982; Parke, Grossman & Tinsley, 1981). African Aka fathers (Hewlett, 1987) and those in New Delhi, India, also tend to play gently with small children (Roopnarine, Hooper, Ahmeduzzaman & Pollack, 1993; Roopnarine, Talokder, Jain, Josh & Srivastav, 1992).

gender-typing
Socialization process by which children, at an early age, learn appropriate gender roles.

Developmental Issues in Infancy

How does a dependent newborn become a child with complex feelings and the abilities to understand and control them? Much of this development revolves around relationships with caregivers.

DEVELOPING TRUST

Erikson (1950) argued that at each stage in the life span, we are faced with a challenge and a complementary risk. Because human babies are dependent upon others to fulfill their basic needs for a far longer period than most mammals, as babies, our first challenge thus involves forming a **basic sense of trust versus mistrust.** The critical element in developing trust is sensitive, responsive, consistent caregiving, and it is formed primarily within the feeding situation. Can the baby count on being fed when hungry, and can the baby therefore trust the mother as a representative of the world? If we are successful, we develop a sense of the reliability of people and objects in our world. We feel safe and loved. The risk, however, is that, instead, we develop a sense of mistrust and feel that those around us cannot be counted on in times of need.

The stage begins in infancy and continues until about 18 months. Ideally, babies develop a balance between trust (which lets them form intimate relationships) and mistrust (which enables them to protect themselves). If trust predominates, as it should, children develop hope and the belief that they can fulfill their needs and obtain their desires (Erikson, 1982). If mistrust predominates, children view the world as unfriendly and unpredictable and have trouble forming quality relationships.

DEVELOPING ATTACHMENTS

When Ahmed's mother is near, he looks at her, smiles at her, babbles to her, and crawls after her. When she leaves, he cries; when she comes back, he squeals with joy. When he is frightened or unhappy, he clings to her. Ahmed has formed his first attachment to another person.

Attachment is a reciprocal, enduring emotional tie between an infant and a caregiver, each of whom contributes to the quality of the relationship. From an evolutionary point of view, attachments have adaptive value for babies, ensuring that their psychosocial as well as physical needs will be met (Ainsworth, Blehar, Waters & Wall, 2015). To ensure this occurs, infants and parents are biologically predisposed to become attached to each other.

Studying Patterns of Attachment The study of attachment owes much to the pioneering work of ethologist John Bowlby (1951). From his knowledge of Harlow's seminal work with rhesus monkeys demonstrating the importance of contact comfort rather than food, and from his observations of disturbed children in a London clinic, Bowlby became convinced of the importance of the mother-baby bond. Mary Ainsworth, a student of Bowlby's, went on to study attachment in African babies in Uganda through naturalistic observation in their homes (Ainsworth, 1967). Ainsworth later devised the **Strange Situation,** a now-classic, laboratory-based technique designed to assess attachment patterns between an infant and an adult. Typically, the adult is the mother and the infant is 10 to 24 months old.

The Strange Situation consists of a sequence of episodes and takes less than half an hour. The episodes are designed to trigger the emergence of attachment-related behaviors. During that time, the mother twice leaves the baby in an unfamiliar room, the first time with a stranger. The second time she leaves the baby alone, and the stranger comes back before the mother does. The mother then encourages the baby to explore and play again and gives comfort if the baby seems to need it (Ainsworth, Blehar, Waters & Wall, 1978). Of particular concern is the baby's response each time the mother returns.

When Ainsworth and her colleagues observed 1-year-olds in the Strange Situation and at home, they found three main patterns of attachment. These are *secure attachment* (the most common category, into which about 60 to 75 percent of low-risk North American babies fall) and two forms of anxious, or insecure, attachment: *avoidant* (15 to 25 percent) and *ambivalent,* or *resistant* (10 to 15 percent) (Vondra & Barnett, 1999).

Babies with **secure attachment** are resilient in the face of stress. They sometimes cry when a caregiver leaves, but they quickly obtain the comfort they need once the caregiver returns. Some babies with secure attachment are comfortable being left with a stranger for a short period of time; however, they clearly indicate they prefer the caregiver to the stranger in the reunion episode, often smiling at, greeting, or approaching the caregiver.

basic sense of trust versus mistrust
Erikson's first stage in psychosocial development, in which infants develop a sense of the reliability of people and objects.

attachment
Reciprocal, enduring tie between two people—especially between infant and caregiver—each of whom contributes to the quality of the relationship.

Strange Situation
Laboratory technique used to study infant attachment.

secure attachment
Pattern in which an infant is highly effective at obtaining comfort from a caregiver when it is needed and trusts that his or her security needs will be met.

Babies with **avoidant attachment,** by contrast, are outwardly unaffected by a caregiver leaving or returning. They generally continue to play in the room, and frequently interact with the stranger. However, upon the caregiver's return, they ignore or reject the caregiver, sometimes deliberately turning away. Avoidantly attached babies tend to show little emotion, either positive or negative. Babies who exhibit **ambivalent (resistant) attachment** are generally anxious even before the caregiver leaves. They are extremely reactive to the caregiver's departure from the room and generally become very upset. Upon the caregiver's return, these babies tend to remain upset for long periods of time, kicking, screaming, refusing to be distracted with toys, and sometimes arching back and away from contact. They show a mix of proximity-seeking and angry behaviors and are very difficult to settle.

Note that in all of these cases what the baby does during the caregiver's *absence* is not diagnostic of attachment categorization. What is diagnostic is what the babies do when the caregiver *returns.* The important component of the attachment relationship is how the babies use a caregiver to obtain comfort while in his or her presence.

These three attachment patterns are universal in all cultures in which they have been studied though the percentage of infants in each category varies (van IJzendoorn & Kroonenberg, 1988; van IJzendoorn & Sagi, 1999). Generally, however, secure attachment is the largest category (van IJzendoorn & Sagi, 1999).

Other research (Main & Solomon, 1986) later identified a fourth pattern, **disorganized-disoriented attachment.** Babies with the disorganized pattern seem to lack a cohesive strategy to deal with the stress of the Strange Situation and are unable to effectively use their attachment figure for comfort. Instead, they show contradictory, repetitive, or misdirected behaviors (such as seeking closeness to the stranger instead of the mother or showing a fear response upon the caregiver's entry). They often seem confused and afraid (Carlson, 1998; van IJzendoorn, Schuengel & Bakermans-Kranenburg, 1999).

Disorganized attachment is thought to occur in at least 10 percent of infants (Vondra & Barnett, 1999). It is most prevalent in babies with mothers who are insensitive, intrusive, or abusive; who are fearful or frightening and thus leave the infant with no one to alleviate the fear the mother arouses; or who have suffered unresolved loss or have unresolved feelings about their childhood attachment to their own parents. The likelihood of disorganized attachment increases in the presence of multiple risk factors, such as maternal insensitivity plus marital discord plus parenting stress. Disorganized attachment is a reliable predictor of later behavioral and adjustment problems (Bernier & Meins, 2008; Solomon & George, 2011; Carlson, 1998; van IJzendoorn & Sagi, 1999).

How Attachment Is Established By the time babies are 1 year old, they have established a characteristic style of attachment. According to Bowlby, attachment styles are the result of repeated interactions with a caregiver. For example, if every time a baby cries the mother responds quickly and sensitively to that bid for comfort, over time the baby comes to expect it. By contrast, if a mother responds inconsistently to crying, babies form a very different set of expectations regarding the likely responses of the mother to their cries.

Bowlby called these sets of expectations working models and theorized that these early working models became the blueprint for the dynamics of that relationship. As long as the mother continues to act the same way, the model holds up. If her behavior changes—not just once or twice but repeatedly—the baby may revise the model, and security of attachment may change. Because the working model emerges as a result of interactions between both partners in the relationship, babies can have different working models (and attachment styles) with different people.

A baby's working model of attachment is related to Erikson's concept of basic trust. Secure attachment reflects trust; insecure attachment, mistrust. Securely attached babies have learned to trust not only their caregivers but also their own ability to get what they need. Not surprisingly, mothers of securely attached infants and toddlers tend to be sensitive and responsive (Ainsworth et al., 1978; Braungart-Rieker, Garwood, Powers & Wang, 2001; NICHD Early Child Care Research Network, 1997). Equally important are mutual interaction, stimulation, a positive attitude, warmth and acceptance, and emotional support (Lundy, 2003).

avoidant attachment
Pattern in which an infant rarely cries when separated from the primary caregiver and avoids contact on his or her return.

ambivalent (resistant) attachment
Pattern in which an infant becomes anxious before the primary caregiver leaves, is extremely upset during his or her absence, and both seeks and resists contact on his or her return.

disorganized-disoriented attachment
Pattern in which an infant, after separation from the primary caregiver, shows contradictory, repetitious, or misdirected behaviors on his or her return.

Alternative Methods of Attachment Study Although much research on attachment has been based on the Strange Situation, some investigators have questioned its validity. The Strange Situation *is* strange; it takes place in a laboratory, and adults follow a script rather than behaving naturally. Also, the Strange Situation may be less valid in some non-Western cultures (Miyake, Chen & Campos, 1985).

To address these concerns, researchers have devised methods to study children in natural settings. The Waters and Deane (1985) Attachment Q-set (AQS) has mothers or other home observers sort a set of descriptive words or phrases ("cries a lot"; "tends to cling") into categories ranging from most to least characteristic of the child and then compare these descriptions with expert descriptions of the prototypical secure child.

In a study using the AQS, mothers in China, Colombia, Germany, Israel, Japan, Norway, and the United States described their children as behaving much like the prototypical "most secure child." Furthermore, the mothers' descriptions of "secure-base" behavior were about as similar across cultures as within cultures. These findings suggest that the tendency to use the mother as a secure base is universal (Posada et al., 1995).

Neurobiological studies may offer another way to study attachment. Functional MRIs given to mothers showed that certain areas of a mother's brain were activated at the sight of her own infant smiling or crying but not at the sight of other infants showing similar behaviors (Strathearn, 2011; Noriuchi, Kikuchi & Senoo, 2008.) Studies such as these suggest that attachment may have a neurological basis.

The Role of Temperament How much does temperament influence attachment and in what ways? Attachment is a relational variable, thus it is not surprising that research has shown that both a mother's sensitivity and her baby's temperament influence attachment patterns (Goldsmith & Alansky, 1987; Seifer, Schiller, Sameroff, Resnick & Riordan, 1996). Neurological or physiological conditions may underlie temperamental differences in attachment. For example, variability in an infant's heart rate is associated with irritability, and heart rate seems to vary more in insecurely attached infants (Izard, Porges, Simons, Haynes & Cohen, 1991).

A baby's temperament may have not only a direct impact on attachment but also an indirect impact through its effect on the parents. In a series of studies in the Netherlands (van den Boom, 1989, 1994), 15-day-old infants classified as irritable were much more likely than nonirritable infants to be insecurely attached at 1 year. However, irritable infants whose mothers received home visits with instruction on how to soothe their babies were as likely to be rated as securely attached as the nonirritable infants. Thus irritability on an infant's part may prevent the development of secure attachment, but not if the mother has the skills to cope with the baby's temperament (Rothbart et al., 2000). Goodness of fit between parent and child may well be a key to understanding security of attachment.

stranger anxiety
Wariness of strange people and places, shown by some infants during the second half of the 1st year.

separation anxiety
Distress shown by someone, typically an infant, when a familiar caregiver leaves.

Maria's reluctance to allow her mother's friend to hold her is a sign of stranger anxiety.
©Christina Kennedy/Alamy Stock Photo

Stranger Anxiety and Separation Anxiety Chloe used to be a friendly baby, smiling at strangers and going to them, continuing to coo happily as long as someone—anyone—was around. Now, at 8 months, she turns away when a new person approaches and howls when her parents try to leave her with a babysitter. Chloe is experiencing both **stranger anxiety,** wariness of a person she does not know, and **separation anxiety,** distress when a familiar caregiver leaves her.

Babies rarely react negatively to strangers before age 6 months but commonly do so by 8 or 9 months (Sroufe, 1997). This change may reflect cognitive development. Chloe's stranger anxiety involves memory for faces, the ability to compare the stranger's appearance with her mother's, and perhaps the recollection of situations in which she has been left with a stranger. If Chloe is allowed to get used to the stranger gradually in a familiar setting, she may react more positively (Lewis, 1997; Sroufe, 1997).

Separation anxiety may be attenuated. When substitute caregivers are warm and responsive and play with 9-month-olds *before* they cry, the babies cry less than when they are with less responsive caregivers (Gunnar, Larson, Hertsgaard, Harris & Brodersen, 1992).

Stability of care is also important. Pioneering work by René Spitz (1945, 1946) on institutionalized children emphasizes the need for substitute care to be as close as possible to good mothering. Research has underlined the value of continuity and consistency in caregiving, so children can form early emotional bonds with their caregivers.

Long-Term Effects of Attachment As attachment theory proposes, security of attachment seems to affect emotional, social, and cognitive competence, presumably through the action of internal working models (Sroufe, Coffino & Carlson, 2010). The more secure a child's attachment to a nurturing adult, the more likely that the child will develop good relationships with others.

Securely attached toddlers tend to have larger, more varied vocabularies than those who are insecurely attached (Meins, 1998) and show less stress in adapting to child care (Ahnert, Gunnar, Lamb & Barthel, 2004). They have more positive interactions with peers, and their friendly overtures are more likely to be accepted (Fagot, 1997). Insecurely attached toddlers tend to show more negative emotions (fear, distress, and anger), whereas securely attached children are more joyful (Kochanska, 2001).

Between ages 3 and 5, securely attached children are likely to be more curious, competent, empathic, resilient, and self-confident, to get along better with other children, and to form closer friendships than children who were insecurely attached as infants (Arend, Gove & Sroufe, 1979; Elicker, Englund & Sroufe, 1992; Jacobson & Wille, 1986; Waters, Wippman & Sroufe, 1979; Youngblade & Belsky, 1992). They interact more positively with parents, preschool teachers, and peers; are better able to resolve conflicts; and tend to have a more positive self-image (Elicker et al., 1992; Verschueren, Marcoen & Schoefs, 1996; Sroufe, Egeland, Carlson & Collins, 2005). In middle childhood and adolescence, securely attached children tend to have the closest, most stable friendships (Schneider, Atkinson & Tardif, 2001; Sroufe, Carlson & Shulman, 1993) and to be socially well adjusted (Jaffari-Bimmel, Juffer, van IJzendoorn, Bakermans-Kranenberg & Mooijaart, 2006). Secure attachment in infancy also influences the quality of attachment to a romantic partner in young adulthood (Simpson, Collins, Tran & Haydon, 2007).

Insecurely attached children, in contrast, often are more likely to have inhibitions and negative emotions in toddlerhood, hostility toward other children at age 5, and dependency during the school years (Calkins & Fox, 1992; Fearon, Bakersmans-Kranenburg, van Ijzendoorn, Lapsley & Roisman, 2010; Kochanska, 2001; Lyons-Ruth, Alpern & Repacholi, 1993; Sroufe, Carlson & Shulman, 1993). They also are more likely to show evidence of externalizing behaviors such as aggression and conduct problems. This appears to be more true for boys, for clinically referred children, and when the attachment assessments are based on observational data (Fearon et al., 2010). Those with disorganized attachment are more likely to have behavior problems at all levels of schooling and psychiatric disorders at age 17 (Carlson, 1998).

Intergenerational Transmission of Attachment Patterns The *Adult Attachment Interview* (AAI) (George, Kaplan, & Main, 1985; Main, 1995; Main, Kaplan & Cassidy, 1985) asks adults to recall and interpret feelings and experiences related to their childhood attachments. Studies using the AAI have found that the way adults recall early experiences with parents or caregivers is related to their emotional well-being and may influence the way they respond to their own children (Dykas & Cassidy, 2011; Adam, Gunnar & Tanaka, 2004). A mother who was securely attached to *her* mother or who understands *why* she was insecurely attached can accurately recognize the baby's attachment behaviors, respond encouragingly, and help the baby form a secure attachment to her (Bretherton, 1990). Mothers who are preoccupied with their past attachment relationships tend to show anger and intrusiveness in interactions with their children. Depressed mothers who dismiss memories of their past attachments tend to be cold and unresponsive to their children (Adam et al., 2004). Parents' attachment history also influences their perceptions of their baby's temperament, and those perceptions may affect the parent-child relationship (Pesonen et al., 2003).

Fortunately, a cycle of insecure attachment can be broken. In one study, mothers who were classified by the AAI as insecurely attached received home visits in which they were given video feedback to enhance sensitive parenting or participated in discussions of their childhood experiences and their current caregiving. After the interventions, these mothers were more sensitive than a control group who had not received the visits. The greatest positive effects were found for infants with highly reactive (negatively emotional) temperaments (Klein-Velderman, Bakermans-Kranenburg, Juffer & van IJzendoorn, 2006).

EMOTIONAL COMMUNICATION WITH CAREGIVERS: MUTUAL REGULATION

The ability of both infant and caregiver to respond appropriately and sensitively to each other's mental and emotional states is known as **mutual regulation.** Ideally, caregivers and infants have high **interactional synchrony**—where both unconsciously coordinate their behavior and affect in a rhythmic back-and-forth manner, responding appropriately and effectively to each other's signals in an interactive dance. Infants take an active part in this by sending behavioral signals, like smiling, that influence the way caregivers behave toward them. Typically, interaction shifts between well-regulated states and poorly regulated states. When an interaction is highly synchronous, the baby tends to be joyful, or at least interested (Tronick, 1989; Lowe et al., 2012). However, when a mother or caregiver is not synchronous in her interaction with the baby—for example, if an invitation to play is ignored or an adult is overly intrusive—the baby can become stressed or physiologically aroused (Haley & Stansbury, 2003). From this process, babies learn over time how to send signals and what to do when their signals are not effective.

Not surprisingly, there are links to later social behaviors. Children whose mothers were high in interactional synchrony when young are more likely later to be better at regulating their behavior, to comply with parental requests, to have higher IQ, to use more words referencing mental states (such as "think"), and to have fewer behavioral problems (Feldman, 2007). It may be that mutual regulation processes help them learn to read others' behavior and to respond appropriately. Research in Action discusses how a mother's depression may contribute to developmental problems in her baby.

SOCIAL REFERENCING

Ann toddles warily toward the new playground and stops at the entrance, staring at the laughing, screaming children scaling the bright structure. Unsure of herself, she turns toward her mother and makes eye contact. Her mother smiles at her, and Ann, emboldened by her mother's response, walks in and starts to climb the structure. When babies check in with their caregivers upon encountering an ambiguous event, they are engaging in **social referencing,** seeking emotional information to guide behavior. In social referencing, one person forms an understanding of how to act in an ambiguous, confusing, or unfamiliar situation by seeking and interpreting another person's perception of it.

Research provides experimental evidence of social referencing at 12 months (Moses, Baldwin, Rosicky & Tidball, 2001). When exposed to jiggling or vibrating toys fastened to the floor or ceiling, both 12- and 18-month-olds moved closer to or farther from the toys depending on the experimenters' expressed emotional reactions ("Yecch!" or "Nice!"). In another experiment (Hertenstein & Campos, 2004), whether 14-month-olds touched plastic creatures that dropped within their reach was related to the positive or negative emotions they had seen an adult express about the same objects an hour before. As children age, social referencing becomes less dependent on facial expression and more dependent on language. Children between the ages of 4 and 5 years are more likely to trust information that comes from their mother than from a stranger (Corriveau et al., 2009).

research in action

POSTPARTUM DEPRESSION AND EARLY DEVELOPMENT

Much media attention has focused on the issue of postpartum depression. Celebrity moms, including Brooke Shields, Hayden Panettiere, and Chrissy Teigen, have spoken publicly about their struggles in an effort to raise awareness, decrease stigma, and advocate for new moms to seek treatment.

Postpartum depression (PPD) includes symptoms of major depressive disorder experienced within 4 weeks of giving birth that interfere with maternal functioning (Vliegen et al., 2014). Between 13 and 19 percent of mothers experience this condition, perhaps in part due to dramatic drops in estrogen and progesterone levels (O'Hara & McCabe, 2013). Significant emotional and lifestyle changes after the birth of a baby may also trigger depressive symptoms. First-time mothers may be especially at risk; they are generally less likely to have experience in taking care of a newborn and thus may struggle with parenting (Leahy-Warren et al., 2012). Other risk factors include prior history of depression, poor partner relationship, parental stress, financial worries, and recent negative life events (Parsons et al., 2012; Vliegen et al., 2014).

Postpartum depression has profoundly negative effects on mother-infant interactions and is linked to long-term disruption in cognitive and emotional outcomes. Depression itself is associated with poor concentration, lethargy, sleep disturbance, and low mood. These symptoms interfere with the ability to carry out child care tasks (Parsons et al., 2012). Depressed mothers are also more irritable and less engaged in parenting, and their social interactions with infants are generally less positive (Field, 2010). Mothers with PPD experience difficulty recognizing and responding to infants' signs of interest (Murray et al., 2014). As early as 2 months, infants look at the depressed mother less often, show less engagement with objects, and have lower activity levels (Earls, 2010). PPD can also interfere in the bonding process. Some mothers report little to no emotional connection with the baby, and attachment issues may persist up to a full year (O'Higgins et al., 2013). Inadequate or inconsistent caregiving practices impact feeding, sleep routines, health care checkups, and safety practices (Field, 2010). In the short term, infants growing up with depressed parents show impaired social interaction and developmental delays (Earls, 2010). Long-term studies highlight emotional and behavioral problems in elementary school (Fihrer et al., 2009; Closa-Monasterolo et al., 2017). Long-term effects were more severe when maternal depressive episodes persisted throughout childhood.

Cognitive-behavioral and interpersonal therapies are recommended for mild-to-moderate cases, while antidepressants may be necessary for more severe conditions (Bobo & Yawn, 2014). Experts argue for increased accessibility to postpartum support professionals (i.e., nurses, midwives, and doulas) to ease emotional and psychological adjustment for new mothers (Field, 2010). New moms traditionally had access to informal social support networks throughout most of world history in the form of close contact with large extended families. Today's modern woman has smaller family networks, with families frequently spread over larger geographic areas, which may preclude access to natural support networks (Hahn-Holbrook & Haselton, 2014). Other techniques show benefits for depressed mothers and babies, including infant massage and interaction coaching, which aims to increase maternal sensitivity and responsiveness to baby's signals (Field, 2010), and moderate aerobic exercise (McCurdy et al., 2017).

Untreated postpartum depression poses a threat to optimal development, with long-lasting effects that may persist throughout childhood. Early intervention is essential to improve children's cognitive, social, and behavioral outcomes (Earls, 2010). Experts advocate for multipronged interventions, including mental health screening for pregnant and postpartum women, parenting practice education, and increased social support and partner involvement for mothers (Field, 2010; O'Hara & McCabe, 2013)

 what's your view
Can you suggest ways to help depressed mothers and babies, other than those mentioned here?

Social referencing, and the ability to retain information gained from it, may play a role in such key developments of toddlerhood as the rise of self-conscious emotions (embarrassment and pride), the development of a sense of self, and the processes of *socialization* and *internalization,* to which we turn in the next section of this chapter.

Developmental Issues in Toddlerhood

About halfway between their 1st and 2nd birthdays, babies become toddlers. This transformation can be seen not only in such physical and cognitive skills as walking and talking, but also in the ways children express their personalities and interact with others.

Let's look at three psychological issues that toddlers—and their caregivers—have to deal with: the emerging *sense of self*; the growth of *autonomy,* or self-determination; and *socialization,* or *internalization of behavioral standards.*

THE EMERGING SENSE OF SELF

self-concept
Sense of self; descriptive and evaluative mental picture of one's abilities and traits.

The **self-concept** is our image of ourselves—our total picture of our abilities and traits. It describes what we know and feel about ourselves and guides our actions (Harter, 1996).

When and how does the self-concept develop? From a jumble of seemingly isolated experiences (say, from one breast-feeding session to another), infants begin to extract consistent patterns that form rudimentary concepts of self and other. Depending on what kind of care the infant receives and how she or he responds, pleasant or unpleasant emotions become connected with experiences that play an important part in the growing concept of the self (Harter, 1998).

By at least 3 months of age, infants pay attention to their mirror image (Courage & Howe, 2002); 4- to 9-month-olds show more interest in images of others than of themselves (Rochat & Striano, 2002). This early *perceptual* discrimination may be the foundation of the *conceptual* self-awareness that develops between 15 and 18 months. Between 4 and 10 months, when infants learn to reach, grasp, and make things happen, they experience a sense of personal *agency,* the realization that they can control external events. At about this time infants develop *self-coherence,* the sense of being a physical whole with boundaries separate from the rest of the world. These developments occur in interaction with caregivers in games such as peekaboo, in which the infant becomes increasingly aware of the difference between self and other.

The emergence of *self-awareness*—conscious knowledge of the self as a distinct, identifiable being—builds on this dawning of perceptual distinction between self and others. Self-awareness can be tested by studying whether an infant recognizes his or her own image. In a classic line of research, investigators dabbed rouge on the noses of 6- to 24-month-olds and sat them in front of a mirror. Three-fourths of 18-month-olds and all 24-month-olds touched their red noses more often than before, whereas babies younger than 15 months never did. This behavior suggests that these toddlers had self-awareness. They knew they did not normally have red noses and recognized the image in the mirror as their own (Lewis, 1997; Lewis & Brooks, 1974). In a later study, 18- and 24-month-olds were about as likely to touch a sticker on their leg, which was visible only in a mirror, as one on their face (Nielsen, Suddendorf & Slaughter, 2006).

By 20 to 24 months, toddlers begin to use first-person pronouns, another sign of self-awareness (Lewis, 1997). Between 19 and 30 months they begin to apply descriptive terms ("big" or "little") and evaluative terms ("good," "naughty," or "strong") to themselves. The rapid development of language enables children to think and talk about the self and to incorporate parents' verbal descriptions ("What a hard worker!") into their emerging self-image (Stipek, Gralinski & Kopp, 1990). Similarly, toddlers of this age demonstrate self-understanding through acknowledging objects that belong to them and those that belong to others (Fasig, 2000).

DEVELOPMENT OF AUTONOMY

As children mature, they are driven to seek independence. "I do it!" is a common refrain as toddlers use their developing muscles and minds to try to do everything on their own—to feed and dress themselves and to explore their world.

Four- to 9-month-olds show more interest in images of others than in images of themselves.
©Zdravinjo/Shutterstock

Erikson (1950) identified the period from about 18 months to 3 years as the second stage in personality development, **autonomy versus shame and doubt,** marked by a shift from external control to self-control. Having come through infancy with a sense of basic trust in the world and an awakening self-awareness, toddlers begin to substitute their own judgment for their caregivers'. The virtue that emerges during this stage is *will*. Because unlimited freedom is neither safe nor healthy, said Erikson, shame and doubt have a necessary place. Toddlers need adults to set appropriate limits, and shame and doubt help them recognize the need for those limits.

In the United States, toddlers often enjoy testing the notions that they are individuals, that they have some control over their world, and that they have new, exciting powers. They are driven to try out their own ideas, exercise their own preferences, and make their own decisions (Brazelton, 2013). This drive often shows itself in the form of *negativism,* the tendency to shout, "No!" just for the sake of resisting authority. Almost all U.S. children show negativism to some degree, commonly described by many caregivers as the "terrible twos." However, the negativism generally begins before age 2, peaks at about 3½ to 4, and declines by age 6. Caregivers who view children's expressions of self-will as a normal, healthy striving for independence, not as stubbornness, can help them learn self-control, contribute to their sense of competence, and avoid excessive conflict. Table 6.2 gives specific, research-based suggestions that can help discourage negativism and encourage socially acceptable behavior during the toddler years.

Many U.S. parents might be surprised to hear that the terrible twos are not universal. In some developing countries, the transition from infancy to early childhood is relatively smooth and harmonious (Mosier & Rogoff, 2003; Window on the World).

Learning to control your temper is a form of self-control.
©Steve Wisbauer/DigitalVision/Getty Images

autonomy versus shame and doubt
Erikson's second stage in psychosocial development, in which children achieve a balance between self-determination and control by others.

TABLE 6.2 Dealing with Toddler Negativism

- *Be flexible.* Learn the child's natural rhythms and special likes and dislikes.
- *Think of yourself as a safe harbor,* with safe limits, from which a child can set out and discover the world and to which the child can keep coming back for support.
- *Make your home child-friendly.* Fill it with unbreakable objects that are safe to explore.
- *Avoid physical punishment.* It is generally ineffective.
- *Offer a choice* to give the child some control. ("Would you like to have your bath now or in five minutes?")
- *Be consistent* in enforcing necessary requests.
- *Don't interrupt an activity unless absolutely necessary.* Try to wait until the child's attention has shifted.
- *If you must interrupt, give warning.* ("We have to leave the playground soon.")
- *Suggest alternative activities* when behavior becomes objectionable. ("Keiko is playing with the truck right now. Want to go swing?")
- *Suggest; don't command.* Accompany requests with smiles or hugs, not criticism, threats, or physical restraint.
- *Link requests with pleasurable activities.* ("It's time to stop playing so that you can go to the store with me.")
- *Remind the child of what you expect:* "When we go to this playground, we *never* go outside the gate."
- *Wait a few moments before repeating a request* when a child doesn't comply immediately.
- *Use a "time-out" to end conflicts.* In a nonpunitive way, remove either yourself or the child from a situation.
- *Expect less self-control during times of stress* (illness, divorce, the birth of a sibling, or a move to a new home).
- *Expect it to be harder for toddlers to comply with "dos" than with "don'ts."* "Clean up your room" takes more effort than "Don't write on the furniture."
- *Keep the atmosphere as positive as possible.* Make your child *want* to cooperate.

Sources: Haswell, Hock, & Wenar, 1981; Kochanska & Aksan, 1995; Kopp, 1982; Kuczynski & Kochanska, 1995; Power & Chapieski, 1986.

on the world

ARE STRUGGLES WITH TODDLERS NECESSARY?

Are the "terrible twos" a normal phase in child development? Many Western parents and psychologists think so, but research shows this phase doesn't appear to be universal.

In Zinacantan, Mexico, toddlers do not typically become demanding and resistant to parental control. Instead, toddlerhood in Zinacantan is a time when children move from being mama's babies toward being "mother's helpers," responsible children who tend a new baby and help with household tasks (Edwards, 1994). A similar developmental pattern seems to occur in Mazahua families in Mexico and among Mayan families in San Pedro, Guatemala. San Pedro parents "do not report a particular age when they expect children to become especially contrary or negative" (Mosier & Rogoff, 2003, p. 1058).

A cross-cultural study compared 16 Mayan families in San Pedro, Guatemala, with 16 American families in Salt Lake City, Utah. Each family had toddlers 14 to 20 months old and older children 3 to 5 years old. Researchers interviewed each mother about her child-raising practices. With the parents and both siblings present, the researchers handed the mother a series of toys (such as a puppet on strings). In the presence of the older sibling, the researchers asked the mother to help the toddler operate the toys. Researchers found striking differences in the way siblings interacted in the two cultures and in the way the mothers viewed and handled sibling conflict.

The older American siblings often tried to take and play with the toys themselves without regard for their younger sibling. By contrast, the older Guatemalan children would often offer to help their younger siblings, or the two children would play with the toys together. When there was a conflict over possession of the toys, the Guatemalan mothers favored the toddlers 94 percent of the time, even taking an object away from the older child if the younger child wanted it. When mothers asked, the older siblings willingly gave the objects to the toddlers or let them have the objects from the start. However, in more than one-third of the American families, the mothers treated both children equally, negotiating with them or suggesting they take turns or share. These observations were consistent with reports of mothers in both cultures as to how they handled such issues at home.

What explains these cultural contrasts? Two differences emerged: the age parents felt children can be held responsible for their actions, and the amount of direct parental supervision children received. Most of the American mothers maintained that by age 1, their toddlers already understood the consequences of their actions. Most Guatemalan mothers placed the age of understanding consequences of actions much later, between 2 and 3 years of age. The American mothers regarded their toddlers as capable of intentional misbehavior and punished them for it; most Guatemalan mothers did not. All of the American children were under direct caregiver supervision. Alternatively, 11 of the 16 Guatemalan children were without supervision much of the time and had more mature household responsibilities.

The researchers suggest that the terrible twos may be a phase specific to societies that place individual freedom before the needs of the group. In societies that place higher value on group needs, freedom of choice exists, but interdependence, responsibility, and expectations of cooperation are more important, research suggests. American parents seem to believe that responsible behavior develops gradually from engaging in fair competition and negotiations. Guatemalan parents seem to believe that responsible behavior develops rapidly when children are old enough to understand the need to respect others' desires as well as their own.

what's your view

From your experience or observation of toddlers, which of the two ways of handling sibling conflict would you expect to be more effective? Can you think of other ways in which independence and interdependence might be expressed in childhood socialization processes?

THE ROOTS OF MORAL DEVELOPMENT: SOCIALIZATION AND INTERNALIZATION

socialization
Development of habits, skills, values, and motives shared by responsible, productive members of a society.

Socialization is the process by which children develop habits, skills, values, and motives that make them responsible, productive members of society. Compliance with parental expectations can be seen as a first step toward compliance with societal standards.

Socialization rests on **internalization** of these standards. Children who are successfully socialized no longer obey rules or commands merely to get rewards or avoid punishment; rather, they have internalized those standards and made them their own (Grusec & Goodnow, 1994; Kochanska, 2002). They follow the rules not because they are afraid of getting in trouble but because they believe them to be right and true.

Developing Self-Regulation Laticia, age 2, is about to poke her finger into an electric outlet. When Laticia hears her father shout, "No!" the toddler pulls her arm back. The next time she goes near an outlet, she starts to poke her finger, hesitates, and then says, "No." She is beginning to show **self-regulation**: control of her behavior to conform to a caregiver's demands or expectations of her, even when the caregiver is not present.

Self-regulation is the foundation of socialization, and it links all domains of development—physical, cognitive, emotional, and social. Until Laticia was physically able to get around on her own, electric outlets posed no hazard. To stop herself from poking her finger into an outlet requires that she consciously remember and understand what her father told her. But memory is not enough; restraining herself also requires emotional control. By reading their parents' emotional responses to their behavior, children continually absorb information about what conduct their parents approve of. The quality of their relationship with their parents affects this emerging skill. Maternal sensitivity, parents' tendency to use mental terms when talking to the child, and support of the child's autonomous behavior are all important influences on self-regulation (Bernier, Carlson & Whipple, 2010).

Before they can control their own behavior, children may need to be able to regulate, or control, their *attentional processes* and to modulate negative emotions (Eisenberg, 2000; Rueda, Posner & Rothbart, 2005). Attentional regulation enables children to develop willpower and cope with frustration (Duckworth, Gendler & Gross, 2014; Sethi, Mischel, Aber, Shoda & Rodriguez, 2000). For example, control of attentional processes might allow a child to distract herself enough that she manages not to steal the cookies temptingly cooling on the counter.

The growth of self-regulation parallels the development of the self-conscious and evaluative emotions, such as empathy, shame, and guilt (Lewis, 1995, 1997, 1998). It requires the ability to wait for gratification. It is correlated with measures of conscience development, such as resisting temptation and making amends for wrongdoing (Eisenberg, 2000). In most children, the full development of self-regulation takes at least 3 years (Rothbart, Sheese, Rueda & Posner, 2011).

Origins of Conscience: Committed Compliance While young children often cooperate with parental dictates because they know they are supposed to, the goal of parenting is development of a **conscience**, which involves both the ability to refrain from certain acts as well as to feel emotional discomfort if they fail to do so.

Kochanska and her colleagues looked for the origins of conscience by studying children ages 26 to 41 months with their mothers playing together with toys (Kochanska & Aksan, 1995). After a free-play period, a mother would give her child 15 minutes to put away the toys. The laboratory where the research occurred had a special shelf with other, unusually attractive toys, such as a bubble gum machine, a walkie-talkie, and a music box. The child was told not to touch anything on that shelf. After about an hour, the experimenter asked the mother to go into an adjoining room, leaving the child alone with the toys. A few minutes later, a woman entered, played with several of the forbidden toys, and then left the child alone again for 8 minutes.

Some children could put the toys away as long as their parents were there to remind them. These children showed what is called **situational compliance.** They needed the extra assistance provided by their parents' presence and prompts to complete the task. However, other children seemed to have internalized their parents' requests more fully. These children showed **committed compliance**—that is, they were committed to following requests and could do so without their parents' direct intervention (Kochanska, Coy & Murray, 2001).

The roots of committed compliance go back to infancy. Committed compliers, most typically girls, tend to be those who, at 8 to 10 months, could refrain from touching

internalization
During socialization, process by which children accept societal standards of conduct as their own.

self-regulation
A child's independent control of behavior to conform to understood social expectations.

conscience
Internal standards of behavior, which usually control one's conduct and produce emotional discomfort when violated.

situational compliance
Kochanska's term for obedience of a parent's orders only in the presence of signs of ongoing parental control.

committed compliance
Kochanska's term for wholehearted obedience of a parent's orders without reminders or lapses.

when told, "No!" (Kochanska, Tjebkes & Forman, 1998). Mothers of committed compliers, as contrasted with mothers of situational compliers, were more sensitive and responsive with their children as infants (Kochanska, Woodard, Kim, Koenig, Yoon & Barry, 2010) and, once the children were toddlers, tended to rely on gentle guidance rather than force, threats, or other forms of negative control (Eisenberg, 2000; Kochanska, Friesenborg, Lange & Martel, 2004). Committed compliance tends to increase with age, whereas situational compliance decreases.

Receptive cooperation goes beyond committed compliance. It is a child's eager willingness to cooperate with a parent, not only in disciplinary situations, but also in a variety of daily interactions, including routines, chores, hygiene, and play. In a longitudinal study of 101 children, those who were prone to anger, who received unresponsive parenting, or who were insecurely attached at 15 months also tended to be low in receptive cooperation in toddlerhood. Children who were securely attached and whose mothers had been responsive to the child during infancy tended to be high in receptive cooperation (Kochanska, Aksan & Carlson, 2005).

Factors in the Success of Socialization Not all children respond in the same way to parental efforts to socialize them. For example, a temperamentally fearful toddler may respond better to gentle reminders than to strong admonitions, whereas a more bold toddler may require more assertive parenting (Kochanska, Aksan & Joy, 2007).

Secure attachment and a warm, mutually responsive, parent-child relationship seem to foster committed compliance and conscience development (Kochanska et al., 2010). In one study, researchers observed mothers and children in lengthy, naturalistic interactions: caregiving routines, preparing and eating meals, playing, relaxing, and doing household chores. Children who had mutually responsive relationships with their mothers at the age of 2 tended in early school age to show *moral emotions* such as guilt and empathy; *moral conduct* in the face of strong temptation to break rules; and *moral cognition,* as judged by their response to hypothetical, age-appropriate moral dilemmas (Kochanska et al., 2002).

Contact with Other Children

Although parents exert a major influence on children's lives, relationships with other children—both in the home and out of it—also are important from infancy on.

SIBLINGS

Sibling relationships play a distinct role in socialization. Sibling conflicts can become a vehicle for understanding social relationships (Ram & Ross, 2001). Lessons and skills learned from interactions with siblings carry over to relationships outside the home (Brody, 1998; Ji-Yeon, McHale, Crouter & Osgood, 2007).

Babies usually become attached to their older siblings. Although rivalry may be present, so is affection. The more securely attached siblings are to their parents, the better they get along with each other (Teti & Ablard, 1989).

Nevertheless, as babies begin to move around and become more assertive, they inevitably come into conflict with siblings—at least in U.S. culture. Sibling conflict increases dramatically after the younger child reaches 18 months (Volling, Kennedy & Jackey, 2010). During the next few months, younger siblings begin to participate more fully in family interactions and become more involved in family disputes. As they do, they become more aware of others' intentions and feelings. They begin to recognize what kind of behavior will upset or annoy an older brother or sister and what behavior is considered "naughty" or "good" (Dunn & Munn, 1985; Recchia & Howe, 2009).

In many non-Western cultures, it is common to see older siblings caring for younger siblings.
©Wigbert Roth/imageBROKER/REX/Shutterstock

receptive cooperation
Kochanska's term for eager willingness to cooperate harmoniously with a parent in daily interactions, including routines, chores, hygiene, and play.

As this cognitive and social understanding grows, sibling conflict tends to become more constructive, and the younger sibling participates in attempts to reconcile. Constructive conflict with siblings helps children recognize each other's needs, wishes, and point of view, and it helps them learn how to fight, disagree, and compromise within the context of a safe, stable relationship (Kramer, 2010; Vandell & Bailey, 1992).

SOCIABILITY WITH NONSIBLINGS

Infants and—even more so—toddlers show interest in people outside the home, particularly people their own size. During the first few months, they look, smile, and coo at other babies (T. M. Field, 1978). From about 6 to 12 months, they increasingly smile at, touch, and babble to them (Hay, Pedersen & Nash, 1982). At about 1 year, as babies are concentrating on learning how to walk and manipulate objects, babies pay less attention to other people (T. M. Field & Roopnarine, 1982). This stage does not last long, though. From about 1½ years to almost 3, children show growing interest in what other children do and an increasing understanding of how to deal with them (Eckerman, Davis & Didow, 1989).

Toddlers learn by imitating one another. Games such as follow-the-leader help toddlers connect with other children and pave the way for more complex games during the preschool years (Eckerman et al., 1989). Imitation of each other's actions leads to more frequent verbal communication (such as "You go in playhouse"), which helps peers coordinate joint activity (Eckerman & Didow, 1996). Cooperative activity develops during the 2nd and 3rd years as social understanding grows (Brownell, Ramani & Zerwas, 2006). As with siblings, conflict also can have a purpose: helping children learn how to negotiate and resolve disputes (Kramer, 2010).

Children of Working Parents

Parents' work determines more than just the family's financial resources. Much of adults' time, effort, and emotional involvement goes into their occupations. How do their work and their child care arrangements affect infants and toddlers?

EFFECTS OF MATERNAL EMPLOYMENT

Labor force participation by mothers of children of all ages has increased dramatically in the past three decades. In 1975, fewer than half of all mothers were working or looking for work. In 2016, more than half (58.6 percent) of mothers of infants in their 1st year of life and 64.7 percent of women with children under age 6 were in the labor force (U.S. Bureau of Labor Statistics, 2017).

How does early maternal employment affect children? Longitudinal data on 900 European American children from the National Institute of Child Health and Human Development (NICHD) Study of Early Child Care showed negative effects on cognitive development at 15 months to 3 years when mothers worked 30 or more hours a week by a child's 9th month. However, maternal sensitivity, a high-quality home environment, and high-quality child care lessened these negative effects (Brooks-Gunn, Han & Waldfogel, 2002).

Similarly, among 6,114 children from the National Longitudinal Survey of Youth (NLSY), those whose mothers worked full-time in the 1st year after giving birth were more likely to show negative cognitive and behavioral outcomes at ages 3 to 8 than children whose mothers worked part-time or not at all during their 1st year. However, children in disadvantaged families showed fewer negative cognitive effects than children in more advantaged families (Hill, Waldfogel, Brooks-Gunn & Han, 2005).

EARLY CHILD CARE

One factor in the impact of a mother's working outside the home is the type of substitute care a child receives. About 61 percent of children under the age of 5 have some sort of regular child care arrangement. Of those children, 42 percent are cared for by relatives, primarily grandparents and fathers. About a third are regularly cared for by nonrelatives, and approximately 12 percent are cared for by a mix of relatives and nonrelatives. Approximately a quarter are cared for in some form of organized care facility. With nonrelative care averaging $143 a week, affordability and quality of care are pressing issues (Laughlin, 2013).

Factors Having an Impact on Child Care The impact of early child care may depend on the type, amount, quality, and stability of care as well as the family's income and the age at which children start receiving nonmaternal care. By 9 months, about 50 percent of U.S. infants are in some kind of regular nonparental child care arrangement, and 86 percent of these infants enter child care before they reach 6 months. More than 50 percent of these babies are in child care more than 30 hours a week (NCES, 2005a).

Temperament and gender of the child make a difference (Crockenberg, 2003). Shy children in child care experience greater stress, as shown by cortisol levels, than sociable children (Watamura, Donzella, Alwin & Gunnar, 2003), and insecurely attached children experience greater stress than securely attached children when introduced to full-time child care (Ahnert et al., 2004). Boys are more vulnerable to stress, in child care and elsewhere, than are girls (Crockenberg, 2003).

A critical factor in determining the effects of child care is the quality of care a child receives. Quality of care can be measured by *structural characteristics,* such as staff training and the ratio of children to caregivers; and by *process characteristics,* such as the warmth, sensitivity, and responsiveness of caregivers and the developmental appropriateness of activities.

Stimulating interactions with responsive adults are crucial to early cognitive, linguistic, and psychosocial development. In one study, warm and caring interactions with staff at home-based day care centers was associated with a lower incidence of problem behavior in children but *not* with decreases in stress hormone activation (as measured by cortisol, the primary stress hormone). By contrast, intrusive and overcontrolling care did lead to increases in cortisol production. The authors suggested that overly structured day cares with multiple transitions overwhelm the children's abilities and lead to heightened stress. However, this is not necessarily maladaptive. We all need to learn how to manage stress during the course of our lives, so this early practice may not be harmful (Gunnar, Kryzer, Van Ryzin & Phillips, 2010).

Low staff turnover is another important factor in quality of care. Infants need consistent caregiving in order to develop trust and secure attachments (Burchinal, Roberts, Nabors & Bryant, 1996; Shonkoff & Phillips, 2000). Stability of care facilitates coordination between parents and child care providers, which may help protect against any negative effects of long hours of care (Ahnert & Lamb, 2003). Table 6.3 provides guidelines for selecting a high-quality child care facility.

The NICHD Study: Isolating Child Care Effects The type of child care a family seeks and can afford is related to many other variables we know impact developmental processes. Thus, it is difficult to pinpoint the effects of child care in isolation from other influences. The most comprehensive attempt to separate child care effects from the effects of factors, such as family characteristics, the child's characteristics, and the care the child receives at home, is a study sponsored by the National Institute of Child Health and Human Development (NICHD).

This longitudinal study of 1,364 children and their families began in 1991 across the United States, shortly after the children's birth. The sample was socioeconomically, educationally, and ethnically diverse. Most infants entered nonmaternal care before 4 months and received, on average, 33 hours of care each week. Child care arrangements varied widely in type and quality. Researchers measured the children's social, emotional, cognitive, and physical development at frequent intervals from age 1 month through 9th grade.

The study showed that the amount and quality of care children received as well as the type and stability of care influenced specific aspects of development. Long days in child care were associated with stress for 3- and 4-year-olds (Belsky et al., 2007; NICHD Early Child Care Research Network, 2003). And the 15 percent of 2- and 3-year-olds who experienced more than one regular child care arrangement were at increased risk of behavior problems and were less likely to help and share (Morrissey, 2009). However, this was not the entire story. Although it was true that, overall, child care was associated with a small increase in externalizing behaviors, good child care quality and small peer group size were important positive influences.

TABLE 6.3 Checklist for Choosing a Good Child Care Facility

- Is the facility licensed? Does it meet minimum state standards for health, fire, and safety?

- Is the facility clean and safe? Does it have adequate indoor and outdoor space?

- Does the facility have small groups, a high adult to child ratio, and a stable, competent, highly involved staff?

- Are caregivers trained in child development?

- Are caregivers warm, affectionate, accepting, responsive, and sensitive? Are they neither too controlling nor merely custodial?

- Does the program promote good health habits?

- Does it provide a balance between age-appropriate structured activities and free play?

- Do the children have access to educational toys and materials that stimulate mastery of cognitive and communicative skills?

- Does the program nurture self-confidence, curiosity, creativity, and self-discipline?

- Does it encourage children to ask questions, solve problems, express feelings and opinions, and make decisions?

- Does it foster self-esteem, respect for others, and social skills?

- Does it help parents improve their child-rearing skills?

- Does it promote cooperation with public and private schools and the community?

Sources: American Academy of Pediatrics (AAP), 1986; Belsky, 1984; Clarke-Stewart, 1987; NICHD Early Child Care Research Network, 1996; Olds, 1989; Scarr, 1998.

Moreover, children in child care centers with low child-staff ratios, small group sizes, and trained, sensitive, responsive caregivers who provided positive interactions and language stimulation scored higher on tests of language comprehension, cognition, and readiness for school than did children in lower-quality care. Their mothers also reported fewer behavior problems (NICHD Early Child Care Research Network, 1999a, 2000, 2002). Children who had received higher-quality care before entering kindergarten had better vocabulary scores in fifth grade (Belsky et al., 2007) and at age 15 (Vandell, Belsky, Burchinal, Steinberg & Vandergrift, 2010) than children who had received lower quality care.

However, factors related to child care were less influential than family characteristics, such as income, the home environment, the amount of mental stimulation the mother provided, and the mother's sensitivity to her child. These characteristics strongly predicted developmental outcomes, regardless of how much time children spent in outside care (Belsky et al., 2007; Marshall, 2004; NICHD Early Child Care Research Network, 2000, 2003).

Did the effects of early child care persist across time? Follow-up studies conducted when the children were 15 years of age suggest that some may have, although effects were small. In general, higher-quality care was associated with increases in cognitive skills, academic achievement, and fewer problem behaviors. Unfortunately, child care also was related to increases in risk-taking behaviors and impulsivity. As before, the magnitude of positive effects was strongest for children in the highest-quality day cares. This suggests that future work should be on increasing day care quality from average to high, rather than from low quality to average (Vandell et al., 2010). Similar findings emerged from a large-scale meta-analyses of more than 69 studies spanning five decades. In this study, maternal employment during infancy and early childhood was associated with higher levels of academic achievement and lower levels of internalizing behaviors, and these findings were most striking for single mothers and for mothers on public assistance (Lucas-Thompson, Goldberg & Prause, 2010).

To sum up, a number of large-scale studies give high-quality child care good marks overall, especially for its impact on cognitive development and interaction with peers. Some observers say that the areas of concern the study pinpointed—stress levels in infants and toddlers and possible behavior problems related to amounts of care and multiple caregiving arrangements—might be counteracted by activities that enhance children's attachment to caregivers and peers, emphasize child-initiated learning and internalized motivation, and focus on group social development (Maccoby & Lewis, 2003).

Maltreatment: Abuse and Neglect

Although most parents are loving and nurturing, some cannot or will not take proper care of their children, and some deliberately harm them. *Maltreatment,* whether perpetrated by parents or others, is deliberate or avoidable endangerment of a child.

Maltreatment can take several specific forms, and the same child can be a victim of more than one type (USDHHS, Administration on Children, Youth and Families, 2008). These types include the following:

- **Physical abuse,** injury to the body through punching, beating, kicking, or burning.
- **Neglect,** failure to meet a child's basic needs, such as food, clothing, medical care, protection, and supervision.
- **Sexual abuse,** any sexual activity involving a child and an older person.
- **Emotional maltreatment,** including rejection, terrorization, isolation, exploitation, degradation, ridicule, or failure to provide emotional support, love, and affection.

State and local child protective service agencies received an estimated 3.4 million referrals for alleged maltreatment of 6.2 million children in 2015, a 9 percent increase from 2011. About 75 percent of children identified as maltreated were neglected, 17.2 percent were physically abused, and 8.4 percent were sexually abused (USDHHS, Administration on Children, Youth, and Families, 2017). Emotional maltreatment was not included in this analysis, however, as it often co-occurs with the other forms of abuse. Younger children are more likely to be victims of abuse than older children, particularly those under the age of 3 years. An estimated 1,670 children died of maltreatment, and the actual number may well have been considerably higher (USDHHS, Administration on Children, Youth, and Families, 2017).

MALTREATMENT IN INFANCY AND TODDLERHOOD

Children are abused and neglected at all ages, but the highest rates of victimization and of death from maltreatment are for age 3 and younger (Child Welfare Information Gateway, 2017; Figure 6.2).

Babies need to form attachments to others as much as they need their basic survival needs taken care of. Babies who do not receive nurturance and affection or who are neglected sometimes suffer from **nonorganic failure to thrive,** slowed or arrested physical growth with no known medical cause, accompanied by poor developmental and emotional functioning. Symptoms may include lack of appropriate weight gain, irritability, excessive sleepiness and fatigue, avoidance of eye contact, lack of smiling or vocalizing, and delayed motor development. In short, they neither grow nor develop normally despite a lack of underlying physical or medical causes. Failure to thrive can result from a combination of inadequate nutrition, difficulties in breast-feeding, improper formula preparation or feeding techniques, and disturbed interactions with parents. Poverty is the greatest single risk factor for failure to thrive worldwide. Infants whose mother or primary caregiver is depressed, abuses alcohol or other substances, is under severe stress, or does not show warmth or affection toward the baby are also at heightened risk (Block, Krebs, the Committee on Child Abuse and Neglect & the Committee on Nutrition, 2005; Lucile Packard Children's Hospital at Stanford, 2009).

Shaken baby syndrome is a form of maltreatment found mainly in children under 2 years old, most often in infants. Because the baby has weak neck muscles and a large, heavy head, shaking makes the brain bounce back and forth inside the skull. This causes bruising, bleeding, and swelling and can lead to permanent and severe brain damage, paralysis, and even death (National Institute of Neurological Disorders and Stroke [NINDS], 2006). The damage is typically worse if the baby is thrown into bed or against a wall. Head trauma is the leading cause of death in child abuse cases in the United States (Dowshen, Crowley & Palusci, 2004). About 20 percent of babies with head trauma die within a few days. Survivors may be left with a wide range of disabilities from learning and behavioral disorders to neurological injuries, paralysis or blindness, or a permanent vegetative state (King, MacKay, Sirnick & The Canadian Shaken Baby Study Group, 2003; NINDS, 2006).

physical abuse
Action taken deliberately to endanger another person, involving potential bodily injury.

neglect
Failure to meet a dependent's basic needs.

sexual abuse
Physically or psychologically harmful sexual activity or any sexual activity involving a child and an older person.

emotional maltreatment
Rejection, terrorization, isolation, exploitation, degradation, ridicule, or failure to provide emotional support, love, and affection; or other action or inaction that may cause behavioral, cognitive, emotional, or mental disorders.

nonorganic failure to thrive
Slowed or arrested physical growth with no known medical cause, accompanied by poor developmental and emotional functioning.

shaken baby syndrome
Form of maltreatment in which shaking an infant or toddler can cause brain damage, paralysis, or death.

CONTRIBUTING FACTORS: AN ECOLOGICAL VIEW

As Bronfenbrenner's bioecological theory would suggest, abuse and neglect are not caused by one thing. The causes of abuse are not in the individual, nor are they in the family, nor are they in the wider social and cultural environment. The causes are in *all* those places, and to understand why it happens, we need to consider *all* the contributing factors.

Characteristics of Abusive and Neglectful Parents and Families Often, abusive adults appear to be just like everyone else; there is no identifying behavior or characteristic that determines who will or will not abuse a child. In 78 percent of cases of maltreatment, the perpetrators are the child's parents. Slightly over 6 percent of perpetrators are other relatives, and almost 4 percent are unmarried partners of parents. Slightly more than half (54.1 percent) are women, and the race of the perpetrator is generally the same as the race of the victim (USDHHS, 2017).

Maltreatment by parents is a symptom of extreme disturbance in child rearing, usually aggravated by other family problems, such as poverty, lack of education, alcoholism, depression, or antisocial behavior. A disproportionate number of abused and neglected children are in large, poor, or single-parent families, which tend to be under stress and to have trouble meeting children's needs (Sedlak & Broadhurst, 1996; USDHHS, 2017; Dubowitz, Kim, Black, Weisbart, Semiatin & Magder, 2011). Yet what pushes one parent over the edge, another may take in stride. Although many neglect cases occur in very poor families, most low-income parents do not neglect their children.

The likelihood that a child will be physically abused has less to do with the child's own characteristics and more to do with the household environment (Jaffee et al., 2004). Abuse may begin when a parent who is already anxious, depressed, or hostile tries to control a child physically but loses self-control and ends up shaking or beating the child. Parents who abuse children tend to have marital problems and to fight physically.

Abuse and neglect sometimes occur in the same families (USDHHS, Administration on Children, Youth, and Families, 2006). Such families tend to have no one to turn to in times of stress and no one to see what is happening (Dubowitz, 1999). Substance abuse is a factor in approximately a quarter of cases of maltreatment (USDHHS, 2017). Sexual abuse often occurs along with other family disturbances such as physical abuse, emotional maltreatment, substance abuse, and family violence (Kellogg & the Committee on Child Abuse and Neglect, 2005).

Community Characteristics and Cultural Values Child abuse is a systems issue, and we cannot ignore the contribution of the local environment on maltreatment. What makes one low-income neighborhood a place where children are highly likely to be maltreated and another, matched for ethnic population and income levels, safer? In one inner-city Chicago neighborhood, the proportion of children who died from maltreatment (1 death for every 2,541 children) was about twice the proportion in another inner-city neighborhood. In the high-abuse community, criminal activity was rampant, and facilities for community programs were dreary. In the low-abuse neighborhood, people described their community as a poor but decent place to live. They painted a picture of a neighborhood with robust social support networks, well-known community services, and strong political leadership. In a community like this, maltreatment is less likely to occur (Garbarino & Kostelny, 1993).

Two cultural factors associated with child abuse are societal violence and physical punishment of children. In countries where violent crime is infrequent and children are rarely spanked, such as Japan, China, and Tahiti, child abuse is rare (Celis, 1990). In the United States, homicide, domestic violence, and rape are common, and many states still permit corporal punishment in schools. While corporal punishment, overall, has been trending down in recent decades, nearly 8 out of 10 parents of preschoolers and nearly half of parents of school-age children still report using physical punishment at home (Zolotor, Theodore, Runyan, Chang & Laskey, 2011).

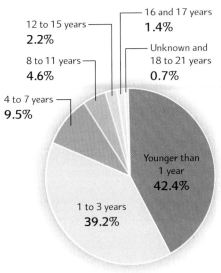

FIGURE 6.2

Deaths from Maltreatment by Age, 2011

More than three-quarters of fatalities are children younger than age 3.

Source: Child Welfare Information Gateway. *Child abuse and neglect fatalities 2011: Statistics and interventions.* Washington, DC: Author, 2013.

HELPING FAMILIES IN TROUBLE

State and local child protective service agencies investigate reports of maltreatment. After making a determination of maltreatment, they determine what steps, if any, need to be taken. Agency staff may try to help the family resolve their problems or arrange for alternative care for children who cannot safely remain at home (USDHHS, Administration on Children, Youth, and Families, 2015). Services for children who have been abused and their parents include shelters, education in parenting skills, and therapy. However, availability of services is often limited (Burns et al., 2004).

When authorities remove children from their homes, the usual alternative is foster care. Foster care removes a child from immediate danger, but it is often unstable, further alienates the child from the family, and may turn out to be another abusive situation. Often a child's basic health and educational needs are not met (David and Lucile Packard Foundation, 2004; National Research Council [NRC], 1993b).

In part because of a scarcity of traditional foster homes and an increasing caseload, a growing proportion of placements are in kinship foster care, under the care of grandparents or other family members (Berrick, 1998; Geen, 2004). Although most foster children who leave the system are reunited with their families, about 28 percent reenter foster care within the next 10 years (Wulczyn, 2004). Children who have been in foster care are more likely than other children to become homeless, to commit crimes, and to become teenage mothers (David and Lucile Packard Foundation, 2004), as well as to suffer mental or physical health problems in adulthood (Zlotnick, Tam & Soman, 2012).

LONG-TERM EFFECTS OF MALTREATMENT

Consequences of maltreatment may be physical, emotional, cognitive, and social, or a combination. A physical blow to a child's head can cause brain damage resulting in cognitive delays and emotional and social problems. Similarly, severe neglect or unloving parents can have traumatic effects on the developing brain (Fries et al., 2005).

Long-term consequences of maltreatment may include poor physical, mental, and emotional health; impaired brain development (Glaser, 2000); cognitive, language, and academic difficulties; problems in attachment and social relationships (National Clearinghouse on Child Abuse and Neglect Information [NCCANI], 2004; Child Welfare Information Gateway, 2013); memory problems (Brunson et al., 2005); and, in adolescence, heightened risks of poor academic achievement, delinquency, teenage pregnancy, alcohol and drug use, and suicide (Dube et al., 2001, 2003; Lansford et al., 2002; NCCANI, 2004). Abuse and neglect in childhood results in an elevated risk that the victims will, when grown, become abusers as well (Child Welfare Information Gateway, 2013).

What are the long-term consequences of sexual abuse? In a study that followed 68 sexually abused children for 5 years, these children showed more disturbed behavior, had lower self-esteem, and were more depressed, anxious, or unhappy than a control group (Swanston, Tebbutt, O'Toole & Oates, 1997). Sexually abused children often become sexually active at an earlier age and tend to have higher numbers of sexual partners than children who were not sexually abused. As adults they tend to be more anxious, depressed, or suicidal, and are more likely to be diagnosed with post-traumatic stress disorder. They are also more likely to abuse drugs and alcohol (Fergusson, McLeod & Horwood, 2013). Moreover, sexual abuse may also compromise physical health: Sexual abuse survivors are more likely to be obese or suffer from stress-related or autoimmune disorders (Wilson, 2010).

Why do some abused children grow up to become antisocial or abusive, while others do not? One possible difference is genetic; some genotypes may be more resistant to trauma than others (Caspi et al., 2002; Jaffee et al., 2005). Many maltreated children show remarkable resilience. Optimism, self-esteem, intelligence, creativity, humor, and independence are also protective factors, as is the social support of a caring adult (NCCANI, 2004). The topic of resilience is so important in development that it is researched extensively.

summary and key terms

Foundations of Psychosocial Development

- Emotional development is orderly; complex emotions seem to develop from earlier, simpler ones.
- Crying, smiling, and laughing are early signs of emotion. Other indices are facial expressions, motor activity, body language, and physiological changes.
- Brain development is closely linked with emotional development.
- Self-conscious and self-evaluative emotions arise after the development of self-awareness.

  personality, emotions, social smiling, anticipatory smiling, self-conscious emotions, self-awareness, self-evaluative emotions, altruistic behavior, empathy, mirror neurons, social cognition

- Many children seem to fall into one of three categories of temperament: "easy," "difficult," and "slow-to-warm-up."
- Temperamental patterns appear to have a biological basis. They are generally stable but can be modified by experience.
- Goodness of fit between a child's temperament and environmental demands aids adjustment.
- Cross-cultural differences in temperament may reflect child-raising practices.

  temperament, "easy" children, "difficult" children, "slow-to-warm-up" children, goodness of fit

- Child-raising practices and caregiving roles vary around the world.
- Infants have strong needs for maternal closeness, warmth, and responsiveness as well as physical care.
- Fathering roles differ in various cultures.
- Although significant gender differences typically do not appear until after infancy, U.S. fathers, especially, promote early gender-typing.

  gender, gender-typing

Developmental Issues in Infancy

- According to Erikson, infants in the first 18 months are in the first stage of personality development, basic sense of trust versus mistrust. Sensitive, responsive, consistent caregiving is the key to successful resolution of this conflict.
- Research based on the Strange Situation has found four patterns of attachment: secure, avoidant, ambivalent (resistant), and disorganized-disoriented.
- Newer instruments measure attachment in natural settings and in cross-cultural research.
- Attachment patterns may depend on a baby's temperament as well as on the quality of parenting and may have long-term implications for development.
- Stranger anxiety and separation anxiety may arise during the second half of the 1st year.
- A parent's memories of childhood attachment can influence his or her own child's attachment.
- Mutual regulation enables babies to play an active part in regulating their emotional states.
- Social referencing has been observed by 12 months.

  basic sense of trust versus mistrust, attachment, Strange Situation, secure attachment, avoidant attachment, ambivalent (resistant) attachment, disorganized-disoriented attachment, stranger anxiety, separation anxiety, mutual regulation, interactional synchrony, social referencing

Developmental Issues in Toddlerhood

- The sense of self arises between 4 and 10 months, as infants begin to perceive a difference between self and others.
- The self-concept builds on the perceptual sense of self and develops between 15 and 24 months with the emergence of self-awareness and self-recognition.
- Erikson's second stage concerns autonomy versus shame and doubt. In U.S. culture, negativism is a normal manifestation of the shift from external control to self-control.
- Socialization, which rests on internalization of societally approved standards, begins with the development of self-regulation.
- A precursor of conscience is committed compliance to a caregiver's demands. Children who show receptive cooperation can be active partners in their socialization.
- Parenting practices, a child's temperament, the quality of the parent-child relationship, and cultural and socioeconomic factors may affect the ease and success of socialization.

  self-concept, autonomy versus shame and doubt, socialization, internalization, self-regulation, conscience, situational compliance, committed compliance, receptive cooperation

Contact with Other Children

- Sibling relationships play a distinct role in socialization and influence relationships outside the home.
- Between ages 1½ and 3 years, children tend to show more interest in and understanding of other children.

Children of Working Parents

- In general, mothers' workforce participation during a child's first 3 years seems to have little impact on development, but cognitive development may suffer when a mother works 30 or more hours a week by her child's 9th month.
- Substitute child care varies in quality. The most important elements include warm, responsive caregivers and low staff turnover.
- Although quality, quantity, stability, and type of care influence psychosocial and cognitive development, the influence of family characteristics seems greater overall.

Maltreatment: Abuse and Neglect

- Forms of maltreatment are physical abuse, neglect, sexual abuse, and emotional maltreatment.
- Most victims of maltreatment are infants and toddlers. Some die due to failure to thrive. Others are victims of shaken baby syndrome.
- Characteristics of the abuser or neglecter, the family, the community, and the larger culture all contribute to child abuse and neglect.
- Maltreatment can interfere with physical, cognitive, emotional, and social development, and its effects can continue into adulthood. Still, many maltreated children show remarkable resilience.
- Preventing or stopping maltreatment may require multifaceted, coordinated community efforts.

  physical abuse, neglect, sexual abuse, emotional maltreatment, nonorganic failure to thrive, shaken baby syndrome

Physical and Cognitive Development in Early Childhood

learning objectives

Identify physical changes in early childhood.

Describe three views of the cognitive changes that occur in early childhood.

Summarize how language develops in early childhood.

Evaluate different approaches to early childhood education.

©gabczi/Shutterstock

In this chapter we look at physical and cognitive development from ages 3 to 6. Children grow more slowly than before, but make enormous progress in muscle development and coordination. We trace their advances in the abilities to think, speak, and remember and consider several health concerns. We end with a discussion of early childhood education.

PHYSICAL DEVELOPMENT
Aspects of Physical Development

In early childhood, children slim down and shoot up. They need less sleep than before and are more likely to develop sleep problems. They get better at running, hopping, skipping, jumping, and throwing balls. They become more proficient at tying shoelaces, drawing with crayons, and pouring cereal; and they show a preference for using either the right or left hand.

BODILY GROWTH AND CHANGE

Children grow rapidly between ages 3 and 6, but less quickly than before. At about 3, children normally begin to lose their babyish roundness and take on the slender, athletic appearance of childhood. As abdominal muscles develop, the toddler potbelly tightens. The trunk, arms, and legs grow longer. The head is still relatively large, but the other parts of the body continue to catch up and body proportions become more adultlike.

The average 3-year-old child will be about 37 to 38 inches tall and between 34 and 35 pounds. Boys have more muscle per pound of body weight, whereas girls have more fatty tissue. Both boys and girls typically grow about 2 to 3 inches a year during early childhood and gain approximately 4 to 6 pounds annually (Table 7.1). Boys have a slight edge in height and weight, which continues until the growth spurt of puberty.

Muscular and skeletal growth progresses, making children stronger. Cartilage turns to bone at a faster rate than before, and bones become harder. These changes, coordinated by the still-maturing brain and nervous system, promote the development of a wide range of motor skills. The increased capacities of the respiratory and circulatory systems build physical stamina and, along with the developing immune system, keep children healthier.

SLEEP PATTERNS AND PROBLEMS

Sleep patterns change throughout the growing-up years (Figure 7.1). Most U.S. children average about 11 hours of sleep at night by age 5 and give up daytime naps (Hoban, 2004). In some other cultures the timing of sleep may vary. Among the Gusii of Kenya, the Javanese in Indonesia, and the Zuni in New Mexico, young children have no regular bedtime and are allowed to stay up until they are sleepy. Among the Canadian Hare, 3-year-olds don't take naps but are put to sleep right after dinner and sleep as long as they wish in the morning (Broude, 1995). And, children from predominantly Asian countries sleep, on average, less than children from predominantly non-Asian countries (Galland, Taylor, Elder & Herbison, 2012).

Estimates are that sleep disorders affect 20 to 30 percent of young children (Bruni & Novelli, 2010). Sleep disturbances may be caused by accidental activation of the brain's

TABLE 7.1 Physical Growth, Ages 3 to 6 (50th percentile*)

	HEIGHT (INCHES)		WEIGHT (POUNDS)	
Age	Boys	Girls	Boys	Girls
3	39.0	36.6	35.3	34.5
4	42.0	41.7	40.8	40.3
5	44.8	44.2	46.6	45.0
6	47.2	46.7	52.8	52.4

*Fifty percent of children in each category are above this height or weight level, and 50 percent are below it.

Source: Fryar, C. D.; Gu, Q.; Ogden, C. L.; & Flegal, K. M. "Anthropometric reference data for children and adults: United States, 2011–2014." *National Center for Health Statistics. Vital Health Stat* 3(39).

FIGURE 7.1
Typical Sleep Requirements in Childhood

Preschoolers get all or almost all their sleep in one long nighttime period. The number of hours of sleep steadily decreases throughout childhood.

Source: Ferber, R. *Solve your child's sleep problems.* New York: Simon & Schuster, 1985.

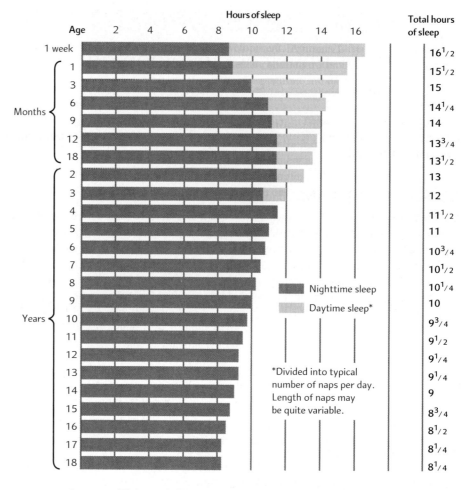

Age	Total hours of sleep
1 week	16¹/₂
1 month	15¹/₂
3 months	15
6 months	14¹/₄
9 months	14
12 months	13³/₄
18 months	13¹/₂
2 years	13
3	12
4	11¹/₂
5	11
6	10³/₄
7	10¹/₂
8	10¹/₄
9	10
10	9³/₄
11	9¹/₂
12	9¹/₄
13	9¹/₄
14	9
15	8³/₄
16	8¹/₂
17	8¹/₄
18	8¹/₄

Legend: Nighttime sleep / Daytime sleep*

*Divided into typical number of naps per day. Length of naps may be quite variable.

motor control system (Hobson & Silvestri, 1999), by incomplete arousal from a deep sleep (Hoban, 2004), or by disordered breathing or restless leg movements (Guilleminault, Palombini, Pelayo & Chervin, 2003). These disturbances tend to run in families (Caylak, 2009) and are associated with separation anxiety (Petit, Touchette, Tremblay, Boivin & Montplaisir, 2007), nasal abnormalities, and overweight (Bixler et al., 2009). In most cases sleep disturbances are occasional and are usually outgrown (Mason & Pack, 2007). (Table 7.2 gives suggestions for helping children sleep.) Persistent sleep problems may indicate an emotional, physiological, or neurological condition that needs to be examined.

A child who experiences *sleep* (or *night*) *terrors* appears to awaken abruptly from a deep sleep in a state of agitation. The child may scream and sit up in bed, staring or thrashing about. Yet he is not really awake, quiets down quickly, and the next morning remembers nothing about the episode. Sleep terrors are common (Petit et al., 2007). They occur mostly between ages 4 and 12 (Mindell & Owens, 2015) and affect boys more often than girls (Nguyen et al., 2008). Walking and talking during sleep are also common in early childhood (Petit et al., 2007). Although sleepwalking itself is harmless, sleepwalkers may be in danger of hurting themselves. It is best not to interrupt sleepwalking or night terrors, as this may confuse or frighten the child (Hoban, 2004).

Nightmares are also common (Petit et al., 2007). The occurrence of nightmares has been related to difficult child temperament, high overall childhood anxiety, and bedtime parenting practices that promote dependency (Moore, 2012). Some studies suggest that overexcitement, perhaps seeing a frightening television show or a video game, is related to nightmares, but results

Nightmares are common in children, and have been related to difficult temperament, anxiety, dependency, and stress.
©Yuliya Evstratenko/Shutterstock

TABLE 7.2 Encouraging Good Sleep Habits

HELPING CHILDREN GO TO SLEEP

- Establish a regular, unrushed bedtime routine of quiet activities, such as reading a story or singing lullabies.
- Allow no scary or loud television shows.
- Avoid highly stimulating, active play before bedtime.
- Keep a small night-light on if it makes the child feel more comfortable.
- Don't feed or rock a child at bedtime.
- Don't yield to requests for "just one more" story, drink of water, or bathroom trip.
- Offer rewards for good bedtime behavior, such as stickers on a chart or simple praise.
- Try sending the child to bed a little later. Sending a child to bed too early may cause sleep problems.

Sources: American Academy of Child and Adolescent Psychiatry (AACAP), 1997; American Academy of Pediatrics (AAP), 1992; L. A. Adams & Rickert, 1989; Graziano & Mooney, 1982.

on this are inconsistent (Schredl, Anders, Hellriegel & Rehm, 2008). Frequent or persistent nightmares may signal excessive stress (Hoban, 2004) and are correlated with emotional, attentional, and conduct problems (Schredl, Frieke-Oerkermann, Mitschke, Wiater & Lehmkuhl, 2009).

Most children stay dry, day and night, by ages 3 to 5, but **enuresis**—repeated, involuntary urination at night by children old enough to be expected to have bladder control—is not unusual. About 10 to 15 percent of 5-year-olds, more commonly boys, wet the bed regularly. More than half outgrow the condition by age 8 without help (Community Paediatrics Committee, 2005). Children (and their parents) need to be reassured that enuresis is common and not serious. The child is not to blame and should not be punished. Enuresis that is particularly persistent is most commonly treated with an antidiuretic hormone or nighttime alarm (Walle, Rittig, Bauer, Eggert, Marschall-Kehrel & Tekgul, 2012).

enuresis
Repeated urination in clothing or in bed.

BRAIN DEVELOPMENT

During the first few years of life, brain development is rapid and profound. At about 5 years of age, the brain is approximately 90 percent of adult size. From ages 3 to 6, the most rapid brain growth occurs in the frontal areas that regulate planning and goal setting. Synapses connecting neighboring neurons continue to form during this time, and the density of synapses in the prefrontal cortex peaks at age 4 (Lenroot & Giedd, 2006). In addition, myelin (a fatty substance that coats the axons of nerve fibers and accelerates neural conduction) continues to form (Giedd & Rapoport, 2010). By age 6, the brain has attained about 95 percent of its peak volume (Giedd et al., 2009). From ages 6 to 11, rapid brain growth occurs in areas that support associative thinking, language, and spatial relations (P. M. Thompson et al., 2000).

The *corpus callosum* is a thick band of nerve fibers that connects both hemispheres of the brain and allows them to communicate more rapidly and effectively with each other (Toga, Thompson, & Sowell, 2006), allowing improved coordination of the senses, attention and arousal, and speech and hearing (Lenroot & Giedd, 2006). The corpus callosum continues to be myelinized throughout childhood and adolescence, with peak volume occurring later in boys than in girls (Luders, Thompson & Toga, 2010).

MOTOR SKILLS

Preschool children make great advances in **gross motor skills** involving the large muscles (Table 7.3). Because their bones and muscles are stronger and their lung capacity is greater, they can run, jump, and climb farther and faster. And, because of the development

gross motor skills
Physical skills that involve the large muscles.

TABLE 7.3 Gross Motor Skills in Early Childhood		
3-Year-Olds	**4-Year-Olds**	**5-Year-Olds**
Cannot turn or stop suddenly or quickly	Have more effective control of stopping, starting, and turning	Can start, turn, and stop effectively
Can jump a distance of 15 to 24 inches	Can jump a distance of 24 to 33 inches	Can make a running jump of 28 to 36 inches
Can ascend a stairway unaided, alternating feet	Can descend a long stairway alternating feet, if supported	Can descend a long stairway unaided, alternating feet
Can hop, using an irregular series of jumps	Can hop four to six steps on one foot	Can easily hop a distance of 16 feet

Source: Corbin, C. *A Textbook of Motor Development.* New York: W. C. Brown Co.; 1973.

of the sensory and motor areas of the cerebral cortex, they are better able to coordinate their motor actions. Children vary in adeptness, depending on their genetic endowment and opportunities to learn and practice motor skills. Physical development flourishes best in active, unstructured free play.

Fine motor skills, such as buttoning shirts and drawing pictures, involve eye-hand and small-muscle coordination. Gains in these skills allow young children to take more responsibility for their personal care.

As they develop motor skills, preschoolers continually merge abilities they already have with those they are acquiring to produce more complex capabilities. Such combinations of skills are known as **systems of action.**

Handedness Handedness, the preference for using one hand over the other, is usually evident by about age 3. Because the left hemisphere of the brain, which controls the right side of the body, is usually dominant, 90 percent of people favor their right side (Coren, 2012). Boys are more likely to be left-handed than are girls (Papadatou-Pastou, Martin, Munafo & Jones, 2008).

Is handedness genetic or learned? Some researchers argue for genetic explanations, citing, for example, high heritability estimates between twins or family members (Medland et al., 2009; Lien, Chen, Hsiao & Tsuang, 2015). Others argue that environmental influences are likely to be key given that such factors as low birth weight, difficult deliveries, and multiples (i.e., twins and triplets) are associated with left-handedness (Alibeik & Angaji, 2010; Vuoksimaa, Koskenvuo, Rose & Kaprio, 2009).

Artistic Development In a landmark study, Rhoda Kellogg (1970) examined more than 1 million drawings by children. She discovered what she believed to be a universal progression of changes, reflecting maturation of the brain as well as of the muscles (Figure 7.2). She found that 2-year-olds *scribble*—not randomly but in patterns, such as vertical and zigzag lines. By age 3, children draw *shapes*—circles, squares, rectangles, triangles, crosses, and Xs—and then begin combining the shapes into more complex *designs*. The *pictorial* stage typically begins between ages 4 and 5. The switch from abstract form and design to depicting real objects marks a fundamental change in the purpose of children's drawing, reflecting the cognitive development of representational ability. In Kellogg's view, the less adults are involved, the better. Kellogg's view that adult intervention has a negative influence on children's drawing, although widely shared by many U.S. educators, is culture-bound. Chinese parents, for example, provide art instruction or models for their children; and Chinese children tend to be more advanced artistically than U.S. children (Braswell, 2006).

As children develop physically, they are better able to make their bodies do what they want. Large-muscle development lets them ride a tricycle or hold securely on to a swing; increasing eye-hand coordination helps them use scissors or chopsticks.
(tricycle): ©Elena Zakh/Shutterstock; (tire swing): ©Ariel Skelley/DigitalVision/Getty Images; (cutting): ©Fertnig/Getty Images

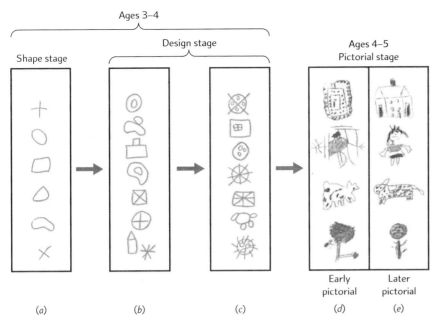

Ages 3–4

Shape stage

Design stage

Ages 4–5
Pictorial stage

Early
pictorial

Later
pictorial

(a)   (b)   (c)   (d)   (e)

(a-e): Source: Rhoda Kellogg, *Analyzing Children's Art.* Mountain View, CA: Mayfield Publishing Co., 1970.

FIGURE 7.2

Artistic Development in Early Childhood

There is a great difference between the very simple shapes shown in (a) and the detailed pictorial drawings in (e).

Health and Safety

Because of widespread immunization, many of what once were the major diseases of childhood are now much less common in Western industrialized countries. In the developing world, however, such vaccine-preventable diseases as measles, pertussis (whooping cough), and tetanus still take a large toll. Even in technologically advanced societies, this is a less healthy time for some children than for others.

PREVENTING OBESITY

Obesity is a serious problem among U.S. preschoolers. In 2011–2014, almost 9 percent of 2- to 5-year-olds had a body mass index (BMI) at or above the 95th percentile for their age; this number was slightly higher in boys than girls. This number was highest in Hispanic children (21.9 percent), followed by African-American (19.5 percent) and white children (14.7 percent), with the lowest obesity rates found in Asian American children (8.6 percent) (Ogden, Carroll, Fryar & Flegal, 2015).

Worldwide, an estimated 41 million children under age 5 were obese in 2015. If current trends continue, 70 million children under age 5 will be overweight or obese by 2025 (World Health Organization, 2017a). While prevalence rates have leveled off in the United States (Ogden et al., 2015), rates continue to rise in developing countries with less income (World Health Organization, 2017a).

A tendency toward obesity can be hereditary, but the main factors driving the obesity epidemic are environmental (AAP, 2004). Excessive weight gain hinges on caloric intake and lack of exercise (Sahoo, Sahoo, Choudhury, Sofi, Kumar & Bhadoria, 2015).

Prevention of obesity in the early years is critical (Quattrin, Liu, Shaw, Shine & Chiang, 2005). Overweight children tend to become obese adults (Singh, Mulder, Twisk, Van Mechelen & Chinapaw, 2008) and excess body mass is a threat to health (Biro & Wein, 2010). Thus early childhood is a good time to treat overweight, when a child's diet is still subject to parental influence or control (Quattrin et al., 2005).

Data suggest that three factors are important in the prevention of obesity: (1) regularly eating an evening meal as a family, (2) getting adequate sleep, and (3) watching less than 2 hours of television a day (Anderson & Whitaker, 2010). Each additional hour of TV above 2 hours increases the likelihood of obesity at age 30 by 7 percent, presumably because each additional hour of television replaces an hour of physical activity (Viner & Cole, 2005).

fine motor skills
Physical skills that involve the small muscles and eye–hand coordination.

systems of action
Increasingly complex combinations of motor skills, which permit a wider or more precise range of movement and more control of the environment.

handedness
Preference for using a particular hand.

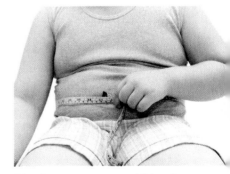

Obesity among young children has increased.
©kwanchai.c/Shutterstock

research in action

FOOD INSECURITY, FOOD DESERTS, AND NUTRIENT DEFICIENCY

Food insecurity occurs when families do not have dependable access to adequate amounts of food to support healthy living. Many American families experience difficulty in supplying sufficient amounts of food due to lack of money or resources. An estimated 15.8 million households in the United States experienced food insecurity during a portion of 2015 (Coleman-Jensen, Rabbit, Gregory & Singh, 2016). Households with very low food security exhibit reduced food intake and disrupted eating patterns, with at least one family member periodically forgoing meals.

About 20 percent of low-income, food-insecure households contain children ages 0 to 5 (Johnson & Markowitz, 2017). When possible, parents attempt to shield young children from disrupted eating and reduced food intake (Coleman-Jensen et al., 2016). When budgets stretch thin, healthy whole grains, lean meats, and fresh vegetables and fruits may be nixed in favor of empty-calorie foods such as highly processed foods and baked goods. Empty calorie foods tend to cost less, but are high in calories and low in nutrients (Drewnowski, 2009). In early childhood, food insecurity and low-quality diet have been linked to vitamin and mineral deficiencies, higher body weight, and reduced cognitive and social-emotional skills (Barroso et al., 2016; Johnson & Markowitz, 2017; Skalicky et al., 2006).

Poor nutrition can also be exacerbated in areas where fresh fruits, vegetables, and other healthful whole foods are not readily available, so called food deserts. Food deserts, typically found in rural and inner city areas, lack geographically accessible supermarkets or grocery stores (Centers for Disease Control and Prevention, 2013a). Instead, food is purchased from convenience stores or fast-food restaurants—each with a preponderance of "junk" food choices. For families on the financial brink, traveling outside of their neighborhood or town to obtain fresh, healthy foods constitutes a time and economic burden (Walker, Keane & Burke, 2010). As a result, families subsist on foods available within their local area. Research shows that children in food deserts have a higher body mass index (Thomsen, Nayga, Alviola & Rouse,

2016) and face greater likelihood of being overweight (Schafft, Jensen & Hinrichs, 2009).

Food accessibility issues uniquely impact young children because of their rapid growth and development. Nutritional deficiency in early childhood has long-lasting consequences for physical growth, brain development, and cognitive and social functioning (Johnson & Markowitz, 2017). It is difficult to estimate the prevalence of certain micronutrient deficiencies because effects do not always show up during routine medical checkups. Estimates suggest that children likely consume inadequate amounts of micronutrients, such as vitamin A, zinc, iron, and iodine (Barrett, 2010). Experts make the specific distinction that children need adequate nutrients, more so than just calories, to support optimal body growth (Lobstein et al., 2015).

Many associate malnutrition with starvation; however, poor nutritional status can also arise through a consistent high-calorie, nutrient-poor diet of "empty foods." This type of diet has been implicated in promoting rapid weight gain during early childhood (Lobstein et al., 2015). For some, excess weight gain leads to onset of childhood obesity. Obese children are likely to stay obese. Recent studies suggest that 55 percent of obese children remain obese in adolescence and around 80 percent of those adolescents become obese adults (Simmonds, Llewellyn, Owen & Woolacott, 2016). Childhood obesity is linked with serious long-term health complications, including greater risk of metabolic syndrome and cardiovascular disease in adulthood (Kelsey, Zaepfel, Bjornstad & Nadeau, 2014). Whether underfed or kept full by low-nutrition foods, either end of the spectrum may lead to problems later in life.

what's
your
view

Federal nutrition programs provide food assistance to low-income children and families. What are the benefits (or drawbacks) of these programs? Are policies or programs useful in alleviating issues related to food deserts or childhood obesity?

UNDERNUTRITION

In 2011, approximately 101 million children were underweight and another 165 million were stunted from lack of adequate nutrients and calories. Undernutrition is an underlying cause in about a third of worldwide deaths for children under 5 (World Health Organization, 2013). South Asia has the highest level of undernutrition; 33 percent of children under age 5 in South Asia are moderately or severely underweight as compared to 22 percent in West and Central Africa, 3 percent in Latin America and the Caribbean, and 15 percent of young children worldwide (UNICEF, 2013a). Even in the United States, 18 percent of children under age 18 lived in food-insecure households in 2015 (Federal Interagency Forum on Child and Family Statistics, 2017). Research in Action has more information about food insecurity.

Because undernourished children usually live in extremely deprived circumstances, the specific effects of poor nutrition are hard to determine. However, taken together, these deprivations may negatively affect not only growth and physical well-being but cognitive and psychosocial development as well (Martorell, Melgar, Maluccio, Stein & Rivera, 2010), and the effects may be long lasting (Liu, Raine, Venables, Dalais, & Mednick, 2003).

Studies suggest effects of undernutrition on growth can be lessened with improved diet (Engle et al., 2007), but the most effective treatments go beyond physical care. For example, a longitudinal study of severely undernourished Jamaican children found that an intervention in which mothers were shown how to make toys and stimulate their children's intellect resulted in significant IQ gains relative to a control group that received only medical care (Grantham-McGregor, Powell, Walker, Chang, & Fletcher, 1994). Similarly, in another study in Mauritia, 3- to 5-year-olds received nutritional supplements and medical examinations and were placed in special preschools with small classes. At age 17, these children had lower rates of antisocial behavior and mental health problems than a control group (Raine, Mellingen, Lui, Venables, & Mednick, 2003).

ALLERGIES

A food allergy is an abnormal immune system response to a specific food. Reactions can range from tingling in the mouth and hives to more serious, life-threatening reactions such as shortness of breath and even death. Ninety percent of food allergies can be attributed to eight foods: milk, eggs, peanuts, tree nuts, fish, soy, wheat, and shellfish (Boyce et al., 2010). Food allergies are more prevalent in children than adults, and most children will outgrow their allergies (Branum & Lukacs, 2008). In 2012, about 6 out of every 100 children suffered from some type of food allergy (Bloom, Jones & Freeman, 2013).

Research on children under age 18 has demonstrated an increase in the prevalence of skin and food allergies over the past 10 years. There is no clear pattern to this increase, and it exists equally for boys and girls and across different races and ethnicities (Branum & Lukacs, 2008; Jackson, Howie & Akinbami, 2013; Figure 7.3). Changes in diet, how foods are processed, and decreased vitamin D based upon less exposure to the sun have all been suggested as contributors to the increase in allergy rates. A theory that society is too clean and that children's immune systems are less mature because they are not exposed to enough dirt and germs has also been explored. Additionally, better awareness by doctors and parents might factor into the reported increases. Although possible explanations abound, not enough evidence exists to pinpoint a cause.

DEATHS AND ACCIDENTAL INJURIES

In 2015, estimates are that approximately 5.9 million children under the age of 5 died worldwide. While large, this number nonetheless represents a 53 percent drop from 1990. Most child deaths are the result of infectious diseases or neonatal complications (You, Hug, Ejdemyr & Beise, 2015). Window on the World discusses children's chances of surviving the first 5 years of life the world over.

In the United States, deaths in childhood are relatively few compared with deaths in adulthood, and accidents are the leading cause of death from the ages of 5 to 12 years (Kochanek, Murphy, Xu & Tejada-Vera, 2016). Most deaths from injuries

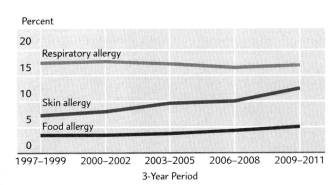

FIGURE 7.3

U.S. Children under Age 18 with a Reported Allergic Condition in Previous 12 Months, 1997–2011

Recent data show that skin and food allergies have increased among children birth to 17 years old.

Source: CDC/NCHS, Health Data Interactive, *National Health Interview Survey.*

wind©w on the world

SURVIVING THE FIRST 5 YEARS OF LIFE

The chances of a child living to his or her 5th birthday have nearly tripled during the past 50 years. Worldwide, more than 17 million children under the age of 5 died in 1970. In 2015, this number dropped to 5.9 million deaths (UNICEF, 2016). Globally the under-5 mortality rate decreased 53 percent from 1990 to 2015 (WHO, 2015).

Causes of deaths among children under 5 years, 2015

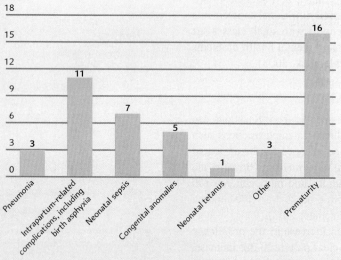

Neonatal (0–27 days)

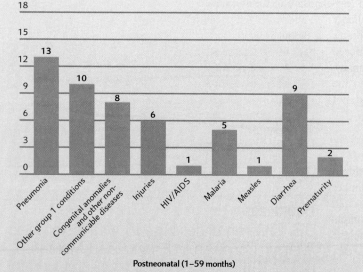

Postneonatal (1–59 months)

Source: Department of Evidence, Information and Research (WHO, Geneva) and Maternal Child Epidemiology Estimation (MCEE), MCEE-WHO methods and data sources for child causes of death 2000-2015. Geneva: World Health Organization, February 2016.

International efforts to improve child health focus on the first 5 years of life because nearly 90 percent of deaths in children under age 15 occur during those years. Worldwide, 70 percent of death in children under the age of 5 is attributed to seven issues: pneumonia, preterm birth complications, intrapartum complications, diarrhea, congenital abnormalities, neonatal sepsis, and malaria. Excluding birth complications, nearly 50 percent of all children's deaths were caused by communicable diseases such as pneumonia, meningitis, tetanus, diarrhea, malaria, measles, sepsis, and AIDS (UNICEF, 2016). Almost all of child deaths (98 percent) occur in the poorest regions of developing countries, where nutrition is inadequate, water is unsafe, and sanitary facilities are lacking (UNICEF, 2015b).

Significant progress was made between 1990 and 2015. East Asia, the Pacific, Latin America, and the Caribbean showed a 66 percent reduction in the under-5 mortality rates. Out of the 196 countries in the world, 62 countries have reduced their under-5 mortality rate by 65 percent or more, and 74 more countries cut their under-5 mortality rate by at least 50 percent. Globally, 70 percent of the countries with available data had at least a 50 percent reduction in under-5 mortality rate (UNICEF, 2016).

In the Latin American region, child deaths dropped 80 percent from 1970 to 1990 and an additional 69 percent since 1990 (Staff, 2016). Haiti still has the highest rate of under-5 mortality in the Western Hemisphere, with a rate of 69 deaths per 1,000 births, although this is a significant decrease from 150 deaths per 1,000 births in 1990 (UNICEF, 2016).

The risk of a child dying by age 5 is still the highest in the sub-Saharan Africa and Southern Asian regions, which account for 81 percent of deaths in 2015 (WHO, 2015). Though significant progress has been made, six of the seven countries with under-5 mortality rates over 100 are African countries. In 2015, Angola had the highest rate of under 5 deaths worldwide at 157 deaths per 1,000 births and Somalia was the second highest with 137 deaths per 1,000 births (UNICEF, 2016)

A global effort is being made to reduce child mortality rates. With the increase of health care and home care for children around the world, great strides are being made. The biggest focus is on improved family care, nutrition supplementation, and breast-feeding practices. These approaches are accompanied by interventions for maternal health, including skilled care during pregnancy and childbirth. Other successful programs focus on vaccinations, antibiotics, and insecticide-treated bed nets (UNICEF, 2015b).

what's your view

Though progress has been made, 5.9 million children died in 2015; it is still too many. What else do you think could help to combat child mortality around the world? What are the responsibilities of individual countries to help decrease child mortality worldwide?

among preschoolers occur in the home—often from fires, drowning in bathtubs, suffocation, poisoning, or falls (Nagaraja et al., 2005). Everyday medications, such as aspirin, acetaminophen, and cough medicine, and even vitamins can be dangerous to inquisitive young children.

U.S. laws requiring the use of car seats, childproof caps on medicine bottles and other dangerous household products, regulation of product safety, mandatory helmets for bicycle riders, and safe storage of medicines have improved child safety.

HEALTH IN CONTEXT: ENVIRONMENTAL INFLUENCES

Why do some children have more illnesses or injuries than others? Some children seem genetically predisposed toward certain medical conditions. In addition, environmental factors play major roles.

Socioeconomic Status and Race/Ethnicity The lower a family's SES, the greater a child's risks of illness, injury, and death (Braveman, Cubbin, Egerter, Williams & Pamuk, 2010; Olson, Diekema, Elliot & Renier, 2010). Poor children are more likely than other children to have chronic conditions and activity limitations, to lack health insurance, and to have unmet medical and dental needs.

Medicaid, a government program that provides medical assistance to eligible low-income persons and families, has been a safety net for many poor children since 1965. However, it had not reached millions of children whose families earned too much to qualify but too little to afford private insurance. In 1993, 14 percent of children did not have health insurance (Federal Interagency Forum on Child and Family Statistics, 2017). In 1997 the federal government created the State Children's Health Insurance Program (SCHIP) to help states extend health care coverage to uninsured children in poor and near-poor families. Legislation passed in 2009 expanded the program and extended the coverage from 7 million to 11 million children (Centers for Medicare & Medicaid Services, 2009). Even with that expansion, there were about 9 million uninsured children in the United States (Devoe, Ray, Krois, & Carlson, 2010). The passage of the Affordable Care Act of 2010 reduced this number. Among the provisions were the expansion of benefits to many previously ineligible poor families, elimination of preexisting condition coverage exclusions, oral and vision coverage for children, and initiatives to prevent and address childhood obesity. In 2015, the number of uninsured children dropped to 4.5 percent (Federal Interagency Forum on Child and Family Statistics, 2017). This number will change if the Affordable Care Act is repealed without a suitable replacement.

Access to quality health care is a particular problem among black and Latino children, especially those who are poor (Flores, 2010). According to the Children's Defense Fund (2014), 1 in 7 Latino children and 1 in 11 black children are uninsured compared with a rate of 1 in 15 for white children. Language and cultural barriers and the need for more Latino care providers may help explain some of these disparities (Betancourt, Green, Carillo & Owusu Ananeh-Firempong, 2016). Even Asian American children, who tend to be in better health than non-Hispanic white children, are less likely to access and use health care, perhaps because of similar barriers (NCHS, 2005; Yu, Huang, & Singh, 2004).

Families with children are the fastest-growing part of the homeless population. Homeless children tend to have more health problems than children with homes.
©Tony Freeman/PhotoEdit

Homelessness Homelessness results from circumstances that force people to choose between food, shelter, and other basic needs. Factors that contribute to homelessness include lack of employment opportunities, declines in public assistance funds, lack of affordable health care, domestic violence, mental illness, and addiction (National Coalition for the Homeless, 2017). In 2011, there were an estimated 1.6 million homeless children in the United States (Bassuk, Murphy, Coupe, Kenney & Beach, 2011).

Families now make up 36 percent of the homeless population on any given night, and the proportion is higher in rural areas (Henry, Cortes & Morris, 2013). In fact, with the economic downturn in the late 2000s, the number of homeless children has increased to about 1 in every 45 children (America's Youngest Outcasts, 2011). Many homeless families are headed by single mothers in their twenties (Park, Metraux, & Culhane, 2010).

Many homeless children spend their early years in unstable, insecure, and often unsanitary environments. They may be cut off from ready access to medical care and schooling. These children suffer more physical health problems than poor children who have homes, and they are more likely to have a low birth weight or need neonatal care in infancy. Homeless children also tend to suffer from depression and anxiety and to have academic and behavior problems (Hwang et al., 2010; Bassuk, Richard & Tsertsvadze, 2015; Herbers et al., 2012; Richards, Merrill & Baksh, 2011). More research is needed on evidence-based interventions to tackle the multitude of risk factors that homeless children are exposed to (Zlotnick, Tam & Zerger, 2012).

Exposure to Smoking, Air Pollution, Pesticides, and Lead Parental smoking is a preventable cause of childhood illness and death. The potential damage caused by exposure to tobacco is greatest during the early years of life (DiFranza et al., 2004). Children exposed to parental smoke are at increased risk of respiratory infections such as bronchitis and pneumonia, ear problems, worsened asthma, and slowed lung growth. In 1988 to 1994, approximately 85 percent of children between the ages of 4 and 11 years showed evidence of exposure to second-hand smoke. In 2011 to 2012, this number dropped to 40 percent (Federal Interagency Forum on Child and Family Statistics, 2017).

Air pollution is associated with increased risks of death and of chronic respiratory disease. Environmental contaminants also may play a role in certain childhood cancers, neurological disorders, attention-deficit/hyperactivity disorder, and mental retardation (Goldman et al., 2004; Woodruff et al., 2004). In 2015, 59 percent of U.S. children up to age 17 lived in counties that failed to meet one or more national air quality standards (Federal Interagency Forum on Child and Family Statistics, 2017).

Children are more vulnerable than adults to chronic pesticide damage (Federal Interagency Forum on Child and Family Statistics, 2017). There is some evidence that pesticide exposure may negatively affect the developing brain (Jurewicz & Hanke, 2008). Pesticide exposure is greater among children in agricultural and inner-city families (Dilworth-Bart & Moore, 2006).

Children can get elevated concentrations of lead from contaminated food or water, from airborne industrial wastes, or from inhaling dust or playing with paint chips in places where there is peeling lead-based paint. Lead poisoning can interfere with cognitive development and can lead to irreversible neurological and behavioral problems (AAP Committee on Environmental Health, 2005; Federal Interagency Forum on Child and Family Statistics, 2017). Very high levels of blood lead concentration may cause headaches, abdominal pain, loss of appetite, agitation, or lethargy and eventually vomiting, stupor, and convulsions (AAP Committee on Environmental Health, 2005).

Children's median blood lead levels have dropped by 89 percent in the United States compared to 1976–1980 levels due to laws mandating removal of lead from gasoline and paints and reducing smokestack emissions (Federal Interagency Forum for Child and Family Statistics, 2005). From 1988 to 1994, approximately 26 percent of children had elevated lead levels in their blood. In 2011 to 2014, this number dropped to 1 percent (Federal Interagency Forum on Child and Family Statistics, 2017).

COGNITIVE DEVELOPMENT

Piagetian Approach: The Preoperational Child

In this chapter we turn our attention to Piaget's second stage, the **preoperational stage.** Lasting from approximately ages 2 to 7, it is characterized by an expansion in symbolic thought. This is most clearly illustrated with the advent of our most profound system of symbolic representation—language. Despite their increasing facility with language, children are not yet ready to engage in logical mental operations. Let's look at some advances and some immature aspects of preoperational thought (Tables 7.4 and 7.5) and at recent research, some of which challenges Piaget's conclusions.

preoperational stage
In Piaget's theory, the second major stage of cognitive development, in which symbolic thought expands but children cannot yet use logic.

ADVANCES OF PREOPERATIONAL THOUGHT

Advances in symbolic thought are accompanied by a growing understanding of space, causality, identities, categorization, and number. Some of these understandings have roots in infancy and toddlerhood; others begin to develop in early childhood but are not fully achieved until middle childhood.

The Symbolic Function "I want ice cream!" announces Gemma, age 4, trudging indoors from the hot, dusty backyard. She has not seen or smelled or tasted anything that triggered this desire. Rather, she has called up the concept from her memories.

Being able to think about something in the absence of sensory or motor cues characterizes the **symbolic function.** Children who have attained symbolic function can use symbols, or mental representations, such as words, numbers, or images to which a person has attached meaning. This is a vital achievement because without symbols people could not communicate verbally, make change, read maps, or treasure photos of distant loved ones. Having symbols for things helps children remember and think about them without having them physically present.

symbolic function
Piaget's term for ability to use mental representations (words, numbers, or images) to which a child has attached meaning.

TABLE 7.4 Cognitive Advances during Early Childhood

Advance	Significance	Example
Use of symbols	Children do not need to be in sensorimotor contact with something in order to think about it.	Simon asks his mother about the elephants they saw on their trip to the circus several months earlier.
	Children can imagine that things are something different than they are.	Rolf pretends that a slice of apple is a vacuum cleaner "vrooming" across the kitchen table.
Understanding of identities	Children are aware that superficial alterations do not change the nature of things.	Antonio knows that his teacher is dressed up as a pirate but is still his teacher underneath the costume.
Understanding of cause and effect	Children realize that events have causes.	Seeing a ball roll from behind a wall, Aneko looks behind the wall for the person who kicked the ball.
Ability to classify	Children organize objects, people, and events into meaningful categories.	Rosa sorts the pinecones she collected on a nature walk into two piles: "big" and "little."
Understanding of number	Children can count and deal with quantities.	Lindsay shares some candy with her friends, counting to make sure that each girl gets the same amount.
Empathy	Children become more able to imagine how others might feel.	Emilio tries to comfort his friend when he sees that his friend is upset.
Theory of mind	Children become more aware of the mental activity of others.	Blanca wants to save some cookies for herself, so she hides them from her brother in a pasta box. She knows her brother will not look in a place where he doesn't expect to find cookies.

TABLE 7.5 Immature Aspects of Preoperational Thought (According to Piaget)

Limitation	Description	Example
Centration: inability to decenter	Children focus on one aspect of a situation and neglect others.	Jacob thinks he has more juice than his sister because his juice box has been poured into a tall, skinny glass, but her equal sized box has been poured into a short, wide glass.
Irreversibility	Children fail to understand that actions can be reversed, restoring the original situation.	Jacob does not realize that the juice in each glass can be poured back into the juice box, contradicting his claim that he has more than his sister.
Focus on states rather than transformations	Children fail to understand the significance of the transformation between states.	Jacob does not understand that transforming the shape of a liquid (pouring it from one container into another) does not change the amount.
Transductive reasoning	Children do not use deductive or inductive reasoning; instead they see cause where none exists.	Luis was mean to his sister. Then she got sick. Luis concludes that he made his sister sick.
Egocentrism	Children assume everyone else thinks, perceives, and feels as they do.	Kara doesn't realize that she needs to turn a book around so that her father can see the picture she is asking him to explain. Instead, she holds the book where only she can see it.
Animism	Children attribute life to objects not alive.	Amanda says that spring is trying to come but winter is saying, "I won't go! I won't go!"
Inability to distinguish appearance from reality	Children confuse what is real with outward appearance.	Courtney is confused by a sponge made to look like a rock. She states that it looks like a rock and it really is a rock.

pretend play
Play involving imaginary people and situations; also called *fantasy play*, *dramatic play*, or *imaginative play*.

transduction
Piaget's term for a preoperational child's tendency to mentally link particular phenomena, whether or not there is logically a causal relationship.

Deferred imitation, in which children imitate an action at some point after having observed it, is related to symbolic function because it requires the child to have kept a mental representation of that action. Deferred imitation becomes more robust after 18 months (Barr, Dowden & Hayne, 1996). Another marker of symbolic function is **pretend play.** In pretend play, also called *fantasy play, dramatic play,* or *imaginary play,* children use an object to represent something else. For example, a child may hold up a remote control to her ear while pretending to talk on a telephone. By far the most extensive use of the symbolic function is language. Language, at its heart, is a system of symbols. For example, the word "key" is a symbol for the class of objects used to open doors. When we see the emergence of language in young children, we have a wide and clear window into their increasing use of the symbolic function.

Understanding of Objects in Space In addition to their growing ability to use the symbolic function, children also slowly begin to be able to understand the symbols that describe physical spaces. It is not until at least age 3 that most children reliably grasp the relationships between pictures, maps, or scale models and the objects or spaces they represent. So, for example, older preschoolers can view a scale model of a room, be shown on that model where a toy is hidden, and then find the toy in the actual room. They can transfer the spatial understanding gained from working with models to the real world and vice versa (DeLoache, 2011).

Understanding of Causality Piaget maintained that preoperational children cannot yet reason logically about cause and effect. Instead, he said, they reason by **transduction.** They mentally link two events, especially events close in time, whether or not there is logically a causal relationship. For example, Luis may think that his "bad" behavior caused his parents' divorce.

Piaget was incorrect in believing that young children could not understand causality. When tested in situations that are appropriate to their overall level of cognitive development, young children do grasp cause and effect. For example, in one study, children were shown two small and one large lights. Pressing on one of the small lights, which was attached to the large light by a wire, caused the large light to illuminate. Four-year-old children were able to understand that a relevant change (switching the wire connection to the other small light) would alter the causal sequence, but an irrelevant change (moving a block near the light) would not (Buchanan & Sobel, 2011). Similarly, naturalistic observations of 2½- to 5-year-olds' everyday language showed flexible causal reasoning. Children listed both physical ("The scissors have to be clean so I can cut better") and social-conventional ("I have to stop now because you said to") causes for their actions (Hickling & Wellman, 2001).

Understanding of Identities and Categorization Preschool children also develop a better understanding of *identities:* the concept that people and many things are fundamentally the same even if they change in outward form, size, or appearance. For example, putting on a wig does not make a person a different person; rather, it is just a surface change in appearance. This understanding underlies the emerging self-concept, and many of the processes involved in understanding the identity of others are mirrored in the understanding of one's own identity.

Categorization, or classification, requires a child to identify similarities and differences. By age 4, many children can classify by two criteria, such as color and shape. Children use this ability to order many aspects of their lives, categorizing people as "good," "bad," "nice," "mean," and so forth.

One type of categorization is the ability to distinguish living from nonliving things. When Piaget asked young children whether the wind and the clouds were alive, their answers led him to think they were confused. The tendency to attribute life to objects that are not alive is called **animism.** However, when later researchers questioned 3- and 4-year-olds about something more familiar to them—differences between a rock, a person, and a doll—the children showed they understood that people are alive and rocks and dolls are not (Gelman, Spelke, & Meck, 1983; Jipson & Gelman, 2007). In general, it appears that children attribute animism to items that share characteristics with living things: things that move, make sounds, or have lifelike features such as eyes (Opfer & Gelman, 2011).

Understanding of Number Multiple lines of research have shown that by the age of 4½ months, infants have a rudimentary concept of number. They seem to know that if one doll is added to another doll, there should be two dolls, not just one (Wynn, 1992a). By 6 months of age, they can "count" higher and know that 8 dots are different from 16 dots (Libertus & Brannon, 2010). Other research has found that *ordinality*—the concept of comparing quantities (*more* or *less, bigger* or *smaller*)—seems to begin at around 9 to 11 months (Suanda, Tompson & Brannon, 2008). The *cardinality* principle, where children understand that the number of items in a set is the same regardless of how they are arranged, and that the last number counted is the total number of items in the set, starts to develop at about 2½ years of age. However, this ability is based in practical situations, such as checking to see which one of two plates has more cookies in it (Gelman, 2006). Not until age 3½ or older do most children consistently apply the cardinality principle in counting (Sarnecka & Carey, 2007; Wynn, 1990). That is, when asked to count six items, children at about 3½ are able to recite the number-names (for example, one through six) and are then able to say how many items there are altogether (six). By age 4, most children have added words for comparing quantities. They can say that one tree is *bigger* than another or one cup holds *more* juice than another. They also can solve simple numerical ordinality problems ("Megan picked six apples, and Joshua picked four apples; which child picked more?") (Byrnes & Fox, 1998). By age 5, most children can count to 20 or more and know the relative sizes of the numbers 1 through 10 (Siegler, 1998).

Children intuitively devise strategies for adding by counting on their fingers or by using other objects (Naito & Miura, 2001). By the time they enter elementary school, most children have developed basic *number sense* (Jordan, Kaplan, Oláh, & Locuniak, 2006). This basic level of number skills includes *counting, number knowledge* (ordinality), *number transformations* (simple addition and subtraction), *estimation* ("Is this group of dots more or less than 5?"), and recognition of *number patterns* (2 plus 2 equals 4, and so does 3 plus 1).

As this girl pretends to listen to the bear's heart, she is showing deferred imitation, the ability to act out a behavior she observed some time before. ©Duplass/Shutterstock

animism
Tendency to attribute life to objects that are not alive.

FIGURE 7.4

Piaget's Three-Mountain Task

A preoperational child is unable to describe the mountains from the doll's point of view—an indication of egocentrism, according to Piaget.

centration
In Piaget's theory, the tendency of preoperational children to focus on one aspect of a situation and neglect others.

decenter
In Piaget's terminology, to think simultaneously about several aspects of a situation.

egocentrism
Piaget's term for inability to consider another person's point of view; a characteristic of young children's thought.

conservation
Piaget's term for awareness that two objects that are equal according to a certain measure remain equal in the face of perceptual alteration so long as nothing has been added to or taken away from either object.

irreversibility
Piaget's term for a preoperational child's failure to understand that an operation can go in two or more directions.

SES and preschool experience affect how rapidly children advance in math. By age 4, children from middle-income families have markedly better number skills than low-SES children, and their initial advantage tends to continue. Children whose preschool teachers do a lot of "math talk" (such as asking children to help count days on a calendar) tend to make greater gains (Klibanoff, Levine, Huttenlocher, Vasilyeva, & Hedges, 2006). Also, playing number board games with children enhances their numerical knowledge and can help low-income children catch up to their middle-income peers (Siegler, 2009). Numerical competence is important; how well children understand numbers in kindergarten predicts their academic performance in math through 3rd grade (Jordan, Kaplan, Raminemi, & Locuniak, 2009).

IMMATURE ASPECTS OF PREOPERATIONAL THOUGHT

One of the main characteristics of preoperational thought is **centration:** the tendency to focus on one aspect of a situation and neglect others. According to Piaget, preschoolers come to illogical conclusions because they cannot **decenter**—think about several aspects of a situation at one time.

Egocentrism **Egocentrism** is a form of centration. According to Piaget, young children center so much on their own point of view that they cannot take in another's. When 3-year-old Luis believes that his "bad thoughts" have made his sister sick, he is thinking egocentrically.

To study egocentrism, Piaget designed the *three-mountain task* (Figure 7.4). A child sits facing a table that holds three large mounds. A doll is placed on a chair at the opposite side of the table. The investigator asks the child how the "mountains" would look to the doll. Piaget found that young children could only describe the mountains from their own perspective. Piaget saw this as evidence that preoperational children cannot imagine a different point of view (Piaget & Inhelder, 1967).

However, posing the problem in a different way can yield different results. In one study, a child was given instructions to select one object from a set by an experimenter who could only see some of the objects. The researchers found that children as young as 3 were able to take the experimenter's perspective. For example, two of the objects were rubber ducks. In one condition, the experimenter could see only one of the rubber ducks. When the child heard the instructions to retrieve the rubber duck, the child more often selected the rubber duck that the experimenter could see even though the child could see both (Nilsen & Graham, 2009). When the question was posed in a familiar, less abstract way, children were able to take others' perspectives.

Conservation Another classic example of centration is the failure to understand **conservation,** the fact that two things that are equal remain so if their appearance is altered, as long as nothing is added or taken away. Piaget found that children do not fully grasp this principle until the stage of concrete operations and that they develop different kinds of conservation at different ages. Table 7.6 shows how various dimensions of conservation have been tested.

In one type of conservation task, conservation of liquid, 5-year-old Justin is shown two identical clear glasses, each short and wide and each holding the same amount of water. Justin is asked, "Is the amount of water in the two glasses equal?" When he agrees, the researcher pours the water in one glass into a third glass, a tall, thin one. Justin is now asked, "Do both glasses contain the same amount of water? Or does one contain more? Why?" In early childhood—even after watching the water being poured or even after pouring it himself—Justin will say that either the taller glass or the wider one contains more water.

Why do children make this error? Their responses are influenced by two immature aspects of thought: centration and **irreversibility.** Centration involves focusing on one dimension while ignoring the other. Preoperational children cannot consider height and width at the same time as they cannot *decenter,* or consider multiple attributes of an object or situation. In addition, children are limited by irreversibility: failure to mentally reverse an action. Because their thinking is concrete, preoperational children cannot realize that the original state of the water can be restored by pouring it back into the

TABLE 7.6 Tests of Various Kinds of Conservation

Conservation Task	What Child Is Shown*	Transformation	Question for Child	Preoperational Child's Usual Answers
Number	Two equal, parallel rows of candies	Space the candies in one row farther apart.	"Are there the same number of candies in each row or does one row have more?"	"The longer one has more."
Length	Two parallel sticks of the same length	Move one stick to the right.	"Are both sticks the same size or is one longer?"	"The one on the right (or left) is longer."
Liquid	Two identical glasses holding equal amounts of liquid	Pour liquid from one glass into a taller, narrower glass.	"Do both glasses have the same amount of liquid or does one have more?"	"The taller one has more."
Matter (mass)	Two balls of clay of the same size	Roll one ball into a sausage shape.	"Do both pieces have the same amount of clay or does one have more?"	"The sausage has more."
Weight	Two balls of clay of the same weight	Roll one ball into a sausage shape.	"Do both weigh the same or does one weigh more?"	"The sausage weighs more."
Area	Two toy rabbits, two pieces of cardboard (representing grassy fields), with blocks or toys (representing barns on the fields); same number of "barns" on each board	Rearrange the blocks on one piece of board.	"Does each rabbit have the same amount of grass to eat or does one have more?"	"The one with the blocks close together has more to eat."
Volume	Two glasses of water with two equal-sized balls of clay in them	Roll one ball into a sausage shape.	"If we put the sausage back in the glass, will the water be the same height in each glass, or will one be higher?"	"The water in the glass with the sausage will be higher."

*Child then acknowledges that both items are equal.

other glass, and thus it must be the same. Preoperational children commonly think as if they were watching a slide show with a series of static frames: They *focus on successive states,* said Piaget, and do not recognize the transformation from one state to another.

DO YOUNG CHILDREN HAVE THEORIES OF MIND?

Theory of mind is the awareness of the broad range of human mental states—beliefs, intents, desires, dreams, and so forth—and the understanding that others have their own distinctive beliefs, desires, and intentions. Having a theory of mind allows us to understand and predict the behavior of others and makes the social world understandable.

Piaget (1929) asked children such questions as "Where do dreams come from?" and "What do you think with?" On the basis of the answers, he concluded that children younger than 6 cannot distinguish between thoughts or dreams and real physical entities and have no theory of mind. However, more recent research indicates that between ages 2 and 5, children's knowledge about mental processes and their ability to distinguish between mental states and reality grows dramatically. For example, at 2 years of age children readily engage in pretend play. At 3 years of age they can use deception in

theory of mind
Awareness and understanding of mental processes.

simple games and predict others' actions on the basis of their desires. And at 4 to 5 years of age they understand that a person can believe something that they themselves know is not true (Frye, 2014). Let's take a closer look at theory of mind.

Knowledge about Thinking and Mental States Between ages 3 and 5, children come to understand that thinking goes on inside the mind; that it can deal with either real or imaginary things, and that thinking is different from seeing, talking, touching, and knowing (Flavell, 2000). They understand that thinking about the past or the future might make someone feel sad or happy (Lagattuta, 2014). They start to expect people to act in accordance with their beliefs, and when asked to explain people's behavior they use words like "want" or "think." They also know that people's expressions might not necessarily match their internal state (Wellman, 2014) and realize that you can manipulate others' mental states to deceive or tease them (Miller, 2009).

However, preschoolers generally believe that mental activity starts and stops. Preschoolers also have little or no awareness that they or other people think in words, or "talk to themselves in their heads" (Flavell, Green, Flavell, & Grossman, 1997). It is not until a few years later that they understand that they can be wrong about what someone else thinks (Miller, 2009) and that the mind is continuously active (Flavell, 2000). And they do not fully realize that they cannot control their dreams until about 11 years of age (Woolley & Boerger, 2002).

The recognition that others have mental states accompanies the decline of egocentrism and the development of empathy (Povinelli & Giambrone, 2001). In the following sections, we will look more closely at some of the abilities related to the understanding of mental states.

False Beliefs and Deception The understanding that people can hold false beliefs flows from the realization that people can hold incorrect mental representations of reality. For example, if you see your mother searching for an umbrella, but you know it's not raining outside, you can understand that she *thinks* it's raining, even if it is not. This ability is generally tested with what is called a false belief task. Although infants as young as 13 months can illustrate some understanding of the mental states of others if asked in an appropriate manner (Scott & Baillargeon, 2009), it is not until about 4 years of age that children consistently pass false belief tasks (Baillargeon, Scott & He, 2010). And, it is not until 5 to 6 years of age that children understand second-order false beliefs—that they may have an incorrect belief about what someone else believes (Miller, 2009).

Three-year-olds' failure to recognize false beliefs may stem from a variety of different processes. Piagetian researchers have suggested it stems from egocentric thinking (Lillard & Curenton, 1999). Other researchers have pointed to general processing mechanisms and predictive abilities (Berthiaume, Shultz & Onishi, 2013). Other researchers have argued that reasoning about false beliefs is likely to be a highly specialized skill with separate processing capabilities (Leslie, Friedman & German, 2004).

There are links between the ability to pass false belief tasks and language (Low, 2010) and attentional and inhibitory processes (Leslie, Friedman & German, 2004). Culturally diverse research has revealed a consistent association between executive functioning ability and theory of mind (Devine & Hughes, 2014). As somewhat different areas of the brain are active during different types of false belief tasks (Schurz, Aichhorn, Martin & Perner, 2013), it may be that a variety of different processes underlie children's developing abilities in this area.

Deception is an effort to plant a false belief in someone else's mind. Not surprisingly, performance on the false belief task has been repeatedly shown to predict the ability to lie (Talwar & Lee, 2008; Bigelow & Dugas, 2009; Russell, Mauthner, Sharpe & Tidswell, 1991). Thus, while most people do not view the ability to lie as a positive trait, it is nonetheless a developmental milestone illustrative of advances.

Generally children become capable of telling simple lies, such as denying looking at a hidden toy they were instructed to avoid, at about 3 years of age. However, when asked follow-up questions to their lie that if answered would reveal their deception, such as what kind of toy it was, young children fail to hide their knowledge (Evans & Lee, 2013). It is not until almost 8 years of age that children become better able to think about what they should and should not know, and thus conceal their transgressions more effectively (Talwar & Lee, 2002). Furthermore, as children age and become more aware of social conventions as well as others' feelings, they become more likely to lie out of politeness or a desire to avoid hurting others' feelings. For example, they are more likely to tell an experimenter that they liked an unattractive gift when in reality they did not (Xu, Bao, Fu, Talwar & Lee, 2010).

Distinguishing between Appearance and Reality According to Piaget, not until about age 5 or 6 do children begin to understand the distinction between what *seems* to be and what *is*. Initial research seemed to support this view; however, more recent studies have found this ability emerging between 3 and 4 years of age.

In one classic series of experiments (Flavell, Green, & Flavell, 1986), 3-year-olds seemed to confuse appearance and reality in a variety of tests. For example, when the children put on special sunglasses that made milk look green, they said the milk *was* green. Similarly, 3-year-olds thought that a sponge that looked like a rock was a rock, even after being shown the sponge in use (Flavell, Flavell & Green, 1983).

Later research showed that 3-year-old children could answer questions about reality and appearance correctly under certain circumstances. For example, when children were asked questions about how to use a sponge that looked like a rock, they answered incorrectly. However, when the experimenter indicated a sponge was needed to clean up some spilled water, the children were able to hand over the correct item (Sapp, Lee & Muir, 2000). Later research showed that if children were presented with two objects, such as an eraser that looked like a chocolate bar and a real chocolate bar, and asked to hand an experimenter "the real one" they were able to select the correct item (Moll & Tomasello, 2012). Similarly, 3-year-old children were able to understand that an adult looking through a yellow screen at a blue object saw it as green, as evidenced by correctly selecting the blue toy after being asked "can you put the green one in the bag for me?" (Moll & Meltzoff, 2011). It may be that children do understand the difference between appearance and reality, but have difficulty displaying their knowledge in traditional tasks that require verbal responses. When you ask them to display their knowledge via their actions, they are better able to do so.

Influences on Individual Differences in Theory-of-Mind Development Some children develop theory-of-mind abilities earlier than others. In part, this development reflects brain maturation and general improvements in cognition. What other influences explain these individual differences?

Infant social attention has been closely linked to theory-of-mind development (Wellman & Liu, 2004). Several lines of research show that infants who are better at paying attention to others as infants show more facility with theory-of-mind tasks at 4 years of age (Wellman, Lopez-Duran, LaBounty, & Hamilton, 2008; Aschersleben, Hofer & Jovanovic, 2008). Social competence also matters and contributes to an understanding of thoughts and emotions (Cassidy, Werner, Rourke, Zubernis, & Balaraman, 2003). Children whose teachers and peers rate them high on social skills are better able to recognize false beliefs, to distinguish between real and pretend emotion, and to take another person's point of view. (Cassidy et al., 2003; Watson, Nixon, Wilson, & Capage, 1999). Findings such as these suggest continuity in social cognition and that skills build on each other over time.

The kind of talk a young child hears at home may affect the child's understanding of mental states. A mother's reference to others' thoughts and knowledge is a consistent predictor of a child's later mental state language (Dunn, 1991, 2006). Being bilingual may also help. Bilingual children do somewhat better on certain theory-of-mind tasks (Kovacs, 2009). Bilingual children know that an object or idea can be represented linguistically in more than one way, and this may help them see that different people may have different perspectives. Bilingual children also recognize the need to match their language to that of their partner, making them more aware of others' mental states (Bialystok & Senman, 2004; Goetz, 2003).

Families that encourage pretend play stimulate the development of theory-of-mind skills. As children play roles, they assume others' perspectives. Talking with children

Is Mickey Mouse real? The ability to distinguish fantasy from reality develops by age 3, but 4- to 6-year-olds may enjoy pretending a character is real nonetheless.
©Broadimage/REX/Shutterstock

about how the characters in a story feel helps them develop social understanding (Lillard & Curenton, 1999). Theory of mind has been positively related to reading storybooks, perhaps because parents and children often discuss characters and their desires, beliefs or emotions (Mar, Tackett & Moore, 2010).

Brain development is also necessary for theory of mind. In particular, neural activity in the prefrontal cortex has been identified as important. In one study, children who were able to correctly reason about the mental states of characters in animated scenarios showed brain wave activation in their left frontal cortex, much as the adults in the study did. However, those children who were not able to correctly pass the task did not (Liu, Sabbagh, Gehring, & Wellman, 2009).

An incomplete or ineffective theory of mind may be a sign of a cognitive or developmental impairment. Individuals with this type of impairment have difficulty determining the intentions of others, lack understanding of how their behavior affects others, and have a difficult time with social reciprocity. Research suggests that children with autism are deficient in theory of mind, and that this is a core feature of autism (Baron-Cohen, Leslie, & Frith, 1985).

Information-Processing Approach: Memory Development

During early childhood, thinking improves in attention, speed, efficiency, and long-term memory. However, some aspects are still immature.

BASIC PROCESSES AND CAPACITIES

Information-processing theorists focus on the processes that affect cognition. According to this view, memory can be described as a filing system that has three steps, or processes: *encoding, storage,* and *retrieval.* **Encoding** is like putting information in a folder to be filed in memory; it attaches a "code" to the information so it will be easier to find when needed. For example, if you were asked to list "things that are red," you might list apples, stop signs, and hearts. Presumably, all these items were tagged in memory with the concept "red" when they were originally encoded. **Storage** is putting the folder away in the filing cabinet. It is where the information is kept. When the information is needed, you access storage, and through the process of **retrieval,** you search for the file and take it out.

The way the brain stores information is believed to be universal (Siegler, 1998). Information-processing models depict the brain as containing three types of storage: *sensory memory, working memory,* and *long-term memory.* **Sensory memory** is a temporary storehouse for incoming sensory information. For example, the light trail that is visible when a sparkler is moved quickly on a dark night illustrates visual sensory memory. Sensory memory shows little change from infancy on (Siegler, 1998). However, without processing (encoding), sensory memories fade quickly.

Information being encoded or retrieved is kept in **working memory,** a short-term storehouse for information a person is actively working on, trying to understand, remember, or think about. Brain imaging studies have found that working memory is located partly in the prefrontal cortex (Nelson et al., 2000). Working memory has a limited capacity. Researchers can assess the capacity of working memory by asking children to recall a series of scrambled digits (for example, 2-8-3-7-5-1 if they heard 1-5-7-3-8-2). The capacity of working memory—the number of digits a child can recall—increases rapidly. At age 4, children typically remember only two digits; at 12 they typically remember six (Zelazo, Müller, Frye, & Marcovitch, 2003). The growth of working memory may permit the development of **executive function,** the conscious control of thoughts, emotions, and actions to accomplish goals or to solve problems (McCabe, Roediger, McDaniel, Balota & Hambrick, 2010). Executive function enables children to plan and carry out goal-directed mental activity (Zelazo & Carlson, 2012). It probably emerges around the end of an infant's 1st year and develops in spurts with age.

Long-term memory is a storehouse of virtually unlimited capacity that holds information for long periods of time. This information is transferred from working memory if it is deemed

encoding
Process by which information is prepared for long-term storage and later retrieval.

storage
Retention of information in memory for future use.

retrieval
Process by which information is accessed or recalled from memory storage.

sensory memory
Initial, brief, temporary storage of sensory information.

working memory
Short-term storage of information being actively processed.

executive function
Conscious control of thoughts, emotions, and actions to accomplish goals or solve problems.

long-term memory
Storage of virtually unlimited capacity that holds information for long periods.

important enough. But who decides its importance? According to a widely used model, a **central executive** controls processing operations in working memory (Baddeley, 1998, 2001). The central executive orders information encoded for transfer to long-term memory, retrieves information from long-term memory for further processing, and can temporarily expand the capacity of working memory by moving information into two separate subsidiary systems while the central executive is occupied with other tasks. One of these subsidiary systems holds verbal information (as in the digit task), and the other holds visual-spatial images.

central executive
In Baddeley's model, element of working memory that controls the processing of information.

RECOGNITION AND RECALL

Recognition and *recall* are types of retrieval. **Recall** is the ability to reproduce knowledge from memory (for example, describing a lost mitten at the lost-and-found desk). **Recognition** is the ability to identify something encountered before (for example, to pick out the missing mitten from a lost-and-found box). Preschool children, like all age groups, do better on recognition than on recall, and both abilities improve with age.

recall
Ability to reproduce material from memory.

recognition
Ability to identify a previously encountered stimulus.

Young children often fail to use strategies for remembering unless reminded, and they sometimes choose inefficient memory strategies (Whitebread at al., 2009). This tendency not to generate efficient strategies may reflect lack of awareness of how a strategy would be useful (Sophian, Wood, & Vong, 1995). Older children, particularly once they begin formal schooling, tend to become more efficient in the spontaneous use of memory strategies (Schneider, 2008).

FORMING AND RETAINING CHILDHOOD MEMORIES

Most of the early conscious childhood memories seem to be short-lived. One investigator has distinguished three types of childhood memory that serve different functions: *generic, episodic,* and *autobiographical* (Nelson, 1993).

Generic memory, which begins at about age 2, produces a **script,** or general outline of a familiar, repeated event, such as riding the bus to preschool. It helps a child know what to expect and how to act.

generic memory
Memory that produces scripts of familiar routines to guide behavior.

script
General remembered outline of a familiar, repeated event, used to guide behavior.

Episodic memory refers to awareness of having experienced a particular event at a specific time and place. Given a young child's limited memory capacity, episodic memories are usually temporary. Unless they recur several times, they last for a few weeks or months and then fade (Nelson, 2005). For example, getting vaccinated at the pediatrician's office might originally be an episodic memory. Over time and repeated visits, a child might form a generic memory of the doctor's office being a place where shots are administered.

episodic memory
Long-term memory of specific experiences or events, linked to time and place.

autobiographical memory
Memory of specific events in one's life.

Autobiographical memory, a type of episodic memory, refers to memories of distinctive experiences that form a person's life history. Autobiographical memories have a special, personal meaning to the child (Fivush, 2011) and generally emerge between ages 3 and 4 (Nelson, 2005).

A suggested explanation for the relatively slow arrival of autobiographical memory is that children cannot store in memory events pertaining to their own lives until they develop a concept of self (Fivush, 2011). Also critical is the emergence of language, which enables children to share memories and organize them into personal narratives (Fivush & Nelson, 2004; Nelson & Fivush, 2004). Last, parents who spend more time reminiscing about and discussing past events have children who form more coherent autobiographical memories (Fivush, Habermas, Waters & Zaman, 2011).

Influences on Memory Retention Why do some memories last longer than others? One important factor is the uniqueness of the event. When events are rare or unusual, children seem to remember them better (Peterson, 2011). Children, as they get older, are also more likely to remember unique details of an event they have a generic script for (Brubacher, Glisic, Powers & Powell, 2011). Moreover, events with emotional impact seem to be remembered better (Buchanan, 2007), although some evidence suggests attention is focused on central aspects of the situation rather than on peripheral details (Levine & Edelstein, 2009). So, for example, if you were frightened by a scary film, you might show enhanced memory for events in the film but forget if you bought candy or who you went with. Still another

"Remember when we all went sledding together last winter?" Young children are most likely to remember unique events and may recall details from a special trip for a year or longer.
©Don Hammond/DesignPics

social interaction model
Model, based on Vygotsky's sociocultural theory, that proposes children construct autobiographical memories through conversation with adults about shared events.

Stanford-Binet Intelligence Scales
Individual intelligence tests for ages 2 and up used to measure fluid reasoning, knowledge, quantitative reasoning, visual-spatial processing, and working memory.

Wechsler Preschool and Primary Scale of Intelligence, Revised (WPPSI-IV)
Individual intelligence test for children ages 2½ to 7 that yields verbal and performance scores as well as a combined score.

factor is children's active participation. Preschoolers tend to remember things they did better than things they merely saw (Murachver, Pipe, Gordon, Owens, & Fivush, 1996).

Finally, the way adults talk with a child about experiences strongly affects autobiographical memory (Fivush et al., 2011; Fivush & Haden, 2006). Why might this be the case? The **social interaction model,** based on Vygotsky's sociocultural approach, provides a rationale. Theorists argue that children collaboratively construct autobiographical memories with parents or other adults as they talk about events (Fivush & Haden, 2006), such as might occur when a mother and child leaf through a photo album and talk about past events.

Parents differ with respect to how they talk about past events (Fivush & Haden, 2006). When a child gets stuck, adults with a *low elaborative style* repeat their own previous statements or questions. Such a parent might ask, "Do you remember how we traveled to Florida?" and then, receiving no answer, ask, "How did we get there? We went in the _____." A parent with a *high elaborative style* would ask a question that elicits more information: "Did we go by car or by plane?" The use of more elaboration on the part of parents results in richer memories for their children (Reese & Newcombe, 2007).

The relationship between elaborative, parent-guided reminiscing and children's autobiographical memory has been replicated widely across cultures. However, mothers in middle-class Western cultures tend to be more elaborative than mothers in non-Western cultures (Fivush & Haden, 2006). In reminiscing with 3-year-olds, U.S. mothers might say, "Do you remember when you went swimming at Nana's? What did you do that was really neat?" Chinese mothers tend to ask leading questions, leaving little for the child to add new information ("What did you play at the place of skiing? Sat on the ice ship, right?") (Nelson & Fivush, 2004).

Intelligence: Psychometric and Vygotskian Approaches

Although the definition of intelligence is controversial, most psychologists agree that intelligence involves the ability to learn from situations, adapt to new experiences, and manipulate abstract concepts.

TRADITIONAL PSYCHOMETRIC MEASURES

Three- to 5-year-old children are more proficient with language than younger children, so intelligence tests for this age group can include more verbal items. These tests, beginning at age 5, tend to be fairly reliable in predicting measured intelligence and school success later in childhood. Two commonly used individual tests are the Stanford-Binet Intelligence Scales and the Wechsler Preschool and Primary Scale of Intelligence.

The **Stanford-Binet Intelligence Scales** are used for ages 2 and up and take 45 to 60 minutes. The child is asked to define words, string beads, build with blocks, identify the missing parts of a picture, trace mazes, and show an understanding of numbers. The child's score is intended to measure fluid reasoning (the ability to solve abstract or novel problems), knowledge, quantitative reasoning, visual-spatial processing, and working memory. The fifth edition, revised in 2003, includes nonverbal methods of testing all five of these dimensions of cognition and permits comparisons of verbal and nonverbal performance. In addition to providing a full-scale IQ, the Stanford-Binet yields separate measures of verbal and nonverbal IQ plus composite scores spanning the five cognitive dimensions.

The **Wechsler Preschool and Primary Scale of Intelligence, Revised (WPPSI-IV)** is an individual test taking 30 to 60 minutes. It has separate levels for ages 2½ to 4 and 4 to 7 and yields verbal, performance, and combined scores. It includes subtests designed to measure both verbal and nonverbal fluid reasoning, receptive versus expressive vocabulary, and processing speed. The WPPSI-IV has been validated for special populations, such as children with intellectual disabilities, developmental delays, language disorders, and autistic disorders.

INFLUENCES ON MEASURED INTELLIGENCE

A common misconception is that IQ scores represent inborn intelligence. In reality, an IQ score is simply a measure of how well a child can do certain tasks in comparison with other children of the same age. Indeed, test scores of children in many industrialized countries have risen steadily since testing began, forcing test developers to raise standardized norms (Flynn, 1984, 1987). This trend reflected better nutrition, preschools, better-educated parents, smaller families in which each child received more attention, and changes in the tests themselves. However, the trend appears to have slowed and even reversed since the 1970s and 1980s, at least in industrialized countries, perhaps because such influences have reached a saturation point (Sundet, Barlaug, & Torjussen, 2004; Teasdale & Owen, 2008).

The degree to which family environment influences a child's intelligence is in question. Some of parents' influence on intelligence comes from their genetic contribution and some results from the fact that they provide a child's earliest environment for learning. Twin and adoption studies suggest that family life has its strongest influence in early childhood, and this influence diminishes greatly by adolescence (Bouchard & McGue, 2003; Haworth et al., 2010).

The correlation between socioeconomic status and IQ is well documented (Strenze, 2007). Family income is associated with cognitive development and achievement in the preschool years and beyond. Family economic circumstances can exert a powerful influence, not so much in themselves as in the way they affect other factors such as health, stress, parenting practices, and the atmosphere in the home (Jenkins, Woolley, Hooper & DeBellis, 2014; NICHD Early Child Care Research Network, 2005a).

The relationship between IQ and socioeconomic status interacts with other variables. For example, children in deprived families tend to have lower IQs. However, poor children with an outgoing temperament, warm mothering, and stimulating activities in the home (which may be influenced by parental IQ) tend to do better than other economically deprived children (Kim-Cohen, Moffitt, Caspi & Taylor, 2004). Environmental differences also seem to matter more for some children than others. Research has shown that children with low IQ show greater negative effects as a result of low socioeconomic status than do those with high IQ (Hanscombe, Trzaskowski, Haworth, Davis, Dale & Plomin, 2012).

By giving suggestions for solving a puzzle until his son can do it on his own, this father supports the child's cognitive progress.
©Africa Studio

TESTING AND TEACHING BASED ON VYGOTSKY'S THEORY

According to Vygotsky, children learn through interactions with others. This interactive learning is most effective in helping children cross the **zone of proximal development (ZPD),** the imaginary psychological space between what children can do or know by themselves and what they could do or know with help. The ZPD can be assessed by *dynamic tests* that provide a better measure of children's intellectual potential than do traditional psychometric tests that measure what children have already mastered. Dynamic tests emphasize potential. Examiners help the child when necessary by asking questions, giving examples or demonstrations, and offering feedback, making the test itself a learning situation.

The ZPD, in combination with the related concept of **scaffolding,** can help parents and teachers more efficiently guide children's cognitive progress. Scaffolding is the supportive assistance that a more sophisticated interaction partner provides, and ideally it should be aimed at the ZPD. For example, consider what happens when you are trying to learn a new skill, such as playing pool. When you play with someone who is worse than you, you are not likely to improve. Likewise, when you play with someone who is a master, their skills are so above yours that they overwhelm you. However, playing with someone who is just a bit better than you is likely to challenge you, illustrate strategies you might be successful at, and result in the greatest amount of learning.

Ideally, scaffolding is lessened as children gain in skills. The less able a child is to do a task, the more scaffolding, or support, an adult must give. As the child can do more and more, the adult helps less and less. When the child can do the job alone, the adult takes away the scaffold that is no longer needed.

Scaffolding helps children learn. For example, when the mothers of 2-year-old children helped maintain their child's interests by scaffolding their attention—by asking questions, making comments, or offering choices—their children tended to show more independence

zone of proximal development (ZPD)
Vygotsky's term for the difference between what a child can do alone and what the child can do with help.

scaffolding
Temporary support to help a child master a task.

and cognitive sophistication at 3½ to 4½ years of age (Landry, Smith, Swank, & Miller-Loncar, 2000). Teachers can also influence children's growing abilities. Prekindergarten children who receive scaffolding are better able to regulate their own learning when they get to kindergarten (Neitzel & Stright, 2003). Teachers who scaffolded the group discussions of their 4th grade classrooms had students who later modeled their behavior on that of the teachers', for example, by remembering to use evidence to support their statements (Jadalla et al., 2011).

Language Development

Young children's growing facility with language helps them express their unique view of the world. Between ages 3 and 6, children make rapid advances in vocabulary, grammar, and syntax.

VOCABULARY

At age 3 the average child knows and can use 900 to 1,000 words. By age 6, a child typically has an expressive (speaking) vocabulary of 2,600 words and understands more than 20,000. With the help of formal schooling, a child's passive, or receptive, vocabulary (words she can understand) will quadruple to 80,000 words by the time she enters high school (Owens, 1996).

This rapid expansion of vocabulary may occur through **fast mapping,** which allows a child to pick up the approximate meaning of a new word after hearing it only once or twice in conversation (Spiegel & Halberda, 2011). Using the context, children seem to form a quick hypothesis about the meaning of the word. For example, suppose a child is at the zoo and encounters an emu for the first time. The mother might point to the emu and say, "Look at the emu over there." The child might use what she knows about the rules for forming words, about the context, and about the subject to form a hypothesis about the meaning of the word *emu.* Names of objects (nouns) seem to be easier to fast map than names of actions (verbs), even across different languages (Imai et al., 2008).

fast mapping
Process by which a child absorbs the meaning of a new word after hearing it once or twice in conversation.

GRAMMAR AND SYNTAX

The ways children combine syllables into words and words into sentences grow increasingly sophisticated during early childhood as their understanding of grammar and syntax becomes more complex. In this context, grammar does not refer to the lessons learned in seventh grade English class; rather, it refers to the deep underlying structure of a language that enables us to both produce and understand utterances. Syntax is a related concept and involves the rules for putting together sentences in a particular language.

At age 3, children typically begin to use plurals, possessives, and past tense and know the difference between *I, you,* and *we.* They can ask and answer what and where questions. However, their sentences are generally short, simple, and declarative ("Kitty wants milk").

Between ages 4 and 5, sentences average four to five words and may be declarative, negative ("I'm not hungry"), interrogative ("Why can't I go outside?"), or imperative ("Catch the ball!"). Four-year-olds use complex, multiclause sentences ("I'm eating because I'm hungry") more frequently if their parents often use such sentences (Huttenlocher, Vasilyeva, Cymerman & Levine, 2002). Children are also affected by their peers. When children interact with peers who have strong language skills, this results in a small but significant positive effect on their own language (Mashburn, Justice, Downer & Pianta, 2009). Children this age tend to string sentences together in long run-on narratives (". . . And then . . . And then . . ."). In some respects, comprehension may be immature. For example, 4-year-old Noah can carry out a command that includes more than one step ("Pick up your toys and put them in the cupboard"). However, if his mother tells him, "You may watch TV after you pick up your toys," he may process the words in the order in which he hears them and think he can first watch television and then pick up his toys.

By ages 5 to 7, children's speech has become adultlike. They speak in longer and more complicated sentences. They use more conjunctions, prepositions, and articles.

Still, although children this age speak fluently, comprehensibly, and fairly grammatically, they have yet to master many fine points of language. They rarely use the passive voice ("I was dressed by Grandpa"), conditional sentences ("If I were big, I could drive the bus"), or the auxiliary verb *have* ("I have seen that lady before") (C. S. Chomsky, 1969).

Young children sometimes make errors because they have not yet learned exceptions to rules. Saying "holded" instead of "held" or "eated" instead of "ate" is a normal sign of linguistic progress. When young children discover a rule, such as adding *-ed* to a verb for past tense, they tend to overgeneralize—to use it even with words that do not conform to the rule. Eventually, they notice that *-ed* is not always used to form the past tense of a verb. Training and practice can help children master such syntactical forms (Vasilyeva, Huttenlocher, & Waterfall, 2006).

PRAGMATICS AND SOCIAL SPEECH

Language is a social process. As children learn vocabulary, grammar, and syntax, they also become more competent in **pragmatics.** Pragmatics involves the practical knowledge of how to use language to communicate. For example, a child is more likely to be successful with a request such as "May I please have a cookie?" than with "Give me a cookie now."

Pragmatics is related to theory of mind because to understand how to use language socially, you must put yourself in other people's shoes. This includes knowing how to ask for things, how to tell a story or joke, how to begin and continue a conversation, and how to adjust comments to the listener's perspective (M. L. Rice, 1982). These are all aspects of **social speech,** speech intended to be understood by a listener.

Most 3-year-olds pay attention to the effect of their speech on others. If people cannot understand them, they try to explain themselves more clearly. Four-year-olds, especially girls, simplify their language and use a higher register when speaking to 2-year-olds. Most 5-year-olds can adapt what they say to what the listener knows. They can now use words to resolve disputes, and they use more polite language and fewer direct commands in talking to adults than to other children. Almost half of 5-year-olds can stick to a conversational topic for about a dozen turns (Owens, 1996; Shatz & Gelman, 1973).

PRIVATE SPEECH

Jenna, age 4, was alone in her room painting. When she finished, she was overheard saying aloud, "Now I have to put the pictures somewhere to dry. I'll put them by the window. They need to get dry now."

Private speech—talking aloud to oneself with no intent to communicate with others—is normal and common in childhood. Piaget (1962) saw private speech as a sign of cognitive immaturity, and he believed that children were simply vocalizing whatever was on their minds. Vygotsky (1962) viewed private speech as a special form of communication: conversation with the self. He believed private speech was part of the learning process.

Research generally supports Vygotsky. There is evidence for the role of private speech in self-regulation (Day & Smith, 2013; Lidstone, Meins & Fernyhough, 2011). Private speech tends to increase when children are trying to solve problems or perform difficult tasks, especially without adult supervision (Berk, 1992). The use of private speech in young children also predicts their autobiographical memory (Al-Namlah, Meins & Fernyhough, 2012), creativity (Daugherty & White, 2008), and spelling proficiency (Aram, Abiri & Elad, 2013). Findings such as these support Vygotsky's view that private speech was part and parcel of learning rather than Piaget's view that it was merely reflecting ongoing mental activity.

DELAYED LANGUAGE DEVELOPMENT

About 5 to 8 percent of preschool children show speech and language delays (U.S. Preventive Services Task Force, 2006). Children who speak late do not necessarily lack linguistic input at home. Hearing problems and head and facial abnormalities may be associated with speech and language delays, as are premature birth, family history, socioeconomic factors, and other developmental delays (Dale et al., 1998; U.S. Preventive

pragmatics
The practical knowledge needed to use language for communicative purposes.

social speech
Speech intended to be understood by a listener.

private speech
Talking aloud to oneself with no intent to communicate with others.

Services Task Force, 2006). Heredity seems to play a role (Kovas, Hayiou-Thomas, Dale, Bishop & Plomin, 2005; Spinath, Price, Dale, & Plomin, 2004). Boys are more likely than girls to be late talkers (U.S. Preventive Services Task Force, 2006).

Many children who speak late—especially those whose comprehension is normal—eventually catch up. About 80 percent of children with language delays at age 2 catch up with their peers by age 7 (Rice, Taylor, & Zubrick, 2008). However, some children with early language delays, if left untreated, may experience far-reaching cognitive, social, and emotional consequences (U.S. Preventive Services Task Force, 2006).

PREPARATION FOR LITERACY

To understand what is on the printed page, children first need to master certain prereading skills. The development of fundamental skills that eventually lead to being able to read is known as **emergent literacy.**

emergent literacy
Preschoolers' development of skills, knowledge, and attitudes that underlie reading and writing.

Prereading skills can be divided into two types: (1) oral language skills, such as vocabulary, syntax, narrative structure, and the understanding that language is used to communicate; and (2) specific phonological skills (linking letters with sounds) that help in decoding the printed word. Each of these types of skills seems to have its own independent effect (NICHD Early Child Care Research Network, 2005b; Lonigan, Burgess, & Anthony, 2000).

Social interaction is an important factor in literacy development. Children are more likely to become good readers and writers if, during the preschool years, parents provide appropriate conversational challenges —if they use a rich vocabulary and read and talk about books, and center dinner-table talk on the day's activities, on mutually remembered past events, or on questions about why people do things and how things work (Reese, 1995; Reese, Sparks & Leyva, 2010).

As children learn the skills they will need to translate the written word into speech, they also learn that writing can express ideas, thoughts, and feelings. Preschool children in the United States pretend to write by scribbling, lining up their marks from left to right (Brenneman, Massey, Machado, & Gelman, 1996). Later they begin using letters, numbers, and letterlike shapes to represent words, syllables, or phonemes. Often their spelling is so inventive that they cannot read it themselves (Whitehurst & Lonigan, 1998, 2001).

Reading to children is one of the most effective paths to literacy. Children who are read to from an early age learn that reading and writing in English move from left to right and from top to bottom and that words are separated by spaces. They also are motivated to learn to read (Whitehurst & Lonigan, 2001; C. E. Baker, 2013).

MEDIA AND COGNITION

Preschool-age children comprehend the symbolic nature of television and can readily imitate behaviors they see. Exposure to television during the first few years of life has been negatively associated with academic outcomes (Pagani, Fitzpatrick, Barnett & Dubow, 2010) and cognitive development, especially when the television is left on for long periods of time or when young children are exposed to high levels of adult programming (Barr, Lauricella, Zack & Calvert, 2010). Some researchers have also found that the fast-paced programming common now in many children's shows negatively impacts executive functioning and the ability to sustain attention in preschool children (Lillard & Peterson, 2011).

While certain kinds of programming do appear to be harmful to young children's cognitive development, the type of television watched is also important, and high-quality children's programming can result in cognitive enhancements (Kirkorian, Wartella & Anderson, 2008). For example, *Sesame Street,* developed specifically to improve school readiness in inner city children, has been repeatedly shown to improve outcomes. Viewing *Sesame Street* is associated with a host of positive outcomes, including cognitive proficiency, literacy, and numeracy (Mares & Pan, 2013). Similar findings have emerged for other educational programming such as *Blue's Clues* and *Dora the Explorer* (Kirkorian et al., 2008). It is clear that program content is an important mediator. Additionally, parents who limit screen time, select well-designed, age-appropriate programs, and view the programs with their children can maximize the benefits of media (Table 7.7).

While for many years television was the most frequently used media source, the use of home computers, tablets, cellular phones, and other such devices has grown rapidly in recent years. Because of the now ubiquitous nature of these devices, the American Academy of Pediatrics (2016) issued new guidelines to encompass usage of all electronics. The recommendations state that children from 2 to 5 years of age should spend no more than an hour a day on any screen media, and that parents should watch programming with their children and discuss it. For children 6 and older, there should be consistent limits and designated media-free times. As with television, the most important variable is content. Children can learn from educational media, but pure entertainment and violent content are negatively associated with cognitive competence and academic achievement (Kirkorian et al., 2008).

TABLE 7.7 Using Media Responsibly

- Limit screen time to the least amount possible.
- Set guidelines for appropriate viewing for all media.
- Protect children from inappropriate media.
- Require that children ask before turning on media.
- Remove TVs, video game systems, and computers from bedrooms.
- Watch and discuss programs and movies together.
- Use media in a positive way to spark imagination and creativity.
- Limit the number of products you purchase for your child that are linked to TV programs.

Source: Teachers Resisting Unhealthy Children's Entertainment (TRUCE). Media action guide, 2008.

Early Childhood Education

Going to preschool is an important step, widening a child's physical, cognitive, and social environment. The transition to kindergarten, the beginning of "real school," is another momentous step. Let's look at both of these transitions.

TYPES OF PRESCHOOLS

Preschools vary greatly in their goals and curriculums. Some programs emphasize academic achievement, and others focus on social and emotional development. Two of the most influential programs, Montessori and Reggio Emilia, were founded on similar philosophical premises.

The Montessori Method As Italy's first female physician, Maria Montessori dedicated herself to finding new and better methods for educating children with disabilities. Based on her success with these children, she was asked to start a school for children living in the slums of Italy. In 1907 Montessori opened Casa dei Bambini and began a movement that has since spread worldwide.

The Montessori method is based on the belief that children's natural intelligence involves rational, spiritual, and empirical aspects (Edwards, 2003). Montessori stresses the importance of children learning independently at their own pace, as they work with developmentally appropriate materials and self-chosen tasks. Children are grouped into multiage classrooms; infancy to age 3 is considered "the unconscious absorbent mind," and age 3 to 6 is considered the "conscious absorbent mind" (Montessori, 1995). Teachers serve as guides, and older children help younger ones. Teachers provide an environment of calm productivity, and the classrooms are organized to be orderly, pleasing environments.

Montessori's approach has proven effective. An evaluation of Montessori education in Milwaukee found that 5-year-old Montessori students were well prepared for elementary school in reading and math, and outperformed children who attended other types of preschools (Lillard & Else-Quest, 2006).

The Reggio Emilia Approach In the late 1940s a group of Italian educators and parents devised a plan to revitalize a crumbling, post-World War II society through a new approach to education for young children. Their goal was to improve the lives of children and families by encouraging nonviolent dialogues and debates, developing problem-solving skills, and forging close, long-term relationships with teachers and classmates. Loris Malaguzzi, the school's founding director, envisioned an "education based on relationships" that supported the child's connections to people, society, and the environment (Malaguzzi, 1993).

Reggio Emilia is a less formal model than Montessori. Teachers follow children's interests and support them in exploring and investigating ideas and feelings through words, movement, dramatic play, and music. Learning is purposeful but less defined than with the Montessori curriculum. Teachers ask questions that draw out children's ideas and then create flexible plans to explore these ideas with the children. Classrooms are carefully constructed to offer complexity, beauty, organization, and a sense of well-being (Ceppi & Zini, 1998; Edwards, 2002).

COMPENSATORY PRESCHOOL PROGRAMS

Compensatory preschool programs are designed to aid children who would otherwise enter school poorly prepared to learn. Generally, research has shown that children who are enrolled in compensatory preschool programs show academic and cognitive gains (Camilli, Vargas, Ryan & Barnett, 2010) and these effects are stronger for children who are low in cognitive potential, have parents with a low educational level, or attend programs for more hours per week (Lee, Zhai, Brooks-Gunn, Han & Waldfogel, 2014; Bitler, Hoynes & Domina, 2014). However, teachers and researchers in early childhood education generally work within a model of the whole child, seeking not just to enhance cognitive skills but also to improve physical health and to foster self-confidence and social skills. The best known of the early intervention programs in the United States is Project Head Start, a federally funded program launched in 1965. Head Start provides medical, dental, and mental health care; social services; and at least one hot meal a day. About 1 out of 3 Head Start children are from non-English-speaking homes (predominantly Hispanic) and a majority live in single-mother homes (Administration for Children and Families [ACF], 2006a).

Has Head Start lived up to its name? Children enrolled in Head Start show academic and social gains in multiple, but not all, target areas immediately following their participation (Camilla, Vargas, Ryan & Barnett, 2010). Head Start children make gains in vocabulary, letter recognition, early writing, early mathematics, and social skills (Figure 7.5). The gap between their vocabulary and early reading scores and national norms narrows significantly. Furthermore, their skills continue to progress in kindergarten. Gains are closely related to parental involvement (ACF, 2006b).

Some reports suggest that these gains are not maintained over time. These reports have been controversial, in part due to the complexity of comparing outcomes of diverse children in varying programs. About half the number of children who apply for but do not get into Head Start find alternative child care arrangements. Thus the control group—those children who did not participate in Head Start—experience a variety of different child care situations rather than the lack of *any* enriching child care experiences. Some researchers argue that this might help explain why many children who do not participate in Head Start seemed to "catch up" to program participants by first grade (National Forum on Early Childhood Policy and Programs, 2010).

An analysis of long-term effects of Head Start suggests that the benefits outweigh the costs (Puma et al., 2012). Children from Head Start and other compensatory programs were less likely to be placed in special education or to repeat a grade and were more likely to finish high school than low-income children who did not attend such programs (Deming, 2009). "Graduates" of similar programs were much less likely to become juvenile delinquents or to become pregnant in their teens (Schweinhart, 2007). There were also differences in long-term outcomes for males and females. At ages 27 and 40, men were less likely to have been involved in criminal

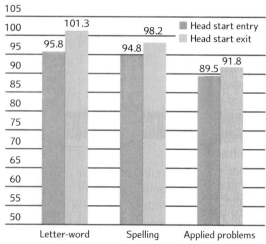

Mean standard score

FIGURE 7.5

Academic Outcomes at the Beginning and End of Head Start

These outcomes represent all children who entered Head Start for the first time in the fall of 2009, completed 1 or 2 years of the program, and entered kindergarten in the fall of either 2010 or 2011. Immediate gains are most striking; however, better outcomes do persist over time.

Source: Aikens, N.; Kopack Klein, A.; Tarullo, L.; & West, J. Getting ready for kindergarten: Children's progress during Head Start. *FACES 2009 Report. OPRE Report 2013-21a.* Washington, DC: Office of Planning, Research and Evaluation, Administration for Children and Families, U.S. Department of Health and Human Services, 2013.

activity and more likely to be employed and have a higher income than controls. For women, there were positive effects on both education and employment at age 19 and 27, and negative effects on criminal activity at age 40 (Heckman et al., 2010; Reynolds, Temple, Ou, Arteaga & White, 2011). Outcomes are best with earlier and longer-lasting intervention through high-quality, center-based programs (Brooks-Gunn, 2003; Zigler & Styfco, 2001). A growing consensus among early childhood educators is that the most effective way to ensure that gains achieved in early intervention and compensatory education programs are maintained is through a systematic program extending from prekindergarten through third grade (Bogard & Takanishi, 2005).

THE CHILD IN KINDERGARTEN

For many years people thought of kindergarten as a transition time between home or preschool and the more academic structure of grade school. Now kindergarten in the United States has become more like first grade and emphasizes academics. Children spend more time on worksheets and preparing to read and less time on self-chosen activities. A successful transition from home or preschool to kindergarten lays the foundation for future academic achievement (Schulting, Malone, & Dodge, 2005).

Although some states do not require kindergarten programs or kindergarten attendance, most 5-year-olds attend kindergarten. Since the late 1970s, an increasing number of kindergarteners spend a full day in school, rather than the traditional half day (Kena et al., 2014). A practical impetus for this trend is the growing number of single-parent and dual-earner households. While full-day kindergarten has been associated with small to moderate increases in reading and math skills when compared to a half-day schedule (Votruba-Drzal, Li-Grining & Maldonado-Carreno, 2008), by the end of third grade these differences disappear (Rathbun, West & Germino-Hausken, 2004).

Findings highlight the importance of the preparation a child receives *before* kindergarten. The resources with which children come to kindergarten—preliteracy skills and the richness of a home literacy environment—predict reading achievement in first grade (Rathbun et al., 2004). Emotional and social adjustment also affect readiness for kindergarten and strongly predict school success. It is important that children have the ability to sit still, follow directions, wait one's turn, and regulate one's own learning (Raver, 2002). Broadly, kindergarten readiness is associated with positive academic and social outcomes for children (Goldstein, McCoach & Yu, 2017; Jones, Greenberg & Crowley, 2015). There are individual differences in children's ability to self-regulate, but the environment can either promote or impede regulatory activity, suggesting the importance of classroom management in academic achievement (Rimm-Kaufman, Curby, Grimm, Nathansan & Brock, 2009). Adjustment to kindergarten can be eased by enabling preschoolers and parents to visit before the start of kindergarten, shortening school days early in the school year, having teachers make home visits, holding parent orientation sessions, and keeping parents informed about what is going on in school (Schulting, Malone & Dodge, 2005).

summary and key terms

PHYSICAL DEVELOPMENT

Aspects of Physical Development

- Physical growth continues during the years from 3 to 6, but more slowly than before. Boys are slightly taller, heavier, and more muscular than girls. Internal body systems are maturing.
- Sleep patterns change during early childhood and are affected by cultural expectations. Occasional sleepwalking, sleep terrors, and nightmares are common, but persistent sleep problems may indicate emotional disturbances.

- Bed-wetting is usually outgrown without special help.
- Brain development continues steadily throughout childhood.
- Children progress rapidly in gross and fine motor skills.
- Handedness is usually evident by age 3.
- According to Kellogg's research, stages of art production are the scribbling stage, shape stage, design stage, and pictorial stage.

enuresis, gross motor skills, fine motor skills, systems of action, handedness

Health and Safety

- Although major contagious illnesses are rare today in industrialized countries, preventable disease continues to be a major problem in the developing world.
- The prevalence of obesity among preschoolers has increased.
- Undernutrition can affect all aspects of development.
- Food allergies are becoming increasingly common.
- Accidents are the leading cause of death in childhood in the United States.
- Environmental factors such as exposure to poverty, homelessness, smoking, air pollution, and pesticides increase the risks of illness or injury. Lead poisoning can have serious physical, cognitive, and behavioral effects.

COGNITIVE DEVELOPMENT

Piagetian Approach: The Preoperational Child

- Children in the preoperational stage show several important advances, as well as some immature aspects of thought.
- The symbolic function enables children to reflect on people, objects, and events that are not physically present. It is shown in deferred imitation, pretend play, and language.
- Symbolic development helps preoperational children make more accurate judgments of spatial relationships. They can link cause and effect with regard to familiar situations, understand the concept of identity, categorize, compare quantities, and understand principles of counting.
- Preoperational children appear to be less egocentric than Piaget thought.
- Centration keeps preoperational children from understanding principles of conservation. Their logic also is limited by irreversibility and a focus on states rather than transformations.
- Theory of mind, which develops markedly between ages 3 and 5, includes awareness of a child's own thought processes, understanding that people can hold false beliefs, ability to deceive, and ability to distinguish appearance from reality.
- Maturational and environmental influences affect individual differences in theory-of-mind development.

preoperational stage, symbolic function, pretend play, transduction, animism, centration, decenter, egocentrism, conservation, irreversibility, theory of mind

Information-Processing Approach: Memory Development

- Information-processing models describe three steps in memory: encoding, storage, and retrieval.
- Although sensory memory shows little change with age, the capacity of working memory increases. The central executive controls the flow of information to and from long-term memory.
- At all ages, recognition is better than recall, but both increase during early childhood.

- Early episodic memory is only temporary; it fades or is transferred to generic memory.
- Autobiographical memory typically begins at about age 3 or 4; it may be related to self-recognition and language development.
- According to the social interaction model, children and adults co-construct autobiographical memories by talking about shared experiences.
- Children are more likely to remember unusual activities that they actively participate in. The way adults talk with children about events influences memory formation.

encoding, storage, retrieval, sensory memory, working memory, executive function, long-term memory, central executive, recall, recognition, generic memory, script, episodic memory, autobiographical memory, social interaction model

Intelligence: Psychometric and Vygotskian Approaches

- The two most commonly used psychometric intelligence tests for young children are the Stanford-Binet Intelligence Scales and the Wechsler Preschool and Primary Scale of Intelligence, Revised (WPPSI-IV).
- Intelligence test scores have risen in industrialized countries.
- Intelligence test scores may be influenced by a number of factors, including the home environment and SES.
- Newer tests based on Vygotsky's concept of the zone of proximal development (ZPD) focus on potential rather than achievement. Such tests, combined with scaffolding, can help parents and teachers guide children's progress.

Stanford-Binet Intelligence Scales, Wechsler Preschool and Primary Scale of Intelligence, Revised (WPPSI-IV), zone of proximal development (ZPD), scaffolding

Language Development

- During early childhood, vocabulary increases greatly, and grammar, syntax, and pragmatics become more sophisticated.
- Private speech is normal and common, and may aid in self-regulation.
- Causes of delayed language development are multiple. If untreated, language delays may have serious cognitive, social, and emotional consequences.
- Interaction with adults can promote emergent literacy.
- Well-designed, age-appropriate programming is associated with enhanced cognitive development.

fast mapping, pragmatics, social speech, private speech, emergent literacy

Early Childhood Education

- Goals of preschool education vary across cultures.
- The academic content of early childhood education programs in the United States has increased.
- Compensatory preschool programs have had positive outcomes, although some gains fade over time. Compensatory programs that start early may have better results.
- Many children today attend full-day kindergarten. Success in kindergarten depends largely on emotional and social adjustment and kindergarten readiness.

Psychosocial Development in Early Childhood

©Big Cheese Photo/Getty Images

In this chapter we discuss preschool children's understanding of themselves and their feelings. We see how their sense of male or female identity arises and how it affects behavior. We describe play, the activity in which children in industrialized countries typically spend most of their time. We consider the influence, for good or ill, of what parents do. Finally, we discuss relationships with siblings and other children.

The Developing Self

"Who in the world am I? Ah, *that's* the great puzzle," said Alice in Wonderland, after her size had abruptly changed—again. Solving Alice's "puzzle" is a lifelong process of getting to know one's self.

THE SELF-CONCEPT AND COGNITIVE DEVELOPMENT

self-concept
Sense of self; descriptive and evaluative mental picture of one's abilities and traits.

The **self-concept** is our total picture of our abilities and traits. It is "a *cognitive construction* . . . a system of descriptive and evaluative representations about the self" that determines how we feel about ourselves and guides our actions (Harter, 1996, p. 207). The sense of self also has a social aspect: Children incorporate into their self-image their growing understanding of how others see them.

The self-concept begins to come into focus in toddlerhood, as children develop self-awareness. It becomes clearer as a person gains in cognitive abilities and deals with the developmental tasks of childhood, of adolescence, and then of adulthood.

Changes in Self-Definition: The 5 to 7 Shift Children's **self-definition**—the way they describe themselves—typically changes between about ages 5 and 7, reflecting self-concept development. At age 4, Jason says,

self-definition
Cluster of characteristics used to describe oneself.

single representations
In neo-Piagetian terminology, first stage in development of self-definition, in which children describe themselves in terms of individual, unconnected characteristics and in all-or-nothing terms.

> My name is Jason and I live in a big house with my mother and father and sister, Lisa. I have a kitty that's orange and a television set in my own room. . . . I like pizza and I have a nice teacher. I can count up to 100, want to hear me? I love my dog, Skipper. I can climb to the top of the jungle gym, I'm not scared! Just happy. You can't be happy *and* scared, no way! I have brown hair, and I go to preschool. I'm really strong. I can lift this chair, watch me! (Harter, 1996, p. 208)

The way Jason describes himself is typical of U.S. children his age. They are very concrete in their thinking. Jason focuses on what he does, what he looks like, things he owns, and the people and animals in his life. He speaks in specifics, mentioning a particular skill (climbing) rather than general abilities (being athletic) and he is unrealistically positive about his abilities. Moreover, he has difficulty understanding how conflicting emotions can exist simultaneously. In a few years at about age 7, Jason will begin to describe himself in terms of generalized traits such as popular, smart, or dumb; recognize that he can have conflicting emotions; and be self-critical while holding a positive overall self-concept.

real self
The self one actually is.

ideal self
The self one would like to be.

representational mappings
In neo-Piagetian terminology, second stage in development of self-definition, in which a child makes logical connections between aspects of the self but still sees these characteristics in all-or-nothing terms.

What specific changes make up this *age 5 to 7 shift?* A neo-Piagetian analysis (Case, 1992; Fischer, 1980) describes this shift in three steps. At 4, Jason is at the first step, **single representations**. His statements about himself are one-dimensional. He cannot consider different aspects of himself at the same time. His thinking about himself is all-or-nothing. He cannot acknowledge that his **real self,** the person he actually is, is not the same as his **ideal self,** the person he would like to be.

At about age 5 or 6, Jason moves to the second step, **representational mappings.** He begins to make logical connections between one aspect of himself and another: "I can run fast, and I can climb high. I'm also strong. I can throw a ball real far, I'm going to be on a team some day!" (Harter, 1996, p. 215). However, his image of himself is still expressed in completely positive, all-or-nothing terms. He cannot see how he might be good at some things and not at others.

self-esteem
The judgment a person makes about his or her self-worth.

The third step, *representational systems,* takes place in middle childhood when children begin to integrate specific features of the self into a general, multidimensional concept. As all-or-nothing thinking declines, Jason's self-descriptions will become more balanced and realistic: "I'm good at hockey but bad at arithmetic."

Jason describes himself in terms of his appearance (brown hair) and his possessions (his dog, Skipper). ©Rob Hainer/Shutterstock

SELF-ESTEEM

Self-esteem is the self-evaluative part of the self-concept, the judgment children make about their overall worth. Self-esteem, in part, is based on children's growing cognitive ability to describe and define themselves.

Developmental Changes in Self-Esteem Children show relative stability in their perceptions of themselves. In a longitudinal study (Verschueren, Buyck, & Marcoen, 2001), 5-year-olds' self-perceptions of variables such as their physical appearance, scholastic and athletic competence, social acceptance, and behavioral conduct predicted their self-perceptions and socioemotional functioning at age 8.

Young children's self-esteem is not firmly based on reality, and most young children wildly overestimate their abilities. One reason for this is that self-esteem is, in part, the result of feedback received from others, and adults tend to give positive feedback (Harter, 1998, 2006). For example, a kindergartener's crude lettering is not generally critiqued as being messy; rather, parents are more likely to praise the child's efforts.

Children's self-esteem also tends to be unidimensional. In other words, children believe they are either all good or all bad (Harter, 1998). You may notice that this is similar to what is found in the self-concept, and presumably the same cognitive constraints underlie both processes. In middle childhood, self-esteem will become more realistic (Harter, 1998).

Contingent Self-Esteem: The "Helpless" Pattern Consider the praise parents give children for succeeding. If a child is generally praised for working hard, and she fails at a task, the logical implication is that she did not try hard enough. That child might then be motivated to work harder next time. If the same child is praised for being smart, and she fails at a task, the implication is far different. Now, the implication is that the child is no longer smart. The motivation for working hard has been stripped away.

If self-esteem is *contingent* on success, children may view failure or criticism as an indictment of their worth and may feel helpless to do better. About one-third to one-half of preschoolers, kindergarteners, and first graders show a "learned helplessness" pattern (Dweck, 2008; Ruble & Dweck, 1995). For example, when given a difficult puzzle, "helpless" children are likely to give up. They assume they will fail, and so do not bother to try. Preschoolers who fail may interpret this as a sign of being "bad," whereas older children who fail may conclude that they are "dumb,"

Children whose self-esteem is contingent on success tend to attribute poor performance or social rejection to personality deficiencies, which they believe they are helpless to change. Children with noncontingent self-esteem, in contrast, tend to attribute failure or disappointment to factors outside themselves or to the need to try harder. If initially unsuccessful or rejected, they persevere, trying new strategies until they find one that works (Harter, 1998; Pomerantz & Saxon, 2001). Children who believe that they can succeed if they try, who enjoy challenges, and who have faith in their ability to meet those challenges tend to have parents who praise their efforts, not their inherent abilities, and who focus on specific, focused feedback rather than generic praise (Gunderson et al., 2013).

UNDERSTANDING AND REGULATING EMOTIONS

At 5-year-old Kayla's birthday party, Kayla opens a present from her grandmother and finds not the doll she was hoping to receive, but a board game. Her face drops as her mother whispers in her ear, "Smile and tell grandma thank you. You don't want to hurt her feelings." Kayla tries, but her smile is unconvincing.

The ability to understand and regulate, or control, one's feelings is one of the key advances of early childhood (Dennis, 2006). Children who can understand their emotions are better able to control the way they show them and to be sensitive to how others feel (Garner & Estep, 2001). Emotional self-regulation helps children guide their behavior (Eisenberg, Fabes & Spinrad, 2006) and contributes to their ability to get along with others (Denham et al., 2003).

In addition to learning how to regulate their emotions, children come to understand emotions in a more sophisticated manner over time. In preschool, children can talk about their feelings and can read the feelings of others. They know that experiences can elicit emotions and are often based on desires (Saarni, Campos, Camras & Witherington, 2006). They understand that people are happy when they get something they want and sad when they do not (Lagattuta, 2005).

This mother's approval of her 3-year-old daughter's artwork is an important contributor to her self-esteem.
©Design Pics/Don Hammond/Getty Images

Understanding Conflicting Emotions Many young children do not understand that they can experience different emotional reactions at the same time ("I'm sad that I can't go to my friend's house, and angry that my mom won't let me go"). Individual differences in understanding conflicting emotions are evident by age 3 (Brown & Dunn, 1996). Over the childhood years, this ability slowly develops, and most children can understand conflicting or ambivalent emotions by 8 to 11 years of age (Harter & Buddin, 1987). One key factor appears to be the types of conversations about emotions children participate in. Children who understand conflicting emotions earlier tend to come from families that often discuss why people behave as they do (Harter, 1996). Research has also supported this relationship experimentally. When children are asked to explain others' emotional responses or listen to an experimenter explain the responses, they later show enhanced emotional understanding (Tenenbaum, Alfierie, Brooks & Dunne, 2008).

Understanding Emotions Directed toward the Self Emotions directed toward the self, such as guilt, shame, and pride, typically develop by the end of the 3rd year, after children gain self-awareness and accept the standards of behavior their parents have set. However, even children a few years older often lack the cognitive sophistication to *recognize* these emotions and what brings them on (Kestenbaum & Gelman, 1995).

In one study (Harter, 1993), 4- to 8-year-olds were told two stories. In the first story, a child takes a few coins from a jar after being told not to do so; in the second story, a child performs a difficult gymnastic feat—a flip on the bars. Each story was presented in two versions: one in which a parent sees the child doing the act and another in which no one sees the child. The children were asked how they and the parent would feel in each circumstance. The answers revealed a gradual progression in understanding of feelings about the self, reflecting the 5 to 7 shift (Harter, 1996). At ages 4 to 5, children did not say that either they or their parents would feel pride or shame. Instead they used such terms as "worried" or "scared" (for the money jar incident) and "excited" or "happy" (about the gymnastic accomplishment). At 5 to 6, children said their parents would be ashamed or proud of them but did not acknowledge feeling these emotions themselves. At 6 to 7, children said they would feel proud or ashamed, but only if they were observed. Not until ages 7 to 8 did children say that they would feel ashamed or proud of themselves even if no one saw them.

Gender

Gender identity, awareness of one's femaleness or maleness and all it implies in one's society of origin, is an important aspect of the developing self-concept. How different are young boys and girls, and why? How do children develop gender identity, and how does it affect them?

GENDER DIFFERENCES

Gender differences are psychological or behavioral differences between males and females. Measurable differences between baby boys and girls are few. Although some gender differences become more pronounced after age 3, boys and girls on average remain more alike than different. Extensive evidence from many studies supports this *gender similarities hypothesis* (Hyde, 2005). Indeed, if gender differences were striking, they would not elicit the controversy they do.

Physically, among the larger gender differences are boys' higher activity level, superior motor performance, especially after puberty, and their greater propensity for physical aggression (Hyde, 2005) beginning by age 2 (Archer, 2004; Baillargeon et al., 2007; Pellegrini & Archer, 2005). These physical differences impact the nature of play. Boys engage in more rough-and-tumble, physically active play than girls do. There are also sex-typed toy preferences; girls prefer to play with dolls and doll accessories, and boys prefer to play with construction and transportation toys (Paterski et al., 2011). Sex-typed play preferences increase between toddlerhood and middle childhood, and the degree of sex-typed behavior exhibited early in life is a strong indicator of later gender-based behavior (Golombok et al., 2008).

gender identity
Awareness, developed in early childhood, that one is male or female.

One clear behavioral difference between young boys and young girls is boys' greater physical aggressiveness. ©RichVintage/iStock/ Getty Images Plus

Cognitive gender differences are few and small (Spelke, 2005). While there are fine-grain differences in particular areas, there do not appear to be gender differences in overall intelligence (Nisbett et al., 2012). Boys and girls do equally well on tasks involving basic mathematical skills and are equally capable of learning math, but show variations in specific abilities. Girls tend to perform better on tests of verbal fluency, mathematical computation, and memory for locations of objects. Boys tend to perform better in verbal analogies, mathematical word problems, and memory for spatial configurations. In most studies, these differences do not emerge until elementary school or later (Spelke, 2005). Also, boys' mathematical abilities vary more than girls', with more boys at both the highest and lowest ends of the ability range (Halpern et al., 2007). In early childhood and again during preadolescence and adolescence, girls tend to use more responsive language, such as praise, agreement, acknowledgment, and elaboration on what someone else has said (Leaper & Smith, 2004). Last, girls tend to show an advantage in school, and as a group tend to earn higher grades, especially in language classes (Voyer & Voyer, 2014).

We need to remember, of course, that gender differences are valid for large groups of boys and girls but not necessarily for individuals. By knowing a child's sex, we cannot predict whether that *particular* boy or girl will be faster, stronger, smarter, more obedient, or more assertive than another child.

PERSPECTIVES ON GENDER DEVELOPMENT

Gender roles are the behaviors, interests, attitudes, skills, and personality traits that a culture considers appropriate for males or females. All societies have gender roles. Historically, in most cultures, women have been expected to devote most of their time to caring for the household and children, while men were providers and protectors. Women were expected to be compliant and nurturing; men, to be active, aggressive, and competitive. Today, gender roles, especially in Western cultures, have become more diverse and more flexible.

Gender-typing, the acquisition of a gender role, takes place early in childhood, but children vary greatly in the degree to which they become gender-typed (Iervolino, Hines, Golombok, Rust & Plomin, 2005). **Gender stereotypes** are preconceived generalizations about male or female behavior: All females are passive and dependent; all males are aggressive and independent. Gender stereotypes appear to some degree in children as young as 2 or 3, increase during the preschool years, and reach a peak at age 5 (Campbell, Shirley & Candy, 2004; Ruble & Martin, 1998).

How do children acquire gender roles, and why do they adopt gender stereotypes? Are these purely social constructs, or do they reflect innate differences between males and females? Let's look at five theoretical perspectives on gender development (summarized in Table 8.1): *biological, evolutionary, psychoanalytic, cognitive,* and *social learning.* All of these perspectives can contribute to our understanding, and none by itself fully explains why boys and girls differ in some respects and not in others.

gender roles
Behaviors, interests, attitudes, skills, and traits that a culture considers appropriate for each sex; differ for males and females.

gender-typing
Socialization process by which children, at an early age, learn appropriate gender roles.

gender stereotypes
Preconceived generalizations about male or female role behavior.

Biological Approach The existence of similar gender roles in many cultures suggests that some gender differences are biologically based. If gender differences were purely cultural inventions, as has sometimes been argued, we would expect to see more variability in male and female roles and characteristics across cultures. Investigators are uncovering evidence of neurological, hormonal, and evolutionary explanations for some gender differences.

Across the life span, and starting early in development, men, on average, have larger brain volume than women (Ruigrok et al., 2014). By age 5, when the brain reaches approximate adult size, boys' brains are about 10 percent larger than girls' brains (Reiss, Abrams, Singer, Ross & Denckla, 1996). However, girls' brains have a higher proportion of gray matter (neurons) and show greater cerebral blood flow, while boys' brains contain more white matter (axons for communication between neurons) (Cosgrove, Mazure & Staley, 2007). What may be even more important is what occurs in the womb when the brain is forming. Hormones in the prenatal environment affect the developing brain. Although levels of the male hormone testosterone do not appear to be directly related to aggressiveness

TABLE 8.1 Five Perspectives on Gender Development

Theories	Major Theorists	Key Processes	Basic Beliefs
Biological Approach		Genetic, neurological, and hormonal activity	Many behavioral differences between the sexes can be traced to biology.
Evolutionary Approach	Charles Darwin	Natural and sexual selection	Gender differences stem from evolutionary differences in reproductive and parenting behaviors for each sex.
Psychoanalytic Approach	Sigmund Freud	Resolution of unconscious emotional conflict	Gender identity occurs when the child identifies with the same-sex parent.
Cognitive Approach/ Cognitive-developmental theory	Lawrence Kohlberg	Self-categorization	Once a child learns she is a girl or he is a boy, the child interprets and uses information about behavior by gender.
Social Learning Approach/Social cognitive theory	Albert Bandura	Observation of models, reinforcement	Child mentally combines observations of gendered behavior and creates own behavioral variations.

in children (Constantino et al., 1993), an analysis of fetal testosterone levels and the development of gender-typical play has shown a link between higher testosterone levels and male-typical play in boys (Auyeng et al., 2009). Additionally, testosterone has been linked to dominance and status striving behavior in humans (Eisenegger, Haushofer & Fehr, 2011).

Some research focuses on girls with a disorder called *congenital adrenal hyperplasia (CAH)*. These girls have high prenatal levels of *androgens* (male sex hormones). They tend to show preferences for boys' toys, rough play, and male playmates, as well as strong spatial skills. *Estrogens* (female sex hormones), on the other hand, seem to have less influence on boys' gender-typed behavior (Paterski et al., 2005).

Perhaps the most dramatic examples of biologically based research have to do with infants born with ambiguous sexual organs that are not clearly male or female. John Money and his colleagues (Money, Hampson & Hampson, 1955) recommended that these children be assigned as early as possible to the gender that holds the potential for the most nearly normal functioning. They based this recommendation on the appearance of the genitals.

However, newer studies demonstrate the profound difficulty of predicting the outcome of sex assignment at birth, particularly on the basis of external genitalia. In one study, 14 genetically male children born without normal penises but with testes were legally and surgically assigned female sex during the 1st month of life and were raised as girls. Ultimately, eight declared themselves male, five declared unwavering female identity but expressed difficulty fitting in with other girls, and one refused to discuss the subject with anyone. Meanwhile, the two boys whose parents had refused the initial sexual assignment remained male (Reiner & Gearhart, 2004). This, and other similar cases, strongly suggest that gender identity is rooted in biological factors and is not easily changed (Meyer-Bahlburg, 2005; Reiner, 2005; Diamond & Sigmundson, 1997). Merely telling a boy or a girl what he or she is is not enough to alter gender identity.

Recently, the issue of transgender children has garnered attention, driven in part by legal challenges regarding which bathroom is appropriate for those individuals who identify with the opposite gender. Transgender people are individuals whose gender identity is different from their biological sex. There are indications that the disparity between gender and sex may be biologically influenced. For example, biological women who later identify as male have markers that suggest high androgen exposure in the womb (Leinung & Wu, 2017; Wu & Leinung, 2015). Additionally, research on twins suggests there may be genetic influences at play as well (Diamond, 2013). While many young children play with their identity—for example, dressing up in different clothes or pretending to be something they are not—children, especially girls, who will later identify as transgender are far more likely to show strong and persistent gender dysphoria early in childhood

(Steensma, McGuire, Kreukels, Beekman & Cohen-Kettenis, 2013). Moreover, the volume of the stria terminalis (an area of the brain involved in sexual behavior) in biological men who later identify as women is more similar to that of other women than to that of other men (Zhou, Hofman, Gooren & Swaab, 1995). The density, but not the volume, of their neurons is more similar to that of biological women as well (Luders at al., 2009). In short, there is emerging evidence that gender identity—a psychological construct housed in the brain—is influenced by biology and is not merely the consequence of biological sex or child-rearing practices. Note that this does not mean the environment does not matter. Gender is complicated and is the result of multiple intersecting lines of influence. More research is needed in this controversial area.

Evolutionary Approach The evolutionary approach sees gendered behavior as adaptive. From this perspective, children's gender roles underlie the evolved mating and child-rearing strategies of adult males and females.

According to Darwin's (1871) **theory of sexual selection,** the selection of sexual partners is a response to the differing reproductive pressures that early men and women confronted in the struggle for survival of the species (Wood & Eagly, 2012). While women *must* invest a great deal in children, including pregnancy and breast-feeding, men may invest minimally via fertilization only. While survival may be more certain if a man invests resources in a child, that investment is not obligatory. This puts into play different reproductive dynamics for each sex. The more widely a man can engage in sexual activity, the greater his chances to pass on his genetic inheritance. Thus, men tend to prefer more sexual partners than women do. They value physical prowess because it enables them to compete for mates and for control of resources and social status, which women value. Because a woman invests more time and energy in pregnancy and can bear only a limited number of children, each child's survival is of utmost importance to her, so she looks for a mate who will remain with her and support their offspring. More sexual activity, for women, does not result in more children. The need to raise each child to reproductive maturity also explains why women tend to be more caring and nurturing than men (Bjorklund & Pellegrini, 2000; Wood & Eagly, 2002).

According to evolutionary theory, male competitiveness and aggressiveness and female nurturance develop during childhood as preparation for these adult roles (Pellegrini & Archer, 2005). Boys play at fighting; girls play at parenting. In caring for children, women often must put a child's needs and feelings ahead of their own. Thus young girls tend to be better able than young boys to control and inhibit their emotions and to refrain from impulsive behavior (Bjorklund & Pellegrini, 2000).

Some people misinterpret evolutionary approaches as being deterministic in nature. If evolution plays a role in the development of gender roles, they assume that means gender roles are preordained, and thus should be inflexible and highly resistant to change. For example, as would be predicted, it is indeed the case that in all cultures women tend to be children's primary caregivers (Wood & Eagly, 2002) and men are overwhelmingly responsible for homicides (Daly & Wilson, 1988). But this does not mean that men never care for children, nor does it mean that women are never aggressive. Rather, it means that evolution has given us a slight "push" in one direction or another that can be minimized or maximized by cultural and environmental influences. It is only when large numbers of individuals are examined that gender differences emerge.

Critics of evolutionary theory argue that society and culture are more important than biology in determining gender roles. But evolutionary theorists have never argued that culture is insignificant. Rather, they have argued that men and women have cognitive adaptations designed to be sensitive to environmental input. Research suggests that men's primary ancestral role was to provide for subsistence while women's was to tend to the children, but this does not mean that we are bound to these roles.

Psychoanalytic Approach "Daddy, where will you live when I grow up and marry Mommy?" asks Mario, age 4. From the psychoanalytic perspective, Mario's question is part of his acquisition of gender identity. That process, according to Freud, is one of

theory of sexual selection
Darwin's theory that gender roles developed in response to men's and women's differing reproductive needs.

identification
In Freudian theory, the process by which a young child adopts characteristics, beliefs, attitudes, values, and behaviors of the parent of the same sex.

identification, the adoption of characteristics, beliefs, attitudes, values, and behaviors of the parent of the same sex. Freud considered identification an important personality development of early childhood.

According to Freud, identification will occur for Mario when he represses or gives up the wish to possess the parent of the other sex (his mother) and identifies with the parent of the same sex (his father). Although this explanation for gender development has been influential, it has been difficult to test and has little research support (Maccoby, 2000). Most developmental psychologists today favor other explanations.

Cognitive Approach Sarah realizes she is a girl because people call her a girl and treat her like a girl. As she continues to observe and think about her world, she concludes that she will always be a girl. She comes to understand gender by actively thinking about and constructing her own gender-typing. This is the heart of Lawrence Kohlberg's (1966) cognitive-developmental theory.

Kohlberg's Cognitive-Developmental Theory In Kohlberg's theory, gender knowledge ("I am a boy") precedes gendered behavior ("so I like to do boy things"). As children begin to realize which gender they belong to, they adopt behaviors they perceive as consistent with being male or female. Thus, 3-year-old Sarah should prefer dolls to trucks because she sees girls playing with dolls and therefore views playing with dolls as consistent with being a girl (Martin & Ruble, 2004).

The acquisition of gender roles, said Kohlberg, hinges on **gender constancy**—a child's realization that his or her gender will always be the same. According to this theory, once this occurs, children are motivated to adopt behaviors appropriate to their gender. Gender constancy seems to develop in three stages: *gender identity, gender stability,* and *gender consistency* (Martin et al., 2002):

gender constancy
Awareness that one will always be male or female.

- *Gender identity:* awareness of one's own gender and that of others typically occurs between ages 2 and 3.

- *Gender stability:* awareness that gender does not change. However, children at this stage base judgments about gender on superficial appearances (clothing or hairstyle) and stereotyped behaviors.

- *Gender consistency:* the realization that a girl remains a girl even if she plays with trucks, and a boy remains a boy even if he has long hair. This typically occurs between ages 3 and 7 once children realize that changes in outward appearance do not affect gender.

Much research challenges Kohlberg's view that gender-typing depends on gender constancy. Long before children attain the final stage of gender constancy, they show gender-typed preferences (Martin & Ruble, 2004). For example, gender preferences in toys and playmates appear as early as 12 months (Jadva, Hines & Golombok, 2010). However, these findings do not challenge Kohlberg's basic insight: that gender concepts influence behavior (Martin et al., 2002).

Today, cognitive-developmental theorists no longer claim that gender constancy must precede gender-typing (Martin et al., 2002). Rather, gender-typing is heightened by the more sophisticated understanding that gender constancy brings (Martin & Ruble, 2004). Each stage of gender constancy increases children's attention toward and memory for gender-relevant information. The achievement of gender identity may motivate children to learn more about gender; whereas gender stability and gender consistency may motivate them to be sure they are acting "like a boy" or "like a girl" (Martin et al., 2002).

gender-schema theory
Theory, proposed by Bem, that children socialize themselves in their gender roles by developing a mentally organized network of information about what it means to be male or female in a particular culture.

Gender-Schema Theory Another cognitive approach is **gender-schema theory.** Like cognitive-developmental theory, it views children as actively extracting knowledge about gender from their environment *before* engaging in gender-typed behavior. However, gender-schema theory places more emphasis on the influence of culture. Once children know what sex they are, they develop a concept of what it means to be male or female *in their culture.* Children then match their behavior to their culture's view of what boys and girls are "supposed" to be and do (Bem, 1993; Martin et al., 2002). According to this theory, gender schemas promote gender stereotypes by influencing judgments about behavior. When meeting a new boy his age, 4-year-old Brandon offers him a toy truck, assuming that the new boy will like the same toys he likes.

Bem suggests that children who show stereotypical behavior may do so as a result of pressure for gender conformity. However, there is little evidence that gender schemas are at the root of stereotyped behavior or that children who are highly gender-typed necessarily feel pressure to conform (Yunger, Carver & Perry, 2004). Indeed, as many parents will attest, it can be difficult to encourage a young child to behave in ways that are not stereotypically masculine or feminine.

Another problem with both gender-schema theory and Kohlberg's theory is that gender-stereotyping does not always become stronger with increased gender knowledge (Bandura & Bussey, 2004; Banse, Gawronski, Rebetez, Gutt & Morton, 2010). In fact, gender-stereotyping rises and then falls in a developmental pattern (Ruble & Martin, 1998; Welch-Ross & Schmidt, 1996). Around ages 4 to 6, when, according to gender-schema theory, children are constructing and consolidating their gender schemas, they notice and remember only information consistent with these schemas. Indeed, they tend to *mis*remember information that challenges gender stereotypes, such as photos of a girl sawing wood or a boy cooking. They are also quick to accept gender labels; when told that an unfamiliar toy is for the other sex, they will drop it like a hot potato (Martin & Ruble, 2004). By ages 5 and 6, children develop rigid stereotypes about gender that they apply to themselves and others. A boy will pay more attention to what he considers boys' toys and a girl to girls' toys. Then, around age 7 or 8, schemas become more complex as children take in and integrate contradictory information, such as the fact that many girls have short hair. At this point, children develop more complex beliefs about gender and become more flexible in their views about gender roles (Martin & Ruble, 2004; Trautner et al., 2005).

Cognitive approaches to gender development have been an important contribution. However, these approaches may not fully explain the link between knowledge and conduct. There is disagreement about precisely what mechanism prompts children to act out gender roles and why some children become more strongly gender-typed than others (Bussey & Bandura, 1992, 1999; Martin & Ruble, 2004). Some investigators point to socialization.

Social Learning Approach According to Walter Mischel (1966), a traditional social learning theorist, children acquire gender roles by imitating models and being rewarded for gender-appropriate behavior. Children may pattern their behavior after a parent, other adults or after peers. Behavioral feedback, together with direct teaching by parents and other adults, reinforces gender-typing. A boy who models his behavior after his father is commended for acting "like a boy." A girl gets compliments on a pretty dress or hairstyle.

Since the 1970s, however, studies have cast doubt on the power of same-sex modeling alone to account for gender differences. As cognitive explanations have come to the fore, traditional social learning theory has lost favor (Martin et al., 2002). Albert Bandura's (1986; Bussey & Bandura, 1999) newer **social cognitive theory,** an expansion of social learning theory, incorporates some cognitive elements.

social cognitive theory
Albert Bandura's expansion of social learning theory; holds that children learn gender roles through socialization.

According to social cognitive theory, observation enables children to actively learn much about gender-typed behaviors before performing them. Instead of viewing the environment as a constant, social cognitive theory recognizes that children select or even create their environments through their choice of playmates and activities. However, critics say that social cognitive theory does not explain how children differentiate between boys and girls before they have a concept of gender, or what initially motivates children to acquire gender knowledge (Martin et al., 2002).

For social cognitive theorists, socialization—the way a child interprets and internalizes experiences with parents, teachers, peers, and cultural institutions—plays a central part in gender development. In the following sections we address three primary sources of social influences on gender development: family, peer, and cultural.

Family Influences Usually, experiences in the family seem to reinforce gender-typical preferences and attitudes. We say *seems* because it is difficult to separate parents' genetic influence from the influence of the environment they create. Also, parents may be responding to rather than encouraging children's gender-typed behavior (Iervolino et al., 2005).

Boys tend to be more strongly gender-socialized concerning play preferences than girls. Parents, especially fathers, generally show more discomfort if a boy plays with a doll than if a girl plays with a truck (Ruble, Martin & Berenbaum, 2006; Sandnabba & Ahlberg, 1999). Girls have more freedom than boys in their clothes, games, and choice of playmates (Fagot, Rogers & Leinbach, 2000; Miedzian, 1991).

The division of labor in a household matters too. Parents who adhere to traditional gender schemas are more likely to have strongly gender-typed children (Tenengaum & Leaper, 2002). There are indications that the father's role in gender socialization is especially important, and that viewing fathers engaged in household and child care work is associated with decreased gender-typing (Deutsch, Servis & Payne, 2001; Turner & Gervai, 1995).

Peer Influences Even in early childhood, the peer group is a major influence on gender-typing. Preschoolers generally play in sex-segregated groups that reinforce gender-typed behavior (Martin, Kornienko et al., 2013), and the influence of the peer group increases with age (Martin et al., 2002). Children who play in same-sex groups (Maccoby, 2002; Martin & Fabes, 2001) or by themselves (Goble, Martin, Hanish & Fabes, 2012) tend to be more gender-typed than children who do not. Additionally, the more children chose to play with particular friends, the more they mutually influence each other (Martin et al., 2013). This illustrates the interactive influence of peer processes and self-socialization. Additionally, peer and parental attitudes also tend to reinforce each other (Bussey & Bandura, 1999).

Cultural Influences When a young girl in Nepal touched the plow that her brother was using, she was scolded. In this way she learned that as a girl she must refrain from acts her brother was expected to perform (D. Skinner, 1989). Social learning theory predicts that the cultural influences around us will influence the degree to which we become gender-typed.

In the United States, television is a major format for the transmission of cultural attitudes toward gender (Collins, 2011). This includes the influences within the content of programming as well as in commercials (Eisend, 2010) and music videos (Wallis, 2011). Theory would predict that those children who watch more television should be more strongly gender-typed. Dramatic supporting evidence emerged from a natural experiment in several Canadian towns. Children who had had relatively unstereotyped attitudes showed marked increases in traditional views 2 years after cable television was introduced to the area (Kimball, 1986). Movies also have an impact. Research has shown that males in G-rated movies are more likely to be main characters, and females are more likely to be portrayed as young and as possessing traits such as intelligence and beauty (Smith, Pieper, Granados & Choueiti, 2010).

Children's books have long been a source of gender stereotypes. Analyses of top-selling and award-winning children's books have uncovered nearly twice as many male as female main characters, greater representation of males in book titles, and strong gender-stereotyping (McCabe, Fairchild, Grauerholz, Pescosolido & Tope, 2011). Female main characters nurtured more, were portrayed in indoor settings, and appeared to have no paid occupations (Hamilton, Anderson, Broaddus & Young, 2006). Fathers were largely absent, and when they appeared, they were shown as withdrawn and ineffectual (Anderson & Hamilton, 2005). Similar results have been found in coloring books, where females are more typically portrayed as children and boys as superheroes, animals, or adults (Fitzpatrick & McPherson, 2010).

Major strengths of the socialization approach include the breadth and multiplicity of processes it examines and the scope for individual differences it reveals. But this very complexity makes it difficult to establish clear causal connections between the way children are raised and the way they think and act. Just what aspects of the home environment and the peer culture promote gender-typing? Does differential treatment *produce* or *reflect* gender differences? Or, as social cognitive theory suggests, is there a bidirectional relationship? Further research may help us see how socializing agents mesh with children's biological tendencies and cognitive understandings with regard to gender-related attitudes and behavior.

THE ADAPTIVE VALUE OF PLAY

Why do children play? Play is ubiquitous, not just in young humans—who take almost any opportunity they can to play—but also in the young of many species, especially intelligent ones (Bjorklund & Pellegrini, 2000; Graham & Burghardt, 2010). Why is this pattern of behavior so common across different species? Why is playing so fun?

Evolutionary psychology can help us answer this question. From an evolutionary standpoint, play serves a purpose. During play, physical attributes plus cognitive and social skills necessary for adult life are practiced. Kittens pounce and stalk, puppies wrestle, horses run and kick. Play is a means of experimenting with new behavioral routines that will be needed in adulthood in a relatively risk-free fashion (Pellegrini, Dupuis & Smith, 2007).

In humans, early locomotor play is believed to support gross motor skill and neuromuscular development (Burdette & Whitaker, 2005). Exercise play increases from early childhood to the early primary school years, and vigorous activity may help develop muscle strength, endurance, efficiency of movement, and athletic coordination (Graham & Burghardt, 2010; Smith & Pellegrini, 2013). Active physical play in outdoor settings offers unique problem-solving and creative thinking opportunities as children interact with varied, unstructured features of the environment (Burdette & Whitaker, 2005).

Object play may serve an evolutionary purpose in the development of tools by enabling children to learn the properties of objects and what can be done with them (Bjorklund & Pellegrini, 2000). In non-Western societies, where children as young as 2 or 3 years old spend time observing adults at work, they begin to emulate their activities through object manipulation and sociodramatic play (Morelli, Rogoff & Angellilo, 2003). As children use objects in pretend play, they display unbounded creativity, substituting the purpose or function of one object with another (Russ & Wallace, 2013).

Social play is abundant in childhood. Children develop and sustain friendships, practice cooperation, negotiate conflict, and build complex social skills in coordination with peers (Jarvis, Newman & Swiniarski, 2014). Across cultures, social play provides an opportunity to learn and practice societal norms of cooperation, competition, power, and social strategies (Kamp, 2001). Pretend play has been linked to cognitive functions, such as creativity, flexible thinking, perspective taking, and exploring bounds of fantasy and reality (Russ & Wallace, 2013). Play fighting, which is often discouraged by adults, has adaptive functions as children innovate story lines, practice controlled physical movements, and experiment with themes of competition and aggression (Hart & Tannock, 2013).

There are cultural differences regarding beliefs about the importance of play. Some cultures actively encourage play, whereas others view play as keeping children busy until they are old enough to assist with work or caregiving (Gaskins, Haight & Lancy, 2007). In Western cultures such as the United States, some argue that adequate amounts of child-directed free play are necessary for optimal development.

Evolutionary psychologists posit for play to be an adaptation, its benefits must outweigh its costs. Potential costs include excess energy expenditure, injury, aggression, and decreased vigilance from predators or other dangers (Graham & Burghardt, 2010). Comparatively, numerous adaptive developmental functions are learned, practiced, and refined through play. Immediate benefits in psychological well-being are noted, with potential lifelong impact on social and emotional health (Hewes, 2014). There is still much more to learn, but one thing seems clear: play is not frivolous activity but time well spent.

From your observations of children's play, what immediate and long-range purposes does it appear to serve? What long-term impacts may be evident from inadequate amounts of free play in childhood? Have you noticed differences in the way boys and girls play together? What might be an evolutionary rationale for that?

Play: The Business of Early Childhood

Play is vitally important to development and has significant current and long-term functions (Whitebread, Basilio, Kuvalja & Verma, 2012; P. K. Smith, 2005b). Play is important to healthy development of body and brain. Play is not what children do to burn off energy so they can get to the real business of learning; rather, it is the context in which much of the most important learning occurs (see Research in Action).

Play contributes to all domains of development. Through play, children stimulate the senses, exercise their muscles, coordinate sight with movement, gain mastery over their bodies, make decisions, and acquire new skills. Indeed, play is so important to children's development that the United Nations High Commissioner for Human Rights (1989) has recognized it as a fundamental right of every child. Children need ample time for free exploratory play.

Researchers categorize children's play in varying ways. One common classification system is by *cognitive complexity*. Another classification is based on the *social dimension* of play.

COGNITIVE LEVELS OF PLAY

Courtney, at 3, talked for a doll, using a deeper voice than her own. Miguel, at 4, wore a kitchen towel as a cape and flew around as Batman. These children were engaged in play involving make-believe people or situations—one of four levels of play Smilansky (1968) identified as showing increasing amounts of cognitive complexity. The categories are *functional play, constructive play, dramatic play,* and *games with rules.* Although certain types of play are more common at particular ages, the types of play can occur anytime.

The simplest level, which begins during infancy, is **functional play** (sometimes called *locomotor play*), consisting of repeated practice of large muscular movements, such as rolling a ball (Bjorklund & Pellegrini, 2002).

The second level, **constructive play** (also called *object play*), is the use of objects or materials to make something, such as a house of blocks or a crayon drawing (Bjorklund & Pellegrini, 2002).

The third level, **dramatic play** (also called *pretend play, fantasy play,* or *imaginative play*), involves imaginary objects, actions, or roles. Dramatic play rests on the symbolic function, which emerges during the last part of the second year (Piaget, 1962). It involves a combination of cognition, emotion, language, and sensorimotor behavior. More advanced cognitive development affords more sophisticated play, but play also helps strengthen the development of dense connections in the brain and promotes later capacity for abstract thought. Play is not just the response to a developing intellect; it is the driver of it as well. For example, studies have found the quality of dramatic play to be associated with social and linguistic competence (Bergen, 2002; Christie, 1998). Pretend play also may further the development of theory-of-mind skills (Smith, 2005b). Pretending that a banana is a telephone, for example, and understanding that you and I both agree on that pretense, can help children begin to understand others' thoughts.

Dramatic play peaks during the preschool years, increasing in frequency and complexity (Bjorklund & Pellegrini, 2002; Smith, 2005a), and then declines as school-age children become more involved in **formal games with rules**—organized games with known procedures and penalties, such as hopscotch and marbles. While most researchers agree on the importance of dramatic play, some theorists have argued that more evidence is needed to establish its causal influence. For example, they argue that dramatic play might be one of many ways to promote positive development, or that, rather than being the driver of development, dramatic play might instead be a secondary consequence of development in other areas (Lillard et al., 2013).

THE SOCIAL DIMENSION OF PLAY

In a classic study done in the 1920s, Mildred B. Parten (1932) identified six types of play ranging from the least to the most social (Table 8.2). She found that as children get older their play tends to become more interactive and cooperative. Although this general progression is common, children of all ages also engage in all of Parten's categories of play (K. H. Rubin, Bukowski, & Parker, 1998).

Parten incorrectly regarded nonsocial play as less mature than social play. She suggested that young children who continue to play alone may develop social, psychological, or educational problems. However, researchers now consider not only *whether* a child plays alone but *why*. Some children may just prefer to play alone. Among 567 kindergartners, teachers, observers, and classmates rated almost 2 out of 3 children who played alone as socially and cognitively competent (Harrist, Zain, Bates, Dodge, & Pettit, 1997).

functional play
Play involving repetitive large muscular movements.

constructive play
Play involving use of objects or materials to make something.

dramatic play
Play involving imaginary people or situations; also called *pretend play, fantasy play,* or *imaginative play.*

formal games with rules
Organized games with known procedures and penalties.

This young "butterfly" is participating in dramatic play.
©Fuse/Corbis/Getty Images

TABLE 8.2 Parten's Categories of Social and Nonsocial Play

Category	Description
Unoccupied behavior	The child does not seem to be playing but watches anything of interest.
Onlooker behavior	The child spends most of the time watching other children play.
Solitary independent play	The child plays alone with toys that are different from those used by nearby children and makes no effort to get close to them.
Parallel play	The child plays alongside other children, but not with other children. The parallel player does not try to influence the other children's play.
Associative play	The child plays with other children. All the children play similarly but there is no organization around a goal. Each child is interested more in being with the other children than in the activity itself.
Cooperative or organized supplementary play	The child plays in a group organized for some goal—to make something, play a formal game, or dramatize a situation. One or two children control who belongs to the group and direct activities. By a division of labor, children take on different roles.

Source: Parten, M. B. "Social play among preschool children." *Journal of Abnormal and Social Psychology*, 27, 1932, 243–269.

On the other hand, solitary play may sometimes be a sign of shyness, anxiety, fearfulness, or social rejection (Coplan, Prakash, O'Neil, & Armer, 2004; Henderson, Marshall, Fox, & Rubin, 2004; Spinrad et al., 2004).

Reticent play, a combination of Parten's unoccupied and onlooker categories, is often a manifestation of shyness (Coplan et al., 2004). Such behaviors as playing near other children, watching what they do, or wandering aimlessly may be a prelude to joining in others' play (Spinrad et al., 2004). In a short-term longitudinal study, reticent children were well-liked and showed few problem behaviors (Spinrad et al., 2004). Nonsocial play, then, seems to be far more complex than Parten imagined.

One kind of play that does become more social during the preschool years is dramatic play (K. H. Rubin et al., 1998). Children typically engage in more dramatic play when playing with someone else than when playing alone (Bjorklund & Pellegrini, 2002). As dramatic play becomes more collaborative, story lines become more complex and innovative, offering rich opportunities to practice interpersonal and language skills and to explore social conventions and roles. In pretending together, children develop joint problem-solving, planning, and goal-seeking skills; gain understanding of other people's perspectives; and construct an image of the social world (Bergen, 2002; Bjorklund & Pellegrini, 2002; P. K. Smith, 2005a).

A common type of dramatic play involves imaginary companions. This normal phenomenon of childhood is seen most often in firstborn and only children, who lack the close company of siblings. Girls are more likely than boys to have imaginary friends, or at least to acknowledge them (Carlson & Taylor, 2005). Children who have imaginary companions can distinguish fantasy from reality (M. Taylor, Cartwright, & Carlson, 1993). They play more imaginatively and cooperatively than other children (D. G. Singer & J. L. Singer, 1990), they do not lack for friends (Gleason, Sebanc & Hartup, 2000), and they perform better on theory-of-mind tasks (such as differentiating appearance and reality and recognizing false beliefs) (M. Taylor & Carlson, 1997). The positive associations with imaginary companions continue through preschool. Although 5½-year-olds with imaginary companions do not have a bigger vocabulary than children without imaginary companions, they tell more elaborate stories about both personal experiences and a storybook (Trionfi & Reese, 2009). These types of results, as a whole, point to the role of play and imagination in the development of essential cognitive and socio-emotional skills.

HOW GENDER INFLUENCES PLAY

As we have mentioned, sex segregation is common among preschoolers and becomes more prevalent in middle childhood. By 3 years of age girls are much more likely to play with

When preschool girls and boys play together they usually play with "masculine" toys such as cars or trains. ©Pixtal/age fotostock

gender segregation
Tendency to select playmates of one's own gender.

dolls and tea sets whereas boys prefer toy guns and trucks (Dunn & Hughes, 2001). Girls and boys also prefer to dress in stereotypically gender typed ways—girls in pink dresses, boys in cowboy hats—and this tendency occurs regardless of the parents' own desires about how their children dress (Halim, Ruble, Tamis-LeMonda, Zosuls, Lurye & Greulich, 2014).

Girls tend to select other girls as playmates, and boys prefer other boys (Maccoby & Jacklin, 1987; Martin & Fabes, 2001), a phenomenon known as **gender segregation.** Boys' tendency to be more active and physically aggressive in their play as compared to girls' more nurturing play styles are major contributors (Martin, Fabes, Hanish, Leonard & Dinella, 2011). Boys engage in higher levels of rough-and-tumble play; girls tend to choose more structured, adult-supervised activities (Fabes, Martin, & Hanish, 2003; P. K. Smith, 2005a). Moreover, this does not seem to be driven by social influences. Regardless of the cultural group they come from, boys tend to engage in more exploratory play, and girls enjoy more symbolic and pretend play (Cote & Bornstein, 2009; P.K. Smith, 2005a). However, the more salient gender is made (for example, with the use of different clothing for men and women, or when children are separated into groups by gender), the more children believe in gender stereotypes and the less they play with other-sex peers (Hillard & Liben, 2010).

Girls' pretend stories generally focus on social relationships and nurturing, and they highlight domestic roles as in playing house (Pellegrini & Archer, 2005; P. K. Smith, 2005a). Boys' pretend play often involves danger or discord and competitive, dominant roles, as in mock battles. Additionally, boys' play is more strongly gender-stereotyped than girls' (Bjorklund & Pellegrini, 2002). Thus, in mixed-sex groups, play tends to revolve around traditionally masculine activities (Fabes et al., 2003).

HOW CULTURE INFLUENCES PLAY

Cultural values affect the play environments adults set up for children, and these environments in turn affect the frequency of specific forms of play across cultures (Bodrova & Leong, 1998, 2005). Additionally, culture also influences development via peer interactions. Children who behave in ways that are contrary to cultural values may be met with rejection from peers, while those who embody those values are likely to be accepted (Chen, 2012).

As one example, Western-style cultures are more likely to value independence and initiative; collectivistic cultures place a higher value on traits such as self-control and group harmony (Chen, 2012; Rogoff, 2003). One observational study compared 48 middle-class Korean American and 48 middle-class Anglo American children in separate preschools (Farver, Kim & Lee, 1995). The Korean American children played more cooperatively, often offering toys to other children—very likely a reflection of their culture's emphasis on group harmony. Anglo American children were more aggressive and often responded negatively to other children's suggestions, reflecting the competitiveness of American culture.

Parenting

Parenting can be a complex challenge. Parents must deal with small people who have independent minds and wills, but who still have a lot to learn about what kinds of behavior work well in society.

FORMS OF DISCIPLINE

discipline
Methods of molding children's character and of teaching them to exercise self-control and engage in acceptable behavior.

In the field of human development, **discipline** refers to methods of molding character and of teaching self-control and acceptable behavior. In casual speech we tend to think of discipline as involving only punishment, but the psychological definition of the word also includes techniques such as rewarding desired behaviors and drawing attention to how actions affect others. Discipline can be a powerful tool for socialization. What forms of discipline work best?

Reinforcement and Punishment "You're such a wonderful helper! Thank you for putting away your toys." Nick's mother smiles warmly at her son as he plops his dump truck into the toy box. Her words and actions provide gentle discipline for her son and teach him that putting away his toys is a positive behavior that should be repeated.

Parents sometimes punish children to stop undesirable behavior, but children usually learn more from being reinforced for good behavior. *External* reinforcements may be tangible (treats, a toy) or intangible (a smile or a word of praise). Whatever the reinforcement, the child must see it as rewarding and must receive it consistently after showing the desired behavior. Eventually, the behavior should provide an *internal* reinforcement: a sense of pleasure or accomplishment.

Sometimes punishment, such as isolation or denial of privileges, can also be effective. Children cannot be permitted to run into traffic or hit another child. In situations such as these, immediate cessation of the behavior is generally the goal. In such situations, punishment, if consistent, immediate, and clearly tied to the offense, may stop the behavior. Punishment should be administered calmly, in private, and aimed at eliciting compliance, not guilt. It is most effective when accompanied by a short, simple explanation (AAP Committee on Psychosocial Aspects of Child and Family Health, 1998; Baumrind, 1996a). It is important to remember that, in addition to punishment for undesired behaviors, the desired behaviors should be made clear. Children need to know what should be substituted for misbehavior.

Punishment that is too harsh can be harmful. Children who are punished harshly and frequently may have trouble interpreting other people's actions and words, and may attribute hostile intentions where none exist (Weiss, Dodge, Bates, & Pettit, 1992). Young children who have been punished harshly also show more externalizing behaviors such as physical aggression and impulsivity (Erath, El-Sheikh & Cummings, 2009). Harsh parenting has also been linked to relational aggression, in which attempts are made to damage another's social status or reputation (Kawabata, Alink, Tseng, Van Ijzendoorn & Crick, 2011).

The influence of harsh parenting is bidirectional; difficult children elicit more coercive parenting on the part of their parents (Pettit & Arsiwalla, 2008). It is also the case that different children respond differently to harsh parenting. For example, children are particularly likely to respond to coercive parenting with behavior problems if they also suffer from attentional issues (Scott, Doolan, Beckett, Harry & Cartwright, 2012). Shyer children may become frightened if parents lose control and may eventually try to avoid a punitive parent, undermining the parent's ability to influence behavior (Grusec & Goodnow, 1994). Essentially, the influence of parenting tactics varies with child temperament, especially with respect to whether or not the child feels guilt or anxiety, a likely prerequisite for the internalization of parental dictates (Kochanska, 1993).

Corporal punishment has been defined as "the use of physical force with the intention of causing a child to experience pain, but not injury, for the purpose of correction or control of the child's behavior" (Straus, 1994, p. 4). It can include spanking, hitting, slapping, pinching, shaking, and other physical acts. Corporal punishment is popularly believed to be more effective than other methods, to instill respect for parental authority, and to be harmless if done in moderation by loving parents (Kazdin & Benjet, 2003). Some researchers have argued that corporal punishment can be one of a number of disciplinary tactics that can be effective under certain circumscribed conditions (Larzelere & Kuhn, 2005). However, a growing body of evidence suggests that it is often counterproductive and should be avoided (Straus, 1999; Gershoff, 2010). Apart from the risk of injury, children who experience corporal punishment may fail to internalize moral messages, develop poor parent-child relationships, and show increased physical aggressiveness or antisocial behavior. As adults they are more likely to suffer from mental health issues, engage in criminal behavior, and abuse their own children (Gershoff, 2013). A link between spanking and externalizing behaviors has been found in children from different cultural and ethnic groups, including white, African American, Latino, and Asian American families (Gershoff, Lansford, Sexton, Davis-Keen & Sameroff, 2012; Berlin et al., 2009). In addition, spanking has been negatively associated with cognitive development (Berlin et al., 2009), and there is no clear line between mild and harsh spanking—mild spanking often leads to the other (Kazdin & Benjet, 2003).

An ongoing debate about the appropriateness of the use of corporal punishment in schools rages in the United States. Twenty states permit the use of corporal punishment in schools. Some educators believe it is an effective deterrent to harmful misbehaviors, like fighting, but others assert that corporal punishment degrades the educational

corporal punishment
Use of physical force with the intention of causing pain but not injury so as to correct or control behavior.

environment. Moreover, critics point to the fact that ethnic minority children and children with disabilities are subject to corporal punishment more frequently (Human Rights Watch, 2010). The American Academy of Pediatrics Committee on Psychosocial Aspects of Child and Family Health (1998) recommends positive reinforcement to encourage desired behaviors and verbal reprimands, time outs (brief isolation to give the child a chance to cool down), or removal of privileges to discourage undesired behaviors.

Inductive Reasoning, Power Assertion, and Withdrawal of Love When Sara took candy from a store, her father explained how the owner of the store would be harmed and how sad he would feel that the candy was gone. He asked Sara how she would feel in the same situation. When he took her back to the store to return the candy, Sara, even though she had not been asked to do so, told the store owner she was sorry she had made him sad.

Inductive techniques, such as those Sara's father used, are designed to encourage desirable behavior or discourage undesirable behavior by setting limits, demonstrating logical consequences of an action, explaining, discussing, negotiating, and getting ideas from the child about what is fair. They also tend to include appeals to consider how one's actions affect how others feel. Inductive techniques are usually the most effective method of getting children to accept parental standards (M. L. Hoffman, 1970; Kerr, Lopez, Olson, & Sameroff, 2004). Inductive reasoning tends to arouse empathy for the victim of wrongdoing as well as guilt on the part of the wrongdoer (Kochanska, Gross, Lin & Nichols, 2002). Parents who use inductive techniques are more likely to have children who see the moral wrongness of behavior that hurts other people (Grusec, 2006; Volling, Mahoney & Rauer, 2009).

Two other broad categories of discipline are *power assertion* and *temporary withdrawal of love*. **Power assertion** is intended to stop or discourage undesirable behavior through physical or verbal enforcement of parental control; it includes demands, threats, withdrawal of privileges, spanking, and other types of punishment. **Withdrawal of love** may include ignoring, isolating, or showing dislike for a child. Neither of these is as effective as inductive reasoning in most circumstances, and both may be harmful (Baumrind, Larzelere, & Owens, 2010; McCord, 1996).

The effectiveness of parental discipline may hinge on how well the child understands and accepts the parent's message. For the child to recognize the message as appropriate, parents need to be fair, clear, and consistent about their expectations. They need to calibrate the discipline to the misdeed and to the child's temperament and cognitive and emotional level (Lansford et al., 2005).

PARENTING STYLES

Parents differ in their approach to parenting. Children interpret and respond to parenting within the context of an ongoing relationship with their parents. Thus the different styles of parenting may affect children's competence in dealing with their world.

Diana Baumrind and the Effectiveness of Authoritative Parenting In pioneering research, Diana Baumrind (1971, 1996b; Baumrind & Black, 1967) studied 103 preschool children from 95 families. Through interviews, testing, and home studies, she measured how the children were functioning, identified three parenting styles, and described typical behavior patterns of children raised according to each. Baumrind's work and the large body of research it inspired established associations between each parenting style and some child behaviors (Baumrind, 1989; Darling & Steinberg, 1993; Pettit, Bates & Dodge, 1997; see Table 8.3).

Authoritarian parenting emphasizes control and obedience. Authoritarian parents insist children conform to a set standard of conduct and punish them for violating it. They are less warm than other parents. Their children tend to be more discontented, withdrawn, and distrustful.

Permissive parenting emphasizes self-expression and self-regulation. Permissive parents make few demands and rarely punish. They are warm, noncontrolling, and undemanding. Their preschool children tend to be immature—the least self-controlled and exploratory.

Authoritative parenting emphasizes a child's individuality as well as social constraints. Authoritative parents are loving yet demand good behavior and have firm standards.

inductive techniques
Disciplinary techniques designed to induce desirable behavior by appealing to a child's sense of reason and fairness.

power assertion
Disciplinary strategy designed to discourage undesirable behavior through physical or verbal enforcement of parental control.

withdrawal of love
Disciplinary strategy that involves ignoring, isolating, or showing dislike for a child.

authoritarian parenting
In Baumrind's terminology, parenting style emphasizing control and obedience.

permissive parenting
In Baumrind's terminology, parenting style emphasizing self-expression and self-regulation.

authoritative parenting
In Baumrind's terminology, parenting style blending respect for a child's individuality with an effort to instill social values.

TABLE 8.3 Parenting Styles

CONTROL		WARMTH	
		High	Low
	High	Authoritative	Authoritarian
	Low	Permissive	Neglectful

They impose limited, judicious punishment when necessary, within the context of a warm, supportive relationship. They favor inductive discipline and encourage verbal give-and-take. Their children know that they are loved and what is expected of them. Preschoolers with authoritative parents tend to be the most self-reliant, self-controlled, self-assertive, exploratory, and content.

Eleanor Maccoby and John Martin (1983) added a fourth parenting style—*neglectful,* or *uninvolved*—to describe parents who, sometimes, perhaps because of stress or depression, focus on their needs rather than on those of the child. Neglectful parenting has been linked with a variety of behavioral disorders in childhood and adolescence (Steinberg, Eisengard & Cauffman, 2006).

Why does authoritative parenting seem to enhance children's social competence? It may be because authoritative parents set sensible and realistic standards. By using clear, consistent rules, they let children know what is expected of them. In authoritarian homes, children are so strictly controlled that often they cannot make independent choices about their own behavior. In permissive homes, children receive so little guidance that they may become uncertain and anxious about whether they are doing the right thing. In authoritative homes, children know when they are meeting expectations and can decide whether it is worth risking parental displeasure to pursue a goal. These children are expected to perform well, fulfill commitments, and participate actively in family duties as well as family fun. They know the satisfaction of accepting responsibilities and achieving success.

Support and Criticisms of Baumrind's Model In research based on Baumrind's work, the benefits of authoritative parenting have repeatedly been supported. This is important because identifying and promoting positive parenting practices is crucial to preventing early-onset problem behavior (Dishion & Stormshak, 2007). Families at high-risk for problem behavior in children who participated in parenting support services were able to improve childhood outcomes by an early focus on positive and proactive parenting practices (Dishion et al., 2008).

Still, Baumrind's model has provoked controversy because it seems to suggest that there is one "right" way to raise children. Additionally, because Baumrind's findings are correlational, they only establish associations between each parenting style and a particular set of child behaviors. They do not show that different styles of child rearing *cause* children to be more or less competent. In addition, Baumrind did not consider innate factors, such as temperament, that might affect children's competence and that clearly exert an influence on parents.

Cultural Differences in Parenting Styles Another concern is that Baumrind's categories reflect the dominant North American view of child development. In countries such as the United States, the traits of independence and initiative are highly valued. Moreover, constraints on behavior are often viewed as being negative by children. Among Asian Americans, obedience and strictness are not necessarily associated with harshness and domination but instead with caring, concern, and involvement. Traditional Chinese culture, with its emphasis on respect for elders, stresses the responsibility to maintain the social order. This obligation is modeled through firm and just control and governance of the child and even by physical punishment if necessary (Zhao, 2002). Although Asian American parenting is frequently described as authoritarian, the warmth and supportiveness that characterize Asian family relationships may more closely resemble Baumrind's authoritative

Traditional Asian culture stresses adults' responsibility to maintain the social order by teaching children socially proper behavior.
©KidStock/ Blend Images/Getty Images

parenting but without the emphasis on the European American values of individuality, choice, and freedom (Chao, 1994) and with stricter parental control (Chao, 2001).

Parenting strategies reflect cultural values. For example, Mexican American families tend to use more authoritarian parenting than white families, perhaps in line with the respect for authority characteristic of Mexican culture (Varela et al., 2004). As another example, in African American families, who tend to use more physical punishment, authoritarian parenting is not related to negative behavioral outcomes, although this relationship does exist for white families (Baumrind, 1972; McLeod, Kruttschnitt & Dornfeld, 1994).

SPECIAL BEHAVIORAL CONCERNS

Three issues of special concern to parents, caregivers, and teachers of preschool children are how to promote altruism, curb aggression, and deal with fears that often arise at this age.

Prosocial Behavior Alex, at 3½, responded to two preschool classmates' complaints that they did not have enough modeling clay, his favorite plaything, by giving them half of his. Alex was showing **altruism:** motivation to help another person with no expectation of reward. Altruism often entails cost, self-sacrifice, or risk. Altruism is at the heart of **prosocial behavior,** voluntary, positive actions to help others.

Even before the 2nd birthday, children often help others, share belongings and food, and offer comfort. Research has revealed three preferences for sharing resources: a preference to share with close relations, reciprocity (a preference to share with people who have shared with you), and indirect reciprocity (a preference to share with people who share with others). In a set of experiments on 3½-year-old children, researchers were able to demonstrate that these preferences are present and functional in young children (Olson & Spelke, 2008). Moreover, there are suggestions that the tendency to be prosocial is akin to a personality trait. Preschoolers who were sympathetic and spontaneously shared with classmates tended to show prosocial understanding and empathic behavior as much as 17 years later (Coplan, Prakash, O'Neil & Armer, 2004).

Early appearing and stable individual differences such as these suggest genetic influences. However, while genes matter, so does the environment. Cultures vary in the degree to which they foster prosocial behavior. Traditional cultures in which people live in extended family groups and share work seem to instill prosocial values more than cultures that stress individual achievement (Eisenberg & Fabes, 1998). The more immediate environment matters as well. Parents who show affection and use positive (inductive) disciplinary strategies encourage their children's natural tendency to prosocial behavior (Knafo & Plomin, 2006). Additionally, parents of prosocial children are typically prosocial themselves. They point out models of prosocial behavior and steer children toward stories, films, and television programs that depict cooperation, sharing, and empathy and encourage sympathy, generosity, and helpfulness (Singer & Singer, 1998), which have been shown to increase children's altruism, cooperation, and even tolerance for others (Wilson, 2008). Relationships with siblings, peers, and teachers also can model and reinforce prosocial behavior (Eisenberg, 1992).

Aggression Noah walks over to Jake, who is playing quietly with a toy car. Noah hits Jake and snatches the car away. He has used aggression as a tool to gain access to a wanted object. This is **instrumental aggression,** or aggression used as an instrument to reach a goal—the most common type of aggression in early childhood. Between ages 2½ and 5, children frequently struggle over toys and control of space. Aggression surfaces mostly during social play; children who fight the most also tend to be the most sociable and competent. In fact, the ability to show some instrumental aggression may be a necessary step in social development.

As children develop more self-control and become better able to express themselves verbally, they typically shift from showing aggression with blows to doing it with words (Coie & Dodge, 1998; Tremblay et al., 2004). However, individual differences remain. In a longitudinal study of 383 preschoolers, 11 percent of the girls and 9 percent of the boys showed high levels of

altruism
Behavior intended to help others out of inner concern and without expectation of external reward; may involve self-denial or self-sacrifice.

prosocial behavior
Any voluntary behavior intended to help others.

instrumental aggression
Aggressive behavior used as a means of achieving a goal.

The goal of instrumental aggression is not to hurt or dominate another child, bur rather to acquire a goal, such as a desired toy.
©Randy Faris/Corbis

aggression between ages 2 and 5 (Hill, Degnan, Calkins & Keane, 2006). Children who, as preschoolers, often engage in violent fantasy play may, at age 6, be prone to violent displays of anger (Dunn & Hughes, 2001).

Gender Differences in Aggression Aggression is an exception to the generalization that boys and girls are more similar than different (Hyde, 2005). In all cultures studied, as among most mammals, boys are more aggressive than girls. This gender difference is apparent by age 2 (Baillargeon et al., 2007; Pellegrini & Archer, 2005). Research with genetically engineered mice suggests that the SRY gene on the Y chromosome may play a role (Gatewood et al., 2006).

However, when aggression is looked at more closely, it becomes apparent that boys and girls also tend to use different kinds of aggression. Boys engage in more **overt (direct) aggression** and tend to openly direct aggressive acts at a target. Girls, by contrast, tend to engage in a form of indirect social aggression known as **relational aggression** (Putallaz & Bierman, 2004). This more subtle kind of aggression consists of damaging or interfering with relationships, reputation, or psychological well-being, often through teasing, manipulation, ostracism, or bids for control. It may include spreading rumors, name-calling, put-downs, or excluding someone from a group. It can be either overt or covert (indirect)—for example, making mean faces or ignoring someone. Among preschoolers, it tends to be direct and face-to-face ("You can't come to my party if you don't give me that toy") (Archer, 2004; Brendgen et al., 2005).

From an evolutionary perspective, boys' greater overt aggressiveness, like their greater size and strength, may prepare them to compete for a mate (Archer, 2004). Males produce many sperm; females generally produce only one ovum at a time. Males can increase their reproductive output by gaining access to females. Thus males are predicted to be more competitive and more likely to take the risks of physical aggression. Females' reproductive output is limited by their own bodies; thus the need for physical aggression as a means by which to compete is diminished (Pellegrini & Archer, 2005).

Influences on Aggression Why are some children more aggressive than others? Temperament may play a part. Children who are intensely emotional and low in self-control, or who have a difficult temperament, tend to express anger aggressively (Eisenberg, Fabes, Nyman, Bernzweig & Pinuelas, 1994; Rubin, Burgess, Dwyer & Hastings, 2003; Yaman, Mesman, van IJzendoorn & Bakermans-Kranenburg, 2010).

Both physical and social aggression have genetic and environmental sources, but their relative influence differs. Among 234 6-year-old twins, physical aggression was 50 to 60 percent heritable; the remainder of the variance was attributable to nonshared environmental influences (unique experiences). Social aggression was much more influenced by the environment; the variance was only 20 percent explained by genetics, 20 percent by shared environmental influences, and 60 percent by nonshared experiences (Brendgen et al., 2005).

Parental behaviors strongly influence aggressiveness. In several longitudinal studies, insecure attachment and lack of maternal warmth and affection in infancy predicted aggressiveness in early childhood (Coie & Dodge, 1998; MacKinnon-Lewis, Starnes, Volling & Johnson, 1997; Rubin, Burgess & Hastings, 2002). Manipulative behaviors such as withdrawal of love and making a child feel guilty or ashamed may foster social aggression (Brendgen et al., 2005).

Aggressiveness may result from a combination of a stressful and unstimulating home atmosphere, harsh discipline, lack of maternal warmth and social support, family dysfunction, exposure to aggressive adults and neighborhood violence, poverty, and transient peer groups, which prevent stable friendships (Dodge, Pettit & Bates, 1994; Grusec & Goodnow, 1994; Romano, Tremblay, Boulerice & Swisher, 2005). For example, children who witness gang activity, drug trafficking, police pursuits and arrests, or people carrying weapons tend to later show symptoms of distress at home and aggressive behavior at school (Farver, Xu, Eppe, Fernandez & Schwartz, 2005).

Culture can influence how much aggressive behavior a child shows. For example, in countries such as Japan and China, there is a cultural emphasis on harmony, self-control, and group cohesiveness. Anger and aggression contradict these cultural values. Thus, Chinese and Japanese mothers are more likely than U.S. mothers to use inductive discipline, pointing

overt (direct) aggression
Aggression that is openly directed at its target.

relational (social or indirect) aggression
Aggression aimed at damaging or interfering with another person's relationships, reputation, or psychological well-being.

A young girl is brave enough to pick up a crab despite the risk of being pinched. ©Johner Images/Getty Images

out how aggressive behavior hurts others. They also show strong disappointment when children fail to meet behavioral standards. Moreover, teachers and peers are more likely to reject or exclude such children, and they are more likely than less aggressive children to have low social status (Zahn-Waxler, Friedman, Cole, Mizuta & Hiruma, 1996; Chen, 2010).

Fearfulness Passing fears are common in early childhood. Many 2- to 4-year-olds are afraid of animals, especially dogs. By age 6, children are more likely to be afraid of the dark. Other common fears are of thunderstorms, doctors, and imaginary creatures (DuPont, 1983; Stevenson-Hinde & Shouldice, 1996).

Young children's fears stem largely from their intense fantasy life and their tendency to confuse appearance with reality. Sometimes their imaginations get carried away, making them worry about being attacked by a lion or being abandoned. Young children are more likely to be frightened by something that looks scary, such as a cartoon monster, than by something capable of doing great harm, such as a nuclear explosion (Cantor, 1994). For the most part, older children's fears are more realistic (being kidnapped) and self-evaluative (failing a test) (Stevenson-Hinde & Shouldice, 1996).

Fears may come from hearing about other people's experiences (Muris, Merckelbach & Collaris, 1997). Additionally, fears are also tied to negative events experienced directly by children. Although they come in contact with knives more frequently than needles, most children pay more attention to and fear needles more, presumably as a result of vaccinations (LoBue, Rakison & DeLoache, 2010). Often fears come from appraisals of danger, such as the likelihood of being bitten by a dog. Children who have lived through an earthquake, kidnapping, war, or some other frightening event may fear that it will happen again (Kolbert, 1994).

It is both normal and appropriate for young children to have fears. It is also normal for these fears to fade as children age. Part of the reason many fears are outgrown is because young children get better at distinguishing the real and the imaginary. Additionally, as children master new skills, they develop an emerging sense of autonomy. When that sense of autonomy is coupled with their increased ability to understand and predict events in their environment, children feel more in control, and thus less frightened (National Scientific Council on the Developing Child, 2010).

Parents can help prevent children's fears by instilling a sense of trust and normal caution without being too protective, and also by overcoming their own unrealistic fears. They can help a fearful child by reassurance and by encouraging open expression of feelings: "I know it is scary, but the thunder can't hurt you." Ridicule ("Don't be such a baby!"), coercion ("Pat the nice doggie—it won't hurt you"), and logical persuasion ("The closest bear is 20 miles away, locked in a zoo!") are not helpful (Cantor, 1994).

Relationships with Other Children

Relationships with siblings and playmates become more important in early childhood. Let's look first at sibling relationships and then at children who have no siblings. Then we will explore relationships with peers and friends.

SIBLING RELATIONSHIPS

The earliest, most frequent, and most intense disputes among siblings are over property rights or access to the mother. Although exasperated adults may not always see it that way, sibling disputes and their settlement are socialization opportunities, in which children learn to stand up for principles and negotiate disagreements, in part because the involuntary nature of the relationship ensures that interactions will continue (Howe, Rinaldi, Jennings & Petrakos, 2002). Another arena for socialization is joint dramatic play. Siblings who frequently play "let's pretend" develop a history of shared understandings that enable them to more easily resolve issues and build on each other's ideas (Howe, Petrakos, Rinaldi & LeFebvre, 2005).

Despite the frequency of conflict, sibling rivalry is *not* the main pattern between brothers and sisters early in life. Affection, interest, companionship, and influence are also prevalent in sibling relationships. Indeed, prosocial and play-oriented behaviors are more common than rivalry, hostility, and competition. Older siblings initiate more behavior, both friendly and unfriendly; while younger siblings tend to imitate the older ones. As the children age, they tend to become less physical and more verbal in showing both aggression and care and affection (Abramovitch, Corter, Pepler & Stanhope, 1986). Because older siblings tend to dominate younger ones, the quality of the relationship is more affected by the emotional and social adjustment of the older child than the younger one (Pike, Coldwell & Dunn, 2005). Generally, same-sex siblings, particularly girls, are closer and play together more peaceably than boy-girl pairs (Kier & Lewis, 1998).

The quality of sibling relationships tends to carry over to relationships with other children. A child who is aggressive with siblings is likely to be aggressive with friends as well (Abramovitch et al., 1986). Siblings who frequently play amicably together tend to develop prosocial behaviors (Pike et al., 2005).

Likewise, friendships can influence sibling relationships. Older siblings who have experienced a good relationship with a friend before the birth of a sibling are likely to treat their younger siblings better and are less likely to develop antisocial behavior in adolescence (Kramer & Kowal, 2005). For a young child at risk for behavioral problems, a positive relationship with *either* a sibling or a friend can buffer the effects of a negative relationship with the other (McElwain & Volling, 2005).

THE ONLY CHILD

In the United States, approximately 21 percent of children under age 18 are only children (Kreider & Fields, 2005). Generally, the stereotype of only children as selfish, lonely, or spoiled appears to be false. A meta-analysis of 115 studies found that most "onlies" do well. With respect to academic outcomes and success in work, they perform slightly better than children with siblings. They tend to be more motivated to achieve and to have slightly higher self-esteem; and they do not differ in emotional adjustment, sociability, or popularity (Mancillas, 2006).

Why do onlies do better on some indices than children with siblings? Some theorists suggest these children do better because parents focus more attention on only children, talk to them more, and expect more of them than do parents with more than one child (Falbo, 2006). Because most children today spend considerable time in play groups, child care, and preschool, only children do not lack opportunities for social interaction with peers.

PLAYMATES AND FRIENDS

Toddlers play alongside or near each other, but not until about age 3 do children begin to have friends. Through friendships with casual playmates, young children learn how to get along with others. They learn that being a friend is the way to have a friend. They learn how to solve problems in relationships and how to put themselves in another person's place, and they see models of various kinds of behavior. They learn moral values and gender-role norms, and they practice adult roles. Children who have frequent positive experiences with each other are most likely to become friends (Rubin et al., 1998; Snyder, West, Stockemer, Gibbons & Almquist-Parks, 1996).

The traits children consider the most important change as children become more developmentally complex. Preschoolers usually like to play with children of the same age and sex. They also prefer prosocial playmates who can provide them with positive experiences (Hartup & Stevens, 1999; C.H. Hart, DeWolf, Wozniak & Burts 1992). Preschoolers reject disruptive, demanding, intrusive, or aggressive children (Ramsey & Lasquade, 1996; Roopnarine & Honig, 1985). As children become older, their preferences become more sophisticated. In one study, 4- to 7-year-olds rated the most important features of friendships as doing things together, liking and caring for each other, sharing and helping one another, and to a lesser degree, living nearby or going to the same school. Younger children rated physical traits, such as appearance and size, higher than older children did and rated affection and support lower (Furman & Bierman, 1983).

Young children learn the importance of being a friend to have a friend. Courtesy Gabriela Martorell

window on the world

AGE SEGREGATION VERSUS MIXED AGES: WHAT ARE THE BENEFITS?

Historically, people of different ages mixed together. Families were bigger, and children and adults often worked and played side by side. If they went to school, children were often assigned to classes based on how much they knew rather than when they were born (Neyfakh, 2014), and particularly in rural areas, many schools consisted of one or a few rooms where children of different ages were taught together.

Today, in families with more than one child, children of different ages still play together and interact often. It is not uncommon for the older children to help care for the younger children. They help their younger siblings learn new skills and accomplish tasks. Some take on similar roles as parents, teaching and interacting with their younger siblings while their parents work. In developed countries, parents sometimes believe that younger and older children do not have much to share and assume that children would prefer to play with others of the same age.

In most developed countries today, as soon as children enter day care or school, many of their activities are structured by age. This is a recent change over the past 100 years and is related to the increased industrialization in society and the advent of compulsory education (Rogoff, 2003; Reese, 1998). Same-age play allows for easier competition and collaboration as both children tend to be at similar levels of developmental complexity. Competition can motivate achievement and push children to work harder to accomplish their goals, and collaboration can help prepare children for later education and careers (Gray, 2011).

However, children of different ages can learn a great deal from each other. For example, in Mexico, one study demonstrated that older siblings exhibited teaching behavior and the younger siblings learned by both observation and direct assistance from their siblings during playtime (Maynard, 2002). In Kenya, another study showed that boys who helped their mothers care for younger siblings were on average kinder, more helpful, and less aggressive than boys who did not have such experience (Gray, 2011). Last, researchers in Samoa found that young children

learned about fishing and politics by observation without any intentional instruction (Odden & Rochat, 2004). Thus, there is evidence that children of mixed ages may benefit and learn from such interactions.

Younger and older children both benefit from age mixing. Younger children learn by watching and modeling the older children's behavior and by participating in activities alongside them. They can learn physical and cognitive skills, hone their social skills, and receive care and emotional support from older children. Older children can develop their leadership abilities and serve as mentors. They expand their comprehension through teaching. This interaction helps to enhance their creativity and allows them to develop their ability to nurture and care for others (Gray, 2011).

If you look at classroom settings, research indicates that academic achievement in mixed-grade classrooms is the same as, or slightly better than, in same-grade classrooms. Children in mixed-age classrooms are self-directed, more likely to cooperate with each other, engage in collaboration and take charge of their own education. In classrooms sorted by age, students are given a common curriculum, allowing teachers to focus on specific skills. The focus is on standardization and imparting knowledge and less on the students' ability to acquire knowledge on their own (Reese, 1998).

"We have a lot to learn from people who are in different phases of life than us," said Barbara Rogoff (Neyfakh, 2014). While children can learn a great deal from those who are similar to them in age, there is also value in interactions with others of different ages. Cultures tend to gravitate toward one or the other dimension, but it may be that the ideal situation is a mix of the two approaches.

what's your view — Which do you think is better for children: mixed-aged play and educational settings or age-segregated play and educational settings?

Well-liked preschoolers and kindergartners and those who are rated by parents and teachers as socially competent generally cope well with anger. They avoid insults and threats. Instead, they respond directly, in ways that minimize further conflict and keep relationships going. Less well-liked children tend to hit back or tattle (Fabes & Eisenberg, 1992).

summary and key terms

The Developing Self

- The self-concept undergoes major change In early childhood. According to a neo-Piagetian model, self-definition shifts from single representations to representational mappings. Young children do not see the difference between the real self and the ideal self.
- Self-esteem in early childhood tends to be global and unrealistic, reflecting adult approval.
- Understanding of emotions directed toward the self and of simultaneous emotions develops gradually.
- According to Erikson, the developmental conflict of early childhood is initiative versus guilt. Successful resolution of this conflict results in the virtue of *purpose*.

self-concept, self-definition, single representations, real self, ideal self, representational mappings, self-esteem, initiative versus guilt

Gender

- Gender identity is an aspect of the developing self-concept.
- The main gender difference in early childhood is boys' greater aggressiveness. Girls tend to be more empathic and prosocial and less prone to problem behavior.
- Children learn gender roles at an early age through gender-typing. Gender stereotypes peak during the preschool years.
- Five major perspectives on gender development are biological, evolutionary, psychoanalytic, cognitive, and social learning.
- Evidence suggests that some gender differences may be biologically based.
- Evolutionary theory sees children's gender roles as preparation for adult mating behavior.
- In Freudian theory, a child identifies with the same-sex parent after giving up the wish to possess the other parent.
- Cognitive-developmental theory maintains that gender identity develops from thinking about one's gender. According to Kohlberg, gender constancy leads to acquisition of gender roles. Gender-schema theory holds that children categorize gender-related information by observing what males and females do in their culture.
- According to social cognitive theory, children learn gender roles through socialization. Parents, peers, and culture influence gender-typing.

gender identity, gender roles, gender-typing, gender stereotypes, theory of sexual selection, identification, gender constancy, gender-schema theory, social cognitive theory

Play: The Business of Early Childhood

- Play has physical, cognitive, and psychosocial benefits. Changes in the types of play children engage in reflect cognitive and social development.
- According to Smilansky, children progress cognitively from functional play to constructive play, dramatic play, and then formal games with rules. Dramatic play and rough-and-tumble play begin during early childhood.

- According to Parten, play becomes more social during early childhood. However, later research has found that nonsocial play is not necessarily immature.
- Children prefer to play with others of their sex.
- Cognitive and social aspects of play are influenced by the culturally approved environments adults create for children.

functional play, constructive play, dramatic play, formal games with rules, gender segregation

Parenting

- Discipline can be a powerful tool for socialization.
- Both positive reinforcement and prudently administered punishment can be appropriate tools of discipline within the context of a positive parent-child relationship.
- Power assertion, inductive techniques, and withdrawal of love are three categories of discipline. Reasoning is generally the most effective and power assertion the least effective. Spanking and other forms of corporal punishment can have negative consequences.
- Baumrind identified three parenting styles: authoritarian, permissive, and authoritative. A fourth style, neglectful or uninvolved, was identified later. Authoritative parents tend to raise more competent children. However, Baumrind's findings may be misleading when applied to some cultures.
- The roots of altruism and prosocial behavior appear early. This may be an inborn disposition, which can be cultivated by parental modeling and encouragement.
- Instrumental aggression—first physical, then verbal—is most common in early childhood.
- Boys tend to practice overt aggression, whereas girls often engage in relational aggression.
- Preschool children show temporary fears of real and imaginary objects and events; older children's fears tend to be more realistic.

discipline, corporal punishment, inductive techniques, power assertion, withdrawal of love, authoritarian parenting, permissive parenting, authoritative parenting, altruism, prosocial behavior, instrumental aggression, overt (direct) aggression, relational aggression

Relationships with Other Children

- Most sibling interactions are positive. Older siblings tend to initiate activities, and younger siblings to imitate. Same-sex siblings, especially girls, get along best.
- Siblings dispute resolution promotes moral development.
- The kind of relationship children have with siblings often carries over into other peer relationships.
- Only children seem to develop at least as well as children with siblings.
- Preschoolers choose playmates and friends who are like them and with whom they have positive experiences.
- Aggressive children are less popular than prosocial children.

Physical and Cognitive Development in Middle Childhood

learning objectives

Describe physical changes and health in school-age children.

Describe cognitive development in school-age children.

Explain how language abilities continue developing in school-age children.

Summarize children's adjustment to school and influences on school achievement.

Describe how schools educate children with special needs.

©Moodboard/age fotostock

In this chapter we look at strength, endurance, motor proficiency, and other physical developments. Cognitively, we examine concrete operations, memory, problem solving, intelligence testing, and literacy. We discuss school achievement, methods of teaching reading, and second-language education. Finally, we look at special needs education.

PHYSICAL DEVELOPMENT
Aspects of Physical Development

Growth during middle childhood slows considerably. Still, although day-by-day changes may not be obvious, they add up to a startling difference between 6-year-olds, who are still small children, and 11-year-olds, many of whom are now beginning to resemble adults.

HEIGHT AND WEIGHT

Children grow about 2 to 3 inches each year between ages 6 and 11 and approximately double their weight during that period (Table 9.1). Girls retain somewhat more fatty tissue than boys, a characteristic that will persist through adulthood. The average 10-year-old weighs about 18 pounds more than 40 years ago—just under 91 pounds for a boy and almost 89 pounds for a girl (Fryar, Gu, Ogden & Flegal, 2016). African American boys and girls tend to grow faster than European American (white) children. By about age 6, African American girls have more muscle and bone mass than white or Mexican American girls, and Mexican American girls have a higher percentage of body fat than white girls the same size (Ellis, Abrams & Wong, 1997).

NUTRITION AND SLEEP

To support their steady growth and constant exertion, schoolchildren need sufficient calories. Depending on activity level, a 4- to 8-year-old boy will need 1,200 to 2,000 calories a day, while a girl of the same age will need 1,200 to 1,800 calories a day. Calorie requirements increase with age (USDA and USDHHS, 2010). Nutritionists recommend a varied diet including plenty of whole grains, fruits, and vegetables and complex carbohydrates.

Sleep needs decline from 12.5 hours a day from 3 to 5 years of age to 10 hours a day from ages 6 to 13 (National Sleep Foundation, 2016). Sleep problems, such as resistance to going to bed, insomnia, and daytime sleepiness, are common in the United States during these years, in part because many children, as they grow older, are allowed to set their own bedtimes (Hoban, 2004). Additionally, the presence of a television in the bedroom can be highly disruptive. At the age of 7, 23 percent of children have a television in their bedroom, and increased television viewing is associated with fewer hours of sleep (Cespedes, Gillman, Kleinman, Rifas-Shiman, Redline & Taveras, 2014). Failure to get adequate sleep is associated with a variety of adjustment problems, and this effect is particularly marked when children are African American or come from homes of low socioeconomic status. Sleep, quite plainly, is necessary for optimal outcomes (El-Sheikh, Kelly, Buckhalt & Hinnant, 2010).

TABLE 9.1 Physical Growth, Ages 6 to 11 (50th percentile*)				
	HEIGHT (INCHES)		WEIGHT (POUNDS)	
Age	Girls	Boys	Girls	Boys
6	46.7	47.2	52.4	52.8
7	49.0	49.8	58.7	61.9
8	51.8	51.9	69.9	69.4
9	54.2	53.7	82.7	74.4
10	56.8	56.3	90.9	88.7
11	59.3	59.2	104.5	107.0

*Fifty percent of children in each category are above this height or weight level and 50 percent are below it.

Source: C. D. Fryar, M. D. Carroll, & C. L. Ogden. *Prevalence of obesity among children and adolescents: United States, trends 1963–1965 through 2009–2010.* National Center for Health Statistics. Health E-Stats, 2012, 1–6.

BRAIN DEVELOPMENT

A number of cognitive advances occur in middle childhood that can be traced back to changes in the brain's structure and functioning. In general, these changes can be characterized as resulting in faster, more efficient information processing and an increased ability to ignore distracting information (Amso & Casey, 2006; Wendelken, Baym, Gazzaley & Bunge, 2011). For example, it becomes easier for children to concentrate on the teacher—even if it's a boring lesson—while filtering out the antics of the class clown.

The study of the brain's structure is complex and depends on the interaction between genetic, epigenetic, and environment factors. The use of new technologies has allowed us a window into this process. For example, one technology, *magnetic resonance imaging* (MRI), enables researchers to observe how the brain changes over time and how these changes vary from one child to another (Giedd & Rapoport, 2010).

MRI technology shows us that the brain consists of both gray matter and white matter. Gray matter is composed of closely packed neurons in the cerebral cortex. White matter is made of glial cells, which provide support for neurons, and of myelinated axons, which transmit information across neurons. Both types of matter are necessary for effective cognition.

The amount of gray matter in the frontal cortex, which is strongly influenced by genetics, is likely linked with differences in IQ (Toga & Thompson, 2005; Deary, Penke & Johnson, 2010). Gray matter volume shows a U-shaped trajectory. The overall volume increases prepuberty and then declines by postpuberty (Gogtay & Thompson, 2010). The decline in overall volume is driven primarily by a *loss in the density of gray matter* (Figure 9.1). Although "less" gray matter may sound negative, the result is actually the opposite. We are born with more connections than we need. The "loss" reflects pruning of unused dendrites. In other words, those connections that are used remain active; the unused connections eventually disappear. The result is that the brain becomes "tuned" to the experiences of the child. In this way, we can calibrate our growing brains to local conditions.

Changes in the volume of gray matter peak at different times in the different lobes. Beneath the cortex, gray matter volume in the caudate—a part of the basal ganglia involved in control of movement and muscle tone and in mediating higher cognitive functions, attention, and emotional states—peaks at age 7 in girls and age 10 in boys (Lenroot & Giedd, 2006). Gray matter volume in the parietal lobes, which deal with spatial understanding, and in the frontal lobes, which handle higher-order functions, peaks at age 11. Gray matter in the temporal lobes, which deal with language, peaks at age 14, while the cerebellum, which regulates motor movements takes longer. Generally, gray matter volume peaks 1 to 2 years earlier in girls than in boys (Gogtay & Thompson, 2010).

The loss in density of gray matter with age is balanced by another change—a steady *increase in white matter*. The connections between neurons thicken and myelinate, beginning with the frontal lobes and moving toward the rear of the brain. Between ages 6 and 13, striking growth occurs in connections between the temporal and parietal lobes. In fact, white matter growth may not begin to drop off until well into adulthood (Giedd & Rapoport, 2010; Kuhn, 2006; Lenroot & Giedd, 2006).

Children's brains also show *changes in the thickness of the cortex*. Overall, the volume of the cortex peaks in late childhood to early adolescence (Raznahan et al., 2011). However,

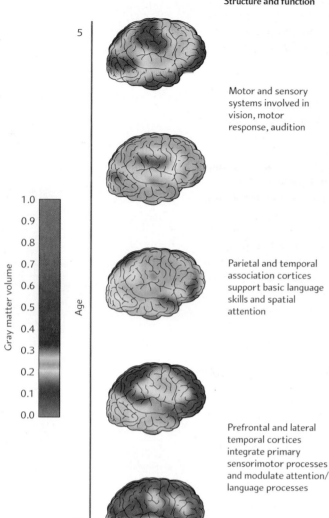

Motor and sensory systems involved in vision, motor response, audition

Parietal and temporal association cortices support basic language skills and spatial attention

Prefrontal and lateral temporal cortices integrate primary sensorimotor processes and modulate attention/language processes

FIGURE 9.1

Gray-Matter Maturation in the Cerebral Cortex, Ages 5 to 20

Losses in gray matter density reflect maturation of various regions of the cortex, permitting more efficient functioning. Blue areas correspond to specific parts of the cortex undergoing loss of gray matter at a given age.

Sources: Amso & Casey, 2006; adapted from Gogtay et al., 2004.

this is not a linear process, and different areas show different rates of change. For example, researchers observed cortical thickening between ages 5 and 11 in regions of the temporal and frontal lobes. At the same time, thinning occurred in the rear portion of the frontal and parietal cortex in the brain's left hemisphere. This change correlated with improved performance on the vocabulary portion of an intelligence test (Toga et al., 2006).

MOTOR DEVELOPMENT AND PHYSICAL PLAY

Motor skills continue to improve in middle childhood (Table 9.2). However, school-age children in the United States spend less time on sports and other outdoor activities than in the early 1980s and more hours on schooling and homework, in addition to time spent on television and on computer activities, which barely existed 20 years ago (Juster, Ono & Stafford, 2004; Basterfield et al., 2011). In 2016, only 21.6 percent of children aged 6 to 19 reached the recommendations for physical activity on 5 out of 7 days in a week (Centers for Disease Control, 2017o).

Recess-Time Play The games children play at recess tend to be informal and spontaneously organized. Most of recess activity involves socializing with peers (Holmes, 2012). Boys play more physically active games, whereas girls favor games that include verbal expression or counting aloud, such as hopscotch and jump rope. Recess-time activities promote growth in agility and social competence and foster adjustment to school (Pellegrini, Kato, Blatchford & Baines, 2002).

Younger children spend more time running and chasing each other (Holmes, 2012). About 10 percent of schoolchildren's free play in the early grades consists of **rough-and-tumble play**—wrestling, kicking, tumbling, grappling, and chasing, often accompanied by laughing and screaming (Bjorklund & Pellegrini, 2002). This kind of play may look like fighting but is done playfully among friends (P. K. Smith, 2005a).

rough-and-tumble play
Vigorous play involving wrestling, hitting, and chasing, often accompanied by laughing and screaming.

Rough-and-tumble play peaks in middle childhood (Bjorklund & Pellegrini, 2002). It seems to be universal, and boys engage in higher levels of it than girls (Pellegrini et al., 2002; P. K. Smith, 2005a). These different play styles help explain sex segregation during play (Maccoby, 2000). From an evolutionary standpoint, rough-and-tumble play has important adaptive benefits: it hones skeletal and muscle development, offers safe practice for hunting and fighting skills, and channels aggression and competition. By age

TABLE 9.2	Motor Development in Middle Childhood
Age	**Selected Behaviors**
6	Girls are superior in movement accuracy; boys in forceful, less complex acts. Skipping is possible. Children can throw with proper weight shift and step.
7	One-footed balancing without looking becomes possible. Children can walk 2-inch-wide balance beams. Children can hop and jump accurately into small squares. Children can execute accurate jumping-jacks.
8	Children have 12-pound pressure on grip strength. The number of games participated in by both sexes is greatest at this age. Children can engage in alternate rhythmic hopping in a 2-2, 2-3, or 3-3 pattern. Girls can throw a small ball 40 feet.
9	Boys can run 16½ feet per second. Boys can throw a small ball 70 feet.
10	Children can judge and intercept pathways of small balls. Girls can run 17 feet per second.
11	A standing broad jump of 5 feet is possible for boys and of 4½ feet for girls.

Source: Adapted from Bryant J. Cratty, *Perceptual and Motor Development in Infants and Children*, 3rd ed. Englewood Cliffs, NJ: Prentice Hall, 1986.

Games at recess, such as jump rope, tend to be informal. They promote both agility and social competence.
©Blue Jean Images/Corbis

body image
Descriptive and evaluative beliefs about one's appearance.

11, it often becomes a way to establish dominance within the peer group (Bjorklund & Pellegrini, 2002; P. K. Smith, 2005b).

Sports and Other Physical Activities In a nationally representative survey of U.S. 9- to 13-year-olds and their parents, 38.5 percent reported participation in organized athletics outside of school hours—most of them in baseball, softball, soccer, or basketball. About twice as many children (77.4 percent) participated in unorganized physical activity, such as bicycling and shooting baskets (Duke, Huhman & Heitzler, 2003).

Besides improving motor skills, regular physical activity has immediate and long-term health benefits: weight control, lower blood pressure, improved cardiorespiratory functioning, and enhanced self-esteem and well-being. Active children tend to become active adults. Thus organized athletic programs should include as many children as possible and should focus on building skills rather than winning games (Council on Sports Medicine and Fitness & Council on School Health, 2006).

Health, Fitness, and Safety

The development of vaccines for major childhood illnesses and modern sanitation has made middle childhood a relatively safe time of life in much of the world. The death rate in these years is the lowest in the life span. Still, too many children are overweight, and some suffer from chronic medical conditions, accidental injuries, or lack of access to health care.

OBESITY AND BODY IMAGE

Obesity in children has become a major health issue worldwide. In the United States, about 17.2 percent of children between the ages of 2 and 19 are obese and another 16.2 percent are overweight. Boys are slightly more likely to be overweight than girls (Fryar, Carroll & Ogden, 2016). Although overweight has increased in all ethnic groups, it is most prevalent among Mexican American boys (28.9 percent) and non-Hispanic black girls (24.8 percent) (Fryar et al., 2012). While Asians show lower rates of overweight and obesity, there are indications that they may have more body fat than Caucasian (white) children, and thus health risks may begin at a lower weight compared to other ethnic groups (Fryar et al., 2016).

Unfortunately, children who try to lose weight are not always the ones who need to do so. Concern with **body image**—how one believes one looks—becomes important early in middle childhood, especially for girls, and may develop into eating disorders in adolescence. In one study of 9- to 12-year-old girls, between 49 and 55 percent were dissatisfied with their weight, with heavier girls experiencing overall higher dissatisfaction (Clark & Tiggeman, 2008). Playing with physically unrealistic dolls, such as Barbie, may be an influence in that direction (Research in Action).

Causes of Obesity Obesity often results from an inherited tendency aggravated by too little exercise and too much or the wrong kinds of food (Sahoo, Sahoo, Choudbury, Sofi, Kumar & Bhadoria, 2015). Children are more likely to be overweight if they have overweight parents or other relatives. Poor nutrition also contributes (Council on Sports Medicine and Fitness & Council on School Health, 2006). Eating out is another culprit; children who eat outside the home consume an estimated 200 more calories a day than when the same foods are eaten at home (French, Story & Jeffery, 2001). On a typical day, over 30 percent of a nationally representative sample of children and adolescents reported eating fast foods high in fat, carbohydrates, and sugar additives (Bowman, Gortmaker, Ebbeling, Pereira & Ludwig, 2004). Children (like adults) should get about 10 percent of their total calories from saturated fat (United States Department of Agriculture, 2010). Sugar, especially in the form of sweetened beverages, should be consumed in limited quantities, as sugar consumption has been linked to weight gain (Malik, Pan, Willet & Hu, 2013; Davis, Bennett, Befort & Nollen, 2011).

Inactivity is another major factor in the sharp rise in overweight. School-age children today spend less time than the children of 20 years ago in outdoor play and sports (Juster et al., 2004). Activity levels decrease significantly as children get older, from an

BARBIE DOLLS AND GIRLS' BODY IMAGE

Barbie has remained the best-selling fashion doll for generations of girls. Although she is marketed as "every girl," Barbie is far from average. Her body proportions present an unrealistic and unattainable female thin-ideal. If she were a real woman, Barbie would have a 39-inch bust, impossibly small 18-inch waist, and 33-inch hips (Dittmar, Halliwell & Ive, 2006; Lind & Brzuzy, 2008).

Barbies act as models for young girls, transmitting cultural ideals of beauty. Girls who do not measure up—which given Barbie's unrealistic proportions includes all girls—may experience body dissatisfaction. Girls may be particularly vulnerable to thin ideal exposure during early childhood, internalizing models used to evaluate their developing bodies. By age 5, girls have internalized thin ideals and express desire for their bodies to look different (Hayes & Tantleff-Dunn, 2010; Tatangelo, McCabe, Mellor & Mealey, 2016).

Rice and colleagues (2016) examined the impact of Barbie on thin ideals and body dissatisfaction among 5- to 8-year-old girls. Barbie's mere presence, whether via photo, physical observation, or play engagement, was associated with higher thin-ideal internalization. This effect extends to judgments made about others as well. Worobey and Worobey (2014) showed preschool-aged girls a variety of Barbie-like dolls of different body types and asked them to assign positive and negative traits to the dolls. The only difference between the dolls was body size, as they had the same head and identical clothing. The results were striking. Positive traits were frequently ascribed to thin and average-sized dolls (i.e., smart, pretty, happy, has a best friend), whereas fat dolls were almost exclusively linked with negative traits (i.e., sad, no friends, gets teased). Nearly two-thirds of the girls said the thin doll was pretty, but failed to ascribe the same trait to the fat doll. Jellinek, Myers, and Keller (2016) asked 6- to 8-year-old girls to play with Barbie or a full-figured Tracey doll. Because the researchers wondered if revealing clothing might exacerbate the effect on girls, the dolls were either fashioned in modest dress or revealing swimwear. The researchers found a main effect for doll type. Girls that played with Barbie reported higher levels of body dissatisfaction, and those that played with Tracey showed lower levels of body dissatisfaction. This was true regardless of what the doll wore. This finding suggests that clothing matters less than the body type of the doll. It also gives credence to the idea that playing with dolls of more realistic proportions may have a positive effect on girls' developing body image.

Although Barbie receives a great deal of critique, other brands of fashion dolls may be just as problematic. Boyd and Murnen (2017) examined 72 popular female dolls available in the United States. Approximately 62 percent of dolls in the sample were also noticeably thin. Barbie has been repeatedly called out in American popular culture for exposing young girls to unrealistic body ideals, but in fact, other types of dolls marketed to girls may share blame in promoting body dissatisfaction.

In response to consumer complaints, Barbie has undergone a series of body proportion makeovers over the years. In 2016, Barbies of three body types premiered—petite, tall, and curvy—with a wider range of skin tones, hair textures, and eye colors to represent a diverse and more inclusive range of beauty. Curvy Barbie has a rounder stomach and wider hips and thighs, but her figure remains slim, though not as unrealistically so (Jarman, 2016). Many are hopeful, but so far no studies have been published to determine if Curvy Barbie can steer young girls away from body dissatisfaction, poor body image, and its ill effects.

what's **your view**
If you had (or have) a young daughter and she requested a Barbie, would you try to discourage her? What proactive measures do you think parents could take to instill healthy body image?

average level of approximately 180 minutes of activity per day for 9-year-olds to 40 minutes per day for 15-year-olds (Nader, Bradley, Houts, McRitchie & O'Brien, 2008).

Childhood Obesity Is a Serious Concern The adverse health effects of obesity for children are similar to those faced by adults. These children are at risk for behavior problems, depression, low self-esteem, and falling behind in physical and social functioning (Datar & Sturm, 2004a; Mustillo et al., 2003; Williams, Wake, Hesketh, Maher & Waters, 2005; Sahoo et al., 2015). They commonly have medical problems, including high blood pressure (discussed in

Promoting an active lifestyle through both informal and organized sports is an important way to combat the problem of childhood obesity.
©Ingram Publishing/Superstock

hypertension
Chronically high blood pressure.

acute medical conditions
Illnesses that last a short time.

chronic medical conditions
Illnesses or impairments that persist for at least 3 months.

asthma
A chronic respiratory disease characterized by sudden attacks of coughing, wheezing, and difficulty in breathing.

the next section), high cholesterol, and high insulin levels (NCHS, 2004; Sorof et al., 2004), or they may develop such diseases at a younger age (Sahoo et al., 2015). Childhood diabetes, discussed later in this chapter, is one of the prime results of rising obesity rates (Perrin, Finkle & Benjamin, 2007). Overweight children often suffer emotionally and may compensate by indulging themselves with treats, making their physical and social problems even worse.

The Centers for Disease Control (2017c) recommends that children and adolescents should get an hour of physical exercise per day. However, almost 80 percent of children and adolescents fail to achieve the goal on 5 out of 7 days a week. Unfortunately school-based activities do not fill this gap, as the average school offers only 85 to 98 minutes each week (National Center for Education Statistics [NCES], 2006a). An additional 60 minutes of physical education per week in kindergarten and first grade could reduce by half the number of overweight girls at that age (Datar & Sturm, 2004b).

Overweight children tend to become obese adults, at risk for **hypertension** (high blood pressure), heart disease, orthopedic problems, diabetes, and other problems (Sahoo et al., 2015). Indeed, childhood obesity may be a stronger predictor of some diseases than adult obesity (AAP, 2004; Baker, Olsen & Sorensen, 2007) and may put children at risk of premature death (Franks et al., 2010). By midcentury, obesity that starts in childhood may shorten life expectancy by 2 to 5 years (Ludwig, 2007).

Prevention and Treatment Preventing weight gain is easier, less costly, and more effective than treating obesity (Council on Sports Medicine and Fitness & Council on School Health, 2006). Parents should encourage healthy eating and activity patterns and address excessive weight gain *before* a child becomes severely overweight. The United States Preventive Services Task Force (USPSTF, 2010) recommends screening children for overweight and obesity starting at the age of 6 years.

Generally, research supports efforts focused on overall lifestyle changes rather than narrowly defined diets or exercise programs. Effective weight-management programs should include efforts of parents, schools, physicians, communities, and the larger culture (Krishnamoorthy, Hart & Jelalian, 2006). Treatment should begin early and promote permanent changes in lifestyle, not weight loss alone (Kitzmann & Beech, 2006; Miller-Kovach, 2003). Less time in front of television and computers, changes in food labeling and advertising, healthier school meals, education to help children make better food choices, and more time spent in physical education and informal exercise with family and friends, such as walking and unorganized sports, would help (AAP, 2004). Parental involvement is a crucial factor. The most effective interventions are those in which parents are helped to change their own behaviors as well as those of their children (Kitzmann et al., 2010).

OTHER MEDICAL CONDITIONS

Illness in middle childhood tends to be brief. **Acute medical conditions**—occasional, short-term conditions, such as infections and warts—are common. Six or seven bouts a year with colds, flu, or viruses are typical as germs pass among children at school or at play (Behrman, 1992).

An estimated 12.8 percent of U.S. children have or are at risk for **chronic medical conditions:** physical, developmental, behavioral, or emotional conditions that persist for 3 months or more (Kogan, Newacheck, Honberg & Strickland, 2005). These rates have been rising, as have the rates of hospital admissions for children with more than one medically complex condition (Burns et al., 2010). Still, most will recover, although children who are males, black, Hispanic, or have overweight mothers are at higher risk (Van Cleave, Gortmaker & Perrin, 2010). Two chronic conditions that have become increasingly common are asthma and diabetes.

Asthma Asthma is a chronic, allergy-based respiratory disease characterized by sudden attacks of coughing, wheezing, and difficulty breathing. Its prevalence in the United States more than doubled between 1980 and 1995 and has remained high (Akinbami,

2006). More than 9.5 percent of U.S. children and adolescents up to age 17 have been diagnosed with asthma at some time (Akinbami et al., 2012). It is 20 percent more likely to be diagnosed in black children than in white children (McDaniel, Paxson & Waldfogel, 2006). Its prevalence has leveled off in developed countries, but is still increasing in developing countries (Asher, 2010).

The causes of the asthma increases are uncertain, but a genetic predisposition is likely to be involved (Eder et al., 2006). For example, researchers have identified a gene variant that increases the risk of developing asthma, an effect that is exacerbated in homes where children are exposed to smoke (Caliskan et al., 2013). Smoke exposure is a major environmental risk factor; allergens such as household pets, molds, and cockroach droppings have also been proposed (Bollinger, 2003; Etzel, 2003). However, findings regarding these proposed causes, except for smoke exposure, are inconclusive. Increasing evidence points to an association between obesity and asthma (Weinmayr et al., 2014). Some researchers have focused on genes that might confer a shared genetic risk for asthma (Melen et al., 2010) while others have argued that the association exists because of an underlying lifestyle factor related to both conditions (Eder et al., 2006).

Diabetes **Diabetes** is one of the most common diseases in school-aged children. In 2015, more than 132,000 children in the United States had diabetes (Centers for Disease Control and Prevention, 2017f). Diabetes is characterized by high levels of glucose in the blood as a result of defective insulin production, ineffective insulin action, or both.

Type 1 diabetes is the result of an insulin deficiency that occurs when insulin-producing cells in the pancreas are destroyed. Type 1 diabetes accounts for 5 to 10 percent of all diabetes cases and for almost all diabetes in children under 10 years of age. Symptoms include increased thirst and urination, hunger, weight loss, blurred vision, and fatigue. Treatment includes insulin administration, nutrition management, and physical activity (National Diabetes Education Program, 2008).

Type 2 diabetes is characterized by insulin resistance and used to be found primarily in overweight and older adults. With the increase in childhood obesity, more and more children are being diagnosed with this form of diabetes. Each year about 3,700 children are diagnosed with type 2 diabetes, and statistics show increased incidence of the disease among African Americans, American Indians, and Latin Americans. Symptoms are similar to type 1 diabetes (Zylke & DeAngelis, 2007). Nutrition management and increased physical activity can be effective treatments, although glucose-lowering medication or insulin may be needed for resistant cases.

ACCIDENTAL INJURIES

As in early childhood, accidental injuries are the leading cause of death among school-age U.S. children (Centers for Disease Control and Prevention, 2017k). An estimated 70 percent of children in the United States ride bicycles, making this one of the most popular forms of outdoor recreation and exercise (Mattei, Bond, Goulart, Sloffer, Morris & Lin, 2012). Unfortunately despite the existence of laws requiring their use in 21 states and the District of Columbia, bicycle helmet use is still low (Kaushik, Krisch, Schroeder, Flick & Nemergut, 2015). An estimated 23,000 children each year suffer serious brain injuries from bicycle accidents, and as many as 88 percent of these injuries could be prevented by using helmets (AAP Council on Injury and Poison Prevention, 2001). Protective headgear also is vital for baseball and softball, football, roller skating, in-line skating, skateboarding, scooter riding, horseback riding, hockey, speed sledding, snowmobiling, skiing, snowboarding, and tobogganing. For soccer, "heading" the ball should be minimized because of the danger of brain injury (AAP Council on Sports Medicine and Fitness, 2001). Also, because of the need for stringent safety precautions and constant supervision for trampoline use, the AAP Council on Injury, Violence and Poison Prevention and the Council on Sports Medicine and Fitness (Briskin et al., 2012) recommend that parents not buy trampolines and that children only be allowed to use trampolines as part of structured training programs.

diabetes
One of the most common diseases of childhood. It is characterized by high levels of glucose in the blood as a result of defective insulin production, ineffective insulin action, or both.

COGNITIVE DEVELOPMENT

Piagetian Approach: The Concrete Operational Child

At about age 7, according to Piaget, children enter the stage of **concrete operations** when they can use mental operations, such as reasoning, to solve concrete (actual) problems. Children can think logically; however, their thinking is still limited to real situations in the here and now. Now we focus on the cognitive advances typical of this stage of development.

COGNITIVE ADVANCES

In the stage of concrete operations, children have a better understanding than preoperational children of spatial concepts, causality, categorization, inductive and deductive reasoning, conservation, and number (Table 9.3).

Spatial Relationships and Causality Eight-year-old Ella stares intently at the map. "The star means we are here," she points, "so that must mean the store is there!" Ella turns to her mother with a smile and they both begin walking.

Ella is now in the stage of concrete operations. She is better able to understand spatial relationships. This allows her to interpret a map, find her way to and from school, estimate the time to get from one place to another, and remember routes and landmarks. Children are more easily able to navigate a physical environment with which they have experience, and training can help improve spatial skills as well (Uttal et al., 2013).

Another key development during middle childhood involves the ability to make judgments about cause and effect. These specific abilities improve as children age. For example, when 5- to 12-year-old children were asked to predict how balance scales worked, the older children gave more correct answers. In addition, earlier in middle childhood they understood that the number of objects on each side of a scale mattered, but it was not until later that they understood that the distance of objects from the center of a scale was also important (Amsel, Goodman, Savoie & Clark, 1996).

TABLE 9.3 Advances in Selected Cognitive Abilities during Middle Childhood

Ability	Example
Spatial thinking	Danielle can use a map or model to help her search for a hidden object. She can find her way to and from school, estimate distances, and judge how long it will take her to get somewhere.
Cause and effect	Douglas knows which physical attributes of objects on a balance scale matter (i.e., number of objects matters but color does not). He does not yet know which spatial factors (e.g., position, placement of the objects) matter.
Categorization	Elena can sort objects into categories, such as shape, color, or both. She knows that a subclass (roses) has fewer members than the class of which it is a part (flowers).
Seriation and transitive inference	Catherine can arrange a group of sticks in order, from the shortest to the longest. She knows that if one stick is longer than a second stick, and the second stick is longer than a third, then the first stick is longer than the third.
Inductive and deductive reasoning	Dominic can solve both inductive and deductive problems and knows that inductive conclusions (based on particular premises) are less certain than deductive conclusions (based on general premises).
Conservation	Felipe, at age 7, knows that a clay ball rolled into a sausage, still contains the same amount of clay (conservation of substance). At age 9, he knows that the ball and the sausage weigh the same. In early adolescence he will understand that they displace the same amount of liquid if dropped in water.
Number and mathematics	Kevin can count in his head, can add by counting up from the smaller number, and can do simple story problems.

Categorization John sits at the table, working on his class project. He is making a timeline of his life. His mother has given him six photographs of himself from infancy to the current time, and John carefully lays them in order from earliest to latest.

Part of the reason John is now able to complete tasks such as this class project is because he is better able to categorize objects. This emerging skill involves a series of relatively sophisticated abilities. One such ability is **seriation,** arranging objects in a series according to one or more dimensions. Children become increasingly better at seriation for dimensions such as time (earliest to latest), length (shortest to longest), or color (lightest to darkest) (Piaget, 1952).

Another emerging ability is that of **transitive inferences** (if a < b and b < c, then a < c). For example, Mateo is shown three sticks: a short yellow stick, a medium-length green stick, and a long blue stick. He is shown that the yellow stick is shorter than the green stick, and is then shown that the green stick is shorter than the blue stick. However, he is not shown all three sticks in order of their length. If Mateo is able to understand transitive inferences, he should be able to quickly and easily infer that the yellow stick is shorter than the blue stick without physically comparing them (Chapman & Lindenberger, 1988; Piaget & Inhelder, 1967).

Class inclusion also becomes easier. **Class inclusion** is the ability to see the relationship between a whole and its parts, and to understand the categories within a whole. For example, Piaget (1964) showed preoperational children 10 flowers—seven roses and three carnations—and asked them whether there were more roses or more flowers. Children in the preoperational stage of development tended to say there were more roses because they were comparing the roses with the carnations rather than the whole bunch of flowers. However, at about age 7 or 8, when children have reached the concrete operations stage, they are able to understand that roses are a subcategory of the flowers, and that there are therefore more flowers than there are roses (Flavell, Miller & Miller, 2002).

Inductive and Deductive Reasoning **Inductive reasoning** involves making observations about particular members of a class of people, animals, objects, or events, and then drawing conclusions about the class as a whole. For example, if one neighbor's dog barks and another neighbor's dog barks, then the conclusion might be that all dogs bark. Inductive reasoning must be tentative, however, because it is always possible to come across new information, such as a dog that does not bark.

Deductive reasoning, by contrast, starts with a general statement—a premise—about a class and applies it to particular members of the class. If a premise is true of the whole class, and the reasoning is sound, then the conclusion must be true. So, for example, if the belief is that all dogs bark, and a new dog comes along, it would be reasonable to conclude that the new dog will also bark.

Piaget believed that children in the concrete operations stage of cognitive development used only inductive reasoning, and deductive reasoning did not develop until adolescence. However, research suggests Piaget underestimated the abilities of children. In one study, researchers gave reasoning problems to kindergarteners, second graders, fourth graders, and sixth graders. Because they did not want the children to use real-world knowledge, they used imaginary terms and words to create both inductive and deductive reasoning problems. For example, one of the inductive problems was "Tombor is a popgop. Tombor wears blue boots. Do all popgops wear blue boots?" The corresponding deductive reasoning problem was "All popgops wear blue boots. Tombor is a popgop. Does Tombor wear blue boots?" Contrary to Piagetian theory, second graders (but not kindergartners) were able to answer both kinds of problems correctly (Galotti, Komatsu & Voelz, 1997; Pillow, 2002). Given age-appropriate testing methods, evidence of inductive and deductive reasoning is present considerably earlier than Piaget predicted.

Conservation In the preoperational stage of development, children are focused on appearances and have difficulty with abstract concepts. For example, Camilla, who is at the preoperational stage of development, is likely to think that if one of two identical clay balls is rolled into a long thin snake, it will now contain more clay because it is

seriation
Ability to order items along a dimension.

transitive inference
Understanding the relationship between two objects by knowing the relationship of each to a third object.

class inclusion
Understanding of the relationship between a whole and its parts.

inductive reasoning
Type of logical reasoning that moves from particular observations about members of a class to a general conclusion about that class.

deductive reasoning
Type of logical reasoning that moves from a general premise about a class to a conclusion about a particular member or members of the class.

A child who has achieved conservation of liquid knows that pouring water from a wide, short glass to a tall, thin glass does not change the volume of water, even though the shape is different.
©Marmaduke St. John/Alamy Stock Photo

longer. She is deceived by appearances and thus fails this conservation task. However, Michael, who is in the stage of concrete operations, will say that the ball and the snake still contain the same amount of clay. What accounts for his ability to understand that the amount of clay remains unchanged regardless of the form it takes?

In solving various types of conservation problems, three primary achievements allow children at this stage to do this. First, they understand the principle of *identity.* For instance, Michael understands that the clay is still the same clay even though it has a different shape because nothing was added or taken away from it. Second, they understand the principle of *reversibility.* Michael can picture what would happen if he went backward in time and rolled the snake back into a ball, thus the snake must still be the same amount of clay. Third, children at this stage can *decenter.* When Camilla looked at the snake, she focused only on its length, ignoring that it was thinner than the ball. She centered on one dimension (length) while excluding the other (thickness). Michael, however, is able to decenter and look at more than one aspect of the two objects at once. Thus, although the ball is shorter than the snake, it is also thicker.

Children do not gain the ability to pass the various types of conservation tasks all at once. Typically, children can solve problems involving conservation of matter, such as the clay task, at about age 7 or 8. By age 8 or 9 children correctly solve conservation of weight tasks in which they are asked, for instance, whether the ball and the snake weigh the same. For conservation of volume—in which children must judge whether the snake and ball displace the same amount of liquid when placed in a glass of water—children rarely answer correctly before age 12. Children's thinking at this stage is so concrete, so closely tied to a particular situation, that they cannot readily transfer what they have learned about one type of conservation to another type, even though the underlying principles are the same.

Number and Mathematics By age 6 or 7, many children can count in their heads. They also learn to *count on:* to add 5 and 3, they start counting at 5 and then go on to 6, 7, and 8. It may take 2 or 3 more years for them to count down for subtraction, but by age 9 most children can count up and down (Resnick, 1989).

Children also become more adept at solving simple story problems, such as "Pedro went to the store with $5 and spent $2 on candy. How much did he have left?" When the original amount is unknown—"Pedro went to the store, spent $2 and had $3 left. How much did he start out with?"—the problem is harder because the operation needed to solve it (addition) is not as clearly indicated. Few children can solve this kind of problem before age 8 or 9 (Resnick, 1989).

Research with minimally schooled people in developing countries suggests that the ability to add can develop through concrete experience in a cultural context (Guberman, 1996; Resnick, 1989). In a study of Brazilian street vendors ages 9 to 15, a researcher said, "I'll take two coconuts." Each coconut cost 40 cruzeiros; she paid with a 500-cruzeiros bill and asked, "What do I get back?" The child counted up from 80: "Eighty, 90, 100. . ." and gave the customer 420 cruzeiros. However, when this same child was given a similar problem in the classroom ("What is 500 minus 80?"), he arrived at the wrong answer by incorrectly using a series of steps learned in school (Carraher, Schliemann & Carraher, 1988). This finding suggests that there are different routes for cultural learning. In cultural contexts in which schooling is not as important, children do not generally use abstract counting strategies.

Some intuitive understanding of fractions seems to exist by age 4, as children show when they deal a deck of cards or distribute portions of pizza (Singer-Freeman & Goswami, 2001; Bialystok & Codd, 2000). However, children tend not to think about the quantity a fraction represents; instead, they focus on the numerals that make it up. Thus they may say that ½ plus ⅓ equals ⅖. It is also difficult for children to grasp that ½ is bigger than ¼—that the smaller fraction (¼) has the larger denominator (Geary, 2006; Sophian & Wood, 1997).

The ability to estimate progresses with age. When asked to place 24 numbers along a line from 0 to 100, kindergartners exaggerate the distances between low numbers and minimize the distances between high numbers. Most second graders produce number lines that are more evenly spaced (Siegler & Booth, 2004). Second, fourth, and sixth graders show a similar progression in producing number lines from 0 to 1,000 (Siegler & Opfer,

2003), most likely reflecting the experience older children gain in dealing with larger numbers (Berteletti, Lucangeli, Piazza Dehaene & Zorzi, 2010). In support of this, children who play board games that include linear sequences show an advantage in their number line estimation (White & Bull, 2008). In addition to improving in *number line estimation,* school-age children also improve in *computational estimation,* such as estimating the sum in an addition problem; *numerosity estimation,* such as estimating the number of candies in a jar; and *measurement estimation,* such as estimating the length of a line (Booth & Siegler, 2006).

INFLUENCES OF NEUROLOGICAL DEVELOPMENT, CULTURE, AND SCHOOLING

Piaget maintained that the shift from the rigid, illogical thinking of younger children to the flexible, logical thinking of older children depends on both neurological development and experience. Research has found support for the existence of neurological changes. For example, changes in the ability to conserve number have been related to the involvement of a parieto-frontal network (Houde et al., 2011), perhaps as a result of an increasing ability to inhibit incorrect assumptions about the pairing of length and quantity (Poirel et al., 2012). Children who had achieved conservation of volume had different brain wave patterns from those who had not yet achieved it, suggesting that they may have been using different brain regions for the task (Stauder, Molenaar & Van der Molen, 1993). In another study, the time needed to categorize plants and animals decreased with age, and the brain wave data suggested this was due to a progressive decrease in the number of neurons needed to make the assessment (Batty & Taylor, 2002).

Piaget believed his theories described universal aspects of child development, but it may be that some abilities depend in part on familiarity. Children can think more logically about things they know something about. Thus understanding may stem from culturally defined experiences. Children are more likely to learn about skills that are valued and required in their culture. For example, West African children, who produce, store, and exchange food in markets, attain proficiency at conservation of liquid tasks at an earlier age than Inuit children, who traditionally lived a hunter-gatherer lifestyle (Dasen, 1984). Similarly, experiences in school may affect the pace of cognitive development. When 10,000 British 11- and 12-year-olds were tested on conservation of volume and weight, their performance was 2 to 3 years behind that of their counterparts 30 years earlier, presumably because teachers were focusing on the three Rs rather than hands-on experience with the way materials behaved (Shayer, Ginsburg & Coe, 2007).

Information-Processing Approach: Planning, Attention, and Memory

As children move through the school years, they make steady progress in the abilities to regulate and sustain attention, process and retain information, and plan and monitor their behavior. All of these interrelated developments contribute to **executive function,** the conscious control of thoughts, emotions, and actions to accomplish goals or solve problems. Executive functioning is involved in the capacity to make good decisions and monitor whether goals are being met.

executive function
Conscious control of thoughts, emotions, and actions to accomplish goals or solve problems.

HOW DO EXECUTIVE SKILLS DEVELOP?

Executive functions allow children to be more thoughtful in their cognition and behavior. We can look at biological and environmental influences as working together to shape the developing child over time.

Executive functioning develops gradually from infancy to adolescence and is accompanied by brain development, most notably in the prefrontal cortex (Lamm, Zelazo & Lewis, 2006). As unneeded synapses are pruned away and pathways become myelinated, processing speed improves dramatically (Camarata & Woodcock, 2006). Faster, more efficient processing increases the amount of information children can keep in working

Contestants in a spelling bee make good use of mnemonic strategies—devices to aid memory—such as rehearsal (repetition), organization, and elaboration.
©Jim Lo Scalzo/EPA/REX/Shutterstock

memory (McAuley & White, 2011). As children develop the ability to mentally juggle more concepts at the same time, they are also able to develop more complex thinking and goal-directed planning (Luna et al., 2004).

In addition to the physical development of the brain, environmental influences also matter. For example, the quality of the family environment—including such factors as available resources, cognitive stimulation, and maternal sensitivity—predicted attentional and memory performance in first grade (NICHD Early Child Care Research Network, 2005c). Moreover, children, particularly those with poor executive control, benefit from training. A wide variety of techniques have been successfully used, including computerized training, physical activity such as martial arts or yoga, and mindfulness (meditation) training (Diamond & Lee, 2011). School impacts this developing ability as well. For example, in a 3-year longitudinal study, the responsibility for planning children's informal activities gradually shifted between second and fourth grades from parent to child, and this change was reflected in children's improved ability to plan classroom work (Gauvain & Perez, 2005).

SELECTIVE ATTENTION

School-age children can concentrate longer than younger children and can focus on the information they need and screen out irrelevant information. For example, in school, it may be necessary for a child to focus on a teacher's less-than-exciting lesson while simultaneously ignoring the antics of the class clown. This growth in *selective attention*—the ability to deliberately direct one's attention and shut out distractions—may hinge on the executive skill of *inhibitory control,* the voluntary suppression of unwanted responses (Luna et al., 2004).

The increasing capacity for selective attention is believed to be due to neurological maturation and is one of the reasons memory improves during middle childhood (Sanders, Stevens, Coch & Neville, 2006; Booth et al., 2003). Older children make fewer mistakes in recall than younger children because they are better able to expect and predict what might be important to remember, to then select and attend to the appropriate stimulus when presented with it, and, when asked, to recall the relevant information from memory while ignoring irrelevant information (Gazzaley & Nobre, 2012).

WORKING MEMORY

Working memory involves the short-term storage of information that is being actively processed, like a mental work space. For example, if you are asked to compute what 42×60 is, you would use your working memory to solve the answer.

The efficiency of working memory increases greatly in middle childhood, laying the foundation for a wide range of cognitive skills. For example, between the ages of 6 and 10 there are improvements in processing speed (how quickly information is processed) and storage capacity (how many things can be simultaneously held in working memory) (Bayliss, Jarrod, Baddeley, Gunn & Leigh, 2005).

Because working memory is necessary for storing information while other material is being mentally manipulated, the capacity of a child's working memory can directly affect academic success (Alloway & Alloway, 2010). For example, children with low working memory struggle with structured learning activities, especially when there are lengthy instructions (Gathercole & Alloway, 2008). Individual differences in working memory capacity are also linked to a child's ability to acquire knowledge and new skills (Alloway, 2006).

Research has indicated that as many as 10 percent of school-age children suffer from poor working memory (Alloway, Gathercole, Kirkwood & Elliot, 2009). Training programs can improve working memory capacity. This is especially true for visuospatial working memory, such as that needed to play concentration games in which pairs of cards must be matched. However, such training effects tend to be short-lived and are not transferable to areas other than the specific form of working memory addressed (Melby-Lervag & Hulme, 2013). Nonetheless, the adoption of tools that assess working memory in the classroom could still influence achievement for these children.

METAMEMORY: UNDERSTANDING MEMORY

Between ages 5 and 7, the brain's frontal lobes undergo significant development and reorganization. These changes may make possible improved **metamemory,** knowledge about the processes of memory (Chua, Schacter, Rand-Giovanetti & Sperling, 2006). Metamemory can be described as thinking about memory. In other words, it involves the knowledge of and reflection about memory processes.

From kindergarten through the elementary school years, children advance steadily in understanding memory (Schneider, 2008). Kindergartners and first graders know that people remember better if they study longer, that people forget things with time, and that relearning something is easier than learning it for the first time. By third grade, children know that some people remember better than others and that some things are easier to remember than others (Flavell et al., 2002).

MNEMONICS: STRATEGIES FOR REMEMBERING

Were you ever taught the saying "please excuse my dear Aunt Sally" as a technique to help you remember the order of operations in solving an equation? This is an example of a **mnemonic device,** a strategy to aid memory. The most common mnemonic device among both children and adults is use of *external memory aids.* Other common mnemonic devices are *rehearsal, organization,* and *elaboration.*

Writing down a telephone number, making a list, setting a timer, and putting a library book by the front door are examples of **external memory aids:** prompts by something outside the person. Saying a telephone number over and over after looking it up, so as not to forget it before dialing, is a form of **rehearsal,** or conscious repetition. **Organization** is mentally placing information into categories (such as animals, furniture, vehicles, and clothing) to make it easier to recall. In **elaboration,** children associate items with something else, such as an imagined scene or story. To remember to buy lemons, ketchup, and napkins, for example, a child might visualize a ketchup bottle balanced on a lemon, with a pile of napkins handy to wipe up any spills.

There are developmental changes in children's ability to use these memory strategies. For example, when young children are taught to use a memory strategy, they tend to use it only in the particular context in which they were taught. Older children, however, are more likely to apply it to other situations (Flavell et al., 2002). This process occurs for spontaneous learning as well. As children grow older, they develop better strategies, use them more effectively (Bjorklund, 1997), and are better at assessing if they are reaching their memory goals (Schneider, 2008). Older children also often use more than one strategy for a task and choose different kinds of strategies for different problems (Bjorklund, Miller, Coyle & Slawinski, 1997).

Although it is difficult to teach young children to use mnemonic strategies, teaching older children about them if they are developmentally ready to learn such skills can result in memory gains. For example, memory can be improved by discussing and modeling the use of different mnemonic strategies and drawing attention to their relative effectiveness. This technique works best if it is integrated into the curricula rather than being taught separately (Schneider, 2008). Some teachers ask students to remember more information than other teachers do, and these students tend to use more mnemonic strategies (Coffman, Ornstein, McCall & Curran, 2008).

Psychometric Approach: Assessment of Intelligence

Psychometrics is a branch of psychology involved in the quantitative measurement of psychological variables. The most widely used psychometric test is the **Wechsler Intelligence Scale for Children (WISC-IV).** This test for ages 6 through 16 measures verbal and performance abilities, yielding separate scores for each as well as a total

metamemory
Understanding of processes of memory.

mnemonic device
Strategy to aid memory.

external memory aids
Mnemonic strategies using something outside the person.

rehearsal
Mnemonic strategy to keep an item in working memory through conscious repetition.

organization
(1) Piaget's term for the creation of categories or systems of knowledge. (2) Mnemonic strategy of categorizing material to be remembered.

elaboration
Mnemonic strategy of making mental associations involving items to be remembered.

Wechsler Intelligence Scale for Children (WISC-IV)
Individual intelligence test for school-age children, which yields verbal and performance scores as well as a combined score.

composite score. The separate subtest scores pinpoint a child's strengths and help diagnose specific problems. For example, if a child does well on verbal tests (such as general information and basic arithmetic operations) but poorly on performance tests (such as doing a puzzle or drawing the missing part of a picture), the child may be slow in perceptual or motor development. A child who does well on performance tests but poorly on verbal tests may have a language problem.

Another commonly used individual test is the Stanford-Binet Intelligence Scales. The Stanford-Binet measures both verbal and nonverbal abilities and consists of five subtests: fluid reasoning, knowledge, quantitative reasoning, visual-spatial processing, and working memory (Becker, 2003).

Otis-Lennon School Ability Test (OLSAT 8)
Group intelligence test for kindergarten through 12th grade.

A popular group test, the **Otis-Lennon School Ability Test (OLSAT8),** has levels for kindergarten through 12th grade. Children are asked to classify items, show an understanding of verbal and numerical concepts, display general information, and follow directions. Separate scores for verbal comprehension, verbal reasoning, pictorial reasoning, figural reasoning, and quantitative reasoning can identify specific strengths and weaknesses (Otis, 1993).

THE IQ CONTROVERSY

The use of psychometric intelligence tests such as those just described is controversial. On the positive side, because IQ tests have been standardized and widely used, there is extensive information about their norms, validity, and reliability. Scores on IQ tests taken during middle childhood are fairly good predictors of school achievement, especially for highly verbal children, and these scores are more reliable than during the preschool years. IQ at age 11 even has been found to predict length of life, functional independence late in life, and dementia (Hart et al., 2003; Whalley & Deary, 2001; Whalley et al., 2000).

On the other hand, critics claim that the tests underestimate the intelligence of children who are in ill health or who do not perform well on tests (Sternberg, 2004). Because the tests are timed, they equate intelligence with speed and penalize a child who works slowly and deliberately. Their appropriateness for diagnosing learning disabilities also has been questioned (Benson, 2003). Moreover, such variables as working memory (Alloway & Alloway, 2010) and self-control (Duckworth, Quinn & Tsukayama, 2012) have also been found to be important in predicting academic achievement.

A more fundamental criticism is that IQ tests do not directly measure native ability; instead, they measure what children already know. Further, the tests are validated against measures of achievement, such as school performance, affected by such factors as schooling and culture. There is also controversy over whether intelligence is a single, general ability or whether there are types of intelligence not captured by IQ tests. For these and other reasons, strong disagreement exists over how accurately these tests assess children's intelligence.

INFLUENCES ON IQ

Both heredity and environment influence intelligence. Keeping in mind the controversy over whether IQ tests actually measure intelligence, let's look more closely at these influences.

Brain Development Brain imaging research shows a moderate correlation between brain size or amount of gray matter and general intelligence (Rushton & Ankney, 2009), especially reasoning and problem-solving abilities (Gray & Thompson, 2004). One study found that the amount of gray matter in the frontal cortex is largely inherited, varies widely among individuals, and is linked with differences in IQ (Thompson et al., 2001).

Some research has found that in children of average IQ, the prefrontal cortex peaks in thickness by age 8, and then gradually thins as unneeded connections are pruned. In the most intelligent 7-year-olds, however, the cortex does not peak in thickness until age 11 or 12 (Shaw et al., 2006). More recent research has found that intelligence is highest in those children whose cortex thins most quickly (Schnack et al., 2014). While the details remain unclear, it does appear that the *pattern* of development is as important as the *amount* of gray matter.

Although reasoning, problem solving, and executive function are linked to the prefrontal cortex, other brain regions under strong genetic influence also contribute to intelligent behavior. So does the speed and reliability of transmission of messages in the brain. Environmental factors, such as the family, schooling, and culture, play a strong role early in life; but heritability of intelligence (an estimate of the degree to which individual differences in intelligence are genetically caused) dramatically increases with age as children select or create environments that fit their genetic tendencies (Davis, Haworth & Plomin, 2009).

Influence of Schooling on IQ Schooling seems to increase tested intelligence (Adey, Csapo, Demetriou, Hautamaki & Shayer, 2007). IQ scores drop during summer vacation and rise again during the academic year (Ceci & Williams, 1997; Huttenlocher, Levine & Vevea, 1998). Additionally, scores attained on various educational assessment tests—which test knowledge, like math and science, unlikely to be learned outside of an educational environment—are strongly correlated with IQ, and this relationship exists in all countries for which data are available (Lynn & Meisenberg, 2010).

IQ scores in children are influenced by a variety of factors, including school. Children's scores drop during summer vacation, and then rise again during the academic year.
©Monkey Business Images/Shutterstock

However, the cognitive gains associated with schooling do not appear to be general in nature, and instead consist of direct gains in specific cognitive skills that are then tapped by IQ tests (Ritchie, Bates & Deary, 2015). Not surprisingly, the type of schooling also matters. Children who are enrolled in schools with an academic focus tend to show greater gains in intellectual performance than children in schools with a vocational focus (Becker, Ludtke, Trautwein, Koller & Baumert, 2012).

Influences of Race/Ethnicity and Socioeconomic Status on IQ Average test scores vary among racial/ethnic groups. Historically, black children scored about 15 points lower than white children and showed a comparable lag on school achievement tests (Neisser et al., 1996). However, these gaps have narrowed by as much as 4 to 7 points in recent years (Dickens & Flynn, 2006). Average IQ scores of Hispanic American children fall between those of black and white children (Ang, Rodgers & Wanstrom, 2010).

What accounts for racial/ethnic differences in IQ? Some researchers have argued for a substantial genetic factor (Herrnstein & Murray, 1994; Jensen, 1969; Rushton & Jensen, 2005). Although there is strong evidence of a genetic influence on *individual* differences in intelligence, there is no direct evidence that IQ differences among ethnic, cultural, or racial *groups* are hereditary (Gray & Thompson, 2004; Neisser et al., 1996; Sternberg et al., 2005). Instead, many studies attribute ethnic differences in IQ to inequalities in environment (Nisbett, 2005; Nisbett et al., 2012)—in income, nutrition, living conditions, health, parenting practices, early child care, intellectual stimulation, schooling, culture, or other circumstances such as the effects of oppression and discrimination that can affect self-esteem, motivation, and academic performance.

The strength of genetic and environmental influences appears to vary with socioeconomic status (Nisbett et al., 2012). For example, one longitudinal study of over 300 twin pairs showed that children from affluent families showed stronger genetic influences on intelligence than those from poorer families (Turkheimer, Haley, Waldron, D'Onofrio & Gottesman, 2003). In another longitudinal study of 8,716 British twin pairs, researchers found that the genetic influences on intelligence were high but relatively similar for twins of low and high SES. However, a different story emerged for environmental influences. Nonshared environmental experiences—those events and influences experienced differently by each twin—had a greater impact on IQ for children of lower SES (Hanscombe et al., 2012). Results such as these have policy implications, as they suggest that the environment may matter more for children of lower SES.

What about Asian Americans, whose scholastic achievements consistently top those of other ethnic groups? Although there is some controversy, most researchers find that these children do not seem to have a significant edge in IQ (Neisser et al., 1996). Instead, Asian American children's strong scholastic achievement seems to be best explained by their culture's emphasis on obedience and respect for elders, the importance Asian American parents place on education as a route to upward mobility, and the devotion of Asian American students to homework and study (Nisbett et al., 2012).

Influence of Culture on IQ Intelligence and culture are inextricably linked, and behavior seen as intelligent in one culture may be viewed as foolish in another (Sternberg, 2004). Thus a test of intelligence developed in one culture may not be equally valid in another. Furthermore, the schooling offered in a culture may prepare a child to do well in certain tasks and not in others, and the competencies taught and tested in school are not necessarily the same as the practical skills needed to succeed in everyday life (Sternberg, 2004, 2005). Intelligence might thus be better defined as the skills and knowledge needed for success within a particular social and cultural context. The mental processes that underlie intelligence may be the same across cultures, but their products may be different—and so should be the means of assessing performance (Sternberg, 2004). Intelligence tests should be culturally relevant and include activities that are common and necessary in that culture.

These arguments have led to assertions that ethnic differences in IQ do not reflect intelligence, but rather are an artifact of cultural bias. It may be that some questions use vocabulary or call for information or skills more familiar to some cultural groups than to others (Sternberg, 1985, 1987). Because these intelligence tests are built around the dominant thinking style and language of white people of European ancestry, minority children are at a disadvantage (Heath, 1989; Helms, 1992; Matsumoto & Juang, 2008).

Test developers have tried to design **culture-free tests**—tests with no culture-linked content—by posing tasks that do not require language, such as tracing mazes, putting the right shapes in the right holes, and completing pictures, but they have been unable to eliminate all cultural influences. Test designers also have found it virtually impossible to produce **culture-fair tests** consisting only of experiences common to people in various cultures. Psychologists continue to work on constructing suitable tests, and on interpreting the meaning of findings on intelligence.

IS THERE MORE THAN ONE INTELLIGENCE?

One critique of IQ tests is that they focus almost entirely on abilities that are useful in school and do not cover other important aspects of intelligent behavior, such as common sense, social skills, creative insight, and self-knowledge. Yet these abilities may become equally or more important in later life and may even be considered separate forms of intelligence.

Gardner's Theory of Multiple Intelligences Is a child who is good at analyzing paragraphs and making analogies more intelligent than one who can play a challenging violin solo or pitch a curve ball at the right time? The answer is no, according to Gardner's (1993, 1998) **theory of multiple intelligences.**

According to Gardner there are eight different types of intelligences, and conventional intelligence tests tap only three of them: *linguistic, logical-mathematical,* and, to some extent, *spatial.* The other five, which are not reflected in IQ scores, are *musical, bodily-kinesthetic, interpersonal, intrapersonal,* and *naturalist* (Table 9.4 gives definitions of each intelligence and examples of fields in which it is most useful).

Gardner argued that high intelligence in one area does not necessarily accompany high intelligence in any of the others. A person may be extremely gifted in art (a spatial ability), precision of movement (bodily-kinesthetic), social relations (interpersonal), or self-understanding (intrapersonal), but not have a traditionally high IQ. Thus an athlete, an artist, and a musician could be equally intelligent, each in a different area.

Gardner (1995) assessed each intelligence directly by observing its products—how well a child can tell a story, remember a melody, or get around in a strange area—and not with typical standardized tests. The type of intelligence being assessed would determine the type of test required.

Critics of Gardner argue that his multiple intelligences are actually more accurately labeled as talents or abilities and assert that *intelligence* is more closely associated with skills that lead to academic achievement. They further question his criteria for defining separate intelligences that largely overlap such as mathematical and spatial intelligence (Willingham, 2004).

culture-free tests
Intelligence tests that, if they were possible to design, would have no culturally linked content.

culture-fair tests
Intelligence tests that deal with experiences common to various cultures, in an attempt to avoid cultural bias.

theory of multiple intelligences
Gardner's theory that each person has several distinct forms of intelligence.

TABLE 9.4 Eight Intelligences, According to Gardner

Intelligence	Definition	Fields or Occupations Where Used
Linguistic	Ability to use and understand words and nuances of meaning	Writing, editing, translating
Logical-mathematical	Ability to manipulate numbers and solve logical problems	Science, business, medicine
Spatial	Ability to find one's way around in an environment and judge relationships between objects in space	Architecture, carpentry, city planning
Musical	Ability to perceive and create patterns of pitch and rhythm	Musical composition, conducting
Bodily-kinesthetic	Ability to move with precision	Dancing, athletics, surgery
Interpersonal	Ability to understand and communicate with others	Teaching, acting, politics
Intrapersonal	Ability to understand the self	Counseling, psychiatry, spiritual leadership
Naturalist	Ability to distinguish species and their characteristics	Hunting, fishing, farming, gardening, cooking

Source: H. Gardner, *Frames of Mind: The Theory of Multiple Intelligences.* New York: Basic Books, 1993 (Original work published 1983); and H. Gardner, "Are there additional intelligences?" In J. Kane (Ed.), *Education, Information, and Transformation: Essays on Learning and Thinking.* Englewood Cliffs, NJ: Prentice Hall, 1998.

Sternberg's Triarchic Theory of Intelligence Gardner segmented intelligence on the basis of areas of ability, whereas Sternberg's (1985, 2004) **triarchic theory of intelligence** focuses on the processes involved in intelligent behavior. In this approach, intelligence consists of three elements: *componential, experiential,* and *contextual* intelligence.

- The **componential element** is the analytic aspect of intelligence; it determines how efficiently people process information. It helps people solve problems, monitor solutions, and evaluate the results. Some people are more effective information processors than others.

- The **experiential element** is insightful or creative; it determines how people approach novel or familiar tasks. It enables people to compare new information with what they already know and to come up with new ways of putting facts together—in other words, to think originally.

- The **contextual element** is practical; it helps people deal with their environment. It is the ability to size up a situation and decide what to do. What actions are most appropriate for a given situation depend on the context.

According to Sternberg, everyone has these three abilities to a greater or lesser extent. The *Sternberg Triarchic Abilities Test* (STAT) (Sternberg, 1993) seeks to measure each of the three aspects of intelligence through multiple-choice and essay questions. Because the ways in which we process information should be applicable across all domains of intelligence, *verbal, quantitative,* and *figural* (or spatial) processes are assessed within each domain. For example, an item to test practical quantitative intelligence might be to solve an everyday math problem having to do with buying tickets to a ball game. A creative verbal item might ask children to solve deductive reasoning problems that start with factually false premises (such as, "Money falls off trees"). An analytical figural item might ask children to identify the missing piece of a figure. Validation studies have found positive correlations between the STAT and several other tests of critical thinking, creativity, and practical problem solving. Additionally, total STAT scores predict academic achievement (Sternberg, Castejon, Prieto, Hautamaki & Grigorenko, 2001; Ekinci, 2014).

Sternberg argued that conventional IQ tests, by focusing only on the componential element and ignoring experiential and contextual elements, have less utility predicting outcomes in the real world. In the real world, book knowledge may not always be helpful. For example, children in many cultures have to learn practical skills, known as

triarchic theory of intelligence
Sternberg's theory describing three elements of intelligence: componential, experiential, and contextual.

componential element
Sternberg's term for the analytic aspect of intelligence.

experiential element
Sternberg's term for the insightful or creative aspect of intelligence.

contextual element
Sternberg's term for the practical aspect of intelligence.

The Kaufman Assessment Battery for Children (K-ABC-II) is designed to evaluate cognitive abilities in children with diverse needs, such as hearing impairments and language disorders.
©JuanSilva 2010/Getty Images

tacit knowledge
Sternberg's term for information that is not formally taught but is necessary to get ahead.

Kaufman Assessment Battery for Children (K-ABC-II)
Nontraditional individual intelligence test designed to provide fair assessments of minority children and children with disabilities.

dynamic tests
Tests based on Vygotsky's theory that emphasize potential rather than past learning.

pragmatics
(1) The practical knowledge needed to use language for communicative purposes. (2) The social context of language.

tacit knowledge, in order to succeed. In studies in Usenge, Kenya, and among Yup'ik Eskimo children in southwestern Alaska, children's tacit knowledge of medicinal herbs, hunting, fishing, and preserving plants showed no correlation with conventional measures of intelligence but were necessary for survival (Grigorenko et al., 2004; Sternberg, 2004).

OTHER DIRECTIONS IN INTELLIGENCE TESTING

Some other diagnostic and predictive tools are based on neurological research and information-processing theory. The second edition of the **Kaufman Assessment Battery for Children (K-ABC-II)** (Kaufman & Kaufman, 1983, 2003), an individual test for ages 3 to 18, is designed to evaluate cognitive abilities in children with diverse needs (such as autism, hearing impairments, and language disorders) and from varying cultural and linguistic backgrounds.

Dynamic tests based on Vygotsky's theories emphasize potential rather than present achievement. The focus in these tests is the child's zone of proximal development (ZPD): the difference between the items a child can answer alone and the items the child can answer with help. Thus, dynamic tests contain items up to 2 years above a child's current level of competence. Examiners help the child when necessary by asking leading questions, giving examples or demonstrations, and offering feedback; thus the test itself is a learning situation (Resing, 2013). By pointing to what a child is ready to learn, dynamic testing may give teachers more useful information than does a psychometric test.

Language and Literacy

Language abilities continue to grow during middle childhood. School-age children are better able to understand and interpret oral and written communication and to make themselves understood.

VOCABULARY, GRAMMAR, AND SYNTAX

As vocabulary grows during the school years, children use increasingly precise verbs. They learn that a word like *run* can have more than one meaning, and they can tell from the context which meaning is intended (Owens, 1996). *Simile* and *metaphor,* figures of speech in which a word or phrase that usually designates one thing is compared or applied to another, become increasingly common and more complex over the school years (Katis & Selimis, 2005). Although grammar is quite complex by age 6, children during the early school years rarely use the passive voice (as in "The sidewalk is being shoveled").

Children's understanding of rules of *syntax* (the deep underlying structure of language that organizes words into understandable phrases and sentences) becomes more sophisticated with age (C. S. Chomsky, 1969). For example, most children under age 5 or 6 think the sentences "John promised Bill to go shopping" and "John told Bill to go shopping" both mean that Bill is the one to go to the store. By age 8 most children can interpret the first sentence correctly and by age 9 virtually all children can. They now look at the meaning of a sentence as a whole instead of focusing on word order alone.

Sentence structure continues to become more elaborate. Older children use more subordinate clauses ("The boy *who delivers the newspapers* rang the doorbell."). Still, some constructions, such as clauses beginning with *however* and *although,* do not become common until early adolescence (Owens, 1996).

PRAGMATICS: KNOWLEDGE ABOUT COMMUNICATION

The major area of linguistic growth during the school years is in **pragmatics:** the social context of language. Pragmatics includes both conversational and narrative skills.

Good conversationalists probe by asking questions before introducing a topic with which the other person may not be familiar. They quickly recognize a breakdown in communication and do something to repair it. There are wide individual differences in such skills; some 7-year-olds are better conversationalists than some adults (Anderson, Clark & Mullin, 1994). There are also gender differences. Boys tend to use more controlling statements, negative interruptions, and competitive statements, whereas girls phrase their remarks in a more tentative, conciliatory way and are more polite and cooperative (Leman, Ahmed & Ozarow, 2005; Cook-Gumperz & Syzmanski, 2001). However, not all children show this gender difference. Both Dutch girls and boys tend to be equally assertive and controlling in their play (Ladegaard, 2004).

Children also improve at telling stories. Most 6-year-olds can retell the plot of a short book, movie, or television show. They are beginning to describe motives and causal links. By second grade, children's stories become longer and more complex. Fictional tales often have conventional beginnings and endings ("Once upon a time . . ." and "They lived happily ever after"). Word use is more varied than before, but characters do not show change, and plots are not fully developed.

Older children usually set the stage with introductory information about the setting and characters, and they clearly indicate changes of time and place during the story. They construct more complex episodes than younger children do, but with less unnecessary detail. They focus more on the characters' motives and thoughts, and they think through how to resolve problems in the plot.

SECOND-LANGUAGE LEARNING

In 2013, 22 percent of U.S. children ages 5 to 17 spoke a language other than English at home. The primary language most of these children spoke was Spanish, and 5 percent had difficulty speaking English (Federal Interagency Forum on Child and Family Statistics, 2015). About 9.4 percent of the public school population are defined as *English-language learners* (ELLs) (NCES, 2017).

Some schools use an **English-immersion approach** (sometimes called ESL, or English as a second language), in which language-minority children are immersed in English from the beginning, in special classes. Other schools have adopted programs of **bilingual education,** in which children are taught in two languages, first learning in their native language and then switching to regular classes in English when they become more proficient. These programs can encourage children to become **bilingual** (fluent in two languages) and to feel pride in their cultural identity.

Advocates of early *English immersion* claim that the sooner children are exposed to English and the more time they spend speaking it, the better they learn it. Proponents of *bilingual* programs claim that children progress faster academically in their native language and later make a smoother transition to all-English classrooms (Padilla et al., 1991).

Statistical analyses of multiple studies conclude that children in bilingual programs typically outperform those in all-English programs on tests of English proficiency (Crawford, 2007; Krashen & McField, 2005). Another, less common approach is **two-way (dual-language) learning,** in which English-speaking and foreign-speaking children learn together in their own and each other's languages. By valuing both languages equally, it reinforces self-esteem and improves school performance. However, less than 2 percent of English-language learners nationwide are enrolled in two-way programs (Crawford, 2007).

BECOMING LITERATE

Learning to read and write gives children access to the ideas and imagination of people in faraway lands and long-ago times. Once children can translate the marks on a page into meaning, they can use written words to express ideas, thoughts, and feelings.

Reading and Writing Think of what must happen in order for a child to learn to read. First, a child must remember the distinctive features of letters—for example, that a "c" consists of a curved half-circle and an "o" is a closed circle. Then a child must be able to recognize the different phonemes by breaking down words into their constituent parts. For example, a child must be able to understand that the word *dog* is composed of three different sounds, the "d," the "o," and the "g." Finally, the child must be able to match the visual features of letters and the phonemes and remember which ones go together. This process is known as **decoding.**

English-immersion approach
Approach to teaching English as a second language in which instruction is presented only in English.

bilingual education
System of teaching non-English-speaking children in their native language while they learn English, and later switching to all-English instruction.

bilingual
Fluent in two languages.

two-way (dual-language) learning
Approach to second-language education in which English speakers and non-English-speakers learn together in their own and each other's languages.

decoding
Process of phonetic analysis by which a printed word is converted to spoken form before retrieval from long-term memory.

phonetic (code-emphasis) approach
Approach to teaching reading that emphasizes decoding of unfamiliar words.

whole-language approach
Approach to teaching reading that emphasizes visual retrieval and use of contextual clues.

visually based retrieval
Process of retrieving the sound of a printed word when seeing the word as a whole.

metacognition
Thinking about thinking, or awareness of one's own mental processes.

Because of the difficulties involved in learning how to read, educators have developed a variety of ways to instruct children. In the traditional approach, called the **phonetic (code-emphasis) approach,** the child sounds out the word, translating it from print to speech before retrieving it from long-term memory. To do this, the child must master the phonetic code that matches the printed alphabet to spoken sounds (as described above). Instruction generally involves rigorous, teacher-directed tasks focused on memorizing sound-letter correspondences.

The **whole-language approach** emphasizes visual retrieval and the use of contextual cues. This approach is based on the belief that children can learn to read and write naturally, much as they learn to understand and use speech. By using **visually based retrieval,** the child simply looks at the word and without analyzing the constituent pieces, pulls it out of memory. Whole-language proponents assert that children learn to read with better comprehension and more enjoyment if they experience written language from the outset as a way to gain information and express ideas and feelings, not as a system of isolated sounds and syllables to be learned by memorization and drill. Whole-language programs tend to feature real literature and open-ended, student-initiated activities.

Despite the popularity of the whole-language approach, research has found little support for its claims. Although humans have brains wired for spoken language, there is no theoretical reason to assume that written language, a relatively new invention in human history, has similar evolutionary roots and thus should be learned as naturally as spoken language. A long line of research supports the view that phonemic awareness and early phonetics training are keys to reading proficiency for most children (Jeynes & Littell, 2000; National Reading Panel, 2000; Jeynes, 2008).

Many experts recommend a blend of the best features of both approaches (National Reading Panel, 2000). Children can learn phonetic skills along with strategies to help them understand what they read. For example, they might be drilled in sound-letter correspondences, but also be asked to memorize certain common words like *the* and *one* that are more difficult to decode. Children who can summon both visually based and phonetic strategies become better, more versatile, readers (Siegler, 1998, 2000).

Metacognition involves thinking about thinking. It can help children monitor their understanding of what they read and develop strategies to address challenges. Children with good metacognitive skills use strategies such as reading more slowly, rereading difficult passages, trying to visualize information, or thinking of additional examples when trying to learn information in a challenging written passage. Metacognitive abilities can be encouraged by having students recall, summarize, and ask questions about what they read (National Reading Panel, 2000).

The acquisition of writing skills goes hand in hand with the development of reading. Older preschoolers begin using letters, numbers, and letterlike shapes as symbols to represent words or parts of words (syllables or phonemes). Often their spelling is quite inventive—so much so that they may not be able to read it themselves (Ouellette & Sénéchal, 2008; Whitehurst & Lonigan, 1998).

Writing is difficult for young children. Unlike conversation, which offers constant feedback, writing requires the child to judge independently whether the communicative goal has been met. The child also must keep in mind a variety of other constraints: spelling, punctuation, grammar, and capitalization, as well as the basic physical task of forming letters (Siegler, 1998).

The Child in School

The earliest school experiences are critical in setting the stage for future success or failure. Let's look at the first-grade experience. Then we'll examine influences on school achievement.

ENTERING FIRST GRADE

First grade is a milestone and marks entry into "real school." To make the most academic progress, a child needs to be involved. Interest, attention, and active participation are positively associated with achievement test scores and teachers' grades from first grade through at least fourth grade (Alexander, Entwisle & Dauber, 1993). For first graders at risk of school failure, teachers can offer support such as frequent literacy instruction, evaluative feedback, engaging students in discussions, responding to students' emotional needs, encouraging responsibility, and creating a positive classroom atmosphere (Hamre & Pianta, 2005).

INFLUENCES ON SCHOOL ACHIEVEMENT

As Bronfenbrenner's bioecological theory would predict, in addition to children's own characteristics, each level of the context of their lives influences how well they do in school. Let's look at this web of influences.

Self-Efficacy Beliefs Think of how you felt the last time you studied for a big exam. Did you feel you could do well as long as you studied, and were you confident in your ability to master the material? Or did you feel that nothing you could do would matter, and that the material was just too hard? Your attitude can be described as involving a construct called *self-efficacy*. Those students high in self-efficacy believe they can master schoolwork and regulate their own learning. They are more likely to succeed than students who do not believe in their abilities (Caprara et al., 2008). Self-regulated learners try hard, persist despite difficulties, and seek help when necessary. Students who do not believe in their ability to succeed tend to become frustrated and depressed—feelings that make success more elusive.

Gender Girls tend to do better in school than boys; they receive better grades, on average, in every subject (Halpern et al., 2007), are less likely to repeat grades, have fewer school problems, and outperform boys in national reading and writing assessments (Freeman, 2004). In addition, girls and women tended to do better than boys and men on timed tests (Camarata & Woodcock, 2006). Differences in mathematical abilities in elementary school, when computational facility is stressed, are small and tend to favor girls. On the other hand, boys do better than girls on science and math tests that are not closely related to material taught in school. Girls' advantage in writing and boys' advantage in science are larger and more reliable. Gender differences tend to become more prominent in high school. A combination of several factors—early experience, biological differences (including differences in brain size and structure), and cultural expectations—helps explain these differences (Halpern et al., 2007).

Interest, attention, and active participation all contribute to a child's academic success in school.
©Andersen Ross/Blend Images/Getty Images

Parenting Practices Parents of high-achieving children create an environment for learning. They provide a place to study and to keep books and supplies; they set times for meals, sleep, and homework; they monitor their children's activities; and they talk with their children about school and are involved in school activities (Hill & Taylor, 2004; Hill & Tyson, 2009).

Generally, regardless of how it is defined, parental involvement has a positive effect on academic achievement (Wilder, 2014; LaRocque, Kleinman & Darling, 2011). However, some forms of involvement appear to be more effective than others. For example, homework assistance has not been consistently related to academic achievement (Hill & Tyson, 2009; McNeal, 2012). School involvement, including parental participation in school events and activities and good communication with teachers, is more strongly associated with strong academic performance (Overstreet, Devine, Bevans & Efreom, 2005; Topor, Keane, Shelton & Calkins, 2010). The strongest effects for parent involvement, however, center on parental expectations. Those parents who expect that their children will do well in school have children who live up to those beliefs (Wilder, 2014, Davis-Keane, 2005) perhaps because children also adopt the same attitude about their abilities (Topor, Keane, Shelton & Calkins, 2010).

Socioeconomic Status Socioeconomic status (SES) can be a powerful factor in educational achievement—not in and of itself, but through its influence on family atmosphere, choice of neighborhood, parenting practices (Evans, 2004; Rouse et al., 2005), and on parents' expectations for children (Davis-Kean, 2005). Generally, achievement gaps between advantaged and disadvantaged students widen from kindergarten to third grade (Rathbun et al., 2004). Summer vacation contributes to these gaps because of differences in the typical home environment and in the summer learning experiences the children have. This can help account for later differences in high school achievement and completion and college attendance (Alexander, Entwisle & Olson, 2007).

SES interacts with parenting practices (Gottfried, Fleming & Gottfried, 1998). One large study found that parents from lower SES tended to use fewer education-oriented practices. Thus, these children were disadvantaged both by the quality of their schools and neighborhood, as well as by their parents' lack of interest in and promotion of academic achievement. However, those parents who were involved in their children's education were able to substantially mitigate the negative characteristics of SES. In other words, parenting practices mattered more in poorer neighborhoods than in more affluent ones.

social capital
Family and community resources on which a person can draw.

In addition to parental influences, another factor that may have an influence is **social capital:** the networks of community resources children and families can draw on (Coleman, 1988). In a 3-year experimental intervention in which working-poor parents received wage supplements and subsidies for child care and health insurance, their school-age children's academic achievement and behavior improved (Huston et al., 2001). Two years after the families had left the program, the impact on school achievement and motivation held steady, especially for older boys (Huston et al., 2005).

Peer Acceptance Children who are disliked by their peers tend to do poorly in school, and this association exists for both boys and girls (Nakamoto & Schwartz, 2010; van Lier, Vitaro, Barker, Brendgen, Tremblay & Boivin, 2012). Among 248 fourth graders, those whose teachers reported that they were not liked by peers had poorer academic self-concepts, more symptoms of anxiety or depression in fifth grade, and lower reading and math grades in sixth grade (Flook, Repetti & Ullman, 2005). It may be that the characteristics of some children, including aggression and oppositional behavior, lead to doing poorly in school *and* not being liked by peers. Then, their academic underachievement and peer victimization lead to anxiety, depression, and further declines in academic performance (van Lier, Vitaro, Barker, Brendgen, Tremblay & Boivin, 2012). Early teacher identification of children who exhibit social problems could lead to interventions that would improve such children's academic as well as emotional and social outcomes (Flook, Repetti & Ullman, 2005).

Class Size Most educators consider small class size a key factor in achievement, especially in the early grades, though findings on this point are mixed (Schneider, 2002). A longitudinal study found lasting academic benefits for students randomly assigned to classes of about 15 students in kindergarten through third grade and—especially for low-SES students—a greater likelihood of finishing high school (Finn, Gerber & Boyd-Zaharias, 2005; Krueger, 2003).

In most places, though, small classes are larger than that. In classroom observations of 890 first graders, classes with 25 students or less tended to be more social and interactive and to enable higher quality instruction and emotional support. Students in these classes tended to score higher on standardized achievement tests and beginning reading skills (NICHD Early Childhood Research Network, 2004b).

Charter Schools and Homeschooling Some parents, unhappy with their public schools or seeking a particular style of education, are choosing charter schools or homeschooling. More than 1.3 million U.S. children now attend charter schools, some privately operated and others under charter from public school boards (Center for Education Reform, 2008). Charter schools tend to be smaller than regular public schools and tend to have a unique philosophy, curriculum, structure, or organizational style. Although parents are generally satisfied with their charter schools, studies of their effects on student outcomes have had mixed results (Braun, Jenkins & Grigg, 2006; Center for Education Reform, 2004; Hoxby, 2004; National Assessment of Educational Progress, 2004; Schemo, 2004).

Homeschooling is legal in all 50 states. In 2012 1.8 million U.S. students representing 3.4 percent of the school-age population were homeschooled (Snyder, de Brey & Dillow, 2016). The main reasons parents give for choosing to homeschool their children is a poor or unsafe learning environment in the schools and the desire to provide

Children who are liked and accepted by peers tend to do better in school.
©Stockbyte/Getty Images

religious or moral instruction (NCES, 2008). While advocates of homeschooling argue that homeschooling is associated with good academic outcomes (Christian Home Educators Association of California, 2013; Ray, 2010) the studies that have been conducted have serious methodological flaws and tend to come from a limited pool of researchers and organizations with potential biases (Kunzman & Gaither, 2013; Lubienski, Puckett & Brewer, 2013). Thus the efficacy of homeschooling remains in question.

Media Use Access to the Internet in public schools has skyrocketed. In 1994 only 4 percent of classrooms had Internet access, compared with 97 percent in 2008 (National Center for Education Statistics, 2016). However, fewer black, Hispanic, and American Indian children than white and Asian children, and fewer poor children than nonpoor children use these technologies. Girls and boys spend about the same amount of time on computer and Internet use (Day, Janus & Davis, 2005; DeBell & Chapman, 2006).

Media influences from home also play a role in children's development. The predominant influence is television. In 2003, 6- to 12-year-old children spent approximately 14 hours per week watching television. Computers also are an influence, although much less time (1 hour and 20 minutes per week) is spent on computers. Of that, the bulk of time is spent on video games, with e-mail, Internet usage, and studying comprising the remainder. This exposure to media has varying influences depending on what type of media is examined as well as the gender of the child. For example, television is associated with the displacement of other more beneficial experiences such as playing or sleeping for all children. Computer usage is associated with increases in achievement and problem-solving abilities for girls. However, for boys, who are more likely to play violent video games, computer usage is associated with increased aggressive behavior problems (Hofferth, 2010).

Computer literacy is an important skill in today's world. However, this tool poses dangers. Foremost is the risk of exposure to harmful or inappropriate material. Also, students need to learn to critically evaluate information they find in cyberspace and to separate facts from opinion and advertising.

Educating Children with Special Needs

Public schools must educate children of varying abilities from many different families and cultural backgrounds, including those children with special needs. When considering special needs, most of us focus on those children who have learning or behavioral disorders (Pastor & Reuben, 2008). However, special needs also include a focus on children who are gifted, talented, or creative, as they have different educational needs than the typical child.

CHILDREN WITH LEARNING PROBLEMS

Just as educators have become more sensitive to teaching children from varied cultural backgrounds, they also have sought to meet the needs of children with special educational needs.

Intellectual Disability **Intellectual disability** is significantly subnormal cognitive functioning. It is indicated by an IQ of about 70 or less, coupled with a deficiency in age-appropriate adaptive behavior (such as communication, social skills, and self-care), appearing before age 18 (American Psychiatric Association, 2013). Intellectual disability is sometimes referred to as cognitive disability or mental retardation. Less than 1 percent of U.S. children are intellectually disabled (NCHS, 2004; Woodruff et al., 2004). Worldwide, about 1 of every 10 people are intellectually disabled (Maulik, Mascarenhas, Mathers, Dua & Saxena, 2011).

In 30 to 50 percent of cases, the cause of intellectual disability is unknown. Known causes include genetic disorders, traumatic accidents, prenatal exposure to infection or alcohol, and environmental exposure to lead or high levels of mercury (Woodruff et al., 2004). Many cases may be preventable through genetic counseling, prenatal care, amniocentesis, routine screening and health care for newborns, and nutritional services for pregnant women and infants.

intellectual disability
Significantly subnormal cognitive functioning. Also referred to as cognitive disability or mental retardation.

Most children with intellectual disabilities can benefit from schooling. Intervention programs have helped many of those mildly or moderately disabled and those considered borderline (with IQs ranging from 70 up to about 85) to hold jobs, live in the community, and function in society. The profoundly disabled need constant care and supervision, usually in institutions.

Learning Disabilities **Learning disabilities (LDs)** are disorders that interfere with specific aspects of school achievement, such as listening, speaking, reading, writing, or mathematics, resulting in performance substantially lower than would be expected given a child's age, intelligence, and amount of schooling. A growing percentage of U.S. children—9.7 percent in 2003—show LDs at some point in their school career (Altarac & Saroha, 2007); 5 percent are served by federally supported programs (National Center for Learning Disabilities, 2004b).

Children with LDs often have near-average to higher-than-average intelligence and normal vision and hearing, but they seem to have trouble processing sensory information. As might be expected, causal influences include both genetic and environmental factors. For example, the genes most responsible for the high heritability of the most common LDs— language impairment, reading disability, and mathematical disability—are also responsible for normal variations in learning abilities (Plomin & Kovas, 2005). Environmental factors may include complications of pregnancy or birth, injuries after birth, nutritional deprivation, and exposure to lead (National Center for Learning Disabilities, 2004b).

About 4 out of 5 children with LDs have been identified as dyslexic. **Dyslexia** is a developmental language disorder in which reading achievement is substantially below the level predicted by IQ or age. It is a chronic, persistent medical condition and tends to run in families (Shaywitz, 1998, 2003). It hinders the development of oral as well as written language skills and may cause problems with writing, spelling, grammar, and understanding speech as well as with reading (National Center for Learning Disabilities, 2004a). Reading disability is more frequent in boys than in girls (Rutter et al., 2004). Although reading and intelligence are related to each other in children without dyslexia, they are not coupled in this fashion for children with dyslexia. In other words, dyslexia is not an issue of intelligence (Ferrer et al., 2010).

Brain imaging studies have found that dyslexia is due to a neurological defect that disrupts recognition of speech sounds (Shaywitz, Mody & Shaywitz, 2006). Several identified genes contribute to this disruption (Kere et al., 2005; Meng et al., 2005). Many children—and even adults—with dyslexia can be taught to read through systematic phonological training, but the process does not become automatic, as it does with most readers (Eden et al., 2004).

Attention-Deficit/Hyperactivity Disorder **Attention-deficit/hyperactivity disorder (ADHD)** has been called the most common mental disorder in childhood (Wolraich et al., 2005). It is a chronic condition usually marked by persistent inattention, distractibility, impulsivity, and low tolerance for frustration. In 2011 about 6.4 million children in the United States were diagnosed with ADHD, a rate of about 11 percent (Centers for Disease Control and Prevention, 2016b). Although the rate of diagnoses of LDs has remained relatively constant, the rate of ADHD increased about 3 percent per year between 1997 and 2006 (Pastor & Reuben, 2008; Figure 9.2).

ADHD has two different but sometimes overlapping types of symptoms, making diagnosis imprecise. Some children are inattentive but not hyperactive; others show the reverse pattern. Because these characteristics appear to some degree in all children, some practitioners question whether ADHD is actually a distinct neurological or psychological disorder (Bjorklund & Pellegrini, 2002; Furman, 2005). However, most experts agree that there is cause for concern when the symptoms are so severe as to interfere with the child's functioning in school and in daily life (AAP Committee on Children with Disabilities and Committee on Drugs, 1996; USDHHS, 1999b).

Imaging studies reveal that brains of children with ADHD show delayed growth in certain regions of the brain, particularly the frontal cortex. These frontal regions enable a person to control movement, suppress inappropriate thoughts and actions, focus attention, remember from moment to moment, and work for rewards—all functions that are often disturbed in children with ADHD. The motor cortex is the only area that matures faster

learning disabilities (LDs)
Disorders that interfere with specific aspects of learning and school achievement.

Dyslexia
Developmental disorder in which reading achievement is substantially lower than predicted by IQ or age.

attention-deficit/hyperactivity disorder (ADHD)
Syndrome characterized by persistent inattention and distractibility, impulsivity, low tolerance for frustration, and inappropriate overactivity.

than normal, and this mismatch may account for the restlessness and fidgeting characteristic of the disorder (P. Shaw et al., 2007).

ADHD seems to have a substantial genetic basis with heritability at about 72 percent for both inattention and hyperactivity (Nikolas & Burt, 2010). Many genes are involved in ADHD, each contributing some small effect (Neale et al., 2008). For example, one gene variant that codes for low levels of dopamine, a brain chemical essential for attention and cognition, is associated with ADHD (Shaw et al., 2007; Volkow et al., 2007). Birth complications also may play a part in ADHD. Prematurity, a prospective mother's alcohol or tobacco use, and oxygen deprivation (Barkley, 1998; Thapar et al., 2003; USDHHS, 1999b; Woodruff et al., 2004) have all been linked to ADHD.

ADHD is often managed with drugs, sometimes combined with behavioral therapy, counseling, training in social skills, and special classroom placement. Interventions with children with ADHD will be most useful if they include behavioral interventions, modification of teaching instructions and student tasks, good communication with parents, and collaboration across school professionals such as teachers and psychologists (DuPaul & Stoner, 2014).

Educating Children with Disabilities In 2014–2015, about 13 percent of public school students in the United States were receiving special educational services under the Individuals with Disabilities Education Act, which ensures a free, appropriate public education for all children with disabilities (United States Department of Education, 2016). Most of these children had learning disabilities or speech or language impairments. An individualized program must be designed for each child, with parental involvement. Children must be educated in the "least restrictive environment" appropriate to their needs—which means, whenever possible, the regular classroom.

Programs in which children with special needs are included in the regular classroom are known as inclusion programs. Here, children with disabilities are integrated with nondisabled children for all or part of the day, sometimes with assistance. In 2014, 62 percent of students with disabilities spent at least 80 percent of their time in regular classrooms (NCES, 2017b).

GIFTED CHILDREN

The traditional criterion of giftedness is high general intelligence as shown by an IQ score of 130 or higher. This definition tends to exclude highly creative children (whose unusual answers often lower their test scores), children from minority groups (whose abilities may not be well developed, though the potential is there), and children with specific aptitudes (who may be only average or even show learning problems in other areas). Thus, all 50 states have moved beyond a single-score definition of giftedness (McClain & Pfeiffer, 2012).

Most states and school districts have adopted a broader definition of creativity which encompasses children who show high intellectual, creative, artistic, or leadership capacity or ability in specific academic fields and who need special educational services and activities to fully develop those capabilities. Generally, multiple criteria are used for admission to programs for the gifted, including achievement test scores, grades,

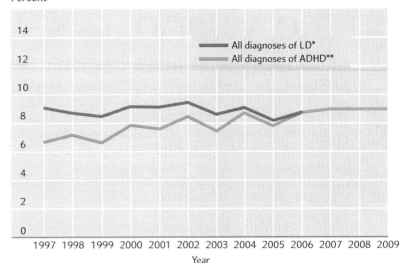

Percent

*Includes LD with and without ADHD.
**Includes ADHD with and without LD.

FIGURE 9.2

U.S. Diagnosis of Attention-Deficit/Hyperactivity Disorder by Year

Diagnosis of learning disabilities has remained constant, but diagnosis of ADHD rose from 1997 to 2009.

Sources: D. Amso and B. J. Casey, "Beyond what develops when: Neuroimaging may inform how cognition changes with development," *Current Directions in Psychological Science,* 15(2006), 24–29; adapted from Gogtay et al., 2004.

It benefits children with disabilities or special needs when accommodations can be made for their inclusion in classrooms with nondisabled or neurotypical children. ©FatCamera/E+/Getty Images

ATTENTION-DEFICIT/HYPERACTIVITY DISORDER (ADHD) AND AUTISM SPECTRUM DISORDER (ASD) WORLDWIDE

Autism spectrum disorders (ASD) and attention-deficit/hyperactivity disorder (ADHD) are common neurodevelopmental disorders in the United States. However, ASD and ADHD are not disorders confined to Western countries. When taking into account cultural differences and definitions of behavior, cases of ADHD and ASD have been found in all areas of the globe (Hughes, 2011; American Psychiatric Association, 2013). Estimates are that worldwide 1 in 160 children have ASD (World Health Organization, 2017) and 7.2 percent of children have ADHD (Thomas, Sanders, Doust, Beller & Glasziou, 2015). The prevalence rates of ADHD reported in the United States are similar and compare with the rates reported in non-U.S. populations (Faraone, Sergeant, Gillberg & Biederman, 2003).

Regardless of country of origin, studies over the past 50 years have indicated the prevalence of ASD, ADHD, and other neurodevelopmental disorders appears to be increasing globally (Environmental Protection Agency, 2015). A study done in Denmark shows a 60 percent rise in the past 30 years in diagnoses of ADHD and ASD and similar rate increases in Finland, Sweden, and Western Australia (Hansen, Schendel & Parner, 2015). The explanations for this global increase include improved awareness, expansion and revision of diagnostic criteria, better diagnostic tools, and improved reporting (World Health Organization, 2017).

Diagnosis of ASD and ADHD is impacted by culture. The Diagnostic and Statistical Manual of Psychological Disorders V (DSM-V) notes that the understanding of behavior is impacted by culture and thus may contribute to differences in estimates across studies (American Psychiatric Association, 2013). Social development in children who grow up in Westernized cultures may not always be the same as that for children who grow up elsewhere. For example, in Eastern cultures, the norms for eye contact, gesturing, social reciprocity, and expressing oneself are greatly different. Using Western criteria with these populations could mistakenly indicate the presence of ASD.

Another issue that impacts prevalence estimates across different cultures is stigma, which can lead to reluctance on the part of parents to classify children as being affected. It is clear that stigma is experienced across many cultures. For example, South Korean mothers of children with ASD reported that they and their children were shut out of social or familial encounters, that they were isolated and excluded, and in some cases, that the diagnosis of their child contributed to divorce (A. Baker, 2013). British parents likewise note stigma, prejudice, and a loss of feelings of "normalcy," although diagnosis allows for treatment and intervention (Russel & Norwich, 2012). Japanese parents and teachers report believing that labeling a child as different and giving them specialized education can disrupt relationships with other children and lead to social harm and prejudice (Hansen, Schendel & Parner, 2015).

Unfortunately, treatment and access to services and support for people with ADHD and ASD is inadequate (World Health Organization, 2017). Globally, parents and health care providers do not always have the resources and tools to face the challenge of caring for people with neurodevelopmental disorders.

what's your view — Do you think ADHD would manifest in the same way in a culture without a formal educational system? How might we reduce stigma for ASD and ADHD?

classroom performance, creative production, parent and teacher nominations, and student interviews. An estimated 6 percent of the student population is considered gifted (National Association for Gifted Children [NAGC], n.d.). In the 2013–2014 academic year, approximately 3.32 million children were enrolled in gifted and talented programs in the United States (United States Department of Education, 2017).

High levels of performance require strong intrinsic motivation and years of rigorous training (Gardner, 1993; Gottfried, Cook, Gottfried & Morris, 2005; Clinkenbeard, 2012). However, motivation and training will not produce giftedness unless a child is endowed with unusual ability (Winner, 2000). Conversely, children with innate gifts are unlikely to show exceptional achievement without motivation and hard work (Achter & Lubinski, 2003).

Gifted children tend to grow up in enriched family environments with intellectual or artistic stimulation. Their parents recognize and often devote themselves to nurturing the children's gifts but also give their children an unusual degree of independence. Parents of gifted children typically have high expectations and are hard workers and high achievers themselves (Winner, 2000; Al-Dhamit & Kreishan, 2016; Garn, Mathews & Jolly, 2010).

Defining and Measuring Creativity One definition of **creativity** is the ability to see things in a new light—to produce something never seen before or to discern problems others fail to recognize and find new and unusual solutions to those problems. High creativity and high academic intelligence (IQ) do not necessarily go hand in hand (Anastasi & Schaefer, 1971; Getzels & Jackson, 1963). However, it does appear that a threshold level of intelligence, which varies with the complexity of the creative activity, is necessary. Once the intelligence threshold is met, personality factors become more important (Jauk, Benedek, Dunst & Neubauer, 2013).

The reason creativity is not highly correlated with traditional IQ tests is because traditional tests are measuring a different kind of thinking than is characteristic of creativity. J. P. Guilford (1956, 1959, 1960, 1967, 1986) distinguished two kinds of thinking: convergent and divergent. **Convergent thinking**—the kind IQ tests measure—seeks a single correct answer. For example, when solving an arithmetic problem, there is one correct answer upon which everyone is expected to converge. **Divergent thinking,** by contrast, involves coming up with a wide array of fresh possibilities, such as when children are asked to list how many different uses there might be for a paper clip or to write down what a sound brings to mind. There is no one right answer. Tests of creativity call for divergent thinking. This ability can be assessed via the *Torrance Tests of Creative Thinking* (TTCT) (Torrance, 1974; Torrance & Ball, 1984), one of the most widely known tests of creativity. While there has been some controversy about the measurement qualities of the test, a 50-year follow-up showed that scores on the TTCT were related to personal achievement, and when IQ was also taken into account, scores were related to public achievement as well (Runco, Miller, Acar & Cramond, 2010).

Educating Gifted Children Programs for gifted children generally stress either enrichment or acceleration. **Enrichment programs** may deepen students' knowledge and skills through extra classroom activities, research projects, field trips, or expert coaching. **Acceleration programs** speed up their education through early school entrance, grade skipping, placement in fast-paced classes, or advanced courses. Other options include ability grouping, which has been found to help children academically and not harm them socially (Vogl & Preckel, 2014); dual enrollment (for example, an eighth grader taking algebra at a nearby high school); magnet schools; and specialized schools for the gifted.

creativity
Ability to see situations in a new way, to produce innovations, or to discern previously unidentified problems and find novel solutions.

convergent thinking
Thinking aimed at finding the one right answer to a problem.

divergent thinking
Thinking that produces a variety of fresh, diverse possibilities.

enrichment programs
Programs for educating the gifted that broaden and deepen knowledge and skills through extra activities, projects, field trips, or mentoring.

acceleration programs
Programs for educating the gifted that move them through the curriculum at an unusually rapid pace.

summary and key terms

PHYSICAL DEVELOPMENT

Aspects of Physical Development

- Physical development is less rapid in middle childhood than in earlier years. Wide differences in height and weight exist.
- Proper nutrition and sleep are essential.
- Changes in brain structure and functioning support cognitive advances.
- Because of improved motor development, boys and girls in middle childhood can engage in a wide range of motor activities.
- Informal recess-time activities help develop physical and social skills. Boys' games tend to be more physical and girls' games more verbal.

- About 10 percent of schoolchildren's play, especially among boys, is rough-and-tumble play.
- Many children engage in organized, competitive sports. A sound physical education program should aim for skill development and fitness.

  rough-and-tumble play

Health, Fitness, and Safety

- Middle childhood is a relatively healthy period; most children are immunized and the death rate is low.
- Overweight entails multiple risks. It is influenced by genetic and environmental factors and is more easily prevented than treated. Many children do not get enough physical activity.

- Hypertension is becoming more common along with the rise in overweight.
- Respiratory infections and other acute medical conditions are common at this age. Chronic conditions such as asthma are most prevalent among poor and minority children. Diabetes is one of the most common childhood chronic conditions.
- Accidents are the leading cause of death in middle childhood. Use of helmets and other protective devices and avoidance of trampolines, snowmobiling, and other dangerous sports can greatly reduce injuries.

body image, hypertension, acute medical conditions, chronic medical conditions, asthma, diabetes

COGNITIVE DEVELOPMENT

Piagetian Approach: The Concrete Operational Child

- A child from about age 7 to age 12 is in the stage of concrete operations. Children are less egocentric than before and are more proficient at tasks requiring logical reasoning, such as spatial thinking, understanding of causality, categorization, inductive and deductive reasoning, and conservation. However, their reasoning is largely limited to the here and now.
- Neurological development, culture, and schooling seem to contribute to the rate of development of Piagetian skills.

concrete operations, seriation, transitive inference, class inclusion, inductive reasoning, deductive reasoning

Information-Processing Approach: Planning, Attention, and Memory

- Executive skills, reaction time, processing speed, selective attention, metamemory, and use of mnemonic devices improve during the school years.

executive function, metamemory, mnemonic device, external memory aids, rehearsal, organization, elaboration

Psychometric Approach: Assessment of Intelligence

- IQ tests are fairly good predictors of school success but may be unfair to some children.
- Differences in IQ among ethnic groups appear to result to a considerable degree from socioeconomic and other environmental differences.
- Schooling increases measured intelligence.
- Attempts to devise culture-free or culture-fair tests have been unsuccessful.
- IQ tests tap only three of the eight intelligences in Howard Gardner's theory of multiple intelligences.
- According to Robert Sternberg's triarchic theory, IQ tests measure mainly the componential element of intelligence, not the experiential and contextual elements.
- Other directions in intelligence testing include the Sternberg Triarchic Abilities Tests (STAT), Kaufman Assessment

Battery for Children (K-ABC-II), and dynamic tests based on Vygotsky's theory.

Wechsler Intelligence Scale for Children (WISC-IV), Otis-Lennon School Ability Test (OLSAT 8), culture-free tests, culture-fair tests, theory of multiple intelligences, triarchic theory of intelligence, componential element, experiential element, contextual element, tacit knowledge, Kaufman Assessment Battery for Children (K-ABC-II), dynamic tests

Language and Literacy

- Use of vocabulary, grammar, and syntax become increasingly sophisticated, but the major area of linguistic growth is in pragmatics.
- Methods of second-language education are controversial.
- Despite the popularity of whole-language programs, early phonetics training is a key to reading proficiency. Mixed approaches may be most effective.

pragmatics, English-immersion approach, bilingual education, bilingual, two-way (dual-language) learning, decoding, phonetic (code-emphasis) approach, whole-language approach, visually based retrieval, metacognition

The Child in School

- Entry into first grade is an important milestone.
- Children's self-efficacy beliefs affect school achievement.
- Girls tend to do better in school than boys.
- Parents influence children's learning by becoming involved in their schooling and transmitting attitudes about academics. Socioeconomic status can influence parental beliefs and practices that, in turn, influence achievement.
- Peer acceptance and class size affect learning.
- Current educational issues and innovations include social promotion, charter schools, homeschooling, and computer literacy.

social capital

Educating Children with Special Needs

- Three frequent sources of learning problems are intellectual disability, learning disabilities (LDs), and attention-deficit/hyperactivity disorder (ADHD). Dyslexia is the most common learning disability.
- In the United States, all children with disabilities are entitled to a free, appropriate education in the least restrictive environment possible, often in the regular classroom.
- An IQ of 130 or higher is a common standard for identifying gifted children.
- Creativity and IQ are *not* closely linked. Tests of creativity seek to measure divergent thinking, but their validity has been questioned.
- Special educational programs for gifted children stress enrichment or acceleration.

intellectual disability, learning disabilities (LDs), dyslexia, attention-deficit/hyperactivity disorder (ADHD), creativity, convergent thinking, divergent thinking, enrichment programs, acceleration programs

Psychosocial Development in Middle Childhood

chapter 10

©Juice Images/Getty Images

In this chapter we see how children develop a more realistic self-concept. Through interacting with peers they make discoveries about their own attitudes, values, and skills. The kind of household a child lives in and the relationships in it can profoundly affect psychosocial development. We look at several mental health problems and at resilient children, who can emerge from stress healthy and strong.

learning objectives

Discuss emotional and personality development in school-age children.

Describe changes in family relationships in the school-age years.

Identify changes in peer relationships among school-age children.

Describe emotional disorders that can develop in school-age children, along with treatment techniques and children's ability to cope with stress.

The Developing Self

The cognitive growth that takes place during middle childhood enables children to develop more complex concepts of themselves and to gain in emotional understanding and control.

SELF-CONCEPT DEVELOPMENT: REPRESENTATIONAL SYSTEMS

"At school I'm feeling pretty smart in certain subjects, Language Arts and Social Studies," says 8-year-old Lisa. "I got As in these subjects on my last report card and was really proud of myself. But I'm feeling really dumb in Arithmetic and Science, particularly when I see how well the other kids are doing. . . . I still like myself as a person, because Arithmetic and Science just aren't that important to me. How I look and how popular I am are more important" (Harter, 1996, p. 208).

Young children have difficulty with abstract concepts and with integrating various dimensions of the self. Their self-concepts focus on physical attributes, possessions, and global descriptions. However, around age 7 or 8, children's judgments about the self become more conscious, realistic, balanced, and comprehensive as children form **representational systems:** broad, inclusive self-concepts that integrate various aspects of the self (Harter, 1993, 1996, 1998). We can see these changes in Lisa's self-description.

INDUSTRY VERSUS INFERIORITY

According to Erikson (1982), a major determinant of self-esteem is children's view of their capacity for productive work, which develops in his fourth stage of psychosocial development: **industry versus inferiority.** As with all of Erikson's stages, there is an opportunity for growth represented by a sense of industry and a complementary risk represented by inferiority.

If children are unable to obtain the praise of others, or lack motivation and self-esteem, they may develop a feeling of low self-worth, and thus develop a sense of inferiority. This is problematic because during middle childhood children must learn skills valued in their society.

Developing a sense of industry, by contrast, involves learning how to work hard to achieve goals. The details may vary across societies: Arapesh boys in New Guinea learn to make bows and arrows and to lay traps for rats; Inuit children of Alaska learn to hunt and fish; and children in industrialized countries learn to read, write, do math, and use computers. If the stage is successfully resolved, children develop a view of themselves as being able to master skills and complete tasks. This can go too far—if children become too industrious, they may neglect social relationships and turn into workaholics.

representational systems
In neo-Piagetian terminology, the third stage in development of self-definition, characterized by breadth, balance, and the integration and assessment of various aspects of the self.

industry versus inferiority
Erikson's fourth stage of psychosocial development, in which children must learn the productive skills their culture requires or else face feelings of inferiority.

In Vietnam, Hie takes geese to market, developing her sense of competence and building her self-esteem. ©Michael Justice/The Image Works

EMOTIONAL GROWTH AND PROSOCIAL BEHAVIOR

As children grow older, they are more aware of their own and other people's feelings. They can better regulate or control their emotions and can respond to others' emotional distress (Saarni et al., 2006). Children learn what makes them angry, fearful, or sad and how other people react to displays of these emotions. They also start to understand that they and others can have conflicting emotions (Zajdel, Bloom, Fireman & Larsen, 2013).

By age 7 or 8, children typically are aware of feeling shame and pride, and they have a clearer idea of the difference between guilt and shame (Olthof, Schouten, Kuiper, Stegge & Jennekens-Schinkel, 2000). Additionally, cultural values affect the expression of these emotions. For example, one study found that children in the United States expressed the most pride, while Japanese children the most shame, and Korean children the most guilt (Furukawa, Tangney & Higashibara, 2012). When parents respond with excessive disapproval or punishment to the expression of emotions, emotions such as anger and fear may become more intense and may impair children's social adjustment (Fabes, Leonard, Kupanoff & Martin, 2001), or children may become secretive and anxious about negative feelings (Almas,

Grusec & Tackett, 2011). Parents who acknowledge children's feelings of distress and help them focus on solving the root problem foster empathy, prosocial development, and social skills (Bryant, 1987; Eisenberg et al., 1996). As children approach early adolescence, emotion may heighten parent-child conflict (Fabes, et al., 2001).

Have you ever received a gift you didn't like or had to hold in your anger to avoid getting in trouble? The ability to fake liking a gift or to smile when you are mad involves emotional self-regulation. Emotional self-regulation is effortful (voluntary) control of emotions, attention, and behavior (Eisenberg et al., 2004). Some children are better than others at emotional self-regulation, but most children get better with age.

Children's ability to exert control over themselves is related to adjustment (Eisenberg et al., 2004). For example, children who, at 3 to 4 years of age, had difficulty in delay-of-gratification tasks were more likely to have behavior problems at 5 to 8 years. Similarly, children who were poor at deliberately slowing down, inhibiting their movements in a game, or paying close attention when young were more likely to have academic difficulties when older (Kim, Nordling, Yoon, Boldt & Kochanska, 2013).

Children tend to become more empathic and more inclined to prosocial behavior in middle childhood. Empathy appears to be "hardwired" into the brains of typical children. As with adults, empathy has been associated with prefrontal activation in children as young as 6 years of age (Light et al., 2009). For example, a study of brain activity in 7- to 12-year-olds found parts of their brains were activated when shown pictures of people in pain (Decety, Michalaska, Akitsuki & Lahey, 2009).

Children with high self-esteem tend to be more willing to volunteer to help those who are less fortunate than they are, and volunteering, in turn, helps build self-esteem (Karafantis & Levy, 2004). Prosocial children tend to act appropriately in social situations, to be relatively free from negative emotion, and to cope with problems constructively (Eisenberg, Fabes & Murphy, 1996). Additionally, classroom interventions have been shown to help children develop empathy for others, increase spontaneous prosocial behavior, and decrease aggressive acts (Schonert-Reichl, Smith, Zaidman-Zait & Hertzman, 2012).

The Child in the Family

School-age children spend more time away from home visiting and socializing with peers than when they were younger. Still, home and the people who live there remain an important part of most children's lives.

FAMILY ATMOSPHERE

Family atmosphere is a key influence on development. One key factor is whether or not conflict is present in the home. Exposure to violence and conflict is harmful to children, both in terms of direct exposure via parental discord (Kaczynski, Lindahl, Malik & Laurenceau, 2006) and via indirect influences on variables like low family cohesion and anger regulation strategies (Houltberg, Henry & Morris, 2012).

Children exposed to family conflict show a variety of responses that can include externalizing or internalizing behaviors. **Internalizing behaviors** include anxiety, fearfulness, and depression—anger turned inward. **Externalizing behaviors** include aggression, fighting, disobedience, and hostility—anger turned outward. Both internalizing behaviors (Fear et al., 2009; Kaczynski et al., 2006) and externalizing behaviors (Houltberg et al., 2012; Kaczynski et al., 2006) are more likely in children who come from families with high levels of discord.

internalizing behaviors
Behaviors by which emotional problems are turned inward; for example, anxiety or depression.

externalizing behaviors
Behaviors by which a child acts out emotional difficulties; for example, aggression or hostility.

Parenting Issues: From Control to Coregulation Babies don't have a lot of say in what happens to them; they experience what their parents decide they should experience. However there is a shift in power as children grow and become more autonomous. Over the course of childhood, control gradually shifts from parents to child. Children begin to request certain types of experiences, demand particular foods, negotiate for desired objects, and communicate their shifting needs to parents.

In middle childhood, social power becomes more equal between parent and child. Parent and child engage in **coregulation,** a stage that can include strategies in which parents exercise oversight but children enjoy moment-to-moment self-regulation (Maccoby, 1984, 1992). For example, with regard to problems among peers, parents might now rely less on direct intervention and more on discussion with their child (Parke & Buriel, 1998).

Coregulation is affected by the overall relationship between parent and child. Children are more apt to follow their parents' wishes when they believe the parents are fair and concerned about the child's welfare and that they may "know better" because of experience. This is particularly true when parents take pains to acknowledge children's maturing judgment and take strong stands only on important issues (Maccoby, 1984, 1992). The shift to coregulation affects the way parents handle discipline (Kochanska, Aksan, Prisco & Adams, 2008). Parents of school-age children are more likely to use inductive techniques. For example, they might explain how their actions affect others, highlight moral values, or let their children experience the natural consequences of their behaviors.

Parents also modify their use of physical discipline (such as spanking) as children age. Parents who use physical punishment tend to decrease its use as children grow older. Generally, the use of physical punishment is associated with negative outcomes for children. Those parents who continue to spank their children past the age of 10 years tend to have worse relationships with their children in adolescence and to have teens with worse behavioral problems (Lansford et al., 2009).

How family conflict is resolved is also important. If family conflict is constructive, it can help children see the need for rules and standards, and learn what issues are worth arguing about and what strategies can be effective (A. R. Eisenberg, 1996). However, as children become preadolescents and their striving for autonomy becomes more insistent, the quality of family problem solving often deteriorates (Vuchinich, Angelelli & Gatherum, 1996).

Although school-age children spend less time at home, family influences continue to be important in their lives.
©Denis Kuvaev/Shutterstock

Cultural differences are also important, and tend to exert complex effects. Generally, researchers find that in cultures that stress family interdependence (such as in Turkey, India, and Latin America) authoritarian parenting, with its high degree of control, is not associated with negative maternal feelings or low self-esteem in children as it is in more individualistic cultures (Rudy & Grusec, 2006). Latino parents, for example, have well adjusted children as often as other groups although they tend to exert more control over their school-age children than European American parents do (Halgunseth et al., 2006) and expectations for girls are even more strict (Domenech Rodriguez, Donovick & Crowley, 2009). However, children in China, also a collectivistic culture, tend to be negatively affected by high control just as are children from the individualistic United States (Pomerantz & Wang, 2009). With respect to low control, children of Iranian (Kazemi, Ardabili & Solokian, 2010), Spanish (Garcia & Garcia, 2009), and some European parents (Calafat, Garcia, Juan, Becona & Fernandez-Hermida, 2014) with a permissive parenting style have good outcomes, contrary to what has been found in American samples (Pinquart, 2017). Thus, the influence of parental control strategies is shaped by the cultural context in which it occurs.

Effects of Parents' Work In 2015, almost 70 percent of U.S. mothers worked either full- or part-time (U.S. Department of Labor, 2016). Most studies of the impact of parents' work on children's well-being have focused on employed mothers. In general, the more satisfied a mother is with her employment status, the more effective she is likely to be as a parent. However, the impact of a mother's work depends on many other factors, including the child's age, sex, temperament, and personality; whether the mother works full-time or part-time; why she is working; whether she has a supportive or unsupportive partner, or none; the family's socioeconomic status; and the type of care the child receives before and/or after school (Parke, 2004a; Gottfried & Gottfried, 2013). Often a single mother must work to stave off economic disaster. How her working affects her children may hinge on how much time and energy she has left to spend with them. How well parents keep track of their children and monitor their activities may be more important than whether the mother works for pay (Fosco, Stormshak, Dishion & Winter, 2012).

When both parents work outside the home, child care arrangements are common. Half of grade school children are in some form of child care outside of school, often with relatives (Laughlin, 2013), while others attend organized programs. These programs vary widely in quality. Two important markers of quality are structural features (such as physical facilities and staff characteristics) and process features (such as the activities available for children and the overall culture of the program). When children are enrolled in high quality programs, they show positive changes in academic outcomes, their attachment to their school, peer relationships, and self-confidence, and show declines in problem behaviors and drug use (Durlak, Mahoney, Bohnert & Parente, 2010).

Approximately 11 percent of school-age children and early adolescents are reported to be in *self-care,* regularly caring for themselves at home without adult supervision (Laughlin, 2013). This arrangement is advisable only for older children who are mature, responsible, and resourceful and know how to get help in an emergency—and, even then, only if a parent can stay in touch by telephone.

Poverty and Parenting About 20 percent of U.S. children up to age 17 lived in poverty in 2015 (Proctor, Semega & Kollar, 2016). The poverty rate for white children was 12 percent. Rates were much higher for black (37 percent) and Hispanic (32 percent) children. Children living with single mothers were about 4 times more likely to be poor than children living with married couples—46 percent as compared with 11 percent (Federal Interagency Forum on Child and Family Statistics, 2016).

Poor children are more likely than other children to have emotional or behavioral problems (Wadsworth, Raviv, Reinhard, Wolff, Santiago & Einhorn, 2008). In addition, their cognitive potential and school performance suffer greatly (Najman et al., 2009).

Poverty can harm children's development through a multitude of pathways. Parents who live in poverty are likely to become anxious, depressed, and irritable and thus may become less affectionate with and responsive to their children. There may be increased levels of parent-child conflict and harsh discipline. Moreover, poverty also affects where children go to school and the neighborhood they live in, features that can exacerbate child stressors. These features in turn also affect parents and their perceived stress. In short, there are cascades of negative interactions that can have a deleterious effect on child outcomes. These outcomes include physical health, behaviors, mental health, and cognitive and intellectual development (Chaudry & Wimer, 2016; Morris et al., 2017; Yoshikawa, Aber & Beardslee, 2012).

Fortunately, this pattern is not inevitable. Effective parenting can buffer children from the effects of poverty. Effective family interventions promote positive parent-child interactions (for example, by encouraging parents to praise their children while also helping them develop reasonable rules and limits) and provide social support for parents (Morris et al., 2017). Parents who can turn to relatives or to community resources for emotional support, help with child care, and child-rearing information often can parent their children more effectively (Brody, Kim, Murry & Brown, 2004).

FAMILY STRUCTURE

Family structure in the United States has changed dramatically. In earlier generations, the vast majority of children grew up in families with two married parents. Today, although about 2 out of 3 children under 18 live with two married biological, adoptive, or stepparents, that proportion represents a dramatic decline—from 85 percent in 1960 to 65 percent in 2015 (Child Trends DataBank, 2015a; Figure 10.1). About 10 percent of two-parent families are stepfamilies resulting from divorce and remarriage, and nearly 4 percent are cohabiting families (Kreider & Fields, 2005). Other increasingly common family types are gay and lesbian families and grandparent-headed families.

Other things being equal, children tend to do better in families with two continuously married parents than in cohabiting, divorced, single-parent, or stepfamilies (S. L. Brown,

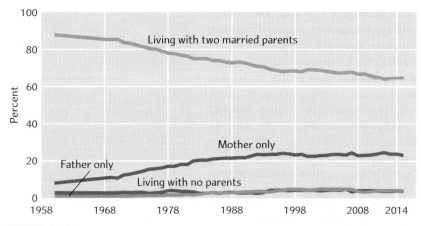

FIGURE 10.1

Living Arrangements of Children Under 18, 1960 to 2015

Most children under 18 in the United States live with two parents.

Source: Child Trends, "Family Structure," *Child Trends DataBank*, 2015.

2004). The distinction is even stronger for children growing up with two *happily* married parents. This suggests that the parents' relationship, the quality of their parenting, and their ability to create a favorable family atmosphere may affect children's adjustment more than their marital status does (Amato, 2005).

With respect to variations in two-parent family structures, there are relatively few differences in child well-being regardless of whether children live with biological cohabitating families, married/cohabitating stepfamilies, or blended families (Artis, 2007). Family instability, however, may be harmful. Children who experience more family transitions, such as a divorce or a remarriage, were more likely to have behavior problems and to engage in delinquent behavior than children in stable families (Fomby & Cherlin, 2007; Magnuson & Berger, 2009). The negative effect of family transitions appears to be stronger if they occur earlier in development, and for boys (Cavanagh & Huston, 2008).

A father's frequent and positive involvement with his child is directly related to the child's well-being and physical, cognitive, and social development (McLanahan, Tach & Schneider, 2013; Cabrera et al., 2000). Unfortunately, in 2014, more than 23.6 percent of children lived in homes without a biological father present (National Fatherhood Initiative, 2016).

When Parents Divorce The United States has one of the highest divorce rates in the world. The divorce rate rose from 1960 (2.2 per 1,000 people) to its peak level in 1980 (3.5 per 1,000 people) (Amato, 2014; Cherlin, 2010). Since then the divorce rate has slowly dropped, and it currently stands at 3.2 per 1,000 people (Centers for Disease Control and Prevention, 2017n). More than 1.5 million children are involved in divorces each year (NIMH, 2002).

Adjusting to Divorce Divorce is stressful for children. First there is the stress of marital conflict and then of parental separation with the departure of one parent, usually the father, and the potential loss of friends if a move is necessary. Children may not fully understand what is happening. Divorce is, of course, stressful for the parents as well and may negatively affect their parenting. The family's standard of living is likely to drop; and, if a parent moves away, a child's relationship with the noncustodial parent may suffer (Kelly & Emery, 2003; Amato, 2014). A parent's remarriage or second divorce after remarriage can increase the stress on children, renewing feelings of loss (Ahrons & Tanner, 2003; Amato, 2003).

Family conflict is a consistently identified risk factor for children (Stallman & Ohan, 2016). Children's emotional or behavioral problems after a divorce may reflect the level of parental conflict *before* the divorce. Children whose parents later divorce show more anxiety, depression, or antisocial behavior prior to the divorce than those whose parents stay married (Strohschein, 2012). In fact, if predivorce parental discord is chronic, overt, or destructive, children may be as well or better off after a divorce (Amato, 2003, 2005). Additionally, the quality of parenting prior to divorce matters as well, with maternal sensitivity and support acting as a protective factor for some children whose families divorced (Weaver & Schofield, 2015).

A child's adjustment to divorce depends in part on the child's age, maturity, gender, temperament, and psychosocial adjustment before the divorce. Children who are younger when their parents divorce tend to suffer from more behavioral problems. By contrast, older children are at higher risk with respect to academic and social outcomes (Lansford, 2009). Although children whose parents divorce are at slightly higher risk for negative outcomes, most do eventually show good adjustment (Amato & Anthony, 2014).

Custody and Co-parenting In most divorce cases, the mother gets custody, though paternal custody is a growing trend. Joint custody, shared by both parents, is another

Children of divorce tend to be better adjusted if they have reliable, frequent contact with the noncustodial parent. ©Eric Audras/ SuperStock

arrangement. When parents have joint legal custody, they share the right and responsibility to make decisions regarding the child's welfare. When they have joint physical custody (which is less common), the child lives part-time with each parent.

All else being equal, the research suggests children do better with joint custody (Warshak, 2014; Baude, Pearson & Drapeau, 2016), perhaps because fathers are more likely to remain involved. Many children of divorce say that losing contact with a father is one of the most painful results of divorce (Fabricius, 2003). When one parent has custody, children do better after divorce if the custodial parent is warm, supportive, and authoritative; monitors the child's activities; and holds age-appropriate expectations. In addition, conflict between the divorced parents needs to be minimal, and the nonresident parent should remain closely involved (Stallman & Ohan, 2016; Ahrons & Tanner, 2003).

Co-parenting is a parenting relationship in which two people who may or may not be romantically involved work together in a cooperative fashion to raise a child. Co-parenting has been consistently linked to positive child outcomes (Teubert & Pinquart, 2010), in part because it is strongly associated with more frequent contact between father and child (Sobolewski & King, 2005). Unfortunately, cooperative parenting is not the norm (Amato, 2005). Parent education programs that teach separated or divorced couples how to prevent or deal with conflict, keep lines of communication open, and help children adjust to divorce have been introduced in many states with measurable success (Ferraro, Malespin, Oeheme, Bruker & Opel, 2016).

Long-Term Effects Most children of divorce adjust well (Amato & Anthony, 2014). However, parental divorce may affect later relationships as children enter adulthood. For example, children whose parents divorced have higher separation and divorce rates themselves (Mustonen, Huurre, Kiviruusu, Huakkala & Aro, 2011). Although these differences are small, as adults, the children of divorce tend to have lower SES, poorer psychological well-being, and a greater chance of having a birth outside marriage. Their marriages tend to be less satisfying and are more likely to end in divorce (Amato, 2005). Additionally, adults whose parents divorced when they were children and who endured multiple or prolonged separation from a parent later show compromised parenting themselves, including lower sensitivity and warmth, and more parent-child conflict and physical punishment (Friesen, Horwood, Fergusson & Woodward, 2017). However, some who saw a high degree of conflict between their parents are able to learn from that negative example and form highly intimate relationships themselves (Shulman, Scharf, Lumer & Maurer, 2001).

Living in a One-Parent Family One-parent families result from divorce or separation, unwed parenthood, or death. With rising rates of divorce and of parenthood outside of marriage, the number of single-parent families in the United States has increased by approximately 3.5 times since 1960 (U.S. Census Bureau, 2016). Currently, about 28 percent of children live in a single-parent household. More than half of all black children live with a single parent, as compared with 21 percent of non-Hispanic white children and 31 percent of Hispanic children (Vespa, Lewis & Kreider, 2013). The issue is even more pressing when low-income families are examined, with 66 percent of African American families and 35 percent of both non-Hispanic and Hispanic white children living in single-parent homes (Mather, 2010). Although children are far more likely to live with a single mother than with a single father, the number of father-only families has more than quadrupled since 1960, apparently due largely to the increase in paternal custody after divorce (U.S. Census Bureau, 2016; Fields, 2004).

Children in single-parent families do fairly well overall but tend to lag socially and educationally behind peers in two-parent families (Waldfogel, Craigie & Brooks-Gunn, 2010; Amato, 2005). Children living with married parents tend to have more daily interaction with their parents, are read to more often, progress more steadily in school, and participate more in extracurricular activities than children living with a single parent (Lugaila, 2003).

However, negative outcomes for children in one-parent families are not inevitable. The child's age and level of development, the family's financial circumstances and educational level, whether there are frequent moves, and a nonresident father's involvement make a difference (Amato, 2005; Seltzer, 2000; Ricciuti, 1999, 2004). One important variable appears to be family stability—children from stable single-parent families fare comparably to those from unstable two-parent families (Heiland & Liu, 2006). Income also matters; many of the negative effects of single-parenthood appear to be driven by lower socioeconomic status. In countries with a more robust welfare support system for single mothers, children families report higher levels of well-being than children in countries who do not provide as much aid to single mothers (Bjarnason et al., 2012).

Living in a Cohabiting Family Approximately 20 percent of births in the United States are to cohabitating couples—in other words, unmarried partners living together (Smock & Greenland, 2010). Cohabiting families are similar in many ways to married families, but the parents tend to be more disadvantaged (Mather, 2010). They traditionally have less income and education, report poorer relationships, and have more mental health problems. Research shows worse emotional, behavioral, and academic outcomes for children living with cohabiting biological parents than for those living with married biological parents (Waldfogel et al., 2010; S. L. Brown, 2004). However, this difference in outcomes is primarily the result of differences in economic resources. In terms of economic disadvantage, cohabitating families are closer to single-parent families than married couples. Parenting differences, by contrast, explain only a small amount of the variation in child outcomes for cohabitating versus married couples (Thomson & McLanahan, 2012).

Cohabiting families are more likely to break up than married families. Although about 40 percent of unwed mothers are living with the child's father at the time of birth, 25 percent of cohabiting parents are no longer together 1 year later, and 31 percent break up after 5 years (Amato, 2005). However, some data suggest that the dissolution of a cohabiting couple does not result in the same risk for negative outcomes as does divorce (Wu, Hou & Schimmele, 2008).

Living in a Stepfamily Most divorced parents eventually remarry, and many unwed mothers marry men who were not the father of their children, forming step-, or blended, families. Sixteen percent of U.S. children live in blended families (Kreider & Ellis, 2011).

Adjusting to a new stepparent may be stressful. Both children and parents have to navigate shifting relationships, adapt to a new power structure in the family, and adjust to household changes. Studies have found small to moderate, but consistent, negative effects for children living in stepparent families when compared to married families (Sweeney, 2010; Hofferth, 2006). Adjustment to the stepparents and the potential negative influence of that on development appear to be influenced by family relationships prior to the formation of the stepfamily. When there is a good relationship with the biological parent (usually the mother) prior to the introduction of a stepparent, children show more positive relationships with their stepparent and better adjustment (King, Amato & Lindstrom, 2015).

Living with Gay or Lesbian Parents An estimated 6 million U.S. children and adolescents have at least one gay or lesbian parent (Gates, 2013). About 25 percent of lesbian couples and 7 percent of gay couples have children living with them (Carpenter & Gates, 2008). Some gays and lesbians are raising children born of previous heterosexual relationships. Others conceive by artificial means, use surrogate mothers, or adopt children.

A considerable body of research has examined the development of children of gays and lesbians and has found no special concerns (APA, 2004b). There is *no* consistent difference between homosexual and heterosexual parents in emotional health or parenting skills and attitudes; and where there are differences, they tend to favor gay and lesbian parents (Golombok et al., 2013; Meezan & Rauch, 2005; Pawelski et al., 2006; Wainright, Russell & Patterson, 2004; Biblarz & Stacey, 2010). Gay or lesbian parents usually have positive relationships with their children, and the children are no more likely than children raised by heterosexual parents to have emotional, social, academic, or psychological problems (APA, 2004b; Perrin, Siegel & Committee on Psychosocial Aspects of Child and Family Health, 2013; Fedewa, Black & Ahn, 2015; Manning, Fettro & Lamidi, 2014; Gartrell, Deck, Rodas, Peyser & Banks, 2005; Meezan & Rauch, 2005). Furthermore, children of gays and lesbians are no more likely to be homosexual or to be confused about their gender than are children of heterosexuals (Fedewa, Black & Ahn, 2015; Meezan & Rauch, 2005; Pawelski et al., 2006; Wainright et al., 2004).

Such findings have social policy implications for legal decisions on custody and visitation disputes, foster care, and adoptions (Manning et al., 2014). In the face of controversy over gay and lesbian marriages or civil unions several states have considered or adopted legislation sanctioning second-parent adoption by same-sex partners. The American Academy of Pediatrics supports a right to civil marriage for gays and lesbians (Pawelski et al., 2006) and legislative and legal efforts to permit a partner in a same-sex couple to adopt the other partner's child (AAP Committee on Psychosocial Aspects of Child and Family Health, 2002).

Research has shown that children living with homosexual parents are no more likely than other children to have social or psychological problems or to turn out to be homosexual themselves. ©Nick Cardillicchio/Corbis/VCG/Getty Images

Adoptive Families Adoption is found in all cultures throughout history. It is not only for infertile people; single people, older people, gay and lesbian couples, and people who already have biological children have become adoptive parents. In 2007, 1.8 million U.S. children under 18 (about 2 percent) lived with at least one adoptive parent (Child Trends DataBank, 2012). and about 136,000 children are adopted annually (Child Welfare Information Gateway, 2011). An estimated 60 percent of legal adoptions are by stepparents or relatives, usually grandparents (Kreider, 2003).

Adoptions usually take place through public or private agencies. Traditionally, agency adoptions were intended to be confidential, with no contact between the birth mother and the adoptive parents. However, independent adoptions, made by direct agreement between birth parents and adoptive parents, have become more common. Often these are *open adoptions,* in which both parties share information or have direct contact with the child (Grotevant, 2012).

While adopted children do tend to have more psychological and academic difficulties than non-adopted children, these differences are small, and most adopted children fall within the normal range of development (Palacios & Brodzinsky, 2010; Haugaard, 1998). Younger children, especially those adopted in infancy, are least likely to have adjustment problems (Julian, 2013; Sharma, McGue & Benson, 1996b). Any problems that do occur may surface during middle childhood, when children become more aware of differences in the way families are formed (Freeark et al., 2005), or in adolescence (Goodman, Emery & Haugaard, 1998; Sharma, McGue & Benson, 1996a), particularly among boys (Freeark et al., 2005).

About 37 percent of adopted children are non-Hispanic white. The remainder are black (23 percent), Hispanic (15 percent), Asian (15 percent), and other (9 percent). Transracial adoptions, where at least one parent is of a different race than the child, are common and comprise about 40 percent of adoptions (Vandivere, Malm & Radel, 2009). Most transracial adoptions involve white parents adopting an Asian or Latin American child (Kreider, 2003).

As the number of babies available for adoption in the United States declined, adoptions of foreign-born children rose by a factor of nearly four since 1978, from 5,315 to 20,679 (Bosch et al., 2003; Crary, 2007). Does foreign adoption entail special problems? Aside from the possibility of malnourishment or medical conditions in children from developing countries (Bosch et al., 2003), a number of studies find no significant problems with the children's psychological adjustment, school adjustment, and performance (Palacios & Brodzinsky, 2010). When foreign adoptees reach adolescence, they may experience feelings of loss of their native culture and growing awareness of racism and discrimination in their adopted culture. Parents who expose their adopted children to experiences that help them identify with their native culture and speak with their children about racism and discrimination may help buffer adopted children from negative effects (Lee, Grotevant, Hellerstedt, Gunnar & The Minnesota International Adoption Project Team, 2006).

SIBLING RELATIONSHIPS

In remote rural areas of Asia, Africa, Oceania, and Central and South America, it is common to see older girls caring for three or four younger siblings (Cicirelli, 1994). This

In many nonindustrialized cultures, children routinely care for their younger siblings.
©Lucian Coman/Shutterstock

pattern is also seen in recent immigrants to industrialized societies such as the United States (Hafford, 2010). However, in most industrialized societies, parents generally try not to "burden" older children with the regular care of siblings (Weisner, 1993).

Sibling relations have both positive and negative aspects to them. Having a warm and supportive sibling relationship is associated with better adjustment, (Noller, 2005), social competence (Kim, McHale, Crouter & Osgood, 2007), and better emotion regulation (Kennedy & Kramer, 2008). Sibling relationships are also marked by conflict. While generally perceived as negative, conflict can nonetheless be a laboratory for conflict resolution. Through these conflicts, siblings learn about others' points of view, negotiation, and problem solving (McHale, Updegraff & Whiteman, 2012).

However, sibling conflict is not always beneficial. High sibling conflict has been associated with internalizing (e.g., depression and anxiety) and externalizing (e.g., deliquency and aggression) problems as well as risky behaviors (Buist, Dekovic & Prinzie, 2012; Solmeyer, McHale & Crouter, 2012). Siblings can also exert a negative effect via modeling antisocial actions, introducing undesirable behaviors to younger siblings, or encouraging antisocial acts or collusion against parents (McHale, Updegraff & Whiteman, 2012). For example, when older siblings use drugs or alcohol, or engage in early sexual activity, their younger siblings are more likely to do so as well (Low, Short & Snyder, 2012; McHale, Bissell & Kim, 2009). Interestingly, there is also another side to the positive effects of sibling warmth. In the presence of antisocial behaviors, sibling warmth can actually be a risk factor (McHale, Bissell & Kim, 2009). For example, an older teen who is abusing substances might be more likely to introduce those substances to a sibling he is close to than to one he is not.

Sibling conflict and warmth are direct influences. However, siblings also influence each other indirectly, through their impact on each other's relationship with their parents. Parents' experience with an older sibling influences their expectations and treatment of a younger one (Brody, 2004). And behavior patterns a child establishes with parents tend to spill over into the child's behavior with siblings. When a parent-child relationship is warm and affectionate, siblings tend to have positive relationships as well. When the parent-child relationship is conflictual, sibling conflict is more likely (Pike et al., 2005).

The Child in the Peer Group

In middle childhood the peer group comes into its own. Groups form naturally among children who live near one another or go to school together and often consist of children of the same racial or ethnic origin and similar socioeconomic status. Children who play together are usually close in age and of the same sex (Hartup, 1992; Pellegrini et al., 2002).

POSITIVE AND NEGATIVE EFFECTS OF PEER RELATIONS

As children begin to move away from parental influence, the peer group opens new perspectives. The peer group helps children learn how to adjust their needs and desires to those of others, when to yield, and when to stand firm. Within the context of peer groups, children develop skills needed for sociability and intimacy, and they gain a sense of belonging. They are motivated to achieve, and they attain a sense of identity.

Same-sex peer groups may help children learn gender-appropriate behaviors and incorporate gender roles into their self-concept. A sense of being typical of one's gender and being content with that gender increases self-esteem and well-being, whereas feeling pressure—from parents, peers, or oneself—to conform to gender stereotypes lessens well-being (Yunger et al., 2004).

prejudice
Unfavorable attitude toward members of certain groups outside one's own, especially racial or ethnic groups.

Unfortunately, peer groups may reinforce **prejudice:** unfavorable attitudes toward outsiders, especially members of certain racial or ethnic groups. Children tend to be biased toward children like themselves. These biases peak at about 5 to 7 years of age and then decrease through late childhood. As children move into adolescence, social context and what children learn from others seem to matter more (Raabe & Beelmann, 2011).

Children can be negatively affected by discrimination. The perception of being discriminated against has been linked to reductions in well-being, self-esteem, and life satisfaction, and increases in anxiety, depression, and conduct problems (Schmitt, Branscombe, Postmes & Garcia, 2014; Brody et al., 2006). However, prejudice is not inevitable. In one study, the degree of bias toward immigrants was related to whether the adolescents in the study had immigrant friends. Those who did were more tolerant of differences and showed less bias toward immigrants (van Zalk & Kerr, 2014). Group norms also matter. Children whose social groups or schools have a norm of inclusion are less likely to show prejudiced behavior (Nesdale, 2011; Tezanos-Pinto, Bratt & Brown, 2010). Intervention programs, including extended contact and the promotion of empathy and perspective-taking, have been moderately successful at reducing prejudice (Beelmann & Heinemann, 2014).

The peer group also can foster antisocial tendencies. While, some degree of conformity to group standards is healthy, it is unhealthy when it becomes destructive or prompts young people to act against their better judgment. It is usually in the company of peers that some children shoplift and begin to use drugs (Dishion & Tipsord, 2011; Hartup, 1992).

POPULARITY

Much of research in child development depends on asking children the right questions in the right way. If a researcher asked schoolchildren to tell her the social ranking of all the children in a classroom, she would most likely be met with a blank stare. However, children can easily say who they like to play with, who they like the most, or who they think other kids like the most. This is known as a *positive nomination.*

Children can also easily describe which children they don't like to play with, like the least, or think other kids don't like—this is a *negative nomination.* By asking these types of questions of every child in a classroom, a researcher can use the aggregated responses to get an overall score, or tally, for each child. The tally may be composed of positive nominations, negative nominations, or no nominations. This measure is known as *sociometric popularity.*

Sociometrically *popular* children receive many positive nominations and few negative nominations. They generally have good cognitive abilities, are high achievers, are good at solving social problems, are kind and help other children, and are assertive without being disruptive or aggressive. Their superior social skills make others enjoy being with them (Cillessen & Mayeux, 2004; LaFontana & Cillessen, 2002)

Children can be *unpopular* in one of two ways. Some children are rejected, and they receive a large number of negative nominations. Other children are neglected and receive few nominations of any kind. Some unpopular children are aggressive; others are hyperactive, inattentive, or withdrawn (Dodge, Coie, Pettit & Price, 1990; LaFontana & Cillessen, 2002; Masten & Coatsworth, 1998). Still others act silly and immature or anxious and uncertain. Unpopular children are often insensitive to other children's feelings and do not adapt well to new situations (Bierman, Smoot & Aumiller, 1993).

Other children can be *average* in their ratings and do not receive an unusual number of either positive or negative nominations. Finally, some children are *controversial* and receive many positive and negative nominations, indicating that some children like them a great deal and some dislike them a great deal. Less is known about outcomes related to average and controversial sociometric categories.

Popularity is important in middle childhood. Schoolchildren whose peers like them are likely to be well adjusted as adolescents. Those who have trouble getting along with peers are more likely to develop psychological problems, drop out of school, or become delinquent (Dishion & Tipsord, 2011; Mrug et al., 2012; Hartup, 1992; Kupersmidt & Coie, 1990). Peer rejection has also been linked to lower levels of classroom participation and low academic achievement (Ladd, Herald-Brown & Reiser, 2008; Wentzel & Muenks, 2016).

FRIENDSHIP

Friends are an important developmental influence. Children look for friends who are like them in age, sex, and interests. The strongest friendships involve equal commitment and mutual give-and-take. Though children tend to choose friends with similar ethnic backgrounds, cross-racial/ethnic friendships are associated with positive developmental outcomes (Kawabata & Crick, 2008).

TABLE 10.1 Selman's Stages of Friendship

Stage	Description	Example
Stage 0: Momentary playmateship (ages 3 to 7)	On this *undifferentiated* level of friendship, children define their friends in terms of physical closeness and value them for material or physical attributes.	"She lives on my street and has a big yard to run in" or "He has the Power Rangers."
Stage 1: One-way assistance (ages 4 to 9)	On this *unilateral* level, a "good friend" does what the child wants the friend to do.	"She's not my friend anymore, because she wouldn't do what I wanted her to" or "He's my friend because he always says yes when I want to borrow his toys."
Stage 2: Two-way fair-weather cooperation (ages 6 to 12)	This *reciprocal* level overlaps stage 1. It involves give-and-take but still serves many separate self-interests, rather than the common interests of the two friends.	"We are friends; we do things for each other" or "A friend is someone who plays with you when you don't have anybody else to play with."
Stage 3: Intimate, mutually shared relationships (ages 9 to 15)	On this *mutual* level, children view a friendship as a committed relationship that incorporates more than doing things for each other. Friends become possessive and demand exclusivity.	"It takes a long time to make a close friend, so you feel bad if you find out that your friend is trying to make other friends too."
Stage 4: Autonomous interdependence (beginning at age 12)	In this *interdependent stage,* children respect friends' needs for both dependency and autonomy.	"A good friendship is a risk you have to take; you have to support and trust and give, but you have to be able to let go too."

Sources: R. L. Selman, *The growth of interpersonal understanding: Developmental and clinical analyses.* New York: Academic Press, 1980.
R. L., Selman & A. P. Selman, *Children's ideas about friendship: A new theory. Psychology Today,* April 1979, pp. 71–80.

With their friends, children learn to communicate and cooperate. They help each other weather stressful situations, such as starting at a new school or adjusting to parents' divorce. The inevitable quarrels help children learn to resolve conflicts. In short, friendships are a means by which children practice and hone social interaction skills (Glick & Rose, 2011; Newcomb & Bagwell, 1995).

Children's concepts of friendship and the ways they act with their friends change with age, reflecting cognitive and emotional growth. Preschool friends play together and have preferred playmates, but they are not friends in the same sense that older children are. Children cannot be or have true friends until they achieve the cognitive maturity to consider other people's views and needs as well as their own (Dodge, Coie & Lynam, 2006; Hartup & Stevens, 1999). On the basis of interviews with people between the ages of 3 and 45, Robert Selman (1980; Selman & Selman, 1979) traced changing conceptions of friendship across development (Table 10.1).

School-age children distinguish among "best friends," "good friends," and "casual friends" on the basis of intimacy and time spent together (Hartup & Stevens, 1999). Children this age typically have three to five best friends but usually play with only one or two at a time (Hartup, 1992; Hartup & Stevens, 1999). School-age girls seem to care less about having many friends than about having a few close friends they can rely on. Boys have more friendships, but they tend to be less intimate and affectionate (Furman & Buhrmester, 1985; Hartup & Stevens, 1999).

AGGRESSION AND BULLYING

Aggression declines and changes in form during the early school years. After age 6 or 7, most children become less aggressive as they grow less egocentric, more empathic, more cooperative, and better able to communicate. They can now put themselves in someone else's place, can understand another person's motives, and can find positive ways of asserting themselves. *Instrumental aggression,* aggression aimed at achieving an objective, becomes much less common. However, as aggression declines overall,

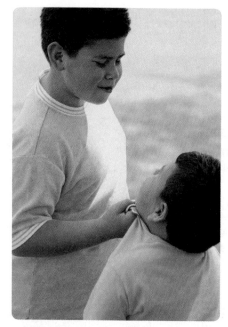

Aggressive boys tend to gain in social status by the end of fifth grade, suggesting that bullying behavior may be seen as cool or glamorous by preadolescents.
©Don Hammond/Design Pics Inc./Alamy Stock Photo

hostile aggression, aggression intended to hurt another person, increases (Dodge, Coie & Lynam, 2006), often taking verbal rather than physical form (Pellegrini & Archer, 2005). Boys continue to engage in more *direct aggression,* and girls are increasingly more likely to engage in *social* or *relational aggression,* although some researchers argue the differences have been overstated (Card, Stucky, Sawalani & Little, 2008).

Generally, those children who are high in physical aggression are disliked, although there are indications that how much these children are disliked is moderated by age. Physically aggressive children sometimes can attain higher social status as they get older (Garandeau, Ahn & Rodkin, 2011; Cillessen & Mayeux, 2004). Relational aggression does not appear to show the same dynamic and has been associated with increased social influence and popularity (Vaillancourt & Hymel, 2006). There is evidence that relationally aggressive children seek out other relationally aggressive children as friends, and that both interaction members then mutually influence each other (Sijtsema et al., 2010; Dijkstra, Berger & Lindenberg, 2011).

Types of Aggression and Social Information Processing What makes children act aggressively? One answer may lie in the way they process social information.

Instrumental, or *proactive,* aggressors view force and coercion as effective ways to get what they want. They act deliberately, not out of anger. For example, such a child might learn that he can force another child to trade lunch items with him by threatening to hit the other child. If that strategy works, the child has been reinforced for his aggressive acts, and his belief in aggression is confirmed.

Other children are more likely to engage in *hostile* or *reactive* aggression. Such a child might, after being accidentally pushed by someone in the lunch line, assume that the bump was on purpose and push back angrily. Children who habitually assume the worst of others in situations such as these are said to have a **hostile attributional bias.** They quickly conclude, in ambiguous situations, that others were acting with ill intent and are likely to strike out in retaliation or self-defense. Generally, other children then respond to this hostility with aggression, thereby confirming the original hostile attributional bias and strengthening it (Crick & Dodge, 1996; de Castro, Veerman, Koops, Bosch & Monshouwer, 2002). Because people often *do* become hostile toward someone who acts aggressively toward them, a hostile bias may become a self-fulfilling prophecy, setting in motion a cycle of aggression (de Castro et al., 2002).

Does Electronic Media Violence Stimulate Aggression? Children spend more time on entertainment media than on any other activities except school and sleeping. On average, children spend about 7 hours and 38 minutes a day in front of a television or computer screen (Rideout, Foehr & Roberts, 2010).

Violence is prevalent in U.S. media. About 6 out of 10 television programs portray violence, usually glamorized, glorified, or trivialized (Yokota & Thompson, 2000). Music videos disproportionately feature violence against women and blacks. The motion picture, music, and video game industries aggressively market violent, adult-rated products to children (AAP Committee on Public Education, 2001).

Evidence from research conducted over the past 50 years on exposure to violence on TV, movies, and video games supports a causal relationship between media violence and violent behavior on the viewer's part (Huesmann, 2007) that, from a public health perspective, is stronger than many other recognized threats to safety (Figure 10.2).

Longitudinal studies have demonstrated that children's exposure to violent media increases their risk for long-term effects based on observational learning, desensitization, and enactive learning (Huesmann, 2007). Children who see characters use violence to achieve their goals are likely to conclude that force is an effective way to resolve conflicts.

hostile attribution bias
Tendency to perceive others as trying to hurt one and to strike out in retaliation or self-defense.

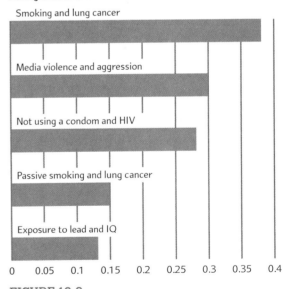

Average correlation

FIGURE 10.2

Effects of Threats to Public Health

The effect of media violence is the same or greater than the effect of many other recognized threats to public health.

Source: B. J., Bushman, & L. Rowell Huesmann, "Effects of televised violence on aggression." In Dorothy G. Singer and Jerome L. Singer (Eds.), *Handbook of Children and the Media.* Thousand Oaks, CA: Sage Publications, 2001, 235.

Research shows that children who see televised violence tend to act aggressively. When the violence is child-initiated, as in video games, the effect may be even stronger.
©Jonathan Nourok/PhotoEdit

Media provides visceral thrills without showing the human cost, leads children to view aggression as acceptable, and desensitizes them to violence (Huesmann & Kirwil, 2007). The more realistically violence is portrayed, the more likely it is to be accepted (AAP Committee on Public Education, 2001; Anderson et al., 2003).

Children are more vulnerable than adults to the influence of televised violence (AAP Committee on Public Education, 2001; Coie & Dodge, 1998). The influence is stronger if the child believes the violence on the screen is real, identifies with the violent character, finds that character attractive, and watches without parental supervision or intervention (Anderson et al., 2003; Coie & Dodge, 1998). Highly aggressive children are more strongly affected by media violence than are less aggressive children (Anderson et al., 2003).

Research on effects of video games and the Internet suggest that long-term increases in violent behavior could be even greater for video games than for TV and movies. Players of violent games are active participants who receive positive reinforcement for violent actions (Huesmann, 2007). Young video game players show less prosocial behavior, higher aggression, and are more likely to respond violently to provocation (Ferguson, 2015; C. Anderson, 2000).

Although the majority of researchers endorse the link between viewing violence and aggression (Bushman, Gollwitzer & Cruz, 2015), some believe the link between media violence and aggression may have been overstated (Ferguson, 2013). For example, some researchers argue that methodological flaws such as a failure to consider confounding variables, difficulty generalizing from laboratory studies of aggression to real-world aggressive acts, and inappropriate statistical modeling call into question some of the claims (Ferguson & Savage, 2012). In support of this assertion are data indicating that youth violence has declined even though exposure to violent media has remained stable (Ferguson, 2013).

Media-induced aggressiveness can be minimized by cutting down on television use and by parental monitoring and guidance of the shows children watch (Anderson et al., 2003). The AAP Committee on Public Education (2001) recommends that parents limit children's media exposure to 1 to 2 hours a day.

bullying
Aggression deliberately and persistently directed against a particular target, or victim, typically one who is weak, vulnerable, and defenseless.

Bullies and Victims Aggression becomes **bullying** when it is deliberately, persistently directed against a particular target: a victim. Bullying can be physical (hitting, punching, kicking, or damaging or taking of personal belongings), verbal (name-calling or threatening), or relational or emotional (isolating and gossiping, often behind the victim's back). Bullying can be *proactive*—done to show dominance, bolster power, or win admiration—or *reactive,* responding to a real or imagined attack. *Cyberbullying*—posting negative comments or derogatory photos of the victim on a website—has become increasingly common (Berger, 2007).

Bullying may reflect a genetic tendency toward aggressiveness combined with environmental influences, such as coercive parents and antisocial friends (Berger, 2007). Most bullies are boys who tend to victimize other boys; female bullies tend to target other girls (Berger, 2007; Pellegrini & Long, 2002; Veenstra et al., 2005). Male bullies tend to use overt, physical aggression; female bullies may use relational aggression (Boulton, 1995; Nansel et al., 2001). Patterns of bullying and victimization may become established as early as kindergarten; as tentative peer groups form, aggressors soon get to know which children make the easiest targets. Physical bullying declines with age, but other forms of bullying increase, especially at ages 11 to 15. Whereas younger children reject an aggressive child, by early adolescence bullies are sometimes dominant, respected, feared, and even liked (Berger, 2007). Both bullies and victims tend to be deficient in social problem-solving skills, and those who also have academic problems are more likely to be bullies than victims (Cook, Williams, Guerra, Kim & Sadek, 2010).

Risk factors for victimization seem to be similar across cultures (Schwartz, Chang & Farver, 2001). Victims do not fit in. They tend to be anxious, depressed, cautious, quiet, and submissive and to cry easily, or to be argumentative and provocative (Hodges,

on the world

BULLYING: A WORLDWIDE PROBLEM

In the United States, 28 percent of U.S. students in grades 6 to 12 report having been bullied, approximately 30 percent of young people admit to bullying others, and 70.6 percent of young people say they have seen bullying in their schools (U.S. Department of Health and Human Services, 2014). How does this compare to other countries? In a global status report UNESCO (2017) examined bullying prevalence rates across a number of countries. In France, 32 percent of students reported being the victim of verbal bullying, and 35 percent were the victims of physical bullying. In Australia, 27 percent of students reported experiencing frequent bullying and 9 percent admitted to bullying others. In Kenya, between 63 and 82 percent of students reported being subjected to various types of bullying, and in South Africa, more than half of respondents had experienced bullying. Reports vary widely—in Sweden, 15 percent reported bullying, while in Lithuania 67 percent of students reported being bullied. Though the statistics vary from country to country, bullying is a global problem and it is having a negative impact on the world's children.

Bullying occurs regardless of whether or not a country is wealthy or poor. In 2014 UNICEF released a report including information collected from approximately 100,000 young people in 18 countries (UNICEF, 2014).

Bullying occurred in every country measured and varied widely. For example, bullying ranged from 7 percent in Tajikistan to a high of 74 percent in Samoa. Wealthy countries likewise showed a similar range, with prevalence rates ranging from a low of 14 percent in the Czech Republic and a high of 69 percent in Latvia and Romania.

Bullying and unsafe environments create a climate of fear and insecurity that can lead to negative developmental outcomes. Cross-cultural research conducted with adults in 30 European countries indicated that those adults who had been bullied as children showed lower life satisfaction (29 percent) than those who had not been bullied (40 percent) (UNESCO, 2017). Health promotion and prevention strategies need to address bullying problems to make the world safer for all.

what's your view

Although the wealth of a country does not seem to account for bullying prevalence rates, there are wide disparities in these rates among countries. What do you think some relevant country-level variables might be? Do you think culture might also impact which characteristics put children at risk of being bullying?

Boivin, Vitaro, & Bukowski, 1999; Veenstra et al., 2005). They have few friends and may live in harsh, punitive family environments (Nansel et al., 2001; Schwartz, Dodge, Pettit, Bates & Conduct Problems Prevention Research Group, 2000). Victims are apt to have low self-esteem, though it is not clear whether low self-esteem leads to or follows from victimization (Boulton & Smith, 1994; Olweus, 1995). Some victims are small, passive, weak, and submissive and may blame themselves for being bullied. Other victims are provocative; they goad their attackers, and they may even attack other children themselves (Berger, 2007; Veenstra et al., 2005). Children who are overweight are more likely to become either victims or bullies (Janssen, Craig, Boyce & Pickett, 2004).

Bullying, especially emotional bullying, is harmful to both bullies and victims (Berger, 2007). Both bullies and victims tend to have conduct problems and lower academic achievement (Golmaryami, Frick, Hemphill, Kahn, Crapanzano & Terranova, 2016; Shetgiri, Espelage & Carroll, 2015). Bullies are at increased risk of delinquency, crime, or alcohol abuse. Victims of chronic bullying tend to develop behavior problems. They may become more aggressive themselves or may become depressed (Schwartz, McFadyen-Ketchum, Dodge, Pettit & Bates, 1998; Veenstra et al., 2005). Furthermore, frequent bullying affects the school atmosphere, leading to widespread underachievement, alienation from school, stomachaches and headaches, reluctance to go to school, and frequent absences (Berger, 2007).

As more and more children gain access to electronic devices and participate in social media at younger and younger ages (Kowalski, Giumetti, Schroeder & Lattanner, 2014), there has been a rise in incidents of cyberbullying. Upward of 70 percent of children report at least one online instance of bullying in the previous year, mostly via instant messaging (Juvonen & Gross, 2008). Research suggests that cyberbullying is often an extension of face-to-face bullying, as cyberbullies also tend to engage in aggressive acts in person as well as online (Modecki, Minchin, Harbaugh, Guerra & Runions, 2014; Kowalski et al., 2014). Cyberbullies tend to believe that aggression is normative and show low empathy for others (Kowalski et al., 2014). While overall, boys cyberbully at higher levels than do girls, girls engage in more cyberbullying in early to mid adolescence, while boys' cyberbullying peaks somewhat later (Barlett & Coyne, 2014). Being a victim of cyberbullying is associated with a wealth of mental health and academic issues, and, for some children, an elevated risk of suicidal ideation and suicide (Van Geel, Vedder & Tanilon, 2014).

The U.S. Department of Health and Human Services has promoted Steps to Respect, a program for grades 3 to 6 that aims to (1) increase staff awareness and responsiveness to bullying, (2) teach students social and emotional skills, and (3) foster socially responsible beliefs. Some research has found a reduction in playground bullying and argumentative behavior and an increase in harmonious interactions among children who participated in the program (Frey et al., 2005). However, other data have indicated the impact on actual bullying behavior is minimal although the programs may enhance students' social competence and self-esteem (Merrell, Gueldner, Ross & Isava, 2008).

Mental Health

Although most children are fairly well adjusted, at least 1 in 10 children and adolescents has a diagnosed mental disturbance severe enough to cause some impairment (Leslie, Newman, Chesney & Perrin, 2005). Let's look at several common emotional disturbances and then at types of treatment.

COMMON EMOTIONAL PROBLEMS

Children with emotional, behavioral, and developmental problems tend to be an underserved group. Only about half of all children in the United States who need services for mental health issues currently receive the help they need (Merikangas et al., 2009).

oppositional defiant disorder (ODD)
Pattern of behavior, persisting into middle childhood, marked by negativity, hostility, and defiance.

conduct disorder (CD)
Repetitive, persistent pattern of aggressive, antisocial behavior violating societal norms or the rights of others.

Disruptive Conduct Disorders Temper tantrums and defiant, argumentative, hostile, or deliberately annoying behavior—common among 4- and 5-year-olds—typically are outgrown by middle childhood as children get better at controlling these behaviors (Miner & Clarke-Stewart, 2009). When such a pattern of behavior persists until age 8, children (usually boys) may be diagnosed with **oppositional defiant disorder (ODD),** a pattern of defiance, disobedience, and hostility toward adult authority figures lasting at least 6 months and going beyond the bounds of normal childhood behavior. Children with ODD constantly fight, argue, lose their temper, snatch things, blame others, and are angry and resentful. They are spiteful and deliberately annoy others. They have few friends, are in constant trouble in school, and test the limits of adults' patience (Matthys & John, 2017).

Some children with ODD may later be diagnosed with **conduct disorder (CD),** a persistent, repetitive pattern, beginning at an early age, of aggressive, antisocial acts, such as truancy, setting fires, habitual lying, fighting, bullying, theft, vandalism, assaults, and drug and alcohol use (Mathys & John, 2017). Between 6 and 16 percent of boys and between 2 and 9 percent of girls under age 18 in the United States have been diagnosed with clinical levels of externalizing behavior or conduct problems (Roosa et al., 2005). Conduct disorder in childhood is strongly predictive of antisocial and criminal behavior in adulthood (Mordre, Groholt, Kjelsberg, Sandstad & Myhre, 2011; Lynam, Caspi, Moffitt, Loeber & Stouthamer-Loeber, 2007).

There are indications that children with conduct disorders have neurological deficits that affect their ability to feel empathy for others, leading to a characteristic callous unemotionality (Lockwood et al., 2013; Michalska, Zeffiro & Decety, 2016). Such deficits may be genetically influenced or may be brought on by adverse environments such as hostile parenting or family conflict, or both (van Goozen, Fairchild, Snoek & Harold, 2007; Miner & Clarke-Stewart, 2009). Also influential are stressful life events and association with deviant peers (Roosa et al., 2005).

School Phobia and Other Anxiety Disorders Some children have **school phobia,** an unrealistic fear of going to school. True school phobia may be a type of **separation anxiety disorder,** a condition involving excessive anxiety for at least 4 weeks concerning separation from home or from people to whom the child is attached. Although separation anxiety is normal in infancy, it is cause for concern when it persists in older children. Separation anxiety disorder affects some 4 percent of children and young adolescents and may persist through the college years. These children often come from close-knit, caring families. They may develop the disorder spontaneously or after a stressful event, such as the death of a pet, an illness, or a move to a new school (American Psychiatric Association, 2000; Harvard Medical School, 2004a).

Sometimes school phobia may be a form of **social phobia,** or *social anxiety:* extreme fear and/or avoidance of social situations such as speaking in class or meeting an acquaintance on the street. Social phobia affects about 5 percent of children. It runs in families, suggesting a genetic component. Often these phobias are triggered by traumatic experiences, such as a child's mind going blank when the child is called on in class (Beidel & Turner, 1998). Social anxiety tends to increase with age, whereas separation anxiety decreases (Costello et al., 2003).

Some children have a **generalized anxiety disorder,** not focused on any specific part of their lives. These children worry about almost everything: school grades, storms, earthquakes, and hurting themselves on the playground. They tend to be self-conscious, self-doubting, and excessively concerned with meeting the expectations of others. They seek approval and need constant reassurance, but their worry seems independent of performance or of how they are regarded by others (Harvard Medical School, 2004a; USDHHS, 1999). Far less common is **obsessive-compulsive disorder (OCD).** Children with this disorder may be obsessed by repetitive, intrusive thoughts, images, or impulses (often involving irrational fears); or may show compulsive behaviors, such as constant hand-washing; or both (American Psychiatric Association, 2000; Harvard Medical School, 2004a).

Childhood Depression **Childhood depression** is a disorder of mood that goes beyond normal, temporary sadness. Depression is estimated to occur in approximately 2.1 percent of children (Perou et al., 2013). Symptoms include inability to have fun or concentrate, fatigue, extreme activity or apathy, crying, sleep problems, weight change, physical complaints, feelings of worthlessness, a prolonged sense of friendlessness, or frequent thoughts about death or suicide. Childhood depression may signal the beginning of a recurrent problem that is likely to persist into adulthood (Cicchetti & Toth, 1998; USDHHS, 1999b; Weissman, Warner, Wickramaratne & Kandel, 1999).

The exact causes of childhood depression are unknown and determined by multiple factors, but depressed children tend to come from families with high levels of parental depression, anxiety, substance abuse, or antisocial behavior. The atmosphere in such families may increase children's risk of depression (USDHHS, 1999b; Bradley et al., 2008). Researchers have also found specific genes related to depression (Aguilera et al., 2009).

Children as young as 5 or 6 can accurately report depressed moods and feelings that forecast later trouble, from academic problems to major depression and ideas of suicide (Ialongo, Edelsohn & Kellam, 2001). Depression often emerges during the transition to middle school and may be related to stiffer academic pressures (Cicchetti & Toth, 1998), weak self-efficacy beliefs, and lack of personal investment in academic success (Rudolph, Lambert, Clark & Kurlakowsky, 2001). Depression becomes more prevalent during adolescence.

TREATMENT TECHNIQUES

Psychological treatment for emotional disturbances can take several forms. In **individual psychotherapy,** a therapist sees a child one-on-one to help the child gain insights into his or her personality and relationships and to interpret feelings and behavior. Such treatment may be helpful at a time of stress, such as the death of a parent or parental divorce.

school phobia
Unrealistic fear of going to school; may be a form of *separation anxiety disorder* or *social phobia.*

separation anxiety disorder
Condition involving excessive, prolonged anxiety concerning separation from home or from people to whom a person is attached.

social phobia
Extreme fear and/or avoidance of social situations.

generalized anxiety disorder
Anxiety not focused on any single target.

obsessive-compulsive disorder (OCD)
Anxiety aroused by repetitive, intrusive thoughts, images, or impulses, often leading to compulsive ritual behaviors.

childhood depression
Mood disorder characterized by such symptoms as a prolonged sense of friendlessness, inability to have fun or concentrate, fatigue, extreme activity or apathy, feelings of worthlessness, weight change, physical complaints, and thoughts of death or suicide.

individual psychotherapy
Psychological treatment in which a therapist sees a troubled person one-on-one.

family therapy
Psychological treatment in which a therapist sees the whole family together to analyze patterns of family functioning.

behavior therapy
Therapeutic approach using principles of learning theory to encourage desired behaviors or eliminate undesired ones; also called *behavior modification.*

art therapy
Therapeutic approach that allows a person to express troubled feelings without words, using a variety of art materials and media.

play therapy
Therapeutic approach that uses play to help a child cope with emotional distress.

drug therapy
Administration of drugs to treat emotional disorders.

In **family therapy,** the therapist sees the family together, observes how members interact, and points out healthy and destructive patterns of family functioning. Therapy can help parents confront their conflicts and begin to resolve them. This is often the first step toward resolving the child's problems as well.

Behavior therapy, or *behavior modification,* uses principles of learning theory to eliminate undesirable behaviors or to develop desirable ones. Behavior therapy is more effective than nonbehavioral methods, and results are best when treatment is targeted to specific problems and desired outcomes (Weisz, Weiss, Han, Granger & Morton, 1995). *Cognitive behavioral therapy,* which seeks to change negative thoughts through gradual exposure, modeling, rewards, or talking to oneself, has proven the most effective treatment for anxiety disorders (Harvard Medical School, 2004a; Hofmann, Asnaani, Volk, Sawyer & Fang, 2012).

When children have limited verbal and conceptual skills or have suffered emotional trauma, **art therapy** can help them describe what is troubling them without the need to put their feelings into words. The child may express deep emotions through his or her choice of colors and subjects to depict (Kozlowska & Hanney, 1999). Art therapy has been demonstrated to be beneficial and is often used in conjunction with other forms of therapy (Slayton, D'Archer & Kaplan, 2010).

Play therapy, in which a child plays freely while a therapist occasionally comments, asks questions, or makes suggestions, has proven effective with a variety of emotional, cognitive, and social problems, especially when consultation with parents or other close family members is part of the process (Lin & Bratton, 2015; Ray, Armstrong, Balkin & Jayne, 2015; Leblanc & Ritchie, 2001).

The use of **drug therapy**—antidepressants, stimulants, tranquilizers, or antipsychotic medications—to treat childhood emotional disorders is controversial. During the past two decades the rate at which antipsychotic medications are prescribed for children and adolescents has risen sharply and at a faster rate than for adults (Olfson, Blanco, Wang, Laje & Correll 2014). For example, from 1999 to 2001 approximately 1 in 650 children were receiving antipsychotic medications; this number rose to 1 in 329 for 2007 (Olfson, Crystal, Huang & Gerhard, 2010). Sufficient research on the effectiveness and safety of many of these drugs, especially for children, is lacking.

STRESS AND RESILIENCE

Stressful events are part of childhood, and most children learn to cope. However, severe stressors may have long-term effects on physical and psychological well-being.

Stresses of Modern Life The pressures of modern life are forcing children to grow up too soon and exposing them to multiple stressors. Anxiety in childhood has increased greatly (Collishaw, 2015; Twenge, 2000). Fears of danger and death are the most consistent fears of children at all ages (Gullone, 2000; Silverman, La Greca & Wasserstein, 1995). This intense anxiety about safety may reflect the high rates of crime and violence in the larger society.

Findings about children's fears have been corroborated in a wide range of developed and developing societies. Poor children tend to be more fearful than children of higher socioeconomic status (Gullone, 2000; Ollendick, Yang, King, Dong & Akande, 1996). Children who grow up constantly surrounded by violence often have trouble concentrating and sleeping. Some become aggressive and come to take brutality for granted. Many do not allow themselves to become attached to other people for fear of more hurt and loss (Garbarino, Dubrow, Kostelny & Pardo, 1992, 1998).

Children are more susceptible than adults to psychological harm from a traumatic event such as war or terrorism, and their reactions vary with age (Garbarino, Governale, Henry & Nesi, 2015; Wexler, Branski & Kerem, 2006; Table 10.2). Younger children, who do not understand why the event occurred, tend to focus on the consequences. Older children are more aware of, and worried about, the underlying forces that caused the event (Hagan et al., 2005).

The impact of a traumatic event is influenced by the type of event, how much exposure children have to it, and how much they and their families

In play therapy, the therapist observes as a child acts out troubled feelings, often using developmentally appropriate materials such as toy animals.
©Photographee.eu/Shutterstock

TABLE 10.2 Children's Age-Related Reactions to Trauma

Age	Typical Reactions
5 years or less	Fear of separation from parent; crying, whimpering, screaming, trembling; immobility or aimless motion; frightened facial expressions; excessive clinging; regressive behaviors (thumbsucking, bed-wetting, fear of dark)
6 to 11 years	Extreme withdrawal; disruptive behavior; inability to pay attention; stomachaches or other symptoms with no physical basis; declining school performance, refusal to go to school; depression, anxiety, guilt, irritability, or emotional numbing; regressive behavior (nightmares, sleep problems, irrational fears, outbursts of anger or fighting)
12 to 17 years	Flashbacks, nightmares; emotional numbing, confusion; avoidance of reminders of the traumatic event; revenge fantasies; withdrawal, isolation; substance abuse; problems with peers, antisocial behavior; physical complaints; school avoidance, academic decline; sleep disturbances; depression, suicidal thoughts

Source: National Institute of Mental Health (NIMH). *Helping children and adolescents cope with violence and disasters: Fact sheet* (NIH Publication No. 01-3518). Bethesda, MD: Author, 2001.

and friends are personally affected. Human-caused disasters, such as terrorism and war, are much harder on children psychologically than natural disasters, such as earthquakes and floods. Exposure to graphic news coverage can worsen the effects (Wexler et al., 2006). Most children who watched news coverage of the September 11, 2001, terrorist attacks on New York and Washington, D.C., experienced profound stress, even if they were not directly affected (Walma van der Molen, 2004).

Children's responses to a traumatic event typically occur in two stages: *first,* fright, disbelief, denial, grief, and relief if their loved ones are unharmed; *second,* several days or weeks later, developmental regression and signs of emotional distress—anxiety, fear, withdrawal, sleep disturbances, pessimism about the future, or play related to themes of the event. If symptoms last for more than a month, the child should receive counseling (Hagan et al., 2005).

Children's responses across different cultures are similar (Navarro et al., 2016). Parents' responses to a violent event or disaster and the way they talk with a child about it strongly influence the child's ability to recover (NIMH, 2001a). Providing parents with strategies for addressing terrorism-related news can reduce threat perceptions and lower anxiety related to potential terrorism attacks (Comer, Furr, Beidas, Weiner & Kendall, 2008; Research in Action). Unfortunately, parents tend to underestimate the amount of stress their children are experiencing (APA, 2009) and thus miss opportunities to intervene.

Coping with Stress: The Resilient Child Much of the early history of psychology was marked by investigations into the various risks that can pull a child into a negative developmental trajectory. However, psychologists have increasingly come to realize that there is also value in examining resilience. **Resilient children** are those who weather circumstances that might blight others, who maintain their composure and competence under challenge or threat, or who bounce back from traumatic events. The two most important **protective factors** that help children and adolescents overcome stress and contribute to resilience are *good family relationships* and *cognitive functioning* (Masten & Coatsworth, 1998).

Resilient children also tend to have high IQs and to be good problem solvers, and their cognitive ability may help them cope with adversity, protect themselves, regulate their behavior, and learn from experience. They may attract the interest of teachers, who can act as guides, confidants, or mentors (Masten & Coatsworth, 1998). They may even have protective genes, which may buffer the effects of an unfavorable environment (Caspi et al., 2002; Kim-Cohen et al., 2004).

Other frequently cited protective factors include the following (Ackerman, Kogos, Youngstrom, Schoff & Izard, 1999; Eisenberg et al., 2004; Masten & Coatsworth, 1998; E. E. Werner, 1993):

- *The child's temperament or personality:* Resilient children are adaptable, friendly, well liked, independent, and sensitive to others. They are competent and have high self-esteem. When under stress, they can regulate their emotions well.

resilient children
Children who weather adverse circumstances, function well despite challenges or threats, or bounce back from traumatic events.

protective factors
(1) Influences that reduce the impact of potentially negative influences and tend to predict positive outcomes. (2) Influences that reduce the impact of early stress and tend to predict positive outcomes.

research in action

CHILDREN'S EXPERIENCES WITH TERRORIST EVENTS

On May 22, 2017, a terrorist attack occurred at singer Ariana Grande's concert in Manchester, England. Many of those injured were children whose parents had taken them to the concert. Hundreds of other children were separated from their parents during the chaos that ensued (Smith & Chan, 2017). Sadly, tragedies like these have become too.

After the devastating 9/11 attacks in 2001, many researchers turned to examine the impact of terrorist events on children. Compared to natural disasters, terrorist events have been associated with higher levels of distress (Hagan et al., 2005), and the intermittent and unpredictable nature of these attacks may contribute to heightened stress and anxiety levels that continue long after the event (Fremont, 2004).

Children experience a wide range of psychological and somatic symptoms after an attack occurs. Children exposed to terrorist attacks have been reported to show elevated post-traumatic stress symptoms for months afterward (Comer, Bry, Poznanski & Golik, 2016). Symptoms are often commensurate with direct threat to life, loss of loved ones, and local community devastation (Drury & Williams, 2012). Sleep disturbances, attention problems, headache and stomachache complaints, school avoidance, or irrational fears are also common (Saraiya, Garakani & Billick, 2013). Even watching recorded TV footage may induce elevated threat perceptions and anxiety symptoms (Comer et al., 2008).

All too often, parents are forced to confront questions from their children about mass violence and terrorism seen in the world around them. Undoubtedly, some parents have no idea what to say or how to explain such unwonted attacks. Although difficult, these are important conversations to have. Children gauge threats based on parental response; therefore, speaking to your child in a calm, reassuring manner can help soothe fears (Pine, Costello & Masten, 2005). The American Academy of Child and Adolescent Psychiatry (2017) issues a few additional pointers:

1. *Listen to children.* Create a time and place for children to ask questions and help them express themselves. Sometimes children are more comfortable drawing pictures or playing with toys rather than talking about their feelings.
2. *Answer their questions.* Be honest when answering tough questions about violence. Use words the child can understand and try not to overload with too much information. You may have to repeat yourself. Be consistent and reassuring.
3. *Provide support.* Children are comfortable with structure and familiarity. Maintain a predictable routine. Avoid exposure to violent images. Watch for physical signs of stress, such as trouble sleeping or separation anxiety, and seek professional help if symptoms are persistent and/or pronounced.

what's your view What would you say to a child to soothe upset emotions and fears regarding terrorist attacks? How might you respond differently to a 6-year-old versus an 11-year-old who have questions about what happened?

- *Compensating experiences:* A supportive school environment or successful experiences in studies, sports, or music or with other children or adults can help make up for a destructive home life.

- *Reduced risk:* Children who have been exposed to only one of a number of factors for psychiatric disorder (such as parental discord, a disturbed mother, a criminal father, and experience in foster care) are often better able to overcome stress than children who have been exposed to more than one risk factor.

This does not mean that bad things that happen in a child's life do not matter. In general, children with unfavorable backgrounds have more adjustment problems than children with more favorable backgrounds, and even some outwardly resilient children may suffer internal distress that may have long-term consequences (Masten & Coatsworth, 1998). Still, what is heartening about these findings is that negative childhood experiences do not necessarily determine the outcome of a person's life and that many children have the strength to rise above the most difficult circumstances.

summary and key terms

The Developing Self

- The self-concept becomes more realistic during middle childhood, when, according to a neo-Piagetian model, children form representational systems.
- According to Erikson, the source of self-esteem is children's competence. This virtue develops through resolution of the fourth psychosocial conflict, industry versus inferiority.
- School-age children have internalized shame and pride and can better understand and regulate negative emotions.
- Empathy and prosocial behavior increase.
- Emotional growth is affected by parents' reactions to displays of negative emotions and involves effortful control.

representational systems, industry versus inferiority

The Child in the Family

- School-age children spend less time with parents and are less close to them than before, but relationships with parents continue to be important. Culture influences family relationships and roles.
- The family environment has two major components: family structure and family atmosphere.
- The emotional tone of the home, the way parents handle disciplinary issues and conflict, the effects of parents' work, and the adequacy of financial resources all contribute to family atmosphere.
- Development of coregulation may affect the way a family handles conflicts and discipline.
- The impact of mothers' employment depends on many factors.
- Poverty can harm children's development indirectly through its effects on parents' well-being and parenting practices.
- Many children today grow up in nontraditional family structures. Other things being equal, children tend to do better in two-parent families than in cohabiting, divorced, single-parent, or stepfamilies.
- Children's adjustment to divorce depends on factors concerning the child, the parents' handling of the situation, custody and visitation arrangements, financial circumstances, contact with the noncustodial parent (usually the father), and a parent's remarriage.
- The amount of conflict in a marriage and after divorce may influence whether children are better off if the parents stay together.
- In most divorces the mother gets custody, though paternal custody is a growing trend.
- Joint custody can be beneficial to children when the parents can cooperate. Joint legal custody is more common than joint physical custody.
- Although parental divorce increases the risk of long-term problems for children, most adjust reasonably well.
- Children living with only one parent are at heightened risk of behavioral and academic problems, largely related to socioeconomic status.
- Studies have found positive developmental outcomes in children living with gay or lesbian parents.
- Adopted children are generally well adjusted, though they face special challenges.
- The roles and responsibilities of siblings in nonindustrialized societies are more structured than in industrialized societies.
- Siblings learn about conflict resolution from their relationships with each other. Relationships with parents affect sibling relationships.

internalizing behaviors, externalizing behaviors, coregulation

The Child in the Peer Group

- The peer group becomes more important in middle childhood. Peer groups generally consist of children who are similar in age, sex, ethnicity, and socioeconomic status and who live near one another or go to school together.
- The peer group helps children develop social skills, allows them to test and adopt values independent of parents, gives them a sense of belonging, and helps develop their self-concept and gender identity. It also may encourage conformity and prejudice.
- Popularity in middle childhood tends to influence future adjustment. Popular children tend to have good cognitive abilities and social skills. Behaviors that affect popularity may be influenced by family relationships and cultural values.
- Intimacy and stability of friendships increase during middle childhood. Boys tend to have more friends, whereas girls tend to have closer friends.
- During middle childhood, aggression typically declines. Instrumental aggression generally gives way to hostile aggression, often with a hostile bias. Highly physically aggressive children tend to be unpopular.
- Aggressiveness is promoted by exposure to media violence and can extend into adult life.
- Middle childhood is a prime time for bullying. Victims tend to be weak and submissive or argumentative and provocative and to have low self-esteem.

prejudice, hostile attribution bias, bullying

Mental Health

- Common emotional and behavioral disorders among school-age children include disruptive behavioral disorders, anxiety disorders, and childhood depression.
- Treatment techniques include individual psychotherapy, family therapy, behavior therapy, art therapy, play therapy, and drug therapy. Often therapies are used in combination.
- As a result of the pressures of modern life, many children experience stress. Children tend to worry about school, health, and personal safety and may be traumatized by exposure to terrorism, war or natural disasters.
- Resilient children are better able than others to withstand stress. Protective factors involve family relationships, cognitive ability, personality, degree of risk, and compensating experiences.

oppositional defiant disorder (ODD), conduct disorder (CD), school phobia, separation anxiety disorder, social phobia, generalized anxiety disorder, obsessive-compulsive disorder (OCD), childhood depression, individual psychotherapy, family therapy, behavior therapy, art therapy, play therapy, drug therapy, resilient children, protective factors

Physical and Cognitive Development in Adolescence

learning objectives

Discuss the nature of adolescence.

Describe the changes involved in puberty, as well as the changes in the adolescent brain.

Identify adolescent problems related to health.

Explain cognitive changes in adolescence.

Summarize key aspects of how schools influence adolescent development.

©moodboard/Alamy Stock Photo

In this chapter, we describe the physical transformations of adolescence and how they affect young people's feelings. We look at the not-yet-mature adolescent brain and discuss health issues associated with this time of life. We examine the Piagetian stage of formal operations, information-processing skills, and linguistic and moral development. Finally, we explore educational and vocational issues.

Adolescence:
A Developmental Transition

This chapter focuses on processes that occur in the long period known as **adolescence**—a developmental transition that involves physical, cognitive, emotional, and social changes and takes varying forms in different social, cultural, and economic settings. In this book, we define adolescence roughly as encompassing the years between 11 and to about 20.

adolescence
Developmental transition between childhood and adulthood entailing major physical, cognitive, and psychosocial changes.

ADOLESCENCE AS A SOCIAL CONSTRUCTION

Adolescence is not a clearly defined physical or biological category—it is a social construction. In traditional and preindustrial cultures, children generally entered the adult world when they matured physically or when they began a vocational apprenticeship. In the Western world, adolescence was first recognized as a unique period in the life span in the twentieth century. Today adolescence is recognized globally, but it may take different forms in different cultures (Window on the World).

In most parts of the world, adolescence lasts longer and is less clear-cut than in the past. There are myriad reasons for this social change. First, puberty generally begins earlier, which means that the period of adolescence begins at a younger age than in the past. In addition, as the world becomes more driven by technology and information, the amount of training required to be eligible for higher-paying occupations has increased.

ADOLESCENCE: A TIME OF OPPORTUNITIES AND RISKS

Any time of transition and change in the life span offers opportunities for both advances and risks. Adolescence is no different. It offers opportunities for growth in cognitive and social competence, autonomy, self-esteem, and intimacy.

However, adolescence is also a time of risk, and adolescents in the United States today face hazards to their well-being (Eaton et al., 2008). Why is adolescence such a risky stage in the life span? Psychologists believe the tendency to engage in risky behaviors may reflect the immaturity of the adolescent brain. Nonetheless, teens can respond to messages about safety and responsibility.

PHYSICAL DEVELOPMENT

Puberty

An important physical change in adolescence is the onset of **puberty**, the process that leads to sexual maturity, or fertility—the ability to reproduce. Puberty involves dramatic biological changes. These changes are part of a long, complex process of maturation that begins even before birth and has psychological ramifications that may continue into adulthood.

puberty
Process by which a person attains sexual maturity and the ability to reproduce.

HOW PUBERTY BEGINS: HORMONAL CHANGES

The advent of puberty results from a cascade of hormonal responses (Figure 11.1). First, the hypothalamus releases elevated levels of gonadotropin-releasing hormone (GnRH). The increased GnRH then triggers a rise in lutenizing hormone (LH) and follicle-stimulating hormone (FSH). These hormones exert their actions differentially on boys and girls. In girls, increased levels of FSH lead to the onset of menstruation. In boys, LH initiates the release of two additional hormones: testosterone and androstenedione (Buck Louis et al., 2008).

Puberty can be broken down into two basic stages: adrenarche and gonadarche. Adrenarche occurs between ages 6 and 8. During this stage, the adrenal glands secrete increasing levels of androgens, most notably dehydroepiandrosterone (DHEA) (Susman & Rogol, 2004). Levels increase gradually but consistently, and by the time a child is

FIGURE 11.1

Regulation of Human Puberty Onset and Progression

HPG (hypothalamus-pituitary-gonadal) activation requires a signal from the central nervous system (CNS) to the hypothalamus, which stimulates the production of LH and FSH from the pituitary.

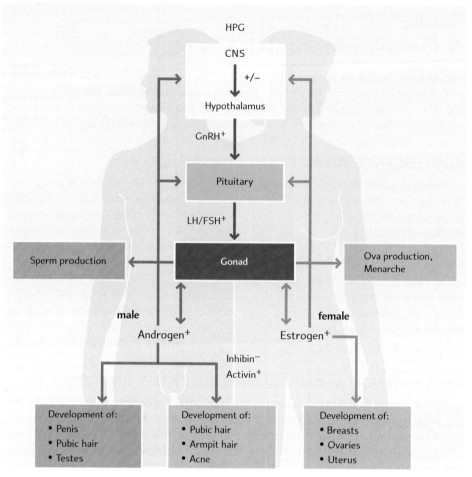

Source: G., Buck Louis, L., Gray, M., Marcus, S., Ojeda, O., Pescovitz, S., Witchel, . . . S. Y. Euling, "Environmental factors and puberty timing: Expert panel research needs." *Pediatrics*, 121, 2008, S192–S207.

10 years of age, the levels of DHEA are 10 times what they were between ages 1 and 4. DHEA influences the growth of pubic, axillary (underarm), and facial hair. It also contributes to faster body growth, oilier skin, and the development of body odor.

The second stage, gonadarche, is marked by the maturing of the sex organs, which triggers a second burst of DHEA production (McClintock & Herdt, 1996). During this time, a girl's ovaries increase their input of estrogen, which in turn stimulates the growth of female genitals, breasts, and the development of pubic and underarm hair. In boys, the testes increase the production of androgens, especially testosterone. This increase leads to the growth of male genitals, muscle mass, and body hair.

One factor in girls involves reaching a critical amount of body fat necessary for successful reproduction. Girls who have a higher percentage of body fat in early childhood tend to show earlier pubertal development (Davison, Susman & Birch, 2003; Lee et al., 2007). Leptin, a hormone associated with obesity, appears to play a role in this process (Kaplowitz, 2008). Increased levels of leptin may signal the pituitary and sex glands to increase their secretion of hormones (Susman & Rogol, 2004). This suggests that leptin may play a permissive role for puberty to start. In other words, leptin may need to be present in sufficient amounts for puberty to occur, but leptin alone does not initiate puberty (Kaplowitz, 2008).

Weight and leptin appear to influence pubertal timing differently in boys. While leptin still plays a permissive role (Clayton et al., 1997), having a high body mass index in childhood or being obese appears to delay puberty rather than accelerate it (Lee et al., 2010; Wang, 2002). Interestingly, recent research has found that being overweight, rather than either thin or obese, results in an earlier start to puberty in boys (J. M. Lee et al., 2016). More research is needed in this area.

Another factor that influences pubertal development is race and ethnicity. African American and Mexican American girls generally enter puberty earlier than white girls (Wu, Mendola & Buck, 2002), although recent data suggest the proportion of white girls who enter puberty early is increasing (Biro et al., 2010). By 7 years of age, 10.4 percent of white girls, 15 percent of Hispanic girls, and 23.4 percent of African American girls are showing signs of entering puberty (Biro et al., 2010).

TIMING, SIGNS, AND SEQUENCE OF PUBERTY AND SEXUAL MATURITY

A wide variation in age at puberty is normative, but puberty generally lasts 3 to 4 years and begins about age 8 in girls and age 9 in boys (Susman & Rogol, 2004). Recently, pediatricians have seen a significant number of girls with breast budding before their eighth birthdays (Slyper, 2006).

Primary and Secondary Sex Characteristics The **primary sex characteristics** are the organs necessary for reproduction. In the female, the sex organs include the ovaries, fallopian tubes, uterus, clitoris, and vagina. In the male, they include the testes, penis, scrotum, seminal vesicles, and prostate gland. During puberty, these organs enlarge and mature.

The **secondary sex characteristics** are physiological signs of sexual maturation that do not directly involve the sex organs, for example, the breasts of females and the broad shoulders of males. Other secondary sex characteristics are changes in the voice and skin texture, muscular development, and the growth of pubic, facial, axillary, and body hair.

These changes unfold in a sequence that is much more consistent than their timing. One girl may develop breasts and body hair at about the same rate; in another girl, body hair may reach adultlike growth a year or so before breasts develop. Similar variations in pubertal status (degree of pubertal development) and timing occur among boys.

Signs of Puberty The first external signs of puberty typically are breast tissue and pubic hair in girls and enlargement of the testes in boys (Susman & Rogol, 2004). A girl's nipples enlarge and protrude, the *areolae* (the pigmented areas surrounding the nipples) enlarge, and the breasts assume first a conical and then a rounded shape. Some adolescent boys experience temporary breast enlargement, much to their distress; this development is normal and generally does not last longer than 18 months.

Pubic hair, at first straight and silky, eventually becomes coarse, dark, and curly. It appears in different patterns in males and females. Adolescent boys are usually happy to see hair on the face and chest; but girls are generally dismayed at the appearance of even a slight amount of hair on the face or around the nipples, though this, too, is normal.

The voice deepens, especially in boys, partly in response to the growth of the larynx and partly in response to the production of male hormones. The skin becomes coarser and oilier, giving rise to pimples and blackheads. Acne is more common in boys and seems related to increased amounts of testosterone.

The Adolescent Growth Spurt The **adolescent growth spurt**—a rapid increase in height, weight, and muscle and bone growth that occurs during puberty—generally begins in girls between ages 9½ and 14½ (usually at about 10) and in boys, between 10½ and 16 (usually at 12 or 13). It typically lasts about 2 years; soon after it ends, the young person reaches sexual maturity. Both growth hormone and the sex hormones (androgens and estrogen) contribute to this normal pubertal growth pattern (Susman & Rogol, 2004).

Because girls' growth spurt usually occurs 2 years earlier than that of boys, girls between ages 11 and 13 tend to be taller, heavier, and stronger than boys the same age. After their growth spurt, boys are again larger. Girls typically reach full height at age 15 and boys at age 17 (Gans, 1990).

primary sex characteristics
Organs directly related to reproduction, which enlarge and mature during adolescence.

secondary sex characteristics
Physiological signs of sexual maturation (such as breast development and growth of body hair) that do not involve the sex organs.

adolescent growth spurt
Sharp increase in height and weight that precedes sexual maturity.

Most girls experience a growth spurt 2 years earlier than most boys, so between ages 11 and 13 girls tend to be taller, heavier, and stronger than boys the same age. © KidStock/Getty Images

Boys and girls also grow differently in form and shape. A boy becomes larger: his shoulders wider, his legs longer relative to his trunk, and his forearms longer relative to his upper arms and his height. A girl's pelvis widens to make childbearing easier, and layers of fat accumulate under her skin, giving her a more rounded appearance. Fat accumulates twice as rapidly in girls as in boys (Susman & Rogol, 2004).

Signs of Sexual Maturity: Sperm Production and Menstruation The maturation of the reproductive organs brings the beginning of menstruation in girls and the production of sperm in boys. The principal sign of sexual maturity in boys is the production of sperm. The first ejaculation, or **spermarche,** occurs at an average age of 13. A boy may wake up to find a wet spot or a hardened, dried spot on the sheets—the result of a *nocturnal emission,* an involuntary ejaculation of semen (commonly referred to as a *wet dream*).

The principal sign of sexual maturity in girls is *menstruation,* a monthly shedding of tissue from the lining of the womb. The first menstruation, called **menarche,** occurs fairly late in the sequence of female development; its normal timing can vary from age 10 to 16½. The average age of menarche in U.S. girls fell from greater than 14 years before 1900 to 12½ years in the 1990s. On average, black girls experience menarche 6 months earlier than white girls (S. E. Anderson, Dallal & Must, 2003).

Influences on and Effects of Timing of Puberty Developmental scientists have found a **secular trend**—a trend that spans several generations—in the onset of puberty: a drop in the ages when puberty begins. The trend, which also involves increases in adult height and weight, began about 100 years ago. It has occurred in such places as the United States, Western Europe, and Japan (S. E. Anderson et al., 2003). This may not be the only change in pubertal processes; recent research indicates that there may be a compensatory delay in pubertal maturation that is associated with earlier puberty. In other words, children may be starting puberty earlier, but spending more time to reach full sexual maturity (Papadimitriou, 2016; Mendle, 2014).

One set of proposed explanations for the secular trend focuses on environmental factors that influence the pace of pubertal development. Children who are healthier, better nourished, and better cared for might be expected to mature earlier and grow bigger (Slyper, 2006). Thus the average age of sexual maturity is earlier in developed countries than in developing countries. Moreover, because of the role of body fat in triggering puberty, a contributing factor in the United States during the last part of the twentieth century may have been the increase in obesity among young girls (S. E. Anderson et al., 2003; Lee et al., 2007). Another environmental explanation focuses on exposure to endocrine-disrupting chemicals, such as those found in some plastics, flame retardants, and pesticides. Research has indicated that exposure to such substances appears to be related to earlier pubertal timing (Lee & Styne, 2013; Ozen & Darcan, 2011). Some of this exposure may be during childhood and adolescence, most commonly through foods and liquids or the inhalation of dust or sprays, and some of it is likely via prenatal exposure in utero (Frye et al., 2012). With respect to prenatal influences, studies have also shown that earlier menarche is associated with maternal smoking during pregnancy (Maisonet et al., 2010).

Genetic factors also appear to influence pubertal timing. Both maternal and paternal pubertal timing are associated with an individual's pubertal timing, although this is less true for girls' breast and pubic hair development (Wohlfahrt-Veje et al., 2016). Additionally, twin studies have documented the heritability of age of menarche (Mendle et al., 2006), and further support for genetic influences is illustrated by the finding that the age of a girl's first menstruation tends to be similar to that of her mother's (Maisonet et al., 2010) if nutrition and standards of living remain stable from one generation to the next (Susman & Rogol, 2004).

But genetics are not the only influence. With respect to mothers, studies have shown that earlier menarche is associated with being the firstborn child (Maisonet et al., 2010) as well as single motherhood (Belsky, Steinberg et al., 2007; Ellis, McFadyen-Ketchum, Dodge, Pettit & Bates, 1999) and harsh maternal parenting practices (Belsky, Steinberg,

spermarche
Boy's first ejaculation.

menarche
Girl's first menstruation.

secular trend
Trend that can be seen only by observing several generations, such as the trend toward earlier attainment of adult height and sexual maturity, which began a century ago in some countries.

Houts, & Halpern-Felsher, 2010). Fathers also play a role. Girls with absent, distant or conflictual relationships with their fathers tend to reach menarche earlier than girls with close supportive paternal relationships (Belsky, Steinberg et al., 2007; Mendle et al., 2006; Ellis et al., 1999; Tither & Ellis, 2008). The unifying theme in these influences is stress, which has been proposed to mediate the above associations. In other words, it is not being firstborn, or being born to a single mother, or having a conflictual relationship per se that influences puberty; rather, it is the presence or absence of high levels of stress. Those children who are exposed to high stress when young tend to reach pubertal milestones earlier than those who are not (Belsky, Ruttle, Boyce, Armstrong & Essex, 2015; Ellis & Del Giuduce, 2014; Bleil et al., 2013).

What difference, if any, does timing of puberty make to psychological well-being? It depends on how the adolescent and others interpret the accompanying changes. Effects of early or late maturation are most likely to be negative when adolescents are much more or less developed than their peers; when they do not see the changes as advantageous; and when several stressful events, such as the advent of puberty and the transition to junior high school, occur about the same time (Petersen, 1993; Simmons, Blyth & McKinney, 1983). Contextual factors such as ethnicity, school, and neighborhood can make a difference. For example, early-maturing girls are more likely to engage in sexual risk-taking (Belsky et al., 2010); and they show more problem behavior in mixed-gender schools than in all-girl schools, and in disadvantaged urban communities than in rural or middle-class urban communities (Caspi, Lynam, Moffitt & Silva, 1993; Dick, Rose, Kaprio & Viken, 2000; Ge, Brody, Conger, Simons & Murry, 2002).

The Adolescent Brain

Dramatic changes in brain structures involved in emotions, judgment, organization of behavior, and self-control take place between puberty and young adulthood (Figure 11.2). An important change in adolescence is a steady increase in white matter (nerve fibers that connect distant portions of the brain). This allows nerve impulses to be transmitted more rapidly and helps neurons synchronize their firing rate (Fields & Stephens-Graham,

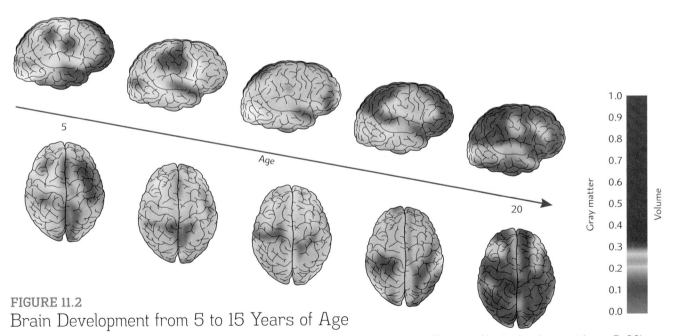

FIGURE 11.2

Brain Development from 5 to 15 Years of Age

Constructed from MRI scans of healthy children and teens, these images compress 15 years of brain development (ages 5–20). Red indicates more gray matter, blue less gray matter.

Source: N., Gogtay, J. N., Giedd, L., Lusk, K. M., Hayashi, D., Greenstein, A. C., Vaituzis, . . . P. M. Thompson, "Dynamic mapping of human cortical development during childhood through early adulthood." *Proceedings of the National Academy of Sciences, USA*, 101, 2004, 8174–8179.

2002), thus improving adolescents' information-processing abilities. This increase is most marked in the corpus callosum, a band of axon fibers that connects the two hemispheres of the brain. During adolescence this band thickens, leading to better communication between hemispheres (Geidd, 2008). This increase in white matter also occurs in the frontal, temporal, and parietal lobes (ACT for Youth, 2002; Blakemore & Choudhury, 2006; Kuhn, 2006; National Institute of Mental Health [NIMH], 2001b; Geidd, 2008) and occurs more rapidly in girls than boys (Hagmann et al., 2010).

There are also marked changes in gray matter composition. A major spurt in production of gray matter in the frontal lobes begins around puberty. After the growth spurt, the density of gray matter declines greatly, particularly in the prefrontal cortex, as unused synapses (connections between neurons) are pruned and those that remain are strengthened (Blakemore & Choudhury, 2006; Kuhn, 2006). This pruning process begins in the rear portions of the brain and moves forward, generally reaching the frontal lobes during adolescence. By middle to late adolescence young people have fewer but stronger, smoother, and more effective neuronal connections, making cognitive processing more efficient (Kuhn, 2006).

Changes in white and gray matter in the amygdala and prefrontal cortex may help explain why teens sometimes make bad choices based on their emotions rather than more reasoned choices based on logic and foresight. The amygdala, broadly, is involved with strong emotional reactions. It matures before the prefrontal cortex. The prefrontal cortex is involved with planning, reasoning, judgment, emotional regulation, and impulse control. The areas of the brain involved with feeling strong emotions mature prior to the area responsible for making thoughtful decisions (Nelson, Thomas & deHann, 2006). Underdevelopment of frontal cortical systems associated with motivation, impulsivity, and addiction may help explain why adolescents tend to seek thrills and novelty and why many of them find it hard to focus on long-term goals (Steinberg, 2010; Bjork et al., 2004; Chambers, Taylor & Potenza, 2003).

Because of the vast amount of brain development occurring during adolescence, the brain is particularly plastic and events experienced at this time affect the shape that development takes (Steinberg, 2010). Some neuronal connections are retained and strengthened, and this in turn supports further cognitive growth in those areas (Kuhn, 2006). Adolescents who "'exercise' their brains by learning to order their thoughts, understand abstract concepts, and control their impulses are laying the neural foundations that will serve them for the rest of their lives" (ACT for Youth, 2002, p. 1). Alternatively, adolescent drug use can have particularly devastating effects, depending on how drugs interact with the growing brain.

Physical and Mental Health

About 1.2 billion people in the world—1 in 6—are adolescents (World Health Organization, 2017). Nine out of ten 11- to 15-year-olds in Western industrialized countries consider themselves healthy (Scheidt, Overpeck, Wyatt & Aszmann, 2000). Still, many adolescents, especially girls, report frequent health problems, such as headache, backache, stomachache, nervousness, and feeling tired, lonely, or low.

Across many countries, adolescents from less affluent families tend to report poorer health and more frequent symptoms. Adolescents from more affluent families tend to have healthier diets and to be more physically active (Elgar et al., 2015; Mullan & Currie, 2000; Scheidt et al., 2000). Let's look at several specific health concerns: physical fitness, sleep needs, eating disorders, drug abuse, depression, and causes of death in adolescence.

EXERCISE

Exercise affects both physical and mental health. The benefits of regular exercise include improved strength and endurance, healthier bones and muscles, weight control, and reduced anxiety and stress, as well as increased self-esteem, school grades, and well-being.

Even moderate physical activity has health benefits if done regularly for at least 30 minutes almost every day. A sedentary lifestyle may result in increased risk of obesity, type 2 diabetes, and an increased likelihood of heart disease and cancer in adulthood (Carnethon, Gulati & Greenland, 2005; Centers for Disease Control and Prevention [CDC], 2000a; National Center for Health Statistics [NCHS], 2004; Nelson & Gordon-Larsen, 2006).

Unfortunately, only about one-third of U.S. high school students engage in the recommended amounts of physical activity, and the proportion of young people who are inactive increases throughout the high school years (Eaton et al., 2008). Adolescents show a steep drop in physical activity upon entering puberty, shifting from an average of 3 hours per day of physical activity at age 9 to an average of only 49 minutes of activity per day at age 15 (Nader et al., 2008). U.S. adolescents exercise less frequently than in past years and less than adolescents in most other industrialized countries (CDC, 2000a; Hickman et al., 2000).

Adolescents who engage in physical activity tend to feel better than those who do not. ©Fuse/Getty Images

SLEEP NEEDS AND PROBLEMS

Sleep deprivation among adolescents has been called an epidemic (Hansen, Janssen, Schiff, Zee & Dubocovich, 2005). A national poll found that 45 percent of adolescents reported getting insufficient sleep, 31 percent were borderline, and only 20 percent slept the recommended amount (Wolfson, Carskadon, Mindell & Drake, 2006).

Children generally go to sleep later and sleep less on school days the older they get. While only 16 percent of U.S. sixth graders report sleeping less than 8 hours a night, by 12th grade, 75 percent do not sleep a full 8 hours, a pattern that is true internationally (Owens & Adolescent Sleep Working Group, 2014). This is particularly distressing as adolescents need as much or more sleep than when they were younger (Hoban, 2004; Iglowstein et al., 2003). Although many teens attempt to catch up with the sleep deficit on weekends (Owens & Adolescent Sleep Working Group, 2014), sleeping in on weekends does not make up for the loss of sleep on school nights (Hoban, 2004).

Sleep deprivation can sap motivation and cause irritability, and concentration and school performance can suffer. Sleepiness also can be deadly for adolescent drivers. Studies have found that young people ages 16 to 29 are most likely to be involved in crashes caused by the driver falling asleep (Millman et al., 2005).

Why do adolescents stay up late? They may need to do homework, listen to music, play video games, or talk to or text friends and surf the web. Such behavior has been clearly linked to the chronic sleep deprivation of modern teenagers (Bartel, Gradisar & Williamson, 2015). However, sleep experts now recognize that biological changes are also behind adolescents' sleep problems (Sadeh et al., 2000). The timing of secretion of the hormone *melatonin* is a gauge of when the brain is ready for sleep. After puberty, this secretion takes place later at night (Carskadon, Acebo, Richardson, Tate & Seifer, 1997; Owens & Adolescent Sleep Working Group, 2014). But adolescents still need just as much sleep as before; so when they go to bed later than younger children, they need to get up later as well. Yet most secondary schools start *earlier* than elementary schools. Their schedules are out of sync with students' biological rhythms (Hoban, 2004). Teenagers tend to be least alert and most stressed early in the morning and more alert in the afternoon (Hansen et al., 2005). Starting school later, or at least offering difficult courses later in the day, would positively influence key outcomes such as student attendance, fatigue, and academic achievement (Adolescent Sleep Working Group, 2014).

NUTRITION AND EATING DISORDERS

Good nutrition is important to support the rapid growth of adolescence and to establish healthy eating habits that will last through adulthood. Unfortunately, U.S. adolescents eat fewer fruits and vegetables and consume more foods that are high in cholesterol, fat, and calories and low in nutrients than adolescents in other industrialized countries (American Heart Association et al., 2006).

Obesity Within high income countries, such as the United States, Canada, Greece, and Italy, approximately a third of teens are overweight, with boys more likely to be overweight

ADOLESCENT OBESITY

Worldwide, obesity in children and adolescents has increased substantially. The prevalence of overweight or obese children and adolescents has increased by nearly 50 percent over the past 30 years. In 2013, more than 22 percent of girls and nearly 24 percent of boys living in developed countries were overweight or obese. Prevalence rates are also increasing in the developing world, where nearly 13 percent of boys and more than 13 percent of girls are overweight or obese. Some of the highest rates of child and adolescent obesity were seen in Middle Eastern and North African countries; the highest numbers were among girls (Murray & Ng, 2017). More than half of the world's 671 million obese (all ages) live in 10 countries: the United States, China, India, Russia, Brazil, Mexico, Egypt, Germany, Pakistan, and Indonesia (Murray & Ng, 2017).

Worldwide, obesity trends are causing serious health concerns. Obesity in childhood and adolescence is associated with a wide range of serious health complications that were previously experienced primarily by adults. These include diabetes, heart disease, metabolic conditions, orthopedic problems, and neurological issues (WHO, 2014). Overweight and obese children are likely to stay obese into adulthood and have a significantly higher risk of mortality. Not surprisingly, there has been an increase in health care costs due to obesity and related issues among children and adolescents over the past 20 years (Raj & Kumar, 2010).

Obesity has multiple causes. A combination of environmental factors, lifestyle preferences, and cultural environment has contributed to the global rise in obesity. Research shows increases in caloric and fat intake, excessive sugar intake, increased portion size, and a decline in physical activity all are factors in the increasing obesity rate in the world's adolescents (Sahoo et al., 2015).

Obesity can profoundly affect adolescent's physical health but also has a large impact on social and emotional well-being. Obesity in adolescents can lead to low self-esteem, eating disorders, depression, anxiety, substance abuse, suicidal thoughts or behaviors, and a lower quality of life. Adolescent obesity is also associated with a higher risk of being bullied, poor academic performance, fewer job prospects, and a lower socioeconomic status in adulthood (Sahoo et al., 2015).

The world has taken notice, and many countries have implemented programs and interventions targeting children and adolescents in the hope of reducing the obesity rates. Health promotion campaigns to encourage parents to provide healthier food options to their children have been implemented in numerous countries, including Canada, Mexico, France, Australia, Denmark, Chile, New Zealand, Spain, and the United States. Improved food labeling campaigns have been launched across Europe and Australia. Bans on advertising of foods and beverages on TV and radio during hours when children are the main audience have been put in place in Chile, Iceland, Ireland, and Mexico. Ireland has launched an obesity action plan including calorie labeling on products and regulating food advertising and marketing. Turkey has implemented several health promotion campaigns, including one called Move for Health, which distributed 275,000 bicycles to schools to get students moving (OECD, 2017).

The most common interventions used with adolescents include increasing physical activity to at least 60 minutes a day, decreasing screen time to under 2 hours per day, and promoting a healthy diet (WHO, 2017).

what's your view

What do you think can be done to fight the obesity epidemic? Do you think the programs that have been implemented in the last few years will make an impact?

than girls (Patton et al., 2012). As countries become more technologically advanced, rates of overweight and obesity are increasing. This trend is being driven by increased consumption of animal fat and protein, refined grains, and added sugar, and concurrent decreases in physical activity. These diet and lifestyle changes are brought about by global trade liberalization, economic growth, and urbanization (Malik, Willett & Hu, 2013). In middle- and especially lower-income countries, undernutrition often co-occurs with overweight. For example, between a fifth to a third of boys in China, the eastern Mediterranean, Latin American countries, Mauritania, Thailand, and the region of Oceania are overweight (Patton et al., 2012).

There are also genetic contributions to obesity. Being born to overweight or obese parents is a risk factor for childhood and adolescent obesity, and overweight and BMI appear to be strongly influenced genetically (Wardle, Carnell, Haworth & Plomin, 2008; Silventoinen, Rokholm, Kaprio & Sorensen, 2010).

In the United States, 13- to 15-year-olds are about twice as likely to be overweight as their age-mates in 14 other industrialized countries (Lissau et al., 2004). About 34 percent of U.S. teens have a body mass index (BMI) at or above the 85th percentile for age and sex. The percentage of U.S. adolescents with BMIs at this level rose from 5 percent in 1980 (Ogden et al., 2010) to over 20 percent in 2014 (National Center for Health Statistics, 2017). Among older adolescents, obesity is 50 percent more prevalent in those from poor families (Miech et al., 2006). Mexican American girls and boys and non-Hispanic black girls, who tend to be poorer than their peers, are more likely to be overweight than non-Hispanic white adolescents (Hernandez & Macartney, 2008; Ogden et al., 2010).

Overweight teenagers tend to be in poorer health than their peers and are more likely to have difficulty attending school or engaging in strenuous activity or personal care (Swallen, Reither, Haas & Meier, 2005). They are at heightened risk of hypertension, diabetes, and cardiac disease (Sahoo et al., 2015; Flynn, 2013; Pulgaron, 2013). One in 5 have abnormal lipid levels, including either too much bad cholesterol, too little good cholesterol, or high blood triglycerides (CDC, 2010). They tend to become obese adults, subject to a variety of physical, social, and psychological risks (Singh, Mulder, Twisk, Van Mechelen & Chinapaw, 2008). Given how many adolescents are overweight today, one research team projects that by 2035 more than 100,000 additional cases of cardiovascular disease will be attributable to an increased prevalence of overweight in young and middle-aged men and women (Bibbins-Domingo, Coxson, Pletcher, Lightwood & Goldman, 2007).

Dieting for adolescents may be counterproductive as interventions in which dieting is encouraged can sometimes result in weight gain for participants (A. E. Field et al., 2003). Programs that use behavioral modification techniques to help adolescents make lifestyle changes have had better success. For example, interventions that have encouraged increases in physical activity, reductions in television viewing, and encouragement of healthier eating habits, either home- or school-based, have been shown to reduce body mass index and other weight-related outcome measures (Wang et al., 2013; Doak, Visscher, Renders & Seidell, 2006).

Body Image and Eating Disorders Eating disorders, including obesity, are most prevalent in industrialized societies, but these disorders appear to be increasing in non-Western countries as well (Makino, Tsuboi & Dennerstein, 2004). Sometimes a concern with **body image** may lead to obsessive efforts at weight control (Davison & Birch, 2001; Vereecken & Maes, 2000). This pattern is more common and less likely to be related to actual weight problems among girls than among boys.

Boys and girls respond differently to the body changes that result from puberty. Overall, boys tend to be more satisfied with their bodies than girls (Makinen, Puukko-Viertomies, Lindberg, Siimes & Aalberg, 2012; Lawler & Nixon, 2011). Because of the normal increase in girls' body fat during puberty, many become unhappy with their appearance, reflecting the cultural emphasis on women's physical attributes (Susman & Rogol, 2004). Girls tend to express the highest levels of body satisfaction when underweight, some dissatisfaction when average weight, and the most dissatisfaction when overweight. Boys express the most dissatisfaction when overweight and underweight, but are more satisfied with an average weight body (Makinen et al., 2012; Lawler & Nixon, 2011). Body satisfaction is important because it has been related to dieting and disordered eating (Bucchianeri et al., 2016).

By age 15, more than half the girls sampled in 16 countries were dieting or thought they should be. The United States was at the top of the list, with 47 percent of 11-year-old girls and 62 percent of 15-year-old girls concerned about their weight (Vereecken & Maes, 2000). Asian American boys and girls have the highest levels of body dissatisfaction, followed by Hispanics, whites, and African Americans (Bucchianeri et al., 2016). African American girls are generally more satisfied with their bodies and less concerned

body image
Descriptive and evaluative beliefs about one's appearance.

People with anorexia, such as this girl, see themselves as fat even when they are emaciated. ©Ted Foxx/Alamy Stock Photo

about weight and dieting than are white girls (Kelly, Wall, Eisenberg, Story & Neumark-Sztainer, 2004; Wardle et al., 2004).

Excessive concern with weight control and body image may be signs of *anorexia nervosa* or *bulimia nervosa,* both of which involve abnormal patterns of food intake. These chronic disorders occur worldwide, mostly in adolescent girls and young women. Table 11.1 outlines some of the symptoms for anorexia and bulimia.

Anorexia Nervosa **Anorexia nervosa,** or *self-starvation,* is potentially life threatening. An estimated 0.3 to 0.5 percent of adolescent girls and young women and a smaller but growing percentage of boys and men in Western countries are known to be affected. People with anorexia have a distorted body image and, though typically severely underweight, think they are too fat. They are often good students but may be withdrawn or depressed and may engage in repetitive, perfectionist behavior. They are extremely afraid of losing control and becoming overweight (AAP Committee on Adolescence, 2003; Wilson, Grilo & Vitousek, 2007). Early warning signs include determined, secret dieting; dissatisfaction after losing weight; setting new, lower weight goals after reaching an initial desired weight; excessive exercising; and interruption of regular menstruation.

Bulimia Nervosa **Bulimia nervosa** affects about 1 to 2 percent of international populations (Wilson et al., 2007). A person with bulimia regularly goes on huge, short-lived eating binges (2 hours or less) and then may try to purge the high caloric intake through self-induced vomiting, strict dieting or fasting, excessively vigorous exercise, or laxatives, enemas, or diuretics. These episodes occur at least once a week for at least 3 months. People with bulimia are not necessarily overweight, but they are obsessed with their weight and shape. They tend to have low self-esteem and may become overwhelmed with shame, self-contempt, and depression (Wilson et al., 2007).

Treatment and Outcomes of Eating Disorders The immediate goal of treatment for anorexia is to get patients to eat and gain weight. One widely used treatment is a form of behaviorally focused, intensive, outpatient family therapy where parents take control

anorexia nervosa
Eating disorder characterized by self-starvation.

bulimia nervosa
Eating disorder in which a person regularly eats huge quantities of food and then purges the body by laxatives, induced vomiting, fasting, or excessive exercise.

TABLE 11.1 Eating Disorders: Risk Factors and Symptoms

SYMPTOMS

Anorexia	Bulimia
• Using laxatives, enemas, or diuretics inappropriately in an effort to lose weight	• Abuse of laxatives, diuretics, or enemas to prevent weight gain
• Binge eating	• Binge eating
• Going to the bathroom right after meals	• Going to the bathroom right after meals
• Exercising compulsively	• Frequent weighing
• Restricting the amount of food eaten	• Self-induced vomiting
• Cutting food into small pieces	• Overachieving behavior
• Dental cavities due to self-induced vomiting	• Dental cavities due to self-induced vomiting
• Confused or slow thinking	
• Blotchy or yellow skin	
• Depression	
• Dry mouth	
• Extreme sensitivity to cold	
• Fine hair	
• Low blood pressure	
• No menstruation	
• Weight loss and wasting away of muscle and body fat	

of their teen's eating patterns, and autonomy over eating is relinquished back to the teen gradually. Alternatively, teens may participate in individual therapy, either inpatient or outpatient. Initially, both family and individual therapy show similar outcomes. However, at 6 to 12 months posttreatment, teens who participated in family therapy show more lasting gains than those who participated in individual therapy (Couturier, Kimber & Szatmari, 2013). Adolescents who show signs of severe malnutrition, are resistant to treatment, or do not make progress on an outpatient basis may be admitted to a hospital, where they can be given 24-hour nursing. Once their weight is stabilized, patients may enter less intensive daytime care (McCallum & Bruton, 2003).

Bulimia is often treated with cognitive behavioral therapy or with medications. In cognitive behavioral therapy, patients keep daily diaries of their eating patterns and are taught ways to avoid the temptation to binge (Wilson et al., 2007). Medications such as fluoxetine and antidepressants are also used to control core symptoms such as binge eating and purging, sometimes in conjunction with therapy. Both cognitive behavioral therapy and medications have been demonstrated to be helpful in the treatment of bulimia (Shapiro et al., 2007).

Mortality rates among those affected with anorexia nervosa have been estimated at about 10 percent of cases. Among the surviving anorexia patients, less than one-half make a full recovery and only one-third improve; 20 percent remain chronically ill (Steinhausen, 2002). It should also be noted that up to one-third of patients drop out of treatment before achieving an appropriate weight (McCallum & Bruton, 2003). Recovery rates from bulimia are a bit better and average 30 to 50 percent after cognitive behavioral therapy (Wilson et al., 2007).

USE AND ABUSE OF DRUGS

Although the great majority of adolescents do not abuse drugs, a significant minority do. **Substance abuse** is harmful use of alcohol or other drugs. Abuse can lead to **substance dependence,** or *addiction,* which may be physiological, psychological, or both and is likely to continue into adulthood. Addictive drugs are especially dangerous because they stimulate parts of the brain that are still developing in adolescence (Crews & Hodge, 2007). About 12 percent of teens ages 13 to 17 will at some point receive treatment for alcohol use and more than 18 percent for illicit drug use (Substance Abuse and Mental Health Services Administration [SAMHSA], 2013a).

substance abuse
Repeated, harmful use of a substance, usually alcohol or other drugs.

substance dependence
Addiction (physical, or psychological, or both) to a harmful substance.

Trends in Illicit Drug Use Nearly half (47 percent) of U.S. adolescents have tried illicit drugs by the time they leave high school (Johnston, O'Malley, Bachman & Schulenberg, 2013). There was an upsurge in drug use during the mid- to late 1990s, then drug use started to go down in the late 90s until 2008, where it once again started to rise. This pattern once again reversed in 2011, and illicit drug use started to decline again, although less so for marijuana (Johnston, O'Malley, Bachman, Schulenberg & Mietch, 2016).

These findings come from the latest in a series of annual government surveys of a nationally representative sample of 8th, 10th, and 12th graders from more than 400 schools across the United States (Figure 11.3). These surveys probably underestimate adolescent drug use because they are based on self-reports and do not reach high school dropouts, who are more likely to use drugs. Continued progress in eliminating drug abuse is slow because new drugs are continually introduced or rediscovered by a new generation, and young people do not necessarily generalize the adverse consequences of one drug to another (Johnston et al., 2016).

A recent trend is the abuse of nonprescription cough and cold medications; 3 percent of 8th graders, 4.7 percent of 10th graders, and 5.6 percent of 12th graders report taking medicines containing dextromethorphan (DXM), a cough suppressant, to get high within the past year (Johnston et al., 2013).

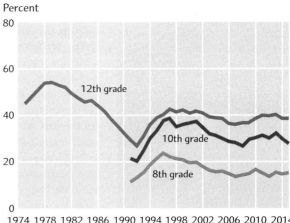

FIGURE 11.3

Trends in High School Students' Use of Illicit Drugs over the Previous 12 Months

Source: L. D., Johnston, P. M., O'Malley, J. G., Bachman, J. E., Schulenberg, & R. A. Miech, *Monitoring the future national survey results on drug use, 1975-2015: Volume II, college students and adults ages 19-55,* Ann Arbor: Institute for Social Research, The University of Michigan, 2016.

In the past two decades, there has also been a general increase in opioid abuse. This involves both prescription and street drugs (Dart et al., 2015; Substance Abuse and Mental Health Services, 2013). With respect to adolescents, use of legal narcotics nearly tripled from 1992 to 2009, and then declined slightly. Use of heroin by children in 8th through 12th grade peaked in the mid to late '90s, and then showed a downward path since that time (Johnston, O'Malley, Miech, Bachman & Schulenberg, 2016). The sharp rise in heroin usage reported in the United States has primarily been limited to older teens and emerging adults, where peak levels of usage were reached in the mid 2000s (Schulenberg et al., 2017).

Alcohol, Marijuana, and Tobacco Alcohol and tobacco use among U.S. teenagers has followed a trend roughly parallel to that of harder drug use, with a dramatic rise during most of the 1990s followed by a smaller, gradual decline. Marijuana has followed this same pattern for the most part; however, its usage has remained higher overall and showed slower declines (Johnston et al., 2013; Johnston et al., 2016). The impact of recent movements to legalize marijuana for recreational use, such as has happened in seven states as of 2017, remains to be seen. There are some indications that the legalization of marijuana in a number of states may lead to increased usage (Johnston, et al., 2016.)

Research shows cigarettes and alcohol are generally the first substances that are tried, often at around sixth grade, followed by inhalants and then marijuana. The initiation period for other illicit drugs tends to occur later in the high school years (Miech, Johnston, O'Malley, Bachman & Shulenberg, 2016). The earlier young people start using a drug, the more frequently they are likely to use it and the greater their tendency to abuse it (Wong et al., 2006).

Alcohol use is a serious problem in many countries (Gabhainn & François, 2000). In 2016, 26 percent of U.S. 8th graders, 47 percent of 10th graders, and 64 percent of 12th graders said they had tried alcohol, and current use (in the past 30 days) is likewise high (Johnston et al., 2016). The majority of high school students who drink engage in **binge drinking**—consuming five or more drinks on one occasion. About 25 percent of high school seniors admit to binge drinking (McQueeny et al., 2009). A recent MRI-based study revealed that binge drinking in teenagers may affect thinking and memory by damaging sensitive "white matter" in the brain (McQueeny et al., 2009). In line with this finding, teenage binge drinkers are more likely than other students to report poor school performance and to engage in other risky behaviors (Miller, Naimi, Brewer & Jones, 2007).

The peak period for first trying alcohol is between 7th and 11th grade, although some children start earlier (Miech et al., 2016). Young people who begin drinking early tend to have behavior problems or to have siblings who are alcohol dependent (Kuperman et al., 2005). Those who start drinking before age 15 are more than 5 times more likely to become alcohol dependent or alcohol abusers than those who do not start drinking until age 21 or later (SAMHSA, 2004a).

Despite the decline in *marijuana* use since 1996–1997, it is still by far the most widely used illicit drug in the United States. In 2012, about 11 percent of 8th graders, 28 percent of 10th graders, and 36 percent of 12th graders admitted to having used it in the past year (Johnston et al., 2013). Approximately 1 in every 17 high school seniors uses marijuana daily (Johnston et al., 2016).

Marijuana potency quadrupled from 1980 to 2014 (ElSohly et al., 2016). Heavy use has been associated with damage to the brain, heart, and lungs. It has been correlated with declines in school performance, memory problems, and increased risk for anxiety and depression. Like any drug, if used while driving, it can contribute to traffic accidents. Given the higher potency of modern marijuana, older studies may not fully capture potential for harm at current levels. Additionally, it is difficult to disentangle the direct effects of marijuana with indirect effects, such as concurrent use of other drugs. The debate about marijuana use is also complicated by the fact that marijuana does have legitimate medical applications and has been used to manage such conditions as nausea, chronic pain, and epilepsy (Volkow, Baler, Compton & Weiss, 2014).

In the United States, approximately 5 percent of 8th graders, 11 percent of 10th graders, and 17 percent of 12th graders are current (past-month) tobacco smokers (Johnston et al., 2013). Although this number is high and cause for concern, there is some

binge drinking
Consuming five or more drinks on one occasion.

Marijuana is the most widely used illicit drug in the United States.
©Doug Menuez/Forrester Images/Photodisc/Getty Images

good news. In the late 1990s, about 28 percent of high school students reported being current smokers. Current data now put this number at 7 percent (Johnston, O'Malley, Miech, Bachman & Schulenberg, 2016). And adolescent tobacco use is a less widespread problem in the United States than in most other industrialized countries (Gabhainn & Françoise, 2000). However, the use of e-cigarettes is increasing. In 2015, e-cigarettes were the most commonly used form of tobacco among middle and high school students (Singh et al., 2016). This is troubling, as there is reason to suspect that e-cigarette users may eventually graduate to cigarettes.

Adolescents exposed to alcohol and drugs before the age of 15 demonstrate an increased risk for substance disorders (Hingson, Heeren & Winter, 2006), risky sexual behavior (Stueve & O'Donnell, 2005), and low educational attainment (King, Meehan, Trim & Chassin, 2006). Moreover, they are at higher risk for continuing substance abuse, sexually transmitted infections, early pregnancy, and crime (Odgers et al., 2008).

Peer influence on substance use has been documented extensively (Monahan, Rhew, Hawkins and Brown, 2014; Cleveland & Wiebe, 2003). As with hard drugs, the influence of older siblings and their friends increases the likelihood of tobacco and alcohol use (Rende, Slomkowski, Lloyd-Richardson & Niaura, 2005). Recent research indicates that peer and sibling influences can also now act via media such as online social media postings and messaging content (Huang et al., 2014).

Rational discussions with parents can counteract harmful influences and discourage or limit drinking (Austin, Pinkleton & Fujioka, 2000). Similarly, adolescents who believe that their parents disapprove of smoking are less likely to smoke (Sargent & Dalton, 2001). However, parents also can be a negative influence. Having an alcoholic parent significantly increases the risk of early alcohol use and later alcohol problems (Wong et al., 2006). The omnipresence of substance use in the media is another important influence. Movies that depict smoking increase early initiation of smoking as well as the overall risk of smoking (Leonardi-Bee, Nderi & Britton, 2016).

DEPRESSION

The prevalence of depression increases during adolescence. In 2016, 12.8 percent of young people ages 12 to 17 experienced at least one episode of major depression, and only 40.9 percent of them had been treated (National Survey on Drug Use and Health [NSDUH], 2017). Rates generally increase with increasing age (Figure 11.4). Depression in young people does not necessarily appear as sadness but as irritability, boredom, or inability to experience pleasure. One reason depression needs to be taken seriously is the danger of suicide (Brent & Birmaher, 2002).

Being female is a risk factor for depression. Adolescent girls, especially early maturing girls, are more likely to be depressed than adolescent boys (Galvao et al., 2014; NSDUH, 2012). This gender difference may be related to biological changes associated with puberty. Other possible factors are the way girls are socialized (Birmaher et al., 1996) and their greater vulnerability to stress in social relationships (Hankin, Mermelstein & Roesch, 2007).

In addition to female gender, risk factors for depression include anxiety, fear of social contact, stressful life events, chronic illnesses such as diabetes or epilepsy, parent-child conflict, abuse or neglect, alcohol and drug use, sexual activity, and having a parent with a history of depression. Alcohol and drug use and sexual activity are more likely to lead to depression in girls than in boys (Hallfors, Waller, Bauer, Ford & Halpern, 2005; NSDUH, 2012; Waller et al., 2006).

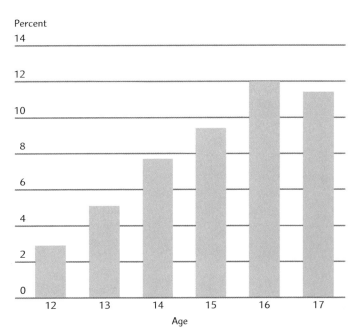

FIGURE 11.4

Depression Rates for 12- to 17-Year-Olds

Source: National Survey on Drug Use and Health (NSDUH). *Results from the 2011 national survey on drug use and health: Mental health findings.* NSDUH Series H-45. HHS Publication No. (SMA) 12-4725. Rockville, MD: Substance Abuse and Mental Health Services Administration, 2012.

Depressed adolescents who do not respond to outpatient treatment or who have substance dependence or psychosis or seem suicidal may need to be hospitalized. At least 1 in 5 persons who experience bouts of depression in childhood or adolescence are at risk for bipolar disorder, in which depressive episodes ("low" periods) alternate with manic episodes ("high" periods) characterized by increased energy, euphoria, grandiosity, and risk-taking (Brent & Birmaher, 2002).

One treatment option for depression is psychotherapy. Studies have found that although it can be effective in the short term, its effects last no more than a year (Weisz, McCarty & Valeri, 2006). Medications, specifically selective serotonin reuptake inhibitors (SSRIs), are also used. Although there are concerns about their safety, research suggests that the benefits outweigh the risks (Bridge et al., 2007). The most effective treatment for depressed adolescents, at least in the short term, seems to be a combination of medications and cognitive behavioral therapy (Dubicka et al., 2010; March & the TADS Team, 2007).

DEATH IN ADOLESCENCE

Worldwide in 2012, a 50-year downward trend for lower adolescent mortality continued, although that number still comprised some 1.3 million teens. The top five causes of death were automobile accidents, HIV, suicide, lower respiratory infection, and violence (World Health Organization, 2016b). In the United States, 63 percent of all deaths among adolescents result from motor vehicle crashes, other unintentional injuries, homicide, and suicide (National Highway Traffic Safety Administration, 2009; Figure 11.5). The mortality rate of 15- to 19-year-old American males is more than twice that of female adolescents (Child Health USA, 2012).

Deaths from Vehicle Accidents and Firearms The frequency of violent and accidental deaths in this age group reflects adolescents' inexperience and immaturity, which can lead to risk-taking and carelessness. Motor vehicle collisions are the leading cause of death among U.S. teenagers, accounting for approximately one-third of all deaths in adolescence (Miniño, 2010). Collisions are more likely to be fatal when teenage passengers are in the vehicle, probably because adolescents tend to drive more recklessly in the presence of peers (Chen, Baker, Braver & Li, 2000). The risk is also higher for males and for new drivers. In the United States, about 1 in 5 teens involved in fatal traffic crashes had been drinking, suggesting that alcohol is a major factor in accident-related fatalities (National Highway Traffic Safety Administration, 2017). Another important risk factor is distracted driving, which includes actions such as texting, talking on a cell phone, or eating. While all drivers risk a crash if distracted, novice drivers are at the highest risk. For example, they are 8 times more likely to crash or have a near miss when dialing a phone in comparison to experienced drivers who are 2 times more likely to do so (Klauer et al., 2014). Despite efforts aimed at increasing seat belt use among teens, observed use among teens and young adults was 61 percent in 2015—the lowest of any age group (Centers for Disease Control, 2017r). In fact, in 2015, 58 percent of young people 16 to 20 years old involved in fatal motor vehicle crashes were unbuckled (National Highway Traffic Safety Administration, 2017).

After automobile accidents, homicides and suicide are the second and third leading causes of death in the United States (Child Trends DataBank, 2015b). Firearm-related deaths are far more common in the United States than in other industrialized countries (Grinshteyn & Hemenway, 2016). Boys are three times more likely to commit suicide and six times more likely to be fatally shot than girls. Race and ethnicity matter as well; the homicide rate for African American male teens is more than 20 times higher than that of white male teens (Child Trends DataBank, 2015b). Gun fatalities make up about one-third of all injury deaths and more than 85 percent of homicides in that age group. The chief reason for these grim statistics seems to be the ease of obtaining a gun in the United States (AAP Committee on Injury and Poison Prevention, 2000). Indeed, having a firearm in the home is strongly associated with an increased risk of completed suicide and being the victim of a homicide (Anglemyer, Horvath & Rutherford, 2014).

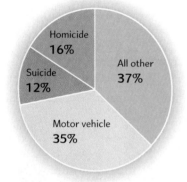

FIGURE 11.5
Leading Causes of Adolescent Deaths

In the United States, motor vehicle crashes are responsible for the most deaths among adolescents.

Source: National Highway Traffic Safety Administration. *Traffic safety facts research note.* Washington, DC: Author, 2009.

Suicide Suicide is the third leading cause of death among U.S. 15- to 19-year-olds (Miniño, 2010). The teenage suicide rate fell by 34 percent between 1990 and 2006, perhaps in part due to restrictions on children's access to firearms (CDC, 2008c; Lubell, Swahn, Crosby & Kegler, 2004). In 2004, however, the suicide rate increased by 8 percent, with the largest increases among teenage girls (Lubell, Kegler, Crosby & Karch, 2007). Rates continued to rise through 2015, with firearms remaining the most common method used (Kegler, 2017).

Although suicide occurs in all ethnic groups, Native American boys have the highest rates and African American girls the lowest. Gay, lesbian, and bisexual youths, who have high rates of depression, also have unusually high rates of suicide and attempted suicide (AAP Committee on Adolescence, 2000).

Young people who consider or attempt suicide tend to have histories of emotional illness. They are likely to be either perpetrators or victims of violence and to have school problems, academic or behavioral. Many have suffered from maltreatment in childhood and have severe problems with relationships. They tend to think poorly of themselves, to feel hopeless, and to have poor impulse control and a low tolerance for frustration and stress. These young people are often alienated from their parents and have no one outside the family to turn to. They also tend to have attempted suicide before, to have friends or family members who did so, or to report suicidal ideation (Borowsky, Ireland & Resnick, 2001; Brent & Mann, 2006; Nock et al., 2013). Substance abuse, especially heroin, is also a risk factor, and that risk increases with the number of illicit substances being used (Wong, Zhou, Goebert & Hishinuma, 2013). Protective factors that reduce the risk of suicide include a sense of connectedness to family and school, emotional well-being, and academic achievement (Taliaferro & Muehlenkamp, 2014; Borowsky et al., 2001).

COGNITIVE DEVELOPMENT
Aspects of Cognitive Maturation

Adolescents not only look different from younger children, but they also think and talk differently. Their speed of information processing continues to increase. Although their thinking may remain immature in some ways, many are capable of abstract reasoning and sophisticated moral judgments and can plan more realistically for the future.

PIAGET'S STAGE OF FORMAL OPERATIONS

Adolescents enter what Piaget called the highest level of cognitive development—**formal operations**—when they move away from their reliance on concrete, real-world stimuli and develop the capacity for abstract thought. This development, usually around age 11, gives them a new, more flexible way to manipulate information. They can use symbols to represent other symbols (for example, letting the letter X stand for an unknown numeral) and thus can learn algebra and calculus. They can better appreciate the hidden messages in metaphor and allegory and thus can find richer meanings in literature. They can think in terms of what *might be,* not just what *is.* They can imagine possibilities and can form and test hypotheses.

formal operations
Piaget's final stage of cognitive development, characterized by the ability to think abstractly.

Hypothetical-Deductive Reasoning **Hypothetical-deductive reasoning** involves a methodical, scientific approach to problem solving, and it characterizes formal operations thinking. It involves the ability to develop, consider, and systematically test hypotheses. To appreciate the difference formal reasoning makes, let's follow the progress of a typical child in dealing with a classic Piagetian problem, the pendulum problem.*

The child, Adam, is shown the pendulum—an object hanging from a string. He is then shown how he can change any of four factors: the length of the string, the weight of the object, the height from which the object is released, and the amount of force he may use to push the object. He is asked to figure out which factor determines how fast the pendulum swings.

hypothetical-deductive reasoning
Ability, believed by Piaget, to accompany the stage of formal operations, to develop, consider, and test hypotheses.

*This description of age-related differences in the approach to the pendulum problem is adapted from H. Ginsburg & Opper, 1979.

When Adam first sees the pendulum, he is not yet 7 years old and is in the preoperational stage. He tries one thing after another in a hit-or-miss manner. First, he puts a light weight on a long string and pushes it; then he tries swinging a heavy weight on a short string; then he removes the weight entirely. He is unable to solve the problem.

Adam next encounters the pendulum at age 10, when he is in the stage of concrete operations. This time, he discovers that varying the length of the string and the weight of the object affects the speed of the swing. However, because he varies both factors at the same time, he cannot tell which is critical or whether both are.

At 15, Adam goes at the pendulum problem systematically. He varies one factor at a time each time holding the other three factors constant. In this way, he is able to solve the problem and determine that only one factor—the length of the string—impacts how fast the pendulum swings. He is now capable of hypothetical-deductive reasoning.

What brings about the shift to formal reasoning? Brain development is required; however, formal education is also necessary. When adolescents in New Guinea and Rwanda were tested on the pendulum problem, none were able to solve it. On the other hand, Chinese children in Hong Kong, who had been to British schools, did at least as well as U.S. or European children. Schoolchildren in Central Java and New South Wales also showed some formal operational abilities (Gardiner & Kosmitzki, 2005). Formal reasoning is a learned ability that is not equally necessary or equally valued in all cultures.

Evaluating Piaget's Theory Psychologists have critiqued Piaget's work on a variety of fronts. The three primary issues are disagreement about the timing; too little attention paid to individual and cultural differences; and a failure to address other, related cognitive advances that influence formal operations reasoning.

Although adolescents *do* tend to think more abstractly than younger children, there is debate about the precise age at which this advance occurs (Eccles, Wigfield & Byrnes, 2003). Piaget's writings provide examples of children displaying aspects of scientific thinking well before adolescence. At the same time, many late adolescents and adults seem incapable of abstract thought as Piaget defined it (Gardiner & Kozmitzki, 2005). Thus the timing of formal operations thought processes does not always correspond to when Piaget argued it occurred.

In most of his early writings, Piaget paid little attention to social and cultural influences. However, neo-Piagetian research suggests that children's cognitive processes are closely tied to the context of a problem and the kinds of information and thought a culture considers important (Kuhn, 2006). So, for example, when children or adolescents are asked to reason within the context of familiar situations or objects, they perform at higher levels, suggesting that prior knowledge affects their ability to reason formally.

Finally, Piaget's theory does not adequately consider such cognitive advances as gains in information-processing capacity, accumulation of knowledge and expertise in specific fields, and the role of *metacognition,* the awareness and monitoring of one's own mental processes and strategies (Flavell et al., 2002). This ability to "think about thinking" and, thus, to manage one's mental processes may be the chief advance of adolescent thought (Kuhn, 2006).

CHANGES IN INFORMATION PROCESSING

Changes in the way adolescents process information reflect the maturation of the brain's frontal lobes. Which neural connections wither and which become strengthened is highly responsive to experience. Thus progress in cognitive processing varies greatly among individual adolescents (Kuhn, 2006).

Information-processing researchers have identified two broad categories of measurable change in adolescent cognition: *structural change* and *functional change* (Eccles, Wigfield & Byrnes, 2003).*

Structural Change *Structural* changes in adolescence include (1) changes in working memory capacity and (2) the increasing amount of knowledge stored in long-term memory.

*The discussion in the following two sections is based on Eccles et al., 2003.

The capacity of working memory, which enlarges rapidly in middle childhood, continues to increase during adolescence. The expansion of working memory may enable older adolescents to deal with complex problems or decisions involving multiple pieces of information.

Information stored in long-term memory can be *declarative, procedural,* or *conceptual.*

- **Declarative knowledge** ("knowing that . . .") consists of all the factual knowledge a person has acquired (for example, knowing that $2 + 2 = 4$ and that George Washington was the first U.S. president).

- **Procedural knowledge** ("knowing how to . . .") consists of all the skills a person has acquired, such as being able to multiply and divide and to drive a car.

- **Conceptual knowledge** ("knowing why . . .") is an understanding of, for example, why an algebraic equation remains true if the same amount is added or subtracted from both sides.

declarative knowledge
Acquired factual knowledge stored in long-term memory.

procedural knowledge
Acquired skills stored in long-term memory.

conceptual knowledge
Acquired interpretive understandings stored in long-term memory.

Functional Change Processes for obtaining, handling, and retaining information are *functional* aspects of cognition. Among these are learning, remembering, and reasoning, all of which improve during adolescence.

Among the most important functional changes are (1) a continued increase in processing speed (Kuhn, 2006) and (2) further development of executive function, which includes such skills as selective attention, decision making, inhibitory control of impulsive responses, and management of working memory. These skills seem to develop at varying rates (Blakemore & Choudhury, 2006; Kuhn, 2006) and they seem to be related. Adolescents reach adult-level performance in response inhibition at age 14, processing speed at 15, and working memory at 19 (Luna et al., 2004). These advances are important as increases in processing speed are associated with improvements in reasoning (Kail, Lervag & Hulne, 2016).

LANGUAGE DEVELOPMENT

In adolescence, vocabulary continues to grow as reading matter becomes more adult. By ages 16 to 18 the average young person knows approximately 80,000 words (Owens, 1996).

With the advent of abstract thought, adolescents can define and discuss such abstractions as *love, justice,* and *freedom.* They more frequently use such terms as *however, otherwise, therefore,* and *probably* to express logical relationships. They become more conscious of words as symbols that can have multiple meanings, and they take pleasure in using irony, puns, and metaphors (Owens, 1996).

Adolescents also become more skilled in social perspective-taking, the ability to tailor their speech to another person's point of view. So, for example, a teen might use simpler words when talking to a child, or swear among friends, and show deference when speaking to an adult. This ability is essential for skilled conversation.

Language is not static; it is fluid and the words and phrases used by people change over time. These changes are striking in the speech of adolescents, who often develop their own specialized terms. Vocabulary may differ by gender, ethnicity, age, geographical region, neighborhood, and type of school (Labov, 1992) and varies from one clique to another. Teenage slang is part of the process of developing an independent identity separate from parents and the adult world. This specialized vocabulary even extends to electronic communication, with its own rules for spelling, abbreviations, and the use of emoticons and emojis to convey emotional content (Haas, Takayoshi, Carr, Hudson & Pollock, 2011).

MORAL REASONING: KOHLBERG'S THEORY

As children attain higher cognitive levels, they become capable of more complex reasoning about moral issues. Adolescents are better able than younger children to take another person's perspective, to solve social problems, to deal with interpersonal relationships, and to see themselves as social beings. All of these tendencies foster, although do not necessarily lead to, moral development.

Let's look at Lawrence Kohlberg's theory of moral reasoning, at Carol Gilligan's work on moral development in women and girls, and at research on prosocial behavior in adolescence.

Heinz's Dilemma A woman is near death from cancer. A druggist has discovered a drug that doctors believe might save her. The druggist is charging $2,000 for a small dose—10 times what the drug costs him to make. The sick woman's husband, Heinz, borrows from everyone he knows but can scrape together only $1,000. He begs the druggist to sell him the drug for $1,000 or let him pay the rest later. The druggist refuses, saying, "I discovered the drug and I'm going to make money from it." Heinz, desperate, breaks into the man's store and steals the drug. Should Heinz have done that? Why or why not? (Kohlberg, 1969).

Heinz's problem is the most famous example of Lawrence Kohlberg's approach to studying moral development. Starting in the 1950s, Kohlberg and his colleagues posed hypothetical dilemmas like this one to 75 boys ages 10, 13, and 16 and continued to question them periodically for more than 30 years. Kohlberg came to believe that moral development was a consequence of moral reasoning, which depended heavily on cognitive development. Moreover, he believed that at the heart of every dilemma was the concept of justice—a universal principle.

Kohlberg's Levels and Stages On the basis of thought processes shown by responses to his dilemmas, Kohlberg (1969) described three levels of moral reasoning, each divided into two stages (Table 11.2):

- *Level I:* **Preconventional morality.** People act under external controls. They obey rules to avoid punishment or reap rewards, or they act out of self-interest.

- *Level II:* **Conventional morality (or morality of conventional role conformity).** People have internalized the standards of authority figures. They are concerned about being "good," pleasing others, and maintaining the social order.

- *Level III:* **Postconventional morality (or morality of autonomous moral principles).** People recognize conflicts between moral standards and make their own judgments on the basis of principles of right, fairness, and justice. People generally do not reach this level of moral reasoning until at least early adolescence, or more commonly in young adulthood, if ever.

In Kohlberg's theory, it is the reasoning underlying a person's response to a moral dilemma, not the response itself, that indicates the stage of moral development. As shown in Table 11.3, two people who give opposite answers may be at the same stage if their reasoning is based on similar factors. Later, Kohlberg proposed a seventh, "cosmic," stage, in which people consider the effect of their actions not only on other people but on the universe as a whole (Kohlberg, 1981; Kohlberg & Ryncarz, 1990).

Evaluating Kohlberg's Theory Kohlberg, building on Piaget, inaugurated a profound shift in the way we look at moral development. Instead of viewing morality solely as the attainment of control over self-gratifying impulses, investigators became interested in how children and adults based moral judgments on their growing understanding of the social world.

For example, neither Piaget nor Kohlberg considered parents important to children's moral development, but more recent research shows that adolescents with supportive, authoritative parents who stimulate them to question and expand on their moral reasoning tend to reason at higher levels. Peers also affect moral reasoning by talking with each other about moral conflicts. Having more close friends, spending quality time with them, and being perceived as a leader are associated with higher moral reasoning (Eisenberg & Morris, 2004).

Initial research supported Kohlberg's theory. The American boys that Kohlberg and his colleagues followed through adulthood progressed through Kohlberg's stages and their moral judgments correlated positively with age, education, IQ, and socioeconomic status (Colby, Kohlberg, Gibbs & Lieberman, 1983). Generally speaking, adolescents who are more advanced in moral reasoning do tend to be more moral in their behavior, and antisocial adolescents tend to use less mature moral reasoning (Eisenberg & Morris, 2004). Recent research, however, has cast doubt on the delineation of some of Kohlberg's stages (Eisenberg & Morris, 2004). For example, some children can reason flexibly about such issues as early as age 6 (Helwig & Jasiobedzka, 2001).

One reason the ages attached to Kohlberg's levels are so variable is that people who have achieved a high level of cognitive development do not always reach a comparably

preconventional morality
First level of Kohlberg's theory of moral reasoning in which control is external and rules are obeyed in order to gain rewards or avoid punishment or out of self-interest.

conventional morality (or morality of conventional role conformity)
Second level in Kohlberg's theory of moral reasoning in which standards of authority figures are internalized.

postconventional morality (or morality of autonomous moral principles)
Third level of Kohlberg's theory of moral reasoning, in which people follow internally held moral principles and can decide among conflicting moral standards.

TABLE 11.2 Kohlberg's Six Stages of Moral Reasoning

Levels	Stages of Reasoning	Typical Answers to Heinz's Dilemma
Level I: Preconventional morality (ages 4 to 10)	*Stage 1: Orientation toward punishment and obedience.* Children obey rules to avoid punishment. They ignore the motives of an act and focus on its consequences.	*Pro:* "He should steal the drug. If he doesn't, his wife might die and he would be lonely."
		Con: "He shouldn't steal the drug. It's a big crime and he might end up in jail."
	Stage 2: Instrumental purpose and exchange. Children conform to rules out of self-interest. They look at an act in terms of the needs it meets and differentiate this value from the act's physical form and consequences.	*Pro:* "It's all right to steal the drug, because his wife needs it and he wants her to live. It isn't that he wants to steal, but that's what he has to do to save her."
		Con: "He shouldn't steal it. The druggist isn't wrong or bad; he just wants to make a profit. That's what you're in business for—to make money."
Level II: Conventional morality (ages 10 to 13 or beyond)	*Stage 3: Maintaining mutual relations, approval of others, the Golden Rule.* Children want to please others, can judge their intentions, and develop their own ideas of what a good person is. They evaluate an act according to motive or the person performing it, and take circumstances into account.	*Pro:* "He should steal the drug because that is the natural thing for a good husband to do and he is doing it out of love. You'd blame him if he didn't love his wife enough to save her."
		Con: "He shouldn't steal. If his wife dies, he can't be blamed. It isn't because he's heartless or that he doesn't love her enough to do everything that he legally can. The druggist is the heartless one."
	Stage 4: Social concern and conscience. People are concerned with doing their duty, showing respect for authority, and maintaining social order. They consider an act always wrong, regardless of motive or circumstances, if it violates a rule.	*Pro:* "You should steal it. If you did nothing, you'd be letting your wife die. It's your responsibility if she dies. You have to take it with the idea of paying the druggist."
		Con: "It is a natural thing for Heinz to want to save his wife, but it's still always wrong to steal."
Level III: Postconventional morality (early adolescence, or not until young adulthood, or never)	*Stage 5: Morality of contract, of individual rights, and of democratically accepted law.* People think in rational terms, valuing the welfare of society. They see these values as best supported by law. While they recognize that there are times when human need and the law conflict, they believe it is better for society if they obey the law.	*Pro:* "The law wasn't set up for these circumstances. Taking the drug in this situation isn't really right, but it's justified."
		Con: "You can't completely blame someone for stealing, but extreme circumstances don't really justify taking the law into your own hands. You can't have people stealing whenever they are desperate. The end may be good, but the ends don't justify the means."
	Stage 6: Morality of universal ethical principles. People do what they as individuals think is right, regardless of legal restrictions or the opinions of others. They act in accordance with internalized standards, knowing that they would condemn themselves if they did not.	*Pro:* "This is a situation that forces him to choose between stealing and letting his wife die. In a situation where the choice must be made, it is morally right to steal. He has to act in terms of the principle of preserving and respecting life."
		Con: "Heinz is faced with the decision of whether to consider the other people who need the drug just as badly as his wife. Heinz ought to consider the value of all the lives involved."

Sources: Adapted from L. Kohlberg, "Stage and sequence: The cognitive-developmental approach to socialization." In D. A. Goslin (Ed.), *Handbook of socialization theory and research.* Chicago: Rand McNally, 1969. Lickona, 1976.

high level of moral development. A certain level of cognitive development is *necessary* but not *sufficient.* In other words, just because a person is capable of moral reasoning does not mean the person actually does so. People may sometimes come up with highly sophisticated and cognitively complex justifications for immoral actions. Thus, moral reasoning and moral behavior are not always linked. Some investigators suggest that moral activity is influenced also by such emotions as empathy, guilt, and distress, and the internalization of prosocial norms (Eisenberg & Morris, 2004; Gibbs, 1991, 1995; Gibbs & Schnell, 1985).

AN ETHIC OF CARE: GILLIGAN'S THEORY

Kohlberg viewed the apex of morality in terms of justice and fairness. Did this view reflect cognitive complexity or Kohlberg's own biases and beliefs about what was most important? This question was addressed by Carol Gilligan (1982/1993), who asserted that Kohlberg's theory was sexist and oriented toward values more important to men than to women. Women, Gilligan argued, held a different set of values that placed caring and avoiding harm as higher goals than justice. Kohlberg's typology unfairly categorized women as less morally and cognitive complex because of the exclusive focus on justice (Eisenberg & Morris, 2004).

Research has found little support for Gilligan's claim of a male bias in Kohlberg's stages (Brabeck & Shore, 2003; Jaffee & Hyde, 2000), and she has since modified her position. Generally, gender differences in moral reasoning are small (Jaffee & Hyde, 2000).

PROSOCIAL BEHAVIOR AND VOLUNTEER ACTIVITY

Some researchers have studied prosocial moral reasoning as an alternative to Kohlberg's justice-based system. Prosocial moral reasoning is reasoning about moral dilemmas in which one person's needs conflict with those of others in situations in which social rules or norms are unclear or nonexistent. For example, a child faced with the dilemma of deciding whether or not to intervene when a friend is being teased might run the risk of becoming a target of the bullies too. Such a child might engage in prosocial moral reasoning when deciding on a course of action. Research has shown that, from childhood to early adulthood, prosocial reasoning based on personal reflection about consequences and on internalized values and norms increases with age, whereas reasoning based on stereotypes such as "it's nice to help" decreases with age (Eisenberg & Morris, 2004).

Prosocial behavior typically increases from childhood through adolescence (Eisenberg & Morris, 2004). Girls tend to show more prosocial behavior and empathic concern than boys (Eisenberg & Fabes, 1998; Van der Graaf et al., 2014), and this difference becomes more pronounced in adolescence (Fabes, Carlo, Kupanoff & Laible, 1999). Cross-culturally, parents of girls emphasize social responsibility more than parents of boys do. This has been validated in Australia, the United States, Sweden, Hungary, Czech Republic, Bulgaria, and Russia (Flannagan, Bowes, Jonsson, Csapo & Sheblanova, 1998). Parents who are warm and sympathetic and who use prosocial reasoning themselves are also more likely to have teens who behave in prosocial ways (Carlo, Mestre, Samper & Armenta, 2011). Peers also matter. Experiments show that peer feedback about the value of prosocial behavior can, depending on whether the peer group is perceived as supporting or disliking such behavior, increase or decrease the occurrence of prosocial behavior (Hoorn, Dijk, Meuwese, Rieffe & Crone, 2016).

Volunteering is a common form of prosocial behavior. About half of adolescents engage in some sort of community service or volunteer activity, although adolescents with high SES volunteer more than those with lower SES (Schmidt, Shumow & Kacker, 2007). Students who do volunteer work tend to be more engaged in their communities than those who do not as adults. In addition, adolescent volunteers tend to have a higher degree of self-understanding and commitment to others (Eccles, 2004) and better academic and civic outcomes (Schmidt, Shumow & Kacker, 2007). The effects of community service also apply to inner city, racial minority youth (Chan, Ou & Reynolds, 2014), suggesting that intervention programs promoting community service might be an important means by which to promote characteristics associated with positive development.

Educational and Vocational Issues

In the United States, as in all other industrialized countries and in some developing countries as well, more students finish high school than ever before, and many enroll in higher education (Eccles et al., 2003; OECD, 2004). In the 2014–2015 academic year, the 4-year graduation rate for U.S. public high school students hit a high of 83 percent.

In the United States, minority status is generally correlated with poverty, and socioeconomic status in turn is strongly associated with school achievement. Thus, we might expect ethnicity to be an important factor. This is indeed the case. High school graduation rates in 2014–2015 were highest for Asian Americans (90 percent), followed by whites (88 percent), Hispanics (78 percent), blacks (75 percent) and Native Americans (72 percent) (National Center for Education Statistics, 2017c).

Among the 35 member countries of the Organisation for Economic Cooperation and Development (OECD, 2008), graduation rates vary—for example, 15 percent in Turkey and 62 percent in Iceland. The United States, with an average of 12.7 years of schooling, is on the high end of this international comparison. However, despite our wealth and technological sophistication, U.S. adolescents remain solidly in the middle with respect to academics. Compared to other countries, U.S. students score average in scientific literacy and reading, and below average in math (OECD, 2016a).

Students who take responsibility for their own learning are likely to do well in school.
©Purestock/Getty Images

INFLUENCES ON SCHOOL ACHIEVEMENT

In adolescence, such factors as parenting practices, socioeconomic status, and the quality of the home environment influence the course of school achievement. Other factors include gender, ethnicity, peer influence, quality of schooling, and students' belief in themselves.

Student Motivation and Self-Efficacy Western educational practices are based on the assumption that students are, or can be, motivated to learn. Educators emphasize the value of intrinsic motivation—the student's desire to learn for the sake of learning—because research has shown this orientation is associated with academic achievement (Cerasoli, Nicklin & Ford, 2014). Unfortunately, many U.S. students are *not* self-motivated, and motivation often declines as they enter high school (Eccles, 2004; Larson & Wilson, 2004).

Students high in *self-efficacy*—who believe that they can successfully achieve academic goals—are likely to do well in school (Komarraju & Nadler, 2013). So, for example, after failing a test, a student with high self-efficacy might conclude that he didn't study enough and that to do well in future tests he should study more. A student with low self-efficacy, by contrast, might conclude that the material was too hard or the test was unfair, a belief system that undermines work ethic and motivation. Similarly, students' beliefs about their ability to self-regulate their learning (Zuffiano et al., 2013) as well as their actual levels of self-discipline (Duckworth & Seligman, 2005) impact academic achievement.

In the United States, where opportunities exist for many children, personal motivation can have a strong effect on how much children learn. But in many cultures, education is based on such factors as duty (India), submission to authority (Islamic countries), and participation in the family and community (sub-Saharan Africa). In the countries of east Asia, students are expected to learn to meet family and societal expectations. Learning is expected to require intense effort, and students who fail or fall behind feel obligated to try again. This expectation may help explain why, in international comparisons in science and math, east Asian students substantially surpass U.S. students. In developing countries, issues of motivation pale in the light of social and economic barriers to education: inadequate or absent schools, the need for child labor to support the family, barriers to schooling for girls, and early marriage (Larson & Wilson, 2004). Thus, as we discuss factors in educational success, which are drawn largely from studies in the United States and other Western countries, we need to remember that they do not apply to all cultures.

Gender Reading tests conducted on 15-year-olds in 72 countries shows an advantage for girls, although the difference in scores for girls and boys narrowed between 2009 and 2015. Although gender differences in science are small, boys are more likely to be top performers in all countries with the exception of Finland (OECD, 2016b). However, despite having a greater proportion of high performers, boys are simultaneously more likely to fail to achieve a baseline of proficiency in reading, mathematics, and science (OECD, 2015). Overall, beginning in adolescence, girls do better on verbal tasks that involve writing and language usage;

boys do better in activities that involve visual and spatial functions helpful in math and science. An evaluation of SAT results and math scores from 7 million students found few gender differences in math performance (Hyde, Lindberg, Linn, Ellis & Williams, 2008).

Why might we expect gender differences? As with all aspects of development, research points to interacting biological and environmental contributions (Hyde & Mertz, 2009). Male and female brains show some differences in structure and organization, and these differences tend to become more pronounced with age. Girls have more gray matter and the growth of gray matter peaks earlier. Their neurons also have more connections (Halpern et al., 2007). The brain structure of girls appears to better integrate verbal and analytic tasks (which occur in the left brain) with spatial and holistic tasks (which occur in the right brain) (Ingalhalikar et al., 2014).

On average, boys have bigger brains (Ruigrok et al., 2014). Boys also have more connective white matter (Ingalhalikar et al., 2014). They also have more cerebrospinal fluid, which cushions the longer paths of nerve impulses. Boys' brains seem to be optimized for activity within each hemisphere—their brains are more modular and seem to show an advantage for visual and spatial performance (Halpern et al., 2007; Ingalhalikar et al., 2014). Earlier reports about sex differences in the size of the corpus callosum (a band of nerve fibers connecting both hemispheres of the brain) appear to be an artifact of overall brain size (Luders, Toga & Thompson, 2014).

Social and cultural forces that influence gender differences include the following (Halpern et al., 2007):

- *Home influences:* Across cultures, parents' educational level and involvement correlates with their children's math achievement. Parents' gender attitudes and expectations also have an effect.
- *School influences:* Subtle differences in the way teachers treat boys and girls, especially in math and science classes, have been documented.
- *Neighborhood influences:* Boys benefit more from enriched neighborhoods and are hurt more by deprived neighborhoods.
- *Women's and men's roles* in society help shape girls' and boys' choices of courses and occupations.
- *Cultural influences:* The size of gender differences in math performance varies among nations and becomes greater by the end of secondary school. These differences correlate with the degree of gender equality in the society.

Parent and Peer Influences *Authoritative parents,* who strike a balance between making demands and being responsive, tend to have teens who do better academically. Both *authoritarian parents,* who tend to use more punishment and harsh control, and *permissive parents,* who seem indifferent to grades, have children who show slightly lower achievement. However, while statistically significant, all of these differences are small to very small (Pinquart, 2016). In other words, they have little predictive value in the real world.

Parental involvement in academic activities is a far better predictor of which teens will do well academically (Castro et al., 2015). Parents who emphasize the value of education, connect academic performance to future goals, and discuss learning strategies have a significant impact on student academic achievement (Hill & Tyson, 2009). Parents' educational level and family income also indirectly affect educational attainment based on how they influence parenting style, sibling relationships, and adolescent academic engagement (Melby, Conger, Fang, Wickrama & Conger, 2008).

There are also peer influences on academic motivation and achievement, which become increasingly important in adolescence as teens interact more with peers and less with family (Brown & Larson, 2009). Generally, academically engaged students associate with others who are also academically engaged (Veronneau & Dishion, 2011), and, especially for girls, this predicts later performance (Crosnoe, Cavanagh & Elder, 2003; Riegle-Crumb, Farkas & Muller, 2006). The quality of peer relationships also seems to be important. Those students who do well tend to be liked by their peers more, and those who do poorly are more likely to be rejected or bullied (Veronneau, Vitaro, Brendgen, Dishion & Tremblay, 2010; Nakamoto & Schwartz, 2010).

The School The quality of schooling strongly influences student achievement. A good school has an orderly and safe environment, adequate resources, a stable teaching staff, and a positive sense of community. The school culture places a strong emphasis on academics and offers opportunities for extracurricular activities. Teachers trust, respect, and care about students and have high expectations for students and confidence in their ability to teach (Eccles, 2004).

In part, the positive effects of a school are a function of the unique peer culture—including both how students relate to each other and what they perceive the academic culture of the school to be (Lynch, Lerner & Leventhal, 2013). If adolescents feel support from teachers and other students, and if the curriculum and instruction are meaningful and appropriately challenging and fit their interests and needs, they are more satisfied with school (Samdal & Dür, 2000) and get better grades (Jia et al., 2009). High teacher expectations are the most consistent positive predictor of students' goals and interests, and negative feedback is the most consistent negative predictor of academic performance and classroom behavior (Wentzel, 2002).

Technology In 2013, approximately 78 percent of teens had a cell phone, 23 percent had a tablet computer, and 93 percent had access to a computer at home (Madden, Lenhart, Duggan, Cortesi & Gassar, 2013). The expansion of technology and the major role it plays in children's lives has affected learning. Teachers often ask students to conduct research online, as well as to access (79 percent) and submit (76 percent) homework and assignments online (Purcell, Heaps, Buchanan & Fried, 2013).

Research indicates that while critical-thinking and analysis skills have declined as a result of the increased use of computers and video games, visual skills have improved. Students are spending more time multitasking with visual media and less time reading for pleasure (Greenfield, 2009). Reading develops vocabulary, imagination, and induction, skills that are critical to solving more complex problems. Multitasking can prevent a deeper understanding of information, and students given access to the Internet during class do not process what was presented as well and perform more poorly than students without access (Greenfield, 2009). See Research in Action for more on multitasking.

DROPPING OUT OF HIGH SCHOOL

As noted, more U.S. youths are completing high school than ever before. The percentage of those who drop out, known as the status dropout rate, includes all people in the 16- to 24-year-old age group who are not enrolled in school and who have not completed a high school program, regardless of when they left school. In 2013, the status dropout rate for this group was 6.4 percent, and it was higher for boys (8.0 percent) than girls (5.6 percent). Average dropout rates are lower for white students (4.7 percent) than for both blacks (9.0 percent) and Hispanics (11.8 percent). Asian students at 2.5 percent are the least likely to drop out (NCES, 2013b).

Why are poor and minority adolescents more likely to drop out? Reasons include low teacher expectations, differential treatment of these students, less teacher support than at the elementary level, and the perceived irrelevance of the curriculum to culturally underrepresented groups. The transition to high school for African American and Latino students seems to be most risky for those students transitioning from smaller, more supportive junior high schools with significant numbers of minority peers to larger, more impersonal high schools with fewer minority peers (Benner & Graham, 2009).

There are consequences both for society and for individuals to dropping out. Society suffers when young people do not finish school. Dropouts are more likely to be unemployed or to have low incomes, to end up on welfare, to become involved with drugs, crime, and delinquency. They also tend to be in poorer health (Laird et al., 2006; NCES, 2001, 2003, 2004).

There are also personal consequences. As young adults, those who successfully complete high school are most likely to obtain postsecondary education, to have jobs, and to be employed. (Finn, 2006; United States Department of Labor, 2013). They are also likely to earn more money. In 2012, the median income of people who did not complete high school was approximately $25,000. However, those with at least a high school degree earned a median income of approximately $46,000. Over a lifetime of work this results in a difference of $670,000 (Stark & Noel, 2015).

research in action

TEENS AND MEDIA MULTITASKING

Multitasking is not a new phenomenon. People have always had to pay attention to more than one thing at once. What has changed dramatically, however, is the impact that electronic media have had on multitasking. Adolescents, who have grown up with portable electronic media at their fingertips, are particularly prone to multitasking (Voorveld & van der Goot, 2013). Studies show that more than 25 percent of adolescents' media consumption occurs using at least two media types simultaneously (Rideout et al., 2010).

Two kinds of media multitasking patterns have been identified: consumption of at least two media types simultaneously (e.g., watching TV while surfing on the Internet) and use of a media during a non-media activity (e.g., instant messaging while completing homework) (Baumgartner et al., 2014). Teenagers are not the only age group to multitask using media, but they are heavy users. Voorveld & van der Goot (2013) found that teens were most likely to media multitask, frequently combining music with online activities. Teenagers are also especially likely to make heavy use of "multitasking facilitators," such as smartphones and instant messaging apps (Pea et al., 2012).

Adolescents may believe that they are producing high-quality work while texting with friends or listening to music, but evidence suggests the opposite. Baumgartner and colleagues (2014) found that adolescents who frequently media multitask report more problems in staying focused, inhibiting inappropriate behavior, and switching effectively between tasks.

Potential deficits in executive function associated with media multitasking may have far-reaching implications in school. Cain and colleagues (2016) were able to demonstrate a link between media multitasking and poorer academic performance on standardized tests in math and English, as well as decreased working memory capacity. These studies were not able to establish cause and effect; it is plausible that teenagers with lower levels of executive functioning are more likely to media multitask. However, they are worthy of note, given the ubiquity of media multitasking.

Equally disturbing are statistics that link media multitasking to distracted driving among adolescents. Distractions come in many forms, but the use of cell phones and texting while driving has been implicated in many adolescent accidents, resulting in injuries and deaths. Carter (2014) reports that 92 percent of adolescents engage in distracted driving behaviors and that teenagers have much higher rates of distracted driving crashes than older drivers. In 2015, 42 percent of high school students who drove in the past 30 days reported sending a text or e-mail while driving (CDC, 2017g). Certainly teenagers are not the only age group to use cell phones while driving, but studies show that dialing and texting in particular are linked to higher risk of crashes among novice drivers (Klauer et al., 2014). Driving inexperience coupled with the visual, manual, and cognitive distraction of cell phone use is considered an especially dangerous combination for adolescent drivers (Garner et al., 2011). In a study comparing cell phone use while driving and drunk driving, impairments while using a cell phone were determined to be as profound as those associated with driving while drunk (Strayer, Drews & Crouch, 2006).

What is your perception of the benefits and risks of teens' use of media multitasking? What actions can be taken to reduce the number of adolescent deaths associated with distracted driving and cell phone use?

what's your view

PREPARING FOR HIGHER EDUCATION OR VOCATIONS

How do young people develop career goals? How do they decide whether to go to college and, if not, how to enter the world of work?

Influences on Students' Aspirations Self-efficacy beliefs help shape the occupational options students consider and the way they prepare for careers (Bandura, Barbaranelli, Caprara & Pastorelli, 2001). In addition, parents' values with regard to academic achievement influence adolescents' values and occupational goals (Jodl, Michael, Malanchuk, Eccles & Sameroff, 2001).

Despite the greater flexibility in career goals today, there are still gender differences in career choices. Women receive more than half of all undergraduate degrees in biology, chemistry, and math. However, they are underrepresented—earning only 20 percent of degrees—in computer science, engineering, and physics (Cheryan, Ziegler, Montoya &

Jiang, 2017). While the reasons for this are varied, one factor is gender-stereotyping, which still influences vocational choice (Eccles et al., 2003). Girls and boys in the United States are now equally likely to plan careers in math and science. However, girls are still more likely to go into fields such as nursing, social welfare professions, and teaching (Eccles et al., 2003). Much the same is true in other industrialized countries (OECD, 2004).

The educational system itself may act as a brake on vocational aspirations. Students who can memorize and analyze tend to do well academically. Students whose strength is in creative or practical thinking—areas critical to success in certain fields—rarely get a chance to show what they can do (Sternberg, 1997). Recognition of a broader range of intelligences and more flexible teaching and career counseling could allow more students to meet their educational goals.

Students whose strength is in creative thinking frequently don't get a chance to show what they can do. ©Jacob Lund/Shutterstock

Guiding Students *Not* Bound for College Adolescents decide to forgo college for a variety of reasons. Some young adults, who tend to come from low-income families and have low academic achievement, have financial constraints that prevent them from attending college despite their desire to do so. A second smaller group is composed of young people who have the financial means to go to college as well as the academic ability, but prefer to begin working and earning money. The remainder of non-college-bound young adults give a wide variety of reasons for their decision not to attend college (Bozick & DeLuca, 2011).

Many industrialized countries offer guidance to non-college-bound students. Germany, for example, has an apprenticeship system in which high school students go to school part-time and spend the rest of the week in paid on-the-job training supervised by an employer-mentor. However, the United States lacks coordinated policies to help non-college-bound youth make a successful transition from high school to the labor market. Most of these young people must get training on the job or in community college courses. Many, ignorant about the job market, do not obtain the skills they need. Others take jobs beneath their abilities. Some do not find work at all (NRC, 1993a).

Adolescents in the Workplace In the United States, about 18 percent of students are employed during a given school year (Child Trends DataBank, 2016), and the vast majority of adolescents are employed at some time during high school, mostly in service and retail jobs. Researchers disagree over whether part-time work is beneficial to high school students (by helping them develop real-world skills and a work ethic) or detrimental (by distracting them from long-term educational and occupational goals). How much time students work matters—those that work more than 20 hours a week generally suffer academically and are more likely to drop out of school (Warren & Lee, 2003).

For high school students who must or choose to work outside of school, the effects are more likely to be positive if they try to limit working hours and remain engaged in school activities. Cooperative educational programs that enable students to work part-time as part of their school program may be especially beneficial (Staff, Mortimer & Uggen, 2004).

summary and key terms

Adolescence: A Developmental Transition

- Adolescence, in modern industrial societies, is the transition from childhood to adulthood. It lasts from about age 11 to about 20.
- Early adolescence involves physical, cognitive, and psychosocial growth, but risks. Risky behavior patterns, such as drinking alcohol, drug abuse, sexual and gang activity, and use of firearms, tend to increase throughout the teenage years, but most young people experience no major problems.

adolescence

PHYSICAL DEVELOPMENT

Puberty

- Puberty is triggered by hormonal changes. Puberty takes about 4 years, typically begins earlier in girls than in boys, and ends when a person can reproduce.
- Puberty is marked by two stages: (1) the activation of the adrenal glands and (2) the maturing of the sex organs a few years later.
- During puberty, both boys and girls undergo an adolescent growth spurt. The reproductive organs enlarge and mature, and secondary sex characteristics appear.

- A secular trend toward earlier attainment of adult height and sexual maturity began about 100 years ago, probably because of improvements in living standards.
- The principal signs of sexual maturity are production of sperm (for males) and menstruation (for females).

puberty, primary sex characteristics, secondary sex characteristics, adolescent growth spurt, spermarche, menarche, secular trend

The Adolescent Brain

- The adolescent brain is not yet fully mature. It undergoes a second wave of overproduction of gray matter, especially in the frontal lobes, followed by pruning of excess nerve cells. Continuing myelination of the frontal lobes facilitates the maturation of cognitive processing.
- Adolescents process information about emotions with the amygdala, whereas adults use the frontal lobe. Thus adolescents tend to make less reasoned judgments.
- Underdevelopment of frontal cortical systems connected with motivation, impulsivity, and addiction may help explain adolescents' tendency toward risk-taking.

Physical and Mental Health

- For the most part, the adolescent years are relatively healthy.
- Many adolescents do not engage in regular vigorous physical activity.
- Many adolescents do not get enough sleep because of electronics use and because the high school schedule is out of sync with their natural body rhythms.
- Concern with body image, especially among girls, may lead to eating disorders.
- Three common eating disorders in adolescence are obesity, anorexia nervosa, and bulimia nervosa. All can have serious long-term effects. Anorexia and bulimia affect mostly girls and young women. Outcomes for bulimia tend to be better than for anorexia.
- Adolescent substance use has lessened in recent years; still, drug use often begins as children move into middle school.
- Marijuana, alcohol, and tobacco are the most popular drugs with adolescents. All involve serious risks. Nonmedical use of prescription and over-the-counter drugs is an increasing problem.
- The prevalence of depression increases in adolescence, especially among girls.
- Leading causes of death among adolescents include motor vehicle accidents, firearm use, and suicide.

body image, anorexia nervosa, bulimia nervosa, substance abuse, substance dependence, binge drinking

COGNITIVE DEVELOPMENT
Aspects of Cognitive Maturation

- Adolescents who reach Piaget's stage of formal operations can engage in hypothetical-deductive reasoning. They can think in terms of possibilities, deal flexibly with problems, and test hypotheses.
- Because environmental stimulation plays an important part in attaining this stage, not all people become capable of formal operations.
- Piaget's proposed stage of formal operations does not take into account such developments as accumulation of knowledge and expertise, gains in information processing, and the growth of metacognition. Piaget also paid little attention to individual differences, between-task variations, and the role of the situation.
- Research has found both structural and functional changes in adolescents' information processing. Structural changes include increases in declarative, procedural, and conceptual knowledge and expansion of the capacity of working memory. Functional changes include progress in deductive reasoning.
- Vocabulary and other aspects of language development, such as social perspective-taking, improve in adolescence. Adolescents enjoy wordplay and create their own dialect.
- According to Kohlberg, moral reasoning progresses from external control to internalized societal standards to personal, principled moral codes.
- Kohlberg's theory has been criticized for failing to credit the roles of emotion, socialization, and parental guidance, and for being biased toward men and Western cultures.
- Prosocial behavior, especially in girls, increases throughout adolescence, and is influenced by parents and peers. It is associated with positive outcomes.

formal operations, hypothetical-deductive reasoning, declarative knowledge, procedural knowledge, conceptual knowledge, preconventional morality, conventional morality (or morality of conventional role conformity), postconventional morality (or morality of autonomous moral principles)

Educational and Vocational Issues

- Self-efficacy beliefs, parental practices, cultural and peer influences, gender, and quality of schooling affect adolescents' educational achievement.
- Although most Americans graduate from high school, the dropout rate is higher among poor, Hispanic, and African American students. However, this racial/ethnic gap is narrowing. Active engagement in studies is an important factor in keeping adolescents in school.
- Educational and vocational aspirations are influenced by several factors, including self-efficacy, parental values, and gender stereotypes.
- High school graduates who do not immediately go on to college can benefit from vocational training.
- Part-time work can have both positive and negative effects on educational, social, and occupational development. The long-term effects tend to be best when working hours are limited.

active engagement

Psychosocial Development in Adolescence

chapter 12

©Glow Asia RF/Alamy Stock Photo

learning objectives

Discuss identity formation in adolescence.

Describe adolescent sexuality.

Characterize changes in adolescents' relationships with family and peers.

Describe adjustment problems of adolescents and strategies for intervention and risk reduction.

In this chapter, we turn to psychosocial aspects of the quest for identity. We discuss how adolescents come to terms with their sexuality. We consider how teenagers' burgeoning individuality expresses itself in relationships with parents, siblings, peers, and friends. We examine sources of antisocial behavior and ways of reducing the risks to adolescents to make it a time of positive growth and expanding possibilities.

The Search for Identity

The search for **identity** comes into focus during the teenage years. Adolescence is a time to figure out exactly who you are.

ERIKSON: IDENTITY VERSUS IDENTITY CONFUSION

The chief task of adolescence, said Erikson (1968), is to confront the crisis of **identity versus identity confusion,** or *identity versus role confusion,* so as to become a unique adult with a coherent sense of self and a valued role in society. At least in Western countries such as the United States, adolescence is a relatively long period of time during which young people begin to take on adult responsibilities but are not fully independent. Erikson believed this time-out period, which he called *psychosocial moratorium,* was ideal for the development of identity and allowed young people the opportunity to search for commitments to which they could be faithful.

Adolescents who resolve the identity crisis satisfactorily, according to Erikson, develop the virtue of **fidelity:** sustained loyalty, faith, or a sense of belonging to a loved one, friends, or companions (Erikson, 1982). Individuals who do not develop a firm sense of their own identity and do not develop fidelity may have an unstable sense of self, be insecure, and fail to plan for themselves and the future. Erikson saw this identity or role confusion as the prime danger of this stage.

Erikson's theory describes male identity development as the norm. According to Erikson, a man is not capable of real intimacy until he has achieved a stable identity, whereas women define themselves through marriage and motherhood. Thus, said Erikson, women (unlike men) develop identity *through* intimacy, not *before* it. As we'll see, this sexist orientation of Erikson's theory has prompted criticism.

MARCIA: IDENTITY STATUS—CRISIS AND COMMITMENT

What does the process of forming an identity look like? Erikson's perspective was extended by work conducted by Marcia (1966, 2002) in identity statuses. Through 30-minute, semistructured *identity-status interviews,* Marcia distinguished four types of identity status: *identity achievement, foreclosure, moratorium,* and *identity diffusion.* The four categories differ according to the presence or absence of **crisis** and **commitment,** the two elements Erikson saw as crucial to forming identity. Marcia defined *crisis* as a period of conscious decision making. Crisis, within the context of Erikson's theories, does not refer to a stressful event such as losing your job or not being able to pay your bills. Rather, it refers to the process of actively grappling with what to believe and who to be.

Commitment, the other aspect of identity formation, involves a personal investment in an occupation or ideology (system of beliefs). Commitments can be held after they have been deeply considered, after crisis, or they can be adopted without much thought put into them. Researchers have found relationships between identity status and personality and family variables (Kroger, 2003). Here is a sketch of young people in each identity status.

- **Identity achievement** (*crisis leading to commitment*). After a crisis period Olivia made thoughtful choices and expresses strong commitment to them. Her parents have encouraged her to make her own decisions. Research suggests she will be more mature and socially competent than people in the other three categories (Kroger, 2003; Marcia, 1993).

- **Foreclosure** (*commitment without crisis*). Isabella has made commitments by uncritically accepting someone else's plans for her life. She is self-assured, but she becomes dogmatic when her opinions are questioned. She has close family ties and is obedient.

- **Moratorium** (*crisis with no commitment yet*). Josh is actively grappling with his identity and trying to decide for himself who he wants to be and the path he wants his life to take. He is lively, talkative, self-confident, but also anxious and fearful. He will probably come out of his crisis with the ability to make commitments and achieve identity.

identity
According to Erikson, a coherent conception of the self, made up of goals, values, and beliefs to which a person is solidly committed.

identity versus identity confusion
Erikson's fifth stage of psychosocial development, in which an adolescent seeks to develop a coherent sense of self, including the role she or he is to play in society. Also called *identity versus role confusion.*

fidelity
Sustained loyalty, faith, or sense of belonging that results from the successful resolution of Erikson's *identity versus identity confusion* psychosocial stage of development.

crisis
Marcia's term for period of conscious decision making related to identity formation.

commitment
Marcia's term for personal investment in an occupation or system of beliefs.

identity achievement
Identity status, described by Marcia, that is characterized by commitment to choices made following a crisis, a period spent in exploring alternatives.

foreclosure
Identity status, described by Marcia, in which a person who has not spent time considering alternatives (that is, has not been in crisis) is committed to other people's plans for his or her life.

moratorium
Identity status, described by Marcia, in which a person is currently considering alternatives (in crisis) and seems headed for commitment.

- **Identity diffusion** (*no commitment, no crisis*). Jayden has not seriously considered options and has avoided commitments. He is unsure of himself and tends to be uncooperative. His parents do not discuss his future with him; they say it's up to him. People in this category tend to be unhappy and often lonely.

identity diffusion
Identity status, described by Marcia, that is characterized by absence of commitment and lack of serious consideration of alternatives.

These categories are not stages; they represent the status of identity development at a particular time, and they may change in any direction as young people continue to develop (Marcia, 1979). Also, because our identity is multidimensional, our identity development is as well. For example, a young person may have decided upon a career path but not yet considered political or religious affiliation. When middle-age people look back on their lives, they most commonly trace a path from foreclosure to moratorium to identity achievement (Kroger & Haslett, 1991). From late adolescence on, as Marcia proposed, more and more people are in moratorium or achievement: seeking or finding their identity. About half of late adolescents remain in foreclosure or diffusion, but when development does occur, it is typically in the direction Marcia described (Kroger, 2003).

GENDER DIFFERENCES IN IDENTITY FORMATION

According to Carol Gilligan (1982/1993, 1987a, 1987b; Brown & Gilligan, 1990), the female sense of self develops not so much through achieving a separate identity as through establishing relationships. Girls and women, says Gilligan, judge themselves on their handling of their responsibilities and on their ability to care for others as well as for themselves.

Some earlier research supports Erikson's view that, for women, identity and intimacy develop together. However, given changes in social structure and the increased role of women in the workplace, it may be that these gender differences are less important than they were previously, and individual differences play more of a role now (Archer, 1993; Marcia, 1993). In other research on Marcia's identity statuses, few gender differences have appeared (Kroger, 2003).

Mastering the challenge of a whitewater course may help this adolescent girl assess her abilities, interests, and desires. ©Michael DeYoung/Blend Images

ETHNIC FACTORS IN IDENTITY FORMATION

For a European American young person growing up in a predominantly white culture, the process of ethnic identity formation is not particularly troublesome. However, for many young people in minority groups, race or ethnicity is central to identity formation. Following Marcia's model, some research has identified four ethnic identity statuses (Phinney, 1998):

1. *Diffused:* Juanita hasn't really thought about her identity. She has done little or no exploration of what her heritage means or what she thinks about it.

2. *Foreclosed:* Caleb has strong feelings about his identity, but those feelings are not really based on any serious exploration of his identity. Rather, he has absorbed the attitudes of other important people in his life. These feelings may be positive or negative.

3. *Moratorium:* Cho-san has begun to think about what her ethnicity means to her but is still confused about it. She asks questions of others, talks about it with her parents, and thinks a great deal about it.

4. *Achieved:* Diego has spent a good deal of time thinking about who he is and what his ethnicity means within that context. He now understands and accepts his ethnicity.

Studies of minority youth have found evidence of all four identity statuses across age groups, although teens are more likely to be in moratorium status than are adults. Regardless of age, teens who are in achieved status are most likely to view race as central to their identity (Yip, Seaton & Sellers, 2006).

Exploration of the meaning of ethnicity, which increases in middle adolescence and may reflect the transition to a more ethnically diverse high school, is an important variable (French, Seidman, Allen & Aber, 2006). Girls may undergo the process of identity formation earlier than boys (Portes, Dunham & Del Castillo, 2000). For example, one study showed that over a 4-year period Latina girls went through exploration, resolution, and affirmation of positive feelings about their ethnic identities, whereas boys showed increases only in affirmation. The increase in exploration—which the boys did not demonstrate—was the only factor tied to increases in self-esteem (Umana-Taylor, Gonzalez-Backen & Guimond, 2009).

THE GLOBALIZATION OF ADOLESCENCE

Adolescence is no longer solely a Western phenomenon. Globalization and modernization have changed the world, leading to urbanization, longer and healthier lives, reduced birthrates, and smaller families. Earlier puberty and later marriage are increasingly common. More women and fewer children work outside the home. Together these changes have brought the extended transitional phase between childhood and adulthood known as adolescence to most parts of the world (Lerner & Steinberg, 2004).

Historically, puberty marked the end of childhood and entry into the adult world of work. In many cultures, there are important rituals such as circumcision or tattooing to mark this entry into adulthood. However, times have changed. In the past 50 years, the markers of adulthood have shifted. For example, many adolescents have postponed entering the job market—and thus fully becoming "adults"—in order to further their education. This process has been driven by the economic realities of the current world. Today adolescents need more schooling and skills to be competitive. Increasingly, it is recognized that to survive and be competitive in this global world, adolescents need to acquire a solid knowledge base, critical-thinking skills, social competencies, and respect for others. They are

Despite the forces of globalization and modernization, preadolescent children in some less-developed societies still follow traditional paths. These 9-year-old schoolgirls in Tehran celebrate the ceremony of Taqlif, which marks their readiness to begin the religious duties of Islam. ©Enric Marti/AP Images

less apt to follow in their parents' footsteps and to be guided by their advice (Larson & Wilson, 2013).

Perceived discrimination during the transition to adolescence can interfere with positive identity formation and lead to conduct problems or depression. As an example, perceptions of discrimination are associated with depressive symptoms, alienation, and a drop in academic performance in Chinese American adolescents (Benner & Kim, 2009) and decreases in self-esteem and increases in depression in Asian American, black and Latino teens (Greene, Way & Pahl, 2006). Although the effect is stronger for males than for females, increases in racial identity over 1 year have been related to a decreased risk of depressive symptoms (Mandara, Gaylord-Harden, Richards & Ragsdale, 2009). Other protective factors are nurturant, involved parenting; secure attachment with parents; prosocial friends; and strong academic performance (Myrick & Martorell, 2011; Brody et al., 2006).

Cultural socialization includes practices that teach children about their racial or ethnic heritage, promote cultural customs and traditions, and foster racial/ethnic and cultural pride. For example, think about the holidays you celebrate. Participating in those traditions and rituals was part of your cultural socialization, and it impacts identity formation. Adolescents who have experienced cultural socialization tend to have stronger and more positive ethnic identities than those who have not (Hughes et al., 2006).

Cultural socialization
Parental practices that teach children about their racial/ethnic heritage and promote cultural practices and cultural pride.

Sexuality

Seeing oneself as a sexual being, recognizing one's sexual orientation, and forming romantic or sexual attachments all are parts of achieving *sexual identity*. Although this process is biologically driven, its expression is in part culturally defined.

In many non-Western countries, adolescent boys and girls live in two separate worlds. In parts of the Middle East, Latin America, Africa, and Asia, 14 percent of girls marry by age 15 and almost 40 percent before they are 18. This limits their chance for education and joining the labor force (Fustos, 2010). Boys, in contrast, have more freedom and mobility.

Gender differences are also apparent in public education in many rural parts of the world. Approximately 66 percent of the 3 million children worldwide without access to education are girls. For example, in Niger, 80 girls for every 100 boys attend school in the urban areas, but only 41 girls for every 100 boys in the rural areas are students. Family beliefs concerning a greater benefit to educating boys are a primary reason. This is unfortunate, as research shows that better-educated girls tend to marry later and have fewer children, enabling them to seek skilled employment in the new technological society (UN, 2003).

Exposure to the values of other cultures can be confusing. For instance, Indian adolescents struggle to find a balance between traditional values and the consumerism of the Western worlds, particularly with respect to the unequitable distribution of material possessions and which Western values they should adopt (Suchday, 2015). Teens in Nepal struggle with a similar set of issues. Nepalese adolescents exposed to Western media and music are provided with information about the wider world beyond the borders of Nepal, and it raises their expectations to unattainable levels. Processes such as these can alienate teens from their own culture and drive a wedge into family relationships (Jensen, Arnett & McKenzie, 2011).

Globalization is here to stay; it will continue to affect teens across the world. The cultural change it engenders can be both liberating and challenging. Learning about other cultures and what teens in distant parts of the world are doing and thinking can be exhilarating for adolescents, expanding their horizons and allowing them to dream of different possible lives. However, this window into other cultures can also be confusing and can lead to behaviors or decisions with adverse immediate and long-term consequences that can affect their health, significant relationships, academic success, or life options. The Internet draws teens into social media, chat rooms, and websites that can include pornography and violence. News, information, and fads sweep almost instantaneously around the planet (Jensen, Arnett & McKenzie, 2011), and can have potentially disastrous consequences for young adults. Globalization is a double-edged sword that wields the ability to both enrich and endanger young adults today.

Source: Larson, R., & Wilson, S. "Adolescents across place and time: Globalization and the changing pathways to adulthood." In R. M. Lerner & L. Steinberg (Eds.), *Handbook of adolescent psychology* (2nd ed., pp. 299–331). Hoboken, NJ: Wiley, 2004.

what's your view Can you think of examples from your experience of how globalization affects adolescents? Why do some countries exert more cultural influence than others?

During the twentieth century a major change in sexual attitudes and behavior in many industrialized countries brought more widespread acceptance of premarital sex, homosexuality, and other previously disapproved forms of sexual activity. The Internet, cell phones, e-mail, and instant messaging make it easy for adolescents to arrange casual sex and engage in sexual risk-taking. On the other hand, the AIDS epidemic and better sexual education programs have led many young people to abstain from sexual activity outside of committed relationships or to engage in safer sexual practices.

SEXUAL ORIENTATION AND IDENTITY

It is in adolescence that a person's **sexual orientation** generally becomes more clear: whether that person will consistently be sexually attracted to persons of the other sex (*heterosexual*), of the same sex (*homosexual*), or of both sexes (*bisexual*). The prevalence of homosexual orientation varies widely according to how questions are worded. Depending on whether it is measured by sexual or romantic *attraction or arousal* or by sexual *behavior* or sexual *identity*, the rate of homosexuality in the U.S. population ranges from 1 to 21 percent (Savin-Williams, 2006).

Many young people have one or more homosexual experiences, but isolated experiences or even occasional attractions or fantasies do not determine sexual orientation. In a national survey, 3 percent of 18- to 19-year-old boys and 8 percent of girls in that age group reported being gay, lesbian, or bisexual, but 4 percent of the boys and 12 percent of the girls reported same-sex sexual behaviors (Guttmacher Institute, 2016). Social

sexual orientation
Focus of consistent sexual, romantic, and affectionate interest, either heterosexual, homosexual, or bisexual.

Attitudes toward sexuality have liberalized in the United States in the past 50 years.
©Leander Baerenz/Media Bakery

stigma may bias such self-reports, underestimating the prevalence of homosexuality and bisexuality.

Origins of Sexual Orientation Although it once was considered a mental illness, several decades of research have found no association between homosexual orientation and emotional or social problems—apart from those caused by societal treatment of homosexuals (APA, n.d.; Meyer, 2003; C. J. Patterson, 1992, 1995a, 1995b). These findings led the psychiatric profession in 1973 to stop classifying homosexuality as a mental disorder.

Sexual orientation seems to be at least partly genetic (Diamond & Savin-Williams, 2003). For example, research has found stretches of DNA on chromosomes 7, 8, 10, and 28 that appear to be involved (Mustanski et al., 2005; Sanders et al., 2015). Twin studies have led to similar conclusions about genetic influences. Researchers have found the concordance rates of monozygotic (identical) twins is always higher than that of dizygotic (fraternal) twins. However, despite having the exact same copy of genes, identical twins are not perfectly concordant for sexual orientation (Ngun & Vilain, 2014). This implies that nongenetic factors must also play a part. One large twin study found that genes explained about 34 percent of the variation in men and 18 percent in women (Långström, Rahman, Carlström & Lichtenstein, 2008). But what of the remaining influence? What are the environmental experiences that might impact sexual orientation?

It is important to note that when discussing environmental influences, researchers are not referring to older, discredited theories about domineering mothers, absent fathers, or sexual abuse as causal factors in the development of homosexual orientation (Ngun & Vilain, 2014). Rather, environmental experiences refer, most commonly, to the 9 months of prenatal influences in the womb. Those experiences have shaped the brain in significant ways that may impact later sexual orientation.

One environmental influence on development involves biological correlates of family structure. The more older biological brothers a man has, the more likely he is to be gay (Blanchard, 2017). Each older biological brother increases the chances of homosexuality in a younger brother by 33 percent (Bogaert, 2006). Furthermore, there are indications that male babies that will later identify as gay are more likely to weigh less at birth and are more likely to have mothers who experience miscarriages (VanderLaan, Blanchard, Wood, Garzon & Zucker, 2015; Skorska, Blanchard, VanderLaan, Zucker & Bogaert, 2017). These phenomena may be a cumulative immune-like response to the presence of successive male fetuses in the womb.

Another variable that has been implicated in sexual orientation is the 2D:4D ratio. This ratio—that of the pointer finger to the ring finger—is, through a quirk of development, affected by hormone exposure in utero. A lower 2D:4D ratio indicates high prenatal androgen exposure and is more typical of men than women. Interestingly, one meta-analysis showed that lesbian women had a significantly more masculinized 2D:4D ratio when compared to heterosexual women, suggesting androgen exposure in utero affected their sexual orientation. Gay men, by contrast, did not appear to have a different 2D:4D ratio than heterosexual men (Grimbos, Dawood, Burriss, Zucker & Putts, 2010). Other research with girls who have a condition called congenital adrenal hyperplasia (CAH) also speaks to the influence of prenatal hormone exposure. Girls with CAH, who are exposed to higher than average levels of androgens in utero, are more likely to later identify as lesbian or bisexual (Bao & Swaab, 2010).

Imaging studies have found similarities of brain structure and function between homosexuals and heterosexuals of the other sex. While correlational, they are intriguing. Brains of gay men and straight women are more symmetrical, whereas in lesbians and straight men the right hemisphere is slightly larger. Also, in gays and lesbians, connections in the amygdala, which is involved in emotion, are more typical of the other sex (Savic & Lindström, 2008). One researcher reported a difference in the size of the hypothalamus, a brain structure that governs sexual activity, in heterosexual and gay men (LeVay, 1991). In brain imaging studies on pheromones, odors that attract mates, the odor of male sweat activated the hypothalamus in gay men much as it did in heterosexual women. Similarly, lesbian women and straight men reacted more positively to female pheromones than to male ones (Savic, Berglund & Lindström, 2005, 2006).

Homosexual and Bisexual Identity Development Despite the increased acceptance of homosexuality in the United States, many adolescents who openly identify as gay, lesbian, or bisexual may feel isolated or subject to discrimination and violence. Others may be reluctant to disclose their sexual orientation, even to their parents, for fear of strong disapproval or a rupture in the family (Hillier, 2002). They may find it difficult to meet and identify potential same-sex partners (Diamond & Savin-Williams, 2003).

Most gay, lesbian and bisexual youth begin to identify as such between the ages of 12 and 17 years (Calzo, Masyn, Austin, Jun & Corliss, 2017). However, because of the lack of socially sanctioned ways to explore their sexuality, many gay and lesbian adolescents experience identity confusion (Sieving, Oliphant & Blum, 2002). Gay, lesbian, and bisexual youth who are unable to establish peer groups that share their sexual orientation may struggle with the recognition of same-sex attractions (Bouchey & Furman, 2003). Moreover, gay and lesbian youth who experience rejection and low support for their sexual orientation from their parents after coming out are more likely to adopt a negative view of their sexuality (Bregman, Malik, Page, Makynen & Lindahl, 2013). Additionally, those gay, lesbian and bisexual youth who do not successfully integrate their sexual identity in their self-concept are at risk for issues with anxiety, depression, or conduct problems (Rosario, Scrimshaw & Hunter, 2011).

SEXUAL BEHAVIOR

According to national surveys, slightly over 41 percent of high school students have had sexual intercourse (Kann, 2016) and 77 percent of young people in the United States have had sex by age 20 (Finer, 2007). Teenage boys historically have been more likely to be sexually experienced than teenage girls; however, trends are shifting. In 2011, 44 percent of 12th grade boys and 51 percent of girls in that age group reported being sexually active (USDHHS, 2012; Figure 12.1). The median age for girls to first have sex is 17.8 years, and boys follow shortly thereafter with a median age of 18.1 years (Finer & Philbin, 2014). African Americans tend to begin sexual activity earlier than white youth (Kaiser Family Foundation, Hoff, Greene & Davis, 2003). While Latino boys are

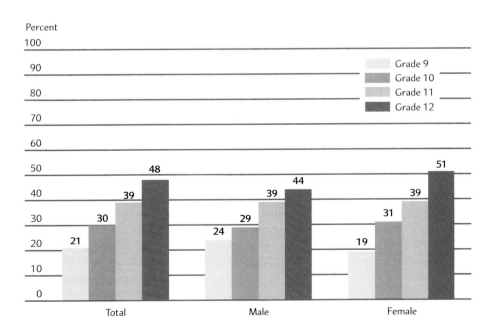

FIGURE 12.1

Percentage of Students in Grades 9 through 12 Who Report They Are Sexually Active

Source: U.S. Department of Health and Human Services (USDHHS). "Youth risk behavior surveillance: United States 2011." *MMWR Surveillance Summaries*, 61(4), 2012, Table 65.

also likely to have sex at an earlier age, Latino girls tend to have sex slightly later than their non-Latino white counterparts (Finer & Philbin, 2014).

Sexual Risk-Taking Two major concerns about adolescent sexual activity are the risks of contracting sexually transmitted infections (STIs) and, for heterosexual activity, of pregnancy. Most at risk are young people who start sexual activity early, have multiple partners, do not use contraceptives regularly, and have inadequate information—or misinformation—about sex (Abma et al., 1997). Other risk factors are living in a socioeconomically disadvantaged community or rural community, being black or Hispanic, substance use, antisocial behavior, and association with deviant peers. Parental monitoring can help reduce these risks (Centers for Disease Control, 2017q; Baumer & South, 2001; Capaldi, Stoolmiller, Clark & Owen, 2002).

Early puberty, poverty, poor school performance, lack of goals, a history of sexual abuse or parental neglect, and cultural or family patterns of early sexual experience may play a part in early and/or risky sexual activity (Klein & AAP Committee on Adolescence, 2005). For example, the absence of a father, especially early in life, is a strong risk factor for early sexual activity (Ellis et al., 2003). One of the most powerful influences is perception of peer group norms. Young people often feel under pressure to engage in sexual activities. Teens are more likely to have sex and to take risks while having sex if they believe their peers are also having and approve of sex, or are pressuring them to have sex (Van de Bongardt, Reitz, Sandfort & Dekovic, 2015)

Generally, an involved and engaged relationship between teens and parents is associated with a decreased risk of early sexual activity. Participating in regular family activities predicts declines in teenaged sexual activity (Coley, Votruba-Drzal & Schindler, 2009), and more parent-child communication is associated with delayed sexual intercourse (Parkes, Henderson, Wight & Nixon, 2011). Teens who have supportive relationships with their parents are more likely to delay intercourse and to use safe sex practices when they finally do so (Deptula, Henry & Shoeny, 2010). Teenagers who have close, warm relationships with their mothers are also likely to delay sexual activity, especially if they perceive that their mothers would disapprove (Jaccard & Dittus, 2000; Sieving, McNeely & Blum, 2000). For those teens in two-parent families, having fathers who know more about their friends and activities is associated with delays in sexual activity (Coley et al., 2009). Common reasons teenagers give for not yet having had sex include that it is against their religion or morals and that they do not want to get (or get a girl) pregnant (Abma et al., 2010).

The percentage of U.S. adolescents who have ever had intercourse has declined over the past few decades (Kann et al., 2014). However, noncoital forms of genital sexual activity, such as oral and anal sex and mutual masturbation, are common. Many heterosexual teens do not regard these activities as "sex" but as substitutes for, or precursors of, sex, or even as abstinence (Remez, 2000). In one national survey, just under half of teenage boys and girls reported having given or received oral sex (Copen, Chandra & Martinez, 2012).

Use of Contraceptives The use of contraceptives among sexually active teenage girls has increased since the 1990s (Abma et al., 2004), and includes the pill and new hormonal and injectable methods or combinations of methods (CDC, 2012b). Teens who, in their first relationship, delay intercourse, discuss contraception before having sex, or use more than one method of contraception are more likely to use contraceptives consistently throughout that relationship (Manlove, Ryan & Franzetta, 2003). By contrast, adolescent girls who do not use contraception during their first sexual encounter are twice as likely to become teenage mothers (Martinez & Abma, 2015). One nationwide study found that 13 percent of currently sexually active teens did not use any form of birth control during their last sexual encounter (Kann et al., 2014).

The best safeguard for sexually active teens is regular use of condoms, which give some protection against STIs as well as against pregnancy. Almost 80 percent of teens who are having sex for the first time use a condom (Martinez, Copen & Abma, 2011). This does not necessarily ensure continued use, however. While condoms are still the most common form of contraception used, almost half of adolescent females and about a third of adolescent males report not using a condom during their last sexual encounter (Martinez & Abma, 2015). Adolescents who start using prescription contraceptives often stop using condoms, in some cases not realizing that they leave themselves unprotected against STIs (Klein & AAP Committee on Adolescence, 2005).

Where Do Teenagers Get Information about Sex? Adolescents get their information about sex primarily from friends, parents, sex education in school, and the media (Kaiser Family Foundation et al., 2003). Adolescents who can talk about sex with older siblings as well as with parents are more likely to have positive attitudes toward safer sexual practices (Kowal & Pike, 2004). However, approximately 22 percent of teen girls and 30 percent of teen boys report that their parents do not talk to them about any sexual or reproductive health topics (Lindberg, Maddow-Zimet & Boonstra, 2016).

Many teenagers get much of their "sex education" from the media, which present a distorted view of sexual activity, associating it with fun, excitement, competition, or violence and rarely showing the risks of unprotected sex. Surprisingly, teens report more exposure to sexual media from television, movies, and music than they do from the Internet (Ybarra, Strasburger & Mitchell, 2014). Teens who watch highly sexual television content are twice as likely to experience a pregnancy compared with lower level or no exposure (Chandra et al., 2008). Additionally, teens exposed to sexual explicit content—including pornography and erotica—are more likely to have oral sex and sexual intercourse at earlier ages (Brown & L'Engle, 2009).

From 2011 to 2013, approximately 80 percent of teens received formal sexual education—generally at a school, church, or community center—on preventing STIs or how to say no to sex. However, only 55 percent of males and 60 percent of females received information on the use of birth control methods (Lindberg, Maddow-Zimet & Boonstra, 2016). This is in part driven by policies promoting abstinence research over more comprehensive programs. Programs that encourage abstinence but also discuss STI prevention and safer sexual practices—known as comprehensive sexual education—have been found to delay sexual initiation and increase contraceptive use (AAP Committee on Psychosocial Aspects of Child and Family Health and Committee on Adolescence, 2001). However, since 1998, federal- and state-funded sex education programs stressing abstinence until marriage as the best option have become common.

Some school programs promote abstinence as the *only* option, even though most abstinence-only courses have not been found to delay sexual activity (AAP Committee on Psychosocial Aspects of Child and Family Health and Committee on Adolescence, 2001; Satcher, 2001; Trenholm et al., 2007). Abstinence-based courses, even when they have been found to reduce some sexual activity, do not reduce pregnancy rates or sexually transmitted infections. This may be because abstinence only programs do not impact whether or not teens use safe sex practices such as condoms (Chin et al., 2012). Thus, if teens do have sex, they are less likely to be protected. Likewise, pledges to maintain virginity have shown little impact on sexual behavior other than a *decrease* in the likelihood to take precautions during sex (Rosenbaum, 2009).

Unfortunately, policies promoting abstinence programs have not only undermined the quality of the information taught in the United States, but also in foreign aid programs. These policies have harmed both family planning and HIV prevention programs in other countries (Santelli et al., 2017). Comprehensive sexual education programs, by contrast, have been shown to be effective in preventing pregnancy and disease across a number of countries (Fonner, Armstrong, Kennedy, O'Reilly & Sweat, 2014).

SEXUALLY TRANSMITTED INFECTIONS (STIS)

Sexually transmitted infections (STIs) are diseases spread by sexual contact. An estimated 19.7 million new STIs are diagnosed each year, over half in young men and women (CDC, 2013b). Approximately 65 million Americans have an uncurable STI (Wildsmith, Schelar, Peterson & Manlove, 2010). An estimated 3.2 million adolescent girls in the United States—about 1 in 4 of those ages 14 to 19—has at least one STI

sexually transmitted infections (STIs) Infections and diseases spread by sexual contact.

(Forhan et al., 2008). The chief reasons for the prevalence of STIs among teenagers include early sexual activity; multiple partners; failure to use condoms or to use them regularly and correctly; and, for women, a tendency to have sex with older partners (CDC, 2000b; Forhan et al., 2008). Additionally, there are often barriers to sexual health services such as lack of transportation to clinics, inability to pay, conflict between school and clinic hours, and concerns about confidentiality (CDC, 2016d). Despite the fact that teens are at higher risk for contracting STIs, they perceive their own personal risk as low (Wildsmith et al., 2010).

STIs in adolescent girls are most likely to develop undetected. In a *single* unprotected sexual encounter with an infected partner, a girl runs a 1 percent risk of acquiring HIV, a 30 percent risk of acquiring genital herpes, and a 50 percent risk of acquiring gonor-rhea (Alan Guttmacher Institute, 1999). Although teenagers tend to view oral sex as less risky than intercourse, a number of STIs, especially pharyngeal gonorrhea, can be trans-mitted in that way (Remez, 2000).

The most common STI, accounting for about half of all STI infections diagnosed in 15- to 24-year-olds each year, is human papilloma virus (HPV), or genital warts, the leading cause of cervical cancer in women (Weinstock et al., 2004). Among girls with three or more partners, the risk jumps to 50 percent (Forhan et al., 2008). In 2006, a vaccine that targets the types of HPV that cause most cases of cervical cancer and genital warts became avail-able. The Centers for Disease Control (2016a) recommends routine vaccination for all female adolescents and young adults starting at age 11 or 12. Vaccination rates are low but growing. In 2010, about half of girls aged 14 to 17 had received at least one dose and only 32 percent had received the recommended three doses (Markowitz et al., 2013). Rates are even lower in adolescent boys; in 2013, only 32.6 percent of teen boys had received at least one dose, and 13.9 percent received the entire series (Lu et al., 2015). Despite low vaccina-tion rates, HPV incidence since the introduction of the vaccine has dropped from 11.5 percent to 5.1 percent, indicating a high level of protection is conferred by the vaccine (Markowitz et al., 2013). Some parents avoid vaccinating their children out of a fear it might lead to increased sexual activity. However, research has shown that vaccination for HPV does not lead to more or riskier sexual behavior in adolescents (Mayhew et al., 2014).

The most common *curable* STIs are chlamydia and gonorrhea. These diseases, if undetected and untreated, can lead to severe health problems, including, in women, pelvic inflammatory disease (PID), a serious abdominal infection. In the United States, close to 1 in 10 teenage girls and 1 in 5 boys are affected by either chlamydia or gonor-rhea, or both (Forhan et al., 2008). The rates of all three STIs have recently increased. In 2015–2016, the reported rate of chlamydia rose by 4 percent in 15- to 19-year-olds, especially in young women. After a period of decline, rates of syphilis (11.3 percent) and gonorrhea (13.0 percent) both rose during the same time period (CDC, 2016d).

Genital herpes simplex is a chronic, recurring, often painful, and highly contagious disease. It can be fatal to a person with a deficiency of the immune system or to the newborn infant of a mother who has an outbreak at the time of delivery. Its incidence has increased dramatically during the past three decades. Hepatitis B remains a promi-nent STI despite the availability, for more than 20 years, of a preventive vaccine. Also common among young people is trichomoniasis, a parasitic infection that may be passed along by moist towels and swimsuits (Weinstock, Berman & Cates, 2004).

The human immunodeficiency virus (HIV), which causes AIDS, is transmitted through bodily fluids, usually by sharing intravenous drug needles or by sexual contact with an infected partner. The virus attacks the body's immune system, leaving a person vulnerable to a variety of fatal diseases. Symptoms of AIDS include extreme fatigue, fever, swollen lymph nodes, weight loss, diarrhea, and night sweats. There were 2.3 million new HIV infections worldwide last year, representing a 33 percent decline from 2001 (UNAIDS, 2013). As of now, AIDS is incurable, but increasingly the related infections that kill people are being stopped with antiviral therapy (UNAIDS, 2013; Weinstock et al., 2004).

Comprehensive sex and STI/HIV education is critical to promoting responsible deci-sion making and controlling the spread of STIs. Evidence for the positive impact of such programs is strong: (Kirby & Laris, 2009).

TEENAGE PREGNANCY AND CHILDBEARING

More than 7 in 100 girls in the United States have been pregnant at least once before age 20 (Kost, Henshaw & Carlin, 2013). More than half (51 percent) of pregnant teenagers in the United States have their babies (Klein & AAP Committee on Adolescence, 2005). Sixty-seven percent of teens who carry the pregnancies to term are between the ages of 18 and 19 years, and 31 percent are 15 to 17 years of age, with 2 percent of live births accounted for by teens under the age of 15 (National Center for Health Statistics, 2009a). Overall, 35 percent of adolescents choose to abort (Figure 12.2) (Klein & AAP Committee on Adolescence, 2005), the lowest percentage recorded since the legalization of abortion in 1973 (Santelli & Melnikas, 2010). Fourteen percent of teen pregnancies end in miscarriage or stillbirth (Klein & AAP Committee on Adolescence, 2005).

A substantial decline in teenage pregnancy has accompanied steady decreases in early intercourse and in sex with multiple partners and an increase in contraceptive use. In 2013, birthrates for teens dropped to their lowest level yet, 22.2 per 1,000 women ages 15 to 19 years (Martin, Hamilton, Osterman, Driscoll & Mathews, 2017).

Programs that focus on teen outreach have had some success. Such programs generally combine comprehensive sex education and access to family planning services. With the use of such a program, California—the only state that refused abstinence-only federal dollars—went from having the highest teen pregnancy rate to showing the steepest decline, effectively halving rates (Boonstra, 2010). Similar results have been found with teen outreach programs that also focus on raising self-esteem, handling emotions, and dealing effectively with peers and adults (Allen & Philliber, 2001).

Although declines in teenage pregnancy and childbearing have occurred among all population groups, birthrates have fallen most sharply among black teenagers. Still, black and Hispanic girls are more likely to have babies than white, American Indian, or Asian American girls (Martin et al., 2012).

More than 90 percent of pregnant teenagers describe their pregnancies as unintended, and 50 percent of teen pregnancies occur within 6 months of sexual initiation (Klein & AAP Committee on Adolescence, 2005). Many of these girls grew up fatherless (Ellis et al., 2003). Research suggests contributing factors include having been physically or sexually abused and/or exposed to parental divorce or separation, domestic violence, substance abuse, or a household member who was mentally ill or engaged in criminal behavior (Madigan, Wade, Tarabulsy, Jenkins & Shouldice, 2014; Hillis et al., 2004). Teenage fathers tend to have limited financial resources, poor academic performance, and high dropout rates. Many teenage parents are themselves products of adolescent pregnancy (Campa & Eckenrode, 2006; Klein & AAP Committee on Adolescence, 2005).

Outcomes of Teenage Pregnancy Teenage pregnancies often have poor outcomes. Many of the mothers are impoverished and poorly educated, and some are drug users. Many do not eat properly, do not gain enough weight, and get inadequate prenatal care or none at all. Their babies are likely to be premature or dangerously small and are at heightened risk of other birth complications (Jeha, Usta, Ghulmiyyah & Nassar, 2015; Wen et al., 2007). They are also at heightened risk for health and academic problems, abuse and neglect, and developmental disabilities that may continue into adolescence (Children's Defense Fund, 2004; Klein & AAP Committee on Adolescence, 2005; Menacker, Martin, MacDorman & Ventura, 2004).

Teenage unwed mothers and their families are likely to suffer financially. Teenage mothers are likely to drop out of school and to have repeated pregnancies, and less likely to go to college. They and their partners may lack the maturity, skills, and social support to be good parents. Their children, in turn, tend to have developmental and academic problems, to be depressed, to engage in substance abuse and early sexual activity, to engage in gang activity, to be unemployed, and to become adolescent parents themselves

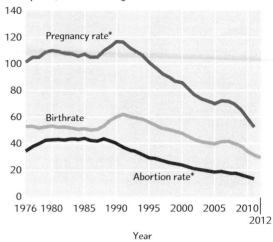

Rate per 1,000 women ages 15–19

*Data not available for 2010–2012.

FIGURE 12.2
Pregnancy, Birth, and Abortion Rates for U.S. Females Ages 15 to 19

Source: Centers for Disease Control and Prevention (CDC). *Pregnancy rates for U.S. women continue to drop,* 2013, Figure 3.

MTV's Teen Mom franchise, originally criticized for glamorizing teen pregnancy, may instead be partially responsible for the recent declines in teenage motherhood. Internet searches for birth control and abortion spiked after episodes of the reality drama aired. (Kearney & Levine, 2015).
©Dfree/Shutterstock

(Basch, 2011; Klein & AAP Committee on Adolescence, 2005; Pogarsky, Thornberry & Lizotte, 2006).

Poor outcomes of teenage parenting are far from inevitable, however. Several long-term studies find that, two decades after giving birth, most former adolescent mothers are not on welfare; many have finished high school and secured steady jobs; and they do not have large families. Comprehensive adolescent pregnancy and home visitation programs seem to contribute to good outcomes (Basch, 2011; Klein & AAP Committee on Adolescence, 2005), as do contact with the father (Howard, Lefever, Borkowski & Whitman, 2006), and involvement in a religious community (Carothers, Borkowski, Lefever & Whitman, 2005).

Preventing Teenage Pregnancy Teenage pregnancy and birthrates in the United States are many times higher than in other industrialized countries, despite similar levels of sexual activity (Guttmacher Institute, 2013). Teenage birthrates are nearly 5 times as high in the United States as in Denmark, Finland, France, Germany, Italy, the Netherlands, Spain, Sweden, and Switzerland and 12 times as high as in Japan (Ventura, Mathews & Hamilton, 2001). Comparisons with the European experience suggest one important distinction between the United States and other countries: U.S. girls are more likely to have multiple sex partners and are less likely to use contraceptives (Darroch et al., 2001).

Europe's industrialized countries have provided universal, comprehensive sex education for a much longer time than the United States. Comprehensive programs encourage young teenagers to delay intercourse and improve contraceptive use. They include education about sexuality, birth control, and responsible sexual decisions, and information about risks and consequences of teenage pregnancy (AAP Committee on Psychosocial Aspects of Child and Family Health and Committee on Adolescence, 2001). Contraceptives are provided free to adolescents in many countries. Sweden showed a fivefold reduction in the teenage birthrate following introduction of birth control education, free access to contraceptives, and free abortion on demand (Bracher & Santow, 1999).

In the United States the provision and content of sex education programs are political issues. Some critics claim that community- and school-based sex education leads to more or earlier sexual activity, even though evidence shows otherwise (Boonstra, 2010; Kirby & Laris, 2009).

The problem of teenage pregnancy requires a multifaceted solution. It must include programs and policies to encourage postponing or refraining from sexual activity, but it also must recognize that many young people do become sexually active and need education and information to prevent pregnancy and STIs. It requires attention to underlying factors that put teenagers and families at risk—reducing poverty, school failure, behavioral and family problems, and expanding employment, skills training, and family life education (CDC, 2013c)—and it should target those young people at highest risk (Klein & AAP Committee on Adolescence, 2005).

Relationships with Family, Peers, and Adult Society

Adolescents spend more time with peers and less with family. However, despite the increased importance of peers, adolescents still need their parents (Offer & Church, 1991). Those adolescents who have the most secure attachment relationships tend to have parents who permit and encourage their strivings for independence while providing a safe haven in times of emotional stress (Allen et al., 2003).

IS ADOLESCENT REBELLION A MYTH?

adolescent rebellion
Pattern of emotional turmoil, characteristic of a minority of adolescents, that may involve conflict with family, alienation from adult society, reckless behavior, and rejection of adult values.

The teenage years have been called a time of **adolescent rebellion.** Yet full-fledged rebellion now appears to be relatively uncommon even in Western societies. Most young people feel close to and positive about their parents, share similar opinions on major issues, and value their parents' approval (Blum & Rinehart, 2000; Offer & Church, 1991). The relatively few deeply troubled adolescents tended to come from disrupted families and, as adults, continued to have unstable family lives and to reject cultural norms (Offer et al., 2002).

Still, adolescence can be a tough time for young people and their parents. Family conflict, depression, and risky behavior are more common than during other parts of the life span (Arnett, 1999; Petersen, 1993). And family conflict can have a significant impact on emotional distress (Chung, Flook & Fuligni, 2009). Negative emotions and mood swings are most intense during early adolescence. By late adolescence, emotionality tends to become more stable (Larson, Moneta, Richards & Wilson, 2002).

Adolescents raised in homes with a positive family atmosphere tend to come through adolescence without serious problems. ©Hero Images/Getty Images

ADOLESCENTS AND PARENTS

Most adolescents report good relations with their parents (Gutman & Eccles, 2007). Still, adolescence brings special challenges. Just as adolescents feel tension between dependency on their parents and the need to break away, parents want their children to be independent yet find it hard to let go.

Individuation, Family Conflict, and Connectedness If you were like most teens, you probably listened to different music from your parents, dressed in a different style of clothing, and felt it was reasonable to keep certain things private from them. This process, called **individuation** by psychologists, begins in infancy and continues throughout adolescence. It involves the struggle for autonomy and differentiation, or personal identity. An important aspect of individuation is carving out boundaries of control between self and parents (Nucci, Hasebe & Lins-Dyer, 2005), and this process may entail family conflict. Somewhat paradoxically, a warm, interconnected relationship with parents can help teens individuate successfully (Ponappa, Bartle-Haring & Day, 2014).

Parents of young adolescents must strike a delicate balance between too much freedom and too much intrusiveness. For instance, seventh and eighth grade students have been found to be at elevated risk because of decreased parental monitoring and involvement, which allows the behavior of antisocial peers to exert increased influence (Van Ryzin, Stormshak & Dishion, 2012). By 11th grade, those young people who see themselves as having a great deal of autonomy tend to spend more time in unsupervised socializing with peers and are at risk for problem behavior. But too little autonomy can also have negative effects. Those students who perceive their parents as highly intrusive in their personal lives are also more likely to be influenced by negative peer interactions (Goldstein, Davis-Kean & Eccles, 2005).

Despite common beliefs about adolescence being a time of great rebellion and chaos, family arguments most often concern control over everyday personal matters—chores, schoolwork, dress, money, curfews, dating, and friends—rather than issues of health and safety or right and wrong (Adams & Laursen, 2001; Steinberg, 2005). Both family conflict and positive identification with parents are highest at age 13 and then diminish until age 17, when they stabilize or increase somewhat. This shift reflects increased opportunities for independent adolescent decision making (Gutman & Eccles, 2007).

There are also cultural differences. One primary distinction is that drawn between collectivistic and individualistic societies. Research in this area shows that connectedness between teens and parents is higher in collectivistic countries such as India, Saudi Arabia, and Algeria than in individualistic Western countries such as France, Poland, and Argentina. In collectivistic cultures, emphasis is placed more on family than on individual desires (Dwairy & Achoui, 2010).

Especially for girls, family relations can affect mental health. Adolescents who are given more decision-making opportunities report higher self-esteem than those who are given fewer such opportunities. In addition, negative family interactions are related to adolescent depression, whereas positive family identification is related to less depression (Gutman & Eccles, 2007). Family conflict predicts multiple adjustment problems in addition to depression, including anxiety, conduct problems, and problems with peers (Cummings, Koss & Davies, 2015). Moreover, family conflict tends to go down over time in warm, supportive families, but increases in hostile, coercive, or critical families

individuation
Adolescents' struggle for autonomy and personal identity.

(Rueter & Conger, 1995). In addition, autonomy support on the part of parents is associated with more adaptive self-regulation of negative emotions and academic engagement (Roth et al., 2009). Last, both individuation and family connectedness during adolescence predict well-being in middle age (Bell & Bell, 2005).

Parenting Styles and Parental Authority Authoritative parenting continues to foster healthy psychosocial development (Baumrind, 2005; Hoskins, 2014). Authoritative parents insist on important rules, norms, and values but are willing to listen, explain, and negotiate. They exercise appropriate control over a child's conduct (*behavioral control*) but not over the child's feelings, beliefs, and sense of self (*psychological control*) (Steinberg & Darling, 1994). So, for example, they might ground their teenage son for breaking a rule, but they would not insist that the teen agree with them about the wisdom of the broken rule. Generally, behavioral control is preferable. Psychological control, exerted through such emotionally manipulative techniques as withdrawal of love, can harm adolescents' psychosocial development and mental health (Steinberg, 2005). For example, withdrawal of love as a control strategy is associated with an increase in resentment toward parents and a decrease in teens' ability to self-regulate negative emotions (Roth et al., 2009). Parents who are psychologically controlling tend to be unresponsive to their children's growing need for *psychological autonomy,* the right to their own thoughts and feelings (Steinberg, 2005). By contrast, parents who are open to new experiences themselves are more likely to allow their teens greater freedom (Denissen et al., 2009).

Problems arise when parents overstep what adolescents perceive as appropriate bounds of legitimate parental authority. The existence of a mutually agreed personal domain in which authority belongs to the adolescent has been found in various cultures and social classes from Japan to Brazil. This domain expands as parents and adolescents continually renegotiate its boundaries (Nucci et al., 2005).

Parental Monitoring and Adolescents' Self-disclosure A large body of research shows that parental monitoring is one of the most consistently identified protective factors for teens (Barnes, Hoffman & Welte, 2006; Racz & McMahon, 2011). Parental monitoring broadly involves keeping track of the young person's activities, for example, by signing the teen up for after-school activities, checking in with parents of their teen's friends, and keeping track of a teen's whereabouts (Barnes et al., 2006).

Part of monitoring involves knowing what a teen is up to. Young people's growing autonomy and the shrinking areas of perceived parental authority redefine the types of behavior adolescents are expected to disclose to parents (Smetana, Crean & Campione-Barr, 2005; Table 12.1). Both adolescents and parents see *prudential* issues, behavior related to health and safety (such as smoking, drinking, and drug use), as most subject to disclosure;

TABLE 12.1 Items Used to Assess Perceived Areas of Parental versus Adolescent Authority

Moral Items	Conventional Items	Prudential Items	Multifaceted Items	Multifaceted Friendship	Personal Items
Stealing money from parents	Not doing chores	Smoking cigarettes	Not cleaning bedroom	When to start dating	Sleeping late on weekends
Hitting siblings	Talking back to parents	Drinking alcohol	Getting multiple ear piercings	Staying over at a friend's house	Choosing how to spend allowance money
Lying to parents	Using bad manners	Doing drugs	Staying out late	Seeing friends parents don't like	Choosing own clothes or hairstyles
Breaking a promise to parents	Cursing	Having sex	Watching cable TV	Seeing friends rather than family	Choice of music

Source: Smetana, J., Crean, H., Campione-Barr, N. Adolescents' and parents' changing conceptions of parental authority. In J. Smetana (Ed.), *Changing boundaries of parental authority during adolescence (New Directions for Child and Adolescent Development,* No. 108, pp. 31–46). San Francisco: Jossey-Bass, 2005.

followed by *moral* issues (such as lying); *conventional* issues (such as bad manners or swearing); and *multifaceted,* or borderline, issues (such as seeing an R-rated movie), which lie at the boundary between personal matters and one of the other categories. Both adolescents and parents see *personal* issues (such as how teens spend their time and money) as least subject to disclosure. However, for each type of behavior parents tend to want more disclosure than adolescents are willing to provide, although this discrepancy diminishes with age (Smetana, Metzger, Gettman & Campione-Barr, 2006).

In a study of 690 Belgian adolescents, teens disclosed more information when parents maintained a warm, responsive family climate and provided clear expectations without being overly controlling (Soenens, Vansteenkiste, Luyckx & Goossens, 2006)—in other words, when parenting was authoritative. This link between warmth and disclosure also has been found in various ethnic groups in the United States, including Chinese, Mexican American, and European American youth (Yau, Tausopoulos-Chan & Smetana, 2009). Adolescents, especially girls, tend to have closer, more supportive relationships with their mothers than with their fathers (Smetana et al., 2006), and girls confide more in their mothers (Yau et al., 2009). Moreover, relationship quality seems to matter more in girls' willingness to confide in their parents. In other words, boys' secret keeping depends less on relationship warmth than does that of girls' (Keijsers et al., 2010).

Family Structure and Family Atmosphere Conflict in the home can affect the process of individuation. Changes in marital distress or conflict predict corresponding changes in adolescents' adjustment (Cui, Conger & Lorenz, 2005). Divorce can affect this process as well. Adolescents whose parents later divorced showed more academic, psychological, and behavioral problems before the breakup than peers whose parents did not later divorce (Sun, 2001).

Adolescents living with their continuously married parents tend to have significantly fewer behavioral problems than those in other family structures (single-parent, cohabiting, or stepfamilies). Divorce negatively impacts outcomes in part via its influence on the paternal relationship. Teens whose parents were still married reported a close relationship with their father 48 percent of the time, whereas those whose parents were divorced reported being close to their father only 25 percent of the time (Scott, Booth, King & Johnson, 2007). High-quality involvement by a nonresident father helps a great deal, but not as much as the involvement of a father living in the home (Carlson, 2006).

Adolescents, especially boys, from single-parent families are at higher risk for problem behaviors such as substance abuse or aggression. However, this risk can be mitigated by other family structures. For example, parental monitoring (Griffin, Botvin, Scheier, Diaz & Miller, 2000) and mother's educational level, family income, and quality of the home environment (Ricciuti, 2004) have been associated with a reduction in risk.

Adolescents in cohabiting families, like younger children, tend to have greater behavioral and emotional problems than adolescents in married families. For adolescents, unlike younger children, these effects are independent of economic resources, parental well-being, or effectiveness of parenting, suggesting that parental cohabitation itself may be more troublesome for adolescents than for younger children (S. L. Brown, 2004).

Adolescents from families headed by gay or lesbian parents do not appear to show differences in a wide variety of outcomes, including cognitive development, gender identity, and adjustment problems (Fedewa, Black & Ahn, 2015). Rather, as with traditional two-parent families, the quality of the relationship—not the sexual orientation of the parents—is the key variable influencing outcomes (Wainright & Patterson, 2006).

Mothers' Employment and Economic Stress The impact of a mother's work outside the home may depend on how many parents are present in the household. Single mothers may find that work affects how much time and energy is left to spend with children or monitor their activities. The type of after-school care and supervision is particularly important. Those teens who are on their own, away from home, tend to become involved in alcohol and drug use and in misconduct in school, especially if they have an early history of problem behavior (Coley, Morris & Hernandez, 2004).

As discussed earlier, a major problem in many single-parent families is lack of money. For example, teens are more likely to drop out of school and show declines in self-esteem and mastery if their mothers have unstable employment or are out of work for 2 years (Kalil & Ziol-Guest, 2005). Job displacement—where employees lose their jobs due to organizational changes such as restructuring, downsizing, or relocating—has also been associated with declines in educational attainment and well-being in adolescents from single-parent families (Brand & Simon Thomas, 2014). Family economic hardship during adolescence affects adult well-being in part because it is stressful, and that stress interferes with family relationships and affects children's educational and occupational attainments (Sobolewski & Amato, 2005).

ADOLESCENTS AND SIBLINGS

There are several trends in sibling relationships across adolescence. In general, siblings spend less time together, their relationships become more equal, and they become more similar in their levels of competence.

Changes in sibling relationships in many ways mirror the changes we see in the relationships of adolescents and their parents. As adolescents spend more time with peers, they spend less time with siblings. Generally, and perhaps as a result of this, adolescents tend to be less close to siblings than to friends and are less influenced by them. This distance grows across adolescence (Laursen, 1996). Moreover, as children move through adolescence, their relationships with their siblings become progressively more equal (Campione-Barr, 2017).

Sibling conflict declines across middle adolescence. Research has shown that sisters report more intimacy than brothers or mixed pairs. Mixed-sex siblings become less intimate between middle childhood and early adolescence, but more so in middle adolescence, a time when most young people become more interested in the other sex (Kim, McHale, Osgood & Courter, 2006). Teens who have opposite-sex siblings report increases in their perceived romantic competence from early adolescence into adulthood (Doughty, Lam, Stanik & McHale, 2015).

Siblings can exert positive or negative effects on each other. Older siblings may influence a younger one to smoke, drink, or use drugs (Pomery et al., 2005; Rende et al., 2005). Younger siblings hanging out with an antisocial older brother are at serious risk for adolescent antisocial behavior, drug use, sexual behavior, and violence (Snyder, Bank & Burraston, 2005; Solmeyer, McHale & Crouter, 2014). However, siblings can also be protective. In single-mother homes, a warm and nurturing relationship with an older sister tended to prevent a younger sister from engaging in substance use and risky sexual behavior (East & Khoo, 2005). And a recent meta-analysis supports the strong connection between warm relationships with little conflict and healthier psychological adjustment in siblings (Buist, Dekovic & Prinzie, 2013).

ADOLESCENTS AND PEERS

In childhood, most peer interactions are *dyadic,* or one-to-one, though larger groupings begin to form in middle childhood. As children move into adolescence, the peer social system becomes more diverse. *Cliques*—structured groups of friends who do things together—become more important. A larger type of grouping, the *crowd,* which does not normally exist before adolescence, is based not on personal interactions but on reputation, image, or identity. Crowd membership is a social construction: for example, the jocks, the nerds, or the stoners. All three levels of peer groupings may exist simultaneously, and some may overlap in membership, which may change over time. Both clique and crowd affiliations tend to become looser as adolescence progresses (B. B. Brown & Klute, 2003).

The influence of peers normally peaks at ages 12 to 13 and declines during middle and late adolescence. Risk-taking, especially in early adolescence, is higher in the company of peers than when alone (Gardner & Steinberg, 2005), even when potential negative consequences are made clear (Smith, Chein & Steinberg, 2014). For example, at age 13 or 14, popular adolescents may engage in mildly antisocial behaviors, such as trying drugs or sneaking into a movie without paying, to demonstrate to their peers their independence from parental rules (Allen, Porter, McFarland, Marsh & McElhaney, 2005).

Sibling relationships become more equal as younger siblings approach or reach adolescence and the relative age difference diminishes. Even so, younger siblings still look up to their older siblings and may try to emulate them.
©Design Pics/Kristy-Anne Glubish/Getty Images

Friendships The intensity of friendships and the amount of time spent with friends may be greater in adolescence than at any other time. Friendships become more reciprocal, equal, and stable. Those that are less satisfying become less important or are abandoned.

Greater intimacy, loyalty, and sharing with friends mark a transition toward adultlike friendships. Adolescents begin to rely more on friends than on parents for intimacy and support, and they share confidences more than younger friends do (Hartup & Stevens, 1999; Nickerson & Nagle, 2005). Girls' friendships tend to be more intimate than boys', with frequent sharing of confidences (B. B. Brown & Klute, 2003).

The increased intimacy of adolescent friendship reflects cognitive as well as emotional development. Adolescents are now better able to express their private thoughts and feelings and consider another person's point of view. Confiding in a friend helps young people explore their own feelings, define their identity, and validate their self-worth.

The capacity for intimacy is related to psychological adjustment and social competence. Adolescents who are more intimate with their friends feel closer to and have less conflict with them (Chow, Ruhl & Buhrmester, 2013). Additionally, they have a high opinion of themselves, do well in school, are sociable, and are unlikely to be hostile, anxious, or depressed (Berndt & Perry, 1990; Buhrmester, 1990; Hartup & Stevens, 1999). They also tend to have established strong bonds with parents (B. B. Brown & Klute, 2003). A bidirectional process seems to be at work: good relationships foster adjustment, which in turn fosters good friendships. Online communication has had both positive and negative effects on adolescents' social relationships (Research in Action).

The increased intimacy of adolescent friendship reflects cognitive as well as emotional development. Closer intimacy means a greater ability and desire to share emotions and feelings. ©Pixtal/age fotostock

Romantic Relationships Romantic relationships are a central part of most adolescents' social worlds. With the onset of puberty, most heterosexual boys and girls begin to think about and interact more with members of the other sex. Typically, they move from mixed groups or group dates to one-on-one romantic relationships that, unlike other-sex friendships, they describe as involving passion and a sense of commitment (Lantagne & Furman, 2017). While they practice interacting with the opposite sex within the context of friendships, opposite-sex friends are unlikely to become romantic partners. Rather, romantic partners tend to come from different friendship networks (Kreager, Molloy, Moody & Feinberg, 2016).

Romantic relationships tend to become more intense and intimate across adolescence. By age 16, adolescents interact with and think about romantic partners more than parents, friends, or siblings (Bouchey & Furman, 2003). Not until late adolescence or early adulthood, though, do romantic relationships begin to serve the full gamut of emotional needs that such relationships can serve and then only in relatively long-term relationships (Furman & Wehner, 1997).

Relationships with parents may affect the quality of romantic relationships. For example, those teens who had a good relationship with their parents as teens had higher self-esteem and better relationship quality as young adults (Johnson & Galambos, 2014). Additionally, parental divorce and marital conflict has been associated with poorer relationship quality in teens, expressed as low commitment, greater endorsement of divorce, and high conflict (Cui & Fincham, 2010; Cui, Fincham & Durtschi, 2011).

Dating Violence Dating violence is a significant problem in the United States. The three common forms of dating violence are:

Physical—when a partner is hit, pinched, shoved, or kicked.

Emotional—when a partner is threatened or verbally abused.

Sexual—when a partner is forced to engage in a nonconsensual sex act.

Statistics indicate that about 10 percent of students have been victims of teen dating violence, including both physical and sexual abuse, but the rate is almost certainly underreported. When analyses are limited to only those students who were dating in the previous year, almost 21 percent of girls and 10.4 percent of boys reported experiencing

research in action

TEEN DATING AND TECHNOLOGY

Adolescent dating is a normative development that typically begins after puberty. Teenagers encounter a variety of romantic experiences, including mutually acknowledged relationships, fantasies, one-sided attractions, and non-relational sexual involvement. These experiences increase steadily over the adolescent years (Collins, Welsh & Furman, 2009). Between texting, messenger apps, and social media sites, adolescents have many outlets to explore early dating experiences, and an overwhelming majority of adolescents agree that technology plays a large role in dating (Vaterlaus, Tulane, Porter & Beckert, 2017).

Social media offer teenagers the opportunity to initiate romantic relationships with partners met online. Recent research suggests that while the majority of teens meet romantic partners in school, some teenagers develop online relationships (Korchmaros, Ybarra & Mitchell, 2015). Teenagers with online romantic partners fall into two camps: those who are popular offline, and those with difficulty forming offline relationships. Popular teens may encounter online partners as a by-product of their gregarious nature and everyday online activity, whereas other teenagers may intentionally seek partners online. LGBTQ adolescents have been identified as especially likely to initiate online relationships, possibly because of a lack of partners or safe, supportive spaces in which to be themselves in real life (Korchmaros et al., 2015).

Social media profiles are often used as a means of "checking out" new romantic interests early in relationships. After a first encounter, exchange of social media information may help gauge continued interest (Subrahmanyam & Greenfield, 2008). Photos and status updates are used to learn more about potential romantic partners. Adolescents also report "signaling" romantic interest by liking older photos and using embedded private messaging tools as a less intimidating means of initiating further communication (Van Ouystel, Van Gool, Walrave, Ponnet & Peeters, 2016).

Teenagers frequently use texting, instant messaging, and social media tools to communicate with existing partners as well. Today, these technologies are rooted in every stage of the relationship cycle—used in daily communication, to convey affection, to referee arguments, and to initiate "breakups and makeups" (Vaterlaus et al, 2017). Teenagers view technology as a means of reinforcing existing relationships (Subrahmanyam & Greenfield, 2008). On Facebook, adolescents report uploading joint photos of themselves as a couple to indirectly broadcast a relationship, rather than making an official status change (Van Ouystel et al., 2016).

Sexually charged conversation may take place using private electronic devices, in which parents may not be able to closely monitor activity (Subrahmanyam & Greenfield, 2008). Concerns abound about "sexting," the exchange of sexually explicit pictures of oneself, between adolescents. Large nationally representative studies suggest that only 4 percent of teenagers send nude or nearly nude photos of themselves via text, instant messaging, or online (Lenhart, 2009). Adolescents who do so tend to be sexually active and intend to share photos privately with a romantic partner (Kletke, Hallford & Mellor, 2014). Sexting has been linked with other risky behaviors, such as higher substance use, having concurrent sexual partners, and more current sexual partners (Ybarra & Mitchell, 2014).

what's your view How do you think social media, text messaging, and other technologies have affected the nature of adolescent dating? Do you think sexting is a form of adolescent risk-taking?

some form of teen dating violence (Vagi, Olsen, Basile & Vivolo-Kantor, 2015). The rates for emotional abuse are even higher: As many as 3 in 10 adolescents report being verbally or psychologically abused (Halpern, Young, Waller, Martin & Kupper, 2003). White students generally report lower levels of teen dating violence than African American or Hispanic students (Vagi et al., 2015).

In addition to the physical harm caused by this type of abuse, teens who are victims of dating violence are more likely to do poorly in school and to engage in risky behaviors such as drug and alcohol use. These students are also subject to eating disorders, depression, and suicide (Mulford & Giordano, 2008).

Risk factors that may predict violence include substance abuse, conflict and/or abuse in the home, antisocial peers, and living in neighborhoods with high rates of crime and drug use (Child Trends DataBank, 2010a, 2010b). Additionally, attitudes about the acceptability of violence within relationships, poor family relationship quality, mental health problems, and the use of aggressive media also predict violence (Vagi, Rothman, Latzman, Tharp, Hall & Breiding, 2013). Unhealthy relationships can last a lifetime as victims carry patterns of violence into future relationships.

Antisocial Behavior and Juvenile Delinquency

What influences young people to enage in—or refrain from—violence or other antisocial acts? What determines whether a juvenile delinquent will grow up to be a hardened criminal? The development of antisocial behavior involves a complex and reciprocal interaction between environment and biological risk factors (Van Goozen & Fairchild, 2008).

GENETIC AND NEUROLOGICAL FACTORS

Antisocial behavior tends to run in families. Analyses of many studies have concluded that genes influence 40 to 56 percent of the variation in antisocial behavior within a population, and 60 to 65 percent of the variation in aggressive antisociality (Ferguson, 2010; Rhee & Waldman, 2002; Tackett, Krueger, Iacono & McGue, 2005). Genes alone, however, are not predictive of antisocial behavior. Recent research findings suggest that although genetics influences delinquency, environmental influences including family, friends, and school affect gene expression (Guo, Roettger & Cai, 2008; Silberg, Maes & Eaves, 2012).

Neurobiological deficits, particularly in the portions of the brain that regulate reactions to stress, may help explain why some children become antisocial. As a result of these neurological deficits, which may result from the interaction of genetic factors or difficult temperament with adverse early environments, children may not receive or heed normal warning signals to restrain impulsive or reckless behavior (Van Goozen & Fairchild, 2008).

FAMILY, PEER, AND COMMUNITY INFLUENCES

Researchers have identified two types of antisocial behavior: an *early-onset* type beginning by age 11, which tends to lead to chronic juvenile delinquency in adolescence, and a milder, *late-onset* type beginning after puberty, which tends to arise temporarily in response to the changes of adolescence: the mismatch between biological and social maturity, increased desire for autonomy, and decreased adult supervision. Late-onset types tend to commit relatively minor offenses (Moffitt, 1993; Schulenberg & Zarrett, 2006).

The early-onset type of antisocial behavior is influenced, as Bronfenbrenner's theory would suggest, by interacting factors ranging from microsystem influences, such as parent-child hostility, poor parenting practices, and peer deviance, to macrosystem influences, such as community structure and neighborhood social support (Buehler, 2006; Tolan, Gorman-Smith & Henry, 2003). Evidence suggests that early-onset offenders are likely different from very early on, explaining both the early onset of their behaviors as well as their persistence into adulthood. For example, such adolescents show poor impulse control, are aggressive, and tend not to think about their future (Barker, Oliver & Maughan, 2010; Monahan, Cauffman & Steinberg, 2009).

Parents of children who become chronically antisocial may have failed to reinforce good behavior in early childhood and may have been harsh or inconsistent in their discipline (Coie & Dodge, 1998; Snyder, Cramer, Afrank & Patterson, 2005). The children may get payoffs for antisocial behavior: When they act up, they may gain attention or get their own way. These early negative patterns pave the way for negative peer influences that promote and reinforce antisocial behavior (B. B. Brown, Mounts, Lamborn & Steinberg, 1993; Collins et al., 2000). When constant criticism, angry coercion, or rude, uncooperative behavior characterizes parent-child interactions, the child tends to show aggressive behavior problems, which worsen the parent-child relationship (Buehler, 2006).

However, when parents show high warmth and low hostility, even delinquent teens tend to reduce their problematic behavior and behave more positively (Williams & Steinberg, 2011). Parents can also inoculate their teens from delinquency by discouraging

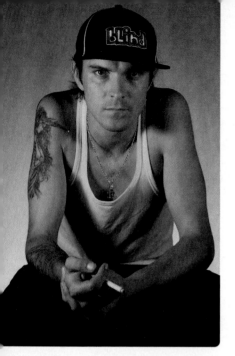

What are the chances this gang member will become a hardened criminal? Teenagers who don't have positive alternatives are more likely to adopt antisocial lifestyles. ©Rene Jansa/Shutterstock

association with deviant peers (Simons et al., 2001). Adolescents whose parents know where they are and what they are doing are less likely to engage in delinquent acts (Laird, Pettit, Bates & Dodge, 2003) or to associate with deviant peers (Lloyd & Anthony, 2003).

The choice of antisocial peers is affected mainly by environmental factors (Iervolino et al., 2002). Young people gravitate to others brought up like themselves who are similar in school achievement, adjustment, and prosocial or antisocial tendencies (Collins et al., 2000). As in childhood, antisocial adolescents tend to have antisocial friends, and their antisocial behavior increases when they associate with each other (Dishion, McCord & Poulin, 1999; Hartup & Stevens, 1999). The way antisocial teenagers talk, laugh, or smirk about rule-breaking and nod knowingly among themselves seems to constitute a sort of "deviancy training" (Dishion et al., 1999). Not all children respond in the same way, however. Teens who are genetically predisposed to antisocial behavior respond more strongly to maladaptive peer group norms than other children (Vitaro, et al., 2015).

Family economic circumstances may influence the development of antisocial behavior. Poor children are more likely than other children to commit antisocial acts, and those whose families are continuously poor tend to become more antisocial with time (Macmillan, McMorris & Kruttschnitt, 2004). Moreover, even within individual children, those whose families rose in and out of poverty showed more delinquent behavior when their families had less money than when they were more financially well off (Rekker et al., 2015). When families rise from poverty while a child is still young, the child is no more likely to develop behavior problems than a child whose family was never poor (Macmillan et al., 2004).

Weak neighborhood social organization in a disadvantaged community can influence delinquency through its effects on parenting behavior and peer deviance (Chung & Steinberg, 2006) as well as on norms about the use of antisocial or violent acts (Stewart & Simons, 2010). *Collective efficacy* is a neighborhood-level influence involving the willingness of individuals in a neighborhood to work together to achieve a common goal, intervene if a problem is apparent, and help each other out in times of need (Sampson, 1997). A combination of nurturant, involved parenting and collective efficacy can discourage adolescents from association with deviant peers (Brody et al., 2001).

PREVENTING AND TREATING DELINQUENCY

Because juvenile delinquency has roots early in childhood, so should preventive efforts that attack the multiple factors that can lead to delinquency. Adolescents who have taken part in certain early childhood intervention programs are less likely to get in trouble than their equally underprivileged peers (Reynolds, Temple, Ou, Arteaga & White, 2011; Yoshikawa, 1994). Effective programs target high-risk urban children and last at least 2 years during the child's first 5 years. They influence children directly, through high-quality day care or education, and at the same time indirectly, by offering families assistance and support geared to their needs (Schweinhart et al., 1993; Yoshikawa, 1994; Zigler et al., 1992).

These programs operate on Bronfenbrenner's mesosystem by affecting interactions between the home and the school or child care center. The programs also go one step further, to the exosystem, by creating supportive parent networks and linking parents with such community services as prenatal and postnatal care and educational and vocational counseling (Yoshikawa, 1994; Zigler et al., 1992; Reynolds et al., 2011). Through their multipronged approach, these interventions have an impact on several early risk factors for delinquency.

Once children reach adolescence, especially in poor, crime-ridden neighborhoods, interventions need to focus on spotting troubled adolescents and preventing gang recruitment (Tolan et al., 2003). Successful programs boost parenting skills through better monitoring, behavioral management, and neighborhood social support. For example, recent research has shown that in early adolescence, maintaining appropriate levels of control and nurturing a close and positive relationship has protective effects against teenage antisocial behaviors later in adolescence, especially for mothers (Vieno, Nation, Pastore & Santinello, 2009).

Programs such as teen hangouts and summer camps for behaviorally disturbed youth can be counterproductive because they bring together groups of deviant youth who tend to reinforce each other's deviancy. Similarly, programs such as Scared Straight, in which at-risk teens visit prisons and speak with inmates, tend to result in higher levels of delinquency and thus have fallen out of favor (Petrosino, Turpin-Petrosino, Hollis-Peel & Lavenberg, 2013). Moving juveniles through the juvenile court system rather than diversion programs (such as counseling referrals) also tends to increase future offending (Petrosino, Guckenburg & Turpin-Petrosino, 2013). More effective programs—Scouts, sports, and church activities—integrate deviant youth into the nondeviant mainstream. Structured, adult-monitored or school-based activities after school, on weekend evenings, and in summer, when adolescents are most likely to be idle and to get in trouble, can reduce their exposure to settings that encourage antisocial behavior (Dodge, Dishion & Lansford, 2006).

Fortunately, the great majority of adolescents do not get into serious trouble. Those who show disturbed behavior can—and should—be helped. With love, guidance, and support, adolescents can avoid risks, build on their strengths, and explore their possibilities as they approach adult life.

summary and key terms

The Search for Identity

- A central concern during adolescence is the search for identity. Erik Erikson described this psychosocial conflict as *identity versus identity confusion*. The virtue that should arise from this conflict is *fidelity*.
- James Marcia described four identity statuses: identity achievement, foreclosure, moratorium, and identity diffusion.
- Researchers differ on whether girls and boys take different paths to identity formation.
- Ethnicity is an important part of identity. Minority adolescents seem to go through stages of ethnic identity development much like Marcia's identity statuses.

identity, identity versus identity confusion, fidelity, identity statuses, crisis, commitment, identity achievement, foreclosure, moratorium, identity diffusion, cultural socialization

Sexuality

- Sexual orientation appears to be influenced by an interaction of biological and environmental factors.
- Because of lack of social acceptance, the course of homosexual identity and relationship development may vary.
- Teenage sexual activity involves risks of pregnancy and sexually transmitted infections. Adolescents at greatest risk are those who begin sexual activity early, have multiple partners, do not use contraceptives, and are ill-informed about sex.
- Regular condom use is the best safeguard for sexually active teens.
- Comprehensive sex education programs delay sexual initiation and encourage contraceptive use. Abstinence-only programs are not as effective.
- Teenage pregnancy and birthrates in the United States have declined.
- Teenage childbearing often has negative outcomes, including ill health and financial hardship, and risk of ineffective parenting.

sexting, sexual orientation, sexually transmitted infections (STIs)

Relationships with Family, Peers, and Adult Society

- Full-scale adolescent rebellion is unusual. For the majority of teens, adolescence is a fairly smooth transition. For the few deeply troubled teens, it can predict a difficult adulthood.
- Adolescents spend an increasing amount of time with peers, but relationships with parents continue to be influential.
- Conflict with parents tends to be greatest during early adolescence. Authoritative parenting is associated with the most positive outcomes.
- Effects of family structure and maternal employment on adolescents' development may depend on such factors as economic resources, the quality of the home environment, and how closely parents monitor adolescents.
- Relationships with siblings tend to become more distant during adolescence, and the balance of power between older and younger siblings becomes more equal.
- The influence of the peer group is strongest in early adolescence. The structure of the peer group becomes more elaborate, involving cliques and crowds as well as friendships.
- Friendships, especially among girls, become more intimate, stable, and supportive in adolescence.
- Romantic relationships meet a variety of needs and develop with age and experience.

adolescent rebellion, individuation

Antisocial Behavior and Juvenile Delinquency

- Chronic delinquency generally stems from early-onset antisociality. It is associated with multiple, interacting risk factors, including ineffective parenting, school failure, peer and neighborhood influence, and low socioeconomic status. Programs that attack risk factors from an early age have had success.

chapter

13

Physical and Cognitive Development in Emerging and Young Adulthood

learning objectives

Describe the transition from adolescence to adulthood.

Summarize physical development in young adults.

Discuss sexuality in young adults.

Characterize cognitive changes in early adulthood.

Identify examples of the roles of experience, culture, and gender in adult moral development.

Explain how emerging adults make the transitions to higher education and work.

©Image Source/Getty Images

In this chapter, we look at emerging and young adults' physical functioning and factors that can affect health, fitness, sexuality, and reproduction. We discuss features of their cognition and how education can stimulate its growth. We examine moral development. Finally, we discuss entering the world of work.

Emerging Adulthood

When does a person become an adult? For most people, three criteria define adulthood: (1) accepting responsibility for oneself, (2) making independent decisions, and (3) becoming financially independent (Arnett, 2006).

In industrialized countries, the achievement of these goals takes longer and follows far more varied routes than in the past. Before the mid-twentieth century, a young man just out of high school typically would seek a stable job, marry, and start a family. For a young woman, the usual route to adulthood was marriage, which occurred as soon as she found a suitable mate.

Since the 1950s, the technological revolution made specialized training increasingly essential. The ages at first marriage and childbirth have shifted sharply upward as both women and men pursued higher education or vocational opportunities and as cohabitation became more acceptable (Furstenberg, Rumbaut & Setterstein, 2005; Lundberg & Pollack, 2014). Today the road to adulthood may be marked by multiple milestones—entering college, working, moving away from home, getting married, and having children—and the order and timing of these transitions vary (Schulenberg, O'Malley, Bachman & Johnston, 2005).

Thus some developmental scientists suggest that, for the many young people in industrialized societies, the late teens through the mid- to late twenties has become a distinct period of the life span now known as **emerging adulthood.** It is a time during which young people are no longer adolescents but have not yet settled into adult roles (Arnett, 2006; Furstenberg et al., 2005). Although the uncertainty and turmoil that can mark this process can be distressing, overall most young people have a positive view of their future and look forward to their adult lives (Arnett, 2007a). It is important to note that this exploratory process is not shared by all young adults in the world. It is largely tied to development in Western countries, especially among relatively affluent young people.

emerging adulthood
Proposed transitional period between adolescence and adulthood commonly found in industrialized countries.

PHYSICAL DEVELOPMENT

Health and Fitness

Young adults in the United States generally enjoy the benefits of good health, but they increasingly suffer from a range of health-related risks tied to modern lifestyles. In the following section, we review some of the more important influences.

HEALTH STATUS AND HEALTH ISSUES

During this period, the foundation for lifelong physical functioning continues to be laid. Behavioral factors—what young adults eat, whether they get enough sleep, how physically active they are, and whether they smoke, drink, or use drugs—contribute greatly to health and well-being. Moreover, these environmental factors can result in epigenetic changes in the expression of particular genes that can have lifelong consequences (Dolinoy & Jirtle, 2008). The habits that young adults develop during this time in the life span tend to become ingrained over time and are highly predictive of the likelihood they will experience good health at older ages (Liu et al., 2012).

Most emerging and young adults in the United States report that they are in good to excellent health (NCHS, 2006). Accidents are the leading cause of death for young Americans aged 20 to 44 (Centers for Disease Control, 2017). Still, mortality rates for this group as a whole have been nearly cut in half in the past 50 years (Kochanek, Murphy, Anderson & Scott, 2004). The health issues of these years mirror those of adolescence; however, rates of injury, homicide, and substance use peak at this time. Whites and Asians are the most likely to be in good health, although whites' health tends to decline as they age into adulthood. The worst health prognosis is generally found for Native Americans, followed by African Americans. Latinos generally occupied a middle position (Harris, Gordon-Larsen, Chantala & Udry, 2006).

Most young adults, like this young man, are in prime physical condition.
©Digital Vision/Getty Images

In the past, young people generally aged out of many social service programs such as Medicaid, Children's Health Insurance Program, or support systems in place within the school system. At the same time, many moved away from home and began living independently. Emerging and young adults have the highest poverty rate and the lowest level of health insurance of any age group, and they often have no regular access to health care (Callahan & Cooper, 2005; Park, Mulye, Adams, Brindis & Irwin, 2006). The implementation of the Affordable Care Act in 2010—including both an individual mandate and the provision allowing children up to age 26 to remain on their parents' insurance—resulted in sharp rises in health care access, health care utilization, and reported health indicators in young adults (Barbaresco, Courtemanche & Qi, 2015; Antwi, Moriya & Simon, 2015; Sommers, Gunja, Finegold & Musco, 2015). The impact of the current administration's policies on health care remains to be seen.

GENETIC INFLUENCES ON HEALTH

The expression of any disorder, including obesity, certain cancers, and mental health conditions (such as alcoholism and depression), is the product of an interaction between genes and environment.

For example, we can examine a person's likelihood of developing symptoms of depression. A genetic variant influences this propensity. However, this variant is highly affected by environmental influences. In the presence of a supportive family environment, depression risk is not elevated. In the absence of such an environment, the gene increases risk (Taylor, Lehman, Kiefe & Seeman, 2006).

BEHAVIORAL INFLUENCES ON HEALTH AND FITNESS

What people know about health affects what they do, and what they do affects how they feel. Yet *knowing* about good (and bad) health habits is not enough. Personality, emotions, and social surroundings often outweigh what people know they should do. In the next section, we look at both direct and indirect influences on health.

Diet and Nutrition   Nutrition is important for physical and mental health. An estimated 365,000 U.S. adults die each year from causes related to poor diet and lack of physical activity (Mokdad, Marks, Stroup & Gerberding, 2005). In one study starting when participants were roughly 13 years old, a Mediterranean diet (high in vegetables and healthy fats, and with moderate meat intake) was associated with healthier heart indices at 36 years of age (Laar et al., 2013).

The World Health Organization recommends a diet rich in fruits, vegetables, whole grains, and unsaturated fats. Although such a diet is associated with reduced risk for a wide variety of different cancers (Couto et al., 2011), that reduced risk may well be the result of other factors: For example, people who eat such a diet tend to live overall healthier lives (Boffetta et al., 2010).

Obesity/Overweight   Between 1980 and 2016, the global obesity rate more than doubled, from 4.8 to 11 percent in men, and from 7.9 to 15 percent in women. Much of this increase can be attributed to unintended consequences of globalization, including increases in the availability of nutrient-poor, high-calorie processed foods and urbanization of the environment (Malik, Willet & Hu, 2012; World Health Organization, 2017; Figure 13.1).

In the United States, the average man or woman is more than 24 pounds heavier than in the early 1960s but is only about 1 inch taller (Flegal, Carroll, Ogden & Curtin, 2010). Over 36 percent of adults 20 years and older were obese in 2014, with a higher rate in women (38.3 percent) than men (34.3 percent). Rates were highest in African Americans (48.1 percent), Hispanics (42.4 percent), and non-Hispanic white (34.5) and lowest in Asian Americans (11.7 percent) (Ogden, Carroll, Fryar & Flegal, 2015).

What explains the obesity epidemic? Experts point to an increase in snacking (Zizza, Siega-Riz & Popkin, 2001), availability of inexpensive fast foods, supersized portions, high-fat diets, labor-saving technologies including highly processed foods, and sedentary recreational pursuits, such as television and computers (Pereira et al., 2005). An inherited

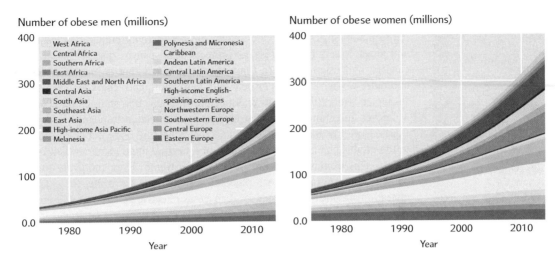

Number of obese men (millions)

West Africa
Central Africa
Southern Africa
East Africa
Middle East and North Africa
Central Asia
South Asia
Southeast Asia
East Asia
High-income Asia Pacific
Melanesia
Polynesia and Micronesia
Caribbean
Andean Latin America
Central Latin America
Southern Latin America
High-income English-
speaking countries
Northwestern Europe
Southwestern Europe
Central Europe
Eastern Europe

Number of obese women (millions)

FIGURE 13.1

Global Trends in Body Mass Index, 1975–2015

Worldwide, obesity is growing. In 1975, approximately 34 million men and 71 million women were medically obese. In 2014, that number rose to 266 million men and 375 million women.

Source: NCD Risk Factor Collaboration. "Trends in adult body-mass index in 200 countries from 1975 to 2014: a pooled analysis of 1698 population-based measurement studies with 19·2 million participants." *The Lancet*, 387(10026), 2016, 1377–1396.

tendency toward obesity may interact with environmental and behavioral factors (Choquet & Meyre, 2011).

Obesity can lead to depression, and vice versa (Markowitz, Friedman & Arent, 2008). It also carries risks of high blood pressure, heart disease, stroke, diabetes, gallstones, arthritis and other muscular and skeletal disorders, and some cancers, and it diminishes quality and length of life (USDHHS, 2013; Harvard Medical School, 2004c; NCHS, 2004; Ogden, Carroll, McDowell & Flegal, 2007). Obesity also impacts health care costs. Estimates are that obesity costs the United States approximately $190 billion a year in health care related costs or some 21 percent of total health care expenditures (Hruby & Hu, 2015).

Lifestyle changes (dietary change plus exercise) or drug treatments have sustained weight-loss targets for 2 or more years (Powell, Calvin & Calvin, 2007), but such losses are difficult for many people to sustain for longer periods of time. People who lose weight must fight both their physiology, which includes altered satiety and metabolic influences, as well as their propensity to return to earlier behaviors that contributed to their weight in the first place (MacLean et al., 2015). Weight-loss maintenance is possible, but requires permanent lifestyle changes and continued behavioral change (Thomas, Bond, Phelan, Hill & Wing, 2014). Unfortunately, many people engage in unhealthy "yo-yo" dieting, which ultimately results in a lowered metabolism, and hence even more difficulty with weight management.

Another option available for weight loss for obese adults is bariatric surgery. Bariatric surgery is any surgery that is carried out to induce weight loss, and it generally involves rerouting or removing parts of the stomach or small intestine. Bariatric surgery results in more consistent and sustained weight loss and a reduction in risk profile for obesity-related disease in most adults than diet or lifestyle changes. However, it does carry risks, and while overall mortality is low, 10 to 17 percent of adults experience complications as a result of the surgery (Chang et al., 2014).

Eating Disorders While eating too much and gaining excessive weight is the more common nutritional issue, eating disorders that focus on attempts to keep weight low also are a problem in many countries (Qian et al., 2013). Overall, lifetime prevalence rates of eating disorders are low, somewhere between 0.3 and 0.6 percent (Favaro, Ferrara & Santonastaso, 2004), but this still represents a substantial amount of pain and suffering, especially as many of those suffering from eating disorders fail to get treatment (Campbell & Peebles, 2014). The most common of the eating disorders are anorexia nervosa and bulimia nervosa.

Incorporating more activity into daily life, say, by biking to work instead of driving, can be as effective as structured exercise.
©LarsZ/Shutterstock

Physical Activity People who are physically active reap many benefits. Aside from helping to maintain desirable body weight, physical activity builds muscles; strengthens heart and lungs; lowers blood pressure; protects against heart disease, stroke, diabetes, several cancers, and osteoporosis (a thinning of the bones that is most prevalent in middle-age and older women); relieves anxiety and depression; and lengthens life (Reiner, Niermann, Jekauc & Woll, 2013; Barnes & Schoenborn, 2003; Bernstein et al., 2005; NCHS, 2004). Moreover, research suggests that exercise is also related to cognitive functioning (Guiney, Lucas, Cotter & Machado, 2015), and that a healthy body is one of the variables related to the establishment and maintenance of a healthy mind (Kramer, Erickson & Colcombe, 2006). This exercise does not have to be extreme. Even moderate exercise has health benefits. Incorporating more physical activity into daily life—for example, by walking instead of driving short distances—can be as effective as structured exercise.

Despite public health recommendations from both the Centers for Disease Control and the American College of Sports Medicine regarding guidelines for appropriate levels of exercise and strength training, Americans have not made substantial progress toward implementing these recommendations (CDC, 2000a). Generally, adults aged 18 to 64 should engage in 75 to 150 minutes of aerobic exercise (depending on intensity levels) and muscle-strengthening activities on at least 2 days a week (CDC, 2017c). Despite the fact that this represents less than half an hour a day of exercise, many Americans do not meet these guidelines.

Stress A growing body of research suggests that our psychological health affects our physical health, and that high levels of chronic stress are related to a host of physical and immunological impairments (Ho, Neo, Chua, Cheak & Mak, 2010).

There are individual differences in how young adults handle stress (Howland, Armeli, Feinn & Tennen, 2017). In some cases, stress may lead young adults to engage in risky behaviors such as drinking or smoking to manage that stress (White et al., 2006; Rice & Van Arsdale, 2010), behaviors that have consequences for their health. Also, stressed out college students are more likely to eat junk food, are less likely to exercise (Hudd et al., 2000), and tend to have poor quality or insufficient sleep (Lund, Reider, Whiting & Prichard, 2010).

There are also gender differences in how young adults typically cope with stress. Emotion-focused coping consists of attempts to manage the emotions associated with experiencing a particular event by such tactics as refusing to think about an issue or reframing the event in a positive light. Problem-focused coping involves addressing an issue head-on and developing action-oriented ways of managing and changing a bad situation (Lazarus & Folkman, 1984). College-age women are more likely to use emotion-focused strategies than are college-age men. Moreover, at the same time, college-age women experience overall higher levels of stress (Brougham et al., 2009). Relationships may help people cope with stress. In one study, individuals who were secure in their relationships with others experienced less interpersonal stress and used more adaptive coping styles (Seiffge-Krenke, 2006).

Sleep Many emerging and young adults often go without adequate sleep. Among college students, family life stress, together with academic stress, is associated with high levels of insomnia (Bernert, Merrill, Braithwaite, Van Orden & Joiner, 2007; Lund et al., 2010).

Sleep deprivation affects not only physical health but cognitive, emotional, and social functioning as well. In a poll by the National Sleep Foundation (2001), respondents said they were more likely to make mistakes, become impatient or aggravated when waiting, or get upset with their children or others when they had not had enough sleep the night before.

The primary cognitive consequence of a lack of sleep is impaired attention and vigilance (Kerkhof & VanDongen, 2010; Lim & Dinges, 2010). However, there are also consequences for verbal learning (Horne, 2000), some aspects of memory (Harrison & Horne, 2000b), high-level decision making (Harrison & Horne, 2000a), inhibitory processes (Anderson & Platten, 2011), and speech articulation (Harrison & Horne, 1997). Sleep deprivation also increases distractibility (Blagrove, Alexander & Horne, 1995) and impulsivity (Anderson & Platten, 2011). Chronic sleep deprivation (less than 6 hours of sleep each night for three or

window on the world

ADULT LIFESTYLE HABITS, EXERCISE, LEISURE, AND NUTRITION AROUND THE WORLD

Globalization has resulted in numerous positive contributions to the developing world. For example, vaccination and clean water campaigns have improved the health status of millions of people, and reproductive health care in particular has benefited many women. However, globalization has a dark side as well. As the world becomes increasingly globalized, the lifestyle patterns found in the developed world are becoming more common in different countries. People across the world are more likely to make unhealthy lifestyle choices, including smoking, drug and alcohol abuse, sedentary behaviors, unhealthy diets, and high stress levels. There is a consequent rise in cardiovascular problems, obesity, joint and skeletal problems, depression, hypertension, type 2 diabetes, and a variety of other preventable physical and mental health conditions (Farhud, 2015).

There is good news; the risk of disease can be reduced by up to 80 percent with a combination of maintaining a healthy weight and diet, not smoking, and engaging in regular exercise (Trovato, 2012). Change is possible. A study in the Netherlands followed a group of adults over a 5-year period and successfully targeted lifestyle factors. Over the 5 years 38 percent of the adults in the study were successful in changing their lifestyle, and showed a 46 to 68 lower risk for cardiovascular problems and up to an 87 percent lower risk for overall mortality (Hulsegge et al., 2016).

Successful interventions have also shown that it is possible to increase people's physical activities. A study conducted in Bourne, England, found that six months after joining a doctor-prescribed exercise program, 70 percent of participants had improved energy levels, 80 percent improved their physical abilities, and 50 percent had achieved weight loss.

Importantly, these changes also resulted in a 90 percent improvement in well-being for participants (Hancock, 2012). In Mexico, a program called Pausa Para Tu Salud ("Break for your health") was created to encourage employees at one company to take a break each day for 30 minutes to engage in exercise. Participants noticed a decrease in waist circumference and in overall blood pressure, as well as reporting higher levels of energy (Hancock, 2012).

As the world changes, our risks have also changed. Research is showing a new global health challenge emerging: too much Internet use. In 2015, 78 percent of adults in Britain used the Internet every day (Office for National Statistics, 2015). A British study indicated too much Internet and social media use causes a decline in physical human contact. This decline is associated with difficulties with basic social skills and appropriate emotional reactions, as well as a short attention span and poor self-control (Paton, 2012). A Swedish study looking at mobile phones use showed that those with high levels of use on their mobile phones reported sleep disturbances and symptoms of depression (Thomee, Harenstam & Hagberg, 2011). Both studies indicated the risk of negative health factors increased with use of more than an hour per day. As the use of technology spreads beyond the borders of the developed world, we can expect to see the influence of this new risk on developing countries as well.

what's your view

What do your lifestyle habits look like? Are there things you need to change to live a healthier life?

---

more nights) can seriously worsen cognitive performance (Van Dongen, Maislin, Mullington & Dinges, 2003). Finally, sleep deprivation has been linked to depression (Murphy & Peterson, 2015), and insomnia and sleep disturbances also are related to the risk of postpartum depression (Wisner, Parry & Piontek, 2002). Sleep deprivation can be dangerous on the road. Indeed, performance impairments related to even partial sleep deprivation have been shown to be similar to those found after drinking alcohol (Elmenhorst et al., 2009).

Adequate sleep improves learning of complex motor skills and consolidates previous learning (Tucker et al., 2017). Compared to adults who did not sleep well the previous night, adults who had a good night's sleep were more engaged with their work the next day (Kuhnel, Zacher, DeBloom & Bledow, 2017). Even a short nap can prevent burnout—oversaturation of the brain's perceptual processing systems (Mednick et al., 2002).

Because smoking is addictive, it is hard to quit despite awareness of health risks. ©Ryan McVay/Photodisc/Getty Images

Smoking Smoking is the leading preventable cause of death worldwide, linked not only to lung cancer but also to increased risks of heart disease, stroke, and chronic lung disease. Smoking is linked to approximately 1 out of every 5 American deaths (CDC, 2017c). Exposure to passive, or secondhand, smoke has been shown to cause circulatory problems and increase the risk of cardiovascular disease (Otsuka et al., 2001) and may increase the risk of cervical cancer (Trimble et al., 2005). In 2000, smoking killed almost 5 million people worldwide, about half in developing countries and half in industrialized countries (Ezzati & Lopez, 2004).

Approximately 17.8 percent of men and 13.9 percent of women over age 18 in the United States are current smokers. Smoking rates are higher in whites (17.8 percent) and African Americans (17.4 percent) and lower in Hispanic adults (10.2 percent) (Clarke, Norris & Schiller, 2017). In recent years, e-cigarettes have become more popular, and currently 3.7 percent of adults smoke e-cigarettes (CDC, 2015).

People start smoking for a variety of reasons; however, the primary reason they continue to do so even when they would prefer to stop is the addictive nature of nicotine, a substance found in tobacco. A tendency to addiction may be genetic (Ware & Munafo, 2015; Lerman et al., 1999; Sabol et al., 1999). And the link between genetic susceptibility and likelihood of addiction is strongest for those who begin to smoke at a young age (Weiss et al., 2008). Smoking is strongly associated with socioeconomic level as well; those adults with less than a high school education are 3 times more likely to be smokers than those with a bachelor's degree or higher (NCHS, 2008).

Giving up smoking reduces the risks of heart disease, cancer, and stroke (USDHHS, 2010). Nicotine chewing gum, nicotine patches, and nicotine nasal sprays and inhalers, especially when combined with counseling, can help addicted persons taper off gradually and safely (Cepeda-Benito, Reynoso & Erath, 2004). Replacing cigarettes with e-cigarettes shows promise as well (Siegel, Tanwar & Wood, 2011; Cahn & Siegel, 2011). Although e-cigarettes are still harmful, they are less so than cigarettes. The use of drugs that help manage cravings without the provision of nicotine also can be helpful (Gonzalez et al., 2006).

Quitting smoking is difficult, and many smoking cessation programs have low success rates. However, most smokers attempt to quit on their own and tend not to use either behavioral therapies or medical support (Shiffman, Brockwell, Pillitteri & Gitchell, 2008). Only about 4 to 7 percent of smokers manage to quit for good on any one attempt, although medication can increase the 6-month success rate to approximately 25 to 33 percent (American Cancer Society, 2011). Many smokers require multiple attempts to quit the habit.

Alcohol Use The United States is a drinking society, and alcohol use peaks in emerging adulthood. Among adults ages 18 to 25, approximately 58 percent reported drinking alcohol in the past month (SAMHSA, 2015). Almost 32 percent of men and 19 percent of women had an episode of binge drinking in the past year (Clarke, Norris & Schiller, 2017).

College is a prime time and place for drinking, and college students tend to drink more frequently and more heavily than their noncollegiate peers. In 2007, nearly 58 percent of full-time college students ages 18 to 22 had used alcohol in the past month as compared to 42 percent of their noncollegiate peers. Moreover 12.5 percent of college students drank heavily; and about 37.9 percent had engaged in binge drinking (NIAAA, 2016; Figure 13.2). Although light to moderate alcohol consumption is not harmful (Ruitenberg et al., 2002), heavy drinking over the years may lead to cirrhosis of the liver, other gastrointestinal disorders (including ulcers), pancreatic disease, certain cancers, heart failure, stroke, damage to the nervous system, psychoses, and other medical problems (NIAAA, 2017; Fuchs et al., 1995).

Alcohol use is associated with other risks characteristic of emerging adulthood, such as traffic accidents, crime, HIV infection (Leigh, 1999), illicit drug and tobacco use (Hingson, Heeren, Winter & Wechsler,

Percent

[Bar chart showing values by age group 18–20 and 21–25]

Category	18–20	21–25
Past month alcohol use	52	69
Binge alcohol use	36	46
Heavy alcohol use	13	14

Age
18–20
21–25

FIGURE 13.2

Current (Past Month) Alcohol Use, Binge Drinking, and Heavy Alcohol Use among Full-Time American College Students Ages 18 to 25

Source: Substance Abuse and Mental Health Services Administration (SAMHSA), Office of Applied Studies. *State estimates of persons aged 18 or older driving under the influence of alcohol or illicit drugs.* NSDUH Report. Rockville, MD: Author, April 18, 2008.

2005), and the likelihood of committing sexual assault (Brecklin & Ullman, 2010). Academic consequences are common for college students (NIAAA, 2016). From 2004 to 2006, an estimated 15 percent of U.S. drivers age 18 or older said that in the past year they drove under the influence of alcohol, and nearly 5 percent said they drove under the influence of drugs (SAMHSA, 2008).

Risky drinking is defined as consuming more than 14 drinks a week or 4 drinks on any single day for men, and more than 7 drinks a week or 3 drinks on any single day for women. Approximately 1 out of 4 people are risky drinkers, at risk for alcoholism and liver disease, as well as physical, mental, and social problems as a result of their drinking (NIAAA, 2016).

risky drinking
Consuming more than 14 drinks a week or 4 drinks on any single day for men, and more than 7 drinks a week or 3 drinks on any single day for women.

Individual variables affect the likelihood of alcohol consumption. For example, race and ethnicity can affect drinking patterns. The group reporting the highest consumption of alcohol is Native Americans, followed by whites, and the lowest levels of use are reported by Central Americans, African Americans, and Asian Americans (Wallace et al., 2005). Gender affects consumption patterns as well, with females generally consuming less alcohol overall as well as having lower levels of binge drinking (NIAAA, 2016). However, this gender gap in alcohol consumption appears to be shrinking (Keyes, Grant & Hasin, 2007).

INDIRECT INFLUENCES ON HEALTH

Indirect influences on health include income, education, and race/ethnicity. Relationships also seem to make a difference, as do the paths young people take into adulthood.

Socioeconomic Status and Race/Ethnicity The connection between socioeconomic status (SES) and health has been widely documented (Williams, Priest & Anderson, 2016). Higher-income people rate their health as better and live longer than lower-income people (NCHS, 2017). Education is important too. The less schooling people have had, the greater the chance that they will develop and die from communicable diseases, injuries, or chronic ailments, or that they will become victims of homicide or suicide (NCHS, 2004; Pamuk, Makuc, Heck, Reuben & Lochner, 1998). Socioeconomic circumstances in both childhood and adulthood are important determinants of risk for cardiovascular disease and, even more so, of stroke (Galobardes, Smith & Lynch, 2006).

This does not mean that income and education *cause* good health; instead, they are related to environmental and lifestyle factors that do. Better-educated and more affluent people tend to have healthier diets and better preventive health care and medical treatment. They exercise more, are less likely to be overweight, smoke less, are less likely to use illicit drugs, and are more likely to use alcohol in moderation (NCHS, 2004; SAMHSA, 2004b). Moreover, the less affluent are more likely to live close to a polluting facility (Mohai, Lantz, Morenoff, House & Mero, 2009) and show elevated levels of lead and other toxins in their blood (Bellinger, 2008).

Race and ethnicity matter as well. However, because many minorities in the United States also tend to have a lower SES, their health issues stem from that rather than from minority status per se (Kiefe et al., 2000). Forty-one percent of African American men and 45 percent of African American women aged 20 years and older suffer from high blood pressure (CDC, 2017l). African Americans also are more likely to be diagnosed with and die from diabetes, (Kirk et al., 2006) and about twice as likely as white people to die in young adulthood, in part because young African American men are far more likely to be victims of homicide (NCHS, 2006).

Factors associated with SES do not tell the whole story, however. For example, although African Americans smoke less than white Americans, they metabolize more nicotine in the blood, face higher risks of lung cancer, and have more trouble breaking the habit (Caraballo et al., 1998; Sellers, 1998). Similarly, even when controlling for SES, African Americans are more likely to suffer from and die of heart disease (Williams et al., 2016). A review of more than 100 studies found that racial/ethnic minorities tend to receive lower-quality health care than white people do, even when insurance status, income, age, and severity of conditions are similar (Smedley, Stith & Nelson, 2002).

Living in poverty, as do this mother and her daughter who share a room in a shelter, can affect health through poor nutrition, substandard housing, and inadequate health care. ©David Wells//The Image Works

Although there is a clear association between relationships and health, it's not clear which is the cause and which the effect.
©Sam Edwards/Glow Images

Relationships and Health Social relationships seem to be vital to health and well-being. Research has identified at least two interrelated aspects of the social environment that can promote health: *social integration* and *social support* (Cohen, 2004).

Social integration is active engagement in a broad range of social relationships, activities, and roles. Social integration has repeatedly been associated with lower mortality rates (Berkman & Glass, 2000; Rutledge et al., 2004). People with wide social networks and multiple social roles are more likely to survive heart attacks and less likely to be anxious or depressed than people with more limited social networks and roles (Cohen, Gottlieb & Underwood, 2000) and even are less susceptible to colds (Cohen, Janicki-Deverts, Turner & Doyle, 2015). In addition, it appears that online social networking sites, such as Facebook, can provide some of those benefits via online interaction and support (Hobbs, Burke, Christakis & Fowler, 2016; Ellison, Steinfield & Lampe, 2007). Some of these processes may be mediated by stress hormones such as cortisol. In other words, the beneficial effects of social integration may in part be due to the decreases in stress levels that strong social ties can engender (Grant, Hamer & Steptoe, 2009).

Social support refers to material, informational, and psychological resources derived from the social network on which a person can rely for help in coping with stress. In highly stressful situations, people who are in touch with others may be more likely to eat and sleep sensibly, get enough exercise, and avoid substance abuse, and are less likely to be distressed, anxious, or depressed or even to die (Cohen, 2004).

Because marriage offers a readily available system for both social integration and social support, it is not surprising that marriage tends to benefit health (Robles, Slatcher, Trombello & McGinn, 2014). Married people, particularly in young adulthood, tend to be healthier physically and psychologically than those who are never-married, cohabiting, widowed, separated, or divorced (Schoenborn, 2004). Dissolving a marriage, or a cohabitation, tends to have negative effects on physical or mental health or both—but so, apparently, does remaining in a bad relationship (Wu & Hart, 2002). People in an unhappy marriage have poorer health than single adults, and even a supportive network of friends and family does not buffer this effect (Holt-Lundstad, Birmingham & Jones, 2008).

However, the effects of marriage and health can be both direct and indirect. Most notably, two-income families are more likely to have access to health insurance, which is in turn related to general health. This can help explain the higher risk for negative health consequences for some people in same-sex relationships, as they are less likely to have health insurance (Buchmueller & Carpenter, 2010). Additionally, passage of same-sex marriage laws seems to result in broad health benefits to gay couples, perhaps as a result of decreasing discrimination and prejudice, and thereby stress (Hatzenbuehler, O'Cleirigh & Bradford, 2012).

MENTAL HEALTH PROBLEMS

The emerging adult transition brings an end to the relatively structured years of high school. The freedom to make life decisions and choose diverse paths is often liberating, but the responsibility to rely on oneself and to become financially self-supporting can be overwhelming (Schulenberg & Zarrett, 2006).

alcoholism
Chronic disease involving dependence on use of alcohol, causing interference with normal functioning and fulfillment of obligations.

Alcoholism Alcohol abuse and dependence are the most prevalent substance disorders, as reported by 6.2 percent of the U.S. adult population (NIAAA, 2016). Alcohol dependence, or **alcoholism,** is a long-term physical condition characterized by compulsive drinking that a person is unable to control. The heritability of a tendency to alcoholism is about 50 percent (Verhulst, Neale & Kendler, 2015). Alcoholism, like other addictions, seems to result from long-lasting changes in patterns of neural signal transmission in the brain. Exposure to alcohol creates a euphoric mental state accompanied by neurological changes that produce feelings of discomfort and craving when it is no longer present. From 6 to 48 hours after the last drink, alcoholics can experience physical withdrawal symptoms (anxiety, agitation, tremors, elevated blood pressure, and sometimes seizures). Alcoholics, like drug addicts, develop a tolerance for the substance and need more and more to get the desired high (NIAAA, 1996).

Treatment for alcoholism may include detoxification (removing all alcohol from the body), hospitalization, medication, individual and group psychotherapy, and referral to a support organization, such as Alcoholics Anonymous. Although not a cure, treatment can give alcoholics new tools to cope with their addiction and lead productive lives.

Drug Use and Abuse Use of illicit drugs peaks at ages 18 to 25; almost 20 percent of this age group report using illicit drugs during the past month. As young adults settle down, get married, and take responsibility for their future, they tend to cut down on drug use. Usage rates drop sharply during the twenties, and then continue to decline, albeit more slowly as people enter later adulthood and old age (SAMHSA, 2013; Figure 13.3).

As in adolescence, marijuana is by far the most popular illicit drug among young adults. In 2006, 18.7 percent of 18- to 25-year-olds had used marijuana within the previous month (SAMHSA, 2013). In general, although a substantial proportion of young adults will experiment with alcohol, cigarettes, or marijuana, a much smaller proportion will try other drugs such as ecstasy, methamphetamines, or heroin; and an even smaller number will become chronic and heavy users of illegal drugs (Johnston, O'Malley, Bachman & Schulenberg, 2013). However, despite the relatively moderate prevalence numbers for heavy abuse, drug abuse still results in significant costs to the user personally and to society at large. Estimates are that illicit drugs cost society some $193 billion a year (U.S. Department of Justice Drug Intelligence Center, 2011).

About 20 percent of persons with substance use disorders also have mood (depression) or anxiety disorders (Grant et al., 2004). Moreover, there is a relationship between the occurrence of personality disorders and the abuse of both illegal drugs and alcohol (Grant et al., 2007). The causal relationship here is unclear. It may be that the use of illegal drugs puts young people at risk for the development of a variety of psychopathologies. Alternatively, it could be the case that those people who suffer from psychological distress self-medicate and thus are more prone to addiction and other risky behaviors.

Depression Adolescence and emerging adulthood appear to be sensitive periods for the onset of depressive disorders. Between ages 15 and 22, the incidence of depression increases gradually (Schulenberg & Zarrett, 2006). Depression is not just being sad. A major depressive disorder is a clinical diagnosis with a specific set of symptoms, is considered to be very serious, and generally requires medical intervention. People who are diagnosed with major depressive disorder often have depressed or irritable moods for most of the day, every day, show reduced interest in and enjoyment of previously pleasurable activities, often either gain or lose significant amounts of weight, have difficulties sleeping too little or too much, and often show a variety of cognitive biases and maladaptive recurrent thoughts.

Generally, young women are more likely to suffer from a major depressive episode, and this difference in prevalence becomes particularly acute after the onset of puberty (Wasserman, 2006). Women are also more likely than men to show atypical symptoms, to have an additional psychopathology along with their depressive disorders, and to attempt (but not succeed in) suicide (Gorman, 2006). In addition, women and men may respond to antidepressants differently, with women showing a greater likelihood of adverse drug reactions (Franconi, Brunelleschi, Steardo & Cuomo, 2007).

Sexual and Reproductive Issues

Sexual and reproductive activities are often a prime preoccupation of emerging and young adulthood. Three such concerns are disorders related to menstruation, sexually transmitted infections (STIs), and infertility.

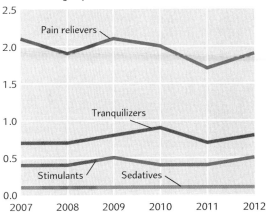

Percent using in past month

FIGURE 13.3

Past Month Nonmedical Use of Types of Psychotherapeutic Drugs among Persons Aged 12 or Older

Source: Substance Abuse and Mental Health Services Administration (SAMHSA). *Results from the 2012 national survey on drug use and health: Summary of national findings.* NSDUH Series H-46, HHS Publication No. (SMA) 13-4795. Rockville, MD: Author, 2013.

SEXUAL BEHAVIOR AND ATTITUDES

Today almost all U.S. adults have had sexual relations before marriage (Lefkowitz & Gillen, 2006). By the age of 20, 75 percent of adults have had premarital sex; and 95 percent have done so by age 44 (Finer, 2007).

Variety in sexual activity is common. Among 25- to 44-year-olds, 97 percent of men and 98 percent of women have had vaginal intercourse; 90 percent of men and 88 percent of women have had oral sex with a partner of the other sex; and 40 percent of men and 35 percent of women have had anal sex with an other-sex partner. About 6.5 percent of men and 11 percent of women have had sex with a same-sex partner (Mosher et al., 2005).

Emerging adults tend to have more sexual partners than in older age groups, but they have sex less frequently. People who become sexually active during emerging adulthood tend to engage in fewer risky behaviors than those who began in adolescence. Condoms are the most commonly used contraceptive, though their use is inconsistent (Lefkowitz & Gillen, 2006).

Casual sex (hooking up) is fairly common, especially on college campuses. Sexual assaults on women are also a problem in this age group. Both are often associated with other, non-sexual risky behaviors such as drinking and drug use (Santelli, Carter, Orr & Dittus, 2007).

By emerging adulthood, most lesbian, gay, bisexual, and transgender persons are clear about their sexual identity. Many first come out to others during this period (Lefkowitz & Gillen, 2006). In general, more recent generations in the United States are coming out at an earlier age, and men are more likely to come out at an earlier age (by approximately 2 years) than women. Ethnic minority youth are equally likely to be open about their sexual orientation to their friends, but they are more likely to keep this information secret from their parents (Grov, Bimbi, Nanin & Parsons, 2006).

SEXUALLY TRANSMITTED INFECTIONS

Sexually transmitted infections (STIs), also known as sexually transmitted diseases (STDs), are illnesses that are transmitted by having sex. Because people can carry infections for years without displaying signs of active disease, STIs is becoming the preferred term.

By far the highest rates of STIs in the United States are among emerging adults ages 18 to 25, especially among those who use alcohol and/or illicit drugs (SAMHSA, 2007b). An estimated 1 in 4 persons who have been sexually active but nearly half of new STI cases are in that age group, and many do not get medical diagnosis and care (Lefkowitz & Gillen, 2006). The risk has been rising—for three years in a row, chlamydia, gonorrhea, and syphilis all showed increases in prevalence (CDC, 2017j). There are also indications that risk is higher among certain ethnic groups. For example, there are elevated rates of STIs for African American and Latino/a young adults (Kaplan, Crespo, Huguet & Marks, 2009).

Worldwide, approximately 34.5 million adults are living with HIV, slightly over half of whom have access to some form of medical treatment. The number of adults newly infected with HIV in 2016 declined for the 10th year in a row, and now numbers approximately 1.8 million people (UNAIDS, 2017).

The number of people living with HIV has risen in every region of the world since 2002, with the steepest increases in East and Central Asia and Eastern Europe. Still, sub-Saharan Africa remains by far the worst affected. Infection can theoretically occur with any transmission of body fluids, although some activities are clearly riskier than others. A growing proportion of new infections occur in women, especially in places where heterosexual transmission is predominant, such as sub-Saharan Africa and the Caribbean. In the United States, most infections occur through drug abusers sharing contaminated hypodermic needles, unprotected sex among gay or bisexual men (who may then pass on the infection to female partners), or commercial sex with prostitutes (UNAIDS/WHO, 2004).

With highly active antiviral therapy, death rates of persons diagnosed with HIV have dropped dramatically, and their average median survival after diagnosis has increased to more than 35 years (Bhaskaran et al., 2008; Lohse et al., 2007). Use of condoms is the most effective means of preventing STIs. Unfortunately, interventions focused on STI transmission for intravenous drug users are not as effective and have not been shown to significantly reduce either needle sharing or risky sexual behaviors in drug addicts (Crepaz et al., 2009; Herbst et al., 2006).

MENSTRUAL DISORDERS

Premenstrual syndrome (PMS) is a disorder that produces physical discomfort and emotional tension for up to 2 weeks before a menstrual period. Symptoms may include fatigue, headaches, swelling and tenderness of the breasts, swollen hands or feet, abdominal bloating, nausea, cramps, constipation, food cravings, weight gain, anxiety, depression, irritability, mood swings, tearfulness, and difficulty concentrating or remembering (ACOG, 2015). Cross-culturally, women report PMS at a rate of about 50 percent, with a range of 10 to 98 percent (Direkvand-Moghadam, Sayehmiri, Delpisheh & Kaikhavandi, 2014).

The cause of PMS is not fully understood, but it appears to be a response to normal monthly surges of the female hormones estrogen and progesterone as well as to levels of the male hormone testosterone and of serotonin, a brain chemical (Biggs & Demuth, 2011). Smoking may put women at increased risk for the development of PMS (Bertone-Johnson, Hankinson, Johnson & Manson, 2008).

The symptoms of PMS can sometimes be alleviated through aerobic exercise, eating frequent small meals, a diet high in complex carbohydrates and low in salt and caffeine, and regular sleep routines. Calcium, magnesium, and vitamin E supplements may help. Medications may relieve specific symptoms—for example, a diuretic for bloating and weight gain (ACOG, 2015).

PMS may include the presence of cramps, but it is not the same thing. PMS can be confused with *dysmenorrhea* (painful menstruation, or "cramps"). Cramps tend to affect younger women, whereas PMS is more typical in women in their thirties or older. Dysmenorrhea is caused by contractions of the uterus, which are set in motion by prostaglandin, a hormone-like substance; it can be treated with prostaglandin inhibitors, such as ibuprofen (Wang et al., 2004). Dysmenorrhea is estimated to affect up to 90 percent of women, and approximately 15 percent experience severe symptoms (Mannix, 2008).

premenstrual syndrome (PMS)
Disorder producing symptoms of physical discomfort and emotional tension for up to 2 weeks before a menstrual period.

INFERTILITY

An estimated 6 percent of U.S. women aged 15 to 44 years old experience **infertility:** the inability to conceive a baby after 12 months of intercourse in the absence of birth control methods (CDC, 2017m). Worldwide, about 1 in 4 couples have difficulty getting pregnant or maintaining a pregnancy to term (Mascarenhas, Flaxman, Boerma, Vanderpoel & Stevens, 2012).

Women's fertility begins to decline in their late twenties, with substantial decreases during their thirties. By their forties, many women are not able to become pregnant without the use of assisted reproductive technology (ART). Men's fertility is less affected by age but begins to decline in the late thirties (Dunson, Colombo & Baird, 2002). Approximately 30 percent of couples are unable to become parents, and they show worse mental health outcomes than those couples who do succeed (Gameiro & Finnigan, 2017).

The most common cause of infertility in men is production of too few sperm. In some instances an ejaculatory duct may be blocked, preventing the exit of sperm, or sperm may be unable to swim well enough to reach the cervix. (O'Flynn O'Brien, Varghese & Agarwal, 2010).

In women, the common causes of infertility include the failure to produce ova or to produce normal ova; mucus in the cervix, which might prevent sperm from penetrating it; or a disease of the uterine lining, which might prevent implantation of the fertilized ovum. A major cause of declining fertility in women after age 30 is deterioration in the quality of ova (CDC, 2017m). However, the most common cause is blockage of the fallopian tubes, preventing ova from reaching the uterus. In about half of these cases, the tubes are blocked by scar tissue from sexually transmitted infections (King, 1996). In addition, some women suffer from physical disorders affecting fertility, such as polycystic ovarian syndrome (Franks, 2009) or primary ovarian insufficiency (Welt, 2008).

In both men and women, modifiable environmental factors are related to infertility. For example, overweight men (Sallmen, Sandler, Hoppin, Blair & Day, 2006) and women (Maheshwari, 2010) are more likely to have issues with

infertility
Inability to conceive a child after 12 months of sexual intercourse without the use of birth control.

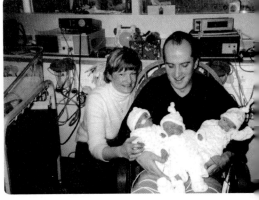

Delayed childbearing, use of fertility drugs, and assisted reproductive techniques such as in vitro fertilization increase the likelihood of multiple, usually premature, births.
©REX/Shutterstock

research in action

ASSISTED REPRODUCTIVE TECHNOLOGY

Assisted reproductive technologies (ARTs) offer hope for those who experience infertility. In vitro fertilization (IVF) is the most common approach, accounting for 99 percent of ARTs (CDC, 2017a). With IVF, women receive fertility drugs to stimulate ova (egg) production. Ova are surgically removed, fertilized with sperm in a laboratory dish, put in a special culture, and monitored for growth. Approximately 3 to 5 days later, the largest and healthiest fertilized eggs—known as blastocysts—are then implanted in the uterus. If successful, the woman's body responds hormonally to the blastocyst, which continues to grow and divide, and pregnancy occurs.

Generally, more fertilized eggs are produced than are used during one cycle. Unused eggs may be frozen and stored for later implantation. Fresh embryo transfers have greater IVF success rates, but frozen-thawed embryo transfers have begun to approach these rates in recent years (Wong, Mastenbroek & Repping, 2014).

IVF can be performed with donor eggs if a woman cannot produce her own viable ova. More recently, women have also been employing cryopreservation, or egg freezing, to extend their years of fertility. Eggs are harvested with the intention of conceiving a child at a later date with the help of IVF. IVF may also be performed to address severe male infertility. Intracytoplasmic sperm injection (ICSI) is used to inject a single sperm into the ovum for fertilization (Brezina & Zhao, 2012).

IVF success rates are not very high. In 2015, approximately 30 percent of IVF procedures using fresh, nondonor eggs resulted in pregnancy (CDC, 2017a). Transfer of multiple embryos increases the odds of IVF success, but also carries risks to mother and baby, including multiple births, preterm delivery, and pregnancy complications (Reddy et al., 2007). Thus, many advocates support single embryo transfers coupled with subsequent frozen-thawed embryo transfers for infertile couples wanting multiple children, and many countries pose restrictions on the number of embryos transferred per IVF cycle (Brezina & Zhao, 2012).

In vitro maturation (IVM), another assisted reproductive technology, involves retrieval of immature eggs from the ovaries. In contrast to IVF, eggs are brought to maturity through the use of hormones in the laboratory rather than in the woman's body. Then, eggs are frozen for later use. This is a promising fertility option for women undergoing cancer treatments, which may damage egg supply, or those with polycystic ovarian syndrome, which interferes with sex hormone cycles and ovulation (Chian, Uzelac & Nargund, 2013).

Gestational surrogacy occurs when fertilized embryos produced in a laboratory are transferred into an unrelated woman's womb to carry throughout pregnancy. Surrogacy is commonly used in absence of a functioning uterus, history of severe obstetric complications, or repeated IVF failure (Soderstrom et al., 2016). Use of gestational carriers has been successful in conjunction with ARTs (Perkins et al., 2016).

Assisted reproduction can result in a tangled web of legal and ethical dilemmas. Should anonymity be maintained with donor eggs or sperm? Who retains ownership of frozen embryos in the event that a couple breaks up? Surrogacy presents other complications. What rights does a surrogate have? What if a surrogate wants to keep the baby? Even the exchange of money is fraught with ethical conflict. Some fear that poor, disadvantaged women may be financially exploited (Soderstrom-Antilla et al., 2016). Additionally, many people object to the creation and/or destruction of embryos in a laboratory on religious grounds. In many ways, our legal system has to play catch up with these new ethical dilemmas created by modern reproductive technologies.

what's your view If you or your partner were infertile, would you seriously consider or undertake one of the methods of assisted reproduction described here? What other ethical dilemmas may be apparent with these technologies?

fertility. Smoking also appears to have a strong negative effect on fertility. Other factors, such as psychological stress, high levels of caffeine and alcohol consumption, and exposure to environmental pollutants have been implicated, but the evidence for their negative effects is less strong (Hoffman, Davies & Norman, 2007).

Sometimes hormone treatment, drug therapy, or surgery may correct the problem. For couples struggling with infertility, science today offers several alternative ways to parenthood; these are discussed in Research in Action.

COGNITIVE DEVELOPMENT

Perspectives on Adult Cognition

Developmentalists have studied cognition from a variety of perspectives. Here, we address three important perspectives on cognition in young adulthood.

NEO-PIAGETIAN APPROACHES

Piaget believed that the pinnacle of cognitive development was formal operations thought. However, some developmental scientists maintain that changes in cognition extend beyond that stage. One line of neo-Piagetian theory and research concerns higher levels of *reflective thinking,* or abstract reasoning. Another line of investigation deals with *post-formal thought,* which combines logic with emotion and practical experience in the resolution of ambiguous problems.

Reflective Thinking **Reflective thinking** was first defined by the American philosopher and educator John Dewey (1997) as "active, persistent, and careful consideration" of information or beliefs. Reflective thinkers continually question facts, draw inferences, and make connections. They are critical thinkers. Reflective thinkers also create complex intellectual systems that reconcile apparently conflicting ideas—for example, by putting together various theories of human development into a single overarching theory that explains many different kinds of behavior (Fischer & Pruyne, 2003).

> **reflective thinking**
> Type of logical thinking that becomes more prominent in adulthood, involving continuous, active evaluation of information and beliefs in the light of evidence and implications.

At approximately 20 to 25 years of age, the brain forms new neurons, synapses, and dendritic connections, and the cortical regions that handle higher-level thinking become fully myelinated. A stimulating environment, such as college, can spur the development of thicker, denser, cortical connections. These physical changes in the brain allow more complex thinking to occur. Although almost all adults develop the *capacity* for becoming reflective thinkers, few attain optimal proficiency in this skill, and even fewer can apply it consistently to various kinds of problems (Fischer & Pruyne, 2003).

Postformal Thought Research and theoretical work since the 1970s suggest that mature thinking is more complex than Piaget described, and that it encompasses more than just the capacity for abstract thought. This higher stage of adult cognition, which tends to emerge in early adulthood, is sometimes called **postformal thought.** As with reflective thinking, exposure to higher education is often a catalyst for the development of this ability (Labouvie-Vief, 2006).

> **postformal thought**
> Mature type of thinking that relies on subjective experience and intuition as well as logic and allows room for ambiguity, uncertainty, inconsistency, contradiction, imperfection, and compromise.

Postformal thought is characterized by the ability to deal with inconsistency, contradiction, and compromise. Life is messy and complex, and some people are better able to deal with its inherent uncertainty. Thus postformal thinking is in some way as much a personality style as it is a mode of thinking.

Another characteristic of postformal thought is its flexibility. At times, formal logical thought is the best tool to solve a problem. But other times, especially in ambiguous circumstances, it is not enough. Postformal thought draws on intuition and emotion as well as logic to help people cope with situations such as social dilemmas, which are often less clearly structured and are often fraught with emotion (Berg & Klaczynski, 1996; Sinnot, 2003).

Postformal thought is also relativistic. Immature thinking tends to be black and white—there is one right answer and one wrong one. Relativistic thought, by contrast, acknowledges that there may be more than one valid way of viewing an issue and that the world is made up of shades of gray. This allows adults to transcend a single logical system and reconcile or choose among conflicting ideas when each of these ideas may have a valid claim as the truth (Sinnott, 2003). Relativistic thinking often develops in response to events or interactions that open up unaccustomed ways of looking at things and challenge a simple, polarized view of the world. Research has found a progression toward postformal thought throughout young and middle adulthood (Blanchard-Fields & Norris, 1994).

STERNBERG: INSIGHT AND KNOW-HOW

Alix, Barbara, and Courtney applied to graduate programs at Yale University. Alix had earned almost straight A's in college and had scored high on the Graduate Record Examination (GRE). Barbara's grades were fair, and her GRE scores were low by Yale's standards, but her letters of recommendation enthusiastically praised her exceptional research and creative ideas. Courtney's grades, GRE scores, and recommendations were good but not among the best.

Alix and Courtney were admitted to the graduate program. Barbara was not admitted but was hired as a research associate and took graduate classes on the side. Alix did very well for the first year or so, but less well after that when asked to develop independent research ideas. Barbara confounded the admissions committee by doing outstanding work. Courtney's performance in graduate school was only fair, but she had the easiest time getting a good job afterward (Trotter, 1986).

This vignette illustrates that doing well in life involves more than just exam grades. The triarchic theory of intelligence is comprised of three elements: *componential, experiential,* and *contextual knowledge* (Sternberg, 1985; 1987). Alix's analytical abilities illustrated componential knowledge, which helped her sail through examinations and receive high grades. However, componential knowledge such as this is not always sufficient to do well in life. Also important are experiential elements (how insightful or creative a person is) and contextual knowledge (the practical aspect of intelligence). In graduate school, where original thinking is expected, Barbara's superior experiential intelligence—her fresh insights and original ideas—began to shine. So did Courtney's practical, contextual intelligence. Courtney knew her way around. She chose hot research topics, submitted papers to the right journals, and knew when and how to apply for jobs.

An important aspect of practical intelligence is **tacit knowledge:** "inside information" or "know-how" that is not formally taught or openly expressed. Tacit knowledge is commonsense knowledge of how to get ahead, such as how to win a promotion or cut through red tape. Sternberg's method of testing tacit knowledge in adults was to compare a test-taker's chosen course of action in hypothetical, work-related situations (such as how best to angle for a promotion) with the choices of experts in the field and with accepted rules of thumb. Tacit knowledge, when measured in this way, is not well correlated with measures of general cognitive ability but does predict managerial success and job performance (Sternberg, Grigorenko & Oh, 2001; Herbig, Büssing & Ewert, 2001; Sternberg, Wagner, Williams & Horvath, 1995).

tacit knowledge
Sternberg's term for information that is not formally taught but is necessary to get ahead.

EMOTIONAL INTELLIGENCE

Peter Salovey and John Mayer (1990) coined the term **emotional intelligence (EI).** It refers to four related skills: the abilities to *perceive, use, understand,* and *manage,* or regulate, emotions—our own and those of others—so as to achieve goals. Emotional intelligence enables a person to harness emotions to deal more effectively with the social environment. It requires awareness of the type of behavior that is appropriate in a given social situation. While mean scores for these four categories differ by country, the test remains valid cross-culturally (Karim & Weisz, 2010).

To measure emotional intelligence, psychologists use the Mayer-Salovey-Caruso Emotional Intelligence Test (MSCEIT) (Mayer, Salovey, Caruso & Sitarenios, 2003), a 40-minute battery of questions that generates a score for each of the four abilities, as well as a total score. The test includes such questions as, "Tom felt anxious and became a bit stressed when he thought about all the work he needed to do. When his supervisor brought him an additional project, he felt (a) overwhelmed, (b) depressed, (c) ashamed, (d) self-conscious, or (e) jittery."

Emotional intelligence affects the quality of personal relationships. Studies have found that college students who score high on the MSCEIT are more likely to report positive relationships with parents and friends (Lopes, Salovey & Straus, 2003), that college-age men who score higher on the MSCEIT engage in less drug and alcohol use and score higher on well-being measures (Brackett, Mayer & Warner, 2004; Lanciano & Curci, 2015), and that close friends of college students who score well on the MSCEIT

emotional intelligence (EI)
Salovey and Mayer's term for the ability to understand and regulate emotions; an important component of effective, intelligent behavior.

rate them as more likely to provide emotional support in time of need (Lopes et al., 2004). College-age couples in which both partners scored high on the MSCEIT reported the happiest relationships, whereas couples who scored low were unhappiest (Brackett, Cox, Gaines & Salovey, 2005). Generally, women score higher on emotional intelligence measures than do men (Lanciano & Curci, 2015).

Emotional intelligence also affects occupational success. Among a sample of employees of a Fortune 500 insurance company, those with higher MSCEIT scores were rated higher by colleagues and supervisors on sociability, interpersonal sensitivity, leadership potential, and ability to handle stress and conflict. High scores also were related to higher salaries and more promotions (Lopes, Grewal, Kadis, Gall & Salovey, 2006).

Moral Reasoning

In Kohlberg's theory, moral development of children and adolescents is closely tied to cognitive maturation. Young people advance in moral judgment as they shed egocentrism and become capable of abstract thought. In adulthood, however, moral judgments become more complex.

Recall that Kohlberg broke moral development into three stages. In the final stage, postconventional morality, Kohlberg believed that people became capable of fully principled moral reasoning, and that they made moral decisions on the basis of universal principles of justice. Kohlberg argued that most people did not reach this level until their twenties, if at all (Kohlberg, 1973). He believed that the acquisition of this was a function of experience. In particular, when young people encounter values that conflict with their own (as might happen in college or foreign travel) and when they are responsible for the welfare of others (as in parenthood), their development of moral reasoning abilities increases.

There is some support for the view that experience can shape moral reasoning. Students who attend church are less likely to cheat on a task than those who attend church less regularly (Bloodgood, Turnley & Mudrack, 2008). On the other hand, people exposed to war (Haskuka, Sunar & Alp, 2008) or who suffer from post-traumatic stress disorder as a result of combat experience (Taylor, 2007) show a reduced tendency to reach Kohlberg's higher levels of moral reasoning. In short, personal experiences can affect the likelihood of engaging in certain types of moral reasoning.

Shortly before his death, Kohlberg proposed an additional seventh state of moral reasoning. He believed it was possible for people to achieve "a sense of unity with the cosmos, nature, or God," which enabled them to see moral issues from "the standpoint of the universe as a whole" (Kohlberg & Ryncarz, 1990, pp. 191, 207). Rather than seeing morality as tied to justice, adults at this stage might instead reflect on the question, "Why be moral?"

CULTURE AND MORAL REASONING

Culture affects the understanding of morality. For example, individualistic cultures like the United States tend to focus on individual autonomy. Collectivistic cultures, such as China, are more concerned with group dynamics and harmony. This may help explain some of the cultural differences in moral reasoning that have been found. Whereas Kohlberg's system is based on justice, the Chinese ethos leans toward conciliation and harmony. In Chinese society, people faced with moral dilemmas are expected to discuss them openly, be guided by community standards, and try to find a way of resolving the problem to please as many parties as possible (Dien, 1982).

This example illustrates a wider critique leveled at Kohlberg's approach. Kohlberg believed that certain cultures were more likely to provide opportunities for people to attain the highest levels of moral reasoning (Jenson, 1997). This underlying belief in the superiority of a particular worldview has been criticized as being too narrow and as being biased toward Western cultural norms of individuality and a nonreligious mind-set. For example, many cultures provide moral dictates focused on divine authority and tradition, and there is no reason for these beliefs to be viewed as morally inferior or as reflecting a less sophisticated form of reasoning (Shweder et al., 2006).

GENDER AND MORAL REASONING

Carol Gilligan was bothered by what she perceived as a male bias in Kohlberg's approach. She believed that women's central dilemma was the conflict between their needs and the needs of others rather than the principles of abstract justice and fairness delineated by Kohlberg. Women's moral reasoning was not less complex than men's, she argued, it merely had a different focus.

In her research, Gilligan (1982/1993) interviewed 29 pregnant women about their decision to continue or end their pregnancies. Gilligan found that the women in her research saw morality in terms of an obligation to exercise care and avoid hurting others rather than independently derived abstract ideals.

The research has been equivocal. Some research has found, contrary to Kohlberg's predictions, that women reason at a higher level than men (Eisenberg, Hofer, Sulik & Liew, 2014). Other research has not found consistent gender differences in moral reasoning (Brabeck & Shore, 2003). Still others argue that although women are more likely to think in terms of care and men in terms of justice these differences are small (Blakemore, Berenbaum & Liben, 2009). It is interesting, however, that in brain imaging studies (Harenski, Antonenko, Shane & Keihl, 2008) women showed more activity in areas of the brain associated with care-based reasoning (the posterior, anterior cingulate, and anterior insula) and men showed more activity in areas of the brain associated with justice-based processing (superior temporal sulcus). Still, the weight of evidence does not appear to back up Gilligan's assertions (L. Walker, 1995).

Education and Work

Unlike young people in past generations, who typically could expect to move directly from school to work and financial independence, many emerging adults today do not have a clear career path. Some alternate between education and work; others pursue both at the same time. Most of those who do not enroll in postsecondary education, or do not finish, enter the job market, but may later seek more schooling (Furstenberg et al., 2005; Hamilton & Hamilton, 2006; NCES, 2005b). Some, especially in the United Kingdom, take a year off from formal education or the workplace—a *gap year*—to gain new skills, do volunteer work, travel, or study abroad (Jones, 2004). And some combine college with marriage and child rearing (Fitzpatrick & Turner, 2007). Many emerging adults who are in school or living in their parents' homes are financially dependent (Schoeni & Ross, 2005).

THE COLLEGE TRANSITION

College is an increasingly important path to adulthood, though it is only one such path and, until recently, not the most common one (Montgomery & Côté, 2003). Between 1975 and 2015, the proportion of U.S. high school graduates who went straight into a 2- or 4-year college grew from about half (51 percent) to more than two-thirds (69 percent; NCES, 2013; NCES, 2017a).

College courses and even complete degree or certificate programs are now widely available by *distance learning,* in which courses are delivered via mail, e-mail, the Internet, or other technological means. About 6.7 million students took at least one online course in 2013, and about 1 in 3 students reported taking at least one online course (Allen & Seaman, 2013). Colleges also are increasingly experimenting with hybrid courses, which utilize a mixture of both online and in-person techniques. In general, research seems to suggest that learning outcomes are similar for online, hybrid, and traditional students, although a wide variety of variables can affect outcomes (Tallent-Runnels et al., 2006).

Some colleges, including Stanford University and MIT, have offered massive, open, online courses (MOOCs) that allow any person with an Internet connection to take the course for free. Although such courses show some promise, especially with respect to opening avenues of affordable knowledge in far-flung locales, they also suffer from high rates of attrition and are subject to cheating (Daniel, 2012). Estimates are that only 6.5 percent of students enrolled in MOOCs finish the course, and the longer the course, the higher the attrition rate (Jordan, 2014). Their effect remains to be determined.

College enrollments in the United States are at an all-time high. More than 2 out of 3 high school graduates go right to college.
©Fuse/Getty Images

Gender, Socioeconomic Status, and Race/Ethnicity U.S. college enrollment reached a high in 2010, and then decreased by 4 percent in 2014 to 20.2 million. However, this number is projected to increase by 15 percent through 2025. In a reversal of the traditional gender gap, women now make up a larger percentage (56 percent) of the student population despite male enrollment increasing at a faster rate (19 percent as compared to 15 percent) (Snyder, de Brey & Dillow, 2016). By comparison, in 1970, women made up only 42 percent of those earning bachelor's degrees (NCES, 2009b). Similarly, women have higher postsecondary enrollment rates than men in most European countries, as well as in Australia, Canada, New Zealand, Japan, and the Russian Federation (Buchmann & DiPrete, 2006; Sen, Partelow & Miller, 2005). Since the mid 1980s, more U.S. women have earned associate's, bachelor's, and master's degrees than men, and since 2005–2006 this has also become true for doctoral degrees (Snyder, de Brey & Dillow, 2016).

In the United States, women remain more likely than men to major in traditionally women's fields, such as education, nursing, English literature, and psychology, and not in math and science (NCES, 2007a). Although women generally do better than men in high school math and science courses, they tend to score lower on standardized college and graduate school entrance tests—a fact that may relate to men's advantage at the upper end of the mathematical, visual, and spatial ability range, or perhaps to differences in the way men and women solve novel problems (Halpern et al., 2007). Even so, women have made gains in almost every field (NCES, 2006b). More women than in the past now earn engineering degrees, though at least 80 percent of bachelor's degrees in that field still go to men (Halpern et al., 2007; NCES, 2007b). The percentage of professional degrees (law, medicine, dentistry, and so forth) awarded to women has risen dramatically since 1970 (NCES, 2005c). In 1960 women earned only 10 percent of postgraduate degrees, averaged across all fields, but women now earn approximately 57 percent of postgraduate degrees (NCES, 2009b).

Socioeconomic status and race/ethnicity affect access to postsecondary education. In 2011, 82 percent of high school graduates from high-income families, as compared with only 52 percent from low-income families, enrolled in college immediately after high school (NCES, 2012a). From the 2004–2005 academic year to the 2014–2015 academic year, prices for tuition, room, and board rose 33 percent at public institutions and 26 percent at private, not-for-profit institutions (Snyder, de Brey & Dillow, 2016), making the attainment of higher education increasingly difficult for low- and middle-income families. Thus many students from more modest circumstances are likely to work while attending college, which often slows their progress (Dey & Hurtado, 1999). In addition, students from wealthier families are less likely to drop out of college before graduating (Hamilton & Hamilton, 2006).

Currently, approximately 72 percent of bachelor's degrees are earned by white students (NCES, 2009b). However, the percentage of college students who are minorities is rising, primarily due to increased numbers of Latinos, Pacific Islanders, and Asian Americans. It is likely, given the current demographic composition of the United States, that this trend will continue. Graduation rates differ by race and ethnicity. Asian Americans (71 percent) are most likely to graduate, followed by white students (63 percent), Hispanics (54 percent), and African Americans (41 percent) (Snyder, de Brey & Dillow, 2016).

Cognitive Growth in College College can be a time of intellectual discovery and personal growth, especially in verbal and quantitative skills, critical thinking, and moral reasoning (Montgomery & Côté, 2003). Students change in response to (1) the curriculum, which offers new insights and new ways of thinking; (2) other students who challenge long-held views and values; (3) the student culture, which is different from the culture of society at large; and (4) faculty members, who provide new role models. In terms of both immediate and long-term benefits, going to college—any college—is more important than which college a person attends (Montgomery & Côté, 2003).

Researchers have found that going to college can result in a fundamental change in the way young people think (Fischer & Pruyne, 2003). In a classic study, William Perry (1970) interviewed 67 Harvard and Radcliffe students throughout their undergraduate years. They found that, overall, their thinking progressed from rigidity to flexibility, and to choosing their own beliefs on the basis of reflection.

Today, more women than men enter college and earn degrees, and many colleges offer support and facilities for students with disabilities. A college education is often the key to a successful career and a healthy, satisfying life.
©Steve Debenport/Getty Images

Ultimately, students achieve what has been called *commitment within relativism*. At this point, students make their own judgments; they decide for themselves, finally, what they want to believe and feel confident in their choices and values and trust in their own opinions.

What drives this change? Overall, exposure to diversity, especially with respect to race (often the most salient dimension), leads to increases in cognitive complexity. This influence is strongest when it takes the form of interpersonal interactions rather than, for example, coursework or workshops (Bowman, 2010; Bowman, 2013). For example, discussions that include mixed-race participants produce greater novelty and complexity of ideas than all-white discussions (Antonio et al., 2004). This has implications for affirmative action and enrollment decisions. Some have argued that a diverse group of students and high academic quality are competing priorities (Bowman, 2010). Research suggests, by contrast, a different story. Those campuses with more diverse student bodies tend to show greater amounts of interracial friendships rather than continued or increased segregation (Fischer, 2008). This integration then contributes to academic achievement and intellectual gains (Gurin, Dey, Gurin & Hurtado, 2003).

Completing College Although college entrance has become more common in the United States, *finishing* college has not. Only 55 percent who start college have received a degree after five years (Snyder, de Brey & Dillow, 2016). A growing number of students, especially men, remain in college more than 5 years or switch from 2-year to 4-year institutions (Horn & Berger, 2004; Peter & Horn, 2005).

Whether a person completes college may depend not only on motivation, academic aptitude and preparation, and ability to work independently, but also on social integration and social support: employment opportunities, financial support, suitability of living arrangements, quality of social and academic interactions, and the fit between what the college offers and what the student wants and needs. Intervention programs for at-risk students have improved college attendance rates by creating meaningful bonds between students and teachers, finding opportunities for students to work while in college, providing academic assistance, and helping students see how college can move them toward a better future (Montgomery & Côté, 2003).

ENTERING THE WORLD OF WORK

By their midtwenties, most emerging adults are either working or pursuing advanced education or both (Hamilton & Hamilton, 2006). Those who enter the workforce face a rapidly shifting landscape. Where previous generations of employees often could expect to remain at a company from their start date until retirement, that pattern of employment is becoming increasingly rare. More and more adults are self-employed, working at home, telecommuting, on flexible work schedules, or acting as independent contractors. These changes, together with a more competitive job market and the demand for a highly skilled workforce, make education and training more vital than ever (Corcoran & Matsudaira, 2005).

Higher education expands employment opportunities and earning power (Figure 13.4) and enhances long-term quality of life for adults worldwide (Centre for Educational Research and Innovation, 2004; Montgomery & Côté, 2003). In the United States, adults with advanced degrees earn 4 times more than those with less than a high school diploma (U.S. Census Bureau, 2007a). For adults without higher education, unemployment rates are high (U.S. Census Bureau, 2006), and it may be difficult to earn enough to establish an independent household. A cross-national survey in Belgium, Canada, Germany, and Italy found a decline in economic self-sufficiency among 18- to 34-year-old men and among women in their early twenties between the mid-1980s and 1995–2000 (Bell, Burtless, Gornick & Smeeding, 2007). And workers in their twenties, especially their early twenties, tend to be concentrated in low-wage, low-skilled positions and frequently change jobs (Hamilton & Hamilton, 2006).

Although income differentials between male and female workers exist at all levels of educational attainment, these gaps have narrowed considerably. In 1980, the average young man with a bachelor's degree

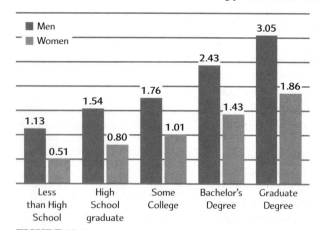

FIGURE 13.4

Median lifetime earnings by highest educational attainment, 2009 dollars

Even considering the cost of an education, higher educational levels mean more lifetime earnings.

Source: Social Security Administration, "Education and Lifetime Earnings," November 2015.

earned 36 percent more than the average young woman; in 2002 the difference was 23 percent (NCES, 2007b). However, a report by the American Association of University Women (2007) found that the earnings gap increases during the 10 years after graduation, so that women at that point earn only 69 percent of what their male counterparts do. Furthermore, one-fourth of the pay gap is unexplained by such factors as hours, occupations, and parenthood, suggesting that it stems from gender discrimination. Data from the last U.S. Census survey reveal that as of 2009 women still earned only 78 cents for every dollar a man earns (Getz, 2010).

Combining Work and Schooling In 2014, about 41 percent of full-time college students and 80 percent of part-time college students worked while attending college (Kena et al., 2016). How does juggling work and study affect cognitive development and career preparation? That depends on a number of factors. One longitudinal study found that during the first 2 years, on- or off-campus work had little or no effect on reading comprehension, mathematical reasoning, or critical-thinking skills. By the 3rd year, part-time work had a positive effect, perhaps because employment forces students to organize their time efficiently and learn better work habits. However, working more than 15 to 20 hours a week tended to have a negative impact (Pascarella, Edison, Nora, Hagedorn & Terenzini, 1998) and is associated with a failure to graduate. Generally, there is a trade-off such that the more time students spend working, the less time they spend on academic pursuits (Greene & Maggs, 2015).

Working during college may also affect the likelihood of attending graduate programs. Although grants and loans are available to some students, many students must work to help support their educational aspirations. Such work cuts into the time they have available to engage in other activities, such as participation in research groups, unpaid internships, and volunteer work. These activities are optional but allow students a more competitive application into graduate school. Therefore, although work itself may not be detrimental to an undergraduate education, it may be related to difficulties meeting criteria for graduate programs.

Cognitive Growth at Work Do people change as a result of the kind of work they do? Some research says yes: People seem to grow in challenging jobs, the kind that are becoming increasingly prevalent today. This research has revealed a reciprocal relationship between the **substantive complexity** of work—the degree of thought and independent judgment it requires—and a person's flexibility in coping with cognitive demands (Kohn, 1980).

substantive complexity
Degree to which a person's work requires thought and independent judgment.

A great deal of development in the frontal lobes occurs in young adulthood (Luciana, 2010). Magnetic resonance imaging shows that the most frontward part of the frontal lobes plays a major role in problem solving and planning. This portion of the brain springs into action when a person needs to put an unfinished task on hold and shift attention to another task. It permits a worker to keep the first task in working memory while attending to the second—for example, to resume reading a report after being interrupted by the telephone (Koechlin, Basso, Pietrini, Panzer & Grafman, 1999). Other aspects of brain development also influence why, as young people enter adulthood, they become less likely to take risks, more responsible, and better able to control their behavior (Luciana, 2010).

Cognitive growth need not stop at the end of the workday. According to the **spillover hypothesis**, cognitive gains from work carry over to nonworking hours. Studies support this hypothesis: Substantive complexity of work strongly influences the intellectual level of leisure activities (Kohn, 1980; K. Miller & Kohn, 1983).

spillover hypothesis
Hypothesis that there is a carryover of cognitive gains from work to leisure that explains the positive relationship between activities in the quality of intellectual functioning.

Smoothing the Transition to the Workplace What does it take to achieve a successful transition from school to work? A review of the literature points to four key factors: (1) competence (in general and at work); (2) personal characteristics such as initiative, flexibility, purposefulness, and a sense of urgency; (3) positive personal relationships; and (4) links between schooling and employment (Blustein, Juntunen & Worthington, 2000).

Some developmental scientists (Furstenberg, Rumbaut & Settersten, 2005; Settersten, 2005) suggest measures to strengthen the links between work and educational institutions, especially community colleges:

- Improve dialogue between educators and employers.
- Modify school and work schedules to adapt to the needs of working students.
- Let employers help design work-study programs.
- Increase availability of temporary and part-time work.

- Relate better what students learn at work and in school.
- Improve training of vocational guidance counselors.
- Make better use of study and support groups and tutoring and mentoring programs.
- Provide scholarships, financial aid, and health insurance to part-time as well as full-time students and employees.

Work affects day-to-day life, not only on the job but at home, and it brings both satisfaction and stress.

summary and key terms

Emerging Adulthood

- For many young people in advanced technological societies, entrance into adulthood is not clearly marked. Some developmental scientists suggest that the late teens through the midtwenties has become a transitional period called emerging adulthood.
- Emerging adulthood consists of multiple milestones or transitions, and their order and timing varies. Passage of these milestones may determine when a young person becomes an adult.

emerging adulthood

PHYSICAL DEVELOPMENT

Health and Fitness

- Physical and sensory abilities are typically at their peak in emerging and young adulthood.
- Accidents are the leading cause of death in this age group.
- The mapping of the human genome is enabling the discovery of genetic bases for certain disorders.
- Lifestyle factors such as diet, obesity, exercise, sleep, smoking, and substance use or abuse can affect health, survival, and may have epigenetic consequences for the regulation of when genes turn on and off.
- Good health is related to higher income and education. Some minorities tend to be less healthy. Although much of this is due to SES, there also are indications that people of different ethnicities sometimes respond differently to environmental influences on health.
- Social relationships, especially marriage, tend to be associated with physical and mental health.
- Mental health is generally good in early adulthood, but certain conditions, such as depression, become more prevalent. Alcohol abuse and alcoholism are the most common substance disorders.

risky drinking, alcoholism

Sexual and Reproductive Issues

- Almost all U.S. young adults have sexual relations before marriage.
- Sexually transmitted infections, menstrual disorders, and infertility can be concerns during young adulthood.
- The highest rates of STIs in the United States are among emerging adults, particularly among young women.
- The most common cause of infertility in men is a low sperm count; the most common cause in women is blockage of the fallopian tubes.

- Infertile couples now have many options for assisted reproduction.

premenstrual syndrome (PMS), infertility

COGNITIVE DEVELOPMENT

Perspectives on Adult Cognition

- Some investigators propose distinctively adult forms of cognition beyond formal operations. Reflective thinking emphasizes complex logic; postformal thought involves intuition and emotion as well.
- According to Sternberg's triarchic theory of intelligence, the experiential and contextual elements become particularly important during adulthood. Tests that measure tacit knowledge can be useful complements to traditional tests.
- Emotional intelligence plays an important part in life success.

reflective thinking, postformal thought, tacit knowledge, emotional intelligence (EI)

Moral Reasoning

- According to Kohlberg, moral development in adulthood depends primarily on experience. Not all cultures support Kohlberg's more advanced stages of moral development.
- Gilligan initially proposed that women have an ethic of care, whereas Kohlberg's theory emphasizes justice. However, later research, including her own, has not supported a distinction between men's and women's moral outlook.

Education and Work

- A majority of emerging adults now go to college. More women than men now go to college, and an increasing percentage pursue advanced degrees even in traditionally male-dominated fields. Minority participation is growing, but more slowly. Many students enter college, but fewer graduate with a degree.
- According to Perry, college students' thinking tends to progress from rigidity to flexibility to freely chosen commitments.
- Research has found a relationship between substantive complexity of work and cognitive growth.
- Changes in the workplace call for higher education or training. Higher education greatly expands workplace opportunities and earnings.
- The transition to the workplace could be eased through measures to strengthen vocational education and its links with work.

substantive complexity, spillover hypothesis

Psychosocial Development in Emerging and Young Adulthood

chapter 14

learning objectives

Describe identity development and the relationship with parents in emerging adulthood.

Summarize theoretical perspectives on adult personality development.

Identify key aspects of intimate relationships and love.

Characterize marital and nonmarital lifestyles.

Discuss parenthood and the pressures on dual-income families.

Identify trends in divorce and remarriage.

©Sam Edwards/age fotostock

Personal choices made in emerging and young adulthood establish a framework for the rest of life. In this chapter, we examine the choices that frame personal and social life: adopting a sexual lifestyle; marrying, cohabiting, or remaining single; having children or not; and establishing and maintaining friendships.

Emerging Adulthood: Patterns and Tasks

VARIED PATHS TO ADULTHOOD

Paths to adulthood are far more varied than in the past. Before the 1960s, young people in the United States typically finished school, left home, got a job, got married, and had children, in that order. Today, a wide variety of paths may be followed on the way to adulthood. What influences affect these varied paths?

Influences on Paths to Adulthood Individual paths to adulthood are influenced by such factors as gender, academic ability, early attitudes toward education, race and ethnicity, expectations in late adolescence, and social class. Increasingly, emerging adults of both sexes extend education and delay parenthood (Osgood, Ruth, Eccles, Jacobs & Barber, 2005), and these decisions are usually keys to future success on the job (Sandefur, Eggerling-Boeck & Park, 2005) as well as to current well-being.

Some emerging adults have more resources—financial and developmental—than others. Much depends on *ego development:* a combination of ability to understand oneself and one's world, to integrate and synthesize what one perceives and knows, and to take charge of planning one's life course. Ego development is influenced by experiences. Young people whose ego development tended to be "stuck" at a less mature level at age 25 were more likely to have had parents who inhibited their autonomy at age 14, devalued them, and were more hostile in conversations (Billings, Hauser & Allen, 2008). Adults who experienced stressful life events earlier in life showed negative effects on ego development as young adults (Alessandri, Eisenberg, Vecchione, Caprara & Milioni, 2016). As a result of these and other influences, some emerging adults have more highly developed egos than others and are therefore more ready to learn to stand alone (Tanner, 2006).

IDENTITY DEVELOPMENT IN EMERGING ADULTHOOD

Adolescence is a time of great change, and Erikson saw the search for identity as a lifelong task focused largely on this stage of the life span. Emerging adulthood, by contrast, offers a moratorium from developmental pressures and allows young people the freedom to experiment with various roles and lifestyles. However, it also represents a turning point during which adult role commitments gradually crystallize. In postindustrialized countries today, the active search for identity is more and more likely to extend into emerging adulthood (Côté, 2006).

recentering
Process that underlies the shift to an adult identity.

Recentering **Recentering** is the primary task of emerging adulthood. It is a three-stage process in which power, responsibility, and decision making gradually shift from the family of origin to the independent young adult (Tanner, 2006):

- At *stage 1,* the individual is still embedded in the family of origin, but expectations for self-reliance and self-directedness increase. So, for example, a young adult might still live at home and attend high school but would be expected to schedule and monitor his own activities during nonschool hours.

- In *stage 2,* the individual remains connected to but no longer embedded within the family of origin. So, for example, an undergraduate student might live in a college dorm but still be supported financially by her parents as she attends school. Exploratory involvements in a variety of college courses, jobs, and intimate partners are common and the individual is moving toward serious commitments.

- In *stage 3,* usually by age 30, the individual moves into young adulthood. This stage is marked by independence from the family of origin (while retaining close ties to it) and commitment to a career, a partner, and possibly children. Here, a young adult might be settling into a career or marriage and live independently but still remain close to his or her parents and family of origin.

The Contemporary Moratorium A fragmented, postindustrial society offers many emerging adults little guidance and less pressure to grow up (Heinz, 2002) and not everyone is equally up to the task (Côté, 2006). Identity status research has found that only about a third of Western youth seem to go through what Marcia named the *moratorium* status, a self-conscious crisis that ideally leads to a resolution and identity achievement status. Approximately 15 percent seem to regress during emerging adulthood, and about half show no significant changes (Kroger, Martinussen & Marcia, 2009). Rather than actively and thoughtfully exploring their identity, many young adults seem to do little active, conscious deliberation, instead taking a passive (diffused) approach or taking the lead from their parents (foreclosure). Nevertheless, about 3 out of 4 eventually settle on some sort of occupational identity by the end of their twenties. Identity confusion persists for 10 to 20 percent, who lack what Erikson called *fidelity:* faith in something larger than themselves (Côté, 2006).

Racial/Ethnic Identity Exploration Identity exploration is different for racial/ethnic minorities than for the majority white population. Ethnic identity can be defined as one's identity as a member of a particular ethnic group (Phinney, 2003) and is part of the wider social identity of an individual (Tajfel, 1981). Many minority youth, often out of economic concerns, must take on adult responsibilities earlier than their peers. At the same time, they tend to value close and interdependent family relations and may feel obligated to assist their families financially. They may be under pressure to marry and have children at an early age, or to enter the workforce immediately rather than spending years in higher education. Thus, for them, some of the processes of emerging adulthood may be curtailed. Simultaneously, they must deal with more complex identity issues regarding their ethnicity (Phinney, 2006).

To achieve a secure ethnic identity, they must come to understand themselves both as part of an ethnic group and as part of the wider, diverse society, and to have a positive view of both the minority and majority cultures in which they live. Multiracial young people have the added challenge of figuring out where they fit in.

As might be expected, the formation of a secure ethnic identity has wide repercussions. For example, secure ethnic identity is related to higher self-esteem (Umana-Taylor & Updegraff, 2006). Because a secure ethnic identity involves positive feelings about both one's own personal identity (Yip, 2014) and the wider culture (Phinney, 1989), it is not surprising to find that secure ethnic identity is related to greater acceptance of other groups (Phinney, Ferguson & Tate, 1997). Presumably, then, such feelings might result in more positive interactions between different groups and reductions in discrimination (Phinney, Jacoby & Silva, 2007).

DEVELOPING ADULT RELATIONSHIPS WITH PARENTS

As young people leave home, they must complete the negotiation of autonomy begun in adolescence and redefine their relationship with their parents as one between adults.

Influences on Relationships with Parents Even though they are no longer children, emerging adults still need parental acceptance, empathy, and support, and attachment to the parents remains a key ingredient of well-being. Financial support from parents, especially for education, enhances emerging adults' chances of success in adult roles (Aquilino, 2006).

Positive parent-child relationships during early adolescence predict warmer and less conflicted relationships with both parents when the children reach age 26 (Belsky, Jaffee, Hsieh & Silva, 2001). When emerging adults have parents who are closely involved, warm, and loving, they have higher levels of self-worth (Nelson, Padilla-Walker & Neilson, 2015). Generally, parents and young adult children get along best when the young adult is following a normative life course but has deferred the responsibility of parenthood until other adult roles are well established (Belsky, Jaffee, Caspi, Moffitt & Silva, 2003).

Although emerging adults may no longer rely on parents for basic sustenance, they still benefit from parental companionship and social support. ©Jupiterimages/Thinkstock/Alamy

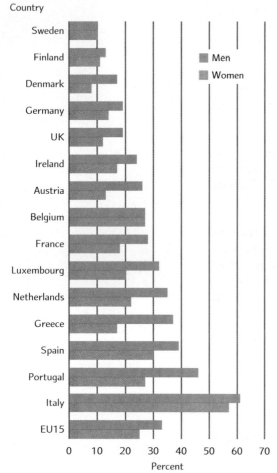

FIGURE 14.1

Percent of European Young Adults Ages 18 to 34 Who Do Not Have Their Own Partners or Children and Are Living with Parents

Many young adults fail to launch from the nest at the expected time or return to it in times of trouble.

Source: Newman, K., & Aptekar, S. "Sticking around: Delayed departure from the parental nest in Western Europe." In S. Danziger & C. Rouse (Eds.), *The price of independence: The economics of early adulthood* (pp. 207–230). New York: Russell Sage Foundation, 2007.

normative-stage models
Theoretical models that describe psychosocial development in terms of a definite sequence of age-related changes.

The quality of the parent-adult child relationship may be affected by the relationship between the mother and father (Aquilino, 2006). When the young adult becomes "caught in the middle" between two conflictual parents there can be negative consequences (Amato & Afifi, 2006). For example, one study showed that such situations resulted in higher levels of internalizing symptoms and depressive thoughts 3 years later (Buehler & Welsh, 2009). This relationship goes both ways; Parents of disruptive young adults may also experience increased distress as a result of their child's actions (McClelland & McKinley, 2016), particularly given the shifting balance of power as young adults become more independent and are less subject to parental control.

Failure to Launch Economic and social changes in the United States—including automation, globalization, and technological change—have made it more difficult for young adults to establish an economically viable independent household (Hill & Holzer, 2007). The view that these young adults who "fail to launch" and do not move out of their parents' homes are selfish slackers who refuse to grow up is largely inaccurate (Arnett, 2007b). Rather, they are forced to remain somewhat dependent out of economic concerns and the need to obtain training or schooling to a greater degree than previous generations. Indeed, the average age at which young adults enter the workplace has risen in past decades, and when compared to previous generations, they do not reach the same earning levels until later in life (Carnevale, Hanson & Gulish, 2013). While staying in the family home can afford the opportunity to continue to work on occupational advancement, it also can result in threats to autonomy and independence for young adults (Burn & Szoeke, 2016).

The trend for emerging adults to live in the parents' home also exists in other countries. In Southern Europe, approximately 60 percent of emerging adults live in the parental home (Newman & Aptekar, 2007). In Hong Kong, the disparity between housing costs and living wages has forced many young people to delay their departure from the family home (Victor, 2015). And in Japan, where children generally live with their parents until they marry, the average age at which young adults marry has risen sharply (Newman, 2008). While living with parents has in the past been associated with lower life satisfaction, this is becoming less true as the practice becomes more widespread. In over half of European families, young adult children living at home is viewed in a positive light (Guerrero, 2001). Indeed, Europeans may be witnessing a new developmental stage, *in-house adulthood,* in which live-in adult children and their parents treat each other as equals (Newman & Aptekar, 2007; Figure 14.1).

Personality Development: Four Views

What is personality? The answer depends in part on how we study and measure it. Four approaches to adult psychosocial development are represented by *normative-stage models,* the *timing-of-events model, trait models,* and *typological models* (Table 14.1).

NORMATIVE-STAGE MODELS

At what age should people marry? Have children? Decide on a career? Every culture has norms about the "right" time for major life events to occur. **Normative-stage models** are theoretical approaches that hold that adults follow a basic sequence of age-related psychosocial changes. The changes are normative in that they are common for most members of a population in a particular culture at a particular time.

TABLE 14.1 Four Views of Personality Development

Models	Questions Asked	Methods Used	Change or Stability
Normative-stage models	Does personality change in typical ways at certain periods throughout the life course?	In-depth interviews, biographical materials	Normative personality changes having to do with personal goals, work, and relationships occur in stages.
Timing-of-events model	When do important life events typically occur? What if they occur earlier or later than usual?	Statistical studies, interviews, questionnaires	Nonnormative timing of life events can cause stress and affect personality development.
Trait models	Do personality traits fall into groups, or clusters? Do these clusters of traits change with age?	Personality inventories, questionnaires, factor analysis	Personality changes substantially until age 30, more slowly thereafter.
Typological models	Can basic personality types be identified, and how well do they predict the life course?	Interviews, clinical judgments, Q-sorts, behavior ratings, self-reports	Personality types tend to show continuity from childhood through adulthood, but certain events can change the life course.

Source: Sternberg, R. J. "A Triangular Theory of Love." *Psychological Review*, 93, 1986, 119–135.

Erikson: Intimacy versus Isolation Erikson argued that at each stage in the life span people address particular crises. The normative crisis of young adulthood is **intimacy versus isolation.**

Erikson believed that young people who develop a strong sense of self during adolescence are in a better position, in early adulthood, to fuse their identity with that of another. In other words, knowing who you are and what you want makes it more likely you will end up with a compatible partner who fulfills your needs. This is important because if adults cannot make deep personal commitments to others, they risk becoming isolated and self-absorbed.

Resolution of this stage results in the virtue of love: mutual devotion between partners who have chosen to share their lives and have children. Erikson believed that a failure to fulfill what he believed to be a natural procreative urge has negative consequences for development. Quite rightly, his theory has been criticized for excluding single, celibate, homosexual, and childless people from his blueprint of healthy development.

Moreover, research has indicated that men and women may follow different developmental trajectories. For example, identity status achievement for men appears to be related to initiation of relationships, whereas for women it is more strongly related to the stability of relationships (Kahn, Zimmerman, Csikszentmihalyi & Getzels, 2014). Additionally, at least early in marriages, women tend to report higher intimacy than do men, which has implications for the health of the marriage later (Boden, Fischer & Niehuis, 2010).

Last, the early work on normative life stages was based on small groups of men and women born in the 1920s, 1930s, and 1940s. Today, young adults follow much more diverse developmental paths and, as a result, may develop differently than did the people in these studies. In addition, the findings of normative-stage research may not apply to other cultures, some of which have very different patterns of life-course development.

Despite these critiques, normative-stage research has nonetheless had an impact on the field. Psychologists, drawing on the work of Erikson, have identified developmental tasks that need to be accomplished for successful adaptation to each stage of life (Roisman, Masten, Coatsworth & Tellegen, 2004). Among the typical developmental tasks of young adulthood are leaving the childhood home for

intimacy versus isolation
Erikson's sixth stage of psychosocial development, in which young adults either form strong, long-lasting bonds with friends and romantic partners or face a possible sense of isolation and self-absorption.

Young adults who have a strong sense of self are likely to be ready for the demands of an intimate relationship, according to Erikson. ©David Lok/Purestock/SuperStock

advanced schooling, work, or military service; developing new and more intimate friendships and romantic relationships; and developing self-reliance and independence (Arnett, 2004; Scharf, Mayseless & Kivenson-Baron, 2004).

TIMING-OF-EVENTS MODEL

Instead of looking at adult personality development purely as a function of age, the **timing-of-events model** (Neugarten, Moore & Lowe, 1965; Neugarten & Neugarten, 1987) holds that the course of development depends on when certain events occur in people's lives. **Normative life events** (also called *normative age-graded events*) are those that typically happen at certain times of life—such events as marriage, parenthood, grandparenthood, and retirement. According to this model, people usually are keenly aware of both their timing and the **social clock**—their society's norms or expectations for the appropriate timing of life events.

If events occur on time, development proceeds smoothly. Stress or depression may come from an unexpected event (such as losing a job), an event that happens off time (being widowed at age 35), or the failure of an expected and wanted event to occur (being unable to have a child) (Rubin, Berntsen & Hutson, 2009). Personality differences influence the way people respond to life events and may even influence their timing. For example, a resilient person is likely to experience an easier transition to adulthood and the tasks and events that lie ahead than an overly anxious person.

The typical timing of events varies from culture to culture and from generation to generation. The timing of the social clock in U.S. culture has shifted somewhat in recent years (Arnett, 2010). The rise in the average age when adults first marry in the United States (U.S. Census Bureau, 2010a) and the trend toward delayed first childbirth (Martin, Hamilton, et al., 2010) are two examples of events for which timing has shifted. The social clock in many Western societies has also become more widely age-graded. Today people are more accepting of 40-year-old first-time parents and 40-year-old grandparents, or 50-year-old retirees and 75-year-old workers.

The timing-of-events model has made an important contribution to our understanding of adult personality by emphasizing the individual life course and challenging the idea of universal, age-related change. However, its usefulness may well be limited to cultures and historical periods in which norms of behavior are stable and widespread.

TRAIT MODELS: COSTA AND MCCRAE'S FIVE FACTORS

Traits can be thought of as mental, emotional, temperamental, or behavioral attributes that vary between people. **Trait models** are psychological models that focus on the measurement and examination of these different traits. One of the best known of these models is Paul T. Costa and Robert R. McCrae's **five-factor model** consisting of factors, or dimensions, that seem to underlie five groups of associated traits, known as the "Big Five." They are *(1) openness to experience (OTE); (2) conscientiousness (C); (3) extraversion (E); (4) agreeableness (A); and (5) neuroticism (N)* (see Figure 14.2).

Continuity and Change in the Five-Factor Model Do people change or stay the same? Overall, average personality changes are small (Cobb-Clark & Schurer, 2012). In analyses of longitudinal and cross-sectional samples of U.S. men and women, Costa and McCrae (1980, 1988, 1994a, 1994b, 2006; Costa et al., 1986; McCrae, 2002; McCrae & Costa, 1984; McCrae, Costa & Busch, 1986) found considerable continuity within people as well as normative developmental change in all five dimensions between adolescence and age 30, with much slower change thereafter. Agreeableness and conscientiousness generally increase in young adults, whereas neuroticism, extraversion, and openness to experience decline (McCrae et al., 2000; Specht, Egloff & Shmukle, 2011). These patterns of age-related change appeared to be universal across cultures and, thus, according to these authors, maturational (McCrae, 2002).

The observation that people's personalities, on average, remain similar does not mean change does not occur (Roberts & Mroczek, 2008; Roberts, Walton & Viechtbauer, 2006a, 2006b). Other research has found changes, almost exclusively in a positive

timing-of-events model
Theoretical model of personality development that describes adult psychosocial development as a response to the expected or unexpected occurrence and timing of important life events.

normative life events
In the timing-of-events model, commonly expected life experiences that occur at customary times.

social clock
Set of cultural norms or expectations for the times of life when certain important events, such as marriage, parenthood, entry into work, and retirement, should occur.

trait models
Theoretical models of personality development that focus on mental, emotional, temperamental, and behavioral traits, or attributes.

five-factor model
Theoretical model of personality, developed and tested by Costa and McCrae, based on the "Big Five" factors underlying clusters of related personality traits: open to new experiences, conscientiousness, extraversion, agreeableness, and neuroticism.

Openness	Conscientiousness	Extraversion	Agreeableness	Neuroticism (emotional stability)
• Imaginative or practical	• Organized or disorganized	• Sociable or retiring	• Softhearted or ruthless	• Calm or anxious
• Interested in variety or routine	• Careful or careless	• Fun-loving or somber	• Trusting or suspicious	• Secure or insecure
• Independent or conforming	• Disciplined or impulsive	• Affectionate or reserved	• Helpful or uncooperative	• Self-satisfied or self-pitying

FIGURE 14.2
Costa and McCrae's Five Factors of Personality

Each factor, or dimension, of personality represents a cluster of related traits. Use the acronym OCEAN to remember the main five: openness, conscientiousness, extraversion, agreeableness, and neuroticism.

Source: Costa, Jr., P. T. & McCrae, R. R. "Still stable after all of these years: Personality as a key to some issues in adulthood and old age." In P. Baltes and O. Brim, Jr. (Eds.), *Life-Span Development and Behavior*. New York: Academic Press, Vol. 3, 1980, 71, Figure 1.

direction, with especially large increases in social dominance (assertiveness, a facet of extraversion), conscientiousness, and emotional stability (Soto, John, Gosling & Potter, 2011; Roberts et al., 2006a).

The Big Five appear to be linked to various aspects of health and well-being. Big Five traits have been associated with marital satisfaction (Gattis, Berns, Simpson & Christensen, 2004), parent-infant relationships (Kochanska, Friesenborg, Lange & Martel, 2004), work-family conflict (Wayne, Musisca, & Fleeson, 2004), and personality disorders. With respect to specific factors, openness to experience has been related to verbal intelligence and creative achievement (DeYoung, Quilty, Peterson & Gray, 2014; Kaufman et al., 2016) as well as better health (Strickhouser, Zell & Krizan, 2017). Conscientiousness has been linked most strongly with health-related behaviors that contribute to long life (Bogg & Roberts, 2013; Strickhouser, Zell & Krizan, 2017). People low in extraversion are prone to agoraphobia (fear of open spaces) and social phobias (Bienvenu et al., 2001), while those high in extraversion tend to be high in well-being (Soto, 2015), but are more likely to engage in more substance use (Atherton, Robins, Rentfrow & Lamb, 2014). Agreeableness has been associated with less negative responses to stress; however, it also appears associated to greater declines in positive affect following a stressor (Leger, Charles, Turiano & Almeida, 2016). Last, people high in neuroticism tend to be subject to anxiety and depression (Bienvenu et al., 2001) and are more likely to be dependent on drugs (Valero et al., 2014).

Evaluating the Five-Factor Model Costa and McCrae's body of work originally made a powerful case for continuity of personality, especially after age 30, as based on maturational processes. More recent research has questioned that conclusion, and Costa and McCrae have now acknowledged that change occurs throughout the life span and that maturational processes may not be as strong of an influence as previously believed.

Some researchers have argued against strong genetic or maturational influences on personality and emphasized life experiences instead. There is growing evidence for this position. While onetime events appear to have little influence on personality change, long-term stressors such as chronic health problems do appear to exert an influence (Elkins, Kassenboehmer & Schurer, 2017). Positive events matter too; people with successful, satisfying careers in young adulthood tend to show disproportionate increases in emotional stability and conscientiousness (Roberts & Mroczek, 2008). Moreover, getting married, divorced, or having a baby can also affect levels of the Big Five traits (Specht, Egloff & Shmukle, 2011). Last, heritability estimates for personality decline with age, suggesting increasingly important environmental influences (Briley & Tucker-Drob, 2017).

It is important to remember that while life events affect personality, personality also affects the probability of particular events occurring. People high in agreeableness are more likely to lose their jobs, highly extraverted people are more likely to move in with a partner, and women high in neuroticism are more likely to marry (Specht, Egloff & Schmukle, 2011). Moroever, effects are interactive. For example, adolescents who are sociable and affable tend to rise faster in their early careers; and, in turn, those who are in higher-status, more satisfying jobs tend to become more sociable and affable over time (Roberts, Caspi & Moffitt, 2003).

TYPOLOGICAL MODELS

Jack Block (1971; Block & Block, 2006) was a pioneer in the **typological approach.** Typological research seeks to complement and expand trait research by looking at personality as a functioning whole.

Researchers have identified three personality types: *ego-resilient, overcontrolled,* and *undercontrolled.* These three types differ in **ego resiliency,** or adaptability under stress, and **ego control,** or self-control. *Ego-resilient* people are well-adjusted, self-confident, independent, articulate, attentive, helpful, cooperative, and task-focused. *Overcontrolled* people are shy, quiet, anxious, and dependable; they tend to keep their thoughts to themselves and to withdraw from conflict, and they are the most subject to depression. *Undercontrolled* people are active, energetic, impulsive, stubborn, and easily distracted.

Ego resiliency interacts with ego control to determine whether or not behavior is adaptive or maladaptive. For example, underrcontrol can lead to creativity and resourcefulness or, if it is excessive, to externalizing and antisocial behaviors. By the same token, overcontrol can help make a person highly focused and planful, or it can lead to an inflexible and inhibited style of behavior. More extreme forms of either overcontrol or undercontrol are generally associated with low levels of ego resilience (Kremen & Block, 1998). For example, a longitudinal study showed that children who were overcontrolled between ages 4 and 6 tended to be shy in late adolescence and emerging adulthood, whereas those who were undercontrolled in early childhood were more aggressive; and these traits became more accentuated between ages 17 and 23. In addition, both overcontrolled and undercontrolled types have more difficulty than more resilient types in assuming adult social roles: leaving the parental home, establishing romantic relationships, and getting part-time jobs (Denissen, Asendorpf & van Aken, 2008). These or similar personality types seem to exist in both sexes, across cultures and ethnic groups, and in children, adolescents, and adults (Caspi, 1998; Hart, Hofmann, Edelstein & Keller, 1997; Pulkkinen, 1996; Robins, John, Caspi, Moffitt & Stouthamer-Loeber, 1996; van Lieshout, Haselager, Riksen-Walraven & van Aken, 1995).

typological approach
Theoretical approach that identifies broad personality types, or styles.

ego resiliency
The ability to adapt flexibly and resourcefully to potential sources of stress.

ego control
Self-control and the self-regulation of impulses.

Foundations of Intimate Relationships

Erikson saw the development of intimate relationships as the crucial task of young adulthood. The need to form strong, stable, close, caring relationships is a powerful motivator of human behavior.

FRIENDSHIP

Friendships during young adulthood are often less stable than in either adolescence or later adulthood, primarily because people in emerging adulthood relocate more frequently (Collins & Van Dulmen, 2006). Nonetheless, many young adults manage to maintain high-quality, committed, long-distance friendships (Johnson, Becker, Craig, Gilchrist & Haigh, 2009), sometimes using social networking sites to keep in touch across geographical distance (Subrahmanyam, Reich, Waecheter & Espinoza, 2008). But regardless of whether the friendships are virtual or not, they tend to center on work and parenting activities, sharing confidences, and advice. Some friendships are intimate and supportive, whereas others are marked by frequent conflict (Hartup & Stevens, 1999).

Young single adults tend to rely on friendships to fulfill their social needs more than young married adults or young parents do. Over the course of young adulthood, the number of friends and the amount of time spent with them gradually decreases, presumably

Intimate relationships involve self-awareness, empathy, and the ability to communicate.
©Creatas/Getty Images

as leisure time decreases and responsibility to others increases. People with friends tend to have a sense of well-being—although it is unclear if friendship causes well-being, or if people who feel good about themselves have an easier time making friends (Myers, 2000).

Women typically have more intimate friendships than men do (Hall, 2011). Women are more likely to share confidences with friends (Rosenbluth & Steil, 1995), to talk with their friends about marital problems, and to receive advice and support (Helms, Crouter & McHale, 2003). Men, by contrast, are more likely to share information and activities (Rosenbluth & Steil, 1995). However, when men do share intimate details, as with women, this results in increased closeness (Bowman, 2009).

Close supportive friendships are sometimes incorporated into family networks. These types of friends are known as **"fictive kin"**—they are treated as family members despite a lack of blood relationship. For example, fictive kinship relationships often develop for gay and lesbian people who have straight friends of the opposite sex, particularly if those friends are unmarried or have an unconventional lifestyle (Muraco, 2006).

fictive kin
Friends who are considered and behave like family members.

In recent years, young adults' use of social networking sites has increased dramatically (Facebook, 2011). In fact, the number of people using such sites doubled between 2008 and 2010 (Hampton, Goulet, Rainie & Purcell, 2011). Some people have argued that such sites can be harmful, and that online relationships can interfere with the formation of high-quality friendships in real life (McPherson, Smith-Lovin & Brashears, 2006). However, social networking sites can have advantages. For example, recent research indicates that social networking sites are often used to maintain and strengthen ties to others (Hampton et al., 2011; Subrahmanyam et al., 2008; Manago, Taylor & Greenfield, 2012), and they are related to increased participation in political discussion and activities (Hampton et al., 2011; Zhang, Johnson, Seltzer & Bichard, 2010).

LOVE

According to Robert J. Sternberg's **triangular theory of love** (1986, 1998a, 2006), the crucial elements of love are intimacy, passion, and commitment. *Intimacy,* the emotional element, involves self-disclosure, which leads to connection, warmth, and trust. *Passion,* the motivational element, is based on inner drives that translate physiological arousal into sexual desire. *Commitment,* the cognitive element, is the decision to love and to stay with the beloved. The degree to which each of the three elements is present determines what type of love people feel.

triangular theory of love
Sternberg's theory that patterns of love hinge on the balance among three elements: intimacy, passion, and commitment.

As adolescents move into adulthood, they tend to feel an increasing amount of intimacy, passion, and commitment in their romantic relationships (Sumter, Valkenburg & Peter, 2013). Their formation of a sense of identity achievement seems to affect the quality of romantic relationships. For example, identity achievement status in young adults is associated with stronger feelings of companionship, worth, affection, and emotional support within romantic relationships (Barry, Madsen, Nelson, Carroll & Badger, 2009). This supports Erikson's (1973) assertions that the formation of a secure sense of identity is necessary for the establishment of high-quality intimate relationships.

While they are more alike than different, men and women show modest differences in intimacy, passion, and commitment within their romantic relationships. Generally, women report greater intimacy in their relationships, while men report greater passion. Levels of commitment, however, appear to be similar in both genders (Sumter, Valkenburg & Peter, 2013). The length of the relationship affects the dynamics of the relationship. Generally, passion is higher at the beginning of the relationship and declines over time as commitment increases (Ahmetoglu, Swami & Chamorro-Premuzic, 2010).

Marital and Nonmarital Lifestyles

In many Western countries, today's rules for socially acceptable lifestyles are more flexible than they were during the first half of the twentieth century. People marry later or have children outside of marriage, and more people end their marriages. Some people remain single, some remarry, and others live with a partner of either sex.

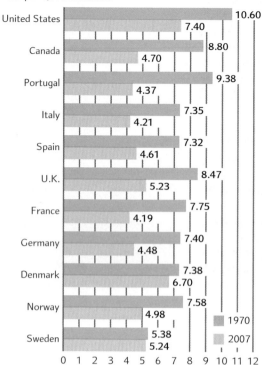

Rate per 1,000 individuals

Country	1970	2007
United States	10.60	7.40
Canada	8.80	4.70
Portugal	9.38	4.37
Italy	7.35	4.21
Spain	7.32	4.61
U.K.	8.47	5.23
France	7.75	4.19
Germany	7.40	4.48
Denmark	7.38	6.70
Norway	7.58	4.98
Sweden	5.38	5.24

0 1 2 3 4 5 6 7 8 9 10 11 12

FIGURE 14.3

Marriage Rates by Country, 1970 and 2007

Source: National Healthy Marriage Resource Center. *Marriage trends in Western culture: A fact sheet.*

SINGLE LIFE

The proportion of young adults ages 25 to 34 in the United States who have not yet married tripled between 1970 and 2005 (U.S. Census Bureau, 2007b) and continued to increase to 54 percent in 2010 (Mather & Lavery, 2012). In 1960, the age at first marriage was 20 years for women and 23 years for men. In 2014, this number has risen to 27 years for women and 29 years for men (Wang & Parker, 2014). This decline in marriage has occurred across all age groups but is most prominent in young adults (Cohn, Passel, Wang & Livingston, 2011). The trend is particularly pronounced among African Americans (Wang & Parker, 2014). Between 1970 and 2007, there has been a significant decline in the marriage rate in almost all countries (Figure 14.3).

Some young adults stay single because they have not found the right mate; others are single by choice. More women today are self-supporting, and there is less social pressure to marry. At the same time, many single adults are postponing marriage and children due to economic instability (Wang & Morin, 2009), a desire to coordinate career goals with long-term relationship goals (Shulman & Connolly, 2013), or out of a desire for self-fulfillment. Some enjoy sexual freedom. Some find the lifestyle exciting. Some just like being alone. And some postpone or avoid marriage because of fear that it will end in divorce.

Since the 1960s, Americans have become more sexually permissive. They are likely to have more sexual partners, have casual sex, and be more accepting of premarital sex (Twenge, Sherman & Wells, 2015). One pattern that has become increasingly common is that of "friends with benefits" (FWB). FWB relationships are relationships in which there is a blend of friendship and physical intimacy, but little commitment. Men are more likely to seek out FWB out of a desire for sexual activity, whereas women are more likely to express a desire for an emotional connection and for the relationship to eventually progress to a committed romantic relationship (Lehmiller, VanderDrift & Kelly, 2011; Gusarova, Fraser & Alderson, 2012). Given these different motivations, it is perhaps not surprising that women report greater levels of deception in FWB relationships (Quirk, Owen & Fincham, 2014). Despite this, both men and women generally report positive emotions about their FWB relationships, although men are more likely to do so (Owen & Fincham, 2011). As a whole, young adults in such relationships do not appear to be at greater risk of psychological distress than their counterparts in committed romantic relationships (Eisenberg, Ackard, Resnick & Neumark-Sztainer, 2009).

On June 26, 2015, the United States Supreme Court legalized same-sex marriage.
©Hinterhaus Productions/ DigitalVision/Getty Images

GAY AND LESBIAN RELATIONSHIPS

In the past 40 years or so, gay and lesbian adults have increasingly come out of the closet and are living openly. Surveys suggest that 40 to 60 percent of gay men and 45 to 80 percent of lesbians in the United States are in romantic relationships, and 8 to 28 percent of these couples have lived together for at least 10 years (Kurdek, 2004). This increasing openness has led to greater societal acceptance of homosexuality. Currently, 87 percent of Americans know someone who is gay or lesbian and about half report a close family member or friend is gay or lesbian (Drake, 2013). It may be that the increasing openness with which gay and lesbian people are living their lives is affecting public opinion. Those who are close to a gay or lesbian person are more likely to be supportive of gay marriage and antidiscrimination laws (Neidorf & Morin, 2011), and a current high of 62 percent of Americans now support gay marriage (Pew Research Center, 2017).

In the United States, gays and lesbians struggled for decades to obtain legal recognition of their unions. They argued that same-sex marriage offered benefits that civil unions did not (Herek, 2006; King & Bartlett,

2006). Research supported their assertion: Gay and lesbian people in those states that had legalized gay marriage and who were thus able to marry showed lower levels of depression, stress, and internalized homophobia and felt they had more meaning in their lives (Riggle, Rotosky & Riggle, 2010). On June 26, 2015, the U.S. Supreme Court legalized gay marriage, ruling that bans on same-sex marriage were unconstitutional. Prior to the Supreme Court decision, approximately 8 percent of gay, lesbian, bisexual, or transgender people were married to a same-sex partner. Currently, this number has risen to slightly over 10 percent (Gallup News, 2017), or some 1.1 million American adults (Romero, 2017).

In most ways, gay and lesbian relationships mirror heterosexual relationships. Gay and lesbian couples tend to be at least as satisfied with their relationships as heterosexual couples (Farr, Forssell & Patterson, 2010). The factors that predict the quality of both homosexual and heterosexual relationships—personality traits, perceptions of the relationship by the partners, ways of communicating and resolving conflicts, and social support—are similar (Kurdek, 2005, 2006). Indeed, committed same-sex relationships are hardly distinguishable in quality from committed heterosexual relationships (Roisman, Clausell, Holland, Fortuna & Elieff, 2008). Just as with heterosexual relationships, support from family and friends is related to how well and how long the relationship lasts (Kurdek, 2008).

Differences between gay and lesbian couples and heterosexual couples also have emerged from research (Kurdek, 2006). First, gay and lesbian couples are more likely than heterosexual couples to negotiate household chores on a more egalitarian basis. Second, they tend to resolve conflicts in a more positive atmosphere than heterosexual couples do. Third, gay and lesbian relationships tend to be less stable than heterosexual relationships, perhaps due to the lack of institutional supports (Pope, Murray & Mobley, 2010).

Beliefs about gay marriage exist in concert with political orientation; however, the striking partisan divisions of the past appear to be lessening. In 2012, approximately 69 percent of Democrats supported same-sex marriage. By contrast, only 32 percent of Republicans supported it (Pew Research Center, 2012). However, only 5 years later, 46 percent of Republicans—a historic high for this group—supported gay marriage. Religion also plays a role. Of those people who characterize themselves as unaffiliated with any religion, 85 percent support gay marriage. While religiously affiliated people are less likely to endorse gay marriage, the number that are in favor of it has also increased. For example, in 2007 approximately 14 percent of white evangelical Christians were in favor of gay marriage. In 2017, that number rose to 35 percent. In addition, age has been implicated in the debate, with younger generations becoming increasingly accepting of same-sex marriage (Pew Research Center, 2017).

Forty-five years ago, same-sex couples were not legally recognized in any country (Saez, 2011). However, shifting attitudes have led to great changes in many countries. Gay marriage is now legal in approximately two dozen countries, concentrated primarily in Europe and the Americas (Masci, Sciupac & Lipka, 2017). However, attitudes vary widely. Countries in Asia and Africa tend to be less tolerant of homosexuality (McGee, 2016).

COHABITATION

Cohabitation is an increasingly common lifestyle in which an unmarried couple involved in a sexual relationship live together.

Types of Cohabitation: International Comparisons The prevalence of cohabitation varies widely across countries. For example, within the Americas, rates are relatively low in Mexico and the United States, and higher in Central America, the Caribbean, and Amazonian areas (Lopez-Gay, Esteve, Lopez-Colas et al., 2014). Surveys in 14 European countries, Canada, New Zealand, and the United States also found wide variations in cohabitation rates, ranging from more than 14 percent in France to less than 2 percent in Italy (Figure 14.4).

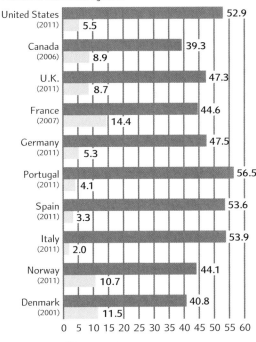

Percent of individuals aged 20+

Country	Married	Cohabiting
United States (2011)	52.9	5.5
Canada (2006)	39.3	8.9
U.K. (2011)	47.3	8.7
France (2007)	44.6	14.4
Germany (2011)	47.5	5.3
Portugal (2011)	56.5	4.1
Spain (2011)	53.6	3.3
Italy (2011)	53.9	2.0
Norway (2011)	44.1	10.7
Denmark (2001)	40.8	11.5

■ Married ▫ Cohabiting (recent estimates)

FIGURE 14.4

Marriage and Cohabitation Rates of Individuals Aged 20+ by Country

Source: Organisation for Economic Co-operation and Development. *Cohabitation rate and prevalence of other forms of partnership* [data report], 2013.

Cohabitation in the United States In 2016 an estimated 7.2 million unmarried couples were living together in the United States. After rising for a decade, the cohabitation rate declined by 2 percent from the levels seen in 2015 (U.S. Census Bureau, 2016), perhaps due to the increased availability of marriage for gay and lesbian couples. The overall increase in cohabitation in the United States has occurred among all racial/ethnic groups and at all educational levels, but people with less education are more likely to cohabit than those with higher education (Fields, 2004; Seltzer, 2004; Manning, 2013). Cohabiters also are likely to be less religious, less traditional, have less confidence in their relationships, be more accepting of divorce, be more negative and aggressive in their interactions with their romantic partners, and communicate less effectively (Jose, O'Leary & Moyer, 2010). About half of cohabitating adults are younger than 35 years of age (Stepler, 2017).

Although U.S. family law currently gives cohabitors few of the legal rights and benefits of marriage, this situation is changing, particularly with regard to protection for children of cohabiting couples (Cherlin, 2004; Seltzer, 2004). Other countries, including the United Kingdom, Australia, Canada, and New Zealand, have enacted legislation giving committed cohabitating couples rights similar to married couples (Waggoner, 2015).

Cohabiting relationships tend to be less satisfying and less stable than marriages (Binstock & Thornton, 2003; Heuveline & Timberlake, 2004; Seltzer, 2004). In particular, cohabiting couples who have divergent expectations about the division of household labor are highly likely to break up (Hohmann-Marriott, 2006).

Some research suggests that cohabiting couples who later marry tend to have unhappier marriages and greater likelihood of divorce than those who wait to live together until marriage (Bramlett & Mosher, 2002; Dush, Cohan & Amato, 2003). However, in a nationally representative cross-sectional survey of 6,577 women ages 15 to 45, women who cohabited or had premarital sex *only with their future husbands* had no special risk of marital dissolution (Teachman, 2003). Many cohabitors who want to marry put off marriage until they feel their economic circumstances permit it (Smock, Manning & Porter, 2005). These young adults are not generally using cohabitation to replace marriage, but rather view it as one step along the way to marriage (Manning, Longmore & Giordano, 2007). Thus, it appears there may be fundamental differences in types of cohabiting couples, with those couples who eventually marry having more stable and happier relationships than those who do not, perhaps as a result of a stronger initial commitment to the relationship (Jose et al., 2010).

Beliefs about cohabitation, cohabitation patterns, and the stability of cohabitation vary among racial/ethnic groups and are very complex in nature. Couples who cohabitate, on average, are younger, black, and less religious (Pew Research Center, 2007a). Perhaps for economic reasons, black and Hispanic couples are less likely than non-Hispanic white couples to regard cohabitation as a trial marriage and more likely to regard it as a substitute for marriage (Phillips & Sweeney, 2005). White couples who cohabit are more likely than other groups to end the relationship; their children have almost 10 times the risk of going through a parental separation (Osborne, Manning & Smock, 2007). Older and younger adults show a distinct difference in their views of the morality of cohabitation, with younger adults much more likely to think living together without being married is not wrong (Pew Research Center, 2012).

Rates of serial cohabitation, especially in disadvantaged groups, rose by almost 40 percent in the late 1990s and early 2000s (Lichter, Turner & Sassler, 2010). Cohabitation after divorce is more common than premarital cohabitation and may function as a form of remarriage mate selection. However, postdivorce cohabitation, especially with serial partners, greatly delays remarriage and contributes to instability in a new marriage (Xu, Hudspeth & Bartkowski, 2006).

MARRIAGE

The United States and other postindustrial societies have seen a weakening of the social norms that once made marriage almost universal. Marriage has been affected by demographic and economic changes. For example, more recent cohorts of young women are likely to have attained a higher educational level than previous generations of women and are generally more economically successful. In 1970, only 4 percent of women 35 to 44 years of age made more money than their husbands, but by 2007 this number had increased to 22 percent. One consequence is that marriage is now associated with increases in economic security for both men and women (Cohn & Fry, 2010). Religious beliefs also affect the marriage rate. Religious people are more likely both to endorse earlier marriage (Fuller, Frost & Burr, 2015) and to marry at earlier ages (Uecker & Stokes, 2008).

What Marriage Means to Emerging and Young Adults Today In the United States, despite the vast demographic changes of the last half-century, some 90 percent of adults will still opt to marry at some point in their lives (Whitehead & Poponoe, 2003). Although the proportion of emerging and young adults who choose to marry is not much different from what it was at the beginning of the twentieth century (Fussell & Furstenberg, 2005), they do seem to think about it differently. Many young adults view traditional marriage with its rigid gender roles as no longer viable in today's world. Instead, they expect greater space for individual interests and pursuits and put more emphasis on friendship and compatibility (Kefalas, Furstenberg & Napolitano, 2005). Indeed, the vast majority of adults in the United States today view the primary purpose of marriage as "the mutual happiness and fulfillment of adults" rather than as being based on parenting and children (Pew Research Center, 2007a).

This mass wedding in India, organized by social workers for members of impoverished families, is an example of the variety of marriage customs around the world. ©Vishal Owe/EPA/REX/Shutterstock

Most young adults plan to marry, but only when they feel ready; and they see getting on their feet financially and establishing themselves in stable jobs or careers as formidable obstacles (Kefalas et al., 2005). This orientation toward marriage includes about 80 percent of young adults and is more characteristic of young adults from urban environments. Rural Americans, by contrast, are more likely to see marriage as an inevitable step toward adulthood, to marry early, and to hold traditional views on marriage (Kefalas, Furstenberg, Carr & Napolitano, 2011).

Entering Matrimony For the reasons just mentioned—as well as because of the increasing enrollment in higher education—the typical marrying age has risen in industrialized countries. Thirty to 50 years ago, most people married in or before their early twenties. In the United States in 2009 the median age of first-time bridegrooms was 28.3 and of first-time brides, 25.8 (Copen, Daniels, Vespa & Mosher, 2012). In England, France, Germany, and Italy, the average marrying age is even higher: 29 or 30 for men and 27 for women (van Dyk, 2005).

Historically and across cultures the most common way of selecting a mate has been through arrangement, either by the parents or by professional matchmakers. Generally, one of the primary beliefs about the role of marriage is focused on the union of two families, rather than on love between two individuals. Given this orientation, it is perhaps not surprising to find that couples in arranged marriages have very different expectations of their spouses. There are decreased expectations of intimacy and love, and responsibility and commitment are emphasized. However, despite these variations in beliefs about what marriage should look like, couples in arranged marriages appear to be equally happy in their relationships (Regan, Lakhanpal & Anguiano, 2012; Myers, Madithil & Tingle, 2005).

In many cultures, the Western ideal of a relationship based on love and personal attraction seems to have changed the nature of arranged marriage, with "semi-arranged" marriages becoming more and more common (Naito & Gielen, 2005). In these situations, parents are heavily involved in the process of finding a marriage partner, but the young adult holds veto power over potential spouses.

The transition to married life brings major changes in sexual functioning, living arrangements, rights and responsibilities, attachments, and loyalties. Among other tasks, marriage partners need to redefine the connection with their original families, balance intimacy with autonomy, and establish a fulfilling sexual relationship.

Extramarital Sexual Activity It is hard to know just how common extramarital sex is, but surveys suggest that it is much less common than is generally assumed. About 18 percent of married people report having had extramarital relations at some time during their married lives. Current extramarital activity is most prevalent among younger adults

window on the world

POPULAR WEDDING TRADITIONS AND WHERE THEY COME FROM

A wedding is a ceremony intended to join two people together in marriage. Most cultures have longstanding traditions that are still practiced today. Often these traditions were designed to ward off evil spirits and bring luck and good fortune to the new couple. Special clothing, symbolic elements, and traditional rites are usually part of the ceremony.

Brides wear white in much of Europe and America. Wearing white is symbolic of purity and virginity of the bride. This tradition began when Queen Victoria wore a white gown to her wedding in 1840. Before this, white was worn as a symbol of mourning; red was the most popular color to be married in (Smithsonian, 2014). In China, brides still wear red, which is considered to be a symbol of good luck and good fortune (Traditional Chinese Weddings, 2014).

In traditional West African weddings, couples would jump a broom together as a symbol of the joining of two families and the couple starting their new life together. This ritual has become a popular part of many African American couples' weddings today as a means of showing respect for their ancestors (African Wedding Traditions, 2013).

Some traditions are widespread but their origins are hard to pin down. For example, one of the most common traditions is to throw rice, oats, wheat, beans, peas, or other seeds at the new couple as they exit the ceremony. It symbolizes new life, fertility, and prosperity for the couple. Other things are used today such as birdseed, confetti, or bubbles. This tradition has been seen in Greece, France, Germany, Czechoslovakia, Spain, Italy, the United States, and numerous other countries (Monger, 2013) but its origin is still unclear.

"Something old, something new, something borrowed, something blue, and a silver sixpence in her shoe" is an old English rhyme that describes things the bride can wear to ward off evil and bring happiness, love, and prosperity to her marriage. This tradition is still practiced in England, Scotland, and much of the United States. Kate Middleton, in her wedding

to Prince William, an heir to the British throne, could be seen taking part in it (Gripper, 2012). It has also been seen in American pop culture during wedding scenes on shows including *Friends*, *Grey's Anatomy*, and *How I Met Your Mother* (The Most Memorable TV Weddings of All Time, 2015).

The wedding veil is also a common tradition used today. Its ancient purpose is to ward off evil spirits by hiding the bride. This was combined with dressing the bridesmaids similarly to the bride to confuse and deter evil spirits. The tradition was also used in arranged marriages in Middle Eastern cultures to hide the bride from her new husband until after the ceremony so he could not change his mind if he did not like what he saw (Monger, 2013). Variations of this tradition include traditional Chinese brides wearing a full red veil to hide their face while being escorted to the ceremony under a red umbrella to ward off evil spirits and encourage fertility and prosperity for the new couple (Traditional Chinese Weddings, 2014).

A wedding reception or party is also common across most cultures. Depending on religion, status, and custom, these can include speeches, a toast, dancing, and traditional wedding foods. This is a time for friends and family to celebrate with the new couple. Length and formality of the reception can vary. For example, in India, the celebration will go on for several days; whereas in Russia the reception lasts 2 hours (Monger, 2013). Marriage is a longstanding tradition, and a wedding ceremony/reception is a common ritual that is performed in almost all countries throughout the world.

what's your view Have you thought about getting married and the traditions that you might follow one day? Where do you think these traditions come from, and what is their meaning?

---

and about twice as common among husbands as among wives (T. W. Smith, 2003). Generally, extramarital activity occurs earlier in the relationship; marriages that last for long periods of time show decreasing risk (DeMaris, 2009). More than half of those engaging in extramarital sex will divorce or separate from their partner (Allen & Atkins, 2012).

Young adults of both sexes have become less permissive in their attitudes toward extramarital sex (Twenge, Sherman & Wells, 2015; T. W. Smith, 2005), and infidelity is disapproved of more than homosexuality or premarital sex in Britain, Ireland, Germany, Sweden, and Poland, though degrees of disapproval differ from one country to another (Scott, 1998).

The changing landscape of technology has led to increased use of the Internet as a means by which to initiate an extramarital affair (Hertlein & Piercy, 2006). While different couples define electronic acts of infidelity differently, they generally include such actions as viewing or participating in pornography, sending or receiving sexually explicit photographs or videos, engaging in sexual activity while online or on the telephone, or messaging inappropriately intimate or sexual content to a person other than the spouse. While online acts of infidelity at times do not consist of actual physical contact, they can nonetheless be perceived as betrayals and result in similar negative consequences for the marital relationship (Whitty, 2003), including a loss of trust, psychological distress, and trauma (Schneider, Weiss & Samenow, 2012).

Marital Satisfaction Married people tend to be happier than unmarried people, though those in unhappy marriages are less happy than those who are unmarried or divorced (Myers, 2000). People who marry and stay married, especially women, tend to become better off financially than those who do not marry or who divorce (Hirschl, Altobelli & Rank, 2003; Wilmoth & Koso, 2002). However, this does not necessarily mean marriage causes wealth; it may be that people who seek wealth and who have characteristics favorable to obtaining it are more likely to marry and to stay married (Hirschl et al., 2003). Nor is it certain that marriage causes happiness; it may be that the greater happiness of married people reflects a greater tendency of happy people to marry (Lucas, Clark, Georgellis & Diener, 2003; Stutzer & Frey, 2006).

Marriages, by and large, seem to be just about as happy as they were a quarter-century ago, but husbands and wives spend less time doing things together. Marital happiness is positively affected by increased economic resources, equal decision making, nontraditional gender attitudes, and support for the norm of lifelong marriage. Marital happiness is negatively affected by premarital cohabitation, extramarital affairs, wives' job demands, and wives' longer working hours. Increases in husbands' share of housework appear to lower marital satisfaction among husbands but improve it among wives (Amato, Johnson, Booth & Rogers, 2003). In fact "sharing household chores" is viewed as very important to marital success by approximately 62 percent of American respondents (Pew Research Center, 2007b). A large difference in wage earning potential between spouses is associated with decreases in happiness (Stuzer & Frey, 2006).

For most couples, sex impacts relationship quality. The frequency of sex, sexual satisfaction, and marital satisfaction are closely related to and predict each other (McNulty, Wenner & Fisher, 2016). Americans have sex less often than media images suggest, and married people have sex more often than singles, though not as often as cohabitors. However, married couples report more emotional satisfaction from sex than single or cohabiting couples (Waite & Joyner, 2000). What may be more important than the actual amount of sex a married couple has is whether or not they both desire roughly similar levels of sexual activity. High discrepancy with respect to the desire for sexual activity is associated with lower relationship satisfaction, lower relationship stability, and greater conflict (Willoughby, Farero & Busby, 2014).

Another factor underlying marital satisfaction may be a difference in what the man and woman expect from marriage. Women tend to place more importance on emotional expressiveness—their own and their husbands'—than men do (Lavee & Ben-Ari, 2004). Empathy, validation and caring are related to feelings of intimacy and better relationship quality (Sullivan, Pasch, Johnson & Bradbury, 2010). Men's efforts to express positive emotion to their wives, to pay attention to the dynamics of the relationship, and to set aside time for activities focused on building the relationship are important to women's perceptions of marital quality (Wilcox & Nock, 2006).

Parenthood

People in industrial societies typically have fewer children today than in earlier generations, and they start having them later in life, in many cases because they spend their emerging adult years getting an education and establishing a career. In 2015 the average age of first births in the United States had risen to 26.4 years (National Vital Statistics Report, 2017;

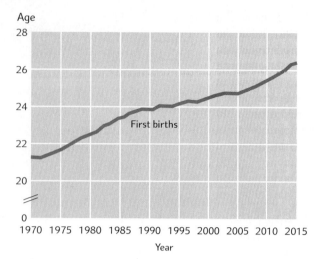

Age

FIGURE 14.5

Mean Age of Mother at First Birth: United States

Many women today start families at a later age than in their parents' generation, raising the average age at first birth.

Source: National Center for Health Statistics, Division of Vital Statistics, *National Vital Statistics Report*, 2016.

Figure 14.5), and the percentage of women who give birth for the first time in their late thirties and even in their forties and fifties has increased dramatically, often with the help of fertility treatments (Martin, Hamilton, Ventura, Osterman & Mathews, 2013).

A woman's age at first birth varies with ethnic and cultural background. In 2015, Asian American and Pacific Islander women had their first babies at an average age of 29.6, whereas American Indian and Alaska Native women gave birth for the first time, on average, at just 23.2 years. Black women and Hispanic women had their first child at about 24.5 years of age, and white women had their first child at 27.2 years (Martin, Hamilton, Osterman, Driscoll & Mathews, 2017).

In 2015, 40.3 percent of U.S. births were to unmarried women, a decline for the seventh straight year from the historic high of 41 percent in 2009 (Martin, Hamilton, Osterman, Driscoll & Mathews, 2017). The U.S. fertility rate is higher than that in several other developed countries, such as Japan and the United Kingdom, where the average age at first birth is about 29 (Martin, Ruble & Szkrybalo, 2002; van Dyk, 2005).

At the same time, an increasing proportion of U.S. couples remain childless. The percentage of households with children fell from 45 percent in 1970 (Fields, 2004) to approximately 28.7 percent in 2016 (Schondelmyer, 2017). The aging of the population as well as delays in marriage and childbearing may help explain these data, but some couples undoubtedly remain childless by choice. Some see marriage primarily as a way to enhance their intimacy, not as an institution dedicated to the bearing and raising of children (Popenoe & Whitehead, 2003). Others may be discouraged by the financial burdens of parenthood and the difficulty of combining parenthood with employment. Better child care and other support services might help couples make truly voluntary decisions.

PARENTHOOD AS A DEVELOPMENTAL EXPERIENCE

Any major life transition is a pivotal time of developmental change that can result in positive or negative outcomes. Among key experiences in life is the birth of a child.

Men's and Women's Involvement in Parenthood Most mothers now work outside the home. The labor force participation rate for mothers with children under the age of 6 years is almost 65 percent, a number that rises to 75 percent when mothers with children up to the age of 18 are included (U.S. Bureau of Labor Statistics, 2017). Despite working outside the home, women spend more time on child care than their counterparts did in the 1960s, when 60 percent of children lived with a breadwinner father and a stay-at-home mother. Today, only about 30 percent of children live in such families. Yet married mothers spent 12.9 hours a week on child care in 2000 compared with 10.6 hours in 1965, and single mothers spent 11.8 hours a week on child care as compared with 7.5 hours in 1965 (Bianchi, Robinson & Milkie, 2006).

What about fathers? Generally, most fathers are not as involved as mothers are (Yeung, Sandberg, Davis-Kean & Hofferth, 2001). However, the amount of time fathers spend with their children has gone up. For example, married fathers spent more than twice as much time with child care (6.5 hours) and housework (9.7 hours) in 2000 than they did in 1965 (Bianchi et al., 2006). On weekends, as their children get older, the time fathers spend with their children is more equal to that of mothers (Yeung et al., 2001). Work affects this as well. Fathers with long working hours report wanting more time to spend with their children but being unable to do so (Milkie et al., 2004).

The impacts of having children are also indirect. In addition to time spent in child care itself, fathers living with dependent children are less likely to be involved in their own independent social activities. However, they are more likely to be engaged in school-

Celebrating a child's birthday is one of the many joys of parenthood.
©Corbis/VCG/Getty Images

related activities, church groups, and community service organizations. The result of this is generally positive—the most involved fathers also report the highest levels of satisfaction (Eggebeen & Knoester, 2001).

How Parenthood Affects Marital Satisfaction How does parenthood affect the relationship between marriage partners? Results are mixed. Some studies show that marital satisfaction typically declines during the child-raising years—and the more children, the greater the decline. Moreover, mothers of young infants tend to feel the effects most strongly. For example, only 38 percent of new mothers report high marital satisfaction compared with 62 percent of childless wives (Twenge, Campbell & Foster, 2003).

Why do these declines occur? New parents are likely to experience stressors that can affect their health and state of mind. Taking care of newborn babies is difficult and often comes with sleep deprivation, uncertainty, and isolation. Nighttime crying, for example, is associated with a decrease in marital satisfaction in the 1st year of the child's life (Meijer & van den Wittenboer, 2007). If the woman was working outside the home and is now staying home, the burden of housework and child care may fall mostly on her. Indeed, the division of household tasks is a common issue among new parents (Schulz, Cowan & Cowan, 2006). Many couples find their relationship becoming more "traditional" following the birth of a child, with the woman often engaging in the bulk of caregiving and housekeeping (Cox & Paley, 2003). The perceptions of unfairness and inequity that result from this process can damage the marital relationship (Dew & Wilcox, 2011).

However, the picture is not all bad. Other studies tell a different story, and it may be that additional variables are needed to truly understand the effect of a new baby. For example, whether or not the couple was happy prior to the pregnancy, whether or not the pregnancy was planned, and the age of parents affects marital satisfaction after the birth of a child (Lawrence, Rothman, Cobb, Rothman & Bradbury, 2008; Nelson, Kushlev, English, Dunn & Lyubomirsky, 2013). Other studies have found no differences in marital satisfaction in the first year of marriage for couples that do and do not have children (McHale & Huston, 1985), and some data indicate that parents have greater happiness, positive emotions, and meaning in life than non-parents (Nelson et al., 2013).

A recent attempt to make sense of these contrasting findings suggests that when studies are examined in concert, a small but significant decrease in marital satisfaction is common 1 to 2 years after the birth of a child. However, this decline is also found in married couples without a child. Thus it may be a general relational process rather than one specific to the parenting transition (Mitnick, Heyman & Slep, 2009).

There are indications, too, that declines in satisfaction are not inevitable. Parents who participate in professionally led couples discussion groups about parenting issues and relationships, beginning in the last trimester of pregnancy, report significantly smaller declines in satisfaction (Schulz et al., 2006). Additionally, the marital relationships of parents who have secure attachments weather the birth of a child more effectively than those who are anxious or avoidant in their relationships (Kohn et al., 2012). Factors outside the home matter as well. A good work-life balance, and the consequent reduction in stress, is also associated with less of a decline in marital satisfaction following the birth of a child (van Steenbergen, Kluwer & Karney, 2011).

HOW DUAL-INCOME FAMILIES COPE

In married family life of the past, men were traditionally viewed as the main providers, and women, if they worked, as secondary providers. These traditional gender roles are changing. In the United States today, slightly over 61 percent of families with children have two working parents (Bureau of Labor Statistics, 2017), and women are providing an increasingly large percentage of family income. For example, in 1973 women's income accounted for only about 26 percent of family income, whereas in 2003 women brought in 35 percent of family income. Moreover, 25 percent of working wives earned *more* than their husbands (Bureau of Labor Statistics, 2005).

How does having two working parents affect families? Generally, combining work and family roles is good for both men's and women's mental and physical health and has positive effects on the strength of their relationship (Barnett & Hyde, 2001). However, juggling multiple roles—partner, parent, and employee—is often difficult. Working couples face extra demands on time and energy, conflict between work and family, possible rivalry between spouses, and anxiety and guilt about meeting children's needs. The family role is most demanding, especially for women, when children are young (Milkie & Peltola, 1999; Warren & Johnson, 1995), and the career role is most demanding when a worker is getting established or being promoted. Therefore, the benefits of these multiple roles depend on how many roles each partner carries, the demands of each role, the success or satisfaction the partners derive from their roles, and the extent to which the couples hold traditional or nontraditional attitudes about gender roles (Barnett & Hyde, 2001; Voydanoff, 2004).

For those parents who are not able to establish a satisfactory work-family balance, negative effects may snowball. The more hours worked, the greater the negative effect on work-family balance (McNamara, Pitt-Catsouphes, Matz-Costa, Brown & Valcour, 2013). Negative effects can either spill over from work to family, or from family to work, although work stress seems to affect family life to a greater degree (Ford, Heinen & Langkamer, 2007; Schulz, Cowan, Cowan & Brennan, 2004). To cope with this, new parents may cut back on working hours, refuse overtime, or turn down jobs that require excessive travel to increase family time and reduce stress (Barnett & Hyde, 2001; Becker & Moen, 1999; Crouter & Manke, 1994). Or a couple may make a trade-off, trading a career for a job, or trading off whose work takes precedence depending on shifts in career opportunities and family responsibilities. Women are more likely to do the scaling back, which usually occurs during the early years of child rearing (Becker & Moen, 1999; Gauthier & Furstenberg, 2005).

Cross-cultural studies have suggested that the general relationship between work-family balance and well-being holds across different countries. However, the effects are stronger in individualistic cultures than collectivistic cultures and in cultures that are more egalitarian with respect to gender roles (Haar, Russo, Sune & Ollier-Malaterre, 2014). To lessen the pressures on dual-income families, most countries have adopted workplace protection for such families (Heymann, Siebert & Wei, 2007). Fathers in 65 countries—but not in the United States—get *paid* paternity leave. (The U.S. Family and Medical Leave Act of 1993 grants 12 weeks of *unpaid* leave.) At least 34 countries—but not the United States—set a maximum length for the workweek. In the United States, approximately 48 percent of workers in the private sector do not have paid leave to care for themselves, and even more lack paid leave to care for other family members such as children. Moreover, even of those who are legally entitled to take family leave, 78 percent do not because they cannot afford to do so (Quamie, 2010). The United States is the only industrialized nation without paid maternity leave, although a few states have adopted paid family plans. President Obama's 2012 budget included $50 million for start-up funds for grants to help states provide paid family leave to workers (Office of Management and Budget, 2011). The future of such grants is uncertain now.

When Marriage Ends

In the United States, the average marriage that ends in divorce does so after 7 or 8 years (Kreider, 2005). Divorce, more often than not, leads to remarriage with a new partner and the formation of a stepfamily, which includes children born to or adopted by one or both partners before the current marriage.

DIVORCE

The U.S. divorce rate hit its lowest point since 1970 in 2014 at 3.2 divorces per 1,000 married women (National Vital Statistics, 2015). About 1 in 5 U.S. adults has been divorced (Kreider, 2005).

Divorce rates vary depending on the age of the cohort examined. The sharpest drop in divorce has occurred among younger cohorts—those born since the mid-1950s (U.S. Census Bureau, 2007b). However, the divorce rate for adults over the age of 35 years has doubled in the past 20 years (Kennedy & Ruggles, 2014). Education matters too. College-educated women, who previously had the most permissive views about divorce, have become less so, whereas women with lower educational levels have become more permissive

INTIMATE PARTNER VIOLENCE

Intimate partner violence (IPV) is the infliction of physical, sexual, or psychological harm by a current or former partner or spouse. Approximately 27 percent of women and 11 percent of men in the United States have experienced some form of physical violence, sexual violence, or stalking by an intimate partner (CDC, 2017h). The true extent of IPV is difficult to ascertain because victims are often too afraid or ashamed to disclose to others or make an official report to legal authorities. Women disproportionately experience multiple forms and more severe levels of IPV in individual relationships and across the life span (CDC, 2017h). Male to female partner violence is more repetitive and is more likely to result in injury or death (Caetano, Shafer, & Cunradi, 2001). More than one-third of female homicides are perpetrated by a current or former intimate partner. Conservative estimates suggest that women are roughly 6 times more likely than men to die at the hands of an intimate partner, with homicide typically occurring as a culmination of a long history of abuse (Stock et al., 2013).

Comparatively, there are far fewer studies examining male IPV victimization. In research studies, men disclose both physical and psychological abuse. Psychological violence was especially likely to go unreported, including threats of blackmail, financial harm, or taking children away. With physical abuse, their partners were especially likely to use objects to inflict injury. Embarrassment and fear of ridicule were among the chief reasons men do not disclose IPV. Serious physical assault incidents were much more likely to be reported to the police, who may not believe the claims or take them seriously (Drijber, Reijnders & Ceelen, 2013).

Same-sex relationships are also affected by IPV. Same-sex IPV rates are similar to those in heterosexual relationships (Edwards, Sylaska & Neal, 2015).

National studies indicate lifetime prevalence of physical violence, rape, or stalking by an intimate partner as comparable among heterosexual and gay men. Bisexual women have a significantly higher prevalence of physical violence, rape, or stalking by an intimate partner than either heterosexual or lesbian women (Black et al., 2011). Although these rates indicate IPV occurrence, much less is known about specific risk factors and patterns of IPV perpetration among sexual minority couples (Edwards, Sylaska & Neal, 2015).

Sometimes victims do not disclose IPV occurrence. Social disclosure is linked to demographic (i.e., age, sex, race), intrapersonal (i.e., feelings of shame, embarrassment, perceptions of control over abuse), and situational factors (i.e., violence frequency and severity, if abuse is witnessed). Research shows that the majority of IPV victims disclose to at least one informal support, most often a friend or female family member (Sylaska & Edwards, 2014). A variety of reactions may be elicited, and not all of them are perceived as positive or supportive (Edwards et al., 2015). Providing emotional support is perceived as the most helpful reaction, and disclosure in general is associated with better mental health outcomes (Sylaska & Edwards, 2014). "Leave" messages are interpreted variably, dependent on the individual's current level of readiness to end the abusive relationship (Edwards et al., 2015).

what's your view

Which individual or psychological factors do you think relate to perpetration and victimization of intimate partner violence? What can be done on an individual and societal level to help protect victims of intimate partner violence?

---

and thus more likely to divorce (Martin & Parashar, 2006). Age at marriage is another predictor of whether a union will last. The decline in divorce may reflect higher educational levels as well as the later age of first marriages, both of which are associated with marital stability (Popenoe & Whitehead, 2004). It also may reflect the rise in cohabitation, which, if it ends, does not end in divorce (Kennedy & Ruggles, 2013). Teenagers, high school dropouts, and nonreligious persons have higher divorce rates (Bramlett & Mosher, 2002; Popenoe & Whitehead, 2004). The rates of marital disruption for black women remain higher than for white or Latino women (Bulanda & Brown, 2007; Sweeney & Phillips, 2004) and, overall, divorce rates are higher for African Americans (Amato, 2010). In addition, interracial couples, particularly those involving white females with Asian or black males, are more likely to divorce than same-race couples (Bratter & King, 2008).

Why Do Marriages Fail? Looking back on their marriages, 130 divorced U.S. women who had been married an average of 8 years showed remarkable agreement on the reasons for the failure of their marriages. The most frequently cited reasons were incompatibility and lack of emotional support; for more recently divorced, presumably younger, women, this included lack of career support. Spousal abuse was third, suggesting that intimate partner violence may be more frequent than is generally realized (Dolan & Hoffman, 1998; Research in Action). Other common risk factors for divorce include premarital cohabitation (Tach & Halpern-Meekin, 2009) and infidelity (Hall & Fincham, 2006).

Economic resources and work are also related to divorce risk. However, effects vary with respect to gender. Husbands' unemployment is associated with a greater risk of divorce (Killewald, 2016). For wives, the relationship is more complex. Risks associated with wives' employment are most notably those linked to tension over the division of labor, a relationship that increases with the number of hours worked by wives. Additionally, greater economic independence means that when they do wish to leave a marriage, women are more able to do so. However, wives' work also has positive effects on marriage stability via the increased income and subsequent reductions in economic concerns generated when women work (Amato, 2010).

Generally, couples are more likely to stay married if they have children (Bernardi & Martinez-Pastor, 2011). However, instead of staying together "for the sake of the children," some embattled spouses conclude that exposing children to continued parental conflict does greater damage (Eisenberg, 1998).

Adjusting to Divorce Ending even an unhappy marriage can be painful for both partners, especially when there are young children in the home. Issues concerning custody and visitation often force divorced parents to maintain contact with each other, and these contacts may be stressful (Williams & Dunne-Bryant, 2006).

Divorce tends to reduce long-term well-being, especially for the partner who did not initiate the divorce or does not remarry (Amato, 2010; Amato, 2000). Especially for men, divorce can have negative effects on physical or mental health or both (Wu & Hart, 2002). Women are more likely than men to experience a sharp reduction in economic resources and living standards after separation or divorce (Kreider & Fields, 2002; Williams & Dunne-Bryant, 2006); however, women in unhappy marriages benefit more from the dissolution of the relationship than men in unhappy marriages (Waite, Luo & Lewin, 2009). People who were—or thought they were—happily married tend to react more negatively and adapt more slowly to divorce (Lucas et al., 2003). On the other hand, when a marriage was highly conflicted, its ending may improve well-being in the long run (Amato, 2000).

An important factor in adjustment is emotional detachment from the former spouse. People who argue with their ex-mates or who have not found a new partner or spouse experience more distress. An active social life, both at the time of divorce and afterward, helps (Amato, 2000; Thabes, 1997).

REMARRIAGE AND STEPPARENTHOOD

In the United States and abroad, rates of remarriage are high and rising (Adams, 2004). More than 1 out of 3 U.S. marriages are remarriages for both bride and groom (Kreider, 2005). Half of those who remarry after divorce from a first marriage do so within 3 to 4 years (Kreider, 2005). Men and women living with children from a previous relationship are most likely to form a new union with someone who also has resident children, thus forming a his-and-hers stepfamily (Goldscheider & Sassler, 2006). And families in which both parents bring children into the marriage are marked by higher levels of conflict (Heatherington, 2006). Remarriages are more likely than first marriages to end in divorce (Adams, 2004).

The more recent the current marriage and the older the stepchildren, the harder stepparenting seems to be. Women, especially, seem to have more difficulties in raising stepchildren than in raising biological children, perhaps because women generally spend more time with the children than men do (MacDonald & DeMaris, 1996). The conflict experienced by stepparents can be mitigated with healthy and open communication between the two partners (Pace, Shafer, Jensen & Larson, 2015). The stepfamily, as any family, has the potential to provide a warm, nurturing atmosphere for children.

summary and key terms

Emerging Adulthood: Patterns and Tasks

- Emerging adulthood is often a time of experimentation before assuming adult roles and responsibilities. Traditional developmental tasks may be postponed until the thirties or even later.
- Paths to adulthood are influenced by gender, academic ability, early attitudes toward education, expectations in late adolescence, social class, and ego development.
- Identity development in emerging adulthood may take the form of recentering, the gradual development of a stable adult identity. For racial/ethnic minorities, the task of identity formation may be accelerated.
- Emerging adulthood offers a moratorium, a period in which young people are free from pressure to make lasting commitments.
- A measure of how successfully emerging adults handle the developmental task of leaving the childhood home is their ability to maintain close but autonomous relationships with their parents.
- Remaining in the parental home is increasingly common among emerging and young adults. This can complicate the negotiation of an adult relationship with parents.

  recentering

Personality Development: Four Views

- Four theoretical perspectives on adult personality development are normative-stage models, the timing-of-events model, trait models, and typological models.
- Normative-stage models hold that age-related social and emotional change emerges in successive periods sometimes marked by crises. In Erikson's theory, the major issue of young adulthood is intimacy versus isolation.
- The timing-of-events model, advocated by Neugarten, proposes that adult psychosocial development is influenced by the occurrence and timing of normative life events.
- The five-factor model of Costa and McCrae is organized around five groupings of related traits: open to new experiences, conscientiousness, extraversion, agreeableness, and neuroticism.
- Typological research, pioneered by Jack Block, has identified personality types that differ in ego resiliency and ego control.

  normative-stage models, intimacy versus isolation, timing-of-events model, normative life events, social clock, trait models, five-factor model, typological approach, ego resiliency, ego control

Foundations of Intimate Relationships

- Young adults seek intimacy in relationships with peers and romantic partners.
- Most young adults have friends but have increasingly limited time to spend with them. Women's friendships tend to be more intimate than men's.
- Many young adults have friends who are considered fictive kin or psychological family.

- Social networking sites may allow some young adults to maintain friendships more easily.
- According to Sternberg's triangular theory of love, love has three aspects: intimacy, passion, and commitment.

  fictive kin, triangular theory of love

Marital and Nonmarital Lifestyles

- Today, more adults postpone marriage or never marry. The trend is particularly pronounced among African American women and people from lower socioeconomic classes.
- Reasons for staying single include career opportunities, travel, sexual and lifestyle freedom, a desire for self-fulfillment, women's greater self-sufficiency, reduced social pressure to marry, financial constraints, fear of divorce, and difficulty in finding a suitable mate.
- The ingredients of long-term satisfaction are similar in homosexual and heterosexual relationships.
- Gays and lesbians in the United States are now able to marry.
- Cohabitation has increased and has become the norm in some countries.
- Cohabitation can be a trial marriage, an alternative to marriage, or, in some places, almost indistinguishable from marriage. Cohabiting relationships in the United States tend to be less stable than marriages.
- Marriage (in a variety of forms) is universal and meets basic economic, emotional, sexual, social, and child-raising needs.
- Mate selection and marrying age vary across cultures. People in industrialized nations now marry later than in past generations.
- Success in marriage may depend on partners' sensitivity to each other, their validation of each other's feelings, and their communication and conflict management skills. Men's and women's differing expectations may be important factors in marital satisfaction.

Parenthood

- Today women in industrialized societies are having fewer children and having them later in life, and an increasing number choose to remain childless.
- Fathers are usually less involved in child raising than mothers, but more so than in previous generations.
- Marital satisfaction typically declines during the childbearing years.
- In most cases, the burdens of a dual-earner lifestyle fall most heavily on the woman.
- Family-friendly workplace policies may help alleviate marital stress.

When Marriage Ends

- Divorce rates in the United States vary depending on the age of the cohort measured. Divorce rates have doubled for those over 35 years of age.
- Adjusting to divorce can be painful.
- Many divorced people remarry within a few years, but remarriages tend to be less stable than first marriages.

Physical and Cognitive Development in Middle Adulthood

learning objectives

Explain how midlife is changing and define *middle adulthood.*

Discuss physical changes in middle adulthood.

Characterize health and well-being in middle age.

Identify cognitive changes in middle adulthood.

Describe creative achievement and the relationship between creativity and age.

Discuss trends in work, retirement, and education in middle adulthood.

©Dima Fadeev/Shutterstock

In this chapter, we examine physical changes during midlife as well as physical, sexual, and mental health issues. We look at factors that affect intelligence, thought processes, and creativity. Finally, we look at work, retirement, and educational pursuits.

Middle Age: A Social Construct

We described adolescence as a social construct. The same is true of midlife (Cohen, 2012). The term *midlife* first came into the dictionary in 1895 (Lachman, 2004) as life expectancy began to lengthen. Today, in industrial societies, middle adulthood is considered to be a distinct stage of life with its own societal norms, roles, opportunities, and challenges. However, some traditional societies, such as upper-caste Hindus in rural India (Menon, 2001) and the Gusii in Kenya, do not recognize a middle stage of adulthood at all.

We define *middle adulthood* in chronological terms as the years between ages 40 and 65. In 2010, approximately 81.5 million people in the United States, or 26.3 percent of the population, were between the ages of 45 and 64 years. This is an increase of 31.5 percent since 2000, making this cohort the fastest growing age group in the United States (Howden & Meyer, 2010).

The Midlife in the United States (MIDUS) study, a comprehensive survey of a national sample of 7,189 adults ages 25 to 75, has enabled researchers to study factors that influence health, well-being, and productivity in midlife (Brim, Ryff & Kessler, 2004). According to the MIDUS data, most middle-age people are in good physical, cognitive, and emotional shape and feel good about the quality of their lives (Lachman, Teshale & Agrigoroaei, 2015; Fleeson, 2004; Figure 15.1). Moreover, the middle years are marked by growing individual differences and a multiplicity of life paths (Lachman, 2004).

PHYSICAL DEVELOPMENT

Physical Changes

Although some physiological changes are direct results of biological aging and genetic makeup, behavioral and lifestyle factors dating from youth strongly affect the likelihood, timing, and extent of physical change.

SENSORY FUNCTIONING

With increasing age, it is common for adults to experience a variety of perceptual declines, including hearing and visual difficulties (Pleis & Lucas, 2009). Age-related visual problems occur mainly in five areas: near vision, dynamic vision (reading moving signs), sensitivity to light, visual search (locating a car in a parking lot), and speed of processing visual information (Kline & Scialfa, 1996).

You may have seen older people using reading glasses, or holding books or newspapers as far out as possible with one arm when trying to focus. As people age, they have difficulty focusing on near objects, a condition known as **presbyopia.** The incidence of **myopia** (nearsightedness) also increases throughout middle age (Rosenthal & Fischer, 2014). Overall, approximately 12 percent of adults age 45 to 64 experience declines in their vision (Pleis & Lucas, 2009). By the age of 65, 36.6 percent of adults will have some form of visual disability (Rosenthal & Fischer, 2014).

Middle-age people often need brighter lighting to see well. Because of changes in the eye, they need about one-third more brightness to compensate for the loss of light reaching the retina. Reading glasses, bifocals, and trifocals are also used to aid the eye in focusing on objects (Rosenthal & Fischer, 2014).

Age-related, gradual hearing loss is known as **presbycusis.** It is rarely noticed earlier in life, but it generally speeds up and becomes noticeable in the 50s (Merrill & Verbrugge, 1999). Presbycusis generally begins with higher-pitched sounds less important for understanding speech and gradually extends into lower pitches. Hearing loss is a significant factor affecting well-being in older adults, as the loss of ability to hear speech effectively

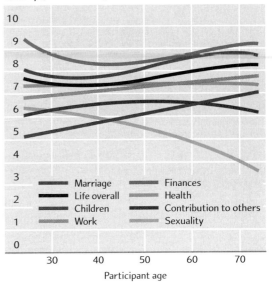

Quality (from 0 to 10)

Legend: Marriage, Finances, Life overall, Health, Children, Contribution to others, Work, Sexuality

Participant age: 30, 40, 50, 60, 70

FIGURE 15.1

How U.S. Adults of Various Ages Rate Aspects of Their Quality of Life and Overall Quality of Life

Source: Fleeson, W. "The quality of American life at the end of the century." In O. G. Brim, C. D. Ryff, & R. C. Kessler (Eds.), *How healthy are we? A national study of well-being at midlife* (pp. 252–272). Chicago: University of Chicago Press, 2004.

presbyopia
Age-related, progressive loss of the eyes' ability to focus on nearby objects due to loss of elasticity in the lens.

myopia
Nearsightedness.

presbycusis
Age-related, gradual loss of hearing, which accelerates after age 55, especially with regard to sounds at higher frequencies.

Though strength and coordination may decline, many middle-age people who remain active show benefits in both psychological and physical health.
©Ronnie Kaufman/Blend Images

can isolate adults and lead to loneliness and depression (Ciorba, Bianchini, Pelucchi & Pastore, 2012).

What factors impact hearing loss? Gender matters; hearing loss proceeds more quickly in men than in women (Ozmeral, Eddins, Frisina & Eddins, 2016). However, the most important factor in hearing loss is environmental noise. Estimates are that, worldwide, 16 percent of hearing loss in adults can be attributed to noise experienced at a work site (Nelson, Nelson, Concha-Barrientos & Fingerhut, 2005). While hearing protectors such as earplugs have decreased the impact of occupational noise, "social noise" (including concerts and personal music players) has increased (Sliwinska-Kowalska & Davis, 2012).

Sensitivity to taste and smell generally begins to decline in midlife (Stevens, Cain, Demarque & Ruthruff, 1991). As the taste buds become less sensitive and the number of olfactory cells diminishes, foods may seem more bland (Merrill & Verbrugge, 1999). Additionally, the use of medicines used to treat many diseases of aging can also have a negative effect on the gustatory senses (Imoscopi, Inelmen, Sergi, Miotto & Manzato, 2012), as can smoking (Vennemann, Hummel & Berger, 2008). Women tend to retain these senses longer than men (Liu, Zong, Doty & Sun, 2016).

PHYSICAL FITNESS

Staying physically active has wide-ranging positive effects on almost every body system, including physical health markers such as reduced cardiovascular risk, psychological markers such as decreased risk of depression, and cognitive markers such as decreased risk of dementia (Bauman, Merom, Bull, Buchner & Fiatarone Singh, 2016). The more people do, the more they *can* do, and the longer they can do it for.

Some loss of muscle strength is usually noticeable by age 45; 10 to 15 percent of maximum strength may be gone by 60. The reason is a loss of muscle fiber, which is replaced by fat (Guralnik, Butterworth, Wadsworth & Kuh, 2006). Still, decline is not inevitable; strength training in middle age can prevent muscle loss and even regain strength (Whitbourne, 2001).

basal metabolism
Use of energy to maintain vital functions.

Basal metabolism is the minimum amount of energy, typically measured in calories, that your body needs to maintain vital functions while resting. As people age, the amount of energy needed to maintain the body goes down, particularly after age 40. So, for example, older people often put on weight later in life despite no change in eating or exercise habits (Merrill & Verbrugge, 1999). Weight gain in early adulthood is predictive of major chronic diseases later (Zheng et al., 2017).

THE BRAIN AT MIDLIFE

In general, the aging brain can be described in two ways: as working more slowly and as having difficulty juggling multiple tasks. This general process affects multiple tasks across many different areas—such as understanding complex language, driving a car skillfully, and learning new skills. What these disparate tasks have in common is the necessity to quickly process complex information and pay attention to relevant stimuli while simultaneously ignoring irrelevant stimuli. In particular, the ability to ignore distractions gradually declines with age, which makes multitasking increasingly challenging (Madden & Langley, 2003; Stevens, Hasher, Chiew & Grady, 2008).

Physical changes in the aging brain contribute to the decline in functioning. Myelin, the fatty sheath that lines nerve axons and helps impulses move more quickly through the brain, begins to break down with age (Bartzokis et al., 2008). Also, when people show atrophy in the left insula, an area of the brain associated with speech production, they more frequently experience the tip-of-the-tongue (TOT) phenomenon (Shafto et al., 2007). In the TOT phenomenon a person knows he knows a word, and can often even specify how many syllables it contains, but cannot access the word.

Although some declines are likely, declines are neither inevitable nor necessarily permanent. Older brains are still flexible and can respond positively. The aging brain compensates for functional declines in part by recruiting a larger number of brain areas to work in concert in order to distribute processing demands more widely for difficult tasks (Davis, Kragel, Madden & Cabeza, 2011).

Overall, keeping the body healthy is associated with retention of cognitive abilities (Doaga & Lee, 2008). For example, when a group of "aging couch potatoes" enrolled in a physical education program, they showed corresponding changes in both gray and white brain matter volume (Colcombe et al., 2006). Aerobic exercise programs result in improvements in attention, processing speed, executive control, and memory (P. J. Smith et al., 2010). Changes in brain health have been documented in the cerebellum (involved in motor coordination and balance), motor cortex (generates voluntary movement), and hippocampus (where memory resides). It is likely that some of the global benefits associated with exercise are due to general processes, such as changes in blood volume or vessels, or changes in gray matter density (Thomas, Dennis, Bandettini & Johansen-Berg, 2012).

Even if declines do occur and the brain's ability to compensate for them has been reached, knowledge based on experience can still offset some problems. For example, middle-age adults are better drivers than younger ones (McFarland, Tune & Welford, 1964), and 60-year-old typists are as efficient as 20-year-olds (Spirduso & MacRae, 1990).

STRUCTURAL AND SYSTEMIC CHANGES

Changes in appearance may become noticeable during the middle years. By the fifth or sixth decade, the skin may become less taut and smooth as the layer of fat below the surface becomes thinner, collagen molecules more rigid, and elastin fibers more brittle. Hair may become thinner due to a slowed replacement rate and grayer as production of melanin, the pigmenting agent, declines. Middle-age people tend to gain weight as a result of accumulation of body fat and lose height due to shrinkage of the intervertebral disks (Merrill & Verbrugge, 1999; Whitbourne, 2001).

Bone density normally peaks in the twenties or thirties. From then on, people typically experience some bone loss as more calcium is absorbed than replaced, causing bones to become thinner and more brittle. Bone loss accelerates in the fifties and sixties; it occurs twice as rapidly in women as in men, sometimes leading to osteoporosis (Merrill & Verbrugge, 1999; Whitbourne, 2001). Smoking, alcohol use, and a poor diet earlier in adulthood tend to speed bone loss; it can be slowed by aerobic exercise, resistance training with weights, increased calcium intake, and vitamin C (Whitbourne, 2001; Yoon, Maalouf & Sakhaee, 2012). Lower childhood socioeconomic level and adult educational attainment have been linked to lower bone mass density in late adulthood. This association may exist because stress, which is higher in people of low socioeconomic status, is damaging to bone health (Crandall et al., 2012). Additionally, accumulated stress may lead to stiffer joints. Exercises that expand range of motion and strengthen the muscles supporting a joint can improve functioning (Whitbourne, 2001).

Large proportions of middle-age and even older adults show little or no decline in organ functioning (Gallagher, 1993). In some, however, the heart begins to pump more slowly and irregularly in the midfifties; by 65, it may lose up to 40 percent of its aerobic power. Arterial walls may become thicker and more rigid. Heart disease becomes more common beginning in the late forties or early fifties. **Vital capacity**—the maximum volume of air the lungs can draw in and expel—may begin to diminish at about age 40 and may drop by as much as 40 percent by age 70 (Merrill & Verbrugge, 1999; Whitbourne, 2001). The body temperature of older people is lower, and they are less able to maintain an appropriate body temperature in extremely hot or cold environments (Blatteis, 2012). Sleep is also affected by age; middle-age adults are less likely to fall asleep in the daytime, need less sleep to maintain alertness, and show reductions in slow wave sleep at night when compared to adolescents and emerging adults (Dijk, Groeger, Stanley & Deacon, 2010).

vital capacity
Amount of air that can be drawn in with a deep breath and expelled.

SEXUALITY AND REPRODUCTIVE FUNCTIONING

Although both sexes experience losses in reproductive capacity during middle adulthood, sexual enjoyment continues throughout adult life. (Changes are summarized in Table 15.1.)

Menopause and Its Meanings **Menopause** takes place when a woman permanently stops ovulating and menstruating and can no longer conceive a child. Most women experience it between 45 and 55 (Avis & Crawford, 2006).

menopause
Cessation of menstruation and of ability to bear children.

TABLE 15.1 Changes in Human Reproductive Systems during Middle Age		
	Female	**Male**
Hormonal change	Drop in estrogen and progesterone	Drop in testosterone
Symptoms	Hot flashes, vaginal dryness, urinary dysfunction	Undetermined
Sexual changes	Less intense arousal, frequent and quicker orgasms	Loss of psychological arousal, less frequent erections, slower orgasms, longer recovery between ejaculations, risk of erectile dysfunction
Reproductive capacity	Ends	Continues; some decrease in fertility occurs

perimenopause
Period of several years during which a woman experiences physiological changes of menopause; includes first year after end of menstruation; also called *climacteric*.

Women of menopausal age report many different symptoms. Physical exercise may alleviate some of them. ©Ty Milford/Aurora Open/Getty Images

TABLE 15.2 Symptoms of Menopause and Aging
Symptom
Hot flashes, night sweats
Vaginal dryness, painful intercourse
Sleep disturbances
Mood disturbances (depression, anxiety, irritability)
Urinary incontinence
Cognitive disturbances (i.e., forgetfulness)
Somatic symptoms (back pain, tiredness, stiff or painful joints)
Sexual dysfunction

Source: National Center for Complementary and Alternative Medicine (NCCAM). *Get the facts: Menopausal symptoms and complementary health practices.* 2008.

Menopause is not a single event; it is a process called the *menopausal transition*. It begins with **perimenopause,** also known as the *climacteric*. During this time, a woman's production of mature ova begins to decline, and the ovaries produce less estrogen. Menstruation becomes less regular, with less flow than before, and there is a longer time between menstrual periods. Eventually, menstruation ceases. The menopausal transition generally begins in the midthirties to midforties, and can take approximately 3 to 5 years.

Symptoms Most women experience some symptoms during the menopausal transition. Some have no symptoms, and racial/ethnic variations exist. Table 15.2 summarizes the current evidence concerning reported symptoms.

Some women find intercourse painful because of thinning vaginal tissues and inadequate lubrication (NIH, 2005), a problem that can be addressed with water-soluble lubricants. Sexual issues can also be alleviated with marital therapy for postmenopausal women and their husbands (Tiznobek, Mirmolaei, Momenimovahed, Kazemnejad & Taheri, 2017).

Treatment of Menopausal Symptoms In 2016 the International Menopause Society (IMS) released an updated set of evidence-based recommendations for the use of menopause hormone therapy (MHT) to address symptoms of menopause. MHT appears to be the most effective intervention for night sweats, hot flashes, and deterioration of the urinary tract and vagina. MHT may also help address other symptoms such as joint and muscle pains, mood swings, problems with sleep, and sexual dysfunction. However, the use of MHT should be the lowest dose possible and considered within the context of other life and health variables, including diet, exercise, family and personal history, and the use of cigarettes and alcohol. Women using MHT should also undergo a yearly health assessment, since the use of hormones is not without risks (Baber, Panay & Fenton, 2016).

Changes in Male Sexual Functioning Men remain fertile throughout the life span and do not go through menopause in the same dramatic fashion as do women. Men do have a biological clock, however, and they also experience age-associated changes. Starting at about age 30, testosterone levels begin to decline at a rate of about 1 percent a year, although there are wide individual variations (Asthana et al., 2004; Lewis, Legato & Fisch, 2006). Men can still father children, but sperm count declines with age, making conception less likely. Moreover, the genetic quality of their sperm declines as well, and advanced paternal age has been implicated as a source of birth defects (Lewis et al., 2006).

Men's changing hormone levels affect more than just their sexual organs. The decline in testosterone has been associated with reductions in bone density and muscle mass (Asthana et al., 2004) as well as decreased energy, lower sex drive, overweight or obesity, emotional irritability, depressed mood, and being a smoker (Lewis et al., 2006; Sartorius et al., 2012). It has also been linked to diabetes and cardiovascular disease and has been theorized to increase mortality (Lewis et al., 2006).

window on the world

CULTURAL DIFFERENCES IN WOMEN'S EXPERIENCE OF MENOPAUSE

Many women accept hot flashes, night sweats, and mood disturbances as normal accompaniments of menopause. Yet women in some cultures rarely or never experience these symptoms. The reasons for the cultural differences are complex and include genetic differences, diet and lifestyle differences, and perceptual differences about aging and what menopause means within the culture (Scheid, 2007).

In a classic study conducted by Margaret Lock, it was found that fewer than 20 percent of Japanese women reported having had hot flashes, compared with about 65 percent of a Canadian sample and 70 percent of a U.S. sample. Furthermore, only about 3 percent of the Japanese women said they experienced night sweats and were less likely than Western women to suffer from insomnia, depression, irritability, or lack of energy (Lock, 1993).

This difference may exist because in many Asian cultures, such as Japan, Singapore, Taiwan, and China, menopause is not regarded as a medical condition. There are no specific terms for "hot flash" in these cultures, although people recognize that there are changes and distinctions among body states. Muscle and joint pains are often reported by women in these countries but are not often interpreted as being related to menopause (Scheid, 2007).

Attitudes toward menopause vary greatly across cultures. Aging is less feared in the East than the West; it is often seen as a welcome event, bringing newfound freedom from reproduction, and taboos of uncleanliness, and respect as an elder. In some cultures, such as that of Mayan women in Mexico or the indigenous women in Australia, menopausal symptoms are rare, with many only noting the cessation of menses (Jones, Jurgenson, Katzenellenbogen & Thompson, 2012).

In the United States, a longitudinal study of women's health looked at the experience and duration of hot flashes. The group consisted of 3,302 women with diverse ethnic backgrounds. Overall, 75 percent of women experienced some hot flashes. No one factor determined what a woman's experience with hot flashes would be. The prevalence of hot flashes was 18 percent in Japanese Americans, 21 percent in Chinese Americans, 35 percent in Hispanic Americans, 46 percent in African Americans, and 53 percent of Caucasian women. Women with early onset of hot flashes were more likely to exhibit depression or anxiety, be in poorer health, smoke, and have a later age at menopause. Those with a later onset of symptoms were more likely to have a higher BMI. Those that experienced low amounts of hot flashes were more likely to be of Asian descent and were in good health. Those that experienced the highest levels and the longest duration of hot flashes were more likely to be African American, use alcohol, and be in poorer health (Tepper et al., 2016).

Research shows that this universal biological event has major variations. A woman's perceptions about menopause as well as her diet, her overall health, her activity levels and her culture all play a factor in her experiences with menopausal symptoms.

 what's your view

What do you think might explain cultural differences in women's experience of menopause? What is a greater influence—changing biology or beliefs about aging, and why?

Some middle-age and older men experience erectile dysfunction (ED; commonly called *impotence*). **Erectile dysfunction** is defined as a persistent inability to achieve or maintain an erect enough penis for satisfactory sexual performance. An estimated 39 percent of 40-year-old men and 67 percent of 70-year-old men experience ED at least sometimes (Feldman, Goldstein, Hatzichristou, Krane & McKinlay, 1994; Goldstein et al., 1998). There are multiple potential causes for ED. Diabetes, hypertension, high cholesterol, kidney failure, depression, neurological disorders, and many chronic diseases have been implicated. In addition, alcohol and drug use, as well as smoking, may contribute. Moreover, the development of ED is also predictive of future health problems, including heart disease and stroke (Dong, Zhang & Qin, 2011). Poor sexual techniques, lack of knowledge, unsatisfying relationships, anxiety, and stress may exacerbate the problem (Lewis et al., 2006; Utiger, 1998).

erectile dysfunction
Inability of a man to achieve or maintain an erect penis sufficient for satisfactory sexual performance.

research in action

ANDROPAUSE AND TESTOSTERONE REPLACEMENT THERAPY

Men have age-related changes in sex hormone levels at midlife, but without the end of reproductive ability that occurs in women (Nieschlag et al., 2004). Sometimes called *andropause,* men experience an estimated 1 percent yearly decrease in testosterone levels beginning around age 30 (Bassil, Alkaade & Morley, 2009). Over time, men may become aware of physical and psychological changes associated with low testosterone levels, including sexual dysfunction, decreased libido, mood disturbances, loss in muscle mass and strength, and decreased bone density (Nieschlag et al., 2004). An expanding waistline is also a symptom, as lower testosterone levels are associated with an increase in body fat (Fui et al., 2016).

Testosterone replacement therapies (TPT) have been used for decades and many men seek these treatments, in part because of aggressive marketing by manufacturers. A recent study estimates that testosterone supplements sales increased 65 percent from 2009 to 2013, with 40- to 60-year-old men accounting for roughly 70 percent of prescriptions (Baillargeon et al., 2013). It has also become common to encounter advertisements for herbal supplements and over-the-counter "medications" marketed to help men regain youthful vitality, athletic performance, and sexual virility.

The U.S. Food and Drug Administration issues stark warnings to consumers interested in boosting aging males' testosterone levels. Testosterone supplements were originally developed for men who produce no endogenous testosterone, and the FDA neither approves nor recommends these products for use to ward off the effects of male aging (U.S. Food and Drug Administration, 2016). A major fear is that testosterone supplementation may further increase men's risk for cardiovascular events, stroke, or death (Garnick, 2015). It is true that studies have shown benefits of TRT's use among middle-age men in terms of improved sexual

function (Corona et al., 2017), decreased frequency of nighttime urination, better sleep quality (Shigehara et al. 2015), and reduced body fat (Fui et al., 2016). However, many studies use small, nonrandomized samples that do not assess long-term treatment risks (U.S. Food and Drug Administration, 2016).

Recent studies have considered these criticisms when examining potential risks. Anderson and colleagues (2015) followed men undergoing testosterone supplementation for a period of 3 years. Results showed that supplementation to reach typical testosterone levels was associated with reduced cardiovascular event rates. However, men with the highest levels of supplementation carried greater risk for stroke. Similarly, Wallis and colleagues (2016) conducted a 5-year longitudinal study of men undergoing TRT. Results showed lower mortality rates and fewer cardiovascular events and prostate cancer diagnoses. However, shorter treatment regimens were associated with higher levels of risk. A recent meta-analysis returned inconclusive results when looking specifically at long-term stroke risk (Loo et al., 2017), suggesting the jury is still out with respect to the use of these supplements over longer periods.

Currently, men with untreated prostate or breast cancer are advised to avoid TRT (Osterberg, Bernie & Ramasamy, 2014). Every drug is a balance of costs and benefits, and TRT is no different. The question is whether the short-term benefits outweigh the potential for health risks potentially leading to an early death.

what's **your view** Do you think *andropause* is analogous to the changes that women undergo in menopause? What advice would you give to a middle-ageman interested in taking testosterone replacement supplements?

Sildenafil (Viagra) and other similar drugs have been found safe and effective in the treatment of ED (Goldstein et al., 1998; Nurnberg et al., 2003; Utiger, 1998), and their use has mushroomed. Testosterone therapy has also been investigated as a treatment; however, its effectiveness is more limited. There is some evidence that men with testosterone levels clearly below average may benefit from testosterone therapy; however, the data are less certain for those men whose testosterone shows the typical age-related drop (Corona et al., 2014; Lewis et al., 2006; Whitbourne, 2001). If there is no apparent physical problem, psychotherapy or sex therapy (with the support and involvement of the partner) may help (NIH, 1992).

Sexual Activity Advances in health care and more liberal attitudes toward sex are making people more aware that sex can be a vital part of life during middle and late adulthood.

Frequency of sexual activity and satisfaction with sex life diminish gradually during the forties and fifties. In the MIDUS study, 61 percent of married or cohabiting premenopausal women but only 41 percent of postmenopausal women reported having sex once a week or more. This decline was related not to menopause but to age and physical condition (Rossi, 2004). Possible physical causes include chronic disease, surgery, medications, and too much food or alcohol. Often, however, a decline in frequency has nonphysiological causes: monotony in a relationship, preoccupation with business or financial worries, mental or physical fatigue, depression, failure to make sex a high priority, fear of failure to attain an erection, or lack of a partner (King, 1996; Weg, 1989). Treating these causes may bring renewed vitality to a couple's sex life.

Physical and Mental Health

Most middle-age Americans, like middle-age people in other industrialized countries, are generally healthy. All but 16 percent of 45- to 54-year-olds and 18.9 percent of 55- to 64-year-olds consider themselves in good to excellent health (National Center for Health Statistics, 2015).

However, baby boomers may be less healthy than previous generations. In a comparison of three birth cohorts—aged 60–69, 70–79, and 80 and older—the younger cohorts showed sharper increases of between 40 and 70 percent in problems with basic activities associated with daily living, performing everyday chores such as making dinner or using a bathroom, and mobility issues. This research suggests that people now entering their sixties could face more disabilities than their counterparts in previous generations (Seeman, Merkin, Crimmins & Karlamangla, 2009). Not surprisingly, research also has shown increases in the use of medical services (Freid & Bernstein, 2010).

HEALTH TRENDS AT MIDLIFE

Many people in midlife, especially those with low SES, experience increasing health problems (Lachman, 2004). The prevalence of physical limitations increases with age. Approximately 17.1 percent of 45- to 54-year-olds and 24.9 percent of 55- to 64-year-olds are limited in activities because of chronic conditions (National Center for Health Statistics, 2015). Middle-age adults are more likely to contract certain diseases, such as hypertension and diabetes, and they take longer to recover from illness or extreme exertion (Merrill & Verbrugge, 1999).

Hypertension (chronically high blood pressure) is an increasingly important concern from midlife on as a risk factor for cardiovascular disease and kidney disease. In the United States, almost 50 percent of men and 37 percent of women ages 45 to 64 are currently diagnosed with uncontrolled hypertension (National Center for Health Statistics, 2017), although these numbers will need to be adjusted in light of new recommendations released in November 2017 (American College of Cardiology, 2017). Previous guidelines defined high blood pressure at 140/90; however, because of research showing an increased risk of disease at lower levels, the recommended cutoff for high blood pressure is now 130/80 (Ettehad et al., 2016).

hypertension
Chronically high blood pressure.

Hypertension is the world's leading preventable cause of early death. Currently, approximately 31 percent of people worldwide have high blood pressure. In high-income countries, rates decreased by 2.6 percent from 2000 to 2010, presumably as a result of better diagnosis and treatment. By contrast, low- and middle-income countries showed an increase of 7.7 percent (Mills et al., 2016). These high rates are troubling given hypertension's status as a risk factor for cardiovascular disease and stroke (Forouzanfar et al., 2015). Currently, these two diseases are the leading causes of global death, and estimates are that 1 in 4 deaths can be attributed to them (Abubakar, Tillman & Bannerjee, 2015).

Some adults can lower their blood pressure with lifestyle modifications, such as weight loss, increases in physical activity, eating a low-salt diet with plentiful fruits and vegetables, increasing potassium intake, and consuming light amounts of alcohol. If lifestyle modifications are not effective, medication is generally used as well (Frisoli, Schmieder, Grodzicki & Messerli, 2011).

diabetes

Disease in which the body does not produce or properly use *insulin*, a hormone that converts sugar, starches, and other foods into energy needed for daily life.

In the United States, cancer has replaced heart disease as the leading cause of death between ages 45 and 64 (National Center for Health Statistics, 2017). Overall, death rates have declined since the 1970s for people in this age bracket, in large part because of improvements in treatment of heart attack patients (Hoyert, Arias, Smith, Murphy & Kochanek, 2001; Rosamond et al., 1998).

The prevalence of **diabetes** doubled in the 1990s (Weinstein et al., 2004). Approximately 13 percent of adults aged 45 to 64 years have been diagnosed with diabetes (National Center for Health Statistics, 2015). The most common type, mature-onset (type 2) diabetes, typically develops after age 30 and becomes more prevalent with age. Unlike juvenile-onset (type 1), or insulin-dependent, diabetes, in which the level of blood sugar rises because the body does not produce enough insulin, in mature-onset diabetes glucose levels rise because the cells lose their ability to use the insulin the body produces. As a result, the body may try to compensate by producing too much insulin. People with mature-onset diabetes often do not realize they have it until they develop such serious complications as heart disease, stroke, blindness, kidney disease, or loss of limbs (American Diabetes Association, 1992).

BEHAVIORAL INFLUENCES ON HEALTH

On average, Americans who smoke, are overweight, and have high blood pressure and high blood sugar have a life expectancy 4 years less than those who do not (Danaei et al., 2010). By the same token, people who do not smoke, who exercise regularly, drink alcohol in moderation, and eat plenty of fruits and vegetables have 4 times less risk of dying in midlife and old age (Khaw et al., 2008). Perhaps more important from a quality of life perspective, people who guard their health not only live longer but also have shorter periods of disability at the end of life (Vita, Terry, Hubert & Fries, 1998).

Weight in particular seems to affect health. Excess weight in middle age increases the risk of impaired health and death (Jee et al., 2006), even in healthy people (Yan et al., 2006) and for those who have never smoked (Adams et al., 2006). Being overweight, which is medically defined as having a body mass index (BMI) of between 25 to 29.9, is a risk factor. However, obesity, defined as a BMI of 30 or more, is an ever greater risk and associated with ever greater mortality (Flegal, Kit, Orpana & Graubard, 2013). Weight also interacts with ethnicity, making some ethnic groups more likely to become overweight or obese. For example, when considering overweight, Hispanics have the highest prevalence rate at 84.2 percent, in comparison to non-Hispanic whites at 70.8 percent and non-Hispanic blacks at 76 percent. By contrast, when considering obesity, non-Hispanic blacks (52.9 percent) demonstrate the highest prevalence rate, with non-Hispanic whites (34.9 percent) and Hispanics (42 percent) at lower risk (Flegal et al., 2010).

Physical activity in midlife is an important protective factor, particularly given that declines in cardiovascular fitness are steep after age 45 (Jackson, Sui, Hébert, Church & Blair, 2009). Physical activity can increase the chances of remaining mobile in old age (Patel et al., 2006), of avoiding weight gain (Lee, Djoussé, & Sesso, 2010), and of staying healthier longer (Jackson et al., 2009). Adults who engage in regular, moderate, or vigorous exercise are about 35 percent less likely to die in the next 8 years than those with a sedentary lifestyle. And those with cardiovascular risk factors, including smoking, diabetes, high blood pressure, and a history of coronary heart disease, benefit the most from being physically active (Richardson, Kriska, Lantz & Hayward, 2004). Last, physical activity is associated with better cognitive functioning at midlife (Hoang et al., 2016) and a decreased risk of dementia in late adulthood (Blondell, Hammersley-Mather & Veerman, 2014; Tolppanen et al., 2015).

Unfortunately, only about a third of U.S. adults show good compliance with health recommendations, most notably with respect to suggested dietary guidelines (Wright, Hirsch & Wang, 2009). Although adhering to a healthy lifestyle throughout life is ideal, changes later in life can reverse some of the damage (Tolppanen et al., 2015).

SOCIOECONOMIC STATUS AND HEALTH

People with low socioeconomic status tend to have poorer health, shorter life expectancy, more activity limitations due to chronic disease, and lower well-being than people with higher SES (National Center for Health Statistics, 2015; Spiro, 2001). In part this is due to the cost of health care. In 2015, almost 39 percent of poor and near poor people either delayed or did not receive medical care because of its expense (National Center for Health Statistics, 2015).

The reasons for the connection between SES and health may also be psychosocial. People with low SES tend to have more negative emotions and thoughts and live in more stressful environments (Gallo & Matthews, 2003). In addition, even when younger, they tend to engage in unhealthy behaviors at higher rates than do those with high SES (Stringhini et al., 2010). People with higher SES, by contrast, tend to have a greater sense of control over what happens to them as they age. They tend to choose healthier lifestyles and to seek medical attention and social support when they need it (Lachman & Firth, 2004; Marmot & Fuhrer, 2004), and they tend to show higher compliance with lifestyle modifications recommended to improve health indices (Wright, Hirsch & Wang, 2009). However, there are wide individual differences in health among low-SES adults. Protective influences include the quality of social relationships and the level of religious engagement from childhood on (Ryff, Singer & Palmersheim, 2004). Negative influences include loneliness, which has a negative effect on both both mental and physical well-being and is a risk factor for poor health and mortality (Cacioppo & Cacioppo, 2014).

RACE/ETHNICITY AND HEALTH

Even though racial and ethnic disparities have decreased in the United States since 1990, substantial differences persist (National Center for Health Statistics, 2015). In trying to determine the cause of these disparities, researchers have looked to the human genome. Research in this area has found distinctive variations in the DNA code among people of European, African, and Chinese ancestry (Hinds et al., 2005). These variations are linked to predispositions to various diseases, from cancer to obesity, and such data may ultimately open the way to targeted treatments of preventive measures.

Although genetics may offer some clues to differences in health as a function of race or ethnicity, by far the most research has focused on correlates of ethnicity, and how those might be related to differences in health. Poverty is most likely the largest single underlying factor in this link. People who live in poverty generally have poorer access to health care, more stressful lives, and greater exposure to potential toxins in their everyday environment. For African Americans, for example, poverty has been related to poor nutrition, substandard housing, and poor access to health care (Smedley & Smedley, 2005).

There are other differences between people of different ethnicities. From young adulthood throughout middle age, African Americans have higher overall death rates and higher incidence of hypertension, obesity, and diabetes (National Center for Health Statistics, 2016). Hispanic Americans, like African Americans, have a disproportionate incidence of stroke, liver disease, diabetes, HIV infection, homicide, and cancers of the cervix and stomach (Office of Minority Health, Centers for Disease Control, 2005; National Center for Health Statistics, 2016). They are also much less likely, particularly if they are limited English proficient, to have health insurance and a regular source of health care (Martorell & Martorell, 2006). Not surprisingly, they are also less likely to be screened for cholesterol and for breast, cervical, and colorectal cancers, or to receive influenza and pneumonia vaccines (Balluz, Okoro & Strine, 2004).

GENDER AND HEALTH

Women have a higher life expectancy than men and lower death rates throughout life (Xu, Kochanek, Murphy & Tejada-Vera, 2016). Women's greater longevity has been attributed to genetic protection given by the second X chromosome (which men do not have) and, before menopause, to beneficial effects of the female hormone estrogen on both cardiovascular and cognitive health (Rodin & Ickovics, 1990; USDHHS, 1992; Pradhan, 2014; Hara, Waters, McEwen & Morrison, 2015). However, psychosocial and cultural factors, such as men's greater propensity for risk-taking, also may play a part (Mahalik et al., 2013; Courtenay, 2011).

Although women live longer, they are slightly more likely to report being in fair or poor health than men. According to the MIDUS survey, middle-age women tend to report more specific symptoms and chronic conditions than men, and they devote more effort to

Women's greater longevity has been attributed to genetic protection given by the second X chromosome (which men do not have) and, before menopause, to beneficial effects of the female hormone estrogen, particularly on cardiovascular health.
©Dave and Les Jacobs/Blend Images LLC

osteoporosis
Condition in which the bones become thin and brittle as a result of rapid calcium depletion.

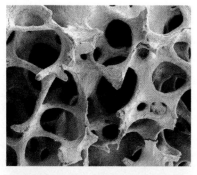

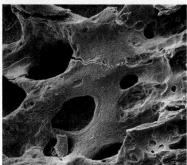

Images of normal (top) and osteoporotic (bottom) bones.
(both): ©Steve Gschmeissner/Science Photo Library/Getty Images

maintaining their health (Cleary, Zaborski & Ayanian, 2004). Men may feel that admitting illness is not masculine and seeking help means a loss of control (Addis & Mahalik, 2003), and they are less likely to seek professional help for health problems or stay overnight in a hospital (National Center for Health Statistics, 2015). They are also more likely to suffer from chronic health problems such as cancer or high blood pressure (Seigel, Miller & Jemal, 2015; Maranon & Reckelhoff, 2013) and to report drug or alcohol problems (Cleary, Zaborski & Ayanian, 2004). Both genders, however, show roughly the same degree of limitations in daily living (12.8 percent for men versus 12.5 percent for women) as a result of chronic health conditions (National Center for Health Statistics, 2015).

As women's lifestyles have become more like men's, so have their health patterns. For example, the gender gap in deaths from heart disease has narrowed primarily because heart attack rates in women have risen. Explanations for this increase rely in part on rising rates of obesity and diabetes in women, and in part on the tendency of doctors to assume heart disease is less likely in women. Thus doctors are more likely to recognize and treat heart disease risk in men, leading to a better focus on controlling risk factors in men than in women (Towfighi, Zheng & Ovbiagele, 2009; Vaccarino et al., 2009). This type of trend may help explain why the difference between women's and men's life expectancy shrank from 7.6 years in 1970 to 4.8 years in 2014 (Xu, Kochanek, Murphy & Tejada-Vera, 2016).

Women are at increased risk for osteoporosis, breast cancer, and heart disease after menopause. With longer life spans, women in many developed countries now can expect to live half their adult lives after menopause. As a result, increasing attention is being paid to women's health issues at this time of life (Barrett-Connor et al., 2002). There has also been more awareness of men's health issues as well. For example, as they age men face an increasing risk of erectile dysfunction, particularly if their health is already poor (Gupta et al., 2011).

For many years, older men were subject to aggressive screening procedures for prostate cancer. Sometimes small cancers would be discovered, and many men were treated for those cancers. However, given the slow growth of prostate cancer, it is likely that many of these growths would never have become dangerous. Thus, new recommendations were recently developed to reduce the emphasis on aggressive screening procedures with the goal of reducing unnecessary medical treatment. Now, unless men meet one of a number of particular risk factors, prostate screening is not always recommended (Moyer, 2012; Heidenreich et al., 2011).

Bone Loss and Osteoporosis In women, bone loss rapidly accelerates in the first 5 to 10 years after menopause as levels of estrogen, which helps in calcium absorption, fall. Extreme bone loss may lead to **osteoporosis** ("porous bones"), a condition in which the bones become thin and brittle as a result of calcium depletion. Common signs of osteoporosis are marked loss in height and a hunchbacked posture that results from compression and collapse of a weakened spinal column. Estimates are that almost half of postmenopausal women have undetected low bone mineral density and 7 percent have osteoporosis (Siris et al., 2001). Osteoporosis is a major cause of broken bones in old age and can greatly affect quality of life and even survival (NIH, 2003).

Almost 3 out of 4 cases of osteoporosis occur in white women, most often in those with fair skin, small frame, low weight and BMI, a family history of the condition, and in those whose ovaries were surgically removed before menopause (NIH Consensus Development Panel, 2001; Siris et al., 2001). Other risk factors, besides age, include smoking, lack of exercise, and alcohol use (Siris et al., 2001; Hannan et al., 2000). A predisposition to osteoporosis seems to have a genetic basis (Prockop, 1998; Uitterlinden et al., 1998), particularly as there are indications that genetic markers may have implications for which drugs will be most effective in an individual (Richards, Zheng & Spector, 2012).

The treatment approaches for osteoporosis have come under scrutiny in recent years (Guallar & Laine, 2014). Previous treatment philosophies assumed increasing available calcium via supplements should increase bone strength. However, research indicated that calcium supplements did not affect the risk of a bone fracture. Moreover, calcium supplements increased the risk of other health issues, including kidney stones, cardiovascular problems, and gastrointestinal issues (Reid, 2014). Additionally, there was also confusion about the role of hormone replacement therapy (HRT) in women. While HRT can ameliorate some of the symptoms of menopause as well as slow bone loss, its use also carries significant risks (De Villiers et al., 2013).

In 2017 the American College of Physicians (ACP) released new, evidence-based guidelines for the treatment and management of osteoporosis in both men and women (Qaseem, Forciea, McLean & Denberg, 2017). Strong recommendations included the use of biphosphonates (drugs that slow or prevent bone loss) such as alendronate, risendronate, zoledronic acid, or denosumab in women who have been diagnosed with osteoporosis. These medications reduce the risk of hip or vertebral fractures in women, but the evidence for their effectiveness in men is weaker. In contrast to earlier recommendations, the ACP strongly recommends HRT not be used for treating osteoporosis in women, as new evidence does not show it to be effective. The ACP also recommends biphosphonate therapy for 5 years; however, bone density monitoring does not appear to confer any additional benefits to patients and is not necessary. Last, the ACP recommends that treatment decisions be holistic and take into account patient preferences and profile, and the financial and medical costs and benefits of medications.

Good lifestyle habits can reduce risk, especially if started early in life (NIH Consensus Development Panel, 2001). Longitudinal studies suggest that exercise can help slow bone density loss (Kemmler, Bebeneck, Kohl & von Stengel, 2015) as well as maintain strength, agility, and balance, and thus be protective against falls that often lead to broken bones (Cosman et al., 2014). Older adults also benefit from proper nutrition and the avoidance of smoking or heavy drinking (Cosman et al., 2014).

Routine mammography to screen for breast cancer is generally recommended for older women. If cancer is detected before it spreads, women have about a 98 percent chance of surviving at least 5 years after diagnosis.
Source: Rhoda Baer/National Cancer Institute (NCI)

Breast Cancer and Mammography One in 8 American women develop breast cancer at some point in their lives (American Cancer Society, 2017). In 2014, almost 42,000 people in the United States died of breast cancer (Xu Kochanek, Murphy & Tejada-Vera, 2016).

About 5 to 10 percent of breast cancer cases are thought to be hereditary, resulting from inherited mutations. The most common of these are mutations of the *BRCA1* and *BRCA2* genes. Women who have a *BRCA1* or *BRCA2* mutation have as much as an 80 percent chance of developing breast cancer (American Cancer Society, 2007).

However, the vast majority of breast cancer cases are environmentally influenced. Once found mostly in affluent countries, breast cancer is becoming a worldwide problem as Western lifestyles move into the developing world (Porter, 2008). Overweight women, those who drink alcohol, those who experience early menarche and late menopause, those with a family history of breast cancer, and those who have no children, did not breast-feed, or who bore children later in life have a greater risk of breast cancer, whereas those who are moderately physically active and eat low-fat, high-fiber diets are at less risk (American Cancer Society, 2017; McTiernan et al., 2003). Weight gain, especially after menopause, increases a woman's risk of breast cancer, and weight loss decreases the risk (Eliassen, Colditz, Rosner, Willett & Hankinson, 2006).

Advances in treatment and early diagnosis have dramatically improved prospects for breast cancer patients. Fully 89 percent of U.S. women with breast cancer now survive at least 5 years past diagnosis. If the cancer is still localized and has not yet spread, the 5-year survival rate is 99 percent (Miller et al., 2016). Cancer can be treated with removal of part or all of the breast, along with radiation or chemotherapy.

The benefits of **mammography,** diagnostic X-ray examination of the breasts, appear to be greatest for women over 50. In 2009, the United States Preventive Services Task Force issued a new set of guidelines recommending that women begin routine screening for breast cancer at 50, rather than at 40 years of age as had been previously suggested. However, adherence to this diagnostic schedule varies, and medical professionals and organizations often disagree with recommended diagnostic guidelines (Corbelli et al., 2014).

Hormone Therapy The most troublesome physical effects of menopause are linked to reduced levels of estrogen, and **hormone therapy (HT)** has been used to address these effects. HT is treatment with artificial estrogen, sometimes in combination with progesterone, to help relieve symptoms of menopause. HT has a complicated pattern of risks and benefits.

mammography
Diagnostic X-ray examination of the breasts.

hormone therapy (HT)
Treatment with artificial estrogen, sometimes in combination with the hormone progesterone, to relieve or prevent symptoms caused by decline in estrogen levels after menopause.

On the positive side, HT is the most effective means of addressing symptoms such as night sweats and hot flashes, especially for women below the age of 60 or who went through menopause less than 10 years ago (De Villiers et al., 2013). However, it is not as effective at managing osteoporosis. HT, when started at menopause and continued for at least 5 years, can slow bone loss after menopause (Barrett-Connor et al., 2002; Lindsay, Gallagher, Kleerekoper & Pickar, 2002). However, bone loss resumes within 3 years if and when HT stops (Heiss et al., 2008). Moreover, as discussed, HT fails to reduce the risk of fracture (Reid, 2014).

Early correlational research suggested that HT cut the risk of heart disease (Ettinger, Friedman, Bush & Quesenberry, 1996; Grodstein, 1996); later research found that hormone treatment either provided no cardiovascular benefit or increased the risks (Grady et al., 2002; Hulley et al., 2002; Petitti, 2002). The most recent research suggests that HT does not not impact the risk of either cardiovascular disease or mortality (Manson et al., 2017; Benkhadra et al., 2015). Because of the complicated risk profile of these drugs, HT should not be used for disease prevention but is appropriate for menopausal symptom management in affected women (Manson et al., 2013). Lifestyle changes such as losing weight and stopping smoking, together with any necessary drugs to lower cholesterol and blood pressure, appear to be wiser courses for heart disease prevention in most women (Manson & Martin, 2001). HT, especially when taken orally, has also been associated with a greater, although still overall small, risk of stroke or blood clot (De Villiers et al., 2013).

As with the cardiac data, the links between HR and breast cancer risk are complex. Heightened risk of breast cancer seems to occur mainly among current or recent estrogen users, if estrogen and progestin are used together, and the risk increases with length of use (Chen, Weiss, Newcomb, Barlow & White, 2002; De Villiers et al., 2013). However, the overall risk is still quite low, with an incidence of less than 1 woman per 1,000 over a year. This risk is comparable to increased risk due to lifestyle factors such as being sedentary or consuming alcohol (De Villiers et al., 2013).

Results on the effects of HT on cognitive function and dementia risk are also difficult to intepret. Some studies have found that HT reduces the risk of cognitive impairment (Zandi et al., 2002), other have found it increases the risk (Espeland et al., 2004; Shumaker et al., 2004). Timing may matter here. HT which begins in early menopause does not seem to have a negative effect on cognition; however, later initiation of HT is associated with increased risk of dementia (De Villiers et al., 2013). Additional research in this area indicates that when women use HT in midlife *only*, they show a lower risk of dementia than women who use HT in early menopause and then continue to do so into late adulthood, and in women who begin using HT in late adulthood. It may be there is a critical window of time where HT is protective, but taken outside of that window, it is damaging (Whitmer, Quesenberry, Zhou & Yaffe, 2011; Shao et al., 2012).

STRESS IN MIDDLE AGE

stress
Physical or psychological demands on a person or organism.

stressors
Perceived environmental demands that may produce stress.

Stress is the damage that occurs when perceived environmental demands, or **stressors,** exceed a person's capacity to cope with them. The body's capacity to adapt to stress involves the brain, which perceives danger (either real or imagined); the adrenal glands, which mobilize the body to fight it; and the immune system, which provides the defenses.

People early in middle age tend to experience higher levels of stress and more frequent stress than other age groups. For example, in a nationally representative study (American Psychological Association, 2017a), 39 percent of U.S. 35- to 55-year-olds reported extreme stress approximately 25 percent of the time. Younger adults (ages 18 to 34) and late middle-age and older adults (age 55 and up) reported lower stress levels, with 29 percent and 25 percent, respectively, reporting high stress. Similar results were found in the MIDUS study, with middle-age adults reporting more frequent, multiple, and severe stressors than older adults (Almeida, Serido & McDonald, 2006).

Since the 2016 election, for the first time, stress about the state of the nation was the highest source of reported stress across all ages, outranking concerns about finances or work. Middle-age and older adults also report great concern about health care. (American Psychological Association, 2017a). Stress in middle age may also come from role changes, career transitions, grown children leaving home, and the renegotiation of family relationships.

Women tend to report more extreme stress than men (35 percent compared to 28 percent) and to be more concerned about stress (American Psychological Association, 2017a). The classic stress response—*fight or flight*—may be more characteristic of men, activated in part by testosterone. Women's response pattern is typically *tend and befriend*—nurturant activities that promote safety and reliance on social networks to exchange resources and responsibilities. These patterns may have evolved through natural selection and may draw on women's involvement in attachment and caregiving (Taylor, 2006).

Women are more likely to tend and befriend as a way of dealing with stress than men are.
©BananaStock/Alamy Stock Photo

EMOTIONS AND HEALTH

There is extensive evidence that positive emotions and well-being are associated with both short- and long-term positive health outcomes (Diener & Chan, 2011; Howell, Kern & Lyubomirsky, 2007) and reduced mortality (Chida & Steptoe, 2008). Negative emotions, such as anxiety and despair, are often associated with poor physical and mental health (Ray, 2004; Salovey, Rothman, Detweiler & Steward, 2000; Spiro, 2001).

Negative moods suppress immune functioning and increase susceptibility to illness; positive moods enhance immune functioning (Salovey et al., 2000). For example, when adult volunteers were exposed to a virus that can cause colds, those with a positive emotional outlook were less likely to get sick (Cohen, Doyle, Turner, Alper & Skoner, 2003). In a study of patients in a large medical practice, two positive emotions—hope and curiosity—were found to lessen the likelihood of having or developing hypertension, diabetes, or respiratory tract infections (Richman et al., 2005). Because people's immune systems become less effective with age (Solomon & Benton, 1994), this process may be particularly important for older adults.

There are also indirect effects of positive emotions on health. A positive emotional outlook motivates people to engage in more healthful practices, such as regular sleep and exercise, and to pay more attention to health-related information. Positive emotions may also affect health indirectly by softening the impact of stressful life events and helping people feel more connected to others (Armenta, Fritz & Lyubomirsky, 2016; Cohen & Pressman, 2006; Richman et al., 2005).

Personality traits are also related to health. In prospective studies, neuroticism and hostility are consistently associated with serious illness and reduced longevity, whereas optimism and conscientiousness are associated with better health and longer life (Kern & Friedman, 2008; Lahey, 2009; T. W. Smith, 2006). Optimism has been related to decreases in risk for coronary heart disease and mortality for postmenopausal women, whereas hostility has been related to the opposite pattern (Tindle et al., 2009).

MENTAL HEALTH

Middle-age adults are more likely to suffer from serious psychological distress than adults of other ages (Pratt, Dey & Cohen, 2007). In 2015, approximately 7.3 million adults in the United States aged 26 to 49 years had a major depressive episode, and slightly over 68 percent of them received treatment for it (Center for Behavioral Health Statistics and Quality, 2016). Depression negatively affects health, making prevention and treatment an important issue (Bromberger, Harlow, Avis, Kravitz & Cordal, 2004).

How Stress Affects Health The stress response system and the immune system are closely linked and work together to keep the body healthy. Chronic stress can lead to persistent inflammation and, over time, to disease (Cohen et al., 2012; Miller & Blackwell, 2006). Moreover, a propensity to respond in a negative fashion to stress may interact with genetic predispositions.

Research has shown a number of life events to be highly stressful, including divorce, the death of a spouse or other family member, or the loss of a job.

A positive outlook may guard against disease and buffer the impact of stress.
©Rolf Bruderer/Blend Images LLC

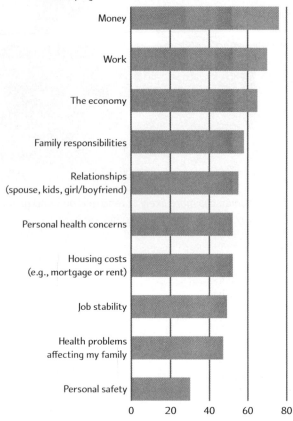

Causes of stress %
somewhat/very significant

FIGURE 15.2

Significant Sources of
Stress, United States,
2010

*Work and money are greater
stressors than relationships or
health, a national survey found.*

Source: American Psychological Association
(APA). *Mental and behavioral health and older
Americans.* 2011.

The more stressful the changes that take place in a person's life, the greater likelihood of serious illness within the next year or 2 (Holmes & Rahe, 1976; Cooper, 2005).

Generally, acute, or short-term, stress, such as the challenge of taking a test or running a competitive race, strengthens the immune system (Segerstrom & Miller, 2004). We are adapted to dealing with such events, and our bodies quickly and efficiently respond and then recover from the event (Sapolsky, 1992). However, intense or prolonged stress, such as might result from poverty or disability, can weaken or break down the body, increasing the susceptibility to disease (Sapolsky, 1992; Segerstrom & Miller, 2004). In support of this assertion, research has found suppressed immune function in breast cancer patients (Compas & Luecken, 2002), abused women, hurricane survivors, and men with a history of post-traumatic stress disorders (PTSD) (Harvard Medical School, 2002). Unsafe neighborhoods with poor-quality housing and few resources also may produce or worsen depression (Cutrona, Wallace & Wesner, 2006). Daily stressors such as irritations, frustrations, and overloads may be less severe in their impact than life changes, but their buildup can also affect health and emotional adjustment (Almeida et al., 2006; American Psychological Association, 2011; Figure 15.2). For minority group members, discrimination and racism can also lead to increased chronic stress and are associated with an increased risk for disease (Thoits, 2010). These processes are of concern because stress has been increasingly recognized as a factor in such age-related diseases as hypertension, heart disease, stroke, diabetes, osteoporosis, peptic ulcers, depression, HIV/AIDS, and cancer (Baum, Caccioppo, Melamed, Gallant & Travis, 1995; Cohen, Janicki-Deverts & Miller, 2007; Levenstein, Ackerman, Kiecolt-Glaser & Dubois, 1999; Light et al., 1999; Sapolsky, 1992; Wittstein et al., 2005).

COGNITIVE DEVELOPMENT

Measuring Cognitive Abilities in Middle Age

The status of cognitive abilities in middle age has been a subject of much debate. Here, we look at two important lines of research, K. Warner Schaie's Seattle Longitudinal Study and Horn and Cattell's studies of fluid and crystallized intelligence.

SCHAIE: THE SEATTLE LONGITUDINAL STUDY

In many respects middle-age people are in their cognitive prime. The Seattle Longitudinal Study of Adult Intelligence (Schaie, 1990, 1994, 1996a, 1996b, 2005; Willis & Schaie, 1999, 2006; Schaie & Willis, 2010) demonstrates this fact.

The study began in 1956 with 500 randomly chosen men and women across a variety of different age brackets ranging from 22 to 67 years of age and involved multiple waves of data collection over 5 decades. The participants were followed longitudinally and assessed every 7 years on timed tests of six primary mental abilities (Table 15.3). By using multiple cohorts—people of different ages, all followed over time—Schaie and his colleagues were able to tease apart the different influences and conduct more sophisticated analyses than either a simple longitudinal or cross-sectional design would have permitted.

Most participants showed remarkable stability over time, and no significant reductions in most abilities until after age 60, and then not in most areas. Virtually no one declined on all fronts, and most people improved in some areas. However, there were wide individual differences. By the age of 74, there were declines in the average scores for all abilities.

Additionally, there were no uniform patterns of age-related change across cognitive abilities. For example, several abilities peaked during middle age, and verbal meaning

TABLE 15.3 Tests of Primary Mental Abilities Given in Seattle Longitudinal Study of Adult Intelligence

Test	Ability Measured	Task	Type of Intelligence*
Verbal meaning	Recognition and understanding of words	Find synonym by matching stimulus word with another word from a list	Crystallized
Word fluency	Retrieving words from long-term memory	Think of as many words as possible beginning with a given letter	Part crystallized, part fluid
Number	Performing computations	Do simple addition problems	Crystallized
Spatial orientation	Manipulating objects mentally in two-dimensional space	Select rotated examples of figure to match stimulus figure	Fluid
Inductive reasoning	Identifying patterns and inferring principles and rules for solving logical problems	Complete a letter series	Fluid
Perceptual speed	Making quick, accurate discriminations between visual stimuli	Identify matching and nonmatching images flashed on a computer screen	Fluid

*Fluid and crystallized intelligence are defined in the next section.

Sources: Schaie, 1989; Willis, S. L., & Schaie, K. W. (1999). Intellectual functioning in midlife. In S. L. Willis & J. D. Reid (Eds.), *Life in the middle: Psychological and social development in middle age* (pp. 233–247). San Diego: Academic Press.

even showed improvements into old age. By contrast, about 13 to 17 percent of adults declined in number, memory recall, or verbal fluency between ages 39 and 53 (Schaie, 1994, 2005; Willis & Schaie, 2006; Schaie & Willis, 2010)

Schaie and his colleagues also found that successive cohorts scored progressively higher at the same ages on most abilities, possibly because of improvements in education, healthy lifestyles, and other positive environmental influences. However, numerical ability showed overall declines after the 1924 cohort, and verbal meaning declined after the 1952 cohort (Willis & Schaie, 2006; Figure 15.3).

Individuals who scored highest tended to be free of cardiovascular and other chronic diseases, to be from higher socioeconomic class, have high educational levels and flexible personalities at midlife, to be in an intact family, to pursue cognitively complex occupations and other activities, to be married to someone more cognitively advanced, to be satisfied with their accomplishments, and to be high in the personality dimension of openness to experience (Schaie, 1994, 2005; Willis & Schaie, 2006; Sharp, Reynolds, Pedersen & Gatz, 2010; Schaie & Willis, 2010). Given the strong cognitive performance of most middle-agers, evidence of substantial cognitive decline in persons younger than 60 may indicate a neurological problem (Schaie, 2005; Willis & Shaie, 1999). In particular, midlife decline in memory recall and verbal fluency (Willis & Schaie, 2006) and perceptual processing speed (Schaie & Willis, 2010) predict cognitive impairment in old age.

HORN AND CATTELL: FLUID AND CRYSTALLIZED INTELLIGENCE

Another set of cognitive researchers, Horn and Cattell (Cattell, 1965; Horn, 1967, 1968, 1970, 1982a, 1982b; Horn & Hofer, 1992), distinguishes between two aspects

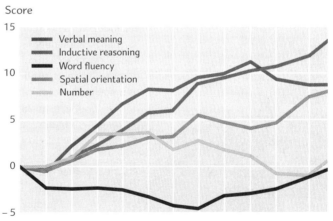

FIGURE 15.3
Cohort Differences in Scores on Tests of Primary Mental Abilities

More recent cohorts scored higher on inductive reasoning, word fluency, and spatial orientation.

Source: Schaie, K. W., *Developmental influences on adult intelligence: The Seattle Longitudinal Study.* New York: Oxford University Press, 2005, Fig. 6.1, p. 137.

fluid intelligence
Type of intelligence, proposed by Horn and Cattell, that is applied to novel problems and is relatively independent of educational and cultural influences.

crystallized intelligence
Type of intelligence, proposed by Horn and Cattell, involving the ability to remember and use learned information; it is largely dependent on education and culture.

of intelligence: *fluid* and *crystallized*. **Fluid intelligence** is the ability to solve novel problems on the fly. Such problems require little or no previous knowledge, such as realizing that a hanger can be used to fix a leaky toilet, or discovering the pattern in a sequence of figures. It involves perceiving relations, forming concepts, and drawing inferences. These abilities are largely determined by neurological status. **Crystallized intelligence,** by contrast, is the ability to remember and use information acquired over a lifetime, such as finding a synonym for a word or solving a math problem. Crystallized intelligence is measured by tests of vocabulary, general information, and responses to social situations and dilemmas—abilities that depend largely on education and cultural experience.

Typically, fluid intelligence has been found to peak in young adulthood. This is particularly true for perceptual speed, which peaks quite early, beginning in the twenties. Working memory capacity also declines with age. However, these changes are gradual and do not generally cause functional impairment (Lachman, 2004; Willis & Schaie, 1999), and regular exercise can slow this process (Singh-Manoux, Hillsdon, Brunner & Marmot, 2005). Morever, the losses in fluid intelligence may be offset by improvements in crystallized intelligence, which increase through middle age and often until near the end of life (Horn, 1982a, 1982b; Horn & Donaldson, 1980).

The Distinctiveness of Adult Cognition

Instead of measuring the same cognitive abilities at different ages, some developmental scientists look for distinctive qualities in the thinking of mature adults.

THE ROLE OF EXPERTISE

Why do mature adults show increasing competence in solving problems in their chosen fields? One answer seems to lie in *specialized knowledge,* or *expertise*—a form of crystallized intelligence.

Because formal education is age-graded, most children learn similar things—such as how to read or complete math problems—at roughly the same time. In adulthood, however, paths of learning diverge, and adults become more or less learned in whatever domain of knowledge they pursue. These advances in expertise continue at least through middle adulthood and, for the most part, are not related to general intelligence. It may take middle-age people longer than younger people to process *new* information. But when it comes to solving problems *within* their field of expertise, their vast base of knowledge compensates for processing declines and allows them to rapidly and effectively solve a problem (Hoyer & Rybash, 1994).

Experts assimilate and interpret new knowledge more efficiently by referring to a rich, highly organized storehouse of mental representations of what they already know. For example, imaging studies show that when completing a task within their domain of expertise, adults show brain activation in areas associated with long-term memory. This allows them to integrate information in long-term memory with working memory in "chunks," and thus perform the task at a higher level than novices (Guida, Gobet, Tardieu & Nicholas, 2012). Experts also sort information on the basis of underlying principles, rather than surface similarities and differences. Also they are more aware of what they do *not* know (Charness & Schultetus, 1999; Goldman, Petrosino & Cognition and Technology Group at Vanderbilt, 1999).

Expertise in interpreting X-rays depends on specialized knowledge. Experts often appear to be guided by intuition and cannot explain how they arrive at conclusions. ©Ron Levine/Getty Images

Studies of people in such diverse occupations as chess players, street vendors, abacus counters, physics experts, hospitality workers, airline counter workers, and airplane pilots illustrate how specific knowledge contributes to superior performance in a particular domain (Billet, 2001) and can help buffer age-related declines in cognitive resources when solving problems in that domain (Morrow, Menard, Stine-Morrow, Teller & Bryant, 2001).

Expert thinking often seems automatic and intuitive. Experts generally are not fully aware of the thought processes that lie behind their decisions (Charness & Schultetus, 1999; Salas, Rosen & DiazGranados, 2010). Such intuitive, experience-based thinking is also characteristic of what has been called postformal thought.

INTEGRATIVE THOUGHT

Although not limited to any particular period of adulthood, postformal thought seems well suited to the complex tasks, multiple roles, and perplexing choices and challenges of midlife, such as the need to synthesize and balance work and family demands (Sinnott, 2003). An important feature of postformal thought is its *integrative* nature (Kallio, 2011). Mature adults integrate logic with intuition and emotion; they put together conflicting facts and ideas; and they compare new information with what they already know. They interpret what they read, see, or hear in terms of its meaning for them. Instead of accepting something at face value, they filter it through their life experience and previous learning.

In one study (C. Adams, 1991), early and late adolescents and middle-age and older adults were asked to summarize a Sufi teaching tale. Adolescents recalled more details of the story than adults did, but their summaries were largely limited to repeating the story line. Adults, especially women, gave summaries that were rich in interpretation, integrating what was in the text with its psychological and metaphorical meaning for them.

Society benefits from this integrative feature of adult thought. Generally, it is mature adults who translate their knowledge about the human condition into inspirational stories to which younger generations can turn for guidance.

Creativity

At about age 40, Frank Lloyd Wright designed Robie House in Chicago. Charles Darwin was 50 when he presented his theory of evolution. Toni Morrison won the Pulitzer Prize for *Beloved,* a novel she wrote at about age 55. Many creative people have reached their greatest achievements in middle age.

CHARACTERISTICS OF CREATIVE ACHIEVERS

Intelligence and creativity are not the same thing. Although a certain baseline general intelligence, or IQ, is needed (Guilford, 1956), creative performance is not strongly related to general intelligence once that threshold is reached (Simonton, 2000). This is true even though the baseline IQ needed for creative performance does rise for more complex creative achievements (Jauk, Benedek, Dunst & Neubauer, 2013). Intelligence also seems to be more strongly influenced by genetic processes than creativity does. Intelligence shows high heritability and its heritability rises with age as individuals get older and seek out more experiences in line with their proclivities (Plomin & Deary, 2015). By contrast, strong genetic contributions have not been found for creative performance (Runco et al., 2011; Reuter, Roth, Holve & Hennig, 2006).

Creativity seems to be the product of particular social contexts as well as individual proclivities. With respect to environment, creativity seems to develop from diverse experiences that weaken conventional constraints and challenging experiences that strengthen the ability to persevere and overcome obstacles (Sternberg & Lubart, 1995).

Individual differences also can make creativity more likely. For example, highly creative people are self-starters and risk-takers. They tend to be independent, nonconformist, unconventional, and they are open to new ideas and experiences. Their thinking processes are often unconscious, leading to sudden moments of illumination (Simonton, 2000; Torrance, 1988). They look at problems more deeply and come up with solutions that do not occur to others (Sternberg & Horvath, 1998). They think in flexible ways and explore many possible solutions to problems (Baas, Nijstad & DeDreu, 2015).

However, this is not enough. Extraordinary creative achievement requires deep, highly organized knowledge of a subject, and a strong emotional attachment to the work, which spurs the creator to persevere in the face of obstacles. A person must first be thoroughly grounded in a field before she or he can see its limitations, envision radical departures, and develop a new and unique point of view (Keegan, 1996).

Not surprisingly, researchers have looked for creative problem-solving correlates in the brain. This research is challenging—creative ideas, by their very nature, are divergent and wide-ranging. One meta-analysis including 34 imaging studies showed that when people were engaged in creative tasks, they showed more activation in the prefrontal cortex

Helen Mirren, long a highly respected, classically trained actress, won the Academy Award for Best Actress at the age of 61 for her portrayal of a proud, aging Queen Elizabeth II in the film The Queen. ©Jamie Rector/EPA/REX/Shutterstock

regardless of what type of creative task they were performing. However, different areas became more active depending on task demands. For example, tasks that required inhibitory processes, fluency, and control were likely to generate activity in the lateral prefrontal cortex; whereas tasks that required the activation of semantic (meaning-based) associations tended to elicit more activity in the superior and inferior central gyri (Gonen-Yaacovi et al., 2013).

CREATIVITY AND AGE

Is there a relationship between creative performance and age? On psychometric tests of divergent thinking, age differences consistently appear. Whether data are cross-sectional or longitudinal, scores peak, on average, around the late thirties (Simonton, 1990). After this, they remain relatively flat for some time, and then decline in the seventies (Massimiliano, 2015). A similar age curve emerges when creativity is measured by variations in output (number of publications, paintings, or compositions). A person in the last decade of a creative career typically produces only about half as much as during the late thirties or early forties, though somewhat more than in the twenties (Simonton, 1990).

However, the age curve varies depending on the field. Poets, mathematicians, and theoretical physicists tend to be most prolific in their late twenties or early thirties. Research psychologists reach a peak around age 40, followed by a moderate decline. Novelists, historians, and philosophers become increasingly productive through their late forties or fifties and then level off. These patterns hold true across cultures and historical periods (Dixon & Hultsch, 1999; Simonton, 1990).

Work and Education

In industrialized societies, occupational roles typically are based on age. Young people are students; young and middle-age adults are workers; older adults organize their lives around retirement and leisure. In postindustrial societies, people make multiple transitions throughout their adult lives (Czaja, 2006).

WORK VERSUS EARLY RETIREMENT

Before 1985, the average age of retirement moved steadily downward. Since then, the trend has reversed. Before bringing their working lives to a complete stop, people may reduce work hours or days, gradually moving into retirement over a number of years. This practice is called *phased retirement.* Or they may switch to another company or a new line of work, a practice called *bridge employment* (Czaja, 2006). A majority of older Americans now remain active in the labor force after retirement from their career job (Cahill, Giandrea & Quinn, 2013). Not surprisingly, those people who have retired or entered partial retirement are generally more interested in volunteering (Tang, 2016).

What has brought about this change? People may continue working to maintain their physical and emotional health and their personal and social roles, or simply because they enjoy the stimulation of work (Czaja, 2006; Sterns & Huyck, 2001). Others work primarily for financial reasons. For example, data show that the implementation of the Affordable Care Act (ACA), which increased the affordability of comprehensive health care for many, led to increased early retirement and increases in part-time work (which does not generally include health benefits) in women and low-income men (Heim & Lim, 2017).

The rise in the Social Security retirement age to 67 for full benefits offers an inducement to keep working. The Age Discrimination in Employment Act, which eliminated mandatory retirement ages for most occupations, and the Americans with Disabilities Act, which requires employers to make reasonable accommodations for workers with disabilities, have helped mature workers to keep their jobs.

WORK AND COGNITIVE DEVELOPMENT

Adults can affect their cognitive development by the occupational choices they make. For example, flexible thinkers tend to seek out and obtain substantively complex work—work that requires thought and independent judgment. In turn, complex work stimulates more flexible thinking, and flexible thinking then increases the ability to do such work (Kohn, 1980). Work need not necessarily be construed in the traditional way, and the same is true of men and women engaged in complex household work, such as planning a budget or making complicated repairs like putting in new plumbing (Caplan & Schooler, 2006). Regardless of the specifics, people who are deeply engaged in complex work or cognitively stimulating lifestyles tend to show stronger cognitive performance and fewer declines than their peers as they age (Avolio & Sosik, 1999; Kohn & Schooler, 1983; Schaie, 1984; Schooler, 1990; La Rue, 2010).

Openness to experience—a personality variable—also affects cognitive performance over time (Sharp et al., 2010). People who are high on openness to experience are more likely to retain their faculties and show high work performance. Similarly, those people who consistently seek more stimulating opportunities are likely to remain mentally sharp (Avolio & Sosik, 1999). Interestingly, this association may work both ways. Older adults enrolled in a cognitive training program for 30 weeks showed increases in openness to experience at the conclusion of the training (Jackson, Hill, Payne, Roberts & Stine-Morrow, 2012).

This suggests that if work, both on the job and at home, could be made meaningful and challenging, more adults might retain or improve their cognitive abilities. This seems to be happening to some extent. The gains in cognitive abilities seen in older cohorts may reflect workplace changes that put a premium on adaptability, initiative, and decentralized decision making.

THE MATURE LEARNER

In 2005, 44 percent of U.S. adults, including 48 percent of 45- to 54-year-olds and 40 percent of 55- to 64-year-olds, reported having participated in adult education, 27 percent in work-related courses (National Center for Education Statistics, 2007; O'Donnell, 2006).

Adult Education and Work Skills Changes in the workplace often entail a need for more training or education. Expanding technology and shifting job markets require a life-span approach to learning. Technological skills are increasingly necessary for success in the modern world and are a major component of work-related adult education. With experience, middle-age people can perform computer-based tasks as well as young adults (Czaja, 2006).

Employers see benefits of workplace education in improved morale, increased quality of work, better teamwork and problem solving, and greater ability to cope with new technology and other changes in the workplace (Conference Board, 1999). Moreover, in addition to the employee benefits, employers increasingly report benefits for the company as a whole, including higher economic returns and improved employee skills (Conference Board, 2000).

Literacy Training **Literacy** is a fundamental requisite for participation not only in the workplace but in all facets of a modern, information-driven society. At the turn of the century, a person with a fourth-grade education was considered literate; today, a high school diploma is barely adequate.

In 2014, 17 percent of U.S. adults could not locate clearly identifiable information in brief English prose, 27 percent could not perform simple numerical operations such as addition, and 23 percent could not use simple technological tools such as e-mail or the Internet. Compared to other countries, the United States ranks about average on literacy tests. However, U.S. adults are clustered at both the high and low ends of the scale (Rampey et al., 2016).

Middle-age and older adults tend to have lower literacy levels than young adults, but the average literacy level of adults ages 50 to 59 has increased since 1992. Adults below basic literacy are less likely to be employed than adults at higher literacy levels (Kutner et al., 2007; Rampey et al., 2016).

Globally, 781 million adults—about 14 percent of the world population—are illiterate, mostly in sub-Saharan Africa and East and South Asia. Women make up 64 percent of illiterate adults worldwide (UNESCO, 2007; 2015). Illiteracy is especially common among women in developing nations, where education typically is considered unimportant for them. In 1990, the United Nations launched literacy programs in such developing countries as Bangladesh, Nepal, and Somalia (Linder, 1990). More recently, the UN named 2003 to 2012 the Literacy Decade and sponsored conferences and programs to promote literacy development. In the United States, the National Literacy Act requires the states to establish literacy training centers with federal funding assistance.

literacy
In an adult, ability to use printed and written information to function in society, achieve goals, and develop knowledge and potential.

summary and key terms

Middle Age: A Social Construct

- The concept of middle age is a social construct. It came into use in industrial societies as an increasing life span led to new roles at midlife.
- The span of middle adulthood is often subjective.
- Most middle-age people are in good physical, cognitive, and emotional condition.

PHYSICAL DEVELOPMENT

Physical Changes

- Although some physiological changes result from aging and genetic makeup, behavior and lifestyle can affect their timing and extent.
- Most middle-age adults compensate well for gradual, minor declines in sensory and psychomotor abilities. Losses in bone density and vital capacity are common.
- Symptoms of menopause and attitudes toward it may depend on cultural factors and natural changes of aging.
- Although men can continue to father children until late in life, many middle-age men experience a decline in fertility and in frequency of orgasm.
- A large proportion of middle-age men experience erectile dysfunction.
- Sexual activity generally diminishes gradually in middle age.

presbyopia, myopia, presbycusis, basal metabolism, vital capacity, menopause, perimenopause, erectile dysfunction

Physical and Mental Health

- Most middle-age people are healthy; however, baby boomers may be less healthy than previous generations at middle age.
- Hypertension is a major health problem beginning in midlife. Cancer has passed heart disease as the number one cause of death in midlife. The prevalence of diabetes has doubled.
- Diet, exercise, alcohol use, and smoking affect present and future health.
- Low income is associated with poorer health.
- Racial and ethnic disparities in health and health care have decreased but still persist.
- Postmenopausal women become more susceptible to heart disease as well as to bone loss leading to osteoporosis. Chances of developing breast cancer also increase with age.
- Mounting evidence suggests that the risks of hormone therapy outweigh its benefits.
- Stress occurs when the body's ability to cope is not equal to the demands on it. Stress is often greatest in middle age. Severe stress can affect immune functioning.

- Role and career changes and other experiences typical of middle age can be stressful, but resilience is common.
- Psychological distress becomes more prevalent in middle age.
- Personality and negative emotionality can affect health. Positive emotions tend to be associated with good health.

hypertension, diabetes, osteoporosis, mammography, hormone therapy (HT), stress, stressors

COGNITIVE DEVELOPMENT

Measuring Cognitive Abilities in Middle Age

- The Seattle Longitudinal Study found that several of the primary mental abilities remain strong during middle age, but there is great individual variability.
- Fluid intelligence declines earlier than crystallized intelligence.

fluid intelligence, crystallized intelligence

The Distinctiveness of Adult Cognition

- Some theorists propose that cognition takes distinctive forms at midlife.
- Expertise allows older adults to perform at high levels in areas they are familiar with despite the processing declines typical of age.
- Postformal thought seems especially useful in situations calling for integrative thinking.

Creativity

- Creative performance depends on personal attributes and environmental forces.
- Creativity is not strongly related to intelligence.
- An age-related decline appears in both psychometric tests of divergent thinking and actual creative output, but peak ages for output vary by occupation.

Work and Education

- A shift away from early retirement and toward more flexible options is occurring.
- Complex work may improve cognitive flexibility.
- Many adults participate in educational activities, often to improve work-related skills and knowledge.
- Literacy training is an urgent need in the United States and globally.

literacy

Psychosocial Development in Middle Adulthood

chapter 16

©Picturenet/Blend Images/age fotostock

learning objectives

Discuss stability and change in development in middle adulthood.

Summarize personality development and psychological adjustment in middle age.

Identify some important aspects of close relationships in middle adulthood.

In this chapter we look at theoretical perspectives and research on psychosocial issues and themes at midlife. We then focus on intimate relationships: marriage, cohabitation, and divorce; gay and lesbian relationships; friendships; and relationships with maturing children, aging parents, siblings, and grandchildren. All these may be woven into the rich texture of the middle years.

Looking at the Life Course in Middle Age

Today it is hard to say what life course, if any, is typical of middle age. Traditionally, early midlife involved caring for children and peak career productivity, and later midlife involved the gradual withdrawal from those roles. However, economic realities have meant that some middle-age adults have had to put off retirement, and that adult children remain in the nest or return (Willis, Martin & Rocke, 2010). The times have changed, and so have the paths of individuals. At 40, some people become parents for the first time, and others become grandparents. At 50, some people are starting new careers, and others are taking early retirement.

Furthermore, lives do not progress in isolation. Individual pathways intersect with those of family members, friends, acquaintances, and strangers. Work and personal roles are interdependent, and those roles are affected by trends in the larger society. Cohort, gender, ethnicity, culture, and socioeconomic status also affect the life course. All these factors, and more, enter into the study of psychosocial development in middle adulthood.

Change at Midlife: Theoretical Approaches

In psychosocial terms, middle adulthood once was considered a relatively stable period of development, where little change occurred. In part because of these assumptions, middle-age adults were rarely the object of direct study. When they were involved in research, such research was more likely to focus on their role as parents and the ways in which they affected their children's development, or on their role as caregivers for elderly parents (Lachman, 2004).

Thus, research on midlife was relatively scarce. When it was conducted, this work utilized primarily cross-sectional designs, in which adults of different ages were compared to each other. This work, while valuable, obscured individual trajectories and patterns of change and stability (Willis, Martin & Rocke, 2010). The research focused primarily on average changes in middle-age adults under the assumption that after the rapid changes of childhood and adolescence and before the declines of late adulthood, development was relatively stable (Schaie, 2005).

However, there is a renewed interest in midlife research. A variety of factors are responsible for this. The changing demographics of countries such as the United States, where large proportions of middle-age adults are moving into late adulthood, has made studying the dynamics of this age more vital. Moreover, the field and the tools available to researchers have changed. Newer work, utilizing previously unavailable longitudinal data and more sophisticated statistical techniques, has allowed researchers to more carefully track individual trajectories of change and stability (Willis, Martin & Rocke, 2010). In the following section, we focus on some of the classic models of middle adulthood that have had the greatest impact on the field as a way to frame our understanding of development in midlife.

TRAIT MODELS

Recall that the best known trait model of personality described the individual differences between people as consisting of five different factors: openness to experience, conscientiousness, extraversion, agreeableness, and neuroticism (Costa & McCrae, 1980). The research in this area originally posited that these traits, known as the Big Five, were relatively continuous and were not believed to change in any appreciable way after the age of 30. More recent data suggest that slow change during the middle and older years is common (Costa & McCrae, 2006), and that significant positive changes during those years are possible (Roberts & Mroczek, 2008).

What specific changes have been noted? Conscientiousness—being deliberate, organized, and disciplined—tends to be highest in middle age (Donnellan & Lucas, 2008), perhaps as a consequence of work experience or because of increases in social maturity and emotional stability (Roberts & Mroczek, 2008).

Individual life trajectories can affect this process as well. For example, compared to people who continue to work, retirees tend to increase in agreeableness—being straightforward, altruistic, and modest—and decrease in activity (Lockenhoff, Terracciano & Costa, 2009). However, those who, against their will, become unemployed show decreases in agreeableness and conscientiousness. This relationship is stronger, especially in men, the longer the unemployment persists (Boyce, Wood, Daly & Sedikides, 2015). Social relationships matter too. Middle-age men who remarry tend to become less neurotic (Roberts & Mroczek, 2008); those who divorce decrease in extraversion (Allemand, Hill & Lehmann, 2015); and increases in extraversion and agreeableness, along with decreases in neuroticism, are associated with high perceived social support (Allemand, Schaffhuser & Martin, 2015).

NORMATIVE-STAGE MODELS

Erik Erikson was the most influential of the normative-stage theorists, and provided a frame of reference for much developmental theory and research on middle adulthood. Erikson believed that the years around age 40 were a time when people entered their seventh normative stage: **generativity versus stagnation. Generativity,** as Erikson defined it, involved finding meaning through contributing to society and leaving a legacy for future generations. The virtue of this period is *care:* "a widening commitment to *take care* of the persons, the products, and the ideas one has learned *to care for*" (Erikson, 1985, p. 67). People who do not find an outlet for generativity run the risk of becoming self-absorbed, self-indulgent, and stagnant. Adults who slide into stagnation may find themselves disconnected from their communities because of their failure to find a way to contribute.

Forms of Generativity What form does generativity take? What does it look like? For many adults, generativity is expressed through parenting, as well as through the generally more leisurely pursuit of grandparenting (Hebblethwaite & Norris, 2011). However, this is not the only path; generativity can derive from involvement in multiple roles (Staudinger & Bluck, 2001; McAdams, 2013). It can be expressed through teaching or mentorship, productivity or creativity, and self-generation or self-development. It can extend to the world or work, to politics, to religion, to hobbies, to art, to music, and to other spheres; or as Erikson called it, "maintenance of the world." Regardless of its form, generativity tends to be associated with prosocial behavior (McAdams, 2006). So, for example, volunteering for community service or for a political cause is an expression of generativity (Hart, Southerland & Atkins, 2003; Matsuba et al., 2012).

High levels of generativity are linked to positive outcomes. For example, highly generative people tend to report greater well-being and satisfaction in midlife (McAdams, 2001) and in later adulthood (Sheldon & Kasser, 2001), perhaps through the sense of having contributed meaningfully to society. Moreover, the positive effects are also physical in nature; generativity is also associated with good health, and a decreased risk of disability or mortality (Gruenewald, Liao & Seeman, 2012).

One possible explanation is that generativity is linked to positive social engagement with others (Cox, Wilt, Olson & McAdams, 2010), which is then associated with positive outcomes. Highly generative people stay continually engaged in life, and this builds competencies, strengthens social bonds, improves self-image, and provides meaning (Kruse & Schmitt, 2012). The direction of effects, however, is unclear. Because such research is correlational, we cannot be sure that generativity causes social engagement and well-being. It could be the case that those people who are happy with their lives and feel connected to others are more likely to be generative (McAdams, 2001).

Generativity, Age, and Gender Erikson believed that generativity was especially salient during midlife because of the demands placed on adults through work and family. Research (Table 16.1) generally supports that middle-age people do indeed score higher on most measures of generativity than do younger and older adults (Beaumont & Pratt, 2011; McAdams, de St. Aubin & Logan, 1993). However, the age at which individuals achieve generativity varies, as does its strength at any particular time, and some people are more generative than others (Keyes & Ryff, 1998; McAdams, 2006; Stewart & Vandewater, 1998).

Given that generativity is often expressed in terms of the next generation, parenting has also been examined to see if it affects this process. Research has shown that women have similar levels of generativity regardless of whether or not they have had a child,

generativity versus stagnation
Erikson's seventh stage of psychosocial development, in which the middle-age adult develops a concern with establishing, guiding, and influencing the next generation or else experiences stagnation (a sense of inactivity or lifelessness).

generativity
Erikson's term for concern of mature adults for finding meaning through contributing to society and leaving a legacy for future generations.

Generativity, a concern for guiding the younger generation, can be expressed through coaching or mentoring. Generativity may be a key to well-being in midlife.
©SW Productions/Getty Images

TABLE 16.1 The Loyola Generativity Scale

- I try to pass along the knowledge I have gained through my experiences.
- I do not feel that other people need me.
- I think I would like the work of a teacher.
- I feel as though I have made a difference to many people.
- I do not volunteer to work for a charity.
- I have made and created things that have had an impact on other people.
- I try to be creative in most things that I do.
- I think that I will be remembered for a long time after I die.
- I believe that society cannot be responsible for providing food and shelter for all homeless people.
- Others would say that I have made unique contributions to society.
- If I were unable to have children of my own, I would like to adopt children.
- I have important skills that I try to teach others.
- I feel that I have done nothing that will survive after I die.
- In general, my actions do not have a positive effect on others.
- I feel as though I have done nothing of worth to contribute to others.
- I have made many commitments to many different kinds of people, groups, and activities in my life.
- Other people say that I am a very productive person.
- I have a responsibility to improve the neighborhood in which I live.
- People come to me for advice.
- I feel as though my contributions will exist after I die.

Source: McAdams, D. P., & de St. Aubin, E. "A theory of generativity and its assessment through self-report, behavioral acts, and narrative themes in autobiography." *Journal of Personality and Social Psychology*, 62(6), 1992, 1003–1015 (from the Appendix, p. 1015).

and that at least early in adulthood, these levels are higher than those of men. For men, however, having a child seems to spur change, and men's levels of generativity rise following the birth of their first child (Karacan, 2014).

By late adulthood, levels of generativity in men and women are more similar (Keyes & Ryff, 1998; Cox, Wilt, Olson & McAdams, 2010). Apparently, even those adults who enter midlife with low levels of generativity can catch up to their peers later (Whitbourne, Sneed & Sayer, 2009). It may be that relief from primary family and work responsibilities frees middle-age and older adults to express generativity on a broader scale (Keyes & Ryff, 1998). This finding underscores Erikson's assertion that positive change is possible at any point in the life span. Because of the centrality of generativity in middle age, we return to generativity later in this chapter.

TIMING OF EVENTS: THE SOCIAL CLOCK

Every culture has a social clock describing the ages at which people are expected to reach certain milestones. Timing of events models suggest that, rather than being based on years lived, development is more affected by *when* events occur in a person's life. In other words, what matters is not that a person turns 65 but that the person retires.

In previous generations, the timing of major events in the social clock were fairly predictable. When occupational patterns were more stable and retirement at age 65 was almost universal, the meaning of work was more similar for all adults nearing retirement age. However, in a time of frequent job changes, downsizing, and either early or delayed retirement, the meaning of work is more variable. Similarly, when most women's lives revolved around bearing and rearing children, the end of the reproductive years meant something different. When people died at younger ages, those who survived into middle age were more likely to feel that they were reaching the end of their life. Today middle-age people may be raising children, being parents to adolescents and young adults, or serving as caregivers to aging parents. Fortunately, despite the multiple challenges and variable events of midlife, most middle-age adults seem well able to handle this life stage (Lachman, 2004).

The Self at Midlife: Issues and Themes

Many issues and themes from research on middle age revolve around the self. Is there such a thing as a midlife crisis? How does identity develop in middle age? What contributes to psychological well-being?

IS THERE A MIDLIFE CRISIS?

The middle-age man who impulsively buys an expensive sports car or the woman who abruptly leaves her job and home to travel to find herself are familiar stereotypes. Often, changes in personality and lifestyle such as these during the early to middle forties are attributed to what has been called a **midlife crisis.** At about this age, many people realize that they will not be able to fulfill the dreams of their youth, or that fulfillment of their dreams has not brought the satisfaction they expected, and they become more aware of their own mortality. The midlife crisis is a supposedly stressful period triggered by this review and reevaluation of one's life.

The term *midlife crisis* is now considered an inaccurate representation of what most people experience in midlife (Wethington, 2000). In fact, its occurrence seems to be fairly unusual (Aldwin & Levenson, 2001; Heckhausen, 2001; Lachman, 2004). Some middle-age people may experience crisis or turmoil, but others feel at the peak of their powers. Still others may fall somewhere in between—with neither a peak nor a crisis—or may experience both crisis and competence at different times or in different domains of life (Lachman, 2004).

It may be best to consider midlife to be one of life's **turning points**—psychological transitions that involve significant change or transformation in the perceived meaning, purpose, or direction of a person's life. Turning points may be triggered by major life events, normative changes, or a new understanding of past experience, either positive or negative, and they may be stressful. However, in the MIDUS survey and a follow-up study of psychological turning points (PTP), many respondents reported positive growth from successful resolution of stressful situations (Wethington et al., 2004; Figure 16.1).

Turning points often involve an introspective review and reappraisal of values and priorities (Helson, 1997; Reid & Willis, 1999; Robinson, Rosenberg & Farrell, 1999; Bauer & McAdams, 2004). The **midlife review** involves recognizing the finiteness of life and can be a time of taking stock, discovering new insights about the self, and spurring midcourse corrections in the design and trajectory of one's life. However, it can also involve regret over failure to achieve a dream or a keener awareness of *developmental deadlines*—time constraints on, say, the ability to have a child or to make up with an estranged friend or family member (Heckhausen, 2001; Heckhausen, Wrosch & Fleeson, 2001).

Whether a turning point becomes a crisis may depend less on age than on individual circumstances and personal resources. People with **ego resiliency**—the ability to adapt flexibly and resourcefully to potential sources of stress—and those who have a sense of mastery and control are more likely to navigate the midlife crossing successfully (Heckhausen, 2001; Klohnen, 1996; Lachman, 2004; Lachman & Firth, 2004). They recover from stress more rapidly (Tugade, Frederickson & Feldman Barrett, 2004)

midlife crisis
In some normative-crisis models, stressful life period precipitated by the review and reevaluation of one's past, typically occurring in the early to middle forties.

turning points
Psychological transitions that involve significant change or transformation in the perceived meaning, purpose, or direction of a person's life.

midlife review
Introspective examination that often occurs in middle age, leading to reappraisal and revision of values and priorities.

ego resiliency
The ability to adapt flexibly and resourcefully to potential sources of stress.

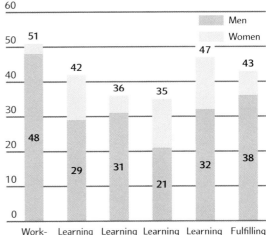

Percentage reporting

FIGURE 16.1

Turning Points Reported by 25- to 74-Year-Olds as Having Occurred in the Past 5 Years

Source: Wethington, E., Kessler, R. C., & Pixley, J. E. "Turning points in adulthood." In O. G. Brim, C. D. Ryff, & R. C. Kessler (Eds.), *How Healthy Are We? A National Study of Well-Being at Midlife*, Chicago: University of Chicago Press, 2004, Figure 3, p. 600.

A midlife review might inspire a woman who senses her biological clock ticking to move forward on her wish to have a child.
©thechatat/Shutterstock

and, for example, are less likely to become depressed after experiencing a trauma (Frederickson, Tugade, Waugh & Larkin, 2003). For people with resilient personalities, even negative events, such as an unwanted divorce, can become springboards for positive growth (Klohnen, 1996; Moen & Wethington, 1999). Table 16.2 outlines qualities considered most and least characteristic of ego-resilient adults.

IDENTITY DEVELOPMENT

Although Erikson defined identity formation as the main concern of adolescence, he noted that identity continues to develop in adulthood.

Generativity and Identity Erikson saw generativity as an aspect of identity formation. Research supports this connection. Successful achievement of identity is associated with generativity, and both together are then associated with other positive outcomes.

A particularly fruitful place to examine the intersection of generativity and identity is in women, and particularly with respect to tensions related to professional success and family life. Working outside the home often requires balancing the demands of home and family, something that is generally more difficult for women than men (Duxbury, Higgins & Lee, 1994; Allen, Herst, Bruck & Sutton, 2000). Demographic changes have led to increasing numbers of women entering the workforce. The process of fulfilling multiple roles, which for women may involve challenging traditional norms and stereotypes, is one that is likely to affect identity processes. Moreover, work and children are areas in which people often seek generative action. Thus, most work in this area has focused on women.

Research has found that for women, inhabiting multiple roles early in life—whether or not they were married, had children, or worked outside the home—impacted identity development. Those women who filled more social roles were more likely to develop a firm sense of identity, and, once developed, their identity balance was associated with generativity, and consequently well-being and psychological health (Vandewater, Ostrove & Stewart, 1997; DeHaan & MacDermid, 1994). Having a firm sense of identity is also helpful in resolving work-family conflict. In one study of college-educated women at midlife, highly generative career-focused women found gratification through generative actions in their work such as mentoring and helping others at their job. Highly generative women not employed outside the home found this same sense of gratification through parenting their children (Peterson & Stewart, 1996).

Once established, generativity appears to pave the way for positive life outcomes. For example, in one study of middle-age women, generativity predicted positive feelings about marriage and motherhood, and was related to successful aging (Peterson & Duncan, 2007). In another study, women who had attained generativity at age 43 reported greater investment 10 years later in their cross-generational roles as daughter and mother and felt less burdened by the care of aging parents (Peterson, 2002). Similarly, in a study of 333 female, mostly white, University of Michigan graduates in their sixties, high levels of generativity went hand in hand with increased certainty about their identity and a sense of confidence in their powers (Zucker, Ostrove & Stewart, 2002). The relationship between identity and generativity may also affect behavior. In a study comparing environmental activists and non-activists, identity maturity was associated with more activism. Presumably, this was because having a mature identity motivated individuals to act in more a generative fashion (Matsuba et al., 2012).

Narrative Psychology: Identity as a Life Story We all carry with us the story of who we are: how we came to be the person we are today, what shaped us over time and how, and who we wish to be in the future. The field of *narrative psychology* views the development of the self as a continuous process of constructing one's life story—a dramatic narrative, or personal

As people get older, they might achieve identity balance as they integrate their self-image of themselves as physically fit with an understanding they need to do more activity to maintain that fitness. ©Igor Palamarchuk/Shutterstock

MIDLIFE CAREER CHANGE

As originally described by Erik Erikson, midlife is characterized as including a period of "life review" that involves evaluating past and present priorities, shifting responsibilities, and seeking out rewarding activities. One area in which people may experience life review relates to their career.

In prior generations, people often stayed employed with the same company from young adulthood to old age. However, this pattern is increasingly rare in today's world. There is now a diverse array of paths toward midlife career change. Corporate restructuring, organizational downsizing, layoffs, and rapid technological change may eliminate certain classes of jobs (Myers & Harper, 2014), and in doing so, prompt a life review focused on occupational identity. For some middle-age adults, appraisal of career satisfaction prompts change and leads them to voluntarily seek out new careers as well-seasoned professionals in midlife.

Research sheds light on motivations for voluntary midlife career change. Personal fulfillment nears the top of the list, including career satisfaction, contributing to greater societal good, increased prestige, or intentionally pursuing career paths put on hold during early adulthood (Etaugh, 2013). Phanse & Kaur (2015) conducted interviews with managers near the peak of their careers who opted for career change. Multiple reasons were cited, but the majority centered around themes of "self-renewal" and desire to perform new, more creative work. Other common reasons include lack of challenge, stress and anxiety due to job insecurity, workplace bullying, and conflicts with management (Barclay, Stoltz & Chung, 2011).

Committing to the idea of career change is a difficult process for those with strong professional identities. Howes & Goodman-Delahunty (2014) zeroed in on teachers and police officers to examine this dynamic, because these jobs are often described as career paths fostered by purpose and a desire to help others. Participants commonly cited passion as a primary factor prompting career entry. For many who later chose to change professions, a strong sense of purpose facilitated career stability, but over many years, feelings of being undervalued or changes perceived to limit meaningful work led to extreme dissatisfaction. While not actively forced out of their jobs, participants described feeling psychologically "shut out" of a once-loved career.

Women face unique challenges in work-life balance that can lead to career transition. For example, middle-age women often assume caregiving roles for aging parents or other relatives. While men are likely to provide financial assistance, women are more likely to provide more time-intensive, hands-on care (Myers & Harper, 2014). Managing daily care, doctor's appointments, or running errands for aging relatives can pose conflicts with work responsibilities. Attempts are often made to negotiate work schedule changes, decrease hours, or take unpaid leave rather than leave the workplace altogether. If unsuccessful, many women seek more flexible employment opportunities (Etaugh, 2013).

Career transition can work out in favor or to the detriment of the career seeker. A failed career transition may result in psychological distress or damage to professional reputation (Barclay, Stoltz & Chung, 2011). "Survival needs," or being able to financially provide for family, are linked to psychological well-being and are a chief area of consideration in midlife career change (Kim et al., 2017). While some pursue a new, clearly defined career interest, for others, options are "fuzzy," taking years to crystallize into a solid career path (Etaugh, 2013). Strong sense of career identity can also cloud vision on work skills that are valuable and applicable across industries, leading people to overlook jobs they might be well suited for (Howes & Goodman-Delahunty, 2014).

Many describe midlife career change as "soul searching" and "stressful," but it can also be rewarding. Self-efficacy and confidence work as catalysts for successful midlife career change (Etaugh, 2013). While many midlifers work through career change independently, career counselors can serve as valuable resources (Barclay, Stoltz & Chung, 2011). A need for more adequate support and assistance is evident, but many professionals lack awareness of how to access career counseling services (Phanse & Kaur, 2015).

what's your view — Would you recommend career counseling services to those seeking a midlife career transition? What approaches could workplaces take in better supporting needs of middle-age professionals?

myth, to help make sense of one's life and connect the past and present with the future (McAdams, 2006). This evolving story provides a person with a "narrative identity" (Singer, 2004). Indeed, some narrative psychologists view identity itself as this internalized *script* or story. People follow the script they have created as they act out their identity (McAdams, Diamond, de St. Aubin & Mansfield, 1997). Midlife often is a time for revision of the life story (McAdams, 1993; Rosenberg, Rosenberg & Farrell, 1999).

Studies in narrative psychology are based on a standardized 2-hour life-story interview. The participant is asked to think of his or her life as a book, to divide the book into chapters, and to recall eight key scenes, each of which includes a turning point. Research using this technique has found that people's scripts tend to reflect their personalities (McAdams, 2006).

Highly generative adults tend to construct *generativity scripts.* These scripts often feature a theme of *redemption,* or deliverance from suffering, and are associated with psychological well-being (McAdams, Reynolds, Lewis, Patten & Bowman, 2001; Bauer, McAdams & Pals, 2008). In one such story, a nurse devotes herself to the care of a good friend during a fatal illness. Although devastated by her friend's death, she comes out of the experience with a renewed sense of confidence and determination to help others (McAdams, 2006). The tendency to develop narratives in which events are generally interpreted as being positive and negative events are closely examined and processed for their meaning is associated with well-being (Lilgendahl & McAdams, 2011).

Gender Identity and Gender Roles As Erikson observed, identity is closely tied to social roles and commitments ("I am a parent," "I am a teacher"). Changing roles and relationships at midlife may affect gender identity (Josselson, 2003).

In many studies during the 1960s, 1970s, and 1980s, middle-age men were more open about feelings, more interested in intimate relationships, and more nurturing—characteristics traditionally labeled as feminine—than at earlier ages, whereas middle-age women became more assertive, self-confident, and achievement-oriented, characteristics traditionally labeled as masculine (Cooper & Gutmann, 1987; Cytrynbaum et al., 1980; Helson & Moane, 1987; Huyck, 1990, 1999; Neugarten, 1968). The psychologist David Gutmann (1975, 1977, 1985, 1987) offered an explanation for this process.

Traditional gender roles, according to Gutmann, evolved to ensure the well-being of growing children: The mother must be the caregiver, the father the provider. Once active parenting is over, there is not just a balancing but a reversal of roles—a **gender crossover.** Men, now free to explore their previously repressed feminine side, become more passive; women, free to explore their masculine side, become more dominant and independent.

These changes may have been normative in the preliterate, agricultural societies Gutmann studied, which had distinct gender roles, but they are not universal (Franz, 1997). In U.S. society today, men's and women's roles are becoming less distinct. In an era in which most young women combine employment with child rearing, when many men take an active part in parenting, and when childbearing may not even begin until midlife, gender crossover in middle age seems less likely (Antonucci & Akiyama, 1997; Barnett, 1997; James & Lewkowicz, 1997). In fact, an analysis of longitudinal studies of men's and women's personality change during the life course found little support for the gender crossover hypothesis (Roberts et al., 2006a, 2006b).

PSYCHOLOGICAL WELL-BEING AND POSITIVE MENTAL HEALTH

Mental health is not just the absence of mental illness. *Positive* mental health involves a sense of psychological well-being, which goes hand in hand with a healthy sense of self (Keyes & Shapiro, 2004). This subjective sense of well-being, or happiness, is a person's evaluation of his or her life (Diener, 2000). How do developmental scientists measure well-being, and what factors affect well-being at midlife?

Emotionality, Personality, and Age Many studies, including the MIDUS survey, have found a gradual average decline in negative emotions through midlife and beyond, though women in the MIDUS study reported slightly more negative emotionality (such as anger, fear, and anxiety) at all ages than men (Mroczek, 2004). According to the MIDUS findings, positive emotionality (such as cheerfulness) increases, on average, among men but falls among women in middle age and then rises sharply for both sexes, but especially men, in late adulthood. The general trends in positive and negative emotionality seem to suggest that as people age they tend to have learned to accept what comes (Carstensen, Pasupathi, Mayr & Nesselroade, 2000) and to regulate their emotions effectively (Lachman, 2004).

The ability to regulate emotions has implications for the stressors of daily life. Younger adults show greater individual variation in emotionality than older adults. In other words, while average levels of emotionality are similar in both younger and older adults, older adults are less variable in their emotionality. They show less of a positive rise in response to positive events, but also less of a negative rise to negative events (Rocke, Li & Smith, 2009). Context matters too. In one study, only physical health had a consistent impact on emotionality in adults of all ages, but two other factors—marital status and education—had significant impacts in middle age. Married people at midlife tended to report more positive emotion and less negative emotion than unmarried people. People with higher education also reported more positive emotion and less negative emotion—but only when stress was controlled (Mroczek, 2004).

The Red Hat Society, whose members go to tea in red hats and purple dresses, began with a few women friends' decision to greet middle age with verve, humor, and élan. ©nano/E+/Getty Images

Subjective well-being (how happy a person feels) also is known to be related to dimensions of personality identified by the five-factor model. In particular, people who are emotionally stable (low in neuroticism), physically and socially active (high in extraversion), and highly conscientious tend to feel happiest (Weiss, Bates & Luciano, 2008).

Life Satisfaction in Midlife In numerous surveys worldwide using various techniques for assessing subjective well-being, most adults of all ages, both sexes, and all races report being satisfied with their lives (Myers, 2000; Myers & Diener, 1995, 1996; Walker, Skowronski & Thompson, 2003). One reason for this general finding of life satisfaction is that the positive emotions associated with pleasant memories tend to persist, whereas the negative feelings associated with unpleasant memories fade. Most people also have good coping skills (Walker et al., 2003). After either especially happy or distressing events, such as marriage or divorce, they generally adapt, and subjective well-being returns to, or close to, its previous level (Lucas et al., 2003; Diener, 2000).

Social support—friends and spouses—and religiosity are important contributors to life satisfaction (Csikszentmihalyi, 1999; Diener, 2000; Myers, 2000). So are certain personality dimensions—extraversion and conscientiousness (Mroczek & Spiro, 2005; Siegler & Brummett, 2000)—and the quality of work and leisure (Csikszentmihalyi, 1999; Diener, 2000; Myers, 2000). Moreover, the relationship between work and life satisfaction is interactive—being happy at work is associated with higher life satisfaction, which then predicts work productivity and occupational commitment (Erdogan, Bauer, Truxillo & Mansfield, 2012). Not surprisingly, income affects life satisfaction as well. Adults who make more money report higher life satisfaction, and this relationship is strongest in middle adulthood (Cheung & Lucas, 2015).

Exercise matters too. In a daily diary study, middle-age and older adults who engaged in more physical activity on a regular basis reported higher life satisfaction than more sedentary adults; this relationship did not exist in younger adults. There were intra-individual differences as well. Study participants of all ages reported higher life satisfaction on days in which they were more active than usual (Maher, Pincus, Ram & Conroy, 2015). It may be that the association between life satisfaction and exercise is driven by overall physical health, as healthier people are more likely to engage in physical activity. In support of this interpretation, among a subsample of middle-age MIDUS respondents, life satisfaction was strongly affected by physical health (Markus, Ryaff, Curhan & Palmershein, 2004).

Enhanced life satisfaction may also be the outcome of a midlife review (Josselson, 2003). For example, in women between ages 37 and 43, those who had midlife regrets—many about educational or work options they had put aside to assume traditional family roles—and changed their lives accordingly had greater well-being and better psychological adjustment in the late forties than those who had regrets but did not make the desired changes (Stewart & Ostrove, 1998; Stewart & Vandewater, 1999).

Does life satisfaction change with age? Although a majority of older adults report rising levels of life satisfaction as they age, this is certainly not the case for every adult. Adults who report poor social relationships and a lack of a sense of control tend to report declines in life satisfaction (Rocke & Lachman, 2008). There are also developmental changes that can best be described as fitting a U-shaped curve. Generally, life satisfaction is lower in early adulthood, rises in mid-adulthood, and then declines again in late adulthood (Maher, Pincus, Ram & Conroy, 2015; Mroczek & Spiro, 2005; Helson & Wink, 1992). This may in part be driven by how adults feel about themselves as self-esteem shows a path similar to that of life satisfaction, suggesting a link between the two. Self-esteem seems to increase until middle adulthood, peak at 60 years of age, and then declines (Orth, Trzesniewski & Robins, 2010).

Multiple Dimensions of Well-Being Within the discipline of psychology, a subjective sense of happiness is characterized as well-being. Although people generally have an overall sense of how happy they are, happiness is multidimensional, and people can be more or less pleased with various aspects of their life. Carol Ryff and colleagues developed a model that includes six dimensions of well-being referred to as the Ryff Well-Being Inventory (Ryff, 1989; Ryff & Keyes, 1995; Ryff & Singer, 1998; Ryff, 2014). The six dimensions of the model are self-acceptance, positive relations with others, autonomy, environmental mastery, purpose in life, and personal growth. Those who score higher on these dimensions may have a stronger sense of well-being than those who score lower.

Studies using Ryff's scale have shown midlife to be a period of generally positive mental health (Ryff & Singer, 1998; Ryff, 2014). The most consistent results have been for an increase in environmental mastery and a decrease in purpose in life and personal growth with age (Ryff, 2014; Springer, Pudrovska & Hauser, 2011). In cross-sectional research, middle-age people were more autonomous than younger adults but somewhat less purposeful and less focused on personal growth—future-oriented dimensions that declined even more sharply in late adulthood. Environmental mastery, on the other hand, increased for all groups over time. Self-acceptance was relatively stable for all age groups. Overall, men's and women's well-being were quite similar, but women had more positive social relationships (Ryff & Singer, 1998).

When Ryff's scale was used to measure the psychological well-being of minority group members, the collective portrait replicated these age-related patterns. However, black and Hispanic women scored lower than black and Hispanic men in several areas, revealing "a wider expanse of compromised well-being among ethnic/minority women of differing ages" (Ryff, Keyes, & Hughes, 2004, p. 417). When employment and marital status were controlled, minority status predicted positive well-being in several areas, even when education and perceived discrimination were accounted for. It may be that such factors as self-regard, mastery, and personal growth are strengthened by meeting the challenges of minority life (Ryff et al., 2004).

Research suggests that more recent immigrants to the United States may be more physically and mentally healthy than those who have been here for two or more generations. Resistance to assimilation may promote well-being in these immigrants, especially in the domains of autonomy, quality of relationships, and purpose in life. Researchers have proposed the term *ethnic conservatism* for this tendency to resist assimilation and cling to familiar values and practices that give meaning to life. Ethnic conservatism is less effective in promoting well-being among the second generation, who may find it harder or more psychologically conflicting to resist the pull of assimilation (Horton & Schweder, 2004).

Relationships at Midlife

It is hard to generalize about the meaning of relationships in middle age today. Not only does that period cover a quarter-century of development; it also embraces a greater multiplicity of life paths than ever before (S. L. Brown, Bulanda & Lee, 2005). However, relationships with others are very important—but perhaps in a different way than earlier in life.

THEORIES OF SOCIAL CONTACT

How do we describe the nature of our social relationships across time? According to **social convoy theory,** people move through life surrounded by *social convoys:* circles of close friends and family members of varying degrees of closeness, on whom they can rely for assistance, well-being, and social support, and to whom they in turn also offer care, concern, and support (Antonucci & Akiyama, 1997; Kahn & Antonucci, 1980). Characteristics of the person (gender, race, religion, age, education, and marital status) together with characteristics of that person's situation (role expectations, life events, financial stress, daily hassles, demands, and resources) influence the size and composition of the convoy, the amount and kinds of social support a person receives, and the satisfaction derived from this support. All of these factors contribute to health and well-being (Antonucci, Akiyama & Merline, 2001).

Generally, the size of the global social network peaks in young adulthood and declines thereafter. The declines in size of the social network in adulthood are primarily seen in friendship networks; the size of the family network remains relatively stable over time. Researchers have variously described this decline in friendship networks as due to changing circumstances (e.g., the increase in time demands of work and family life) or motivational goals (e.g., staying most close to people who help us regulate emotions). Other relationships, such as those with coworkers or neighbors, tend to be important during particular times. For example, when changing jobs or moving, people in the social network may drop out, or new people may be included (Wrzus, Hanel, Wagner & Neyer, 2013).

Middle-age people in industrialized countries tend to have the largest convoys because they are likely to be married, to have children, to have living parents, and to be in the workforce unless they have retired early (Antonucci et al., 2001). Women's convoys, particularly the inner circle, tend to be larger than men's (Antonucci & Akiyama, 1997).

Laura Carstensen's (1991, 1995, 1996; Carstensen, Isaacowitz & Charles, 1999) **socioemotional selectivity theory** offers a life-span perspective on how people choose with whom to spend their time. According to Carstensen, social interaction has three main goals: (1) it is a source of information; (2) it helps people develop and maintain a sense of self; and (3) it is a source of pleasure and comfort, or emotional well-being. In infancy, the third goal, the need for emotional support, is paramount. From childhood through young adulthood, information-seeking comes to the fore. As young people strive to learn about their society and their place in it, strangers may well be the best sources of knowledge. By middle age, although information-seeking remains important (Fung, Carstensen & Lang, 2001), the original, emotion-regulating function of social contacts begins to reassert itself. In other words, middle-age people increasingly seek out others who help them feel good (Figure 16.2). In support of this, although their social networks were smaller than those of younger adults, older adults described their social network members more positively and less negatively. In other words, older adults chose to limit their interactions to those people whom they found to be emotionally fulfilling and supportive of them (English & Carstensen, 2014).

RELATIONSHIPS, GENDER, AND QUALITY OF LIFE

For most middle-age adults, relationships are key to well-being (Markus et al., 2004). They can be a major source of health and satisfaction (Lachman, 2004). For example, social support from spouses, and to a lesser extent from children and friends, is related to well-being in retired adults (Chen & Feeley, 2014), and social support is related to life satisfaction at all ages (Siedlecki, Salthouse, Oishi & Jeswani, 2014). According to two national surveys, having a partner and being in good health were the biggest factors in well-being for women in their fifties. Being single, divorced, or widowed, however, was associated with depression, loneliness, and decreases in happiness (Koropeckyj-Cox, Pienta & Brown, 2007).

However, relationships can also present stressful demands (Lachman, 2004), which tend to fall most heavily on women. A sense of responsibility

social convoy theory
Theory, proposed by Kahn and Antonucci, that people move through life surrounded by concentric circles of intimate relationships on which they rely for assistance, well-being, and social support.

socioemotional selectivity theory
Theory, proposed by Carstensen, that people select social contacts on the basis of the changing relative importance of social interaction as a source of information, as an aid in developing and maintaining a self-concept, and as a source of emotional well-being.

Importance of motives for social contact

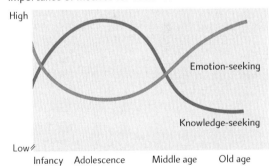

FIGURE 16.2

How Motives for Social Contact Change across the Life Span

According to socioemotional selectivity theory, infants seek social contact primarily for emotional comfort. In adolescence and young adulthood, people tend to be most interested in seeking information from others. From middle age on, emotional needs increasingly predominate.

Source: Carstensen, L. L., Gross, J. J. & Fung, H. H. "The social context of emotional experience." In K. Warner Schaie and M. Powell Lawton (Eds.), *Annual Review of Gerontology and Geriatrics,* 17, p. 1997, 331, Figure 12.2.

and concern for others may impair a woman's well-being when problems or misfortunes beset others; men are less likely to be affected in this way. This greater concern for the welfare of others may help explain why middle-age women tend to be unhappier with their marriages than are men (Antonucci & Akiyama, 1997; S. P. Thomas, 1997).

In studying midlife social relationships, then, we need to keep in mind that their effects can be both positive and negative. In the remaining sections of this chapter, we examine how intimate relationships develop during the middle years. We look first at relationships with spouses, cohabiting partners, homosexual partners, and friends; next at bonds with maturing children; and then at ties with aging parents, siblings, and grandchildren.

Consensual Relationships

Marriages, cohabitations, homosexual unions, and friendships typically involve two people of the same generation who mutually choose each other. How do these relationships fare in middle age?

MARRIAGE

Midlife marriage is very different from what it used to be. When life expectancies were shorter, couples who remained together for 25, 30, or 40 years were rare. The most common pattern was for marriages to be broken by death and for survivors to remarry. For example, maternal mortality was high, and childbirth was a dangerous enterprise for women (Loudon, 1992). Still, people had many children and expected them to live at home until they married. It was unusual for a middle-age husband and wife to be alone together. Today, more marriages end in divorce, but couples who stay together can often look forward to 20 or more years of married life after the last child leaves home.

Marriages generally follow a developmental sequence. In one study, more than 1,000 individuals were followed for the first 10 years of their marriage. For most people, marital quality declined in the first few years of marriage. Following this, there was a stabilization period, after which marriage quality declined once again. Not surprisingly, the people who divorced during the course of the study reported lower marital satisfaction (Kurdek, 1999).

What happens to the quality of marriages that last longer than 10 years? An analysis of two surveys of 8,929 men and women in first marriages found a U-shaped curve. During the first 20 to 24 years of marriage, the longer a couple had been married, the less satisfied they tended to be. Then the association between marital satisfaction and length of marriage begins to turn positive. At 35 to 44 years of marriage, a couple tends to be even more satisfied than during the first 4 years (Orbuch, House, Mero & Webster, 1996).

Why do we see these changes in marital satisfaction? Marital satisfaction generally hits bottom early in middle age, when many couples have teenage children and are heavily involved in careers. Satisfaction usually reaches a height when children are grown; many people are retired or entering retirement, and a lifetime accumulation of assets helps ease financial worries (Orbuch et al., 1996).

Sexual satisfaction affects marital satisfaction and stability. Those couples who are satisfied with their sex lives tend to be satisfied with their marriages, and better marital quality leads to longer marriages for both men and women (Yeh, Lorenz, Wickrama, Conger & Elder, 2006). Similar results have been found in Brazil, Germany, Spain, Japan, and the United States (Heiman et al., 2011). Communication patterns matter as well. When couples communicate effectively, sexual satisfaction and marital satisfaction are not associated. However, when communication breaks down, declines in sexual satisfaction predict declines in marital satisfaction (Litzinger & Gordon, 2005).

COHABITATION

Cohabitation has increased greatly in the United States. Overall, estimates are that in 2010 there were approximately 7.5 million cohabiting opposite-sex adults (U.S. Census Bureau, 2010). While cohabitation has generally been less common in midlife than in young adulthood

(Blieszner & Roberto, 2006), with the aging of the baby boom generation, it is becoming more common (S. L. Brown et al., 2005). For instance, in 2010 among women 40 to 44 years of age, 65 percent had cohabited at some point in their life, representing a 195 percent increase since 1987. This was the largest percent increase among all age groups measured (Manning, 2013). When older adults do cohabitate, their relationships are generally more stable than those of younger cohabiting adults; and cohabitation is more often viewed as an alternative to marriage rather than a prelude to it (Brown, Bulanda & Lee, 2012).

What explains the rise in cohabitation for older adults? One of the reasons is a desire for an intimate companion without the commitment of formal marriage—a commitment that, in middle age, may come to mean the possibility of having to care for an infirm partner. Indeed, cohabiting adults with disabled or ill partners, as a whole, provide less care than do married partners in the same situation (Noel-Miller, 2011). This process appears to be most relevant for widowed women (Davidson, 2001). Aging men, alternatively, may be motivated to cohabitate because they anticipate needing the kind of care that wives traditionally provide and may worry about not getting it otherwise (S. L. Brown et al., 2005).

Do cohabitants reap the same rewards as married people? Although there is little research on cohabitation among middle-age and older people, one study suggests that the answer, at least for men in the United States, is no. Among 18,598 Americans over age 50, cohabiting men (but not cohabiting women) were more likely to be depressed than their married counterparts, even when such variables as physical health, social support, and economic resources were controlled. Indeed, cohabiting men were about as likely to be depressed as men without partners (S. L. Brown et al., 2005). However, the outcomes of cohabitation differ by country. While cohabitation does not provide the same level of health benefits as marriage in the United States, Britain, and Australia, cohabiting adults and married adults are equally healthy in Norway and Germany. In Australia, cohabiting women, but not men, are as healthy as married people (Perelli-Harris et al., 2017).

DIVORCE

Although divorce in midlife is more common than in the past (Aldwin & Levenson, 2001; Blieszner & Roberto, 2006), the breakup can still be traumatic. In an American Association of Retired Persons (AARP) survey of adults who had been divorced at least once in their forties, fifties, or sixties, most respondents described the experience as more emotionally devastating than losing a job and about as devastating as a major illness, though less devastating than a spouse's death. Midlife divorce seems especially hard for women, who are more negatively affected psychologically by divorce at any age than men are (Marks & Lambert, 1998; Montenegro, 2004). With respect to physical health, marital dissolution is associated with an elevated chance of chronic health conditions in both sexes, but especially in men (Hughes & Waite, 2009; Amato, 2010). Luckily, most middle-age divorced people bounce back eventually. On average, the AARP respondents rated their outlook on life as highly as does the general over-45 population and higher than that of singles in their age group. Three out of four said that ending their marriage was the right decision. About 1 out of 3 (32 percent) had remarried—6 percent to their former spouses—and their outlook was better than that of those who had not remarried (Montenegro, 2004).

Long-standing marriages may be less likely to break up than more recent ones. Why might this be the case? One possible explanation lies with the concept of **marital capital**. The longer a couple is married, the more likely they are to have built up joint financial assets, to share the same friends, to go through important experiences together, and to get used to the emotional benefits that marriage can provide. This accumulated "capital" can be difficult to give up (Becker, 1991; Jones, Tepperman & Wilson, 1995).

Another important factor that keeps many couples from divorcing is finances. After the first decade of marriage, educated couples who have accumulated marital assets have much to lose financially from divorce and are less likely to divorce or separate (Hiedemann, Suhomilinova & O'Rand, 1998). Supporting this view, research has shown that marriage stability and consumer debt are associated; stable marriages are more likely to have low debt (Dew, 2011). One interpretation of this is that healthy marriages are more likely to

marital capital
Financial and emotional benefits built up during a long-standing marriage, which tend to hold a couple together.

have healthy finances, and thus presumably more to lose in the event of divorce. And when marriage does end, middle-age divorcees, especially women who do not remarry, tend to be less financially secure than those who remain married (Wilmoth & Koso, 2002) and may have to work outside of the home, perhaps for the first time (Huyck, 1999).

When they do divorce, why do middle-age people do so? The number one reason given is partner abuse—verbal, physical, or emotional. Other frequent reasons are differing values or lifestyles, infidelity, alcohol or drug abuse, and simply falling out of love (Marks & Lambert, 1998).

Divorce does not eliminate stress, although it may change the source of it. Nearly half (49 percent) of the AARP respondents, especially women, said they suffered greatly from stress and 28 percent from depression. These proportions are similar to the rates among singles the same age (Montenegro, 2004).

The sense of violated expectations may be diminishing as midlife divorce becomes more common (Marks & Lambert, 1998; Norton & Moorman, 1987). Even in long marriages, the increasing number of years that people can expect to live in good health after child rearing ends may make the dissolution of a marginal marriage an attractive option and, at least for women, growing economic independence makes it more practical to consider as well (Hiedemann et al., 1998). Moreover, while it may be stressful, divorce can also lead to personal growth (Aldwin & Levenson, 2001; Helson & Roberts, 1994). Older adults' better emotional regulatory strategies and greater life knowledge may make them better able to weather the storms of marriage dissolution. A longitudinal study of almost 7,000 young and middle-age adults showed that in almost all respects, middle-age people showed more adaptability than younger people in the face of separation or divorce (Marks & Lambert, 1998).

MARITAL STATUS AND HEALTH

As in young adulthood, marriage offers major benefits. In cross-sectional studies, married people appear to be healthier, both physically and mentally, in middle age and they tend to live longer than single, separated, or divorced people (S. L. Brown et al., 2005; Kaplan & Kronick, 2006; Zhang, 2006). Overall, married people enjoy better health, lower mortality, and better cardiovascular health than their single counterparts (Robles, Slatcher, Trombello & McGinn, 2014). But why would marriage (a social relationship) affect health (a biological state)? Two classes of theories have been advanced to explain these findings. The first posits that marriage is associated with the encouragement of health-promoting behaviors. So, for example, a husband might persuade or encourage his wife to stop smoking. The second theory focuses on the stress response system. In this view, the social support provided by marriage buffers individuals against life stressors. As chronic stress negatively affects health, married people are thus protected against some of its effects (Robles et al., 2014). Some of this may be mediated by immune function. Long-term stress depresses immune system functioning (Dhabhar, 2014). Being in a good marriage, with its protective social support, can thus bolster the immune system (Graham, Christian & Kiecolt-Glaser, 2006).

Marital quality appears to be a key factor. In one study, adults in high quality marriages had lower blood pressure, lower stress, less depression, and higher life satisfaction than single adults (Holt-Lunstad, Birmingham & Jones, 2008). In a longitudinal study, women in highly satisfying marital or cohabiting relationships had lower risk factors for cardiovascular disease than single women or women in unsatisfying relationships (Gallo et al., 2003). While a good marital relationship can buffer people against life stressors, a poor marital relationship can make people more vulnerable to them. For example, marital strains increased both men's and women's aging-related declines in health, and this effect was stronger the older a couple was (Umberson, Williams, Powers, Liu & Needham, 2006). In addition, women who are in unsatisfying married or cohabiting relationships are at higher risk for cardiovascular disease and other health problems, especially if marital conflict is involved (Gallo et al., 2003; Kiecolt-Glaser & Newton, 2001).

What about single adults? In comparison to their married peers, single adults show a disadvantage. In the MIDUS sample, single people, especially men, were more likely to be anxious, sad, or restless and to be less generative than their younger counterparts.

Formerly married, noncohabiting women and men reported more negative emotionality than those still in a first marriage (Marks, Bumpass & Jun, 2004). And those who never marry may be at the highest risk for cardiovascular and other disease (Kaplan & Kronick, 2006). However, being single may be better than being in a bad marriage. For example, the blood pressure of adults in low quality marriages was higher than that of single adults (Holt-Lunstad et al., 2008).

GAY AND LESBIAN RELATIONSHIPS

The cohort of gays and lesbians now in middle age grew up at a time when homosexuality was not as accepted as it is now and was sometimes considered a mental illness. At that time, homosexuals tended to be isolated not only from the larger community but also from each other. It was not until the 1990s that acceptance of homosexual relationships began to increase sharply, and the general public's negative perception of gays and lesbians became more positive (Keleher & Smith, 2012; Hicks & Lee, 2006).

One factor that seems to affect relationship quality in gays and lesbians is whether or not they have internalized society's negative views on homosexuality. Overall, homosexual people who have internalized a negative view of their sexuality report lower relationship quality (Otis, Rostosky, Riggle & Hamrin, 2006; Frost & Meyer, 2009). This may be because when faced with an episode of discrimination—which is common for sexual minorities—gays and lesbians who have internalized negative beliefs about themselves are more likely to respond with anxiety or depression than those who have not internalized those beliefs (Feinstein, Goldfried & Davila, 2012). Even in the absence of precipitating events, gays and lesbians who have internalized the homophobic attitudes held by others are more likely to show symptoms of depression, presumably because these attitudes affect their overall self-concept. And when depressive symptoms increase, so do relationship issues (Frost & Meyer, 2009).

Coming out can be a challenging process. Some middle-age gays and lesbians may be associating openly for the first time and establishing relationships. Many are still working out conflicts with parents and other family members (sometimes including spouses) or hiding their homosexuality from them. Some move to cities with large homosexual populations where they can more easily seek out and form relationships. While times have changed and society is more accepting of homosexual relationships, many older gays and lesbians are still reluctant to fully come out of the closet. For example, one recent study showed that about a third of older adults still feared being completely open about their sexuality (Gardner, deVries & Mockus, 2014).

On June 26, 2015, same-sex marriage became the law of the land in the United States. While the American Medical Association had released a statement in 2009 arguing that exclusion from marriage might be contributing to health disparities between homosexual and heterosexual couples (American Medical Association, 2009), there was a paucity of research on the possible benefits of marriage for gays and lesbians. Given the already established findings for heterosexual couples, did the same dynamics exist in gay and lesbian couples?

While more work needs to be done, initial data on marriage equality show that, as in heterosexual couples, gay and lesbian couples also benefit from marriage. In one study of 1,166 adults, married gay, lesbian, and bisexual couples reported less distress than their single counterparts, as did married heterosexuals when compared to single adults (Wight, LeBlanc & Lee Badgett, 2013). Earlier research suggested gay and lesbian couples were more likely to break up than heterosexual couples, but as marriage was unavailable to many, data were scarce. This resulted in methodological problems; samples were small and often compared cohabiting couples or those in civil unions rather than marriage (Kalmijn, Loeve & Manting, 2007; Balsam, Beauchaine, Rothblum & Solomon, 2008). More recent nationally representative U.S. data suggest that both heterosexual and homosexual couples have similar rates of relationship duration and stability (Rosenfeld, 2014).

Midlife friendships often have a special importance for homosexuals. Lesbians are more likely to get emotional support from lesbian friends, lovers, and

Some gay men and women do not come out until well into adulthood and so may develop intimate relationships later in life than their heterosexual counterparts.
©Lars A. Niki

even ex-lovers than from relatives. Gay men, too, rely on friendship networks, or *fictive kin*, which they actively create and maintain. Friendship networks for gays and lesbians provide solidarity and contact with younger people, which middle-age heterosexuals normally get through family rather than friendship networks.

FRIENDSHIPS

As Carstensen's theory predicts, social networks tend to become smaller and more intimate at midlife. Still, friendships persist and are a strong source of emotional support and well-being, especially for women (Adams & Allan, 1998; Antonucci et al., 2001). Midlife baby boomers have as many as seven good friends on average (Blieszner & Roberto, 2006). Friendships often revolve around work and parenting; others are based on neighborhood contacts or on association in volunteer organizations (Antonucci et al., 2001; Hartup & Stevens, 1999).

The quality of midlife friendships often makes up for what they lack in quantity of time spent. Especially during a crisis, such as a divorce or a problem with an aging parent, adults turn to friends for emotional support, practical guidance, comfort, companionship, and talk (Antonucci & Akiyama, 1997; Hartup & Stevens, 1999; Suitor & Pillemer, 1993). The quality of such friendships can affect health, as can lack of friendships. Loneliness, for example, is predictive of increases in blood pressure, even when such variables as age, gender, race, and cardiovascular risk factors are taken into account (Hawkley, Thisted, Masi & Cacioppo, 2010). Friendship quality impacts psychological variables as well. While in early adulthood, loneliness, depression, well-being, and social integration are affected by the number of friends a person has, in late adulthood, the quality of friends is what matters. Those older adults with higher quality friendships have better psychosocial well-being (Carmichael, Reis & Duberstein, 2015). This is especially true in times of crisis: Depressed adults with high-quality friendships have a lower suicide risk than those who do not have good friends (Marver et al., 2017). However, sometimes friendships themselves can be stressful. Conflicts with friends often center on differences in values, beliefs, and lifestyles; yet friends usually can talk out these conflicts while maintaining mutual dignity and respect (Hartup & Stevens, 1999).

Relationships with Maturing Children

Parenthood is in some ways a process of letting go, and this process usually approaches or reaches its climax during the parents' middle age (Marks et al., 2004). It is true that, with contemporary trends toward delayed marriage and parenthood, some middle-age people face such issues as finding a good day care or helping their grade-school child with math homework. However, most parents in middle age must cope with a different set of issues that arise from living with children who will soon be leaving home. Once children become adults and have their own children, the intergenerational family multiplies in number. Increasingly, middle-age parents have to deal with an adult child's continuing to live in the family home or leaving it only to return.

ADOLESCENT CHILDREN: ISSUES FOR PARENTS

Ironically, the people at the two times of life popularly linked with emotional crises—adolescence and midlife—often live in the same household. It is usually middle-age adults who are the parents of adolescent children.

Theorists from a variety of perspectives have described this period as one of questioning, reappraisal, or diminished well-being for parents, but this is not inevitable. In the MIDUS study, being a parent was associated with more psychological distress than being child-free, but it also brought greater psychological wellness and generativity, especially to men (Marks et al., 2004). Generally, most parents at midlife express they are happy with their parenting role. However, contextual and relational variables affect happiness. For example, parents are more likely to report happiness when they are financially secure, healthy, close to their child, retired, or younger parents (Mitchell, 2010). Parenting satisfaction is also positively related to parental education level and marital status, and negatively related to conflict between the parents (Downing-Matibag, 2009).

Negative emotions are also possible. Although research contradicts the stereotype of adolescence as a time of inevitable turmoil and rebellion, some rejection of parental authority is necessary, and this can be difficult for parents. An important task for parents is to accept maturing children as they are, not as what the parents had hoped they would be. When parents perceive of their children as mature and approve of their life choices, this process is easier. By contrast, when parents do not approve of their child's choices, they are more likely to perceive their child's striving for autonomy as hostile or immature (Kloep & Hendry, 2010). Parental satisfaction declines when parents perceive their adolescent children as being involved in negative behaviors or failing to meet the challenges of life (Downing-Matibag, 2009). Fortunately, the parent-child relationship often improves with age (Blieszner & Roberto, 2006).

WHEN CHILDREN LEAVE: THE EMPTY NEST

Research is challenging popular ideas about the **empty nest**—a supposedly difficult transition, especially for women, that occurs when the youngest child leaves home. Although some parents do have problems in adjusting to the empty nest, they are far outnumbered by those who find the departure liberating (Antonucci et al., 2001; Chiriboga, 1997; Helson, 1997). Generally, parents whose children have left the nest report higher levels of well-being, at least when their children stay in frequent contact with them (Gorchoff, John & Helson, 2008; White & Edwards, 1990). They can pursue their own interests as they enjoy their grown children's accomplishments.

When children are not accomplished, however, this process may be more difficult. Typically, when adult children have greater needs, parents provide more material and financial support to them (Fingerman, Miller, Birditt & Zarit, 2009). Given this tendency, it is not surprising to also find that such parents are likely to feel torn between wanting their adult children to assert their independence and a desire to step in and help. Men, in particular, seem to be more affected by their children's successes and failures (Birditt, Fingerman & Zarit, 2010). Some ambivalence during these situations is standard, but far more stress results when there is already tension in the relationship (Birditt, Miller, Fingerman & Lefkowitz, 2009) or when grown children return home (Thomas, 1997).

The effects of the empty nest on a marriage depend on its quality and length. In a good marriage, the departure of grown children may usher in a second honeymoon. The departure of children from the family home generally increases marital satisfaction, perhaps because of the additional time partners now have to spend with each other (Gorchoff, John & Helson, 2008; White & Edwards, 1990). The empty nest may be harder on couples whose identity is dependent on the parental role, or who now must face marital problems they had previously pushed aside under the press of parental responsibilities (Antonucci et al., 2001).

The empty nest does not signal the end of parenthood. It is a transition to a new stage: the relationship between parents and adult children.

PARENTING GROWN CHILDREN

Even after children have left home for good, parents are still parents. The midlife role of parent to young adults raises new issues on the part of both generations (Marks et al., 2004).

Middle-age parents generally give their children more help and support than they get from them as the young adults establish careers and families (Antonucci et al., 2001). Parents give the most help to children who need it most, typically those who are single or are single parents (Blieszner & Roberto, 2006). Some parents have difficulty treating their offspring as adults, and many young adults have difficulty accepting their parents' continuing concern about them. In a warm, supportive family environment, such conflicts can be managed by an open airing of feelings (Putney & Bengtson, 2001). However, at the same time adult children's problems do have the potential to reduce their parents' well-being (Greenfield & Marks, 2006).

empty nest
Transitional phase of parenting following the last child's leaving the parents' home.

Most young adults and their middle-age parents enjoy each other's company and get along well. However, intergenerational families do not all fit one mold. An estimated 25 percent of intergenerational families are *tight-knit,* both geographically and emotionally; they have frequent contact with mutual help and support. Another 25 percent are *sociable,* but with less emotional affinity or commitment. About 16 percent have *obligatory* relationships, with much interaction but little emotional attachment; and 17 percent are *detached,* both emotionally and geographically. An in-between category consists of those who are *intimate but distant* (16 percent), spending little time together but retaining warm feelings that might lead to a renewal of contact and exchange. Adult children tend to be closer to their mothers than to their fathers (Bengtson, 2001; Silverstein & Bengtson, 1997).

PROLONGED PARENTING: THE "CLUTTERED NEST"

What happens if the nest does not empty when it normally should, or unexpectedly refills? Since the 1980s, in most Western nations, more and more adult children have delayed leaving home until the late twenties or beyond (Mouw, 2005). Furthermore, the **revolving door syndrome,** sometimes called the *boomerang phenomenon,* has become more common. Increasing numbers of young adults, especially men, return to their parents' home, sometimes more than once, and sometimes with their own families (Aquilino, 1996; Blieszner & Roberto, 2006; Putney & Bengtson, 2001).

Prolonged parenting may lead to intergenerational tension when it contradicts parents' normative expectations. As children move from adolescence to young adulthood, parents typically expect them to become independent, and children expect to do so. As the timing-of-events model would predict, then, a grown child's delayed departure from the nest or return to it may produce family stress (Antonucci et al., 2001; Aquilino, 1996). From the adult child's point of view, living with parents can provide much needed financial and emotional support, but can threaten a sense of independence (Burn & Szoeke, 2016). When adult children live with parents, relations tend to be smoother when the parents see the adult child moving toward autonomy—for example, by enrolling in college (Antonucci et al., 2001).

However, the nonnormative experience of parent-child coresidence is becoming less so, especially for parents with more than one child. Rather than an abrupt leave-taking, the empty nest transition is coming to be seen as a more prolonged process of separation, often lasting several years (Aquilino, 1996; Putney & Bengtson, 2001). Coresidence with adult children may be seen as an expression of family solidarity, an extension of the normative expectation of assistance from parents to young adult children.

VOLUNTARY CHILDLESSNESS

Increasing numbers of men and women in the United do not have children. Currently, approximately 30.8 percent of women have never given birth to a child, an increase of 4 percentage points since 2006. While this number does not account for women who will go on to have children, especially given recent trends toward delayed child rearing, it is nonetheless a significant demographic change in the United States (U.S. Census Bureau, 2017). Similar trends have been found in other countries as well, including Germany, the United Kingdom, Austria, the Netherlands, and Switzerland, and to a lesser extent Central and Eastern Europe (Kreyenfeld & Konietzka, 2017).

While involuntary childlessness—or infertility—has a negative effect on well-being (Luk & Loke, 2015), voluntary childlessness does not. Generally, people who are childless by choice have higher well-being and better psychological health than parents, especially those who had children when young; and empty nesters (Koropeckyj-Cox, Pienta & Brown, 2007; Hansen, 2012; Umberson, Pudrovska & Reczek, 2010; Bures, Koropeckyj-Cox & Loree, 2009). This same pattern is found across a number of countries, although it is less pronounced in countries that have stronger norms regarding parenthood (Huijts, Kraaykam & Subramanian, 2012).

Because people are living longer and there are more childless adults, researchers have investigated the effect of being childless in later adulthood. Generally, research has shown that childless women fare well, but childless men are more vulnerable. For example, in one

revolving door syndrome
Tendency for young adults who have left home to return to their parents' household in times of financial, marital, or other trouble.

study never married, divorced, or widowed men were at higher risk for depression than their female counterparts (Zhang & Hayward, 2001). Similarly, research conduced in Austria, Finland, and the Netherlands showed that divorced childless men were at risk for poor health, while divorced childless women were not (Kendig, Dykstra, van Gaalen & Melkas, 2007). In considering this gender difference, one possible explanation focuses on social connections. Childless older women tend to be very active socially and have particularly robust social networks and community connections. Married childless men often depend on their wives to link them to this support network. Thus, when both unmarried and childless, these men are more prone to difficulties (Wenger, Dykstra, Melkas & Knipscheer, 2007).

Other Kinship Ties

Except in times of need, ties with the family of origin—parents and siblings—tend to recede in importance during young adulthood, when work, spouses or partners, and children take precedence. At midlife, these earliest kinship ties may reassert themselves, as the responsibility for care and support of aging parents may begin to shift to their middle-agd children. In addition, a new relationship often begins at this time of life: grandparenthood.

RELATIONSHIPS WITH AGING PARENTS

The middle years may bring dramatic, though gradual, changes in parent-child relationships. Many middle-age people look at their parents more objectively than before, seeing them as individuals with both strengths and weaknesses.

Contact and Mutual Help Most commonly, help and assistance continues to flow from adults to their own children rather than to their parents. The majority of help consists of assistance with everyday needs and, less commonly, emergencies and crises. This pattern is true of most families; however, the dynamics change in situations in which parents are disabled or experience some sort of crisis themselves. Not surprisingly, in these cases, adult children often provide resources to their middle-age parents (Fingerman et al., 2010).

Even when they do not live close to each other, most middle-age adults and their parents have warm, affectionate relationships based on frequent contact, mutual help, feelings of attachment, and shared values. Daughters and older mothers tend to be especially close (Bengtson, 2001; Fingerman & Dolbin-MacNab, 2006; Willson, Shuey & Elder, 2003). Positive relationships with parents contribute to a strong sense of self and to emotional well-being at midlife (Blieszner & Roberto, 2006).

However, family relations in middle and late adulthood can be complex. With increasing longevity, middle-age couples with limited emotional and financial resources may need to allocate them among two sets of aging parents as well as provide for their own (and possibly their own adult children's) needs. Not surprisingly, many adult children express a sense of ambivalence toward the care of their aging parents or in-laws (Willson et al., 2003). Ambivalence may emerge out of the struggles found in trying to juggle competing needs. Generally, the allocation of assistance to aging parents involves trade-offs and often depends on family lineage. Most couples are willing to contribute time or money, but not both, and few have the necessary resources or inclination to support both sets of parents. Couples tended to respond more readily to the needs of the wife's parents, presumably because of her greater closeness to them. African American and Hispanic couples are more likely than white couples to provide consistent assistance of all types to parents on each side of the family (Shuey & Hardy, 2003).

Becoming a Caregiver for Aging Parents With the changing demographics of the United States, particularly the lengthening of the life span, many middle-age adults gradually take on more responsibilities for their parents over time. For example, a son might realize that his mother is no longer able to drive and might decide to stop by the grocery store once a week for her, or a daughter might realize her father is no longer able to remember to pay bills unassisted and set up payments for him. This normative development

Most middle-age adults and their aging parents have warm, affectionate relationships. ©Hero/Corbis/Glow Images

filial crisis
In Marcoen's terminology, normative development of middle age, in which adults learn to balance love and duty to their parents with autonomy within a two-way relationship.

is seen as the healthy outcome of a **filial crisis,** in which adults learn to balance love and duty to their parents with autonomy in a two-way relationship. Although striking this balance can be challenging, most middle-age people willingly accept their obligations to their parents (Antonucci et al., 2001).

The generations typically get along best while parents are healthy and vigorous. When older people become infirm, the burden of caring for them may strain the relationship (Antonucci et al., 2001; Marcoen, 1995). Given the high cost of nursing homes and most older people's reluctance to stay in them, many dependent elders receive long-term care in their own home or that of a caregiver.

The world over, caregiving is typically a female function (Kinsella & Velkoff, 2001). When an ailing mother is widowed or a divorced woman can no longer manage alone, it is most likely that a daughter will take on the caregiving role (Pinquart & Sörensen, 2006; Schulz & Martire, 2004). Sons do contribute to caregiving, but they are less likely to provide primary, personal care (Blieszner & Roberto, 2006; Marks, 1996).

Strains of Caregiving Caregiving can be stressful. Many caregivers find the task a physical, emotional, and financial burden, especially if they work full-time, have limited financial resources, or lack support and assistance (Lund, 1993a; Schulz & Martire, 2004). It is hard for women who work outside the home to assume an added caregiving role, and reducing work hours or quitting a job to meet caregiving obligations can increase financial stress. Flexible work schedules and family and medical leave could help alleviate this problem.

Emotional strain may come not only from caregiving itself but also from the need to balance it with the many other responsibilities of midlife (Antonucci et al., 2001; Climo & Stewart, 2003). Elderly parents may become dependent at a time when middle-age adults need to launch their children or, if parenthood was delayed, to raise them. Caregiving can also lead to marriage problems. Adult caregivers report less marital happiness, great marital inequality, more hostility, and, for women, a greater degree of depressive symptomatology and depression over time (Bookwala, 2009). Members of this generation in the middle, sometimes called the **sandwich generation,** may be caught in a squeeze between these competing needs and their limited resources of time, money, and energy. Also, a middle-age child, who may be preparing to retire, can ill afford the additional costs of caring for a frail older person or may have health problems of his or her own (Kinsella & Velkoff, 2001).

sandwich generation
Middle-age adults squeezed by competing needs to raise or launch children and to care for elderly parents.

Estimates are that approximately 59 percent of family caregivers are caring for a parent with physical impairments. Caring for a person with physical impairments is hard. It can be even more difficult to care for someone with dementia, a situation faced by 26 percent of caregivers. Moreover, 37 percent of care recipients have more than one condition or illness (National Alliance for Caregiving, 2015).

Dementia and related conditions are among the hardest to cope with. In addition to being unable to carry on basic functions of daily living, people with dementia may be incontinent, suspicious, agitated or depressed, subject to hallucinations, likely to wander about at night, dangerous to self and others, and in need of constant supervision (Schulz & Martire, 2004). Sometimes the caregiver becomes physically or mentally ill under the strain (Pinquart & Sörensen, 2007; Schulz & Martire, 2004; Vitaliano, Zhang & Scanlan, 2003). Because women are more likely than men to give personal care, their mental health and well-being may be more likely to suffer (Amirkhanyan & Wolf, 2006; Climo & Stewart, 2003; Pinquart & Sörensen, 2006). Sometimes the stress created by the incessant, heavy demands of caregiving is so great as to lead to abuse, neglect, or even abandonment of the dependent elderly person.

caregiver burnout
Condition of physical, mental, and emotional exhaustion affecting adults who provide continuous care for sick or aged persons.

A result of these and other strains may be **caregiver burnout,** a physical, mental, and emotional exhaustion that can affect adults who care for aged relatives (Barnhart, 1992). Even the most patient, loving caregiver may become frustrated, anxious, or resentful under the constant strain of meeting an older person's seemingly endless needs. Often families and friends fail to recognize that caregivers have a right to feel discouraged, frustrated, and put upon. Caregivers need a life of their own, beyond the loved one's disability or disease. Sometimes other arrangements, such as institutionalization, assisted living, or a division of responsibilities among siblings, must be made (Shuey & Hardy, 2003).

Community support programs can reduce the strains and burdens of caregiving. Support services may include meals and housekeeping; transportation and escort services; and adult day care centers, which provide supervised activities and care while caregivers work or attend to personal needs. *Respite care* (substitute supervised care by visiting nurses or home health aides) gives regular caregivers some time off. Through counseling, support, and self-help groups, caregivers can share problems, gain information about community resources, and improve skills.

Some family caregivers, looking back, regard the experience as uniquely rewarding. If a caregiver deeply loves an infirm parent; cares about family continuity; looks at caregiving as a challenge; and has adequate personal, family, and community resources to meet that challenge, caregiving can be an opportunity for personal growth in competence, compassion, self-knowledge, and self-transcendence (Bengtson, 2001; Bengtson, Rosenthal & Burton, 1996; Biegel, 1995; Climo & Stewart, 2003; Lund, 1993a).

RELATIONSHIPS WITH SIBLINGS

Sibling ties are the longest-lasting relationships in most people's lives. In some cross-sectional research, sibling relationships over the life span look like an hourglass, with the most contact at the two ends—childhood and middle to late adulthood—and the least contact during the child-raising years. After establishing careers and families, siblings may renew their ties (White, 2001; Cicirelli, 1995; Putney & Bengtson, 2001). Other studies indicate a decline in contact throughout adulthood. Sibling conflict tends to diminish with age—perhaps because siblings who do not get along see each other less (Putney & Bengtson, 2001).

Relationships with siblings who remain in contact can be central to psychological well-being in midlife (Antonucci et al., 2001; Spitze & Trent, 2006). As in young adulthood, sisters tend to be closer than brothers (Blieszner & Roberto, 2006; Spitze & Trent, 2006). Sibling relationships may be particularly beneficial for those adults who did not have children (Pinquart, 2003).

Dealing with the care of aging parents can bring siblings closer together but also can cause resentment and conflict (Blieszner & Roberto, 2006; Ingersoll-Dayton, Neal, Ha & Hammer, 2003). Disagreements may arise over the division of care or over an inheritance, especially if the sibling relationship has not been good.

GRANDPARENTHOOD

Often grandparenthood begins before the end of active parenting. Adults in the United States become grandparents, on average, around age 45 (Blieszner & Roberto, 2006). In 2014, the United States had a population of 65 million grandparents (U.S. Census Bureau, 2014). By the age of 65, 80 percent of people have grandchildren, and about a third of them list grandparenting as the most valued aspect of getting older (Livingston & Parker, 2010).

Grandparenthood today is different in other ways from grandparenthood in the past. Most U.S. grandparents have fewer grandchildren than their parents or grandparents did (Blieszner & Roberto, 2006). With the rising incidence of midlife divorce, about 1 in 5 grandparents is divorced, widowed, or separated (Davies & Williams, 2002), and many are stepgrandparents. Middle-age grandparents tend to be married, active in their communities, and employed and thus less available to help out with their grandchildren. They also are likely to be raising one or more children of their own (Blieszner & Roberto, 2006).

The Grandparent's Role In many developing societies, such as those in Latin America and Asia, extended-family households predominate, and grandparents play an integral role in child raising and family decisions. In Asian countries such as Thailand and Taiwan, about 40 percent of the population ages 50 and older lives in

In many Asian countries, grandparents live in the same home as their grandchildren, playing an important role in their lives. ©Kohei Hara/Getty Images

on the world

IS THE SANDWICH GENERATION A GLOBAL PHENOMENON?

In recent years researchers have called those in their forties and fifties who are squeezed between caring for both their own children and their aging parents the sandwich generation. Parents are living longer, and young adult children need support for longer periods, bringing new challenges for middle-age adults. As the worldwide aging population increases, balancing the roles of how to care for aging parents as well as children will become an increasingly important global issue. The responsibility can be overwhelming at times and it is often perceived as a financial and emotional burden.

According to the Pew Research Center, 47 percent of middle-age adults are part of the sandwich generation in the United States. About 15 percent of U.S. middle-age adults are providing financial support in some way to both a parent and a child. In addition, 61 percent of these adults are also providing emotional support and day-to-day assistance to both their aging parents and their own children (Parker & Patten, 2013). About 29 percent of adult children up to age 30 still live with their parents or have returned home after college, being at least partially supported by their parents (Parker, 2012).

Similar trends have been found in other parts of the world as well. It is estimated that by 2050, worldwide there will be three times more people in the sandwich generation caring for approximately 2 billion aging parents (UN Staff, 2007). In Australia 2.6 million people are considered "sandwich carers"; in the United Kingdom an additional 2.4 million fall into this group (Carers UK Staff, 2012; Carers Australia Staff, 2012).

In many parts of the world, particularly in developing countries, it is common for multiple generations of families to live together. For example, in Japan, nearly 50 percent of elders live with their children (NIH Staff, 2007), and in China 35 to 45 percent of the elderly live with their children (Ren & Treiman, 2014). Even if elders do not live with their children, family support is very important in Japan and China, and adult children are often available for daily care and assistance.

Regardless of living situation, the sandwich generation is growing and the responsibility for caring for loved ones is falling onto the shoulders of middle-age adults. They are often responsible for helping with day-to-day functions; medical services; and financial, emotional, and legal issues of both their aging parents and their own children. This can be a daunting, stressful, and sometimes overwhelming task. A study by the American Psychological Association found that 40 percent of adults in the 35 to 55 age range who are caregivers for both parents and children reported extreme levels of stress, stating that family was the top source of their stress. This stress takes a toll on family relationships and the well-being of the caretakers themselves (APA Staff, 2007). It is important for caretakers to recharge and take care of themselves physically and mentally. Though it may feel like a challenge at times, those being cared for are usually the people that are most important to the caretakers, and their care is an act of dedicated love for their family members.

what's your view How would you handle the responsibilities of caring for aging parents? What can you do to support a loved one who finds himself or herself in this situation?

the same household with a minor grandchild, and half of those with grandchildren age 10 or younger—usually grandmothers—provide care for the child (Kinsella & Velkoff, 2001).

In the United States, the extended family household is common in some minority communities, but the dominant household pattern is the nuclear family. When children grow up, they typically leave home and establish new, autonomous nuclear families. Although 68 percent of the grandparents in an AARP survey see at least one grandchild every 1 or 2 weeks, 45 percent live too far away to see their grandchildren regularly (Davies & Williams, 2002). However, distance does not necessarily affect the quality of relationships with grandchildren (Kivett, 1991, 1993, 1996).

In general, grandmothers have closer, warmer, more affectionate relationships with their grandchildren (especially granddaughters) than grandfathers do, and see them more (Putney & Bengtson, 2001). Grandparents who have frequent contact with their grandchildren, feel good about grandparenthood, attribute importance to the role, and have high self-esteem tend to be more satisfied with being grandparents (Reitzes & Mutran, 2004). Grandparents sometimes have difficulty balancing their connection with their grandchildren and allowing their children to parent their family in accordance with their own beliefs and values (Breheny, Stephens & Spilsbury, 2013).

About 15 percent of U.S. grandparents provide child care for working parents (Davies & Williams, 2002). Indeed, grandparents are almost as likely to be child care providers as organized child care centers or preschools; 30 percent of children under age 5 with employed mothers are under a grandparent's care while the mothers are at work (U.S. Census Bureau, 2008b). In countries where the government spends more funds on child care assistance, grandparent care is less common. For example, in Denmark and Sweden, approximately 2 percent of families use grandparent care, contrasted with 15 percent in Germany and around 30 percent in Italy and Spain (Del Boca, 2015). Geographical proximity of grandparents who are willing to assist with child care, including both regular care and unanticipated "emergency" care, has a positive effect on the probability of women working outside the home (Compton & Pollak, 2014).

Grandparenting after Divorce and Remarriage One result of the rise in divorce and remarriage is a growing number of grandparents and grandchildren whose relationships are endangered or severed. After a divorce, because the mother usually has custody, her parents tend to have more contact and stronger relationships with their grandchildren, and the paternal grandparents tend to have less (Cherlin & Furstenberg, 1986; Myers & Perrin, 1993; Doyle, O'Dywer & Timonen, 2010). When fathers have primary custody or share custody, paternal grandparents continue to have contact with their grandchildren, and the degree of contact may even increase if the divorced father needs assistance (Jappens & Van Bavel, 2016). A divorced mother's remarriage typically reduces her need for support from her parents, but not their contact with their grandchildren. For paternal grandparents, however, the new marriage increases the likelihood that they will be displaced or that the family will move away, making contact more difficult (Cherlin & Furstenberg, 1986).

Before 1965, grandparents had no legal rights to see their grandchildren in the event of a divorce or death of their adult child. Because ties with grandparents are important to children's development, every state has given grandparents (and in some states, great-grandparents, siblings, and others) the right to visitation after a divorce or the death of a parent if a judge finds it in the best interest of the child (Mason, 2011). However, a few state courts have struck down such laws for being too broad and potentially infringing on parental rights (Greenhouse, 2000), and some legislatures have restricted grandparents' visitation rights. Currently, the laws vary state by state, and the burden of proof is generally on the grandparents.

Raising Grandchildren Many grandparents are their grandchildren's sole or primary caregivers. One reason, in developing countries, is the migration of rural parents to urban areas to find work. These *skip-generation* families exist in all regions of the world, particularly in Afro-Caribbean countries. In sub-Saharan Africa, the AIDS epidemic has left many orphans whose grandparents step into the parents' place (Kinsella & Velkoff, 2001).

In the United States, about 1 in 10 grandparents is raising a grandchild, and this number is rising (Livingston & Parker, 2010). Many are serving as *parents by default* for children whose parents are unable to care for them—often as a result of teenage pregnancy, substance abuse, illness, divorce, or death. Surrogate parenting by grandparents is a well-established pattern in African American and Latino families. It is more common in grandmothers, especially those living in poverty (Allen et al., 2000; Blieszner & Roberto, 2006; Dolbin-McNab & Hayslip, 2014).

Unexpected surrogate parenthood can be a physical, emotional, and financial drain on middle-age or older adults (Blieszner & Roberto, 2006). They may have to quit their jobs, shelve their retirement plans, drastically reduce their leisure pursuits and social life, and endanger their health.

Most grandparents who take on the responsibility to raise their grandchildren do it because they do not want their grandchildren placed in a stranger's foster home.

Grandparents often have to deal with a sense of guilt because the adult children they raised have failed their own children and also with the rancor they may feel toward these adult children. For some caregiver couples, the strains produce tension in their relationship. If one or both parents resume their normal roles, it may be emotionally wrenching to return the child (Crowley, 1993; Larsen, 1990–1991).

Taking over the full care of grandchildren can be psychologically and physically taxing (Hadfield, 2014). With respect to physical health, studies have indicated custodial grandparents are at higher risk of poor physical health (Neely-Barnes, Graff & Washington, 2010; Minkler & Fuller-Thomson, 2001; Musil et al., 2010). Custodial grandparents also report higher levels of anxiety, stress, and particularly depression, and those who are caring for children with social, behavioral, or emotional problems are particularly at risk (Doley, Bell, Watt & Simpson, 2015; Minkler & Fuller-Thomson, 2001; Neely-Barnes, Graff & Washington, 2010). High levels of social support can help grandparents deal with the difficulties of parenting their grandchildren and are associated with better psychological health (Hayslip, Blumenthal & Garner, 2014).

kinship care
Care of children living without parents in the home of grandparents or other relatives, with or without a change of legal custody.

Grandparents providing **kinship care** who do not become foster parents or gain custody have no legal status and few rights. They may face many practical problems, from enrolling the child in school and gaining access to academic records to obtaining medical insurance for the child. Grandchildren are usually not eligible for coverage under employer-provided health insurance even if the grandparent has custody. Moreover, kinship families are not legally entitled to as many benefits as foster families (Lin, 2014), despite research showing that kinship care allows children to remain connected to their family networks and cultural traditions (Kiraly & Humphreys, 2013). Like working parents, working grandparents need good, affordable child care and family-friendly workplace policies, such as time off to care for a sick child. The federal Family and Medical Leave Act of 1993 does cover grandparents who are raising grandchildren, but many do not realize it.

Grandparents can be sources of guidance, companions in play, links to the past, and symbols of family continuity. They express generativity, a longing to transcend mortality by investing themselves in the lives of future generations. Men and women who do not become grandparents may fulfill generative needs by becoming foster grandparents or volunteering in schools or hospitals. By finding ways to develop what Erikson called the virtue of *care,* adults prepare themselves to enter the culminating period of adult development.

summary and key terms

Looking at the Life Course in Middle Age

- Developmental scientists view midlife psychosocial development both objectively, in terms of trajectories or pathways, and subjectively, in terms of people's sense of self and the way they actively construct their lives.
- Change and continuity must be seen in context and in terms of the whole life span.

Change at Midlife: Theoretical Approaches

- There is a growing consensus that midlife development shows change as well as stability.

- Costa and McCrae's five-factor model shows slowed change after age 30. Other trait research has found more significant positive change with individual differences.
- Erikson's seventh psychosocial stage is generativity versus stagnation. Generativity is most commonly expressed through parenting, but can be expressed in other ways. The virtue of this period is *care.*
- The greater fluidity of the life cycle today has partly undermined the assumption of a "social clock."

  individuation, generativity versus stagnation, generativit

The Self at Midlife: Issues and Themes

- Key psychosocial issues and themes during middle adulthood concern the existence of a midlife crisis, identity development (including gender identity), and psychological well-being.

- Research does not support a normative midlife crisis. It is more accurate to refer to a transition that may be a psychological turning point.
- Generativity is an aspect of identity development.
- Narrative psychology describes identity development as a continuous process of constructing a life story. Highly generative people tend to focus on a theme of redemption.
- Some research has found increasing "masculinization" of women and "feminization" of men at midlife, but this may be largely a cohort effect. Research does *not* support Gutmann's proposed gender crossover.
- Emotionality and personality are related to psychological well-being.
- Research based on Ryff's six-dimensional scale has found that midlife is generally a period of positive mental health and well-being, though socioeconomic status is a factor.

midlife crisis, turning points, midlife review, ego resiliency, identity process theory (IPT), identity schemas, identity assimilation, identity accommodation, identity balance, gender crossover

Relationships at Midlife

- Two theories of the changing importance of relationships are Kahn and Antonucci's social convoy theory and Carstensen's socioemotional selectivity theory.
- Relationships at midlife are important to physical and mental health but also can present stressful demands.

social convoy theory, socioemotional selectivity theory

Consensual Relationships

- Research on the quality of marriage suggests a dip in marital satisfaction during the years of child rearing, followed by an improved relationship after the children leave home.
- Cohabitation has become more common. It may negatively affect men's well-being.
- Divorce at midlife can be stressful and life changing. Marital capital tends to dissuade midlife divorce.
- Divorce today may be less threatening to well-being in middle age than in young adulthood.
- Married people tend to be happier at middle age than people with any other marital status.
- Because some gays and lesbians delayed coming out, at midlife they may be just establishing intimate relationships.
- Middle-age people tend to invest less time in friendships than younger adults do but depend on friends for emotional support.

marital capital

Relationships with Maturing Children

- Parents of adolescents have to come to terms with a loss of control over their children's lives.
- The emptying of the nest is liberating for many women but may be stressful for couples whose identity is dependent on the parental role or those who now must face previously submerged marital problems.
- Middle-age parents tend to remain involved with their adult children. Conflict may arise over grown children's need to be treated as adults and parents' continuing concern about them.
- Today, more young adults are delaying departure from their childhood home or are returning to it. Adjustment tends to be smoother if the parents see the adult child as moving toward autonomy.
- Increasing numbers of adults are choosing to not have children. Generally, childlessness is associated with high well-being.

empty nest, revolving door syndrome

Other Kinship Ties

- Relationships between middle-age adults and their parents are usually characterized by a strong bond of affection. Aid flows mostly from parents to children.
- As life lengthens, more aging parents become dependent for care on their middle-age children. Acceptance of these dependency needs is the mark of filial maturity and may be the outcome of a filial crisis.
- The chances of becoming a caregiver to an aging parent increase in middle age, especially for women.
- Caregiving can be a source of considerable stress but also of satisfaction. Community support programs can help prevent caregiver burnout.
- Although siblings tend to have less contact at midlife than before and after, most middle-age siblings remain in touch, and their relationships are important to well-being.
- Most U.S. adults become grandparents in middle age and have fewer grandchildren than in previous generations.
- Divorce and remarriage of an adult child can affect grandparent-grandchild relationships.
- A growing number of grandparents are raising grandchildren whose parents are unable to care for them. Raising grandchildren can create physical, emotional, and financial strains.

filial crisis, sandwich generation, caregiver burnout, kinship care

Physical and Cognitive Development in Late Adulthood

learning objectives

Discuss the causes and impact of the aging population.

Characterize longevity and discuss biological theories of aging.

Describe physical changes in late adulthood.

Identify factors that influence health and well-being in late adulthood.

Describe the cognitive functioning of older adults.

©Ariel Skelley/DigitalVision/GettyImages

In this chapter, we begin by sketching demographic trends among today's older population. We look at the increasing length and quality of life in late adulthood and at causes of biological aging. We examine physical changes and health. We then turn to cognitive development: changes in intelligence and memory, the emergence of wisdom, and the influence of continuing education in late life.

Old Age Today

In Japan, old age is a status symbol; travelers checking into hotels there are often asked their age to ensure that they will receive proper deference. In the United States, by contrast, aging is generally seen as undesirable. In research, the most consistent stereotypes that have emerged regarding the elderly are that while older people are generally seen as warm and loving, they are incompetent and of low status (Cuddy, Norton & Fiske, 2005). These stereotypes about aging, internalized in youth and reinforced for decades by societal attitudes, may unconsciously affect older people's expectations about themselves and act as self-fulfilling prophecies (Levy, 2003).

Today, efforts to combat **ageism**—prejudice or discrimination based on age—are making headway. Reports about aging achievers appear more frequently in the media. In media, older people are less often portrayed as dotards and more often as level-headed, respected, and wise, a shift that may be important in the reduction of negative stereotypes about the elderly (Bodner, 2009).

We need to look beyond distorted images of age to its true, multifaceted reality. What does today's older population look like?

ageism
Prejudice or discrimination against a person (most commonly an older person) based on age.

THE GRAYING OF THE POPULATION

The global population is aging. In 2015, 617 million people worldwide were age 65 or older, and by 2050 the total population in that age group is projected to reach 1.6 billion (He, Goodkind & Kowal, 2016). The most rapid increases will be in developing countries, where the number of older people is projected to increase more than 250 percent by 2050 (National Institute on Aging, 2011; Figure 17.1). Aging populations result from declines in fertility accompanied by economic growth, better nutrition, healthier lifestyles, improved control of infectious disease, safer water and sanitation facilities, and advances in science, technology, and medicine (He et al., 2016; Dobriansky, Suzman & Hodes, 2007).

The aged population itself is aging. In many parts of the world, the fastest-growing age group consists of people in their eighties and older. The population of people 80 and older is projected to almost triple between 2015 and 2050, from 126.5 million to 446.6 million. By contrast, the percentage rate increase predicted for adults aged 65 and older is about 1.5 times the current numbers, and there is an almost flat percentage change predicted in people under the age of 20 (He et al., 2016). In the United States, the graying of the population is due to high birthrates and high immigration rates during the early to mid-twentieth century and a trend toward smaller families, which has reduced the relative size of younger age groups. It is also due to aging of baby boomers—the surge of people born following World War II. Since 1900, the proportion of Americans age 65 and up has more than tripled, from 4.1 to 15 percent. The first of the baby boomers turned 65 in 2011, and around 21 percent of Americans are likely to be 65 and older in 2030, about twice as many as in 2000. However, after 2030, as most baby boomers pass 65 years of age, the rapid growth in the elderly should level off (Administration on Aging, 2010; Federal Interagency Forum on Aging-Related Statistics, 2016).

Ethnic diversity among older adults is increasing. In 2014, 34.3 percent of older Americans were members of minority groups; by 2060, 45 percent will be. The older Hispanic population is projected to grow most rapidly, from 3.6 percent of the over-65 population in 2014 to almost 22 percent in 2060 (Federal Interagency Forum on Aging-Related Statistics, 2016).

The growing visibility of such active, healthy older adults as actress Diana Rigg is changing the perception of old age. At age 75, she played the role of brilliant, sharp-tongued Lady Olenna Tyrell on the popular fantasy drama, Game of Thrones.
©HBO/Kobal/REX/Shutterstock

YOUNG OLD TO OLDEST OLD

The economic impact of a graying population depends on the proportion of the population that is healthy and able-bodied. In this regard, the trend is encouraging. Many problems that we used to think were the result of age have been determined to be due to lifestyle factors or disease.

Primary aging is a gradual, inevitable process of bodily deterioration that begins early in life and continues through the years irrespective of what people do to stave it off. In

primary aging
Gradual, inevitable process of bodily deterioration throughout the life span.

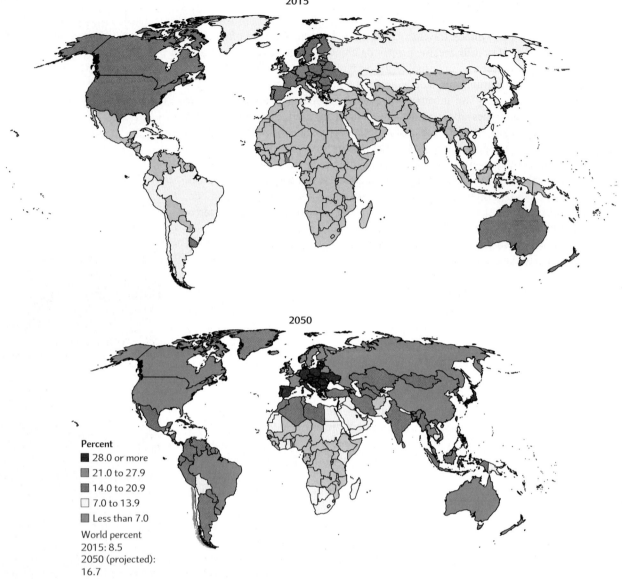

2015

2050

Percent
- 28.0 or more
- 21.0 to 27.9
- 14.0 to 20.9
- 7.0 to 13.9
- Less than 7.0

World percent
2015: 8.5
2050 (projected):
16.7

FIGURE 17.1

Percentage of Population age 65 and older: 2015 and 2050

The growth of the population age 65 and up is projected to increase rapidly in coming decades. Growth will be greatest in much of the developing world.

Source: He, W., Goodkind, D., & Kowal, P. *U.S. Census Bureau, International Population Reports, P95/16-1, An Aging World: 2015.* Washington, DC: U.S. Government Publishing Office, 2016.

secondary aging
Aging processes that result from disease and bodily abuse and disuse and are often preventable.

this view, aging is an unavoidable consequence of getting older. **Secondary aging** results from disease, abuse, and disuse—factors that are often within a person's control (Horn & Meer, 1987). These two philosophies of aging can be likened to the familiar nature-nurture debate. Primary aging is a nature process governed by biology. Secondary aging is the result of nurture, the environmental insults that accrue over the course of a lifetime. As always, the truth lies somewhere in between and both factors matter.

Today, social scientists who specialize in the study of aging refer to three groups of older adults: the "young old," "old old," and "oldest old." These terms represent social constructions similar to the concept of adolescence. Chronologically, *young old* generally

Countries that have programs supporting the elderly are already trying to adjust to the population change. The number of people eligible for such programs is growing and the duration that people are in these programs is also increasing.

The Global Age Watch Index ranks countries based on how well older people are doing. It measures four aspects of elder welfare: income security, health status, capability, and the enabling environment (aspects that help elders to independently care for themselves). In 2015, data were available for and used to rank 96 out of the 195 countries of the world. Switzerland (1), Norway (2), and Sweden (3) top the list with Afghanistan (96), Malawi (95), and Mozambique (94) at the bottom. In North America, the United States ranked ninth, Canada fifth, and Mexico 33rd. Most of the European countries were in the top half, and the bottom 20 countries consisted mostly of African, Middle Eastern, and Southeast Asian countries (HelpAge International Staff, 2015).

About one-fourth of Switzerland's population is over 60 years old. Despite the large proportion of elderly people, Switzerland secured the top ranking because of its many programs promoting health, capability, and activity for the aging population, as well as universal health care and pension plans for all citizens. Nearly one-third of Japan's population is over 60, yet at the number eight ranking, it is considered one of the oldest and healthiest countries in the world. Not surprisingly, Japan has comprehensive policies in place for the elderly, including universal health care and pension plans (HelpAge International Staff, 2015).

India (71) and China (52) have the highest populations of elderly in the world. Both countries have mixed access to health care. While approximately 75 percent of elderly adults feel they can get secure health care when needed, there are major disparities with respect to the quality of health care that is provided. In India, 80 percent of the elderly live in rural areas and 40 percent live below the poverty line; there is no official social security or pension plan for the elderly. Chinese elders fare somewhat better with both physical and mental health. The discrepancies are worse in both countries for those older than 75 (HelpAge International Staff, 2015).

Malawi and Mozambique have very few programs for elders. They rank lowest in income security and as a result 95 percent of the elder population still work. There are no universal pension programs and access to health care is very limited. In both countries chronic diseases are rampant. Elder abuse is common, and it includes financial, physical, and sexual abuse. Many elderly people report feeling unsafe and devalued (HelpAge International Staff, 2015).

Inequality in health care, income, education, and opportunities is apparent between the top and bottom ranked countries. In the highest-income countries, nearly all people older than 65 receive some sort of pension and health care. In the low- and middle-income countries, about 25 percent receive a pension or quality health care. Much still needs to be done to equalize elder care worldwide.

what's your view In countries with limited budgets, what priority should the elderly hold when considering funding for social services? Are they equally, more, or less important than other age groups? Why?

refers to people ages 65 to 74, who are usually active, vital, and vigorous. The *old old,* ages 75 to 84, and the *oldest old,* age 85 and above, are more likely to be frail and infirm and to have difficulty managing **activities of daily living (ADL).** As a result, the oldest old consume a disproportionate number of resources such as pensions or health care costs given their population size (Kinsella & He, 2009).

A more meaningful classification is **functional age:** how well a person functions in a physical and social environment in comparison with others of the same chronological age. For example, a person of 90 who is still in good health and can live independently may be functionally younger than a 75-year-old suffering the effects of dementia.

The use of these terms and age distinctions has arisen out of research and service needs. **Gerontology** is the study of the aged and aging processes. Gerontologists are interested in differences between elderly people because these differences can influence outcomes. Likewise, researchers and service providers in **geriatrics,** the branch of medicine concerned with aging, are concerned with differences among the elderly. Understanding differences among the elderly is vital for the provision of support services for different age groups.

activities of daily living (ADL)
Essential activities that support survival, such as eating, dressing, bathing, and getting around the house.

functional age
Measure of a person's ability to function effectively in his or her physical and social environment in comparison with others of the same chronological age.

gerontology
Study of the aged and the process of aging.

geriatrics
Branch of medicine concerned with processes of aging and medical conditions associated with old age.

PHYSICAL DEVELOPMENT

Longevity and Aging

life expectancy
Age to which a person in a particular cohort is statistically likely to live (given his or her current age and health status), on the basis of average longevity of a population.

longevity
Length of an individual's life.

life span
The longest period that members of a species can live.

Life expectancy is the age to which a person born at a certain time and place is statistically likely to live, given his or her current age and health status. Life expectancy is based on the average **longevity,** or actual length of life, of members of a population. Gains in life expectancy reflect declines in *mortality rates,* or death rates (the proportions of a total population or of certain age groups who die in a given year). The human **life span** is the longest period that members of our species can live. The longest documented life span thus far is that of Jeanne Clement, a French woman who died at 122 years of age.

TRENDS AND FACTORS IN LIFE EXPECTANCY

The average American is getting older, a phenomenon that has been called "the graying of the population." This reflects a rapid rise in life expectancy. A baby born in the United States in 2015 can expect to live to 78.8 years, about 29 years longer than a baby born in 1900 and more than 4 times longer than a baby born at the dawn of human history (National Center for Health Statistics, 2017; Wilmoth, 2000; Figure 17.2).

Gender Differences Nearly all over the world, women typically live longer and have lower mortality rates at all ages than men. By the age of 65, there are approximately 80.3 men for every 100 women, by age 85 there are only 50 men for every 100 women, and by age 100 women outnumber men by 4 to 1 (He et al., 2016). The gender gap is widest in high-income industrialized nations, where female mortality dropped sharply with improvements in prenatal and obstetric care. Women's longer lives also have been attributed to their greater tendency to take care of themselves and to seek medical care, the higher level of social support they enjoy, and the rise in women's socioeconomic status in recent decades. Further, men are more likely to smoke, drink, and be exposed to dangerous toxins (Kinsella & He, 2009).

In the United States, women's life expectancy in 1900 was only 2 years longer than men's. The gender gap widened to 7.8 years in the late 1970s, mainly because more men were dying from smoking-related illnesses (heart disease and lung cancer) and fewer women were dying in childbirth. Since then the gap has narrowed to just under 5 years (National Center for Health Statistics, 2017), largely because more women are smoking (Gorman & Read, 2007). With the exception of Eastern Europe and the former Soviet Union, similar trends have been noted in other developed countries (Kinsella & He, 2009). The gender disparity in the United States mirrors the global rates. At the age of 65, there are approximately 79.6 men for every 100 women. This disparity increases with advancing age; by the age of 85, there are 52 men for every 100 women (Federal Interagency Forum on Aging-Related Statistics, 2016a).

Regional and Racial/Ethnic Differences The gap in life expectancies between developed and developing countries is vast. In the African nation of Sierra Leone, a man born in 2009 could expect to live 49.3 years, as compared to 86.8 years for a woman born in Japan (World Health Organization, 2016a). On average, a child born in a developed country can expect to live for 14 years more than a child born in a developing country (Kinsella & He, 2009). The most dramatic improvements in life expectancy between 2000 and 2015 occurred in Africa, where improvements in child survival and the treatment of malaria and HIV increased life expectancy by 9.4 years (World Health Organization, 2016a).

Wide racial/ethnic, socioeconomic, and geographic disparities in life expectancy exist in the United States. In contrast to the upward national

Years

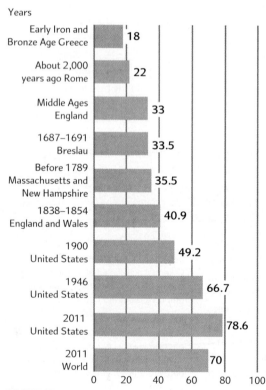

FIGURE 17.2

Changes in Life Expectancy from Ancient to Modern Times

Source: Adapted from Katchadourian, 1987; 2011 U.S. and World data from World Bank, n.d., and WHO, n.d., respectively.

trend, life expectancy has stagnated or even declined since 1983 in many of the nation's poorest counties, mainly in the Deep South, along the Mississippi River, in Appalachia, and in Texas and the southern Plains region (Ezzati, Friedman, Kulkarni & Murray, 2008). On average, white Americans live about 3.5 years longer than African Americans (National Center for Health Statistics, 2017). African Americans, especially men, are more vulnerable than white Americans to illness and death from infancy through middle adulthood. Somewhat surprisingly, Hispanic Americans have the highest life expectancy (82 years), an advantage of approximately 3 years over white Americans and 6.5 years over African Americans (National Center for Health Statistics, 2017); Table 17.1). The reasons for this are somewhat unclear but may include cultural lifestyle issues or migration effects (e.g., those who migrate to the United States tend to be healthier) (Arias, 2010).

A new way to look at life expectancy is in terms of the number of years a person can expect to live in good health, free of disabilities. Globally, healthy life expectancy (HLE) is 61.5 years for men and 64.6 years for women (World Health Organization, 2016a). In the United States, HLE is currently estimated to be 69.1 years of age (World Health Organization, 2015c).

TABLE 17.1 Life Expectancy in Years for . . .	
	At Birth
Hispanic men	79.3
Hispanic women	84.3
White men	76.6
White women	81.3
African American men	72.2
African American women	78.5

Source: Arias, E., Heron, M., & Xu, J. "United States Life Tables, 2012," *National Vital Statistics Reports,* 65, 2016.

WHY PEOPLE AGE

As we get older, we move slower, we become wrinkled, and we may feel the effects of various chronic conditions or diseases. This process is known as **senescence,** the decline in body functioning associated with aging. Why does senescence occur? Most theories about biological aging fall into one of two categories *genetic-programming theories* and *variable-rate theories.*

Genetic-Programming Theories Is aging an inevitable biological process? **Genetic-programming theories** hold that this is indeed the case. These theories propose that people's bodies age according to instructions built into the genes, and that aging is a normal part of development.

Twin studies have shown that genetic differences account for about one-fourth of the variance in the adult human life span. The genetic influences on aging appear to become stronger over time, especially after age 60 (Molofsky et al., 2006; Willcox et al., 2008; Finkel, Gerritson, Reynolds, Dahl & Pedersen, 2014). With the exception of some rare genetic disorders, there is not "a" gene for aging. Rather, aging in typical people involves many gene variants, each with small effects.

Aging also may be influenced by specific genes "switching off," after which age-related losses (such as declines in vision, hearing, and motor control) occur. This process, broadly described as *epigenesis,* involves genes being turned on and off by molecular "tags," or instructions. Epigenetic changes do not involve changes in the underlying genetic code; rather, they involve changes in how genes are expressed. The accumulation of epigenetic changes is partly responsible for aging (D'Aquila, Rose, Bellizi & Passarino, 2013: Sierra, Fernandez & Fraga, 2015; Skulachev et al., 2009). Because epigenetic changes are dynamic and modifiable by environmental influences, positive interventions may be able to combat the effects of aging (Gravina & Vijg, 2010). For example, diet and lifestyle changes can change our epigenetic expression and slow the rate of decline (Pal & Tyler, 2016).

Another cellular process involves *telomeres,* the repetitive fragments of DNA on the tips of chromosomes. Every time a cell divides, replicating its genetic code, the telomeres become shorter. Some theorists argue that cells can only divide a fixed number of times— eventually they run out of telomeres. Leonard Hayflick (1974) found that human cells will divide in the laboratory no more than 50 times. This is called the **Hayflick limit,** and it has been shown to be genetically controlled. Hayflick (1981) argued cells go through the same process in the body as in a laboratory culture. Once cells can no longer replicate, the body loses its ability to repair damaged tissue, and thus begins to age.

In support of this theory, research shows that telomeres shorten with age, and that the rate of telomere shortening is related to the rate of aging (Shammas, 2011). Shorter telomeres result in accelerated aging and risk of early death, and they are associated with increased risk

senescence
Period of the life span marked by declines in physical functioning usually associated with aging; begins at different ages for different people.

Genetic-programming theories
Theories that explain biological aging as resulting from a genetically determined developmental timeline.

Hayflick limit
Genetically controlled limit, proposed by Hayflick, on the number of times cells can divide in members of a species.

This Japanese woman's active lifestyle has contributed to her long healthy life. ©Rob Van Petten/ Photoplay/Media Bakery

variable-rate theories
Theories that explain biological aging as a result of processes that involve damage to biological systems and that vary from person to person.

free radicals
Unstable, highly reactive atoms or molecules, formed during metabolism, that can cause internal bodily damage.

of cancer, stroke, diabetes, dementia, chronic obstructive pulmonary disease, and skin disorders (Chilton, O'Brien & Charchar, 2017). Additionally, people who have genetic disorders in which they age prematurely also have shorter telomere length (Burtner & Kennedy, 2010; Decker, Chavez, Vulto & Landsdorp, 2009). Telomere change is also affected by environmental factors that are known to be associated with disease and mortality, such as stress (Epel et al., 2004), smoking, overweight, alcohol use, and physical inactivity (Shalev et al., 2013; Huzen et al., 2014; Strandberg et al., 2012; Latifovic, Peacock, Massey & King, 2016).

According to *endocrine theory,* the biological clock acts through genes that control hormonal changes. Loss of muscle strength, accumulation of fat, and atrophy of organs may be related to declines in hormonal activity (Lamberts, van den Beld & van der Lely, 1997). For example, mutations in the genes that code for hormones involved in the regulation of blood sugar have been linked in various other species to either increased or decreased life span, and it is likely they function similarly in humans (Van Heemst, 2010). *Immunological theory* proposes a similar process; that certain genes may cause problems in the immune system (Holliday, 2004; Kiecolt-Glaser & Glaser, 2001) that then leads to an increased susceptibility to diseases, infections, and cancer (DiCarlo, Fuldner, Kaminski & Hodes, 2009).

According to the *evolutionary theory of aging,* reproductive fitness is the primary aim of natural selection. Therefore, natural selection acts most strongly on the young, who have many years of potential reproduction ahead of them. If a trait favoring reproductive output in the young is present, it will be spread throughout the population, even if the effects are damaging to the individual later in life (Hamilton, 1966; Baltes, 1997). Moreover, natural selection results in energy resources being allocated to protect and maintain the body until reproduction, but not necessarily after. After reproduction has ceased, the molecular integrity of the body cells and systems eventually deteriorate beyond the body's ability to repair them (Hayflick, 2004). This deterioration occurs because there is no selective pressure to prevent it once genes have been passed on to the next generation.

Variable-Rate Theories Why might one older adult suffer from arthritis, poor health, and declining perceptual abilities and another remain active and engaged? According to **variable-rate theories,** aging is the result of random processes that vary from person to person. They are also called *error theories* because these processes often involve damage due to chance errors in, or environmental assaults on, biological systems.

One such theory, *wear-and-tear theory,* holds that the body ages as a result of accumulated damage to the system at the molecular level. Like an old car, the parts of the body eventually wear out (Jin, 2010). Some theorists have argued that while this sounds commonsensical, there is no fundamental reason bodies could not be made to continually regenerate, as they do in youth (Mitteldorf, 2010).

Another theory of aging, known as the *free-radical theory,* proposes that aging results from the formation of **free radicals,** a by-product of metabolic processes (Harman, 1956). Free radicals are molecules with unpaired electrons. This makes them very reactive because they seek to pair their electrons and will "steal" electrons from neighboring atoms. According to the theory, this process can ultimately damage cell membranes, structures and proteins, fats, carbohydrates, and even DNA. Moreover, free-radical damage accumulates with age and has been associated with cardiovascular disease, cancer, inflammatory diseases such as arthritis, heart disease, neurological disorders such as Parkinson's disease and Alzheimer's disease, gastric ulcers, and many others (Lobo, Patil, Phatak & Chandra, 2010).

This theory was expanded to the *mitochondrial theory of aging.* Mitochondria—tiny organisms that generate chemical energy for cells and tissues—play an important role in helping cells survive under stress and powering the body. However, when mitochondria generate energy, they also create free radicals as by-products of that process. These free radicals can negatively affect surrounding tissues, including their own mitochondrial DNA. This leads to even more free radical release, more damage, and the aging process (Harman, 2006; 1992; 1983). In this view, the action of free radicals affects the rate of aging, but it does so via damage to mitochondrial genes.

Free radicals, while potentially damaging, may also have a signaling role to play by helping regulate genes necessary for cell growth and differentiation (Wojcik, Burzynska-Pedziwiatr & Wozniak, 2010; Schieber & Chandel, 2014).

The *rate-of-living theory* postulates that there is a balance between metabolism, or energy use, and life span. The faster a body's metabolism, the shorter its life span, and vice versa (Pearl, 1928). So, for example, a hummingbird would be predicted to have a far shorter life than a sloth. While this theory is useful in describing some phenomena, for example, when broadly comparing small and large animals to each other, it does not explain many aspects of aging. For example, exercise, which increases metabolic activity, would be predicted to shorten life span. In reality, it has the opposite effect (Hulbert, Pamplona, Buffenstein & Buttemer, 2007).

Genetic-programming and variable-rate theories have practical implications. If human beings are programmed to age at a certain rate, they can do little to retard the process. If, on the other hand, aging is variable, then lifestyle practices may influence it.

Some researchers have suggested that rather than focusing on how to extend the human life span, it makes more sense to consider how we can improve human health *while* aging (Partridge, 2010). Still, interest in increasing the life span remains. Controllable environmental and lifestyle factors may interact with genetic factors to determine how long a person lives and in what condition. And epigenetic processes are also likely to be at play here (Migliore & Coppede, 2008).

HOW FAR CAN THE LIFE SPAN BE EXTENDED?

Most people understand that more people survive to the age of 40 than to 60, and that more people survive to the age of 60 than to 80. When translated into statistical terms, this concept is known as a **survival curve.** A survival curve represents the percentage of people or animals alive at various ages. Survival curves support the idea of a biological limit to the life span because more members of a species die as they approach the upper limit. With respect to humans, the curve currently ends around age 100, meaning few people survive past this age.

survival curve
A curve on a graph showing the percentage of people or animals alive at various ages.

Because genetics plays at least a partial role in human longevity (Coles, 2004), some believe the idea of an exponential increase in the human life span is unrealistic. It has been assumed that gains in life expectancy since the 1970s have come from reductions in age-related diseases, such as heart disease, cancer, and stroke. Thus, further gains should be far more difficult to achieve unless scientists find ways to modify the basic processes of aging—a feat some gerontologists consider impossible (Hayflick, 2004; Holliday, 2004).

However, this assumption is now being questioned (Vaupel, 2010). Scientists have extended the healthy life spans of worms, fruit flies, and mice through slight genetic mutations (Ishii et al., 1998; Kolata, 1999; Lin, Seroude & Benzer, 1998; Parkes et al., 1998; Pennisi, 1998). Such research suggests the possibility of delayed senescence and a significant increase in the average and maximum life spans (Arking, Novoseltsev & Novoseltseva, 2004). In human beings, of course, genetic control of a biological process may be far more complex. Because no single gene or process seems responsible for senescence and the end of life, we are less likely to find genetic quick fixes for human aging (Holliday, 2004). Moreover, techniques that show promise in shorter-lived species may not apply to humans.

Optimists, however, point to data showing continued increase in longevity. In the United States, the number of centenarians increased from roughly 50,000 people in 2000 to approximately 72,000 in 2014 (Xu, 2016). Data show that while different dynamics are playing out in different countries, the increase in longevity is not uncommon (World Health Organization, 2016a). In the countries with the highest life expectancy, longevity has increased by 2.5 years every decade, and it does not appear to be leveling off (Oeppen & Vaupel, 2002). Interestingly, death rates actually *decrease* after 100 (Coles, 2004). People at 110 are no more likely to die in a given year than people in their 80s (Vaupel et al., 1998). In other words, people hardy enough to reach a certain age are likely to go on living a while longer (Administration on Aging, 2016).

When people who live to be very old are examined, it appears that morbidity—or being in a state of disease—is being compressed. In other words, these people are reaching old age in relatively good health. However, once they begin to deteriorate, they do so very quickly. So while the overall rate of aging is unchanged, the process of aging itself seems to have been postponed, presumably because of good health (Andersen, Sebastiani, Dworkis, Feldman & Perls, 2012). Given this finding, the question then

Jeanne Calment was a French woman with the longest confirmed human life span. She lived a total of 122 years and 164 days.
©Pascal Parrot/Sygma via Getty Images

research in action

THE OLDEST OLD AND SUCCESSFUL AGING

Some people will far outlive the average life expectancy of 78.8 years for Americans (CDC, 2017i). Research has increasingly been able to pinpoint factors that keep the "oldest-old" alive, often decades longer, than their peers.

Nearly no one reaches advanced age without health issues, but a characteristic shared by the oldest-old is resilience against disease. Their bodies are subject to extended aging processes, much greater risk for disease than younger people, and they are more likely to be frail or dependent (Sole-Auro & Crimmins, 2013). However, they are still around.

What accounts for the extreme longevity of some people? Genetics appears to be important and can explain about 25 percent of the variation in human longevity (Passarino, De Rango & Montesanto, 2016). Centenarians and supercentenarians appear to possess longevity-assuring genes. These genes seem to counteract age-related molecular damage, loss in function, and cognitive decline (Arai et al., 2014, Arai, 2017). While discovering the genetic variants that lead to longevity might provide us with clues to help us the research is challenging to conduct. Sample sizes are only as large as the minority of individuals who reach exceptionally old age (Santos-Lozano et al., 2016).

Lifestyle factors are also key influencers of longevity and successful aging. Health status in old age represents a lifetime accumulation of behaviors (Sole-Auro & Crimmins, 2013). Avoidance of obesity and smoking and engaging in regular exercise are critical lifestyle factors for healthy aging (Ferdows, Jensen & Tarraf, 2017).

The most important lifestyle factor is likely to be exercise. Exercise is clearly beneficial from a physical point of view by, for example, reducing the risk of obesity and cardiovascular disease. However, it is perhaps even more important with respect to the maintenance of cognitive abilities. Blondell and colleagues' (2014) meta-analysis examined the longitudinal impact of physical activity on cognitive decline and found that physical activity was associated with a long-term 18 percent

reduction in risk of dementia. Benefits have also been found among the "young-old" who continue to exercise (Kirk-Sanchez & McGough, 2014). Exercise is linked to increased oxygen consumption and cerebral brain flow, which may explain why it helps preserve brain health and cognitive performance (Blondell et al., 2014).

Successful aging also has much to do with psychosocial factors. Cho, Martin, and Poon (2015) highlighted the role of positive affect, which was linked to social interactions. While all people benefitted from social interaction, those who had greatest levels of education and better cognitive functioning were able to engage in more frequent and intense social interactions, which, in turn, contributed to higher levels of positive affect. Family contact, specifically when such interaction is positive, may help stave off depressive symptoms and promote well-being (Fuller-Iglesias, Webster & Antonucci, 2015).

Jeste and colleagues (2013) suggest that older adults may not use the same yardstick that younger people do when they consider their well-being. They suggested that older people are more likely to accept their physical limitations, have more realistic appraisals of their abilities, be more content with life accomplishments, reduce their degree of social comparison, and experience greater emotional stability, despite worsening physical and cognitive functioning. When asked what constitutes a "good" old age, oldest old describe living independently, preferably in their homes, a pain-free existence, and for a quick, peaceful death (Nosraty, Jylha, Raittila & Lumme-Sandt, 2015).

what's **your view**

Have you ever known someone who lived past 100 years old? To what did that person attribute his or her longevity?

becomes: Can we postpone aging even more, delay aging until even later, and thus increase the life span? This has been termed the longevity riddle (Vaupel, 2010).

While the answer to this question remains to be seen, it raises important issues. It suggests that increasing the healthy life span—a goal worthy in itself—may itself increase life expectancy. It also suggests the most fruitful area for longevity interventions should be focused on risk reduction and living a healthy lifestyle (Fries, Bruce & Chakravarty, 2011). There are possible economic benefits to this approach. Morbidity compression could lead to people living longer lives, while simultaneously decreasing medical costs because of the compression of poor health at the tail end of the life span (Cutler, Ghosh & Landrum, 2013).

One line of research—inspired by rate-of-living theories that view energy use as the crucial determinant of aging—is on dietary restriction. Drastic caloric reduction has been found to greatly extend life in worms, fish, and monkeys—in fact, in nearly all animal species on which it has been tried (Colman et al., 2014; Heilbronn & Ravussin, 2003). A review of 15 years of research suggests that calorie restriction can have beneficial effects on human aging and life expectancy (Fontana & Klein, 2007). Calorie-restricted monkeys also show less of the brain atrophy that sometimes accompanies aging (Colman et al., 2009), a promising finding that may have implications for brain health.

The Calorie Restriction Society practices voluntary caloric restriction, avoiding processed foods rich in refined carbohydrates and partially hydrogenated oils. In comparison with control groups eating a typical Western diet, society members do show a low percentage of body fat and a decreased incidence of diabetes, cancer, and age-related disease. However, the optimal amount of caloric restriction in humans is not known, nor it is known if there are any adverse effects of such extreme restriction. In addition, it is unclear if exercise-induced leanness has the same positive benefits as leanness resulting from mere calorie restriction.

For these reasons, and because a very-low-calorie diet takes great discipline to maintain, there is increasing interest in developing drugs that mimic the effects of caloric restriction (Fontana, Klein & Holloszy, 2010). Additionally, intermittent fasting, where food is eaten only during some hours of the day, holds some promise as well. Research suggests it may exert a similar effect on metabolic processes as calorie restriction (Martin, Mattson & Maudsley, 2006) while being easier to maintain on a long-term basis. Last, a more general and holistic approach to aging, with medications used *before* the advent of aging-related disease, might show more promise for extending life in humans (Partridge, 2010).

Physical Changes

Some physical changes typically associated with aging are obvious to a casual observer. Older skin tends to become paler and less elastic; and, as fat and muscle shrink, the skin may wrinkle. The hair on the head thins and turns gray and then white, and body hair becomes sparser. Older adults become shorter as the disks between their spinal vertebrae atrophy. In addition, the chemical composition of the bones changes, creating a greater risk of fractures. Less visible but equally important changes affect internal organs and body systems; the brain; and sensory, motor, and sexual functioning.

ORGANIC AND SYSTEMIC CHANGES

Changes in organic and systemic functioning are highly variable. Some body systems decline rapidly, others hardly at all (Figure 17.3). There are, however, typical age-related declines in most people. The lungs, for example, become less effective because of reductions in lung volume, atrophy in the muscles involved with breathing, and reductions in the ability of cilia (hairlike structures that clear mucus and dirt out of the lungs) to function effectively (Lowery, Brubaker, Kuhlmann & Kovacs, 2013). While there are normative age-related declines in immune system functioning, stress can exacerbate this process, making older people more susceptible to respiratory infections (Kiecolt-Glaser & Glaser, 2001). Heart health suffers as well. Elderly adults are more likely to suffer from arrhythmia (irregular heartbeat), the muscle walls of the heart may thicken, and the valves that control the flow of blood in and out of the heart may no longer open completely. These heart changes result in impaired capacity for pumping blood, and thus decreases in cardiovascular fitness (Lee, Huang & Shen, 2011). Chronic stress in older adults is also related to chronic low-grade inflammation, making older adults more vulnerable to disease (Bauer, Jeckel & Luz, 2009; Heffner, 2011). Problems with swallowing food, gastric reflux, indigestion, irritable bowel syndrome, constipation,

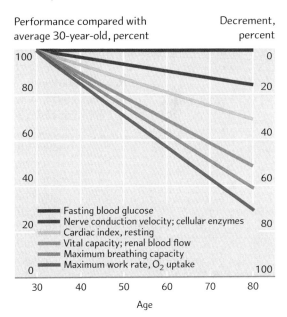

FIGURE 17.3

Declines in Organ Functioning

Differences in functional efficiency of various internal body systems are typically slight in young adulthood but widen by old age.

Source: Katchadourian, H. *Fifty: Midlife in perspective.* New York: W. H. Freeman, 1987.

and reduced absorption of nutrients become more common with age (Grassi et al., 2011). This puts elderly people at higher risk of malnutrition (Harris, Davies, Ward & Haboubi, 2008), especially if they have chronic diseases or are dependent on others for assistance in daily activities (Ulger et al., 2010; Saka, Kaya, Ozturk, Erten & Karan, 2010).

Reserve capacity is the backup capacity that helps body systems function to their utmost limits in times of stress. With age, reserve levels tend to drop, and many older people cannot respond to extra physical demands as they once did. For example, a person who used to be able to shovel snow from the entire driveway easily may become exhausted from shoveling just the front entry.

reserve capacity
The backup capacity that helps body systems function to their utmost limits in times of stress.

THE AGING BRAIN

As people become older, there are declines in the brain's ability to process information rapidly, in executive functioning, and in episodic memory (Fjell & Walhovd, 2010). However, in normal, healthy people, changes in the aging brain are generally subtle and make little difference in functioning. This is because the brain retains a significant degree of plasticity and can compensate for the challenges of aging by reorganizing neural circuitry and working around the problem (Park & Gutchess, 2006). This way, the declines seen in the aging brain are not as severe. For example, there are age-related changes in functional connectivity, the ways in which different areas of the brain coordinate with each other during a task. In general, imaging studies have found reduced functional connectivity during tasks. However, there is more diffuse activation (more brain areas are used for completing tasks) to compensate. This is particularly true when tasks are challenging (Sala-Llonch, Bartres-Faz & Junque, 2015; Geerligs, Renken, Saliasi, Maurits & Lorist, 2014). Some areas of the brain may even become more active with age. For example, there are increases in prefrontal activity (associated with effortful, controlled tasks) with age (Eyler, Sherzai, Kaup & Jeste, 2011; Park & Reuter-Lorenz, 2009).

In late adulthood, the brain gradually diminishes in volume and weight, particularly in the frontal and temporal regions (Fjell & Walhovd, 2010; Lockhart & DeCarli, 2014). The hippocampus—the seat of memory—also shrinks (Raz, Ghisletta, Rodrigue, Kennedy & Lindenberger, 2010). There is also a reduction in cortical thickness (Lemaitre et al., 2012). This gradual shrinkage was formerly attributed to a loss of neurons (nerve cells). However, most researchers now agree that—except in certain specific brain areas, such as the cerebellum, which coordinates sensory and motor activity—neuronal loss is not substantial and does not affect cognition (Burke & Barnes, 2006; Finch & Zelinski, 2005). When the pace of these brain changes increases, however, cognitive declines are increasingly likely (Carlson et al., 2008).

Another typical change is a decrease in the number, or density, of dopamine neurotransmitters due to losses of synapses (neuronal connections). Dopamine receptors are important as they help in regulating attention (Park & Reuter-Lorenz, 2009). This decline generally results in slowed response time.

Beginning in the midfifties, the myelin sheathing that enables neuronal impulses to travel rapidly between brain regions begins to thin (Natrajan et al., 2015; Hinman & Abraham, 2007). This deterioration of the brain's myelin, or white matter, is associated with cognitive and motor declines (Andrews-Hanna et al., 2007; Finch & Zelinski, 2005).

Changes in the brain can have social as well as cognitive consequences. Loss of executive function in the frontal cortex can lessen the ability to inhibit irrelevant or unwanted thoughts; thus older adults may not realize if they are talking too much or if their conversation partner is uninterested. On the positive side, the amygdala, the seat of emotions, shows lessened response to negative, but not positive, events; thus older adults tend to be more constructive in resolving conflicts than are younger adults (von Hippel, 2007).

Postmortem examinations of brain tissue have found significant DNA damage in certain genes that affect learning and memory in most very old people and some middle-age people (Lu et al., 2004). Such changes are associated with neurodegenerative disorders and dementia (Madabhushi, Pan & Tsai, 2014). Although adults over the age of 90 years are more than 25 times more likely to develop dementia than adults aged 65 to 69 years (Brayne, 2007), such deterioration is not inevitable.

Not all changes in the brain are destructive. Researchers have discovered that older brains can grow new nerve cells from stem cells—something once thought impossible. Evidence of cell division has been found in the hippocampus, a portion of the brain involved in learning and memory (Spalding et al., 2013). It appears likely that in humans, physical activity paired with cognitive challenges may be most effective in promoting the growth of new cells in the hippocampus (Kempermann, 2015; Fabel & Kempermann, 2008).

SENSORY AND PSYCHOMOTOR FUNCTIONING

Individual differences in sensory and motor functioning increase with age. Some older people experience sharp declines; others find their abilities virtually unchanged. Visual and hearing problems may deprive them of social relationships and independence, and motor impairments may limit everyday activities.

Vision and Hearing Older eyes need more light to see, are more sensitive to glare, and may have trouble locating and reading signs. Thus driving may become hazardous, especially at night. Older adults may have difficulty with depth or color perception or with such daily activities as reading, sewing, shopping, and cooking (Desai et al., 2001). Losses in visual contrast sensitivity can cause difficulty reading very small or very light print (Owsley, 2011). Vision problems also can cause accidents and falls (Lord, Smith & Menant, 2010). Many community-dwelling older adults report difficulty with bathing, dressing, and walking around the house, in part because they are visually impaired (Desai et al., 2001; Kempen, Ballemans, Ranchor, van Rens & Zijlstra, 2012).

People with moderate visual losses often can be helped by corrective lenses or changes in the environment. Still, 17 percent of U.S. older adults and 30 percent of those 85 and older have trouble seeing, even when wearing glasses or contact lenses (Schoenborn, Vickerie & Powell-Griner, 2006), and women are generally more impaired than are men, at least until age 85 (Schoenborn & Heyman, 2009).

Cataracts, cloudy or opaque areas in the lens of the eye, are common in older adults and eventually cause blurred vision (Schaumberg et al., 2004). Approximately 26 million Americans are currently affected by cataracts (Wittenborn & Rein, 2014), and worldwide, 94 million people are visually impaired and 20 million are blind because of cataracts (Mariotti, 2012). Surgery to remove cataracts is one of the most frequent operations among older Americans and is generally quite successful (National Guidance Alliance, 2017). Cataract surgery is associated with a reduction in mortality risk of up to 60 percent, as recently reported in a 20-year longitudinal study of over 74,000 women (Tseng et al., 2017). Presumably the reduction in mortality risk results from a number of factors tied to vision, such as greater ease and accuracy in taking medications, greater likelihood of staying physically active, and lower accident risk. Similar research has shown the same effects in men (Tseng, Yu, Lum & Coleman, 2016).

The leading cause of visual impairment in older adults is **age-related macular degeneration.** The macula is a small spot in the center of the retina that helps us keep objects directly in our line of sight in sharp focus. In the most common form of macular degeneration, the retinal cells in this area degenerate over time, and the center of the retina gradually loses the ability to sharply distinguish fine details. Activities such as reading and driving become extremely problematic, as the exact area in which a person focuses becomes blurry. In some cases, treatments using antioxidant and zinc supplements and drugs that block the growth of abnormal blood vessels under the retina can prevent further vision loss, but cannot reverse loss that has already occurred. For people with severe degeneration, implantation of a tiny "telescope" that magnifies and focuses central retinal content to other areas of the retina that are still healthy can be used (Foundation Fighting Blindness, 2017).

Glaucoma is irreversible damage to the optic nerve caused by increased pressure in the eye. Glaucoma can be treated with eye drops, pills, or surgery. If left untreated, it can cause blindness, but early treatment can lower elevated pressure in the eye and delay the onset of the condition. However, even with treatment, 10 percent of people who get glaucoma will eventually go blind. In the United States, approximately 120,000 people

cataracts
Cloudy or opaque areas in the lens of the eye, which cause blurred vision.

age-related macular degeneration
Condition in which the center of the retina gradually loses its ability to discern fine details; leading cause of irreversible visual impairment in older adults.

glaucoma
Irreversible damage to the optic nerve caused by increased pressure in the eye.

In age-related macular degeneration the center of the retina gradually loses visual acuity. In these photos, the left is an image as seen by a person with normal vision and the right is the same image as seen by a person with macular degeneration.
(both): Source: National Eye Institute, National Institutes of Health

are blind from glaucoma (Glaucoma Research Foundation, 2017). Worldwide, glaucoma is the leading cause of blindness, and in 2013 approximately 64.3 million people were affected by glaucoma (Tham et al. 2014).

Globally, about 328 million adults have disabling hearing loss—a permanent hearing loss in the better ear of more than 40 decibels (World Health Organization, 2017). In the United States, approximately 37.5 million adults have some form of hearing loss (Blackwell, Lucas & Clarke, 2014).

Hearing impairments increase with age. About 2 percent of adults aged 45 to 54 have disabling hearing loss. By 55 to 64 years, the proportion of affected adults rises to 8.5 percent, then to 25 percent by ages 65 to 74, and 50 percent for people 75 and older. Men are approximately twice as likely to experience a hearing impairment, and white people are more likely to be affected than those of other ethnicities (National Institute on Deafness and Other Communication Disorders, 2016). Hearing loss may contribute to a false perception of older people as distractible, absentminded, and irritable and tends to have a negative impact on the well-being not only of the impaired person but also of his or her spouse or partner (Wallhagen, Strawbridge, Shema & Kaplan, 2004). Hearing aids can help but are expensive and may magnify background noises as well as the sounds a person wants to hear. Only 1 in 3 adults aged 70 or older who would benefit from the use of hearing aids uses them (National Institute on Deafness and Other Communication Disorders, 2016).

Changes in environmental design, such as brighter reading lights, a closed captioning option on television sets, and built-in telephone amplifiers can help many older adults with sensory limitations.

Strength, Endurance, Balance, and Reaction Time Generally, aging results in a variety of changes related to physical abilities, including increases in body fat and declines in muscle strength, aerobic capacity, flexibility, and agility (Milanovic et al., 2013). Adults generally lose about 10 to 20 percent of their strength up to age 70 and more after that (Van Heuvelen, Kempen, Ormel & Rispens, 1998). Generally, the loss of strength is greater for lower than for upper limbs. The declines are related to aging as well as to the decreases in physical activity that are often associated with aging (Milanovic, et al., 2013). Aerobic capacity (based upon both lung and heart health) declines about 10 percent a year (Hollenberg, Yang, Haight & Tager, 2006). Flexibility also declines, although less so for women than for men (Araujo, 2008).

Falls, and the injuries that often occur as a result, are the leading cause of hospitalization in the elderly (Centers for Disease Control & Merck Company Foundation, 2007). Many falls and fractures are preventable by eliminating hazards commonly found in the home (Agency for Healthcare Research and Quality and CDC, 2002; Table 17.2). Additionally, some of the physical changes of age contributing to falls can be reversed

TABLE 17.2 Safety Checklist for Preventing Falls in the Home	
Stairways, hallways, and pathways	Free of clutter Good lighting, especially at top of stairs Light switches at top and bottom of stairs Tightly fastened handrails on both sides and full length of stairs Carpets firmly attached and not frayed; rough-textured or abrasive strips to secure footing
Bathrooms	Grab bars conveniently located inside and outside of tubs and showers and near toilets Nonskid mats, abrasive strips, or carpet on all surfaces that may get wet Night lights
Bedrooms	Telephones and night lights or light switches within easy reach of beds
All living areas	Electrical cords and telephone wires out of walking paths Rugs and carpets well secured to floor No exposed nails or loose threshold trim Furniture and other objects in familiar places and not in the way; rounded or padded table edges Couches and chairs proper height to get into and out of easily

Source: National Institute on Aging (NIA). *Bound for good health: A collection of age pages.* Washington, DC: U.S. Government Printing Office, 1993.

or slowed. A recent review showed that exercise interventions using multiple-component exercises, resistance training, balance training, and endurance training reduced the risk of falls and improved balance, endurance, and elderly people's ease of walking (Cadore, Rodriguez-Manas, Sinclair & Izquierdo, 2013).

The World Health Organization (2015a) has made the promotion of functional ability a priority in its advocacy and research, and global fitness trends show increased interest in functional fitness training (Thompson, 2016). **Functional fitness** refers to exercises or activities that improve daily activity. While it has implications for all ages, it is perhaps most relevant to elderly adults, who may have increasing difficulty in performing the activities of daily living necessary for independence. Levels of functional fitness decline with age in concert with physical activity in a bidirectional fashion (Milanovic et al., 2013). In other words, becoming less physically active over time results in declines in functional fitness. Those functional fitness declines then lead to less physical activity as movements become harder to execute.

While intervention programs using resistance training in the elderly have shown that it is possible to increase muscle strength, how these increases in strength transfer to everyday movements and disability are less clear (Latham, Bennett, Stretton & Anderson, 2004). It is not enough to just be strong. Thus, functional fitness interventions have become more common and are showing more success. The exercises used in intervention programs are designed to mimic the desired action. For example, an elderly person might be coached by being asked to sit down and rise from a chair while wearing a weighted vest (Liu, Shiroy, Jones & Clark, 2014). A recent meta-analysis of 13 studies on functional fitness intervention programs showed that such programs were effective in increasing functional performance in everyday life, and that they were more effective than merely focusing on muscle strength (Liu et al., 2014).

Part of the reason for these gains is that the primary factor in older adults is likely to be a training-induced adaptation in the brain's ability to coordinate motor and brain activity (Voss et al., 2010; Barry & Carson, 2004). For example, vacuuming requires muscle strength in the arms and legs, dynamic balance, control of range of motion, gross and fine motor movements, and the coordination of all movements together (Liu et al., 2014). Thus, it is as much a cognitive exercise as a physical one. Exercise programs hold as much promise for the prevention of cognitive declines in older adults as they do for physical health (Bherer, Erickson & Liu-Ambrose, 2013; Voelcker-Rehage, Godde & Staudinger, 2010).

functional fitness
Exercises or activities that improve daily activity.

SLEEP

Older people tend to sleep and dream less than before. Their hours of deep sleep are more restricted, and they may awaken more easily and earlier in the morning (Pace-Schott

& Spencer, 2014). To some extent, this is driven by normative changes in circadian (daily) rhythms. However, the assumption that sleep problems are normal in old age can be dangerous (Mattis & Sehgal, 2016). Poor sleep quality or chronic insomnia can contribute to depression, neurodegenerative disorders such as dementia, and cognitive declines (Baglioni et al., 2011; Lee et al., 2013; Mattis & Sehgal, 2016; Miyata ct al., 2013). Either too much sleep or too little sleep is associated with an increased risk of mortality (Gangwisch et al., 2008; Chen, Su & Chou, 2013).

The American College of Physicians (ACP) recommends that the first line of defense against insomnia and sleep disorders is the use of cognitive behavioral therapy (Qaseem, Kansagara, Forciea, Cooke & Denberg, 2016). Such therapy may include instructions on, for example, staying in bed only when asleep, getting up at the same time each morning, and learning about false beliefs pertaining to sleep needs. This type of therapy has produced improvements, with or without drug treatment (Lovato, Lack, Wright & Kennaway, 2014; Reynolds, Buysse & Kupfer, 1999). However, if it is not effective, the ACP recommends short-term use medications be considered. The most commonly prescribed drugs include benzodiazepines (e.g., Halcion, Ativan), non-benzodiazepine hypnotics (e.g., Ambien), and suvorexant (e.g., Belsomra), a drug that works via altering the signalling of neurotransmitters that regulate sleep.

SEXUAL FUNCTIONING

The most important factor in maintaining sexual functioning is consistent sexual activity over the years. In a national survey, 53 percent of U.S. adults ages 65 to 74 and 26 percent of those ages 75 to 85 reported being sexually active. Men are much more likely than women to remain sexually active in old age, largely because, being less numerous, they are more likely to have a spouse or partner (Lindau et al., 2007). Men retain more sexual desire; however, both men and women report a decline in sexual desire with age (Aggarwal, 2013) and women report a greater decline in sexual activity (Lee, Nazroo, O'Connor, Blake & Pendleton, 2016). Ageism and stereotypes about the elderly may negatively influence sexual desire in older adults (Heywood et al., 2017).

Sex is different in late adulthood from what it was earlier. Men typically take longer to develop an erection and to ejaculate, may need more manual stimulation, may experience longer intervals between erections, or may have difficult achieving an erection. Women report more difficulties with becoming aroused and experiencing orgasm, breast engorgement and other signs of sexual arousal are less intense than before, and they may experience issues with lubrication (Lee et al., 2016; Lindau et al., 2007). Health problems are more likely to affect the sex life of women than men, but poor mental health and relationship dissatisfaction are associated with sexual dysfunction in both men and women (Laumann, Das & Waite, 2008).

Sexual activity in older people is normal and healthy. Housing arrangements and care providers should consider the sexual needs of elderly people. Satisfaction with life, cognitive functioning, and psychological well-being are all strongly related to interest in and having sex (Trudel, Villeneuve, Anderson & Pilon, 2008). Physicians should avoid prescribing drugs that interfere with sexual functioning if alternatives are available and, when such a drug must be taken, should alert the patient to its effects.

Physical and Mental Health

Increasing life expectancy is raising pressing questions about the relationship between longevity and health, both physical and mental. How healthy are older adults today, and how can they stave off declines in health?

HEALTH STATUS

Poor health is not an inevitable consequence of aging. About 78 percent of U.S. adults age 65 and older consider themselves in good to excellent health (Federal Interagency

Forum on Aging-Related Statistics, 2016). As earlier in life, poverty is strongly related to poor health and to limited access to, and use of, health care (Schoenborn & Heyman, 2009). For instance, poverty is related to a higher incidence of arthritis, diabetes, high blood pressure, heart disease, depression, and stroke in the elderly (Menec, Shooshtari, Nowicki & Fournier, 2010). Adults who live in poverty are less likely to engage in such healthy behaviors as leisure-time physical activity, avoidance of smoking, and maintenance of appropriate body weight (Schoenborn & Heyman, 2009).

CHRONIC CONDITIONS AND DISABILITIES

More than 2 out of 3 Americans have multiple chronic conditions. People with chronic health conditions are likely to have a lower quality of life and are at risk of disability and death (Gill & Moore, 2013).

Common Chronic Conditions In 2016, the six top leading causes of death in the United States—heart disease, cancer, chronic lower respiratory disease, stroke, Alzheimer's disease, and diabetes—were chronic conditions (Federal Interagency Forum on Aging-Related Statistics, 2016). More than two-thirds of health care costs involve the management of chronic disease (Centers for Disease Control and Prevention, 2013d). Worldwide, the leading causes of death at age 60 and above are heart disease, stroke, chronic pulmonary disease, lower respiratory infections, and lung cancer (WHO, 2003). Many of these deaths could be prevented through healthier lifestyles. If Americans were to quit smoking, eat a healthier diet, and engage in higher levels of physical activity, estimates are that approximately 35 percent of deaths could be prevented in the elderly (Centers for Disease Control & Merck Company Foundation, 2007). The overall need for health care services for this population is expected to increase markedly over the next two decades (Centers for Disease Control and Prevention, 2013d).

Rates of death as a result of diabetes declined recently, although it is still the sixth leading cause of death. Approximately 23 percent of men and 19 percent of women report being diagnosed with diabetes in the United States. Hypertension increased in prevalence, affecting about 55 percent of men and 58 percent of women (Federal Interagency Forum on Aging-Related Statistics, 2016). Hypertension, which can affect blood flow to the brain, is related to declines in attention, learning, memory, executive functions, psychomotor abilities, and visual, perceptual, and spatial skills and is a risk factor for stroke.

Aside from hypertension and diabetes, the most common chronic conditions are arthritis (43 percent of men and 54 percent of women), heart disease (35 percent of men and 25 percent of women), and cancer (26 percent of men and 21 percent of women). Women are more likely to report hypertension, asthma, chronic bronchitis, emphysema, and arthritis, whereas men are more likely to have heart disease, cancer, stroke, and diabetes (Federal Interagency Forum on Aging-Related Statistics, 2016).

Chronic conditions vary by race/ethnicity. For example, in 2013–2014, 71 percent of older blacks had hypertension, compared with 54 percent of older whites and Hispanics. Older blacks and Hispanics were significantly more likely than older whites to have diabetes—both 32 percent, as compared with 18 percent for older whites (Federal Interagency Forum on Aging-Related Statistics, 2016).

Disabilities and Activity Limitations The proportion of older adults in the United States with chronic physical disabilities or activity limitations has declined since the late 1990s (Federal Interagency Forum on Aging-Related Statistics, 2016), perhaps due in part to the increasing number of older people who are educated and knowledgeable about preventive measures. However, the proportion of people who have difficulty with functional activities rises sharply with age (NCHS, 2010). Approximately 34 percent of people aged 65 to 74 have functional impairments, compared with 48 percent of those aged 75 to 84 and 74 percent of those aged 85 and above (Federal Interagency Forum on Aging-Related Statistics, 2016).

In the presence of chronic conditions and loss of reserve capacity, even a minor illness or injury can have serious repercussions. In one study looking at older adults hospitalized

Exercise helps these women live longer, healthier lives, and the social aspect of their shared activities keep them mentally healthy. ©Ariel Skelley/ DigitalVision/Getty Images

after a fall, those adults were more likely to die or be placed in a nursing home than adults admitted to the hospital for reasons unrelated to a fall (Aitken, Burmeister, Lang, Chaboyer & Richmond, 2010).

LIFESTYLE INFLUENCES ON HEALTH AND LONGEVITY

The chances of remaining healthy and fit in late life often depend on lifestyle choices, especially related to smoking, heavy drinking, and exercise (Vu, Liu, Garside & Daviglus, 2009).

Physical Activity A lifelong program of exercise may prevent many physical changes once associated with normal aging. Regular exercise can strengthen the heart and lungs and decrease stress. It can protect against hypertension, hardening of the arteries, heart disease, osteoporosis, and diabetes. It helps maintain speed, stamina, strength, and endurance, and such basic functions as circulation and breathing. It reduces the chance of injuries by making joints and muscles stronger and more flexible, and it helps prevent or relieve lower-back pain and symptoms of arthritis. It can enable people with such conditions as lung disease and arthritis to remain independent and can help prevent the development of limitations on mobility. In addition, it may improve mental alertness and cognitive performance, help relieve anxiety and mild depression, and enhance feelings of mastery and well-being (Bauman, Merom, Bull, Buchner & Fiatarone Singh, 2016; Agency for Healthcare Research and Quality & CDC, 2002; Butler, Davis, Lewis, Nelson & Strauss, 1998a, 1998b; Kramer et al., 1999; Kritchevsky et al., 2005; Netz, Wu, Becker & Tenenbaum, 2005).

*In*activity contributes to heart disease, diabetes, colon cancer, and high blood pressure. It may lead to obesity, which affects the circulatory system, the kidneys, and sugar metabolism; contributes to degenerative disorders; and tends to shorten life. An analysis of many studies found that aerobic activity of moderate intensity was most beneficial to well-being (Netz et al., 2005). Unfortunately, many older adults do not do even this much. Current recommendations call for a minimum of 150 minutes of moderate aerobic activity over the course of a week, or slightly more than 20 minutes a day. Additional exercise is ideal, but anything is better than nothing (Centers for Disease Control and Prevention, 2014). Twenty-eight percent of adults 50 years and older without a chronic disease are physically inactive. Moreover, adults who have chronic diseases are 30 percent less likely to be physically active (Centers for Disease Control and Prevention, 2016).

Nutrition Almost 80 percent of Americans aged 71 and older fail to meet the criteria for a healthy diet, most notably by eating too many empty calories (Krebs-Smith, Guenther, Subar, Kirkpatrick & Dodd, 2010). Generally, older women (when compared to older men) (Ervin, 2008) and people of higher economic status (Wang et al., 2014) consume a healthier diet.

Nutrition plays a large part in susceptibility to such chronic illnesses as atherosclerosis, heart disease, and diabetes as well as functional and activity limitations. Excessive body fat, particularly from a diet heavy in red and processed meats and alcohol, has been linked to several types of cancer (World Cancer Research Fund, 2007). However, while weight gain is not healthy for older adults, neither is excessive weight loss. Excessive weight loss can lead to muscle weakness and general frailty, and it can be as debilitating to older adults as weight gain (Schlenker, 2010).

A healthy diet can reduce risks of obesity as well as of high blood pressure and cholesterol (Federal Interagency Forum on Aging-Related Statistics, 2016). A diet high in olive oil, whole grains, vegetables, and nuts has been found to reduce cardiovascular risk (Esposito et al., 2004) and—in combination with physical activity, moderate alcohol use, and refraining from smoking—cut 10-year mortality from all causes in healthy 70- to 90-year-old Europeans by nearly two-thirds (Rosamond et al., 2008). Eating fruits and vegetables—especially those rich in vitamin C, citrus fruits and juices, green leafy vegetables, broccoli, cabbage, cauliflower, and brussels sprouts—lowers the risk of cancer and heart disease (Takachi et al., 2007).

Periodontal disease is a chronic inflammation of the gums caused by the bacteria in plaque. It can result in tender or bleeding gums and eventual tooth loss. Although more aging Americans are keeping their natural teeth than ever before, 16 percent of adults aged 65 to 74 and 31 percent of adults aged 75 and above have no teeth (Federal Interagency Forum on Aging-Related Statistics, 2016). Those older adults with fewer than 20 teeth may suffer from malnutrition (Hassan et al., 2017) as a result of the increased difficulty in adequately chewing food. Periodontal disease has also been related to cognitive declines (Kaye et al., 2010) and cardiovascular disease (Blaizot, Vergnes, Nuwwareh, Amar & Sixou, 2009). Some suggest it may impair the regulation of blood sugar as well (Zadik, Bechor, Galor & Levin, 2010).

MENTAL AND BEHAVIORAL PROBLEMS

Only 6.3 percent of Americans 75 years and older report frequent mental distress (Centers for Disease Control, 2013d). However, mental and behavioral disturbances that do occur can result in functional impairment in major life activities as well as cognitive decline (van Hooren et al., 2005).

Many older people with mental and behavioral problems tend not to seek help for their issues. The primary reason older people do not seek help is difficulty accessing needed support services (Mackenzie, Scott, Mather & Sareen, 2008). Indeed, there is a shortage of trained mental health professionals for the elderly, and this shortage is likely to increase in line with projected increases in the elderly population (American Psychological Association, 2011).

Depression Rates of reported depressive symptomatology have stayed relatively stable since the late 1990s. In 2016, 11 percent of older men and 16 percent of older women in the United States reported symptoms of clinical depression (Federal Interagency Forum on Aging-Related Statistics, 2016). Heredity may account for 40 to 50 percent of the risk for major depression (Bouchard, 2004; Harvard Medical School, 2004c). Vulnerability seems to result from the influence of multiple genes interacting with environmental factors. Special risk factors in late adulthood include chronic illness or disability, cognitive decline, and divorce, separation, or widowhood (Harvard Medical School, 2003; Mueller et al., 2004). Genetic factors linking poor health to depression may be more important in men than women (Petkus et al., 2017). Depression plays a more pervasive role in mental functional status, disability, and quality of life than do physical ailments such as diabetes or arthritis (Noël et al., 2004).

Depression can be treated by antidepressant drugs, psychotherapy, or both, and antidepressant drugs appear to work equally as well as they do at younger ages (Blazer, 2009). Regular exercise can reduce symptoms of mild to moderate depression (Stanton & Reaburn, 2014; Dunn, Trivedi, Kampert, Clark & Chambliss, 2005), although this may not be true for very frail older adults (Underwood et al., 2013).

Dementia **Dementia** is the general term for physiologically caused cognitive and behavioral decline sufficient to interfere with daily activities. Cognitive decline becomes increasingly common with advanced age, affecting 11 percent of men and 13 percent of women aged 75 to 84, and 24 percent of men and 30 percent of women 85 and over (Federal Interagency Forum on Aging-Related Statistics, 2016).

Although there are about 50 causes of dementia of known origin, the vast majority of cases (about two-thirds) are caused by **Alzheimer's disease,** a progressive, degenerative brain disorder (Gatz, 2007). **Parkinson's disease,** the second most common disorder involving progressive neurological degeneration, is characterized by tremor, stiffness, slowed movement, and unstable posture (Nussbaum, 1998). These two diseases, together with *multi-infarct dementia (MD),* which is caused by a series of small strokes, account for at least 8 out of 10 cases of dementia, all irreversible.

Dementia is not inevitable. A variety of factors protect people from developing dementia. Certain personality traits seem to confer protection. In particular, high conscientiousness and low neuroticism offer advantages (Low, Harrison & Lackersteen, 2013). Cognitive characteristics can also buffer a person. Education is protective (Xu et al., 2016; Sharp & Gatz,

dementia
Deterioration in cognitive and behavioral functioning due to physiological causes.

Alzheimer's disease
Progressive, irreversible, degenerative brain disorder characterized by cognitive deterioration and loss of control of bodily functions, leading to death.

Parkinson's disease
Progressive, irreversible degenerative neurological disorder, characterized by tremor, stiffness, slowed movement, and unstable posture.

2011), as is a challenging job (Smart, Gow & Deary, 2014; Seidler et al., 2004), and bilingualism, even in those who are illiterate (Bialystok, Craik & Freeman, 2007; Alladi et al., 2013). Essentially, an active mind stays healthy longer. Drinking small amounts of alcohol has been associated with a decrease in risk (Peters, Peters, Warner, Beckett & Bulpitt, 2008). Staying engaged with others may be beneficial, but results are unclear. Some studies, particularly those that look at adults of different ages, show reductions in dementia risk with social interaction and engagement. Other studies, particularly longitudinal work, show little effect of social networks on dementia (Baumgart et al., 2015; Marioni et al., 2015).

Cognitive impairment is more likely in people with poor health, especially those who experience strokes or diabetes (Tilvis et al., 2004). A lack of regular physical activity puts people at risk for later dementia (Baumgart et al., 2015), and instituting an exercise program even late in life may help reverse some of the early signs of cognitive impairment in otherwise healthy adults (Lautenschlager et al., 2008).

Alzheimer's Disease Alzheimer's disease (AD) is one of the most common and most feared terminal illnesses among aging persons. It gradually robs patients of intelligence, awareness, and even the ability to control their bodily functions—and finally kills them. The disease affects 46.8 million people throughout the world, and its incidence is expected to double every 20 years (Prince, 2015).

An estimated 5.5 million people in the United States are living with AD, approximately 200,000 of whom are under 65 and may have an early-onset form of the disease. The risk rises dramatically with age; thus increases in longevity mean that more people will survive to an age when the risk of AD is greatest (Alzheimer's Association, 2017). In the United States, AD was the sixth leading cause of death in 2015 (Murphy, Xu, Kochanek, Curtin & Arias, 2017).

Symptoms The classic symptoms of Alzheimer's disease are memory impairment, deterioration of language, and deficits in visual and spatial processing. The most prominent early symptom is inability to recall recent events or take in new information. A person may repeat questions that were just answered or leave an everyday task unfinished. These early signs may be overlooked because they look like ordinary forgetfulness or may be interpreted as signs of normal aging.

Personality changes—for instance, rigidity, apathy, egocentricity, and impaired emotional control—tend to occur early in the disease's development (Balsis, Carpenter & Storandt, 2005). There are indications that these personality changes may be useful in predicting which healthy adults might be at risk of developing dementia (Duchek, Balota, Storandt & Larsen, 2007). More symptoms follow: irritability, anxiety, depression, and, later, delusions, delirium, and wandering. Long-term memory, judgment, concentration, orientation, and speech all become impaired, and patients have trouble handling basic activities of daily life. By the end, the patient cannot understand or use language, does not recognize family members, cannot eat without help, cannot control the bowels and bladder, and loses the ability to walk, sit up, and swallow solid food. Death usually comes within 8 to 10 years after symptoms appear (Cummings, 2004).

Causes and Risk Factors Accumulation of an abnormal protein called *beta amyloid peptide* appears to be the main culprit contributing to the development of Alzheimer's disease (Gatz et al., 2006). The brain of a person with AD contains excessive amounts of **neurofibrillary tangles** (twisted masses of dead neurons) and large waxy clumps of **amyloid plaque** (nonfunctioning tissue formed by beta amyloid in the spaces between neurons). Because these plaques are insoluble, the brain cannot clear them away. They may become dense, spread, and destroy surrounding neurons.

There is growing evidence that one of the primary mechanisms driving the progression of neurodegenerative disease is the breakdown of myelin, the fatty substance that coats axons and allows neural impulses to travel more rapidly. Myelin affords our brains some of their great complexity, but it also makes us vulnerable to neurodegenerative disease in old age, particularly in late developing areas of the brain (Bartzokis, Lu & Mintz, 2007; Bartzokis, 2004). In this theory, neurodegenerative disease results from the brain's efforts to repair broken-down myelin, which result in the release of neurofibrillary tangles and amyloid plaques. These substances can damage neurons directly, but the brain is also affected by the compromised myelin (Papuc & Rejdak, 2017; Amlien &

neurofibrillary tangles
Twisted masses of protein fibers found in brains of persons with Alzheimer's disease.

amyloid plaque
Waxy chunks of insoluble tissue found in brains of persons with Alzheimer's disease.

Fjell, 2014). When attempts to restore myelin are successful, disease progression is slow. However, when this process fails, neurodegenerative disease progresses (Bartzokis, 2011).

Alzheimer's disease is strongly heritable (Gatz et al., 2006). A variant of the *APOE* gene has been found to contribute to susceptibility to both early- and late-onset AD (Van Cauwenberghe, Van Broeckhoven & Sleegers, 2015; Gatz, 2007). Sex modifies this association; the gene puts women at greater risk than men (Altmann, Tian, Henderson & Greicius, 2014). A variant of another gene called *SORL1* was found to stimulate the formation of amyloid plaque (Reitz et al., 2011; Meng et al., 2007). Another gene variant involved in the manufacture of amyloid precursors, Cathepsin D, moderately increases the risk as well (Schuur et al., 2011). However, identified genes are thought to explain no more than half of all AD cases. Epigenetic modifications that determine whether a particular gene is activated may play a part (Lord & Cruchaga, 2014).

Although a number of lifestyle factors have been studied regarding their potential impact on AD, results are mixed and conclusions difficult to reach. However, some general lifestyle factors, such as diet and physical activity, have been implicated, especially for persons who are not at genetic risk (Gatz, 2007). Foods rich in vitamin E, vitamin B-12, omega-3 fatty acids, and unhydrogenated unsaturated fats—such as nuts, seeds, fish, and eggs—may be protective against AD, whereas foods high in saturated and transunsaturated fats, such as red meats, butter, and ice cream, may be harmful. Vegetables, legumes, fruits, and whole grains should be the base of a diet, and exercise should be incorporated into a routine (Barnard et al., 2014; Morris, 2004). Smokers have increased risk of AD (Saito, Diaz, Chung & McMurtray, 2017; Durazzo, Mattsson, Weiner, & Alzheimer's Disease Neuroimaging Initiative, 2014). Nonsteroidal anti-inflammatory drugs such as aspirin and ibuprofen were originally thought to cut the risk of AD (Vlad, Miller, Kowall & Felson, 2008); however, randomized controlled studies have not found an association (Wang et al., 2015).

Education and cognitively stimulating activities have been associated with reduced risk of the disorder (Sattler, Toro, Schonknecht & Schroder, 2012; Wilson, Scherr, Schneider, Tang & Bennett, 2007). The protective effect may be due not to education itself, but rather to the fact that educated people tend to be cognitively active (Wilson & Bennett, 2003). Cognitive activity may build **cognitive reserve** and thus delay the onset of dementia (Stern, 2012). Cognitive reserve, like organ reserve, may enable a deteriorating brain to continue to function under stress, up to a point, without showing signs of impairment.

Although, a NIH Consensus Development statement (Daviglus et al., 2010) stated that no firm conclusions could be drawn about lifestyle modifications that might decrease risk for AD, a recent report by the Alzheimer's Association (Baumgart et al., 2015) argued there is enough evidence to provide some general guidelines. Regular physical activity and the management of cardiovascular risk factors (diabetes, obesity, hypertension, and smoking), a healthy diet, and remaining cognitively active throughout the life span all offer a protective advantage.

Diagnosis AD is generally diagnosed via medical assessment. A medical history of the patient is taken, including mental status, mood testing, a physical and neurological exam, and blood and imaging tests in order to rule out alternative explanations (Alzheimer's Association, 2017). Until relatively recently, the only definitive way to diagnose AD, however, was a post-mortem examination of the affected brain. Current efforts are focused on diagnosing the disease early in the process, when signs of cognitive deficits are mild. Recommendations are that a medical assessment be used clinically, and that imaging and biomarker status be used in clinical trials and research (Albert et al., 2011).

Neuroimaging has been useful in excluding alternative causes of dementia (Cummings, 2004) and in allowing researchers to see brain lesions indicative of AD in a living patient (Shoghi-Jadid et al., 2002). Noninvasive PET (positron emission tomography) scanning has been used to detect the plaques and tangles characteristic of Alzheimer's, and the results were as good as those obtained by autopsy (Reitz & Mayeux, 2014; Mosconi et al., 2008). Whatever the technique used, the identification of AD prior to symptom onset has a variety of important applications, from assessing those individuals at risk of developing dementia to monitoring interventions and drug treatments of affected people to allowing people time to plan for their future.

Esther Lipman Rosenthal's battle with Alzheimer's disease is evident in her artwork. She created the picture on the top, showing her husband golfing, at age 55 and the picture on the bottom, showing him on cross-country skis, at age 75, during the early and middle stages of her disease. Photos courtesy of Linda Goldman.
(both): Artwork by Esther Lipman Rosenthal. Photos©Linda Lee Goldman

cognitive reserve
Hypothesized fund of energy that may enable a deteriorating brain to continue to function normally.

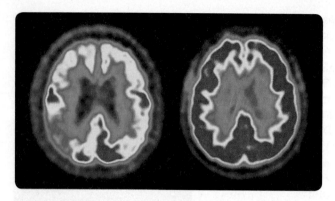

These PET (positron emission tomography) scans show significant decrease of glucose cerebral metabolism and reduced activity (left) in a patient with Alzheimer's disease, compared to the greater activity levels seen in a normal brain (right). ©ISM/Centre Jean PERRIN/Medical Images

Another diagnostic approach has focused on finding biomarkers—a measurable indicator of a biological process—in order to diagnose early manifestations of the disease, perhaps even before the presence of symptoms. Currently, three biomarkers have been strongly associated with dementia risk: tau proteins, amyloid plaques, and neurofilament light chains (NFLs). Tau proteins help deliver materials to neurons; however, in AD they become twisted into neurofibrillary tangles. Amyloid is a protein found throughout the body that in AD results in plaques of sticky buildup. And NFL is a protein released when myelin is tangled. Researchers have used technology to detect all three substances in the cerebral and spinal fluid of people with AD (Olsson et al., 2016; Georganopoulou et al., 2005). Importantly, biomarker tests also show promise for ruling out AD in people showing impairment (Molinuevo et al., 2014).

Despite the identification of several genes associated with AD (Kim et al., 2014), genetic testing so far has a limited role in prediction and diagnosis. Still, it may be useful in combination with cognitive tests, brain scans, and clinical evidence of symptoms. There is evidence that people alter their health behaviors if told they have genes making them vulnerable to dementia (Chao et al., 2008), so such information may someday become part of the way in which the medical profession addresses risk in individuals. Genetic profiles may also offer a means by which to predict which drugs might be most effective in different individuals (Roses et al., 2014).

Treatment Although no cure has yet been found, early diagnosis and treatment can slow the progress of Alzheimer's disease and improve quality of life. Currently, the U.S. Food and Drug Administration has approved five drugs that have been shown to slow, though not stop, the progression of Alzheimer's disease for up to a year (Alzheimer's Association, 2017). One medication is memantine (commercially known as Namenda). Daily doses of memantine taken for as long as a year reduced deterioration in patients with moderate to severe AD without significant adverse effects (Reisberg et al., 2006).

Another experimental approach involved immunotherapy (Solomon & Frenkel, 2010). In this approach, a "vaccine" was developed that trained the immune system to attack amyloid plaques. While there was some success in early trials, they were halted because some patients developed meningoencephalitis, or swelling of their brain tissue, and others showed little change (Panza, Logroscino, Imbimbo & Solfrizzi, 2014).

In the absence of a cure, management of the disease is critical. In the early stages, cognitive training interventions have been demonstrated to result in gains in both cognitive and behavioral areas (Sitzer, Twamley & Jeste, 2006). Behavioral therapies can slow deterioration, improve communication, and reduce disruptive behavior (Barinaga, 1998). Drugs can relieve agitation, lighten depression, and help patients sleep. Proper nourishment and fluid intake together with exercise, physical therapy, and control of other medical conditions are important, and cooperation between the physician and the caregiver is essential (Cummings, 2004).

COGNITIVE DEVELOPMENT
Aspects of Cognitive Development

Let's look first at intelligence and general processing abilities, then at memory, and then at wisdom, which is popularly associated with the later years.

INTELLIGENCE AND PROCESSING ABILITIES

Does intelligence diminish in late adulthood? The answer depends on what abilities are being measured and how. Some abilities, such as speed of mental processes and abstract reasoning, may decline in later years, but other abilities tend to improve throughout most of adult life.

Measuring Older Adults' Intelligence To measure the intelligence of older adults, researchers often use the **Wechsler Adult Intelligence Scale (WAIS).** The WAIS is a standardized measure that allows assessment of a person's intellectual functioning at different ages. Scores on the WAIS subtests yield a verbal IQ, a performance IQ, and a total IQ. Older adults tend not to perform as well as younger adults on the WAIS, but the difference is primarily in processing speed and nonverbal performance. On the five subtests in the performance scale (such as identifying the missing part of a picture or mastering a maze), scores drop with age, but on the six tests making up the verbal scale—particularly tests of vocabulary, information, and comprehension—scores fall only slightly (Figure 17.4). This is called the *classic aging pattern* (Botwinick, 1984). This age disparity in performance, particularly for processing speed, is smaller in more recent cohorts (Miller, Myers, Prinzi & Mittenberg, 2009). Variability in scores—meaning that some people score higher than others—increases with age, and particularly in those areas in which average declines are more apparent (Wisdom, Mignogna & Collins, 2012).

This pattern is likely a consequence of muscular and neurological slowing. For tasks that do not require speed, declines are less likely. For example, verbal items that hold up with age are based on knowledge and do not require the test-taker to figure out or do anything new. The performance tasks involve the processing of new information and require perceptual speed and motor skills.

The Seattle Longitudinal Study: Use It or Lose It In some ways, the mind can be thought of as a muscle. It too responds to use, and it too declines if not engaged in the world around us. This "use it or lose it" dynamic is illustrated with research from the Seattle Longitudinal Study of Adult Intelligence. Researchers measured six primary mental abilities: verbal meaning, word fluency, number (computational ability), spatial orientation, inductive reasoning, and perceptual speed. In general, fluid abilities decline more rapidly than crystallized abilities. Consistent with other studies, perceptual speed tends to decline earliest and most rapidly. Cognitive decline in other respects is slower and more variable. Very few people weaken in all abilities, and many improve in some areas. Most fairly healthy older adults show only small losses until the late sixties or seventies. Not until the eighties do they consistently fall below the average performance of younger adults, and even then, only in about half of people, and less so in verbal abilities and reasoning (Schaie & Willis, 2010; Schaie, 2005).

The most striking feature of the Seattle findings is the tremendous variation among individuals. Some participants show declines during their forties, but a few maintain full functioning very late in life. Those most likely to show declines are men who have low educational levels, are dissatisfied with their success in life, and exhibit a significant decrease in flexibility of personality. Some health-related variables are also important, most notably, hypertension and diabetes. Participants who engage in cognitively complex work, who are in good health, and who exercise tended to retain their abilities longer. Engaging in activities that challenge cognitive skills promotes the retention or growth of those skills and, as we mentioned earlier, may protect against dementia (Schaie & Willis, 2010; Willis & Schaie, 2005; Lindwall et al., 2012).

Cognitive deterioration, then, often may be related to disuse. Much as many aging athletes can call on physical reserves, older people who get training, practice, and social support seem to be able to draw on mental reserves.

Everyday Problem Solving The purpose of intelligence, of course, is not to take tests but to deal with the challenges of daily life. In many studies, the quality of practical decisions (such as what car to buy or how to compare insurance policies) bore only a modest relationship, if any, to performance on tasks like those on intelligence tests (Blanchard-Fields, 2007; Meyer et al., 1995). Similarly, much research on everyday problem solving (such as what to do about a flooded basement) has not found as

Wechsler Adult Intelligence Scale (WAIS) Intelligence test for adults that yields verbal and performance scores as well as a combined score.

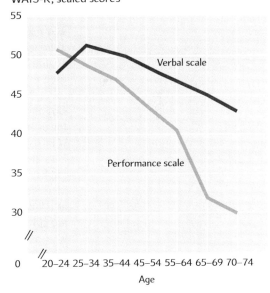

FIGURE 17.4

Classic Aging Pattern on the Revised Version of the Wechsler Adult Intelligence Scale (WAIS-R)

Scores on the performance subtests decline far more rapidly with age than scores on the verbal subtests.

Source: Botwinick, J. *Aging and behavior* (3rd ed.). New York: Springer, 1984.

early a decline as is often seen in measures of fluid intelligence, and some research has found marked improvement (Blanchard-Fields, Stein & Watson, 2004; Mienaltwoski, 2011), particularly when the contexts being assessed are those that older people are familiar with (Artistico, Orom, Cervone, Krauss & Houston, 2010).

Age differences are reduced in studies that focus on *interpersonal* problems—such as how to deal with a new mother who insists on showing her older mother-in-law how to hold the baby—rather than on *instrumental* problems—such as how to return defective merchandise (Thornton & Dumke, 2005). Older adults have more extensive repertoires of strategies to apply to interpersonal situations than younger adults do, they tend to minimize tension and disagreement and emphasize positive emotions, and they are more likely to chose a highly effective strategy than are younger adults (Blanchard-Fields, Mienaltowski & Seay, 2007; Fingerman & Charles, 2010).

Changes in Processing Abilities In many older adults, a general slowdown in central nervous system functioning is a major contributor to losses of efficiency of information processing and changes in cognitive abilities. Speed of processing, one of the first abilities to decline, is related to health status, balance, and gait and to performance of activities of daily living, such as looking up phone numbers and counting out change (Ball, Edwards & Ross, 2007; Bezdicek, Stepankova, Novakova & Kopacek, 2016).

One ability that tends to slow with age is ease in switching attention from one task to another (Bucur & Madden, 2010). This finding may help explain why many older adults have difficulty driving, which requires rapid attentional shifts (Duley & Adams, 2013; Bialystok, Craik, Klein & Viswanathan, 2004). In studies of several training programs—which involved practice, feedback, and learning task-specific strategies—participants who started with the worst performance made the most gains. This research underlines the brain's plasticity even with regard to a basic fluid ability, speed of processing (Ball et al., 2007).

Although age-related declines in processing abilities occur, it is not inevitable in daily life. Older adults use their vast reservoirs of knowledge to work around problems and compensate for declines that do occur (Peters, Hess, Västfjäll & Auman, 2007). Generally, older adults tend to do better on tasks that depend on ingrained habits and knowledge (Bialystok et al., 2004). It is likely that older adults are using alternative, although complementary, neural circuits for more difficult tasks, and it may be that cognitive interventions are exerting their influence here by restructuring the pathways used to complete such tasks (Park & Reuter-Lorenz, 2009).

Cognitive Abilities, Health, and Mortality Psychometric intelligence may be a predictor of how long and in what condition adults will live. In one longitudinal study, people who scored high in intelligence as children were less likely to suffer from poor health or have chronic health conditions at age 50 (Wraw, Deary, Gale & Der, 2015). Other longitudinal work showed high intelligence in childhood was associated with a lower risk of mortality at age 79 (Cukic, Brett, Calvin, Batty & Deary, 2017). Cognitive performance is also linked to physical health in adulthood as well. For example, physically frail older adults are at higher risk for cognitive impairment (Robertson, Savva & Kenny, 2013), and people who have been critically ill often show cognitive impairments for up to year after they recover (Pandharipande et al., 2013).

Recently researchers have begun to wonder if the intelligence mortality link is an artifact of methodological confounds in research. For example, studies that include childhood adversity within the models are less likely to find a link between intelligence and mortality (Kilgour, Starr & Whalley, 2010). Socioeconomic status (SES) may also matter. Some studies have found that childhood SES does not seem to attenuate the link between intelligence and health (Der, Batty & Deary, 2009). However, when adult SES is included in models, the strength of the relationship between health and intelligence is lessened (Calvin et al., 2010). Yet another interpretation is that, as many diseases such as diabetes and hypertension may lead *both* to cognitive declines earlier in life *and* an earlier death, data showing a link between the two may reflect the action of the disease instead of an association between IQ and mortality (Batty, Deary & Gottfredson, 2007).

MEMORY: HOW DOES IT CHANGE?

An estimated 1 in 5 adults over age 70 has some degree of memory impairment short of dementia (Plassman et al., 2008). To understand age-related memory decline, we need to review the various memory systems that enable the brain to process information for use later. These systems are traditionally classified as "short-term" and "long-term."

Short-Term Memory Researchers assess short-term memory by asking a person to repeat a sequence of numbers, either in the order in which they were presented (*digit span forward*) or in reverse order (*digit span backward*). Digit span forward ability holds up well with advancing age (Craik & Jennings, 1992; Wingfield & Stine, 1989) but digit span backward performance does not (Craik & Jennings, 1992; Lovelace, 1990). Why? One reason may involve the differentiation of sensory and working memory. **Sensory memory** involves the brief storage of sensory information. For example, when you see the trail left behind by a Fourth of July sparkler, you are seeing the trace left by your sensory memory. **Working memory** involves the short-term storage of information being actively processed, such as when you calculate the tip for a restaurant bill in your head. Some theorists argue that forward repetition requires only sensory memory, which retains efficiency throughout life. Therefore, declines in this area are more rare. However, backward repetition requires the manipulation of information in working memory, which gradually shrinks in capacity with age (Hale et al., 2011).

A key factor in memory performance is the complexity of the task (Park & Reuter-Lorenz, 2009). Tasks that require only *rehearsal,* or repetition, show very little decline. Tasks that require *reorganization* or *elaboration* show greater falloff (Emery, Heaven, Paxton & Braver, 2008). If you are asked to verbally rearrange a series of items (such as "Band-Aid, elephant, newspaper") in order of increasing size ("Band-Aid, newspaper, elephant"), you must call to mind your previous knowledge of Band-Aids, newspapers, and elephants (Cherry & Park, 1993). More mental effort is needed to keep this additional information in mind, using more of the limited capacity of working memory.

Long-Term Memory Information-processing researchers divide long-term memory into three major systems: *episodic memory, semantic memory,* and *procedural memory.*

Do you remember what you had for breakfast this morning? Such information is stored in **episodic memory,** the long-term memory system most likely to deteriorate with age (Park & Gutchess, 2005; Tromp, Dufour, Lithfous, Pebayle & Despres, 2015). Episodic memory is linked to specific events; you retrieve an item by reconstructing the original experience in your mind. Older adults are less able than younger people to do so, perhaps because they focus less on context (where something happened, who was there), and rely more on gist than details (Dodson & Schacter, 2002). Because of this, they have fewer connections to jog their memory (Lovelace, 1990). Also, older people have had many similar experiences that tend to run together. When older people perceive an event as distinctive, they can remember it nearly as well as younger people (Geraci, McDaniel, Manzano & Roediger, 2009).

Some types of long-term memories remain vigorous as people age. **Semantic memory** consists of meanings, facts, and concepts accumulated over a lifetime of learning. Semantic memory shows little decline with age, although infrequently used or highly specific information may sometimes be difficult to retrieve (Luo & Craik, 2008). Indeed, some aspects of semantic memory, such as vocabulary and knowledge of rules of language, may even increase with age (Camp, 1989).

Another long-term memory system that remains relatively unaffected is procedural memory. **Procedural memory** includes motor skills (like riding a bike) and habits (like taking a particular street home) that, once learned, take little conscious effort. It is relatively unaffected by age (Fleischman, Wilson, Gabrieli, Bienias & Bennett, 2004; Lezak, Howieson, Bigler & Tranel, 2012). Moreover, new procedural memories that are formed in old age may be retained for at least 2 years (Smith et al., 2005) even though they may take a bit more time to learn initially (Iaria, Palermo, Committeri & Barton, 2009).

Speech and Memory: Effects of Aging As people become older, they often begin to have minor difficulties with language. However, these experiences are not generally due

sensory memory
Initial, brief, temporary storage of sensory information.

working memory
Short-term storage of information being actively processed.

episodic memory
Long-term memory of specific experiences or events, linked to time and place.

semantic memory
Long-term memory of general factual knowledge, social customs, and language.

procedural memory
Long-term memory of motor skills, habits, and ways of doing things, which can be recalled without conscious effort.

Riding a bicycle requires procedural memory. Once learned, procedural skills can be activated without conscious effort, even after a long period of disuse.
©Blend Images/Granger Wootz/Getty Images

to issues related to language per se but rather are the result of problems accessing and retrieving information from memory. The core language processes remain relatively unchanged across age (Shafto & Tyler, 2014). Thus issues are considered memory problems rather than language problems.

For example, have you ever been unable to come up with a word that you knew perfectly well? This is known as the tip-of-the-tongue (TOT) phenomenon; it occurs in people of all ages but becomes more common in late adulthood (Burke & Shafto, 2004). Presumably, the TOT phenomenon results from a failure in working memory (Schwartz, 2008). Other problems in verbal retrieval include errors in naming pictures of objects aloud, more ambiguous references and slips of the tongue in everyday speech, more use of nonfluencies (such as "um" and "er") in speech, and a tendency to misspell words (such as *indict*) that are spelled differently than they sound (Burke & Shafto, 2004).

Why Do Some Memory Systems Decline? What explains older adults' memory losses? Investigators have offered several hypotheses. One approach focuses on biological structures and the other on the processing of information.

Neurological Change The decline in processing speed described earlier in this chapter seems to be a fundamental contributor to age-related memory loss. In one study, controlling for processing speed eliminated most of the age-related drop in memory performance (Hedden, Lautenschlager & Park, 2005). Theory suggests that declines in cognitive performance are associated with structural changes in the brain, which research has generally confirmed. For example, myelin in the brain allows for faster conduction of nerve impulses, which should theoretically affect processing speed. Research has shown that processing speed and myelin integrity follow a similar trajectory: a U-shaped curve peaking a midlife (Bartzokis et al., 2010).

Different memory systems depend on different brain structures. Thus a disorder that damages a particular brain structure may impair the type of memory associated with it. For example, Alzheimer's disease disrupts working memory (located in the prefrontal cortex at the front of the frontal lobes) as well as semantic and episodic memory (located in the frontal and temporal lobes); Parkinson's disease affects procedural memory, located in the cerebellum, basal ganglia, and other areas (Budson & Price, 2005).

The main structures involved in normal memory processing and storage include the *frontal lobes* and the *hippocampus.* The *frontal lobes* are active in both encoding and retrieval of episodic memories. Dysfunction of the frontal lobes may cause false memories—"remembering" events that never occurred. Early decline in the prefrontal cortex may underlie such common problems as inability to concentrate or pay attention and difficulty in performing a task with several steps. The *hippocampus,* a small, centrally located structure deep in the temporal lobe, seems critical to the ability to store new information in episodic memory. Lesions in the hippocampus or other brain structures involved in episodic memory may result in loss of recent memories (Budson & Price, 2005).

The brain often compensates for age-related declines in specialized regions by tapping other regions to help. Younger adults are more likely to use localized areas of the brain during challenging tasks, while older adults are more likely to use more diffuse activation and utilize more or different brain areas as compensatory mechanisms for declines (Reuter-Lorenz, Stanczak & Miller, 1999; Reuter-Lorenz et al., 2000; Park & Reuter-Lorenz, 2009). The brain's ability to shift functions may help explain why symptoms of Alzheimer's disease often do not appear until the disease is well advanced and previously unaffected regions of the brain, which have taken over for impaired regions, lose their own working capacity ("Alzheimer's Disease, Part I," 1998; Finch & Zelinski, 2005). By the time signs of damage show, the disease has likely existed for decades.

Problems in Encoding, Storage, and Retrieval Episodic memory is particularly vulnerable to the effects of aging, an effect that is aggravated as memory tasks become more complex or demanding (Cansino, 2009). Older adults seem to have more difficulty *encoding* new episodic memories, presumably because of difficulties in forming and later recalling a coherent and cohesive episode (Naveh-Benjamin, Brav & Levy, 2007). They tend to be less efficient and precise than younger adults in the use of strategies to make it easier to remember—for example, by arranging material alphabetically or creating mental associations (Craik & Byrd, 1982). Most studies have found that older and younger adults are about equally knowledgeable as to effective encoding strategies but that older adults tend to use them less frequently (Salthouse, 1991). Some research has found that training older adults in memory strategies results in fewer age-related declines and that the larger the number of strategies taught, the larger the effect on memory (Gross et al., 2012; Naveh-Benjamin et al., 2007). However, other researchers have argued that the memory gains are limited, do not generalize to tasks other than those participants are trained in, and do not result in improvements in general memory performance (Bellander, Eschen et al., 2017).

Another hypothesis is that material in *storage* may deteriorate to the point where retrieval becomes difficult or impossible. Some research suggests that a small increase in "storage failure" may occur with age (Lustig & Flegal, 2008). However, traces of decayed memories are likely to remain, and it may be possible to reconstruct them, or at least to relearn the material speedily (Camp & McKitrick, 1989; Chafetz, 1992). In particular, it appears as if memories that contain an emotional component are more resistant to the effects of decay (Kensinger, 2009). For example, studies have found that older adults are motivated to preserve memories that have positive emotional meaning to them (Reed, Chan & Mikels, 2014; Carstensen & Mikels, 2005). Thus emotional factors need to be considered in studying memory changes in old age.

We should keep in mind that most of the research on encoding, storage, and retrieval has been done in the laboratory and that results may not transfer to the real world (Kempe, Kalicinski & Memmert, 2015). For example, in daily diary studies, older adults were more likely to report memory failures on days when they experienced stress, suggesting stress is relevant (Neupert, Almeida, Mroczek & Spiro, 2006). As another example, memory failures of older adults in daily life often include prospective memory failures. Prospective memory involves remembering to do something in the future, such as remembering to call a friend later. Prospective memory declines with age and is a significant issue for many older adults. However, the research in this area is incomplete and does not illuminate the central processes that govern failure (Kliegel et al., 2016).

WISDOM

Wisdom has been defined as "exceptional breadth and depth of knowledge about the conditions of life and human affairs and reflective judgment about the application of this knowledge. It may involve insight and awareness of the uncertain, paradoxical nature of reality and may lead to *transcendence,* detachment from preoccupation with the self" (Kramer, 2003, p. 132). Quite simply, wisdom is the ability to navigate the messiness of life. It involves understanding how people work and how to accomplish goals. People who are wise, according to psychologists, are also comfortable with uncertainty and understand that different people have different viewpoints and that sometimes there is no one right answer.

The most extensive research on wisdom as a cognitive ability has been done by the late Paul Baltes and his colleagues. In a series of studies, they asked adults of various ages and occupations to think aloud about hypothetical dilemmas. Responses were rated according to whether they showed rich factual and procedural knowledge about the human condition and about dealing with life's problems. Other criteria were awareness that contextual circumstances can influence problems, that problems tend to lend themselves to multiple interpretations and solutions, and that choices of solutions depend on individual values, goals, and priorities (Baltes & Staudinger, 2000; Pasupathi, Staudinger & Baltes, 2001).

Wisdom is not necessarily a property of old age—or of any age. Instead, it appears to be a rather rare and complex phenomenon that shows relative stability or slight growth in certain individuals (Staudinger & Baltes, 1996; Staudinger, Smith & Baltes, 1992). A variety of factors, including personality, life experience, and self-reflective tendencies (Weststrate & Gluck, 2017; Wink & Staudinger, 2016; Shedlock & Cornelius, 2003), affect the propensity to be wise.

Research on physical functioning, cognition, and aging is more encouraging than some might expect. Older adults tend to make the most of their abilities, often exploiting gains in one area to offset declines in another. Research highlights the widely varying paths of physical and cognitive development among individuals.

summary and key terms

Old Age Today

- Efforts to combat ageism are making headway.
- The proportion of older people in the United States and world populations is greater than ever before and is expected to continue to grow. People over 80 are the fastest-growing age group.
- Although effects of primary aging may be beyond people's control, they often can avoid effects of secondary aging.
- Specialists in the study of aging sometimes refer to people between ages 65 and 74 as the *young old*, those over 75 as the *old old*, and those over 85 as the *oldest old*. However, these terms may be more useful when used to refer to functional age.

ageism, primary aging, secondary aging, activities of daily living (ADL), functional age, gerontology, geriatrics

PHYSICAL DEVELOPMENT

Longevity and Aging

- Life expectancy has increased dramatically.
- In general, life expectancy is greater in developed countries than in developing countries, among Hispanics and white Americans than among African Americans, and among women as compared to men.
- Recent gains in life expectancy come largely from progress toward reducing death rates from diseases affecting older people.
- Many older people are staying healthier longer, but then decline rapidly once their health starts to fail. This is known as morbidity compression and may offer clues to increasing life expectancy.
- Theories of biological aging fall into two categories: genetic-programming theories and variable-rate, or error, theories.
- Research on extension of the life span through genetic manipulation or caloric restriction has challenged the idea of a biological limit to the life span.

life expectancy, longevity, life span, senescence, genetic-programming theories, Hayflick limit, variable-rate theories, free radicals, survival curve

Physical Changes

- Changes in body systems and organs are highly variable. Reserve capacity declines.
- Although the brain changes with age, the changes are usually modest. They include loss of volume and weight and a slowing of responses. However, the brain can compensate for some problems by changing how it processes information.
- Vision and hearing problems may interfere with daily life but often can be corrected. Irreversible damage may result from age-related macular degeneration or glaucoma. Losses in taste and smell may lead to poor nutrition.
- Functional fitness interventions show promise. Training can improve muscular strength, balance, and reaction time. Older adults tend to be susceptible to accidents and falls.
- Older people tend to sleep less and dream less than before. Chronic insomnia or poor sleep can contribute to health problems.

- Many older adults remain sexually active.

reserve capacity, cataracts, age-related macular degeneration, glaucoma, functional fitness

Physical and Mental Health

- Most older people are reasonably healthy. Many have chronic conditions, but these usually do not greatly limit activities or interfere with daily life. Chronic conditions are less likely with a healthy lifestyle.
- Exercise and diet are important influences on health. Loss of teeth can seriously affect nutrition.
- Most older people are in good mental health. Depression, alcoholism, and many other conditions can be reversed with treatment; a few, such as Alzheimer's disease, are irreversible.
- Alzheimer's disease becomes more prevalent with age. It is highly heritable, but diet, exercise, and other lifestyle factors may play a part. Cognitive activity may be protective by building up a cognitive reserve that enables the brain to function under stress. Behavioral and drug therapies can slow deterioration. Mild cognitive impairment can be an early sign of the disease, and researchers are developing tools for early diagnosis.

dementia, Alzheimer's disease, Parkinson's disease, neurofibrillary tangles, amyloid plaque, cognitive reserve

COGNITIVE DEVELOPMENT

Aspects of Cognitive Development

- Older adults do better on the verbal portion of the Wechsler Adult Intelligence Scale than on the performance portion.
- The Seattle Longitudinal Study found that cognitive functioning in late adulthood is highly variable. Few people decline in all or most areas, and many people improve in some.
- Older adults are more effective in solving practical problems.
- A general slowdown in central nervous system functioning may affect the speed of information processing.
- Intelligence may be a predictor of longevity.
- Sensory memory, semantic memory, and procedural memory appear nearly as efficient in older adults as in younger adults. The capacity of working memory and episodic memory are often less efficient.
- Older adults have more problems with oral word retrieval and spelling than younger adults. Grammatical complexity and content of speech decline.
- Neurological changes and problems in encoding, storage, and retrieval may account for much of the decline in memory functioning in older adults. However, the brain can compensate for some age-related declines.
- Older people show considerable plasticity in cognitive performance and can benefit from training.
- According to Baltes's studies, wisdom is not age-related, but people of all ages give wiser responses to problems affecting their own age group.

Wechsler Adult Intelligence Scale (WAIS), sensory memory, working memory, episodic memory, semantic memory, procedural memory

Psychosocial Development in Late Adulthood

chapter 18

©Blend Images - KidStock/Getty Images

learning objectives

Discuss theories and research on personality changes in late adulthood.

Identify strategies and resources that contribute to older adults' well-being and mental health.

Discuss aging and adaptation to work and retirement.

Characterize the social relationships of aging adults.

In this chapter, we look at theory and research on psychosocial development in late adulthood and discuss such late-life options as work, retirement, and living arrangements and their impact on society's ability to support and care for an aging population. Finally, we look at relationships with families and friends, which greatly affect the quality of these last years.

Jimmy Carter, one of the most active ex-presidents in American history, won the Nobel Prize at age 78 for his continuing work in human rights, education, preventive health research, and conflict resolution.
©Nir Levy/Shutterstock

ego integrity versus despair
According to Erikson, the eighth and final stage of psychosocial development, in which people in late adulthood either achieve a sense of integrity of the self by accepting the lives they have lived, and thus accept death, or yield to despair that their lives cannot be relived.

Theory and Research on Personality Development

Most theorists view late adulthood as a developmental stage with its own special issues and tasks. It is a time when people can reexamine their lives, complete unfinished business, and decide how best to channel their energies and spend their remaining days, months, or years. Many older adults experience this last stage of life as a positive one.

Let's see what theory and research can tell us about personality in this final phase of the life span and about the psychosocial challenges and opportunities of aging.

ERIK ERIKSON: NORMATIVE ISSUES AND TASKS

For Erikson, the crowning achievement of late adulthood is a sense of *ego integrity*, or integrity of the self. In the eighth and final stage of the life span, **ego integrity versus despair,** older adults need to evaluate and accept their lives so as to accept death. Building on the outcomes of the seven previous stages, they struggle to achieve a sense of coherence and wholeness, rather than give way to despair over their inability to relive the past differently (Erikson, Erikson & Kivnick, 1986). People who succeed in this final, integrative task gain a sense of the meaning of their lives within the larger social order. The virtue that may develop during this stage is *wisdom,* an "informed and detached concern with life itself in the face of death itself" (Erikson, 1985, p. 61).

Wisdom, said Erikson, means accepting the life one has lived, without major regrets: without dwelling on "might-have-beens." It means accepting imperfection in the self, in parents, in children, and in life.

Although integrity must outweigh despair if this stage is to be resolved successfully, Erikson maintained that some despair is inevitable. People need to mourn—not only for their own misfortunes and lost chances but for the vulnerability and transience of the human condition.

Yet, Erikson believed, even as the body's functions weaken, people must maintain a "vital involvement" in society. On the basis of studies of life histories of people in their eighties, he concluded that ego integrity comes not just from reflecting on the past but also from continued stimulation and challenge—whether through political activity, fitness programs, creative work, or relationships with grandchildren (Erikson et al., 1986).

THE FIVE-FACTOR MODEL: PERSONALITY TRAITS IN OLD AGE

Does personality change in late life? What is the average pattern of personality change across the life course?

According to Erikson, ego integrity in late adulthood requires continuing stimulation and challenge, which, for this sculptor, come from creative work.
©kali9/ E+/Getty Images

Personality Stability and Change in Late Adulthood Generally, personality stability follows an inverted U-shaped curve. It is lowest in adolescence, peaks in mid-adulthood, and then declines slightly in late adulthood (Specht, Egloff & Schmukle, 2011; Terracciano, McCrae & Costa, 2010). Most of the personality changes seen in late adulthood are in the direction of increased stability, adaptability, and adjustment (Soto, John, Gosling & Potter, 2011; Hopwood et al., 2011).

While Costa and McCrae reported long-term stability in their data, the stability was in terms of *average levels* of various traits within a population, and people generally maintained their rank order. In other words, particularly outgoing people were likely to remain more outgoing than their peers, even if everyone became slightly more so over time.

Longitudinal and cross-sectional studies using a modified version of their original model have found continued change in late adulthood. Research has found decreases in neuroticism over time (Soto et al., 2011; Allemand, 2007); increases in agreeableness, self-confidence, warmth, and emotional stability (Soto et al., 2011; Roberts & Mroczek, 2008); and increases in conscientiousness (Soto et al., 2011; Donnellan

& Lucas, 2008) and declines in social vitality (gregariousness) and openness to experience (Roberts & Mroczek, 2008). Contrary to stereotypes of the elderly as rigid and set in their ways, there appear to be no age-related trends in inflexibility. In fact, more recent cohorts, as a whole, seem to be more flexible (that is, less rigid) than previous cohorts (Schaie, 2005).

Why do people show normative changes in personality characteristics? Some researchers argue that these processes are driven primarily by intrinsic genetic differences between people that unfold over time (Costa & McCrae, 2013). Other researchers argue that life experiences—getting married, joining the workforce, and so on—are the primary drivers of personality change (Roberts, Wood & Smith, 2005). Still others argue explicitly for a consideration both of genetic and environmental influences (Hopwood et al., 2011).

Personality as a Predictor of Emotionality, Health, and Well-Being Personality is a strong predictor of emotionality and subjective well-being—stronger in most respects than social relationships and health (Isaacowitz & Smith, 2003). Personality change can also have implications for physical and cognitive health. For example, people who remain stable on openness to experience and neuroticism enjoy better reasoning abilities and faster reaction time than those individuals whose levels change (Graham & Lachman, 2012).

In a 23-year longitudinal study, self-reported *negative* emotions such as restlessness, boredom, loneliness, unhappiness, and depression decreased with age. At the same time, *positive* emotionality—excitement, interest, pride, and a sense of accomplishment—tended to remain stable until late life and then declined only slightly and gradually (Charles, Reynolds & Gatz, 2001).

One explanation for this generally positive picture comes from socioemotional selectivity theory: As people get older, they tend to seek out activities and people that give them emotional gratification (English & Carestensen, 2014). Older adults are also better at regulating their emotions, thus they tend to be happier and more cheerful than younger adults and to experience negative emotions less often and more fleetingly (Urry & Gross, 2010; Jacques, Bessette-Symons & Cabeza, 2009). Additionally, older adults also show a bias in their information processing known as the positivity effect. Older adults are more likely to pay attention to, and then later remember, positive events than negative events (Reed, Chan & Mikels, 2014). Last, emotions are part and parcel of personality. For example, neuroticism is in many respects a characteristically negative way of viewing the world. Therefore, it is not surprising that personality variables might be related to general well-being and satisfaction with life (Lucas & Diener, 2009).

Two of the Big Five personality traits—extraversion and neuroticism—demonstrate this relationship. As Costa and McCrae (1980) predicted, people with *extraverted* personalities (outgoing and socially oriented) tend to report especially high levels of positive emotion initially and are more likely than others to retain their positivity throughout life (Charles et al., 2001; Isaacowitz & Smith, 2003). Subsequent brain imaging research has shown that positive affect appears to be a core feature of extraversion (Hermes, Hagemann, Naumann & Walter, 2011).

People with *neurotic* personalities (moody, touchy, anxious, and restless) tend to report negative and not positive emotions, and they tend to become even less positive as they age (Charles et al., 2001; Isaacowitz & Smith, 2003). Neuroticism is a far more powerful predictor of moods and mood disorders than variables such as age, health status, education, or gender (Siedlecki, Tucker-Drop, Oishi & Salthouse, 2008). Highly neurotic people who become more neurotic as they age have low survival rates, possibly because they are likely to smoke or use alcohol or drugs to help calm their negative emotions and because they are ineffective in managing stress (Mroczek & Spiro, 2007). In contrast, *conscientiousness,* or dependability, has been found to predict health and mortality, most likely because conscientious people tend to avoid risky behaviors and to engage in activities that promote their health (Friedman & Kern, 2014; Martin, Friedman & Schwartz, 2007). The riskiest combination appears to be when individuals are both high in neuroticism as well as low in conscientiousness, as both these patterns are associated with a higher risk of inflammatory responses in the body (Sutin et al., 2010).

Well-Being in Late Adulthood

In general, older adults have fewer mental disorders and are happier and more satisfied with life than younger adults (Mroczek & Kolarz, 1998; Yang, 2008). In fact, a recent study of 340,000 adults showed that happiness is high at approximately 18 years of age, declines until people reach 50 years of age, and then tends to rise again until 85 years of age—at that point reaching levels even higher than in the teenage years (Stone, Schwartz, Broderick & Deaton, 2010). However, for some adults there is a sharp and rapid decline in well-being and life satisfaction approximately 3 to 5 years before death (Gerstorf et al., 2010; St. John, Mackenzie & Menec, 2015).

The rise in happiness later in life may in part reflect the value of a mature outlook, but it also may reflect the selective survival of happier people. Still, some cohort variations and social disparities exist. For example, baby boomers report lower levels of happiness than do earlier and later cohorts, perhaps due to the immense size of their generation and the resulting competitive strains for schooling, jobs, and economic security, as well as the turbulent societal events of their formative years. Gender, racial/ethnic, and educational disparities in happiness have narrowed or, in the case of gender, disappeared, especially since the mid-1990s. Furthermore, social disparities may have less impact in old age as biological changes, life events, the ability to cope with stress, and access to social welfare and support services play a more important role (Yang, 2008).

With respect to the sharp "terminal drop" in well-being shortly before death, a variety of explanations have been proposed. For example, it has been argued that events more common in the last years of life—the loss of a spouse, increasing mobility limitations, deteriorating health, or the knowledge that the end of life is drawing near—may lead to the declines (Gerstorf et al., 2010). Researchers have also pointed out that satisfaction with various parts of life need to be examined separately. For example, satisfaction with health, housing, and recreation has not been found to be associated with mortality risk, while low satisfaction with religion, self-esteem, and finances has (St. John, Mackenzie & Menec, 2015).

COPING AND MENTAL HEALTH

coping
Adaptive thinking or behavior aimed at reducing or relieving stress that arises from harmful, threatening, or challenging conditions.

Coping is adaptive thinking or behavior aimed at reducing or relieving stress that arises from harmful, threatening, or challenging conditions. It is an important aspect of mental health. Let's look at two theoretical approaches to the study of coping: adaptive defenses and the cognitive-appraisal model. Then we'll examine a support system to which many older adults turn: religion.

George Vaillant: Adaptive Defenses What makes for positive mental health in old age? According to prospective studies covering more than 70 years, an important predictive factor is the use of mature *adaptive defenses* in coping with problems earlier in life.

Vaillant (2000) looked at the survivors of his earlier studies as well as at a subsample of women from Terman's study of gifted California schoolchildren born about 1910. Those who, in old age, showed the best psychosocial adjustment were those who, earlier in adulthood, had used such mature adaptive defenses as altruism, humor, suppression (keeping a stiff upper lip), anticipation (planning for the future), and sublimation (redirecting negative emotions into productive pursuits).

How do adaptive defenses work? According to Vaillant (2000), they can change people's perceptions of realities they are powerless to change. For example, in the studies just mentioned, the use of adaptive defenses predicted *subjective* physical functioning even though it did not predict *objective* physical health as measured by physicians.

cognitive-appraisal model
Model of coping, proposed by Lazarus and Folkman, that holds that, on the basis of continuous appraisal of their relationship with the environment, people choose appropriate coping strategies to deal with situations that tax their normal resources.

Adaptive defenses may be unconscious or intuitive. In contrast, the cognitive-appraisal model, to which we turn now, emphasizes consciously chosen coping strategies.

Cognitive-Appraisal Model In the **cognitive-appraisal model** (Lazarus & Folkman, 1984), people respond to stressful or challenging situations on the basis of two types of analyses. In *primary appraisal,* people analyze a situation and decide, at some level, whether or not the situation is a threat to their well-being. In *secondary appraisal,* people evaluate what can be done to prevent harm and choose a coping strategy to handle the situation. Coping includes anything an individual thinks or does in trying to adapt to stress, regardless of how well it works. Choosing the most appropriate strategy and adapting to the various stressors of life requires a continuous reappraisal of the relationship between person and environment.

Coping Strategies: Problem-Focused versus Emotion-Focused Coping strategies may be either problem-focused or emotion-focused. **Problem-focused coping** involves the use of *instrumental,* or action-oriented, strategies to eliminate, manage, or improve a stressful condition. For example, some students may feel they are capable of learning the relevant material and can do well on an upcoming exam if they try hard enough. To achieve this, they may use such problem-focused coping strategies as going to the professor for extra help or spending more time studying. By addressing the source of stress, people using problem-focused coping seek to lessen any harm to the self.

Emotion-focused coping, by contrast, involves attempting to manage the emotional response to a stressful situation to relieve its physical or psychological impact. People are more likely to use this coping strategy when they conclude that little or nothing can be done about the situation itself. Thus they direct their energy toward "feeling better" rather than toward any actions meant to change the situation. For example, when faced with a difficult test, some students may select coping strategies that focus on emotions rather than actions. They might ignore the upcoming test and go out with friends instead of studying, decide the class is not important after all, or become angry with the professor for being unfair. There are two types of emotion-focused coping: *proactive* (confronting or expressing one's emotions or seeking social support) and *passive* (avoidance, denial, suppression of emotions, or acceptance of the situation as it is).

Age Differences in Choice of Coping Styles Older adults tend to do more emotion-focused coping than younger people (Blanchard-Fields, 2007; Trouillet, Doan-Van-Hay, Launay & Martin, 2011; Melendez, Mayordomo, Sancho & Tomas, 2012); this is particularly true when looking at the oldest old (Martin et al., 2008). Generally, emotion-focused coping is less adaptive than problem-focused coping, but this is only true when something can realistically be done about the problem. When a solution is not available, it may be more adaptive to control negative or unpleasant emotions. When both emotion- and problem-focused coping are used together, a wider and more flexible range of responses to stressful events is possible.

In studies in which young, middle-age, and older adults were asked how they would deal with various kinds of problems, participants, regardless of age, most often picked problem-focused strategies. Adults of all ages were more likely to use emotion-focused coping in highly emotional or stressful situations (such as that of a divorced man who is only allowed to see his child on weekends but who wants more contact), but older adults chose emotion-focused strategies (such as doing nothing, waiting until the child is older, or trying not to worry about it) more often than younger adults did (Blanchard-Fields et al., 2004).

Emotion-focused coping can be useful in coping with what the family therapist Pauline Boss (2007) calls **ambiguous loss.** Boss applies that term to losses that are not clearly defined or do not bring closure, such as the loss of a still-living loved one to Alzheimer's disease or the loss of a homeland, which elderly immigrants may feel as long as they live. In such situations, experience may teach people to accept what they cannot change—a lesson often reinforced by religion.

Coping styles are also related to physical well-being. In general, happier people are healthier. Why does this link exist? Research suggests that adaptive coping is related to health via stress hormone pathways (Carver, 2007). In one study of more than 500 older adults, those adults who used problem-focused coping strategies and sought social support in the face of stressful events showed lower levels of cortisol, a stress hormone, over the course of the day (O'Donnell, Badrick, Kumari & Steptoe, 2008). This is important because higher cortisol can lead to declines in health over time. For instance, in another study, older adults who did not use adaptive coping strategies *and* who had

---

problem-focused coping

In the cognitive-appraisal model, coping strategy directed toward eliminating, managing, or improving a stressful situation.

emotion-focused coping

In the cognitive-appraisal model, coping strategy directed toward managing the emotional response to a stressful situation so as to lessen its physical or psychological impact.

ambiguous loss

A loss that is not clearly defined or does not bring closure.

Religious activity seems to help many people cope with stress and loss in later life, and some research suggests that its effect on health and well-being may be real. ©ESB Professional/Shutterstock

high cortisol showed more functional disabilities (i.e., more problems with activities of daily life) over time. Neither those adults who had high cortisol and coped effectively, nor those adults who had low cortisol showed similar declines (Wrosch, Miller & Schulz, 2009).

Does Religion or Spirituality Affect Health and Well-Being? As a whole, older adults today are more religious than younger adults. For example, 38 percent of younger millennials (born between 1990 and 1996) say that religion is very important in their lives. However, 59 percent of baby boomers (born from 1946 to 1964) say the same, and for those over the age of 72, the number rises to 67 percent (Pew Research Center, 2015). Religion seems to play a supportive role for many older people and can be part of their coping strategy (Melendez, Mayordomo, Sancho & Tomas, 2012). Religion may benefit older people by providing social support, encouraging a healthy lifestyle, giving the perception of control over life through prayer, fostering positive emotional states, reducing stress, and using faith in God as a way of interpreting misfortunes (Seybold & Hill, 2001). But does religion actually improve health and well-being?

Many studies suggest a positive link between religion or spirituality and health (Lawler-Row & Elliott, 2009). In fact, a review of studies with relatively sound methodology found a 25 percent reduction in risk of mortality among healthy adults who attended religious services weekly (Powell, Shahabi & Thoresen, 2003). Other research has found positive associations between religiosity or spirituality and measures of health, well-being, marital satisfaction, and psychological functioning, and negative associations with depression, suicide, delinquency, criminality, and drug and alcohol use (Koenig, 2012; Seybold & Hill, 2001; Bjorklof, Engedal, Selbaek, Kouwenhoven & Helvik, 2013; Green & Elliott, 2010). It seems that part of the reason for the positive links between health and spirituality is because people who belong to a church are more likely to engage in healthy behaviors and have higher levels of social support (Lawler-Row & Elliott, 2009).

Relatively little of the research on religion and spirituality has been done with racial/ethnic minorities. In one such study, older Mexican Americans who attended church once a week had a 32 percent lower mortality risk than those who never attended (Hill, Angel, Ellison & Angel, 2005). Similar results have been found for Chinese people, with a 21 percent reduction in mortality risk for frequent church attendees as compared to infrequent attendees (Zeng, Gu & George, 2011). For elderly black people, religion is closely related to life satisfaction and well-being (Coke & Twaite, 1995; Krause, 2004a). A special factor is the belief held by many black people that the church helps sustain them in confronting racial injustice (Ellison, Musick, & Henderson, 2008).

MODELS OF "SUCCESSFUL," OR "OPTIMAL," AGING

With a growing number of active, healthy older adults, the concept of aging has shifted. *Successful,* or *optimal, aging* has largely replaced the idea that aging results from inevitable, intrinsic processes of loss and decline. Given that modifiable factors play a role in at least some aspects of aging, it follows that some people may age more successfully than others (Rowe & Kahn, 1997).

A considerable body of work has identified three main components of successful aging: (1) avoidance of disease or disease-related disability, (2) maintenance of high physical and cognitive functioning, and (3) sustained, active engagement in social and productive activities (activities, paid or unpaid, that create social value). Successful agers tend to have social support, both emotional and material, which aids mental health; and they tend to stay active and productive and to perceive low levels of stress in their lives (Rowe & Kahn, 1997; Moore et al., 2015). Another approach emphasizes subjective well-being and satisfaction with life (Jopp & Smith, 2006; Cho, Martin, Poon, & Georgia Centenarian Study, 2014). Agreement on what constitutes successful aging is surprisingly absent (Martinson & Berridge, 2014). However, a meta-analysis of studies that included quantitative data as well as a definition of "successful aging" found that approximately one-third of adults over the age of 60 engage in successful aging (Depp & Jeste, 2009).

Many people argue that the definitions of *successful,* or *optimal, aging* are value-laden. These terms may put pressure on elderly people to meet standards they cannot or do not wish to meet. The concept of successful aging, according to these critics, does not pay enough attention to the constraints that may limit lifestyle choices. Not all adults have the good genes, education, and favorable circumstances to "construct the kind of life they choose." An unintended result of labeling older adults as "successful" or "unsuccessful" may be to blame the victims and drive them to self-defeating, antiaging, strategies. It also tends to demean old age itself and to deny the importance of accepting, or adapting to, what cannot be changed (Holstein & Minkler, 2003). Moreover, the concept of successful aging is culturally bound. Western ideals such as independence, autonomy, control, and continued productivity are presented as the ideal. However, different cultures may not view these traits in the same way (Lamb, 2014).

Keeping these concerns in mind, let's look at some classic and current theories and research about aging well.

Disengagement Theory versus Activity Theory Who is making a healthier adjustment to old age: a person who peacefully watches the world go by from a rocking chair or one who keeps busy from morning till night? According to **disengagement theory,** a normal part of aging involves a gradual reduction in social involvement and greater preoccupation with the self. According to **activity theory,** the more active older people remain, the better they age.

Disengagement theory was one of the first theories in gerontology. Its proponents (Cumming & Henry, 1961) regarded disengagement as a normative, or typical, part of aging. They argued that awareness of the approach of death and declines in physical functioning resulted in a gradual, inevitable withdrawal from social roles. Moreover, because society stops providing useful roles for the older adult, the disengagement is mutual—others do not try to stop it. Introspection and a quieting of the emotions also accompany disengagement.

For a time this approach was influential, but more than five decades of research has provided little support for disengagement theory, and its influence has largely waned (Achenbaum & Bengtson, 1994). This approach may have reflected beliefs about aging at the time it was developed (Moody, 2009) rather than describing a normative and healthy developmental process.

The second approach, *activity theory,* takes the opposing viewpoint. In this theory, we are what we do (Moody, 2009). Rather than retreating from life, adults who age successfully tend to remain engaged with social roles and connections. The more active they remain in those roles, the more satisfied with life they are likely to be. When they lose a role, such as when they retire, they find a substitute role, such as volunteering (Lemon, Bengstun & Peterson, 1972; Neugarten, Havinghurst & Tobin, 1968). Research generally supports this approach, showing that people who retain their major role identities tend to report greater well-being and better mental health (Greenfield & Marks, 2004). For example, retired adults who continued or began to volunteer during the course of one longitudinal study were less likely to show the declines in well-being that other adults did (Wahrendorf & Siegrist, 2010).

How has this theory held up? As originally framed, activity theory is now regarded as overly simplistic. Moreover, research did not provide strong empirical support for the major postulates (Bengtson & DeLiema, 2016). For example, while early research did suggest that activity was associated with life satisfaction (Neugarten et al., 1968), the interpretation of this finding may have been flawed. Rather than activity driving satisfaction, it may have been relationships that were responsible for the effect. People who remain active are more likely to maintain high-quality social relationships, and the presence of these relationships is likely to positively affect life satisfaction (Litwin & Shiovitz-Ezra, 2006). In addition, a good proportion of disengaged people are nonetheless happy with their lives, and recent research suggests that disengagement and activity theory may both speak to successful aging. Specifically, adults who believed themselves to be aging successfully struck a balance between self-acceptance and being happy with themselves as they were and remaining simultaneously engaged and involved with life (Reichstadt, Sengupta, Depp, Palinkas & Jeste, 2010). Findings such as these suggest that activity may work best for most people but disengagement may be appropriate for others, and that it may be unwise to make generalizations about a particular pattern of successful aging (Moen, Dempster-McClain & Williams, 1992; Musick, Herzog & House, 1999).

disengagement theory
Theory of aging that holds that successful aging is characterized by mutual withdrawal of the older person and society.

activity theory
Theory of aging that holds that to age successfully a person must remain as active as possible.

Older people who feel useful to others, as this grandparent does to his grandson, are more likely to age successfully.
©Steve Mason/ Photodisc/GettyImages

Continuity Theory Are you happiest being out and about, visiting friends, and staying busy? Or do you prefer a quiet night spent watching a movie by yourself? What you prefer prior to the later stages of life may influence what you prefer when you reach them. In other words, if you are happy being active now, you are likely to be happy being active later. However, if you are happy being less active now, you may prefer a quieter lifestyle later in life too (Pushkar et al., 2009). This is the primary premise of **continuity theory** (Atchley, 1989). In this approach, people's need to maintain a connection between past and present is emphasized, and activity is viewed as important, not for its own sake but because it represents continuation of a previous lifestyle. For example, many retired people are happiest pursuing work or leisure activities similar to those they enjoyed in the past (Pushkar et al., 2010). For example, many professors, when given the choice, will opt not to retire (Dorfman, 2009). Moreover, even after they retire, the majority remain involved in professional activities similar to those they participated in when working (Dorfman & Kolarik, 2005). People who, in middle age, enjoyed leisure activities such as reading books, pursuing a hobby, or gardening tended to engage in these activities in old age as well (Agahi, Ahacic & Parker, 2006).

Continuity in activities is not always possible because some older adults must cut back on participation in favorite events due to visual, motor, or cognitive impairments. Additionally, sometimes the environment is such that they do not have a choice. For example, sometimes older adults retire not because they want to, but because they are forced to do so. Older adults are likely to be happier, however, if they can maintain their favorite activities to some extent. So, for instance, if adults who are forced to retire are able to find bridge employment (a job following retirement), they tend to show fewer declines in well-being (Dingemans & Henkenls, 2015).

The Role of Productivity Some researchers focus on productive activity, any action that provides a contribution to society, as a key to aging well. Productive activity, whether paid or unpaid, has been found to have positive effects on older adults. For example, a recent meta-analysis found that across 73 studies, volunteering was associated with a host of positive outcomes, including reduced depression, better health and functional ability, and lower mortality risk. The authors suggest that participating in volunteering keeps older adults physically, cognitively, and socially active, and this increased engagement then positively affects health indices (Anderson et al., 2014). Generally, the more activities adults are involved in, and the more time spent on them, the greater the positive effects (Vozikaki, Linardakis, Micheli & Philalithis, 2017; Baker, Cahalin, Gerst & Burr, 2005). Similar effects have been found for working, but not for caregiving activities (Choi, Stewart & Dewey, 2013; Stav, Hallenen, Lane & Arbesman, 2012; Pinquart & Sorenson, 2003).

Some research suggests that frequent participation in leisure activities can be as beneficial to health and well-being as participation in productive activities, although this effect may be stronger for women (Agahi & Parker, 2008). Social relationships appear to be important here (Stav et al., 2012). Those adults who perceive their social relationships as positive are more likely to engage in leisure activities, and leisure activities are then associated with better health outcomes (Chang, Wray & Lin, 2014). However, this does not mean that leisure activities that are more solitary in nature do not have any benefits. For example, both gardening (Wang & MacMillan, 2013) and reading (Menec, 2003) have been associated with well-being as well.

Why do some older adults not engage in productive activities? Some may merely not be interested. However, it is also the case that discriminatory attitudes and stereotypes about the elderly, as well as social program structures and policies, sometimes make it difficult to get older people engaged. This is unfortunate; elderly people have a great deal of wisdom, experience, and often time to contribute. Both society and aging adults would benefit from greater inclusion and their participation in productive engagement (Gonzales, Matz-Costa & Morrow-Howell, 2015).

Selective Optimization with Compensation According to Paul Baltes and his colleagues (Baltes, 1997), successful aging involves strategies that enable people to adapt to the changing balance of growth and decline throughout life. In childhood, resources are primarily used for growth, and in early adulthood resources are used to maximize reproductive fitness. In old age, resources are increasingly directed toward the maintenance of health and the management of loss (Baltes & Smith, 2004; Jopp & Smith, 2006). Older adults allocate these resources via a process called **selective optimization with compensation (SOC).** SOC involves developing abilities that allow for maximum gain, as well as developing abilities that compensate for decline and could lead to loss. According to SOC, older adults conserve their resources by:

- *Selecting* fewer and more meaningful activities or goals.
- *Optimizing,* or making the most of, the resources they have to achieve their goals.
- *Compensating* for losses by using resources in alternative ways to achieve their goals.

For example, the celebrated concert pianist Arthur Rubenstein gave his farewell concert at age 89. He was able to compensate for his age-related memory loss by selecting a smaller repertoire of material to play and by practicing longer each day to optimize his performance. He also compensated for declines in motor abilities by slowing down his playing immediately before fast movements, thus heightening the contrast and making the music sound faster (Baltes & Baltes, 1990).

The same life-management strategies apply to psychosocial development. According to Carstensen's (1991, 1995, 1996) socioemotional selectivity theory, older adults become more selective about social contacts, keeping up with friends and relatives who can best meet their current needs for emotional satisfaction. In this way, even though older adults may have fewer friends, the friends that they do have are closer and provide more rewarding social contact (English & Carstenson, 2014).

Research has found that use of SOC is associated with positive developmental outcomes, including greater well-being (Baltes & Smith, 2004). Eventually, though, older people may reach the limit of their available resources, and compensatory efforts may no longer seem to work. In a 4-year longitudinal study of 762 adults, compensatory efforts increased up to age 70 but then declined. Adjusting one's personal standards to changes in what is possible to achieve may be essential to maintaining a positive outlook on life (Rothermund & Brandtstädter, 2003). The argument about what constitutes successful or optimal aging and what contributes to well-being in old age is far from settled and may never be. One thing is clear: People differ greatly in the ways they can and do live—and want to live—in the later years of life.

Practical and Social Issues Related to Aging

Whether and when to retire are among the most crucial lifestyle decisions people make as they approach late adulthood. These decisions affect their financial situation and emotional state, as well as the ways they spend their waking hours and the ways they relate to family and friends. The need to provide financial support for large numbers of retired older people also has serious implications for society, especially as the baby boom generation starts to retire. Another social issue is the need for appropriate living arrangements and care for older people who can no longer manage on their own. (Window on the World reports on stereotypes of older people worldwide.)

WORK AND RETIREMENT

Retirement took hold in many industrialized countries during the late nineteenth and early twentieth centuries as life expectancy increased. In the United States, the creation of the Social Security system in the 1930s, together with company-sponsored pension plans negotiated by labor unions, made it possible for many older workers to retire with financial security. Eventually, mandatory retirement at age 65 became almost universal. However, in 1983, an amendment was passed in which the age for full eligibility for Social Security retirement benefits was raised to 67 years for people born in 1960 or later, and more stringent penalties were instituted for early retirement at age 62. Despite these changes, the number of people receiving benefits continued to rise in concert with the changing demographics of the United States (Duggan, Singleton & Song, 2007), reaching a peak in 2003 and remaining relatively stable from that point on. In 2013, the average age of retirement for men was 64 years and for women 62 years (Munnell, 2015).

Today, compulsory retirement has been virtually outlawed in the United States as a form of age discrimination (except for certain occupations, such as airline pilots), and the line between work and retirement is not as clear as it used to be. There are no longer strong norms concerning the timing of retirement, how to plan for it, and what to do afterward. The biggest factors in the decision usually are health and financial considerations (Kim & Moen, 2001). However, there are multiple interrelated issues, including marital status, current assets and liabilities, the status of dependents, the nature of the work and whether or not age will make that challenging, and the current state of the job market (Gibaldi, 2013). Only 40 percent of those older adults who stop working in their fifties and sixties stop for good; the remainder go back to work either part- or full-time before permanently exiting the workforce (Maestas, 2010).

Trends in Late-Life Work and Retirement In the United States, most adults who *can* retire *do* retire; and, with increasing longevity, they spend more time in retirement than in the past (Dobriansky et al., 2007). However, the proportion of workers older than 65 years of age has increased sharply. This graying of the working population is expected to continue to increase through 2024 and is the fastest growing labor participation group. Projections suggest that by that time, 41 million people aged 55 and older, 13 million of whom will be 65 and older, will be in the workforce (U.S. Bureau of Labor Statistics, 2017).

How Does Age Affect Attitudes toward Work and Job Performance? Prior to the economic downturn that began in 2007, people who continued to work after age 65 typically liked their work and did not find it unduly stressful. They tended to be better educated and in better health than those who retired earlier (Kiefer, Summer & Shirey, 2001; Kim & Moen, 2001). However, the changing economic climate has meant that many older workers now work not because they want to but because they are forced to by their financial situation and escalating medical costs (Sterns, 2010).

Contrary to ageist stereotypes, older workers can be as productive as younger workers. Although they may work more slowly than younger people, they are more accurate and perform equally well on most jobs (Czaja & Sharit, 1998; Salthouse & Maurer, 1996; McDaniel, Pesta & Banks, 2012). A key factor may be experience rather than age: When older people perform better, it may be because they have been on a job, or have done similar work, longer (Cleveland & Lim, 2007). The greatest declines in productivity for older workers are seen when problem solving, learning, or speed are important. When experience or verbal abilities matter more, productivity of older workers matches or even exceeds that of younger workers (McDaniel et al., 2012; Skirbekk, 2008).

In the United States, the Age Discrimination in Employment Act (ADEA), which applies to firms with 20 or more employees, protects workers ages 40 and older from being denied a job, fired, paid less, or forced to retire because of age. Still, many employers exert subtle pressures on older employees (Landy, 1994) and age discrimination is still a factor in employment for older adults (Neumark, 2008). More than 80 percent of older workers experience at least one instance of age discrimination a year (Chou & Choi, 2011).

Life after Retirement Retirement is not a single event but a dynamic adjustment process that is best conceptualized as a form of decision making. There are five broad categories of resources that help determine how well a person adjusts to retirement: (1) individual attributes such as health and financial status; (2) preretirement job-related variables such as job stress; (3) family-related variables such as marriage quality and dependents; (4) retirement transition-related variables such as retirement planning; and (5) postretirement activities such as bridge employment and volunteer work (Wang, Henkens & van Solinge, 2011).

The research on adjustment to retirement has supported this model. For example, those adults in better health at retirement tend to, not surprisingly, have better health after retirement. Preretirement financial planning leads to a greater likelihood of savings and a better

on the world

AGING AND AGEISM: STEREOTYPES WORLDWIDE

In America, Australia, the United Kingdom, and many other countries around the world, youth and beauty are idealized and the elderly are often seen as frail, useless, childlike, and a burden to society. In the media, elders are often portrayed as sick, lonely, and mentally incompetent. Late adulthood is thought of as a time of decline, worry, fear, and loss. The idea that the elderly should have hope or anything helpful to contribute to society is rarely considered (Quine, Morrell & Kendig, 2007).

These negative age stereotypes endorse segregation and discrimination in society, especially in the workplace and health care facilities. Ageism directly undermines political support for programs benefitting older people, including access to health care and medical treatments (Cheng & Heller, 2009). Ageism can directly affect the elderly as they often internalize societal views, hastening physical and mental decline. It has been found that adopting these negative stereotypes can decrease life span up to 7.5 years (Scheve & Venzon, 2017).

One American study found that 84 percent of elders still in the work force reported being subjected to ageism at work. Reports include insulting jokes, patronizing behavior, disrespectful attitudes or gestures, and comments about being slow, frail, and sickly (Roscigno, Mong, Bryon & Tester, 2007). A similar study was done in Slovenian countries and found that older employees were stereotyped as being less motivated, less adaptable, not innovative, and slower (Rozman, Treven & Cancer, 2016). Though the negative stereotypes are present, both studies concluded that older employees are often better workers, showing less absenteeism, higher commitment, more knowledge, more professionalism, and loyalty to their companies (Roscigno et al., 2007; Rozman et al., 2016).

The belief that elders are treated with reverence and respect in other cultures penetrates our knowledge of Asian countries and many less industrialized nations. However, research shows that there are both positive and negative beliefs about the elderly in these countries (Vauclair, Hanke, Haung & Dominic, 2017). Although elders are often looked upon for their wisdom, social class, gender, and income all play a role in how elders are treated. Cultures with high levels of poverty or with harsh living conditions provide less care for the elderly. The treatment of elders depends much on their usefulness and contributions they can provide to others (McGuire, 2017). Elder abuse is common and often seen as the norm. In parts of India elderly widows are considered "ill omens" and are sent to live in widow villages, isolated from their family and society (Cheng & Heller, 2009).

The way we view the aging process influences how we age. For example, in the Tarahumara society in Mexico the belief is that people get stronger as they age. Many elders are still able to run great distances and lead very healthy active lives (Scheve & Venzon, 2017). Another example is 106-year-old Fauja Singh. The Indian ran his first marathon in his late eighties. His advice: "Exercise daily, eat less, and resist meaningless temptations; with time my vision and hearing have deteriorated, but I'm very fit for my age" (Singh, 2017). Research has shown that elders with positive attitudes about aging show lower rates of mental illness, quicker recovery times from illness and stress, and less cognitive decline, and they live longer (McGuire, 2017).

Social policies are being created focused on increasing education, developing positive images of the elderly and supporting the continuation of independence and resources for elders. The goals are to increase hope for the future and reduce fears among the elderly and include assisting with financial and health struggles (Quine, Morrell & Kendig, 2007).

what's your view

What do you think we can do to combat negative stereotypes about the elderly? How can you challenge your own beliefs about the elderly?

established long-term budgeting plan. Moreover, married retirees generally report higher levels of well-being, although this is true only while one partner continues to work. Upon retirement, retirees in happy marriages and with fewer dependents show higher levels of well-being than other groups. For example, those retirees who lose a partner in retirement show lower well-being. The voluntariness of retirement also matters; those retirees who retire earlier than planned or against their will also show declines in well-being (Wang & Shi, 2014).

About 500,000 older Americans volunteer through the Senior Corps program. These volunteers are building a home for a low-income family through Habitat for Humanity. ©Hill Street Studios/Blend Images/Getty Images

Volunteer work is closely tied to well-being during retirement (Hao, 2008). Volunteering during retirement has been positively associated with good health and negatively associated with depression, functional limitations, and mortality (Wahrendorf, Blane, Matthews & Siegrist, 2016). Volunteering also predicts positive emotionality and protects against declines in well-being associated with major role-identity losses (Greenfield & Marks, 2004) and declines in mental health (Hao, 2008). While older adults who volunteer are more likely to be higher in resources than those who do not (Li & Ferraro, 2005), it nonetheless does appear that volunteering has a positive effect on older adults.

HOW DO OLDER ADULTS FARE FINANCIALLY?

Since the 1960s, Social Security has provided the largest share of older Americans' income—33 percent in 2017 (Social Security Administration, 2018). Other sources of income include income from assets (13 percent), private pensions (19 percent), and earnings (30 percent) (Federal Interagency Forum on Aging-Related Statistics, 2010). Dependence on Social Security and asset income rises dramatically with age and decreases with income level (Federal Interagency Forum on Aging-Related Statistics, 2016).

Social Security and other government programs, such as Medicare, which covers basic health insurance for U.S. residents who are 65 or older or are disabled, have enabled today's older Americans, as a group, to live fairly comfortably. The proportion of older adults living in poverty has fallen from 35 percent in 1959, to 29 percent in 1966, and then to 10 percent in 2014 (Administration on Aging, 2016; Federal Interagency Forum on Aging-Related Statistics, 2016). The poverty rate for older adults, while still lower than that of the total population, was the only demographic group to show an increase in 2016 (Semega, Fontenot & Kollar, 2017). As the U.S. population grays, and as proportionately fewer workers contribute to the Social Security system, it seems likely that benefits will decline, though the timing and severity of the problem are in dispute (Sawicki, 2005).

Women—especially if they are single, widowed, separated, or divorced or if they were previously poor or worked only part-time in middle age—are more likely (12 percent) than men (7 percent) to live in poverty in old age (Federal Interagency Forum on Aging-Related Statistics, 2016). There are also ethnic differences. Older African Americans and Hispanic Americans, at rates of 23 and 17 percent, respectively, are more likely to live in poverty than older white Americans at 7.4 percent (Federal Interagency Forum on Aging-Related Statistics, 2010).The highest poverty rates are among older Hispanic women (20 percent) and older African American women (21 percent) who live alone (Federal Interagency Forum on Aging-Related Statistics, 2016).

LIVING ARRANGEMENTS

In developing countries, older adults typically live with adult children and grandchildren in multigenerational households, though this custom is declining. In developed countries, most older people live alone or with a partner or spouse (Kinsella & Phillips, 2005).

In the United States, in 2014, about 7 percent of adults aged 65 and older live in senior housing of various types, generally taking advantage of supportive services. Because of women's greater life expectancy, about 70 percent of noninstitutionalized men but only about 45 percent of noninstitutionalized women lived with a spouse. Twenty percent of the men and 36 percent of the women lived alone, although the proportion living alone increases with advancing age. Approximately 10 percent of the men and 19 percent of the women lived with other relatives or nonrelatives, including partners and children (Federal Interagency Forum on Aging-Related Statistics, 2016; Figure 18.1).

Aging in Place Most older adults in industrialized countries prefer, if possible, to stay in their own homes and communities (Aurand, Miles & Usher, 2014). This option, called **aging in place,** makes sense for those who can manage on their own or with minimal help. Most informal caregivers, such as family, who provide aging in place care do so willingly,

aging in place
Remaining in one's own home, with or without assistance, in later life.

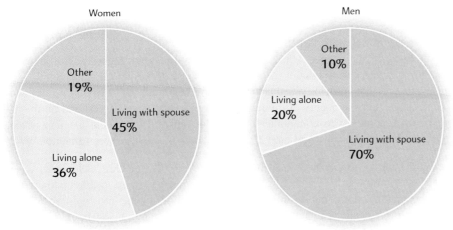

Women

Men

Other
19%

Living with spouse
45%

Living alone
36%

Other
10%

Living alone
20%

Living with spouse
70%

FIGURE 18.1

Living Arrangements of Noninstitutionalized Men and Women Age 65 and Over, United States, 2015

Women are more likely to live alone (especially as they get older), whereas men are more likely to live with a spouse. The "Other" category includes those living with adult children, other relatives, or nonrelatives.

Source: Federal Interagency Forum on Aging-Related Statistics. *Older Americans update 2016: Key indicators of well-being.* Washington, DC: U.S. Government Printing Office, 2016.

but it can be a significant source of stress and worry for them (Sanders, Stone, Meador & Parker, 2010). Partially in response to this, naturally occurring retirement communities (NORCs) are neighborhoods in which a large proportion of residents happen to be older adults. In general, NORCs are not the result of deliberate planning; rather, they are the result of the simultaneous aging of community residents or migration of large numbers of older adults to a particular location. A national initiative of the U.S. Administration on Aging seeks to enhance supportive services for people living in NORCs (Bernstein, 2008), a process that is likely to be of growing importance with the graying of the population.

For older people with impairments that make it hard to get along entirely on their own, minor support—such as meals, transportation, and home health aides—often can help them stay put. So can ramps, grab bars, and other modifications within the home (Newman, 2003). Most older people do not need much help; and those who do can often remain in the community if they have at least one person to depend on. In fact, the single most important factor keeping people out of institutions is being married (Nihtilä & Martikainen, 2008). Increasingly, technological aids such as activity monitoring, wandering detection, and e-health applications are being used to help keep older adults physically safe and connected to others (Peek et al., 2014).

Living Alone The growth of elderly single-person households has been spurred by greater longevity, increased benefits and pensions, increased home ownership, more elder-friendly housing, more availability of community support, and reduced public assistance with nursing home costs. Because women live longer than men and are more likely to be widowed, older women in the most developed countries are more likely than older men to live alone (Kinsella & Phillips, 2005). Older people living alone are more likely than older people with spouses to be poor (Administration on Aging, 2016) and to end up in institutions (Kasper, Pezzin & Rice, 2010).

It might seem that older people who live alone, particularly the oldest old, would be lonely. However, such factors as personality, cognitive abilities, physical health, and a depleted social network may play a greater role in loneliness (Martin, Kliegel, Rott, Poon & Johnson, 2007). Social activities, such as volunteer work, can help an older person living alone stay connected to the community (Carr, Kail, Matz-Costa & Shavit, 2017). Additionally, technology-based interventions using computers and the Internet to address social and emotional needs have also been shown to reduce loneliness (Choi, Kong & Jung, 2012).

Living with Adult Children Historically, older people in many African, Asian, and Latin American societies could expect to live and be cared for in their children's or grandchildren's homes, but this pattern is changing. Most older people in developed countries, even when in difficult circumstances, prefer not to live with their children (Kinsella & Phillips, 2005). They are reluctant to burden their families and to give up their freedom. The parent may feel useless, bored, and isolated from friends. If the adult child is married and the spouse and parent do not get along well, or caregiving duties become too burdensome, the marriage may be threatened (Shapiro & Cooney, 2007). Often, moving in with adult children is a consequence of economic pressures; parents move in not because they want to, but because they have little choice (Isengard & Szydlik, 2012).

Adults, especially women, who move in with relatives are at higher risk of loneliness than those that are able to continue to live with a spouse or partner (Henning-Smith, 2016; Greenfield & Russell, 2011). Whether or not living with adult children will be successful depends largely on the quality of the relationship that existed in the past and on the ability of both generations to communicate fully and frankly. Parents and children need to respect each other's dignity and autonomy and accept their differences (Shapiro, 1994).

Living in Institutions The use of nonfamily institutions for care of the frail elderly varies greatly around the world. Institutionalization has been rare in developing regions but is becoming more common even in countries such as Japan with traditions of elder care. Moreover, declines in fertility have resulted in a rapidly aging population and a shortage of family caregivers (World Health Organization, 2012).

In all countries, the likelihood of living in a nursing home increases with age—in the United States, from about 1 percent at ages 65 to 74 to 9 percent at age 85 and over (Administration on Aging, 2016). Most older nursing home residents worldwide and almost 3 out of 4 in the United States are women (Federal Interagency Forum on Aging-Related Statistics, 2004; Kinsella & Velkoff, 2001). In addition to gender, being poor and living alone significantly increase the risk of entering long-term care (Martikainen et al., 2009).

In 2014, there were approximately 1.4 million older adults living in nursing homes (Harris-Kojetin et al., 2016). Such care is expensive: The average cost for a private room in a nursing home in the United States is $7,698 per month (U.S. Department of Health and Human Services, 2016). High costs, among other factors, have spurred a shift from institutionalization to less expensive alternative living options (discussed in the next section) and home health care. Nonetheless, as the baby boom generation ages and if current nursing home usage rates continue, the number of residents is projected to rise sharply (Seblega et al., 2010). Such growth would greatly burden Medicaid, the national health insurance program for low-income persons and the major source of payments for nursing home usage (Ness & Aronow, 2004).

Federal law sets strict requirements for nursing homes and gives residents the right to choose their own doctors, to be fully informed about their care and treatment, and to be free from physical or mental abuse, corporal punishment, involuntary seclusion, and physical or chemical restraints. An essential element of good care is the opportunity for residents to make decisions and exert some control over their lives. When elderly people are allowed more autonomy, they are more motivated to participate in activities and have higher well-being (Philippe & Vallerand, 2008).

Older adults in a retirement village with supportive living facilities keep their minds active. These women are taking a computer class in cooperation with a nearby community college. ©KatarzynaBialasiewicz/Getty Images

Alternative Housing Options Many older adults are utilizing a relatively new but growing segment of the housing market known as age-qualified active adult communities. In these communities, limited to people age 55 and older, residents can walk out their front door and find a variety of leisure opportunities, such as fitness centers, tennis courts, and golf courses, close by.

One popular option is *assisted living,* housing specifically for older adults. Assisted-living facilities enable tenants to live in their own homelike space while giving them easy 24-hour access to needed personal and health care services. In most of these facilities a person can move, when and if necessary, from relative independence (with housekeeping and meals provided) to help with bathing, dressing, managing medications, and using a wheelchair to get around. Assisted-living facilities vary widely in accommodations, operation, philosophy, and rates, and those offering adequate privacy and services are generally not affordable for moderate- and low-income persons (Hawes et al., 2003). Indeed, facilities are disproportionately found in areas with more educated residents and higher incomes (Stevenson & Grabowski, 2010).

Elder Abuse Elder abuse can be defined as "a single, or repeated act, or lack of appropriate action, occurring within any relationship where there is an expectation of trust, which causes harm or distress to an older person"

(World Health Organization, 2015a). It can take various forms, including physical abuse, sexual abuse or abusive sexual contact, emotional or psychological abuse, and neglect. Elder abuse can also include financial abuse or exploitation, which involves the use of an older person's resources, such as savings accounts or Social Security payments, for personal gain (Centers for Disease Control, 2018). Global estimates are that 15.7 percent of people aged 60 years and older were subjected to some kind of abuse in the past year (World Health Organization, 2017e). In the United States, the prevalence rate is approximately 10 percent (Lachs & Pillemer, 2015).

A number of factors increase the risk of elder abuse, including being female, having difficulty with activities of daily living, poor health, poverty, and having previously been victimized. Dementia and cognitive impairment are also strong predictors of the likelihood of abuse (Burnes et al., 2015; Friedman, Santos, Leibel, Russ & Conwell, 2015; Acierno et al., 2010). Perpetrators of abuse are most likely to be family members, male, to have a history of mental or physical illness, substance abuse, physical abuse or violence, and to be unemployed or suffering from economic strain (Lachs & Pillemer, 2015). Abuse can also occur within the context of nursing homes or residential care communities (US Government Accounting Office, 2008).

In most states, physicians are obligated to screen for elder abuse (Hoover & Polson, 2014). Unfortunately, evidence has not shown that such screenings have an effect on the incidence of elder abuse (Moyer, 2013). Thus, intervention services may have more utility. While some studies have shown mixed results (Ploeg, Fear, Hutchison, McMillan & Bolan, 2009), others have shown success. For example, one community-based intervention program utilizing law enforcement, supportive social services, and coaching of at-risk older adults showed promise in reducing risk factors for abuse over the course of the study (Mariam, McClure, Robinson & Yang, 2015). The Research in Action box addresses this issue in greater detail.

Personal Relationships in Late Life

Our stereotypes often lead us to believe that old age is a time of loneliness and isolation. In some ways it can be; older adults report only half as many people in their social networks as younger adults do (Lang, 2001), with men's social networks even smaller than those of women (McLaughlin, Vagenas, Pachana, Begum & Dobson, 2010). However, research suggests that even though age may result in a shrinking of the size of social networks, older adults nonetheless retain a close circle of confidants (Cornwell et al., 2008). Furthermore, the relationships older adults *do* maintain are more important to their well-being than ever (Charles & Carstensen, 2007) and help keep their minds and memories sharp (Crooks, Lubben, Petitti, Little & Chiu, 2008; Ertel, Glymour & Berkman, 2008).

THEORIES OF SOCIAL CONTACT AND SOCIAL SUPPORT

According to *social convoy theory,* aging adults maintain their level of social support by identifying members of their social network who can best help them and avoiding those who are not supportive. As former coworkers and casual friends drop away, most older adults retain a stable inner circle of social convoys: close friends and family members on whom they can rely and who strongly affect their well-being (Antonucci & Akiyama, 1995).

A somewhat different explanation of changes in social contact comes from *socioemotional selectivity theory* (Carstensen, 1991, 1995, 1996). As remaining time becomes short, older adults choose to spend time with people and in activities that meet immediate emotional needs. For example, an older adult may be less willing to spend precious time with a friend who gets on her nerves.

Thus, even though older adults may have smaller social networks than younger adults do, they tend to have as many very close relationships (Cornwell et al., 2008) and tend to be quite satisfied with those they have (Fiori, Smith & Antonucci, 2007). Their positive feelings toward old friends are as strong as those of young adults, and their positive feelings toward family members are stronger (Charles & Piazza, 2007). While older adults tend to see friends less often, they see family about as frequently as before (Shaw, Krause, Liang & Bennett, 2007).

research in action

MISTREATMENT OF THE ELDERLY

Mickey Rooney was a legendary actor, rising to fame in the Golden Age of Hollywood. He is immortalized on the Hollywood Walk of Fame. He was also a victim of elder abuse. He was granted a restraining order against his stepchildren, alleging emotional and financial abuse. At the age of 90, Rooney testified in front of a Senate Special Committee on Aging, advocating for better legal protections for elders (Cohen, 2011).

There are several categories of elder mistreatment: (1) *physical abuse*—causing bodily injury, pain, or impairment; (2) *emotional abuse*—infliction of anguish or distress through verbal or nonverbal means; (3) *sexual abuse*—nonconsensual sexual contact; (4) *exploitation*—illegal or improper use of funds, property, or assets; (5) *neglect*—failure to provide food, shelter, health care, or protection; and (6) *abandonment*—desertion of responsibility for care or custody of a vulnerable elder (NCEA, 2017).

Elder abuse is not uncommon. National studies estimate a prevalence rate of approximately 10 percent (Pillemer et al., 2015). For every reported case, an estimated 23 cases of elder abuse remain undetected (CDC, 2017d). Often perpetrators are spouses or family members. Abuse may correspond with long-standing patterns of poor relationships or onset due to high caregiver stress levels (Cooper, Selwood & Livingston, 2008). Elders may wrestle with feelings of shame, intimidation, and fear of retaliation, which may prompt them to remain silent (Castle, Ferguson-Rome & Teresi, 2013).

Self-neglect abuse is the most frequently reported concern to adult protective services. Some individuals are unable to care for themselves due to conditions such as declining health, dementia, or drug and alcohol dependency (Hildebrand, Taylor & Bradway, 2013; NCEA, 2017). Self-neglect results when people are not able to take care of basic needs such as personal hygiene, taking medications on schedule, or clothing and feeding themselves. It is not typically a willful refusal of care, but rather the result of physical or cognitive declines that inhibit the ability to perform self-care behaviors (Reyes-Ortiz, Burnett, Flores, Halphen & Dyer, 2014). Self-neglect abuse is when the caregiver does not adequately provide assistance for these tasks.

Elder abuse also occurs in nursing homes or assisted-living facilities. Nursing aides and direct care workers provide hands-on care in institutional settings. Low pay, long hours, physical demands, and minimal education and training may contribute to job burnout, demoralization, and high stress levels among staff members. Unfavorable work conditions, coupled with problem behaviors or negative interactions with residents, may lead to mistreatment. Residents may also inflict violence on staff members, which increases odds of neglect or retaliation (Castle, Ferguson-Rome & Teresi, 2013). Residents also harm one another, as documented in a recent study of elders living in nursing homes. Approximately 20 percent of residents reported at least one instance of mistreatment from another elder. While verbal mistreatment was most common, physical altercations occurred among residents as well (Lachs et al., 2016). Sexual abuse also occurs, with common perpetrators as staff or other residents (Malmedal, Iversen & Kilvik, 2015).

Financial abuse often goes unreported. Exploitation of power of attorney (POA) privileges is a common occurrence. A trusted party is granted legal ability to make financial decisions in the elders' best interests. Instead, the party withdraws funds or makes financial decisions to benefit themselves. Sometimes, individuals acquire POA privileges through physical threat or intimidation (IOM & NRC, 2014). Not only are these cases difficult to detect, but these crimes often go unprosecuted as well (Gibson & Greene, 2013).

In 2015, the White House hosted a Conference on Aging, which rallied for more extensive research, better coordination of elder care services, and staff training opportunities, and defined legislative policy to reduce elder mistreatment (Pillemer, Connolly, Breckman, Spreng & Lachs, 2015). It remains to be seen what the future holds for elder care under the current administration.

what's **your** **view** — What actions or measures do you support to prevent or reduce elder mistreatment? What can be done to empower senior citizens, family members, or institutions to report abuse or mistreatment to authorities?

THE IMPORTANCE OF SOCIAL RELATIONSHIPS

Humans are a profoundly social species. Most of us want and need the support and love of others around us, and we are happier when part of a social community. Even if the size of that community might shrink with age, we need interaction. Because of this need, social isolation—or loneliness—is an important outcome variable that affects both psychological and physical health. Indeed, strong social relationships are as important for health and mortality as smoking, being obese, and abusing alcohol (Holt-Lunstad, Smith & Layton, 2010).

People who are socially isolated tend to show more rapid physical and cognitive declines than those who are not isolated, even very late in life (Cherry et al., 2013; Hawkley & Cacioppo, 2007; Holtzman et al., 2004). Moreover, the feeling of being useless to others is a strong factor for disabilities and mortality (Tilvis, Laitala, Routasalo, Strandberg & Pitkala, 2012; Gruenewald, Karlamangla, Greendale, Singer & Seeman, 2007). To be beneficial, however, relationships must be of good quality. If they are marked by criticism, rejection, competition, violation of privacy, or lack of reciprocity, they can serve as chronic stressors (Krause & Rook, 2003).

Strong, positive social ties can literally be a lifesaver. One longitudinal study showed that socially isolated men were 53 percent more likely than the most socially connected men to die of cardiovascular disease and more than twice as likely to die from accidents or suicide (Eng, Rimm, Fitzmaurice & Kawachi, 2002). Similar data with women showed that older women who received the most social support were 2 times less likely to die during a 10-year period than those who received the least such support (Lyyra & Heikkinen, 2006).

THE MULTIGENERATIONAL FAMILY

The late-life family has special characteristics. Historically, families rarely spanned more than three generations. Today, many families in developed countries can include four or more generations, making it possible for a person to be both a grandparent and a grandchild at the same time (Costanzo & Hoy, 2007).

The presence of so many family members can be enriching (McIlvane, Ajrouch & Antonucci, 2007) but also can create special pressures. While there is great variability, older adults are as a group more likely to suffer from debilitating disease or infirmity, and this care can be physically and emotionally draining (Gonyea, 2013). Given the rapid growth in the population of adults 85 and older (Ortman, Velkoff & Hogan, 2014), many people in their late sixties or beyond, whose own health and energy may be faltering, may find themselves serving as caregivers. Generally, the burden of this intergenerational care falls to women (Gonyea, 2013) due in part to gender role norms of women as caregivers.

The ways families deal with these issues often have cultural roots. People from cultures that strongly focus on familial bonds are, not surprisingly, more receptive to the needs of their aging parents and more likely to offer support than are people from more individualistic cultures (Kalmijn & Saraceno, 2008; Tomassini, Glaser & Stuchbury, 2007). For example, the nuclear family and the desire of older adults to live apart from their children reflect dominant U.S. values of individualism, autonomy, and self-reliance, while Hispanic and Asian American cultures traditionally emphasize *lineal,* or intergenerational, obligations (C. L. Johnson, 1995). One consequence of differing cultural values is that ethnic minority group members are less likely to institutionalize aging parents suffering from dementia, as well as show different patterns of response to the stressors of caring for aging parents in the home (Dilworth-Anderson, Williams & Gibson, 2002; Napoles, Chadiha, Eversley & Moreno-John, 2010). There are suggestions that the accelerating pace of globalization will result in a movement away from the more traditionally oriented family bonds found in many countries and toward the individualistic style more characteristic of more economically stable nations (Costanzo & Hoy, 2007).

Marital Relationships

Unlike other family relationships, marriage—at least in contemporary Western cultures—is generally formed by mutual consent. Thus its effect on well-being has characteristics of both friendship and kinship ties (Antonucci & Akiyama, 1995). It can provide both the highest emotional highs and the lowest lows a person experiences. What happens to marital quality in late life?

Many couples who are still together late in life say they are happier in marriage than they were in their younger years. Important benefits of marriage include intimacy, sharing, and a sense of belonging to one another. ©Stockbyte/Getty Images

LONG-TERM MARRIAGE

Because women usually marry older men and outlive them and because men are more likely to remarry after divorce or widowhood, a higher proportion of men than women throughout the world are married in late life (Federal Interagency Forum on Aging-Related Statistics, 2012; Figure 18.2).

Married couples who are still together in late adulthood are more likely than middle-age couples to report higher satisfaction and fewer adjustment problems in their marriages (Orathinkal & Vansteenwegen, 2007). This may be because spouses who remain together are likely to have worked out their differences. Marriage satisfaction is important because it has been related not just to psychological well-being (Carr, Friedman, Cornman & Schwarz, 2014), but also to multiple positive health indices (Robles, Slatcher, Trombello & McGinn, 2014).

The way couples resolve conflicts is key to marital satisfaction throughout adulthood. Married people with more discord in their marriages tend to be anxious and depressed, whereas those with less discordant marriages tend to have higher self-esteem (Whisman, Uebelacker, Tolejko, Chatav & McKelvie, 2006) and report higher levels of marital satisfaction (Schmitt, Kliegel & Shapiro, 2007). Patterns of conflict resolution tend to remain fairly constant throughout a marriage, and those couples who believe strongly in marriage, share responsibility for decision making, and share household chores are more likely to report low levels of conflict and high levels of happiness in their marriage (Kamp Dush & Taylor, 2012). The way emotions are handled matters as well. Marriage partners, especially wives, who are able to successfully regulate negative emotions and communicate effectively are more likely to report high marriage satisfaction (Bloch, Haase & Levenson, 2014).

Late-life marriage can be severely tested by advancing age and physical ills, though a close marital relationship can moderate the negative psychological effects of functional disabilities by reducing anxiety and depression and increasing self-esteem (Mancini & Bonanno, 2006). Spouses who care for disabled partners may feel isolated, angry, and frustrated, especially if they are in poor health themselves. Such couples may be caught in a vicious cycle: The illness puts strains on the marriage, and these strains may then aggravate the illness (Karney & Bradbury, 1995), putting the caregiver's health and well-being at risk (Graham et al., 2006). For example, when one spouse is hospitalized, the other's risk of death increases (Christakis & Allison, 2006). This iterative process is exacerbated by age (Umberson, Williams, Powers, Liu & Needham, 2006).

Spousal caregiving late in life often ends with the institutionalization or death of one partner. A longitudinal study of over 2,000 older couples captured the fragile nature of spousal caregiving in late life. At the beginning of the study, all couples were living independently in the community. Eight years later, 20.7 percent of the husbands and 18.1 percent of the wives had been institutionalized. Moreover, 17.1 percent of husbands and 33.1 percent of wives became widowed over the course of the study (Noel-Miller, 2010).

WIDOWHOOD

With increasing age, death of a spouse becomes more common, and more so in women than in men. Women tend to outlive their husbands and are less likely than men to marry again. As Figure 18.2 shows, U.S. women age 65 and over are far more likely than men of the same age to be widowed. By the age of 65, women are 4 times as likely as men to be widowers (Federal Interagency Forum on Aging-Related Statistics, 2012). In most countries, more than half of older women are widows (Kinsella & Velkoff, 2001).

Widowhood has been repeatedly associated with increased mortality, with the sharpest declines seen in the first 6 months following the death of a spouse (Moon, Kondo, Glymour & Subramanian, 2011) and for unexpected deaths (Sullivan & Fenelon, 2014). While becoming widowed is a risk for both men and women, men appear to be affected more strongly by the loss of a spouse. For example, older widowed men are far more likely to be institutionalized than older widowed women following the death of a spouse (Nihtila & Martikainen, 2008). Additionally, while women's mortality risk following the death of a spouse is 15 percent, men's increased risk is 27 percent (Shor et al., 2012).

DIVORCE AND REMARRIAGE

Divorce in middle-age and older adults, although rare, has risen. In 1980, approximately 5 percent of men and 4 percent of women aged 65 and older reported being divorced. By 2008, these numbers had risen sharply, to 10 percent in men and 12 percent in women (Manning & Brown, 2011). This rise can be attributed to a variety of factors. First, increasing life expectancy increases the risk of divorce as people may be unwilling to spend long periods of time with a spouse they find unsuitable. As a correlate to this, remarriages, which become also more common with increasing age, are more likely to result in divorce than first marriages. Also, as divorce becomes more common, it also becomes more acceptable. Last, women's participation in the workforce has given them more economic security and hence lessened the financial burden of divorce for many women (Brown & Lin, 2012).

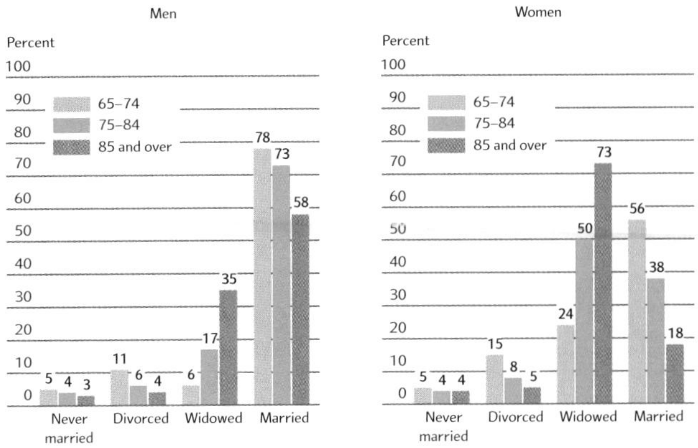

In 2013, 67 percent of adults aged 55 to 64 years, and 50 percent of those 65 and above remarried, an increase from previous years. Men are somewhat more likely to remarry, a difference that emerges sometime in middle age. This gender gap has decreased since the 1960s and most strikingly for younger cohorts. In 1960, the gender gap was +29 for adults 55 to 64 years of age, and +28 for adults over 65. These numbers are now, respectively, +8 and +26 (Livingston, 2014). Remarriage in late life may have a special character. People in late-life remarriages seemed more trusting and accepting and less in need of deep sharing of personal feelings than in earlier marriages. Men, but not women, tend to be more satisfied in late-life remarriages than in midlife remarriages (Bograd & Spilka, 1996).

FIGURE 18.2

Marital Status of the U.S. Population Age 65 and Over by Age Group and Sex, 2010

Because of women's greater longevity, they are more likely than men to be widowed in late life, whereas men are more likely to be married or remarried in late life.

Note: Married includes married, spouse present; married, spouse absent; and separated. These data refer to the civilian noninstitutionalized population.

Source: Federal Interagency Forum on Aging-Related Statistics. *Older Americans 2012: Key indicators of well-being.* Washington, DC: U.S. Government Printing Office, 2012.

Nonmarital Lifestyles and Relationships

SINGLE LIFE

In the United States, the number of single older adults has risen in the past few decades. These adults may be single either because of never marrying, divorce, or widowhood. These demographic changes reflect a number of influences, including a decision to delay or forgo marriage, liberalization of divorce, cohabitation, and unmarried parenthood. In the United States, approximately 33 percent of baby boomers, who began to turn 65 in 2011, are unmarried (Lin & Brown, 2012).

In most countries, 5 percent or less of older men and 10 percent or less of older women have never married. In Europe, this gender difference may reflect the toll on marriageable men taken by World War II, when today's older cohort were of marrying age. In some Latin American and Caribbean countries, proportions of never-marrieds are higher, probably due to the prevalence of consensual unions (Kinsella & Phillips, 2005). In the United States, approximately 4 percent of Americans 65 years or older have never been married (He, Sengupta, Velkoff & DeBarros, 2005).

When compared to divorced or widowed people, older never-married adults in the United States are more likely to prefer single life and less likely to be lonely (Dykstra, 1995), even though they are most likely to live alone and receive the least social support. They are less likely to experience "single strain"—chronic practical and emotional stressors attributed to the lack of an intimate partner (Pudrovska, Schieman & Carr, 2006).

However, when compared to married adults, never-married people, especially men, are disadvantaged (Lin & Brown, 2012). They do not benefit from the protective effects of marriage on morbidity and mortality discussed earlier, and they are as likely to have poor health (Tamborini, 2007) and be at higher risk of death as divorced or widowed adults (Rendall, Weden, Favreault & Waldron, 2011). Moreover, they are more likely to live in poverty than married couples, as well as divorced and widowed older adults (Tamborini, 2007).

Approximately 14 percent of single adults aged 57 to 85 years are in a dating relationship (Brown & Shinohara, 2013). Previously married older men are more likely to date than previously married older women, probably because of the greater availability of women in this age group. Men prefer to date women who are younger than they are, while women show a preference for older men until age 75, after which they prefer younger men as well (Alterovitz & Mendelsohn, 2009). Many elderly daters are sexually active but do not expect to marry. Among both whites and blacks, men are more interested in romantic involvement than women, who may fear getting locked into traditional gender roles (Bulcroft & Bulcroft, 1991; Tucker, Taylor & Mitchell-Kernan, 1993).

COHABITATION

Cohabitation rates have risen sharply for older adults. In 2007, approximately 2.3 million adults 50 years and older were cohabitating. By 2016, this number had risen to 4 million, a 75 percent increase (Stepler, 2017). While younger adults sometimes view cohabitation as a prelude to marriage, older adults are more likely to view it as an alternative to marriage (Brown, Bulanda & Lee, 2012). Approximately 9 out of 10 cohabitating older adults were previously married (Brown, Lee & Bulanda, 2006).

Generally cohabitating relationship tend to be quite stable in older adults and are relatively unlikely to lead to separation, a finding that is especially true for women 65 years and older (Brown, Bulanda & Lee, 2012; Vespa, 2012). This may be because such relationships tend to be at least as satisfying as marriage. Research has shown that cohabitators report equal levels of emotional satisfaction, pleasure, openness, time spent together, criticism, and demands (Brown & Kawamura, 2010).

In younger adults, cohabitation is often the result of economic concerns. However, this does not seem to be the case in older adults. Factors such as wealth (Vespa, 2012), owning a home, receiving Social Security payments or a pension, or having private health insurance (Brown, Bulanda & Lee, 2012) do not seem to affect the likelihood that a couple will choose to cohabitate. Perhaps older adults, particularly women, are hesitant to marry and prefer to cohabitate because of the possibility of having to provide care to a disabled or sick partner later in life (Noel-Miller, 2011).

Intimacy is important to older gay men, as it is to older heterosexual adults. Contrary to stereotype, homosexual relationships in late life are strong and supportive.
©Thinkstock/Stockbyte/Getty Images

GAY AND LESBIAN RELATIONSHIPS

There is little research on homosexual relationships in old age, largely because the current cohort of older adults grew up at a time when living openly as a homosexual was rare (Fredriksen-Goldsen & Muraco, 2010). For aging gays and lesbians who recognized their homosexuality before the rise of the gay liberation movement in the late 1960s, their self-concept tended to be shaped by the then-prevailing stigma against homosexuality. Those who came of age after the liberation movement was in full swing are more likely to view their homosexuality simply as a characteristic of the self like any other (Rosenfeld, 1999).

Gay and lesbian relationships in late life tend to be strong, supportive, and diverse. Many homosexuals have children from earlier marriages; others have adopted children. Friendship networks or support groups may substitute for the traditional family (Reid, 1995). Those who have maintained close relationships and strong involvement in the homosexual community tend to adapt to aging with relative ease (Friend, 1991; Reid, 1995).

The main problems of many older gays and lesbians grow out of societal attitudes: strained relationships with the family of origin, discrimination in nursing homes and elsewhere, lack of medical or social services and social support, insensitive policies of social agencies, and, when a partner falls ill or dies, dealing with health care providers, bereavement and inheritance issues, and lack of access to a partner's Social Security benefits (Knochel, Quam & Croghan, 2011; Rawlings, 2012; Addis, Davies, Greene, MacBride-Stewart & Shepherd, 2009).

FRIENDSHIPS

Maintaining friendships is important for well-being. Most older people have close friends, and, as in early and middle adulthood, those with an active circle of friends tend to be healthier and happier (Golden, Conroy & Lawlor, 2009; Huxhold, Miche & Schuz, 2013). Emotional closeness seems to be a key factor. When emotional closeness is lacking, more frequent contact with friends does not impact feelings of loneliness (Drageset, Kirkevold & Espehaug, 2011). However, regardless of closeness, those people who are not getting as much contact as they desire are more likely to feel lonely (Nicolaisen & Thorsen, 2017). People who can confide their feelings and thoughts and can talk about their worries and pain with friends tend to deal better with the changes and crises of aging (Genevay, 1986) and to live longer (Steinbach, 1992).

The element of choice in friendship may be especially important to older people (Golden et al., 2009), who may feel their control over their lives slipping away (R. G. Adams, 1986). Friendship may also help older adults deal with some of the role losses of late life; those with friends tend to be happier (Adams & Taylor, 2015).

Some research has shown that many older people enjoy spending time with their friends more than time spent with their families. As earlier in life, friendships tend to revolve around pleasure and leisure, whereas family relationships tend to involve everyday needs and tasks (Antonucci & Akiyama, 1995). People usually rely on relatives for long-term commitments, such as caregiving, but friends may, on occasion, fulfill this function. Although friends cannot replace a spouse or partner, they can help compensate for the lack of one (Hartup & Stevens, 1999) by playing the role of fictive kin, a psychological family. When family relationships are poor, older adults tend to have closer relationships with friends, and this in turn is associated with well-being (Wrzus, Wagner & Neyer, 2012). For example, never married, divorced, and widowed older adults who receive high levels of emotional and practical support from friends are less likely to be lonely (Dykstra, 1995).

In line with social convoy and socioemotional selectivity theories, longtime friendships often persist into very old age (Hartup & Stevens, 1999) and older adults tend to have stronger positive feelings about old friends than about new friends (Charles & Piazza, 2007). Sometimes, however, relocation, illness, or disability make it hard to keep up with old friends. This is a particularly pressing issue for women, who are more likely to survive their husbands (d'Epinay, Cavalli & Guinett, 2010). Although many older people do make new friends, even after age 85 (C. L. Johnson & Troll, 1994), older adults are more likely than younger adults to attribute the benefits of friendship (such as affection and loyalty) to specific individuals, who cannot easily be replaced if they die, go into a nursing home, or move away (de Vries, 1996).

Nonmarital Kinship Ties

Some of the most lasting and important relationships in late life come not from mutual choice (as marriages, cohabitations, homosexual partnerships, and friendships do) but from kinship bonds. Let's look at these.

RELATIONSHIPS WITH ADULT CHILDREN

Parent-child bonds remain strong in old age. Children provide a link with other family members, especially grandchildren. Parents who have good relationships with their adult children are less likely to be lonely or depressed than those whose parent-child relationships are not as good (Koropeckyj-Cox, 2002).

Most older people have living children, but, because of global trends toward smaller families, have fewer of them than in previous generations (Dobriansky et al., 2007; Kinsella & Phillips, 2005). In European countries, almost half of adults in their sixties live within 15 miles of their adult children, and about one-third live with an adult child (Hank, 2007). Coresidence commonly results from economic pressures (Isengard & Szydlik, 2012) and is less common in countries with strong welfare services. It is most common in the more traditional Mediterranean countries (Greece, Italy, and Spain) and least common in the

Scandinavian countries (Denmark and Sweden). About half of older parents below age 80 report contact with a child, most often a daughter, at least once a week (Hank, 2007). The mother-daughter relationship tends to be especially close (Lefkowitz & Fingerman, 2003). In the United States, immigrants who arrived as older adults are most likely to live with adult children and to be dependent on them (Glick & Van Hook, 2002). The trend toward smaller families means fewer potential family caregivers for ailing, aging parents (Kinsella & Phillips, 2005), increasing the strains on those who do serve as caregivers—strains that may lead to mistreatment of a "difficult" frail patient.

The balance of mutual aid between parents and their adult children tends to shift as parents age, with children providing a greater share of support (Bengtson et al., 1990, 1996). Mothers'—but not fathers'—willingness to ask adult children for help reflects their earlier parenting styles. Warm, responsive mothers are more likely to ask for financial help or personal advice than mothers who were more dominant or restrictive during their children's adolescence and young adulthood (Schooler, Revell & Caplan, 2007). While the provision of support to aging parents can result in declines in well-being for both parents and adult children, a close, high-quality relationship can buffer against this (Merz & Consedine, 2009; Merz, Consedine, Schulze & Schuengel, 2009).

Older parents who can do so often continue to provide financial support to children. In less-developed countries, older parents contribute through housekeeping, child care, and socialization of grandchildren (Kinsella & Phillips, 2005). Older parents continue to show strong concern about their children (Bengtson et al., 1996). Adults with children doing less well than they would like often have conflicted feelings—they are concerned and want to help, but at the same time may feel a desire to be free of responsibility toward adult children or want to encourage independence and autonomy (Birditt, Fingerman & Zarit, 2010; Smith, 2012). They tend to be distressed if their children have serious problems and may consider such problems a sign of their failure as parents (G. R. Lee, Netzer & Coward, 1995; Pillemer & Suitor, 1991; Suitor, Pillemer, Keeton & Robison, 1995; Troll & Fingerman, 1996). Many older people whose adult children are mentally ill, retarded, physically disabled, or stricken with serious illnesses serve as primary caregivers for as long as both parent and child live (Greenberg & Becker, 1988; Ryff & Seltzer, 1995). The strain of this caregiving adds up over time. In middle age, parents of children with intellectual or developmental disabilities have a similar profile to parents of neurotypical children. However, as they enter old age, parents of disabled children have worse physical and mental health (Seltzer, Floyd, Song, Greenberg & Hong, 2011). Additionally, the generally unexpected loss of an adult child can result in deep psychological distress and unresolved grief (Van Humbeeck et al., 2013). For example, mothers who have outlived their children show elevated levels of depression relative to fathers and older adults with living adult children (Bures, Koropeckkyj-Cox & Loree, 2009).

RELATIONSHIPS WITH SIBLINGS

Brother and sisters play an important role in older people's support networks. Siblings, more than other family members, tend to provide companionship as older adults. They also, more than friends, tend to provide emotional support (Bedford, 1995). Although siblings often engage in conflict when young, overt rivalry generally decreases with age, especially for sisters (Cicirelli, 1995).

Sibling commitment, meaning the degree to which siblings keep in contact with and help each other out, is relatively stable across the life span (Rittenour, Myers & Brann, 2007). Most older siblings say they stand ready to provide tangible help and would turn to a sibling for such help as needed, although relatively few actually do so unless facing an emergency (Cicirelli, 1995). For those that do, however, both giving support (Gierveld & Dykstra, 2008) and receiving support (Thomas, 2010) are associated with positive outcomes such as reductions in loneliness. Surviving siblings with a poor relationship are at higher risk of depression (Cicirelli, 2009).

Bessie and Sadie Delany were best friends all their lives. Elderly siblings are an important part of each other's support network, and sisters are especially vital in maintaining family relationships. ©Hans L Bonnevier, Johner/Getty Images

The nearer older people live to their siblings and the more siblings they have, the more they are likely to confide in them (Connidis & Davies, 1992). Reminiscing about shared early experiences becomes more frequent in old age and may help in reviewing a life and putting the significance of family relationships into perspective (Cicirelli, 1995; Eaves, McQuiston & Miles, 2005).

Sisters are especially vital in maintaining family relationships and well-being, perhaps because of women's emotional expressiveness and traditional role as nurturers (Bedford, 1995; Cicirelli, 1995). Older people who are close to their sisters feel better about life and worry less about aging than those without sisters or without close ties to them (Cicirelli, 1989).

Although the death of a sibling in old age may be understood as normative and becomes increasingly common with advanced age (d'Epinay, Cavalli & Guillet, 2010), survivors may grieve intensely and become lonely or depressed (Cicirelli, 2009). The loss of a sibling represents not only a loss of someone to lean on and a shift in the family constellation, but perhaps even a partial loss of identity. To mourn for a sibling is to mourn for the lost completeness of the original family within which one came to know oneself and can bring home one's own nearness to death (Cicirelli, 1995).

BECOMING GREAT-GRANDPARENTS

As grandchildren grow up, grandparents generally see them less often. Then, when grandchildren become parents, grandparents move into a new role: great-grandparenthood.

Because of age, declining health, and the scattering of families, great-grandparents tend to be less involved than grandparents in a child's life; and, because four- or five-generation families are relatively new, there are few generally accepted guidelines for what great-grandparents are supposed to do (Cherlin & Furstenberg, 1986). Still, most great-grandparents find the role fulfilling (Pruchno & Johnson, 1996). Great-grandparenthood offers a sense of personal and family renewal, a source of diversion, and a mark of longevity. Adults who are close to their great-grandchildren are likely to live nearby and be close to the children's parents and grandparents as well, often helping out with loans, gifts, and babysitting. (Doka & Mertz, 1988).

Grandparents and great-grandparents are important to their families. They are sources of wisdom, companions in play, links to the past, and symbols of the continuity of family life. They are engaged in the ultimate generative function: expressing the human longing to transcend mortality by investing themselves in the lives of future generations.

summary and key terms

Theory and Research on Personality Development

- Erik Erikson's final stage, ego integrity versus despair, culminates in the virtue of *wisdom*.
- Erikson believed that people must maintain a vital involvement in society.
- Personality traits tend to remain fairly stable in late adulthood, depending on how they are measured.
- Emotionality tends to become more positive and less negative in old age, but personality traits can modify this pattern.

ego integrity versus despair

Well-Being in Late Adulthood

- George Vaillant found that the use of mature adaptive defenses earlier in adulthood predicts psychosocial adjustment in late life.
- In research based on the cognitive-appraisal model, adults of all ages generally prefer problem-focused coping, but older adults use more emotion-focused coping than younger adults.
- Religion is an important source of emotion-focused coping for many older adults. Links have been found between religion or spirituality and health, longevity, and well-being.

- The concept of successful, or optimal, aging reflects the growing number of healthy, vital older adults, but there is dispute over how to define and measure it and over the validity of the concept.
- Two contrasting early models of *successful,* or *optimal,* aging are disengagement theory and activity theory. Disengagement theory has little support, and findings on activity theory are mixed. Newer refinements of activity theory include continuity theory and an emphasis on productive activity.
- Baltes and his colleagues suggest that successful aging, in the psychosocial as well as the cognitive realm, may depend on selective optimization with compensation.

coping, cognitive-appraisal model, problem-focused coping, emotion-focused coping, ambiguous loss, disengagement theory, activity theory, continuity theory, selective optimization with compensation (SOC)

Practical and Social Issues Related to Aging

- Some older adults continue to work for pay, but most are retired. However, many retired people start new careers or do part-time paid or volunteer work. Often retirement is a phased process.
- Age has both positive and negative effects on job perfor-mance, and individual differences are more significant than age differences.
- Retirement is an ongoing process. Personal, economic, and social resources may affect morale.
- The financial situation of older Americans has improved, and fewer live in poverty. Women, Hispanic Americans, and African Americans are most likely to be poor in old age.
- In developing countries, the elderly often live with children or grandchildren. In developed countries, most older people live with a spouse or live alone. Minority elders are more likely than white elders to live with extended family members.
- Most older adults in industrialized nations prefer to age in place. Most can remain in the community if they can depend on a spouse or someone else for help.
- Older women are more likely than older men to live alone.
- Older adults in developed countries typically do not expect to live with adult children and do not wish to do so.
- Institutionalization is rare in developing countries. Its extent varies in developed countries.
- Fast-growing alternatives to institutionalization include assisted-living facilities and other types of group housing.
- Elder abuse is a significant problem. Women, and adults with physical limitations or health problems, living in poverty, or who were previous victims of abuse are at increased risk. Dementia is a particularly strong risk factor as well. Intervention programs may help.

aging in place

Personal Relationships in Late Life

- Relationships are important to older people, even though frequency of social contact declines in old age.
- According to social convoy theory, reductions or changes in social contact in late life do not impair well-being because a stable inner circle of social support is maintained. According to socioemotional selectivity theory, older people choose to spend time with people who enhance their emotional well-being.
- Social interaction is associated with good health and life satisfaction, and isolation is a risk factor for mortality.
- The way multigenerational late-life families function often has cultural roots.

Marital Relationships

- As life expectancy increases, so does the potential longevity of marriage. More men than women are married in late life. Marriages that last into late adulthood tend to be relatively satisfying.
- Although a growing proportion of men are widowed, women tend to outlive their husbands and are less likely to marry again.
- Divorce is uncommon among older people, and most older adults who have been divorced are remarried. Remarriages may be more relaxed in late life.

Nonmarital Lifestyles and Relationships

- A small but increasing percentage of adults reach old age without marrying. Never-married adults are less likely to be lonely than divorced or widowed ones.
- Older adults are more likely to cohabit after a prior marriage than before marriage, and these unions are generally quite stable.
- Many gays and lesbians adapt to aging with relative ease, particularly if they maintain relationships as well as involve-ment in the gay community.
- Most older adults have close friends, and those who do are healthier and happier.
- Older people enjoy time spent with friends more than with family, but the family is the main source of emotional and practical support.

Nonmarital Kinship Ties

- Older parents and their adult children frequently see or contact each other, are concerned about each other, and offer each other assistance. Many older parents are caregiv-ers for adult children, grandchildren, or great-grandchildren.
- Often siblings offer each other emotional support and sometimes more tangible support as well. Sisters, in particular, maintain sibling ties.
- Great-grandparents are usually less involved in children's lives than grandparents are, but most find the role fulfilling.

Dealing with Death and Bereavement

©Con Tanasiuk/Design Pics/age fotostock

learning objectives

Describe the cultural and historical contexts of death and dying.

Discuss death and bereavement as well as attitudes about death and dying across the life span.

Identify the challenges of coping with the death of another person.

Evaluate issues involved in decisions about death.

In this chapter we discuss how people of different cultures and ages think and feel about death and dying. We examine patterns of grief and how people cope with significant loss. We look at questions raised about life support and examine whether people have the right to die. Finally, we consider how confronting death can give life greater purpose.

The Many, Changing Meanings of Death and Dying

Death is a biological fact, but it also has social, cultural, historical, religious, legal, psychological, developmental, medical, and ethical aspects, and often these are closely intertwined.

Let's look more closely at death and mourning in their cultural and historical context.

THE CULTURAL CONTEXT

Customs concerning disposal and remembrance of the dead, transfer of possessions, and even expression of grief vary greatly from culture to culture and often are governed by religious or legal prescriptions that reflect a society's view of what death is and what happens afterward. Cultural aspects of death include care of and behavior toward the dying and the dead, the setting where death usually takes place, and mourning customs and rituals—from the all-night Irish wake, at which friends and family toast the memory of the dead person, to the weeklong Jewish *shiva,* during which family members gather at home and receive visitors. Some cultural conventions, such as flying a flag at half-mast after the death of a public figure, are codified in law.

Although there are wide variations in customs surrounding death, there are nonetheless some commonalities in the experience across cultures. Expressions of grief, anger and fear are common across different cultures, and most cultures have a socially sanctioned way of expressing these emotions within the context of mourning or funeral practices (Parkes, Laungani & Young, 2015). Beliefs about the dead also show some commonalities. In one study, participants from Europe, Central America, Asia, the Caribbean, and South America all shared beliefs that the "soul" of the dead person would pass on to some sort of afterlife, and they had rituals or ceremonies intended to facilitate this transition (Lobar, Youngblut & Brooten, 2006).

THE MORTALITY REVOLUTION

Until the twentieth century, in all societies throughout history, death was a frequent, expected event, sometimes welcomed as a peaceful end to suffering. Caring for a dying loved one at home was a common experience, as it still is in some rural communities.

Great historical changes regarding death and dying have taken place since the late nineteenth century. Advances in medicine and sanitation, new treatments for many once-fatal illnesses, and a better-educated, more health-conscious population have brought about a *mortality revolution.* Women today are less likely to die in childbirth, infants are more likely to survive their 1st year, children are more likely to grow to adulthood, young adults are more likely to reach old age, and older people often can overcome illnesses they grew up regarding as fatal. The top causes of death in the United States in the 1900s were diseases that most often affected children and young people: pneumonia and influenza, tuberculosis, diarrhea, and enteritis. Today, despite recent increases in apparently drug-related deaths of people in their twenties and in early middle age as well as a spike in midlife suicide, nearly three-quarters of deaths in the United States still occur among people age 65 and over; and close to one-half of deaths are from heart disease, cancer, and stroke—the three leading causes of death in late adulthood (Xu, Kochanek, Murphy & Tejada-Vera, 2010).

Amid all this progress in improving health and lengthening life, something important may have been lost. Looking death in the eye, bit by bit, day by day, people growing up in traditional societies absorbed an important truth: dying is part of living. As death increasingly became a phenomenon of late adulthood, it became "invisible and abstract" (Fulton & Owen, 1987–1988, p. 380). Care of the dying and the dead became largely a task for professionals. Such social conventions as placing the dying person in a hospital or nursing home and refusing to openly discuss his or her condition reflected and perpetuated attitudes of avoidance and denial of death. Death—even of the very old—came to be regarded as a failure of medical treatment rather than as a natural end to life (McCue, 1995; Waldrop, 2011).

UNIQUE FUNERAL CEREMONIES AND RITUALS AROUND THE WORLD

Funerals in America or Europe are generally held at a church or funeral home. People dress in black, a service is held, and the deceased is either buried or cremated. There is often a visitation before the service and a gathering held at the home or church of the family. Though this is the common tradition in much of the Westernized world, it is not the only tradition. Different cultures have unique funeral traditions or rituals to honor their deceased loved ones.

In traditional Islamic burials, the deceased must be buried as soon as possible after death, usually within 24 hours, to free the soul from the body. The body is washed and a burial shroud is placed over it. The deceased is laid on the right side facing Mecca, without a casket, if allowed. Burial sites are marked by a simple flat marker or not marked at all. The mourning period is 3 days where the family says daily prayers for the loved one (Rahman, 2011).

For the Toraja in Indonesia, the funeral is a celebration of life. Funerals are elaborate and expensive and the whole community takes part. There are a series of ceremonies that must take place, and while this happens the deceased is embalmed and stays with the family. The person is symbolically fed and cared for, remaining part of the family until the final burial takes place on the 11th day of the ceremonies. Each year during a ritual called Ma' Nene, the bodies are exhumed, cleaned, and dressed in new clothes and walked around the village (Holloway, 2014).

In Tibet, burial rituals are based on the Buddhist belief that the spirit leaves the body the moment a person dies. The body should be returned to the earth and recycled. The sky burial is the preferred ritual. In the sky burial the body is dissected and placed on a high cliff, it is offered up to hungry vultures, a final act of kindness to other creatures, contributing to the life cycle (Kerala, 2005).

Cremation has become more common in South Korea due to lack of space to bury the dead. Rather than storing ashes, many people are choosing to turn their loved ones' remains into beads. The beads are colorful and are stored in glass containers to keep their loved ones close (The Week Staff, 2012).

In Mexico and Latin America, a traditional ceremony is given at a church or the family home with a final ceremony at the burial site. Each family member, including children, throws a handful of dirt on the coffin before the grave is filled. They light a candle at church for 9 days following the death. Every year on November 2nd, the Day of the Dead, families gather to remember and honor those who have passed. It is often celebrated with festivals; families eat, sing, and tell stories about deceased loved ones. Families may visit the gravesite or create an altar for the family member, decorating it with candles, flowers, and the favorite foods of the deceased (Benedetti, 2017).

Rituals and practices intended to honor the dead and help people mourn the loss of loved ones are deeply engrained into every culture.

what's your view

Do you think it is important to honor the dead? What are the traditions in your culture?

Today, this picture again is changing. **Thanatology,** the study of death and dying, is arousing interest, and educational programs have been established to help people deal with death. Because of the prohibitive cost of extended hospital care that cannot save the terminally ill, many more deaths are now occurring at home, as they once did the world over.

thanatology
Study of death and dying.

CARE OF THE DYING

Along with a growing tendency to face death more honestly, movements have arisen to make dying more humane. Primary among these movements is the establishment of **hospice care** for dying persons. Hospice care is personal, patient- and family-centered, compassionate care for the terminally ill. Hospice facilities generally provide **palliative care,** which includes relief of pain and suffering, control of symptoms, alleviation of stress, and attempts to maintain a satisfactory quality of life. However, palliative care is not intended to cure or reverse the course of disease.

hospice care
Personal, patient- and family-centered care for a person with a terminal illness.

palliative care
Care aimed at relieving pain and suffering and allowing the terminally ill to die in peace, comfort, and dignity.

Hospice care seeks to ease patients' pain and treat their symptoms to keep them as comfortable and alert as possible. It also helps families deal with illness and death.

©Ron Nickel/Design Pics/Corbis

terminal drop
A frequently observed decline in cognitive abilities near the end of life. Also called *terminal decline*.

Hospice facilities offer a specialized type of palliative care for people whose life expectancy is 6 months or less. The goal is to allow the person to die in peace and dignity, while minimizing any pain and suffering, and it often includes self-help support groups for both dying people and their families.

Hospice care may take place at home, but such care can also be given in a hospital or another institution, at a hospice center, or through a combination of home and institutional care. Family members often take an active part. Palliative care also can be introduced earlier in an illness that is not yet terminal, and it may lead to increases in quality of life. For example, in one study tracking newly diagnosed advanced metastatic lung cancer patients, those that began to receive palliative care immediately at the time of diagnosis had a higher quality of life, better emotional state, and even longer median survival time than patients who received standard oncological care only (Temel et al., 2010).

What does it mean to preserve the dignity of a patient who is dying? One research team decided to ask patients themselves. From interviews with 50 Canadian patients with advanced terminal cancer, researchers concluded that dignity-conserving care depends not only on how patients are treated but also on how they are regarded: "When dying patients are seen, and know that they are seen, as being worthy of honor and esteem by those who care for them, dignity is more likely to be maintained" (Chochinov, Hack, McClement, Harlos & Kristjanson, 2002, p. 2259).

Facing Death and Loss

Death is an important chapter in human development. What changes do people undergo shortly before death? How do they come to terms with its imminence? How do people handle grief? How do attitudes toward death change across the life span?

PHYSICAL AND COGNITIVE CHANGES PRECEDING DEATH

Even without any identifiable illness, people around the age of 100 tend to experience functional declines, lose interest in eating and drinking, and die a natural death (Johansson et al., 2004; Singer, Verhaeghen, Ghisletta, Lindenberger & Baltes, 2003; Small, Fratiglioni, von Strauss & Bäckman, 2003). There also appear to be changes in life satisfaction that precede death (Gerstorf et al., 2010; Gerstorf, Ram, Rocke, Lindenberger & Smith, 2008). Such changes also have been noted in younger people whose death is near. In a 22-year longitudinal study of 1,927 men, life satisfaction showed steep declines within 1 year before death, regardless of self-rated health (Mroczek & Spiro, 2005).

Terminal drop, or *terminal decline,* refers specifically to a widely observed decline in cognitive abilities shortly before death, even when factors such as demographics and health are controlled for (Weatherbee & Allaire, 2008). This effect has been found in longitudinal studies in various countries—not only of the very old (Johansson et al., 2004; Singer et al., 2003; Small et al., 2003), but also of adults of a wide range of ages (Rabbitt et al., 2002; Small et al., 2003) with no signs of dementia. Losses of perceptual speed have been found to predict death nearly 15 years later (Thorvaldsson et al., 2008), although most declines start at about 7.7 years before death occurs (Muniz-Terrera, van den Hout, Piccinin, Matthews & Hofer, 2013). Declines in verbal ability, spatial reasoning, and everyday cognition are other important markers of terminal drop (Rabbitt et al., 2002; Thorvaldsson et al., 2008).

Some people who have come close to dying report *near-death experiences (NDE),* often involving a sense of being out of the body or sucked into a tunnel and visions of bright lights or mystical encounters. These types of experiences have been reported in many different cultures, both in modern times and in written and oral histories of nonindustrialized cultures (Tassell-Matamua, 2013). Skeptics generally interpret these reports as resulting from physiological changes that accompany the process of dying. Some researchers argue that near-death experiences reflect the common bodily structures affected by the process of dying (Mobbs & Watt, 2011), in particular, the oxygen deprivation that occurs in 9 out of 10 dying persons (Woerlee, 2005). Research in rats shows that a cardiac arrest, which brings about oxygen deprivation, also results in brain waves indicating an aroused, highly functioning brain shortly before death. This suggests humans might experience a similar type of conscious information processing during clinical death (Borjigin et al., 2013). However, not everyone who experiences oxygen deprivation experiences a NDE. In one study of cardiac patients who were "brought back" after clinical death, only about 21 percent reported a NDE (Klemenc-Ketis, Kersnik & Grmec, 2010). Therefore, anoxia cannot be the sole cause of NDEs.

NDEs are generally experienced as positive, an effect that has been proposed to occur as a result of the release of endorphins that are released during stressful experiences (Agrillo, 2011). Some people who experience NDEs report spiritual growth as one consequence, and the degree of spiritual transformation is related to the depth of the NDE (Greyson & Khanna, 2014). NDEs are predicted to occur more frequently in the coming years as survival rates continue to improve with modern resuscitation techniques (Agrillo, 2011; van Lommel, 2011).

CONFRONTING ONE'S OWN DEATH

The psychiatrist Elisabeth Kübler-Ross, in her pioneering work with dying people, found that most of them welcomed an opportunity to speak openly about their condition and were aware of being close to death, even when they had not been told. After speaking with some 500 terminally ill patients, Kübler-Ross (1969, 1970) outlined five stages in coming to terms with death: (1) *denial* ("This can't be happening to me!"); (2) *anger* ("Why me?"); (3) *bargaining for extra time* ("If I can only live to see my daughter married, I won't ask for anything more"); (4) *depression;* and ultimately (5) *acceptance.* She also proposed a similar progression in the feelings of people facing imminent bereavement (Kübler-Ross, 1975).

Kübler-Ross's model has been criticized and modified by other professionals who work with dying patients. Although the emotions she described are common, not everyone goes through all five stages and not necessarily in the same sequence. A person may go back and forth between anger and depression, for example, or may feel both at once.

Dying, like living, is an individual experience. For some people, denial or anger may be a healthier way to face death than calm acceptance. Kübler-Ross's findings, valuable as they are in helping us understand the feelings of those who are facing the end of life, should not be considered the sole model or criterion for a "good death."

PATTERNS OF GRIEVING

The death of a loved one is a difficult thing. First, there is **grief,** the emotional response that generally follows closely on the heels of death. This is followed by **bereavement.** Bereavement is a response to the loss of someone to whom a person feels close. But bereavement is not just an event, and it is not just grief—it is also a process of adjustment.

Bereavement often brings about a change in role or status. For example, a person may have to adjust to becoming a widow after previously being a wife, or as an orphan after previously being a son or daughter. There may be social or economic consequences as well—a loss of friends and sometimes of income. In short, bereavement can affect practically all aspects of a person's life.

The Classic Grief Work Model How do people grieve? A classic pattern of grief is three stages in which the bereaved person accepts the painful reality of the loss, gradually lets go of the bond with the dead person, and readjusts to life by developing new interests and relationships. This process of **grief work,** often takes the following path—though, as with Kübler-Ross's stages, it may vary (J. T. Brown & Stoudemire, 1983; R. Schulz, 1978).

1. *Shock and disbelief.* Immediately following a death, survivors often feel lost and confused. As awareness of the loss sinks in, the initial numbness gives way to overwhelming feelings of sadness and frequent crying. This first stage may last several weeks, especially after a sudden or unexpected death.

2. *Preoccupation with the memory of the dead person.* In the second stage, which may last 6 months to 2 years or so, the survivor tries to come to terms with the death

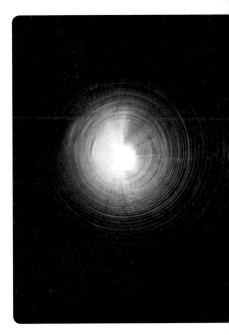

When a brain is deprived of oxygen, certain images arise due to alterations in the visual cortex and can result in the perception of a tunnel, like the images reported by people who have had near-death experiences.
©Mark Gibbons/Alamy Stock Photo

grief
Emotional response experienced in the early phases of bereavement.

bereavement
Loss, due to death, of someone to whom one feels close and the process of adjustment to the loss.

grief work
Working out of psychological issues connected with grief.

but cannot yet accept it. These experiences diminish with time, though they may recur—perhaps for years—on such occasions as the anniversary of the marriage or of the death.

3. *Resolution.* The final stage has arrived when the bereaved person renews interest in everyday activities. Memories of the dead person bring fond feelings mingled with sadness rather than sharp pain and longing.

Some people recover quickly from the loss of a loved one; others never do. ©Spohn Matthieu/PhotoAlto Agency RF Collections/Getty Images

Grieving: Multiple Variations Although the pattern of grief work just described is common, grieving does not necessarily follow a straight line from shock to resolution. In the *commonly expected* pattern, the mourner goes from high to low distress. In the *absent grief* pattern, the mourner does not experience intense distress, either immediately or later. In the *chronic grief* pattern, the mourner remains distressed for a long time (Wortman & Silver, 1989). Chronic grief may be especially painful and acceptance most difficult when a loss is *ambiguous,* as when a loved one is missing and presumed dead.

Sometimes the assumption is made that something is wrong if a bereaved person shows only mild distress and moves on quickly from the death of a loved one. However, research suggests this is a common pattern. A series of studies (Boerner, Wortman & Bonanno, 2005; Bonanno, Wortman & Nesse, 2004) showed that approximately 46 percent of participants reported *resilience:* a low and gradually diminishing level of distress following the death of a loved one. The resilient mourners expressed acceptance of death as a natural process. While many expressed yearning and emotional pangs in the first 6 months, after this point they spent relatively little time thinking about or searching for meaning in it. They demonstrate that "'doing well' after a loss is not necessarily a cause for concern but rather a normal response for many older adults" (Boerner et al., 2005, p. P72).

The knowledge that grief takes varied forms and patterns has important implications for helping people deal with loss (Boerner et al., 2004, 2005; Bonanno et al., 2002). Table 19.1 lists suggestions for helping those who have lost a loved one. It may be unnecessary and even harmful to urge or lead mourners to work through a loss or to expect them to follow a set pattern of emotional reactions. While bereavement therapy may help some people, the evidence suggests that many people will recover on their own if given time (Neimeyer & Currier, 2009).

ATTITUDES ABOUT DEATH AND DYING ACROSS THE LIFE SPAN

There is no single way of viewing death at any age. As the timing-of-events model suggests, death probably does not mean the same thing to an 85-year-old man with excruciatingly painful arthritis, a 56-year-old woman at the height of a brilliant legal career who discovers she has breast cancer, and a 15-year-old who dies of an overdose of drugs.

TABLE 19.1 Helping Someone Who Has Lost a Loved One

- *Share the sorrow.* Allow—or encourage—the bereaved person to talk about feelings of loss and share memories of the deceased person.

- *Don't offer false comfort.* Saying such things as "It's all for the best" or "You'll get over it in time" is not helpful. Instead, simply express sorrow—and take time to listen.

- *Offer practical help.* Babysitting, cooking, and running errands are ways to help someone who is grieving.

- *Be patient.* It can take a long time to recover from a significant loss. Be available to talk and listen.

- *Suggest professional help when necessary.* Don't hesitate to recommend professional help when it appears that someone is experiencing too much pain to cope alone.

Source: National Mental Health Association. (n.d.). *Coping with loss—bereavement and grief* [Fact sheet]. Alexandria, VA: Author.

Childhood and Adolescence According to early neo-Piagetian research (Speece & Brent, 1984), sometime between ages 5 and 7 most children come to understand that death is *irreversible*—that a dead person, animal, or flower cannot come to life again; that it is *universal* (all living things die) and therefore *inevitable;* and that a dead person is *nonfunctional* (all life functions end at death). These understandings usually develop during the shift from preoperational to concrete operational thinking, when concepts of causation become more mature.

More recent research suggests that children may acquire a partial understanding of what happens after death as early as age 4. In a series of studies preschoolers and kindergartners expressed knowledge that a dead mouse will never be alive again or grow up to be an old mouse, but 54 percent said the mouse might still need to eat. By age 7, 91 percent of the children were consistent in their knowledge that such biological processes as eating and drinking cease at death. Yet when similar questions were put in psychological terms ("Is he still hungry?"), children this age and younger were less consistent. Only 21 percent of kindergartners and 55 percent of early elementary students knew, for example, that a dead mouse would no longer feel sick, compared with 75 percent of late elementary students ages 11 to 12. And only 30 percent of the late elementary group correctly answered questions about whether thoughts, feelings, and desires persist after death (Bering & Bjorklund, 2004). Additionally, being taught about an afterlife can result in a U-shaped curve for some of these beliefs. One study of British schoolchildren found that 10- to 11-year-olds gave explanations about death not being final that were couched in their belief in an afterlife. In other words, these children argued that people continued to exist in some way despite dying, but their beliefs did not reflect cognitive immaturity; rather, they reflected explicit spiritual beliefs they had been taught (Hopkins, 2014).

Children can better understand death if they are introduced to the concept at an early age and are encouraged to talk about it. For example, the death of a pet or knowing another child that dies may provide an opportunity. For children with terminal illnesses, the need to understand death may be more pressing and more concrete. Yet parents often avoid bringing up the subject. In so doing, they may miss an opportunity for the child and family to prepare emotionally for what is to come (Wolfe, 2004). Not surprisingly, children who have had experience with the death of a loved one have a more realistic view of death than children who have not experienced such an event (Bonoti, Leondari & Mastora, 2013; Hunter & Smith, 2008). However, whether or not children have been raised in a secular or religious fashion does not seem to impact understanding of death (Bering, Blasi & Bjorkland, 2005).

If children are old enough to love, they are old enough to grieve. However, they may have difficulty expressing or understanding their grief. Like their understanding of death, this depends on cognitive and emotional development. Children sometimes express grief through anger, acting out, or refusal to acknowledge a death, as if the pretense that a person is still alive will make it so. They may be confused by adults' euphemisms: that someone "passed on" or that the family "lost" someone or that someone is "asleep" and will never awaken.

Adjusting to loss is more difficult if a child had a troubled relationship with the person who died; if a surviving parent depends too much on the child; if the death was unexpected, especially if it was a murder or suicide; if the child has had previous behavioral or emotional problems; or if family and community support are lacking (AAP Committee on Psychosocial Aspects of Child and Family Health, 1992).

Parents and other adult caregivers can help children deal with bereavement by explaining that death is final and inevitable and that they did not cause the death by their misbehavior or thoughts. Children need reassurance that they will continue to receive care from loving adults. It is usually advisable to make as few changes as possible in a child's environment, relationships, and daily activities; to answer questions simply and honestly; and to encourage the child to talk about his or her feelings and about the person who died (Schonfeld, Demaria & Committee on Psychosocial Aspects of Child and Family Health, 2016).

For adolescents, while they are capable of a mature understanding of death, it is not something they normally think much about unless they are directly faced with it. Most teens are at the beginning of their lives, and generally their contact with death involves the death of a loved one rather than their own mortality.

In the event of a close death, teens benefit from talking about it, although support and assistance for them is not always present (Schonfeld et al., 2016). Often teens may turn to peers for such support (Dopp & Cain, 2012). At the same time teens must process their own grief they are often also asked to take on more adult responsibilities, such as helping take care of younger siblings or providing emotional support to a surviving parent (Schonfeld et al., 2016). The bereavement process can lead to academic problems, especially for juniors and seniors in high school (Schonfeld & Quackenbush, 2010), and mental health issues, particularly depression, conduct disorder, and increased likelihood of substance abuse (Brent, Melhem, Donohoe & Walker, 2009; Kaplow, Saunders, Angold & Costello, 2010).

Fortunately, much of the grief response in both children and adolescents declines over time. However, a subset of young people experience persistent or even increasing grief over time (Melhem, Porta, Shamsseddeen, Payne & Brent, 2011). A recent meta-analysis showed that while the effect size was small to moderate, therapeutic interventions could have positive effects on the bereavement process that persisted over time. The most promising treatment approaches were musical therapy and brief psychotherapy (Rosner, Kruse & Hagl, 2010).

Adulthood Young adults who have finished their education and have embarked on careers, marriage, or parenthood are generally eager to live the lives they have been preparing for. If they are suddenly struck by a potentially fatal illness or injury, they are likely to be extremely frustrated and angry. People who develop terminal illnesses in their twenties or thirties must face issues of death and dying at an age when they normally would be dealing with such issues of young adulthood as establishing an intimate relationship. Rather than having a long lifetime of losses as gradual preparation for the final loss of life, they find their entire world collapsing at once.

In middle age, most adults' bodies send them signals that they are not as young, agile, and hearty as they once were. More and more they think about how many years they may have left and how to make the most of those years (Neugarten, 1967). Often—especially after the death of both parents—there is a new awareness of being the older generation or the next in line to die (Scharlach & Fredriksen, 1993). Middle-age and older adults may prepare for death emotionally as well as in practical ways by making a will, planning their funerals, and discussing their wishes with family and friends.

Older adults may have mixed feelings about the prospect of dying. Physical losses and other problems may diminish their pleasure in living and their will to live (McCue, 1995). Some older adults give up on achieving unfulfilled goals. Others push harder to do what they can with life in the time they have left. Many try to extend their remaining time by adopting healthier lifestyles or struggle to live even when they are profoundly ill (Cicirelli, 2002). When they think or talk of their impending death, some older adults express fear or anxiety. The larger the discrepancy between how long they want to live and how long they think they have left, the greater the distress (Cicirelli, 2006).

Terror Management Theory Regardless of age, the awareness of death is distressing and has the potential to result in declines in well-being and increases in anxiety (Juhl & Routledge, 2016). One approach—Terror Management Theory (TMT)—proposes that humans' unique understanding of death, in concert with self-preservation needs and capacity for fear, results in common emotional and psychological responses when mortality, or thoughts of death, are made salient.

One common response to thoughts of death is to become more committed to a cultural worldview (Rosenblatt, Greenberg, Solomon, Pyszczynski & Lyon, 1989). For example, when death is made salient, people are more likely to endorse their religious beliefs and they believe more strongly in the afterlife (Vail et al., 2010; Lehto & Stein, 2009). This stronger adherence to a religious ideology provides psychological comfort. Another implication of TMT is that high self-esteem should buffer people against anxiety and fear over death. Feeling significant and valuable to others can help people believe they are more

When death is made salient, stronger adherence to a religious ideology can provide psychological comfort. ©Design Pics/Don Hammond

than their physical body. Generally, research has supported a link between high self-esteem and less anxiety regarding death (Burke, Martens & Faucher, 2010). Last, mortality salience has been associated with attachment processes. Seeking comfort from loved ones is a common response in humans undergoing threat. Therefore, those people who have more secure attachment relationships would be predicted to show less anxiety in the face of death, a finding that has been verified in research (Mikulincer & Florian, 2000).

Significant Losses

Especially difficult losses that may occur during adulthood are the deaths of a spouse, a parent, or a child.

SURVIVING A SPOUSE

Because women tend to live longer than men and to be younger than their husbands, they are more likely to be widowed. They also tend to be widowed at an earlier age. Some 34 percent of U.S. women, but only 12 percent of U.S. men, lose their spouse by age 65 (Federal Interagency Forum on Aging-Related Statistics, 2010).

The stress of widowhood often affects physical and mental health. Bereavement can lead to headaches, memory problems, difficulty with concentration, dizziness, indigestion, loss of appetite, or chest pain. It also entails higher risks of disability, drug use, anxiety, depression, insomnia, hospitalization, and even death (Stroebe, Schut, & Stroebe, 2007). A meta-analysis of mortality risk including data from over 500 million people showed that becoming a widowed person is associated with a 22 percent increase in risk of death when compared to married people, and that this risk is higher for men (27 percent) than women (15 percent) (Moon, Kondo, Glymour & Subramanian, 2011). The risk of either natural death or suicide is greatest in the early months after a loss and is higher for younger adults. These reactions may range from fairly short and mild to extreme and long lasting, sometimes even for years (Stroebe et al., 2007).

The loss of companionship may help explain why a widowed person, especially a widower, may soon follow the spouse to the grave (Ray, 2004). However, a more practical explanation also may apply; after the death of a spouse, there may be no one to remind an older widow to take her pills or to make sure a widowed man adheres to a special diet. Those who receive such reminders (say, from children or health workers) tend to improve in health habits and reported health (Williams, 2004).

The quality of the marital relationship that has been lost may affect the degree to which widowhood affects mental health. Higher relationship quality during the marriage has been associated with greater anger, more anxiety, and feelings of yearning 6 months after the loss of the spouse (Carr & Boerner, 2009; Carr et al., 2000).

Widowhood can create practical problems too. For women, the main consequences of widowhood are more likely to be economic strain, whereas for men the chief consequences are more likely to be social isolation and loss of emotional intimacy (Pudrovska et al., 2006). Women whose husbands were the chief breadwinners may experience economic hardship or fall into poverty (Hungerford, 2001). Older widows are more likely than older widowers to stay in touch with friends from whom they receive social support (Kinsella & Velkoff, 2001).

Ultimately, the distress of loss can be a catalyst for introspection and growth (Lieberman, 1996). In one study, widows continued to talk and think about their deceased husbands decades after the loss, but these thoughts rarely upset them. Instead, these women said they had become stronger and more self-confident as a result of their loss (Carnelley, Wortman, Bolger & Burke, 2006).

LOSING A PARENT IN ADULTHOOD

The loss of a parent at any time is difficult, even in adulthood (Marks, Jun & Song, 2007). The majority of bereaved adult children still experience emotional distress—ranging from sadness and crying to depression and thoughts of suicide—after 1 to 5 years, especially

Older widows are more likely than older widowers to stay in touch with friends and benefit from the support of a social network.
© Belushi/Shutterstock

following loss of a mother (Scharlach & Fredriksen, 1993). Still, the death of a parent can be a maturing experience. It can push adults into resolving important developmental issues: achieving a stronger sense of self and a more pressing, realistic awareness of their own mortality, along with a greater sense of purpose, responsibility, commitment, and interconnectedness to others (Pope, 2005; Moss & Moss, 1989; Scharlach & Fredriksen, 1993).

Conflict between siblings is common when a parent is dying. Thus, whether and how a parent planned for death can impact their relationships. When adult parents leave instructions for the type of medical treatment they desire at the end of life, this generally results in less stressful decision making for their children (Tilden, Tolle, Nelson & Fields, 2001). However, regardless of the wishes of the dying parent, if siblings disagree on the treatment provided, this can damage their relationship. Siblings are less likely to engage in conflict over end-of-life care when parents designate someone outside of the family as the person who will make decisions about end of life care (Khodyakov & Carr, 2009; Kramer, Boelk & Auer, 2006)

The impact of a parent's death on siblings is equivocal. Some research suggests that following the death of a parent, siblings tend to grow less close. This may be because the link that bound them together in their adult life—a parent—is gone (Walker, Allen & Connidis, 2005), or it may be because of conflict following parental death about such aspects as funeral arrangements or distribution of assets (Umberson, 2003). Other research suggests that parental death may lead to more close relationships. A bereaved adult child may assume more responsibility for the surviving parent and for keeping the family together (Aldwin & Levenson, 2001). Additionally, the intense emotions of bereavement may draw siblings closer, and their parent's death may eliminate previous sources of dissent and disagreement over care and medical decisions (Umberson, 2003).

The death of a second parent can have especially great impact. The adult child may feel a sharpened sense of mortality now that the buffer of the older generation is gone (Aldwin & Levenson, 2001). This awareness can be an opportunity for growth, leading to a more mature outlook on life and a greater appreciation of the value of personal relationships (Scharlach & Fredriksen, 1993).

LOSING A CHILD

A parent is rarely prepared emotionally for the death of a child. Such a death, no matter at what age, comes as a cruel, unnatural shock, an untimely event that, in the normal course of things, should never happen. The parents may feel they have failed, no matter how much they loved and cared for the child, and they may find it hard to let go. If a marriage is strong, the couple may draw closer together, supporting each other in their shared loss. In other cases, the loss weakens and eventually destroys the marriage (Brandt, 1989). Parents who have lost a child are at heightened risk of being depressed or hospitalized for mental illness (Rogers, Floyd, Seltzer, Greenberg & Hong, 2008; Li, Laursen, Precht, Olsen & Mortensen, 2005). The stress of a child's loss may even hasten a parent's death (Li, Precht, Mortensen & Olsen, 2003). Those parents who are able to make some sense of the loss generally show less intense grief (Keesee, Currier & Neimeyer, 2008). However, even decades later, most parents express lasting grief (Rogers et al., 2008).

Many parents hesitate to discuss a terminally ill child's impending death with the child, but those who do so tend to achieve a sense of closure that helps them cope after the loss. In one study, approximately one-third of the parents said they had talked with their children about their impending death, and none of these parents regretted having done so, whereas 27 percent of those who had not brought up the subject regretted it (Kreicbergs, Valdimarsdottir, Onelov, Henter & Steineck, 2004).

The impact of parental bereavement may vary depending on such factors as the age of the child, the cause of death, and the number of remaining children a couple has. In a longitudinal study, 219 Dutch couples who had lost a child were followed for 20 months after the death. Grief was greater the older the child (up to age 17). Parents whose child had died a traumatic death grieved more than those whose child had died of an illness or disorder or those who experienced a stillbirth or neonatal death. Parents who had expected the death and those who had other children expressed the least grief. Mothers tended to grieve more than fathers. As time went by, grief tended to diminish, especially among couples who became pregnant again (Wijngaards-de Meij et al., 2005).

Although each bereaved parent must cope with grief in his or her own way, some have found that plunging into work, interests, and other relationships or joining a support group eases the pain. Some well-meaning friends tell parents not to dwell on their loss, but remembering the child in a meaningful way may be exactly what they need to do. When asked what most helped them cope with the end of their child's life, 73 percent of parents whose children died in intensive-care units gave religious or spiritual responses. They mentioned prayer, faith, discussions with clergy, or a belief that the parent-child relationship endures beyond death. Parents also said they were guided by insight and wisdom, inner values, and spiritual virtues such as hope, trust, and love (Robinson, Thiel, Backus & Meyer, 2006).

MOURNING A MISCARRIAGE

Estimates are that somewhere around one in three pregnancies end in miscarriage (Smith, Rissel, Richters, Grulich & Visser, 2003). Families, friends, and health professionals tend to avoid talking about such losses, which often are considered insignificant compared with the loss of a living child (Van, 2001). Grief can be more wrenching without social support.

How do prospective parents cope with the loss of a child they never knew? Each person's or couple's experience of loss is unique, although grief, especially in women, is the most common response (Brier, 2008). In one small study, 11 men whose child had died in utero reported being overcome with frustration and helplessness during and after the delivery, but several found relief in supporting their partners (Samuelsson, Radestad & Segesten, 2001). In another study, grieving parents perceived their spouses and extended families as most helpful and their doctors as least helpful. Some bereaved parents benefitted from a support group, and some not (DiMarco, Menke & McNamara, 2001). Whether married or living together, couples who experience a miscarriage prior to 20 weeks gestation are 22 percent more likely to break up than couples who have a successful pregnancy. When the miscarriage occurs after 20 weeks gestation, that risk is elevated by as much as 40 percent (Gold, Sen & Hayward, 2010).

Medical, Legal, and Ethical Issues: The "Right to Die"

Do people have a right to die? Should a terminally ill person who wants to commit suicide be allowed or helped to do so? Who decides that a life is not worth prolonging?

SUICIDE

Although suicide is no longer a crime in modern societies, there is still a stigma against it, based in part on religious prohibitions and in part on society's interest in preserving life. A person who expresses suicidal thoughts may be mentally ill, and the desire to die may be temporary and disappear when mental illness abates or circumstances change. On the other hand, a growing number of people consider a mature adult's deliberate choice of a time to end his or her life a rational decision and a right to be defended.

Suicide rates in the United States peaked in 1977 at 13.7 deaths per 100,000 people. Despite some variation, including a slight increase in the late 1980s, it slowly declined to a low of 10.4 in 2000. Since that time, however, the rate has begun to increase again, and as of 2014 was 13.0 deaths per 100,000 people (Xu, Kochanek et al., 2010; Curtin, Warner & Hedegaard, 2016). In the United States, over 42,000 people committed suicide in 2014 (Kochanek, Murphy, Xu & Tejada-Vera, 2016). Still, this rate is lower than in many other industrialized countries (Kinsella & Velkoff, 2001).

Statistics probably understate the number of suicides; many go unreported and some (such as traffic "accidents" and "accidental" medicinal overdoses) are not recognized as

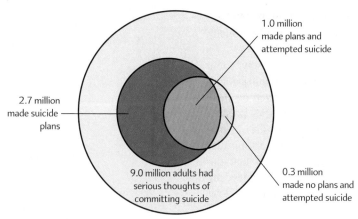

2.7 million
made suicide
plans

1.0 million
made plans and
attempted suicide

9.0 million adults had
serious thoughts of
committing suicide

0.3 million
made no plans and
attempted suicide

FIGURE 19.1

About 1.3 million people attempted suicide in 2012.

Source: Substance Abuse and Mental Health Services Administration, *Results from the 2012 National Survey on Drug Use and Health: Mental Health Findings*, NSDUH Series H-47, HHS Publication No. (SMA) 13-4805. Rockville, MD: Substance Abuse and Mental Health Services Administration, 2013, fig. 3.2.

The highest rate of suicide is among white men age 75 and over; the risk rises among men 85 and older. Older people are more likely than younger people to be depressed and socially isolated.
©Anna Lurye/Shutterstock

such. Also, the figures on suicides often do not include suicide *attempts;* an estimated 20 to 60 percent of people in the United States who commit suicide have tried before, and about 10 percent of people who attempt suicide will kill themselves within 10 years (Harvard Medical School, 2003).

In most nations, suicide rates rise with age and are higher among men than among women (Curtin et al., 2016; Kinsella & Velkoff, 2001; Nock et al., 2008), though more women consider or attempt suicide (Figure 19.1). Young, unmarried women with little education and those who are unusually impulsive, anxious, or depressed are most at risk for suicidal thoughts and behavior (Nock et al., 2008). Historically males were far more likely to succeed in taking their own life, but this gap has greatly diminished in recent years and males are only marginally more likely to attempt suicide (National Survey on Drug Use and Health, 2009). Men's suicide rates are higher mainly because they are far more likely to use reliable methods, such as firearms, whereas women are more likely to choose other means, such as poisoning or hanging. More than half of completed suicides are by gunshot (CDC, 2007a; Kung et al., 2008; Miniño et al., 2007), and the rates of suicide using firearms are much higher in the United States than in other similar industrialized nations (Richardson & Hemenway, 2010), presumably because of easy accessibility to firearms (Anglemyer, Horvath & Rutherford, 2014). Suicide by suffocation has increased recently; approximately 1 in 4 suicides in 2014 were the result of suffocation (Curtin et al., 2016).

Suicide rates vary among ethic and racial lines. Native American and Alaskan Natives have the highest rates, at 19.89 per 100,000 people. They are followed by whites (18.12), Asian/Pacific Islanders (6.66), African Americans (5.78), and Hispanics (5.84) (Centers for Disease Control, 2016f). While older blacks are only about one-third as likely to commit suicide as older whites (NCHS, 2006), suicide rates among black people, especially those who are younger and less educated, have increased significantly since the mid-1980s (Joe, Baser, Breeden, Neighbors & Jackson, 2006).

Due to a jump in midlife suicide (Table 19.2), U.S. suicide rates now reach a high for adults in their forties and early fifties and then subside and rise again after age 75 (Xu et al., 2010).

TABLE 19.2 Changes in Suicide Rates by Age, United States, 2000–2014

SUICIDE RATE, PER 100,000 PEOPLE		
Age Group	Rate in 2000	Rate in 2014
15 to 24	10.2	11.6
25 to 34	12.0	15.1
35 to 44	14.5	16.6
45 to 54	14.4	20.2
55 to 64	12.1	18.8
65 to 74	12.5	15.6
75 to 84	17.6	17.5
85 and over	19.6	19.3

Source: Kochanek, K. D., Murphy, S. L., Xu, J., & Tejada-Vera, B. (2016). *Deaths: final data for 2014. National vital statistics reports: from the Centers for Disease Control and Prevention, National Center for Health Statistics, National Vital Statistics System*, 65(4), 1-122.

Although some people intent on suicide carefully conceal their plans, most give warning signs. These may include talking about death or suicide; giving away prized possessions; abusing drugs or alcohol; and personality changes, such as unusual anger, sadness, boredom, or apathy. People who are about to kill themselves may neglect their appearance and sleep or eat much more or less than usual. They often show signs of depression, such as unusual difficulty concentrating, loss of self-esteem, and feelings of helplessness, hopelessness, or panic (American College of Emergency Physicians, 2008; Harvard Medical School, 2003). Table 19.3 lists warning signs of suicide and steps to take if someone threatens suicide.

Survivors of people who take their own lives have been called "suicide's other victims." Many blame themselves for failing to recognize the signs. They "obsessively replay the events leading up to the death, imagining how they could have prevented it and berating themselves for their failure to do so" (Goldman & Rothschild, n.d.). Because of the stigma attached to suicide, these survivors often struggle with their emotions alone rather than share them with others who might understand (Schomerus et al., 2015).

HASTENING DEATH

Medical technology has outpaced our legal system and ethics way. Until recent decades, the idea of helping a suffering loved one hasten death was virtually unheard of. Changing

TABLE 19.3 Preventing Suicide

WARNING SIGNS OF SUICIDE:

- Feeling depressed, down, or excessively sad.
- Feelings of hopelessness, worthlessness, or having no purpose in life, along with a loss of interest or pleasure in doing things.
- Preoccupation with death, dying, or violence, or talking about wanting to die.
- Seeking access to medications, weapons, or other means of committing suicide.
- Wide mood swings—feeling extremely up one day and terribly down the next.
- Feelings of great agitation, rage, or uncontrolled anger, or wanting to get revenge.
- Changes in eating and sleeping habits, appearance, behavior, or personality.
- Risky or self-destructive behavior, such as driving recklessly or taking illegal drugs.
- Sudden calmness (a sign that a person has made the decision to attempt suicide).
- Life crises, trauma, or setbacks, including school, work, or relationship problems, job loss, divorce, death of a loved one, financial difficulties, diagnosis of a terminal illness.
- Putting one's affairs in order, including giving away belongings, visiting family members and friends, drawing up a will, or writing a suicide note.

IF SOMEONE THREATENS SUICIDE:

- Stay calm.
- Take the threat seriously.
- Don't leave the person alone. Prevent access to firearms, knives, medications, or any other item the person may use to commit suicide.
- Don't try to handle the situation alone. Call 911 or the local emergency response number. Phone the person's doctor, the police, a local crisis intervention team, or others who are trained to help.
- While waiting for help, listen closely to the person. Let the person know you're listening by maintaining eye contact, moving closer, or holding his or her hand, if appropriate.
- Ask questions to determine what method of suicide the person is considering and whether he or she has an organized plan.
- Remind the person that help is available.
- If the person does attempt suicide, immediately call for emergency medical assistance and administer first aid, if necessary.

Source: American College of Emergency Physicians. (2008, March 10). *Know suicide's warning sign*. Irving, TX: Author.

attitudes toward hastening death can be attributed largely to revulsion against technologies that keep patients alive against their will despite intense suffering, and sometimes even after the brain has stopped functioning.

Euthanasia *Euthanasia* means "good death" and is intended to end suffering or to allow a terminally ill person to die with dignity. People differ in their beliefs about this process, and some draw distinctions between the types of euthanasia used. **Passive euthanasia** involves withholding or discontinuing treatment that might extend the life of a terminally ill patient, such as medication, life support systems, or feeding tubes. Many people would characterize turning off the life support systems as passive euthanasia. Passive euthanasia is generally legal. **Active euthanasia** (sometimes called *mercy killing*) involves action taken directly or deliberately to shorten a life, and it is generally illegal. An important question regarding either form of euthanasia is whether it is done at the direct request, or to carry out the express wishes, of the person whose death results.

Advance Directives Some of the issues surrounding how much medical technology should be used to keep a person alive near the end of life can be addressed if people's wishes are made clear before they are incapacitated. The U.S. Supreme Court held that a person whose wishes are clearly known has a constitutional right to refuse or discontinue life-sustaining treatment (*Cruzan v. Director, Missouri Department of Health,* 1990). A mentally competent person's wishes can be spelled out in advance in a document called an **advance directive (living will),** which contains instructions for when and how to discontinue futile medical care. All 50 states have since legalized some form of advance directive or adopted other provisions governing the making of end-of-life decisions. However, only about 35 percent of people report having written down their wishes for end-of-life care and 27 percent say they have given no thought to it at all (Duggan, 2014).

A *living will* may contain specific provisions with regard to circumstances in which treatment should be discontinued, what extraordinary measures—if any—should be taken to prolong life, and what kind of pain management is desired. A person also may specify, through a donor card or a signature on the back of his or her driver's license, that his or her organs be donated to someone in need of an organ transplant.

Some living will legislation applies only to terminally ill patients, not to those who are incapacitated by illness or injury but may live many years in severe pain. Thus, advance directives may not help them. Similarly, advance directives may not help patients in comas or in persistent vegetative states. Such situations can be covered by a **durable power of attorney,** which appoints another person to make decisions if the maker of the document becomes incompetent to do so. A number of states have adopted a simple form known as a *medical durable power of attorney* expressly for decisions about health care.

Advance care planning is beneficial not just to the dying person, but also to the family. Having a plan of action when death is imminent leads to improved end-of-life care and results in higher levels of family satisfaction, and reductions in stress, anxiety, and depression in family members of the terminally ill patient (Detering, Hancock, Reade & Silvester, 2010). Unfortunately, even with advance planning, directives are not always followed. Often they are unavailable during a crisis, or the wishes of the ill or dying adult are overruled in the moment (Perkins, 2007). Plans for end-of-life are more likely to be followed if the decisions for care are made within the context of coordinated interventions where medical personnel, family members, and trained facilitators work together to determine a course of action (Brinkman-Stoppelenburg, Rietjens & van der Heide, 2014).

Assisted Suicide: Pros and Cons **Assisted suicide**—in which a physician or someone else helps a person bring about a self-inflicted death by, for example, prescribing or obtaining drugs or enabling a patient to inhale a deadly gas—commonly refers to situations in which people with incurable, terminal illnesses request help in ending their lives. Assisted suicide is still illegal in most places but in recent years has come to the forefront of public debate. It may be similar in principle to voluntary active euthanasia, in which, for example, a patient asks for, and receives, a lethal injection; but in assisted suicide the person who wants to die performs the actual deed.

---

passive euthanasia
Withholding or discontinuation of life-prolonging treatment of a terminally ill person in order to end suffering or allow death with dignity.

active euthanasia
Deliberate action taken to shorten the life of a terminally ill person in order to end suffering or to allow death with dignity; also called *mercy killing*.

advance directive (living will)
Document specifying the type of care wanted by the maker in the event of an incapacitating or terminal illness.

durable power of attorney
Legal instrument that appoints an individual to make decisions in the event of another person's incapacitation.

assisted suicide
Suicide in which a physician or someone else helps a person take his or her own life.

As of June 2018, assisted suicide is legal in seven states (California, Oregon, Washington, Colorado, Montana, Hawaii, and Vermont) and Washington, D.C. (Death with Dignity, 2018). The American College of Physicians (Sulmasy & Mueller, 2017) and the American Medical Association (American Medical Association, 2018) opposes physician aid in dying as contrary to a practitioner's oath to "do no harm." The American Psychological Association takes no position, neither endorsing nor opposing assisted suicide (American Psychological Association, 2017b). The American public is split with respect to the issue; 47 percent are in favor of laws to legalize assisted suicide, 49 percent are opposed (Duggan, 2014).

The *ethical arguments for* assisted suicide are based on the principles of autonomy and self-determination: that mentally competent persons should have the right to control the quality of their own lives and the timing and nature of their death. Proponents of assisted suicide place a high value on preserving the dignity and personhood of the dying human being. *Medical arguments* hold that a doctor is obligated to take all measures necessary to relieve suffering. Additionally, in assisted suicide the patient, not the doctor, is the one who takes the actual step to end life. A *legal argument* is that legalizing assisted suicide would permit the regulation of practices that now occur anyway out of compassion for suffering patients. It is argued that adequate safeguards against abuse can be put in place through a combination of legislation and professional regulation (APA Online, 2001).

Some ethical and legal scholars go further: They favor legalizing all forms of *voluntary euthanasia* with safeguards against involuntary euthanasia. The key issue, according to these scholars, is not how death occurs but who makes the decision. They see no difference in principle between pulling the plug on a respirator, pulling out feeding tubes, giving a lethal injection, or prescribing an overdose of pills at the patient's request. They maintain that aid in dying, if openly available, would reduce fear and helplessness by enabling patients to control their own fate (APA Online, 2001; Orentlicher, 1996).

Ethical arguments against assisted suicide center on two principles: (1) the belief that taking a life, even with consent, is wrong; and (2) concern for protection of the disadvantaged. Opponents of aid-in-dying point out that autonomy is often limited by poverty or disability or membership in a stigmatized social group, and they fear that persons in these categories may be subtly pressured into choosing suicide with cost containment as an underlying factor. *Medical arguments* against assisted suicide include the possibility of misdiagnosis, the potential future availability of new treatments, the likelihood of incorrect prognosis, and the belief that helping someone die is incompatible with a physician's role as healer and that adequate safeguards are not possible. *Legal arguments* against assisted suicide include concerns about enforceability of safeguards and about lawsuits when family members disagree about the propriety of terminating a life (APA Online, 2001).

Some opponents contend that physician-assisted suicide would lead to voluntary active euthanasia (Groenewoud et al., 2000). The next step on the slippery slope, some warn, would be involuntary euthanasia—not only for the terminally ill but for others, such as people with disabilities, whose quality of life is perceived as diminished. The opponents also claim that people who want to die are often temporarily depressed and might change their minds with treatment or palliative care (APA Working Group on Assisted Suicide and End-of-Life Decisions, 2005; Quill et al., 1997).

Legalizing Physician Aid in Dying Since 1997, when a unanimous U.S. Supreme Court left regulation of physician aid-in-dying up to the states, measures to legalize assisted suicide for the terminally ill have been introduced in several states. Oregon was the first state to pass such a law, the Death with Dignity Act (DWDA). In 1994, Oregonians voted to let mentally competent patients, who have been told by two doctors that they have less than 6 months to live, request a lethal prescription with strong safeguards to make sure the request is serious and voluntary and that all other alternatives have been considered.

What has been the experience under the Oregon law? The legalization of assisted suicide has resulted in improvements of palliative care and an increased number of deaths occurring at home rather than in the hospital (Steinbrook, 2008). In the years 1997 to 2015, 1,545 terminally ill patients were reported to state health officials to have taken their lives, 218 of them in 2015. The concerns most frequently mentioned by patients who requested and used lethal prescriptions were loss of ability to participate in activities that make life enjoyable (96.2 percent), loss of autonomy (92.4 percent), and loss of dignity (75.4 percent). The median age at death was 73 years, and most who chose to end their lives were white and well-educated (Oregon Public Health Division, 2016).

Active euthanasia remains illegal in the United States but not in the Netherlands, where in 2002 a law permitting voluntary euthanasia for patients in a state of continuous, unbearable, and incurable suffering went into effect. In such cases, doctors can now inject a lethal dose of medication. Estimates are that somewhere around 1.8 to 2.9 percent of deaths in the Netherlands result from euthanasia or assisted suicide (Steck, Egger, Maessen, Reisch & Zwahlen, 2013).

Currently, euthanasia or physician-assisted suicide is also legal in Belgium, Luxembourg, Colombia, and Canada, with public support growing in Western Europe but declining in Central and Eastern Europe. In no areas, including the United States, does data indicate that vulnerable patients such as the disabled have been receiving physician-assisted suicide or euthanasia at higher rates than the general population (Radbruch et al., 2016).

End-of-Life Decisions and Cultural Attitudes Most Americans—62 percent—believe there is a moral right to end one's life in the event of great pain with no hope of improvement. This belief varies with respect to a number of demographic variables. Race and ethnicity matter; whites are more likely (65 percent) to support this statement than Hispanics (58 percent) and African Americans (52 percent). Religion also plays a role. Only 43 percent of white Evangelicals and black Protestants agree on the morality of suicide in the event of intractable pain. By contrast, white mainline Protestants (71 percent), Catholics (63 percent), and religiously unaffiliated adults (85 percent) believe it is a moral right (Pew Research Center, 2013). Roughly 84 percent of Americans support a terminally ill person's right to decide whether or not to be kept alive with medical treatment, and approximately 70 percent agree that there are some circumstances in which a person should be allowed to die (Parker, 2009a). Perhaps as a response to the dialogue surrounding end-of-life care, the belief that everything possible should always be done to save the life of a patient has risen from 22 percent in 2009 (Parker, 2009a) to 31 percent in 2013 (Pew Research Center, 2013).

The first representative study of end-of-life decisions in six European countries (Belgium, Denmark, Italy, the Netherlands, Sweden, and Switzerland) found important cultural differences. In all six countries, physicians reported withholding or withdrawing life-prolonging treatment—most typically medication, followed by hydration or nutrition—but the frequency varied greatly, from 41 percent of deaths in Switzerland to 6 percent in Italy (Bosshard et al., 2005). Active forms of physician-assisted death were most prevalent in the Netherlands and Belgium (van der Heide et al., 2003). In a later survey of physicians in the same six countries, direct physician-assisted deaths were rare, but in one-quarter to one-half of all deaths (23 percent in Italy, 51 percent in Switzerland), physicians made death-hastening decisions, such as deep sedation, sometimes accompanied by withdrawal of artificial nutrition and hydration (Bilsen, Cohen & Deliens, 2007).

End-of-Life Options and Diversity Concerns One beneficial result of the aid-in-dying controversy has been to call attention to the need for better palliative care and closer attention to patients' motivation and state of mind. When doctors talk openly with patients about their physical and mental symptoms, their expectations, their fears and goals, their options for end-of-life care, their family concerns, and their need for meaning and quality of life, ways may be found to diminish these concerns without the taking of life (Bascom & Tolle, 2002).

In the United States, with its ethnically diverse population, issues of social and cultural diversity need to be addressed in end-of-life decision making. Planning for death is inconsistent with traditional Navajo values, which avoid negative thinking and talk. Chinese families may seek to protect a dying person from unfavorable information, including knowledge of his or her impending death. Recent Mexican or Korean

research in action

PHYSICIAN-ASSISTED SUICIDE AND DEATH WITH DIGNITY LAWS

Brittany Maynard sparked national debate on physician-assisted suicide after a diagnosis of stage 4 malignant brain cancer. At 29 years old, she was given 6 months to live. Rather than waiting for cancer to slowly overtake her brain, Brittany moved from California to Oregon, where physician-assisted suicide was legal through Oregon's Death with Dignity law. She launched an online campaign in support of expansion of legalized physician-assisted suicide for the terminally ill; her video describing her situation and decision process received over 12 million views (https://www.youtube.com/watch?annotation_id=annotation_1855568639&feature=iv&src_vid=1lHXH0Zb2QI&v=yPfe3rCcUeQ). She died as she wished: peacefully, at home, with her husband and family (Bever, 2014).

Physician-assisted suicide (PAS), involves a formal patient request for prescription of a lethal dosage of medication with the intent of ending life (Sulmasy et al., 2017). The patient is the one who administers the fatal dose.

Over the years, public attitudes toward PAS have shifted dramatically. About 66 percent of Americans support permitting patients a means of ending one's life in the event of terminal illness (Emanuel et al., 2016). Oregon became the first state to legalize PAS in 1997. Six other states followed: Washington, Montana, Vermont, California, Colorado, and the District of Columbia (Sulmasy et al., 2017).

PAS opponents reject deliberate termination of life, often on moral grounds. Proponents argue for patients' autonomy, self-determination, and a compassionate end to human suffering (Levy et al., 2013; Pormeister, Finley & Rohack, 2017). The typical PAS recipient is a white male, over the age of 65, college-educated, with a terminal cancer diagnosis (Emanuel et al., 2016; Sulmasy et al., 2017). Use of PAS remains relatively rare, despite increasing state legalization, accounting for only 0.3 to 4.6 percent of all deaths in legal jurisdictions (Emanuel et al., 2016).

The American Medical Association views PAS in opposition to aims of health restoration for the sick (Yang et al., 2016). Physicians are bound by social justice principles, protecting human rights of society's most vulnerable members: the sick, disabled, poor, and minorities. Questions are raised whether these groups may be disproportionately affected by legalized PAS (Sulmasy et al., 2017).

Physicians endorse current standards of care, including patient right to refusal of treatment and further expansion of hospice and palliative care services. Palliative services deliver holistic care to patients, caregivers, and relatives with the goal of easing pain and suffering, increasing psychological and spiritual well-being, family adjustment, and a dignified transition to death (De Lima et al., 2017). Kelley and Morrison (2015) report that over 90 percent of American adults are unaware of the existence of palliative care services, but when educated, many desire these services for end of life.

Awareness of advanced planning options and compassionate physician care are deemed essential in supporting terminally ill patients. Physicians unfortunately experience challenges in providing intensive end-of-life care in time-pressured health care environments (Sulmasy et al., 2017). Many argue for universal accessibility to palliative care services, addressing physical, emotional, and psychological needs of dying patients and their families. Medical technology is essential to prolong life, but preservation of quality at the end of life is equally important to patients.

what's your view Do you support expansion of Death with Dignity laws to legalize physician-assisted suicide? What kinds of safeguards can be put into place to further protect patients?

---

immigrants may believe less in individual autonomy than is customary in the dominant U.S. culture. Among some ethnic minorities, the value of longevity may take priority over health. Both African Americans and Hispanics, for example, are more likely than European Americans to prefer life-sustaining treatment regardless of the state of the disease and of their educational level (Pew Research Center, 2013; APA Working Group on Assisted Suicide, 2005).

Issues of hastening death will become more pressing as the population ages. In years to come, both the courts and the public will be forced to come to terms with these issues as increasing numbers of people claim a right to die with dignity and with help.

Finding Meaning and Purpose in Life and Death

The struggle to find meaning in life and in death—often dramatized in books and movies—has been borne out by research. Studies examining religion and death have found that such beliefs are generally beneficial for the dying (Edmondson, Park, Chaudoir & Wortmann, 2008). According to Kübler-Ross (1975), facing the reality of death is a key to living a meaningful life:

> It is the denial of death that is partially responsible for [people] living empty, purpose-less lives; for when you live as if you'll live forever, it becomes too easy to postpone the things you know that you must do. In contrast, when you fully understand that each day you awaken could be the last you have, you take the time that day to grow, to become more of who you really are, to reach out to other human beings. (p. 164)

REVIEWING A LIFE

life review
Reminiscence about one's life in order to see its significance.

Life review is a process of reminiscence that enables a person to see the significance of his or her life. Life review can, of course, occur at any time. However, it may have special meaning in old age, when it can foster ego integrity—according to Erikson, the final critical task of the life span. As the end of their journey approaches, people may look back over their accomplishments and failures and ask themselves what their lives have meant. Awareness of mortality may be an impetus for reexamining values and seeing one's experiences and actions in a new light. Some people find the will to complete unfinished tasks, such as reconciling with estranged family members or friends, and thus to achieve a satisfying sense of closure.

Life review therapy and reminiscence interventions can help focus the natural process of life review and make it more conscious, purposeful, and efficient (Westerhof & Bohlmeijer, 2014; M. I. Lewis & Butler, 1974). Such interventions have been shown to reduce symptoms of depression and result in greater ego integrity (Pinquart & Forstmeier, 2012). Methods often used for uncovering memories in life review therapy include recording an autobiography; constructing a family tree; spending time with scrapbooks, photo albums, old letters, and other memorabilia; making a trip back to scenes of childhood and young adulthood; reuniting with former classmates or colleagues or distant family members; describing ethnic traditions; and summing up one's life's work.

DEVELOPMENT: A LIFELONG PROCESS

In his late seventies, the artist Pierre-Auguste Renoir had crippling arthritis and chronic bronchitis and had lost his wife. He spent his days in a wheelchair, and his pain was so great that he could not sleep through the night. He was unable to hold a palette or grip a brush: His brush had to be tied to his right hand. Yet he continued to produce brilliant paintings, full of color and vibrant life. Finally, stricken by pneumonia, he lay in bed, gazing at some anemones his attendant had picked. He gathered enough strength to sketch the form of these beautiful flowers, and then—just before he died—lay back and whispered, "I think I am beginning to understand something about it" (Hanson, 1968).

Even dying can be a developmental experience. As one health practitioner put it, "There are things to be gained, accomplished in dying. Time with and for those whom we are close to, achieving a final and enduring sense of self-worth, and a readiness to let go are priceless elements of a good death" (Weinberger, 1999).

Within a limited life span, no person can realize all capabilities, gratify all desires, explore all interests, or experience all the richness that life has to offer. The tension between possibilities for growth and a finite time in which to do the growing defines human life. By choosing which possibilities to pursue and by continuing to follow them as far as possible, even up to the very end, each person contributes to the unfinished story of human development.

Sharing memories evoked by a photo album is one way to review a life. Life review can help people recall important events and can motivate them to rebuild damaged relationships or complete unfinished tasks. ©Corbis/VCG/Getty Images

summary and key terms

The Many, Changing Meanings of Death and Dying

- Death has biological, social, cultural, historical, religious, legal, psychological, developmental, medical, and ethical aspects.
- Customs surrounding death and mourning vary greatly from one culture to another. Some modern customs have evolved from ancient beliefs and practices.
- Death rates dropped drastically during the twentieth century, especially in developed countries.
- Nearly three-quarters of deaths in the United States occur among the elderly, and the top causes of death are diseases that primarily affect older adults.
- As death became primarily a phenomenon of late adulthood, it became largely "invisible," and care of the dying took place in isolation, by professionals.
- There is now an upsurge of interest in understanding and dealing realistically and compassionately with death. Examples of this tendency are a growing interest in hospice care and palliative, or comfort, care.

thanatology, hospice care, palliative care

Facing Death and Loss

- People often undergo cognitive and functional declines shortly before death.
- Some people who come close to dying have "near-death" experiences that may result from physiological changes in the brain.
- Elisabeth Kübler-Ross proposed five stages in coming to terms with dying: denial, anger, bargaining, depression, and acceptance. These stages, and their sequence, are not universal.
- There is no universal pattern of grief. The most widely studied pattern moves from shock and disbelief to preoccupation with the memory of the dead person and finally to resolution. However, research has found wide variations and resilience.
- Children's understanding of death develops gradually. Young children can better understand death if it is part of their own experience.
- Adolescents generally do not think much about death, but benefit from talking to others, especially peers, in the event of the death of a loved one.
- Realization and acceptance of the inevitability of death increases throughout adulthood.
- Terror Management Theory states that mortality salience is a consequence of our ability to understand death and our self-preservation instincts. Research suggests that people may be buffered against the resulting anxiety by strong cultural beliefs, high self-esteem or secure attachment.

terminal drop, grief, bereavement, grief work

Significant Losses

- Women are more likely to be widowed, and widowed younger, than men, and they may experience widowhood somewhat differently. Physical and mental health tend to decline after widowhood, but for some people widowhood can ultimately become a positive developmental experience.
- Death of a parent can precipitate changes in the self and in relationships with others.
- The loss of a child can be especially difficult because it is not typical for most families.
- Because miscarriage and stillbirth are not generally considered significant losses in U.S. society, those who experience such losses are often left to deal with them with little social support.

Medical, Legal, and Ethical Issues: The "Right to Die"

- Although suicide is no longer illegal in many modern societies, there is still a stigma attached to it. Some people maintain a "right to die," especially for people with long-term degenerative illness or pain.
- The number of suicides is probably underestimated. It is often related to depression, isolation, family conflict, financial troubles, and debilitating ailments. There are many more suicide attempts than actual deaths.
- Euthanasia and assisted suicide involve controversial ethical, medical, and legal issues.
- To avoid unnecessary suffering through artificial prolongation of life, passive euthanasia is generally permitted with the patient's consent or with advance directives. However, such directives are not consistently followed.
- Active euthanasia and assisted suicide are generally illegal, but public support for physician aid-in-dying has increased. Seven states and the District of Columbia have laws permitting physician-assisted suicide for the terminally ill. European countries vary with respect to the beliefs about and legality of euthanasia and assisted suicide.
- The assisted suicide controversy has focused more attention on the need for better palliative care and understanding of patients' state of mind. Issues of social and cultural diversity need to be considered.

passive euthanasia, active euthanasia, advance directive (living will), durable power of attorney, assisted suicide

Finding Meaning and Purpose in Life and Death

- The more meaning and purpose people find in their lives, the less they tend to fear death.
- Life review can help people prepare for death and give them a last chance to complete unfinished tasks.
- Even dying can be a developmental experience.

life review

glossary

acceleration programs Programs for educating the gifted that move them through the curriculum at an unusually rapid pace.

accommodation Piaget's term for changes in a cognitive structure to include new information.

acquired immune deficiency syndrome (AIDS) Viral disease that undermines effective functioning of the immune system.

active engagement Personal involvement in schooling, work, family, or other activity.

active euthanasia Deliberate action taken to shorten the life of a terminally ill person in order to end suffering or to allow death with dignity; also called *mercy killing.*

activities of daily living (ADL) Essential activities that support survival, such as eating, dressing, bathing, and getting around the house.

activity theory Theory of aging that holds that to age successfully a person must remain as active as possible.

acute medical conditions Illnesses that last a short time.

adaptation Piaget's term for adjustment to new information about the environment, achieved through processes of assimilation and accommodation.

adolescence Developmental transition between childhood and adulthood entailing major physical, cognitive, and psychosocial changes.

adolescent growth spurt Sharp increase in height and weight that precedes sexual maturity.

adolescent rebellion Pattern of emotional turmoil, characteristic of a minority of adolescents, that may involve conflict with family, alienation from adult society, reckless behavior, and rejection of adult values.

advance directive (living will) Document specifying the type of care wanted by the maker in the event of an incapacitating or terminal illness.

age-related macular degeneration Condition in which the center of the retina gradually loses its ability to discern fine details; leading cause of irreversible visual impairment in older adults.

ageism Prejudice or discrimination against a person (most commonly an older person) based on age.

aging in place Remaining in one's own home, with or without assistance, in later life.

alcoholism Chronic disease involving dependence on use of alcohol, causing interference with normal functioning and fulfillment of obligations.

alleles Two or more alternative forms of a gene that occupy the same position on paired chromosomes and affect the same trait.

altruism Behavior intended to help others out of inner concern and without expectation of external reward; may involve self-denial or self-sacrifice.

altruistic behavior Activity intended to help another person with no expectation of reward.

Alzheimer's disease Progressive, irreversible, degenerative brain disorder characterized by cognitive deterioration and loss of control of bodily functions, leading to death.

ambiguous loss A loss that is not clearly defined or does not bring closure.

ambivalent (resistant) attachment Pattern in which an infant becomes anxious before the primary caregiver leaves, is extremely upset during his or her absence, and both seeks and resists contact on his or her return.

amyloid plaque Waxy chunks of insoluble tissue found in brains of persons with Alzheimer's disease.

animism Tendency to attribute life to objects that are not alive.

anorexia nervosa Eating disorder characterized by self-starvation.

anoxia Lack of oxygen, which may cause brain damage.

anticipatory smiling Infant smiles at an object and then gazes at an adult while still smiling.

Apgar scale Standard measurement of a newborn's condition; it assesses appearance, pulse, grimace, activity, and respiration.

art therapy Therapeutic approach that allows a person to express troubled feelings without words, using a variety of art materials and media.

assimilation Piaget's term for incorporation of new information into an existing cognitive structure.

assisted suicide Suicide in which a physician or someone else helps a person take his or her own life.

asthma A chronic respiratory disease characterized by sudden attacks of coughing, wheezing, and difficulty in breathing.

attachment Reciprocal, enduring tie between two people—especially between infant and caregiver—each of whom contributes to the quality of the relationship.

attention-deficit/hyperactivity disorder (ADHD) Syndrome characterized by persistent inattention and distractibility, impulsivity, low tolerance for frustration, and inappropriate overactivity.

authoritarian parenting In Baumrind's terminology, parenting style emphasizing control and obedience.

authoritative parenting In Baumrind's terminology, parenting style blending respect for a child's individuality with an effort to instill social values.

autobiographical memory Memory of specific events in one's life.

autonomy versus shame and doubt Erikson's second stage in psychosocial development, in which children achieve a balance between self-determination and control by others.

autosomes In humans, the 22 pairs of chromosomes not related to sexual expression.

avoidant attachment Pattern in which an infant rarely cries when separated from the primary caregiver and avoids contact on his or her return.

basal metabolism Use of energy to maintain vital functions.

basic sense of trust versus mistrust Erikson's first stage in psychosocial development, in which infants develop a sense of the reliability of people and objects.

Bayley Scales of Infant and Toddler Development Standardized test of infants' and toddlers' mental and motor development.

behavior therapy Therapeutic approach using principles of learning theory to encourage desired behaviors or eliminate undesired ones; also called *behavior modification.*

behavioral genetics Quantitative study of relative hereditary and environmental influences on behavior.

behaviorism Learning theory that emphasizes the predictable role of environment in causing observable behavior.

behaviorist approach Approach to the study of cognitive development that is concerned with basic mechanics of learning.

bereavement Loss, due to death, of someone to whom one feels close and the process of adjustment to the loss.

bilingual Fluent in two languages.

bilingual education System of teaching non-English-speaking children in their native language while they learn English, and later switching to all-English instruction.

binge drinking Consuming five or more drinks on one occasion.

bioecological theory Bronfenbrenner's approach to understanding processes and contexts of human development that identifies five levels of environmental influence.

body image Descriptive and evaluative beliefs about one's appearance.

Brazelton Neonatal Behavioral Assessment Scale (NBAS) Neurological and behavioral test to measure neonate's responses to the environment.

bulimia nervosa Eating disorder in which a person regularly eats huge quantities of food and then purges the body by laxatives, induced vomiting, fasting, or excessive exercise.

bullying Aggression deliberately and persistently directed against a particular target, or victim, typically one who is weak, vulnerable, and defenseless.

canalization Limitation on variance of expression of certain inherited characteristics.

caregiver burnout Condition of physical, mental, and emotional exhaustion affecting adults who provide continuous care for sick or aged persons.

case study Study of a single subject, such as an individual or family.

cataracts Cloudy or opaque areas in the lens of the eye, which cause blurred vision.

cell death In brain development, normal elimination of excess brain cells to achieve more efficient functioning.

central executive In Baddeley's model, element of working memory that controls the processing of information.

central nervous system Brain and spinal cord.

centration In Piaget's theory, the tendency of preoperational children to focus on one aspect of a situation and neglect others.

cephalocaudal principle Principle that development proceeds in a head-to-tail direction, that is, that upper parts of the body develop before lower parts of the trunk.

cesarean delivery Delivery of a baby by surgical removal from the uterus.

child-directed speech (CDS) Form of speech often used in talking to babies or toddlers; includes slow, simplified speech, a high-pitched tone, exaggerated vowel sounds, short words and sentences, and much repetition; also called *parentese* or *motherese*.

childhood depression Mood disorder characterized by such symptoms as a prolonged sense of friendlessness, inability to have fun or concentrate, fatigue, extreme activity or apathy, feelings of worthlessness, weight change, physical complaints, and thoughts of death or suicide.

chromosomes Coils of DNA that consist of genes.

chronic medical conditions Illnesses or impairments that persist for at least 3 months.

circular reactions Piaget's term for processes by which an infant learns to reproduce desired occurrences originally discovered by chance.

class inclusion Understanding of the relationship between a whole and its parts.

classical conditioning Learning based on associating a stimulus that does not ordinarily elicit a response with another stimulus that does elicit the response.

code mixing Use of elements of two languages, sometimes in the same utterance, by young children in households where both languages are spoken.

code switching Changing one's speech to match the situation, as in people who are bilingual.

cognitive development Pattern of change in mental abilities, such as learning, attention, memory, language, thinking, reasoning, and creativity.

cognitive neuroscience Study of links between neural processes and cognitive abilities.

cognitive neuroscience approach Approach to the study of cognitive development that links brain processes with cognitive ones.

cognitive perspective View that thought processes are central to development.

cognitive reserve Hypothesized fund of energy that may enable a deteriorating brain to continue to function normally.

cognitive-appraisal model Model of coping, proposed by Lazarus and Folkman, that holds that, on the basis of continuous appraisal of their relationship with the environment, people choose appropriate coping strategies to deal with situations that tax their normal resources.

cognitive-stage theory Piaget's theory that children's cognitive development advances in a series of four stages involving qualitatively distinct types of mental operations.

cohort A group of people born at about the same time.

commitment Marcia's term for personal investment in an occupation or system of beliefs.

committed compliance Kochanska's term for wholehearted obedience of a parent's orders without reminders or lapses.

componential element Sternberg's term for the analytic aspect of intelligence.

conceptual knowledge Acquired interpretive understandings stored in long-term memory.

concordant Term describing tendency of twins to share the same trait or disorder.

concrete operations Third stage of Piagetian cognitive development (approximately ages 7 to 12), during which children develop logical but not abstract thinking.

conduct disorder (CD) Repetitive, persistent pattern of aggressive, antisocial behavior violating societal norms or the rights of others.

conscience Internal standards of behavior, which usually control one's conduct and produce emotional discomfort when violated.

conservation Piaget's term for awareness that two objects that are equal according to a certain measure remain equal in the face of perceptual alteration so long as nothing has been added to or taken away from either object.

constructive play Play involving use of objects or materials to make something.

contextual element Sternberg's term for the practical aspect of intelligence.

contextual perspective View of human development that sees the individual as inseparable from the social context.

continuity theory Theory of aging, described by Atchley, that holds that in order to age successfully people must maintain a balance of continuity and change in both the internal and external structures of their lives.

control group In an experiment, a group of people, similar to those in the experimental group, who do not receive the treatment under study.

conventional morality (or morality of conventional role conformity) Second level in Kohlberg's theory of moral reasoning in which standards of authority figures are internalized.

convergent thinking Thinking aimed at finding the one right answer to a problem.

coping Adaptive thinking or behavior aimed at reducing or relieving stress that arises from harmful, threatening, or challenging conditions.

coregulation Transitional stage in the control of behavior in which parents exercise general supervision and children exercise moment-to-moment self-regulation.

corporal punishment Use of physical force with the intention of causing pain but not injury so as to correct or control behavior.

correlational study Research design intended to discover whether a statistical relationship between variables exists.

creativity Ability to see situations in a new way, to produce innovations, or to discern previously unidentified problems and find novel solutions.

crisis Marcia's term for period of conscious decision making related to identity formation.

critical period Specific time when a given event or its absence has a specific impact on development.

cross-modal transfer Ability to use information gained by one sense to guide another.

cross-sectional study Study designed to assess age-related differences, in which people of different ages are assessed on one occasion.

crystallized intelligence Type of intelligence, proposed by Horn and Cattell, involving the ability to remember and use learned information; it is largely dependent on education and culture.

cultural socialization Parental practices that teach children about their racial/ ethnic heritage and promote cultural practices and cultural pride.

culture A society's or group's total way of life, including customs, traditions, beliefs, values, language, and physical products—all learned behavior, passed on from parents to children.

culture-fair tests Intelligence tests that deal with experiences common to various cultures, in an attempt to avoid cultural bias.

culture-free tests Intelligence tests that, if they were possible to design, would have no culturally linked content.

decenter In Piaget's terminology, to think simultaneously about several aspects of a situation.

declarative knowledge Acquired factual knowledge stored in long-term memory.

decoding Process of phonetic analysis by which a printed word is converted to spoken form before retrieval from long-term memory.

deductive reasoning Type of logical reasoning that moves from a general premise about a class to a conclusion about a particular member or members of the class.

deferred imitation Piaget's term for reproduction of an observed behavior after the passage of time by calling up a stored symbol of it.

dementia Deterioration in cognitive and behavioral functioning due to physiological causes.

Denver Developmental Screening Test Screening test given to children 1 month to 6 years old to determine whether they are developing normally.

deoxyribonucleic acid (DNA) Chemical that carries inherited instructions for the development of all cellular forms of life.

dependent variable In an experiment, the condition that may or may not change as a result of changes in the independent variable.

depth perception Ability to perceive objects and surfaces three-dimensionally.

diabetes (1) One of the most common diseases of childhood. It is characterized by high levels of glucose in the blood as a result of defective insulin production, ineffective insulin action, or both. (2) Disease in which the body does not produce or properly use *insulin,* a hormone that converts sugar, starches, and other foods into energy needed for daily life.

differentiation Process by which cells acquire specialized structures and functions.

"difficult" children Children with irritable temperament, irregular biological rhythms, and intense emotional responses.

discipline Methods of molding children's character and of teaching them to exercise self-control and engage in acceptable behavior.

disengagement theory Theory of aging that holds that successful aging is characterized by mutual withdrawal of the older person and society.

dishabituation Increase in responsiveness after presentation of a new stimulus.

disorganized-disoriented attachment Pattern in which an infant, after separation from the primary caregiver, shows contradictory, repetitious, or misdirected behaviors on his or her return.

divergent thinking Thinking that produces a variety of fresh, diverse possibilities.

dizygotic twins Twins conceived by the union of two different ova with two different sperm cells; also called *fraternal twins;* they are no more alike genetically than any other siblings.

dominant inheritance Pattern of inheritance in which, when a child receives different alleles, only the dominant one is expressed.

doula An experienced mentor who furnishes emotional support and information for a woman during labor.

Down syndrome Chromosomal disorder characterized by moderate-to-severe mental retardation and by such physical signs as a downward-sloping skin fold at the inner corners of the eyes. Also called *trisomy-21.*

dramatic play Play involving imaginary people or situations; also called *pretend play, fantasy play, or imaginative play.*

drug therapy Administration of drugs to treat emotional disorders.

dual representation hypothesis Proposal that children under age 3 have difficulty grasping spatial relationships because of the need to keep more than one mental representation in mind at the same time.

durable power of attorney Legal instrument that appoints an individual to make decisions in the event of another person's incapacitation.

dynamic systems theory (DST) Esther Thelen's theory, which holds that motor development is a dynamic process of active coordination of multiple systems within the infant in relation to the environment.

dynamic tests Tests based on Vygotsky's theory that emphasize potential rather than past learning.

dyslexia Developmental disorder in which reading achievement is substantially lower than predicted by IQ or age.

early intervention Systematic process of providing services to help families meet young children's developmental needs.

"easy" children Children with a generally happy temperament, regular biological rhythms, and a readiness to accept new experiences.

ecological theory of perception Theory developed by Eleanor and James Gibson, which describes developing motor and perceptual abilities as interdependent parts of a functional system that guides behavior in varying contexts.

ego control Self-control and the self-regulation of impulses.

ego integrity versus despair According to Erikson, the eighth and final stage of psychosocial development, in which people in late adulthood either achieve a sense of integrity of the self by accepting the lives they have lived, and thus accept death, or yield to despair that their lives cannot be relived.

ego resiliency (1) Dynamic capacity to modify one's level of ego control in response to environmental and contextual influences. (2) The ability to adapt flexibly and resourcefully to potential sources of stress.

egocentrism Piaget's term for inability to consider another person's point of view; a characteristic of young children's thought.

elaboration Mnemonic strategy of making mental associations involving items to be remembered.

electronic fetal monitoring Mechanical monitoring of fetal heartbeat during labor and delivery.

elicited imitation Research method in which infants or toddlers are induced to imitate a specific series of actions they have seen but not necessarily done before.

embryonic stage   Second stage of gestation (2 to 8 weeks), characterized by rapid growth and development of major body systems and organs.

emergent literacy   Preschoolers' development of skills, knowledge, and attitudes that underlie reading and writing.

emerging adulthood   Proposed transitional period between adolescence and adulthood commonly found in industrialized countries.

emotion-focused coping   In the cognitive-appraisal model, coping strategy directed toward managing the emotional response to a stressful situation so as to lessen its physical or psychological impact.

emotional intelligence (EI)   Salovey and Mayer's term for the ability to understand and regulate emotions; an important component of effective, intelligent behavior.

emotional maltreatment   Rejection, terrorization, isolation, exploitation, degradation, ridicule, or failure to provide emotional support, love, and affection; or other action or inaction that may cause behavioral, cognitive, emotional, or mental disorders.

emotions   Subjective reactions to experience that are associated with physiological and behavioral changes.

empathy   Ability to put oneself in another person's place and feel what the other person feels.

empty nest   Transitional phase of parenting following the last child's leaving the parents' home.

encoding   Process by which information is prepared for long-term storage and later retrieval.

English-immersion approach   Approach to teaching English as a second language in which instruction is presented only in English.

enrichment programs   Programs for educating the gifted that broaden and deepen knowledge and skills through extra activities, projects, field trips, or mentoring.

enuresis   Repeated urination in clothing or in bed.

environment   Totality of nonhereditary, or experiential, influences on development.

epigenesis   Mechanism that turns genes on or off and determines functions of body cells.

episodic memory   Long-term memory of specific experiences or events, linked to time and place.

equilibration   Piaget's term for the tendency to seek a stable balance among cognitive elements; achieved through a balance between assimilation and accommodation.

erectile dysfunction   Inability of a man to achieve or maintain an erect penis sufficient for satisfactory sexual performance.

ethnic group   A group united by ancestry, race, religion, language, or national origins, which contribute to a sense of shared identity.

ethnographic study   In-depth study of a culture, which uses a combination of methods including participant observation.

ethology   Study of distinctive adaptive behaviors of species of animals that have evolved to increase survival of the species.

evolutionary psychology   Application of Darwinian principles of natural selection and survival of the fittest to individual behavior.

evolutionary/sociobiological perspective   View of human development that focuses on evolutionary and biological bases of behavior.

executive function   Conscious control of thoughts, emotions, and actions to accomplish goals or solve problems.

experiential element   Sternberg's term for the insightful or creative aspect of intelligence.

experiment   Rigorously controlled, replicable procedure in which the researcher manipulates variables to assess the effect of one on the other.

experimental group   In an experiment, the group receiving the treatment under study.

explicit memory   Intentional and conscious memory, generally of facts, names, and events.

extended family   Multigenerational kinship network of parents, children, and other relatives, sometimes living together in an extended-family household.

external memory aids   Mnemonic strategies using something outside the person.

externalizing behaviors   Behaviors by which a child acts out emotional difficulties; for example, aggression or hostility.

family therapy   Psychological treatment in which a therapist sees the whole family together to analyze patterns of family functioning.

fast mapping   Process by which a child absorbs the meaning of a new word after hearing it once or twice in conversation.

fertilization   Union of sperm and ovum to produce a zygote; also called *conception*.

fetal alcohol syndrome (FAS)   Combination of mental, motor, and developmental abnormalities affecting the offspring of some women who drink heavily during pregnancy.

fetal stage   Final stage of gestation (from 8 weeks to birth), characterized by increased differentiation of body parts and greatly enlarged body size.

fictive kin   Friends who are considered and behave like family members.

fidelity   Sustained loyalty, faith, or sense of belonging that results from the successful resolution of Erikson's *identity versus identity confusion* psychosocial stage of development.

filial crisis   In Marcoen's terminology, normative development of middle age, in which adults learn to balance love and duty to their parents with autonomy within a two-way relationship.

fine motor skills   Physical skills that involve the small muscles and eye–hand coordination.

five-factor model   Theoretical model of personality, developed and tested by Costa and McCrae, based on the "Big Five" factors underlying clusters of related personality traits: neuroticism, extraversion, openness to experience, conscientiousness, and agreeableness.

fluid intelligence   Type of intelligence, proposed by Horn and Cattell, that is applied to novel problems and is relatively independent of educational and cultural influences.

foreclosure   Identity status, described by Marcia, in which a person who has not spent time considering alternatives (that is, has not been in crisis) is committed to other people's plans for his or her life.

formal games with rules   Organized games with known procedures and penalties.

formal operations   Piaget's final stage of cognitive development, characterized by the ability to think abstractly.

free radicals   Unstable, highly reactive atoms or molecules, formed during metabolism, that can cause internal bodily damage.

functional age   Measure of a person's ability to function effectively in his or her physical and social environment in comparison with others of the same chronological age.

functional fitness   Exercises or activities that improve daily activity.

functional play   Play involving repetitive large muscular movements.

gender   Significance of being male or female.

gender constancy   Awareness that one will always be male or female.

gender crossover   Gutmann's term for reversal of gender roles after the end of active parenting.

gender identity   Awareness, developed in early childhood, that one is male or female.

gender roles   Behaviors, interests, attitudes, skills, and traits that a culture considers appropriate for each sex; differ for males and females.

gender segregation Tendency to select playmates of one's own gender.

gender stereotypes Preconceived generalizations about male or female role behavior.

gender-schema theory Theory, proposed by Bem, that children socialize themselves in their gender roles by developing a mentally organized network of information about what it means to be male or female in a particular culture.

gender-typing Socialization process by which children, at an early age, learn appropriate gender roles.

generalized anxiety disorder Anxiety not focused on any single target.

generativity Erikson's term for concern of mature adults for finding meaning through contributing to society and leaving a legacy for future generations.

generativity versus stagnation Erikson's seventh stage of psychosocial development, in which the middle-age adult develops a concern with establishing, guiding, and influencing the next generation or else experiences stagnation (a sense of inactivity or lifelessness).

generic memory Memory that produces scripts of familiar routines to guide behavior.

genes Small segments of DNA located in definite positions on particular chromosomes; functional units of heredity.

genetic code Sequence of bases within the DNA molecule; governs the formation of proteins that determine the structure and functions of living cells.

genetic counseling Clinical service that advises prospective parents of their probable risk of having children with hereditary defects.

genetic-programming theories Theories that explain biological aging as resulting from a genetically determined developmental timeline.

genotype Genetic makeup of a person, containing both expressed and unexpressed characteristics.

genotype-environment correlation Tendency of certain genetic and environmental influences to reinforce each other; may be passive, reactive (evocative), or active. Also called *genotype-environment covariance.*

genotype-environment interaction The portion of phenotypic variation that results from the reactions of genetically different individuals to similar environmental conditions.

geriatrics Branch of medicine concerned with processes of aging and medical conditions associated with old age.

germinal stage First 2 weeks of prenatal development, characterized by rapid cell division, blastocyst formation, and implantation in the wall of the uterus.

gerontology Study of the aged and the process of aging.

gestation Period of development between conception and birth.

gestational age Age of an unborn baby, usually dated from the first day of an expectant mother's last menstrual cycle.

glaucoma Irreversible damage to the optic nerve caused by increased pressure in the eye.

goodness of fit Appropriateness of environmental demands and constraints to a child's temperament.

grief Emotional response experienced in the early phases of bereavement.

grief work Working out of psychological issues connected with grief.

gross motor skills Physical skills that involve the large muscles.

guided participation Adult's participation in a child's activity that helps to structure it and bring the child's understanding of it closer to the adult's.

habituation Type of learning in which familiarity with a stimulus reduces, slows, or stops a response.

handedness Preference for using a particular hand.

haptic perception Ability to acquire information about properties of objects, such as size, weight, and texture, by handling them.

Hayflick limit Genetically controlled limit, proposed by Hayflick, on the number of times cells can divide in members of a species.

heredity Inborn traits or characteristics inherited from the biological parents.

heritability Statistical estimate of contribution of heredity to individual differences in a specific trait within a given population.

heterozygous Possessing differing alleles for a trait.

historical generation A group of people strongly influenced by a major historical event during their formative period.

holophrase Single word that conveys a complete thought.

Home Observation for Measurement of the Environment (HOME) Instrument to measure the influence of the home environment on children's cognitive growth.

homozygous Possessing two identical alleles for a trait.

hormone therapy (HT) Treatment with artificial estrogen, sometimes in combination with the hormone progesterone, to relieve or prevent symptoms caused by decline in estrogen levels after menopause.

hospice care Personal, patient- and family-centered care for a person with a terminal illness.

hostile attribution bias Tendency to perceive others as trying to hurt one and to strike out in retaliation or self-defense.

human development Scientific study of processes of change and stability throughout the human life span.

human genome Complete sequence of genes in the human body.

hypertension Chronically high blood pressure.

hypotheses Possible explanations for phenomena, used to predict the outcome of research.

hypothetical-deductive Ability, believed by Piaget to accompany the stage of formal operations, to develop, consider, and test hypotheses.

ideal self The self one would like to be.

identification In Freudian theory, the process by which a young child adopts characteristics, beliefs, attitudes, values, and behaviors of the parent of the same sex.

identity According to Erikson, a coherent conception of the self, made up of goals, values, and beliefs to which a person is solidly committed.

identity accommodation Whitbourne's term for adjusting the self-concept to fit new experience.

identity achievement Identity status, described by Marcia, that is characterized by commitment to choices made following a crisis, a period spent in exploring alternatives.

identity assimilation Whitbourne's term for effort to fit new experience into an existing self-concept.

identity balance Whitbourne's term for a tendency to balance assimilation and accommodation.

identity diffusion Identity status, described by Marcia, that is characterized by absence of commitment and lack of serious consideration of alternatives.

identity process theory (IPT) Whitbourne's theory of identity development based on processes of assimilation and accommodation.

identity schemas Accumulated perceptions of the self shaped by incoming information from intimate relationships, work-related situations, and community and other experiences.

identity status Marcia's term for states of ego development that depend on the presence or absence of crisis and commitment.

identity versus identity confusion Erikson's fifth stage of psychosocial development, in which an adolescent seeks to develop a coherent sense of self, including the role she or he is to play in society. Also called *identity versus role confusion.*

implantation The attachment of the blastocyst to the uterine wall, occurring at about day 6.

implicit memory Unconscious recall, generally of habits and skills; sometimes called *procedural memory.*

imprinting Instinctive form of learning in which, during a critical period in early development, a young animal forms an attachment to the first moving object it sees, usually the mother.

incomplete dominance Pattern of inheritance in which a child receives two different alleles, resulting in partial expression of a trait.

independent variable In an experiment, the condition over which the experimenter has direct control.

individual differences Differences in characteristics, influences, or developmental outcomes.

individual psychotherapy Psychological treatment in which a therapist sees a troubled person one-on-one.

individuation (1) Adolescents' struggle for autonomy and personal identity. (2) Jung's term for emergence of the true self through balancing or integration of conflicting parts of the personality.

inductive reasoning Type of logical reasoning that moves from particular observations about members of a class to a general conclusion about that class.

inductive techniques Disciplinary techniques designed to induce desirable behavior by appealing to a child's sense of reason and fairness.

industry versus inferiority Erikson's fourth stage of psychosocial development, in which children must learn the productive skills their culture requires or else face feelings of inferiority.

infant mortality rate Proportion of babies born alive who die within the 1st year.

infertility Inability to conceive a child after 12 months of sexual intercourse without the use of birth control.

information-processing approach (1) Approach to the study of cognitive development by observing and analyzing the mental processes involved in perceiving and handling information. (2) Approach to the study of cognitive development that analyzes processes involved in perceiving and handling information.

instrumental aggression Aggressive behavior used as a means of achieving a goal.

integration Process by which neurons coordinate the activities of muscle groups.

intellectual disability Significantly subnormal cognitive functioning. Also referred to as cognitive disability or mental retardation.

intelligent behavior Behavior that is goal oriented and adaptive to circumstances and conditions of life.

interactional synchrony The synchronized coordination of behavior and affect between a caregiver and infant.

internalization During socialization, process by which children accept societal standards of conduct as their own.

internalizing behaviors Behaviors by which emotional problems are turned inward; for example, anxiety or depression.

intimacy versus isolation Erikson's sixth stage of psychosocial development, in which young adults either form strong, long-lasting bonds with friends and romantic partners or face a possible sense of isolation and self-absorption.

invisible imitation Imitation with parts of one's body that one cannot see.

IQ (intelligence quotient) tests Psychometric tests that seek to measure intelligence by comparing a test-taker's performance with standardized norms.

irreversibility Piaget's term for a preoperational child's failure to understand that an operation can go in two or more directions.

kangaroo care Method of skin-to-skin contact in which a newborn is laid face down between the mother's breasts for an hour or so at a time after birth.

Kaufman Assessment Battery for Children (K-ABC-II) Nontraditional individual intelligence test designed to provide fair assessments of minority children and children with disabilities.

kinship care Care of children living without parents in the home of grandparents or other relatives, with or without a change of legal custody.

laboratory observation Research method in which all participants are observed under the same controlled conditions.

language Communication system based on words and grammar.

language acquisition device (LAD) In Chomsky's terminology, an inborn mechanism that enables children to infer linguistic rules from the language they hear.

lateralization Tendency of each of the brain's hemispheres to have specialized functions.

learning disabilities (LDs) Disorders that interfere with specific aspects of learning and school achievement.

learning perspective View of human development that holds that changes in behavior result from experience or from adaptation to the environment.

life expectancy Age to which a person in a particular cohort is statistically likely to live (given his or her current age and health status), on the basis of average longevity of a population.

life review Reminiscence about one's life in order to see its significance.

life span The longest period that members of a species can live.

life-span development Concept of human development as a lifelong process which can be studied scientifically.

linguistic speech Verbal expression designed to convey meaning.

literacy (1) Ability to read and write. (2) In an adult, ability to use printed and written information to function in society, achieve goals, and develop knowledge and potential.

long-term memory Storage of virtually unlimited capacity that holds information for long periods.

longevity Length of an individual's life.

longitudinal study Study designed to assess age changes in a sample over time.

low-birth-weight babies Weight of less than 5½ pounds (2,500 grams) at birth because of prematurity or being small for date.

mammography Diagnostic X-ray examination of the breasts.

marital capital Financial and emotional benefits built up during a long-standing marriage, which tend to hold a couple together.

maturation Unfolding of a natural sequence of physical and behavioral changes.

mechanistic model Model that views human development as a series of predictable responses to stimuli.

menarche Girl's first menstruation.

menopause Cessation of menstruation and of ability to bear children.

metacognition Thinking about thinking, or awareness of one's own mental processes.

metamemory Understanding of processes of memory.

midlife crisis In some normative-crisis models, stressful life period precipitated by the review and reevaluation of one's past, typically occurring in the early to middle forties.

midlife review Introspective examination that often occurs in middle age, leading to reappraisal and revision of values and priorities.

mirror neurons Neurons that fire when a person does something or observes someone else doing the same thing.

mnemonic device Strategy to aid memory.

monozygotic twins Twins resulting from the division of a single zygote after fertilization; also called *identical twins*; they are genetically similar.

moratorium Identity status, described by Marcia, in which a person is currently considering alternatives (in crisis) and seems headed for commitment.

multifactorial transmission Combination of genetic and environmental factors to produce certain complex traits.

mutation Permanent alteration in genes or chromosomes that may produce harmful characteristics.

mutual regulation Process by which infant and caregiver communicate emotional states to each other and respond appropriately.

myelination Process of coating neural pathways with a fatty substance called myelin, which enables faster communication between cells.

myopia Nearsightedness.

nativism Theory that human beings have an inborn capacity for language acquisition.

natural childbirth Method of childbirth that seeks to prevent pain by eliminating the mother's fear through education about the physiology of reproduction and training in breathing and relaxation during delivery.

naturalistic observation Research method in which behavior is studied in natural settings without intervention or manipulation.

neglect Failure to meet a dependent's basic needs.

neonatal jaundice Condition, in many newborn babies, caused by immaturity of liver and evidenced by yellowish appearance; can cause brain damage if not treated promptly.

neonatal period First 4 weeks of life, a time of transition from intrauterine dependency to independent existence.

neonate Newborn baby, up to 4 weeks old.

neurofibrillary tangles Twisted masses of protein fibers found in brains of persons with Alzheimer's disease.

neurons Nerve cells.

niche-picking Tendency of a person, especially after early childhood, to seek out environments compatible with his or her genotype.

nonnormative Characteristic of an unusual event that happens to a particular person or a typical event that happens at an unusual time of life.

nonorganic failure to thrive Slowed or arrested physical growth with no known medical cause, accompanied by poor developmental and emotional functioning.

nonshared environmental effects The unique environment in which each child grows up, consisting of distinctive influences or influences that affect one child differently than another.

normative Characteristic of an event that occurs in a similar way for most people in a group.

normative life events In the timing-of-events model, commonly expected life experiences that occur at customary times.

normative-stage models Theoretical models that describe psychosocial development in terms of a definite sequence of age-related changes.

nuclear family Two-generational kinship, economic, and household unit consisting of one or two parents and their biological children, adopted children, or stepchildren.

obesity Extreme overweight in relation to age, sex, height, and body type as defined by having a body mass index at or above the 95th percentile.

object permanence Piaget's term for the understanding that a person or object still exists when out of sight.

observational learning Learning through watching the behavior of others.

obsessive-compulsive disorder (OCD) Anxiety aroused by repetitive, intrusive thoughts, images, or impulses, often leading to compulsive ritual behaviors.

operant conditioning (1) Learning based on association of behavior with its consequences. (2) Learning based on reinforcement or punishment.

operational definition Definition stated solely in terms of the operations or procedures used to produce or measure a phenomenon.

oppositional defiant disorder (ODD) Pattern of behavior, persisting into middle childhood, marked by negativity, hostility, and defiance.

organismic model Model that views human development as internally initiated by an active organism and as occurring in a sequence of qualitatively different stages.

organization (1) Piaget's term for the creation of categories or systems of knowledge. (2) Mnemonic strategy of categorizing material to be remembered.

osteoporosis Condition in which the bones become thin and brittle as a result of rapid calcium depletion.

Otis-Lennon School Ability Test (OLSAT 8) Group intelligence test for kindergarten through 12th grade.

overt (direct) aggression Aggression that is openly directed at its target.

palliative care Care aimed at relieving pain and suffering and allowing the terminally ill to die in peace, comfort, and dignity.

Parkinson's disease Progressive, irreversible degenerative neurological disorder, characterized by tremor, stiffness, slowed movement, and unstable posture.

participant observation Research method in which the observer lives with the people or participates in the activity being observed.

parturition The act or process of giving birth.

passive euthanasia Withholding or discontinuation of life-prolonging treatment of a terminally ill person in order to end suffering or allow death with dignity.

perimenopause Period of several years during which a woman experiences physiological changes of menopause; includes first year after end of menstruation; also called *climacteric*.

permissive parenting In Baumrind's terminology, parenting style emphasizing self-expression and self-regulation.

personality The relatively consistent blend of emotions, temperament, thought, and behavior that makes a person unique.

phenotype Observable characteristics of a person.

phonetic (code-emphasis) approach Approach to teaching reading that emphasizes decoding of unfamiliar words.

physical abuse Action taken deliberately to endanger another person, involving potential bodily injury.

physical development Development of the body and brain, including patterns of change in sensory capacities, motor skills, and health.

Piagetian approach Approach to the study of cognitive development that describes qualitative stages in cognitive functioning.

plasticity (1) Range of modifiability of performance. (2) Modifiability, or "molding," of the brain through experience.

play therapy Therapeutic approach that uses play to help a child cope with emotional distress.

polygenic inheritance Pattern of inheritance in which multiple genes at different sites on chromosomes affect a complex trait.

postconventional morality (or morality of autonomous moral principles) Third level of Kohlberg's theory of moral reasoning, in which people follow internally held moral principles and can decide among conflicting moral standards.

postformal thought Mature type of thinking that relies on subjective experience and intuition as well as logic and allows room for ambiguity, uncertainty, inconsistency, contradiction, imperfection, and compromise.

postmature A fetus not yet born as of 2 weeks after the due date or 42 weeks after the mother's last menstrual period.

power assertion Disciplinary strategy designed to discourage undesirable behavior through physical or verbal enforcement of parental control.

pragmatics (1) The practical knowledge needed to use language for communicative purposes. (2) The social context of language.

preconventional morality First level of Kohlberg's theory of moral reasoning in which control is external and rules are obeyed in order to gain rewards or avoid punishment or out of self-interest.

prejudice Unfavorable attitude toward members of certain groups outside one's own, especially racial or ethnic groups.

prelinguistic speech Forerunner of linguistic speech; utterance of sounds that are not words. Includes crying, cooing, babbling, and accidental and deliberate imitation of sounds without understanding their meaning.

premenstrual syndrome (PMS) Disorder producing symptoms of physical discomfort and emotional tension for up to 2 weeks before a menstrual period.

preoperational stage In Piaget's theory, the second major stage of cognitive development, in which symbolic thought expands but children cannot yet use logic.

prepared childbirth Method of childbirth that uses instruction, breathing exercises, and social support to induce controlled physical responses to uterine contractions and reduce fear and pain.

presbycusis Age-related, gradual loss of hearing, which accelerates after age 55, especially with regard to sounds at higher frequencies.

presbyopia Age-related, progressive loss of the eyes' ability to focus on nearby objects due to loss of elasticity in the lens.

pretend play Play involving imaginary people and situations; also called *fantasy play, dramatic play,* or *imaginative play.*

preterm (premature) infants Infants born before completing the 37th week of gestation.

primary aging Gradual, inevitable process of bodily deterioration throughout the life span.

primary sex characteristics Organs directly related to reproduction, which enlarge and mature during adolescence.

private speech Talking aloud to oneself with no intent to communicate with others.

problem-focused coping In the cognitive-appraisal model, coping strategy directed toward eliminating, managing, or improving a stressful situation.

procedural knowledge Acquired skills stored in long-term memory.

procedural memory Long-term memory of motor skills, habits, and ways of doing things, which can be recalled without conscious effort; sometimes called *implicit memory.*

prosocial behavior Any voluntary behavior intended to help others.

protective factors (1) Influences that reduce the impact of potentially negative influences and tend to predict positive outcomes. (2) Influences that reduce the impact of early stress and tend to predict positive outcomes.

proximodistal principle Principle that development proceeds from within to without, that is, that parts of the body near the center develop before the extremities.

psychoanalytic perspective View of human development as shaped by unconscious forces that motivate human behavior.

psychometric approach Approach to the study of cognitive development that seeks to measure intelligence quantitatively.

psychosexual development In Freudian theory, an unvarying sequence of stages of childhood personality development in which gratification shifts from the mouth to the anus and then to the genitals.

psychosocial development (1) Pattern of change in emotions, personality, and social relationships. (2) In Erikson's eight-stage theory, the socially and culturally influenced process of development of the ego, or self.

puberty Process by which a person attains sexual maturity and the ability to reproduce.

punishment The process by which a behavior is weakened, decreasing the likelihood of repetition.

qualitative change Discontinuous changes in kind, structure, or organization.

qualitative research Research that focuses on nonnumerical data, such as subjective experiences, feelings, or beliefs.

quantitative change Changes in number or amount, such as in height, weight, size of vocabulary, or frequency of communication.

quantitative research Research that deals with objectively measurable data.

random assignment Assignment of participants in an experiment to groups in such a way that each person has an equal chance of being placed in any group.

random selection Selection of a sample in such a way that each person in a population has an equal and independent chance of being chosen.

reaction range Potential variability, depending on environmental conditions, in the expression of a hereditary trait.

real self The self one actually is.

recall Ability to reproduce material from memory.

recentering Process that underlies the shift to an adult identity.

receptive cooperation Kochanska's term for eager willingness to cooperate harmoniously with a parent in daily interactions, including routines, chores, hygiene, and play.

recessive inheritance Pattern of inheritance in which a child receives identical recessive alleles, resulting in expression of a nondominant trait.

reciprocal determinism Bandura's term for bidirectional forces that affect development.

recognition Ability to identify a previously encountered stimulus.

reflective thinking Type of logical thinking that becomes more prominent in adulthood, involving continuous, active evaluation of information and beliefs in the light of evidence and implications.

reflex behaviors Automatic, involuntary, innate responses to stimulation.

rehearsal Mnemonic strategy to keep an item in working memory through conscious repetition.

reinforcement The process by which a behavior is strengthened, increasing the likelihood that the behavior will be repeated.

relational (social or indirect) aggression Aggression aimed at damaging or interfering with another person's relationships, reputation, or psychological well-being.

representational ability Piaget's term for capacity to store mental images or symbols of objects and events.

representational mappings In neo-Piagetian terminology, second stage in development of self-definition, in which a child makes logical connections between aspects of the self but still sees these characteristics in all-or-nothing terms.

representational systems In neo-Piagetian terminology, the third stage in development of self-definition, characterized by breadth, balance, and the integration and assessment of various aspects of the self.

reserve capacity   The backup capacity that helps body systems function to their utmost limits in times of stress.

resilient children   Children who weather adverse circumstances, function well despite challenges or threats, or bounce back from traumatic events.

retrieval   Process by which information is accessed or recalled from memory storage.

revolving door syndrome   Tendency for young adults who have left home to return to their parents' household in times of financial, marital, or other trouble.

risk factors   Conditions that increase the likelihood of a negative developmental outcome.

risky drinking   Consuming more than 14 drinks a week or 4 drinks on any single day for men, and more than 7 drinks a week or 3 drinks on any single day for women.

rough-and-tumble play   Vigorous play involving wrestling, hitting, and chasing, often accompanied by laughing and screaming.

sample   Group of participants chosen to represent the entire population under study.

sandwich generation   Middle-age adults squeezed by competing needs to raise or launch children and to care for elderly parents.

scaffolding   Temporary support to help a child master a task.

schemes   Piaget's term for organized patterns of thought and behavior used in particular situations.

schizophrenia   Mental disorder marked by loss of contact with reality; symptoms include hallucinations and delusions.

school phobia   Unrealistic fear of going to school; may be a form of *separation anxiety disorder* or *social phobia.*

scientific method   System of established principles and processes of scientific inquiry, which includes identifying a problem to be studied, formulating a hypothesis to be tested by research, collecting data, analyzing the data, forming tentative conclusions, and disseminating findings.

script   General remembered outline of a familiar, repeated event, used to guide behavior.

secondary aging   Aging processes that result from disease and bodily abuse and disuse and are often preventable.

secondary sex characteristics   Physiological signs of sexual maturation (such as breast development and growth of body hair) that do not involve the sex organs.

secular trend   Trend that can be seen only by observing several generations, such as the trend toward earlier attainment of adult height and sexual maturity, which began a century ago in some countries.

secure attachment   Pattern in which an infant cries or protests when the primary caregiver leaves and actively seeks out the caregiver on his or her return.

selective optimization with compensation (SOC)   Enhancing overall cognitive functioning by using stronger abilities to compensate for those that have weakened.

self-awareness   Realization that one's existence and functioning are separate from those of other people and things.

self-concept   Sense of self; descriptive and evaluative mental picture of one's abilities and traits.

self-conscious emotions   Emotions, such as embarrassment, empathy, and envy, that depend on self-awareness.

self-definition   Cluster of characteristics used to describe oneself.

self-efficacy   Sense of one's capability to master challenges and achieve goals.

self-esteem   The judgment a person makes about his or her self-worth.

self-evaluative emotions   Emotions, such as pride, shame, and guilt, that depend on both self-awareness and knowledge of socially accepted standards of behavior.

self-regulation   A child's independent control of behavior to conform to understood social expectations.

semantic memory   Long-term memory of general factual knowledge, social customs, and language.

senescence   Period of the life span marked by declines in physical functioning usually associated with aging; begins at different ages for different people.

sensitive periods   Times in development when a person is particularly open to certain kinds of experiences.

sensorimotor stage   Piaget's first stage in cognitive development, in which infants learn through senses and motor activity.

sensory memory   Initial, brief, temporary storage of sensory information.

separation anxiety   Distress shown by someone, typically an infant, when a familiar caregiver leaves.

separation anxiety disorder   Condition involving excessive, prolonged anxiety concerning separation from home or from people to whom a person is attached.

sequential study   Study design that combines cross-sectional and longitudinal techniques.

seriation   Ability to order items along a dimension.

sex chromosomes   Pair of chromosomes that determines sex: XX in the normal human female, XY in the normal human male.

sex-linked inheritance   Pattern of inheritance in which certain characteristics carried on the X chromosome inherited from the mother are transmitted differently to her male and female offspring.

sexting   The sharing or sending of sexually explicit or suggestive photos or videos to others.

sexual abuse   Physically or psychologically harmful sexual activity or any sexual activity involving a child and an older person.

sexual orientation   Focus of consistent sexual, romantic, and affectionate interest, either heterosexual, homosexual, or bisexual.

sexually transmitted infections (STIs)   Infections and diseases spread by sexual contact.

shaken baby syndrome   Form of maltreatment in which shaking an infant or toddler can cause brain damage, paralysis, or death.

single representations   In neo-Piagetian terminology, first stage in development of self-definition, in which children describe themselves in terms of individual, unconnected characteristics and in all-or-nothing terms.

situational compliance   Kochanska's term for obedience of a parent's orders only in the presence of signs of ongoing parental control.

"slow-to-warm-up" children   Children whose temperament is generally mild but who are hesitant about accepting new experiences.

small-for-date (small-for-gestational-age) infants   Infants whose birth weight is less than that of 90 percent of babies of the same gestational age, as a result of slow fetal growth.

social capital   Family and community resources on which a person can draw.

social clock   Set of cultural norms or expectations for the times of life when certain important events, such as marriage, parenthood, entry into work, and retirement, should occur.

social cognition   The ability to understand that others have mental states and to gauge their feelings and actions.

social cognitive theory   Albert Bandura's expansion of social learning theory; holds that children learn gender roles through socialization.

social construction   A concept or practice that may appear natural and obvious to those who accept it, but that in reality is an invention of a particular culture or society.

social convoy theory   Theory, proposed by Kahn and Antonucci, that people move through life surrounded by concentric circles of intimate relationships on which they rely for assistance, well-being, and social support.

social interaction model   Model, based on Vygotsky's sociocultural theory, that proposes children construct autobiographical memories through conversation with adults about shared events.

social learning theory   Theory that behaviors are learned by observing and imitating models. Also called *social cognitive theory.*

social phobia   Extreme fear and/or avoidance of social situations.

social referencing   Understanding an ambiguous situation by seeking another person's perception of it.

social smiling   Beginning in the 2nd month, newborn infants gaze at their parents and smile at them, signaling positive participation in the relationship.

social speech   Speech intended to be understood by a listener.

social-contextual approach   Approach to the study of cognitive development that focuses on environmental influences, particularly parents and other caregivers.

socialization   Development of habits, skills, values, and motives shared by responsible, productive members of a society.

sociocultural theory   Vygotsky's theory of how contextual factors affect children's development.

socioeconomic status (SES)   Combination of economic and social factors describing an individual or family, including income, education, and occupation.

socioemotional selectivity theory   Theory, proposed by Carstensen, that people select social contacts on the basis of the changing relative importance of social interaction as a source of information, as an aid in developing and maintaining a self-concept, and as a source of emotional well-being.

spermarche   Boy's first ejaculation.

spillover hypothesis   Hypothesis that there is a carryover of cognitive gains from work to leisure that explains the positive relationship between activities in the quality of intellectual functioning.

spontaneous abortion   Natural expulsion from the uterus of an embryo that cannot survive outside the womb; also called *miscarriage.*

Stanford-Binet Intelligence Scales   Individual intelligence tests for ages 2 and up used to measure fluid reasoning, knowledge, quantitative reasoning, visual-spatial processing, and working memory.

state of arousal   An infant's physiological and behavioral status at a given moment in the periodic daily cycle of wakefulness, sleep, and activity.

stillbirth   Death of a fetus at or after the 20th week of gestation.

storage   Retention of information in memory for future use.

Strange Situation   Laboratory technique used to study infant attachment.

stranger anxiety   Wariness of strange people and places, shown by some infants during the second half of the 1st year.

stress   Physical or psychological demands on a person or organism.

stressors   Perceived environmental demands that may produce stress.

substance abuse   Repeated, harmful use of a substance, usually alcohol or other drugs.

substance dependence   Addiction (physical, or psychological, or both) to a harmful substance.

substantive complexity   Degree to which a person's work requires thought and independent judgment.

sudden infant death syndrome (SIDS)   Sudden and unexplained death of an apparently healthy infant.

survival curve   A curve on a graph showing the percentage of people or animals alive at various ages.

symbolic function   Piaget's term for ability to use mental representations (words, numbers, or images) to which a child has attached meaning.

syntax   Rules for forming sentences in a particular language.

systems of action   Increasingly complex combinations of motor skills, which permit a wider or more precise range of movement and more control of the environment.

tacit knowledge   Sternberg's term for information that is not formally taught but is necessary to get ahead.

telegraphic speech   Early form of sentence use consisting of only a few essential words.

temperament   Characteristic disposition, or style of approaching and reacting to situations.

teratogen   Environmental agent, such as a virus, a drug, or radiation, that can interfere with normal prenatal development and cause developmental abnormalities.

terminal drop   A frequently observed decline in cognitive abilities near the end of life. Also called *terminal decline.*

thanatology   Study of death and dying.

theory   Coherent set of logically related concepts that seeks to organize, explain, and predict data.

theory of mind   Awareness and understanding of mental processes.

theory of multiple intelligences   Gardner's theory that each person has several distinct forms of intelligence.

theory of sexual selection   Darwin's theory that gender roles developed in response to men's and women's differing reproductive needs.

timing-of-events model   Theoretical model of personality development that describes adult psychosocial development as a response to the expected or unexpected occurrence and timing of important life events.

trait models   Theoretical models of personality development that focus on mental, emotional, temperamental, and behavioral traits, or attributes.

transduction   Piaget's term for a preoperational child's tendency to mentally link particular phenomena, whether or not there is logically a causal relationship.

transitive inference   Understanding the relationship between two objects by knowing the relationship of each to a third object.

triangular theory of love   Sternberg's theory that patterns of love hinge on the balance among three elements: intimacy, passion, and commitment.

triarchic theory of intelligence   Sternberg's theory describing three elements of intelligence: componential, experiential, and contextual.

turning points   Psychological transitions that involve significant change or transformation in the perceived meaning, purpose, or direction of a person's life.

two-way (dual-language) learning   Approach to second-language education in which English speakers and non-English-speakers learn together in their own and each other's languages.

typological approach   Theoretical approach that identifies broad personality types, or styles.

ultrasound   Prenatal medical procedure using high-frequency sound waves to detect the outline of a fetus and its movements, so as to determine whether a pregnancy is progressing normally.

variable-rate theories   Theories that explain biological aging as a result of processes that involve damage to biological systems and that vary from person to person.

violation of expectations Research method in which dishabituation to a stimulus that conflicts with experience is taken as evidence that an infant recognizes the new stimulus as surprising.

visible imitation Imitation with parts of one's body that one can see.

visual cliff Apparatus designed to give an illusion of depth and used to assess depth perception in infants.

visual guidance Use of the eyes to guide movements of the hands or other parts of the body.

visual preference Tendency of infants to spend more time looking at one sight than another.

visual recognition memory Ability to distinguish a familiar visual stimulus from an unfamiliar one when shown both at the same time.

visually based retrieval Process of retrieving the sound of a printed word when seeing the word as a whole.

vital capacity Amount of air that can be drawn in with a deep breath and expelled.

Wechsler Adult Intelligence Scale (WAIS) Intelligence test for adults that yields verbal and performance scores as well as a combined score.

Wechsler Intelligence Scale for Children (WISC-IV) Individual intelligence test for school-age children, which yields verbal and performance scores as well as a combined score.

Wechsler Preschool and Primary Scale of Intelligence, Revised (WPPSI-IV) Individual intelligence test for children ages 2½ to 7 that yields verbal and performance scores as well as a combined score.

whole-language approach Approach to teaching reading that emphasizes visual retrieval and use of contextual clues.

withdrawal of love Disciplinary strategy that involves ignoring, isolating, or showing dislike for a child.

working memory Short-term storage of information being actively processed.

zone of proximal development (ZPD) Vygotsky's term for the difference between what a child can do alone and what the child can do with help.

zygote One-celled organism resulting from fertilization.

25th Annual Children's Africana Book Awards. (2017). Retrieved from Africa Access: http://africaaccessreview.org/caba-2017

Abma, J. C., Chandra, A., Mosher, W. D., Peterson, L., & Piccinino, L. (1997). Fertility, family planning, and women's health: New data from the 1995 National Survey of Family Growth. *Vital Health Statistics, 23*(19). Washington, DC: National Center for Health Statistics.

Abma, J. C., Martinez, G. M., & Copen, C. E. (2010). Teenagers in the United States: Sexual activity, contraceptive use, and childbearing, National Survey of Family Growth 2006-2008. *Vital Health Statistics, 23*(30). Washington, DC: National Center for Health Statistics.

Abma, J. C., Martinez, G. M., Mosher, W. D., & Dawson, B. S. (2004). Teenagers in the United States: Sexual activity, contraceptive use, and childbearing, 2002. *Vital Health Statistics, 23*(24). Washington, DC: National Center for Health Statistics.

Abramovitch, R., Corter, C., Pepler, D., & Stanhope, L. (1986). Sibling and peer interactions: A final follow-up and comparison. *Child Development, 57,* 217-229.

Abubakar, I. I., Tillmann, T., & Banerjee, A. (2015). Global, regional, and national age-sex specific all-cause and cause-specific mortality for 240 causes of death, 1990-2013: A systematic analysis for the Global Burden of Disease Study 2013. *Lancet, 385*(9963), 117-171.

Achenbaum, W. A., & Bengtson, V. L. (1994). Re-engaging the disengagement theory of aging: On the history and assessment of theory development in gerontology. *Gerontologist, 34,* 756-763.

Achter, J. A., & Lubinski, D. (2003). Fostering exceptional development in intellectually talented populations. In W. B. Walsh (Ed.), *Counseling psychology and optimal human functioning* (pp. 279-296). Mahwah, NJ: Erlbaum.

Acierno, R., Hernandez, M. A., Amstadter, A. B., Resnick, H. S., Steve, K., Muzzy, W., & Kilpatrick, D. G. (2010). Prevalence and correlates of emotional, physical, sexual, and financial abuse and potential neglect in the United States: The National Elder Mistreatment Study. *American Journal of Public Health, 100*(2), 292-297.

Ackerman, B. P., Kogos, J., Youngstrom, E., Schoff, K., & Izard, C. (1999). Family instability and the problem behaviors of children from economically disadvantaged families. *Developmental Psychology, 35*(1), 258-268.

ACT for Youth Upstate Center of Excellence. (2002). *Adolescent brain development. Research facts and findings* [A collaboration of Cornell University, University of Rochester, and the NYS Center for School Safety]. Retrieved from www.human.cornell.edu/actforyouth

Adam, E. K., Gunnar, M. R., & Tanaka, A. (2004). Adult attachment, parent emotion, and observed parenting behavior: Mediator and moderator models. *Child Development, 75,* 110-122.

Adams, B. N. (2004). Families and family study in international perspective. *Journal of Marriage and Family, 66,* 1076-1088.

Adams, C. (1991). Qualitative age differences in memory for text: A life-span developmental perspective. *Psychology and Aging, 6,* 323-336.

Adams, K. F., Schatzkin, A., Harris, T. B., Kipnis, V., Mouw, T., Ballard-Barbash, R., . . . Leitzmann, M. F. (2006). Overweight, obesity, and mortality in a large prospective cohort of persons 50 to 71 years old. *New England Journal of Medicine, 355,* 763-778.

Adams, R. G. (1986). Friendship and aging. *Generations, 10*(4), 40-43.

Adams, R. G., & Allan, G. (1998). *Placing friendship in context.* Cambridge, MA: Cambridge University Press.

Adams, R. G., & Taylor, E. M. (2015). Friendship and happiness in the third age. In *Friendship and happiness* (pp. 155-169). Amsterdam: Springer.

Adams, R., & Laursen, B. (2001). The organization and dynamics of adolescent conflict with parents and friends. *Journal of Marriage and the Family, 63,* 97-110.

Addis, M. E., & Mahalik, J. R. (2003). Men, masculinity, and the contexts of help seeking. *American Psychologist, 58,* 5-14.

Addis, S., Davies, M., Greene, G., MacBride-Stewart, S., & Shepherd, M. (2009). The health, social care and housing needs of lesbian, gay, bisexual and transgender older people: A review of the literature. *Health & Social Care in the Community, 17*(6), 647-658.

Adey, P., Csapó, B., Demetriou, A., Hautamäki, J., & Shayer, M. (2007). Can we be intelligent about intelligence? Why education needs the concept of plastic general ability. *Educational Research Review, 2*(2), 75-97.

Administration for Children and Families. (2006a). *FACES 2003 research brief and program quality in Head Start.* Washington, DC: Author.

Administration for Children and Families. (2006b). *FACES findings: New research on Head Start outcomes and program quality.* Washington, DC: Author.

Administration on Aging. (2010). *Aging statistics.* Retrieved from www.aoa.gov/AoARoot/Aging_Statistics/index.aspx

Administration on Aging. (2016). *A profile of older Americans: 2016.* Retrieved from www.acl.gov/sites/default/files/Aging%20and%20Disability%20in%20America/2016-Profile.pdf

Adolescent Sleep Working Group. (2014). School start times for adolescents. *Pediatrics, 134*(3), 642-649.

Adolph, K. E. (2008). Learning to move. *Current Directions in Psychological Science, 17,* 213-218.

Adolph, K. E., & Eppler, M. A. (2002). Flexibility and specificity in infant motor skill acquisition. In J. Fagen & H. Hayne (Eds.), *Progress in infancy research* (Vol. 2, pp. 121-167). Mahwah, NJ: Erlbaum.

Adolph, K. E., Vereijken, B., & Shrout, P. E. (2003). What changes in infant walking and why. *Child Development, 74,* 475-497.

African Wedding Traditions. (2013). *Jumping the broom ceremony & African wedding traditions.* Retrieved from African Wedding Traditions: http://africanweddingtraditions.com/jumping-the-broom-ceremony.html

Agahi, N., & Parker, M. G. (2008). Leisure activities and mortality: Does gender matter? *Journal of Aging and Health, 20*(7), 855-871.

Agahi, N., Ahacic, K., & Parker, M. G. (2006). Continuity of leisure participation from middle age to old age. *Journal of Gerontology: Social Sciences, 61B,* S340-S346.

Agency for Healthcare Research and Quality and the Centers for Disease Control. (2002). *Physical activity and older Americans: Benefits and strategies.* Retrieved from www.ahrq.gov/ppip/activity.htm

Aggarwal, K. K. (2013). Sexual desire and sexual activity of men and women across their lifespan. *Indian Journal of Clinical Practice, 24*(3).

Agrillo, C. (2011). Near-death experience: out-of-body and out-of-brain? *Review of General Psychology, 15*(1), 1.

Aguilera, M., Arias, B., Wichers, M., Barrantes-Vidal, N., Moya, J., Villa, H., . . . & Fañanás, L. (2009). Early adversity and 5-HTT/BDNF genes: new evidence of gene-environment interactions on depressive symptoms in a general population. *Psychological Medicine, 39*(9), 1425-1432.

Ahmetoglu, G., Swami, V., & Chamorro-Premuzic, T. (2010). The relationship between dimensions of love, personality, and relationship length. *Archives of Sexual Behavior, 39*(5), 1181-1190.

Ahnert, L., & Lamb, M. E. (2003). Shared care: Establishing a balance between home and child care settings. *Child Development, 74,* 1044-1049.

Ahnert, L., Gunnar, M. R., Lamb, M. E., & Barthel, M. (2004). Transition to child care: Associations with infant-mother attachment, infant negative emotion and corticol elevation. *Child Development, 75,* 639-650.

Ahrons, C. R., & Tanner, J. L. (2003). Adult children and their fathers: Relationship changes 20 years after parental divorce. *Family Relations, 52,* 340-351.

Ainsworth, M. D. S. (1967). *Infancy in Uganda: Infant care and the growth of love.* Baltimore: Johns Hopkins University Press.

Ainsworth, M. D. S., Blehar, M. C., Waters, E., & Wall, S. (1978). *Patterns of attachment: A psychological study of the strange situation.* Hillsdale, NJ: Erlbaum.

Ainsworth, M. D. S., Blehar, M. C., Waters, E., & Wall, S. N. (2015). *Patterns of attachment: A psychological study of the strange situation.* New York: Psychology Press.

Aitken, L., Burmeister, E., Lang, J., Chaboyer, W., & Richmond, T. S. (2010). Characteristics and outcomes of injured older adults after hospitalization. *Journal of the American Geriatrics Society, 58*(3), 442–449.

Akinbami, L. (2006). The state of childhood asthma, United States, 1980–2005. *Advance Data from Vital and Health Statistics, 381.* Hyattsville, MD: National Center for Health Statistics.

Akinbami, O. J., Moorman, J. E., Bailey, C., Zahran, H. S., King, M., Johnson, C. A., & Liu, X. (2012). Trends in asthma prevalence, health care use, and mortality in the United States, 2001–2010. *NCHS Data Brief, 94.*

Al-Namlah, A. S., Meins, E., & Fernyhough, C. (2012). Self-regulatory private speech relates to children's recall and organization of autobiographical memories. *Early Childhood Research Quarterly, 27*(3), 441–446.

Alan Guttmacher Institute (AGI). (1999). *Facts in brief: Teen sex and pregnancy.* Retrieved from www.agi_usa.org/pubs/fb_teen_sex.html#sfd

Alati, R., Al Mamun, A., Williams, G. M., O'Callaghan, M., Najman, J. M., & Bor, W. (2006). In utero alcohol exposure and prediction of alcohol disorders in early adulthood: A birth cohort study. *Archives of General Psychiatry, 63*(9), 1009–1016.

Albert, M. S., DeKosky, S. T., Dickson, D., Dubois, B., Feldman, H. H., Fox, N. C., . . . & Snyder, P. J. (2011). The diagnosis of mild cognitive impairment due to Alzheimer's disease: Recommendations from the National Institute on Aging-Alzheimer's Association workgroups on diagnostic guidelines for Alzheimer's disease. *Alzheimer's & Dementia, 7*(3), 270–279.

Aldwin, C. M., & Levenson, M. R. (2001). Stress, coping, and health at midlife: A developmental perspective. In M. E. Lachman (Ed.), *Handbook of midlife development* (pp. 188–214). New York: Wiley.

Alessandri, G., Eisenberg, N., Vecchione, M., Caprara, G. V., & Milioni, M. (2016). Ego-resiliency development from late adolescence to emerging adulthood: A ten-year longitudinal study. *Journal of Adolescence, 50,* 91–102.

Alexander, K. L., Entwisle, D. R., & Dauber, S. L. (1993). First-grade classroom behavior: Its short- and long-term consequences for school performance. *Child Development, 64,* 801–814.

Alexander, K. L., Entwisle, D. R., & Olson, L. S. (2007). Lasting consequences of the summer learning gap. *American Sociological Review, 72,* 167–180.

Alibeik, H., & Angaji, S. A. (2010). Developmental aspects of left handedness. *Australian Journal of Basic and Applied Sciences, 4*(5), 881–977.

All Children Reading: A grand challenge for development. (2017). Retrieved from All Children Reading: https://allchildrenreading.org/about-us/literacy-statistics

Alladi, S., Bak, T. H., Duggirala, V., Surampudi, B., Shailaja, M., Shukla, A. K., . . . & Kaul, S. (2013). Bilingualism delays age at onset of dementia, independent of education and immigration status. *Neurology, 81*(22), 1938–1944.

Allemand, M. (2007). Cross-sectional age differences and longitudinal age changes of personality in middle adulthood and old age. *Journal of Personality, 75*(2), 323–358.

Allemand, M., Hill, P. L., & Lehmann, R. (2015). Divorce and personality development across middle adulthood. *Personal Relationships, 22*(1), 122–137.

Allemand, M., Schaffhuser, K., & Martin, M. (2015). Long-term correlated change between personality traits and perceived social support in middle adulthood. *Personality and Social Psychology Bulletin, 41*(3), 420–432.

Allen, E. S., & Atkins, D. C. (2012). The association of divorce and extramarital sex in a representative US sample. *Journal of Family Issues, 33*(11), 1477–1493.

Allen, I. E., & Seaman, J. (2013). *Changing course: Ten years of tracking online education in the United States.* Newburyport, MA: Sloan Consortium.

Allen, J. P., & Philliber, S. (2001). Who benefits most from a broadly targeted prevention program? Differential efficacy across populations in the Teen Outreach Program. *Journal of Community Psychology, 29,* 637–655.

Allen, J. P., McElhaney, K. B., Land, D. J., Kuperminc, G. P., Moore, C. W., O'Beirner-Kelly, H., & Kilmer, S. L. (2003). A secure base in adolescence: Markers of attachment security in the mother-adolescent relationship. *Child Development, 74,* 292–307.

Allen, J. P., Porter, M. R., McFarland, F. C., Marsh, P., & McElhaney, K. B. (2005). The two faces of adolescents' success with peers: Adolescent popularity, social adaptation, and deviant behavior. *Child Development, 76*(3), 747–760.

Allen, K. R., Blieszner, R., & Roberto, K. A. (2000). Families in the middle and later years: A review and critique of research in the 1990s. *Journal of Marriage and Family, 62,* 911–926.

Allen, T. D., Herst, D. E., Bruck, C. S., & Sutton, M. (2000). Consequences associated with work-to-family conflict: a review and agenda for future research. *Journal of Occupational Health Psychology, 5*(2), 278.

Alloway, T. P. (2006). How does working memory work in the classroom? *Education Research and Reviews, 1,* 134–139.

Alloway, T. P., & Alloway, R. G. (2010). Investigating the predictive roles of working memory and IQ in academic attainment. *Journal of Experimental Child Psychology, 106*(1), 20–29.

Alloway, T. P., Gathercole, S. E., Kirkwood, H., & Elliot, J. (2009). The cognitive and behavioral characteristics of children with low working memory. *Child Development, 80*(2), 606–621.

Almas, A. N., Grusec, J. E., & Tackett, J. L. (2011). Children's disclosure and secrecy: Links to maternal parenting characteristics and children's coping skills. *Social Development, 20*(3), 624–643.

Almeida, D. M., & Horn, M. C. (2004). Is daily life more stressful during adulthood? In O. G. Brim, C. D. Riff, & R. C. Kessler (Eds.), *How healthy are we? A national study of well-being at midlife* (pp. 425–451). Chicago: University of Chicago Press.

Almeida, D. M., Serido, J., & McDonald, D. (2006). Daily life stressors of early and late baby boomers. In S. K. Whitbourne & S. L. Willis (Eds.), *The baby boomers grow up: Contemporary perspectives on midlife* (pp. 165–183). Mahwah, NJ: Erlbaum.

Almli, C. R., Ball, R. H., & Wheeler, M. E. (2001). Human fetal and neonatal movement patterns: Gender differences and fetal-to-natal continuity. *Developmental Psychobiology, 38*(4), 252–273.

Altarac, M., & Saroha, E. (2007). Lifetime prevalence of learning disabilities among U.S. children. *Pediatrics, 119*(Suppl. 1), S77–S83.

Alterovitz, S. S. R., & Mendelsohn, G. A. (2009). Partner preferences across the life span: Online dating by older adults. *Psychology and Aging, 24*(2), 513.

Altmann, A., Tian, L., Henderson, V. W., & Greicius, M. D. (2014). Sex modifies the APOE-related risk of developing Alzheimer disease. *Annals of Neurology, 75*(4), 563–573.

Altschul, I., Oyserman, D., & Bybee, D. (2006). Racial-ethnic identity in mid-adolescence: Content and change as predictors of academic achievement. *Child Development, 77,* 1155–1169.

Alzheimer's Association. (2017a). Diagnosis of Alzheimer's Disease and dementia. Retrieved from www.alz.org/alzheimers_disease_diagnosis.asp

Alzheimer's Association. (2017b). *Alzheimer's disease: Facts and figures.* Retrieved from www.alz.org/documents_custom/2017-facts-and-figures.pdf

Alzheimer's Disease: The search for causes and treatments—Part I. (1998, August). *Harvard Mental Health Letter, 15*(2).

Al-Dhamit, Y., & Kreishan, L. (2016). Gifted students' intrinsic and extrinsic motivations and parental influence on their motivation: from the self-determination theory perspective. *Journal of Research in Special Educational Needs, 16*(1), 13–23.

Amato, P. R. (2000). The consequences of divorce for adults and children. *Journal of Marriage and Family, 62,* 1269–1287.

Amato, P. R. (2003). Reconciling divergent perspectives: Judith Wallerstein, quantitative family research, and children of divorce. *Family Relations, 52,* 332–339.

Amato, P. R. (2005). The impact of family formation change on the cognitive, social, and emotional well-being of the next generation. *Future of Children, 15,* 75–96.

Amato, P. R. (2010). Research on divorce: Continuing trends and new developments. *Journal of Marriage and Family, 72*(3), 650–666.

Amato, P. R. (2014). The consequences of divorce for adults and children: An update. *Drustvena Istrazivanja, 23*(1), 5.

Amato, P. R., & Afifi, T. D. (2006). Feeling caught between parents: Adult children's relations with parents and subjective well-being. *Journal of Marriage and Family, 68,* 222–235.

Amato, P. R., & Anthony, C. J. (2014). Estimating the effects of parental divorce and death with fixed effects models. *Journal of Marriage and Family, 76*(2), 370–386.

Amato, P. R., Johnson, D. R., Booth, A., & Rogers, S. J. (2003). Continuity and change in marital quality between 1980 and 2000. *Journal of Marriage and Family, 65,* 1–22.

American Academy of Child and Adolescent Psychiatry (2017). Terrorism and war: How to talk to your children. Retrieved from www.aacap.org/AACAP/Families_and_Youth/Facts_for_Families/FFF-Guide/Talking-To-Children-About-Terrorism-And-War-087.aspx

American Academy of Pediatrics & Fetus and Newborn Committee. (2006). Prevention and management of pain in the neonate: an update. *Pediatrics, 118*(5), 2231–2241.

American Academy of Pediatrics (AAP) Committee on Adolescence. (2000). Suicide and suicide attempts in adolescents. *Pediatrics, 105*(4), 871–874.

American Academy of Pediatrics (AAP) Committee on Adolescence. (2003). Policy statement: Identifying and treating eating disorders. *Pediatrics, 111,* 204–211.

American Academy of Pediatrics (AAP) Committee on Bioethics. (1992, July). Ethical issues in surrogate motherhood. *AAP News,* pp. 14–15.

American Academy of Pediatrics (AAP) Committee on Children with Disabilities and Committee on Drugs. (1996). Medication for children with attentional disorders. *Pediatrics, 98,* 301–304.

American Academy of Pediatrics (AAP) Committee on Drugs. (2001). The transfer of drugs and other chemicals into human milk. *Pediatrics, 108*(3), 776–789.

American Academy of Pediatrics (AAP) Committee on Environmental Health. (2005). Lead exposure in children: Prevention, detection, and management. *Pediatrics, 116,* 1036–1046.

American Academy of Pediatrics (AAP) Committee on Injury and Poison Prevention. (2000). Firearm-related injuries affecting the pediatric population. *Pediatrics, 105*(4), 888–895.

American Academy of Pediatrics (AAP) Committee on Nutrition. (2003). Prevention of pediatric overweight and obesity. *Pediatrics, 112,* 424–430.

American Academy of Pediatrics (AAP) Committee on Nutrition. (2006). Dietary recommendations for children and adolescents: A guide for practitioners. *Pediatrics, 117*(2), 544–559.

American Academy of Pediatrics (AAP) Committee on Practice and Ambulatory Medicine and Section on Ophthalmology. (2002). Use of photoscreening for children's vision screening. *Pediatrics, 109,* 524–525.

American Academy of Pediatrics (AAP) Committee on Psychosocial Aspects of Child and Family Health and Committee on Adolescence. (2001). Sexuality education for children and adolescence. *Pediatrics, 108*(2), 498–502.

American Academy of Pediatrics (AAP) Committee on Psychosocial Aspects of Child and Family Health. (1998). Guidance for effective discipline. *Pediatrics, 101,* 723–728.

American Academy of Pediatrics (AAP) Committee on Psychosocial Aspects of Child and Family Health. (2002). Coparent or second-parent adoption by same-sex parents. *Pediatrics, 109*(2), 339–340.

American Academy of Pediatrics (AAP) Committee on Public Education (2001). Policy statement: Children, adolescents, and television. *Pediatrics, 107,* 423–426.

American Academy of Pediatrics (AAP) Committee on Substance Abuse. (2001). Tobacco's toll: Implications for the pediatrician. *Pediatrics, 107,* 794–798.

American Academy of Pediatrics (AAP) Council on Injury and Poison Prevention. (2001). Bicycle helmets. *Pediatrics, 108*(4), 1030–1032.

American Academy of Pediatrics (AAP) Council on Sports Medicine and Fitness. (2001). Risk of injury from baseball and softball in children. *Pediatrics, 107*(4), 782–784.

American Academy of Pediatrics (AAP) Section on Breastfeeding. (2005). Breastfeeding and the use of human milk. *Pediatrics, 115,* 496–506.

American Academy of Pediatrics (AAP) Task Force on Sudden Infant Death Syndrome. (2005). The changing concept of sudden infant death syndrome: Diagnostic coding shifts, controversies regarding sleeping environment, and new variables to consider in reducing risk. *Pediatrics, 116,* 1245–1255.

American Academy of Pediatrics (AAP), Stirling, J., Jr., and the Committee on Child Abuse and Neglect and Section on Adoption and Foster Care; American Academy of Child and Adolescent Psychiatry, Amaya-Jackson, L.; & National Center for Child Traumatic Stress, Amaya-Jackson, L. (2008). Understanding the behavioral and emotional consequences of child abuse. *Pediatrics, 122*(3), 667–673.

American Academy of Pediatrics (AAP). (2004, September 30). *American Academy of Pediatrics (AAP) supports Institute of Medicine's (IOM) childhood obesity recommendation* [Press release].

American Academy of Pediatrics. (2011). Media use by children under age 2. *Pediatrics, 128,* 1040–1045.

American Academy of Pediatrics. (2013). Children, adolescents, and the media. *Pediatrics, 132,* 958–961.

American Academy of Pediatrics. (2016). *American Academy of Pediatrics announces new guidelines for children's media use.* Retrieved from www.aap.org/en-us/about-the-aap/aap-press-room/pages/american-academy-of-pediatrics-announces-new-recommendations-for-childrens-media-use.aspx

American Association of University Women. (2007). *Behind the pay gap.* Washington, DC: AAUW Educational Foundation.

American Cancer Society. (2007). What are the risk factors for breast cancer? *Cancer Reference Information.* Oklahoma City, OK: Author.

American Cancer Society. (2011). *Guide to quitting smoking.* Retrieved from www.cancer.org/docroot/PED/content/PED_10_13X_Guide_for_Quitting_Smoking.asp?from=fast

American Cancer Society. (2017a). *How common is breast cancer?* [information sheet]. Retrieved from www.cancer.org/cancer/breast-cancer/about/how-common-is-breast-cancer.html

American Cancer Society. (2017b). *Lifestyle-related breast cancer risk factors* [information sheet]. Retrieved from www.cancer.org/cancer/breast-cancer/risk-and-prevention/lifestyle-related-breast-cancer-risk-factors.html

American College of Cardiology. (2017). New *ACC/AHA high blood pressure guidelines lower definition of hypertension* [news release]. Retrieved from www.acc.org/latest-in-cardiology/articles/2017/11/08/11/47/mon-5pm-bp-guideline-aha-2017

American College of Emergency Physicians. (2008, March 10). *Know suicide's warning sign* [Press release]. Irving, TX: Author.

American College of Nurse-Midwives. (2016). *Position statement: Planned home births.* Silver Spring, MD: Author.

American College of Obstetricians and Gynecologists (ACOG). (2000). Premenstrual syndrome. *ACOG Practice Bulletin, No. 15.* Washington, DC: Author.

American College of Obstetricians and Gynecologists (ACOG). (2015). *Premenstrual syndrome.* Retrieved from www.acog.org/Patients/FAQs/Premenstrual-Syndrome-PMS

American College of Obstetricians and Gynecologists. (2013). Weight gain during pregnancy. Committee Opinion No. 548. *Obstet Gynecol, 121,* 210–212.

American College of Obstetricians and Gynecologists. (2015, May). Early pregnancy loss. Practice Bulletin No. 150. *Obstet Gynecol, 125*(5), 1258–67.

American College of Obstetricians and Gynecologists. (2017). Planned home birth. Committee Opinion No. 697. *Obstet Gynecol, 129,* e117–e122.

American College of Obstetricians and Gynecologists. (2016). *Exercise during pregnancy.* Retrieved from www.acog.org/Patients/FAQs/Exercise-During-Pregnancy#precautions

American Diabetes Association. (1992). *Diabetes facts.* Alexandria, VA: Author.

American Heart Association (AHA). (1995). *Silent epidemic: The truth about women and heart disease.* Dallas: Author.

American Heart Association, Gidding, S. S., Dennison, B. A., Birch, L. L., Daniels, S. R., Gilman, M. W., Lichtenstein, A. H., . . . & Van Horn, L. (2006). Dietary recommendations for children and adolescents: a guide for practitioners. *Pediatrics, 117*(2), 544–559.

American Medical Association House of Delegates. (2008, June). *Resolution 205: Home deliveries.* Proceedings of the American Medical Association House of Delegates, Fifteenth Annual Meeting, Chicago, IL. Retrieved from www.ama-assn.org/ama1/pub/upload/mm/471/205.doc

American Medical Association. (2009). *AMA policy regarding sexual orientation: H-65.973 health care disparities in same-sex partner households.* Houston, TX: Retrieved from www.ama-assn.org/ama/pub/about-ama/our-people/member-groups-sections/glbt-advisory-committee/ama-policy-regarding-sexual-orientation.page.

American Medical Association. (2018). Physician assisted suicide: Permitting physicians to engage in assisted suicide would ultimately cause more harm than good [position statement]. Retrieved from www.ama-assn.org/delivering-care/physician-assisted-suicide

American Psychiatric Association. (2000). *Diagnostic and statistical manual of mental disorders* (4th ed., Text Revision). Washington, DC: Author.

American Psychiatric Association. (2013). *Diagnostic and statistical manual of mental disorders: DSM-5.* Washington, DC: Author.

American Psychological Association (APA) Online. (2001). *End-of-life issues and care.* Retrieved from www.apa.org/pi/eol/arguments.html

American Psychological Association (APA) Working Group on Assisted Suicide and End-of-Life Decisions. (2005). *Orientation to end-of-life decision-making.* Retrieved from www.apa.org/pi/aseol/section1.html

American Psychological Association (APA). (2002). Ethical principles of psychologists and code of conduct. *American Psychologist, 57,* 1060–1073.

American Psychological Association (APA). (2004b, July). *Resolution on sexual orientation, parents, and children.* Retrieved from www.apa.org/pi/lgbc/policy/parents.html

American Psychological Association (APA). (2009). *Stress in America.* Retrieved from www.apa.org/news/press/releases/stress-exec-summary.pdf

American Psychological Association (APA). (2011). *Mental and behavioral health and older Americans.* Retrieved from www.apa.org/about/gr/issues/aging/mental-health.aspx

American Psychological Association (APA). (2017a). *Stress in America.* Retrieved from www.apa.org/news/press/releases/stress/2017/state-nation.pdf

American Psychological Association (2017b). *Resolution on assisted dying.* Retrieved from: www.apa.org/about/policy/assisted-dying-resolution.aspx.

American Psychological Association (APA). (n.d.). *Answers to your questions about sexual orientation and homosexuality* [Brochure]. Washington, DC: Author.

American Public Health Association. (2004). *Disparities in infant mortality* [Fact sheet]. Retrieved from www.medscape.com/viewarticle/472721

America's youngest outcasts 2010. (2011). National Center on Family Homelessness, Needham, MA. Retrieved from www.HomelessChildrenAmerica.org

Amirkhanyan, A. A., & Wolf, D. A. (2006). Parent care and the stress process: Findings from panel data. *Journal of Gerontology: Social Sciences, 61B,* S248–S255.

Amlien, I. K., & Fjell, A. M. (2014). Diffusion tensor imaging of white matter degeneration in Alzheimer's disease and mild cognitive impairment. *Neuroscience, 276,* 206–215.

Amsel, E., Goodman, G., Savoie, D., & Clark, M. (1996). The development of reasoning about causal and noncausal influences on levers. *Child Development, 67,* 1624–1646.

Amso, D., & Casey, B. J. (2006). Beyond what develops when: Neuroimaging may inform how cognition changes with development. *Current Directions in Psychological Science, 15,* 24–29.

Anastasi, A. (1988). *Psychological testing* (6th ed.). New York: Macmillan.

Anastasi, A., & Schaefer, C. E. (1971). Note on concepts of creativity and intelligence. *Journal of Creative Behavior, 3,* 113–116.

Andersen, S. L., Sebastiani, P., Dworkis, D. A., Feldman, L., & Perls, T. T. (2012). Health span approximates life span among many supercentenarians: Compression of morbidity at the approximate limit of life span. *Journals of Gerontology Series A: Biomedical Sciences and Medical Sciences, 67*(4), 395–405.

Anderson, A. H., Clark, A., & Mullin, J. (1994). Interactive communication between children: Learning how to make language work in dialog. *Journal of Child Language, 21,* 439–463.

Anderson, C. (2000). *The impact of interactive violence on children.* Statement before the Senate Committee on Commerce, Science, and Transportation, 106th Congress, 1st session.

Anderson, C. A., Berkowitz, L., Donnerstein, E., Huesmann, L. R., Johnson, J. D., Linz, D., Malamuth, N. M., & Wartella, E. (2003). The influence of media violence on youth. *Psychological Science in the Public Interest, 4,* 81–110.

Anderson, C., & Platten, C. R. (2011). Sleep deprivation lowers inhibition and enhances impulsivity to negative stimuli. *Behavioural Brain Research, 217*(2), 463–466.

Anderson, D. A., & Hamilton, M. (2005). Gender role stereotyping of parents in children's picture books: The invisible father. *Sex Roles, 52,* 145–151.

Anderson, J.L., May, H.T., Lappe, D.L., Bair, T., Le, V., Carlquist, J.F., & Muhlestein, J.B. (2015). Impact of testosterone replacement on myocardial infarction, stroke, and death in men with low testosterone concentrations in an integrated health care system. *American Journal of Cardiology, 117,* 794–799.

Anderson, N. D., Damianakis, T., Kröger, E., Wagner, L. M., Dawson, D. R., Binns, M. A., . . . & Cook, S. L. (2014). The benefits associated with volunteering among seniors: A critical review and recommendations for future research. *Psychological Bulletin, 140*(6), 1505.

Anderson, S. E., & Whitaker, R. C. (2010). Household routines and obesity in US preschool-aged children. *Pediatrics, 125*(3), 420–428. doi: 10.1542/peds.2009-0417

Anderson, S. E., Dallal, G. E., & Must, A. (2003). Relative weight and race influence average age at menarche: Results from two nationally representative surveys of U.S. girls studied 25 years apart. *Pediatrics, 111,* 844–850.

Andrews-Hanna, J. R., Snyder, A. Z., Vincent, J. L., Lustig, C., Head, D., Raichle, M. E., & Buckner, R. L. (2007). Disruption of large-scale brain systems in advanced aging. *Neuron, 56,* 924–935.

Ang, S., Rodgers, J. L., & Wanstrom, L. (2010). The Flynn Effect within subgroups in the U.S.: Gender, race, income, education, and urbanization differences in the NLSY-Children data. *Intelligence, 38*(4), 367–384.

Anglemyer, A., Horvath, T., & Rutherford, G. (2014). The accessibility of firearms and risk for suicide and homicide victimization among household members: A systematic review and meta-analysis. *Annals of Internal Medicine, 160*(2), 101–110.

Antonio, A. L., Chang, M. J., Hakuta, K., Kenny, D. A., Levin, S., & Milem, J. F. (2004). Effects of racial diversity on complex thinking in college students. *Psychological Science, 15,* 507–510.

Antonucci, T. C., & Akiyama, H. (1995). Convoys of social relations: Family and friendships within a life-span context. In R. Blieszner & V. Hilkevitch (Eds.), *Handbook of aging and the family* (pp. 355–371). Westport, CT: Greenwood Press.

Antonucci, T. C., Akiyama, H., & Merline, A. (2001). Dynamics of social relationships in midlife. In M. E. Lachman (Ed.), *Handbook of midlife development* (pp. 571–598). New York: Wiley.

Antonucci, T., & Akiyama, H. (1997). Concern with others at midlife: Care, comfort, or compromise? In M. E. Lachman & J. B. James (Eds.), *Multiple paths of midlife development* (pp. 145–169). Chicago: University of Chicago Press.

Antwi, Y. A., Moriya, A. S., & Simon, K. I. (2015). Access to health insurance and the use of inpatient medical care: evidence from the Affordable Care Act young adult mandate. *Journal of Health Economics, 39,* 171–187.

APA Staff. (2007). *Sandwich generation moms feeling the squeeze.* Retrieved from American Psychological Association: www.apa.org/helpcenter/sandwich-generation.aspx

Apgar, V. (1953). A proposal for a new method of evaluation of the newborn infant. *Current Research in Anesthesia and Analgesia, 32,* 260–267.

Aquilino, W. S. (1996). The returning adult child and parental experience at midlife. In C. Ryff & M. M. Seltzer (Eds.), *The parental experience in midlife* (pp. 423–458). Chicago: University of Chicago Press.

Aquilino, W. S. (2006). Family relationships and support systems in emerging adulthood. In J. J. Arnett & J. L. Tanner (Eds.), *Emerging adults in America: Coming of age in the 21st century* (pp. 193–217). Washington, DC: American Psychological Association.

Araújo, C. G. S. D. (2008). Flexibility assessment: normative values for flexitest from 5 to 91 years of age. *Arquivos Brasileiros de Cardiologia, 90*(4), 280-287.

Araújo, J. R., Martel, F., Borges, N., Araújo, J. M., & Keating, E. (2015). Folates and aging: Role in mild cognitive impairment, dementia and depression. *Ageing Research Reviews, 22*, 9-19.

Arai, Y. (2017). The prevalence and risk factors of dementia in centenarians. *Brain Nerve, 69*, 771-780.

Arai, Y., Inagaki, H., Takayama, M., Abe, Y., Saito, Y., Takebayashi, T., Gondo, Y., & Hirose, N. (2014). Physical independence and mortality at the extreme limit of life span: Supercentenarians study in Japan. *Journals of Gerontology, 69*, 486-494.

Aram, D., Abiri, S., & Elad, L. (2014). Predicting early spelling: the contribution of children's early literacy, private speech during spelling, behavioral regulation, and parental spelling support. *Reading and Writing, 27*(4), 685-707.

Archer, J. (2004). Sex differences in aggression in real-world settings: A meta-analytic review. *Review of General Psychology, 8*, 291-322.

Archer, S. L. (1993). Identity in relational contexts: A methodological proposal. In J. Kroger (Ed.), *Discussions on ego identity* (pp. 75-99). Hillsdale, NJ: Erlbaum.

Arend, R., Gove, F., & Sroufe, L. A. (1979). Continuity of individual adaptation from infancy to kindergarten: A predictive study of ego-resiliency and curiosity in preschoolers. *Child Development, 50*(4), 950-959.

Arias, E. (2010). United States life tables by Hispanic origin. *Vital Health Statistics, 2*(152), 1-33. Hyattsville, MD: National Center for Health Statistics.

Arias, E., MacDorman, M. F., Strobino, D. M., & Guyer, B. (2003). Annual summary of vital statistics—2002. *Pediatrics, 112*, 1215-1230.

Arking, R., Novoseltsev, V., & Novoseltseva, J. (2004). The human life span is not that limited: The effect of multiple longevity phenotypes. *Journal of Gerontology: Biological Sciences, 59A*, 697-704.

Armenta, C. N., Fritz, M. M., & Lyubomirsky, S. (2016). Functions of positive emotions: Gratitude as a motivator of self-improvement and positive change. *Emotion Review* doi: 10.1177/1754073916669596.

Arner, P. (2000). Obesity—a genetic disease of adipose tissue? *British Journal of Nutrition, 83*(1), 9-16.

Arnestad, M., Crotti, L., Rognum, T. O., Insolia, R., Pedrazzini, M., Ferrandi, C., . . . Schwartz, P. J. (2007). Prevalence of long-qt syndrome gene variants in sudden infant death syndrome. *Circulation, 115*, 361-367.

Arnett, J. J. (1999). Adolescent storm and stress, reconsidered. *American Psychologist, 54*, 317-326.

Arnett, J. J. (2004). *Emerging adulthood.* New York: Oxford University Press.

Arnett, J. J. (2006). Emerging adulthood: Understanding the new way of coming of age. In J. J. Arnett & J. L. Tanner (Eds.), *Emerging adults in America: Coming of age in the 21st century* (pp. 3-19). Washington, DC: American Psychological Association.

Arnett, J. J. (2007a). Emerging adulthood: What is it, and what is it good for? *Child Development Perspectives, 1*, 68-73.

Arnett, J. J. (2007b). Suffering, selfish slackers? Myths and reality about emerging adults. *Journal of Youth and Adolescence, 36*, 23-39.

Arnett, J. J. (2010). Oh, grow up! Generational grumbling and the new life stage of emerging adulthood. *Perspectives on Psychological Science, 5*, 89-92.

Artis, J. E. (2007). Maternal cohabitation and child well-being among kindergarten children. *Journal of Marriage and Family, 69*(1), 222-236.

Artistico, D., Orom, H., Cervone, D., Krauss, S., & Houston, E. (2010). Everyday challenges in context: The influence of contextual factors on everyday problem solving among young, middle-aged and older adults. *Experimental Aging Research, 36*(2), 230-247.

Aschersleben, G., Hofer, T., & Jovanovic, B. (2008). The link between infant attention to goal-directed action and later theory of mind abilities. *Developmental Science, 11*(6), 862-868.

Asher, M. I. (2010). Recent perspectives on global epidemiology of asthma in childhood. *Allergologia et immunopathologia, 38*(2), 83-87.

Associated Press. (2017). Oldest American celebrates 114th birthday. Retrieved from https://nypost.com/2017/08/18/oldest-american-celebrates-114th-birthday/

Asthana, S., Bhasin, S., Butler, R. N., Fillit, H., Finkelstein, J., Harman, S. M., . . . Urban, R. (2004). Masculine vitality: Pros and cons of testosterone in treating the andropause. *Journal of Gerontology: Medical Sciences, 59A*, 461-466.

Atchley, R. C. (1989). A continuity theory of normal aging. *Gerontologist, 29*, 183-190.

Atherton, O. E., Robins, R. W., Rentfrow, P. J., & Lamb, M. E. (2014). Personality correlates of risky health outcomes: Findings from a large Internet study. *Journal of Research in Personality, 50*, 56-60.

Attili, G., Vermigli, P., & Roazzi, A. (2010). Children's social competence, peer status, and the quality of mother-child and father-child relationships. *European Psychologist.*

Attili, G., Vermigli, P., & Roazzi, A. (2011). Rearing styles, parents' attachment mental state, and children's social abilities: The link to peer acceptance. *Child Development Research, 2011.*

Aurand, A., Miles, R., & Usher, K. (2014). Local environment of neighborhood Naturally Occurring Retirement Communities (NORCs) in a mid-sized US city. *Journal of Housing for the Elderly, 28*(2), 133-164.

Austin, E. W., Pinkleton, B. E., & Fujioka, Y. (2000). The role of interpretation processes and parental discussion in the media's effects on adolescents' use of alcohol. *Pediatrics, 105*(2), 343-349.

Ausubel, N. (1964). *The book of Jewish knowledge.* New York: Crown.

Auyeng, B., Baron-Cohen, S., Ashwin, E., Kinckmeyer, R., Taylor, K., Hackett, G., & Hines, M. (2009). Fetal testosterone predicts sexually differentiated childhood behavior in girls and in boys. *Psychological Science, 20*, 144-148.

Avis, N. E. (1999). Women's health at midlife. In S. L. Willis & J. D. Reid (Eds.), *Life in the middle: Psychological and social development in middle age* (pp. 105-146). San Diego: Academic Press.

Avis, N. E., & Crawford, S. (2006). Menopause: Recent research findings. In S. K. Whitbourne & S. L. Willis (Eds.), *The baby boomers grow up: Contemporary perspectives on midlife* (pp. 75-109). Mahwah, NJ: Erlbaum.

Avolio, B. J., & Sosik, J. J. (1999). A life-span framework for assessing the impact of work on white-collar workers. In S. L. Willis & J. D. Reid (Eds.), *Life in the middle: Psychological and social development in middle age.* San Diego: Academic Press.

Bönsch, D., Wunschel, M., Lenz, B., Janssen, G., Weisbrod, M., & Sauer, H. (2012). Methylation matters? Decreased methylation status of genomic DNA in the blood of schizophrenic twins. *Psychiatry Research, 198*(3), 533-537.

Baas, M., Nijstad, B. A., & De Dreu, C. K. (2015). The cognitive, emotional and neural correlates of creativity. *Frontiers in Human Neuroscience, 9.*

Baber, R. J., Panay, N., & Fenton, A. (2016). 2016 IMS Recommendations on women's midlife health and menopause hormone therapy. *Climacteric, 19*(2), 109-150.

Bachmann, C. J., Aagaard, L., Burcu, M., Glaeske, G., Kalverdijk, L. J., Petersen, I., . . . & Hoffmann, F. (2016). Trends and patterns of antidepressant use in children and adolescents from five western countries, 2005-2012. *European Neuropsychopharmacology, 26*(3), 411-419.

Baddeley, A. (1998). Recent developments in working memory. *Current Opinion in Neurobiology, 8*, 234-238.

Baddeley, A. D. (2001). Is working memory still working? *American Psychologist, 56*, 851-864.

Baer, J. S., Sampson, P. D., Barr, H. M., Connor, P. D., & Streissguth, A. P. (2003). A 21-year longitudinal analysis of the effects of prenatal alcohol exposure on young adult drinking. *Archives of General Psychiatry, 60*, 377-385.

Baglioni, C., Battagliese, G., Feige, B., Spiegelhalder, K., Nissen, C., Voderholzer, U., . . . & Riemann, D. (2011). Insomnia as a predictor of depression: A meta-analytic evaluation of longitudinal epidemiological studies. *Journal of Affective Disorders, 135*(1), 10-19.

Baillargeon, J., Urban, R.J., Ottenbacher, K.J., Pierson, K.S. & Goodwin, J.S. (2013). Trends in androgen prescribing in the United States, 2001 to 2011. *JAMA Internal Medicine, 173*, 1465-1466.

Baillargeon, R. (1999). Young infants' expectations about hidden objects. *Developmental Science, 2*, 115-132.

Baillargeon, R. H., Zoccolillo, M., Keenan, K., Côté, S., Pérusse, D., Wu, H.-X., . . . Tremblay, R. E. (2007). Gender differences in physical aggression: A prospective population-based survey of children before and after 2 years of age. *Developmental Psychology, 43*, 13-26.

Baillargeon, R., Li, J., Gertner, Y., & Wu, D. (2011). How do infants reason about physical events. *The Wiley-Blackwell Handbook of Childhood Cognitive Development* (2nd ed., pp. 11–48). Hoboken, NJ: Wiley.

Baillargeon, R., Scott, R. M., & He, Z. (2010). False-belief understanding in infants. *Trends in Cognitive Sciences, 14*(3), 110–118.

Baker, A. (2013, June 30). Working to combat the stigma of autism. Retrieved from nytimes.com: www.nytimes.com/2013/07/01/nyregion/in-queens-an-effort-to-combat-autisms-stigma-among-korean-americans.html?mcubz=1

Baker, C. E. (2013). Fathers' and mothers' home literacy involvement and children's cognitive and social emotional development: Implications for family literacy programs. *Applied Developmental Science, 17*(4), 184–197.

Baker, J. L., Olsen, L. W., & Sørensen, T. I. A. (2007). Childhood body-mass index and the risk of coronary heart disease in adulthood. *New England Journal of Medicine, 357,* 2329–2336.

Baker, L. A., Cahalin, L. P., Gerst, K., & Burr, J. A. (2005). Productive activities and subjective well-being among older adults: The influence of number of activities and time commitment. *Social Indicators Research, 73*(3), 431–458.

Ball, K., Edwards, J. D., & Ross, L. A. (2007). The impact of speed of processing training on cognitive and everyday functions [Special issue I]. *Journal of Gerontology: Psychological Sciences, 62B,* 19–31.

Balluz, L. S., Okoro, C. A., & Strine, T. W. (2004). Access to health-care preventive services among Hispanics and non-Hispanics—United States, 2001–2002. *Morbidity and Mortality Weekly Report, 53,* 937–941.

Balsam, K. F., Beauchaine, T. P., Rothblum, E. D., & Solomon, S. E. (2008). Three-year follow-up of same-sex couples who had civil unions in Vermont, same-sex couples not in civil unions, and heterosexual married couples. *Developmental Psychology, 44*(1), 102.

Balsis, S., Carpenter, B. D., & Storandt, M. (2005). Personality change precedes clinical diagnosis of dementia of the Alzheimer type. *Journal of Gerontology: Psychological Sciences, 60B,* P98–P101.

Baltes, P. B. (1987). Theoretical propositions of life-span development psychology: On the dynamics between growth and decline. *Developmental Psychology 23*(5), 611–626.

Baltes, P. B. (1997). On the incomplete architecture of human ontogeny: Selection, optimization, and compensation as foundation of developmental theory. *American Psychologist, 52,* 366–380.

Baltes, P. B., & Baltes, M. M. (1990). Psychological perspectives on successful aging: The model of selective optimization with compensation. In P. B. Baltes & M. M. Baltes (Eds.), *Successful aging: Perspectives from the behavioral sciences* (pp. 1–34). New York: Cambridge University Press.

Baltes, P. B., & Smith, J. (2004). Lifespan psychology: From developmental contextualism to developmental biocultural co-constructivism. *Research in Human Development, 1,* 123–144.

Baltes, P. B., & Staudinger, U. M. (2000). Wisdom: A metaheuristic (pragmatic) to orchestrate mind and virtue toward excellence. *American Psychologist, 55,* 122–136.

Baltes, P. B., Lindenberger, U., & Staudinger, U. M. (1998). Life-span theory in developmental psychology. In R. M. Lerner (Ed.), *Handbook of child psychology: Vol. 1. Theoretical models of human development* (pp. 1029–1143). New York: Wiley.

Bandura, A. (1977). *Social learning theory.* Englewood Cliffs, NJ: Prentice Hall.

Bandura, A. (1986). *Social foundations of thought and action: A social cognitive theory.* Englewood Cliffs, NJ: Prentice Hall.

Bandura, A. (1989). Social cognitive theory. In R. Vasta (Ed.), *Annals of child development* (Vol. 6, pp. 1–60). Greenwich, CT: JAI.

Bandura, A., & Bussey, K. (2004). On broadening the cognitive, motivational, and sociostructural scope of theorizing about gender development and functioning: Comment on Martin, Ruble, and Szkrybalo (2002). *Psychological Bulletin, 130*(5), 691–701.

Bandura, A., & Walters, R. H. (1963). *Social learning and personality development.* New York: Holt, Rinehart & Winston.

Bandura, A., Barbaranelli, C., Caprara, G. V., & Pastorelli, C. (2001). Self-efficacy beliefs as shapers of children's aspirations and career trajectories. *Child Development 72*(1), 187–206.

Banse, R., Gawronski, B., Rebetez, C., Gutt, H., & Bruce Morton, J. (2010). The development of spontaneous gender stereotyping in childhood: Relations to stereotype knowledge and stereotype flexibility. *Developmental Science, 13*(2), 298–306.

Banta, D., & Thacker, S. B. (2001). Historical controversy in health technology assessment: The case of electronic fetal monitoring. *Obstetrical and Gynecological Survey, 56*(11), 707–719.

Bao, A. M., & Swaab, D. F. (2010). Sex differences in the brain, behavior, and neuropsychiatric disorders. *The Neuroscientist, 16*(5), 550–565.

Barbaresco, S., Courtemanche, C. J., & Qi, Y. (2015). Impacts of the Affordable Care Act dependent coverage provision on health-related outcomes of young adults. *Journal of Health Economics, 40,* 54–68.

Barclay, S.R., Stoltz, K.B., & Chung, Y.B. (2011). Voluntary midlife career change: Integrating the transtheoretical model and the life-span, life-space approach. *The Career Development Quarterly, 59,* 386–399.

Barinaga, M. (1998). Alzheimer's treatments that work now. *Science, 282,* 1030–1032.

Barker, E. D., Oliver, B. R., & Maughan, B. (2010). Co-occurring problems of early onset persistent, childhood limited, and adolescent onset conduct problem youth. *Journal of Child Psychology and Psychiatry, 51*(11), 1217–1226.

Barkley, R. A. (1998, September). Attention-deficit hyperactivity disorder. *Scientific American,* pp. 66–71.

Barlett, C., & Coyne, S. M. (2014). A meta-analysis of sex differences in cyber-bullying behavior: The moderating role of age. *Aggressive Behavior, 40*(5), 474–488.

Barnard, N. D., Bush, A. I., Ceccarelli, A., Cooper, J., de Jager, C. A., Erickson, K. I., . . . & Morris, M. C. (2014). Dietary and lifestyle guidelines for the prevention of Alzheimer's disease. *Neurobiology of Aging, 35,* S74–S78.

Barnes, G. M., Hoffman, J. H., & Welte, J. W. (2006). Effects of parental monitoring and peer deviance in substance abuse and delinquency. *Journal of Marriage and Family, 68,* 1084–1104.

Barnes, P. M., & Schoenborn, C. A. (2003). Physical activity among adults: United States, 2000. *Advance Data from Vital and Health Statistics, 133.* Hyattsville, MD: National Center for Health Statistics.

Barnett, R. C. (1997). Gender, employment, and psychological well-being: Historical and life-course perspectives. In M. E. Lachman & J. B. James (Eds.), *Multiple paths of midlife development* (pp. 325–343). Chicago: University of Chicago Press.

Barnett, R. C., & Hyde, J. S. (2001). Women, men, work, and family. *American Psychologist, 56,* 781–796.

Barnett, W. S., Jung, K., Yarosc, D. J., Thomas, J., Hornbeck, A., Stechuk, R. A., & Burns, M. S. (2008). Educational effects of the tools of the mind curriculum: A randomized trial. *Early Childhood Research Quarterly, 23*(3), 299–313.

Barnhart, M. A. (1992, Fall). Coping with the Methuselah syndrome. *Free Inquiry, 19*–22.

Baron-Cohen, S., Leslie, A. M., & Frith, U. (1985). Does the autistic child have a "theory of mind"? *Cognition, 21*(1), 37–46.

Barr, R., Danziger, C., Hilliard, M., Andolina, C., & Ruskis, J. (2010). Amount, content and context of infant media exposure: A parental questionnaire and diary analysis. *International Journal of Early Years Education, 18,* 107–122.

Barr, R., Dowden, A., & Hayne, H. (1996). Developmental changes in deferred imitation by 6-to 24-month-old infants. *Infant Behavior and Development, 19*(2), 159–170.

Barr, R., Lauricella, A., Zack, E., & Calvert, S. L. (2010). Infant and early childhood exposure to adult-directed and child-directed television programming: Relations with cognitive skills at age four. *Merrill-Palmer Quarterly, 56*(1), 21–48.

Barrett, A. E., & Turner, R. J. (2005). Family structure and mental health: The mediating effects of socioeconomic status, family process, and social stress. *Journal of Health and Social Behavior, 46*(2), 156–169.

Barrett, C. B. (2010). Measuring food insecurity. *Science, 327,* 825–828.

Barrett-Connor, E., Hendrix, S., Ettinger, B., Wenger, N. K., Paoletti, R., Lenfant, C. J. M., & Pinn, V. W. (2002). *Best clinical practices: Chapter 13. International position paper on women's health and menopause: A comprehensive approach.* Washington, DC: National Heart, Lung, and Blood Institute.

Barroso, C. S., Roncacio, A., Moramarco, M. W., Hinojosa, M. B., Davila, Y. R., Mendias, E., & Reifsnider, E. (2016). Food security, maternal feeding practices, and child weight-for-length. *Applied Nursing Research, 29,* 31–36.

Barry, B. K., & Carson, R. G. (2004). The consequences of resistance training for movement control in older adults. *Journal of Gerontology: Medical Sciences, 59A*, 730-754.

Barry, C. M., Madsen, S. D., Nelson, L. J., Carroll, J. S., & Badger, S. (2009). Friendship and romantic relationship qualities in emerging adulthood: Differential associations with identity development and achieved adulthood criteria. *Journal of Adult Development, 16*(4), 209-222.

Bartel, K. A., Gradisar, M., & Williamson, P. (2015). Protective and risk factors for adolescent sleep: a meta-analytic review. *Sleep Medicine Reviews, 21*, 72-85.

Bartick, M., & Reinhold, A. (2010). The burden of suboptimal breastfeeding in the United States: A pediatric cost analysis. *Pediatrics, 125*, e1048-e1056.

Bartzokis, G. (2004). Age-related myelin breakdown: A developmental model of cognitive decline and Alzheimer's disease. *Neurobiology of Aging, 25*(1), 5-18.

Bartzokis, G. (2011). Alzheimer's disease as homeostatic responses to age-related myelin breakdown. *Neurobiology of Aging, 32*(8), 1341-1371.

Bartzokis, G., Lu, P. H., & Mintz, J. (2007). Human brain myelination and amyloid beta deposition in Alzheimer's disease. *Alzheimer's & Dementia, 3*(2), 122-125.

Bartzokis, G., Lu, P. H., Tingus, K., Mendez, M. F., Richard, A., Peters, D. G., . . . & Thompson, P. M. (2010). Lifespan trajectory of myelin integrity and maximum motor speed. *Neurobiology of Aging, 31*(9), 1554-1562.

Basch, C. E. (2011). Teen pregnancy and the achievement gap among urban minority youth. *Journal of School Health, 81*(10), 614-618.

Basch, C. H., Zybert, P., Reeves, R., Basch, C. E. (2017). What do popular Youtube videos say about vaccines? *Child: Care, Health and Development, 43*, 499-503.

Bascom, P. B., & Tolle, S. W. (2002). Responding to requests for physician-assisted suicide: "These are uncharted waters for both of us. . . ." *Journal of the American Medical Association, 288*, 91-98.

Bassil, N., Alkaade, S., & Morley, J.E. (2009). The benefits and risks of testosterone replacement therapy: A review. *Therapeutics and Clinical Risk Management, 5*, 427-448.

Bassuk, E. L., Murphy, C., Coupe, N. T., Kenney, R. R., Beach, C. A. (2011). America's youngest outcasts 2010: State report card on child homelessness. *The National Center on Family Homelessness.* Retrieved from www.homelesschildrenamerica.org/media/NCFH_AmericaOutcast2010_web.pdf

Bassuk, E. L., Richard, M. K., & Tsertsvadze, A. (2015). The prevalence of mental illness in homeless children: A systematic review and meta-analysis. *Journal of the American Academy of Child & Adolescent Psychiatry, 54*(2), 86-96.

Baste, V., Moen, B. E., Oftedal, G., Strand, L. Å., Bjørge, L., & Mild, K. H. (2012). Pregnancy outcomes after paternal radiofrequency field exposure aboard fast patrol boats. *Journal of Occupational and Environmental Medicine, 54*(4), 431-438.

Basterfield, L., Adamson, A. J., Frary, J. K., Parkinson, K. N., Pearce, M. S., Reilly, J. J., & Gateshead Millennium Study Core Team. (2011). Longitudinal study of physical activity and sedentary behavior in children, *Pediatrics, 127*(1), e24-e30.

Batty, G. D., Deary, I. J., & Gottfredson, L. S. (2007). Premorbid (early life) IQ and later mortality risk: Systematic review. *Annals of Epidemiology, 17*(4), 278-288.

Batty, M., & Taylor, M. J. (2002). Visual categorization during childhood: an ERP study. *Psychophysiology, 39*(4), 482-490.

Baude, A., Pearson, J., & Drapeau, S. (2016). Child adjustment in joint physical custody versus sole custody: A meta-analytic review. *Journal of Divorce & Remarriage, 57*(5), 338-360.

Bauer, J. J., & McAdams, D. P. (2004). Personal growth in adults' stories of life transitions. *Journal of Personality, 72*(3), 573-602.

Bauer, J. J., McAdams, D. P., & Pals, J. L. (2008). Narrative identity and eudaimonic well-being. *Journal of Happiness Studies, 9*(1), 81-104.

Bauer, M. E., Jeckel, C. M. M., & Luz, C. (2009). The role of stress factors during aging of the immune system. *Annals of the New York Academy of Sciences, 1153*, 39-152. doi: 10.1111/j.1749-6632.2008.03966.x

Bauer, P. J. (2002). Long-term recall memory: Behavioral and neurodevelopmental changes in the first 2 years of life. *Current Directions in Psychological Science, 11*, 137-141.

Bauer, P. J., DeBoer, T., & Lukowski, A. F. (2007). In the language of multiple memory systems, defining and describing developments in long-term explicit memory. In L. M. Oakes & P. J. Bauer (Eds.). *Short- and long-term memory in infancy and early childhood* (pp. 240-270). New York: Oxford University Press.

Bauer, P. J., Wenner, J. A., Dropik, P. L., Wewerka, S. S., & Howe, M. L. (2000). Parameters of remembering and forgetting in the transition from infancy to early childhood. *Monographs of the Society for Research in Child Development,* i-213.

Bauer, P. J., Wiebe, S. A., Carver, L. J., Waters, J. M., & Nelson, C. A. (2003). Developments in long-term explicit memory late in the first year of life: Behavioral and electrophysiological indices. *Psychological Science, 14*, 629-635.

Baum, A., Cacioppo, J. T., Melamed, B. G., Gallant, S. J., & Travis, C. (1995). *Doing the right thing: A research plan for healthy living.* Washington, DC: American Psychological Association Science Directorate.

Bauman, A., Merom, D., Bull, F. C., Buchner, D. M., & Fiatarone Singh, M. A. (2016). Updating the evidence for physical activity: summative reviews of the epidemiological evidence, prevalence, and interventions to promote "Active Aging." *The Gerontologist, 56*(Suppl_2), S268-S280.

Baumer, E. P., & South, S. J. (2001). Community effects on youth sexual activity. *Journal of Marriage and Family, 63*, 540-554.

Baumgart, M., Snyder, H. M., Carrillo, M. C., Fazio, S., Kim, H., & Johns, H. (2015). Summary of the evidence on modifiable risk factors for cognitive decline and dementia: A population-based perspective. *Alzheimer's & Dementia, 11*(6), 718-726.

Baumgartner, S. E., Weeda, W. D., van der Heijden, L. L., & Huizinga, M. (2014). The relationship between media multitasking and executive function in early adolescents. *Journal of Early Adolescence, 34*, 1120-1144.

Baumrind, D. (1971). Harmonious parents and their preschool children. *Developmental Psychology, 41*, 92-102.

Baumrind, D. (1972). An exploratory study of socialization effects on black children: Some black-white comparisons. *Child Development,* 261-267.

Baumrind, D. (1989). Rearing competent children. In W. Damon (Ed.), *Child development today and tomorrow* (pp. 349-378). San Francisco: Jossey-Bass.

Baumrind, D. (1996a). A blanket injunction against disciplinary use of spanking is not warranted by the data. *Pediatrics, 88*, 828-831.

Baumrind, D. (1996b). The discipline controversy revisited. *Family Relations, 45*, 405-414.

Baumrind, D. (2005). Patterns of parental authority and adolescent autonomy. In J. Smetana (Ed.), *Changing boundaries of parental authority during adolescence* (New Directions for Child and Adolescent Development, No. 108, pp. 61-70). San Francisco: Jossey-Bass.

Baumrind, D., & Black, A. E. (1967). Socialization practices associated with dimensions of competence in preschool boys and girls. *Child Development, 38*, 291-327.

Baumrind, D., Larzelere, R. E., & Owens, E. B. (2010). Effects of preschool parents' power assertive patterns and practices on adolescent development. *Parenting: Science and Practice, 10*(3), 157-201.

Bayley, N. (1969). *Bayley Scales of Infant Development.* New York: Psychological Corporation.

Bayley, N. (1993). *Bayley Scales of Infant Development: II.* New York: Psychological Corporation.

Bayley, N. (2005). *Bayley Scales of Infant Development, Third Ed. (Bayley-III).* New York: Harcourt Brace.

Bayliss, D. M., Jarrold, C., Baddeley, A. D., Gunn, D. M., & Leigh, E. (2005). Mapping the developmental constraints on working memory span performance. *Developmental Psychology, 41*(4), 579-597.

Beal, S. J., & Crockett, L. J. (2010). Adolescents' occupational and educational aspirations and expectations: Links to high school activities and adult educational achievement. *Developmental Psychology, 46*(1), 258-265.

Beauchamp, G. K., & Mennella, J. A. (2011). Flavor perception in human infants: development and functional significance. *Digestion, 83*(Suppl. 1), 1-6.

Beauchesne, M.A., Kelley, B.R., Patsdaughter, C.A., & Pickard, J. (2002). Attack on America: Children's reactions and parents' responses. *Journal of Pediatric Health Care*, 16, 213-221.

Beaumont, S. L., & Pratt, M. M. (2011). Identity processing styles and psychosocial balance during early and middle adulthood: The role of identity in intimacy and generativity. *Journal of Adult Development*, 18(4), 172-183.

Becker, G. S. (1991). *A treatise on the family* (Enlarged ed.). Cambridge, MA: Harvard University Press.

Becker, K. A. (2003). History of the Stanford-Binet intelligence scales: Content and psychometrics. *Stanford-Binet Intelligence Scales, Fifth Edition Assessment Service Bulletin, 1.*

Becker, M., Lüdtke, O., Trautwein, U., Köller, O., & Baumert, J. (2012). The differential effects of school tracking on psychometric intelligence: Do academic-track schools make students smarter? *Journal of Educational Psychology*, 104(3), 682.

Becker, P. E., & Moen, P. (1999). Scaling back: Dual-earner couples' work-family strategies. *Journal of Marriage and Family*, 61, 995-1007.

Beckett, C., Maughan, B., Rutter, M., Castle, J., Colvert, E., Groothues, C., ... Sonuga-Barke, E. J. S. (2006). Do the effects of severe early deprivation on cognition persist into early adolescence? Findings from the English and Romanian adoptees study. *Child Development*, 77, 696-711.

Bedford, V. H. (1995). Sibling relationships in middle and old age. In R. Blieszner & V. Hilkevitch (Eds.), *Handbook of aging and the family* (pp. 201-222). Westport, CT: Greenwood Press.

Beelmann, A., & Heinemann, K. S. (2014). Preventing prejudice and improving intergroup attitudes: A meta-analysis of child and adolescent training programs. *Journal of Applied Developmental Psychology*, 35(1), 10-24.

Behne, R., Carpenter, M., Call, J., & Tomasello, M. (2005). Unwilling versus unable: Infants' understanding of intentional action. *Developmental Psychology*, 41, 328-337.

Behne, T., Liszkowski, U., Carpenter, M., & Tomasello, M. (2012). Twelve-month-olds' comprehension and production of pointing. *British Journal of Developmental Psychology*, 30(3), 359-375.

Behnke, M., Smith, V. C., & Committee on Substance Abuse. (2013). Prenatal substance abuse: short-and long-term effects on the exposed fetus. *Pediatrics*, 131(3), e1009-e1024.

Behrman, R. E. (1992). *Nelson textbook of pediatrics* (13th ed.). Philadelphia: Saunders.

Beidel, D. C., & Turner, S. M. (1998). *Shy children, phobic adults: Nature and treatment of social phobia.* Washington, DC: American Psychological Association.

Bell, J. F., Zimmerman, F. J., & Diehr, P. K. (2008). Maternal work and birth outcome disparities. *Maternal & Child Health Journal*, 12, 415-426.

Bell, J. T. & Spector, T. D. (2011). A twin approach to unraveling epigenetics. *Trends in Genetics*, 27, 116-125.

Bell, J. T., & Saffery, R. (2012). The value of twins in epigenetic epidemiology. *International Journal of Epidemiology*, 41(1), 140-150.

Bell, L. G., & Bell, D. C. (2005). Family dynamics in adolescence affect midlife well-being. *Journal of Family Psychology*, 19, 198-207.

Bell, L., Burtless, G., Gornick, J., & Smeedling, T. M. (2007). A cross-national survey of trends in the transition to economic independence. In S. Danzinger & C. Rouse (Eds.), *The price of independence: The economics of early adulthood* (pp. 27-55). New York: Russell Sage Foundation.

Bell, M. A. (2012). A psychobiological perspective on working memory performance at 8 months of age. *Child Development*, 83(1), 251-265.

Bell, M. A., & Fox, N. A. (1992). The relations between frontal brain electrical activity and cognitive development during infancy. *Child Development*, 63,1142-1163.

Bellander, M., Eschen, A., Lövdén, M., Martin, M., Bäckman, L., & Brehmer, Y. (2017). No evidence for improved associative memory performance following process-based associative memory training in older adults. *Frontiers in Aging Neuroscience*, 8, 326.

Bellieni, C. V., & Buonocore, G. (2012). Is fetal pain a real evidence? *The Journal of Maternal-Fetal & Neonatal Medicine*, 25(8), 1203-1208.

Bellinger, D. C. (2008). Lead neurotoxicity and socioeconomic status: Conceptual and analytic issues. *NeuroToxicology*, 29(5), 828-832.

Belsky, J. (2005). Differential susceptibility to rearing influence: An evolutionary hypothesis and some evidence. In B. J. Ellis & D. F. Bjorklund (Eds.), *Origins of the social mind: Evolutionary psychology and child development* (pp. 139-163). New York: Guilford Press.

Belsky, J., & Pluess, M. (2009). Beyond diathesis stress: Differential susceptibility to environmental influences. *Psychological Bulletin*, 135(6), 885-908. doi: 10.1037/a0017376

Belsky, J., Fish, M., & Isabella, R. (1991). Continuity and discontinuity in infant negative and positive emotionality: Family antecedents and attachment consequences. *Developmental Psychology*, 27, 421-431.

Belsky, J., Jaffee, S. R., Caspi, A., Moffitt, T., & Silva, P. A. (2003). Intergenerational relationships in young adulthood and their life course, mental health, and personality correlates. *Journal of Family Psychology*, 17, 460-471.

Belsky, J., Jaffee, S., Hsieh, K., & Silva, P. A. (2001). Childrearing antecedents of intergenerational relations in young adulthood: A prospective study. *Developmental Psychology*, 37, 801-814.

Belsky, J., Ruttle, P. L., Boyce, W. T., Armstrong, J. M., & Essex, M. J. (2015). Early adversity, elevated stress physiology, accelerated sexual maturation, and poor health in females. *Developmental Psychology*, 51(6), 816.

Belsky, J., Steinberg, L. D., Houts, R. M., Friedman, S. L., DeHart, G., Cauffman, E., ... NICHD Early Child Care Research Network. (2007). Family rearing antecedents of pubertal timing. *Child Development*, 78(4), 1302-1321.

Belsky, J., Steinberg, L., Houts, R. M., & Halpern-Felsher, B. L. (2010). The development of reproductive strategy in females: Early maternal harshness—earlier menarch—increased sexual risk taking. *Developmental Psychology*, 46(1), 120-128.

Bem, S. L. (1993). *The lenses of gender: Transforming the debate on sexual inequality.* New Haven, CT: Yale University Press.

Bender, P. K., Reinholdt-Dunne, M. L., Esbjørn, B. H., & Pons, F. (2012). Emotion dysregulation and anxiety in children and adolescents: Gender differences. *Personality and Individual Differences*, 53(3), 284-288.

Benedetti, A. M. (2017, December 6). *5 Dia De Los Muertos questions you were too afraid to ask.* Retrieved from Huffingtonpost.com: www.huffingtonpost.com/2013/11/01/dia-de-los-muertos_n_4184636.html

Benes, F. M., Turtle, M., Khan, Y., & Farol, P. (1994). Myelination of a key relay zone in the hippocampal formation occurs in the human brain during childhood, adolescence, and adulthood. *Archives of General Psychiatry*, 51, 447-484.

Bengtson, V. L. (2001). Beyond the nuclear family: The increasing importance of multigenerational bonds. *Journal of Marriage and Family*, 63, 1-16.

Bengtson, V. L., & DeLiema, M. (2016). Theories of aging and social gerontology: Explaining how social factors influence well-being in later life. *Gerontology: Changes, Challenges, and Solutions [2 volumes]: Changes, Challenges, and Solutions*, 25.

Bengtson, V. L., Rosenthal, C. J., & Burton, L. M. (1990). Families and aging: Diversity and heterogeneity. In R. Binstock & L. George (Eds.), *Handbook of aging and the social sciences* (3rd ed., pp. 263-287). San Diego: Academic Press.

Bengtson, V. L., Rosenthal, C., & Burton, L. (1996). Paradoxes of families and aging. In R. H. Binstock & L. K. George (Eds.), *Handbook of aging and the social sciences* (4th ed., pp. 253-282). San Diego: Academic Press.

Benkhadra, K., Mohammed, K., Al Nofal, A., Carranza Leon, B. G., Alahdab, F., Faubion, S., ... & Murad, M. H. (2015). Menopausal hormone therapy and mortality: A systematic review and meta-analysis. *The Journal of Clinical Endocrinology & Metabolism*, 100(11), 4021-4028.

Benner, A. D., & Graham, S. (2009). The transition to high schools as a developmental process among multiethnic urban youth. *Child Development*, 80(2), 356-376.

Benner, A. D., & Kim, S. Y. (2009). Experiences of discrimination among Chinese American adolescents and the consequences for socioemotional and academic development. *Developmental Psychology*, 45(6), 1682-1694.

Benson, E. (2003). Intelligent intelligence testing. *Monitor on Psychology*, 43(2), 48-51.

Berg, C. A., & Klaczynski, P. A. (1996). Practical intelligence and problem solving: Search for perspectives. In F. Blanchard-Fields & T. M. Hess (Eds.), *Perspectives on cognitive change in adulthood and aging* (pp. 323-357). New York: McGraw-Hill.

Bergelson, E., & Swingley, D. (2012). At 6-9 months, human infants know the meanings of many common nouns. *Proceedings of the National Academy of Sciences of the United States of America*, 109, 3253-3259.

Bergeman, C. S., & Plomin, R. (1989). Genotype-environment interaction. In M. Bornstein & J. Bruner (Eds.), *Interaction in human development* (pp. 157-171). Hillsdale, NJ: Erlbaum.

Bergen, D. (2002). The role of pretend play in children's cognitive development. *Early Childhood Research & Practice, 4*(1). Retrieved from http://ecrp.uiuc.edu/v4n1/bergen.html

Berger, K. S. (2007). Update on bullying at school: Science forgotten? *Developmental Review, 27*, 91-92.

Bering, J. M., & Bjorklund, D. F. (2004). The natural emergence of reasoning ability about the afterlife as a developmental regularity. *Developmental Psychology, 40*, 217-233.

Bering, J. M., Blasi, C. H., & Bjorklund, D. F. (2005). The development of afterlife beliefs in religiously and secularly schooled children. *British Journal of Developmental Psychology, 23*(4), 587-607.

Berk, L. E. (1992). Children's private speech: An overview of theory and the status of research. In R. M. Diaz & L. E. Berk (Eds.), *Private speech: From social interaction to self-regulation* (pp. 17-53). Hillsdale, NJ: Erlbaum.

Berkman, L. F., & Glass, T. (2000). Social integration, social networks, social support, and health. In L. F. Berkman & I. Kawachi (Eds.), *Social epidemiology* (pp. 137-173). New York: Oxford University Press.

Berlin, L. J., Ispa, J. M., Fine, M. A., Malone, P. S., Brooks-Gunn, J., Brady-Smith, C., . . . & Bai, Y. (2009). Correlates and consequences of spanking and verbal punishment for low-income white, African American, and Mexican American toddlers. *Child Development, 80*(5), 1403-1420.

Bernardi, F., & Martinez-Pastor, J. I. (2011). Divorce risk factors and their variation over time in Spain. *Demographic Research, 24*, 771-800.

Berndt, T. J., & Perry, T. B. (1990). Distinctive features and effects of early adolescent friendships. In R. Montemayor, G. R. Adams, & T. P. Gullotta (Eds.), *From childhood to adolescence: A transitional period?* (Vol. 2, pp. 269-287). Newbury Park, CA: Sage.

Bernert, R. A., Merrill, K. A., Braithwaite, S. R., Van Orden, K. A., & Joiner, T. E. (2007). Family life stress and insomnia symptoms in a prospective evaluation of young adults. *Journal of Family Psychology, 21*, 58-66.

Bernier, A., & Meins, E. (2008). A threshold approach to understanding the origins of attachment disorganization. *Developmental Psychology, 44*, 969-982.

Bernier, A., Carlson, S. M., & Whipple, N. (2010). From external regulation to self-regulation: Early parenting precursors of young children's executive functioning. *Child Development, 81*, 326-339. doi: 10.1111/ j.1467-8624.2009.01397.x

Bernstein, L., Patel A. V., Sullivan-Halley, J., Press, M. F., Deapen, D., Berlin, J. A., . . . Spirtas, R. (2005). Lifetime recreational exercise activity and breast cancer risk among black women and white women. *Journal of the National Cancer Institute, 97*, 1671-1679.

Bernstein, N. (2008). *"Aging in place" communities offer seniors independence and support.* Retrieved from www.caring.com/articles/aging-in-place

Berrick, J. D. (1998). When children cannot remain home: Foster family care and kinship care. *Future of Children, 8*, 72-87.

Berry, M., Dylla, D. J., Barth, R. P., & Needell, B. (1998). The role of open adoption in the adjustment of adopted children and their families. *Children and Youth Services Review, 20*, 151-171.

Berteletti, I., Lucangeli, D., Piazza, M., Dehaene, S., & Zorzi, M. (2010). Numerical estimation in preschoolers. *Developmental Psychology, 46*(2), 545.

Bertenthal, B. I., Campos, J. J., & Kermoian, R. (1994). An epigenetic perspective on the development of self-produced locomotion and its consequences. *Current Directions in Psychological Science, 3*(5), 140-145.

Berthiaume, V. G., Shultz, T. R., & Onishi, K. H. (2013). A constructivist connectionist model of transitions on false-belief tasks. *Cognition, 126*(3), 441-458.

Berthier, N. E., & Carrico, R. L. (2010). Visual information and object size in infant reaching. *Infant Behavior and Development, 33*(4), 555-566.

Bertone-Johnson, E. R., Hankinson, S. E., Johnson, S. R., & Manson, J. E. (2008). Cigarette smoking and the development of premenstrual syndrome. *American Journal of Epidemiology, 168*(8), 938-945.

Betancourt, J. R., Green, A. R., Carrillo, J. E., & Owusu Ananeh-Firempong, I. I. (2016). Defining cultural competence: a practical framework for addressing racial/ethnic disparities in health and health care. *Public Health Reports*.

Bethell, C. D., Read, D., & Blumberg, S. J. (2005). Mental health in the United States: Health care and well-being of children with chronic emotional, behavioral, or developmental problem—United States, 2001. *Morbidity and Mortality Weekly Report, 54*, 985-989.

Bevan, S., Traylor, M., Adib-Samii, P., Malik, R., Paul, N. L., Jackson, C., . . . & Markus, H. S. (2012). Genetic heritability of ischemic stroke and the contribution of previously reported candidate gene and genomewide associations. *Stroke, 43*(12), 3161-3167.

Bever, L. (2014, November 2). Brittany Maynard, as promised, ends her life at 29. *The Washington Post*. Retrieved from www.washingtonpost.com/

Bezdicek, O., Stepankova, H., Novakova, L. M., & Kopecek, M. (2016). Toward the processing speed theory of activities of daily living in healthy aging: Normative data of the Functional Activities Questionnaire. *Aging Clinical and Experimental Research, 28*(2), 239-247.

Bhaskaran, K., Hamouda, O., Sannesa, M., Boufassa, F., Johnson, A. M., Lambert, P. C., & Porter, K., for the CASCADE Collaboration. (2008). Changes in the risk of death after HIV seroconversion compared with mortality in the general population. *Journal of the American Medical Association, 300*, 51-59.

Bherer, L., Erickson, K. I., & Liu-Ambrose, T. (2013). A review of the effects of physical activity and exercise on cognitive and brain functions in older adults. *Journal of Aging Research*.

Bhutta, Z. A., Yakoob, M. Y., Lawn, J. E., Rizvi, A., Friberg, I. K., Weissman, E., . . . & Lancet's Stillbirths Series steering committee. (2011). Stillbirths: What difference can we make and at what cost? *The Lancet, 377*(9776), 1523-1538.

Bialystok, E., & Codd, J. (2000). Representing quantity beyond whole numbers: Some, none, and part. *Canadian Journal of Experimental Psychology/Revue canadienne de psychologie expérimentale, 54*(2), 117.

Bialystok, E., & Senman, L. (2004). Executive processes in appearance-reality tasks: The role of inhibition of attention and symbolic representation. *Child Development, 75*, 562-579.

Bialystok, E., Craik, F. I. M., & Freeman, M. (2007). Bilingualism as a protection against the onset of symptoms of dementia. *Neuropsychologia, 45*(2), 459-464.

Bialystok, E., Craik, F. I. M., Klein, R., & Viswanathan, M. (2004). Bilingualism, aging, and cognitive control: Evidence from the Simon task. *Psychology and Aging, 19*, 290-303.

Bianchi, S., Robinson, J., & Milkie, M. (2006). *The changing rhythms of American family life.* New York: Russell Sage Foundation.

Biason-Lauber, A., Konrad, D., Navratil, F., & Schoenle, E. J. (2004). A WNT4 mutation associated with Mullerian-duct regression and virilization in a 46, XX woman. *New England Journal of Medicine, 351*, 792-798.

Bibbins-Domingo, K., Coxson, P., Pletcher, M. J., Lightwood, J., & Goldman, L. (2007). Adolescent overweight and future adult coronary heart disease. *New England Journal of Medicine, 357*, 2371-2379.

Biblarz, T. J., & Stacey, J. (2010). How does the gender of parents matter? *Journal of Marriage and Family, 72*(1), 3-22.

Biegel, D. E. (1995). Caregiver burden. In G. E. Maddox (Ed.), *The encyclopedia of aging* (2nd ed., pp. 138-141). New York: Springer.

Bienvenu, O. J., Nestadt, G., Samuels, J. F., Costa, P. T., Howard, W. T., & Eaton, W. W. (2001). Phobic, panic, and major depressive disorders and the five-factor model of personality. *Journal of Mental Diseases, 189*, 154-161.

Bierman, K. L., Smoot, D. L., & Aumiller, K. (1993). Characteristics of aggressive rejected, aggressive (nonrejected), and rejected (nonaggressive) boys. *Child Development, 64*, 139-151.

Bigelow, A. E., & Dugas, K. (2009). Relations among preschool children's understanding of visual perspective taking, false belief, and lying. *Journal of Cognition and Development, 9*(4), 411-433.

Biggs, W. S., & Demuth, R. H. (2011). Premenstrual syndrome and premenstrual dysphoric disorder. *American Family Physician, 84*(8).

Billet, S. (2001). Knowing in practice: Reconceptualising vocational expertise. *Learning and Instruction, 11*, 431-452.

Billings, R. L., Hauser, S. T., & Allen, J. P. (2008). Continuity and change from adolescence to emerging adulthood: Adolescence-limited vs. life-course-persistent profound ego development arrests. *Journal of Youth and Adolescence, 37*(10), 1178-1192.

Bilsen, J., Cohen, J., & Deliens, L. (2007). End of life in Europe: An overview of medical practices. *Populations and Societies* (No. 430). Paris: INED.

Binstock, G., & Thornton, A. (2003). Separations, reconciliations, and living apart in cohabiting and marital units. *Journal of Marriage and Family, 65*, 432–443.

Birditt, K. S., Fingerman, K. L., & Zarit, S. H. (2010). Adult children's problems and successes: Implications for intergenerational ambivalence. *Journals of Gerontology Series B: Psychological Sciences and Social Sciences, 65*(2), 145–153.

Birditt, K. S., Miller, L. M., Fingerman, K. L., & Lefkowitz, E. S. (2009). Tensions in the parent and adult child relationship: Links to solidarity and ambivalence. *Psychology and Aging, 24*(2), 287–295.

Birmaher, B., Ryan, N. D., Williamson, D. E., Brent, D. A., Kaufman, J., Dahl, R. E., Perel, J., & Nelson, B. (1996). Childhood and adolescent depression: A review of the past 10 years. *Journal of the American Academy of Child and Adolescent Psychiatry, 35*, 1427–1440.

Biro, F. M., & Wien, M. (2010). Childhood obesity and adult morbidities. *The American Journal of Clinical Nutrition, 91*(5), 1499S–1505S.

Biro, F. M., Galvez, M. P., Greenspan, L. C., Succop, P. A., Vangeepuram, N., Pinney, S. N., . . . Wolff, M. S. (2010). Pubertal assessment method and baseline characteristics in a mixed longitudinal study of girls. *Pediatrics, 126*(3), e583–590.

Bitler, M. P., Hoynes, H. W., & Domina, T. (2014). *Experimental evidence on distributional effects of Head Start* (No. w20434). Cambridge, MA: National Bureau of Economic Research.

Bittles, A. H., Bower, C., Hussain, R., & Glasson, E. J. (2006). The four ages of Down syndrome. *European Journal of Public Health, 17*(2), 221–225.

Bixler, E. O., Vgontzas, A. N., Lin, H. M., Liao, D., Calhoun, S., Vela-Bueno, A., . . . & Graff, G. (2009). Sleep disordered breathing in children in a general population sample: prevalence and risk factors. *Sleep, 32*(6), 731–736.

Bjarnason, T., Bendtsen, P., Arnarsson, A. M., Borup, I., Iannotti, R. J., Löfstedt, P., . . . & Niclasen, B. (2012). Life satisfaction among children in different family structures: a comparative study of 36 western societies. *Children & Society, 26*(1), 51–62.

Bjelakovic, G., Nikolova, D., Gluud, L. L., Simonetti, R. G., & Gluud, C. (2008). Antioxidant supplements for prevention of mortality in healthy participants and patients with various diseases. *Cochrane Database of Systematic Reviews, 2008*(2), CD007176.

Bjork, J. M., Knutson, B., Fong, G. W., Caggiano, D. M., Bennett, S. M., & Hommer, D. W. (2004). Incentive-elicited brain activities in adolescents: Similarities and differences from young adults. *Journal of Neuroscience, 24*, 1793–1802.

Bjørkløf, G. H., Engedal, K., Selbæk, G., Kouwenhoven, S. E., & Helvik, A. S. (2013). Coping and depression in old age: a literature review. *Dementia and Geriatric Cognitive Disorders, 35*(3–4), 121–154.

Bjorklund, D. F. (1997). The role of immaturity in human development. *Psychological Bulletin, 122*, 153–169.

Bjorklund, D. F., & Causey, K. B. (2017). *Children's thinking: Cognitive development and individual differences* (pp. 572). Thousand Oaks, CA: Sage.

Bjorklund, D. F., & Pellegrini, A. D. (2000). Child development and evolutionary psychology. *Child Development, 71*, 1687–1708.

Bjorklund, D. F., & Pellegrini, A. D. (2002). *The origins of human nature: Evolutionary developmental psychology.* Washington, DC: American Psychological Association.

Bjorklund, D. F., Miller, P. H., Coyle, T. R., & Slawinski, J. L. (1997). Instructing children to use memory strategies: Evidence of utilization deficiencies in memory training studies. *Developmental Review, 17*(4), 411–441.

Black, M.C., Basile, K.C., Breiding, M.J., Smith, S.G., Walters, M.L., Merrick, M.T., Chen, J., & Stevens, M.R. (2011). The National Intimate Partner and Sexual Violence Survey (NISVS): 2010 Summary Report. National Center for Injury Prevention and Control, Centers for Disease Control and Prevention. Retrieved from www.cdc.gov/violenceprevention/pdf/nisvs_report2010-a.pdf

Blackwell, D. L., Lucas, J. W., & Clarke, T. C. (2014). Summary health statistics for US adults: National health interview survey, 2012. *Vital and Health Statistics. Series 10, Data from the National Health Survey,* (260), 1–161.

Blagrove, M., Alexander, C., & Horne, J. A. (1995). The effects of chronic sleep reduction on the performance of cognitive tasks sensitive to sleep deprivation. *Applied Cognitive Psychology, 9*, 21–40.

Blaizot, A., Vergnes, J. N., Nuwwareh, S., Amar, J., & Sixou, M. (2009). Periodontal diseases and cardiovascular events: Meta-analysis of observational studies. *International Dental Journal, 59*(4), 197–209.

Blakemore, J. E. O., Berenbaum, S. A., & Liben, L. S. (2009). *Gender development.* New York: Psychology Press.

Blakemore, S., & Choudhury, S. (2006). Development of the adolescent brain: Implications for executive function and social cognition. *Journal of Child Psychology and Psychiatry, 47*(3), 296–312.

Blanchard, R. (2017). Fraternal birth order, family size, and male homosexuality: Meta-analysis of studies spanning 25 years. *Archives of Sexual Behavior*, 1–15.

Blanchard-Fields, F. (2007). Everyday problem solving and emotion: An adult developmental perspective. *Current Directions in Psychological Science, 16*(1), 26–31.

Blanchard-Fields, F., & Norris, L. (1994). Causal attributions from adolescence through adulthood: Age differences, ego level, and generalized response style. *Aging and Cognition, 1*, 67–86.

Blanchard-Fields, F., Mienaltowski, A., & Seay, R. B. (2007). Age differences in everyday problem-solving effectiveness: Older adults select more effective strategies for interpersonal problems. *Journal of Gerontology: Psychological Sciences, 62B*, P61–P64.

Blanchard-Fields, F., Stein, R., & Watson, T. L. (2004). Age differences in emotion-regulation strategies in handling everyday problems. *Journal of Gerontology: Psychological Sciences, 59B*, P261–P269.

Blatteis, C. M. (2012). Age-dependent changes in temperature regulation–a mini review. *Gerontology, 58*(4), 289–295.

Blazer, D. G. (2009). Depression in late life: Review and commentary. *Focus, 7*(1), 118–136.

Bleil, M. E., Adler, N. E., Appelhans, B. M., Gregorich, S. E., Sternfeld, B., & Cedars, M. I. (2013). Childhood adversity and pubertal timing: Understanding the origins of adulthood cardiovascular risk. *Biological Psychology, 93*(1), 213–219.

Blieszner, R., & Roberto, K. (2006). Perspectives on close relationships among the baby boomers. In S. K. Whitbourne & S. L. Willis (Eds.), *The baby boomers grow up: Contemporary perspectives on midlife* (pp. 261–279). Mahwah, NJ: Erlbaum.

Bloch, L., Haase, C. M., & Levenson, R. W. (2014). Emotion regulation predicts marital satisfaction: More than a wives' tale. *Emotion, 14*(1), 130.

Block, J. (1971). *Lives through time.* Berkeley, CA: Bancroft.

Block, J., & Block, J. H. (2006). Venturing a 30-year longitudinal study. *American Psychologist, 61*, 315–327.

Block, R. W., Krebs, N. F., Committee on Child Abuse and Neglect, & Committee on Nutrition. (2005). Failure to thrive as a manifestation of child neglect. *Pediatrics, 116*(5), 1234–1237.

Blondell, S. J., Hammersley-Mather, R., & Veerman, J. L. (2014). Does physical activity prevent cognitive decline and dementia?: A systematic review and meta-analysis of longitudinal studies. *BMC Public Health, 14*(1), 510.

Bloodgood, J. M., Turnley, W. H., & Mudrack, P. (2008). The influence of ethics instruction, religiosity and ethics on cheating behavior. *Journal of Business Ethics, 82*(3), 0167–4544.

Bloom, B., Jones, L. I., & Freeman, G. (2013). Summary health statistics for US children: National Health Interview Survey, 2012. *National Center for Health Statistics, 10*(258).

Blum, R., & Reinhart, P. (2000). *Reducing the risk: Connections that make a difference in the lives of youth.* Minneapolis: University of Minnesota, Division of General Pediatrics and Adolescent Health.

Blustein, D. L., Juntunen, C. L., & Worthington, R. L. (2000). The school-to-work transition: Adjustment challenge for the forgotten half. In S. D. Brown & R. W. Lent (Eds.), *Handbook of counseling psychology* (pp. 435–470). New York: Wiley.

Bobo, W. V., & Yawn, B. P. (2014). Concise review for physicians and other clinicians: Postpartum depression. *Mayo Clinic Proceedings, 89*, 835–844.

Bochukova, E. G., Huang, N., Keogh, J., Henning, E., Plurmann, C., Blaszczyk, K., . . . Faroqui, I. S. (2009). Large, rare chromosomal deletions associated with severe early-onset obesity. *Nature, 463,* 666-670.

Bocskay, K. A., Tang, D., Orjuela, M. A., Liu, X., Warburton, D. P., & Perera, F. P. (2005). Chromosomal aberrations in cord blood are associated with prenatal exposure to carcinogenic polycyclic aromatic hydrocarbons. *Cancer Epidemiology Biomarkers and Prevention, 14,* 506-511.

Boden, J. M., Fergusson, D. M., & Horwood, L. J. (2008). Early motherhood and subsequent life outcomes. *Journal of Child Psychology and Psychiatry, 49*(2), 151-160.

Boden, J. S., Fischer, J. L., & Niehuis, S. (2010). Predicting marital adjustment from young adults' initial levels and changes in emotional intimacy over time: A 25-year longitudinal study. *Journal of Adult Development, 17*(3), 121-134.

Bodner, E. (2009). On the origins of ageism in older and younger workers. *International Psychogeriatrics, 21,* 1003-1014.

Bodrova, E., & Leong, D. J. (1998). Adult influences on play: The Vygotskian approach. In D. P. Fromberg & D. Bergen (Eds.), *Play from birth to twelve and beyond: Contexts, perspectives, and meanings* (pp. 277-282). New York: Garland.

Bodrova, E., & Leong, D. J. (2005). High quality preschool programs: What would Vygotsky say? *Early Education & Development, 16*(4), 437-446.

Boerner, K., Schulz, R., & Horowitz, A. (2004). Positive aspects of caregiving and adaptation to bereavement. *Psychology and Aging, 19,* 668-675.

Boerner, K., Wortman, C. B., & Bonanno, G. A. (2005). Resilient or at risk? A 4-year study of older adults who initially showed high or low distress following conjugal loss. *Journal of Gerontology: Psychological Sciences, 60B,* P67-P73.

Boffetta, P., Couto, E., Wichman, J., Ferrari, P., Trichopoulos, D., Bas Bueno-de-Mesquita, H., . . . Trichopoulou, A. (2010). Fruit and vegetable intake and overall cancer risk in the European Prospective Investigation into Cancer and Nutrition (EPIC). *Journal of the National Cancer Institute, 102*(8), 529-537.

Bogaert, A. F. (2006). Biological versus nonbiological older brothers and men's sexual orientation. *Proceedings of the National Academy of Sciences, 103,* 10771-10774.

Bogard, K., & Takanishi, R. (2005). Pre-K through 3: An aligned and coordinated approach to education for children 3-8 years old. *Social Policy Report, 19*(3).

Bogg, T., & Roberts, B. W. (2013). The case for conscientiousness: Evidence and implications for a personality trait marker of health and longevity. *Annals of Behavioral Medicine, 45*(3), 278-288.

Boggess, A., Faber, S., Kern, J., Kingston, H.M.S. (2016). Mean serum-level of common organic pollutants is predictive of behavioral severity in children with autism spectrum disorders. *Scientific Reports, 6,* 26185. http://doi.org/10.1038/srep26185

Bograd, R., & Spilka, B. (1996). Self-disclosure and marital satisfaction in mid-life and late-life remarriages. *International Journal of Aging and Human Development, 42*(3), 161-172.

Bollinger, M. B. (2003). Involuntary smoking and asthma severity in children: Data from the Third National Health and Nutrition Examination Survey (NHANES III). *Pediatrics, 112,* 471.

Bonanno, G. A. (2005). Resilience in the face of potential trauma. *Current Directions in Psychological Science, 14,* 135-138.

Bonanno, G. A., Galea, S., Bucciarelli, A., & Vlahov, D. (2006). Psychological resilience after disaster. *Current Directions in Psychological Science, 17,* 181-186.

Bonanno, G. A., Wortman, C. B., & Nesse, R. M. (2004). Prospective patterns of resilience and maladjustment during widowhood. *Psychology and Aging, 19,* 260-271.

Bonanno, G. A., Wortman, C. B., Lehman, D. R., Tweed, R. G., Haring, M., Sonnega, J., . . . Nesse, R. M. (2002). Resilience to loss and chronic grief: A prospective study from preloss to 18-month postloss. *Journal of Personality and Social Psychology,* 1150-1164.

Bonham, V. L., Warshauer-Baker, E., & Collins, F. S. (2005). Race and ethnicity in the genome era: the complexity of the constructs. *American Psychologist, 60*(1), 9.

Bonny, J. W., & Lourenco, S. F. (2013). The approximate number system and its relation to early math achievement: Evidence from the preschool years. *Journal of Experimental Child Psychology, 114*(3), 375-388.

Bonoti, F., Leondari, A., & Mastora, A. (2013). Exploring children's understanding of death: Through drawings and the death concept questionnaire. *Death Studies, 37*(1), 47-60.

Bookwala, J. (2009). The impact of adult care on marital quality and well-being in adult daughters and sons. *Journal of Gerontology, 64B*(3), 339-347.

Boonstra, H. D. (2010). Winning campaign: California's concerted effort to reduce its teen pregnancy rate. *Gottmacher Policy Review, 13*(2), 18-24.

Booth, J. L., & Siegler, R. S. (2006). Developmental and individual differences in pure numerical estimation. *Developmental Psychology, 41,* 189-201.

Booth, J. R., Burman, D. D., Meyer, J. R., Lei, Z., Trommer, B. L., Davenport, D., . . . Mesulam, M. M. (2003). Neural development of selective attention and response inhibition. *Neuroimage, 20,* 737-751.

Borjigin, J., Lee, U., Liu, T., Pal, D., Huff, S., Klarr, D., . . . & Mashour, G. A. (2013). Surge of neurophysiological coherence and connectivity in the dying brain. *Proceedings of the National Academy of Sciences, 110*(35), 14432-14437.

Bornstein, M. H., & Cote, L. R., with Maital, S., Painter, K., Park, S. Y., Pascual, L., . . . Vyt, A. (2004). Cross-linguistic analysis of vocabulary in young children: Spanish, Dutch, French, Hebrew, Italian, Korean, and American English. *Child Development, 75,* 1115-1139.

Bornstein, M. H., Haynes, O. M., O'Reilly, A. W., & Painter, K. (1996). Solitary and collaborative pretense play in early childhood: Sources of individual variation in the development of representational competence. *Child Development, 67,* 2910-2929.

Bornstein, M. H., Putnick, D. L., Cote, L. R., Haynes, O. M., & Suwalsky, J. T. D. (2015). Mother-infant contingent vocalization in eleven countries. *Psychological Science, 26,* 1272-1284.

Bornstein, M. H., Putnick, D. L., Gartstein, M. A., Hahn, C. S., Auestad, N., & O'Connor, D. L. (2015). Infant temperament: stability by age, gender, birth order, term status, and socioeconomic status. *Child Development, 86*(3), 844-863.

Borowsky, I. A., Ireland, M., & Resnick, M. D. (2001). Adolescent suicide attempts: Risks and protectors. *Pediatrics, 107*(3), 485-493.

Borse, N. N., Gilchrist, J., Dellinger, A. M., Rudd, R. A., Ballesteros, M. F., & Sleet, D. A. (2008). *CDC childhood injury reports: Patterns of unintentional injuries among 0-19 year olds in the United States, 2000-2006.* Atlanta, GA: Centers for Disease Control and Prevention, National Center for Injury Prevention and Control.

Bosch, J., Sullivan, S., Van Dyke, D. C., Su, H., Klockau, L., Nissen, K., . . . Eberly, S. S. (2003). Promoting a healthy tomorrow here for children adopted from abroad. *Contemporary Pediatrics, 20*(2), 69-86.

Boss, P. (2007). Ambiguous loss theory: Challenges for scholars and practitioners. *Family Relations, 56*(2), 105-111.

Bosshard, G., Nilstun, T., Bilsen, J., Norup, M., Miccinesi, G., vanDelden, J. J. M., . . . van der Heide, A., for the European End-of-Life (EURELD) Consortium. (2005). Forgoing treatment at the end of life in 6 European countries. *Archives of Internal Medicine, 165,* 401-407.

Botwinick, J. (1984). *Aging and behavior* (3rd ed.). New York: Springer.

Bouchard, T. J. (2004). Genetic influence on human psychological traits: A survey. *Current Directions in Psychological Science, 13,* 148-154.

Bouchard, T. J. (2013). The Wilson effect: The increase in heritability of IQ with age. *Twin Research and Human Genetics, 16*(5), 923-930.

Bouchard, T. J., & McGue, M. (2003). Genetic and environmental influences on human psychological differences. *Developmental Neurobiology, 54*(1), 4-45.

Bouchey, H. A., & Furman, W. (2003). Dating and romantic experiences in adolescence. In G. R. Adams & M. D. Berzonsky (Eds.), *Blackwell handbook of adolescence* (pp. 313-329). Oxford, UK: Blackwell.

Boulton, M. J. (1995). Playground behaviour and peer interaction patterns of primary school boys classified as bullies, victims and not involved. *British Journal of Educational Psychology, 65,* 165-177.

Boulton, M. J., & Smith, P. K. (1994). Bully/victim problems in middle school children: Stability, self-perceived competence, peer perception, and peer acceptance. *British Journal of Developmental Psychology, 12,* 315-329.

Bowlby, J. (1951). Maternal care and mental health. *Bulletin of the World Health Organization, 3,* 355-534.

Bowlby, J. (1969). *Attachment and loss: Vol. I. Attachment.* London: Hogarth Press & the Institute of Psychoanalysis.

Bowman, J. M. (2009). Gender role orientation and relational closeness: Self-disclosive behavior in same-sex male friendships. *The Journal of Men's Studies, 16*(3), 316-330.

Bowman, N. (2013). College diversity experiences and cognitive development: A meta-analysis. *Educational Studies,* (2), 88-132.

Bowman, N. A. (2010). College diversity experiences and cognitive development: A meta-analysis. *Review of Educational Research, 80*(1), 4-33.

Bowman, S. A., Gortmaker, S. L., Ebbeling, C. B., Pereira, M. A., & Ludwig, D. S. (2004). Effects of fast food consumption on energy intake and diet quality among children in a national household survey. *Pediatrics, 113,* 112-118.

Boyce, C. J., Wood, A. M., Daly, M., & Sedikides, C. (2015). Personality change following unemployment. *Journal of Applied Psychology, 100*(4), 991.

Boyce, J. A., Assa'ad, A., Burks A. W., et al. (2010). Guidelines for the diagnosis and management of food allergy in the United States: Report of the NIAID-sponsored expert panel. *Journal of Allergy and Clinical Immunology, 126* (suppl 6), S1-S58.

Boyd, H., & Murnen, S. K. (2017). Thin and sexy vs muscular and dominant: Prevalence of gendered body ideals in popular dolls and action figures. *Body Image, 21,* 90-96.

Boyles, S. (2002, January 27). Toxic landfills may boost birth defects. *WebMD Medical News.* Retrieved from www.webmd.com/content/article/25/3606_1181.htm

Bozick, R., & DeLuca, S. (2011). Not making the transition to college: School, work, and opportunities in the lives of American youth. *Social Science Research, 40*(4), 1249-1262.

Brabeck, M. M., & Shore, E. L. (2003). Gender differences in intellectual and moral development? The evidence refutes the claims. In J. Demick & C. Andreoletti (Eds.), *Handbook of adult development* (pp. 351-368). New York: Plenum Press.

Bracher, G., & Santow, M. (1999). Explaining trends in teenage childbearing in Sweden. *Studies in Family Planning, 30,* 169-182.

Brackett, M. A., Cox, A., Gaines, S. O., & Salovey, P. (2005). Emotional intelligence and relationship quality among heterosexual couples. Unpublished data, Yale University.

Brackett, M. A., Mayer, J. D., & Warner, R. M. (2004). Emotional intelligence and the prediction of behavior. *Personality and Individual Differences, 36,* 1387-1402.

Bradbery, D. (2012). Using children's literature to build concepts of teaching about global citizenship. Retrieved from eric.ed.gov: http://files.eric.ed.gov/fulltext/ED544512.pdf

Bradbury, M., Peterson, M. N., & Liu, J. (2014). Long-term dynamics of household size and their environmental implications. *Population and Environment, 36*(1), 73-84.

Braddick, O., & Atkinson, J. (2011). Development of human visual function. *Vision Research, 51*(13), 1588-1609.

Bradley, R. G., Binder, E. B., Epstein, M. P., Tang, Y., Nair, H. P., Liu, W., . . . & Stowe, Z. N. (2008). Influence of child abuse on adult depression: moderation by the corticotropin-releasing hormone receptor gene. *Archives of General Psychiatry, 65*(2), 190-200.

Bradley, R. H. (1989). Home measurement of maternal responsiveness. In M. H. Bornstein (Ed.), *Maternal responsiveness: Characteristics and consequences* (New Directions for Child Development, No. 43). San Francisco: Jossey-Bass.

Bradley, R. H., Corwyn, R. F., Burchinal, M., McAdoo, H. P., & Coll, C. G. (2001). The home environment of children in the United States: Part II: Relations with behavioral development through age thirteen. *Child Development, 72*(6), 1868-1886.

Bradley, R. H., Corwyn, R. F., McAdoo, H. P., & Coll, C. G. (2001). The home environment of children in the United States: Part I: Variation by age, ethnicity, and poverty status. *Child Development, 72*(6), 1844-1867.

Bradley, R., & Caldwell, B. (1982). The consistency of the home environment and its relation to child development. *International Journal of Behavioral Development, 5,* 445-465.

Braine, M. (1976). Children's first word combinations. *Monographs of the Society for Research in Child Development, 41*(1, Serial No. 164).

Bramlett, M. D., & Mosher, W. D. (2002). Cohabitation, marriage, divorce, and remarriage in the United States. *Vital Health Statistics, 23*(22). Hyattsville, MD: National Center for Health Statistics.

Brand, J. E., & Simon Thomas, J. (2014). Job displacement among single mothers: Effects on children's outcomes in young adulthood. *American Journal of Sociology, 119*(4), 955-1001.

Brandt, B. (1989). A place for her death. *Humanistic Judaism, 17*(3), 83-85.

Branum, A., & Lukacs, S. L. (2008). *Food allergy among U.S. children: Trends in prevalence and hospitalizations* (Data Brief No. 10). Hyattsville, MD: National Center for Health Statistics.

Brass, L. M., Isaacsohn, J. L., Merikangas, K. R., & Robinette, C. D. (1992). A study of twins and stroke. *Stroke, 23*(2), 221-223.

Braswell, G. S. (2006). Sociocultural contexts for the early development of semiotic production. *Psychological Bulletin, 132,* 877-894.

Bratter, J. L., & King, R. B. (2008). "But will it last?": Marital instability among interracial and same-race couples. *Family Relations, 57*(2), 160-171.

Braun, H., Jenkins, F., & Grigg, W. (2006). *A closer look at charter schools using hierarchical linear modeling* (NCES 2006-460). Washington, DC: U.S. Government Printing Office.

Braungart, J. M., Plomin, R., DeFries, J. C., & Fulker, D. W. (1992). Genetic influence on tester-rated infant temperament as assessed by Bayley's Infant Behavior Record: Nonadoptive and adoptive siblings and twins. *Developmental Psychology, 28,* 40-47.

Braungart-Rieker, J. M., Garwood, M. M., Powers, B. P., & Wang, X. (2001). Parental sensitivity, infant affect, and affect regulation: Predictors of later attachment. *Child Development, 72*(1), 252-270.

Braveman, P. A., Cubbin, C., Egerter, S., Williams, D. R., & Pamuk, E. (2010). Socioeconomic disparities in health in the United States: What the patterns tell us. *American Journal of Public Health, 100*(S1), S186-S196.

Brayne, C. (2007). The elephant in the room—Healthy brains in later life, epidemiology and public health. *Neuroscience, 8*(3), 233-239.

Brazelton, T. B. (1973). *Neonatal Behavioral Assessment Scale.* Philadelphia: Lippincott.

Brazelton, T. B. (1984). *Neonatal Behavioral Assessment Scale* (2nd ed.). Philadelphia: Lippincott.

Brazelton, T. B. (2013). *Toddlers and parents: A declaration of independence.* New York: Dell.

Brazelton, T. B., & Nugent, J. K. (1995). *Neonatal Behavioral Assessment Scale* (3rd ed.). Cambridge: Cambridge University Press.

Brazelton, T. B., & Nugent, J. K. (2011). *Neonatal Behavioral Assessment Scale* (4th ed.). Hoboken, NJ: Wiley.

Breastfeeding and HIV International Transmission Study Group. (2004). Late postnatal transmission of HIV-1 in breast-fed children: An individual patient data meta-analysis. *Journal of Infectious Diseases, 189,* 2154-2166.

Brecklin, L. R., & Ullman, S. E. (2010). The roles of victim and offender substance use in sexual assault outcomes. *Journal of Interpersonal Violence, 25*(8), 1503-1522. doi: 0886260509354584

Bregman, H. R., Malik, N. M., Page, M. J., Makynen, E., & Lindahl, K. M. (2013). Identity profiles in lesbian, gay, and bisexual youth: The role of family influences. *Journal of Youth and Adolescence, 42*(3), 417-430.

Breheny, M., Stephens, C., & Spilsbury, L. (2013). Involvement without interference: How grandparents negotiate intergenerational expectations in relationships with grandchildren. *Journal of Family Studies, 19*(2), 174-184.

Brendgen, M., Dionne, G., Girard, A., Boivin, M., Vitaro, F., & Perusse, D. (2005). Examining genetic and environmental effects on social aggression: A study of 6-year-old twins. *Child Development, 76,* 930-946.

Brenneman, K., Massey, C., Machado, S. F., & Gelman, R. (1996). Young children's plans differ for writing and drawing. *Cognitive Development, 11,* 397-419.

Brent, D. A., & Birmaher, B. (2002). Adolescent depression. *New England Journal of Medicine, 347,* 667-671.

Brent, D. A., & Mann, J. J. (2006). Familial pathways to suicidal behavior—Understanding and preventing suicide among adolescents. *New England Journal of Medicine, 355,* 2719-2721.

Brent, D., Melhem, N., Donohoe, M. B., & Walker, M. (2009). The incidence and course of depression in bereaved youth 21 months after the loss of a parent to suicide, accident, or sudden natural death. *American Journal of Psychiatry, 166*(7), 786-794.

Brent, M. R., & Siskind, J. M. (2001). The role of exposure to isolated words in early vocabulary development. *Cognition, 81,* 33-34.

Bretherton, I. (1990). Communication patterns, internal working models, and the intergenerational transmission of attachment relationships. *Infant Mental Health Journal, 11*(3), 237-252.

Brezina, P.R. & Zhao, Y. (2012). The ethical, legal, and social issues impacted by modern assisted reproductive technologies. *Obstetrics and Gynecology International.* doi:10.1155/2012/686253

Bridge, J. A., Iyengar, S., Salary, C. B., Barbe, R. P., Birmaher, B., Pincus, H. A., . . . Brent, D. A. (2007). Clinical response and risk for reported suicidal ideation and suicide attempts in pediatric antidepressant treatment: A meta-analysis of randomized controlled trials. *Journal of the American Medical Association, 297,* 1683-1696.

Brier, N. (2008). Grief following miscarriage: A comprehensive review of the literature. *Journal of Women's Health, 17*(3), 451-464.

Briggs, G. G., Freeman, R. K., & Yaffe, S. J. (2012). *Drugs in pregnancy and lactation: A reference guide to fetal and neonatal risk.* Baltimore, MD: Lippincott Williams & Wilkins.

Briggs, J. L. (1970). *Never in anger.* Cambridge, MA: Harvard University Press.

Briley, D. A., & Tucker-Drob, E. M. (2014). Genetic and environmental continuity in personality development: A meta-analysis. *Psychological Bulletin, 140*(5), 1303.

Briley, D. A., & Tucker-Drob, E. M. (2017). Comparing the developmental genetics of cognition and personality over the life span. *Journal of Personality, 85*(1), 51-64.

Brim, O. G., Ryff, C. D., & Kessler, R. C. (2004). The MIDUS National Survey: An overview. In O. G. Brim, C. D. Ryff, & R. C. Kessler (Eds.), *How healthy are we? A national study of well-being at midlife.* Chicago: University of Chicago Press.

Brinkman-Stoppelenburg, A., Rietjens, J. A., & van der Heide, A. (2014). The effects of advance care planning on end-of-life care: A systematic review. *Palliative Medicine, 28*(8), 1000-1025.

Briskin, S., LaBotz, M., Brenner, J. S., Benjamin, H. J., Cappetta, C. T., Demorest, R. A., . . . & Martin, S. S. (2012). Trampoline safety in childhood and adolescence. *Pediatrics, 130*(4), 774-779.

Brody, E. M. (2004). *Women in the middle: Their parent care years* (2nd ed.). New York: Springer.

Brody, G. H. (1998). Sibling relationship quality: Its causes and consequences. *Annual Review of Psychology, 49,* 1-24.

Brody, G. H., Chen, Y.-F., Murry, V. M., Ge, X., Simons, R. L., Gibbons, F. X., . . . Cutrona, C. E. (2006). Perceived discrimination and the adjustment of African American youths: A five-year longitudinal analysis with contextual moderation effects. *Child Development, 77*(5), 1170-1189.

Brody, G. H., Ge., X., Conger, R., Gibbons, F. X., Murry, V. M., Gerrard, M., & Simons, R. L. (2001). The influence of neighborhood disadvantage, collective socialization, and parenting on African American children's affiliation with deviant peers. *Child Development, 72*(4), 1231-1246.

Brody, G. H., Kim, S., Murry, V. M., & Brown, A. C. (2004). Protective longitudinal paths linking child competence to behavioral problems among African American siblings. *Child Development, 75,* 455-467.

Broesch, T. L., & Bryant, G. A. (2015). Prosody in infant-directed speech is similar across western and traditional cultures. *Journal of Cognition and Development, 16,* 31-43.

Broidy, L. M., Tremblay, R. E., Brame, B., Fergusson, D., Horwood, J. L., Laird, R., . . . Vitaro, F. (2003). Developmental trajectories of childhood disruptive behaviors and adolescent delinquency: A six-site cross-national study. *Developmental Psychology, 39,* 222-245.

Bromberger, J. T., Harlow, S., Avis, N., Kravitz, H. M., & Cordal, A. (2004). Racial/ethnic differences in the prevalence of depressive symptoms among middle-aged women: The study of women's health across the nation (SWAN). *American Journal of Public Health, 94,* 1378-1385.

Bronfenbrenner, U. (1979). *The ecology of human development.* Cambridge, MA: Harvard University Press.

Bronfenbrenner, U. (1986). Ecology of the family as a context for human development: Research perspectives. *Developmental Psychology, 22,* 723-742.

Bronfenbrenner, U. (1994). Ecological models of human development. In T. Husen & T. N. Postlethwaite (Eds.), *International encyclopedia of education* (Vol. 3, 2nd ed., pp. 1643-1647). Oxford: Pergamon Press/Elsevier Science.

Bronfenbrenner, U., & Morris, P. A. (1998). The ecology of developmental processes. In W. Damon (Series Ed.) & R. Lerner (Vol. Ed.), *Handbook of child psychology: Vol. 1. Theoretical models of human development* (5th ed., pp. 993-1028). New York: Wiley.

Bronstein, P. (1988). Father-child interaction: Implications for gender role socialization. In P. Bronstein & C. P. Cowan (Eds.), *Fatherhood today: Men's changing role in the family.* New York: Wiley.

Brooks, R., & Meltzoff, A. N. (2005). The development of gaze following and its relation to language. *Developmental Science, 8,* 535-543.

Brooks, R., & Meltzoff, A. N. (2008). Infant gaze following and pointing predict accelerated vocabulary growth through two years of age: A longitudinal, growth curve modeling study. *Journal of Child Language, 35*(1), 207-220.

Brooks-Gunn, J. (2003). Do you believe in magic? What can we expect from early childhood intervention programs? *SRCD Social Policy Report, 17*(1).

Brooks-Gunn, J., Han, W.-J., & Waldfogel, J. (2002). Maternal employment and child cognitive outcomes in the first three years of life: The NICHD study of early child care. *Child Development, 73,* 1052-1072.

Broude, G. J. (1995). *Growing up: A crosscultural encyclopedia.* Santa Barbara, CA: ABC-CLIO.

Brougham, R. R., Zail, C. M., Mendoza, C. M., & Miller, J. R. (2009). Stress, sex differences, and coping strategies among college students. *Current Psychology, 28*(2), 85-97.

Brousseau, E. (2006, May). *The effect of maternal body mass index on efficacy of dinoprostone vaginal insert for cervical ripening.* Paper presented at the annual meeting of the American College of Obstetricians and Gynecologists, Washington, DC.

Brown, A. S. (2012). Epidemiologic studies of exposure to prenatal infection and risk of schizophrenia and autism. *Developmental Neurobiology, 72*(10), 1272-1276.

Brown, B. B., & Klute, C. (2003). Friendships, cliques, and crowds. In G. R. Adams & M. D. Berzonsky (Eds.), *Blackwell handbook of adolescence* (pp. 330-348). Malden, MA: Blackwell.

Brown, B. B., & Larson, J. (2009). *Peer relationships in adolescents.* In Steinberg, R. M. L. (Ed.), Handbook of adolescent psychology, Contextual influences on adolescent development (Vol. 2, 3rd ed., pp. 74-103). Hoboken, NJ: John Wiley & Sons.

Brown, B. B., Mounts, N., Lamborn, S. D., & Steinberg, L. (1993). *Parenting practices and peer group affiliation in adolescence* (pp. 245-270). Cambridge, UK: Cambridge University Press.

Brown, J. D., & L'Engle, K. L. (2009). X-rated: Sexual attitudes and behaviors associated with US early adolescents' exposure to sexually explicit media. *Communication Research, 36*(1), 129-151.

Brown, J. R., & Dunn, J. (1996). Continuities in emotion understanding from three to six years. *Child Development, 67,* 789-802.

Brown, J. T., & Stoudemire, A. (1983). Normal and pathological grief. *Journal of the American Medical Association, 250,* 378-382.

Brown, L. M., & Gilligan, C. (1990, April). *The psychology of women and the development of girls.* Paper presented at the Laurel-Harvard Conference on the Psychology of Women and the Education of Girls, Cleveland, OH.

Brown, S. L. (2004). Family structure and child well-being: The significance of parental cohabitation. *Journal of Marriage and Family, 66,* 351-367.

Brown, S. L., & Kawamura, S. (2010). Relationship quality among cohabitors and marrieds in older adulthood. *Social Science Research, 39*(5), 777-786.

Brown, S. L., & Lin, I. F. (2012). The gray divorce revolution: Rising divorce among middle-aged and older adults, 1990-2010. *The Journals of Gerontology: Series B, 67*(6), 731-741.

Brown, S. L., & Shinohara, S. K. (2013). Dating relationships in older adulthood: A national portrait. *Journal of Marriage and Family, 75*(5), 1194-1202.

Brown, S. L., Bulanda, J. R., & Lee, G. R. (2005). The significance of nonmarital cohabitation: Marital status and mental health benefits among middle-aged and older adults. *Journal of Gerontology: Social Sciences, 60B,* S21-S29.

Brown, S. L., Bulanda, J. R., & Lee, G. R. (2012). Transitions into and out of cohabitation in later life. *Journal of Marriage and Family, 74*(4), 774-793.

Brown, S. L., Lee, G. R., & Bulanda, J. R. (2006). Cohabitation among older adults: A national portrait. *Journal of Gerontology: Social Sciences, 61B,* S71–S79.

Brown, S. L., Manning, W. D., & Stykes, J. B. (2015). Family structure and child well-being: Integrating family complexity. *Journal of Marriage and Family, 77*(1), 177–190.

Brownell, C. A., Ramani, G. B., & Zerwas, S. (2006). Becoming a social partner with peers: Cooperation and social understanding in one- and two-year-olds. *Child Development, 77,* 803–821.

Brubacher, S. P., Glisic, U., Roberts, K. P., & Powell, M. (2011). Children's ability to recall unique aspects of one occurrence of a repeated event. *Applied Cognitive Psychology, 25*(3), 351–358.

Bruer, J. T. (2001). A critical and sensitive period primer. In D. B. Bailey, J. T. Bruer, F. J. Symons, & J. W. Lichtman (Eds.), *Critical thinking about critical periods: A series from the National Center for Early Development and Learning* (pp. 289–292). Baltimore, MD: Paul Brooks Publishing.

Bruni, O., & Novelli, L. (2010). Sleep disorders in children. *BMJ Clinical Evidence, 2010.*

Brunson, K. L., Kramar, E., Lin, B., Chen, Y., Colgin, L. L., Yanagihara, T. K., Lynch, G., & Baram, T. Z. (2005). Mechanisms of late-onset cognitive decline after early-life stress. *Journal of Neuroscience, 25*(41), 9328–9338.

Bryant, B. K. (1987). Mental health, temperament, family, and friends: Perspectives on children's empathy and social perspective taking. In N. Eisenberg & J. Strayer (Eds.), *Empathy and its development of competence in adolescence* (pp. 245–270). Cambridge, UK: Cambridge University Press.

Bucchianeri, M. M., Fernandes, N., Loth, K., Hannan, P. J., Eisenberg, M. E., & Neumark-Sztainer, D. (2016). Body dissatisfaction: Do associations with disordered eating and psychological well-being differ across race/ethnicity in adolescent girls and boys? *Cultural Diversity and Ethnic Minority Psychology, 22*(1), 137.

Buchanan, D. W., & Sobel, D. M. (2011). Mechanism-based causal reasoning in young children. *Child Development, 82*(6), 2053–2066.

Buchanan, T. W. (2007). Retrieval of emotional memories. *Psychological Bulletin, 133*(5), 761.

Buchmann, C., & DiPrete, T. A. (2006). The growing female advantage in college completion: The role of family background and academic achievement. *American Sociological Review, 71,* 515–541.

Buchmueller, T., & Carpenter, C. (2010). Disparities in health insurance coverage, access and outcomes for individuals in same-sex versus different-sex relationships, 2000–2007. *American Journal of Public Health, 100*(3), 489–495.

Buck Louis, G., Gray, L., Marcus, M., Ojeda, S., Pescovitz, O., Witchel, S., . . . Euling, S. Y. (2008). Environmental factors and puberty timing: Expert panel research needs. *Pediatrics, 121,* S192–S207.

Buck-Morss, S. (1975). Social-economic bias in Piaget's theories and its implication for cross-cultural study. *Human Development, 18*(1–2), 35–49.

Bucur, B., & Madden, D. J. (2010). Effects of adult age and blood pressure on executive function and speech of processing. *Experimental Aging Research, 36*(2), 153–168.

Budson, A. E., & Price, B. H. (2005). Memory dysfunction. *New England Journal of Medicine, 352,* 692–699.

Buehler, C. (2006). Parents and peers in relation to early adolescent problem behavior. *Journal of Marriage and Family, 68,* 109–124.

Buehler, C., & Welsh, D. P. (2009). A process model of adolescents' triangulation into parents' marital conflict: The role of emotional reactivity. *Journal of Family Psychology, 23*(2), 167–180.

Buell, J. S., Scott, T. M., Dawson-Hughes, B., Dallal, G. E., Rosenberg, I. H., Folstein, M. F., & Tucker, K. L. (2009). Vitamin D is associated with cognitive function in elders receiving home health services. *Journals of Gerontology, 64A*(8), 888–895.

Buhrmester, D. (1990). Intimacy of friendship, interpersonal competence, and adjustment during preadolescence and adolescence. *Child Development, 61,* 1101–1111.

Buist, K. L., Deković, M., & Prinzie, P. (2013). Sibling relationship quality and psychopathology of children and adolescents: A meta-analysis. *Clinical Psychology Review, 33*(1), 97–106.

Bulanda, J. R., & Brown, S. L. (2007). Race-ethnic differences in marital quality and divorce. *Social Science Research, 36*(3), 945–967.

Bulcroft, R. A., & Bulcroft, K. A. (1991). The nature and function of dating in later life. *Research on Aging, 13,* 244–260.

Burchinal, M. R., Roberts, J. E., Nabors, L. A., & Bryant, D. M. (1996). Quality of center child care and infant cognitive and language development. *Child Development, 67,* 606–620.

Burdette, H. L., & Whitaker, R. C. (2005). Resurrecting free play in young children. *Archives of Pediatrics and Adolescent Medicine, 159,* 46–50.

Bureau of Labor Statistics. (2005). *Data on unemployment rate.* Retrieved from www.bls.gov/cps/home.htm

Bureau of Labor Statistics. (2017). *Employment characteristics of families* [news release]. Retrieved from www.bls.gov/news.release/pdf/famee.pdf

Bures, R. M., Koropeckyj-Cox, T., & Loree, M. (2009). Childlessness, parenthood, and depressive symptoms among middle-aged and older adults. *Journal of Family Issues, 30*(5), 670–687.

Burke, B. L., Martens, A., & Faucher, E. H. (2010). Two decades of terror management theory: A meta-analysis of mortality salience research. *Personality and Social Psychology Review, 14*(2), 155–195.

Burke, D. M., & Shafto, M. A. (2004). Aging and language production. *Current Directions in Psychological Science, 13,* 81–84.

Burke, S. N., & Barnes, C. A. (2006). Neural plasticity in the ageing brain. *Nature Review Neuroscience, 7,* 30–40.

Burn, K., & Szoeke, C. (2016). Boomerang families and failure-to-launch: Commentary on adult children living at home. *Maturitas, 83,* 9–12.

Burnes, D., Pillemer, K., Caccamise, P. L., Mason, A., Henderson, C. R., Berman, J., . . . & Salamone, A. (2015). Prevalence of and risk factors for elder abuse and neglect in the community: A population-based study. *Journal of the American Geriatrics Society, 63*(9), 1906–1912.

Burns, B. J., Phillips, S. D., Wagner, H. R., Barth, R. P., Kolko, D. J., Campbell, Y., & Landsverk, J. (2004). Mental health need and access to mental health services by youths involved with child welfare: A national survey. *Journal of the American Academy of Child & Adolescent Psychiatry, 43,* 960–970.

Burns, K. H., Casey, P. H., Lyle, R. E., Mac Bird, T., Fussell, J. J., & Robbins, J. M. (2010). Increasing prevalence of medically complex children in US hospitals. *Pediatrics, 126*(4), 638–646.

Burtner, C. R., & Kennedy, B. K. (2010). Progeria syndromes and ageing: What is the connection? *Nature Reviews Molecular Cell Biology, 11*(8), 567–578.

Bushman, B. J., Gollwitzer, M., & Cruz, C. (2015). There is broad consensus: Media researchers agree that violent media increase aggression in children, and pediatricians and parents concur. *Psychology of Popular Media Culture, 4*(3), 200.

Bushnell, E. W., & Boudreau, J. P. (1993). Motor development and the mind: The potential role of motor abilities as a determinant of aspects of perceptual development. *Child Development, 64,* 1005–1021.

Bussey, K. (2011). Gender identity development. In S. J. Schwarts, K. Luyckx, & V. L. Vignoles (Eds.), *Handbook of identity theory and research: Vol. 1. Structures and processes* (pp. 603–628). New York: Springer.

Bussey, K., & Bandura, A. (1992). Self-regulatory mechanisms governing gender development. *Child Development, 63,* 1236–1250.

Bussey, K., & Bandura, A. (1999). Social cognitive theory of gender development and differentiation. *Psychological Review, 106,* 676–713.

Butler, R. N., Davis, R., Lewis, C. B., Nelson, M. E., & Strauss, E. (1998a). Physical fitness: Benefits of exercise for the older patient. *Geriatrics 53,* 46, 49–52, 61–62.

Butler, R. N., Davis, R., Lewis, C. B., Nelson, M. E., & Strauss, E. (1998b). Physical fitness: How to help older patients live stronger and longer. *Geriatrics, 53,* 26–28, 31–32, 39–40.

Byers, T. (2006). Overweight and mortality among baby boomers—Now we're getting personal. *New England Journal of Medicine, 355,* 758–760.

Byers-Heinlein, K., Burns, T. C., & Werker, J. F. (2010). The roots of bilingualism in newborns. *Psychological Science, 21*(3), 343–348. doi:10.1177/0956797609360758

Byrne, M., Agerbo, E., Ewald, H., Eaton, W. W., & Mortensen, P. B. (2003). Parental age and risk of schizophrenia. *Archives of General Psychiatry, 60,* 673–678.

Byrnes, J. P., & Fox, N. A. (1998). The educational relevance of research in cognitive neuroscience. *Educational Psychology Review, 10,* 297–342.

Bystron, I., Rakic, P., Molnar, Z., & Blakemore, C. (2006). The first neurons of the human cerebral cortex. *Nature Neuroscience, 9*(7), 880–886.

Caballero, B. (2006). Obesity as a consequence of undernutrition. *Journal of Pediatrics, 149*(5, Suppl. 1), 97–99.

Cabeza, R., Anderson, N. D., Locantore, J. K., & McIntosh, A. R. (2002). Aging gracefully: compensatory brain activity in high-performing older adults. *Neuroimage, 17*(3), 1394–1402.

Cabrera, N. J., Tamis-LeMonda, C. S., Bradley, R. H., Hofferth, S., & Lamb, M. E. (2000). Fatherhood in the twenty-first century. *Child Development, 71,* 127–136.

Cacioppo, J. T., & Cacioppo, S. (2014). Social relationships and health: The toxic effects of perceived social isolation. *Social and Personality Psychology Compass, 8*(2), 58–72.

Cadore, E. L., Rodríguez-Mañas, L., Sinclair, A., & Izquierdo, M. (2013). Effects of different exercise interventions on risk of falls, gait ability, and balance in physically frail older adults: A systematic review. *Rejuvenation Research, 16*(2), 105–114.

Caetano, R., Schafer, J., & Cunradi, C.B. (2001). Alcohol-related intimate partner violence among White, Black, and Hispanic couples in the United States. Retrieved from https://pubs.niaaa.nih.gov/publications/arh25-1/58-65.htm

Cahill, K. E., Giandrea, M. D., & Quinn, J. F. (2013). *Bridge employment.* In M. Wang (Ed.), The Oxford handbook of retirement (pp. 293–310). New York, NY: Oxford University Press.

Cahn, Z., & Siegel, M. (2011). Electronic cigarettes as a harm reduction strategy for tobacco control: A step forward or a repeat of past mistakes? *Journal of Public Health Policy, 32,* 16–31. doi: 10.1057/jphp2010.41

Cain, M.S., Leonard, J.A., Gabrieli, J.D.E., & Finn, A.S. (2016). Media multitasking in adolescence. *Psychonomic Bulletin & Review,* 23, 1932–1941.

Calafat, A., García, F., Juan, M., Becoña, E., & Fernández-Hermida, J. R. (2014). Which parenting style is more protective against adolescent substance use? Evidence within the European context. *Drug and alcohol dependence, 138,* 185-192.

Caldwell, B. M., & Bradley, R. H. (1984). *Home observation for measurement of the environment.* Unpublished manuscript, University of Arkansas at Little Rock.

Çalışkan, M., Bochkov, Y. A., Kreiner-Møller, E., Bønnelykke, K., Stein, M. M., Du, G., . . . & Nicolae, D. L. (2013). Rhinovirus wheezing illness and genetic risk of childhood-onset asthma. *New England Journal of Medicine, 368*(15), 1398–1407.

Calkins, S. D., & Fox, N. A. (1992). The relations among infant temperament, security of attachment, and behavioral inhibition at twenty-four months. *Child Development, 63,* 1456–1472.

Callahan, S. T., & Cooper, W. O. (2005). Uninsurance and health care access among young adults in the United States. *Pediatrics, 116,* 88–95.

Calvin, C. M., Deary, I. J., Fenton, C., Roberts, B. A., Der, G., Leckenby, N., & Batty, G. D. (2010). Intelligence in youth and all-cause-mortality: systematic review with meta-analysis. *International Journal of Epidemiology, 40*(3), 626–644.

Calzo, J. P., Masyn, K. E., Austin, S. B., Jun, H. J., & Corliss, H. L. (2017). Developmental latent patterns of identification as mostly heterosexual versus lesbian, gay, or bisexual. *Journal of Research on Adolescence, 27*(1), 246–253.

Camarata, S., & Woodcock, R. (2006). Sex differences in processing speed: Developmental effects in males and females. *Intelligence, 34*(3), 231–252.

Camarota, S. A., & Zeigler, K. (2016, October). *Immigrants in the United States: A profile of the foreign-born using 2014 and 2015 Census Bureau data.* Retrieved from Center for Immigration Studies: http://cis.org/sites/cis.org/files/immigrant-profile_0.pdf

Cameron, L., Rutland, A., Brown, R., & Douch, R. (2006). Changing children's intergroup attitudes towards refugees: Testing different models of extended contact. *Child Development, 77,* 1208–1219.

Camilli, G., Vargas, S., Ryan, S., & Barnett, W. S. (2010). Meta-analysis of the effects of early education interventions on cognitive and social development. *Teachers College Record, 112*(3), 579–620.

Camp, C. J. (1989). World-knowledge systems. In L. W. Poon, D. C. Rubin, & B. A. Wilson (Eds.), *Everyday cognition in adulthood and late life.* Cambridge, UK: Cambridge University Press.

Camp, C. J., & McKitrick, L. A. (1989). The dialectics of remembering and forgetting across the adult lifespan. In D. Kramer & M. Bopp (Eds.), *Dialectics and contextualism in clinical and developmental psychology: Change, transformation, and the social context* (pp. 169–187). New York: Springer.

Campa, M. J., & Eckenrode, J. J. (2006). Pathways to intergenerational adolescent childbearing in a high-risk sample. *Journal of Marriage and Family, 68,* 558–572.

Campbell, A., Shirley, L., & Candy, J. (2004). A longitudinal study of gender-related cognition and behaviour. *Developmental Science, 7,* 1–9.

Campbell, A., Shirley, L., Heywood, C., & Crook, C. (2000). Infants' visual preference for sex-congruent babies, children, toys, and activities: A longitudinal study. *British Journal of Developmental Psychology, 18,* 479–498.

Campbell, F. A., Ramey, C., Pungello, E., Sparling, J., & Miller-Johnson, S. (2002). Early childhood education: Young adult outcomes from the Abecedarian Project. *Applied Developmental Science, 6*(1), 42–57.

Campbell, K., & Peebles, R. (2014). Eating disorders in children and adolescents: State of the art review. *Pediatrics, 134*(3), 582–592.

Campione-Barr, N. (2017). The changing nature of power, control, and influence in sibling relationships. *New Directions for Child and Adolescent Development, 2017*(156), 7–14.

Campos, J. J., Sorce, J. F., Emde, R. N., & Svejda, M. (2013). Emotions as behavior regulators: Social referencing in infancy. *Emotions in Early Development,* 57.

Cansino, S. (2009). Episodic memory decay along the adult lifespan: A review of behavioral and neurophysiological evidence. *International Journal of Psychophysiology, 71*(1), 64–69.

Cantor, J. (1994). Confronting children's fright responses to mass media. In D. Zillman, J. Bryant, & A. C. Huston (Eds.), *Media, children, and the family: Social scientific, psychoanalytic, and clinical perspectives* (pp. 139–150). Hillsdale, NJ: Erlbaum.

Cao, A., & Kan, Y. W. (2013). The prevention of thalassemia. *Cold Spring Harbor perspectives in medicine, 3*(2), a011775.

Cao, A., Rosatelli, M. C., Monni, G., & Galanello, R. (2002). Screening for thalassemia. *Obstetrics and Gynecology Clinics, 29*(2), 305–328.

Capaldi, D. M., Stoolmiller, M., Clark, S., & Owen, L. D. (2002). Heterosexual risk behaviors in at-risk young men from early adolescence to young adulthood: Prevalence, prediction, and STD contraction. *Developmental Psychology, 38,* 394–406.

Caplan, L. J., & Schooler, C. (2006). Household work complexity, intellectual functioning, and self-esteem in men and women. *Journal of Marriage and Family, 68,* 883–900.

Caprara, G. V., Fida, R., Vecchione, M., Del Bove, G., Vecchio, G. M., Barbaranelli, C., & Bandura, A. (2008). Longitudinal analysis of the role of perceived self-efficacy for self-regulated learning in academic continuance and achievement. *Journal of Educational Psychology, 100*(3), 525–534.

Caraballo, R. S., Giovino, G. A., Pechacek, T. F., Mowery, P. D., Richter, P. A., Strauss, W. J., . . . Maurer, K. R. (1998). Racial and ethnic differences in serum cotinine levels of cigarette smokers. *Journal of the American Medical Association, 280,* 135–139.

Card, N., Stucky, B., Sawalani, G., & Little, T. (2008). Direct and indirect aggression during childhood and adolescence: A meta-analytic review of gender differences, intercorrelations, and relations to maladjustment. *Child Development, 79*(5), 1185–1229.

Carers Australia Staff. (2012, September 28). *Carers caught in the 'sandwich generation'.* Retrieved from Carers Australia: www.carersaustralia.com.au/media-centre/article/?id=carers-caught-in-the-sandwich-generation

Carers UK Staff. (2012, November 29). *Sandwich Caring.* Retrieved from carersUK: www.carersuk.org/for-professionals/policy/policy-library/sandwich-caring

Carlo, G., Mestre, M. V., Samper, P., Tur, A., & Armenta, B. E. (2011). The longitudinal relations among dimensions of parenting styles, sympathy, prosocial moral reasoning, and prosocial behaviors. *International Journal of Behavioral Development, 35*(2), 116–124.

Carlson, E. A. (1998). A prospective longitudinal study of attachment disorganization/disorientation. *Child Development, 69*(4), 1107-1128.

Carlson, M. J. (2006). Family structure, father involvement, and adolescent behavioral outcomes. *Journal of Marriage and Family, 68,* 137-154.

Carlson, N. E., Moore, M. M., Dame, A., Howieson, D., Silbert, L. C., Quinn, J. F., & Kaye, J. A. (2008). Trajectories of brain loss in aging and the development of cognitive impairment. *Neurology, 79*(11), 828-833.

Carlson, S. M., & Taylor, M. (2005). Imaginary companions and impersonated characters: Sex differences in children's fantasy play. *Merrill-Palmer Quarterly, 51*(1), 93-118.

Carmichael, C. L., Reis, H. T., & Duberstein, P. R. (2015). In your 20s it's quantity, in your 30s it's quality: The prognostic value of social activity across 30 years of adulthood. *Psychology and Aging, 30*(1), 95.

Carnelley, K. B., Wortman, C. B., Bolger, N., & Burke, C. T. (2006). The time course of grief reactions to spousal loss: Evidence from a national probability sample. *Journal of Personality and Social Psychology, 91,* 476-492.

Carnethon, M. R., Gulati, M., & Greenland, P. (2005). Prevalence and cardiovascular disease correlates of low cardiorespiratory fitness in adolescents and adults. *Journal of the American Medical Association, 294,* 2981-2988.

Carnevale, A. P., Hanson, A. R., & Gulish, A. (2013). *Failure to Launch: Structural Shift and the New Lost Generation.* Washington, DC: Georgetown University Center on Education and the Workforce.

Carothers, S. S., Borkowski, J. G., Lefever, J. B., & Whitman, T. L. (2005). Religiosity and the socioemotional adjustment of adolescent mothers and their children. *Journal of Family Psychology, 19,* 263-275.

Carpenter, C., & Gates, G. J. (2008). Gay and lesbian partnership: Evidence from California. *Demography, 45,* 573-590.

Carr, D. C., Kail, B. L., Matz-Costa, C., & Shavit, Y. Z. (2017). Does becoming a volunteer attenuate loneliness among recently widowed older adults? *The Journals of Gerontology: Series B.*

Carr, D., & Boerner, K. (2009). Do spousal discrepancies in marital quality assessments affect psychological adjustment to widowhood? *Journal of Marriage and Family, 71*(3), 495-509.

Carr, D., Freedman, V. A., Cornman, J. C., & Schwarz, N. (2014). Happy marriage, happy life? Marital quality and subjective well-being in later life. *Journal of Marriage and Family, 76*(5), 930-948.

Carr, D., House, J. S., Kessler, R. C., Nesse, R. M., Sonnega, J., & Wortman, C. (2000). Marital quality and psychological adjustment to widowhood among older adults: A longitudinal analysis. *Journal of Gerontology: Social Sciences, 55B,* S197-S207.

Carraher, T. N., Schliemann, A. D., & Carraher, D. W. (1988). Mathematical concepts in everyday life. In G. B. Saxe & M. Gearhart (Eds.), *Children's mathematics* (New Directions in Child Development, No. 41, pp. 71-87). San Francisco: Jossey-Bass.

Carrel, L., & Willard, B. F. (2005). X-inactivation profile reveals extensive variability in X-linked gene expression in females. *Nature, 434,* 400-404.

Carskadon, M. A., Acebo, C., Richardson, G. S., Tate, B. A., & Seifer, R. (1997). Long nights protocol: Access to circadian parameters in adolescents. *Journal of Biological Rhythms, 12,* 278-289.

Carstensen, L. L. (1991). Selectivity theory: Social activity in life-span context. In *Annual Review of Gerontology and Geriatrics* (Vol. 11, pp. 195-217). New York: Springer.

Carstensen, L. L. (1995). Evidence for a life-span theory of socioemotional selectivity. *Current Directions in Psychological Science, 4,* 150-156.

Carstensen, L. L. (1996). Socioemotional selectivity: A life-span developmental account of social behavior. In M. R. Merrens & G. G. Brannigan (Eds.), *The developmental psychologists: Research adventures across the life span* (pp. 251-272). New York: McGraw-Hill.

Carstensen, L. L., & Mikels, J. A. (2005). At the intersection of emotion and cognition: Aging and the positivity effect. *Current Directions in Psychological Science, 11,* 117-122.

Carstensen, L. L., Isaacowitz, D. M., & Charles, S. T. (1999). Taking time seriously: A theory of socioemotional selectivity. *American Psychologist, 54,* 165-181.

Carstensen, L. L., Pasupathi, M., Mayr, U., & Nesselroade, J. (2000). Emotional experience in everyday life across the adult life span. *Journal of Personality and Social Psychology, 79,* 644-655.

Carter, P.M., Bingham, C.R., Zakrajsek, J.S., Shope, J.T., & Sayer, T.B. (2014). Social norms and risk perception: predictors of distracted driving behavior among novice adolescent drivers. *Journal of Adolescent Health,* 54, S32-S41.

Carter, R. C., Jacobson, S. W., Molteno, C. D., Chiodo, L. M., Viljoen, D., & Jacobson, J. L. (2005). Effects of prenatal alcohol exposure on infant visual acuity. *Journal of Pediatrics, 147*(4), 473-479.

Carver, C. S. (2007). Stress, coping, and health. In H. S. Friedman, & R. C. Silver (Eds.), *Foundations of health psychology* (pp. 117-144). New York: Oxford University Press.

Case, R. (1992). Neo-Piagetian theories of child development. In R. Sternberg & C. Berg (Eds.), *Intellectual development* (pp. 161-196). New York: Cambridge University Press.

Caspi, A. (1998). Personality development across the life course. In W. Damon (Series Ed.) & N. Eisenberg (Vol. Ed.), *Handbook of child psychology: Vol. 3. Social, emotional, and personality development* (5th ed., pp. 311-388). New York: Wiley.

Caspi, A. (2000). The child is father of the man: Personality continuity from childhood to adulthood. *Journal of Personality and Social Psychology, 78,* 158-172.

Caspi, A., Lynam, D., Moffitt, T. E., & Silva, P. A. (1993). Unraveling girls' delinquency: Biological, dispositional, and contextual contributions to adolescent misbehavior. *Developmental Psychology, 29*(1), 19-30.

Caspi, A., McClay, J., Moffitt, T. E., Mill, J., Martin, J., Craig, I. W., . . . Poulton, R. (2002). Role of genotype in the cycle of violence in maltreated children. *Science, 297,* 851-854.

Caspi, A., Sugden, K., Moffitt, T. E., Taylor, A., Craig, I. W., Harrington, H., . . . Poulton, R. (2003). Influence of life stress on depression: Moderation by a polymorphism in the 5-HTT gene. *Science, 301,* 386-389.

Cassidy, K. W., Werner, R. S., Rourke, M., Zubernis, L. S., & Balaraman, G. (2003). The relationship between psychological understanding and positive social behaviors. *Social Development, 12,* 198-221.

Castle, N., Ferguson-Rome, J.C., & Teresi, J.A. (2013). Elder abuse in residential long-term care: An update to the 2003 National Research Council Report. *Journal of Applied Gerontology,* 34, 407-433.

Castro, M., Expósito-Casas, E., López-Martín, E., Lizasoain, L., Navarro-Asencio, E., & Gaviria, J. L. (2015). Parental involvement on student academic achievement: A meta-analysis. *Educational Research Review, 14,* 33-46.

Cattell, R. B. (1965). *The scientific analysis of personality.* Baltimore: Penguin Books.

Caughey, A. B., Hopkins, L. M., & Norton, M. E. (2006). Chorionic villus sampling compared with amniocentesis and the difference in the rate of pregnancy loss. *Obstetrics and Gynecology, 108,* 612-616.

Cavanagh, S. E., & Huston, A. C. (2008). The timing of family instability and children's social development. *Journal of Marriage and Family, 70*(5), 1258-1270.

Caylak, E. (2009). The genetics of sleep disorders in humans: Narcolepsy, restless legs syndrome, and obstructive sleep apnea syndrome. *American Journal of Medical Genetics Part A, 149*(11), 2612-2626.

Ceci, S. J., & Williams, W. M. (1997). Schooling, intelligence, and income. *American Psychologist, 52*(10), 1051-1058.

Celis, W. (1990). More states are laying school paddle to rest. *The New York Times,* pp. A1, B12.

Center for Behavioral Health Statistics and Quality. (2016). *Key substance use and mental health indicators in the United States: Results from the 2015 National Survey on Drug Use and Health* (HHS Publication No. SMA 16-4984, NSDUH Series H-51). Retrieved from www.samhsa.gov/data/

Center for Education Reform. (2004, August 17). *Comprehensive data discounts account; reveals charter schools performing at or above traditional schools* [Press release]. Retrieved from http://edreform.com/indexcfm?fuseAction=document&documentID=1806

Center for Education Reform. (2008, October 23). *Charter school numbers 2008: Count 'em up* [Press release]. Retrieved from http://www.edreform.com/Press_Box/Press_releases/?Charter_School_Numbers_2008_Count_Em_Up&year=2008

Center for Substance Abuse Treatment. (2008). Medication-assisted treatment for opioid addiction during pregnancy. *SAHMSA/CSAT treatment improvement protocols.* Rockville, MD: Substance Abuse and Mental Health Services Administration. Available at www.ncbi.nlm.nih.gov/books/NBK26113

Centers for Disease Control and Prevention (2017a). *2015 Assisted Reproductive Technology National Summary Report.* Retrieved from www.cdc.gov/art/pdf/2015-report/ART-2015-National-Summary-Report.pdf

Centers for Disease Control and Prevention (CDC). (2000a). *CDC's guidelines for school and community programs: Promoting lifelong physical activity.* Retrieved from www.cdc.gov/nccdphp/dash/phactaag.htm

Centers for Disease Control and Prevention. (2017b). *CDC National Health Report Highlights.* Retrieved from www.cdc.gov/healthreport/publications/compendium.pdf

Centers for Disease Control and Prevention (CDC). (2000b). *Tracking the hidden epidemic: Trends in STDs in the U.S., 2000.* Washington, DC: Author.

Centers for Disease Control and Prevention (CDC). (2006a). Achievements in public health: Reduction in perinatal transmission of HIV infection—United States, 1985–2005. *Morbidity and Mortality Weekly Report, 55*(21), 592–597.

Centers for Disease Control and Prevention (CDC). (2007a, Summer). *Suicide: Facts at a Glance.* Retrieved from www.cdc.gov/ncipc/dvp/Suicide/SuicideDataSheet.pdf

Centers for Disease Control and Prevention (CDC). (2008c). *Surveillance summaries.* Atlanta, GA: Author.

Centers for Disease Control and Prevention (CDC). (2010). *Mortality among teenagers aged 12–19 years: United States, 1999–2006.* NCHS Data Brief. Retrieved from www.cdc.gov/nchs/data/databriefs/db37.htm

Centers for Disease Control and Prevention (CDC). (2012a). *Death rates for suicide, by sex, race, Hispanic origin, and age: United States, selected years 1950–2010.* Retrieved from www.cdc.gov/nchs/data/hus/2012/035.pdf

Centers for Disease Control and Prevention (CDC). (2012b). Sexual experience and contraceptive use among female teens—United States, 1995, 2002, and 2006–2010. *Morbidity and Mortality Weekly Report, 61*(17), 297–301.

Centers for Disease Control and Prevention (CDC). (2013c). *Reducing teen pregnancy: Engaging communities.* Retrieved from www.cdc.gov/Features/TeenPregnancy/

Centers for Disease Control and Prevention (CDC). (2017c). *Current physical activity guidelines.* Retrieved from www.cdc.gov/cancer/dcpc/prevention/policies_practices/physical_activity/guidelines.htm

Centers for Disease Control and Prevention and The Merck Company Foundation. (2007). *The state of aging and health care in America.* Whitehouse Station, NJ: The Merck Company Foundation. Retrieved from www.cdc.gov/Aging/pdf/saha_2007.pdf

Centers for Disease Control and Prevention, National Center for Injury Prevention and Control. (2017d). *Elder abuse: Consequences.* Retrieved from www.cdc.gov/violenceprevention/elderabuse/consequences.html

Centers for Disease Control and Prevention. (2013a). *Food desert.* Retrieved from www.cdc.gov/healthcommunication/toolstemplates/entertainmented/tips/fooddesert.html

Centers for Disease Control and Prevention. (2013b). *Incidence, prevalence and cost of sexually transmitted infections in the United States.* Retrieved from www.cdc.gov/std/stats/STI-Estimates-Fact-Sheet-Feb-2013.pdf

Centers for Disease Control and Prevention. (2014a). *U.S. infant vaccinations rates still high: Unvaccinated still vulnerable.* Retrieved from www.cdc.gov/media/releases/2014/p0828-infant-vaccination.html

Centers for Disease Control and Prevention. (2016a). *CDC recommends only two HPV shots for younger adolescents.* Retrieved from www.cdc.gov/media/releases/2016/p1020-hpv-shots.html

Centers for Disease Control and Prevention. (2016b). *Key Findings: Trends in the Parent-Report of Health Care Provider-Diagnosis and Medication Treatment for ADHD: United States, 2003–2011.* Retrieved from www.cdc.gov/ncbddd/adhd/features/key-findings-adhd72013.html

Centers for Disease Control and Prevention. (2016c). Physical inactivity among adults 50 years and older: MMWR data highlights [data report]. *Centers for Disease Control and Prevention. State Indicator Report on Physical Activity, 2014.* Atlanta, GA: U.S. Department of Health and Human Services, 2014

Centers for Disease Control and Prevention. (2016d). *STDs in adolescents and young adults.* Retrieved from www.cdc.gov/std/stats16/adolescents.htm

Centers for Disease Control and Prevention. (2017e). *10 leading causes of death by age group: United States—2015.* Retrieved from www.cdc.gov/injury/wisqars/pdf/leading_causes_of_death_by_age_group_2015-a.pdf

Centers for Disease Control and Prevention. (2017f). *National diabetes statistics report: estimates of diabetes and its burden in the United States, 2017.* Atlanta, GA: US Department of Health and Human Services.

Centers for Disease Control and Prevention. (2017g). *Distracted Driving.* Retrieved from www.cdc.gov/motorvehiclesafety/distracted_driving/index.html.

Centers for Disease Control and Prevention. (2017h). *Intimate Partner Violence.* Retrieved from www.cdc.gov/violenceprevention/intimatepartnerviolence/index.html

Centers for Disease Control and Prevention. (2017i). *National Center for Health Statistics: Deaths and mortality.* Retrieved from www.cdc.gov/nchs/fastats/deaths.htm

Centers for Disease Control and Prevention. (2017j). *Sexually Transmitted Disease Surveillance 2016.* Atlanta: U.S. Department of Health and Human Services.

Centers for Disease Control and Prevention. (2014b). *State indicator report on physical activity, 2014.* Atlanta, GA: U.S. Department of Health and Human Services.

Centers for Disease Control and Prevention. (2013d). *The state of aging and health in America 2013.* Atlanta, GA: Centers for Disease Control and Prevention, U.S. Department of Health and Human Services.

Centers for Disease Control and Prevention. (2015). *Electronic cigarette use among adults: United States, 2014.* Retrieved from www.cdc.gov/nchs/data/databriefs/db217.htm

Centers for Disease Control and Prevention. (2016e). Community Report on Autism 2016. Retrieved from www.cdc.gov/ncbddd/autism/documents/community_report_autism.pdf

Centers for Disease Control and Prevention. (2016f). Fatal injury reports, national and regional, 1999-2014 [interactive data file]. Retrieved from https://webappa.cdc.gov/sasweb/ncipc/mortrate10_us.html

Centers for Disease Control and Prevention. (2017k). 10 leading causes of death by age group, United States- 2015 [data graphic]. Retrieved from www.cdc.gov/injury/images/lc-charts/leading_causes_of_death_age_group_2015_1050w740h.gif

Centers for Disease Control and Prevention. (2017l). *Fast Stats: Health of Black or African American non-Hispanic population.* Retrieved fromwww.cdc.gov/nchs/fastats/black-health.htm

Centers for Disease Control and Prevention. (2017m). *Infertility FAQs* [Fact sheet]. Retrieved from www.cdc.gov/reproductivehealth/infertility/index.htm

Centers for Disease Control and Prevention. (2017n). *National marriage and divorce rate trends: 2000-2015.* [Data file]. Retrieved from www.cdc.gov/nchs/data/dvs/national_marriage_divorce_rates_00-15.pdf

Centers for Disease Control and Prevention. (2017o). *Physical activity facts.* Retrieved from www.cdc.gov/healthyschools/physicalactivity/facts.htm

Centers for Disease Control and Prevention. (2017p). Preconception health and health care. Retrieved from www.cdc.gov/preconception/index.html

Centers for Disease Control and Prevention. (2017q). Social determinants and eliminating disparities in teen pregnancy. Retrieved from www.cdc.gov/teenpregnancy/about/social-determinants-disparities-teen-pregnancy.htm

Centers for Disease Control and Prevention. (2017r). Teen drivers: Get the facts. Retrieved from www.cdc.gov/motorvehiclesafety/teen_drivers/teendrivers_factsheet.html

Centers for Disease Control and Prevention. (2018). Elder abuse: Definitions [fact sheet]. Retrieved from www.cdc.gov/violenceprevention/elderabuse/definitions.html

Centers for Medicare and Medicaid Services. (2009). *Low cost health insurance for families and children.* Retrieved from www.cms.hhs.gov/lowcosthealthinsfamchild/

Central Intelligence Agency. (2015). *Country comparison to the world*. Retrieved from: www.cia.gov/library/publications/the-world-factbook/fields/2223.html

Centre for Educational Research and Innovation. (2004). Education at a Glance: OECD indicators—2004. *Education and Skills, 2004*(14), 1–456.

Cepeda-Benito, A., Reynoso, J. T., & Erath, S. (2004). Meta-analysis of the efficacy of nicotine replacement therapy for smoking cessation: Differences between men and women. *Journal of Consulting and Clinical Psychology, 72*, 712–722.

Ceppi, G., & Zini, M. (1998). *Children, spaces, relations: Metaproject for an environment for young children*. Eggio Emilia, Italy: Municipality of Reggio Emilia Inanzia ricerca.

Cerasoli, C. P., Nicklin, J. M., & Ford, M. T. (2014). Intrinsic motivation and extrinsic incentives jointly predict performance: A 40-year meta-analysis. *Psychological Bulletin, 140*(4), 980.

Cespedes, E. M., Gillman, M. W., Kleinman, K., Rifas-Shiman, S. L., Redline, S., & Taveras, E. M. (2014). Television viewing, bedroom television, and sleep duration from infancy to mid-childhood. *Pediatrics, 133*(5), e1163–e1171.

Chafetz, M. D. (1992). *Smart for life*. New York: Penguin Books.

Chambers, R. A., Taylor, J. R., & Potenza, M. N. (2003). Developmental neurocircuitry of motivation in adolescence: A critical period of addiction vulnerability. *American Journal of Psychiatry, 160*, 1041–1052.

Champagne, F. A. (2014). Epigenetics and developmental plasticity across species. *Developmental Psychobiology, 55*, 33–41.

Champagne, F. A., & Mashoodh, R. (2009). Genes in context: Gene-environment interactions and the origins of individual differences in behavior. *Current Directions in Psychological Science, 18*(3), 127–131.

Chan, W. Y., Ou, S. R., & Reynolds, A. J. (2014). Adolescent civic engagement and adult outcomes: An examination among urban racial minorities. *Journal of Youth and Adolescence, 43*(11), 1829–1843.

Chandra, A., Martin, S., Collins, R., Elliott, M., Berry, S., Kanouse, D., & Miu, A. (2008). Does watching sex on television predict teen pregnancy? Findings from a National Longitudinal Survey of Youth. *Pediatrics, 122*(5), 1047–1054.

Chang, P. J., Wray, L., & Lin, Y. (2014). Social relationships, leisure activity, and health in older adults. *Health Psychology, 33*(6), 516.

Chang, S. H., Stoll, C. R., Song, J., Varela, J. E., Eagon, C. J., & Colditz, G. A. (2014). The effectiveness and risks of bariatric surgery: an updated systematic review and meta-analysis, 2003-2012. *JAMA Surgery, 149*(3), 275–287.

Chao, R. K. (1994). Beyond parental control and authoritarian parenting style: Understanding Chinese parenting through the cultural notion of training. *Child Development, 65*, 1111–1119.

Chao, R. K. (2001). Extending research on the consequences of parenting style for Chinese Americans and European Americans. *Child Development, 72*, 1832–1843.

Chao, S., Roberts, J. S., Marteau, T. M., Silliman, R., Cupples, L. A., & Green, R. C. (2008). Health behavior changes after genetic risk assessment for Alzheimer disease: The REVEAL study. *Alzheimer Disease Association, 22*(1), 94–97.

Chapman, M., & Lindenberger, U. (1988). Functions, operations, and décalage in the development of transitivity. *Developmental Psychology, 24*, 542–551.

Charles, S. T., & Piazza, J. R. (2007). Memories of social interactions: Age differences in emotional intensity. *Psychology and Aging, 22*, 300–309.

Charles, S. T., & Carstensen, L. L. (2007). Emotion regulation and aging. In J. J. Gross (Ed.), *Handbook of emotion regulation* (pp. 307–330). New York: Guilford Press.

Charles, S. T., Reynolds, C. A., & Gatz, M. (2001). Age-related differences and change in positive and negative affect over 23 years. *Journal of Personality and Social Psychology, 80*, 136–151.

Charness, N., & Schultetus, R. S. (1999). Knowledge and expertise. In F. T. Durso (Ed.), *Handbook of applied cognition* (pp. 57–81). Chichester, England: Wiley.

Chaudry, A., & Wimer, C. (2016). Poverty is not just an indicator: the relationship between income, poverty, and child well-being. *Academic Pediatrics, 16*(3), S23–S29.

Chen, C. L., Weiss, N. S., Newcomb, P., Barlow, W., & White, E. (2002). Hormone replacement therapy in relation to breast cancer. *Journal of the American Medical Association, 287*, 734–741.

Chen, H. C., Su, T. P., & Chou, P. (2013). A nine-year follow-up study of sleep patterns and mortality in community-dwelling older adults in Taiwan. *Sleep, 36*(8), 1187–1198.

Chen, H., Chauhan, S. P., Ananth, C. V., Vintzileos, A. M., & Abuhamad, A. Z. (2013). Electronic fetal heart rate monitoring and its relationship to neonatal and infant mortality in the United States. *American Journal of Obstetrics and Gynecology, 204*(6), 491–501.

Chen, L. W., Wu, Y., Neelakantan, N., Chong, M. F. F., Pan, A., & van Dam, R. M. (2014). Maternal caffeine intake during pregnancy is associated with risk of low birth weight: a systematic review and dose-response meta-analysis. *BMC Medicine, 12*(1), 174.

Chen, L., Baker, S. B., Braver, E. R., & Li, G. (2000). Carrying passengers as a risk factor for crashes fatal to 16- and 17-year-old drivers. *Journal of the American Medical Association, 283*(12), 1578–1582.

Chen, P. C., & Wang, J. D. (2006). Parental exposure to lead and small for gestational age births. *American Journal of Industrial Medicine, 49*(6), 417–422.

Chen, X. (2010). Socioemotional development in Chinese children. In M. H. Bond (Ed.), *Handbook of Chinese psychology* (pp. 37–52). Oxford: Oxford University Press.

Chen, X. (2012). Culture, peer interaction, and socioemotional development. *Child Development Perspectives, 6*(1), 27–34.

Chen, X., Cen, G., Li, D., & He, Y. (2005). Social functioning and adjustment in Chinese children: The imprint of historical time. *Child Development, 76*, 182–195.

Chen, X., Wang, L., & Wang, Z. (2009). Shyness-sensitivity and social, school, and psychological adjustment in rural migrant and urban children in China. *Child Development, 80*(5), 1499–1513.

Chen, Y., & Feeley, T. H. (2014). Social support, social strain, loneliness, and well-being among older adults: An analysis of the Health and Retirement Study. *Journal of Social and Personal Relationships, 31*(2), 141–161.

Cheng, S., & Heller, K. (2009). *Global aging: Challenges for community psychology*. Retrieved from dx.doi.org: doi:http://dx.doi.org/10.1007/s10464-009-9244-x

Cherlin, A. (2004). The deinstitutionalization of American marriage. *Journal of Marriage and Family, 66*, 848–861.

Cherlin, A. J. (2010). Demographic trends in the United States: A review of research in the 2000s. *Journal of Marriage and Family, 72*(3), 403–419.

Cherlin, A., & Furstenberg, F. F. (1986). *The new American grandparent*. New York: Basic Books.

Cherry, K. E., & Park, D. C. (1993). Individual differences and contextual variables influence spatial memory in younger and older adults. *Psychology and Aging, 8*, 517–526.

Cherry, K. E., Walker, E. J., Brown, J. S., Volaufova, J., LaMotte, L. R., Welsh, D. A., . . . & Frisard, M. I. (2013). Social engagement and health in younger, older, and oldest-old adults in the Louisiana healthy aging study. *Journal of Applied Gerontology, 32*(1), 51–75.

Cheryan, S., Ziegler, S. A., Montoya, A. K., & Jiang, L. (2017). Why are some STEM fields more gender balanced than others? *Psychological Bulletin, 143*(1), 1.

Cheung, F., & Lucas, R. E. (2015). When does money matter most? Examining the association between income and life satisfaction over the life course. *Psychology and Aging, 30*(1), 120.

Chian, R., Uzelac, P.S., & Nargund, G. (2013). In vitro maturation of human immature oocytes for fertility preservation. *Fertility and Sterility, 99*, 1173–1181.

Chida, Y., & Steptoe, A. (2008). Positive psychological well-being and mortality: A quantitative review of prospective observational studies. *Psychosomatic Medicine, 70*(7), 741–756.

Child Health USA. (2012). Adolescent mortality. Retrieved from https://mchb.hrsa.gov/chusa12/hs/hsa/pages/am.html

Child Trends DataBank. (2012). *Number and percentage distribution of all children and adopted children, ages 0-17, by selected characteristics, United States, 2007.* [Data file]. Retrieved from www.childtrends.org/wp-content/uploads/2012/08/113_appendix1.pdf

Child Trends DataBank. (2015a). *Family structure: Indicators of child and youth well-being.* Retrieved from www.childtrends.org/wp-content/uploads/2015/12/59_Family_Structure.pdf

Child Trends DataBank. (2015b). *Teen homicide, suicide and firearm deaths.* Retrieved from www.childtrends.org/wp-content/uploads/2015/12/70_Homicide_Suicide_Firearms.pdf

Child Trends Databank. (2015c). Late or no prenatal care [report]. Retrieved from www.childtrends.org/?late-or-no-prenatal-care

Child Trends DataBank. (2016). *Youth employment.* Retrieved from www.childtrends.org/?indicators=youth-employment

Child Trends DataBank. (2010a). *Children in poverty.* Retrieved from www.childtrendsdatabank.org/?q=node/221

Child Trends DataBank. (2010b). *Physical Fighting by Youth.* Retrieved from www.childtrendsdatabank.org/?q=node/136

Child Welfare Information Gateway. (2011). *How many children were adopted in 2007 and 2008?* Washington, DC: U.S. Department of Health and Human Services, Children's Bureau.

Child Welfare Information Gateway. (2013). *Long-term consequences of child abuse and neglect.* Washington, DC: U.S. Department of Health and Human Services, Children's Bureau.

Child Welfare Information Gateway. (2017). *Child abuse and neglect fatalities 2015: Statistics and interventions.* Washington, DC: U.S. Department of Health and Human Services, Children's Bureau.

Children's Defense Fund (CDF). (2004). *The state of America's children, 2004.* Washington, DC: Author.

Children's Defense Fund. (2017). *Ending child poverty now.* Retrieved from www.childrensdefense.org/library/PovertyReport/EndingChildPovertyNow.html

Children's Defense Fund. (2014). *The state of America's children 2014.* Retrieved from www.childrensdefense.org/library/state-of-americas-children/2014-soac.pdf?utm_source=2014-SOAC-PDF&utm_medium=link&utm_campaign=2014-SOAC

Children in U.S. immigrant families. (2015). Retrieved from Migration Policy Institute: www.migrationpolicy.org/programs/data-hub/charts/children-immigrant-families

Chilton, W., O'Brien, B., & Charchar, F. (2017). Telomeres, aging and exercise: guilty by association? *International Journal of Molecular Sciences, 18*(12), 2573.

Chin, H. B., Sipe, T. A., Elder, R., Mercer, S. L., Chattopadhyay, S. K., Jacob, V., . . . & Chuke, S. O. (2012). The effectiveness of group-based comprehensive risk-reduction and abstinence education interventions to prevent or reduce the risk of adolescent pregnancy, human immunodeficiency virus, and sexually transmitted infections: Two systematic reviews for the Guide to Community Preventive Services. *American Journal of Preventive Medicine, 42*(3), 272–294.

Chiriboga, C. A., Brust, J. C. M., Bateman, D., & Hauser, W. A. (1999). Dose-response effect of fetal cocaine exposure on newborn neurologic function. *Pediatrics, 103,* 79–85.

Chiriboga, D. A. (1997). Crisis, challenge, and stability in the middle years. In M. E. Lachman & J. B. James (Eds.), *Multiple paths of midlife development* (pp. 293–322). Chicago: University of Chicago Press.

Cho, J., Martin, P., & Poon, L.W. (2015). Successful aging and subjective well-being among oldest-old adults. *The Gerontologist, 55,* 132–143.

Cho, J., Martin, P., Poon, L. W., & Georgia Centenarian Study. (2014). Successful aging and subjective well-being among oldest-old adults. *The Gerontologist, 55*(1), 132–143.

Chochinov, H. M., Hack, T., McClement, S., Harlos, M., & Kristjanson, L. (2002). Dignity in the terminally ill: A developing empirical model. *Social Science Medicine, 54,* 433–443.

Choi, K. S., Stewart, R., & Dewey, M. (2013). Participation in productive activities and depression among older Europeans: Survey of Health, Ageing and Retirement in Europe (SHARE). *International Journal of Geriatric Psychiatry, 28*(11), 1157–1165.

Choi, M., Kong, S., & Jung, D. (2012). Computer and internet interventions for loneliness and depression in older adults: A meta-analysis. *Healthcare Informatics Research, 18*(3), 191–198.

Chomitz, V. R., Cheung, L. W. Y., & Lieberman, E. (1995). The role of lifestyle in preventing low birth weight. *Future of Children, 5*(1), 121–138.

Chomsky, C. S. (1969). *The acquisition of syntax in children from five to ten.* Cambridge, MA: MIT Press.

Chomsky, N. (1957). *Syntactic structures.* The Hague: Mouton.

Chomsky, N. (1972). *Language and mind* (2nd ed.). New York: Harcourt Brace Jovanovich.

Chomsky, N. (1995). *The minimalist program.* Cambridge, MA: MIT Press.

Choquet, H., & Meyre, D. (2011). Genetics of obesity: what have we learned? *Current Genomics, 12*(3), 169–179.

Chorpita, B. P., & Barlow, D. H. (1998). The development of anxiety: The role of control in the early environment. *Psychological Bulletin, 124,* 3–21.

Chou, R. J. A., & Choi, N. G. (2011). Prevalence and correlates of perceived workplace discrimination among older workers in the United States of America. *Ageing & Society, 31*(6), 1051–1070.

Chow, C. M., Ruhl, H., & Buhrmester, D. (2013). The mediating role of interpersonal competence between adolescents' empathy and friendship quality: A dyadic approach. *Journal of Adolescence, 36*(1), 191–200.

Christakis, D. A. (2014). Interactive media use at younger than the age of 2 years: Time to rethink the American Academy of Pediatrics Guideline? *JAMA Pediatrics, 168,* 399–400.

Christakis, D. A., Zimmerman, F. J., DiGiuseppe, D. L., & McCarty, C. A. (2004). Early television exposure and subsequent attentional problems in children. *Pediatrics, 113,* 708–713.

Christakis, N. A., & Allison, P. D. (2006). Mortality after the hospitalization of a spouse. *New England Journal of Medicine, 354,* 719–730.

Christian Home Educators Association of California. (2013). *Considering homeschooling?* Norwalk, CA: Christian Home Educators Association of California. Retrieved from http://www.cheaofca.org/index.cfm?fuseaction=Page.viewPage&pageId=1033

Christian, M. S., & Brent, R. L. (2001). Teratogen update: Evaluation of the reproductive and developmental risks of caffeine. *Teratology, 64*(1), 51–78.

Christie, J. F. (1998). Play as a medium for literacy development. In D. P. Fromberg & D. Bergen (Eds.), *Play from birth to 12 and beyond: Contexts, perspectives, and meanings* (pp. 50–55). New York: Garland.

Chu, S. Y., Bachman, D. J., Callaghan, W. M., Whitlock, E. P., Dietz, P. M., Berg, C. J., . . . Hornbrook, M. C. (2008). Association between obesity during pregnancy and increased use of health care. *New England Journal of Medicine, 358,* 1444–1453.

Chua, E. F., Schacter, D. L., Rand-Giovanetti, E., & Sperling, R. A. (2006). Understanding metamemory: Neural correlates of the cognitive process and subjective level of confidence in recognition memory. *Neuroimage, 29*(4), 1150–1160.

Chung, G. H., Flook, L., & Fuligni, A. J. (2009). Daily family conflict and emotional distress among adolescents from Latin American, Asian and European backgrounds. *Developmental Psychology, 45*(5), 1406–1415.

Chung, H. L., & Steinberg, L. (2006). Relations between neighborhood factors, parenting behaviors, peer deviance, and delinquency among serious juvenile offenders. *Developmental Psychology, 42,* 319–331.

Church, T. S., Earnest, C. P. Skinner, J. S., & Blair, S. N. (2007). Effects of different doses of physical activity on cardiorespiratory fitness among sedentary, overweight or obese post-menopausal women with elevated blood pressure. *Journal of the American Medical Association, 297,* 2081–2091.

CIA. (2015). Literacy rates. *CIA World Factbook.* Retrieved from Central Intelligence Agency: www.cia.gov/library/publications/the-world-factbook/fields/2103.html

Cicchetti, D., & Toth, S. L. (1998). The development of depression in children and adolescents. *American Psychologist, 53,* 221–241.

Cicchino, J. B., & Rakison, D. H. (2008). Producing and processing self-propelled motion in infancy. *Developmental Psychology, 44,* 1232–1241.

Cicirelli, V. G. (1989). Feelings of attachment to siblings and well-being in later life. *Psychology and Aging, 4*(2), 211–216.

Cicirelli, V. G. (1994). Sibling relationships in cross-cultural perspective. *Journal of Marriage and Family, 56,* 7–20.

Cicirelli, V. G. (1995). *Sibling relationships across the life span.* New York: Plenum Press.

Cicirelli, V. G. (2006). Fear of death in mid-old age. *The Journals of Gerontology Series B: Psychological Sciences and Social Sciences, 61*(2), P75–P81.

Cicirelli, V. G. (2009). Sibling death and death fear in relation to depressive symptomatology in older adults. *Journals of Gerontology Series B: Psychological Sciences and Social Sciences, 64*(1), 24–32.

Cicirelli, V. G. (Ed.). (2002). *Older adults' views on death.* New York: Springer.

Cillessen, A. H. N., & Mayeux, L. (2004). From censure to reinforcement: Developmental changes in the association between aggression and social status. *Child Development, 75,* 147–163.

Ciorba, A., Bianchini, C., Pelucchi, S., & Pastore, A. (2012). The impact of hearing loss on the quality of life of elderly adults. *Clinical Interventions in Aging, 7*, 159.

Clark, L., & Tiggeman, M. (2008). Sociocultural and individual psychology predictors of body image in young girls: A prospective study. *Developmental Psychology, 44,* 1124–1134.

Clarke, T.C., Norris, T. & Schiller, J.S. (2017). *Early release of selected estimates based on data from 2016 National Health Interview Survey. National Center for Health Statistics. May 2017.* Retrieved from www.cdc.gov/nchs/nhis.htm.

Clayton, P. E., Gill, M. S., Hall, C. M., Tillmann, V., Whatmore, A. J., & Price, D. A. (1997). Serum leptin through childhood and adolescence. *Clinical Endocrinology, 46*(6), 727–733.

Cleary, P. D., Zaborski, L. B., & Ayanian, J. Z. (2004). Sex differences in health over the course of midlife. In O. G. Brim, C. E. Ryff, & R. C. Kessler (Eds.), *How healthy are we? A national study of well-being at midlife.* Chicago: University of Chicago Press.

Clements, M. L., Stanley, S. M., & Markman, H. J. (2004). Before they said "I do": Discriminating among marital outcomes over 13 years. *Journal of Marriage and Family, 66,* 613–626.

Clemmons, N. S., Gastanaduy, P. A., Fiebelkorn, A. P., Redd, S. B., Wallace, G. S., & Centers for Disease Control and Prevention (CDC). (2015). Measles—United States, January 4–April 2, 2015. *MMWR Morb Mortal Wkly Rep, 64*(14), 373–376.

Cleveland, H. H., & Wiebe, R. P. (2003). The moderation of adolescent-to-peer similarity in tobacco and alcohol use by school level of substance use. *Child Development, 74,* 279–291.

Cleveland, J. N., & Lim, A. S. (2007). Employee age and evaluation in organizations. In K. S. Shultz & G. A. Adams (Eds.), *Aging and work in the 21st century* (pp. 109–137). Mahwah, NJ: Lawrence Erlbaum.

Climo, A. H., & Stewart, A. J. (2003). Eldercare and personality development in middle age. In J. Demick & C. Andreoletti (Eds.), *Handbook of adult development.* New York: Plenum Press.

Clinkenbeard, P. R. (2012). Motivation and gifted students: Implications of theory and research. *Psychology in the Schools, 49*(7), 622–630.

Cloak, C. C., Ernst, T., Fujii, L., Hedemark, B., & Chang, L. (2009). Lower diffusion in white matter of children with prenatal methamphetamine exposure. *Neurology, 72*(24), 2068–2975. doi: 10.1212/01.wnl.0000346516.49126.20 Ch. 3

Closa-Monasterolo, R., Gispert-Llaurado, M., Canals, J., Luque, V., Zaragoza-Jordana, M., Koletzko, B., Grote, V., Weber, M., Gruszfeld, D., Scott, K., Verduci, E., ReDionigi, A., Hoyos, J., Brasselle, G., & Escribano Subias, J. (2017). The effect of postpartum depression and current mental health problems of the mother on child behavior at eight years. *Maternal and Child Health Journal, 21,* 1563–1572.

Cobb-Clark, D. A., & Schurer, S. (2012). The stability of big-five personality traits. *Economics Letters, 115*(1), 11–15.

Coffman, J. L., Ornstein, P. A., McCall, L. W., & Curran, P. J. (2008). Linking teachers' memory-relevant language and the development of children's memory skills. *Developmental Psychology, 44,*1640–1654.

Cohen, L. B., & Amsel, L. B. (1998). Precursors to infants' perception of the causality of a simple event. *Infant Behavior and Development, 21,* 713–732.

Cohen, L. B., & Marks, K. S. (2002). How infants process addition and subtraction events. *Developmental Science, 5,* 186–201.

Cohen, L. B., Chaput, H. H., & Cashon, C. H. (2002). A constructivist model of infant cognition. *Cognitive Development, 17,* 1323–1343.

Cohen, P. (2012). *In our prime: The invention of middle age.* New York: Simon and Schuster.

Cohen, S. (2004). Social relationships and health. *American Psychologist, 59,* 676–684.

Cohen, S., & Pressman, S. D. (2006). Positive affect and health. *Current Directions in Psychological Science, 15,* 122–125.

Cohen, S., Doyle, W. J., Skoner, D. P., Rabin, B. S., & Gwaltney, J. M., Jr. (1997). Social ties and susceptibility to the common cold. *Journal of the American Medical Association, 277,* 1940–1944.

Cohen, S., Doyle, W. J., Turner, R. B., Alper, C. M., & Skoner, D. P. (2003). Emotional style and susceptibility to the common cold. *Psychosomatic Medicine, 65,* 652–657.

Cohen, S., Gottlieb, B., & Underwood, L. (2000). Social relationships and health. In S. Cohen, L. Underwood, & B. Gottlieb (Eds.), *Measuring and intervening in social support* (pp. 3–25). New York: Oxford University Press.

Cohen, S., Janicki-Deverts, D., & Miller, G. E. (2007). Psychological stress and disease. *JAMA, 298*(14), 1685–1687.

Cohen, S., Janicki-Deverts, D., Doyle, W. J., Miller, G. E., Frank, E., Rabin, B. S., & Turner, R. B. (2012). Chronic stress, glucocorticoid receptor resistance, inflammation, and disease risk. *Proceedings of the National Academy of Sciences, 109*(16), 5995-5999.

Cohen, S., Janicki-Deverts, D., Turner, R. B., & Doyle, W. J. (2015). Does hugging provide stress-buffering social support? A study of susceptibility to upper respiratory infection and illness. *Psychological Science, 26*(2), 135–147.

Cohen, T. (2011). Mickey Rooney tells Senate panel he was a victim of elder abuse. Retrieved from CNN: www.cnn.com/2011/SHOWBIZ/03/02/rooney.elderly.abuse/index.html

Cohn, D., & Passel, J. S. (2016). *Record 60.6 million Americans live in multigenerational households.* Pew Research Center, Fact Tank.

Cohn, D., & Fry, R. (2010). *Women, men and the new economics of marriage.* Retrieved from http://pewsocialtrends.org/2010/01/19/women-men-and-the-new-economics-of-marriage/

Cohn, D., Passel, J. S., Wang, W., & Livingston, G. (2011). *Barely half of U.S adults are married—a record low.* Pew Research Center. Retrieved from www.pewsocialtrends.org/2011/12/14/barely-half-of-u-s-adults-are-married-a-record-low/

Coie, J. D., & Dodge, K. A. (1998). Aggression and antisocial behavior. In W. Damon (Series Ed.) & N. Eisenberg (Vol. Ed.), *Handbook of child psychology: Vol. 3. Social, emotional, and personality development* (5th ed., pp. 780–862). New York: Wiley.

Coke, M. M., & Twaite, J. A. (1995). *The black elderly: Satisfaction and quality of later life.* New York: Haworth.

Colby, A., Kohlberg, L., Gibbs, J., & Lieberman, M. (1983). A longitudinal study of moral development. *Monographs of the Society for Research in Child Development, 48*(1–2, Serial No. 200).

Colby, S. L., & Ortman, J. M. (2014). *Projections of the size and composition of the U.S. population: 2014 to 2060, current population reports, P25-1143.* Washington, DC: U.S. Census Bureau.

Colcombe, S. J., Erickson, K. I., Scalf, P. E., Kim, J. S., Prakash, R., McAuley, E., . . . Kramer, A. F. (2006). Aerobic exercise training increases brain volume in aging humans. *Journals of Gerontology. Series A, 61*(11), 1166–1170.

Cole, P. M., Barrett, K. C., & Zahn-Waxler, C. (1992). Emotion displays in two-year-olds during mishaps. *Child Development, 63,* 314–324.

Cole, S. W. (2009). Social regulation of human gene expression. *Current Directions in Psychological Science, 18*(3), 132–137.

Coleman, J. S. (1988). Social capital in the creation of human capital. *American Journal of Sociology, 94*(Suppl. 95), S95–S120.

Coleman-Jensen, A., Rabbit, M. P., Gregory, C. A., & Singh, A. (2016). *Household food security in the United States in 2015, ERR-215.* Washington, DC: United States Department of Agriculture, Economic Research Service.

Coles, L. S. (2004). Demography of human supercentenarians. *Journal of Gerontology: Biological Sciences, 59A,* 579–586.

Coley, R. L., Morris, J. E., & Hernandez, D. (2004). Out-of-school care and problem behavior trajectories among low-income adolescents: Individual, family, and neighborhood characteristics as added risks. *Child Development, 75,* 948–965.

Coley, R. L., Votruba-Drzal, E., & Schindler, H. S. (2009). Fathers' and mothers' parenting predicting and responding to adolescent sexual risk behaviors. *Child Development, 80*(3), 808–827.

Coll, C. G., Crnic, K., Lamberty, G., Wasik, B. H., Jenkins, R., Garcia, H. V., & McAdoo, H. P. (1996). An integrative model for the study of developmental competencies in minority children. *Child Development, 67*(5), 1891–1914.

Collins, R. L. (2011). Content analysis of gender roles in media: Where are we now and where should we go? *Sex Roles, 64*(3–4), 290–298.

Collins, W. A., & van Dulmen, M. (2006). Friendships and romance in emerging adulthood: Assessing the distinctiveness in close relationships. In J. J. Arnett & J. L. Tanner (Eds.), *Emerging adults in America: Coming of age in the 21st century* (pp. 219–234). Washington DC: American Psychological Association.

Collins, W. A., Maccoby, E. E., Steinberg, L., Hetherington, E. M., & Bornstein, M. H. (2000). Contemporary research in parenting: The case for nature and nurture. *American Psychologist, 55,* 218-232.

Collins, W.A., Welsh, D.P., & Furman, W, (2009). Adolescent romantic relationships. *Annual Review of Psychology,* 60, 631-652.

Collishaw, S. (2015). Annual research review: secular trends in child and adolescent mental health. *Journal of Child Psychology and Psychiatry,* 56(3), 370-393.

Colman, R. J., Anderson, R. M., Johnson, S. C., Kastman, E. K., Kosmatka, K. J., Beasley, T. M., . . . Weindruch, R. (2009). Caloric restriction delays disease onset and mortality in Rhesus monkeys. *Science, 325*(5937), 201-204.

Colman, R. J., Beasley, T. M., Kemnitz, J. W., Johnson, S. C., Weindruch, R., & Anderson, R. M. (2014). Caloric restriction reduces age-related and all-cause mortality in rhesus monkeys. *Nature Communications,* 5, 3557.

Colombo, J. (2002). Infant attention grows up: The emergence of a developmental cognitive neuroscience perspective. *Current Directions in Psychological Science, 11,* 196-200.

Colombo, J., Kannass, K. N., Shaddy, J., Kundurthi, S., Maikranz, J. M., Anderson, C. J., . . . Carlson, S. E. (2004). Maternal DHA and the development of attention in infancy and toddlerhood. *Child Development, 75,* 1254-1267.

Colombo, J., Shaddy, D. J., Anderson, C. J., Gibson, L. J., Blaga, O. M., & Kannass, K. N. (2010). What habituates in infant visual habituation? A psychophysiological analysis. *Infancy, 15*(2), 107-124.

Colonnesi, C., Stams, G. J. J., Koster, I., & Noom, M. J. (2010). The relation between pointing and language development: A meta-analysis. *Developmental Review,* 30(4), 352-366.

Comer, J., Furr, J., Beidas, R., Weiner, C., & Kendall, P. (2008). Children and terrorism related news: Training parents in coping and media literacy. *Journal of Consulting and Clinical Psychology, 76*(4), 568-578.

Comer, J.S., Bry, L.J., Poznanski, B., & Golik, A.M. (2016). Children's mental health in the context of terrorist attacks, ongoing threats, and possibilities of future terrorism. *Current Psychiatry Reports,* 18. https://doi.org/10.1007/s11920-016-0722-1

Comer, J.S., Furr, J.M., Beidas, R.S., Weiner, C.L., & Kendall, P.C. (2008). Children and terrorism-related news: Training parents in coping and media literacy. *Journal of Consulting and Clinical Psychology,* 76, 568-578.

Committee on Obstetric Practice. (2002). ACOG committee opinion: Exercise during pregnancy and the postpartum period. *International Journal of Gynecology & Obstetrics, 77*(1), 79-81.

Community Paediatrics Committee, Canadian Paediatrics Society. (2005). Management of primary nocturnal enuresis. *Paediatrics and Child Health, 10,* 611-614.

Compas, B. E., & Luecken, L. (2002). Psychological adjustment to breast cancer. *Current Directions in Psychological Science, 11,* 111-114.

Compton, J., & Pollak, R. A. (2014). Family proximity, childcare, and women's labor force attachment. *Journal of Urban Economics, 79,* 72-90.

Conde-Agudelo, A., Rosas-Bermúdez, A., & Kafury-Goeta, A. C. (2006). Birth spacing and risk of adverse perinatal outcomes: A meta-analysis. *Journal of the American Medical Association, 295,* 1809-1823.

Conference Board. (1999, June 25). Workplace education programs are benefiting U.S. corporations and workers [Press release]. Retrieved from www.newswise.com/articles/1999/6/WEP.TCB.html

Connidis, I. A., & Davies, L. (1992). Confidants and companions: Choices in later life. *Journal of Gerontology: Social Sciences, 47*(30), S115-S122.

Consideration of Deferred Action for Childhood Arrivals (DACA), 2016. Retrieved from official website of the Department of Homeland Security: www.uscis.gov/humanitarian/consideration-deferred-action-childhood-arrivals-daca

Constantino, J. N., Grosz, D., Saenger, P., Chandler, D. W., Nandi, R., & Earls, F. J. (1993). Testosterone and aggression in children. *Journal of the Academy of Child and Adolescent Psychiatry, 32,* 1217-1222.

Cook, C. R., Williams, K. R., Guerra, N. G., Kim, T. E., & Sadek, S. (2010). Predictors of bullying and victimization in childhood and adolescence: A meta-analytic investigation. *Social Psychology Quarterly, 25*(2), 65-83.

Cook-Gumperz, J., & Szymanski, M. (2001). Classroom "families": Cooperating or competing-Girls' and boys' interactional styles in a bilingual classroom. *Research on Language and Social Interaction, 34*(1), 107-130.

Cooper, C., Selwood, A., & Livingston, G. (2008). The prevalence of elder abuse and neglect: A systematic review. *Age and Ageing,* 37, 151-160.

Cooper, C. L. (2005). *Handbook of stress medicine and health.* London, England: CRC Press

Cooper, K. L., & Gutmann, D. L. (1987). Gender identity and ego mastery style in middle-aged, pre- and post-empty nest women. *Gerontologist, 27*(3), 347-352.

Cooper, R. P., & Aslin, R. N. (1990). Preference for infant-directed speech in the first month after birth. *Child Development, 61,* 1584-1595.

Cooper, W. O., Hernandez-Diaz, S., Arbogast, P. G., Dudley, J. A., Dyer, S., Gideon, P. S., Hall, K., & Ray, W. A. (2006). Major congenital formations after first-trimester exposure to ACE inhibitors. *New England Journal of Medicine, 354,* 2443-2451.

Copen, C. E., Chandra, A., & Martinez, G. (2012). *Prevalence and timing of oral sex with opposite-sex partners among females and males aged 15-24 years: United States, 2007-2010.* Washington, DC: U.S. Department of Health and Human Services, Centers for Disease Control and Prevention, National Center for Health Statistics.

Copen, C. E., Daniels, K., Vespa, J., & Mosher, W. D. (2012). First marriages in the United States: Data from the 2006-2010 National Survey of Family Growth. *National Health Statistics Reports, 49.* Hyattsville, MD: National Center for Health Statistics.

Coplan, R. J., Prakash, K., O'Neil, K., & Armer, M. (2004). Do you "want" to play? Distinguishing between conflicted-shyness and social disinterest in early childhood. *Developmental Psychology, 40,* 244-258.

Corbelli, J., Borrero, S., Bonnema, R., McNamara, M., Kraemer, K., Rubio, D., . . . & McNeil, M. (2014). Physician adherence to U.S. Preventive Services Task Force mammography guidelines. *Women's Health Issues, 24*(3), e313-e319.

Corcoran, M., & Matsudaira, J. (2005). Is it getting harder to get ahead? Economic attainment in early adulthood for two cohorts. In R. A. Settersten Jr., F. F. Furstenberg Jr., & R. G. Rumbaut (Eds.), *On the frontier of adulthood: Theory, research, and public policy* (pp. 356-395). Chicago: University of Chicago Press.

Coren, S. (2012). *The left-hander syndrome: The causes and consequences of left-handedness.* New York: Simon and Schuster.

Cornwell, B., Laumann, E. O., & Schumm, L. P. (2008). The social connectedness of older adults: A national profile. *American Sociological Review, 73,* 185-203.

Corona, G., Isidori, A. M., Buvat, J., Aversa, A., Rastrelli, G., Hackett, G., . . . & Maggi, M. (2014). Testosterone supplementation and sexual function: A meta-analysis study. *The Journal of Sexual Medicine, 11*(6), 1577-1592.

Corona, G., Rastrelli, G., Morgentaler, A., Sforza, A., Mannucci, E., & Maggi, M. (2017). Meta-analysis of results of testosterone therapy on sexual function based on international index of erectile function scores. *European Urology.* http://dx.doi.org/10.1016/j.eururo.2017.03.032

Correa, A., Botto, L., Liu, V., Mulinare, J., & Erickson, J. D. (2003). Do multivitamin supplements attenuate the risk for diabetes-associated birth defects? *Pediatrics, 111,* 1146-1151.

Correa, A., Gilboa, S. M., Besser, L. M., Botto, L. D., Moore, C. A., Hobbs, C. A., . . . Reece, E. A. (2008). Diabetes mellitus and birth defects. *American Journal of Obstetrics & Gynecology, 199*(237), e1-e9.

Corriveau, K. H., Harris, P. L., Meins, E., Fernyhough, C., Arnott, B., Elliott, L., . . . deRosnay, M. (2009). Young children's trust in their mother's claims: Longitudinal links with attachment security in infancy. *Child Development, 80*(3), 750-761.

Cosgrove, K. P., Mazure, C. M., & Staley, J. K. (2007). Evolving knowledge of sex differences in brain structure, function, and chemistry. *Biological Psychiatry, 62*(8), 847-855.

Cosman, F., De Beur, S. J., LeBoff, M. S., Lewiecki, E. M., Tanner, B., Randall, S., & Lindsay, R. (2014). Clinician's guide to prevention and treatment of osteoporosis. *Osteoporosis International, 25*(10), 2359-2381.

Costa, P. T., Jr., & McCrae, R. R. (2013). *Personality in adulthood: A five-factor theory perspective.* Abingdon-on-Thames, England: Routledge.

Costa, P. T., Jr., & McCrae, R. R. (1980). Still stable after all these years: Personality as a key to some issues in adulthood and old age. In P. B. Baltes Jr. & O. G. Brim (Eds.), *Lifespan development and behavior* (Vol. 3, pp. 65–102). New York: Academic Press.

Costa, P. T., Jr., & McCrae, R. R. (1988). Personality in adulthood: A six-year longitudinal study of self-reports and spouse ratings on the NEO Personality Inventory. *Journal of Personality and Social Psychology, 54,* 853–863.

Costa, P. T., Jr., & McCrae, R. R. (1994a). Set like plaster? Evidence for the stability of adult personality. In T. F. Heatherton & J. L. Weinberger (Eds.), *Can personality change?* (pp. 21–41). Washington, DC: American Psychological Association.

Costa, P. T., Jr., & McCrae, R. R. (1994b). Stability and change in personality from adolescence through adulthood. In C. F. Halverson, G. A. Kohnstamm, & R. P. Martin (Eds.), *The developing structure of temperament and personality from infancy to adulthood.* Hillsdale, NJ: Erlbaum.

Costa, P. T., Jr., & McCrae, R. R. (2006). Age changes in personality and their origins: Comments on Roberts, Walton, and Viechtbauer (2006). *Psychological Bulletin, 1,* 26–28.

Costa, P. T., Jr., McCrae, R. R., Zonderman, A. B., Barbano, H. E., Lebowitz, B., & Larson, D. M. (1986). Cross-sectional studies of personality in a national sample: 2. Stability in neuroticism, extraversion, and openness. *Psychology and Aging, 1,* 144–149.

Costanzo, P. R., & Hoy, M. B. (2007). Intergenerational relations: Themes, prospects, and possibilities. *Journal of Social Issues, 63*(4), 885–902.

Costello, E. J., Compton, S. N., Keeler, G., & Angold, A. (2003). Relationship between poverty and psychopathology: A natural experiment. *Journal of the American Medical Association, 290,* 2023–2029.

Côté, J. E. (2006). Emerging adulthood as an institutionalized moratorium: Risks and benefits to identity formation. In J. J. Arnett & J. L. Tanner (Eds.), *Emerging adults in America: Coming of age in the 21st century* (pp. 85–116). Washington, DC: American Psychological Association.

Cote, L. R., & Bornstein, M. H. (2009). Child and mother play in three U.S. cultural groups: Comparisons and associations. *Journal of Family Psychology, 23*(3), 355–363.

Council on Sports Medicine and Fitness & Council on School Health. (2006). Active healthy living: Prevention of childhood obesity through increased physical activity. *Pediatrics, 117,* 1834–1842.

Courage, M. L., & Howe, M. L. (2002). From infant to child: The dynamics of cognitive change in the second year of life. *Psychological Bulletin, 128,* 250–277.

Courage, M.L., & Howe, M.L. (2010). To watch or not to watch: Infants and toddlers in a brave new electronic world. *Developmental Review, 30,* 101–115.

Courtenay, W. (2011). *Dying to be men: Psychosocial, environmental, and biobehavioral directions in promoting the health of men and boys.* Abingdon-on-Thames, England: Routledge.

Couto, E., Boffetta, P., Lagiou, P., Ferrari, P., Buckland, G., et al. (2011). Mediterranean dietary pattern and cancer risk in the EPIC cohort. *British Journal Cancer, 104*(9), 1493–1499.

Couturier, J., Kimber, M., & Szatmari, P. (2013). Efficacy of family-based treatment for adolescents with eating disorders: A systematic review and meta-analysis. *International Journal of Eating Disorders, 46*(1), 3–11.

Cox, K. S., Wilt, J., Olson, B., & McAdams, D. P. (2010). Generativity, the Big Five, and psychosocial adaptation in midlife adults. *Journal of Personality, 78*(4), 1185–1208.

Cox, M. J., & Paley, B. (2003). Understanding families as systems. *Current Directions in Psychological Science, 12*(5), 193–196.

Craik, F. I. M., & Byrd, M. (1982). Aging and cognitive deficits: The role of attentional resources. In F. I. M. Craik & S. Trehub (Eds.), *Aging and cognitive processes* (pp. 191–221). New York: Plenum Press.

Craik, F. I. M., & Jennings, J. M. (1992). Human memory. In F. I. M. Craik & T. A. Salthouse (Eds.), *Handbook of aging and cognition* (pp. 51–110). Hillsdale, NJ: Erlbaum.

Crandall, C. J., Merkin, S. S., Seeman, T. E., Greendale, G. A., Binkley, N., & Karlamangla, A. S. (2012). Socioeconomic status over the life-course and adult bone mineral density: the Midlife in the US Study. *Bone, 51*(1), 107–113.

Crary, D. (2007, January 6). After years of growth, foreign adoptions by Americans decline sharply. *Associated Press.* Retrieved from www.chron.com/disp/story.mpl/nation/4452317.html

Crawford, J. (2007). The decline of bilingual education: How to reverse a troubling trend? *International Multilingual Research Journal, 1*(1), 33–38.

Crepaz, N., Lyles, C. M., Passin, R. J., Rama, S. M., Herbst, J. H., Malow, R. W., & Stal, R. (2009). Do prevention interventions reduce HIV risk behaviours among people living with HIV? A meta-analytic review of controlled trials. *AIDS, 20*(2), 143–157.

Crews, F., He, J., & Hodge, C. (2007). Adolescent cortical development: a critical period of vulnerability for addiction. *Pharmacology Biochemistry and Behavior, 86*(2), 189–199.

Crick, N. R., & Dodge, K. A. (1996). Social information-processing mechanisms in reactive and proactive aggression. *Child Development, 67,* 993–1002.

Crick, N. R., & Grotpeter, J. K. (1995). Relational aggression, gender, and social psychological adjustment. *Child Development, 66,* 710–722.

Crippen, M. (2017). The value of children's literature. Retrieved from Luther College: www.luther.edu/oneota-reading-journal/archive/2012/the-value-of-childrens-literature

Crockenberg, S. C. (2003). Rescuing the baby from the bathwater: How gender and temperament influence how child care affects child development. *Child Development, 74,* 1034–1038.

Crooks, V. C., Lubben, J., Petitti, D. B., Little, D., & Chiu, V. (2008). Social network, cognitive function, and dementia incidence among elderly women. *American Journal of Public Health, 98,* 1221–1227.

Crosnoe, R., Cavanagh, S., & Elder Jr, G. H. (2003). Adolescent friendships as academic resources: The intersection of friendship, race, and school disadvantage. *Sociological Perspectives, 46*(3), 331–352.

Crouter, A. C., & Manke, B. (1994). The changing American workplace: Implications for individuals and families. *Family Relations, 43,* 117–124.

Crowley, S. L. (1993, October). Grandparents to the rescue. *AARP Bulletin,* pp. 1, 16–17.

Cruzan v. Director, Missouri Department of Health, 110 S. Ct. 2841 (1990).

Csikszentmihalyi, M. (1999). If we are so rich, why aren't we happy? *American Psychologist, 54,* 821–827.

Cuddy, A. J. C., Norton, M. I., & Fiske, S. T. (2005). This old stereotype: The pervasiveness and persistence of the elderly stereotype. *Journal of Social Issues, 61*(2), 267–285.

Cuevas, K., & Bell, M. A. (2010). Developmental progression of looking and reaching performance on the A-not-B task. *Developmental Psychology, 46*(5), 1363.

Cui, M., & Fincham, F. D. (2010). The differential effects of parental divorce and marital conflict on young adult romantic relationships. *Personal Relationships, 17*(3), 331–343.

Cui, M., Conger, R. D., & Lorenz, F. O. (2005). Predicting change in adolescent adjustment from change in marital problems. *Developmental Psychology, 41,* 812–823.

Cui, M., Fincham, F. D., & Durtschi, J. A. (2011). The effect of parental divorce on young adults' romantic relationship dissolution: What makes a difference? *Personal Relationships, 18*(3), 410–426.

Cumming, E., & Henry, W. (1961). *Growing old.* New York: Basic Books.

Cummings, E. M., Koss, K. J., & Davies, P. T. (2015). Prospective relations between family conflict and adolescent maladjustment: Security in the family system as a mediating process. *Journal of Abnormal Child Psychology, 43*(3), 503–515.

Cummings, J. L. (2004). Alzheimer's disease. *New England Journal of Medicine, 351,* 56–67.

Curtin, S. C., Warner, M., & Hedegaard, H. (2016). *Increase in suicide in the United States, 1999-2014.* Washington, DC: U.S. Department of Health and Human Services, Centers for Disease Control and Prevention, National Center for Health Statistics.

Cutler, D. M., Ghosh, K., & Landrum, M. B. (2013). *Evidence for significant compression of morbidity in the elderly US population* (No. w19268). Cambridge, MA: National Bureau of Economic Research.

Cutrona, C. E., Wallace, G., & Wesner, K. A. (2006). Neighborhood characteristics and depressions: An examination of stress processes. *Current Directions in Psychological Science, 15,* 188–192.

Cytrynbaum, S., Bluum, L., Patrick, R., Stein, J., Wadner, D., & Wilk, C. (1980). Midlife development: A personality and social systems perspective. In L. Poon (Ed.), *Aging in the 1980s.* Washington, DC: American Psychological Association.

Czaja, A. J., & Sharit, J. (1998). Ability-performance relationships as a function of age and task experience for a data entry task. *Journal of Experimental Psychology–Applied, 4,* 332–351.

Czaja, S. J. (2006). Employment and the baby boomers: What can we expect in the future? In S. K. Whitbourne & S. L. Willis (Eds.), *The baby boomers grow up: Contemporary perspectives on midlife* (pp. 283-298). Mahwah, NJ: Erlbaum.

Çalışkan, M., Bochkov, Y. A., Kreiner-Møller, E., Bønnelykke, K., Stein, M. M., Du, G., . . . & Nicolae, D. L. (2013). Rhinovirus wheezing illness and genetic risk of childhood-onset asthma. *New England Journal of Medicine, 368*(15), 1398-1407.

Čukić, I., Brett, C. E., Calvin, C. M., Batty, G. D., & Deary, I. J. (2017). Childhood IQ and survival to 79: Follow-up of 94% of the Scottish Mental Survey 1947. *Intelligence, 63*, 45-50.

D'Epinay, C. J. L., Cavalli, S., & Guillet, L. A. (2010). Bereavement in very old age: impact on health and relationships of the loss of a spouse, a child, a sibling, or a close friend. *OMEGA-Journal of Death and Dying, 60*(4), 301-325.

Dale, P. S., Simonoff, E., Bishop, D. V. M., Eley, T. C., Oliver, B., Price, T. S., . . . Plomin, R. (1998). Genetic influence on language delay in two-year-old children. *Nature Neuroscience, 1*, 324-328.

Daly, M., & Wilson, M. (1988). *Homicide.* Hawthorne, NY: Aldine de Gruyter.

Daly, R. (2005). Drop in youth antidepressant use prompts call for FDA monitoring. *Psychiatric News, 40*(19), 18.

Danaei, G., Rimm, E. B., Oza, S., Kulkarni, S. C., Murray, C. J. L., & Ezzati, M. (2010). The promise of prevention: The effects of four preventable risk factors on national life expectancy and life expectancy disparities by race and county in the United States. *PLoS Medicine, 7*(3) e1000248. doi:10.1371/journal.pmed.1000248

Daniel, J. (2012). Making sense of MOOCs: Musing in a maze of myth, paradox and possibility. *Journal of Interactive Media in Education, 18*(3), 1-20.

Darling, N., & Steinberg, L. (1993). Parenting style as context: An integrative model. *Psychological Bulletin, 113*, 487-496.

Darling, N., Kolasa, M., & Wooten, K. G. (2008). National, state, and local area vaccination coverage among children aged 19-35 months—United States, 2007. *Morbidity & Mortality Weekly Report, 57*(35), 961-966.

Darroch, J. E., Singh, S., Frost, J. J., & the Study Team. (2001). Differences in teenage pregnancy rates among five developed countries: The roles of sexual activity and contraceptive use. *Family Planning Perspectives, 33*, 244-250, 281.

Dart, R. C., Surratt, H. L., Cicero, T. J., Parrino, M. W., Severtson, S. G., Bucher-Bartelson, B., & Green, J. L. (2015). Trends in opioid analgesic abuse and mortality in the United States. *New England Journal of Medicine, 372*(3), 241-248.

Dasen, P. R. (1984). The cross-cultural study of intelligence: Piaget and the Baoule. *International Journal of Psychology, 19*(1-4), 407-434.

Datar, A., & Sturm, R. (2004a). Childhood overweight and parent- and teacher-reported behavior problems. *Archives of Pediatric and Adolescent Medicine, 158*, 804-810.

Datar, A., & Sturm, R. (2004b). Duke physical education in elementary school and body mass index: Evidence from the Early Childhood Longitudinal Study. *American Journal of Public Health, 94*, 1501-1507.

Daugherty, M., & White, C. S. (2008). Relationships among private speech and creativity in Head Start and low-socioeconomic status preschool children. *Gifted Child Quarterly, 52*(1), 30-39.

David and Lucile Packard Foundation. (2004). Children, families, and foster care: Executive summary. *Future of Children, 14*(1). Retrieved from www.futureofchildren.org

Davidson, K. (2001). Late life widowhood, selfishness and new partnership choices: A gendered perspective. *Ageing & Society, 21*(3), 297-317.

Davidson, N. E. (1995). Hormone-replacement therapy—Breast versus heart versus bone. *New England Journal of Medicine, 332*, 1638-1639.

Davidson, R. J., Jackson, D. C., & Kalin, N. H. (2000). Emotion, plasticity, context, and regulation: perspectives from affective neuroscience. *Psychological Bulletin, 126*(6), 890.

Davies, C., & Williams, D. (2002). *The grandparent study 2002 report.* Washington, DC: American Association of Retired Persons.

Daviglus, M. L., Bell, C. C., Berrettini, W., Bowen, P. E., Connolly, E. S., Cox, N. J., . . . Trevisan, M. (2010). Preventing Alzheimer's disease and cognitive decline. *NIH Consensus State-of-the-Science Statements, 27*(4), 1-30.

Davis, A. M., Bennett, K. J., Befort, C., & Nollen, N. (2011). Obesity and related health behaviors among urban and rural children in the United States: data from the National Health and Nutrition Examination Survey 2003-2004 and 2005-2006. *Journal of Pediatric Psychology, 36*(6), 669-676.

Davis, A. S. (2008). Children with Down syndrome: Implications for assessment and intervention in the school. *School Psychology Quarterly, 23*, 271-281.

Davis, M., & Emory, E. (1995). Sex differences in neonatal stress reactivity. *Child Development, 66*, 14-27.

Davis, O. S. P., Haworth, C. M. A., & Plomin, R. (2009). Dramatic increases in heritability of cognitive development from early to middle childhood: An 8-year longitudinal study of 8,700 pairs of twins. *Psychological Science, 20*(10), 1301-1308.

Davis, S. W., Kragel, J. E., Madden, D. J., & Cabeza, R. (2011). The architecture of cross-hemispheric communication in the aging brain: linking behavior to functional and structural connectivity. *Cerebral Cortex, 22*(1), 232-242.

Davis-Kean, P. E. (2005). The influence of parent education and family income on child achievement: The indirect role of parental expectation and the home environment. *Journal of Family Psychology, 19*(2), 294-304.

Davison, K. K., & Birch, L. L. (2001). Weight status, parent reaction, and self-concept in 5-year-old girls. *Pediatrics, 107*, 46-53.

Davison, K. K., Susman, E. J., & Birch, L. L. (2003). Percent body fat at age 5 predicts earlier pubertal development among girls at age 9. *Pediatrics, 111*, 815-821.

Dawson, M. A., & Kouzarides, T. (2012). Cancer epigenetics: from mechanism to therapy. *Cell, 150*(1), 12-27.

Day, J. C., Janus, A., & Davis, J. (2005). Computer and Internet use in the United States: 2003. *Current Population Reports*, P23-208. Washington, DC: U.S. Census Bureau.

Day, K. L., & Smith, C. L. (2013). Understanding the role of private speech in children's emotion regulation. *Early Childhood Research Quarterly, 28*(2), 405-414.

de Castro, B. O., Veerman, J. W., Koops, W., Bosch, J. D., & Monshouwer, H. J. (2002). Hostile attribution of intent and aggressive behavior: A meta-analysis. *Child Development, 73*, 916-934.

de Kieviet, J. F., Piek, J. P., Aarnoudse-Moens, C. S., & Oosterlaan, J. (2009). Motor development in very preterm and very-low-birth-weight children from birth to adolescence. *Journal of the American Medical Association, 302*(20), 2235-2242. doi: 10.1001/jama.2009.1708

De Lima, L., Woodruff, R., Pettus, K., Downing, J., Buitrago, R., Munyoro, E., Venkateswaran, C., Bhatnagar, S., & Radbruch, L. (2017). International Association for Hospice and Palliative Care position statement: Euthanasia and physician-assisted suicide. *Journal of Palliative Medicine, 20*, 8-14.

De Villiers, T. J., Gass, M. L. S., Haines, C. J., Hall, J. E., Lobo, R. A., Pierroz, D. D., & Rees, M. (2013). Global consensus statement on menopausal hormone therapy. *Climacteric, 16*(2), 203-204.

de Vries, B. (1996). The understanding of friendship: An adult life course perspective. In C. Magai & S. H. McFadden (Eds.), *Handbook of emotion, adult development, and aging* (pp. 249-269). San Diego: Academic Press.

Deary, I. J., Penke, L., & Johnson, W. (2010). The neuroscience of human intelligence differences. *Nature reviews. Neuroscience, 11*(3), 201.

Death with Dignity. (2018). Take action: Death with dignity around the U.S. [map]. Retrieved from www.deathwithdignity.org/take-action/

Deave, T., Heron, J., Evans, J., & Emond, A. (2008). The impact of maternal depression in pregnancy on early child development. *BJOG: An International Journal of Obstetrics & Gynaecology, 115*(8), 1043-1051.

DeBell, M., & Chapman, C. (2006). *Computer and Internet use by students in 2003: Statistical analysis report* (NCES 2006-065). Washington, DC: National Center for Education Statistics.

Debnath, M., Venkatasubramanian, G., & Berk, M. (2015). Fetal programming of schizophrenia: select mechanisms. *Neuroscience & Biobehavioral Reviews, 49*, 90-104.

DeCasper, A. J., Lecanuet, J. P., Busnel, M. C., Granier-Deferre, C., & Maugeais, R. (1994). Fetal reactions to recurrent maternal speech. *Infant Behavior and Development, 17*, 159-164.

Decety, J., Michalska, K., Akitsuki, Y., & Lahey, B. (2009). Atypical empathetic responses in adolescents with aggressive conduct disorder: A functional MRI investigation. *Biological Psychology, 80,* 203–211.

Decker, M. L., Chavez, E., Vulto, I., & Lansdorp, P. M. (2009). Telomere length in Hutchinson-Gilford progeria syndrome. *Mechanisms of Ageing and Development, 130*(6), 377–383.

Dee, T. S., & Jacob, B. (2011). The impact of No Child Left Behind on student achievement. *Journal of Policy Analysis and management, 30*(3), 418–446.

DeHaan, L. G., & MacDermid, S. M. (1994). Is women's identity achievement associated with the expression of generativity? Examining identity and generativity in multiple roles. *Journal of Adult Development, 1,* 235–247.

Del Boca, D. (2015). *Child care arrangements and labor supply* (No. IDB-WP-569). IDB Working Paper Series.

Deli, E., Bakle, I., & Zachopoulou, E. (2006). Implementing intervention movement programs for kindergarten children. *Journal of Early Childhood Research, 4*(1), 5–18.

DeLoache, J. S. (2011). Early development of the understanding and use of symbolic artifacts. *The Wiley-Blackwell Handbook of Childhood Cognitive Development* (pp. 312–336). Hoboken, NJ: Wiley.

DeLoache, J. S., LoBue, V., Vanderborght, M., & Chiong, C. (2013). On the validity and robustness of the scale error phenomenon in early childhood. *Infant Behavior and Development, 36*(1), 63–70.

DeLoache, J. S., Pierroutsakos, S. L., & Uttal, D. H. (2003). The origins of pictorial competence. *Current Directions in Psychological Science, 12,* 114–118.

DeLoache, J. S., Uttal, D. H., & Rosengren, K. S. (2004). Scale errors offer evidence for a perception-action dissociation early in life. *Science, 304,* 1027–1029.

DeLoache, J., & Gottlieb, A. (2000). If Dr. Spock were born in Bali: Raising a world of babies. In J. DeLoache & A. Gottlieb (Eds.), *A world of babies: Imagined childcare guides for seven societies* (pp. 1–27). New York: Cambridge University Press.

DeMaris, A. (2009). Distal and proximal influences on the risk of extramarital sex: A prospective study of longer duration marriages. *Journal of Sex Research, 46*(6), 597–607.

Deming, D. (2009). Early childhood intervention and life-cycle skill development: Evidence from Head Start. *American Economic Journal: Applied Economics, 1*(3), 111–134.

Deng, K., Liu, Z., Lin, Y., Mu, D., Chen, X., Li, J., . . . & Li, S. (2013). Periconceptional paternal smoking and the risk of congenital heart defects: A case-control study. *Birth Defects Research Part A: Clinical and Molecular Teratology, 97*(4), 210–216.

Deng, W., Aimone, J. B., & Gage, F. H. (2010). New neurons and new memories: How does adult hippocampal neurogenesis affect learning and memory? *Nature reviews. Neuroscience, 11*(5), 339.

Denham, S. A., Blair, K. A., DeMulder, E., Levitas, J., Sawyer, K., Auerbach-Major, S., & Queenan, P. (2003). Preschool emotional competence: Pathway to social competence? *Child Development, 74,* 238–256.

Denissen, J. J. A., Asendorpf, J. B., & van Aken, M. A. G. (2008). Childhood personality predicts long-term trajectories of shyness and aggressiveness in the context of demographic transitions in emerging adulthood. *Journal of Personality, 76,* 67–99.

Denissen, J. J. A., van Aken, M. A. G., & Dubas, J. S. (2009). It takes two to tango: How parents' and adolescents' personalities link to the quality of their mutual relationship. *Developmental Psychology, 45*(4), 928–941.

Dennis, T. (2006). Emotional self-regulation in preschoolers: The interplay of child approach reactivity, parenting, and control capacities. *Developmental Psychology, 42,* 84–97.

Department of Immunization, Vaccines, and Biologicals, World Health Organization; United Nations Children's Fund; Global Immunization Division, National Center for Immunization and Respiratory Diseases (proposed); & McMorrow, M. (2006). Vaccine preventable deaths and the global immunization vision and strategy, 2006–2015. *Morbidity and Mortality Weekly Report, 55,* 511–515.

Depp, C. A., & Jeste, D. V. (2009). Definitions and predictors of successful aging: A comprehensive review of larger quantitative studies. *Focus, 7,* 137–150.

Deptula, D. P., Henry, D. B., & Schoeny, M. E. (2010). How can parents make a difference? Longitudinal associations with adolescent sexual behavior. *Journal of Family Psychology, 24*(6), 731.

Der, G., Batty, G. D., & Deary, I. J. (2009). The association between IQ in adolescence and a range of health outcomes at 40 in the 1979 US National Longitudinal Study of Youth. *Intelligence, 37*(6), 573–580.

Desai, M., Pratt, L. A., Lentzner, H., & Robinson, K. N. (2001). Trends in vision and hearing among older Americans. *Aging Trends,* No. 2. Hyattsville, MD: National Center for Health Statistics.

Detering, K. M., Hancock, A. D., Reade, M. C., & Silvester, W. (2010). The impact of advance care planning on end of life care in elderly patients: Randomised controlled trial. *British Medical Journal, 340,* 1345. doi:10.1136/bmj.c1345

Deutsch, F. M., Servis, L. J., & Payne, J. D. (2001). Paternal participation in child care and its effects on children's self-esteem and attitudes toward gender roles. *Journal of Family Issues, 22*(8), 1000–1024.

Devine, R. T., & Hughes, C. (2014). Relations between false belief understanding and executive function in early childhood: A meta-analysis. *Child Development, 85*(5), 1777–1794.

Devoe, J. E., Ray, M., Krois, L., & Carlson, M. J. (2010). Uncertain health insurance coverage and unmet children's health care needs. *Family Medicine, 42*(2), 121–132.

Dew, J. (2011). The association between consumer debt and the likelihood of divorce. *Journal of Family and Economic Issues, 32*(4), 554–565.

Dew, J., & Wilcox, W. B. (2011). If Momma ain't happy: Explaining declines in marital satisfaction among new mothers. *Journal of Marriage and Family, 73*(1), 1–12.

Dewey, J. (1997). *How we think.* North Chelmsford, MA: Courier Corporation.

Dey, E. L., & Hurtado, S. (1999). Students, colleges and society: Considering the interconnections. In P. G. Altbach, R. O. Berndahl, & P. J. Gumport (Eds.), *American higher education in the twenty-first century: Social, political and economic challenges* (pp. 298–322). Baltimore, MD: Johns Hopkins University Press.

DeYoung, C. G., Quilty, L. C., Peterson, J. B., & Gray, J. R. (2014). Openness to experience, intellect, and cognitive ability. *Journal of Personality Assessment, 96*(1), 46–52.

Dhabhar, F. S. (2014). Effects of stress on immune function: the good, the bad, and the beautiful. *Immunologic Research, 58*(2–3), 193–210.

Diamond, A. (1991). Neuropsychological insights into the meaning of object concept development. In S. Carey & R. Gelman (Eds.), *Epigensis of mind* (pp. 67–110). Hillsdale, NJ: Erlbaum.

Diamond, A. (2002). Normal development of prefrontal cortex from birth to young adulthood: Cognitive functions, anatomy, and biochemistry. In D. T. Strauss & R. T. Knight (Eds.), *Principles of frontal lobe function* (pp. 466–503). New York: Oxford University Press.

Diamond, A., & Lee, K. (2011). Interventions shown to aid executive function development in children 4 to 12 years old. *Science, 333*(6045), 959–964.

Diamond, L. M., & Savin-Williams, R. C. (2003). The intimate relationships of sexual-minority youths. In G. R. Adams & M. D. Berzonsky (Eds.), *Blackwell handbook of adolescence* (pp. 393–412). Malden, MA: Blackwell.

Diamond, M. (2013). Transsexuality among twins: Identity concordance, transition, rearing, and orientation. *International Journal of Transgenderism, 14*(1), 24–38.

Diamond, M., & Sigmundson, H. K. (1997). Sex reassignment at birth: Longterm review and clinical implications. *Archives of Pediatric and Adolescent Medicine, 151,* 298–304.

DiCarlo, A. L., Fuldner, R., Kaminski, J., & Hodes, R. (2009). Aging in the context of immunological architecture, function and disease outcomes. *Trends in Immunology, 30*(7), 293–294.

Dick, D. M., Rose, R. J., Kaprio, J., & Viken, R. (2000). Pubertal timing and substance use: Associations between and within families across late adolescence. *Developmental Psychology, 36,* 180–189.

Dickens, W. T., & Flynn, J. R. (2006). Black Americans reduce the racial IQ gap: Evidence from standardization samples. *Psychological Science, 17*(10), 913–920.

Dien, D. S. F. (1982). A Chinese perspective on Kohlberg's theory of moral development. *Developmental Review, 2,* 331–341.

Diener, E. (2000). Subjective well-being: The science of happiness and a proposal for a national index. *American Psychologist, 55*, 34–43.

Diener, E., & Chan, M. Y. (2011). Happy people live longer: Subjective well-being contributes to health and longevity. *Applied Psychology: Health and Well-Being, 3*(1), 1–43.

Dietert, R. R. (2005). Developmental immunotoxicology (DIT): Is DIT testing necessary to ensure safety? *Proceedings of the 14th Immunotoxicology Summer School, Lyon, France, October 2005, 246–257.*

DiFranza, J. R., Aligne, C. A., & Weitzman, M. (2004). Prenatal and postnatal environmental tobacco smoke exposure and children's health. *Pediatrics, 113*, 1007–1015.

Dijk, D. J., Groeger, J. A., Stanley, N., & Deacon, S. (2010). Age-related reduction in daytime sleep propensity and nocturnal slow wave sleep. *Sleep, 33*(2), 211–223.

Dijkstra, J. K., Berger, C., & Lindenberg, S. (2011). Do physical and relational aggression explain adolescents' friendship selection? The competing roles of network characteristics, gender, and social status. *Aggressive Behavior, 37*(5), 417–429.

Dilworth-Anderson, P., Williams, I. C., & Gibson, B. E. (2002). Issues of race, ethnicity, and culture in caregiving research: A 20-year review (1980–2000). *The Gerontologist, 42*(2), 237–272.

Dilworth-Bart, J. E., & Moore, C. F. (2006). Mercy mercy me: Social injustice and the prevention of environmental pollutant exposures among ethnic minority and poor children. *Child Development, 77*(2), 247–265.

DiMarco, M. A., Menke, E. M., & McNamara, T. (2001). Evaluating a support group for perinatal loss. *MCN American Journal of Maternal and Child Nursing, 26*, 135–140.

Dingemans, E., & Henkens, K. (2015). How do retirement dynamics influence mental well-being in later life? A 10-year panel study. *Scandinavian Journal of Work, Environment & Health, 41*(1), 16–23.

DiPietro, J. A. (2004). The role of prenatal maternal stress in child development. *Current Directions in Psychological Science, 13*(2), 71–74.

DiPietro, J. A., Bornstein, M. H., Costigan, K. A., Pressman, E. K., Hahn, C. S., Painter, K., Smith, B. A., & Yi, L. J. (2002). What does fetal movement predict about behavior during the first two years of life? *Developmental Psychobiology, 40*(4), 358–371.

DiPietro, J. A., Kivlighan, K. T., Costigan, K. A., Rubin, S. E., Shiffler, D. E., Henderson, J. L., & Pillion, J. P. (2010). Prenatal antecedents of newborn neurological maturation. *Child Development, 81*(1), 115–130. doi: 10.1111/j.1467-8624.2009.01384.x

DiPietro, J. A., Novak, M. F. S. X., Costigan, K. A., Atella, L. D., & Reusing, S. P. (2006). Maternal psychological distress during pregnancy in relation to child development at age 2. *Child Development, 77*(3), 573–587.

Direkvand-Moghadam, A., Sayehmiri, K., Delpisheh, A., & Kaikhavandi, S. (2014). Epidemiology of Premenstrual Syndrome (PMS): A systematic review and meta-analysis study. *Journal of Clinical and Diagnostic Research: JCDR, 8*(2), 106.

Dirix, C. E. H., Nijhuis, J. G., Jongsma, H. W., & Hornstra, G. (2009). Aspects of fetal learning and memory. *Child Development, 80*(4), 1251–1258.

Dishion, T. J., & Stormshak, E. (2007). *Intervening in children's lives: An ecological, family-centered approach to mental healthcare.* Washington, DC: APA Books.

Dishion, T. J., & Tipsord, J. M. (2011). Peer contagion in child and adolescent social and emotional development. *Annual Review of Psychology, 62*, 189–214.

Dishion, T. J., McCord, J., & Poulin, F. (1999). When intervention harms. *American Psychologist, 54*, 755–764.

Dishion, T. J., Shaw, D., Connell, A., Gardner, F., Weaver, C., & Wilson, M. (2008). The family check-up with high-risk indigent families: Preventing problem behavior by increasing parents' positive behavior support in early childhood. *Child Development, 79*, 1395–1414.

Dittmar, H., Halliwell, E., & Ive, S. (2006). Does Barbie make girls want to be thin? The effect of experimental exposure to images of dolls on the body image of 5- to 8-year-old girls. *Developmental Psychology, 42*, 283–292.

Dixon, R. A., & Hultsch, D. F. (1999). Intelligence and cognitive potential in late life. In J. C. Cavanaugh & S. K. Whitbourne (Eds.), *Gerontology: An interdisciplinary perspective.* New York: Oxford University Press.

Doaga, D., & Lee, T. (2008). What could be behind your elderly patient's subjective memory complaints? *Journal of Family Practice, 57*(3), 333–334.

Doak, C. M., Visscher, T. L. S., Renders, C. M., & Seidell, J. C. (2006). The prevention of overweight and obesity in children and adolescents: a review of interventions and programmes. *Obesity Reviews, 7*(1), 111–136.

Dobriansky, P. J., Suzman, R. M., & Hodes, R. J. (2007). *Why population aging matters: A global perspective.* Washington, DC: U.S. Department of State and Department of Health and Human Services, National Institute on Aging, & National Institutes of Health.

Dodge, K. A., Coie, J. D., & Lynam, D. (2006). Aggression and antisocial behavior in youth. In N. Eisenberg, W. Damon, & R. Lerner (Eds.), *Handbook of Child Psychology: Vol. 3, Social, emotional and personality development* (6th ed., pp. 719–788). Hoboken, NJ: Wiley.

Dodge, K. A., Coie, J. D., Pettit, G. S., & Price, J. M. (1990). Peer status and aggression in boys' groups: Developmental and contextual analysis. *Child Development, 61*, 1289–1309.

Dodge, K. A., Pettit, G. S., & Bates, J. E. (1994). Socialization mediators of the relation between socioeconomic status and child conduct problems. *Child Development, 65*, 649–665.

Dodson, C. S., & Schacter, D. L. (2002). Aging and strategic retrieval processes: Reducing false memories with a distinctiveness heuristic. *Psychology and Aging, 17*(3), 405–415.

Doherty, W. J., Kouneski, E. F., & Erickson, M. F. (1998). Responsible fathering: An overview and conceptual framework. *Journal of Marriage and Family, 60*, 277–292.

Doka, K. J., & Mertz, M. E. (1988). The meaning and significance of great-grandparenthood. *Gerontologist, 28*(2), 192–197.

Dolan, M. A., & Hoffman, C. D. (1998). Determinants of divorce among women: A reexamination of critical influences. *Journal of Divorce and Remarriage, 28*, 97–106.

Dolbin-MacNab, M. L., & Hayslip Jr, B. (2014). Grandparents raising grandchildren. *Family Problems: Stress, Risk, and Resilience,* 133–149.

Doley, R., Bell, R., Watt, B., & Simpson, H. (2015). Grandparents raising grandchildren: investigating factors associated with distress among custodial grandparent. *Journal of Family Studies, 21*(2), 101–119.

Dolinoy, D. C., & Jirtle, R. L. (2008). Environmental epigenomics in human health and disease. *Environmental and Molecular Mutagenesis, 49*, 4–8.

Domènech Rodriguez, M. M., Donovick, M. R., & Crowley, S. L. (2009). Parenting styles in a cultural context: Observations of "protective parenting" in first-generation Latinos. *Family Process, 48*(2), 195–210.

Dong, J. Y., Zhang, Y. H., & Qin, L. Q. (2011). Erectile dysfunction and risk of cardiovascular disease: meta-analysis of prospective cohort studies. *Journal of the American College of Cardiology, 58*(13), 1378–1385.

Donnellan, M. B., & Lucas, R. E. (2008). Age differences in the big five across the life span: Evidence from two national samples. *Psychology and Aging, 23*(3), 558–566.

Dopp, A. R., & Cain, A. C. (2012). The role of peer relationships in parental bereavement during childhood and adolescence. *Death Studies, 36*(1), 41–60.

Dorfman, L. T. (2009). Ten years later: A follow-up study of professors still working after age 70. *Educational Gerontology, 35*(11), 1032–1045.

Dorfman, L. T., & Kolarik, D. C. (2005). Leisure and the retired professor: Occupation matters. *Educational Gerontology, 31*(5), 343–361.

Doughty, S. E., Lam, C. B., Stanik, C. E., & McHale, S. M. (2015). Links between sibling experiences and romantic competence from adolescence through young adulthood. *Journal of Youth and Adolescence, 44*(11), 2054–2066.

Downing-Matibag, T. (2009). Parents' perceptions of their adolescent children, parental resources, and parents' satisfaction with the parent-child relationship. *Sociological Spectrum, 29*(4), 467–488.

Dowshen, S., Crowley, J., & Palusci, V. J. (2004). *Shaken baby/shaken impact syndrome.* Retrieved from www.kidshealth.org/parent/medical/brain/shaken.html

Doyle, M., O'Dywer, C., & Timonen, V. (2010). "How can you just cut off a whole side of the family and say move On?" The reshaping of paternal grandparent-grandchild relationships following divorce or separation in the middle generation. *Family Relations, 59*(5), 587–598.

Drageset, J., Kirkevold, M., & Espehaug, B. (2011). Loneliness and social support among nursing home residents without cognitive impairment: A questionnaire survey. *International Journal of Nursing Studies, 48*(5), 611-619.

Drake, B. (2013). As more Americans have contacts with gays and lesbians, social acceptance rises. *Pew Research Center.*

Drewnowski, A. (2009). Obesity, diets, and social inequalities. *Nutrition Reviews, 67,* S36-S39.

Dreyfus, H. L. (1993-1994, Winter). What computers still can't do. *Key Reporter,* 4-9.

Drijber, B. C., Reijnders, U. J. L., & Ceelen, M. (2013). Male victims of domestic violence. *Journal of Family Violence, 28,* 173-178.

Drury, J., & Williams, R. (2012). Children and young people who are refugees, internally displaced persons or survivors or perpetrators of war, mass violence and terrorism. *Current Opinion in Psychiatry, 25,* 277-284.

Dube, S. R., Anda, R. F., Felitti, V. J., Chapman, D. P., Williamson, D. F., & Giles, W. H. (2001). Childhood abuse, household dysfunction, and the risk of attempted suicide throughout the life span: Findings from the Adverse Childhood Experiences Study. *Journal of the American Medical Association, 286*(24), 3089-3096.

Dube, S. R., Felitti, V. J., Dong, M., Chapman, D. P., Giles, W. H., & Anda, R. F. (2003, March). Childhood abuse, neglect, and household dysfunction and the risk of illicit drug use: The Adverse Childhood Experiences Study. *Pediatrics, 111*(3), 564-572.

Dubicka, B., Elvins, R., Roberts, C., Chick, G., Wilkinson, P., & Goodyer, I. M. (2010). Combined treatment with cognitive-behavioural therapy in adolescent depression: meta-analysis. *The British Journal of Psychiatry, 197*(6), 433-440.

Dubowitz, H. (1999). The families of neglected children. In M. E. Lamb (Ed.), *Parenting and child development in "nontraditional" families* (pp. 327-345). Mahwah, NJ: Erlbaum.

Dubowitz, H., Kim, J., Black, M. M., Weisbart, C., Semiatin, J., & Magder, L. S. (2011). Identifying children at high risk for a child maltreatment report. *Child Abuse & Neglect, 35*(2), 96-104.

Duchek, J. M., Balota, D. A., Storandt, M., & Larsen, R. (2007). The power of personality in discriminating between healthy aging and early-stage Alzheimer's disease. *Journals of Gerontology, 62*(6, Series A), 353-361.

Duckworth, A. L., Gendler, T. S., & Gross, J. J. (2014). Self-control in school-age children. *Educational Psychologist, 49*(3), 199-217.

Duckworth, A. L., Quinn, P. D., & Tsukayama, E. (2012). What No Child Left Behind leaves behind: The roles of IQ and self-control in predicting standardized achievement test scores and report card grades. *Journal of Educational Psychology, 104*(2), 439.

Duckworth, A., & Seligman, M. E. P. (2005). Self-discipline outdoes IQ in predicting academic performance of adolescents. *Psychological Science, 26,* 939-944.

Duff, J. (2014). *Why the increase in autism (ASD), ADHD and neurodevelopmental disorders?* Retrieved from Australian Autism ADHD Foundation: www.autism-adhd.org.au/autism_prevalence

Duggan, M. (2014). 5 facts about Americans' views on life-and-death issues. *Pew Research Center.* Retrieved from www.pewresearch.org/fact-tank/2014/01/07/5-facts-about-americans-views-on-life-and-death-issues/

Duggan, M., Singleton, P., & Song, J. (2007). Aching to retire? The rise in the full retirement age and its impact on the Social Security disability rolls. *Journal of Public Economics, 91*(7-8), 1327-1350.

Duke, J., Huhman, M., & Heitzler, C. (2003). Physical activity levels among children aged 9-13 years—United States, 2002. *Morbidity and Mortality Weekly Report, 52,* 785-788.

Duley, J., & Adams, R. (2013). Aging and driving II: Implications of cognitive changes. *Human Performance, Situation Awareness, and Automation: Current Research and Trends HPSAA II.*

Duncan, J. R., Paterson, D. S., Hoffman, J. M., Mokler, D. J., Borenstein, N. S., Belliveau, R. A., . . . Kinney, H. C. (2010). Brainstem serotonergic deficiency in sudden infant death syndrome. *Journal of the American Medical Association, 303*(5), 430-437. doi: 10.1001/jama.2010.45

Dunfield, K. A., & Kuhlmeier, V. A. (2013). Classifying prosocial behavior: Children's responses to instrumental need, emotional distress, and material desire. *Child Development, 84*(5), 1766-1776.

Dunfield, K., Kuhlmeier, V. A., O'Connell, L., & Kelley, E. (2011). Examining the diversity of prosocial behavior: Helping, sharing, and comforting in infancy. *Infancy, 16*(3), 227-247.

Dunham, P., Dunham, F., & O'Keefe, C. (2000). Two-year-olds' sensitivity to a parent's knowledge state: Mind reading or contextual cues? *British Journal of Developmental Psychology, 18*(4), 519-532.

Dunn, A. L., Trivedi, M. H., Kampert, J. B., Clark, C. G., & Chambliss, H. O. (2005). Exercise treatment for depression: Efficacy and dose response. *American Journal of Preventive Medicine, 28,* 1-8.

Dunn, J. (1991). Young children's understanding of other people: Evidence from observations within the family. In D. Frye & C. Moore (Eds.), *Children's theories of mind: Mental states and social understanding.* Hillsdale, NJ: Erlbaum.

Dunn, J. (2006). Moral development in early childhood and social interaction in the family. In M. Killen & J. Smetana (Eds.), *Handbook of moral development* (pp. 331-350). Mahwah, NJ: Earlbaum.

Dunn, J., & Hughes, C. (2001). "I got some swords and you're dead!": Violent fantasy, antisocial behavior, friendship, and moral sensibility in young children. *Child Development, 72,* 491-505.

Dunn, J., & Munn, P. (1985). Becoming a family member: Family conflict and the development of social understanding in the second year. *Child Development, 56,* 480-492.

Dunson, D. B., Colombo, B., & Baird, D. D. (2002). Changes with age in the level and duration of fertility in the menstrual cycle. *Human Reproduction, 17,* 1399-1403.

DuPaul, G. J., & Stoner, G. (2014). *ADHD in the schools: Assessment and intervention strategies.* New York: Guilford Publications.

DuPont, R. L. (1983). Phobias in children. *Journal of Pediatrics, 102,* 999-1002.

Durazzo, T. C., Mattsson, N., Weiner, M. W., & Alzheimer's Disease Neuroimaging Initiative. (2014). Smoking and increased Alzheimer's disease risk: a review of potential mechanisms. *Alzheimer's & Dementia, 10*(3), S122-S145.

Durga, J., van Boxtel, M. P. J., Schouten, E. G., Kok, F. J., Jolles, J., Katan, M. B., & Verhoef, P. (2007). Effect of 3-year folic acid supplementation on cognitive function in older adults in the FACIT trial: A randomized, double blind controlled study. *Lancet, 369,* 208-216.

Durlak, J. A., Mahoney, J. L., Bohnert, A. M., & Parente, M. E. (2010). Developing and improving after-school programs to enhance youth's personal growth and adjustment: A special issue of AJCP. *American Journal of Community Psychology, 45*(3-4), 285-293.

Dush, C. M. K., Cohan, C. L., & Amato, P. R. (2003). The relationship between cohabitation and marital quality and stability: Change across cohorts? *Journal of Marriage and Family, 65,* 539-549.

Duxbury, L., Higgins, C., & Lee, C. (1994). Work-family conflict: A comparison by gender, family type, and perceived control. *Journal of Family Issues, 15*(3), 449-466.

Dwairy, M., & Achoui, M. (2010). Adolescents-family connectedness: A first cross-cultural research on parenting and psychological adjustment of children. *Journal of Child and Family Studies, 19*(1), 8-15.

Dweck, C. S. (2008). Mindsets: How praise is harming youth and what can be done about it. *School Library Medical Activities Monthly, 24*(5), 55-58.

Dwyer, T., Ponsonby, A. L., Blizzard, L., Newman, N. M., & Cochrane, J. A. (1995). The contribution of changes in the prevalence of prone sleeping position to the decline in sudden infant death syndrome in Tasmania. *Journal of the American Medical Association, 273,* 783-789.

Dye, J. L. (2010). *Fertility of American women: 2008.* Retrieved from www.census.gov/prod/2010pubs/p20-563.pdf

Dye, J. L., & Johnson, T. D. (2009). A child's day: 2006 (selected indicators of child well-being). *Current Population Reports,* P70-118. Washington, DC: U.S. Census Bureau.

Dykas, M. J., & Cassidy, J. (2011). Attachment and the processing of social information across the life span: theory and evidence. *Psychological Bulletin, 137*(1), 19.

Dykstra, P. A. (1995). Loneliness among the never and formerly married: The importance of supportive friendships and a desire for independence. *Journal of Gerontology: Social Sciences, 50B,* S321-S329.

D'Aquila, P., Rose, G., Bellizzi, D., & Passarino, G. (2013). Epigenetics and aging. *Maturitas, 74*(2), 130-136.

Earls, M. (2010). Incorporating recognition and management of perinatal and postpartum depression into pediatric practice. *Pediatrics, 126,* 1032-1039.

East, P. L., & Khoo, S. T. (2005). Longitudinal pathways linking family factors and sibling relationship qualities to adolescent substance use and sexual risk behaviors. *Journal of Family Psychology, 19,* 571-580.

Eaton, D. K., Kann, L., Kinchen, S., Shanklin, S., Ross, J., Hawkins, J., . . . Wechsler, H. (2008). Youth risk behavior surveillance—United States, 2007. *Morbidity and Mortality Weekly Report, 57*(SS-4), 1-131.

Eaves, Y. D., McQuiston, C., & Miles, M. S. (2005). Coming to terms with adult sibling grief: When a brother dies from AIDS. *Journal of Hospice & Palliative Nursing, 7*(3), 139-149.

Eccles, J. S. (2004). Schools, academic motivation, and stage-environment fit. In R. M. Lerner & L. Steinberg (Eds.), *Handbook of adolescent development* (2nd ed., pp. 125-153). Hoboken, NJ: Wiley.

Eccles, J. S., Wigfield, A., & Byrnes, J. (2003). Cognitive development in adolescence. In I. B. Weiner (Series Ed.), R. M. Lerner, M. A. Easterbrooks, & J. Mistry (Vol. Eds.), *Handbook of psychology: Vol. 6. Developmental psychology.* New York: Wiley.

Ecker, J. L., & Frigoletto, F. D., Jr. (2007). Cesarean delivery and the risk-benefit calculus. *New England Journal of Medicine, 356,* 885-888.

Eckerman, C. O., & Didow, S. M. (1996). Nonverbal imitation and toddlers' mastery of verbal means of achieving coordinated action. *Developmental Psychology, 32,* 141-152.

Eckerman, C. O., Davis, C. C., & Didow, S. M. (1989). Toddlers' emerging ways of achieving social coordination with a peer. *Child Development, 60,* 440-453.

Eddleman, K. A., Malone, F. D., Sullivan, L., Dukes, K., Berkowitz, R. L., Kharbutli, Y., . . . D'Alton, M. E. (2006). Pregnancy loss rates after midtrimester amniocentesis. *Obstetrics and Gynecology, 108*(5), 1067-1072.

Eddy, K. T., Dorer, D. J., Franko, D. L., Tahilani, K., Thompson-Brenner, H., & Herzog, D. B. (2008). Diagnostic crossover in anorexia nervosa and bulimia nervosa: implications for DSM-V. *American Journal of Psychiatry, 165*(2), 245-250.

Eden, G. F., Jones, K. M., Cappell, K., Gareau, L., Wood, F. B., Zeffiro, T. A., . . . Flowers, D. L. (2004). Neural changes following remediation in adult developmental dyslexia. *Neuron, 44,* 411-422.

Eder, W., Ege, M. J., & von Mutius, E. (2006). The asthma epidemic. *New England Journal of Medicine, 355,* 2226-2235.

Edmondson, D., Park, C. L., Chaudoir, S. R., & Wortman, J. H. (2008). Death without God: Religious struggle, death concerns, and depression in the terminally ill. *Psychological Science, 19*(8), 754-758.

Edwards, C. P. (1994, April). *Cultural relativity meets best practice, or, anthropology and early education, a promising friendship.* Paper presented at the meeting of the American Educational Research Association, New Orleans.

Edwards, C. P. (2002). Three approaches from Europe: Waldorf, Montessori, and Reggio Emilia. *Early Childhood Research and Practice, 4*(1), 14-38.

Edwards, C. P. (2003). "Fine designs" from Italy: Montessori education and the Reggio Emilia approach. *Montessori Life: Journal of the American Montessori Society, 15*(1), 33-38.

Edwards, K.M., Dardis, C.M., Sylaska, K.M., & Gidycz, C.A. (2015). Informal social reactions to college women's disclosure of intimate partner violence: Associations with psychological and relational variables. *Journal of Interpersonal Violence, 30,* 25-44.

Edwards, K.M., Sylaska, K.M., & Neal, A.M. (2015). Intimate partner violence among sexual minority populations: A critical review of the literature and agenda for future research. *Psychology of Violence, 5,* 112-121.

Eggebeen, D. J., & Knoester, C. (2001). Does fatherhood matter for men? *Journal of Marriage and Family, 63,* 381-393.

Eggebeen, D. J., & Sturgeon, S. (2006). Demography of the baby boomers. In S. K. Whitbourne & S. L. Willis (Eds.), *The baby boomers grow up: Contemporary perspectives on midlife* (pp. 3-21). Mahwah, NJ: Erlbaum.

Ehrenreich, B., & English, D. (2005). *For her own good: Two centuries of the experts' advice to women.* New York: Anchor.

Eidelman, A. I., Schanler, R. J., Johnston, M., Landers, S., Noble, L., Szucs, K., & Viehmann, L. (2012). Breastfeeding and the use of human milk. *Pediatrics, 129*(3), e827-e841.

Eimas, P., Siqueland, E., Jusczyk, P., & Vigorito, J. (1971). Speech perception in infants. *Science, 171,* 303-306.

Einarson, A., & Boskovic, R. (2009). Use and safety of antipsychotic drugs during pregnancy. *Journal of Psychiatric Practice, 15*(3), 183-192.

Eisenberg, A. R. (1996). The conflict talk of mothers and children: Patterns related to culture, SES, and gender of child. *Merrill-Palmer Quarterly, 42,* 438-452.

Eisenberg, L. (1998). Is the family obsolete? *Bulletin of the American Academy of Arts and Sciences, 52*(1), 33-46.

Eisenberg, M. E., Ackard, D. M., Resnick, M. D., & Neumark-Sztainer, D. (2009). Casual sex and psychological health among young adults: Is having "friends with benefits" emotionally damaging? *Perspectives on Sexual and Reproductive Health, 41*(4), 231-237.

Eisenberg, N. (1992). *The caring child.* Cambridge, MA: Harvard University Press.

Eisenberg, N. (2000). Emotion, regulation, and moral development. *Annual Review of Psychology, 51,* 665-697.

Eisenberg, N., & Fabes, R. A. (1998). Prosocial development. In W. Damon (Series Ed.) & N. Eisenberg (Vol. Ed.), *Handbook of child psychology: Vol. 3. Social, emotional, and personality development* (5th ed., pp. 701-778). New York: Wiley.

Eisenberg, N., & Morris, A. D. (2004). Moral cognitions and prosocial responding in adolescence. In R. M. Lerner & L. Steinberg (Eds.), *Handbook of adolescent psychology* (2nd ed., pp. 155-188). Hoboken, NJ: Wiley.

Eisenberg, N., Fabes, R. A., & Murphy, B. C. (1996). Parents' reactions to children's negative emotions: Relations to children's social competence and comforting behavior. *Child Development, 67,* 2227-2247.

Eisenberg, N., Fabes, R. A., & Spinrad, T. L. (2006). Prosocial development. In W. Damon & R. M. Lerner (Series Eds.) & N. Eisenberg (Vol. Ed.), *Handbook of child psychology: Vol 3. Social, emotional and personality development* (6th ed., pp. 646-718). Hoboken: NJ: Wiley.

Eisenberg, N., Fabes, R. A., Nyman, M., Bernzweig, J., & Pinuelas, A. (1994). The relations of emotionality and regulation to children's anger-related reactions. *Child Development, 65,* 109-128.

Eisenberg, N., Hofer, C., Sulik, M. J., & Liew, J. (2014). The development of prosocial moral reasoning and a prosocial orientation in young adulthood: Concurrent and longitudinal correlates. *Developmental Psychology, 50*(1), 58.

Eisenberg, N., Spinrad, T. L., Fabes, R. A., Reiser, M., Cumberland, A., Shepard, S. A., . . . Thompson, M. (2004). The relations of effortful control and impulsivity to children's resiliency and adjustment. *Child Development, 75,* 25-46.

Eisend, M. (2010). A meta-analysis of gender roles in advertising. *Journal of the Academy of Marketing Science, 38*(4), 418-440.

Eisenegger, C., Haushofer, J., & Fehr, E. (2011). The role of testosterone in social interaction. *Trends in Cognitive Sciences, 15*(6), 263-271.

Ekinci, B. (2014). The relationships among Sternberg's Triarchic Abilities, Gardner's multiple intelligences, and academic achievement. *Social Behavior and Personality: an international journal, 42*(4), 625-633.

El-Sheikh, M., Kelly, R. J., Buckhalt, J. A., & Hinnant, J. B. (2010). Children's sleep and adjustment over time: The role of socioeconomic context. *Child Development, 81,* 870-883. doi: 10.1111/j.1467-8624.2010.01439.x

Elgar, F. J., Pförtner, T. K., Moor, I., De Clercq, B., Stevens, G. W., & Currie, C. (2015). Socioeconomic inequalities in adolescent health 2002-2010: a time-series analysis of 34 countries participating in the Health Behaviour in School-aged Children study. *The Lancet, 385*(9982), 2088-2095.

Eliassen, H., Colditz, G. A., Rosner, B., Willett, W. C., & Hankinson, S. E. (2006). Adult weight change and risk of postmenopausal breast cancer. *Journal of the American Medical Association, 296,* 193-201.

Elicker, J., Englund, M., & Sroufe, L. A. (1992). Predicting peer competence and peer relationships in childhood from early parent-child relationships. In R. Parke & G. Ladd (Eds.), *Family peer relationships: Modes of linkage* (pp. 77-106). Hillsdale, NJ: Erlbaum.

Elkins, R. K., Kassenboehmer, S. C., & Schurer, S. (2017). The stability of personality traits in adolescence and young adulthood. *Journal of Economic Psychology, 60,* 37–52.

Ellis, A., & Oakes, L. M. (2006). Infants flexibly use different dimensions to categorize objects. *Developmental Psychology, 42,* 1000–1011.

Ellis, B. J., & Del Giudice, M. (2014). Beyond allostatic load: Rethinking the role of stress in regulating human development. *Development and Psychopathology, 26*(1), 1–20.

Ellis, B. J., Bates, J. E., Dodge, K. A., Fergusson, D. M., Horwood, L. J., Pettit, G. S., & Woodward, L. (2003). Does father-absence place daughters at special risk for early sexual activity and teenage pregnancy? *Child Development, 74,* 801–821.

Ellis, B. J., McFadyen-Ketchum, S., Dodge, K. A., Pettit, G. S., & Bates, J. E. (1999). Quality of early family relationships and individual differences in the timing of pubertal maturation in girls: A longitudinal test of an evolutionary model. *Journal of Personality and Social Psychology, 77,* 387–401.

Ellis, K. J., Abrams, S. A., & Wong, W. W. (1997). Body composition of a young, multiethnic female population. *American Journal of Clinical Nutrition, 65,* 724–731.

Ellison, C. G., Musick, M. A., & Henderson, A. K. (2008). Balm in Gilead: Racism, religious involvement, and psychological distress among African American adults. *Journal for the Scientific Study of Religion, 47,* 291–309.

Ellison, N. B., Steinfield, C., & Lampe, C. (2007). The benefits of Facebook "friends": Social capital and college students' use of online social network sites. *Journal of Computer-Mediated Communication, 12*(4), 1143–1168.

Elmenhorst, D., Elmenhorst, E., Luks, N., Maass, H., Mueller, E., Vejvoda, M., . . . Samuel, A. (2009). Performance impairment after four days partial sleep deprivation compared with acute effects of alcohol and hypoxia. *Sleep Medicine, 10,* 189–197.

Else-Quest, N. M., Hyde, J. S., Goldsmith, H. H., & Van Hulle, C. A. (2006). Gender differences in temperament: a meta-analysis. *Psychological Bulletin, 132*(1), 33.

ElSohly, M. A., Mehmedic, Z., Foster, S., Gon, C., Chandra, S., & Church, J. C. (2016). Changes in cannabis potency over the last 2 decades (1995–2014): Analysis of current data in the United States. *Biological Psychiatry, 79*(7), 613–619.

Emanuel, E.J., Onwuteaka-Philipsen, B.D., Urwin, J.W., & Cohen, J. (2016). Attitudes and practices of euthanasia and physician-assisted suicide in the United States, Canada, and Europe. *Journal of the American Medical Association*, 316, 79–90.

Emde, R. N., Plomin, R., Robinson, J., Corley, R., DeFries, J., Fulker, D. W., . . . Zahn-Waxler, C. (1992). Temperament, emotion, and cognition at 14 months: The MacArthur Longitudinal Twin Study. *Child Development, 63,* 1437–1455.

Emery, L., Heaven, T. J., Paxton, J. L., & Braver, T. S. (2008). Age-related changes in neural activity during performance matched working memory manipulation. *NeuroImage, 42*(4), 1577–1586.

Eng, P. M., Rimm, E. B., Fitzmaurice, G., & Kawachi, I. (2002). Social ties and change in social ties in relation to subsequent total and cause-specific mortality and coronary heart disease incidence in men. *American Journal of Epidemiology, 155,* 700–709.

Engle, P. L., & Breaux, C. (1998). Fathers' involvement with children: Perspectives from developing countries. *Social Policy Report, 12*(1), 1–21.

Engle, P. L., Black, M. M., Behrman, J. R., de Mello, M. C., Gertler, P. J., Kapiriri, L., Martorell, R., & Young, M. E. (2007). Strategies to avoid the loss of developmental potential in more than 200 million children in the developing world. *The Lancet, 369*(9557), 20–26.

English, T., & Carstensen, L. L. (2014). Selective narrowing of social networks across adulthood is associated with improved emotional experience in daily life. *International Journal of Behavioral Development, 38*(2), 195–202.

Environmental Protection Agency. (2015). *Neurodevelopmental disorders.* Retrieved from www.epa.gov/sites/production/files/2015-10/documents/ace3_neurodevelopmental.pdf

Epel, E. S., Blackburn, E. H., Lin, J., Dhabhar, F. S., Adler, N. E., Morrow, J. D., & Cawthon, R. M. (2004). Accelerated telomere shortening in response to life stress. *Proceedings of the National Academy of Sciences, 101,* 17312–17315.

Erath, S. A., El-Sheikh, M., & Cummings, E. M. (2009). Harsh parenting and child externalizing behavior: Skin conductance level reactivity as a moderator. *Child Development, 80*(2), 578–592.

Erdogan, B., Bauer, T. N., Truxillo, D. M., & Mansfield, L. R. (2012). Whistle while you work: A review of the life satisfaction literature. *Journal of Management, 38*(4), 1038–1083.

Erikson, E. H. (1950). *The life cycle completed.* New York: Norton.

Erikson, E. H. (1968). *Identity: Youth and crisis.* New York: Norton.

Erikson, E. H. (1973). The wider identity. In K. Erikson (Ed.), *In search of common ground: Conversations with Erik H. Erikson and Huey P. Newton.* New York: Norton.

Erikson, E. H. (1982). *The life cycle completed.* New York: Norton.

Erikson, E. H. (1985). *The life cycle completed* (Paperback reprint ed.). New York: Norton.

Erikson, E. H., Erikson, J. M., & Kivnick, H. Q. (1986). *Vital involvement in old age: The experience of old age in our time.* New York: Norton.

Ertel, K. A., Glymour, M. M., & Berkman, L. F. (2008). Effects of social integration on preserving memory function in a nationally representative elderly population. *American Journal of Public Health, 98,* 1215–1220.

Ervin, R. B. (2008). Healthy Index Eating scores among adults, 60 years of age and over, by sociodemographic and health characteristics: United States, 1999–2002. *Advance Data from Vital and Health Statistics,* No. 395. Hyattsville, MD: National Center for Health Statistics.

Eryigit Madzwamuse, S., Baumann, N., Jaekel, J., Bartmann, P., & Wolke, D. (2015). Neurocognitive performance of very preterm or very low birth weight adults at 26 years. *Journal of Child Psychology and Psychiatry, 56*(8), 857–864.

Espeland, M. A., Rapp, S. R., Shumaker, S. A., Brunner, R., Manson, J. E., Sherwin, B. B., . . . Hays, J., for the Women's Health Initiative Memory Study Investigators. (2004). Conjugated equine estrogens and global cognitive function in postmenopausal women: Women's Health Initiative Memory Study. *Journal of the American Medical Association, 21,* 2959–2968.

Esposito, K., Marfella, R., Ciotola, M., DiPalo, C., Giugliano, F., Giugliano, G., . . . Giugliano, D. (2004). Effects of a Mediterranean-style diet on endothelial dysfunction and markers of vascular inflammation in the metabolic syndrome: A randomized trial. *Journal of the American Medical Association, 292,* 1440–1446.

Estes, K. G., & Hurley, K. (2013). Infant-directed prosody helps infants map sounds to meanings. *Infancy, 18,* 797–824.

Etaugh, C.A. (2013). Midlife career transitions for women. In W. Patton (Ed.), *Conceptualising women's working lives: Moving the boundaries of discourse* (pp. 105–118). Rotterdam: Sense Publishers.

Ettehad, D., Emdin, C. A., Kiran, A., Anderson, S. G., Callender, T., Emberson, J., . . . & Rahimi, K. (2016). Blood pressure lowering for prevention of cardiovascular disease and death: a systematic review and meta-analysis. *The Lancet, 387*(10022), 957–967.

Ettinger, B., Friedman, G. D., Bush, T., & Quesenberry, C. P. (1996). Reduced mortality associated with long-term postmenopausal estrogen therapy. *Obstetrics & Gynecology, 87,* 6–12.

Etzel, R. A. (2003). How environmental exposures influence the development and exacerbation of asthma. *Pediatrics, 112*(1), 233–239.

Evans, A. D., & Lee, K. (2013). Emergence of lying in very young children. *Developmental Psychology, 49*(10), 1958.

Evans, G. W. (2004). The environment of childhood poverty. *American Psychologist, 59,* 77–92.

Eyler, L. T., Sherzai, A., Kaup, A. R., & Jeste, D. V. (2011). A review of functional brain imaging correlates of successful cognitive aging. *Biological Psychiatry, 70*(2), 115–122.

Ezzati, M., & Lopez, A. D. (2004). Regional, disease specific patterns of smoking-attributable mortality in 2000. *Tobacco Control, 13,* 388–395.

Ezzati, M., Friedman, A. B., Kulkarni, S. C., & Murray, C. J. L. (2008). The reversal of fortunes: Trends in country mortality and cross-country mortality disparities in the United States. *PloS Medicine, 5*(4), e66. doi: 10:1371/journal.pmed.0050066

Fabel, K., & Kempermann, G. (2008). Physical activity and the regulation of neurogenesis in the adult and aging brain. *Neuromolecular Medicine, 10*(2), 59–66.

Fabes, R. A., & Eisenberg, N. (1992). Young children's coping with interpersonal anger. *Child Development, 63,* 116-128.

Fabes, R. A., Carlo, G., Kupanoff, K., & Laible, D. (1999). Early adolescence and prosocial/moral behavior: I. The role of individual processes. *Journal of Early Adolescence, 19,* 5-16.

Fabes, R. A., Leonard, S. A., Kupanoff, K., & Martin, C. L. (2001). Parental coping with children's negative emotions: Relations with children's emotional and social responding. *Child Development, 72,* 907-920.

Fabes, R. A., Martin, C. L., & Hanish, L. D. (2003). Young children's play qualities in same-, other-, and mixed-gender peer groups. *Child Development, 74*(3), 921-932.

Fabricius, W. V. (2003). Listening to children of divorce: New findings that diverge from Wallerstein, Lewis, and Blakeslee. *Family Relations, 52,* 385-394.

Facebook. (2011). *Statistics.* Retrieved from www.facebook.com/press/info.php?statistics

Fagan, J. F., Holland, C. R., & Wheeler, K. (2007). The prediction, from infancy, of adult IQ. *Intelligence, 35,* 225-231.

Fagot, B. I. (1997). Attachment, parenting, and peer interactions of toddler children. *Developmental Psychology, 33,* 489-499.

Fagot, B. I., Rogers, C. S., & Leinbach, M. D. (2000). Theories of gender socialization. In T. Eckes & H. M. Trautner (Eds.), *The developmental social psychology of gender.* Mahwah, NJ: Earlbaum.

Falbo, T. (2006). *Your one and only: Educational psychologist dispels myths surrounding only children.* Retrieved from www.utexas.edu/features/archive/2004/single.htm

Falbo, T., & Poston, D. L. (1993). The academic, personality, and physical outcomes of only children in China. *Child Development, 64,* 18-35.

Fantz, R. L. (1963). Pattern vision in newborn infants. *Science, 140,* 296-297.

Fantz, R. L. (1964). Visual experience in infants: Decreased attention to familiar patterns relative to novel ones. *Science, 146,* 668-670.

Fantz, R. L. (1965). Visual perception from birth as shown by pattern selectivity. In H. E. Whipple (Ed.), *New issues in infant development. Annals of the New York Academy of Science, 118,* 793-814.

Fantz, R. L., & Nevis, S. (1967). Pattern preferences and perceptual-cognitive development in early infancy. *Merrill-Palmer Quarterly, 13,* 77-108.

Fantz, R. L., Fagen, J., & Miranda, S. B. (1975). Early visual selectivity. In L. Cohen & P. Salapatek (Eds.), *Infant perception: From sensation to cognition: Vol. 1. Basic visual processes* (pp. 249-341). New York: Academic Press.

Faraone, S. V., Sergeant, J., Gillberg, C., & Biederman, J. (2003, June). The worldwide prevalence of ADHD: is it an American condition. Retrieved from World Psychiatry: www.ncbi.nlm.nih.gov/pmc/articles/PMC1525089

Farhud, D. D. (2015, November). *Impact of Lifestyle of Health.* Retrieved from U.S. National Library of Medicine National Institutes of Health: www.ncbi.nlm.nih.gov/pmc/articles/PMC4703222/

Farr, R. H., Forssell, S. L., & Patterson, C. J. (2010). Gay, lesbian, and heterosexual adoptive parents: Couple and relationship issues. *Journal of GLBT Family Studies, 6*(2), 199-213.

Farver, J. A. M., Kim, Y. K., & Lee, Y. (1995). Cultural differences in Korean and Anglo-American preschoolers' social interaction and play behavior. *Child Development, 66,* 1088-1099.

Farver, J. A. M., Xu, Y., Eppe, S., Fernandez, A., & Schwartz, D. (2005). Community violence, family conflict, and preschoolers' socioemotional functioning. *Developmental Psychology, 41,* 160-170.

Fasig, L. (2000). Toddlers' understanding of ownership: Implications for self-concept development. *Social Development, 9,* 370-382.

Favaro, A., Ferrara, S., & Santonastaso, P. (2004). The spectrum of eating disorders in young women: A prevalence study in a general population sample. *Psychosomatic Medicine, 65,* 701-708.

Fear, J. M., Champion, J. E., Reeslund, K. L., Forehand, R., Colletti, C., Roberts, L., & Compas, B. E. (2009). Parental depression and interparental conflict: Children and adolescents' self-blame and coping responses. *Journal of Family Psychology, 23*(5), 762-766. doi:10.1037/a0016381

Fearon, P., O'Connell, P., Frangou, S., Aquino, P., Nosarti, C., Allin, M., . . . Murray, R. (2004). Brain volume in adult survivors of very low birth weight: A sibling-controlled study. *Pediatrics, 114,* 367-371.

Fearon, R. P., Bakermans-Kranenburg, M. J., Van IJzendoorn, M. H., Lapsley, A.-M., & Roisman, G. I. (2010). The significance of insecure attachment and disorganization in the development of children's externalizing behavior: A meta-analytic study. *Child Development, 81,* 435-456. doi: 10.1111/j.1467-8624.2009.01405.x

Federal Interagency Forum on Aging-Related Statistics. (2004). *Older Americans 2004: Key indicators of well-being.* Washington, DC: U.S. Government Printing Office.

Federal Interagency Forum on Aging-Related Statistics. (2010). *Older Americans 2010: Key indicators of well-being.* Washington, DC: U.S. Government Printing Office.

Federal Interagency Forum on Aging-Related Statistics. (2012). *Older Americans 2012: Key indicators of well-being.* Washington, DC: U.S. Government Printing Office.

Federal Interagency Forum on Aging-Related Statistics. (2016a). *Older Americans 2016: Key indicators of well-being.* Washington, DC: U.S. Government Printing Office.

Federal Interagency Forum on Aging-Related Statistics. (2016b). *Older Americans update 2016: Key indicators of well-being.* Washington, DC: U.S. Government Printing Office.

Federal Interagency Forum on Child and Family Statistics. (2005). *America's children: Key national indicators of well-being, 2005.* Washington, DC: U.S. Government Printing Office.

Federal Interagency Forum on Child and Family Statistics. (2015). *America's children: Key national indicators of well-being, 2015.* Retrieved from www.childstats.gov/pdf/ac2015/ac_15.pdf

Federal Interagency Forum on Child and Family Statistics. (2017). *America's children: Key national indicators of well-being, 2017.* Washington, DC: U.S. Government Printing Office.

Federal Interagency Forum on Child and Family Statistics. (2016). *America's Children in Brief: Key National Indicators of Well-Being, 2016.* Washington, DC: U.S. Government Printing Office.

Fedewa, A. L., Black, W. W., & Ahn, S. (2015). Children and adolescents with same-gender parents: A meta-analytic approach in assessing outcomes. *Journal of GLBT Family Studies, 11*(1), 1-34.

Feinstein, B. A., Goldfried, M. R., & Davila, J. (2012). The relationship between experiences of discrimination and mental health among lesbians and gay men: An examination of internalized homonegativity and rejection sensitivity as potential mechanisms. *Journal of Consulting and Clinical Psychology, 80*(5), 917.

Feldman, H. A., Goldstein, I., Hatzichristou, D. G., Krane, R. J., & McKinlay, J. B. (1994). Impotence and its medical and psychosocial correlates: Results of the Massachusetts Male Aging Study. *Journal of Urology, 151,* 54-61.

Feldman, R. (2007). Parent-infant synchrony: Biological foundations and developmental outcomes. *Current Directions in Psychological Science, 16*(6), 340-345.

Ferber, S. G., & Makhoul, I. R. (2004). The effect of skin-to-skin contact (Kangaroo Care) shortly after birth on the neuro-behavioral responses of the term newborn: A randomized, controlled trial. *Pediatrics, 113,* 858-865.

Ferdows, N.B., Jensen, G.A., & Tarraf, W. (2017). Healthy aging after age 65: A lifespan health production function approach. *Research on Aging.* Retrieved from https://doi.org/10.1177/0164027517713312

Ferguson, C. J. (2010). Genetic contributions to antisocial personality and behavior: A meta-analytic review from an evolutionary perspective. *The Journal of Social Psychology, 150*(2), 160-180.

Ferguson, C. J. (2013). Violent video games and the Supreme Court: Lessons for the scientific community in the wake of Brown vs. Entertainment Merchant's Association. *American Psychologist, 68*(2), 57-74.

Ferguson, C. J. (2015). Do angry birds make for angry children? A meta-analysis of video game influences on children's and adolescents' aggression, mental health, prosocial behavior, and academic performance. *Perspectives on Psychological Science, 10*(5), 646-666.

Ferguson, C. J., & Savage, J. (2012). Have recent studies addressed methodological issues raised by five decades of televised violence research? A critical review. *Aggression and Violent Behavior, 17,* 129-139.

Fergusson, D. M., McLeod, G. F., & Horwood, L. J. (2013). Childhood sexual abuse and adult developmental outcomes: Findings from a 30-year longitudinal study in New Zealand. *Child Abuse & Neglect, 37*(9), 664–674.

Fernald, A., & Morikawa, H. (1993). Common themes and cultural variations in Japanese and American mothers' speech to infants. *Child Development, 64,*637–656.

Fernald, A., Perfors, A., & Marchman, V. A. (2006). Picking up speed in understanding: Speech processing efficiency and vocabulary growth across the second year. *Developmental Psychology, 42,* 98–116.

Fernald, A., Swingley, D., & Pinto, J. P. (2001). When half a word is enough: Infants can recognize spoken words using partial phonetic information. *Child Development, 72,* 1003–1015.

Ferraro, A. J., Malespin, T., Oehme, K., Bruker, M., & Opel, A. (2016). Advancing co-parenting education: Toward a foundation for supporting positive post-divorce adjustment. *Child and Adolescent Social Work Journal, 33*(5), 407–415.

Ferrer, E., Shaywitz, B. A., Holahan, J. M., Marchione, K., & Shaywitz, S. E. (2010). Uncoupling of reading and IQ over time: Empirical evidence for a definition of dyslexia. *Psychological Science, 21*(1), 93–101.

Ferry, A. L., Hespos, S. J., & Waxman, S. R. (2010). Categorization in 3"and 4"month"old infants: an advantage of words over tones. *Child Development, 81*(2), 472–479.

Field, A. E., Austin, S. B., Taylor, C. B., Malspeis, S., Rosner, B., Rockett, H. R., . . . Colditz, G. A. (2003). Relation between dieting and weight change among preadolescents and adolescents. *Pediatrics, 112*(4), 900–906.

Field, T. (2010). Postpartum depression effects on early interactions, parenting, and safety practices: A review. *Infant Behavior and Development, 33,* 1–6.

Field, T. M. (1978). Interaction behaviors of primary versus secondary caretaker fathers. *Developmental Psychology, 14,* 183–184.

Field, T. M., & Roopnarine, J. L. (1982). Infant-peer interaction. In T. M. Field, A. Huston, H. C. Quay, L. Troll, & G. Finley (Eds.), *Review of human development.* New York: Wiley.

Field, T., Diego, M., & Hernandez-Reif, M. (2007). Massage therapy research. *Developmental Review, 27,* 75–89.

Fields, J. (2004). America's families and living arrangements: 2003. *Current Population Reports,* P20-553. Washington, DC: U.S. Census Bureau.

Fields, R. D., & Stevens-Graham, B. (2002). New insights into neuron–glia communication. *Science, 298,* 556–562.

Fihrer, I., McMahon, C. A., & Taylor, A. J. (2009). The impact of postnatal and concurrent maternal depression on child behaviour during the early school years. *Journal of Affective Disorders, 119,* 116–123.

Finch, C. E., & Zelinski, E. M. (2005). Normal aging of brain structure and cognition: Evolutionary perspectives. *Research in Human Development, 2,* 69–82.

Finer, L. B. (2007). Trends in premarital sex in the United States, 1954–2003. *Public Health Reports, 122,* 73–78.

Finer, L. B., & Philbin, J. M. (2014). Trends in ages at key reproductive transitions in the United States, 1951–2010. *Women's Health Issues, 24*(3), e271–e279.

Fingerman, K. L., & Charles, S. T. (2010). It takes two to tango: Why older people have the best relationships. *Current Directions in Psychological Science, 19*(3), 172–176.

Fingerman, K. L., Pitzer, L. M., Chan, W., Birditt, K., Franks, M. M., & Zarit, S. (2010). Who gets what and why? Help middle-aged adults provide to parents and grown children. *Journal of Gerontology, 10,* 1–12.

Fingerman, K., & Dolbin-MacNab, M. (2006). The baby boomers and their parents: Cohort influences and intergenerational ties. In S. K. Whitbourne & S. L. Willis (Eds.), *The baby boomers grow up: Contemporary perspectives on midlife* (pp. 237–259). Mahwah, NJ: Erlbaum.

Fingerman, K., Miller, L., Birditt, K., & Zarit, S. (2009). Giving to the good and to the needy: Parental support of grown children. *Journal of Marriage and Family, 71,* 1220–1233.

Finkel, D., Gerritsen, L., Reynolds, C. A., Dahl, A. K., & Pedersen, N. L. (2014). Etiology of individual differences in human health and longevity. *Annual Review of Gerontology and Geriatrics, 34*(1), 189–227.

Finkelstein, J. S., Lee, H., Burnett-Bowie, S. M., Pallais, J. C., Yu, E. W., Borges, L. F., Jones, B. F., Barry, C. V., Wuczyn, K. E., Thomas, B. J., & Leder, B. Z. (2013). Gonadal steroids and body composition, strength, and sexual function in men. *New England Journal of Medicine, 369,* 1011–1022.

Finn, J. D. (2006). *The adult lives of at-risk students: The roles of attainment and engagement in high school* (NCES 2006-328). Washington, DC: U.S. Department of Education, National Center for Education Statistics.

Finn, J. D., Gerber, S. B., & Boyd-Zaharias, J. (2005). Small classes in the early grades, academic achievement, and graduating from high school. *Journal of Educational Psychology, 97,* 214–223.

Fiori, K. L., Smith, J., & Antonucci, T. C. (2007). Social network types among older adults: A multidimensional approach. *Journals of Gerontology, 62*(6, Series A), 322–330.

First 30 days. (2008). *The change report* (Research conducted by Southeastern Institute of Research). Retrieved from www.first30days.com/pages/the_change_report.html

Fischer, K. (1980). A theory of cognitive development: The control and construction of hierarchies of skills. *Psychological Review, 87,* 477–531.

Fischer, K. W. (2008). Dynamic cycles of cognitive and brain development: Measuring growth in mind, brain, and education. In A. M. Battro, K. W. Fischer, & P. Léna (Eds.), *The educated brain* (pp. 127–150). Cambridge UK: Cambridge University Press.

Fischer, K. W., & Pruyne, E. (2003). Reflective thinking in adulthood. In J. Demick & C. Andreoletti (Eds.), *Handbook of adult development.* New York: Plenum Press.

Fitzpatrick, M. D., & Turner, S. E. (2007). Blurring the boundary: Changes in the transition from college participation to adulthood. In S. Danziger & C. Rouse (Eds.), *The price of independence: The economics of early adulthood* (pp. 107–137). New York: Russell Sage Foundation.

Fitzpatrick, M. J., & McPherson, B. J. (2010). Coloring within the lines: Gender stereotypes in contemporary coloring books. *Sex Roles, 62*(1–2), 127–137.

Fivush, R. (2011). The development of autobiographical memory. *Annual Review of Psychology, 62,* 559–582.

Fivush, R., & Haden, C. A. (2006). Elaborating on elaborations: Role of maternal reminiscing style in cognitive and socioemotional development. *Child Development, 77,* 1568–1588.

Fivush, R., & Nelson, K. (2004). Culture and language in the emergence of autobiographical memory. *Psychological Science, 15,* 573–577.

Fivush, R., Habermas, T., Waters, T. E., & Zaman, W. (2011). The making of autobiographical memory: Intersections of culture, narratives and identity. *International Journal of Psychology, 46*(5), 321–345.

Fjell, A. M., & Walhovd, K. B. (2010). Structural brain changes in aging: Courses, causes and cognitive consequences. *Reviews in the Neurosciences, 21*(3), 187–222.

Flannagan, C. A., Bowes, J. M., Jonsson, B., Csapo, B., & Sheblanova, E. (1998). Ties that bind: Correlates of adolescents' civic commitment in seven countries. *Journal of Social Issues, 54,* 457–475.

Flavell, J. H. (2000). Development of children's knowledge about the mental world. *International Journal of Behavioral Development, 24*(1), 15–23.

Flavell, J. H., Flavell, E. R., & Green, F. L. (1983). Development of the appearance-reality distinction. *Cognitive Psychology, 15*(1), 95–120.

Flavell, J. H., Green, F. L., & Flavell, E. R. (1986). Development of knowledge about the appearance-reality distinction. *Monographs of the Society for Research in Child Development, 51*(1, Serial No. 212).

Flavell, J. H., Green, F. L., Flavell, E. R., & Grossman, J. B. (1997). The development of children's knowledge about inner speech. *Child Development, 68,* 39–47.

Flavell, J. H., Miller, P. H., & Miller, S. A. (2002). *Cognitive development.* Englewood Cliffs, NJ: Prentice Hall.

Fleeson, W. (2004). The quality of American life at the end of the century. In O. G. Brim, C. D. Ryff, & R. C. Kessler (Eds.), *How healthy are we? A national study of well-being at midlife* (pp. 252–272). Chicago: University of Chicago Press.

Flegal, K. M., Carroll, M. D., Ogden, C. L., & Curtin, L. R. (2010). Prevalence and trends in obesity among U.S. adults, 1999–2008. *Journal of the American Medical Association, 303,* 235–241.

Flegal, K. M., Kit, B. K., Orpana, H., & Graubard, B. I. (2013). Association of all-cause mortality with overweight and obesity using standard body mass index categories: a systematic review and meta-analysis. *JAMA, 309*(1), 71–82.

Fleischman, D. A., Wilson, R. S., Gabrieli, J. D. E., Bienias, J. L., & Bennett, D. A. (2004). A longitudinal study of implicit and explicit memory in old persons. *Psychology and Aging, 19*(4), 617–625. doi: 10.1037/0882-7974. 19.4.617

Flook, L., Repetti, R. L., & Ullman, J. B. (2005). Classroom social experiences as predictors of academic performance. *Developmental Psychology, 41*, 319–327.

Flores, G. (2010). Technical report—racial and ethnic disparities in the health and health care of children. *Pediatrics*, peds-2010.

Flynn, J. (2013). The changing face of pediatric hypertension in the era of the childhood obesity epidemic. *Pediatric Nephrology, 28*(7), 1059–1066.

Flynn, J. R. (1984). The mean IQ of Americans: Massive gains 1932 to 1978. *Psychological Bulletin, 95*, 29–51.

Flynn, J. R. (1987). Massive IQ gains in 14 nations: What IQ tests really measure. *Psychological Bulletin, 101*, 171–191.

Fomby, P., & Cherlin, A. J. (2007). Family instability and child well-being. *American Sociological Review, 72*(2), 181–204.

Fong, A., King, E., Duffy, J., Wu, E., Pan, D., & Ogunyemi, D. (2016). Declining VBAC rates despite improved delivery outcomes compared to repeat cesarean delivery [20Q]. *Obstetrics & Gynecology, 127*, 144S.

Fonner, V. A., Armstrong, K. S., Kennedy, C. E., O'Reilly, K. R., & Sweat, M. D. (2014). School based sex education and HIV prevention in low- and middle-income countries: A systematic review and meta-analysis. *PloS one, 9*(3), e89692.

Fontana, L., & Klein, S. (2007). Aging, adiposity, and calorie restriction. *Journal of the American Medical Association, 297*, 986–994.

Fontana, L., Klein, S., & Holloszy, J. (2010). Effects of long-term calorie restriction and endurance exercise on glucose tolerance, insulin action, and adipokine production. *Age, 32*(1), 97–108. doi: 10.1007/s11357-009-9118-z

Fontanel, B., & d'Harcourt, C. (1997). *Babies, history, art and folklore.* New York: Abrams.

Ford, M. T., Heinen, B. A., & Langkamer, K. L. (2007). Work and family satisfaction and conflict: A meta-analysis of cross-domain relations. *Journal of Applied Psychology, 92*(1), 57–80.

Ford, P. (2002, April 10). In Europe, marriage is back. *Christian Science Monitor*, 1.

Forget-Dubois, N., Dionne, G., Lemelin, J.-P., Pérusse, D., Tremblay, R. E., & Boivin, M. (2009). Early child language mediates the relation between home environment and school readiness. *Child Development, 80,* 736–749. doi: 10.1111/j.1467-8624.2009.01294.x

Forhan, S. E., Gottlieb, S. L., Sternberg, M. R., Xu, F., Datta, D., Berman, S., & Markowitz, L. E. (2008, March 13). *Prevalence of sexually transmitted infections and bacterial vaginosis among female adolescents in the United States: Data from the National Health and Nutritional Examination Survey (NHANES) 2003–2004.* Oral presentation at the meeting of the 2008 National STD Prevention Conference, Chicago.

Forouzanfar, M. H., Alexander, L., Anderson, H. R., Bachman, V. F., Biryukov, S., Brauer, M., . . . & Delwiche, K. (2015). Global, regional, and national comparative risk assessment of 79 behavioural, environmental and occupational, and metabolic risks or clusters of risks in 188 countries, 1990–2013: A systematic analysis for the Global Burden of Disease Study 2013. *The Lancet, 386*(10010), 2287–2323.

Forray, A., & Foster, D. (2015). Substance use in the perinatal period. *Current Psychiatry Reports, 17.* doi: 10.1007/s11920-015-0626-5.nytimes.com

Fosco, G. M., Stormshak, E. A., Dishion, T. J., & Winter, C. E. (2012). Family relationships and parental monitoring during middle school as predictors of early adolescent problem behavior. *Journal of Clinical Child & Adolescent Psychology, 41*(2), 202–213.

Foster, E. M., & Watkins, S. (2010). The value of reanalysis: TV viewing and attention problems. *Child Development, 81*(1), 368–375. doi: 10.1111/j.1467-8624.2009.01400.x

Foundation Fighting Blindness. (2017). *Macular degeneration: available treatments.* Retrieved from www.blindness.org/macular-degeneration#available-treatments

Foundation for Child Development. (2015). *Children's experience with parental employment insecurity and income inequality.* Retrieved from www.fcd-us.org/childrens-experience-parental-employment-insecurity-family-income-inequality/

Fox, M. K., Pac, S., Devaney, B., & Jankowski, L. (2004). Feeding Infants and Toddlers Study: What foods are infants and toddlers eating? *Journal of the American Dietetic Association, 104*, 22–30.

Fox, N. A., Hane, A. A., & Pine, D. S. (2007). Plasticity for affective neurocircuitry: How the environment affects gene expression. *Current Directions in Psychological Science, 16*(1), 1–5.

Fox, N. A., Henderson, H. A., Rubin, K. H., Calkins, S. D., & Schmidt, L. A. (2001). Continuity and discontinuity of behavioral inhibition and exuberance: Psychophysiological and behavioral influences across the first four years of life. *Child Development, 72*(1), 1–21.

Fraga, M. F., Ballestar, E., Paz, M. F., Ropero, S., Setien, F., Ballestar, M. L., Heine-Suner, D., Cigudosa, J. C., Urioste, M., Benitez, J., Boix-Chornet, M., Sanchez-Aguilera, A., Ling, C., Carlsson, E., Poulson, P., Vaag, A., Stephan, Z., Spector, T. D., Wu, Y., Plass, C., Esteller, M. (2005). Epigenetic differences arise during the lifetime of monozygotic twins. *Proceedings of the National Academy of Sciences of the United States of America, 102*, 10604–10609.

Fraga, M. F., Ballestar, E., Paz, M. F., Ropero, S., Setien, F., Ballestar, M. L., . . . Esteller, M. (2005). Epigenetic differences arise during the lifetime of monozygotic twins. *Proceedings of the National Academy of Sciences, USA, 102*, 10604–10609.

Franconi, F., Brunelleschi, S., Steardo, L., & Cuomo, V. (2007). Gender differences in drug responses. *Pharmacological Research, 55*, 81–95.

Frank, D. A., Augustyn, M., Knight, W. G., Pell, T., & Zuckerman, B. (2001). Growth, development, and behavior in early childhood following prenatal cocaine exposure. *Journal of the American Medical Association, 285*, 1613–1625.

Frankenburg, W. K., Dodds, J. B., Fandal, A. W., Kazuk, E., & Cohrs, M. (1975). *The Denver Developmental Screening Test: Reference manual.* Denver: University of Colorado Medical Center.

Frankenburg, W. K., Dodds, J., Archer, P., Bresnick, B., Maschka, P., Edelman, N., & Shapiro, H. (1992). *Denver II training manual.* Denver: Denver Developmental Materials.

Franks, P. W., Hanson, R. L., Knowler, W. C., Sievers, M. L., Bennett, P. H., & Looker, H. C. (2010). Childhood obesity, other cardiovascular risk factors and premature death. *New England Journal of Medicine, 362*(6), 485–493.

Franks, S. (2009). Polycystic ovary syndrome. *Medicine, 37*(9), 441–444.

Frans, E. M., Sandin, S., Reichenberg, A., Lichtenstein, P., Långström, N., & Hultman, C. M. (2008). Advancing paternal age and bipolar disorder. *Archives of General Psychiatry, 65*, 1034–1040.

Franz, C. E. (1997). Stability and change in the transition to midlife: A longitudinal study of midlife adults. In M. E. Lachman & J. B. James (Eds.), *Multiple paths of mid-life development* (pp. 45–66). Chicago: University of Chicago Press.

Fredricks, J. A., & Eccles, J. S. (2010). Breadth of extracurricular participation and adolescent adjustment among African-American and European-American youth. *Journal of Research on Adolescence, 20*(2), 307–333.

Fredrickson, B. L., Tugade, M. M., Waugh, C. E., & Larkin, G. R. (2003). What good are positive emotions in crisis? A prospective study of resilience and emotions following the terrorist attacks on the United States on September 11th, 2001. *Journal of Personality and Social Psychology, 84*(2), 365.

Fredriksen-Goldsen, K. I., & Muraco, A. (2010). Aging and sexual orientation: A 25-year review of the literature. *Research on Aging, 32*(3), 372–413.

Freeark, K., Rosenberg, E. B., Bornstein, J., Jozefowicz-Simbeni, D., Linkevich, M., & Lohnes, K. (2005). Gender differences and dynamics shaping the adoption life cycle: Review of the literature and recommendations. *American Journal of Orthopsychiatry, 75*, 86–101.

Freeman, C. (2004). *Trends in educational equity of girls & women: 2004* (NCES 2005-016). Washington, DC: National Center for Education Statistics.

Freid, V. M., & Bernstein, A. B. (2010). Health care utilization among adults aged 55–64 years: How has it changed over the past 10 years? *NCHS Data Brief, 32.* Hyattsville, MD: National Center for Health Statistics.

Fremont, W.P. (2004). Childhood reactions to terrorism-induced trauma: A review of the past 10 years. *Journal of the American Academy of Child and Adolescent Psychiatry, 43*, 381–392

Fremont, W.P., Pataki, C., & Beresin, E.V. (2005). The impact of terrorism on children and adolescents: Terror in the skies, terror on television.

Child and Adolescent Psychiatric Clinics of North America, 14, 429–451.

French, R. M., Mareschal, D., Mermillod, M., & Quinn, P. C. (2004). The role of bottom-up processing in perceptual categorization by 3- to 4-month old infants: Simulations and data. *Journal of Experimental Psychology: General*, 133(3), 382–397.

French, S. A., Story, M., & Jeffery, R. W. (2001). Environmental influences on eating and physical activity. *Annual Review of Public Health, 22*, 309–335.

French, S. E., Seidman, E., Allen, L., & Aber, J. L. (2006). The development of ethnic identity during adolescence. *Developmental Psychology, 42*, 1–10.

Freud, S. (1953). *A general introduction to psychoanalysis* (J. Rivière, Trans.). New York: Permabooks. (Original work published 1935)

Freud, S. (1964a). New introductory lectures on psychoanalysis. In J. Strachey (Ed. & Trans.), *The standard edition of the complete psychological works of Sigmund Freud* (Vol. 22). London: Hogarth. (Original work published 1933)

Freud, S. (1964b). An outline of psychoanalysis. In J. Strachey (Ed. & Trans.), *The standard edition of the complete psychological works of Sigmund Freud* (Vol. 23). London: Hogarth. (Original work published 1940)

Frey, K. S., Hirschstein, M. K., Snell, J. L., Edstrom, L. V. S., MacKenzie, E. P., & Broderick, C. J. (2005). Reducing playground bullying and supporting beliefs: An experimental trial of the Steps to Respect program. *Developmental Psychology, 41*, 479–491.

Fried, P. A. (2002). Adolescents prenatally exposed to marijuana: examination of facets of complex behaviors and comparisons with the influence of in utero cigarettes. *The Journal of Clinical Pharmacology, 42*(S1).

Friederici, A. D. (2011). The brain basis of language processing: From structure to function. *Physiological Reviews, 91*(4), 1357–1392.

Friedman, B., Santos, E. J., Liebel, D. V., Russ, A. J., & Conwell, Y. (2015). Longitudinal prevalence and correlates of elder mistreatment among older adults receiving home visiting nursing. *Journal of Elder Abuse & Neglect, 27*(1), 34–64.

Friedman, H. S., & Kern, M. L. (2014). Personality, well-being, and health. *Annual Review of Psychology, 65*.

Friend, R. A. (1991). Older lesbian and gay people: A theory of successful aging. In J. A. Lee (Ed.), *Gay midlife and maturity* (pp. 99–118). New York: Haworth.

Fries, A. B. W., Ziegler, T. E., Kurian, J. R., Jacoris, S., & Pollak, S. D. (2005). Early experiences in humans is associated with changes in neuropeptides critical for regulating social behavior. *Proceedings of the National Academy of Sciences, USA, 102*, 17237–17240.

Fries, J. F., Bruce, B., & Chakravarty, E. (2011). Compression of morbidity 1980–2011: A focused review of paradigms and progress. *Journal of Aging Research, 2011*.

Friesen, M. D., Horwood, L. J., Fergusson, D. M., & Woodward, L. J. (2017). Exposure to parental separation in childhood and later parenting quality as an adult: evidence from a 30-year longitudinal study. *Journal of Child Psychology and Psychiatry, 58*(1), 30–37.

Frisoli, T. M., Schmieder, R. E., Grodzicki, T., & Messerli, F. H. (2011). Beyond salt: lifestyle modifications and blood pressure. *European Heart Journal, 32*(24), 3081–3087.

Froehlich, T. E., Lanphear, B. P., Auinger, P., Hornung, R., Epstein, J. N., Braun, J., & Kahn, R. S. (2009). Association of tobacco and lead exposures with attention-deficit/hyperactivity disorder. *Pediatrics, 124*(6), e1054–e1063. Doi: 10.1542/peds.2009-0738

Frost, D. M., & Meyer, I. H. (2009). Internalized homophobia and relationship quality among lesbians, gay men and bisexuals. *Journal of Counseling Psychology, 56*(1), 97–109.

Fryar, C. D., Carroll, M. D., & Ogden, C. (2016). Prevalence of overweight and obesity among children and adolescents aged 2–19 years: United States, 1963–1965 through 2013–2014. *Health E-Stats*.

Fryar, C. D., Carroll, M. D., & Ogden, C. L. (2012). Prevalence of obesity among children and adolescents: United States, trends 1963–1965 through 2009–2010. National Center for Health Statistics. *Health E-Stats*, 1–6.

Fryar, C. D., Gu, Q., Ogden, C. L., Flegal, K. M. (2016). Anthropometric reference data for children and adults: United States, 2011–2014. National Center for Health Statistics. *Vital Health Stat 3*(39).

Frye, C., Bo, E., Calamandrei, G., Calza, L., Dessi-Fulgheri, F., Fernández, M., . . . & Patisaul, H. B. (2012). Endocrine disrupters: a review of some sources, effects, and mechanisms of actions on behaviour and neuroendocrine systems. *Journal of Neuroendocrinology, 24*(1), 144–159.

Frye, D. (2014). *Children's theories of mind: Mental states and social understanding*. London: Psychology Press.

Fuchs, C. S., Stampfer, M. J., Colditz, G. A., Giovannucci, E. L., Manson, J. E., Kawachi, I., . . . Willett, W. C. (1995). Alcohol consumption and mortality among women. *New England Journal of Medicine, 332*, 1245–1250.

Fui, M.N.T., Prendergast, L.A., Dupuis, P., Raval, M., Strauss, B.J., Zajac, J.D., & Grossmann, M. (2016). Effects of testosterone treatment on body fat and lean mass in obese men on a hypocaloric diet: A randomized controlled trial. *BMC Medicine*, 14. https://doi.org/10.1186/s12916-016-0700-9

Fuligni, E. Barber, & Clements.(2001). Early adolescent peer orientation and adjustment during high school. *Developmental Psychology, 37*(1), 28–36.

Fuller, J. N., Frost, A. M., & Burr, B. K. (2015). Exploring the impact of religiosity and socioeconomic factors on perceived ideal timing of marriage in young adults. *Journal of Student Research, 4*(1), 120–129.

Fuller-Iglesias, H.R., Webster, N.J., Antonucci, T.C. (2015). The complex nature of family support across the lifespan: Implications for psychological well-being. *Developmental Psychology*, 51, 277–288.

Fulton, R., & Owen, G. (1987–1988). Death and society in twentieth-century America. *Omega: Journal of Death and Dying, 18*(4), 379–395.

Fung, H. H., Carstensen, L. L., & Lang, F. R. (2001). Age-related patterns in social networks among European-Americans and African-Americans: Implications for socioemotional selectivity across the life span. *International Journal of Aging and Human Development, 52*, 185–206.

Furman, L. (2005). What is attention-deficit hyperactivity disorder (ADHD)? *Journal of Child Neurology, 20*, 994–1003.

Furman, W., & Bierman, K. L. (1983). Developmental changes in young children's conception of friendship. *Child Development, 54*, 549–556.

Furman, W., & Buhrmester, D. (1985). Children's perceptions of the personal relationships in their social networks. *Developmental Psychology, 21*, 1016–1024.

Furman, W., & Wehner, E. A. (1997). Adolescent romantic relationships: A developmental perspective. In S. Shulman & A. Collins (Eds.), *Romantic relationships in adolescence: Developmental perspectives* (New Directions for Child and Adolescent Development, No. 78, pp. 21–36). San Francisco: Jossey-Bass.

Furstenberg, F. F., Jr., Rumbaut, R. G., & Settersten, R. A., Jr. (2005). On the frontier of adulthood: Emerging themes and new directions. In R. A. Settersten Jr., F. F. Furstenberg Jr., & R. G. Rumbaut (Eds.), *On the frontier of adulthood: Theory, research, and public policy* (pp. 3–25). Chicago: University of Chicago Press.

Furukawa, E., Tangney, J., & Higashibara, F. (2012). Cross-cultural continuities and discontinuities in shame, guilt, and pride: A study of children residing in Japan, Korea and the USA. *Self and Identity, 11*(1), 90–113.

Fussell, E., & Furstenberg, F. (2005). The transition to adulthood during the twentieth century: Race, nativity, and gender. In R. A. Settersten Jr., F. F. Furstenberg Jr., & R. G. Rumbaut (Eds.), *On the frontier of adulthood: Theory, research, and public policy* (pp. 29–75). Chicago: University of Chicago Press.

Fustos, K. (2010, April). *Despite wide-ranging benefits, girls' education and empowerment overlooked in developing countries*. Retrieved from Population Reference Bureau: www.prb.org/Publications/Articles/2010/girlseducation.aspx

Gabhainn, S., & François, Y. (2000). Substance use. In C. Currie, K. Hurrelmann, W. Settertobulte, R. Smith, & J. Todd (Eds.), *Health behaviour in school-aged children: A WHO cross-national study (HBSC) international report* (pp. 97–114). *WHO Policy Series: Healthy Policy for Children and Adolescents, Series No. 1*. Copenhagen, Denmark: World Health Organization Regional Office for Europe.

Gaffney, M., Gamble, M., Costa, P., Holstrum, J., & Boyle, C. (2003). Infants tested for hearing loss—United States, 1999–2001. *Morbidity and Mortality Weekly Report, 51*, 981–984.

Gagne, J. R., & Saudino, K. J. (2010). Wait for it! A twin study of inhibitory control in early childhood. *Behavioral Genetics, 40*(3), 327-337.

Galal, M., Symonds, I., Murray, H., Petraglia, F., & Smith, R. (2012). Postterm pregnancy. *Facts, Views & Vision in ObGyn, 4*(3), 175.

Gallagher, W. (1993, May). Midlife myths. *Atlantic Monthly*, pp. 51-68.

Galland, B. C., Taylor, B. J., Elder, D. E., & Herbison, P. (2012). Normal sleep patterns in infants and children: A systematic review of observational studies. *Sleep Medicine Reviews, 16*(3), 213-222.

Gallo, L. C., & Matthews, K. A. (2003). Understanding the association between socioeconomic status and physical health: Do negative emotions play a role? *Psychological Bulletin, 129*, 10-51.

Gallo, L. C., Troxel, W. M., Matthews, K. A., & Kuller, L. H. (2003). Marital status and quality in middle-aged women: Associations with levels and trajectories of cardiovascular risk factors. *Health Psychology, 22*, 453-463.

Gallup News. (2017). *In U.S., 10.2 % or LGBT adults now married to same-sex couple.* Retrieved from http://news.gallup.com/poll/212702/lgbt-adults-married-sex-spouse.aspx?utm_source=alert&utm_medium=email&utm_content=morelink&utm_campaign=syndication

Galobardes, B., Smith, G. D., & Lynch, J. W. (2006). Systematic review of the influence of childhood socioeconomic circumstances on risk for cardiovascular disease in adulthood. *Annals of Epidemiology, 16*, 91-104.

Galotti, K. M., Komatsu, L. K., & Voelz, S. (1997). Children's differential performance on deductive and inductive syllogisms. *Developmental Psychology, 33*, 70-78.

Galvao, T. F., Silva, M. T., Zimmermann, I. R., Souza, K. M., Martins, S. S., & Pereira, M. G. (2014). Pubertal timing in girls a nd depression: a systematic review. *Journal of Affective Disorders, 155*, 13-19.

Gameiro, S., & Finnigan, A. (2017). Long-term adjustment to unmet parenthood goals following ART: a systematic review and meta-analysis. *Human Reproduction Update, 23*(3), 322-337.

Ganger, J., & Brent, M. R. (2004). Reexamining the vocabulary spurt. *Developmental Psychology, 40*, 621-632.

Gangwisch, J. E., Heymsfield, S. B., Boden-Albala, B., Buijs, R. M., Kreier, F., Opler, M. G., . . . Pickering, T. G. (2008). Sleep duration associated with mortality in elderly, but not middle-aged, adults in a large U.S. sample. *Sleep, 31*(8), 1087-1096.

Gans, J. E. (1990). *America's adolescents: How healthy are they?* Chicago: American Medical Association.

Garandeau, C. F., Ahn, H. J., & Rodkin, P. C. (2011). The social status of aggressive students across contexts: the role of classroom status hierarchy, academic achievement, and grade. *Developmental Psychology, 47*(6), 1699.

Garbarino, J., & Kostelny, K. (1993). Neighborhood and community influences on parenting. In T. Luster & L. Okagaki (Eds.), *Parenting: An ecological perspective* (pp. 203-226). Hillsdale, NJ: Erlbaum.

Garbarino, J., Dubrow, N., Kostelny, K., & Pardo, C. (1992). *Children in danger: Coping with the consequences of community violence.* San Francisco: Jossey-Bass.

Garbarino, J., Governale, A., Henry, P., & Nesi, D. (2015). Children and terrorism. *Social Policy Report, 29*(2).

Garces, A., McClure, E., Chomba, E., Patel, A., Pasha, O., Tshefu, A., et al. (2011, November 18). Home birth attendants in low income countries: who are they and what do they do? Retrieved from BMC Pregnancy and Childbirth: https://bmcpregnancychildbirth.biomedcentral.com/articles/10.1186/1471-2393-12-34

Garcia, F., & Gracia, E. (2009). Is always authoritative the optimum parenting style? Evidence from Spanish families. *Adolescence, 44*(173), 101.

Gardiner, H. W., & Kosmitzki, C. (2005). *Lives across cultures: Cross-cultural human development.* Boston: Allyn & Bacon.

Gardner, A. T., de Vries, B., & Mockus, D. S. (2014). Aging out in the desert: Disclosure, acceptance, and service use among midlife and older lesbians and gay men. *Journal of Homosexuality, 61*(1), 129-144.

Gardner, H. (1993). *Frames of mind: The theory of multiple intelligences.* New York: Basic Books. (Original work published 1983)

Gardner, H. (1995). Reflections on multiple intelligences: Myths and messages. *Phi Delta Kappan*, 200-209.

Gardner, H. (1998). Are there additional intelligences? In J. Kane (Ed.), *Education, information, and transformation: Essays on learning and thinking.* Englewood Cliffs, NJ: Prentice Hall.

Gardner, H. (1999). Are there additional intelligences? The case for naturalist, spiritual, and existential intelligences. *Education, information, and transformation*, 111-131. Upper Saddle River, NJ: Prentice Hall.

Gardner, H. *Frames of mind: The theory of multiple intelligences.* New York: Basic Books (Original work published 1983).

Gardner, M., & Steinberg, L. (2005). Peer influence on risk taking, risk preference, and risky decision making in adolescence and adulthood: An experimental study. *Developmental Psychology, 41*, 625-635.

Garlick, D. (2003). Integrating brain science research with intelligence research. *Current Directions in Psychological Science, 12*, 185-192.

Garn, A. C., Matthews, M. S., & Jolly, J. L. (2010). Parental influences on the academic motivation of gifted students: A self-determination theory perspective. *Gifted Child Quarterly, 54*(4), 263-272.

Garner, A.A., Fine, P.R., Franklin, C.A., Sattin, R.W., & Stavrinos, D. (2011). Distracted driving among adolescents: Challenges and opportunities. *Injury Prevention*, 17, 285.

Garner, P. W., & Estep, K. M. (2001). Emotional competence, emotional socialization, and young children's peer-related social competence. *Early Education & Development, 12*(1), 29-48.

Garnick, M.B. (2015). Testosterone replacement therapy faces FDA scrutiny. *JAMA*, 313, 563.

Gartrell, N., Deck, A., Rodas, C., Peyser, H., & Banks, A. (2005). The National Lesbian Family Study: Interviews with the 10-year-old children. *American Journal of Orthopsychiatry, 75*, 518-524.

Gaskins, S., Haight, W., & Lancy, D. F. (2007). The cultural construction of play. In A. Goncu & S. Gaskins (Eds.) *Play and development: Evolutionary, sociocultural and functional perspectives (pp. 179-202).* Hillsdale, NJ: Lawrence Erlbaum.

Gates, G. J. (2013). *LBGT parenting in the United States.* Retrieved from http://williamsinstitute.law.ucla.edu/wp-content/uploads/LGBT-Parenting.pdf

Gatewood, J. D., Wills, A., Shetty, S., Xu, J., Arnold, A. P., Burgoyne, P. S., & Rissman, E. F. (2006). Sex chromosome complement and gonadal sex influence aggressive and parental behaviors in mice. *Journal of Neuroscience, 26*, 2335-2342.

Gathercole, S. E., & Alloway, T. P. (2008). *Working memory and learning: A practical guide.* Thousand Oaks, CA: Sage.

Gattis, K. S., Berns, S., Simpson, L. E., & Christensen, A. (2004). Birds of a feather or strange birds? Ties among personality dimensions, similarity, and marital quality. *Journal of Family Psychology, 18*, 564-574.

Gatz, M. (2007). Genetics, dementia, and the elderly. *Current Directions in Psychological Science, 16*, 123-127.

Gatz, M., Reynolds, C. A., Fratiglioni, L., Johansson, B., Mortimer, J. A., Berg, S., . . . Pederson, N. L. (2006). Role of genes and environments for explaining Alzheimer disease. *Archives of General Psychiatry, 63*, 168-174.

Gauthier, A. H., & Furstenberg, F. F., Jr. (2005). Historical trends in patterns of time use among young adults in developed countries. In R. A. Settersten Jr., F. F. Furstenberg Jr., & R. G. Rumbaut (Eds.), *On the frontier of adulthood: Theory, research, and public policy* (pp. 150-176). Chicago: University of Chicago Press.

Gauvain, M., & Perez, S. M. (2005). Parent-child participation in planning children's activities outside of school in European American and Latino families. *Child Development, 76*, 371-383.

Gazzaley, A., & Nobre, A. C. (2012). Top-down modulation: bridging selective attention and working memory. *Trends in Cognitive Sciences, 16*(2), 129-135.

Ge, X., Brody, G. H., Conger, R. D., Simons, R. L., & Murry, V. (2002). Contextual amplification of pubertal transitional effect on African American children's problem behaviors. *Developmental Psychology, 38*, 42-54.

Geary, D. C. (2006). Development of mathematical understanding. In W. Damon (Ed.), & D. Kuhl & R. S. Siegler (Vol. Eds.), *Handbook of child psychology: Cognition, perception, and language, Vol 2.* (6th ed., pp. 777-810). Hoboken, NJ: Wiley.

Gedo, J. (2001). *The enduring scientific contributions of Sigmund Freud.* Retrieved from www.pep-web.org/document.php?id=AOP.029.0105A

Geen, R. (2004). The evolution of kinship care: Policy and practice. *Future of Children, 14*(1). (David and Lucile Packard Foundation.) Retrieved from www.futureofchildren.org

Geerligs, L., Renken, R. J., Saliasi, E., Maurits, N. M., & Lorist, M. M. (2014). A brain-wide study of age-related changes in functional connectivity. *Cerebral Cortex, 25*(7), 1987–1999.

Geidd, J. N. (2008). The teen brain: Insights from neuroimaging. *Journal of Adolescent Health, 42,* 321–323.

Gelman, R. (2006). Young natural-number mathematicians. *Current Directions in Psychological Science, 15,* 193–197.

Gelman, R., Spelke, E. S., & Meck, E. (1983). What preschoolers know about animate and inanimate objects. In D. R. Rogers & J. S. Sloboda (Eds.), *The acquisition of symbolic skills* (pp. 297–326). New York: Plenum Press.

Genesee, F., Nicoladis, E., & Paradis, J. (1995). Language differentiation in early bilingual development. *Journal of Child Language, 22,* 611–631.

Genevay, B. (1986). Intimacy as we age. *Generations, 10*(4), 12–15.

Georganopoulou, D. G., Chang, L., Nam, J.-M., Thaxton, C. S., Mufson, E. J., Klein, W. L., & Mirkin, C. A. (2005). Nanoparticle-based detection in cerebral spinal fluid of a soluble pathogenic biomarker for Alzheimer's disease. *Proceedings of the National Academy of Sciences, 102,* 2273–2276.

George, C., Kaplan, N., & Main, M. (1985). *The Berkeley Adult Attachment Interview.* [Unpublished protocol]. Department of Psychology, University of California, Berkeley.

Geraci, L., McDaniel, M. A., Manzano, I., & Roediger, H. L. (2009). The influence of age on memory for distinctive events. *Memory & Cognition, 37*(2), 175–180.

Gershoff, E. T. (2010). More harm than good: A summary of scientific research on the intended and unintended effects of corporal punishment on children. *Law and Contemporary Problems, 73*(2), 31–56.

Gershoff, E. T. (2013). Spanking and child development: We know enough now to stop hitting our children. *Child Development Perspectives, 7*(3), 133–137.

Gershoff, E. T., Lansford, J. E., Sexton, H. R., Davis-Kean, P., & Sameroff, A. J. (2012). Longitudinal links between spanking and children's externalizing behaviors in a national sample of white, black, Hispanic, and Asian American families. *Child Development, 83*(3), 838–843.

Gerstorf, D., Ram, N., Mayraz, G., Hidajat, M., Lindenberger, U., Wagner, G. G., & Schupp, J. (2010). Late-life decline in well-being across adulthood in Germany, the United Kingdom, and the United States: Something is seriously wrong at the end of life. *Psychology and Aging, 25*(2), 477.

Gerstorf, D., Ram, N., Röcke, C., Lindenberger, U., & Smith, J. (2008). Decline in life satisfaction in old age: longitudinal evidence for links to distance-to-death. *Psychology and Aging, 23*(1), 154.

Gervain, J., & Mehler, J. (2010). Speech perception and language acquisition in the first year of life. *Annual Review of Psychology, 61,* 191–218.

Gest, S. D. (1997). Behavioral inhibition: Stability and associations with adaptation from childhood to early adulthood. *Journal of Personality and Social Psychology, 72*(2), 467.

Getz, D. (2010). *American community survey briefs: Men's and women's earnings for states and metropolitan statistical areas: 2009* (ACSBR/09-3). Washington DC: U.S. Census Bureau. Retrieved from www.census.gov/prod/2010pubs /acsbr09-3.pdf

Getzels, J. W., & Jackson, P. W. (1963). The highly intelligent and the highly creative adolescent: A summary of some research findings. In C. W. Taylor & F. Baron (Eds.), *Scientific creativity: Its recognition and development* (pp. 161–172). New York: Wiley.

Gibaldi, C. P. (2013). The changing trends of retirement: Baby boomers leading the charge. *Review of Business, 34*(1), 50.

Gibbs, J. C. (1991). Toward an integration of Kohlberg's and Hoffman's theories of moral development. In W. M. Kurtines & J. L. Gewirtz (Eds.), *Handbook of moral behavior and development: Advances in theory, research, and application* (Vol. 1). Hillsdale, NJ: Erlbaum.

Gibbs, J. C. (1995). The cognitive developmental perspective. In W. M. Kurtines & J. L. Gewirtz (Eds.), *Moral development: An introduction.* Boston: Allyn & Bacon.

Gibbs, J. C., & Schnell, S. V. (1985). Moral development "versus" socialization. *American Psychologist, 40*(10), 1071–1080.

Gibson, E. J. (1969). *Principles of perceptual learning and development.* New York: Appleton-Century-Crofts.

Gibson, E. J., & Pick, A. D. (2000). *An ecological approach to perceptual learning and development.* New York: Oxford University Press.

Gibson, E. J., & Walker, A. S. (1984). Development of knowledge of visual tactual affordances of substance. *Child Development, 55,* 453–460.

Gibson, J. J. (1979). *The ecological approach to visual perception.* Boston: Houghton-Mifflin.

Gibson, S.C. & Greene, E. (2013). Assessing knowledge of elder financial abuse: A first step in enhancing prosecutions. *Journal of Elder Abuse and Neglect, 25,* 162–182.

Giedd, J. N., & Rapoport, J. L. (2010). Structural MRI of pediatric brain development: What have we learned and where are we going? *Neuron, 67*(5), 728–734.

Giedd, J. N., Lalonde, F. M., Celano, M. J., White, S. L., Wallace, G. L., Lee, N. R., & Lenroot, R. K. (2009). Anatomical brain magnetic resonance imaging of typically developing children and adolescents. *Journal of the American Academy of Child and Adolescent Psychiatry, 48*(5), 465.

Gierveld, J. D. J., & Dykstra, P. A. (2008). Virtue is its own reward? Support-giving in the family and loneliness in middle and old age. *Ageing and Society, 28*(2), 271–287.

Gilboa, S., Correa, A., Botto, L., Rasmussen, S., Waller, D., Hobbs, C., . . . Riehle-Colarusso, T. J. (2009). Association between prepregnancy body mass index and congenital heart defects. *American Journal of Obstetrics and Gynecology, 202*(1), 51–61.

Gill, J., & Moore, M. J. (2013). Centers for Disease Control and Prevention. (2013). The state of aging and health in America 2013. *Atlanta, GA: Centers for Disease Control and Prevention, US Department of Health and Human Services.*

Gilligan, C. (1982/1993). *In a different voice: Psychological theory and women's development.* Cambridge, MA: Harvard University Press.

Gilligan, C. (1987a). Adolescent development reconsidered. In E. E. Irwin (Ed.), *Adolescent social behavior and health.* San Francisco: Jossey-Bass.

Gilligan, C. (1987b). Moral orientation and moral development. In E. F. Kittay & D. T. Meyers (Eds.), *Women and moral theory* (pp. 19–33). Totowa, NJ: Rowman & Littlefield.

Gilmore, J., Lin, W., Prastawa, M. W., Looney, C. B., Vetsa, Y. S. K., Knickmeyer, R. C., . . . Gerig, G. (2007). Regional gray matter growth, sexual dimorphism, and cerebral asymmetry in the neonatal brain. *Journal of Neuroscience, 27*(6), 1255–1260.

Giordano, P. C., Cernkovich, S. A., & DeMaris, A. (1993). The family and peer relations of black adolescents. *Journal of Marriage and Family, 55,* 277–287.

Giscombé, C. L., & Lobel, M. (2005). Explaining disproportionately high rates of adverse birth outcomes among African Americans: The impact of stress, racism, and related factors in pregnancy. *Psychological Bulletin, 131,* 662–683.

Glaser, D. (2000). Child abuse and neglect and the brain: A review. *Journal of Child Psychiatry, 41,* 97–116.

Glass, H. C., Costarino, A. T., Stayer, S. A., Brett, C., Cladis, F., & Davis, P. J. (2015). Outcomes for extremely premature infants. *Anesthesia and Analgesia, 120*(6), 1337.

Glaucoma Research Foundation. (2017). Four key facts about glaucoma. Retrieved from www.glaucoma.org/glaucoma/glaucoma-facts-and-stats.php

Gleason, T. R., Sebanc, A. M., & Hartup, W. W. (2000). Imaginary companions of preschool children. *Developmental Psychology, 36,* 419–428.

Glenn, N., & Marquardt, E. (2001). *Hooking up, hanging out, and hoping for Mr. Right: College women on dating and mating today.* New York: Institute for American Values.

Glick, G. C., & Rose, A. J. (2011). Prospective associations between friendship adjustment and social strategies: Friendship as a context for building social skills. *Developmental Psychology, 47*(4), 1117.

Glick, J. E., & Van Hook, J. (2002). Parents' co-residence with adult children: Can immigration explain racial and ethnic variation? *Journal of Marriage and Family, 64,* 240–253.

Goble, P., Martin, C. L., Hanish, L. D., & Fabes, R. A. (2012). Children's gender-typed activity choices across preschool social contexts. *Sex Roles, 67*(7–8), 435–451.

Goertz, C., Lamm, B., Graf, F., Kolling, T., Knopf, M., & Keller, H. (2011). Deferred imitation in 6-month-old German and Cameroonian Nso infants. *Journal of Cognitive Education and Psychology, 10*(1), 44.

Goetz, P. J. (2003). The effects of bilingualism on theory of mind development. *Bilingualism: Language and Cognition, 6*, 1-15.

Gogtay, N., & Thompson, P. M. (2010). Mapping gray matter development: Implications for typical development and vulnerability to psychopathology. *Brain and Cognition, 72*(1), 6-15.

Gold, K. J., Sen, A., & Hayward, R. A. (2010). Marriage and cohabitation outcomes after pregnancy loss. *Pediatrics, 125*(5), e1202-e1207.

Goldberg, W. A., Prause, J. A., Lucas-Thompson, R., & Himsel, A. (2008). Maternal employment and children's achievement in context: A meta-analysis of four decades of research. *Psychological Bulletin, 134*, 77-108.

Golden, J., Conroy, R. M., & Lawlor, B. A. (2009). Social support network structure in older people: Underlying dimensions and association with psychological and physical health. *Psychology, Health & Medicine, 14*(3), 280-290.

Goldenberg, R. L., Kirby, R., & Culhane, J. F. (2004). Stillbirth: A review. *Journal of Maternal-Fetal & Neonatal Medicine, 16*(2), 79-94.

Goldin-Meadow, S. (2007). Pointing sets the stage for learning language—And creating language. *Child Development, 78*(3), 741-745.

Goldman, L. L., & Rothschild, J. (n.d.). *Healing the wounded with art therapy.* Unpublished manuscript.

Goldman, L., Falk, H., Landrigan, P. J., Balk, S. J., Reigart, J. R., & Etzel, R. A. (2004). Environmental pediatrics and its impact on government health policy. *Pediatrics, 113*, 1146-1157.

Goldman, S. R., Petrosino, A. J., & Cognition and Technology Group at Vanderbilt. (1999). Design principles for instruction in content domains: Lessons from research on expertise and learning. In F. T. Durso (Ed.), *Handbook of applied cognition* (pp. 595-627). Chichester, England: Wiley.

Goldscheider, F., & Sassler, S. (2006). Creating stepfamilies: Integrating children into the study of union formation. *Journal of Marriage and Family, 68*, 275-291.

Goldschmidt, L., Richardson, G. A., Cornelius, M. D., & Day, N. L. (2004). Prenatal marijuana and alcohol exposure and academic achievement at age 10. *Neurotoxicology and Teratology, 26*(4), 521-532.

Goldsmith, H. H., & Alansky, J. A. (1987). Maternal and infant predictors of attachment: A meta-analytic review. *Journal of Consulting and Clinical Psychology, 55*, 805-816.

Goldstein, I., Padma-Nathan, H., Rosen, R. C., Steers, W. D., & Wicker, P. A., for the Sildenafil Study Group. (1998). Oral sildenafil in the treatment of erectile dysfunction. *New England Journal of Medicine, 338*, 1397-1404.

Goldstein, J., McCoach, D. B., & Yu, H. (2017). The predictive validity of kindergarten readiness judgments: Lessons from one state. *The Journal of Educational Research, 110*(1), 50-60.

Goldstein, M. H., Schwade, J. A., & Bornstein, M. H. (2009). The value of vocalizing: Five-month-old infants associate their own noncry vocalizations with responses from caregivers. *Child Development, 80*(3), 636-644.

Goldstein, M., King, A., & West, M. (2003). Social interaction shapes babbling: Testing parallels between birdsong and speech. *Proceedings of the National Academy of Sciences, USA, 100*, 8030-8035.

Goldstein, S. E., Davis-Kean, P. E., & Eccles, J. E. (2005). Parents, peers, and problem behavior: A longitudinal investigation of the impact of relationship perceptions and characteristics on the development of adolescent problem behavior. *Developmental Psychology, 2*, 401-413.

Golinkoff, R. M., & Hirsh-Pasek, K. (2006). Baby wordsmith. *Current Directions in Psychological Science, 15*, 30-33.

Golinkoff, R. M., Can, D. D., Soderstrom, M., & Hirsh-Pasek, K. (2015). (Baby) talk to me: The social context of infant-directed speech and its effects on early language acquisition. *Current Directions in Psychological Science, 24*(5), 339-344.

Golmaryami, F. N., Frick, P. J., Hemphill, S. A., Kahn, R. E., Crapanzano, A. M., & Terranova, A. M. (2016). The social, behavioral, and emotional correlates of bullying and victimization in a school-based sample. *Journal of Abnormal Child Psychology, 44*(2), 381-391.

Golombok, S., Mellish, L., Jennings, S., Casey, P., Tasker, F., & Lamb, M. E. (2013). Adoptive gay father families: Parent–child relationships and children's psychological adjustment. *Child Development.* doi: 10.1111/cdev.12155

Golombok, S., Rust, J., Zervoulis, K., Croudace, T., Golding, J., & Hines, M. (2008). Developmental trajectories of sex-typed behaviors in boys and girls: A longitudinal general population study of children aged 2.5-8 years. *Child Development, 79*, 1583-1593.

Gómez-Robles, A., Hopkins, W. D., & Sherwood, C. C. (2013, June). Increased morphological asymmetry, evolvability and plasticity in human brain evolution. In *Proc. R. Soc. B* (Vol. 280, No. 1761, p. 20130575). The Royal Society.

Göncü, A., Mistry, J., & Mosier, C. (2000). Cultural variations in the play of toddlers. *International Journal of Behavioral Development, 24*(3), 321-329.

Gonen-Yaacovi, G., de Souza, L. C., Levy, R., Urbanski, M., Josse, G., & Volle, E. (2013). Rostral and caudal prefrontal contribution to creativity: A meta-analysis of functional imaging data. *Frontiers in Human Neuroscience, 7*.

Gonyea, J. G. (2013). Changing family demographics, multigenerational bonds, and care for the oldest old. *Public Policy and Aging Report, 23*(2), 11-15.

Gonzales, E., Matz-Costa, C., & Morrow-Howell, N. (2015). Increasing opportunities for the productive engagement of older adults: A response to population aging. *The Gerontologist, 55*(2), 252-261.

Gonzales, N. A., Cauce, A. M., & Mason, C. A. (1996). Interobserver agreement in the assessment of parental behavior and parent-adolescent conflict: African American mothers, daughters, and independent observers. *Child Development, 67*, 1483-1498.

Gonzalez, D., Rennard, S. I., Nides, M., Oncken, C., Azouley, S., Billing, C., . . . Reeves, K. R. (2006). Vereniicline, an α4β2 nicotinic acetylcholine receptor partial agonist, vs. sustained-release bupropion and placebo for smoking cessation. *Journal of the American Medical Association, 296*, 47-55.

Goodman, G. S., Emery, R. E., & Haugaard, J. J. (1998). Developmental psychology and law: Divorce, child maltreatment, foster care, and adoption. In W. Damon (Series Ed.), I. E. Sigel & K. A. Renninger (Vol. Eds.), *Handbook of Child Psychology* (Vol. 4, pp. 775-874). New York: Wiley.

Gorchoff, S. M., John, O. P., & Helson, R. (2008). Contextualizing change in marital satisfaction during middle age. *Psychological Science, 19*(11), 1194-1200.

Gordon, L., Joo, J. E., Andronikos, R., Ollikainen, M., Wallace, E. M., Umstad, M. P., Permezel, M., Oshlack, A., Morley, R., Carlin, J. B., Saffrey, R., Smyth, G. K., & Craig, J. M. (2011). Expression discordance of monozygotic twins at birth: Effect of intrauterine environment and a possible mechanism for fetal programming. *Epigenetics, 6*, 579-592.

Gorman, B. K., & Read, J. G. (2007). Why men die younger than women. *Geriatrics and Aging, 10*, 182-191.

Gorman, J. (2006). Gender differences in depression and response to psychotropic medication. *Gender Medicine, 3*(2), 93-109.

Gostin, L. O. (2006). Physician-assisted suicide. *Journal of the American Medical Association, 295*, 1941-1943.

Gottfried, A. E., & Gottfried, A. W. (Eds.). (2013). *Maternal employment and children's development: Longitudinal research.* Berlin: Springer Science & Business Media.

Gottfried, A. E., Fleming, J. S., & Gottfried, A. W. (1998). Role of cognitively stimulating home environment in children's academic intrinsic motivation: A longitudinal study. *Child Development, 69*, 1448-1460.

Gottfried, A. W., Cook, C. R., Gottfried, A. E., & Morris, P. E. (2005). Educational characteristics of adolescents with gifted academic intrinsic motivation: A longitudinal investigation from school entry through early adulthood. *Gifted Child Quarterly, 49*(2), 172-186.

Gottlieb, G. (1991). Experiential canalization of behavioral development theory. *Developmental Psychology, 27*(1), 4-13.

Gottlieb, G. (1997). *Synthesizing nature-nurture: Prenatal roots of instinctive behavior.* Mahwah, NJ: Erlbaum.

Goubet, N., & Clifton, R. K. (1998). Object and event representation in 6½-month-old infants. *Developmental Psychology, 34*, 63-76.

Gould, E., Reeves, A. J., Graziano, M. S. A., & Gross, C. G. (1999). Neurogenesis in the neocortex of adult primates. *Science, 286*, 548-552.

Grady, D. (2010, July 21). New guidelines seek to reduce repeat caesareans. *The New York Times.* Retrieved from www.nytimes.com/2010/07/22/health/22birth.html?_r=1&emc=eta1

Grady, D., Herrington, D., Bittner, V., Blumenthal, R., Davidson, M., Hlatky, M., . . . Wenger, N. (2002). Cardiovascular disease outcomes during 6.8 years of hormone therapy: Heart and Estrogen/Progestin Replacement Study follow-up (HERS II). *Journal of the American Medical Association, 288,* 49–57.

Graham, E. K., & Lachman, M. E. (2012). Personality stability is associated with better cognitive performance in adulthood: Are the stable more able? *Journals of Gerontology Series B: Psychological Sciences and Social Sciences, 67*(5), 545–554.

Graham, J. E., Christian, L. M., & Kiecolt-Glaser, J. K. (2006). Marriage, health and immune function: A review of key findings and the role of depression. In S. Beach & M. Wimboldt (Eds.), *Relational processes in mental health* (Vol. 11, pp. 61–76). Arlington, VA: American Psychiatric Publishing.

Graham, K. L., & Burghardt, G. M. (2010). Current perspectives on the biological study of play: Signs of progress. *The Quarterly Review of Biology, 85,* 393–418.

Grant, B. F., Stinson, F. S., Chou, D. A., Raun, P., June, W., & Pickering, R. P. (2007). Co-occurrence of 12-month alcohol and drug use disorders and personality disorders in the United States: Results from the National Epidemiologic Survey on alcohol and related conditions. *Alcohol Research and Health, 29*(2), 121–130.

Grant, B. F., Stinson, F. S., Dawson, D. A., Chou, S. P., Dufour, M. C., Compton, W., Pickering, R. P., & Kaplan, K. (2004). Prevalence and co-occurrence of substance use disorders and independent mood and anxiety disorders: Results from the National Epidemiologic Survey on Alcohol and Related Conditions. *Archives of General Psychiatry, 61,* 807–816.

Grant, N., Hamer, M., & Steptoe, A. (2009). Social isolation and stress-related cardiovascular, lipid, and cortisol responses. *Annals of Behavioral Medicine, 37*(1), 29–37.

Grantham-McGregor, S., Powell, C., Walker, S., Chang, S., & Fletcher, P. (1994). The long-term follow-up of severely malnourished children who participated in an intervention program. *Child Development, 65,* 428–439.

Grassi, M., Petraccia, L., Mennuni, G., Fontana, M., Scarno, A., Sabetta, S., & Fraioli, A. (2011). Changes, functional disorders, and diseases in the gastrointestinal tract of elderly. *Nutricion Hospitalaria, 26*(4).

Gravina, S., & Vijg, J. (2010). Epigenetic factors in aging and longevity. *Pflugers Archives, European Journal of Physiology, 459*(2), 241–258. doi: 10.1007/s00424-009-0730-7 Ch. 17

Gray, J. R., & Thompson, P. M. (2004). Neurobiology of intelligence: Science and ethics. *Neuroscience, 5,* 471–492.

Gray, P. (2011). The special value of children's age-mixed play. *American Journal of Play,* 500–522.

Green, M., & Elliott, M. (2010). Religion, health, and psychological well-being. *Journal of Religion and Health, 49*(2), 149–163.

Greenberg, J., & Becker, M. (1988). Aging parents as family resources. *Gerontologist, 28*(6), 786–790.

Greene, K. M., & Maggs, J. L. (2015). Revisiting the time trade-off hypothesis: Work, organized activities, and academics during college. *Journal of Youth and Adolescence, 44*(8), 1623–1637.

Greene, M. L., Way, N., & Pahl, K. (2006). Trajectories of perceived adult and peer discrimination among black, Latino, and Asian American adolescents: patterns and psychological correlates. *Developmental Psychology, 42*(2), 218.

Greenfield, E. A., & Marks, N. F. (2004). Formal volunteering as a protective factor for older adults' psychological well-being. *Journal of Gerontology: Social Sciences, 59B,* S258–S264.

Greenfield, E. A., & Marks, N. F. (2006). Linked lives: Adult children's problems and their parents' psychological and relational well-being. *Journal of Marriage and Family, 68,* 442–454.

Greenfield, E. A., & Russell, D. (2011). Identifying living arrangements that heighten risk for loneliness in later life: Evidence from the US National Social Life, Health, and Aging Project. *Journal of Applied Gerontology, 30*(4), 524–534.

Greenfield, P. M. (2009). Technology and informal education: What is taught, what is learned. *Science, 323*(5910), 69–71. doi: 10.1126/science.1167190

Greenfield, P. M., & Childs, C. P. (1978). Understanding sibling concepts: A developmental study of kin terms in Zinacanten. In P. R. Dasen (Ed.), *Piagetian psychology* (pp. 335–358). New York: Gardner.

Greenhouse, L. (2000, June 6). Justices reject visiting rights in divided case: Ruling favors mother over grandparents. *The New York Times* (National ed.), A1, A15.

Greenhouse, L. (2005, February 23). Justices accept Oregon case weighing assisted suicide. *The New York Times,* A1.

Greenwood, D. C., Thatcher, N. J., Ye, J., Garrard, L., Keogh, G., King, L. G., & Cade, J. E. (2014). Caffeine intake during pregnancy and adverse birth outcomes: a systematic review and dose-response meta-analysis. *European Journal of Epidemiology, 29*(10), 725.

Grenier, A. (2014, April 11). *Majority of U.S. patents granted to foreign individuals.* Retrieved from American Immigration Council Immigration Impact: http://immigrationimpact.com/2014/04/11/majority-of-u-s-patents-granted-to-foreign-individuals/

Greyson, B., & Khanna, S. (2014). Spiritual transformation after near-death experiences. *Spirituality in Clinical Practice, 1*(1), 43.

Griffin, K. W., Botvin, G. J., Scheier, L. M., Diaz, T., & Miller, N. L. (2000). Parenting practices as predictors of substance use, delinquency, and aggression among urban minority youth: Moderating effects of family structure and gender. *Psychology of Addictive Behaviors: Journal of the Society of Psychologists in Addictive Behaviors, 14*(2), 174.

Grigorenko, E. L., Meier, E., Lipka, J., Mohatt, G., Yanez, E., & Sternberg, R. J. (2004). Academic and practical intelligence: A case study of the Yup'ik in Alaska. *Learning and Individual Differences, 14*(4), 183–207.

Grigoriadis, S., VonderPorten, E. H., Mamisashvili, L., Tomlinson, G., Dennis, C. L., Koren, G., . . . & Martinovic, J. (2013). The impact of maternal depression during pregnancy on perinatal outcomes: A systematic review and meta-analysis. *J Clin Psychiatry, 74*(4), e321–e341.

Grimbos, T., Dawood, K., Burriss, R. P., Zucker, K. J., & Puts, D. A. (2010). Sexual orientation and the second to fourth finger length ratio: a meta-analysis in men and women. *Behavioral Neuroscience, 124*(2), 278–287.

Grinshteyn, E., & Hemenway, D. (2016). Violent death rates: I US compared with other high-income OECD countries, 2010. *The American Journal of Medicine, 129*(3), 266–273.

Gripper, A. (2012, March 2). *Kate Middleton's something old, new, borrowed and blue for royal wedding revealed.* Retrieved from Mirror: www.mirror.co.uk/news/uk-news/kate-middletons-something-old-new-179096

Grodstein, F. (1996). Postmenopausal estrogen and progestin use and the risk of cardiovascular disease. *New England Journal of Medicine, 335,* 453.

Groen, R. S., Bae, J. Y., & Lim, K. J. (2012). Fear of the unknown: ionizing radiation exposure during pregnancy. *American Journal of Obstetrics and Gynecology, 206*(6), 456–462.

Groenewoud, J. H., van der Heide, A., Onwuteaka-Philipsen, B. D., Willems, D. L., van der Maas, P. J., & van der Wal, G. (2000). Clinical problems with the performance of euthanasia and physician-assisted suicide in the Netherlands. *New England Journal of Medicine, 342,* 551–556.

Gross, A. L., Parisi, J. M., Spira, A. P., Kueider, A. M., Ko, J. Y., Saczynski, J. S., . . . & Rebok, G. W. (2012). Memory training interventions for older adults: A meta-analysis. *Aging & Mental Health, 16*(6), 722–734.

Grotevant, H. D., McRoy, R. G., Eide, C. L., & Fravel, D. L. (1994). Adoptive family system dynamics: Variations by level of openness in the adoption. *Family Process, 33*(2), 125–146.

Grotevant, H. D., McRoy, R. G., Wrobel, G. M., & Ayers-Lopez, S. (2013). Contact between adoptive and birth families: Perspectives from the Minnesota/Texas Adoption Research Project. *Child Development Perspectives, 7*(3), 193–198.

Grotevant, H.D. (2012). What works in open adoption. In P. A. Curtis & G. Alexander (Eds). *What works in child welfare.* Washington, DC: Child Welfare League of America.

Grov, C., Bimbi, D. S., Nanin, J. E., & Parsons, J. T. (2006). Race, ethnicity, gender and generational factors associated with the coming-out process among gay, lesbian and bisexual individuals. *Journal of Sex Research, 43*(2), 115–121.

Gruenewald, T. L., Karlamangla, A. S., Greendale, G. A., Singer, B. H., & Seeman, T. E. (2007). Feelings of usefulness to others, disability, and mortality in older adults: The MacArthur Study of Successful Aging. *Journal of Gerontology: Psychological Sciences, 62B,* P28–P37.

Gruenewald, T. L., Liao, D. H., & Seeman, T. E. (2012). Contributing to others, contributing to oneself: Perceptions of generativity and health in later life. *Journals of Gerontology Series B: Psychological Sciences and Social Sciences, 67*(6), 660–665.

Grusec, J. E. (2006). The development of moral behavior and conscience from a socialization perspective. *Handbook of Moral Development,* 243–265.

Grusec, J. E., & Goodnow, J. J. (1994). Impact of parental discipline methods on the child's internalization of values: A reconceptualization of current points of view. *Developmental Psychology, 30,* 4–19.

Guallar, E., & Laine, C. (2014). Controversy over clinical guidelines: listen to the evidence, not the noise. *Annals of Internal Medicine, 160*(5), 361–362.

Guberman, S. R. (1996). The development of everyday mathematics in Brazilian children with limited formal education. *Child Development, 67,* 1609–1623.

Guendelman, S., Kosa, J. L., Pearl, M., Graham, S., Goodman, J., & Kharrazi, M. (2009). Juggling work and breastfeeding: Effects of maternity leave and occupational characteristics. *Pediatrics, 123,* e38–e46.

Guerrero, T. J. (2001). *Youth in transition: Housing, employment, social policies and families in France and Spain.* Aldershot, Hants, England: Ashgate.

Guida, A., Gobet, F., Tardieu, H., & Nicolas, S. (2012). How chunks, long-term working memory and templates offer a cognitive explanation for neuroimaging data on expertise acquisition: A two-stage framework. *Brain and Cognition, 79*(3), 221–244.

Guilford, J. P. (1956). Structure of intellect. *Psychological Bulletin, 53,* 267–293.

Guilford, J. P. (1959). Three faces of intellect. *American Psychologist, 14,* 469–479.

Guilford, J. P. (1960). Basic conceptual problems of the psychology of thinking. *Proceedings of the New York Academy of Sciences, 91,* 6–21.

Guilford, J. P. (1967). *The nature of human intelligence.* New York: McGraw-Hill.

Guilford, J. P. (1986). *Creative talents: Their nature, uses and development.* Buffalo, NY: Bearly.

Guilleminault, C., Palombini, L., Pelayo, R., & Chervin, R. D. (2003). Sleeping and sleep terrors in prepubertal children: What triggers them? *Pediatrics, 111,* e17–e25.

Guiney, H., Lucas, S. J., Cotter, J. D., & Machado, L. (2015). Evidence cerebral blood-flow regulation mediates exercise–cognition links in healthy young adults. *Neuropsychology, 29*(1), 1.

Gullone, E. (2000). The development of normal fear: A century of research. *Clinical Psychology Review, 20,* 429–451.

Gunderson, E. A., Gripshover, S. J., Romero, C., Dweck, C. S., Goldin-Meadow, S., & Levine, S. C. (2013). Parent praise to 1- to 3-year-olds predicts children's motivational frameworks 5 years later. *Child Development, 84*(5), 1526–1541.

Gunnar, M. R., Kryzer, E., Van Ryzin, M. J., & Phillips, D. A. (2010). The rise in cortisol in family day care: Associations with aspects of care quality, child behavior, and child sex. *Child Development, 81,* 851–869. doi: 10.1111/j.1467-8624.2010.01438.x

Gunnar, M. R., Larson, M. C., Hertsgaard, L., Harris, M. L., & Brodersen, L. (1992). The stressfulness of separation among 9-month-old infants: Effects of social context variables and infant temperament. *Child Development, 63,* 290–303.

Guo, G., Roettger, M., & Cai, T. (2008). The integration of genetic propensities into social-control models of delinquency and violence among male youths. *American Sociological Review, 73,* 543–568.

Gupta, B. P., Murad, M. H., Clifton, M. M., Prokop, L., Nehra, A., & Kopecky, S. L. (2011). The effect of lifestyle modification and cardiovascular risk factor reduction on erectile dysfunction: a systematic review and meta-analysis. *Archives of Internal Medicine, 171*(20), 1797–1803.

Guralnik, J. M., Butterworth, S., Wadsworth, M. E. J., & Kuh, D. (2006). Childhood socioeconomic status predicts physical functioning a half century later. *Journal of Gerontology: Medical Sciences, 61A,* 694–701.

Gurin, P. Y., Dey, E. L., Gurin, G., & Hurtado, S. (2003). How does racial/ethnic diversity promote education? *Western Journal of Black Studies, 27*(1), 20.

Gusarova, I., Fraser, V., & Alderson, K. G. (2012). A quantitative study of "friends with benefits" relationships. *The Canadian Journal of Human Sexuality, 21*(1), 41.

Gutman, L. M., & Eccles, J. S. (2007). Stage-environment fit during adolescence: Trajectories of family relations and adolescent outcomes. *Developmental Psychology, 43,* 522–537.

Gutmann, D. (1975). Parenting: A key to the comparative study of the life cycle. In N. Datan & L. H. Ginsberg (Eds.), *Life-span developmental psychology: Normative life crises.* New York: Academic Press.

Gutmann, D. (1977). The cross-cultural perspective: Notes toward a comparative psychology of aging. In J. E. Birren & K. W. Schaie (Eds.), *Handbook of the psychology of aging* (pp. 302–326). New York: Van Nostrand Reinhold.

Gutmann, D. (1985). The parental imperative revisited. In J. Meacham (Ed.), *Family and individual development.* Basel, Switzerland: Karger.

Gutmann, D. L. (1987). *Reclaimed powers: Toward a new psychology of men and women in later life.* New York: Basic Books.

Guttmacher Institute. (2013). *Facts on American teens' sexual and reproductive health.* Retrieved from www.guttmacher.org/pubs/FB-ATSRH.html#6

Guttmacher Institute. (2016). American teens' sexual and reproductive health [fact sheet]. Retrieved from www.guttmacher.org/fact-sheet/american-teens-sexual-and-reproductive-health-old

Haar, J. M., Russo, M., Suñe, A., & Ollier-Malaterre, A. (2014). Outcomes of work–life balance on job satisfaction, life satisfaction and mental health: A study across seven cultures. *Journal of Vocational Behavior, 85*(3), 361–373.

Haas, C., Takayoshi, P., Carr, B., Hudson, K., & Pollock, R. (2011). Young people's everyday literacies: The language features of instant messaging. *Research in the Teaching of English,* 378–404.

Haber, C. (2004). Life extension and history: The continual search for the Fountain of Youth. *Journal of Gerontology: Biological Sciences, 59A,* 515–522.

Hack, M., Youngstrom, E. A., Cartar, L., Schluchter, M., Taylor, H. G., Flannery, D., . . . Borawski, E. (2004). Behavioral outcomes and evidence of psychopathology among very low birth weight infants at age 20 years. *Pediatrics, 114,* 932–940.

Hadfield, J. C. (2014). The health of grandparents raising grandchildren: A literature review. *Journal of Gerontological Nursing, 40*(4), 32–42.

Hafford, C. (2010). Sibling caretaking in immigrant families: Understanding cultural practices to inform child welfare practice and evaluation. *Evaluation and Program Planning, 33*(3), 294–302.

Hagan, Jr., J.F., Committee of Psychosocial Aspects of Child and Family Health, & Task Force on Terrorism (2005). Psychosocial implications of disaster or terrorism on children: A guide for the pediatrician. *Pediatrics, 116,* 787–795.

Hagmann, P., Sporns, O., Madan, N., Cammoun, L., Pienaar, R., Wedeen, V. J., . . . & Grant, P. E. (2010). White matter maturation reshapes structural connectivity in the late developing human brain. *Proceedings of the National Academy of Sciences, 107*(44), 19067–19072.

Hahn-Holbrook, J., & Haselton, M. (2014). Is postpartum depression a disease of modern civilization? *Current Directions in Psychological Science, 23,* 395–400.

Haider, B. A., & Bhutta, Z. A. (2012). Multiple-micronutrient supplementation for women during pregnancy. *Cochrane Database Syst Rev, 11.*

Haith, M. M. (1986). Sensory and perceptual processes in early infancy. *Journal of Pediatrics, 109*(1), 158–171.

Haith, M. M. (1998). Who put the cog in infant cognition? Is rich interpretation too costly? *Infant Behavior and Development, 21*(2), 167–179.

Haith, M. M., & Benson, J. B. (1998). Infant cognition. In D. Kuhn & R. S. Siegler (Eds.), *Handbook of child psychology: Vol. 2. Cognition, perception, and language* (5th ed., pp. 199–254). New York: Wiley.

Hale, S., Rose, N. S., Myerson, J., Strube, M. J., Sommers, M., Tye-Murray, N., & Spehar, B. (2011). The structure of working memory abilities across the adult life span. *Psychology and Aging, 26*(1), 92.

Haley, D. W., & Stansbury, K. (2003). Infant stress and parent responsiveness: regulation of physiology and behavior during still-face and reunion. *Child Development, 74*(5), 1534–1546.

Halgunseth, L. C., Ispa, J. M., & Rudy, D. (2006). Parental control in Latino families: An integrated review of the literature. *Child Development, 77*, 1282–1297.

Halim, M. L., Ruble, D. N., Tamis-LeMonda, C. S., Zosuls, K. M., Lurye, L. E., & Greulich, F. K. (2014). Pink frilly dresses and the avoidance of all things "girly": Children's appearance rigidity and cognitive theories of gender development. *Developmental Psychology, 50*(4), 1091.

Hall, J. A. (2011). Sex differences in friendship expectations: A meta-analysis. *Journal of Social and Personal Relationships, 28*(6), 723–747.

Hall, J. H., & Fincham, F. D. (2006). Relationship dissolution after infidelity. In M. Fine & J. Harvey (Eds.), *Handbook of divorce and relationship dissolution* (pp. 153–168). Hillsdale, NJ: Erlbaum.

Hallfors, D. D., Waller, M. W., Bauer, D., Ford, C. A., & Halpern, C. T. (2005). Which comes first in adolescence—Sex and drugs or depression? *American Journal of Preventive Medicine, 29*, 1163–1170.

Halpern, C., Young, M., Waller, M., Martin, S., & Kupper, L. (2003). Prevalence of partner violence in same-sex romantic and sexual relationships in a national sample of adolescents. *Journal of Adolescent Health, 35*(2), 124–131.

Halpern, D. F., Benbow, C. P., Geary, D. C., Gur, R. C., Hyde, J. S., & Gernsbacher, M. A (2007). The science of sex differences in science and mathematics. *Psychological Science in the Public Interest, 8*, 1–51.

Hamilton, B. E., & Ventura, S. J. (2012). *Birth rates for US teenagers reach historic lows for all age and ethnic groups* (Vol. 89). US Department of Health and Human Services, Centers for Disease Control and Prevention, National Center for Health Statistics.

Hamilton, S. F., & Hamilton, M. A. (2006). School, work, and emerging adulthood. In J. J. Arnett & J. L. Tanner (Eds.). *Emerging adults in America: Coming of age in the 21st century* (pp. 257–277). Washington, DC: American Psychological Association.

Hamilton, W. D. (1966). The moulding of senescence by natural selection. *Journal of Theoretical Biology, 12*(1), 12–45.

Hammad, T. A., Laughren, T., & Racoosin, J. (2006). Suicidality in pediatric patients treated with antidepressant drugs. *Archives of General Psychiatry, 63*, 332–339.

Hampton, K. N., Goulet, L. S., Rainie, L., & Purcell, K. (2011). *Social networking sites and our lives.* Pew Research Center's Internet and American Life Project. Retrieved from www.namingandtreating.com/wp-content/uploads/2011/07/PIP-Social-networking-sites-and-our-lives.pdf

Hamre, B. K., & Pianta, R. C. (2005). Can instructional and emotional support in the first-grade classroom make a difference for children at risk of school failure? *Child Development, 76*, 949–967.

Hancock, C. (2012, Septempter). *The benefits of physical activity for health and well-being (2nd ed).* Retrieved from Collaborating For Health: C3: www.c3health.org/wp-content/uploads/2017/07/C3-review-of-physical-activity-and-health-v-2-a-20121011.pdf

Handmaker, N. S., Rayburn, W. F., Meng, C., Bell, J. B., Rayburn, B. B., & Rappaport, V. J. (2006). Impact of alcohol exposure after pregnancy recognition on ultrasonographic fetal growth measures. *Alcoholism: Clinical and Experimental Research, 30*, 892–898.

Hank, K. (2007). Proximity and contacts between older parents and their children: A European comparison. *Journal of Marriage and Family, 69*, 157–173.

Hankin, B. L., Mermelstein, R., & Roesch, L. (2007). Sex differences in adolescent depression: Exposure and reactivity models. *Child Development, 78*, 279–295.

Hannan, M. T., Felson, D. T., Dawson-Hughes, B., Tucker, K. L., Cupples, L. A., Wilson, P. W., & Kiel, D. P. (2000). Risk factors for longitudinal bone loss in elderly men and women: The Framingham Osteoporosis Study. *Journal of Bone and Mineral Research, 15*(4), 710–720.

Hannigan, J. H., & Armant, D. R. (2000). Alcohol in pregnancy and neonatal outcome. *Seminars in Neonatology, 5*, 243–254.

Hanscombe, K. B., Trzaskowski, M., Haworth, C. M., Davis, O. S., Dale, P. S., & Plomin, R. (2012). Socioeconomic status (SES) and children's intelligence (IQ): In a UK-representative sample SES moderates the environmental, not genetic, effect on IQ. *PLoS One, 7*(2), e30320.

Hansen, M., Janssen, I., Schiff, A., Zee, P. C., & Dubocovich, M. L. (2005). The impact of school daily schedule on adolescent sleep. *Pediatrics, 115*, 1555–1561.

Hansen, S. N., Schendel, D. E., & Parner, E. T. (2015). Explaining the increase in the prevalence of autism spectrum disorders: the proportion attributable to changes in reporting practices. *JAMA Pediatrics, 169*(1), 56–62.

Hansen, S. N., Schendel, D. E., & Parner, E. T. (2015, January). Explaining the increase in the prevalence of autism spectrum disorders: The proportion attributable to changes in reporting practices. Retrieved from *The JAMA Network:* http://jamanetwork.com/journals/jamapediatrics/fullarticle/1919642

Hansen, T. (2012). Parenthood and happiness: A review of folk theories versus empirical evidence. *Social Indicators Research, 108*(1), 29-64.

Hanson, L. (1968). *Renoir: The man, the painter, and his world.* New York: Dodd, Mead.

Hao, Y. (2008). Productive activities and psychological well-being among older adults. *Journals of Gerontology, 63*(2, Series A), S64–S72.

Hara, Y., Waters, E. M., McEwen, B. S., & Morrison, J. H. (2015). Estrogen effects on cognitive and synaptic health over the lifecourse. *Physiological Reviews, 95*(3), 785–807.

Hardway, C., & Fuligni, A. J. (2006). Dimensions of family connectedness among adolescents with Mexican, Chinese, and European backgrounds. *Developmental Psychology, 42*, 1246–1258.

Harenski, C. L., Antonenko, O., Shane, M. S., & Keihl, K. A. (2008). Gender differences in neural mechanisms underlying moral sensitivity. *Social Cognitive and Affective Neuroscience, 3*, 313–321.

Harlow, H. F., & Harlow, M. K. (1962). The effect of rearing conditions on behavior. *Bulletin of the Menninger Clinic, 26*, 213–224.

Harman, D. (1956). Aging: a theory based on free radical and radiation chemistry. *Journal of Gerontology, 11*(3), 298–300.

Harman, D. (1983). Free radical theory of aging: consequences of mitochondrial aging. *Age, 6*(3), 86–94.

Harman, D. (1992). Free radical theory of aging. *Mutation Research/DNAging, 275*(3-6), 257–266.

Harman, D. (2006). Free radical theory of aging: An update. *Annals of the New York Academy of Sciences, 1067*(1), 10–21.

Harper, S., Lynch, J., Burris, S., & Smith, G. D. (2007). Trends in the black-white life expectancy gap in the United States, 1983-2003. *Journal of the American Medical Association, 297*, 1224–1232.

Harrell, S. P. (2000). A multidimensional conceptualization of racism-related stress: Implications for the well-being of people of color. *American Journal of Orthopsychiatry, 70*(1), 42–57.

Harris, D. G., Davies, C., Ward, H., & Haboubi, N. Y. (2008). An observational study of screening for malnutrition in elderly people living in sheltered accommodation. *Journal of Human Nutrition and Dietetics, 21*(1), 3–9.

Harris, K. M., Gordon-Larsen, P., Chantala, K., & Udry, J. R. (2006). Longitudinal trends in race/ethnic disparities in leading health indicators from adolescence to young adulthood. *Archives of Pediatric and Adolescent Medicine, 160*, 74–81.

Harris-Kojetin, L., Sengupta, M., Park-Lee, E., Valverde, R., Caffrey, C., Rome, V., & Lendon, J. (2016). Long-term care providers and services users in the United States: Data from the National Study of Long-Term Care Providers, 2013-2014. *National Center for Health Statistics. Vital Health Stat, 3*(38).

Harrison, Y., & Horne, J. A. (1997). Sleep deprivation affects speech. *Sleep, 20*, 871–877.

Harrison, Y., & Horne, J. A. (2000a). Impact of sleep deprivation on decision making: A review. *Journal of Experimental Psychology, 6*, 236–249.

Harrison, Y., & Horne, J. A. (2000b). Sleep loss and temporal memory. *Quarterly Journal of Experimental Psychology: Human Experimental Psychology, 53A*, 271–279.

Harrist, A. W., Zain, A. F., Bates, J. E., Dodge, K. A., & Pettit, G. S. (1997). Subtypes of social withdrawal in early childhood: Sociometric status and social-cognitive differences across four years. *Child Development, 68*, 278–294.

Hart, C. H., DeWolf, M., Wozniak, P., & Burts, D. C. (1992). Maternal and paternal disciplinary styles: Relations with preschoolers' playground behavioral orientation and peer status. *Child Development, 63*, 879–892.

Hart, C. L., Taylor, M. D., Smith, G. D., Whalley, L. J., Starr, J. M., Hole, D. J., . . . & Deary, I. J. (2003). Childhood IQ, social class, deprivation, and their relationships with mortality and morbidity risk in later life: prospective observational study linking the Scottish Mental Survey 1932 and the Midspan studies. *Psychosomatic Medicine, 65*(5), 877-883.

Hart, D., Hofmann, V., Edelstein, W., & Keller, M. (1997). The relation of childhood personality types to adolescent behavior and development: A longitudinal study of Icelandic children. *Developmental Psychology, 33*, 195-205.

Hart, D., Southerland, N., & Atkins, R. (2003). Community service and adult development. In J. Demick & C. Andreoletti (Eds.), *Handbook of adult development* (pp. 585-597). New York: Plenum Press.

Hart, J. L., & Tannock, M. T. (2013). Young children's play fighting and use of war toys. In R. E. Tremblay, M. Boivin, & R. Peters (Eds.), *Encyclopedia on early childhood development* [online]. www.child-encyclopedia.com/play/according-experts/learning-through-play

Harter, S. (1993). Developmental changes in self-understanding across the 5 to 7 shift. In A. Sameroff & M. Haith (Eds.), *Reason and responsibility: The passage through childhood* (pp. 207-236). Chicago: University of Chicago Press.

Harter, S. (1996). Developmental changes in self-understanding across the 5 to 7 shift. In A. J. Sameroff & M. M. Haith (Eds.), *The five to seven year shift: The age of reason and responsibility* (pp. 207-235). Chicago: University of Chicago Press.

Harter, S. (1998). The development of self-representations. In W. Damon (Series Ed.) & N. Eisenberg (Vol. Ed.), *Handbook of child psychology: Vol. 3. Social, emotional, and personality development* (5th ed., pp. 553-617). New York: Wiley.

Harter, S. (2006). The self. In W. Damon & R. M. Lerner (Series Eds.) & N. Eisenberg (Vol. Ed.), *Handbook of child psychology: Vol 3. Social, emotional and personality development* (pp. 505-570). Hoboken: NJ: Wiley.

Harter, S., & Buddin, B. (1987). Children's understanding of the simultaneity of two emotions: A five-stage developmental acquisition sequence. *Developmental Psychology, 23*, 388-439.

Hartshorn, K., Rovee-Collier, C., Gerhardstein, P., Bhatt, R. S., Wondoloski, R. L., Klein, P., . . . Campos-de-Carvalho, M. (1998). The ontogeny of long-term memory over the first year-and-a-half of life. *Developmental Psychobiology, 32*, 69-89.

Hartup, W. W. (1992). Peer relations in early and middle childhood. In V. B. Van Hasselt & M. Hersen (Eds.), *Handbook of social development: A lifespan perspective* (pp. 257-281). New York: Plenum Press.

Hartup, W. W., & Stevens, N. (1999). Friendships and adaptation across the life span. *Current Directions in Psychological Science, 8*, 76-79.

Harvard Medical School. (2002). The mind and the immune system—Part I. *Harvard Mental Health Letter, 18*(10), 1-3.

Harvard Medical School. (2003, May). Confronting suicide—Part I. *Harvard Mental Health Letter, 19*(11), 1-4.

Harvard Medical School. (2004a, December). Children's fears and anxieties. *Harvard Mental Health Letter, 21*(6), 1-3.

Harvard Medical School. (2004c, May). Women and depression: How biology and society may make women more vulnerable to mood disorders. *Harvard Mental Health Letter, 20*(11), 1-4.

Haskuka, M., Sunar, D., & Alp, I. E. (2008). War exposure, attachment and moral reasoning. *Journal of Cross Cultural Psychology, 39*(4), 381-401.

Hassan, N. M. M., Akhter, R., Staudinger, L., Tarpey, N., Basha, S., Cox, S., & Kashiwazaki, H. (2017). Oral disease and malnutrition in the elderly—Impact of oral cancer. *Current Oral Health Reports, 4*(2), 64-69.

Hatzenbuehler, M. L., O'Cleirigh, C., & Bradford, J. (2012). Effect of same-sex marriage laws on health care use and expenditures on sexual minority men: A quasi-natural experiment. *American Journal of Public Health, 102*(2), 285-291.

Haugaard, J. J. (1998). Is adoption a risk factor for the development of adjustment problems? *Clinical Psychology Review, 18*, 47-69.

Hawes, C., Phillips, C. D., Rose, M., Holan, S., & Sherman, M. (2003). A national survey of assisted living facilities. *Gerontologist, 43*, 875-882.

Hawkley, L. C., & Cacioppo, J. T. (2007). Aging and loneliness: Downhill quickly? *Current Directions in Psychological Science, 16*, 187-191.

Hawkley, L. C., Thisted, R. A., Masi, C. M., & Cacioppo, J. T. (2010). Loneliness predicts increased blood pressure: 5-year cross-lagged analyses in middle-aged and older adults. *Psychology and Aging, 25*(1), 132.

Haworth, C. M., Wright, M. J., Luciano, M., Martin, N. G., De Geus, E. J. C., Van Beijsterveldt, C. E. M., . . . & Kovas, Y. (2010). The heritability of general cognitive ability increases linearly from childhood to young adulthood. *Molecular Psychiatry, 15*(11), 1112.

Hay, C., Meldrum, R. C., Widdowson, A. O., & Piquero, A. R. (2017). Early aggression and later delinquency: considering the redirecting role of good parenting. *Youth Violence and Juvenile Justice, 15*(4), 374-395.

Hay, D. F., Pawlby, S., Waters, C. S., Perra, O., & Sharp, D. (2010). Mothers' antenatal depression and their children's antisocial outcomes. *Child Development, 81*(1), 149-165.

Hay, D. F., Pedersen, J., & Nash, A. (1982). Dyadic interaction in the first year of life. In K. H. Rubin & H. S. Ross (Eds.), *Peer relationships and social skills in children.* New York: Springer.

Hay, E. L., & Diehl, M. (2010). Reactivity to daily stressors in adulthood: The importance of stressor type in characterizing risk factors. *Psychology and Aging, 25*(1), 118.

Hayes, S. & Tantleff-Dunn, S. (2010). Am I too fat to be a princess? Examining the effects of popular children's media on young girls' body image. *British Journal of Developmental Psychology, 28*, 413-426.

Hayflick, L. (1974). The strategy of senescence. *Gerontologist, 14*(1), 37-45.

Hayflick, L. (1981). Intracellular determinants of aging. *Mechanisms of Aging and Development, 28*, 177.

Hayflick, L. (2004). "Anti-aging" is an oxymoron. *Journal of Gerontology: Biological Sciences, 59A*, 573-578.

Hayslip Jr., B., Blumenthal, H., & Garner, A. (2014). Social support and grandparent caregiver health: One-year longitudinal findings for grandparents raising their grandchildren. *Journals of Gerontology Series B: Psychological Sciences and Social Sciences, 70*(5), 804-812.

He, W., Goodkind, D., & Kowal, P. R. (2016). *An aging world: 2015.* Washington, DC: United States Census Bureau.

He, W., Sengupta, M., Velkoff, V. A., & DeBarros, K. A. (2005). *65+ in the United States: 2005* (pp. 23-209). Washington, DC: U.S. Department of Commerce, Economics and Statistics Administration, Bureau of the Census.

He, Y., Chen, Z. J., & Evans, A. C. (2007). Small-world anatomical networks in the human brain revealed by cortical thickness from MRI. *Cerebral Cortex, 17*(10), 2407-2419.

Healy, A. J., Malone, F. D., Sullivan, L. M., Porter, T. F., Luthy, D. A., Comstock, C. H., . . . D'Alton, M. E. (2006). Early access to prenatal care: Implications for racial disparity in perinatal mortality. *Obstetrics and Gynecology, 107*, 625-631.

Heath, S. B. (1989). Oral and literate tradition among black Americans living in poverty. *American Psychologist, 44*, 367-373.

Heatherington, E. M. (2006). The influence of conflict, marital problem solving and parenting on children's adjustment in nondivorced, divorced and remarried families. In A. Clarke-Stewart & J. Dunn (Eds.), *Families count: Effects on child and adolescent development* (pp. 203-237). New York: Cambridge University Press.

Hebblethwaite, S., & Norris, J. (2011). Expressions of generativity through family leisure: Experiences of grandparents and adult grandchildren. *Family Relations, 60*(1), 121-133.

Heckhausen, J. (2001). Adaptation and resilience in midlife. In M. E. Lachman (Ed.), *Handbook of midlife development* (pp. 345-394). New York: Wiley.

Heckhausen, J., Wrosch, C., & Fleeson, W. (2001). Developmental regulation before and after a developmental deadline: The sample case of biological clock for childbearing. *Psychology and Aging, 16*, 400-413.

Heckman, J. J., Moon, S. H., Pinto, R., Savelyev, P. A., & Yavitz, A. (2010). The rate of return to the High/Scope Perry Preschool Program. *Journal of Public Economics, 94*(1), 114-128.

Hedden, T., Lautenschlager, G., & Park, D. C. (2005). Contributions of processing ability and knowledge to verbal memory tasks across the adult life-span. *Quarterly Journal of Experimental Psychology. A Human Experimental Psychology, 58*(1), 169-190.

Heffner, K. L. (2011). Neuroendocrine effects of stress on immunity in the elderly: implications for inflammatory disease. *Immunology and Allergy Clinics of North America, 31*(1), 95-108.

Heffner, L. J. (2004). Advanced maternal age—How old is too old? *New England Journal of Medicine, 351*, 1927–1929.

Heidenreich, A., Bellmunt, J., Bolla, M., Joniau, S., Mason, M., Matveev, V., . . . & Zattoni, F. (2011). EAU guidelines on prostate cancer. Part 1: screening, diagnosis, and treatment of clinically localised disease. *European Urology, 59*(1), 61–71.

Heiland, F., & Liu, S. H. (2006). Family structure and wellbeing of out-of-wedlock children: The significance of the biological pare'ts' relationship. *Demographic Research, 15*, 61–104.

Heilbronn, L. K., & Ravussin, E. (2003). Calorie restriction and aging: Review of the literature and implications for studies in humans. *American Journal of Clinical Nutrition, 78*, 361–369.

Heim, B. T., & Lin, L. (2017). Does health reform lead to an increase in early retirement? Evidence from Massachusetts. *ILR Review, 70*(3), 704–732.

Heiman, J. R., Long, J. S., Smith, S. N., Fisher, W. A., Sand, M. S., & Rosen, R. C. (2011). Sexual satisfaction and relationship happiness in midlife and older couples in five countries. *Archives of Sexual Behavior, 40*(4), 741–753.

Heinz, W. (2002). Self-socialization and post-traditional society. *Advances in Life Course Research, 7*, 41–64.

Heiss, G., Wallace, R., Anderson, G. L., Aragaki, A., Beresford, S. A. A., Brzyski, R., . . . Stefanick, M. L., for the WHI Investigators. (2008). Health risks and benefits 3 years after stopping randomized treatment with estrogen and progestin. *Journal of the American Medical Association, 299*, 1036–1045.

Helms, H. M., Crouter, A. C., & McHale, S. M. (2003). Marital quality and spouses' marriage work with close friends and each other. *Journal of Marriage and Family, 65*, 963–977.

Helms, J. E. (1992). Why is there no study of cultural equivalence in standardized cognitive ability testing? *American Psychologist, 47*, 1083–1101.

Helms, J. E., Jernigan, M., & Mascher, J. (2005). The meaning of race in psychology and how to change it: A methodological perspective. *American Psychologist, 60*, 27–36.

HelpAge International Staff. (2015). *Global AgeWatch Index 2015: Insight report.* Retrieved from age international: www.ageinternational. org.uk/Documents/Global_AgeWatch_Index_2015_HelpAge.pdf

Helson, R. (1997). The self in middle age. In M. E. Lachman & J. B. James (Eds.), *Multiple paths of midlife development* (pp. 21–43). Chicago: University of Chicago Press.

Helson, R., & Moane, G. (1987). Personality change in women from college to midlife. *Journal of Personality and Social Psychology, 53*, 176–186.

Helson, R., & Roberts, B. W. (1994). Ego development and personality change in adulthood. *Journal of Personality and Social Psychology, 66*, 911–920.

Helson, R., & Wink, P. (1992). Personality change in women from the early 40s to the early 50s. *Psychology and Aging, 7*(1), 46–55.

Helwig, C. C., & Jasiobedzka, U. (2001). The relation between law and morality: Children's reasoning about socially beneficial and unjust laws. *Child Development, 72*, 1382–1393.

Henderson, H. A., Marshall, P. J., Fox, N. A., & Rubin, K. H. (2004). Psychophysiological and behavioral evidence for varying forms and functions of nonsocial behavior in preschoolers. *Child Development, 75*, 251–263.

Henning-Smith, C. (2016). Quality of life and psychological distress among older adults: The role of living arrangements. *Journal of Applied Gerontology, 35*(1), 39–61.

Henry, M., Cortes, A., & Morris, S. (2013). *The 2013 annual homeless assessment report (AHAR) to congress.* Washington. DC: U.S. Department of Housing and Urban Development.

Hepach, R., Vaish, A., & Tomasello, M. (2012). Young children are intrinsically motivated to see others helped. *Psychological Science, 23*(9), 967–972.

Herbers, J. E., Cutuli, J. J., Supkoff, L. M., Heistad, D., Chan, C. K., Hinz, E., & Masten, A. S. (2012). Early reading skills and academic achievement trajectories of students facing poverty, homelessness, and high residential mobility. *Educational Researcher, 41*(9), 366–374.

Herbig, B., Büssing, A., & Ewert, T. (2001). The role of tacit knowledge in the work context of nursing. *Journal of Advanced Nursing, 34*, 687–695.

Herbst, J. H., Kay, L. S., Passin, W. F., Lyles, C. M., Crepaz, N., & Marin, B. V. (2006). A systematic review and meta-analysis of behavioral interventions to reduce HIV risk behaviors of Hispanics in the United States and Puerto Rico. *AIDS and Behavior, 11*(1), 25–47.

Herek, G. M. (2006). Legal recognition of same-sex unions in the United States: A social science perspective. *American Psychologist, 61*, 607–621.

Hermes, M., Hagemann, D., Naumann, E., & Walter, C. (2011). Extraversion and its positive emotional core—Further evidence from neuroscience. *Emotion, 11*(2), 367.

Hernandez, D. J., & Macartney, S. E. (2008, January). *Racial-ethnic inequality in child wellbeing from 1985–2004: Gaps narrowing, but persist* (No. 9). New York: Foundation for Child Development.

Hernandez, S. J. (2004, Summer). Demographic change and the life circumstances of immigrant families. *Future of Children 14*(2).

Heron, M. P., Hoyert, D. L., Murphy, S. L., Xu, J. Q., Kochanek, K. D., & Tejada-Vera, B. (2009). Deaths: Final data for 2006. *National Vital Statistics Reports, 57*(14). Hyattsville, MD: National Center for Health Statistics.

Heron, M. P., Hoyert, D. L., Xu, J., Scott, C., & Tejada-Vera, B. (2008). Deaths: Preliminary data for 2006. *National Vital Statistics Reports, 56*(16). Hyattsville, MD: National Center for Health Statistics.

Herrnstein, R. J., & Murray, C. (1994). *The bell curve: Intelligence and class structure in American life.* New York: Free Press.

Hertenstein, M. J., & Campos, J. J. (2004). The retention effects of an adult's emotional displays on infant behavior. *Child Development, 75*, 595–613.

Hertlein, K. M., & Piercy, F. P. (2006). Internet infidelity: A critical review of the literature. *The Family Journal, 14*(4), 366–371.

Hesketh, T., Lu, L., & Xing, Z. W. (2005). The effect of China's one-child policy after 25 years. *New England Journal of Medicine, 353*, 1171–1176.

Hespos, S. J., & Baillargeon, R. (2008). Young infants' actions reveal their developing knowledge of support variables: Converging evidence for violation-of-expectation findings. *Cognition, 107*(1), 304–316.

Hess, S. Y., & King, J. C. (2009). Effects of maternal zinc supplementation on pregnancy and lactation outcomes. *Food and Nutrition Bulletin, 30*(1), 60–78.

Hesso, N. A., & Fuentes, E. (2005). Ethnic differences in neonatal and postneonatal mortality. *Pediatrics, 115*, e44–e51.

Hetherington, E. M., Reiss, D., & Plomin, R. (Eds.). (2013). *Separate social worlds of siblings: The impact of nonshared environment on development.* New York: Routledge.

Heuveline, P., & Timberlake, J. M. (2004). The role of cohabitation in family formation: The United States in comparative perspective. *Journal of Marriage and Family, 66*, 1214–1230.

Hewes, J. (2014). Seeking balance in motion: The role of spontaneous free play in promoting social and emotional health in early childhood care and education. *Children, 1*, 280–301.

Hewlett, B. S. (1987). Intimate fathers: Patterns of paternal holding among Aka pygmies. In M. E. Lamb (Ed.), *The father's role: Cross-cultural perspectives* (pp. 295–330). Hillsdale, NJ: Erlbaum.

Hewlett, B. S. (1992). Husband-wife reciprocity and the father-infant relationship among Aka pygmies. In B. S. Hewlett (Ed.), *Father-child relations: Cultural and biosocial contexts* (pp. 153–176). New York: de Gruyter.

Hewlett, B. S., Lamb, M. E., Shannon, D., Leyendecker, B., & Schölmerich, A. (1998). Culture and early infancy among central African foragers and farmers. *Developmental Psychology, 34*(4), 653–661.

Heymann, J., Siebert, W. S., & Wei, X. (2007). The implicit wage costs of family friendly work practices. *Oxford Economic Papers, 59*(2), 275–300.

Heywood, W., Minichiello, V., Lyons, A., Fileborn, B., Hussain, R., Hinchliff, S., . . . & Dow, B. (2017). The impact of experiences of ageism on sexual activity and interest in later life. *Ageing & Society.*

Hickling, A. K., & Wellman, H. M. (2001). The emergence of children's causal explanations and theories: Evidence from everyday conversations. *Developmental Psychology, 37*(5), 668–683.

Hickman, M., Roberts, C., & de Matos, M. G. (2000). Exercise and leisure time activities. In C. Currie, K. Hurrelmann, W. Settertobulte, R. Smith, & J. Todd (Eds.), *Health and health behaviour among young people: A WHO cross-national study (HBSC) international report* (pp. 73–82). *WHO Policy Series: Health Policy for Children and Adolescents, Series No. 1.* Copenhagen, Denmark: World Health Organization Regional Office for Europe.

Hicks, G. R., & Lee, T. T. (2006). Public attitudes toward gays and lesbians: Trends and predictors. *Journal of Homosexuality, 51*(2), 57-77.

Hiedemann, B., Suhomilinova, O., & O'Rand, A. M (1998). Economic independence, economic status, and empty nest in midlife marital disruption. *Journal of Marriage and Family, 60,* 219-231.

Hildebrand, C., Taylor, M., & Bradway, C. (2013). Elder self-neglect: The failure of coping because of cognitive and functional impairments. *Journal of the American Association of Nurse Practitioners, 26,* 452-462.

Hill, A. L., Degnan, K. A., Calkins, S. D., & Keane, S. P. (2006). Profiles of externalizing behavior problems for boys and girls across preschool: The roles of emotional regulation and inattention. *Developmental Psychology, 42,* 913-928.

Hill, C., & Holzer, H. (2007). Labor market experiences and the transition to adulthood. In S. Danziger & C. Rouse (Eds.), *The price of independence: The economics of early adulthood* (pp. 141-169). New York: Russell Sage Foundation.

Hill, D. A., Gridley, G., Cnattingius, S., Mellemkjaer, L., Linet, M., Adami, H.-O., . . . Fraumeni, J. F. (2003). Mortality and cancer incidence among individuals with Down syndrome. *Archives of Internal Medicine, 163,* 705-711.

Hill, J. L., Waldfogel, J., Brooks-Gunn, J., & Han, W.-J. (2005). Maternal employment and child development: A fresh look using newer methods. *Developmental Psychology, 41,* 833-850.

Hill, N. E., & Taylor, L. C. (2004). Parental school involvement and children's academic achievement: Pragmatics and issues. *Current Directions in Psychological Science, 13,* 161-168.

Hill, N., & Tyson, D. (2009). Parental involvement in middle school: A meta-analytical assessment of the strategies that promote achievement. *Developmental Psychology, 45*(3), 740-763.

Hill, T. D., Angel, J. L., Ellison, C. G., & Angel, R. J. (2005). Religious attendance and mortality: An 8-year follow-up of older Mexican Americans. *Journal of Gerontology: Social Sciences, 60B,* S102-S109.

Hilliard, L. J., & Liben, L. S. (2010). Differing levels of gender salience in preschool classrooms: Effects on children's gender attitudes and intergroup bias. *Child Development, 81*(6), 1787-1798.

Hillier, L. (2002). "It's a catch-22": Same-sex-attracted young people on coming out to parents. In S. S. Feldman & D. A. Rosenthal (Eds.), *Talking sexuality* (New Directions for Child and Adolescent Development, No. 97, pp. 75-91). San Francisco: Jossey-Bass.

Hillis, S. D., Anda, R. F., Dubé, S. R., Felitti, V. J., Marchbanks, P. A., & Marks, J. S. (2004). The association between adverse childhood experiences and adolescent pregnancy, long-term psychosocial consequences, and fetal death. *Pediatrics, 113,* 320-327.

Hinds, D. A., Stuve, L. L., Nilsen, G. B., Halperin, E., Eskin, E., Ballinger, D. G., . . . Cox, D. R. (2005). Whole-genome patterns of common DNA variation in three human populations. *Science, 307,* 1072-1079.

Hingson, R. W., Heeren, T., & Winter, M. R. (2006). Age at drinking onset and alcohol dependence: Age at onset, duration, and severity. *Archivers of Pediatrics & Adolescent Medicine, 160,* 739-746.

Hingson, R., Heeren, T., Winter, M., & Wechsler, H. (2005). Magnitude of alcohol-related mortality and morbidity among U.S. college students ages 18-24: Changes from 1998-2001. *Annual Reviews, 26,* 259-279.

Hinman, J. D., & Abraham, C. R. (2007). What's behind the decline? The role of white matter in brain aging. *Neurochemical Research, 32*(12), 2023-2031.

Hirschl, T. A., Altobelli, J., & Rank, M. R. (2003). Does marriage increase the odds of affluence? Exploring the life course probabilities. *Journal of Marriage and Family, 65,* 927-938.

Hitzert, M. M., Van Braeckel, K. N., Bos, A. F., Hunnius, S., & Geuze, R. H. (2014). Early visual attention in preterm and fullterm infants in relation to cognitive and motor outcomes at school age: an exploratory study. *Frontiers in Pediatrics, 2.*

Hjelmborg, J., Iachine, I., Skytthe, A., Vaupel, J., McGue, M., et al. (2006). Genetic influence on human lifespan and longevity. *Human Genetics 199*(3), 312-321.

Ho, R. C. M., Neo, L. F., Chua, A. N. C., Cheak, A. A. C., & Mak, A. (2010). Research on psychoneuroimmunology: Does stress influence immunity and coronary artery disease? *Annals Academy of Medicine Singapore, 39,* 191-196.

Hoang, T. D., Reis, J., Zhu, N., Jacobs, D. R., Launer, L. J., Whitmer, R. A., . . . & Yaffe, K. (2016). Effect of early adult patterns of physical activity and television viewing on midlife cognitive function. *JAMA Psychiatry, 73*(1), 73-79.

Hoban, T. F. (2004). Sleep and its disorders in children. *Seminars in Neurology, 24,* 327-340.

Hobbs, W. R., Burke, M., Christakis, N. A., & Fowler, J. H. (2016). Online social integration is associated with reduced mortality risk. *Proceedings of the National Academy of Sciences, 113*(46), 12980-12984.

Hobson, J. A., & Silvestri, L. (1999, February). Parasomnias. *Harvard Mental Health Letter,* 3-5.

Hodges, E. V. E., Boivin, M., Vitaro, F., & Bukowski, W. M. (1999). The power of friendship: Protection against an escalating cycle of peer victimization. *Developmental Psychology, 35,* 94-101.

Hodnett, E. D., Gates, S., Hofmeyr, G. J., & Sakala, C. (2005). Continuous support for women during childbirth (Cochrane Review). *The Cochrane Library, 1.*

Hoff, E. (2003). The specificity of environmental influence: Socioeconomic status affects early vocabulary development via maternal speech. *Child Development, 74,* 1368-1378.

Hoff, E. (2006). How social contexts support and shape language development. *Developmental Review, 26,* 55-88.

Hofferth, S. L. (2006). Residential father family type and child well-being: Investment versus selection. *Demography, 43*(1), 53-77.

Hofferth, S. L. (2010). Home media and children's achievement and behavior, *Child Development, 81,* 1598-1619. doi: 10.1111/j.1467-8624.2010.01494.x

Hoffman, G. F., Davies, M., & Norman, R. (2007). The impact of lifestyle factors on reproductive perfomance in the general population and those undergoing infertility treatment: A review. *Human Reproduction Update, 13*(3), 209-223.

Hoffman, M. L. (1970). Conscience, personality, and socialization techniques. *Human Development, 13,* 90-126.

Hofman, P. L., Regan, F., Jackson, W. E., Jefferies, C., Knight, D. B., Robinson, E. M., & Cutfield, W. S. (2004). Premature birth and later insulin resistance. *New England Journal of Medicine, 351,* 2179-2186.

Hofmann, S. G., Asnaani, A., Vonk, I. J., Sawyer, A. T., & Fang, A. (2012). The efficacy of cognitive behavioral therapy: A review of meta-analyses. *Cognitive Therapy and Research, 36*(5), 427-440.

Hogge, W. A. (2003). The clinical use of karyotyping spontaneous abortions. *American Journal of Obstetrics and Gynecology, 189,* 397-402.

Hohmann-Marriott, B. E. (2006). Shared beliefs and the union stability of married and cohabiting couples. *Journal of Marriage and Family, 68,* 1015-1028.

Hollenberg, M., Yang, J., Haight, T. J., & Tager, I. B. (2006). Longitudinal changes in aerobic capacity: implications for concepts of aging. *The Journals of Gerontology Series A: Biological Sciences and Medical Sciences, 61*(8), 851-858.

Holliday, R. (2004). The multiple and irreversible causes of aging. *Journal of Gerontology: Biological Sciences, 59A,* 568-572.

Holloway, A. (2014, January 24). *The Toraja people and the most complex funeral rituals in the world.* Retrieved from Ancient Origins: http://www.ancient-origins.net/ancient-places-asia/toraja-people-and-most-complex-funeral-rituals-world-001268

Holmes, R. M. (2012). The outdoor recess activities of children at an urban school: Longitudinal and intraperiod patterns. *American Journal of Play, 4*(3), 327.

Holmes, T. H., & Rahe, R. H. (1976). The social readjustment rating scale. *Journal of Psychosomatic Research, 11,* 213.

Holstein, M. B., & Minkler, M. (2003). Self, society, and the "New Gerontology." *Gerontologist, 43,* 787-796.

Holt-Lunstad, J., Birmingham, W., & Jones, B. Q. (2008). Is there something unique about marriage? The relative impact of marital status, relationship quality, and network social support on ambulatory blood pressure and mental health. *Annals of Behavioral Medicine, 35*(2), 239-244.

Holt-Lunstad, J., Smith, T. B., & Layton, J. B. (2010). Social relationships and mortality risk: A meta-analytic review. *PLoS Medicine, 7*(7), e1000316. doi:10.1371/journal.pmed.1000316

Holtzman, R. E., Rebok, G. W., Saczynski, J. S., Kouzis, A. C., Doyle, K. W., & Eaton, W. W. (2004). Social network characteristics and cognition in middle-aged and older adults. *Journal of Gerontology: Psychological Sciences, 59B,* 278-284.

Honein, M. A., Paulozzi, L. J., Mathews, T. J., Erickson, J. D., & Wong, L.-Y. C. (2001). Impact of folic acid fortification of the U.S. food supply on the occurrence of neural tube defects. *Journal of the American Medical Association, 285,* 2981-2986.

Hoorn, J., Dijk, E., Meuwese, R., Rieffe, C., & Crone, E. A. (2016). Peer influence on prosocial behavior in adolescence. *Journal of Research on Adolescence, 26*(1), 90-100.

Hoover, R. M., & Polson, M. (2014). Detecting elder abuse and neglect: assessment and intervention. *American Family Physician, 89*(6).

Hopkins, B., & Westra, T. (1988). Maternal handling and motor development: An intracultural study. *Genetic, Social and General Psychology Monographs, 14,* 377-420.

Hopkins, B., & Westra, T. (1990). Motor development, maternal expectations and the role of handling. *Infant Behavior and Development, 13,* 117-122.

Hopkins, M. (2014). *The development of children's understanding of death.* Doctoral dissertation, University of East Anglia.

Hopwood, C. J., Donnellan, M. B., Blonigen, D. M., Krueger, R. F., McGue, M., Iacono, W. G., & Burt, S. A. (2011). Genetic and environmental influences on personality trait stability and growth during the transition to adulthood: a three-wave longitudinal study. *Journal of Personality and Social Psychology, 100*(3), 545.

Horn, J. C., & Meer, J. (1987, May). The vintage years. *Psychology Today,* pp. 76-90.

Horn, J. L. (1967). Intelligence—Why it grows, why it declines. *Transaction, 5*(1), 23-31.

Horn, J. L. (1968). Organization of abilities and the development of intelligence. *Psychological Review, 75,* 242-259.

Horn, J. L. (1970). Organization of data on lifespan development of human abilities. In L. R. Goulet & P. B. Baltes (Eds.), *Life-span developmental psychology: Theory and research* (pp. 424-466). New York: Academic Press.

Horn, J. L. (1982a). The aging of human abilities. In B. B. Wolman (Ed.), *Handbook of developmental psychology* (pp. 847-870). Englewood Cliffs, NJ: Prentice Hall.

Horn, J. L. (1982b). The theory of fluid and crystallized intelligence in relation to concepts of cognitive psychology and aging in adulthood. In F. I. M. Craik & S. Trehub (Eds.), *Aging and cognitive processes* (pp. 237-278). New York: Plenum Press.

Horn, J. L., & Donaldson, G. (1980). Cognitive development: 2. Adulthood development of human abilities. In O. G. Brim & J. Kagan (Eds.), *Constancy and change in human development.* Cambridge, MA: Harvard University Press.

Horn, J. L., & Hofer, S. M. (1992). Major abilities and development in the adult. In R. J. Sternberg & C. A. Berg (Eds.), *Intellectual development.* New York: Cambridge University Press.

Horn, L., & Berger, R. (2004). *College persistence on the rise? Changes in 5-year completion and postsecondary persistence rates between 1994 and 2000* (NCES 2005-156). Washington, DC: U.S. Department of Education, National Center for Education Statistics.

Horne, J. (2000). Neuroscience: Images of lost sleep. *Nature, 403,* 605-606.

Horowitz, B. N., Neiderhiser, J. M., Ganiban, J. M., Spotts, E. L., Lichtenstein, P., & Reiss, D. (2010). Genetic and environmental influences on global family conflict. *Journal of Family Psychology, 24*(2), 217-220.

Horton, R., & Shweder, R. A. (2004). Ethnic conservatism, psychological well-being, and the downside of mainstreaming: Generational differences. In O. G. Brim, C. D. Ryff, & R. C. Kessler (Eds.), *How healthy are we? A national study of well-being at midlife* (pp. 373-397). Chicago: University of Chicago Press.

Hoskins, D. H. (2014). Consequences of parenting on adolescent outcomes. *Societies, 4*(3), 506-531.

Houdé, O., Pineau, A., Leroux, G., Poirel, N., Perchey, G., Lanoë, C., . . . & Delcroix, N. (2011). Functional magnetic resonance imaging study of Piaget's conservation-of-number task in preschool and school-age children: A neo-Piagetian approach. *Journal of Experimental Child Psychology, 110*(3), 332-346.

Houltberg, B. J., Henry, C. S., & Morris, A. S. (2012). Family interactions, exposure to violence, and emotion regulation: Perceptions of children and early adolescents at risk. *Family Relations, 61,* 283-296. doi: 10.1111/j.1741-3729.2011.00699.x

Hourcade, J. P., Mascher, S. L., Wu, D., & Pantoja, L. (2015). Look, my baby is using an iPad! An analysis of YouTube videos of infants and toddlers using tablets. Proceedings of the 33rd Annual ACM Conference on Human Factors in Computing Systems. doi: 10.1145/2702123.2702266

Howard, K. S., Lefever, J. B., Borkowski, J. G., & Whitman, T. L. (2006). Fathers' influence in the lives of children with adolescent mothers. *Journal of Family Psychology, 20,* 468-476.

Howden, L. M., & Meyer, J. A. (2010). Age and sex composition: 2010. *2010 Census Briefs.* Washington, DC: U.S. Department of Commerce, Economics and Statistics Administration. U.S. Census Bureau.

Howe, N., Petrakos, H., Rinaldi, C. M., & LeFebvre, R. (2005). "This is a bad dog, you know . . ." : Constructing shared meanings during sibling pretend play. *Child Development, 76,* 783-794.

Howe, N., Rinaldi, C. M., Jennings, M., & Petrakos, H. (2002). "No! The lambs can stay out because they got cozies": Constructive and destructive sibling conflict, pretend play, and social understanding. *Child Development, 73*(5), 1460-1473.

Howell, R. T., Kern, M. L., & Lyubomirsky, S. (2007). Health benefits: Meta-analytically determining the impact of well-being on objective health outcomes. *Health Psychology Review, 1*(1), 83-136.

Howes, L.M., & Goodman-Delahunty, J. (2014). Life course research design: Exploring career change experiences of former school teachers and police officers. *Journal of Career Development,* 41, 62-84.

Howland, M., Armeli, S., Feinn, R., & Tennen, H. (2017). Daily emotional stress reactivity in emerging adulthood: Temporal stability and its predictors. *Anxiety, Stress, & Coping, 30*(2), 121-132.

Hoxby, C. M. (2004). *Achievement in charter schools and regular public schools in the United States: Understanding the differences.* Cambridge, MA: Department of Economics, Harvard University.

Hoyer, W. J., & Rybash, J. M. (1994). Characterizing adult cognitive development. *Journal of Adult Development, 1*(1), 7-12.

Hoyert, D. L., Arias, E., Smith, B. L., Murphy, S. L., & Kochanek, K. D. (2001). Deaths: Final data for 1999. *National Vital Statistics Reports, 49*(8). Hyattsville, MD: National Center for Health Statistics.

Hoyert, D. L., Mathews. T. J., Menacker, F., Strobino, D. M., & Guyer, B. (2006). Annual summary of vital statistics, 2004. *Pediatrics, 117,* 168-183.

Hruby, A., & Hu, F. B. (2015). The epidemiology of obesity: a big picture. *Pharmacoeconomics, 33*(7), 673-689.

Huang, G. C., Unger, J. B., Soto, D., Fujimoto, K., Pentz, M. A., Jordan-Marsh, M., & Valente, T. W. (2014). Peer influences: the impact of online and offline friendship networks on adolescent smoking and alcohol use. *Journal of Adolescent Health, 54*(5), 508-514.

Hudak, M. L., & Tan, R. C. (2012). Neonatal drug withdrawal. *Pediatrics, 129*(2), e540-e560.

Hudd, S., Dumlao, J., Erdmann-Sager, D., Murray, D., Phan, E., & Soukas, N. (2000). Stress at college: Effects on health habits, health status and self-esteem. *College Students Journal, 34*(2), 217-227.

Huesmann, L. R., & Kirwil, L. (2007). Why observing violence increases the risk of violent behavior in the observer. In D. Flannery, A. Vazinsyi, & I. Waldman (Eds.), *The Cambridge handbook of violent behavior and agression* (pp. 545-570). Cambridge, UK: Cambridge University Press.

Huesmann, L. R., Moise-Titus, J., Podolski, C. L., & Eron, L. D. (2003). Longitudinal relations between children's exposure to TV violence and their aggressive and violent behavior in young adulthood: 1977-1992. *Developmental Psychology, 39,* 201-221.

Huesmann, R. (2007). The impact of electronic media violence: Scientific theory and research. *Journal of Adolescent Health, 41,* S6-S13.

Hughes, D., Rodriguez, J., Smith, E. P., Johnson, D. J., Stevenson, H. C., & Spicer, P. (2006). Parents' ethnic-racial socialization practices: A review of research and directions for future study. *Developmental Psychology, 42,* 747-770.

Hughes, I. A. (2004). Female development—All by default? *New England Journal of Medicine, 351,* 748-750.

Hughes, M. E., & Waite, L. J. (2009). Marital biography and health at mid-life. *Journal of Health and Social Behavior, 50,* 344-358.

Hughes, V. (2011, April 7). Researchers track down autism rates across the globe. Retrieved from Spectrum: https://spectrumnews.org/news/researchers-track-down-autism-rates-across-the-globe

Huijts, T., Kraaykamp, G., & Subramanian, S. V. (2011). Childlessness and psychological well-being in context: A multilevel study on 24 European countries. *European Sociological Review, 29*(1), 32–47.

Huizink, A., Robles de Medina, P., Mulder, E., Visser, G., & Buitelaar, J. (2002). Psychological measures of prenatal stress as predictors of infant temperament. *Journal of the American Academy of Child and Adolescent Psychiatry, 41*, 1078–1085.

Hujoel, P. P., Bollen, A. M., Noonan, C. J., & del Aguila, M. A. (2004). Antepartum dental radiography and infant low birth weight. *Journal of the American Medical Association, 291*, 1987–1993.

Hulbert, A. J., Pamplona, R., Buffenstein, R., & Buttemer, W. A. (2007). Life and death: metabolic rate, membrane composition, and life span of animals. *Physiological Reviews, 87*(4), 1175–1213.

Hulley, S., Furberg, C., Barrett-Connor, E., Cauley, J., Grady, D., Haskell, W., . . . Hunninghake, D. (2002). Non-cardiovascular disease outcomes during 6.8 years of hormone therapy. *Journal of the American Medical Association, 288*, 58–66.

Hulsegge, G., Looman, M., Smit, H. A., Daviglus, M. L., Schouw, Y., & Verschuren, M. (2016, January 16). *Lifestyle changes in young adulthood and middle age and risk of cardiovascular disease and all-cause mortality: The Doetinchem Cohort Study.* Retrieved from U.S. National Library of Medicine National Institutes of Health: www.ncbi.nlm.nih.gov/pmc/articles/PMC4859361/

Human Rights Watch. (2010). *Corporal punishment and its effect on students' academic performance.* Retrieved from www.hrw.org/news/2010/04/15/corporal-punishment-schools-and-its-effect-academic-success-joint-hrw/aclu-statement

Hunger Notes. (2016). *2016 World Hunger and Poverty Facts and Statistics.* Retrieved from worldhunger.org: www.worldhunger.org/2015-world-hunger-and-poverty-facts-and-statistics/#progress

Hungerford, T. L. (2001). The economic consequences of widowhood on elderly women in the United States and Germany. *Gerontologist, 41*, 103–110.

Hunt, C. E. (1996). Prone sleeping in healthy infants and victims of sudden infant death syndrome. *Journal of Pediatrics, 128*, 594–596.

Hunter, S. B., & Smith, D. E. (2008). Predictors of children's understandings of death: Age, cognitive ability, death experience and maternal communicative competence. *OMEGA-Journal of Death and Dying, 57*(2), 143–162.

Hupp, J. M., Smith, J. L., Coleman, J. M., & Brunell, A. B. (2010). That's a boy's toy: Gender-typed knowledge in toddlers as a function of mother's marital status. *The Journal of Genetic Psychology, 171*(4), 389–401.

Huston, A. C., Duncan, G. J., McLoyd, V. C., Crosby, D. A., Ripke, M. N., Weisner, T. S., &

Eldred, C. A. (2005). Impacts on children of a policy to promote employment and reduce poverty for low-income parents: New hope after 5 years. *Developmental Psychology, 41*, 902–918.

Huston, H. C., Duncan, G. J., Granger, R., Bos, J., McLoyd, V., Mistry, R., . . . Ventura, A. (2001). Work-based antipoverty programs for parents can enhance the performance and social behavior of children. *Child Development, 72*(1), 318–336.

Hutchinson, E. A., De Luca, C. R., Doyle, L. W., Roberts, G., Anderson, P. J., & Victorian Infant Collaborative Study Group. (2013). School-age outcomes of extremely preterm or extremely low birth weight children. *Pediatrics*, peds-2012.

Huttenlocher, J., Levine, S., & Vevea, J. (1998). Environmental input and cognitive growth: A study using time period comparisons. *Child Development, 69*, 1012–1029.

Huttenlocher, J., Vasilyeva, M., Cymerman, E., & Levine, S. (2002). Language input and child syntax. *Cognitive Psychology, 45*, 337–374.

Huxhold, O., Miche, M., & Schüz, B. (2013). Benefits of having friends in older ages: Differential effects of informal social activities on well-being in middle-aged and older adults. *Journals of Gerontology Series B: Psychological Sciences and Social Sciences, 69*(3), 366–375.

Huyck, M. H. (1990). Gender differences in aging. In J. E. Birren & K. W. Schaie (Eds.), *Handbook of the psychology of aging* (3rd ed., pp. 124–132). San Diego: Academic Press.

Huyck, M. H. (1999). Gender roles and gender identity in midlife. In S. L. Willis & J. D. Reid (Eds.), *Life in the middle: Psychological and social development in middle age* (pp. 209–232). New York: Academic Press.

Huzen, J., Wong, L. S. M., Veldhuisen, D. J., Samani, N. J., Zwinderman, A. H., Codd, V., . . . & Bakker, S. J. L. (2014). Telomere length loss due to smoking and metabolic traits. *Journal of Internal Medicine, 275*(2), 155–163.

Hwang, S. W., Ueng, J. J., Chiu, S., Kiss, A., Tolomiczenko, G., Cowan, L., . . . & Redelmeier, D. A. (2010). Universal health insurance and health care access for homeless persons. *American Journal of Public Health, 100*(8), 1454–1461.

Hyde, J. S. (2005). The gender similarity hypothesis. *American Psychologist, 60*, 581–592.

Hyde, J. S., & Mertz, J. E. (2009). Gender, culture, and mathematics performance. *Proceedings of the National Academy of Sciences, 106*(22), 8801–8807.

Hyde, J., Lindberg, S., Linn, M., Ellis, A., & Williams, C. (2008). Gender similarities characterize math performance. *Science, 321*, 494–495.

Iacoboni, M. (2008). *Mirroring people: The new science of how we connect with others.* New York: Farrar, Straus, & Giroux.

Iacoboni, M., & Mazziotta, J. C. (2007). Mirror neuron system: Basic findings and clinical applications. *Annals of Neurology, 62*, 213–218.

Ialongo, N. S., Edelsohn, G., & Kellam, S. G. (2001). A further look at the prognostic power of young children's reports of depressed mood and feelings. *Child Development, 72*, 736–747.

Iaria, G., Palermo, L., Committeri, G., & Barton, J. J. S. (2009). Age differences in the formation and use of cognitive maps. *Behavioural Brain Research, 196*(2), 187–191.

Iervolino, A. C., Hines, M., Golombok, S. E., Rust, J., & Plomin, R. (2005). Genetic and environmental influences on sex-types behavior during the preschool years. *Child Development, 76*, 826–840.

Iervolino, A. C., Pike, A., Manke, B., Reiss, D., Hetherington, E. M., & Plomin, R. (2002). Genetic and environmental influences in adolescent peer socialization: Evidence from two genetically sensitive designs. *Child Development, 73*(1), 162–174.

Iglowstein, I., Jenni, O. G., Molinari, L., & Largo, R. H. (2003). Sleep duration from infancy to adolescence: Reference values and generational trends. *Pediatrics, 111*, 302–307.

Imada, T., Zhang, Y., Cheour, M., Taulu, S., Ahonen, A., & Kuhl, P. (2006). Infant speech perception activates Broca's area: A developmental magnetoencephalography study. *NeuroReport, 17*, 957–962.

Imai, M., Li, L., Haryu, E., Okada, H., Hirsh-Pasek, K., Golinkoff, R. M., & Shigematsu, J. (2008). Novel noun and verb learning in Chinese-, English-, and Japanese-speaking children. *Child Development, 79*(4), 979–1000.

Imdad, A., & Bhutta, Z. A. (2011). Effect of balanced protein energy supplementation during pregnancy on birth outcomes. *BMC Public Health, 11*(3), S17.

Imoscopi, A., Inelmen, E. M., Sergi, G., Miotto, F., & Manzato, E. (2012). Taste loss in the elderly: epidemiology, causes and consequences. *Aging Clinical and Experimental Research, 24*(6), 570–579.

Ingalhalikar, M., Smith, A., Parker, D., Satterthwaite, T. D., Elliott, M. A., Ruparel, K., . . . & Verma, R. (2014). Sex differences in the structural connectome of the human brain. *Proceedings of the National Academy of Sciences, 111*(2), 823–828.

Ingersoll-Dayton, B., Neal, M. B., Ha, J., & Hammer, L. B. (2003). Redressing inequity in parent care among siblings. *Journal of Marriage and Family, 65*, 201–212.

Institute of Medicine and National Research Council. (2014). *Elder abuse and its prevention: Workshop summary.* Washington, DC: The National Academies Press.

Isaacowitz, D. M., & Smith, J. (2003). Positive and negative affect in very old age. *Journal of Gerontology: Psychological Sciences, 58B*, P143–P152.

Isengard, B., & Szydlik, M. (2012). Living apart (or) together? Coresidence of elderly parents and their adult children in Europe. *Research on Aging, 34*(4), 449–474.

Ishida, M., & Moore, G. E. (2013). The role of imprinted genes in humans. *Molecular aspects of medicine, 34*(4), 826–840.

Ishii, N., Fujii, M., Hartman, P. S., Tsuda, M., Yasuda, K., Senoo-Matsuda, N., . . . Suzuki, K. (1998). A mutation in succinate dehydrogenase cytochrome b causes oxidative stress and ageing in nematodes. *Nature, 394*, 694–697.

Izard, C. E., Porges, S. W., Simons, R. F., Haynes, O. M., & Cohen, B. (1991). Infant cardiac activity: Developmental changes and relations with attachment. *Developmental Psychology, 27*, 432–439.

Jaccard, J., & Dittus, P. J. (2000). Adolescent perceptions of maternal approval of birth control and sexual risk behavior. *American Journal of Public Health, 90*, 1426–1430.

Jackson, A. S., Sui, X., Hébert, J. R., Church, T. S., & Blair, S. N. (2009). Role of lifestyle and aging on the longitudinal change in cardiorespiratory fitness. *Archives of Internal Medicine, 169*(19), 1781–1787.

Jackson, J. J., Hill, P. L., Payne, B. R., Roberts, B. W., & Stine-Morrow, E. A. (2012). Can an old dog learn (and want to experience) new tricks? Cognitive training increases openness to experience in older adults. *Psychology and Aging, 27*(2), 286.

Jackson, K. D., Howie, L. D., & Akinbami, L. J. (2013). *Trends in allergic conditions among children: United States, 1997–2011.* NCHS Data Brief No 121. Hyattsville, MD: National Center for Health Statistics.

Jackson, R. D., LaCroix, A. Z., Gass, M., Wallace, R. B., Robbins, J., Lewis, C. E., . . . Women's Health Initiative Invesigators. (2006). Calcium plus vitamin D supplementation and the risk of fractures. *New England Journal of Medicine, 354*, 669–683.

Jacobi, T. (2012, April 17). Without immigrant labor, the economy would crumble. *New York Times.* Retrieved from www.nytimes.com/roomfordebate/2011/08/17/could-farms-survive-without-illegal-labor/without-immigrant-labor-the-economy-would-crumble

Jacobson, J. L., & Wille, D. E. (1986). The influence of attachment pattern on developmental changes in peer interaction from the toddler to the preschool period. *Child Development, 57*, 338–347.

Jacques, P. L. S., Bessette-Symons, B., & Cabeza, R. (2009). Functional neuroimaging studies of aging and emotion: fronto-amygdalar differences during emotional perception and episodic memory. *Journal of the International Neuropsychological Society, 15*(6), 819–825.

Jadallah, M., Anderson, R. C., Nguyen-Jahiel, K., Miller, B. W., Kim, I. H., Kuo, L. J., . . . & Wu, X. (2011). Influence of a teacher's scaffolding moves during child-led small-group discussions. *American Educational Research Journal, 48*(1), 194–230.

Jadva, V., Hines, M., & Golombok, S. (2010). Infants' preferences for toys, colors, and shapes: Sex differences and similarities. *Archives of Sexual Behavior, 39*(6), 1261–1273.

Jaffari-Bimmel, N., Juffer, F., van IJzendoorn, M. H., Bakermans-Kranenburg, M. J., & Mooijaart, A. (2006). Social development from infancy to adolescence: Longitudinal and concurrent factors in an adoption sample. *Developmental Psychology, 42*, 1143–1153.

Jaffee, S. R., Caspi, A., Moffitt, T. E., Dodge, K. A., Rutter, M., Taylor, A., & Tully, L. A. (2005). Nature x nature: Genetic vulnerabilities interact with physical maltreatment to promote conduct problems. *Developmental Psychopathology, 17*, 67–84.

Jaffee, S. R., Caspi, A., Moffitt, T. E., Polo-Tomas, M., Price, T. S., & Taylor, A. (2004). The limits of child effects: Evidence for genetically mediated child effects on corporal punishment but not on physical maltreatment. *Developmental Psychology, 40*, 1047–1058.

Jaffee, S., & Hyde, J. S. (2000). Gender differences in moral orientation: A meta-analysis. *Psychological Bulletin, 126*, 703–726.

James, J. B., & Lewkowicz, C. J. (1997). Themes of power and affiliation across time. In M. E. Lachman & J. B. James (Eds.), *Multiple paths of midlife development* (pp. 109–143). Chicago: University of Chicago Press.

Jankowiak, W. (1992). Father-child relations in urban China. In B. S. Hewlett (Ed.), *Father-child relations: Cultural and bi-social contexts* (pp. 345–363). New York: de Gruyter.

Jankowski, J. J., Rose, S. A., & Feldman, J. F. (2001). Modifying the distribution of attention in infants. *Child Development, 72*, 339–351.

Janssen, I., Craig, W. M., Boyce, W. F., & Pickett, W. (2004). Associations between overweight and obesity with bullying behaviors in school-aged children. *Pediatrics, 113*, 1187–1194.

Jansson, L. M., & Velez, M. (2012). Neonatal abstinence syndrome. *Current Opinion in Pediatrics, 24*(2), 252–258.

Jappens, M., & Van Bavel, J. (2016). Parental divorce, residence arrangements, and contact between grandchildren and grandparents. *Journal of Marriage and Family, 78*(2), 451–467.

Jardri, R., Houfflin-Debarge, V., Delion, P., Pruvo, J. P., Thomas, P., & Pins, D. (2012). Assessing fetal response to maternal speech using a noninvasive functional brain imaging technique. *International Journal of Developmental Neuroscience, 30*(2), 159–161.

Jarman, H. (2016). Curvy Barbie: A step in the right direction, but is it far enough? *Journal of Aesthetic Nursing, 5*, 396–397.

Jarvis, P., Newman, S., & Swiniarski, L. (2014). On becoming social: The importance of collaborative free play in childhood. *International Journal of Play, 3*, 53–68.

Jauk, E., Benedek, M., Dunst, B., & Neubauer, A. C. (2013). The relationship between intelligence and creativity: New support for the threshold hypothesis by means of empirical breakpoint detection. *Intelligence, 41*(4), 212–221.

Javaid, M. K., Crozier, S. R., Harvey, N. C., Gale, C. R., Dennison, E. M., Boucher, B. J., . . . Princess Anne Hospital Study Group. (2006). Maternal vitamin D status during pregnancy and childhood bone mass at age 9 years: A longitudinal study. *Lancet, 367*(9504), 36–43.

Jee, S. H., Sull, J. W., Park, J., Lee, S., Ohrr, H., Guallar, E., & Samet, J. M. (2006). Body-mass index and mortality in Korean men and women. *New England Journal of Medicine, 355*, 779–787.

Jeha, D., Usta, I., Ghulmiyyah, L., & Nassar, A. (2015). A review of the risks and consequences of adolescent pregnancy. *Journal of Neonatal-Perinatal Medicine, 8*(1), 1–8.

Jellinek, R. D., Myers, T. A. & Keller, K. L. (2016). The impact of doll style of dress and familiarity on body dissatisfaction in 6- to 8-year-old girls. *Body Image, 18*, 78–85.

Jenkins, J. V. M., Woolley, D. P., Hooper, S. R., & De Bellis, M. D. (2014). Direct and indirect effects of brain volume, socioeconomic status and family stress on child IQ. *Journal of Child and Adolescent Behavior, 1*(2).

Jensen, A. R. (1969). How much can we boost IQ and scholastic achievement? *Harvard Educational Review, 39*, 1–123.

Jensen, L. A., Arnett, J. J., & McKenzie, J. (2011). Globalization and cultural identity. In S. J. Schwartz, *Handbook of identity theory and research* (pp. 285–301). New York: Springer.

Jenson, L. A. (1997). Different worldviews, different morals: America's culture war divide. *Human Development, 40*, 325–344.

Jeste, D.V., Savla, G.N., Thompson, W.K., Vahia, I.V., Glorioso, D.K., Martin, A.S., Palmer, B.W., Rock, D., Golshan, S., Kraemer, H.C., Depp, C.A. (2013). Older age is associated with more successful aging: Role of resilience and depression. *American Journal of Psychiatry, 170*, 188–196.

Jeynes, W. H. (2008). A meta-analysis of the relationship between phonics instruction and minority elementary school student academic achievement. *Education and Urban Society, 40*(2), 151–166.

Jeynes, W. H., & Littell, S. W. (2000). A meta-analysis of studies examining the effect of whole language instruction on the literacy of low-SES students. *Elementary School Journal, 101*(1), 21–33.

Ji, B. T., Shu, X. O., Linet, M. S., Zheng, W., Wacholder, S., Gao, Y. T., . . . Jin, F. (1997). Paternal cigarette smoking and the risk of childhood cancer among offspring of nonsmoking mothers. *Journal of the National Cancer Institute, 89*, 238–244.

Ji-Yeon, K., McHale, S. M., Crouter, A. C., & Osgood, D. W. (2007). Longitudinal linkages between sibling relationships and adjustment from middle childhood through adolescence. *Developmental Psychology, 43*(4), 960–973.

Jia, Y., Way, N., Ling, G., Yoshikawa, H., Chen, X., Hughes, D., . . . Lu, Z. (2009). The influence of student perceptions of school climate on socioemotional and academic adjustment: A comparison of Chinese and American adolescents. *Child Development, 80*(5), 1514–1530.

Jiang, Y., Ekono, M., &Skinner, C. (2015). *Basic facts about low-income children: Children aged 12 through 17 years, 2013.* Retrieved from www.nccp.org/publications/pub_1099.html

Jiao, S., Ji, G., & Jing, Q. (1996). Cognitive development of Chinese urban only children and children with siblings. *Child Development, 67*, 387–395.

Jin, K. (2010). Modern biological theories of aging. *Aging and Disease, 1*(2), 72.

Jipson, J. L., & Gelman, S. A. (2007). Robots and rodents: Children's inferences about living and nonliving kinds. *Child Development, 78*(6), 1675–1688.

Jodl, K. M., Michael, A., Malanchuk, O., Eccles, J. S., & Sameroff, A. (2001). Parents' roles in shaping early adolescents' occupational aspirations. *Child Development, 72*(4), 1247–1265.

Joe, S., Baser, R. E., Breeden, G., Neighbors, H. W., & Jackson, J. S. (2006). Prevalence of and risk factors for lifetime suicide attempts among blacks in the United States. *Journal of the American Medical Association, 296*, 2112–2123.

Johannes, C. B., Araujo, A. B., Feldman, H. A., Derby, C. A., Kleinman, K. P., & McKinlay, J. B. (2000). Incidence of erectile dysfunction in men 40 to 69 years old: Longitudinal results from the Massachusetts male aging study. *The Journal of Urology, 163*(2), 460–463.

Johansson, B., Hofer, S. M., Allaire, J. C., Maldonado-Molina, M. M., Piccinin, A. M., Berg, S., . . . McClearn, G. E. (2004). Change in cognitive capabilities in the oldest old: The effects of proximity to death in genetically related individuals over a 6-year period. *Psychology and Aging, 19*, 145–156.

Johnson, A. D., & Markowitz, A. J. (2017). Associations between household food insecurity in early childhood and children's kindergarten skills. *Child Development.* doi: 10.1111/cdev.12764

Johnson, A. J., Becker, J. A. H., Craig, E. A., Gilchrist, E. S., & Haigh, M. M. (2009). Changes in friendship commitment: Comparing geographically close and long-distance young-adult friendships. *Communication Quarterly, 57*(4), 395–415.

Johnson, C. L. (1995). Cultural diversity in the late-life family. In R. Blieszner & V. Hilkevitch (Eds.), *Handbook of aging and the family* (pp. 307–331). Westport, CT: Greenwood Press.

Johnson, C. L., & Troll, L. E. (1994). Constraints and facilitators to friendships in late late life. *Gerontologist, 34*, 79–87.

Johnson, K., Caskey, M., Rand, K., Tucker, R., & Vohr, B. (2014). Gender differences in adult-infant communication in the first months of life. *Pediatrics, 134*, 1603–1610.

Johnson, M. D., & Galambos, N. L. (2014). Paths to intimate relationship quality from parent-adolescent relations and mental health. *Journal of Marriage and Family, 76*(1), 145–160.

Johnston, L. D., O'Malley, P. M., Bachman, J. G., & Schulenberg, J. E. (2013). *Monitoring the Future: National results on drug use: 2012 Overview, key findings on adolescent drug use.* Ann Arbor: Institute for Social Research, The University of Michigan.

Johnston, L. D., O'Malley, P. M., Bachman, J. G., Schulenberg, J. E., & Miech, R. A. (2016). *Monitoring the future national survey results on drug use, 1975–2015: Volume II, college students and adults ages 19–55.* Ann Arbor: Institute for Social Research, The University of Michigan.

Johnston, L. D., O'Malley, P. M., Miech, R. A., Bachman, J. G., & Schulenberg, J. E. (2016). *Monitoring the Future national survey results on drug use, 1975–2015: Overview, key findings on adolescent drug use.* Ann Arbor: Institute for Social Research, The University of Michigan. Retrieved from www.monitoringthefuture.org/pubs/monographs/mtf-overview2015.pdf - PDF

Jones, A M. (2004). *Review of gap year provisions.* London: Department of Education and Skills.

Jones, C. L., Tepperman, L., & Wilson, S. J. (1995). *The future of the family.* Englewood Cliffs, NJ: Prentice Hall.

Jones, D. E., Greenberg, M., & Crowley, M. (2015). Early social-emotional functioning and public health: The relationship between kindergarten social competence and future wellness. *Journal Information, 105*(11).

Jones, E. K., Jurgenson, J. R., Katzenellenbogen, J. M., & Thompson, S. C. (2012, December). *Menopause and the influence of culture: Another gap for Indigenous Australian women?* Retrieved from U.S. National Library of Medicine National Institutes of Health: www.ncbi.nlm.nih.gov/pmc/articles/PMC3554544/

Jones, K. M., Whitbourne, S. K., & Skultety, K. M. (2006). Identity processes and the transition to midlife among baby boomers. In S. K. Whitbourne & S. L. Willis (Eds.), *The baby boomers grow up: Contemporary perspectives on midlife* (pp. 149–164). Mahwah, NJ: Erlbaum.

Jopp, D., & Smith, J. (2006). Resources and life management strategies as determinants of successful aging: On the protective effect of selection, optimization, and compensation. *Psychology and Aging, 21*, 253–265.

Jordan, K. (2014). Initial trends in enrolment and completion of massive open online courses. *The International Review of Research in Open and Distributed Learning, 15*(1).

Jordan, N. C., Kaplan, D., Oláh, L. N., & Locuniak, M. N. (2006). Number sense growth in kindergarten: A longitudinal investigation of children at risk for mathematics difficulties. *Child Development, 77*, 153–175.

Jordan, N. C., Kaplan, D., Raminemi, C., & Locuniak, M. N. (2009). Early math matters: Kindergarten number competence and later mathematics outcomes. *Developmental Psychology, 45*(3), 850–867.

Jose, A., O'Leary, K. D., & Moyer, A. (2010). Does premarital cohabitation predict subsequent marital stability and marital quality? A meta-analysis. *Journal of Marriage and Family, 72*(1), 105–116.

Josselson, R. (2003). Revisions: Processes of development in midlife women. In J. Demick & C. Andreoletti (Eds.), *Handbook of adult development.* New York: Plenum Press.

Juhl, J., & Routledge, C. (2016). Putting the terror in terror management theory: Evidence that the awareness of death does cause anxiety and undermine psychological well-being. *Current Directions in Psychological Science, 25*(2), 99–103.

Julian, M. M. (2013). Age at adoption from institutional care as a window into the lasting effects of early experiences. *Clinical Child and Family Psychology Review, 16*(2), 101–145.

Jung, C. G. (1933). *Modern man in search of a soul.* New York: Harcourt Brace.

Jung, C. G. (1953). The stages of life. In H. Read, M. Fordham, & G. Adler (Eds.), *Collected works* (Vol. 2). Princeton, NJ: Princeton University Press. (Original work published 1931)

Jung, C. G. (1966). Two essays on analytic psychology. In *Collected works* (Vol. 7). Princeton, NJ: Princeton University Press.

Jung, C. G. (1969). *The structure and dynamics of the psyche.* Princeton, NJ: Princeton University Press.

Jung, C. G. (1971). Aion: Phenomenology of the self (the ego, the shadow, the syzgy: Anima/animus). In J. Campbell (Ed.), *The portable Jung.* New York: Viking Penguin.

Jurewicz, J., & Hanke, W. (2008). Prenatal and childhood exposure to pesticides and neurobehavioral development: Review of epidemiological studies. *International Journal of Occupational Medicine and Environmental Health, 21*(2), 121–132.

Jusczyk, P. W., & Hohne, E. A. (1997). Infants' memory for spoken words. *Science, 277*, 1984–1986.

Juster, F. T., Ono, H., & Stafford, F. P. (2004). *Changing times of American youth: 1981–2003* (Child Development Supplement). Ann Arbor, MI: University of Michigan Institute for Social Research.

Juvonen, J., & Gross, E. F. (2008). Extending the school grounds?—Bullying experiences in cyberspace. *Journal of School Health, 78*(9), 496–505.

Kabali, H. K., Irigoyen, M. M., Nunez-Davis, R., Budacki, J. G., Mohanty, S. H., Leister, K. P., Bonner, Jr., R. L. (2015). Exposure and use of mobile media devices by young children. *Pediatrics, 136.* doi: 10.1542/peds.2015-2151

Kaczynski, K. J., Lindahl, K. M., Malik, N. M., & Laurenceau, J. (2006). Marital conflict, maternal and paternal parenting, and child adjustment: A test of mediation and moderation. *Journal of Family Psychology, 20*, 199–208.

Kagan, J. (1997). Temperament and the reactions to unfamiliarity. *Child Development, 68*, 139–143.

Kagan, J. (2008). In defense of qualitative changes in development. *Child Development, 79,* 1606–1624.

Kagan, J., & Snidman, N. (2004). *The long shadow of temperament.* Cambridge, MA: Belknap Press.

Kagan, J., Reznick, J. S., Clarke, C., Snidman, N., & Garcia-Coll, C. (1984). Behavioral inhibition to the unfamiliar. *Child Development,* 2212–2225.

Kagan, J., Reznick, J. S., Snidman, N., Gibbons, J., & Johnson, M. O. (1988). Childhood derivatives of inhibition and lack of inhibition to the unfamiliar. *Child Development,* 1580–1589.

Kahn, R. L., & Antonucci, T. C. (1980). Convoys over the life course: Attachment, roles, and social support. In P. B. Baltes & O. G. Brim Jr. (Eds.), *Life-span development and behavior* (pp. 253–286). New York: Academic Press.

Kahn, S., Zimmerman, G., Csikszentmihalyi, M., & Getzels, J. W. (2014). Relations between identity in young adulthood and intimacy at midlife. In *Applications of flow in human development and education* (pp. 327–338). Amsterdam: Springer Netherlands.

Kail, R. V., Lervåg, A., & Hulme, C. (2016). Longitudinal evidence linking processing speed to the development of reasoning. *Developmental Science, 19*(6), 1067-1074.

Kaiser Family Foundation, Hoff, T., Greene, L., & Davis, J. (2003). *National survey of adolescents and young adults: Sexual health knowledge, attitudes and experiences.* Menlo Park, CA: Henry J. Kaiser Foundation.

Kaiser Family Foundation. (2017). OECD Health Data: Health status: Health status indicators. *OECD Health Statistics database.*

Kalil, A., & Ziol-Guest, K. M. (2005). Single mothers' employment dynamics and adolescent well-being. *Child Development, 76*, 196-211.

Kalkbrenner, A. E., Schmidt, R. J., & Penlesky, A. C. (2014). Environmental chemical exposures and autism spectrum disorders: A review of the epidemiological evidence. *Current Problems in Pediatric Adolescent Health Care, 44*, 277-318.

Kallio, E. (2011). Integrative thinking is the key: An evaluation of current research into the development of adult thinking. *Theory & Psychology, 21*(6), 785-801.

Kalmijn, M., & Saraceno, C. (2008). A comparative perspective on intergenerational support: Responsiveness to parental needs in individualistic and familialistic cultures. *European Societies, 10*(3), 479-508.

Kalmijn, M., Loeve, A., & Manting, D. (2007). Income dynamics in couples and the dissolution of marriage and cohabitation. *Demography, 44*(1), 159-179.

Kalmuss, D., Davidson, A., & Cushman, L. (1992). Parenting expectations, experiences, and adjustment to parenthood: A test of the violated expectations framework. *Journal of Marriage and Family, 54*(3), 516-526.

Kamp Dush, C. M., & Taylor, M. G. (2012). Trajectories of marital conflict across the life course: Predictors and interactions with marital happiness trajectories. *Journal of Family Issues, 33*(3), 341-368.

Kamp, K.A. (2001). Where have all the children gone? The archaeology of childhood. *Journal of Archaeological Method and Theory, 8*, 1-34.

Kann, L. (2016). Youth risk behavior surveillance–United States, 2015. *MMWR. Surveillance Summaries, 65.*

Kann, L., Kinchen, S., Shanklin, S. L., Flint, K. H., Hawkins, J., Harris, W. A., . . . & Whittle, L. (2014). Youth risk behavior surveillance—United States, 2013. *MMWR. Surveillance Summaries, 63.*

Kaplan, H., & Dove, H. (1987). Infant development among the Ache of East Paraguay. *Developmental Psychology, 23*, 190-198.

Kaplan, M. K., Crespo, C. J., Huguet, N., & Marks, G. (2009). Ethnic/racial homogeneity and sexually transmitted diseases: A study of 77 Chicago Community Areas. *Sexually Transmitted Diseases, 36*(2), 108-111.

Kaplan, R. M., & Kronick, R. G. (2006). Marital status and longevity in the United States population. *Journal of Epidemiological Community Health, 60*, 760-765.

Kaplow, J. B., Saunders, J., Angold, A., & Costello, E. J. (2010). Psychiatric symptoms in bereaved versus nonbereaved youth and young adults: a longitudinal epidemiological study. *Journal of the American Academy of Child & Adolescent Psychiatry, 49*(11), 1145-1154.

Kaplowitz, P. B. (2008). The link between body fat and the timing of puberty. *Pediatrics, 121* (2, Suppl. 3), S208-S217.

Karacan, E. (2014). Timing of parenthood and generativity development: An examination of age and gender effects in Turkish sample. *Journal of Adult Development, 21*(4), 207-215.

Karafantis, D. M., & Levy, S. R. (2004). The role of children's lay theories about the malleability of human attributes in beliefs about and volunteering for disadvantaged groups. *Child Development, 75*, 236-250.

Karasik, L. B., Tamis-LeMonda, C. S., & Adolph, K. E. (2011). Transition from crawling to walking and infants' actions with objects and people. *Child Development, 82*(4), 1199-1209.

Karim, J., & Weisz, R. (2010). Cross-cultural research on the reliability and validity of the Mayer-Salovey-Caruso Emotional Intelligence Test (MSCEIT). *Cross-Cultural Research, 44*(4), 374-404.

Karney, B. R., & Bradbury, T. N. (1995). The longitudinal course of marital quality and stability: A review of theory, method, and research. *Psychological Bulletin, 118*, 3-34.

Kashimada, K., & Koopman, P. (2010). Sry: the master switch in mammalian sex determination. *Development, 137*(23), 3921-3930.

Kasper, J. D., Pezzin, L. E., & Rice, J. B. (2010). Stability and changes in living arrangements: Relationship to nursing home admission and timing of placement. *Journals of Gerontology, 65B*(Series B), 783-791.

Katis, D., & Selimis, S. (2005, June). The development of metaphoric motion: Evidence from Greek child'en's narratives. In *Annual Meeting of the Berkeley Linguistics Society* (Vol. 31, No. 1, pp. 205-216).

Katzman, R. (1993). Education and prevalence of Alzheimer's disease. *Neurology, 43*, 13-20.

Kaufman, A. S., & Kaufman, N. L. (1983). *Kaufman Assessment Battery for Children: Administration and scoring manual.* Circle Pines, MN: American Guidance Service.

Kaufman, A. S., & Kaufman, N. L. (2003). *Kaufman Assessment Battery for Children* (2nd ed.). Circle Pines, MN: American Guidance Service.

Kaufman, S. B., Quilty, L. C., Grazioplene, R. G., Hirsh, J. B., Gray, J. R., Peterson, J. B., & DeYoung, C. G. (2016). Openness to experience and intellect differentially predict creative achievement in the arts and sciences. *Journal of Personality, 84*(2), 248-258.

Kaushik, R., Krisch, I. M., Schroeder, D. R., Flick, R., & Nemergut, M. E. (2015). Pediatric bicycle-related head injuries: a population-based study in a county without a helmet law. *Injury Epidemiology, 2*(1), 16.

Kawabata, Y., & Crick, N. (2008). The roles of cross-racial/ethnic friendships in social adjustment. *Developmental Psychology, 44*(4), 1177-1183.

Kawabata, Y., Alink, L. R., Tseng, W. L., Van Ijzendoorn, M. H., & Crick, N. R. (2011). Maternal and paternal parenting styles associated with relational aggression in children and adolescents: A conceptual analysis and meta-analytic review. *Developmental Review, 31*(4), 240-278.

Kaye, E. K., Valencia, A., Baba, N., Spiro, A., Dietrich, T., & Garcia, R. I. (2010). Tooth loss and periodontal disease predict poor cognitive function in older men. *Journal of the American Geriatrics Society, 58*(4), 713-718.

Kazdin, A. E., & Benjet, C. (2003). Spanking children: Evidence and issues. *Current Directions in Psychological Science, 12*, 99-103.

Kazemi, A., Ardabili, H. E., & Solokian, S. (2010). The association between social competence in adolescents and mothers' parenting style: A cross sectional study on Iranian girls. *Child and Adolescent Social Work Journal, 27*(6), 395-403.

Keegan, R. T. (1996). *Creativity from childhood to adulthood: A difference of degree and not of kind* (New Directions for Child Development, No. 72, pp. 57-66). San Francisco: Jossey-Bass.

Keesee, N. J., Currier, J. M., & Neimeyer, R. A. (2008). Predictors of grief following the death of one's child: The contribution of finding meaning. *Journal of Clinical Psychology, 64*(10), 1145-1163.

Kefalas, M. J., Furstenberg, F. F., Carr, P. J., & Napolitano, L. (2011). "Marriage is more than being together": The meaning of marriage for young adults. *Journal of Family Issues, 32*(7), 845-875.

Kefalas, M., Furstenberg, F., & Napolitano, L. (2005, September). *Marriage is more than being together: The meaning of marriage among young adults in the United States.* Network on Transitions to Adulthood Research Working Paper.

Kegler, S. R. (2017). Trends in suicide by level of urbanization—United States, 1999-2015. *Morbidity and Mortality Weekly Report, 66.*

Keijsers, L., Branje, S. J. T., Frijns, T., Finkenauer, C., & Meeus, W. (2010). Gender differences in keeping secrets from parents in adolescence. *Developmental Psychology, 46*(1), 293-298.

Keleher, A., & Smith, E. R. (2012). Growing support for gay and lesbian equality since 1990. *Journal of Homosexuality, 59*(9), 1307-1326.

Keller, B. (1999, February 24). *A time and place for teenagers.* Retrieved from www.edweek.org/ew/vol-18/24studen.h18

Kelley, A.S., & Morrison, R.S. (2015). Palliative care for the seriously ill. *New England Journal of Medicine, 373*, 747-755.

Kelley, M. L., Smith, T. S., Green, A. P., Berndt, A. E., & Rogers, M. C. (1998). Importance of fathers' parenting to African-American toddlers' social and cognitive development. *Infant Behavior & Development, 21*, 733-744.

Kellman, P. J., & Arterberry, M. E. (1998). *The cradle of knowledge: Development of perception in infancy.* Cambridge, MA: MIT Press.

Kellogg, N., & the Committee on Child Abuse and Neglect. (2005). The evaluation of sexual abuse in children. *Pediatrics, 116*(2), 506-512.

Kellogg, R. (1970). Understanding children's art. In P. Cramer (Ed.), *Readings in developmental psychology today.* Delmar, CA: CRM.

Kelly, A. M., Wall, M., Eisenberg, M., Story, M., & Neumark-Sztainer, D. (2004). High body satisfaction in adolescent girls: Association with demographic, socio-environmental, personal, and behavioral factors. *Journal of Adolescent Health, 34,* 129.

Kelly, J. B., & Emery, R. E. (2003). Children's adjustment following divorce: Risk and resiliency perspectives. *Family Relations, 52,* 352–362.

Kelsey, M. M., Zaepfel, A., Bjornstad, P., & Nadeau, K. J. (2014). Age-related consequences of childhood obesity. *Gerontology, 60,* 222–228.

Kemmler, W., Bebenek, M., Kohl, M., & von Stengel, S. (2015). Exercise and fractures in postmenopausal women. Final results of the controlled Erlangen Fitness and Osteoporosis Prevention Study (EFOPS). *Osteoporosis International, 26*(10), 2491–2499.

Kempe, M., Kalicinski, M., & Memmert, D. (2015). Naturalistic assessment of everyday memory performance among older adults. *Experimental Aging Research, 41*(4), 426–445.

Kempen, G. I., Ballemans, J., Ranchor, A. V., van Rens, G. H., & Zijlstra, G. R. (2012). The impact of low vision on activities of daily living, symptoms of depression, feelings of anxiety and social support in community-living older adults seeking vision rehabilitation services. *Quality of Life Research, 21*(8), 1405–1411.

Kempermann, G. (2015). Activity dependency and aging in the regulation of adult neurogenesis. *Cold Spring Harbor Perspectives in Biology, 7*(11), a018929.

Kena, G., Aud, S., Johnson, F., Wang, X., Zhang, J., Rathbun, A., Wilkinson-Flicker, S., and Kristapovich, P. (2014). *The condition of education 2014 (NCES 2014-083).* Washington, DC: U.S. Department of Education, National Center for Education Statistics. Retrieved from http://nces.ed.gov/pubsearch

Kena, G., Hussar, W., McFarland, J., de Brey, C., Musu-Gillette, L., Wang, X., . . . & Barmer, A. (2016). The condition of education 2016. NCES 2016-144. *National Center for Education Statistics.*

Kendig, H., Dykstra, P. A., van Gaalen, R. I., & Melkas, T. (2007). Health of aging parents and childless individuals. *Journal of Family Issues, 28*(11), 1457–1486.

Kennedy, D. E., & Kramer, L. (2008). Improving emotion regulation and sibling relationship quality: The more fun with sisters and brothers program. *Family Relations, 57*(5), 567–578.

Kennedy, S., & Ruggles, S. (2013). *Breaking up is Hard to Count: The Rise of Divorce and Cohabitation Instability in the United States, 1980-2010.* Working Paper 2013-01. Minneapolis: University of Minnesota, Minnesota Population Center.

Kennedy, S., & Ruggles, S. (2014). Breaking up is hard to count: The rise of divorce in the United States, 1980-2010. *Demography, 51*(2), 587–598.

Kensinger, E. A. (2009). How emotion affects older adults' memories for event details. *Memory, 17*(2), 208–219.

Keppel, K. G., Pearcy, J. N., & Wagener, D. K. (2002). Trends in racial and ethnic-specific rates for the health status indicators: United States, 1990-1998. *Statistical Notes,* No. 23. Hyattsville, MD: National Center for Health Statistics.

Kerala, N. (2005, September 1). *After death, Tibetans still prefer sky burial.* Retrieved from The Buddhist Channel: www.buddhistchannel. tv/index.php?id=1,1614,0,0,1,0#.Wjb-nN-nGCi

Kere, N., Hannula-Jouppi, K., Kaminen-Ahola, N., Taipale, M., Eklund, R., Nopola-Hemmi, J., & Kaariainen, H. (2005, October). *Identification of the dyslexia susceptibility gene for DYX5 on chromosome 3.* Paper presented at the meeting of the American Society of Human Genetics, Salt Lake City, UT.

Kerkhof, G. A., & Van Dongen, H. P. A. (2010). Effects of sleep deprivation on cognition. *Human Sleep and Cognition: Basic Research, 185,* 105.

Kern, M. L., & Friedman, H. S. (2008). Do conscientious individuals live longer?: A quantitative review. *Health Psychology, 27*(5), 505–512.

Kerns, K. A., Don, A., Mateer, C. A., & Streissguth, A. P. (1997). Cognitive deficits in nonretarded adults with fetal alcohol syndrome. *Journal of Learning Disabilities, 30,* 685–693.

Kerr, D. C. R., Lopez, N. L., Olson, S. L., & Sameroff, A. J. (2004). Parental discipline and externalizing behavior problems in early childhood: The roles of moral regulation and child gender. *Journal of Abnormal Child Psychology, 32*(4), 369–383.

Kestenbaum, R., & Gelman, S. A. (1995). Preschool children's identification and understanding of mixed emotions. *Cognitive Development, 10,* 443–458.

Keyes, C. L. M., & Ryff, C. D. (1998). Generativity in adult lives: Social structural contours and quality of life consequences. In D. P. McAdams & E. de St. Aubin (Eds.), *Generativity and adult development* (pp. 227–263). Washington, DC: American Psychological Association.

Keyes, C. L. M., & Shapiro, A. D. (2004). Social well-being in the United States: A descriptive epidemiology. In O. G. Brim, C. D. Ryff, & R. C. Kessler (Eds.), *How healthy are we? A national study of well-being at midlife* (pp. 350–372). Chicago: University of Chicago Press.

Keyes, K. M., Grant, B. M., & Hasin, D. S. (2007). Evidence for a closing gender gap in alcohol use, abuse and dependence in the United States population. *Drug and Alcohol Dependence, 93,* 21–29.

Khashan, A. S., Abel, K. M., McNamee, R., Pedersen, M. G., Webb, R. T., Baker, P. N., . . . Mortensen, P. B. (2008). Higher risk of offspring schizophrenia following antenatal maternal exposure to severe adverse life events. *Archives of General Psychiatry, 65,* 146–152.

Khaw, K. T., Wareham, N., Bingham, S., Welch, A., Luben, R., & Day, N. (2008). Combined impact of health behaviours and mortality in men and women: The EPIC-Norfolk Prospective Population Study. *PLoS Medicine, 5*(1), e12. doi: 10.1371/journal.pmed.0050012

Khodyakov, D., & Carr, D. (2009). The impact of late-life parental death on adult sibling relationships: Do parents' advance directives help or hurt? *Research on Aging, 31*(5), 495–519.

Kiecolt-Glaser, J. K., & Glaser, R. (2001). Stress and immunity: Age enhances the risks. *Current Directions in Psychological Science, 10,* 18–21.

Kiecolt-Glaser, J. K., & Newton, T. L. (2001). Marriage and health: His and hers. *Psychological Bulletin, 127,* 472–503.

Kiefe, C. I., Williams, O. D., Weissman, N. W., Schreiner, P. J., Sidney, S., & Wallace, D. D. (2000). Changes in U.S. health care access in the 90s: Race and income differences from the CARDIA study. Coronary artery risk development in young adults. *Ethnicity and Disease, 10,* 418–431.

Kiefer, K. M., Summer, L., & Shirey, L. (2001). What are the attitudes of young retirees and older workers? *Data Profiles: Young Retirees and Older Workers,* 5.

Kier, C., & Lewis, C. (1998). Preschool sibling interaction in separated and married families: Are same-sex pairs or older sisters more sociable? *Journal of Child Psychology and Psychiatry, 39,* 191–201.

Kilgour, A. H., Starr, J. M., & Whalley, L. J. (2010). Associations between childhood intelligence (IQ), adult morbidity and mortality. *Maturitas, 65*(2), 98–105.

Killewald, A. (2016). Money, work, and marital stability: Assessing change in the gendered determinants of divorce. *American Sociological Review, 81*(4), 696–719.

Kim, D. H., Yeo, S. H., Park, J. M., Choi, J. Y., Lee, T. H., Park, S. Y., . . . & Cha, H. J. (2014). Genetic markers for diagnosis and pathogenesis of Alzheimer's disease. *Gene, 545*(2), 185–193.

Kim, J. E., & Moen, P. (2001). Moving into retirement: Preparation and transitions in late midlife. In M. E. Lachman (Ed.), *Handbook of midlife development* (pp. 487–527). New York: Wiley.

Kim, J. Y., McHale, S. M., Crouter, A. C., & Osgood, D. W. (2007). Longitudinal linkages between sibling relationships and adjustment from middle childhood through adolescence. *Developmental Psychology, 43*(4), 960.

Kim, J., McHale, S. M., Osgood, D. W., & Crouter, A. C. (2006). Longitudinal course and family correlates of sibling relationships from childhood through adolescence. *Child Development, 77,* 1746–1761.

Kim, S., Nordling, J. K., Yoon, J. E., Boldt, L. J., & Kochanska, G. (2013). Effortful control in "hot" and "cool" tasks differentially predicts children's behavior problems and academic performance. *Journal of Abnormal Child Psychology, 41*(1), 43–56.

Kim, S.Y., Fouad, N., Maeda, H., Xie, H., & Nazan, N. (2017). Midlife work and psychological well-being: A test of the psychology of working theory. *Journal of Career Assessment,* 1–12. doi: 10.1177/1069072717714538

Kim-Cohen, J., Moffitt, T. E., Caspi, A., & Taylor, A. (2004). Genetic and environmental processes in young children's resilience and vulnerability to socioeconomic deprivation. *Child Development, 75,* 651–668.

Kimball, M. M. (1986). Television and sex-role attitudes. In T. M. Williams (Ed.), *The impact of television: A natural experiment in three communities* (pp. 265–301). Orlando, FL: Academic Press.

King, B. M. (1996). *Human sexuality today.* Englewood Cliffs, NJ: Prentice Hall.

King, K. M., Meehan, B. T., Trim, R. S., & Chassin, L. (2006). Market or mediator? The effects of adolescent substance use on young adult educational attainment. *Addiction, 101,* 1730–1740.

King, M., & Bartlett, A. (2006). What same sex civil partnerships may mean for health. *Journal of Epidemiology and Community Health, 60,* 188–191.

King, V., Amato, P. R., & Lindstrom, R. (2015). Stepfather–adolescent relationship quality during the first year of transitioning to a stepfamily. *Journal of Marriage and Family, 77*(5), 1179–1189.

King, W. J., MacKay, M., Sirnick, A., & The Canadian Shaken Baby Study Group. (2003). Shaken baby syndrome in Canada: Clinical characteristics and outcomes of hospital cases. *Canadian Medical Association Journal, 168,* 155–159.

Kinsella, K., & He, W. (2009). *An aging world: 2008. International Population Reports* (P95/09-1). Washington, DC: U.S. Government Printing Office.

Kinsella, K., & Phillips, P. (2005, March). Global aging: The challenges of success. *Population Bulletin,* No. 1. Washington, DC: Population Reference Bureau.

Kinsella, K., & Velkoff, V. A. (2001). *An aging world: 2001* (U.S. Census Bureau, Series P95/01-1). Washington, DC: U.S. Government Printing Office.

Kiraly, M., & Humphreys, C. (2013). Family contact for children in kinship care: A literature review. *Australian Social Work, 66*(3), 358–374.

Kirby, D., & Laris, B. (2009). Effective curriculum-based sex and STD/HIV education programs for adolescents. *Child Development Perspectives, 3,* 21–29.

Kirk, J. K., D'Agostino, R. B., Jr., Bell, R. A., Passmore, L. V., Bonds, D. E., Karter, A. J., & Narayan, K. M. V. (2006). Disparities in HbA1c levels between African-American and Non-Hispanic white adults with diabetes: A meta-analysis. *Diabetes Care, 29*(9), 2130–2136.

Kirk-Sanchez, N. & McGough, E.L. (2014). Physical exercise and cognitive performance in the elderly: Current perspectives. *Clinical Interventions in Aging, 9,* 51–62.

Kirkorian, H. L., Wartella, E. A., & Anderson, D. R. (2008). Media and young children's learning. *The Future of Children, 18*(1), 39–61.

Kisilevsky, B. S., & Haines, S. M. J. (2010). Exploring the relationship between fetal heart rate and cognition. *Infant and Child Development, 19,* 60–75.

Kisilevsky, B. S., Muir, D. W., & Low, J. A. (1992). Maturation of human fetal responses to vibroacoustic stimulation. *Child Development, 63,* 1497–1508.

Kitzmann, K. M., & Beech, B. (2006). Family-based interventions for pediatric obesity: Methodological and conceptual challenges from family psychology. *Journal of Family Psychology, 20,* 175–189.

Kitzmann, K. M., Dalton, W. T., III, Stanley, C. M., Beech, B. M., Reeves, T. P., Bescemi, J., . . . Midgett, E. L. (2010). Lifestyle interventions for youth who are overweight: A meta-analytic review. *Health Psychology, 29*(1), 91–101.

Kivett, V. R. (1991). Centrality of the grandfather role among older rural black and white men. *Journal of Gerontology: Social Sciences, 46*(5), S250–S258.

Kivett, V. R. (1993). Racial comparisons of the grandmother role: Implications for strengthening the family support system of older black women. *Family Relations, 42,* 165–172.

Kivett, V. R. (1996). The saliency of the grandmother-granddaughter relationship: Predictors of association. *Journal of Women and Aging, 8,* 25–39.

Klauer, S. G., Guo, F., Simons-Morton, B. G., Ouimet, M. C., Lee, S. E., & Dingus, T. A. (2014). Distracted driving and risk of road crashes among novice and experienced drivers. *New England Journal of Medicine, 370*(1), 54–59.

Klein, J. D., & the American Academy of Pediatrics Committee on Adolescence. (2005). Adolescent pregnancy: Current trends and issues. *Pediatrics, 116,* 281–286.

Klein-Velderman, M., Bakermans-Kranenburg, M. J., Juffer, F., & van IJzendoorn, M. H. (2006). Effects of attachment-based interventions on maternal sensitivity and infant attachment: Differential susceptibility of highly reactive infants. *Journal of Family Psychology, 20,* 266–274.

Klemenc-Ketis, Z., Kersnik, J., & Grmec, S. (2010). The effect of carbon dioxide on near-death experiences in out-of-hospital cardiac arrest survivors: A prospective observational study. *Critical Care, 14*(2), R56.

Kletke, B., Hallford, D.J., & Mellor, D.J. (2014). Sexting prevalence and correlates: A systematic literature review. *Clinical Psychology Review, 34,* 44–53.

Klibanoff, R. S., Levine, S. C., Huttenlocher, J., Vasilyeva, M., & Hedges, L. V. (2006). Preschool children's mathematical knowledge: The effect of teacher "math talk." *Developmental Psychology, 42,* 59–69.

Kliegel, M., Ballhausen, N., Hering, A., Ihle, A., Schnitzspahn, K. M., & Zuber, S. (2016). Prospective memory in older adults: Where we are now and what is next. *Gerontology, 62*(4), 459–466.

Kline, D. W., & Scialfa, C. T. (1996). Visual and auditory aging. In J. E. Birren & K. W. Schaie (Eds.), *Handbook of the psychology of aging* (pp. 191–208). San Diego: Academic Press.

Kloep, M., & Hendry, L. B. (2010). Letting go or holding on? Parents' perceptions of their relationships with their children during emerging adulthood. *British Journal of Developmental Psychology, 28*(4), 817–834.

Klohnen, E. C. (1996). Conceptual analysis and measurement of the construct of ego-resiliency. *Journal of Personality and Social Psychology, 70,* 1067–1079.

Knafo, A., & Plomin, R. (2006). Parental discipline and affection and children's prosocial behavior: Genetic and environmental links. *Journal of Personality and Social Psychology, 90,* 147–164.

Knecht, S., Drager, B., Deppe, M., Bobe, L., Lohmann, H., Floel, A., Ringelstein, E. B., & Henningsen, H. (2000). Handedness and hemispheric language dominance in healthy humans. *Brain: A Journal of Neurology, 123*(12), 2512–2518.

Knickmeyer, R. C., Gouttard, S., Kang, C., Evans, D., Wilber, K., Smith, J. K., . . . Gilmore, J. H. (2008). A structural MRI study of human brain development from birth to 2 years. *Journal of Neuroscience, 28*(47), 12176–12182.

Knochel, K. A., Quam, J. K., & Croghan, C. F. (2011). Are old lesbian and gay people well served? Understanding the perceptions, preparation, and experiences of aging services providers. *Journal of Applied Gerontology, 30*(3), 370–389.

Ko, T. J., Tsai, L. Y., Chu, L. C., Yeh, S. J., Leung, C., Chen, C. Y., . . . & Hsieh, W. S. (2014). Parental smoking during pregnancy and its association with low birth weight, small for gestational age, and preterm birth offspring: a birth cohort study. *Pediatrics & Neonatology, 55*(1), 20–27.

Kochanek, K. D., Murphy, S. L., Xu, J. Q. & Tejada-Vera, B. (2016). Deaths: Final data for 2014. *National Vital Statistics Reports, 65*(4).

Kochanek, K. D., Murphy, S. L., Anderson, R. N., & Scott, C. (2004). Deaths: Final data for 2002. *National Vital Statistics Reports, 53*(5). Hyattsville, MD: National Center for Health Statistics.

Kochanek, K. D., Murphy, S. L., Xu, J. & Tejada-Vera, B. (2016). *Deaths: final data for 2014.* Retrieved from https://stacks.cdc.gov/view/cdc/40133

Kochanek, K. D., Murphy, S. L., Xu, J., & Tejada-Vera, B. (2016). Deaths: final data for 2014. *National Vital Statistics Reports: from the Centers for Disease Control and Prevention, National Center for Health Statistics, National Vital Statistics System, 65*(4), 1–122.

Kochanska, G. (1993). Toward a synthesis of parental socialization and child temperament in early development of conscience. *Child Development, 64*(2), 325–347.

Kochanska, G. (2001). Emotional development in children with different attachment histories: The first three years. *Child Development, 72,* 474–490.

Kochanska, G., & Aksan, N. (1995). Mother-child positive affect, the quality of child compliance to requests and prohibitions, and maternal control as correlates of early internalization. *Child Development, 66,* 236–254.

Kochanska, G., Aksan, N., & Carlson, J. J. (2005). Temperament, relationships, and young children's receptive cooperation with their parents. *Developmental Psychology, 41*, 648–660.

Kochanska, G., Aksan, N., & Joy, M. E. (2007). Children's fearfulness as a moderator of parenting in early socialization: Two longitudinal studies. *Developmental Psychology, 43*, 222–237.

Kochanska, G., Askan, N., Prisco, T. R., & Adams, E. E. (2008). Mother-child and father-child mutually responsive orientation in the first two years and children's outcomes at preschool age: Mechanisms of influence. *Child Development, 79*, 30–44.

Kochanska, G., Coy, K. C., & Murray, K. T. (2001). The development of self-regulation in the first four years of life. *Child Development, 72*(4), 1091–1111.

Kochanska, G., Friesenborg, A. E., Lange, L. A., & Martel, M. M. (2004). Parents' personality and infants' temperament as contributors to their emerging relationship. *Journal of Personality and Social Psychology, 86*, 744–759.

Kochanska, G., Gross, J. N., Lin, M. H., & Nichols, K. E. (2002). Guilt in young children: Development, determinants, and relations with a broader system of standards. *Child Development, 73*(2), 461–482.

Kochanska, G., Tjebkes, T. L., & Forman, D. R. (1998). Children's emerging regulation of conduct: Restraint, compliance, and internalization from infancy to the second year. *Child Development, 69*(5), 1378–1389.

Kochanska, G., Woodard, J., Kim, S., Koenig, J. L., Yoon, J. E., & Barry, R. A. (2010). Positive socialization mechanisms in secure and insecure parent–child dyads: Two longitudinal studies. *Journal of Child Psychology and Psychiatry, 51*(9), 998–1009.

Kocherlakota, P. (2014). Neonatal abstinence syndrome. *Pediatrics, 134*(2), e547–e561.

Koechlin, E., Basso, G., Pietrini, P., Panzer, S., & Grafman, J. (1999). The role of the anterior prefrontal cortex in human cognition. *Nature, 399*, 148–151.

Koenig, H. G. (2012). Religion, spirituality, and health: the research and clinical implications. *ISRN Psychiatry, 2012*.

Koetse, M. (2017, March 18). Top 5 of popular children's books in China after crackdown on foreign storybooks. Retrieved from Whats on Weibo: www.whatsonweibo.com/top-5-popular-childrens-books-china-crackdown-foreign-story-books

Kogan, M. D., Newacheck, P. W., Honberg, L., & Strickland, B. (2005). Association between underinsurance and access to care among children with special health care needs in the United States. *Pediatrics, 116*, 1162–1169.

Kohlberg, L. (1966). A cognitive-developmental analysis of children's sex role concepts and attitudes. In E. E. Maccoby (Ed.), *The development of sex differences.* Stanford, CA: Stanford University Press.

Kohlberg, L. (1969). Stage and sequence: The cognitive-developmental approach to socialization. In D. A. Goslin (Ed.), *Handbook of socialization theory and research.* Chicago: Rand McNally.

Kohlberg, L. (1973). Continuities in childhood and adult moral development revisited. In P. Baltes & K. W. Schaie (Eds.), *Life-span developmental psychology: Personality and socialization* (pp. 180–207). New York: Academic Press.

Kohlberg, L. (1981). *Essays on moral development.* San Francisco: Harper & Row.

Kohlberg, L., & Ryncarz, R. A. (1990). Beyond justice reasoning: Moral development and consideration of a seventh stage. In C. N. Alexander & E. J. Langer (Eds.), *Higher stages of human development* (pp. 191–207). New York: Oxford University Press.

Kohn, J. L., Rholes, S. W., Simpson, J. A., Martin III, A. M., Tran, S., & Wilson, C. L. (2012). Changes in marital satisfaction across the transition to parenthood: The role of adult attachment orientations. *Personality and Social Psychology Bulletin, 38*(11), 1506–1522.

Kohn, M. L. (1980). Job complexity and adult personality. In N. J. Smelser & E. H. Erikson (Eds.), *Themes of work and love in adulthood.* Cambridge, MA: Harvard University Press.

Kohn, M. L., & Schooler, C. (1983). The cross-national universality of the interpretive model. In M. L. Kohn & C. Schooler (Eds.), *Work and personality: An inquiry into the impact of social stratification* (pp. 281–295). Norwood, NJ: Ablex.

Kolata, G. (1999, March 9). Pushing limits of the human life span. *The New York Times.* Retrieved from www.nytimes.com/library/national/science/030999sci-aging.html

Kolb, B., Mychasiuk, R., Muhammad, A., Li, Y., Frost, D. O., & Gibb, R. (2012). Experience and the developing prefrontal cortex. *Proceedings of the National Academy of Sciences, 109*(Supplement 2), 17186–17193.

Kolbert, E. (1994, January 11). Canadians curbing TV violence. *The New York Times,* pp. C15, C19.

Komarraju, M., & Nadler, D. (2013). Self-efficacy and academic achievement: Why do implicit beliefs, goals, and effort regulation matter?. *Learning and Individual Differences, 25*, 67–72.

Korchmaros, J.D., Ybarra, M.L., & Mitchell, K.J. (2015). Adolescent online romantic relationship initiation: Differences by sexual and gender identification. *Journal of Adolescence, 40*, 54–64.

Koren, G., Pastuszak, A., & Ito, S. (1998). Drugs in pregnancy. *New England Journal of Medicine, 338*, 1128–1137.

Koropeckyj-Cox, T. (2002). Beyond parental status: Psychological well-being in middle and old age. *Journal of Marriage and Family, 64*, 957–971.

Koropeckyj-Cox, T., Pienta, A. M., & Brown, T. H. (2007). Women of the 1950s and the "normative" life course: The implications of childlessness, fertility timing, and marital status for psychological well-being in late midlife. *The International Journal of Aging and Human Development, 64*(4), 299–330.

Kost, K., Henshaw, S., & Carlin, L. (2013). *U.S. teenage pregnancies, births and abortions: National and state trends and trends by race and ethnicity, 2010.* Retrieved from www.guttmacher.org/pubs/USTPtrends.pdf

Kosterman, R., Graham, J. W., Hawkins, J. D., Catalano, R. F., & Herrenkohl, T. I. (2001). Childhood risk factors for persistence of violence in the transition to adulthood: A social development perspective. *Violence & Victims. Special Issue: Developmental Perspectives on Violence and Victimization, 16*(4), 355–369.

Kovács, Á. M. (2009). Early bilingualism enhances mechanisms of false-belief reasoning. *Developmental Science, 12*(1), 48–54.

Kovas, Y., Hayiou-Thomas, M. E., Dale, P. S., Bishop, D. V. M., & Plomin, R. (2005). Genetic influences in different aspects of language development: The etiology of language skills in 4.5-year-old twins. *Child Development, 76*, 632–651.

Kowal, A. K., & Pike, L. B. (2004). Sibling influences on adolescents' attitudes toward safe sex practices. *Family Relations, 53*, 377–384.

Kowalski, R. M., Giumetti, G. W., Schroeder, A. N., & Lattanner, M. R. (2014). Bullying in the digital age: A critical review and meta-analysis of cyberbullying research among youth. *Psychological Bulletin, 140*(4), 1073–1137.

Kozlowska, K., & Hanney, L. (1999). Family assessment and intervention using an interactive art exercise. *Australia and New Zealand Journal of Family Therapy, 20*(2), 61–69.

Kramer, A. F., Erickson, K. I., & Colcombe, S. J. (2006). Exercise, cognition and the aging brain. *Journal of Applied Physiology, 101*, 1237–1242.

Kramer, A. F., Hahn, S., McAuley, E., Cohen, N. J., Banich, M. T., Harrison, C., . . . Vakil, E. (1999). Ageing, fitness and neurocognitive function. *Nature, 400*, 418–419.

Kramer, B. J., Boelk, A. Z., & Auer, C. (2006). Family conflict at the end of life: Lessons learned in a model program for vulnerable older adults. *Journal of Palliative Medicine, 9*(3), 791–801.

Kramer, D. A. (2003). The ontogeny of wisdom in its variations. In J. Demick & C. Andreolett (Eds.), *Handbook of adult development* (pp. 131–151). New York: Plenum Press.

Kramer, L. (2010). The essential ingredients of successful sibling relationships: An emerging framework for advancing theory and practice. *Child Development Perspectives, 4*(2), 80–86.

Kramer, L., & Kowal, A. K. (2005). Sibling relationship quality from birth to adolescence: The enduring contributions of friends. *Journal of Family Psychology, 19*, 503–511.

Krashen, S., & McField, G. (2005). What works? Reviewing the latest evidence on bilingual education. *Language Learner 1*(2), 7–10, 34.

Krause, N. (2004a). Common facets of religion, unique facets of religion, and life satisfaction among older African Americans. *Journal of Gerontology: Social Sciences, 59B*, S109–S117.

Krause, N. (2004b). Lifetime trauma, emotional support, and life satisfaction among older adults. *Gerontologist, 44*, 615–623.

Krause, N., & Rook, K. S. (2003). Negative interaction in late life: Issues in the stability and generalizability of conflict across relationships. *Journal of Gerontology: Psychological Sciences, 58B*, P88–P99.

Kreager, D. A., Molloy, L. E., Moody, J., & Feinberg, M. E. (2016). Friends first? The peer network origins of adolescent dating. *Journal of Research on Adolescence, 26*(2), 257–269.

Krebs-Smith, S. M., Guenther, P. M., Subar, A. F., Kirkpatrick, S. I., & Dodd, K. W. (2010). Americans do not meet federal dietary recommendations. *The Journal of Nutrition, 140*(10), 1832–1838.

Kreicbergs, U., Valdimarsdóttir, U., Onelöv, E., Henter, J. I., & Steineck, G. (2004). Talking about death with children who have severe malignant disease. *New England Journal of Medicine, 351*(12), 1175–1186.

Kreider, R. M. (2003). Adopted children and stepchildren: 2000. *Census 2000 Special Reports.* Washington, DC: U.S. Bureau of the Census.

Kreider, R. M. (2005). Number, timing, and duration of marriages and divorces: 2001. *Household Economic Studies,* P70–97. Washington, DC: U.S. Census Bureau.

Kreider, R. M., & Ellis, R. (2011). Living arrangements of children: 2009. *Current Population Reports,* P70–126. Washington, DC: U.S. Census Bureau.

Kreider, R. M., & Fields, J. (2005). Living arrangements of children: 2001. *Current Population Reports,* P70104. Washington, DC: U.S. Census Bureau.

Kreider, R. M., & Fields, J. M. (2002). Number, timing, and duration of marriages and divorces: Fall 1996. *Current Population Reports,* P70–80. Washington, DC: U.S. Census Bureau.

Kremen, A. M., & Block, J. (1998). The roots of ego-control in young adulthood: Links with parenting in early childhood. *Journal of Personality and Social Psychology, 75*(4), 1062–1075.

Kreyenfeld, M., & Konietzka, D. (2017). Analyzing childlessness. In *Childlessness in Europe: Contexts, causes, and consequences* (pp. 3–15). New York: Springer International Publishing.

Krishnamoorthy, J. S., Hart, C., & Jelalian, E. (2006). The epidemic of childhood obesity: Review of research and implications for public policy. *Society for Research in Child Development (SRCD) Social Policy Report, 20*(2).

Kritchevsky, S. B., Nicklas, B. J., Visser, M., Simonsick, E. M., Newman, A. B., Harris, T. B., . . . Pahor, M. (2005). Angiotensin-converting enzyme insertion/deletion genotype, exercise, and physical decline. *Journal of the American Medical Association, 294,* 691–698.

Kroger, J. (2003). Identity development during adolescence. In G. R. Adams & M. D. Berzonsky (Eds.), *Blackwell handbook of adolescence* (pp. 205–226). Malden, MA: Blackwell.

Kroger, J., & Haslett, S. J. (1991). A comparison of ego identity status transition pathways and change rates across five identity domains. *International Journal of Aging and Human Development, 32,* 303–330.

Kroger, J., Martinussen, M., & Marcia, J. E. (2009). Identity status change during adolescence and young adulthood: A meta-analysis. *Journal of Adolescence, 33*(5), 683–698.

Krueger, A. B. (2003, February). Economic considerations and class size. *Economic Journal, 113,* F34–F63.

Kruse, A., & Schmitt, E. (2012). Generativity as a route to active ageing. *Current Gerontology and Geriatrics Research, 2012.*

Kübler-Ross, E. (1969). *On death and dying.* New York: Macmillan.

Kübler-Ross, E. (1970). *On death and dying* [Paperback]. New York: Macmillan.

Kübler-Ross, E. (Ed.). (1975). *Death: The final stage of growth.* Englewood Cliffs, NJ: Prentice Hall.

Kuczmarski, R. J., Ogden, C. L., Grummer-Strawn, L. M., Flegal, K. M., Guo, S. S., Wei, R., . . . Johnson, C. L. (2000). *CDC growth charts: United States* (Advance Data, No. 314). Washington, DC: Centers for Disease Control and Prevention, U.S. Department of Health and Human Services.

Kuhl, P. K. (2004). Early language acquisition: Cracking the speech code. *Nature Reviews Neuroscience, 5,* 831–843.

Kuhl, P. K. (2010). Brain mechanisms in early language acquisition. *Neuron, 67*(5), 713–727.

Kuhl, P. K., Andruski, J. E., Chistovich, I. A., Chistovich, L. A., Kozhevnikova, E. V., Ryskina, V. L., . . . Lacerda, F. (1997). Cross-language analysis of phonetic units in language addressed to infants. *Science, 277,* 684–686.

Kuhl, P. K., Conboy, B. T., Padden, D., Nelson, T., & Pruitt, J. (2005). Early speech perception and later language development: Implications for the "critical period." *Language Learning and Development, 1,* 237–264.

Kuhl, P. K., Williams, K. A., Lacerda, F., Stevens, K. N., & Lindblom, B. (1992). Linguistic experience alters phonetic perception in infants by 6 months of age. *Science, 255,* 606–608.

Kuhl, P., & Rivera-Gaxiola, M. (2008). Neural substrates of language acquisition. *Annual Review of Neuroscience, 31,* 511–534.

Kuhn, D. (2006). Do cognitive changes accompany developments in the adolescent brain? *Perspectives on Psychological Science, 1,* 59–67.

Kühnel, J., Zacher, H., De Bloom, J., & Bledow, R. (2017). Take a break! Benefits of sleep and short breaks for daily work engagement. *European Journal of Work and Organizational Psychology, 26*(4), 481–491.

Kumwenda, N. I., Hoover, D. R., Mofenson, L. M., Thigpen, M. C., Kafulafula, G., Li, Q., . . . Taha, T. E. (2008). Extended antiretroviral prophylaxis to reduce breast-milk HIV-1 transmission. *New England Journal of Medicine, 359,* 119–129.

Kung, H.-C., Hoyert, D. L., Xu, J., & Murphy, S. L. (2008). Deaths: Final data for 2005. *National Vital Statistics Reports, 56*(10). Hyattsville, MD: National Center for Health Statistics.

Kunzman, R., & Gaither, M. (2013). Homeschooling: A comprehensive survey of the research. *Other Education, 2*(1), 4–59.

Kuperman, S., Chan, G., Kramer, J. R., Bierut, L., Buckholz, K. K., Fox, L., . . . Schuckit, M. A. (2005). Relationship of age of first drink to child behavioral problems and family psychopathology. *Alcoholism: Clinical and Experimental Research, 29*(10), 1869–1876.

Kupersmidt, J. B., & Coie, J. D. (1990). Preadolescent peer status, aggression, and school adjustment as predictors of externalizing problems in adolescence. *Child Development, 61,* 1350–1362.

Kurdek, L. A. (1999). The nature and predictors of the trajectory of change in marital quality for husbands and wives over the first 10 years of marriage. *Developmental Psychology, 35*(5), 1283.

Kurdek, L. A. (2004). Are gay and lesbian cohabiting couples really different from heterosexual married couples? *Journal of Marriage and Family, 66,* 880–900.

Kurdek, L. A. (2005). What do we know about gay and lesbian couples? *Current Directions in Psychological Science, 5,* 251–254.

Kurdek, L. A. (2006). Differences between partners from heterosexual, gay, and lesbian cohabiting couples. *Journal of Marriage and Family, 68,* 509–528.

Kurdek, L. A. (2008). A general model of relationship commitment: Evidence from same-sex partners. *Personal Relationships, 15*(3), 391–405.

Kutner, M., Greenberg, E., Jin, Y., Boyle, B., Hsu, Y., & Dunleavy, E. (2007). *Literacy in everyday life: Results from the 2003 National Assessment of Adult Literacy* (NCES 2007-480). Washington, DC: U.S. Department of Education, National Center for Education Statistics.

Långström, N., Rahman, Q., Carlström, E., & Lichtenstein, P. (2008). Genetic and environmental effects on same-sex sexual behavior: A population study of twins in Sweden. *Archives of Sexual Behavior.* Retrieved from https://commerce.metapress.com/content/2263646523551487/-resource-secured/?target5fulltext.pdf&sid5ur4ndr55ssgnkk550wsdrbuz&sh5www.springerlink.-com. doi: 10.1007/s10508-008-9386-1

La Rue, A. (2010). Healthy brain aging: role of cognitive reserve, cognitive stimulation, and cognitive exercises. *Clinics in Geriatric Medicine, 26*(1), 99–111.

Laar, R. J. J., Stehouwer, C. D. A., Bussel, B. C. T., Prins, M. H., Twisk, J. W. R., & Ferreira, I. (2013). Adherence to a Mediterranean dietary pattern in early life is associated with lower arterial stiffness in adulthood: the Amsterdam Growth and Health Longitudinal Study. *Journal of Internal Medicine, 273*(1), 79–93.

Labouvie-Vief, G. (2006). Emerging structures of adult thought. In J. J. Arnett & J. L. Tanner (Eds.), *Emerging adults in America: Coming of age in the 21st century* (pp. 59–84). Washington, DC: American Psychological Association.

Labov, T. (1992). Social and language boundaries among adolescents. *American Speech, 67,* 339–366.

Lachman, M. E. (2004). Development in midlife. *Annual Review of Psychology, 55,* 305–331.

Lachman, M. E., & Firth, K. M. P. (2004). The adaptive value of feeling in control during midlife. In O. G. Brim, C. D. Ryff, & R. C. Kessler (Eds.), *How healthy are we? A national study of well-being at midlife* (pp. 320–349). Chicago: University of Chicago Press.

Lachman, M. E., Teshale, S., & Agrigoroaei, S. (2015). Midlife as a pivotal period in the life course: Balancing growth and decline at the crossroads of youth and old age. *International Journal of Behavioral Development, 39*(1), 20-31.

Lachs, M., & Pillemer, K. (2015). Elder abuse. *New England Journal of Medicine, 373,* 1947-56. doi: 10.1056/NEJMra1404688

Lachs, M.S., Teresi, J.A., Ramirez, M., van Haitsma, K., Silver, S., Eimicke, J.P., Boratgis, G., Sukha, G., Kong, J., Besas, A.M., Luna, M.R., Pillemer, K.A. (2016). The prevalence of resident-to-resident elder mistreatment in nursing homes. *Annals of Internal Medicine, 165,* 229-236.

Ladd, G. W., Herald-Brown, S. L., & Reiser, M. (2008). Does chronic classroom peer rejection predict the development of children's classroom participation during the grade school years? *Child Development, 79*(4), 1001-1015.

Ladegaard, H. J. (2004). Politeness in young children's speech: Context, peer group influence and pragmatic competence. *Journal of Pragmatics, 36*(11), 2003-2022.

LaFontana, K. M., & Cillessen, A. H. N. (2002). Children's perceptions of popular and unpopular peers: A multi-method assessment. *Developmental Psychology, 38,* 635-647.

Lagattuta, K. H. (2005). When you shouldn't do what you want to do: Young children's understanding of desires, rules, and emotions. *Child Development, 76,* 713-733.

Lagattuta, K. H. (2014). Linking past, present, and future: Children's ability to connect mental states and emotions across time. *Child Development Perspectives, 8*(2), 90-95.

Lahey, B. B. (2009). Public health significance of neuroticism. *American Psychologist, 64*(4), 241-256.

Laird, J., Lew, S., DeBell, M., & Chapman, C. (2006). *Dropout rates in the United States: 2002 and 2003* (NCES 2006-062). Washington, DC: U.S. Department of Education, National Center for Education Statistics.

Laird, R. D., Pettit, G. S., Bates, J. E., & Dodge, K. A. (2003). Parents' monitoring relevant knowledge and adolescents' delinquent behavior: Evidence of correlated developmental changes and reciprocal influences. *Child Development, 74,* 752-768.

Lake, A. (2015, November). *For every child, a fair chance: The promise of equity.* Retrieved from UNICEF: https://www.unicef.org/publications/files/For_every_child_a_fair_chance.pdf

Lamb, M. E. (1981). The development of father-infant relationships. In M. E. Lamb (Ed.), *The role of the father in child development* (2nd ed.). New York: Wiley.

Lamb, M. E., Frodi, A. M., Frodi, M., & Hwang, C. P. (1982). Characteristics of maternal and paternal behavior in traditional and non-traditional Swedish families. *International Journal of Behavior Development, 5,* 131-151.

Lamb, S. (2014). Permanent personhood or meaningful decline? Toward a critical anthropology of successful aging. *Journal of Aging Studies, 29,* 41-52.

Lamberts, S. W. J., van den Beld, A. W., & van der Lely, A. (1997). The endocrinology of aging. *Science, 278,* 419-424.

Lamm, C., & Majdandžić, J. (2015). The role of shared neural activations, mirror neurons, and morality in empathy-a critical comment. *Neuroscience Research, 90,* 15-24.

Lamm, C., Zelazo, P. D., & Lewis, M. D. (2006). Neural correlates of cognitive control in childhood and adolescence. Disentangling the contributions of age and executive function. *Neuropsychologia, 44,* 2139-2148.

Lanciano, T., & Curci, A. (2015). Does emotions communication ability affect psychological well-being? A study with the Mayer–Salovey–Caruso Emotional Intelligence Test (MSCEIT) v2. 0. *Health Communication, 30*(11), 1112-1121.

Lancy, D. F. (2016). Playing with knives: The socialization of self-initiated learners. *Child Development, 87*(3), 654-665.

Landon, M. B., Hauth, J. C., Leveno, K. J., Spong, C. Y., Leindecker, S., Varner, M. W., . . . Gabbe, S. G., for the National Institute of Child Health and Human Development Maternal-Fetal Medicine Units Network. (2004). Maternal and perinatal outcomes associated with a trial of labor after prior cesarean delivery. *New England Journal of Medicine, 351,* 2581-2589.

Landry, S. H., Smith, K. E., Swank, P. R., & Miller-Loncar, C. L. (2000). Early maternal and child influences on children's later independent cognitive and social functioning. *Child Development, 71,* 358-375.

Landy, F. J. (1994, July-August). Mandatory retirement age: Serving the public welfare? *Psychological Science Agenda* (Science Directorate, American Psychological Association), 10-11, 20.

Lang, F. R. (2001). Regulation of social relationships in later adulthood. *Journal of Gerontology: Psychological and Social Sciences, 56B,* P321-P326.

Langley, K., Heron, J., Smith, G. D., & Thapar, A. (2012). Maternal and paternal smoking during pregnancy and risk of ADHD symptoms in offspring: testing for intrauterine effects. *American Journal of Epidemiology, 176*(3), 261-268.

Lansford, J. E. (2009). Parental divorce and children's adjustment. *Perspectives on Psychological Science, 4*(2), 140-152.

Lansford, J. E., Chang, L., Dodge, K. A., Malone, P. S., Oburu, P., Palmérus, K., . . . Quinn, N. (2005). Physical discipline and children's adjustment: Cultural normativeness as a moderator. *Child Development, 76,* 1234-1246.

Lansford, J. E., Criss, M. M., Dodge, K. A., Shaw, D. S., Pettit, G. S., & Bates, J. E. (2009). Trajectories of physical discipline: Early childhood antecedents and developmental outcomes. *Child Development, 80*(5), 1385-1402. doi: 10.1111/j.1467-8624.2009.01340.x

Lansford, J. E., Dodge, K. A., Pettit, G. S., Bates, J. E., Crozier, J., & Kaplow, J. (2002). A 12-year prospective study of the long-term effects of early child physical maltreatment on psychological, behavioral, and academic problems in adolescence. *Archives of Pediatric and Adolescent Medicine, 156*(8), 824-830.

Lantagne, A., & Furman, W. (2017). Romantic relationship development: The interplay between age and relationship length. *Developmental Psychology, 53*(9), 1738.

Lapierre, M. A., Piotrowski, J. T., & Linebarger, D. L. (2012). Background television in the homes of U.S. children. *Pediatrics, 130.* doi: 10.1542/peds/2011-2581

LaRocque, M., Kleiman, I., & Darling, S. M. (2011). Parental involvement: The missing link in school achievement. *Preventing School Failure, 55*(3), 115-122.

Larsen, D. (1990, December-1991, January). Unplanned parenthood. *Modern Maturity,* 32-36.

Larson, R. W. (1997). The emergence of solitude as a constructive domain of experience in early adolescence. *Child Development, 68,* 80-93.

Larson, R. W. (2001). How US children and adolescents spend time: What it does (and doe'sn't) tell us about their development. *Current Directions in Psychological Science, 10*(5), 160-164.

Larson, R. W., & Verma, S. (1999). How children and adolescents spend time across the world: Work, play, and developmental opportunities. *Psychological Bulletin, 125*(6), 701-736.

Larson, R. W., Moneta, G., Richards, M. H., & Wilson, S. (2002). Continuity, stability, and change in daily emotional experience across adolescence. *Child Development, 73,* 1151-1165.

Larson, R., & Wilson, S. (2004). Adolescents across place and time: Globalization and the changing pathways to adulthood. In R. M. Lerner & L. Steinberg (Eds.), *Handbook of adolescent psychology* (2nd ed., pp. 299-331). Hoboken, NJ: Wiley.

Larson, R., & Wilson, S. (2013). Adolescence across place and time: Globalization and the changing pathways to adulthood. In *Handbook of adolescent psychology* (2nd ed., pp. 297-330). New York: Wiley.

Larzelere, R. E., & Kuhn, B. R. (2005). Comparing child outcomes of physical punishment and alternative disciplinary tactics: A meta-analysis. *Clinical Child and Family Psychology Review, 8*(1), 1-37.

Latham, N. K., Bennett, D. A., Stretton, C. M., & Anderson, C. S. (2004). Systematic review of progressive resistance strength training in older adults. *The Journals of Gerontology Series A: Biological Sciences and Medical Sciences, 59*(1), M48-M61.

Latifovic, L., Peacock, S. D., Massey, T. E., & King, W. D. (2016). The influence of alcohol consumption, cigarette smoking, and physical activity on leukocyte telomere length. *Cancer Epidemiology and Prevention Biomarkers, 25*(2), 374-380.

Laughlin, L. (2013). Who's minding the kids? Child care arrangements: Spring 2011. *Current Population Reports,* P70-135. Washington, DC: U.S. Census Bureau.

Laumann, E. O., Das, W., & Waite, L. J. (2008). Sexual dysfunction among older adults: Prevalence and risk factors from a nationally representative U.S. probability sample of men and women 57-85 years of age. *Journal of Sexual Medicine, 5*(10), 2300-2311.

Lauricella, A. R., Wartella, E., & Rideout, V. J. (2015). Young children's screen time: The complex role of parent and child factors. *Journal of Applied Developmental Psychology, 36,* 11-17.

Laursen, B. (1996). Closeness and conflict in adolescent peer relationships: Interdependence with friends and romantic partners. In W. M. Bukowski, A. F. Newcomb, & W. W. Hartup (Eds.), *The company they keep: Friendship in childhood and adolescence* (pp. 186-210). New York: Cambridge University Press.

Lautenschlager, N. T., Cox, K. L., Flicker, L., Foster, J. K., van Bockxmeer, F. M., Xiao, J., . . . Almeida, O. P. (2008). Effects of physical activity on cognitive function in older adults at risk for Alzheimer's disease. *Journal of the American Medical Association, 300*(9), 1027-1037.

Lavee, Y., & Ben-Ari, A. (2004). Emotional expressiveness and neuroticism: Do they predict marital quality? *Journal of Marriage and Family, 18,* 620-627.

Lavenex, P., & Lavenex, P. B. (2013). Building hippocampal circuits to learn and remember: insights into the development of human memory. *Behavioural Brain Research, 254,* 8-21.

Lavie, C. J., Kuruvanka, T., Milani, R. V., Prasad, A., & Ventura, H. O. (2004). Exercise capacity in adult African-Americans referred for exercise stress testing: Is fitness affected by race? *Chest, 126,* 1962-1968.

Lawler, M., & Nixon, E. (2011). Body dissatisfaction among adolescent boys and girls: the effects of body mass, peer appearance culture and internalization of appearance ideals. *Journal of Youth and Adolescence, 40*(1), 59-71.

Lawler-Row, K. A., & Elliott, J. (2009). The role of religious activity and spirituality in the health and well-being of older adults. *Journal of Health Psychology, 14*(1), 43-52.

Lawn, J. E., Gravett, M. G., Nunes, T. M., Rubens, C. E., Stanton, C., & the Gapps Review Group. (2010). Global report on preterm birth and stillbirth (1 of 7): Definitions, description of the burden and opportunities to improve data. *BMS Pregnancy and Childbirth, 10* (Suppl. 1), S1. doi: 10.1186/1471-2393-10-S1-S1

Lawrence, E., Rothman, A. D., Cobb, R., Rothman, M. T., & Bradbury, T. (2008). Marital satisfaction across the transition to parenthood. *Journal of Family Psychology, 22*(1), 41-50.

Lazarus, R. S., & Folkman, S. (1984). *Stress, appraisal, and coping.* New York: Springer.

Le Bourdais, C., & LaPierre-Adamcyk, E. (2004). Changes in conjugal life in Canada: Is cohabitation progressively replacing marriage? *Journal of Marriage and Family, 66,* 929-942.

Le, H. N. (2000). Never leave your little one alone: Raising an Ifaluk child. In J. DeLoache & A. Gottlieb (Eds.), *A world of babies: Imagined child-care guides for seven societies* (pp. 199-222). New York: Cambridge University Press.

Leahy-Warren, P., McCarthy, G., & Corcoran, P. (2012). First-time mothers: Social support, maternal parental self-efficacy and postnatal depression. *Journal of Clinical Nursing, 21,* 388-397.

Leaper, C., & Smith, T. E. (2004). A meta-analytic review of gender variations in children's language use: Talkativeness, affiliative speech, and assertive speech. *Developmental Psychology, 40,* 993-1027.

Leaper, C., Anderson, K. J., & Sanders, P. (1998). Moderators of gender effects on parents' talk to their children: A meta-analysis. *Developmental Psychology, 34*(1), 3-27.

Leavell, A. S., Tamis-LeMonda, C. S., Ruble, D. N., Zosuls, K. M., & Cabrera, N. J. (2012). African American, White and Latino fathers' activities with their sons and daughters in early childhood. *Sex Roles, 66*(1-2), 53-65.

Leblanc, M., & Ritchie, M. (2001). A meta-analysis of play therapy outcomes. *Counseling Psychology Quarterly, 14,* 149-163.

Lederberg, A. R., Schick, B., & Spencer, P. E. (2013). Language and literacy development of deaf and hard-of-hearing children: Successes and challenges. *Developmental Psychology, 49*(1), 15.

Lee, D. M., Nazroo, J., O'Connor, D. B., Blake, M., & Pendleton, N. (2016). Sexual health and well-being among older men and women in England: Findings from the English Longitudinal Study of Ageing. *Archives of Sexual Behavior, 45*(1), 133-144.

Lee, E., Cho, H. J., Olmstead, R., Levin, M. J., Oxman, M. N., & Irwin, M. R. (2013). Persistent sleep disturbance: A risk factor for recurrent depression in community-dwelling older adults. *Sleep, 36*(11), 1685-1691.

Lee, G. R., Netzer, J. K., & Coward, R. T. (1995). Depression among older parents: The role of intergenerational exchange. *Journal of Marriage and Family, 57,* 823-833.

Lee, G. Y., & Kisilevsky, B. S. (2014). Fetuses respond to father's voice but prefer mother's voice after birth. *Developmental Psychobiology, 56*(1), 1-11.

Lee, H. C., Huang, K. T., & Shen, W. K. (2011). Use of antiarrhythmic drugs in elderly patients. *Journal of Geriatric Cardiology: JGC, 8*(3), 184.

Lee, I., Djoussé, L., & Sesso, H. D. (2010). Physical activity and weight gain prevention. *Journal of the American Medical Association, 303*(12), 1173-1179.

Lee, J. M., Appugliese, D., Kaciroti, N., Corwyn, R. F., Bradley, R., & Lumeng, J. C. (2007). Weight status in young girls and the onset of puberty. *Pediatrics, 119,* e624-e630.

Lee, J. M., Kaciroti, N., Appugliese, D., Corwyn, R. F., Bradley, R. H., & Lumeng, J. C. (2010). Body mass index and timing of pubertal initiation in boys. *Archives of Pediatrics & Adolescent Medicine, 164*(2), 139-144.

Lee, J. M., Wasserman, R., Kaciroti, N., Gebremariam, A., Steffes, J., Dowshen, S., . . . & Reiter, E. (2016). Timing of puberty in overweight versus obese boys. *Pediatrics,* peds-2015.

Lee, J. T., & Bartolomei, M. S. (2013). X-inactivation, imprinting, and long noncoding RNAs in health and disease. *Cell, 152*(6), 1308-1323.

Lee, J., & Reeves, T. (2012). Revisiting the impact of NCLB high-stakes school accountability,

capacity, and resources: State NAEP 1990-2009 reading and math achievement gaps and trends. *Educational Evaluation and Policy Analysis, 34*(2), 209-231.

Lee, R. M., Grotevant, H. D., Hellerstedt, W. L., Gunnar, M. R., & The Minnesota International Adoption Project Team. (2006). Cultural socialization in families with internationally adopted children. *Journal of Family Psychology, 20*(4), 571-580.

Lee, R., Zhai, F., Brooks-Gunn, J., Han, W. J., & Waldfogel, J. (2014). Head Start participation and school readiness: Evidence from the early childhood longitudinal study-birth cohort. *Developmental Psychology, 50*(1), 202.

Lee, S. J., Ralston, H. J. P., Drey, E. A., Partridge, J. C., & Rosen, M. A. (2005). Fetal pain: A systematic multidisciplinary review of the evidence. *Journal of the American Medical Association, 294,* 947-954.

Lee, Y., & Styne, D. (2013). Influences on the onset and tempo of puberty in human beings and implications for adolescent psychological development. *Hormones and Behavior, 64*(2), 250-261.

Leerkes, E. M., Blankson, A. N., & O'Brien, M. (2009). Differential effects of maternal sensitivity to infant distress and nondistress on social-emotional functioning. *Child Development, 80*(3), 762-775.

Leerkes, E. M., Weaver, J. M., & O'Brien, M. (2012). Differentiating maternal sensitivity to infant distress and non-distress. *Parenting, 12*(2-3), 175-184.

Lefkowitz, E. S., & Fingerman, K. L. (2003). Positive and negative emotional feelings and behaviors in mother-daughter ties in late life. *Journal of Family Psychology, 17,* 607-617.

Lefkowitz, E. S., & Gillen, M. M. (2006). "Sex is just a normal part of life": Sexuality in emerging adulthood. In J. J. Arnett & J. L. Tanner (Eds.), *Emerging adults in America: Coming of age in the 21st century* (pp. 235-255). Washington, DC: American Psychological Association.

Leger, K. A., Charles, S. T., Turiano, N. A., & Almeida, D. M. (2016). Personality and stressor-related affect. *Journal of Personality and Social Psychology, 111*(6), 917.

Lehmiller, J. J., VanderDrift, L. E., & Kelly, J. R. (2011). Sex differences in approaching friends with benefits relationships. *Journal of Sex Research, 48*(2-3), 275-284.

Lehto, R., & Stein, K. (2009). Death anxiety: An analysis of an evolving concept. *Research and Theory for Nursing Practice: An International Journal, 23,* 23-41.

Leigh, B. C. (1999). Peril, chance, adventure: Concepts of risk, alcohol use, and risky behavior in young adults. *Addiction, 94*(3), 371-383.

Leinung, M., & Wu, C. (2017). The biologic basis of transgender identity: 2D:4D finger length ratios implicate a role for prenatal androgen activity. *Endocrine Practice, 23*(6), 669-671.

Lemaitre, H., Goldman, A. L., Sambataro, F., Verchinski, B. A., Meyer-Lindenberg, A., Weinberger, D. R., & Mattay, V. S. (2012). Normal age-related brain morphometric changes: Nonuniformity across cortical thickness, surface area and gray matter volume? *Neurobiology of Aging, 33*(3), 617-e1.

Leman, P. J., Ahmed, S., & Ozarow, L. (2005). Gender, gender relations, and the social dynamics of children's conversations. *Developmental Psychology, 41*, 64-74.

Lemon, B. W., Bengtson, V. L., & Peterson, J. A. (1972). An exploration of the activity theory of aging: Activity types and life satisfaction among in-movers to a retirement community. *Journal of Gerontology, 27*(4), 511-523.

Lenhart, A. (2009). Teens and sexting. Retrieved from Pew Research Center: www.pewinternet.org/2009/12/15/teens-and-sexting/

Lenroot, R. K., & Giedd, J. N. (2006). Brain development in children and adolescents: Insights from anatomical magnetic resonance imaging. *Neuroscience & Biobehavioral Reviews, 30*(6), 718-729.

Leonardi-Bee , J., Nderi, M., & Britton, J. (2016). Smoking in movies and smoking initiation in adolescents: Systematic review and meta-analysis. *Addiction, 111*(10), 1750-1763.

Lerman, C., Caporaso, N. E., Audrain, J., Main, D., Bowman, E. D., Lockshin, B., . . . Shields, P. G. (1999). Evidence suggesting the role of specific genetic factors in cigarette smoking. *Health Psychology, 18*, 14-20.

Lerner, R., & Steinberg, L. (2004). Adolescents across place and time: Globalization and the changing pathways to adulthood. In R. W. Larson, & S. Wilson, *Handbook of adolescent psychology* (pp. 299-330). New York: Wiley.

Lesgold, A., Glaser, R., Rubinson, H., Klopfer, D., Feltovich, P., & Wang, Y. (1988). Expertise in a complex skill: Diagnosing X-ray pictures. In M. T. H. Chi, R. Glaser, & M. J. Farr (Eds.), *The nature of expertise* (pp. 311-342). Hillsdale, NJ: Erlbaum.

Leslie, A. M. (1995). A theory of agency. In D. Sperber, D. Premack, & A. J. Premack (Eds.), *Causal cognition* (pp. 121-149). Oxford: Clarendon Press.

Leslie, A. M., Friedman, O., & German, T. P. (2004). Core mechanisms in 'theory of mind.' *Trends in Cognitive Sciences, 8*(12), 528-533.

Leslie, L. K., Newman, T. B., Chesney, J., & Perrin, J. M. (2005). The Food and Drug Administration's deliberations on antidepressant use in pediatric patients. *Pediatrics, 116*, 195-204.

Lester, B. M., & Boukydis, C. F. Z. (1985). *Infant crying: Theoretical and research perspectives.* New York: Plenum Press.

LeVay, S. (1991). A difference in hypothalamic structure between heterosexual and homosexual men. *Science, 253*, 1034-1037.

Levenstein, S., Ackerman, S., Kiecolt-Glaser, J. K., & Dubois, A. (1999). Stress and peptic ulcer disease. *Journal of the American Medical Association, 281*, 10-11.

Levine, L. J., & Edelstein, R. S. (2009). Emotion and memory narrowing: A review and goal-relevance approach. *Cognition and Emotion, 23*(5), 833-875.

LeVine, R. A. (1994). *Child care and culture: Lessons from Africa.* Cambridge, UK: Cambridge University Press.

Levy, B. R. (2003). Mind matters: Cognitive and physical effects of aging self-stereotypes. *Journal of Gerontology: Psychological Sciences, 58B*, P203-P211.

Levy, T. B., Azar, S., Huberfeld, R., Siegel, A. M., & Strous, R.D. (2013). Attitudes towards euthanasia and assisted suicide: A comparison between psychiatrists and other physicians. *Bioethics, 27*, 402-408.

Lewis, B. H., Legato, M., & Fisch, H. (2006). Medical implications of the male biological clock. *Journal of the American Medical Association, 19*, 2369-2371.

Lewis, M. (1995). Self-conscious emotions. *American Scientist, 83*, 68-78.

Lewis, M. (1997). The self in self-conscious emotions. In S. G. Snodgrass & R. L. Thompson (Eds.), *The self across psychology: Self-recognition, self-awareness, and the self-concept: Vol. 818.* New York: New York Academy of Sciences.

Lewis, M. (1998). Emotional competence and development. In D. Pushkar, W. Bukowski, A. E. Schwartzman, D. M. Stack, & D. R. White (Eds.), *Improving competence across the life-span* (pp. 27-36). New York: Plenum Press.

Lewis, M. (2007). Early emotional development. In A. Slater & M. Lewis (Eds.), *Introduction to infant development.* Malden, MA: Blackwell.

Lewis, M. I., & Butler, R. N. (1974). Life-review therapy: Putting memories to work in individual and group psychotherapy. *Geriatrics, 29*, 165-173.

Lewis, M., & Brooks, J. (1974). Self, other, and fear: Infants' reaction to people. In H. Lewis & L. Rosenblum (Eds.), *The origins of fear: The origins of behavior* (Vol. 2). New York: Wiley.

Lezak, M. D., Howieson, D. B., Bigler, E. D., & Tranel, D. (2012). *Neuropsychological Assessment* (5th ed.). New York: Oxford University Press.

Li, J., Laursen, T. M., Precht, D. H., Olsen, J., & Mortensen, P. B. (2005). Hospitalization for mental illness among parents after the death of a child. *New England Journal of Medicine, 352*, 1190-1196.

Li, J., Precht, D. H., Mortensen, P. B., & Olsen, J. (2003). Mortality in parents after death of a child in Denmark: A nationwide follow-up study. *Lancet, 361*, 363-367.

Li, R., Chase, M., Jung, s., Smith, P. J. S., & Loeken, M. R. (2005). Hypoxic stress in diabetic pregnancy contributes to impaired embryo gene expression and defective development by inducing oxidative stress. *American Journal of Physiology: Endocrinology and Metabolism, 289*, 591-599.

Li, Y., & Ferraro, K. F. (2005). Volunteering and depression in later life: Social benefit or selection processes? *Journal of Health and Social Behavior, 46*(1), 68-84.

Li, Y., Putallaz, M., & Su, Y. (2011). Interparental conflict styles and parenting behaviors: Associations with overt and relational aggression among Chinese children. *Merrill-Palmer Quarterly, 57*(4), 402-428.

Libertus, M. E., & Brannon, E. M. (2010). Stable individual differences in number discrimination in infancy. *Developmental Science, 13*(6), 900-906.

Lichter, D. T., Turner, R. N., & Sassler, S. (2010). National estimates of the rise in serial cohabitation. *Social Science Research, 39*(5), 754-765.

Lickliter, R., & Honeycutt, H. (2003). Developmental dynamics: Toward a biologically plausible evolutionary psychology. *Psychological Bulletin, 129*, 819-835.

Lidstone, J., Meins, E., & Fernyhough, C. (2011). Individual differences in children's private speech: Consistency across tasks, timepoints, and contexts. *Cognitive Development, 26*(3), 203-213.

Lieberman, M. (1996). *Doors close, doors open: Widows, grieving and growing.* New York: Putnam.

Lien, Y. J., Chen, W. J., Hsiao, P. C., & Tsuang, H. C. (2015). Estimation of heritability for varied indexes of handedness. *Laterality: Asymmetries of Body, Brain and Cognition, 20*(4), 469-482.

Light, K. C., Girdler, S. S., Sherwood, A., Bragdon, E. E., Brownley, K. A., West, S. G., & Hinderliter, A. L. (1999). High stress responsivity predicts later blood pressure only in combination with positive family history and high life stress. *Hypertension, 33*, 1458-1464.

Light, S. N., Coan, J. A., Zahn-Waxler, C., Frye, C., Goldsmith, H. H., & Davidson, R. J. (2009). Empathy is associated with dynamic change in prefrontal brain electrical activity during positive emotion in children. *Child Development, 80*, 1210-1231. doi: 10.1111/j.1467-8624.2009.01326.x

Lilgendahl, J. P., & McAdams, D. P. (2011). Constructing stories of self-growth: How individual differences in patterns of autobiographical reasoning relate to well-being in midlife. *Journal of Personality, 79*(2), 391-428.

Lillard, A. S., & Peterson, J. (2011). The immediate impact of different types of television on young children's executive function. *Pediatrics, 128*(4), 644-649.

Lillard, A. S., Lerner, M. D., Hopkins, E. J., Dore, R. A., Smith, E. D., & Palmquist, C. M. (2013). The impact of pretend play on children's development: A review of the evidence. *Psychological Bulletin, 139*(1), 1.

Lillard, A., & Curenton, S. (1999). Do young children understand what others feel, want, and know? *Young Children, 54*(5), 52-57.

Lillard, A., & Else-Quest, N. (2006). The early years: Evaluating Montessori education. *Science, 313*, 1893-1894.

Lim, J., & Dinges, D. F. (2010). A meta-analysis of the impact of short-term sleep deprivation on cognitive variables. *Psychological Bulletin, 136*(3), 375-389.

Lin, C. H. (2014). Evaluating services for kinship care families: A systematic review. *Children and Youth Services Review, 36*, 32-41.

Lin, I. F., & Brown, S. L. (2012). Unmarried boomers confront old age: A national portrait. *The Gerontologist, 52*(2), 153-165.

Lin, S., Hwang, S. A., Marshall, E. G., & Marion, D. (1998). Does paternal occupational lead exposure increase the risks of low birth weight or prematurity? *American Journal of Epidemiology, 148*, 173-181.

Lin, Y. W., & Bratton, S. C. (2015). A meta-analytic review of child-centered play therapy approaches. *Journal of Counseling & Development, 93*(1), 45–58.

Lin, Y., Seroude, L., & Benzer, S. (1998). Extended life-span and stress resistance in the Drosophila mutant methuselah. *Science, 282,* 943–946.

Lind, A. & Brzuzy, S. (2008). *Battleground: Women, gender, and sexuality.* Westport, CT: Greenwood Publishing Group.

Lindau, S. T., Schumm, P., Laumann, E. O., Levinson, W., O'Muircheartaigh, C. A., & Waite, L. J. (2007). A study of sexuality and health among older adults in the United States. *New England Journal of Medicine, 357,* 762–774.

Lindberg, L. D., Maddow-Zimet, I., & Boonstra, H. (2016). Changes in adolescents' receipt of sex education, 2006–2013. *Journal of Adolescent Health, 58*(6), 621–627.

Linder, K. (1990). *Functional literacy projects and project proposals: Selected examples.* Paris: United Nations Educational, Scientific, and Cultural Organization.

Lindsay, R., Gallagher, J. C., Kleerekoper, M., & Pickar, J. H. (2002). Effect of lower doses of conjugated equine estrogens with and without medroxyprogesterone acetate on bone in early postmenopausal women. *Journal of the American Medical Association, 287,* 2668–2676.

Lindwall, M., Cimino, C. R., Gibbons, L. E., Mitchell, M. B., Benitez, A., Brown, C. L., . . . & MacDonald, S. W. (2012). Dynamic associations of change in physical activity and change in cognitive function: coordinated analyses of four longitudinal studies. *Journal of Aging Research, 2012.*

Linnet, K. M., Wisborg, K., Obel, C., Secher, N. J., Thomsen, P. H., Agerbo, E., & Henriksen, T. B. (2005). Smoking during pregnancy and the risk of hyperkinetic disorder in offspring. *Pediatrics, 116,* 462–467.

Lissau, I., Overpeck, M. D., Ruan, J., Due, P., Holstein, B. E., Hediger, M. L., & Health Behaviours in School-Aged Children Obesity Working Group. (2004). Body mass index and overweight in adolescents in 13 European countries, Israel, and the United States. *Archives of Pediatric and Adolescent Medicine, 158,* 27–33.

Liszkowski, U., Carpenter, M., & Tomasello, M. (2008). Twelve-month-olds communicate helpfully and appropriately for knowledgeable and ignorant partners. *Cognition, 108,* 732–739.

Litt, J. S., Gerry Taylor, H., Margevicius, S., Schluchter, M., Andreias, L., & Hack, M. (2012). Academic achievement of adolescents born with extremely low birth weight. *Acta Paediatrica, 101*(12), 1240–1245.

Littleton, H., Breitkopf, C., & Berenson, A. (2006, August 13). *Correlates of anxiety symptoms during pregnancy and association with perinatal outcomes: A meta-analysis.* Presentation at the 114th annual convention of the American Psychological Association, New Orleans.

Litwin, H., & Shiovitz-Ezra, S. (2006). The association between activity and well-being in later life: What really matters? *Aging and Society, 26*(2), 225–242.

Litzinger, S., & Gordon, K. C. (2005). Exploring relationships among communication, sexual satisfaction, and marital satisfaction. *Journal of Sex & Marital Therapy, 31*(5), 409–424.

Liu, C. J., Shiroy, D. M., Jones, L. Y., & Clark, D. O. (2014). Systematic review of functional training on muscle strength, physical functioning, and activities of daily living in older adults. *European Review of Aging and Physical Activity, 11*(2), 95.

Liu, D., Sabbagh, M. A., Gehring, W. J., & Wellman, H. M. (2009). Neural correlates of children's theory of mind development. *Child Development, 80*(2), 318–326.

Liu, G., Zong, G., Doty, R. L., & Sun, Q. (2016). Prevalence and risk factors of taste and smell impairment in a nationwide representative sample of the US population: a cross-sectional study. *BMJ Open, 6*(11), e013246.

Liu, J., Raine, A., Venables, P. H., Dalais, C., & Mednick, S. A. (2003). Malnutrition at age 3 years and lower cognitive ability at age 11 years. *Archives of Pediatric and Adolescent Medicine, 157,* 593–600.

Liu, K., Daviglus, M. L., Loria, C. M., Colangelo, L. A., Spring, B., Moller, A. C., & Lloyd-Jones, D. M. (2012). Healthy lifestyle through young adulthood and the presence of low cardiovascular disease risk profile in middle age. *Circulation, 125*(8), 996–1004.

Livingston, G. (2014). Chapter 2: The demographics of remarriage. Pew Research Center [report]. Retrieved from www.pewsocialtrends.org/2014/11/14/chapter-2-the-demographics-of-remarriage/

Livingston, G., & Parker, K. (2010, September 9). *Since the start of the Great Recession, more children raised by grandparents.* Retrieved from http://pewsocialtrends.org/2010/09/09/since-the-start-of-the-great-recession-more-children-raised-by-grandparents/

Lloyd, J. J., & Anthony, J. C. (2003). Hanging out with the wrong crowd: How much difference can parents make in an urban environment? *Journal of Urban Health, 80,* 383–399.

Lobar, S. L., Youngblut, J. M., & Brooten, D. (2006). Cross-cultural beliefs, ceremonies, and rituals surrounding death of a loved one. *Pediatric Nursing, 32*(1), 44.

Lobo, V., Patil, A., Phatak, A., & Chandra, N. (2010). Free radicals, antioxidants and functional foods: Impact on human health. *Pharmacognosy Reviews, 4*(8), 118.

Lobstein, T., Jackson-Leach, R., Moodie, M. L., Hall, K. D., Gortmaker, S. L., Swinburn, B. A., James, W. P. T., Wang, Y., & McPherson, K. (2015). Child and adolescent obesity: Part of a bigger picture. *Lancet, 385,* 2510–2520.

LoBue, V., & DeLoache, J. (2011). Pretty in pink: The early development of gender-stereotyped colour preferences. *British Journal of Developmental Psychology, 29*(3), 656–667. doi: 10.1111/j.2044-835X.2011.02027.x

LoBue, V., Rakison, D. H., & DeLoache, J. S. (2010). Threat perception across the life span: Evidence for multiple converging pathways. *Current Directions in Psychological Science, 19*(6), 375–379.

Lock, A., Young, A., Service, V., & Chandler, P. (1990). Some observations on the origin of the pointing gesture. In V. Volterra & C. J. Erting (Eds.), *From gesture to language in hearing and deaf children.* New York: Springer.

Lock, M. M. (1993). *Encounters with aging: mythologies of menopause in Japan and North America.* London: University of California Press.

Lockenhoff, C. E., Terracciano, A., & Costa, P. T. (2009). Five-factor model personality traits and the retirement transition: Longitudinal and cross-sectional associations. *Psychology and Aging, 24*(3), 722–728.

Lockhart, S. N., & DeCarli, C. (2014). Structural imaging measures of brain aging. *Neuropsychology Review, 24*(3), 271–289.

Lockwood, P. L., Sebastian, C. L., McCrory, E. J., Hyde, Z. H., Gu, X., De Brito, S. A., & Viding, E. (2013). Association of callous traits with reduced neural response to others' pain in children with conduct problems. *Current Biology, 23*(10), 901–905.

Lohse, N., Hansen, A. E., Pedersen, G., Kronborg, G., Gerstoft, J., Sørensen, H. T., . . . Obel, N. (2007). Survival of persons with and without HIV infection in Denmark, 1995–2005. *Annals of Internal Medicine, 146,* 87–95.

Loke, Y. L., Novaknovic, R., Ollikainen, M., & Wallace, E. M. (2013). The Peri/Postnatal Epigenetic Twins Study (PETS). *Twin Research and Human Genetics, 16,* 13–20.

Lonczak, H. S., Abbott, R. D., Hawkins, J. D., Kosterman, R., & Catalano, R. F. (2002). Effects of the Seattle Social Development Project on sexual behavior, pregnancy, birth, and sexually transmitted disease. *Archives of Pediatric and Adolescent Medicine, 156,* 438–447.

Lonigan, C. J., Burgess, S. R., & Anthony, J. L. (2000). Development of emergent literacy and early reading skills in preschool children: Evidence from a latent-variable longitudinal study. *Developmental Psychology, 36,* 593–613.

Loo, S.Y., Chen, B.Y., Yu, O.H.Y., Azoulay, L., & Renoux, C. (2017). Testosterone replacement therapy and the risk of stroke in men: A systematic review. *Maturitas, 106,* 31–37.

Lopes, P. N., Brackett, M. A., Nezlek, J. B., Schütz, A., Sellin, L., & Salovey, P. (2004). Emotional intelligence and social interaction. *Personality and Social Psychology Bulletin, 30,* 1018–1034.

Lopes, P. N., Grewal, D., Kadis, J., Gall, M., & Salovey, P. (2006). Evidence that emotional intelligence is related to job performance and affect and attitudes at work. *Psicothema, 18*(Suppl. 1), 132–138.

Lopes, P. N., Salovey, P., & Straus, R. (2003). Emotional intelligence, personality, and the perceived quality of social relationships. *Personality and Individual Differences, 35,* 641–658.

Lopez-Gay, A., Esteve, A., López-Colás, J., Permanyer, I., Turu, A., Kennedy, S., . . . & Lesthaeghe, R. (2014). A geography of unmarried cohabitation in the Americas. *Demographic Research, 30,* 1621.

Lord, J., & Cruchaga, C. (2014). The epigenetic landscape of Alzheimer's disease. *Nature Neuroscience, 17*(9), 1138–1140.

Lord, S. R., Smith, S. T., & Menant, J. C. (2010). Vision and falls in older people: risk factors and intervention strategies. *Clinics in Geriatric Medicine, 26*(4), 569-581.

Lorenz, K. (1957). Comparative study of behavior. In C. H. Schiller (Ed.), *Instinctive behavior.* New York: International Universities Press.

Loudon, I. (1992). The transformation of maternal mortality. *BMJ: British Medical Journal, 305*(6868), 1557.

Lovato, N., Lack, L., Wright, H., & Kennaway, D. J. (2014). Evaluation of a brief treatment program of cognitive behavior therapy for insomnia in older adults. *Sleep, 37*(1), 117-126.

Lovelace, E. A. (1990). Basic concepts in cognition and aging. In E. A. Lovelace (Ed.), *Aging and cognition: Mental processes, self-awareness, and interventions* (pp. 1-28). Amsterdam: North-Holland, Elsevier.

Low, J. (2010). Preschoolers' implicit and explicit false-belief understanding: Relations with complex syntactical mastery. *Child Development, 81*(2), 597-615.

Low, L. F., Harrison, F., & Lackersteen, S. M. (2013). Does personality affect risk for dementia? A systematic review and meta-analysis. *The American Journal of Geriatric Psychiatry, 21*(8), 713-728.

Low, S., Shortt, J. W., & Snyder, J. (2012). Sibling influences on adolescent substance use: The role of modeling, collusion, and conflict. *Development and Psychopathology, 24*(1), 287-300.

Lowe, J. R., MacLean, P. C., Duncan, A. F., Aragón, C., Schrader, R. M., Caprihan, A., & Phillips, J. P. (2012). Association of maternal interaction with emotional regulation in 4-and 9-month infants during the Still Face Paradigm. *Infant Behavior and Development, 35*(2), 295-302.

Lowery, E. M., Brubaker, A. L., Kuhlmann, E., & Kovacs, E. J. (2013). The aging lung. *Clinical Interventions in Aging, 8*, 1489.

Lu, P. J., Yankey, D., Jeyarajah, J., O'Halloran, A., Elam-Evans, L. D., Smith, P. J., . . . & Dunne, E. F. (2015). HPV vaccination coverage of male adolescents in the United States. *Pediatrics*, peds-2015.

Lu, T., Pan, Y., Kao, S.-Y., Li, C., Cohane, I., Chan, J., & Yankner, B. A. (2004). Gene regulation and DNA damage in the ageing human brain. *Nature, 429*,883-891.

Lubell, K. M., Kegler, S. R., Crosby, A. E., & Karch, M. D. (2007). Suicide trends among youths and young adults aged 10-24 years—United States, 1990-2004. *Morbidity and Mortality Weekly Report, 56*(35), 905-908.

Lubell, K. M., Swahn, M. H., Crosby, A. E., & Kegler, S. R. (2004). Methods of suicide among persons aged 10-19 years—United States, 1992-2001. *Morbidity and Mortality Weekly Report, 53,* 471-474.

Lubienski, C., Puckett, T., & Brewer, T. J. (2013). Does homeschooling "work"? A critique of the empirical claims and agenda of advocacy organizations. *Peabody Journal of Education, 88*(3), 378-392.

Luby, J. L. (2015). Poverty's most insidious damage: the developing brain. *JAMA Pediatrics, 169*(9), 810-811.

Lucas, R. E., & Diener, E. (2009). Personality and subjectivity of well-being. In E. Diener (Ed.), *The science of well-being: The collected works of Ed Diener* (pp. 75-102). New York: Springer.

Lucas, R. E., Clark, A. E., Georgellis, Y., & Diener, E. (2003). Reexamining adaptation and the set point model of happiness: Reactions to changes in marital status. *Journal of Personality and Social Psychology, 84,* 527-539.

Lucas-Thompson, R. G., Goldberg, W. A., & Prause, J. (2010). Maternal work early in the lives of children and its distal associations with achievement and behavior problems: A meta-analysis. *Psychological Bulletin, 136* (6), 915-942.

Luciana, M. (2010). Adolescent brain development: Introduction to the special issue. *Brain and Cognition, 72*(1), 1-5.

Lucile Packard Children's Hospital at Stanford. (2009). *Failure to thrive.* Retrieved from www.lpch.org/DiseaseHealthInfo/Health/Library/growth/thrive.html

Luders, E., Sánchez, F. J., Gaser, C., Toga, A. W., Narr, K. L., Hamilton, L. S., & Vilain, E. (2009). Regional gray matter variation in male-to-female transsexualism. *Neuroimage, 46*(4), 904-907.

Luders, E., Thompson, P. M., & Toga, A. W. (2010). The development of the corpus callosum in the healthy human brain. *Journal of Neuroscience, 30*(33), 10985-10990.

Luders, E., Toga, A. W., & Thompson, P. M. (2014). Why size matters: differences in brain volume account for apparent sex differences in callosal anatomy: The sexual dimorphism of the corpus callosum. *Neuroimage, 84*, 820-824.

Ludwig, D. S. (2007). Childhood obesity—The shape of things to come. *New England Journal of Medicine, 357*, 2325-2327.

Lugaila, T. A. (2003). A child's day: 2000 (Selected indicators of child well-being). *Current Population Reports,* P70-89. Washington, DC: U.S. Census Bureau.

Luk, B. H. K., & Loke, A. Y. (2015). The impact of infertility on the psychological well-being, marital relationships, sexual relationships, and quality of life of couples: A systematic review. *Journal of Sex & Marital Therapy, 41*(6), 610-625.

Luna, B., Garver, K. E., Urban, T. A., Lazar, N. A., & Sweeney, J. A. (2004). Maturation of cognitive processes from late childhood to adulthood. *Child Development, 75,* 1357-1372.

Lund, D. A. (1993a). Caregiving. In R. Kastenbaum (Ed.), *Encyclopedia of adult development* (pp. 57-63). Phoenix, AZ: Oryx Press.

Lund, H. D., Reider, B. D., Whiting, A. B., & Prichard, J. R. (2010). Sleep patterns and predictors of disturbed sleep in a large population of college students. *Journal of Adolescent Health, 46*(2), 125-132.

Lundberg, S., & Pollak, R. A. (2014). Cohabitation and the uneven retreat from marriage in the United States, 1950-2010. In *Human capital in history: The American record* (pp. 241-272). Chicago: University of Chicago Press.

Lundy, B. L. (2003). Father—and mother—infant face-to-face interactions: Differences in mind-related comments and infant attachment? *Infant Behavior and Development, 26*(2), 200-212.

Luo, L., & Craik, F. I. M. (2008). Aging and memory: A cognitive approach. *Canadian Journal of Psychiatry, 53*(6), 346-353.

Lustig, C., & Flegal, K. (2008). Age differences in memory: Demands on cognitive control and association processes. *Advances in Psychology, 139,* 137-149.

Luthar, S. S., & Latendresse, S. J. (2005). Children of the affluent: Challenges to well-being. *Current Directions in Psychological Science, 14,* 49-53.

Lynam, D. R., Caspi, A., Moffitt, T. E., Loeber, R., & Stouthamer-Loeber, M. (2007). Longitudinal evidence that psychopathy scores in early adolescence predict adult psychopathy. *Journal of Abnormal Psychology, 116*(1), 155.

Lynch, A. D., Lerner, R. M., & Leventhal, T. (2013). Adolescent academic achievement and school engagement: An examination of the role of school-wide peer culture. *Journal of Youth and Adolescence, 42*(1), 6-19.

Lynn, R., & Meisenberg, G. (2010). National IQs calculated and validated for 108 nations. *Intelligence, 38*(4), 353-360.

Lyons-Ruth, K., Alpern, L., & Repacholi, B. (1993). Disorganized infant attachment classification and maternal psychosocial problems as predictors of hostile-aggressive behavior in the preschool classroom. *Child Development, 64,* 572-585.

Lyyra, T., & Heikkinen, R. (2006). Perceived social support and mortality in older people. *Journal of Gerontology: Social Sciences, 61B,* S147-S152.

Mäkinen, M., Puukko-Viertomies, L. R., Lindberg, N., Siimes, M. A., & Aalberg, V. (2012). Body dissatisfaction and body mass in girls and boys transitioning from early to mid-adolescence: additional role of self-esteem and eating habits. *BMC Psychiatry, 12*(1), 35.

Ma, W., Golinkoff, R. M., Houston, D. M., & Hirsh-Pasek, K. (2011). Word learning in infant- and adult-directed speech. *Language Learning and Development, 7,* 185-201.

Maccoby, E. (1980). *Social development.* New York: Harcourt Brace Jovanovich.

Maccoby, E. (2000). A developmental account. *Psychology of Education: Major Themes,* 323.

Maccoby, E. E. (1984). Middle childhood in the context of the family. In W. A. Collins (Ed.), *Development during middle childhood.* Washington, DC: National Academy.

Maccoby, E. E. (1992). The role of parents in the socialization of children: A historical overview. *Developmental Psychology, 28*(6), 1006-1017.

Maccoby, E. E. (2000). Perspectives on gender development. *International Journal of Behavioral Development, 24*(4), 398-406.

Maccoby, E. E. (2002). Gender and group process: A developmental perspective. *Current Directions in Psychological Science, 11,* 54-58.

Maccoby, E. E., & Jacklin, C. N. (1987). Gender segregation in childhood. *Advances in Child Development and Behavior, 20,* 239-287.

Maccoby, E. E., & Lewis, C. C. (2003). Less day care or different day care? *Child Development, 74,* 1069-1075.

Maccoby, E. E., & Martin, J. A. (1983). Socialization in the context of the family: Parent-child interaction. In P. H. Mussen (Series Ed.) & E. M. Hetherington (Vol. Ed.), *Handbook of child psychology: Vol. 4. Socialization, personality, and social development* (pp. 1-101). New York: Wiley.

MacDonald, W. L., & DeMaris, A. (1996). Parenting stepchildren and biological children. *Journal of Family Issues, 17,* 5-25.

MacDorman, M. F., & Gregory, E. C. (2015). Fetal and perinatal mortality: United States, 2013. *National Vital Statistics Reports: from the Centers for Disease Control and Prevention, National Center for Health Statistics, National Vital Statistics System, 64*(8), 1-24.

MacDorman, M. F., & Kirmeyer, S. (2009). Fetal deaths and perinatal mortality. United States, 2005. *National Vital Statistics Reports, 57*(8). Hyattsville, MD: National Center for Health Statistics.

MacDorman, M. F., & Mathews, T. J. (2009). Behind international rankings of infant mortality: How the United States compares with Europe. *NCHS Data Brief, 23.* Hyattsville, MD: National Center for Health Statistics.

MacDorman, M. F., Menacker, F., & Declercq, E. (2010). Trends and characteristics of home and other out-of-hospital births in the United States, 1990-2006. *National Vital Statistics Reports, 58*(11), 1-14, 16.

Machaalani, R., & Waters, K. A. (2014). Neurochemical abnormalities in the brainstem of the sudden infant death syndrome (SIDS). *Paediatric Respiratory Reviews, 15*(4), 293-300.

Mackenzie, C. S., Scott, T., Mather, A., & Sareen, J. (2008). Older adults' help-seeking attitudes and treatment beliefs concerning mental problems. *American Journal of Geriatric Psychiatry, 16*(12), 1010-1019.

MacKinnon-Lewis, C., Starnes, R., Volling, B., & Johnson, S. (1997). Perceptions of parenting as predictors of boys' sibling and peer relations. *Developmental Psychology, 33,* 1024-1031.

MacLean, P. S., Wing, R. R., Davidson, T., Epstein, L., Goodpaster, B., Hall, K. D., . . . & Rothman, A. J. (2015). NIH working group report: innovative research to improve maintenance of weight loss. *Obesity, 23*(1), 7-15.

Macmillan, R., McMorris, B. J., & Kruttschnitt, C. (2004). Linked lives: Stability and change in maternal circumstances and trajectories of antisocial behavior in children. *Child Development, 75,* 205-220.

Madabhushi, R., Pan, L., & Tsai, L. H. (2014). DNA damage and its links to neurodegeneration. *Neuron, 83*(2), 266-282.

Madden, D. J., & Langley, I. K. (2003). Age-related changes in selective attention and perceptual load during visual search. *Psychology & Aging, 18,* 54-67.

Madden, M., Lenhart, A., Duggan, M., Cortesi, S., & Gasser, U. (2013). *Teens and technology 2013* (pp. 1-19). Washington, DC: Pew Internet & American Life Project.

Madigan, S., Wade, M., Tarabulsy, G., Jenkins, J. M., & Shouldice, M. (2014). Association between abuse history and adolescent pregnancy: a meta-analysis. *Journal of Adolescent Health, 55*(2), 151-159.

Maestas, N. (2010). *Encouraging work at older ages. Testimony presented before the Senate Finance Committee on July 15, 2010* (CT-350). Rand Corporation. Retrieved from http://finance. senate.gov/imo/media/doc/071510nmtest.pdf

Magnuson, K., & Berger, L. M. (2009). Family structure states and transitions: associations with children's well-being during middle childhood. *Journal of Marriage and Family, 71*(3), 575-591.

Mahalik, J. R., Levine Coley, R., McPherran Lombardi, C., Doyle Lynch, A., Markowitz, A. J., & Jaffee, S. R. (2013). Changes in health risk behaviors for males and females from early adolescence through early adulthood. *Health Psychology, 32*(6), 685.

Maher, J. P., Pincus, A. L., Ram, N., & Conroy, D. E. (2015). Daily physical activity and life satisfaction across adulthood. *Developmental Psychology, 51*(10), 1407.

Maheshwari, A. (2010). Overweight and obesity in infertility: Cost and consequences. *Human Reproductive Updates, 16*(3), 229-230.

Main, M. (1995). Recent studies in attachment: Overview, with selected implications for clinical work. In S. Goldberg, R. Muir, & J. Kerr (Eds.), *Attachment theory: Social, developmental, and clinical perspectives* (pp. 407-470). Hillsdale, NJ: Analytic Press.

Main, M., & Solomon, J. (1986). Discovery of an insecure, disorganized/disoriented attachment pattern: Procedures, findings, and implications for the classification of behavior. In M. Yogman & T. B. Brazelton (Eds.), *Affective development in infancy.* Norwood, NJ: Ablex.

Main, M., Kaplan, N., & Cassidy, J. (1985). Security in infancy, childhood and adulthood: A move to the level of representation. In I. Bretherton & E. Waters (Eds.), *Growing points in attachment. Monographs of the Society for Research in Child Development, 50*(1-20), 66-104.

Maisonet, M., Christensen, K. Y., & Rubin, C., Holmes, A., Flanders, A. H., Heron, J., . . . Ong, K. K. (2010). Role of prenatal characteristics and early growth on pubertal attainment of British girls. *Pediatrics, 126*(3), 591-600.

Makino, M., Tsuboi, K., & Dennerstein, L. (2004). Prevalence of eating disorders: A comparison of Western and non-Western countries. *Medscape General Medicine, 6*(3). Retrieved from www.medscape.com/ viewarticle/487413

Malabarey, O. T., Balayla, J., Klam, S. L., Shrim, A., & Abenhaim, H. A. (2012). Pregnancies in young adolescent mothers: a population-based study on 37 million births. *Journal of Pediatric and Adolescent Gynecology, 25*(2), 98-102.

Malaguzzi, L. (1993). For an education based on relationships. *Young Children, 49*(1), 9-12.

Malaspina, D., Harlap, S., Fennig, S., Heiman, D., Nahon, D., Feldman, D., & Susser, E. S. (2001). Advancing paternal age and the risk of schizophrenia. *Archives of General Psychiatry, 58,* 361-371.

Malik, V. S., Pan, A., Willett, W. C., & Hu, F. B. (2013). Sugar-sweetened beverages and weight gain in children and adults: A systematic review and meta-analysis. *The American Journal of Clinical Nutrition, 98*(4), 1084-1102.

Malik, V. S., Willett, W. C., & Hu, F. B. (2012). Global obesity: Trends, risk factors and policy implications. *Nature Reviews: Endocrinology, 9*(1), 13-27. doi:10.1038/nrendo.2012.199/.

Malloy, M. H. (2008). Impact of Cesarean section on neonatal mortality rates among very preterm infants in the United States, 2000-2003. *Pediatrics, 122,* 285-292.

Malmedal, W., Iversen, M.H., & Kilvik, A. (2015). Sexual abuse of older nursing home residents: A literature review. *Nursing Research and Practice.* http://dx.doi.org/10.1155/2015/902515

Malone, F. D., Canick, J. A., Ball, R. H., Nyberg, D. A., Comstock, C. H., Bukowski, R., . . . D'Alton, M. E. (2005). First-trimester or second-trimester screening, or both, for Down's syndrome. *New England Journal of Medicine, 353,* 2001-2011.

Malone, J. C., Cohen, S., Liu, S. R., Vaillant, G. E., & Waldinger, R. J. (2013). Adaptive midlife defense mechanisms and late-life health. *Personality and individual differences, 55*(2), 85-89.

Mampe, B., Friederici, A. D., Christophe, A., & Wermke, K. (2009). Newborns' cry melody is shaped by their native language. *Current Biology, 19*(23), 1994-1997. doi: 10.1016/j. cub.2009.09.064

Manago, A. M., Taylor, T., & Greenfield, P. M. (2012). Me and my 400 friends: The anatomy of college students' Facebook networks, their communication patterns, and well-being. *Developmental Psychology, 48*(2), 369.

Mancillas, A. (2006). Challenging the stereotypes about only children: A review of the literature and implications for practice. *Journal of Counseling & Development, 84*(3), 268-275.

Mancini, A. D., & Bonanno, G. A. (2006). Marital closeness, functional disability, and adjustment in late life. *Psychology and Aging, 21,* 600-610.

Mandara, J., Gaylord-Harden, N. K., Richards, M. H., & Ragsdale, B. L. (2009). The effects of change in racial identity and self-esteem on changes in African American adolescents' mental health. *Child Development, 80*(6), 1660-1675.

Mandler, J. M. (1998). Representation. In D. Kuhn & R. S. Siegler (Eds.), *Handbook of child psychology: Vol. 2. Cognition, perception, and language* (5th ed., pp. 255-308). New York: Wiley.

Mandler, J. M. (2007). On the origins of the conceptual system. *American Psychologist, 62,* 741-751.

Manlove, J., Ryan, S., & Franzetta, K. (2003). Patterns of contraceptive use within teenagers' first sexual relationships. *Perspectives on Sexual and Reproductive Health, 35,* 246-255.

Manning, W. D. (2013). Trends in cohabitation: Over twenty years of change, 1987–2010. *NCFMR Family Profiles, 54,* 29–41.

Manning, W. D., & Brown, S. L. (2011). The demography of unions among older Americans, 1980–present: A family change approach. In *Handbook of sociology of aging* (pp. 193–210). New York: Springer.

Manning, W. D., Fettro, M. N., & Lamidi, E. (2014). Child well-being in same-sex parent families: Review of research prepared for American Sociological Association Amicus Brief. *Population Research and Policy Review, 33*(4), 485–502.

Manning, W. D., Longmore, M. A., & Giordano, P. C. (2007). The changing institution of marriage: Adolescents' expectations to cohabit and to marry. *Journal of Marriage and Family, 69*(3), 559–575.

Mannix, L. J. (2008). Menstrual-related pain conditions: Dysmenorrhea and migraine. *Journal of Women's Health, 17*(5), 879–891. doi:10.1089/jwh.2007.0440

Manson, J. E., & Martin, K. A. (2001). Postmenopausal hormone-replacement therapy. *New England Journal of Medicine, 345,* 34–40.

Manson, J. E., Aragaki, A. K., Rossouw, J. E., Anderson, G. L., Prentice, R. L., LaCroix, A. Z., . . . & Lewis, C. E. (2017). Menopausal hormone therapy and long-term all-cause and cause-specific mortality: The Women's Health Initiative randomized trials. *JAMA, 318*(10), 927–938.

Manson, J. E., Chlebowski, R. T., Stefanick, M. L., Aragaki, A. K., Rossouw, J. E., Prentice, R. L., . . . & Wactawski-Wende, J. (2013). Menopausal hormone therapy and health outcomes during the intervention and extended poststopping phases of the Women's Health Initiative randomized trials. *JAMA, 310*(13), 1353–1368.

Mar, R. A., Tackett, J. L., & Moore, C. (2010). Exposure to media and theory-of-mind development in preschoolers. *Cognitive Development, 25*(1), 69–78.

Maranon, R., & Reckelhoff, J. F. (2013). Sex and gender differences in control of blood pressure. *Clinical Science, 125*(7), 311–318.

March of Dimes Birth Defects Foundation. (2004a). *Cocaine use during pregnancy* [Fact sheet]. Retrieved from www.marchofdimes.com/professionals/681_1169.asp

March of Dimes Foundation. (2012). *Toxoplasmosis* [Fact sheet]. Wilkes-Barre, PA: Author.

March of Dimes. (2014, October). *Low birthweight.* Retrieved from: www.marchofdimes.org/complications/low-birthweight.aspx

March, J., & the TADS Team. (2007). The Treatment for Adolescents with Depression Study (TADS): Long-term effectiveness and safety outcomes. *Archives of General Psychiatry, 64,* 1132–1143.

Marchman, V. A., & Fernald, A. (2008). Speed of word recognition and vocabulary knowledge in infancy predict cognitive and language outcomes in later childhood. *Developmental Science, 11,* F9–16.

Marcia, J. E. (1966). Development and validation of ego identity status. *Journal of Personality and Social Psychology, 3*(5), 551–558.

Marcia, J. E. (1979, June). *Identity status in late adolescence: Description and some clinical implications.* Address given at symposium on identity development, Rijksuniversitat Gronlngen, Netherlands.

Marcia, J. E. (1993). The relational roots of identity. In J. Kroger (Ed.), *Discussions on ego identity* (pp. 101–120). Hillsdale, NJ: Erlbaum.

Marcoen, A. (1995). Filial maturity of middle-aged adult children in the context of parent care: Model and measures. *Journal of Adult Development, 2,* 125–136.

Mares, M. L., & Pan, Z. (2013). Effects of Sesame Street: A meta-analysis of children's learning in 15 countries. *Journal of Applied Developmental Psychology, 34*(3), 140–151.

Mariam, L. M., McClure, R., Robinson, J. B., & Yang, J. A. (2015). Eliciting Change in At-Risk Elders (ECARE): Evaluation of an elder abuse intervention program. *Journal of Elder Abuse & Neglect, 27*(1), 19–33.

Marioni, R. E., Proust-Lima, C., Amieva, H., Brayne, C., Matthews, F. E., Dartigues, J. F., & Jacqmin-Gadda, H. (2015). Social activity, cognitive decline and dementia risk: a 20-year prospective cohort study. *BMC Public Health, 15*(1), 1089.

Mariotti, S. P. (2012). Global data on visual impairment 2010. *World Health Organization, 20.*

Mark, K., Desai, A., & Terplan, M. (2016). Marijuana use and pregnancy: prevalence, associated characteristics, and birth outcomes. *Archives of Women's Mental Health, 19*(1), 105.

Markant, J., & Amso, D. (2014). Leveling the playing field: Attention mitigates the effects of intelligence on memory. *Cognition, 131*(2), 195–204.

Markowitz, L. E., Hariri, S., Lin, C., Dunne, E. F., Steinau, M., McQuillan, G., & Unger, E. R. (2013). Reduction in human papillomavirus (HPV) prevalence among young women following HPV vaccine introduction in the United States, National Health and Nutrition Examination Surveys, 2003–2010. *The Journal of Infectious Diseases, 208*(3), 385–393.

Markowitz, S., Friedman, M. A., & Arent, S. M. (2008). Understanding the relation between obesity and depression: Causal mechanisms and duplications for treatment. *Clinical Psychology: Science and Practice, 15,* 1–20.

Marks, H. M. (2000). Student engagement in instructional activity: Patterns in the elementary, middle, and high school years. *American Educational Research Journal, 37*(1), 153–184.

Marks, N. F. (1996). Caregiving across the life-span: National prevalence and predictors. *Family Relations, 45,* 27–36.

Marks, N. F., & Lambert, J. D. (1998). Marital status continuity and change among young and midlife adults. *Journal of Family Issues, 19,* 652–686.

Marks, N. F., Bumpass, L. L., & Jun, H. (2004). Family roles and well-being during the middle life course. In O. G. Brim, C. D. Ryff, & R. C. Kessler (Eds.), *How healthy are we? A national study of well-being at midlife* (pp. 514–549). Chicago: University of Chicago Press.

Marks, N. F., Jun, H., & Song, J. (2007). Death of parents and adult psychological and physical well-being: A prospective U.S. national study. *Journal of Family Issues, 28*(12), 1611–1638.

Markus, H. R., Ryff, C. D., Curhan, K. B., & Palmersheim, K. A. (2004). In their own words: Well-being at midlife among high school-educated and college-educated adults. In O. G. Brim, C. D. Ryff, & R. C. Kessler (Eds.), *How healthy are we? A national study of well-being at midlife* (pp. 273–319). Chicago: University of Chicago Press.

Marmot, M. G., & Fuhrer, R. (2004). Socioeconomic position and health across midlife. In O. G. Brim, C. D. Ryff, & R. C. Kessler (Eds.), *How healthy are we? A national study of well-being at midlife.* Chicago: University of Chicago Press.

Marshall, B.L. (2007). Climacteric redux? (Re)medicalizing the male menopause. *Men and Masculinities, 9,* 509–529.

Marshall, N. L. (2004). The quality of early child care and children's development. *Current Directions in Psychological Science, 13,* 165–168.

Martinez-Ortega, J. M., Carretero, M. D., Gutiérrez-Rojas, L., Díaz-Atienza, F., Jurado, D., & Gurpegui, M. (2011). Winter birth excess in schizophrenia and in non-schizophrenic psychosis: Sex and birth-cohort differences. *Progress in Neuro-Psychopharmacology and Biological Psychiatry, 35*(7), 1780–1784.

Martikainen, P., Moustgaard, H., Murphy, M., Einio, E. K., Koskinen, S., Martelin, T., & Noro, A. (2009). Gender, living arrangements, and social circumstances as determinants of entry into and exit from long-term institutional care at older ages: A 6-year follow-up study of older Finns. *The Gerontologist, 49*(1), 34–45.

Martin, B., Mattson, M. P., & Maudsley, S. (2006). Caloric restriction and intermittent fasting: Two potential diets for successful brain aging. *Ageing Research Reviews, 5*(3), 332–353.

Martin, C. E., Longinaker, N., & Terplan, M. (2015). Recent trends in treatment admissions for prescription opioid abuse during pregnancy. *Journal of Substance Abuse Treatment, 48*(1), 37–42.

Martin, C. E., Longinaker, N., Mark, K., Chisolm, M. S., & Terplan, M. (2015). Recent trends in treatment admissions for marijuana use during pregnancy. *Journal of Addiction Medicine, 9*(2), 99–104.

Martin, C. L., & Fabes, R. A. (2001). The stability and consequences of young children's same-sex peer interactions. *Developmental Psychology, 37,* 431–446.

Martin, C. L., & Ruble, D. (2004). Children's search for gender cues: Cognitive perspectives on gender development. *Current Directions in Psychological Science, 13,* 67–70.

Martin, C. L., Fabes, R. A., Hanish, L., Leonard, S., & Dinella, L. M. (2011). Experienced and expected similarity to same-gender peers: Moving toward a comprehensive model of gender segregation. *Sex Roles, 65*(5-6), 421–434.

Martin, C. L., Kornienko, O., Schaefer, D. R., Hanish, L. D., Fabes, R. A., & Goble, P. (2013). The role of sex of peers and gender-typed activities in young children's peer affiliative networks: A longitudinal analysis of selection and influence. *Child Development, 84*(3), 921–937.

Martin, C. L., Ruble, D. N., & Szkrybalo, J. (2002). Cognitive theories of early gender development. *Psychological Bulletin, 128,* 903–933.

Martin, G. M. (2005). Epigenetic drift in aging identical twins. *Proceedings of the National Academy of Sciences of the United States of America, 102.* doi: 10.1073/pnas.0504743102

Martin, J. A., Hamilton B. E., & Osterman, M. J. K. (2012). *Three decades of twin births in the United States, 1980–2009.* NCHS Data Brief No 80. Hyattsville, MD: National Center for Health Statistics.

Martin, J. A., Hamilton, B. E., Osterman, M. J., Driscoll, A. K., & Mathews, T. J. (2017). Births: Final data for 2015. *National Vital Statistics Report, 66*(1), 1. Hyattsville, MD: National Center for Health Statistics.

Martin, J. A., Hamilton, B. E., Sutton, P. D., Ventura, S. J., Mathews, T. J., & Ostermam M. J. K. (2010). Births: Final data for 2008. *National Vital Statistics Reports, 59*(1). Hyattsville, MD: National Center for Health Statistics.

Martin, J. A., Hamilton, B. E., Sutton, P. D., Ventura, S. J., Mathews, T. J., Kirmeyer, S., & Osterman, M. J. (2010). Births: final data for 2007. *National Vital Statistics Reports, 59*(1), 1–72.

Martin, J. A., Hamilton, B. E., Sutton, P. D., Ventura, S. J., Menacker, F., & Munson, M. L. (2005). Births: Final data for 2003. *National Vital Statistics Reports, 54*(2). Hyattsville, MD: National Center for Health Statistics.

Martin, J. A., Hamilton, B. E., Sutton, P. D., Ventura, S. J., Menacker, F., Kirmeyer, S., & Mathews, T. J. (2009). Births: Final data for 2006. *National Vital Statistics Reports, 57*(7). Hyattsville, MD: National Center for Health Statistics.

Martin, J. A., Hamilton, B. E., Sutton, P. D., Ventura, S. J., Menacker, F., Kirmeyer, S., & Munson, M. (2007). Births: Final data for 2005. *National Vital Statistics Reports, 56*(6). Hyattsville, MD: National Center for Health Statistics.

Martin, J. A., Hamilton, B. E., Ventura, S. J., Osterman, M. J. K., & Mathews, M. S. (2013). Births: Final data for 2011. *National Vital Statistics Reports, 62*(1). Hyattsville, MD: National Center for Health Statistics.

Martin, J. A., Kirmeyer, S., Osterman, M., & Shepherd, R. A. (2009). Born a bit too early: Recent trends in later preterm births. *NCHS Data Brief, 24,* Hyattsville, MD: National Center for Health Statistics.

Martin, L. R., Friedman, H. S., & Schwartz, J. E. (2007). Personality and mortality risk across the life span: The importance of conscientiousness as a biopsychosocial attribute. *Health Psychology, 26*(4), 428–436.

Martin, N., & Montgomery, G. (2002, March 18). *Is having twins, either identical or fraternal, in someone's genes? Is there a way to increase your chances of twins or is having twins just luck?* Retrieved from http://genepi.qimr.edu.au/ Scientific American Twins.html

Martin, P., Kliegel, M., Rott, C., Poon, L. W., & Johnson, M. A. (2007). Personality and coping among centenarians. In L. W. Poon & T. T. Perls (Eds.), *Annual review of gerontology and geriatrics, vol. 27: Biopsychosocial approaches to longevity* (pp. 89–106). New York: Springer.

Martin, P., Kliegel, M., Rott, C., Poon, L. W., & Johnson, M. A. (2008). Age differences and changes of coping behavior in three age groups: Findings from the Georgia Centenarian Study. *International Journal of Aging & Human Development, 66*(2), 97–114.

Martin, R., Noyes, J., Wisenbaker, J., & Huttunen, M. (2000). Prediction of early childhood negative emotionality and inhibition from maternal distress during pregnancy. *Merrill-Palmer Quarterly, 45,* 370–391.

Martin, S. P., & Parashar, S. (2006). Women's changing attitudes toward divorce, 1974–2002: Evidence for an educational crossover. *Journal of Marriage and Family, 68,* 29–40.

Martinez, G., and Abma, J. C. (2015). *Sexual activity, contraceptive use, and childbearing of teenagers aged 15-19 in the United States.* Washington, DC: National Center for Health Statistics. Retrieved May 4, 2016, from www.cdc.gov/mmwr/pdf/ss/ss6304.pdf - PDF

Martinez, G., Copen, C. E., & Abma, J. C. (2011). Teenagers in the United States: Sexual activity, contraceptive use, and childbearing, 2006–2010. National Survey of Family Growth. National Center for Health Statistics. *Vital Health Statistics, 23*(31).

Martino, D., Loke, Y.J., Gordon, L., Ollikainen, M., Cruickshank, M. N., Saffrey, R., Craig, J. M. (2013). Longitudinal, genome-scale analyses of DNA methylation in twins from birth to 18 months of age reveals rapid epigenetic change in early life and pair-specific effects of discordance. *Genome Biology, 14,* R42. http://doi.org/10.1186/gb-2013-14-5-r4

Martinson, M., & Berridge, C. (2014). Successful aging and its discontents: A systematic review of the social gerontology literature. *The Gerontologist, 55*(1), 58–69.

Martorell, R. (2010). Physical growth and development of the malnourished child: contributions from 50 years of research at INCAP. *Food and Nutrition Bulletin, 31*(1), 68–82.

Martorell, R. (2016). Improved nutrition in the first 1000 days and adult human capital and health. *American Journal of Human Biology,* 1–12.

Martorell, R., Melgar, P., Maluccio, J. A., Stein, A. D., & Rivera, J. A. (2010). The nutrition intervention improved adult human capital and economic productivity. *The Journal of Nutrition, 140*(2), 411–414.

Martorell, S., & Martorell, G. (2006). Bridging uncharted waters: Down syndrome association of Atlanta outreach to Latino/a families. *American Journal of Community Psychology, 37,* 219–225.

Marver, J. E., Galfalvy, H. C., Burke, A. K., Sublette, M. E., Oquendo, M. A., Mann, J. J., & Grunebaum, M. F. (2017). Friendship, depression, and suicide attempts in adults: Exploratory analysis of a longitudinal follow-up study. *Suicide and Life-Threatening Behavior.*

Mascarenhas, M. N., Flaxman, S. R., Boerma, T., Vanderpoel, S., & Stevens, G. A. (2012). National, regional, and global trends in infertility prevalence since 1990: a systematic analysis of 277 health surveys. *PLoS Medicine, 9*(12), e1001356.

Masci, D., Sciupac, E., & Lipka, M. (2017). *Gay marriage around the world.* Washington, DC: Pew Research Center. Retrieved from www.pewforum.org/2017/08/08/gay-marriage-around-the-world-2013/

Mashburn, A. J., Justice, L. M., Downer, J. T., & Pianta, R. C. (2009). Peer effects on children's language achievement during prekindergarten. *Child Development, 80*(3), 686–702.

Mason, M. A. (2011). The roller coaster of child custody law over the last half century. *J. Am. Acad. Matrimonial Law, 24,* 451.

Mason, T. B., & Pack, A. I. (2007). Pediatric parasomnias. *Sleep, 30*(2), 141–151.

Massimiliano, P. (2015). The effects of age on divergent thinking and creative objects production: A cross-sectional study. *High Ability Studies, 26*(1), 93–104.

Masten, A. S., & Coatsworth, J. D. (1998). The development of competence in favorable and unfavorable environments: Lessons from research on successful children. *American Psychologist, 53,* 205–220.

Mastin, J. D.. & Vogt, P. (2016). Infant engagement and early vocabulary development: A naturalistic observation study of Mozambican infants from 1;1 to 2;1. *Journal of Child Language, 43,* 235–264.

Mather, M. (2010). *U.S. children in single-mother families.* Washington, DC: Population Reference Bureau.

Mather, M., & Lavery, D. (2012). *In U.S., proportion married at lowest recorded levels.* Population Reference Bureau. Retrieved from www.prb.org/Publications/Articles/2010/

Mathews, T. J., & Hamilton, B. E. (2016). Mean age of mothers is on the rise: United States, 2000-2014. *NCHS Data Brief,* (232), 1–8.

Mathews, T. J., & MacDorman, M. F. (2008). Infant mortality statistics from the 2005 period linked birth/infant death data set. *National Vital Statistics Report, 57*(2).

Mathews, T. J., MacDorman, M. F., Thoma, M. E. (2015). Infant mortality statistics from the 2013 period linked birth/infant death data set. *National Vital Statistics Reports, 64*(9).

Mathie, A., & Carnozzi, A. (2005). *Qualitative research for tobacco control: A how-to introductory manual for researchers and development practitioners.* Ottawa, Ontario, Canada: International Development Research Centre.

Matsuba, M. K., Pratt, M. W., Norris, J. E., Mohle, E., Alisat, S., & McAdams, D. P. (2012). Environmentalism as a context for expressing identity and generativity: Patterns among activists and uninvolved youth and midlife adults. *Journal of Personality, 80*(4), 1091-1115.

Matsumoto, D., & Juang, L. (2008). *Culture and psychology* (4th ed.). Belmont, CA: Wadsworth, Cengage Learning.

Mattanah, J. F., Ayers, J. F., Brand, B. L., Brooks, L. J., Quimby, J. L., & McNary, S. W. (2010). A social support intervention to ease the college transition: Exploring main effects and moderators. *Journal of College Student Development, 51*(1), 93-108.

Mattei, T. A., Bond, B. J., Goulart, C. R., Sloffer, C. A., Morris, M. J., & Lin, J. J. (2012). Performance analysis of the protective effects of bicycle helmets during impact and crush tests in pediatric skull models. *Journal of Neurosurgery: Pediatrics, 10*(6), 490-497.

Matthys, W., & John, E. (2017). *Oppositional defiant disorder and conduct disorder in childhood.* Hoboken, NJ: Wiley & Sons.

Mattis, J., & Sehgal, A. (2016). Circadian rhythms, sleep, and disorders of aging. *Trends in Endocrinology & Metabolism, 27*(4), 192-203.

Maulik, P. K., Mascarenhas, M. N., Mathers, C. D., Dua, T., & Saxena, S. (2011). Prevalence of intellectual disability: a meta-analysis of population-based studies. *Research in Developmental Disabilities, 32*(2), 419-436.

Maurer, D., & Lewis, T. L. (1979). Peripheral discrimination by three-month-old infants. *Child Development, 50,* 276-279.

Mayer, J. D., Salovey, P., Caruso, D. R., & Sitarenios, G. (2003). Measuring emotional intelligence with the MSCEIT V2. 0. *Emotion, 3*(1), 97.

Mayhew, A., Mullins, T. L. K., Ding, L., Rosenthal, S. L., Zimet, G. D., Morrow, C., & Kahn, J. A. (2014). Risk perceptions and subsequent sexual behaviors after HPV vaccination in adolescents. *Pediatrics,* peds-2013.

Maynard, A. E. (2002). Cultural teaching: The development of teaching skills in Maya sibling interactions. *Child Development, 73*(3), 969-982.

Mayo Foundation for Medical Education and Research. (2009, January). Beyond the human genome: Meet the epigenome. *Mayo Clinic Health Letter, 27*(1), pp. 4-5.

Mazzio, E. A., & Soliman, K. F. (2012). Basic concepts of epigenetics: impact of environmental signals on gene expression. *Epigenetics, 7*(2), 119-130.

McAdams, D. (1993). *The stories we live by.* New York: Morrow.

McAdams, D. P. (2001). Generativity in mid-life. In M. E. Lachman (Ed.), *Handbook of midlife development* (pp. 395-443). New York: Wiley.

McAdams, D. P. (2006). The redemptive self: Generativity and the stories Americans live by. *Research in Human Development, 3,* 81-100.

McAdams, D. P. (2013). The positive psychology of adult generativity: Caring for the next generation and constructing a redemptive life. In *Positive Psychology* (pp. 191-205). New York: Springer.

McAdams, D. P., de St. Aubin, E. D., & Logan, R. L. (1993). Generativity among young, midlife, and older adults. *Psychology and Aging, 8*(2), 221.

McAdams, D. P., Diamond, A., de St. Aubin, E., & Mansfield, E. (1997). Stories of commitment: The psychosocial construction of generative lives. *Journal of Personality and Social Psychology, 72,* 678-694.

McAdams, D. P., Reynolds, J., Lewis, M., Patten, A. H., & Bowman, P. J. (2001). When bad things turn good and good things turn bad: Sequences of redemption and contamination in life narrative and their relation to psychosocial adaptation in midlife adults and in students. *Personality and Social Psychology Bulletin, 27*(4), 474-485.

McAuley, T., & White, D. A. (2011). A latent variables examination of processing speed, response inhibition, and working memory during typical development. *Journal of Experimental Child Psychology, 108*(3), 453-468.

McCabe, D. P., Roediger III, H. L., McDaniel, M. A., Balota, D. A., & Hambrick, D. Z. (2010). The relationship between working memory capacity and executive functioning: evidence for a common executive attention construct. *Neuropsychology, 24*(2), 222.

McCabe, J., Fairchild, E., Grauerholz, L., Pescosolido, B. A., & Tope, D. (2011). Gender in twentieth-century children's books: Patterns of disparity in titles and central characters. *Gender & Society, 25*(2), 197-226.

McCallum, K. E., & Bruton, J. R. (2003). The continuum of care in the treatment of eating disorders. *Primary Psychiatry, 10*(6), 48-54.

McClain, M. C., & Pfeiffer, S. (2012). Identification of gifted students in the United States today: A look at state definitions, policies, and practices. *Journal of Applied School Psychology, 28*(1), 59-88.

McClelland, E., & McKinney, C. (2016). Disruptive behavior and parenting in emerging adulthood: Mediational effect of parental psychopathology. *Journal of Child and Family Studies, 25*(1), 212-223.

McClintock, M. K., & Herdt, G. (1996). Rethinking puberty: The development of sexual attraction. *Current Directions in Psychological Science, 5*(6), 178-183.

McCord, J. (1996). Unintended consequences of punishment. *Pediatrics, 98*(4), 832-834.

McCrae, R. R. (2002). Cross-cultural research on the five-factor model of personality. In W. J. Lonner, D. L. Dinnel, S. A. Hayes, & D. N. Sattler (Eds.), *Online readings in psychology and culture* (Unit 6, Chapter 1). Bellingham, WA: Center for Cross-Cultural Research, Western Washington University.

McCrae, R. R., & Costa, P. T., Jr. (1984). *Emerging lives, enduring dispositions.* Boston: Little, Brown.

McCrae, R. R., Costa, P. T., Jr., & Busch, C. M. (1986). Evaluating comprehensiveness in personality systems: The California Q-set and the five-factor model. *Journal of Personality, 54,* 430-446.

McCrae, R. R., Costa, P. T., Jr., Ostendorf, F., Angleitner, A., Hebríckova, M., Avia, M. D., . . . Smith, P. B. (2000). Nature over nurture: Temperament, personality, and lifespan development. *Journal of Personality and Social Psychology, 78,* 173-186.

McCrink, K., & Wynn, K. (2004). Large-number addition and subtraction by 9-month-old infants. *Psychological Science, 15,* 776-781.

McCue, J. D. (1995). The naturalness of dying. *Journal of the American Medical Association, 273,* 1039-1043.

McCurdy, A. P., Boule, N. G., Sivak, A., Davenport, M. H. (2017). Effects of exercise on mild-to-moderate depressive symptoms in the postpartum period: A meta-analysis. *Obstetrics and Gynecology, 129,* 1087-1097.

McDaniel, M. A., Pesta, B. J., & Banks, G. C. (2012). Job performance and the aging worker. *The Oxford Handbook of Work and Aging, 15,* 280-citation_lastpage.

McDaniel, M., Paxson, C., & Waldfogel, J. (2006). Racial disparities in childhood asthma in the United States: Evidence from the National Health Interview Survey, 1997 to 2003. *Pediatrics, 117,* 868-877.

McDowell, D. J., & Parke, R. (2009). Parental correlates of children's peer relations: An empirical test of a tripartite model. *Developmental Psychology, 45*(1), 224-235.

McDowell, M., Fryar, C., Odgen, C., & Flegal, K. (2008). Anthropometric reference data for children and adults: United States, 2003-2006. *National Health Statistics Report* (No. 10). Hyattsville, MD: National Center for Health Statistics.

McElwain, N. L., & Volling, B. L. (2005). Preschool children's interactions with friends and older siblings: Relationship specificity and joint contributions to problem behavior. *Journal of Family Psychology, 19,* 486-496.

McFarland, R. A., Tune, G. B., & Welford, A. (1964). On the driving of automobiles by older people. *Journal of Gerontology, 19,* 190-197.

McGee, R. W. (2016). In which countries is homosexuality most (and least) acceptable? A ranking of 98 countries. [Data report]. Social Science Research Network. Retrieved from https://papers.ssrn.com/sol3/papers.cfm?abstract_id=2799845.

McGuffin, P., Riley, B., & Plomin, R. (2001). Toward behavioral genomics. *Science, 291,* 1232-1249.

McGuire, S. L. (2017, September 27). *Aging education: A worldwide imperative.* Retrieved from Scientific Research Publishing: http://file.scirp.org/pdf/CE_2017092615440943.pdf

McHale, S. M., & Huston, T. L. (1985). The effect of the transition to parenthood on the marriage relationship. *Journal of Family Issues, 6*(4), 409-433.

McHale, S. M., Bissell, J., & Kim, J. Y. (2009). Sibling relationship, family, and genetic factors in sibling similarity in sexual risk. *Journal of Family Psychology, 23*(4), 562.

McHale, S. M., Updegraff, K. A., & Whiteman, S. D. (2012). Sibling relationships and influences in childhood and adolescence. *Journal of Marriage and Family, 74*(5), 913-930.

McIlvane, J. M., Ajrouch, K. J., & Antonucci, T. C. (2007). Generational structure and social resources in mid-life influences on health and well-being. *Journal of Social Issues, 63,* 759-774.

McLanahan, S., Tach, L., & Schneider, D. (2013). The causal effects of father absence. *Annual Review of Sociology, 39*, 399–427.

McLaughlin, D., Vagenas, D., Pachana, N. A., Begum, N., & Dobson, A. (2010). Gender differences in social network size and satisfaction in adults in their 70s. *Journal of Health Psychology, 15*(5), 671–679.

McLeod, J. D., Kruttschnitt, C., & Dornfeld, M. (1994). Does parenting explain the effects of structural conditions on children's antisocial behavior? A comparison of blacks and whites. *Social Forces, 73*(2), 575–604.

McLeod, R., Boyer, K., Karrison, T., Kasza, K., Swisher, C., Roizen, N., . . . Toxoplamosis Study Group. (2006). Outcome of treatment for congenital toxoplasmosis, 1981–2004: The national collaborative Chicago-based, congenital toxoplasmosis study. *Clinical Infectious Diseases: An Official Publication of the Infectious Diseases Society of America, 42*(10), 1383–1394.

McNamara, T. K., Pitt-Catsouphes, M., Matz-Costa, C., Brown, M., & Valcour, M. (2013). Across the continuum of satisfaction with work–family balance: Work hours, flexibility-fit, and work–family culture. *Social Science Research, 42*(2), 283-298.

McNeal Jr, R. B. (2012). Checking in or checking out? Investigating the parent involvement reactive hypothesis. *The Journal of Educational Research, 105*(2), 79–89.

McNulty, J. K., Wenner, C. A., & Fisher, T. D. (2016). Longitudinal associations among relationship satisfaction, sexual satisfaction, and frequency of sex in early marriage. *Archives of Sexual Behavior, 45*(1), 85–97.

McPhate, M. (2016, May 9). Bartenders can't refuse pregnant women alcohol, New York City says. *The New York Times.* Retrieved from www.nytimes.com/2016/05/10/nyregion/bartenders-cant-refuse-pregnant-women-alcohol-new-york-city-says.html

McPherson, M., Smith-Lovin, L., & Brashears, M. E. (2006). Social isolation in America: Changes in core discussion networks over two decades. *American Sociological Review, 71*, 353–375.

McQueeny, T., Schweinsburg, B. C., Schweinsburg, A. D., Jacobus, J., Bava, S., Frank, L. R., & Tapert, S. F. (2009). Altered white matter integrity in adolescent binge drinkers. *Alcoholism: Clinical and Experimental Research, 33*(7), 1278–1285.

McTiernan, A., Kooperberg, C., White, E., Wilcox, S., Coates, R., Adams-Campbell, L. L., . . . Ockene, J. (2003). Recreational physical activity and the risk of breast cancer in postmenopausal women: The Women's Health Initiative Cohort Study. *Journal of the American Medical Association, 290*, 1331–1336.

Mears, B. (2005, March 1). *High court: Juvenile death penalty unconstitutional: Slim majority cites "evolving standards" in American society.* Retrieved from http://cnn.com./2005/LAW/03/01/scotus.death.penalty

Medland, S. E., Duffy, D. L., Wright, M. J., Geffen, G. M., Hay, D. A., Levy, F., . . . & Hewitt, A. W. (2009). Genetic influences on handedness: Data from 25,732 Australian and Dutch twin families. *Neuropsychologia, 47*(2), 330–337.

Mednick, S. C., Nakayama, K., Cantero, J. L., Atienza, M., Levin, A. A., Pathak, N., & Stickgold, R. (2002). The restorative effect of naps on perceptual deterioration. *Nature Neuroscience, 5*, 677–681.

Meezan, W., & Rauch, J. (2005). Gay marriage, same-sex parenting, and America's children. *Future of Children, 15*, 97–115.

Meier, R. (1991, January–February). Language acquisition by deaf children. *American Scientist, 79*, 60–70.

Meijer, A. M., & van den Wittenboer, G. L. H. (2007). Contributions of infants' sleep and crying to marital relationship of first-time parent couples in the 1st year after childbirth. *Journal of Family Psychology, 21*, 49–57.

Meins, E. (1998). The effects of security of attachment and maternal attribution of meaning on children's linguistic acquisitional style. *Infant Behavior and Development, 21*, 237–252.

Melén, E., Himes, B. E., Brehm, J. M., Boutaoui, N., Klanderman, B. J., Sylvia, J. S., & Lasky-Su, J. (2010). Analyses of shared genetic factors between asthma and obesity in children. *Journal of Allergy and Clinical Immunology, 126*(3), 631–637.

Meléndez, J. C., Mayordomo, T., Sancho, P., & Tomás, J. M. (2012). Coping strategies: Gender differences and development throughout life span. *The Spanish Journal of Psychology, 15*(3), 1089–1098.

Melby, J., Conger, R., Fang, S., Wickrama, K., & Conger, K. (2008). Adolescent family experiences and educational attainment during early adulthood. *Developmental Psychology, 44*(6), 1519–1536.

Melby-Lervåg, M., & Hulme, C. (2013). Is working memory training effective? A meta-analytic review. *Developmental Psychology, 49*(2), 270.

Melhem, N. M., Porta, G., Shamseddeen, W., Payne, M. W., & Brent, D. A. (2011). Grief in children and adolescents bereaved by sudden parental death. *Archives of General Psychiatry, 68*(9), 911–919.

Meltzoff, A. N. (2007). "Like me": A foundation for social cognition. *Developmental Science, 10*, 126–134.

Meltzoff, A. N., & Moore, M. K. (1989). Imitation in newborn infants: Exploring the range of gestures imitated and the underlying mechanisms. *Developmental Psychology, 25*, 954–962.

Menacker, F., Martin, J. A., MacDorman, M. F., & Ventura, S. J. (2004). Births to 10–14 year-old mothers, 1990–2002: Trends and health outcomes. *National Vital Statistics Reports, 53*(7). Hyattsville, MD: National Center for Health Statistics.

Mendle, J. (2014). Beyond pubertal timing: New directions for studying individual differences in development. *Current Directions in Psychological Science, 23*(3), 215–219.

Mendle, J., Turkheimer, E., D'Onofrio, B. M., Lynch, S. K., Emery, R. E., Slutske, W. S., &

Martin, N. G. (2006). Family structure and age at menarche: A children-of-twins approach. *Developmental Psychology, 42*, 533–542.

Menec, V. H. (2003). The relation between everyday activities and successful aging: A 6-year longitudinal study. *The Journals of Gerontology Series B: Psychological Sciences and Social Sciences, 58*(2), S74–S82.

Menec, V. H., Shooshtari, S., Nowicki, S., & Fournier, S. (2010). Does the relationship between neighborhood socioeconomic status and health outcomes persist into very old age? A population-based study. *Journal of Aging and Health, 22*(1), 27–47.

Menegaux, F., Baruchel, A., Bertrand, Y., Lescoeur, B., Leverger, G., Nelken, B., . . . Clavel, J. (2006). Household exposure to pesticides and risk of childhood acute leukaemia. *Occupational and Environmental Medicine, 63*(2), 131–134.

Meng, H., Smith, S. D., Hager, K., Held, M., Liu, J., Olson, R. K., . . . Gruen, J. R. (2005, October). *A deletion in DCDC2 on 6p22 is associated with reading disability.* Paper presented at the American Society of Human Genetics meeting, Salt Lake City, UT.

Meng, Y., Lee, J. H., Cheng, R., St. George-Hyslop, P., Mayeux, R., & Farrer, L. A. (2007). Association between SORL1 and Alzheimer's disease in a genome-wide study. *NeuroReport, 18*(17), 1761–1764.

Mennella, J. A. (2014). Ontogeny of taste preferences: basic biology and implications for health. *The American Journal of Clinical Nutrition, 99*(3), 704S–711S.

Mennella, J. A., & Beauchamp, G. K. (1996). The early development of human flavor preferences. In E. D. Capaldi (Ed.), *Why we eat what we eat: The psychology of eating* (pp. 83–112). Washington DC: American Psychological Association.

Menon, U. (2001). Middle adulthood in cultural perspective: The imagined and the experienced in three cultures. In M. E. Lachman (Ed.), *Handbook of midlife development* (pp. 40–74). New York: Wiley.

Merikangas, K. D., He, J-P., Brody, D., Fisher, P. W., Bourdon, K., & Koretz, D. S. (2010). Prevalence and treatment of mental disorders among U.S. children in the 2001–2004 NHANES. *Pediatrics, 125*(1), 75–81. doi: 10.1542/peds.2008-2598

Merrell, K., Gueldner, B., Ross, S., & Isava, D. (2008). How effective are school bullying intervention programs? A meta-analysis of intervention research. *School Psychology Quarterly, 23*(1), 26–42.

Merrill, S. S., & Verbrugge, L. M. (1999). Health and disease in midlife. In S. L. Willis & J. D. Reid (Eds.), *Life in the middle: Psychological and social development in middle age* (pp. 78–103). San Diego: Academic Press.

Merz, E. M., & Consedine, N. S. (2009). The association of family support and wellbeing in later life depends on adult attachment style. *Attachment & Human Development, 11*(2), 203–221.

Merz, E. M., Consedine, N. S., Schulze, H. J., & Schuengel, C. (2009). Wellbeing of adult children and ageing parents: Associations with intergenerational support and relationship quality. *Ageing & Society, 29*(5), 783–802.

Messinger, D. S., Bauer, C. R., Das, A., Seifer, R., Lester, B. M., Lagasse, L. L., . . . Poole, W. K. (2004). The maternal lifestyle study: Cognitive, motor, and behavioral outcomes of cocaine-exposed and opiate-exposed infants through three years of age. *Pediatrics, 113*, 1677–1685.

Metz, T. D., & Stickrath, E. H. (2015). Marijuana use in pregnancy and lactation: a review of the evidence. *American Journal of Obstetrics and Gynecology, 213*(6), 761–778.

Meyer, B. J. F., Russo, C., & Talbot, A. (1995). Discourse comprehension and problem solving: Decisions about the treatment of breast cancer by women across the life-span. *Psychology in Aging, 10*, 84–103.

Meyer, I. H. (2003). Prejudice, social stress, and mental health in lesbian, gay, and bisexual populations: Conceptual issues and research evidence. *Psychological Bulletin, 129*, 674–697.

Meyer-Bahlburg, H. F. (2005). Gender identity outcome in female-raised 46, XY persons with penile agenesis, cloacal exstrophy of the bladder, or penile ablation. *Archives of Sexual Behavior, 34*(4), 423–438.

Michalska, K. J., Zeffiro, T. A., & Decety, J. (2016). Brain response to viewing others being harmed in children with conduct disorder symptoms. *Journal of Child Psychology and Psychiatry, 57*(4), 510–519.

Miech, R. A., Johnston, L. D., O'Malley, P. M., Bachman, J. G., & Schulenberg, J. E. (2016). *Monitoring the Future national survey results on drug use, 1975-2015: Volume I, Secondary school students.* Ann Arbor: Institute for Social Research, The University of Michigan.

Miech, R. A., Kumanyika, S. K., Stettler, N., Link, B., Phelan, J. C., & Chang, V. W. (2006). Trends in the association of poverty with overweight among US adolescents, 1971–2004. *Journal of the American Medical Association, 295*, 2385–2393.

Miedzian, M. (1991). *Boys will be boys: Breaking the link between masculinity and violence.* New York: Doubleday.

Mienaltowski, A. (2011). Everyday problem solving across the adult life span: Solution diversity and efficacy. *Annals of the New York Academy of Sciences, 1235*(1), 75–85.

Migeon, B. R. (2006). The role of X inactivation and cellular mosaicism in women's health and sex-specific disorders. *Journal of the American Medical Association, 295*, 1428–1433.

Migliore, L., & Coppede, F. (2008). Genetics, environmental factors, and the emerging role of epigenetics in neurodegenerative disease. *Mutation Research/Fundamental and Molecular Mechanisms of Mutagenesis, 667*, 82–97.

Mikulincer, M., & Florian, V. (2000). Exploring individual differences in reactions to mortality salience: Does attachment style regulate terror management mechanisms? *Journal of Personality and Social Psychology, 79*(2), 260.

Milanović, Z., Pantelić, S., Trajković, N., Sporiš, G., Kostić, R., & James, N. (2013). Age-related decrease in physical activity and functional fitness among elderly men and women. *Clinical Interventions in Aging, 8*, 549.

Milkie, M. A., & Peltola, P. (1999). Playing all the roles: Gender and the work-family balancing act. *Journal of Marriage and Family, 61*, 476–490.

Milkie, M. A., Mattingly, M. J., Nomaguchi, S. M., Bianchi, S. M., & Robinson, J. P. (2004). The time squeeze: Parental statuses and feelings about time with children. *Journal of Marriage and Family, 66*, 739–761.

Miller, B., Messias, E., Miettunen, J., Alaräisänen, A., Järvelin, M. R., Koponen, H., . . . & Kirkpatrick, B. (2011). Meta-analysis of paternal age and schizophrenia risk in male versus female offspring. *Schizophrenia Bulletin, 37*(5), 1039–1047.

Miller, G. E., & Blackwell, E. (2006). Turning up the heat. *Current Directions in Psychological Science, 15*, 269–272.

Miller, J. W., Naimi, T. S., Brewer, R. D., & Jones, S. E. (2007). Binge drinking and associated health risk behaviors among high school students. *Pediatrics, 119*, 76–85.

Miller, K. D., Siegel, R. L., Lin, C. C., Mariotto, A. B., Kramer, J. L., Rowland, J. H., . . . & Jemal, A. (2016). Cancer treatment and survivorship statistics, 2016. *CA: a cancer journal for clinicians, 66*(4), 271–289.

Miller, K., & Kohn, M. (1983). The reciprocal effects of job condition and the intellectuality of leisure-time activities. In M. L. Kohn & C. Schooler (Eds.), *Work and personality: An inquiry into the impact of social stratification* (pp. 217–241). Norwood, NJ: Ablex.

Miller, L. J., Myers, A., Prinzi, L., & Mittenberg, W. (2009). Changes in intellectual functioning associated with normal aging. *Archives of Clinical Neuropsychology, 24*(7), 681–688. doi: 10.1093/arclin/acp072

Miller, M. A., & Rahe, R. H. (1997). Life changes scaling for the 1990s. *Journal of Psychosomatic Research, 43*, 279–292.

Miller, S. A. (2009). Children's understanding of second-order mental states. *Psychological Bulletin, 135*(5), 749.

Miller-Kovach, K. (2003). *Childhood and adolescent obesity: A review of the scientific literature* (Weight Watchers International). Unpublished manuscript.

Millman, R. P., Working Group on Sleepiness in Adolescents/Young Adults, & AAP Committee on Adolescents. (2005). Excessive sleepiness in adolescents and young adults: Causes, consequences, and treatment strategies. *Pediatrics, 115*, 1774–1786.

Mills, K. T., Bundy, J. D., Kelly, T. N., Reed, J. E., Kearney, P. M., Reynolds, K., . . . & He, J. (2016). Global disparities of hypertension prevalence and control. *Circulation, 134*(6), 441–450.

Min, J., Chiu, D. T., & Wang, Y. (2013). Variation in the heritability of body mass index based on diverse twin studies: a systematic review. *Obesity Reviews, 14*(11), 871–882.

Mindell, J. A., & Owens, J. A. (2015). *A clinical guide to pediatric sleep: diagnosis and management of sleep problems.* Philadelphia, PA: Lippincott Williams & Wilkins.

Mindell, J. A., Sadeh, A., Wiegand, B., How, T. H., & Goh, D. Y. T. (2010). Cross-cultural differences in infant and toddler sleep. *Sleep Medicine, 11*, 274–289.

Miner, J. L., & Clarke-Stewart, A. (2009). Trajectories of externalizing behaviors from age 2 to age 9: Relations with gender, temperament, ethnicity, parenting and rater. *Developmental Psychology, 44*(3), 771–786.

Miniño, A. M. (2010). Mortality among teenagers aged 12-19 years: United States, 1999-2006. *NCHS Data Brief, 37.* Hyattsville, MD: National Center for Health Statistics.

Miniño, A. M., Heron, M. P., Murphy, S. L., & Kochanek, K. D. (2007). Deaths: Final data for 2004. *National Vital Statistics Reports, 55*(19). Hyattsville, MD: National Center for Health Statistics.

Minkler, M., & Fuller-Thomson, D. E. (2001). Physical and mental health status of American grandparents providing extensive child care to their grandchildren. *Journal of the American Medical Women's Association (1972), 56*(4), 199–205.

Mintz, T. H. (2005). Linguistic and conceptual influences on adjective acquisition in 24- to 36-month-olds. *Developmental Psychology, 41*, 17–29.

Miranda, L., Dixon, V., & Reyes, C. (2015). How states handle drug use during pregnancy. *ProPublica.* https://projects.propublica.org/graphics/maternity-drug-policies-by-state

Mischel, W. (1966). A social learning view of sex differences in behavior. In E. Maccoby (Ed.), *The development of sex differences* (pp. 57–81). Stanford, CA: Stanford University Press.

Mitchell, B. A. (2010). Happiness in midlife parental roles: A contextual mixed methods analysis. *Family Relations, 59*(3), 326–339.

Mitchell, K. J., Finkelhor, D., Jones, L. M., & Wolak, J. (2012). Prevalence and characteristics of youth sexting: A national study. *Pediatrics, 129*(1), 13–20.

Mitnick, D. M., Heyman, R. E., & Slep, A. M. S. (2009). Changes in relationship satisfaction across the transition to parenthood: A meta-analysis. *Journal of Family Psychology, 23*(6), 848–852.

Mitteldorf, J. (2010). Aging is not a process of wear and tear. *Rejuvenation Research, 13*(2–3), 322–326.

Mix, K. S., Huttenlocher, J., & Levine, S. C. (2002). Multiple cues for quantification in infancy: Is number one of them? *Psychological Bulletin, 128*, 278–294.

Miyake, K., Chen, S., & Campos, J. (1985). Infants' temperament, mothers' mode of interaction and attachment in Japan: An interim report. In I. Bretherton & E. Waters (Eds.), *Growing points of attachment theory and research. Monographs of the Society for Research in Child Development, 50*(1–2, Serial No. 109), 276–297.

Miyata, S., Noda, A., Iwamoto, K., Kawano, N., Okuda, M., & Ozaki, N. (2013). Poor sleep quality impairs cognitive performance in older adults. *Journal of Sleep Research, 22*(5), 535–541.

Mobbs, D., & Watt, C. (2011). There is nothing paranormal about near-death experiences: How neuroscience can explain seeing bright lights, meeting the dead, or being convinced you are one of them. *Trends in Cognitive Sciences, 15*(10), 447–449.

Modecki, K. L., Minchin, J., Harbaugh, A. G., Guerra, N. G., & Runions, K. C. (2014). Bullying prevalence across contexts: A meta-analysis measuring cyber and traditional bullying. *Journal of Adolescent Health, 55*(5), 602–611.

Moen, P., & Wethington, E. (1999). Midlife development in a life course context. In S. L. Willis & J. D. Reid (Eds.), *Life in the middle: Psychological and social development in middle age* (pp. 1–23). San Diego: Academic Press.

Moen, P., Dempster-McClain, D., & Williams, R. M., Jr. (1992). Successful aging: Life-course perspective on women's multiple roles and health. *American Journal of Sociology, 97,* 1612–1638.

Moffitt, T. E. (1993). Adolescence-limited and life-course-persistent antisocial behavior: a developmental taxonomy. *Psychological Review, 100*(4), 674.

Mohai, P., Lantz, P. M., Morenoff, J., House, J. S., & Mero, R. P. (2009). Racial and socioeconomic disparities in residential proximity to polluting industrial facilities: Evidence from the Americans' Changing Lives study. *American Journal of Public Health, 99,* S649–S656.

Mokdad, A. H., Marks, J. S., Stroup, D. F., & Gerberding, J. L. (2005). Correction: Actual causes of death in the United States, 2000. *Journal of the American Medical Association, 293,* 293–294.

Moline, M. L., & Zendell, S. M. (2000). Evaluating and managing premenstrual syndrome. *Medscape General Medicine, 2.* Retrieved from www.medscape.com/viewarticle/408913_print

Molinuevo, J. L., Blennow, K., Dubois, B., Engelborghs, S., Lewczuk, P., Perret-Liaudet, A., . . . & Parnetti, L. (2014). The clinical use of cerebrospinal fluid biomarker testing for Alzheimer's disease diagnosis: A consensus paper from the Alzheimer's Biomarkers Standardization Initiative. *Alzheimer's & Dementia, 10*(6), 808–817.

Moll, H., & Meltzoff, A. N. (2011). How does it look? Level 2 perspective-taking at 36 months of age. *Child Development, 82*(2), 661–673.

Moll, H., & Tomasello, M. (2012). Three-year-olds understand appearance and reality—just not about the same object at the same time. *Developmental Psychology, 48*(4), 1124.

Mollenkopf, J., Waters, M. C., Holdaway, J., & Kasinitz, P. (2005). Ethnic and racial diversity in the transition to adulthood. In R. A. Settersten Jr., F. F. Furstenberg Jr., & R. G. Rumbaut (Eds.), *On the frontier of adulthood: Theory, research, and public policy* (pp. 454–497). Chicago: University of Chicago Press.

Molofsky, A. V., Slutsky, S. G., Joseph, N. M., He, S., Pardal, R., Krishnamurthy, J., . . . Morrison, S. J. (2006). Increasing p16INK4a expression decreases forebrain progenitors and neurogenesis during ageing. *Nature, 443,* 448–452.

Monahan, K. C., Cauffman, E., & Steinberg, L. (2009). Affiliation with antisocial peers, susceptibility to peer influence, and antisocial behavior during the transition to adulthood. *Developmental Psychology, 45*(6), 1520–1530.

Monahan, K. C., Rhew, I. C., Hawkins, J. D., & Brown, E. C. (2014). Adolescent pathways to co-occurring problem behavior: The effects of peer delinquency and peer substance use. *Journal of Research on Adolescence, 24*(4), 630–645.

Mondschein, E. R., Adolph, K. E., & Tamis-LeMonda, C. S. (2000). Gender bias in mothers' expectations about infant crawling. *Journal of Experimental Child Psychology* (Special Issue on Gender), *77,* 304–316.

Money, J., Hampson, J. G., & Hampson, J. L. (1955). Hermaphroditism: Recommendations concerning assignment of sex, change of sex and psychologic management. *Bulletin of the Johns Hopkins Hospital, 97*(4), 284–300.

Monger, G. P. (2013). *Marriage customs of the world: An encyclopedia of dating customs and wedding traditions.* Santa Barbara: ABC-CLIO, LLC.

Montenegro, X. P. (2004). *The divorce experience: A study of divorce at midlife and beyond.* Washington, DC: American Association of Retired Persons.

Montessori, M. (with Chattin-McNichogls, J.). (1995). *The absorbent mind.* New York: Holt.

Montgomery, M. J., & Côté, J. E. (2003). College as a transition to adulthood. In G. R. Adams & M. D. Berzonsky (Eds.), *Blackwell handbook of adolescence.* Malden, MA: Blackwell.

Moody, H. R. (2009). *Aging: Concepts and controversies.* Thousand Oaks, CA: Pine Forge/Sage.

Mook-Kanamori, D. O., Steegers, E. A., Eilers, P. H., Raat, H., Hofman, A., & Jaddoe, V. W. (2010). Risk factors and outcomes associated with first-trimester fetal growth restriction. *Journal of the American Medical Association, 303*(6), 527–534. doi: 10.1001/jama.2010.78

Moon, J. R., Kondo, N., Glymour, M. M., & Subramanian, S. V. (2011). Widowhood and mortality: A meta-analysis. *PLoS One, 6*(8), e23465.

Moore, M. (2012). Behavioral sleep problems in children and adolescents. *Journal of Clinical Psychology in Medical Settings, 19*(1), 77–83.

Moore, R. C., Eyler, L. T., Mausbach, B. T., Zlatar, Z. Z., Thompson, W. K., Peavy, G., . . . & Jeste, D. V. (2015). Complex interplay between health and successful aging: role of perceived stress, resilience, and social support. *The American Journal of Geriatric Psychiatry, 23*(6), 622–632.

Moore, S. E., Cole, T. J., Poskitt, E. M. E., Sonko, B. J., Whitehead, R. G., McGregor, I. A., & Prentice, A. M. (1997). Season of birth predicts mortality in rural Gambia. *Nature, 388,* 434.

Mordre, M., Groholt, B., Kjelsberg, E., Sandstad, B., & Myhre, A. M. (2011). The impact of ADHD and conduct disorder in childhood on adult delinquency: A 30 years follow-up study using official crime records. *BMC Psychiatry, 11*(1), 57.

Morelli, G. A., Rogoff, B., & Angellilo, C. (2003). Cultural involvement in young children's access to work or involvement in specialized child-focused activities. *International Journal of Behavioral Development, 27,* 264–274.

Morin, R. (2009, May 28). *Most middle-aged adults are rethinking retirement plans: The threshold generation.* Retrieved from http://pewresearch.org/pubs/1234/the-threshold-generation

Morris, A. S., Robinson, L. R., Hays-Grudo, J., Claussen, A. H., Hartwig, S. A., & Treat, A. E. (2017). Targeting parenting in early childhood: A public health approach to improve outcomes for children living in poverty. *Child Development, 88*(2), 388–397.

Morris, M. C. (2004). Diet and Alzheimer's disease: What the evidence shows. *Medscape General Medicine, 6,* 1–5.

Morris, M. S., Jacques, P. F., Rosenberg, I. H., & Selhub, J. (2007). Folate and vitamin B-12 status in relation to anemia, macrocytosis, and cognitive impairment in older Americans in the age of folic acid fortification. *American Journal of Clinical Nutrition, 85*(1), 193–200.

Morrissey, T. W. (2009). Multiple child-care arrangements and young children's behavioral outcomes. *Child Development, 80,* 59–76.

Morrow, D. G., Menard, W. W. E., Stine-Morrow, E. A. L., Teller, T., & Bryant, D. (2001). The influence of expertise and task factors on age differences in pilot communication. *Psychology and Aging, 16,* 31–46.

Mosconi, L., Tsui, W. H., Herholz, K., Pupi, A., Drzezga, A., Lucignani, G., . . . de Leon, M. J. (2008). Multicenter standardized 18F-FDG PET diagnosis of mild cognitive impairment, Alzheimer's disease, and other dementias. *Journal of Nuclear Medicine, 49,* 390–398.

Moses, L. J., Baldwin, D. A., Rosicky, J. G., & Tidball, G. (2001). Evidence for referential understanding in the emotions domain at twelve and eighteen months. *Child Development, 72,* 718–735.

Mosher, W. D., Chandra, A., & Jones, J. (2005). Sexual behavior and selected health measures: Men and women 15–44 years of age, United States, 2002. *Advance Data from Vital and Health Statistics,* No. 362. Hyattsville, MD: Centers for Disease Control and Prevention, National Center for Health Statistics.

Mosier, C. E., & Rogoff, B. (2003). Privileged treatment of toddlers: Cultural aspects of individual choice and responsibility. *Developmental Psychology, 39,* 1047–1060.

Moss, M. S., & Moss, S. Z. (1989). The death of a parent. In R. A. Kalish (Ed.), *Midlife loss: Coping strategies.* Newbury Park, CA: Sage.

Moster, D., Lie, R. T., & Markestad, T. (2008). Long-term medical and social consequences of preterm birth. *New England Journal of Medicine, 359,* 262–273.

Moulson, M. C., Fox, N. A., Zeanah, C. H., & Nelson, C. A. (2009). Early adverse experiences and the neurobiology of facial emotion processing. *Developmental Psychology, 45,* 17-30.

Mouw, T. (2005). Sequences of early adult transition: A look at variability and consequences. In R. A. Settersten Jr., F. F. Furstenberg Jr., & R. G. Rumbaut (Eds.), *On the frontier of adulthood: Theory, research, and public policy* (pp. 256-291). Chicago: University of Chicago Press.

Moyer, V. A. (2012). Screening for prostate cancer: U.S. Preventive Services Task Force recommendation statement. *Annals of Internal Medicine, 157*(2), 120-134.

Moyer, V. A. (2013). Screening for intimate partner violence and abuse of elderly and vulnerable adults: US preventive services task force recommendation statement. *Annals of Internal Medicine, 158*(6), 478-486.

Mroczek, D. K. (2004). Positive and negative affect at midlife. In O. G. Brim, C. D. Ryff, & R. C. Kessler (Eds.), *How healthy are we? A national study of well-being at midlife* (pp. 205-226). Chicago: University of Chicago Press.

Mroczek, D. K., & Kolarz, C. M. (1998). The effect of age on positive and negative affect: A developmental perspective on happiness. *Journal of Personality and Social Psychology, 75*(5), 1333-1349.

Mroczek, D. K., & Spiro, A. (2005). Change in life satisfaction during adulthood: Findings from the Veterans Affairs Normative Aging Study. *Journal of Personality and Social Psychology, 88,* 189-202.

Mroczek, D. K., & Spiro, A., III. (2007). Personality change influences mortality in older men. *Psychological Science, 18*(5), 371-376.

Mrug, S., Molina, B. S., Hoza, B., Gerdes, A. C., Hinshaw, S. P., Hechtman, L., & Arnold, L. E. (2012). Peer rejection and friendships in children with attention-deficit/hyperactivity disorder: Contributions to long-term outcomes. *Journal of Abnormal Child Psychology, 40*(6), 1013-β1026.

MTA Cooperative Group. (1999). A 14-month randomized clinical trial of treatment strategies for attention-deficit/hyperactivity disorder. *Archives of General Psychiatry, 56,* 1073-1986.

Mueller, T. I., Kohn, R., Leventhal, N., Leon, A. C., Solomon, D., Coryell, W., . . . Keller, M. B. (2004). The course of depression in elderly patients. *American Journal of Psychiatry, 12,* 22-29.

Muentener, P., & Carey, S. (2010). Infants' causal representations of state change events. *Cognitive Psychology, 61*(2), 63-86.

Mulford, C., & Giordano, P. (2008). Teen dating violence: A closer look at adolescent romantic relationships. *National Institute of Justice Journal, 261,* 34-41.

Mullan, D., & Currie, C. (2000). Socioeconomic equalities in adolescent health. In C. Currie, K. Hurrelmann, W. Settertobulte, R. Smith, & J. Todd (Eds.), *Health and health behaviour among young people: A WHO cross-national study (HBSC) international report* (pp. 65-72). (WHO Policy Series: Healthy Policy for Children and Adolescents, Series No. 1.) Copenhagen, Denmark: World Health Organization Regional Office for Europe.

Munakata, Y., McClelland, J. L., Johnson, M. J., & Siegler, R. S. (1997). Rethinking infant knowledge: Toward an adaptive process account of successes and failures in object permanence tasks. *Psychological Review, 104,* 686-714.

Muniz-Terrera, G., van den Hout, A., Piccinin, A. M., Matthews, F. E., & Hofer, S. M. (2013). Investigating terminal decline: Results from a UK population-based study of aging. *Psychology and Aging, 28*(2), 377.

Munnell, A. H. (2015). The average retirement age-an update. *Notes, 1920,* 1960-1980.

Murachver, T., Pipe, M., Gordon, R., Owens, J. L., & Fivush, R. (1996). Do, show, and tell: Children's event memories acquired through direct experience, observation, and stories. *Child Development, 67,* 3029-3044.

Muraco, A. (2006). Intentional families: Fictive kin ties between cross-gender, different sexual orientation friends. *Journal of Marriage and Family, 68,* 1313-1325.

Muris, P., Merckelbach, H., & Collaris, R. (1997). Common childhood fears and their origins. *Behaviour Research and Therapy, 35,* 929-937.

Murphy, M. J., & Peterson, M. J. (2015). Sleep disturbances in depression. *Sleep Medicine Clinics, 10*(1), 17-23.

Murphy, S. L., Xu, J., Kochanek, K. D., Curtin, S. C., & Arias, E. (2017). Deaths: Final data for 2015. *National Vital Statistics Reports: from the Centers for Disease Control and Prevention, National Center for Health Statistics, National Vital Statistics System, 66*(6), 1-75.

Murray, C. J., & Ng, M. (2017). Nearly one-third of the world's population is obese or overweight, new data show. Retrieved from Institute for Health Metrics and Evaluation: www.healthdata.org/news-release/nearly-one-third-world%E2%80%99s-population-obese-or-overweight-new-data-show

Murray, L., Cooper, P., & Fearon, P. (2014). Parenting difficulties and postnatal depression: Implications for primary healthcare assessment and intervention. *Community Practitioner, 87,* 34-38.

Musick, M. A., Herzog, A. R., & House, J. S. (1999). Volunteering and mortality among older adults: Findings from a national sample. *Journal of Gerontology: Psychological Sciences, 54B,* S173-S180.

Musil, C. M., Gordon, N. L., Warner, C. B., Zauszniewski, J. A., Standing, T., & Wykle, M. (2010). Grandmothers and caregiving to grandchildren: Continuity, change, and outcomes over 24 months. *The Gerontologist, 51*(1), 86-100.

Mustanski, B. S., DuPree, M. G., Nievergelt, C. M., Bocklandt, S., Schork, N. J., & Hamer, D. H. (2005). A genomewide scan of male sexual orientation. *Human Genetics, 116,* 272-278.

Mustillo, S., Worthman, C., Erkanli, A., Keeler, G., Angold, A., & Costello, E. J. (2003). Obesity and psychiatric disorder: Developmental trajectories. *Pediatrics, 111,* 851-859.

Mustonen, U., Huurre, T., Kiviruusu, O., Haukkala, A., & Aro, H. (2011). Long-term impact of parental divorce on intimate relationship quality in adulthood and the mediating role of psychosocial resources. *Journal of Family Psychology, 25*(4), 615.

Myers, D. G. (2000). The funds, friends, and faith of happy people. *American Psychologist, 55,* 56-67.

Myers, D. G., & Diener, E. (1996). The pursuit of happiness. *Scientific American, 274,* 54-56.

Myers, D., & Diener, E. (1995). Who is happy? *Psychological Science, 6,* 10-19.

Myers, J. E., & Perrin, N. (1993). Grandparents affected by parental divorce: A population at risk? *Journal of Counseling and Development, 72,* 62-66.

Myers, J. E., Madathil, J., & Tingle, L. R. (2005). Marriage satisfaction and wellness in India and the United States: A preliminary comparison of arranged marriages and marriages of choice. *Journal of Counseling and Development, 83*(2), 183-190.

Myers, J.E., & Harper, M.C. (2014). Midlife concerns and caregiving experiences: Intersecting life issues affecting mental health. In R.C. Talley, G.L. Fricchione, & B.G. Druss (Eds.), *The challenges of mental health caregiving* (pp. 123-142). New York: Springer.

Myrick, S. E., & Martorell, G. A. (2011). Sticks and stones may break my bones: Protective factors for the effects of perceived discrimination on social competence in adolescence. *Personal Relationships, 18*(3), 487-501.

Nader, P. R., Bradley, R. H., Houts, R. M., McRitchie, S. L., & O'Brien, M. (2008). Moderate-to-vigorous physical activity from ages 9 to 15 years. *Journal of the American Medical Association, 300,* 295-305.

Nagaraja, J., Menkedick, J., Phelan, K. J., Ashley, P., Zhang, X., & Lanphear, B. P. (2005). Deaths from residential injuries in US children and adolescents, 1985-1997. *Pediatrics, 116,* 454-461.

Naito, M., & Miura, H. (2001). Japanese childrens' numerical competencies: Age and school-related influences on the development of number concepts and addition skills. *Developmental Psychology, 37,* 217-230.

Naito, T., & Geilen, U. P. (2005). The changing Japanese family: A psychological portrait. In J. L. Roopnarine & U. P. Gielen (Eds.), *Families in global perspective* (pp. 63-84). Boston, MA: Allyn & Bacon.

Najman, J. M., Hayatbakhsh, M. R., Heron, M. A., Bor, W., O'Callaghan, M. J., & Williams, G. M. (2009). The impact of episodic and chronic poverty on child cognitive development. *Journal of Pediatrics, 154*(2), 284-289.

Nakamoto, J., & Schwartz, D. (2010). Is peer victimization associated with academic achievement? A meta-analytic review. *Social Development, 19*(2), 221-242.

Nansel, T. R., Overpeck, M., Pilla, R. S., Ruan, W. J., Simons-Morton, B., & Scheidt, P. (2001). Bullying behaviors among U.S. youth: Prevalence and association with psychosocial adjustment. *Journal of the American Medical Association, 285,* 2094-2100.

Napoles, A. M., Chadiha, L., Eversley, R., & Moreno-John, G. (2010). Reviews: Developing culturally sensitive dementia caregiver interventions: Are we there yet? *American Journal of Alzheimer's Disease & Other Dementias, 25*(5), 389–406.

Nardone, S., & Elliott, E. (2016). The interaction between the immune system and epigenetics in the etiology of autism spectrum disorders. *Frontiers in Neuroscience, 10,* 329. http://doi.org/10.3389/fnins.2016.00329

Nathanielsz, P. W. (1995). The role of basic science in preventing low birth weight. *Future of Our Children, 5*(1), 57–70.

National Alliance for Caregiving. (2015). 2015 report: Caregiving in the U.S. [report]. Retrieved from www.caregiving.org/wp-content/uploads/2015/05/2015_CaregivingintheUS_Final-Report-June-4_WEB.pdf

National Assessment of Educational Progress: The Nation's Report Card. (2004). *America's charter schools: Results from the NAEP 2003 pilot study* (NCES 2005-456). Jessup, MD: U.S. Department of Education.

National Association for Gifted Children [NAGC]. (n.d.). Frequently asked questions. Retrieved from ww.nagc.org/index.aspx?id5548

National Center for Complementary and Alternative Medicine (NCCAM). (2008). *Get the facts: Menopausal symptoms and complementary health practices.* Retrieved from http://nccam.nih.gov/sites/nccam.nih.gov/files/ Get_The_Facts_Menopause_09-19-2013.pdf

National Center for Education Statistics (NCES). (2001). *The condition of education 2001* (NCES 2001-072). Washington, DC: U.S. Government Printing Office.

National Center for Education Statistics (NCES). (2003). *The condition of education, 2003* (NCES 2003-067). Washington, DC: Author.

National Center for Education Statistics (NCES). (2004). *The condition of education 2004* (NCES 2004-077). Washington, DC: U.S. Government Printing Office.

National Center for Education Statistics (NCES). (2005a). *Children born in 2001—First results from the base year of Early Childhood Longitudinal Study, Birth Cohort* (ECLS-B). Retrieved from http://nces.ed.gov/pubs2005/children/index.asp

National Center for Education Statistics (NCES). (2005b). *The condition of education 2005* (NCES 2005-094). Washington, DC: U.S. Government Printing Office.

National Center for Education Statistics (NCES). (2005c). *Trends in educational equity of girls & women 2004.* Retrieved from http://nces.ed.gov/pubsearch/pubsinfo.asp?pubid52005016

National Center for Education Statistics (NCES). (2006a). *Calories in, calories out: Food and exercise in public elementary schools, 2005* (NCES 2006-057). Washington, DC: Author.

National Center for Education Statistics (NCES). (2006b). *The condition of education 2006* (NCES 2006-071). Washington, DC: U.S. Government Printing Office.

National Center for Education Statistics (NCES). (2007a). *College enrollment rate of recent high school completers, by sex: 1960 through 2006. Table 191*[Digest of Education Statistics]. Retrieved from http://nces.ed.gov/programs/digest/d07/tables/dt07_191.asp

National Center for Education Statistics (NCES). (2007b). *The condition of education 2007.* (NCES 2007-064). Washington DC: Author.

National Center for Education Statistics (NCES). (2007c). *The Nation's Report Card: Mathematics 2007* (NCES 2007-494). Washington, DC: Author.

National Center for Education Statistics (NCES). (2007d). *The Nation's Report Card: Reading 2007* (NCES 2007-496). Washington, DC: Author.

National Center for Education Statistics (NCES). (2008). *1.5 million homeschooled students in the United States in 2007* (NCES 2009-030). Washington, DC: Author.

National Center for Education Statistics (NCES). (2009a). *Bachelor's degrees conferred by degree-granting institutions, by race/ethnicity and sex of student: Selected years, 1976–77 through 2006–07. Table 284* [Digest of Education Statistics: 2008]. Retrieved from http://nces.ed.gov/programs/digest/d08/tables/dt08_284.asp?referrer=report

National Center for Education Statistics (NCES). (2009b). *The condition of education 2009* (NCES 2009-081). Washington, DC: Author.

National Center for Education Statistics (NCES). (2012a). *The condition of education 2012.* (NCES 2012-045), Table A-47-2.

National Center for Education Statistics (NCES). (2013a). *The condition of education 2013* (NCES 2013-037). Immediate Transition to College.

National Center for Education Statistics (NCES). (2017). *The condition of education 2017* (NCES 2017-144). Washington, DC: Author.

National Center for Education Statistics. (2013b). Trends in high school dropout and completion rates in the Unites States. Retrieved from https://nces.ed.gov/programs/dropout/ind_03.asp

National Center for Education Statistics. (2016). Number and internet access of instructional computers and rooms in public schools, by selected school characteristics: Selected years, 1995 through 2008 [Data file]. Retrieved from https://nces.ed.gov/programs/digest/d15/tables/dt15_218.10.asp?

National Center for Education Statistics. (2017a). *Fast facts: Immediate transition to college.* Retrieved from https://nces.ed.gov/fastfacts/display.asp?id551

National Center for Education Statistics. (2017b). The condition of education: Children and Youth with Disabilities. Retrieved from https://nces.ed.gov/programs/coe/indicator_cgg.asp

National Center for Education Statistics. (2017c). The condition of education: Public high school graduation rates. Retrieved from https://nces.ed.gov/programs/coe/indicator_coi.asp

National Center for Elder Abuse. (2017). *Frequently asked questions: What is elder abuse?* Retrieved from https://ncea.acl.gov/faq/index.html#faq1

National Center for Health Statistics (NCHS). (1999). *Abstract adapted from Births: Final Data for 1999 by Mid-Atlantic Parents of Multiples.* Retrieved from www.orgsites.com/va/mapom/_pgg1.php3

National Center for Health Statistics (NCHS). (2004). *Health, United States, 2004 with chartbook on trends in the health of Americans* (DHHS Publication No. 2004-1232). Hyattsville, MD: Author.

National Center for Health Statistics (NCHS). (2005). *Health, United States, 2005* (DHHS Publication No. 2005-1232). Hyattsville, MD: Author.

National Center for Health Statistics (NCHS). (2006). *Health, United States, 2006.* Hyattsville, MD: Author.

National Center for Health Statistics (NCHS). (2007). *Health, United States, 2007 with chartbook on trends in the health of Americans.* Hyattsville, MD: Author.

National Center for Health Statistics (NCHS). (2008). *Health, United States, 2008, with chartbook.* Retrieved from www.cdc.gov/nchs/data/hus/hus08.pdf

National Center for Health Statistics (NCHS). (2010). Table 68. Hypertension and elevated blood pressure among persons 20 years of age and over, by selected characteristics: United States, 1988–1994, 1999–2002, and 2003–2006. *Health, United States, 2009: With special feature on medical technology* (DHHS Publication No. 2010-1232). Hyattsville, MD: Author. Retrieved from http://www.cdc.gov/nchs/data/hus/hus09.pdf#068

National Center for Health Statistics (US). (2016). *Health, United States, 2015: with special feature on racial and ethnic health disparities.* Retrieved from www.ncbi.nlm.nih.gov/pubmed/27308685

National Center for Health Statistics. (2015a). Tables of Summary Health Statistics [data tables]. Retrieved from www.cdc.gov/nchs/nhis/SHS/tables.htm

National Center for Health Statistics. (2015b). The public use natality file. Retrieved from ftp://ftp.cdc.gov/pub/Health_Statistics/NCHS/Dataset_Documentation/DVS/natality/UserGuide2015.pdf

National Center for Health Statistics. (2017). *Health, United States report 2016: With chartbook on long term trends in health.* Retrieved from www.cdc.gov/nchs/data/hus/hus16.pdf

National Center for Learning Disabilities (2004b). *LD at a glance* [Fact sheet]. Retrieved from www.ld.org/LDInfoZone/InfoZone_FactSheet_LD.cfm

National Center for Learning Disabilities. (2004a). *Dyslexia: Learning disabilities in reading* [Fact sheet]. Retrieved from www.ld.org/LDInfoZone/InfoZone_FactSheet_Dyslexia.cfm

National Clearinghouse on Child Abuse and Neglect Information (NCCANI). (2004). *Long-term consequences of child abuse and neglect.* Retrieved from http://nccanch.acf.hhs.gov/pubs/factsheets/longtermconsequences.cfm

National Coalition for the Homeless. (2017). *Homelessness in America.* Retrieved from http://nationalhomeless.org/about-homelessness/

National Fatherhood Initiative. (2016). *Father Facts 7*. Retrieved from www.fatherhood.org/father-absence-statistics-2016?

National Forum on Early Childhood Policy and Programs (2010). *Understanding the Head Start Impact Study*. Retrieved from www.developingchild.harvard.edu/

National Guidance Alliance. (2017). *Cataracts in adults: Management*. Retrieved from www.ncbi.nlm.nih.gov/pubmed/29106797

National Highway Traffic Safety Administration. (2009). *Traffic safety facts research note*. Washington, DC: Author.

National Highway Traffic Safety Administration. (2017). Teen driving. Retrieved from www.nhtsa.gov/road-safety/teen-driving

National Institute of Child Health and Development. (2008). *Facts about Down syndrome*. Retrieved from www.nichd.nihgov/publications/pubs/downsyndrome.cfm

National Institute of Child Health and Human Development (NICHD). (2017). *Phenylketonuria (PKU)*. Retrieved from https://www.nichd.nih.gov/health/topics/pku/Pages/default.aspx

National Institute of Mental Health (NIMH). (2001a). *Helping children and adolescents cope with violence and disasters: Fact sheet* (NIH Publication No. 01-3518). Bethesda, MD: Author.

National Institute of Mental Health (NIMH). (2001b). *Teenage brain: A work in progress*. Retrieved from www.nimh.gov/publicat/teenbrain.cfm

National Institute of Mental Health (NIMH). (2002). *Preventive sessions after divorce protect children into teens*. Retrieved from www.nimh.nih.gov

National Institute of Neurological Disorders and Stroke (NINDS). (2006, January 25). *NINDS shaken baby syndrome information page*. Retrieved from www.ninds.nih.gov/disorders/shakenbaby/shakenbaby.htm

National Institute on Aging (NIA). (2011). *Global health and aging*. Retrieved from www.nia.nih.gov/sites/default/files/nia-who_report_booklet_oct-2011_a4__1-12-12_5.pdf

National Institute on Alcohol Abuse and Alcoholism (NIAAA). (1996, July). *Alcohol alert* (No. 33-1996 [PH 366]). Bethesda, MD: Author.

National Institute on Alcohol Abuse and Alcoholism. (2016). *Alcohol facts and statistics*. Retrieved from www.niaaa.nih.gov/alcohol-health/overview-alcohol-consumption/alcohol-facts-and-statistics

National Institute on Alcohol Abuse and Alcoholism. (2017). *Beyond hangovers: Understanding alcohol's impact on your health* [fact sheet]. Retrieved from https://pubs.niaaa.nih.gov/publications/Hangovers/beyondHangovers.htm

National Institute on Deafness and Other Communication Disorders. (2016). *Quick statistics about hearing*. Retrieved from www.nidcd.nih.gov/health/statistics/quick-statistics-hearing

National Institutes of Health (NIH) Consensus Development Panel. (2001). National Institutes of Health Consensus Development conference statement: Phenyl-ketonuria screening and management. October 16–18, 2000. *Pediatrics, 108*(4), 972–982.

National Institutes of Health (NIH). (1992, December 7–9). Impotence. *NIH Consensus Statement, 10*(4). Washington, DC: U.S. Government Printing Office.

National Institutes of Health (NIH). (2003). The low-down on osteoporosis: What we know and what we don't. *Word on health*. Bethesda, MD: Author.

National Institutes of Health (NIH). (2005). NIH state-of-the-science conference statement: Management of menopause-related symptoms. *Annals of Internal Medicine, 142*(12, Pt.1), 1003–1013.

National Institutes of Health (NIH). (2010a, February 4). *NIH scientists identify maternal and fetal genes that increase preterm birth risk* [Press release]. Retrieved from http://www.nih.gov/news/health/feb2010/nichd-04.htm

National Institutes of Health (NIH). (2010b, March 8–10). *Consensus Development Conference on Vaginal Birth after Cesarean: New insights*. Bethesda, MD: Author. Retrieved from http://consensus.nih.gov/2010/vbac.htm

National Reading Panel. (2000). *Report of the National Reading Panel. Teaching children to read: An evidence-based assessment of the scientific research literature on reading and its implications for reading instruction: Reports of the subgroups*. Washington, DC: National Institute of Child Health and Human Development.

National Research Council (NRC). (1993a). *Losing generations: Adolescents in high risk settings*. Washington, DC: National Academy Press.

National Research Council (NRC). (1993b). *Understanding child abuse and neglect*. Washington, DC: National Academy Press.

National Scientific Council on the Developing Child. (2010). *Persistent fear and anxiety can affect young children's learning and development: Working paper #9*. Retrieved from www.developingchild.net

National Sleep Foundation. (2001). *2001 Sleep in America poll*. Retrieved from https://sleepfoundation.org/publications/2001poll.html

National Sleep Foundation. (2016). *National Sleep Foundation recommends new sleep times*. Retrieved from https://sleepfoundation.org/press-release/national-sleep-foundation-recommends-new-sleep-times/page/0/1

National Survey on Drug Use and Health (NSDUH). (2009, September 17). *Suicidal thoughts and behaviors among adults*. Retrieved from www.oas.samhsa.gov/2k9/165/Suicide.htm

National Survey on Drug Use and Health (NSDUH). (2012). *Results from the 2011 national survey on drug use and health: Mental health findings*. NSDUH Series H-45. HHS Publication No. (SMA) 12-4725. Rockville, MD: Substance Abuse and Mental Health Services Administration. Retrieved from http://www.samhsa.gov/data/NSDUH/2k11MH_FindingsandDetTables/2K11MHFR/NSDUHmhfr2011.htm

National Vital Statistics Report. (2017). *Births: Final data for 2015* [data table]. Retrieved from https://www.cdc.gov/nchs/data/nvsr/nvsr66/nvsr66_01_tables.pdf

National Vital Statistics. (2015). National marriage and divorce rates trends [data table] Retrieved from https://www.cdc.gov/nchs/nvss/marriage_divorce_tables.htm

Natrajan, M. S., de la Fuente, A. G., Crawford, A. H., Linehan, E., Nuñez, V., Johnson, K. R., . . . & Franklin, R. J. (2015). Retinoid X receptor activation reverses age-related deficiencies in myelin debris phagocytosis and remyelination. *Brain, 138*(12), 3581–3597.

Navarro, J., Pulido, R., Berger, C., Arteaga, M., Osofsky, H. J., Martinez, M., . . . & Hansel, T. C. (2016). Children's disaster experiences and psychological symptoms: An international comparison between the Chilean earthquake and tsunami and Hurricane Katrina. *International Social Work, 59*(4), 545–558.

Naveh-Benjamin, M., Brav, T., & Levy, O. (2007). The associative memory deficit of older adults: The role of strategy utilization. *Psychology and Aging, 22*(1), 202–208.

Neale, B. M., Lasky-Su., J., Anney, R., Franke, B., Zhou, K., Maller, J. B., . . . Faraone, S. V. (2008). Genome-wide association scan of attention deficit hyperactivity disorder. *American Journal of Medical Genetics Part B: Neuropsychiatric Genetics, 147B* (8), 1337–1344.

Nedrow, A., Miller, J., Walker, M., Nygren, P., Huffman, L. H., & Nelson, H. D. (2006). Complementary and alternative therapies for the management of menopause-related symptoms. *Archives of Internal Medicine, 166*, 1453–1465.

Neely-Barnes, S. L., Graff, J. C., & Washington, G. (2010). The health-related quality of life of custodial grandparents. *Health & Social Work, 35*(2), 87-97.

Neidorf, S., & Morin, R. (2011). *Four-in-ten Americans have close friends or relatives who are gay*. Retrieved from http://pewresearch.org/pubs/485/friends-who-are-gay

Neimeyer, R. A., & Currier, J. M. (2009). Grief therapy: Evidence of efficacy and emerging directions. *Current Directions in Psychological Science, 18*(6), 352–356.

Neisser, U., Boodoo, G., Bouchard, T. J., Jr., Boykin, A. W., Brody, N., Ceci, S. J., . . . Urbina, S. (1996). Intelligence: Knowns and unknowns. *American Psychologist, 51*(2), 77–101.

Neitzel, C., & Stright, A. D. (2003). Relations between parents' scaffolding and children's academic self-regulation: Establishing a foundation of self-regulatory competence. *Journal of Family Psychology, 17*, 147–159.

Nelson, C. A. (1995). The ontogeny of human memory: A cognitive neuroscience perspective. *Developmental Psychology, 31*, 723–738.

Nelson, C. A., Monk, C. S., Lin, J., Carver, L. J., Thomas, K. M., & Truwit, C. L. (2000). Functional neuroanatomy of spatial working memory in children. *Developmental Psychology, 36*, 109–116.

Nelson, C. A., Thomas, K. M., & deHaan, M. (2006). Neural bases of cognitive development. In W. Damon & R. Lerner (Eds.), *Handbook of child psychology* (6th ed.). Hoboken, NJ: Wiley.

Nelson, D. I., Nelson, R. Y., Concha-Barrientos, M., & Fingerhut, M. (2005). The global burden of occupational noise-induced hearing loss. *American Journal of Industrial Medicine, 48*(6), 446–458.

Nelson, K. (1993). The psychological and social origins of autobiographical memory. *Psychological Science, 47*, 7–14.

Nelson, K. (2005). Evolution and development of human memory systems. In B. J. Ellis and D. F. Bjorklund (Eds.), *Origins of the social mind: Evolutionary psychology and child development* (pp. 354–382). New York: Guilford Press.

Nelson, K., & Fivush, R. (2004). The emergence of autobiographical memory: A social cultural developmental theory. *Psychological Bulletin, 111*, 486–511.

Nelson, L. J., Padilla-Walker, L. M., & Nielson, M. G. (2015). Is hovering smothering or loving? An examination of parental warmth as a moderator of relations between helicopter parenting and emerging adults' indices of adjustment. *Emerging Adulthood, 3*(4), 282–285.

Nelson, M. C., & Gordon-Larsen, P. (2006). Physical activity and sedentary behavior patterns are associated with selected adolescent risk behaviors. *Pediatrics, 117*, 1281–1290.

Nelson, S. K., Kushlev, K., English, T., Dunn, E. W., & Lyubomirsky, S. (2013). In defense of parenthood: Children are associated with more joy than misery. *Psychological Science, 24*(1), 3–10.

Nesdale, D. (2011). Social groups and children's intergroup prejudice: Just how influential are social group norms? *Anales de Psicología/Annals of Psychology, 27*(3), 600–610.

Ness, J., Ahmed, A., & Aronow, W. S. (2004). Demographics and payment characteristics of nursing home residents in the United States: A 23-year trend. *Journal of Gerontology: Medical Sciences, 59A*, 1213–1217.

Netz, Y., Wu, M., Becker, B. J., & Tenenbaum, G. (2005). Physical activity and psychological well-being in advanced age: A meta-analysis of intervention studies. *Psychology and Aging, 20*, 272–284.

Neugarten, B. L. (1967). The awareness of middle age. In R. Owen (Ed.), *Middle age.* London: BBC.

Neugarten, B. L., & Neugarten, D. A. (1987, May). The changing meanings of age. *Psychology Today,* pp. 29–33.

Neugarten, B. L., Havinghurst, R. & Tobin, S. (1968). Personality and patterns of aging. In B. Neugarten (Ed.). *Middle age and aging.* Chicago: University of Chicago Press.

Neugarten, B. L., Moore, J. W., & Lowe, J. C. (1965). Age norms, age constraints, and adult socialization. *American Journal of Sociology, 70*, 710–717.

Neumark, D. (2008). *Reassessing the age discrimination in employment act* (Research Report No. 2008–09). Washington, DC: AARP Public Policy Institute. Retrieved from http://www.socsci.uci.edu/~dneumark/2008_09_adea.pdf

Neupert, S. D., Almeida, D. M., Mroczek, D. K., & Spiro, A. (2006). Daily stressors and memory failures in a naturalistic setting; Findings from the VA Normative Aging Study. *Psychology and Aging, 21*, 424–429.

Newcomb, A. F., & Bagwell, C. L. (1995). Children's friendship relations: A meta-analytic review. *Psychological Bulletin, 117*(2), 306–347.

Newman, D. L., Caspi, A., Moffitt, T. E., & Silva, P. A. (1997). Antecedents of adult interpersonal functioning: Effects of individual differences in age 3 temperament. *Developmental Psychology, 33*, 206–217.

Newman, K. S. (2008, December). Ties that bind: Cultural interpretations of delayed adulthood in Western Europe and Japan. In *Sociological Forum* (Vol. 23, No. 4, pp. 645-669). Hoboken, NJ: Blackwell Publishing Ltd.

Newman, K., & Aptekar, S. (2007). Sticking around: Delayed departure from the parental nest in Western Europe. In S. Danziger & C. Rouse (Eds.), *The price of independence: The economics of early adulthood* (pp. 207–230). New York: Russell Sage Foundation.

Newman, R. S. (2005). The cocktail party effect in infants revisited: Listening to one's name in noise. *Developmental Psychology, 41*, 352–362.

Newman, S. (2003). The living conditions of elderly Americans. *Gerontologist, 43*, 99–109.

Newton, K. M., Reed, S. D., LaCroix, A. Z., Grothaus, L. C., Ehrlich, K., & Guiltinan, J. (2006). Treatment of vasomotor symptoms of menopause with black cohosh, multibotanicals, soy, hormone therapy, or placebo: A randomized trial. *Annals of Internal Medicine, 145*(12), 869–879.

Neyfakh, L. (2014, August 31). What "age segregation" does to America. *Boston Globe.* Retrieved from www.bostonglobe.com/ideas/2014/08/30/what-age-segregation-does-america/o568E8xoAQ7VG6F4grjLxH/story.html

Ng, M., De Montigny, J. G., Ofner, M., Do, M. T. (2017). Environmental factors associated with autism spectrum disorder: A scoping review for the years 2003-2013. *Health Promotion and Chronic Disease Prevention in Canada, 37,* 1–23.

Ngun, T. C., & Vilain, E. (2014). The biological basis of human sexual orientation: Is there a role for epigenetics. *Adv. Genet, 86*, 167–184.

Nguyen, B. H., Pérusse, D., Paquet, J., Petit, D., Boivin, M., Tremblay, R. E., & Montplaisir, J. (2008). Sleep terrors in children: a prospective study of twins. *Pediatrics, 122*(6), e1164–e1167.

NICHD Early Child Care Research Network. (1997). The effects of infant child care on infant-mother attachment security: Results of the NICHD Study of Early Child Care. *Child Development,* 860–879.

NICHD Early Child Care Research Network. (1999a). Child outcomes when child care center classes meet recommended standards for quality. *American Journal of Public Health, 89,* 1072–1077.

NICHD Early Child Care Research Network. (2000). The relation of child care to cognitive and language development. *Child Development, 71*, 960–980.

NICHD Early Child Care Research Network. (2002). Child-care structure, process, and outcome: Direct and indirect effects of child-care quality on young children's development. *Psychological Science, 13*, 199–206.

NICHD Early Child Care Research Network. (2003). Does amount of time spent in child care predict socioemotional adjustment during the transition to kindergarten? *Child Development, 74*, 976–1005.

NICHD Early Child Care Research Network. (2004b). Does class size in first grade relate to children's academic and social performance or observed classroom processes? *Developmental Psychology, 40*, 651–664.

NICHD Early Child Care Research Network. (2005a). Duration and developmental timing of poverty and children's cognitive and social development from birth through third grade. *Child Development, 76*, 795–810.

NICHD Early Child Care Research Network. (2005b). Pathways to reading: The role of oral language in the transition to reading. *Developmental Psychology, 41*, 428–442.

NICHD Early Child Care Research Network. (2005c). Predicting individual differences in attention, memory, and planning in first graders from experiences at home, child care, and school. *Developmental Psychology, 41*, 99–114.

Nickerson, A. B., & Nagel, R. J. (2005). Parent and peer attachment in late childhood and early adolescence. *Journal of Early Adolescence, 25,* 223–249.

Nicolaisen, M., & Thorsen, K. (2017). What are friends for? Friendships and loneliness over the lifespan—From 18 to 79 years. *The International Journal of Aging and Human Development, 84*(2), 126–158.

Nielsen, M., Suddendorf, T., & Slaughter, V. (2006). Mirror self-recognition beyond the face. *Child Development, 77*, 176–185.

Nieschlag, E., Behre, H.M., Bouchard, P., Corrales, J.J., Jones, T.H., Stalla, G.K., Webb, S.M., & Wu, F.C.W. (2004). Testosterone replacement therapy: Current trends and future directions. *Human Reproduction Update*, 10, 409–419.

Nieuwenhuijsen, M. J., Dadvand, P., Grellier, J., Martinez, D., & Vrijheid, M. (2013). Environmental risk factors of pregnancy outcomes: a summary of recent meta-analyses of epidemiological studies. *Environmental Health, 12*(1), 6.

NIH Staff. (2007, March). *Why populations aging matters: A global perspective.* Retrieved from National Institute on Aging: www.nia.nih.gov/sites/default/files/2017-06/WPAM.pdf

Nihtilä, E., & Martikainen, P. (2008). Why older people living with a spouse are less likely to be institutionalized: The role of socioeconomic factors and health characteristics. *Scandinavian Journal of Public Health, 36*, 35–43.

Nikolas, M. A., & Burt, S. A. (2010). Genetic and environmental influences on ADHD symptom dimensions of inattention and hyperactivity: a meta-analysis. *Journal of abnormal psychology, 119*(1), 1.

Nilsen, E. S., & Graham, S. A. (2009). The relations between children's communicative perspective-taking and executive functioning. *Cognitive Psychology, 58,* 220-249.

Nirmala, A., Reddy, B. M., & Reddy, P. P. (2008). Genetics of human obesity: An overview. *International Journal of Human Genetics, 8,* 217-226.

Nisbett, R. E. (2005). Heredity, environment, and race differences in IQ: A commentary on Rushton and Jensen (2005). *Psychology, Public Policy, and Law, 11,* 302-310.

Nisbett, R. E., Aronson, J., Blair, C., Dickens, W., Flynn, J., Halpern, D. F., & Turkheimer, E. (2012). Group differences in IQ are best understood as environmental in origin. *American Psychologist, 67,* 503-504. doi:10.1037/a0029772

Nisbett, R. E., Aronson, J., Blair, C., Dickens, W., Flynn, J., Halpern, D. F., & Turkheimer, E. (2012). Intelligence: new findings and theoretical developments. *American Psychologist, 67*(2), 130.

Nobes, G., Panagiotaki, G., & Pawson, C. (2009). The influence of negligence, intentions and outcome on children's moral judgments. *Journal of Experimental Child Psychology, 104*(4), 382-397.

Noble, Y., & Boyd, R. (2012). Neonatal assessments for the preterm infant up to 4 months corrected age: a systematic review. *Developmental Medicine & Child Neurology, 54*(2), 129-139.

Nock, M. K., Borges, G., Bromet, E. J., Alonso, J., Angermeyer, M., Beautrais, A., . . . Williams, D. (2008). Cross-national prevalence and risk factors for suicidal ideation, plans and attempts. *British Journal of Psychiatry, 192,* 98-105.

Nock, M. K., Green, J. G., Hwang, I., McLaughlin, K. A., Sampson, N. A., Zaslavsky, A. M., & Kessler, R. C. (2013). Prevalence, correlates, and treatment of lifetime suicidal behavior among adolescents: results from the National Comorbidity Survey Replication Adolescent Supplement. *JAMA Psychiatry, 70*(3), 300-310.

Noël, P. H., Williams, J. W., Unutzer, J., Worchel, J., Lee, S., Cornell, J., . . . Hunkeler, E. (2004). Depression and comorbid illness in elderly primary care patients: Impact on multiple domains of health status and well-being. *Annals of Family Medicine, 2,* 555-562.

Noël-Miller, C. (2010). Spousal loss, children, and the risk of nursing home admission. *Journals of Gerontology Series B: Psychological Sciences and Social Sciences, 65*(3), 370-380.

Noël-Miller, C. M. (2011). Partner caregiving in older cohabiting couples. *Journals of Gerontology Series B: Psychological Sciences and Social Sciences, 66*(3), 341-353.

Noller, P. (2005). Sibling relationships in adolescence: Learning and growing together. *Personal Relationships, 12*(1), 1-22.

Noriuchi, M., Kikuchi, Y., & Senoo, A. (2008). The functional neuroanatomy of maternal love: Mother's response to infant's attachment behaviors. *Biological Psychiatry, 63,* 415-423.

Northwestern University Center on Human Development. (2014). Revised parenting in the age of digital technology: A national survey. Retrieved from http://cmhd.northwestern.edu/wp-content/uploads/2015/06/Parenting AgeDigitalTechnology.REVISED.FINAL_.2014.pdf

Norton, A. J., & Moorman, J. E. (1987). Current trends in marriage and divorce among American women. *Journal of Marriage and the Family, 49*(1), 3-14.

Norton, D. E. (2010). *Through the eyes of a child: An introduction to children's literature* (8th ed.). Boston: Prentice-Hall.

Nosraty, L., Jylha, M., Raittila, T. & Lumme-Sandt, K. (2015). Perceptions by the oldest old of successful aging, Vitality 90+ study. *Journal of Aging Studies, 32,* 50-58.

Nucci, L., Hasebe, Y., & Lins-Dyer, M. T. (2005). Adolescent psychological well-being and parental control. In J. Smetana (Ed.), *Changing boundaries of parental authority during adolescence* (New Directions for Child and Adolescent Development, No. 108, pp. 17-30). San Francisco: Jossey-Bass.

Nurnberg, H. G., Hensley, P. L., Gelenberg, A. J., Fava, M., Lauriello, J., & Paine, S. (2003). Treatment of antidepressant- associated sexual dysfunction with sildenafil. *Journal of the American Medical Association, 289,* 56-64.

Nussbaum, R. L. (1998). Putting the parkin into Parkinson's. *Nature, 392,* 544-545.

Oberman, L. M., & Ramachandran, V. S. (2007). The simulating social mind: The role of the mirror neuron system and simulation in the social and communicative deficits of autism spectrum disorders. *Psychological Bulletin, 133,* 310-327.

Obradovic, J., Stamperdahl, J., Bush, N. R., Adler, N. E., & Boyce, W. T. (2010). Biological sensitivity to context: The interactive effects of stress reactivity and family adversity on socioemotional behavior and school readiness. *Child Development, 81,* 270-289.

Odden, H., & Rochat, P. (2004). Observational learning and enculturation. *Educational and Child Psychology, 21*(2), 39-50.

Odgers, C., Caspi, A., Nagin, D., Piquero, A., Slutske, W., Milne, B., . . . Moffitt, T. E. (2008). Is it important to prevent early exposure to drugs and alcohol among adolescents? *Psychological Science, 19*(10), 1037-1044.

Organization for Economic Cooperation and Development (OECD). (2017). *Obesity Update 2017.* Retrieved from www.oecd.org/els/health-systems/Obesity-Update-2017.pdf

Oeppen, J., & Vaupel, J. W. (2002). Broken limits to life expectancy. *Science, 296*(5570), 1029-1031.

Offer, D., & Church, R. B. (1991). Generation gap. In R. M. Lerner, A. C. Petersen, & J. Brooks-Gunn (Eds.), *Encyclopedia of adolescence* (pp. 397-399). New York: Garland.

Offer, D., Kaiz, M., Ostrov, E., & Albert, D. B. (2002). Continuity in family constellation. *Adolescent and Family Health, 3,* 3-8.

Offer, D., Offer, M. K., & Ostrov, E. (2004). *Regular guys: 34 years beyond adolescence.* Dordrecht, The Netherlands: Kluwer-Academic.

Office for National Statistics. (2015, August 06). *Internet access–households and individuals 2015.* Retrieved from Office for National Statistics: http://webarchive.nationalarchives.gov.uk/20160106051923/; http://www.ons.gov.uk/ons/dcp171778_412758.pdf

Office of Management and Budget. (2011). *Fiscal year 2012 budget of the U.S. government.* Washington, DC: Executive Office of the President.

Office of Minority Health, Centers for Disease Control and Prevention. (2005). Health disparities experienced by Black or African Americans–United States. *Morbidity and Mortality Weekly Report, 54,* 1-3.

Offit, P. A., Quarles, J., Gerber, M. A., Hackett, C. J., Marcuse, E. K., Kollman, T. R., . . . Landry, S. (2002). Addressing parents' concerns: Do multiple vaccines overwhelm or weaken the infant's immune system? *Pediatrics, 109,* 124-129.

Ofori, B., Oraichi, D., Blais, L., Rey, E., & Berard, A. (2006). Risk of congenital anomalies in pregnant users of non-steroidal anti-inflammatory drugs: A nested case-control study. *Birth Defects Research Part B: Developmental and Reproductive Toxicology, 77*(4), 268-279.

Ogden, C. L., Carroll, M. D., Curtin, L. R., Lamb, M. M., & Flegal, K. M. (2010). Prevalence of high body mass index in U.S. children and adolescents, 2007-2008. *Journal of the American Medical Association, 303*(3), 242-249.

Ogden, C. L., Carroll, M. D., Fryar, C. D., & Flegal, K. M. (2015). *Prevalence of obesity among adults and youth: United States, 2011-2014* (pp. 1-8). Washington, DC: US Department of Health and Human Services, Centers for Disease Control and Prevention, National Center for Health Statistics.

Ogden, C. L., Carroll, M. D., McDowell, M. A., & Flegal, K. M. (2007). Obesity among adults in the United States: No change since 2003-2004. *NCHS Data Brief.* Hyattsville, MD: National Center for Health Statistics.

M., Blanco, C., Wang, S., Laje, G., & Correll, C. U. (2014). National trends in the mental health care of children, adolescents, and adults by office-based physicians. *JAMA Psychiatry, 71*(1), 81-90.

Olfson, M., Crystal, S., Huang, C., & Gerhard, T. (2010). Trends in antipsychotic drug use by very young, privately insured children. *Journal of Child and Adolescent Psychiatry, 49*(1), 13-23.

Ollendick, T. H., Yang, B., King, N. J., Dong, Q., & Akande, A. (1996). Fears in American, Australian, Chinese, and Nigerian children and adolescents: A cross-cultural study. *Journal of Child Psychology and Psychiatry, 37,* 213-220.

Olshansky, S. J., Passaro, D. J., Hershow, R. C., Layden, J., Carnes, B. A., Brody, J., . . . Ludwig, D. S. (2005). A potential decline in life expectancy in the United States in the 21st century. *New England Journal of Medicine, 352,* 1138-1145.

Olson, K. R., & Spelke, E. S. (2008). Foundations of cooperation in young children. *Cognition, 108,* 222-231.

Olson, M. E., Diekema, D., Elliott, B. A., & Renier, C. M. (2010). Impact of income and income inequality on infant health outcomes in the United States. *Pediatrics, 126*(6), 1165-1173.

Olsson, B., Lautner, R., Andreasson, U., Öhrfelt, A., Portelius, E., Bjerke, M., . . . & Wu, E. (2016). CSF and blood biomarkers for the diagnosis of Alzheimer's disease: a systematic review and meta-analysis. *The Lancet Neurology, 15*(7), 673-684.

Olthof, T., Schouten, A., Kuiper, H., Stegge, H., & Jennekens-Schinkel, A. (2000). Shame and guilt in children: Differential situational antecedents and experiential correlates. *British Journal of Developmental Psychology, 18*, 51-64.

Olweus, D. (1995). Bullying or peer abuse at school: Facts and intervention. *Current Directions in Psychological Science, 4*, 196-200.

Ono, M., & Harley, V. R. (2013). Disorders of sex development: new genes, new concepts. *Nature Reviews Endocrinology, 9*(2), 79-91.

Oostenbroek, J., Suddendorf, T., Nielsen, M., Redshaw, J., Kennedy-Costantini, S., Davis, J., . . . & Slaughter, V. (2016). Comprehensive longitudinal study challenges the existence of neonatal imitation in humans. *Current Biology, 26*(10), 1334-1338.

Opfer, J. E., & Gelman, S. A. (2011). Development of the animate-inanimate distinction. *The Wiley-Blackwell handbook of childhood cognitive development* (2nd ed., pp. 213-238). Hoboken, NJ: Wiley.

Orathinkal, J., & Vansteenwegen, A. (2007). Do demographics affect marital satisfaction? *Journal of Sex & Marital Therapy, 33*(1), 73-85.

Orbuch, T. L., House, J. S., Mero, R. P., & Webster, P. S. (1996). Marital quality over the life course. *Social Psychology Quarterly, 59*, 162-171.

Oregon Public Health Division. (2016). Oregon death with dignity act: 2015 data summary [report]. Retrieved from www.oregon.gov/oha/ph/ProviderPartnerResources/EvaluationResearch/DeathwithDignityAct/Documents/year18.pdf

Orenstein, P. (2002, April 21). Mourning my miscarriage. *The New York Times.* Retrieved from www.NYTimes.com

Orentlicher, D. (1996). The legalization of physician-assisted suicide. *New England Journal of Medicine, 335*, 663-667.

Organization for Economic Cooperation and Development (OECD). (2008). *Education at a glance.* Paris, France: Author.

Organization for Economic Cooperation and Development. (2015). The ABC of gender equity in education: Aptitude, behavior, confidence. Retrieved from www.oecd.org/pisa/keyfindings/pisa-2012-results-gender-eng.pdf

Organization for Economic Cooperation and Development. (2016a). Country note: Key findings from the PISA 2015 from the United States. Retrieved from www.oecd.org/pisa/PISA-2015-United-States.pdf

Organization for Economic Cooperation and Development. (2016b). PISA 2015 results in focus. Retrieved from www.oecd.org/pisa/pisa-2015-results-in-focus.pdf

Organization for Economic Cooperation and Development (OCED). (2004). Education at a glance: OECD indicators—2004. *Education & Skills, 2004*(14), 1-456.

Orth, U., Trzesniewski, K. H., & Robins, R. W. (2010). Self-esteem development from young adulthood to old age: A cohort-sequential longitudinal study. *Journal of Personality and Social Psychology, 98*, 645-658. doi: 10.1037/a0018769

Ortman, J. M., Velkoff, V. A., & Hogan, H. (2014). *An aging nation: the older population in the United States,* P25-1140. Washington, DC: United States Census Bureau, Economics and Statistics Administration, U.S. Department of Commerce.

Osborne, C., Manning, W. D., & Smock, P. J. (2007). Married and cohabiting parents' relationship stability: A focus on race and ethnicity. *Journal of Marriage and Family, 69*(5), 1345-1366.

Osgood, D. W., Ruth, G., Eccles, J., Jacobs, J., & Barber, B. (2005). Six paths to adulthood: Fast starters, parents without careers, educated partners, educated singles, working singles, and slow starters. In R. A. Settersten Jr., F. F. Furstenberg Jr., & R. G. Rumbaut (Eds.), *On the frontier of adulthood: Theory, research, and public policy* (pp. 320-355). Chicago: University of Chicago Press.

Ossorio, P., & Duster, T. (2005). Race and genetics: Controversies in biomedical, behavioral, and forensic sciences. *American Psychologist, 60*, 115-128.

Osterberg, E.C., Bernie, A.M., & Ramasamy, R. (2014). Risks of testosterone replacement therapy in men. *Indian Journal of Urology*, 30, 2-7.

Osterman, M. J., & Martin, J. A. (2011). Epidural and spinal anesthesia use during labor: 27-state reporting area, 2008. *National Vital Statistics Reports: from the Centers for Disease Control and Prevention, National Center for Health Statistics, National Vital Statistics System, 59*(5), 1-13.

Ostfeld, B. M., Esposity, L., Perl, H., & Hegyl, T. (2010). Concurrent risks in sudden infant death syndrome. *Pediatrics, 125*(3), 447-453.

Otis, A. S. (1993). *Otis-Lennon School Ability Test: OLSAT.* New York: The Psychological Corp.

Otis, M. D., Rostosky, S. S., Riggle, E. D., & Hamrin, R. (2006). Stress and relationship quality in same-sex couples. *Journal of Social and Personal Relationships, 23*(1), 81-99.

Otsuka, R., Watanabe, H., Hirata, K., Tokai, K., Muro, T., Yoshiyama, M., Takeuchi, K., & Yoshikawa, J. (2001). Acute effects of passive smoking on the coronary circulation in healthy young adults. *Journal of the American Medical Association, 286*, 436-441.

Ouellette, G. P., & Sénéchal, M. (2008). A window into early literacy: Exploring the cognitive and linguistic underpinnings of invented spelling. *Scientific Studies of Reading, 12*(2), 195-219.

Overstreet, S., Devine, J., Bevans, K., & Efreom, Y. (2005). Predicting parental involvement in children's schooling within an economically disadvantaged African American sample. *Psychology in the Schools, 42*(1), 101-111.

Owen, J., & Fincham, F. D. (2011). Effects of gender and psychosocial factors on "friends with benefits" relationships among young adults. *Archives of Sexual Behavior, 40*(2), 311-320.

Owens, J., & Adolescent Sleep Working Group. (2014). Insufficient sleep in adolescents and young adults: An update on causes and consequences. *Pediatrics, 134*(3), e921-e932.

Owens, R. E. (1996). *Language development* (4th ed.). Boston: Allyn & Bacon.

Owsley, C. (2011). Aging and vision. *Vision Research, 51*(13), 1610-1622.

Ozmeral, E. J., Eddins, A. C., Frisina, D. R., & Eddins, D. A. (2016). Large cross-sectional study of presbycusis reveals rapid progressive decline in auditory temporal acuity. *Neurobiology of Aging, 43*, 72-78.

Ozonoff, S., Young, G.S., Carter, A., Messinger, D., Yirimiya, N., Zwaigenbaum, L., . . . & Stone, W.L. (2011). Recurrence risk for autism spectrum disorders: A baby siblings research consortium study. *Pediatrics, 128.* doi: 10.1542/peds. 2010-2825

O'Brien, C. M., & Jeffery, H. E. (2002). Sleep deprivation, disorganization and fragmentation during opiate withdrawal in newborns. *Pediatric Child Health, 38*, 66-71.

O'Connor, T., Heron, J., Golding, J., Beveridge, M., & Glover, V. (2002). Maternal antenatal anxiety and children's behavioural/emotional problems at 4 years. *British Journal of Psychiatry, 180*, 502-508.

O'Donnell, K. (2006). *Adult education participation in 2004-06* (NCES 2006-077). Washington, DC: National Center for Education Statistics.

O'Donnell, K., Badrick, E., Kumari, M., & Steptoe, A. (2008). Psychological coping styles and cortisol over the day in healthy older adults. *Psychoneuroendocrinology, 33*(5), 601-611.

O'Flynn O'Brien, K. L., Varghese, A. C., & Agarwal, A. (2010). The genetic causes of male factor infertility: A review. *Fertility and Sterility, 93*, 1-12.

O'Hara, M. W., & McCabe, J. E. (2013). Postpartum depression: Current status and future directions. *Annual Review of Clinical Psychology, 9, 379-407.*

O'Higgins, M., Roberts, I. S., Glover, V., & Taylor, A. (2013). Mother-child bonding at 1 year: Associations with symptoms of postnatal depression and bonding in the first few weeks. *Archives of Women's Mental Health, 16*, 381-389.

O'Keefe, L. (2014, June 24). Parents who read to their children nurture more than literary skills. Retrieved from AAP News: www.aappublications.org/content/early/2014/06/24/aap-news.20140624-2

Özçalışkan, Ş., & Goldin-Meadow, S. (2010). Sex differences in language first appear in gesture. *Developmental Science, 13*(5), 752-760.

Özen, S., & Darcan, Ş. (2011). Effects of environmental endocrine disruptors on pubertal development. *Journal of Clinical Research in Pediatric Endocrinology, 3*(1), 1.

Pace, G. T., Shafer, K., Jensen, T. M., & Larson, J. H. (2015). Stepparenting issues and relationship quality: The role of clear communication. *Journal of Social Work, 15*(1), 24-44.

Pace-Schott, E. F., & Spencer, R. M. (2014). Sleep loss in older adults: Effects on waking performance and sleep-dependent memory consolidation with healthy aging and insomnia. In *Sleep deprivation and disease* (pp. 185-197). New York: Springer.

Padilla, A. M., Lindholm, K. J., Chen, A., Duran, R., Hakuta, K., Lambert, W., & Tucker, G. R. (1991). The English-only movement: Myths, reality, and implications for psychology. *American Psychologist, 46*(2), 120-130.

Pagani, L. S., Fitzpatrick, C., Barnett, T. A., & Dubow, E. (2010). Prospective associations between early childhood television exposure and academic, psychosocial, and physical well-being by middle childhood. *Archives of Pediatrics & Adolescent Medicine, 164*(5), 425-431.

Pal, S., & Tyler, J. K. (2016). Epigenetics and aging. *Science Advances, 2*(7), e1600584.

Palacios, J., & Brodzinsky, D. (2010). Adoption research: Trends, topics, outcomes. *International Journal of Behavioral Development, 34*(3), 270-284.

Paley, B., & O'Connor, M. J. (2011). Behavioral interventions for children and adolescents with Fetal Alcohol Spectrum Disorders. *Alcohol Research and Health, 34,* 64-75.

Pamuk, E., Makuc, D., Heck, K., Reuben, C., & Lochner, K. (1998). Socioeconomic status and health chartbook. In *Health, United States, 1998.* Hyattsville, MD: National Center for Health Statistics.

Pan, B. A., Rowe, M. L., Singer, J. D., & Snow, C. E. (2005). Maternal correlates of growth in toddler vocabulary production in low-income families. *Child Development, 76,* 763-782.

Pandharipande, P. P., Girard, T. D., Jackson, J. C., Morandi, A., Thompson, J. L., Pun, B. T., . . . & Moons, K. G. (2013). Long-term cognitive impairment after critical illness. *New England Journal of Medicine, 369*(14), 1306-1316.

Panigrahy, A., Filiano, J., Sleeper, L. A., Mandell, F., Valdes-Dapena, M., Krous, H. F., . . . Kinney, H. C. (2000). Decreased serotonergic receptor binding in rhombic lip-derived regions of the medulla oblongata in the sudden infant death syndrome. *Journal of Neuropathology and Experimental Neurology, 59,* 377-384.

Panza, F., Logroscino, G., Imbimbo, B. P., & Solfrizzi, V. (2014). Is there still any hope for amyloid-based immunotherapy for Alzheimer's disease? *Current Opinion in Psychiatry, 27*(2), 128-137.

Papadatou-Pastou, M., Martin, M., Munafo, M., & Jones, G. (2008). Sex differences in left-handedness: A meta-analysis of 144 studies. *American Psychological Association Bulletin, 134*(5), 677-699.

Papadimitriou, A. (2016). Timing of puberty and secular trend in human maturation. In *Puberty* (pp. 121-136). New York: Springer International Publishing.

Papuć, E., & Rejdak, K. (2017). Does myelin play the leading role in Alzheimer's disease pathology. *J Alzheimers Dis Parkinsonism, 7*(321), 2161-0460.

Park, D. C., & Gutchess, A. H. (2005). Long-term memory and aging: A cognitive neuroscience perspective. In R. Cabeza, L. Nyberg, & D. C. Park (Eds.), *Cognitive neuroscience of aging: linking cognitive and cerebral aging* (pp. 218-245). New York: Oxford University Press.

Park, D. C., & Reuter-Lorenz, P. (2009). The adaptive brain: Aging and neurocognitive scaffolding. *Annual Review of Psychology, 60*(1), 173-176.

Park, D., & Gutchess, A. (2006). The cognitive neuroscience of aging and culture. *Current Directions in Psychological Science, 15,* 105-108.

Park, J. M., Metraux, S., & Culhane, D. P. (2010). Behavioral health services use among heads of homeless and housed poor families. *Journal of Health Care for the Poor and Underserved, 21*(2), 582-590.

Park, M. J., Mulye, T. P., Adams, S. H., Brindis, C. D., & Irwin, C. E. (2006). The health status of young adults in the United States. *Journal of Adolescent Health, 39,* 305-317.

Park, S., Belsky, J., Putnam, S., & Crnic, K. (1997). Infant emotionality, parenting, and 3-year inhibition: Exploring stability and lawful discontinuity in a male sample. *Developmental Psychology, 33,* 218-227.

Parke, R. D. (2004a). Development in the family. *Annual Review of Psychology, 55,* 365-399.

Parke, R. D. (2004b). The Society for Research in Child Development at 70: Progress and promise. *Child Development, 75,* 1-24.

Parke, R. D., & Buriel, R. (1998). Socialization in the family: Ethnic and ecological perspectives. In W. Damon (Series Ed.) & N. Eisenberg (Vol. Ed.), *Handbook of child psychology: Vol. 3. Social, emotional, and personality development* (5th ed., pp. 463-552). New York: Wiley.

Parke, R. D., Grossman, K., & Tinsley, R. (1981). Father-mother-infant interaction in the newborn period: A German-American comparison. In T. M. Field, A. M. Sostek, P. Viete, & P. H. Leideman (Eds.), *Culture and early interaction.* Hillsdale, NJ: Erlbaum.

Parker, J. D., Woodruff, T. J., Basu, R., & Schoendorf, K. C. (2005). Air pollution and birth weight among term infants in California. *Pediatrics, 115,* 121-128.

Parker, K. (2009a). *End-of-life decisions: How Americans cope.* Retrieved from www.pewresearch.org/

Parker, K. (2012, March 15). *The Boomerang Generation: Feeling OK about Living with Mom and Dad.* Retrieved from Pew Research Center: http://www.pewsocialtrends.org/2012/03/15/the-boomerang-generation/

Parker, K., & Patten, E. (2013, January 30). *The Sandwich Generation: Rising Financial Burdens for Middle-Aged Americans.* Retrieved from Pew Research Center: http://www.pewsocialtrends.org/2013/01/30/the-sandwich-generation/

Parker, S. E., Mai, C. T., Canfield, M. A., Rickard, R., Wang, Y., Meyer, R. E., . . . & Correa, A. (2010). Updated national birth prevalence estimates for selected birth defects in the United States, 2004-2006. *Birth Defects Research Part A: Clinical and Molecular Teratology, 88*(12), 1008-1016.

Parkes, A., Henderson, M., Wight, D., & Nixon, C. (2011). Is parenting associated with teenagers' early sexual risk-taking, autonomy and relationship with sexual partners? *Perspectives on Sexual and Reproductive Health, 43*(1), 30-40.

Parkes, C. M., Laungani, P., & Young, W. (Eds.). (2015). *Death and bereavement across cultures.* Abingdon-on-Thames, England: Routledge.

Parkes, T. L., Elia, A. J., Dickinson, D., Hilliker, A. J., Phillips, J. P., & Boulianne, G. L. (1998). Extension of Drosophila lifespan by overexpression of human SOD1 in motorneurons. *Nature Genetics, 19,* 171-174.

Parsons, C. E., Young, K. S., Rochat, T. J., Kringelbach, M. L., & Stein, A. (2012). Postnatal depression and its effects on child development: A review of evidence from low- and middle-income countries. *British Medical Bulletin, 101,* 57-79.

Partanen, E., Kujala, T., Näätänen, R., Liitola, A., Sambeth, A., & Huotilainen, M. (2013). Learning-induced neural plasticity of speech processing before birth. *Proceedings of the National Academy of Sciences, 110*(37), 15145-15150.

Parten, M. B. (1932). Social play among preschool children. *Journal of Abnormal and Social Psychology, 27,* 243-269.

Partridge, L. (2010). The new biology of ageing. *Philosophical Transactions, 365*(1537), 147-154.

Partridge, S., Balayla, J., Holcroft, C. A., & Abenhaim, H. A. (2012). Inadequate prenatal care utilization and risks of infant mortality and poor birth outcome: a retrospective analysis of 28,729,765 US deliveries over 8 years. *American Journal of Perinatology, 29*(10), 787-794.

Pascarella, E. T., Edison, M. I., Nora, A., Hagedorn, L. S., & Terenzini, P. T. (1998). Does work inhibit cognitive development during college? *Educational Evaluation and Policy Analysis, 20,* 75-93.

Passarino, G., De Rango, F., & Montesanto, A. (2016). Human longevity: Genetics or lifestyle? It takes two to tango. *Immunity and Aging,* 13. doi: 10.1186/s12979-016-0066-z

Pasterski, V. L., Geffner, M. E., Brain, C., Hindmarsh, P., Brook, C., & Hines, M. (2005). Prenatal hormones and postnatal socialization by parents as determinants of male-typical toy play in girls with congenital adrenal hyperplasia. *Child Development, 76*(1), 264-278.

Pasterski, V., Geffner, M. E., Brain, C., Hindmarsh, P., Brook, C., & Hines, M. (2011). Prenatal hormones and childhood sex segregation: playmate and play style preferences in girls with congenital adrenal hyperplasia. *Hormones and Behavior, 59*(4), 549-555.

Pastor, P. N., & Reuben, C. A. (2008). Diagnosed attention deficit hyperactivity disorder and learning disability, United States, 2004-2006. *Vital and Health Statistics, 10*(237). Hyattsville, MD: National Center for Health Statistics.

Pasupathi, M., Staudinger, U. M., & Baltes, P. B. (2001). Seeds of wisdom: Adolescents' knowledge and judgment about difficult life problems. *Developmental Psychology, 37*(3), 351-361.

Patel, H., Rosengren, A., & Ekman, I. (2004). Symptoms in acute coronary syndromes: Does sex make a difference? *American Heart Journal, 148,* 27-33.

Patel, K. V., Coppin, A. K., Manini, T. M., Lauretani, F., Bandinelli, S., Ferrucci, L., & Guralnik, J. M. (2006, August 10). Midlife physical activity and mobility in older age: The InCHIANTI Study. *American Journal of Preventive Medicine, 31*(3), 217-224.

Paton, G. (2012, October 26). Overexposure to technology 'makes children miserable'. Retrieved from *The Telegraph:* www.telegraph.co.uk/education/educationnews/9636862/Overexposure-to-technology-makes-children-miserable.html#disqus_thread uk/201601060

Patrick, S. W., & Schiff, D. M. (2017). A public health response to opioid use in pregnancy. *Pediatrics*, e20164070.

Patterson, C. J. (1992). Children of lesbian and gay parents. *Child Development, 63,* 1025-1042.

Patterson, C. J. (1995a). Lesbian mothers, gay fathers, and their children. In A. R. D'Augelli & C. J. Patterson (Eds.), *Lesbian, gay, and bisexual identities over the lifespan: Psychological perspectives* (pp. 293-320). New York: Oxford University Press.

Patterson, C. J. (1995b). Sexual orientation and human development: An overview. *Developmental Psychology, 31,* 3-11.

Patterson, T. (2017, June 15). *Why does America have so many hungry kids?* Retrieved from CNN: http://www.cnn.com/2017/06/09/health/champions-for-change-child-hunger-in-america/index.html

Patton, G. C., Coffey, C., Cappa, C., Currie, D., Riley, L., Gore, F., . . . & Mokdad, A. (2012). Health of the world's adolescents: a synthesis of internationally comparable data. *The Lancet, 379*(9826), 1665-1675.

Patton, G. C., Coffey, C., Sawyer, S. M., Viner, R. M., Haller, D. M., Bose, K. (2009, September 12). Global patterns of mortality in young people: A systematic analysis of population health data. Retrieved from *The Lancet:* http://www.thelancet.com/journals/lancet/article/PIIS0140-6736(09)60741-8/fulltext

Pauen, S. (2002). Evidence for knowledge-based category discrimination in infancy. *Child Development, 73,* 1016-1033.

Pawelski, J. G., Perrin, E. C., Foy, J. M., Allen, C. E., Crawford, J. E., Del Monte, M., . . . Vickers, D. L. (2006). The effects of marriage, civil union, and domestic partnership laws on the health and well-being of children. *Pediatrics, 118,* 349-364.

Pea, R., Nass, C., Meheula, L., Rance, M., Kumar, A., Bamford, H., Nass, M., Simha, A., Stillerman, B., Yang, S., & Zhou, M. (2012). Media use, face-to-face communication, media multitasking, and social well-being among 8- to 12-year old girls. *Developmental Psychology, 48,* 327-336.

Pearl, R. (1928). *The rate of living.* New York: Alfred A. Knopf.

Pedersen, M., Giorgis-Allemand, L., Bernard, C., Aguilera, I., Andersen, A. M. N., Ballester, F., . . . & Dedele, A. (2013). Ambient air pollution and low birthweight: a European cohort study (ESCAPE). *The Lancet Respiratory Medicine, 1*(9), 695-704.

Peek, S. T., Wouters, E. J., van Hoof, J., Luijkx, K. G., Boeije, H. R., & Vrijhoef, H. J. (2014). Factors influencing acceptance of technology for aging in place: a systematic review. *International Journal of Medical Informatics, 83*(4), 235-248.

Pegg, J. E., Werker, J. F., & McLeod, P. J. (1992). Preference for infant-directed over adult-directed speech: Evidence from 7 week old infants. *Infant Behavior and Development, 15,* 325-345.

Pellegrini, A. D., & Archer, J. (2005). Sex differences in competitive and aggressive behavior: A view from sexual selection theory. In B. J. Ellis & D. F. Bjorklund (Eds.), *Origins of the social mind: Evolutionary psychology and child development* (pp. 219-244). New York: Guilford Press.

Pellegrini, A. D., & Long, J. D. (2002). A longitudinal study of bullying, dominance, and victimization during the transition from primary school through secondary school. *British Journal of Developmental Psychology, 20,* 259-280.

Pellegrini, A. D., Dupuis, D., & Smith, P.K. (2007). Play in evolution and development. *Developmental Review, 27,* 261-276.

Pellegrini, A. D., Kato, K., Blatchford, P., & Baines, E. (2002). A short-term longitudinal study of children's playground games across the first year of school: Implications for social competence and adjustment to school. *American Educational Research Journal, 39,* 991-1015.

Pelphrey, K. A., Reznick, J. S., Davis Goldman, B., Sasson, N., Morrow, J., Donahoe, A., & Hodgson, K. (2004). Development of visuo-spatial short-term memory in the second half of the 1st year. *Developmental Psychology, 40*(5), 836.

Pennington, B. F., Moon, J., Edgin, J., Stedron, J., & Nadel, L. (2003). The neuropsychology of Down syndrome: Evidence for hippocampal dysfunction. *Child Development, 74,* 75-93.

Pennisi, E. (1998). Single gene controls fruit fly life-span. *Science, 282,* 856.

Pennsylvania Department of Aging (2017). Wolf administration honors America's oldest resident, Pennsylvanian Delphine Gibson. Retrieved from www.prnewswire.com/news-releases/wolf-administration-honors-americas-oldest-resident-pennsylvanian-delphine-gibson-300415348.html

Pepper, S. C. (1942). *World hypotheses.* Berkeley: University of California Press.

Pepper, S. C. (1961). *World hypotheses.* Berkeley: University of California Press.

Pereira, M. A., Kartashov, A. I., Ebbeling, C. B., Van Horn, L., Slattery, M. L., Jacobs, D. R., Jr., & Ludwig, D. S. (2005). Fast-food habits, weight gain, and insulin resistance (the CARDIA study): 15-year prospective analysis. *Lancet, 365,* 36-42.

Perelli-Harris, B., Styrc, M. E., Addo, F., Hoherz, S., Lappegard, T., Sassler, S., & Evans, A. (2017). Comparing the benefits of cohabitation and marriage for health in mid-life: Is the relationship similar across countries? ESRC Centre for Population Change working paper 84.

Perera, F. P., Rauh, V., Whyatt, R. M., Tsai, W. Y., Bernert, J. T., Tu, Y.-H., . . . Tang, D. (2004). Molecular evidence of an interaction between prenatal environmental exposures and birth outcomes in a multiethnic population. *Environmental Health Perspectives, 112,* 626-630.

Perera, F., Tang, W-y., Herbstman, J., Tang, D., Levin, L., Miller, R., & Ho, S.-m. (2009). Relation of DNA methylation of 5'-CpG island of *ACSL3* to transplacental exposure to airborne polycyclic aromatic hydrocarbons and childhood asthma. *PloS ONE, 4,* e44-e48.

Perkins, H. S. (2007). Controlling death: The false promise of advance directives. *Annals of Internal Medicine, 147*(1), 51-57.

Perkins, K.M., Boulet, S.L., Jamieson, D.J., & Kissin, D.M. (2016). Trends and outcomes of gestational surrogacy in the United States. *Fertility and Sterility,* 106, 435-442.

Perou, R., Bitsko, R. H., Blumberg, S. J., Pastor, P., Ghandour, R. M., Gfroerer, J. C., . . . & Parks, S. E. (2013). Mental health surveillance among children—United States, 2005-2011. *MMWR Surveill Summ, 62*(Suppl 2), 1-35.

Perrin, E. C., Siegel, B. S., & Committee on Psychosocial Aspects of Child and Family Health. (2013). Promoting the well-being of children whose parents are gay or lesbian. *Pediatrics, 131*(4), e1374-e1383.

Perrin, E. M., Finkle, J. P., & Benjamin, J. T. (2007). Obesity prevention and the primary care pediatrician's office. *Current Opinion in Pediatrics, 19*(3), 354-361.

Perry, W. G. (1970). *Forms of intellectual and ethical development in the college years: A scheme.* New York: Holt, Rinehart and Winston. Cerca con Google.

Pesonen, A., Raïkkönen, K., Keltikangas-Järvinen, L., Strandberg, T., & Järvenpää, A. (2003). Parental perception of infant temperament: Does parents' joint attachment matter? *Infant Behavior and Development, 26,* 167-182.

Peter, K., & Horn, L. (2005). *Gender differences in participation and completion of undergraduate education and how they have changed over time* (NCES 2005-169). Washington, DC: U.S. Government Printing Office.

Peters, E., Hess, T. M., Västfjäll, D., & Auman, C. (2007). Adult age differences in dual information processes: Implications for the role of affective and deliberative processes in older adults' decision making. *Perspectives on Psychological Science, 2*(1), 1-23.

Peters, R., Peters, J., Warner, J., Beckett, N., & Bulpitt, C. (2008). Alcohol, dementia and cognitive decline in the elderly: A systematic review. *Age and Ageing, 37*(5), 505-512.

Petersen, A. C. (1993). Presidential address: Creating adolescents: The role of context and process in developmental transitions. *Journal of Research on Adolescents, 3*(1), 1-18.

Peterson, B. E. (2002). Longitudinal analysis of midlife generativity, intergenerational roles, and caregiving. *Psychology and Aging, 17,* 161-168.

Peterson, B. E., & Duncan, L. E. (2007). Midlife women's generativity and authoritarianism: Marriage, motherhood and 10 years of aging. *Psychology and Aging, 22*(3), 411-419.

Peterson, B. E., & Stewart, A. J. (1996). Antecedents and contexts of generativity motivation at midlife. *Psychology and Aging, 11*(1), 21.

Peterson, C. (2011). Children's memory reports over time: Getting both better and worse. *Journal of Experimental Child Psychology, 109*(3), 275-293.

Petit, D., Touchette, E., Tremblay, R. E., Boivin, M., & Montplaisir, J. (2007). Dyssomnias and parasomnias in early childhoold. *Pediatrics, 119*(5), e1016-e1025.

Petitti, D. B. (2002). Hormone replacement therapy for prevention: More evidence, more pessimism. *Journal of the American Medical Association, 288*, 99-101.

Petitto, L. A., & Kovelman, I. (2003). The bilingual paradox: How signing-speaking bilingual children help us to resolve it and teach us about the brain's mechanisms underlying all language acquisition. *Learning Languages, 8*, 5-18.

Petitto, L. A., & Marentette, P. F. (1991). Babbling in the manual mode: Evidence for the ontogeny of language. *Science, 251*, 1493-1495.

Petitto, L. A., Holowka, S., Sergio, L., & Ostry, D. (2001). Language rhythms in babies' hand movements. *Nature, 413*, 35-36.

Petkus, A. J., Beam, C. R., Johnson, W., Kaprio, J., Korhonen, T., McGue, M., . . . & IGEMS Consortium. (2017). Gene-environment interplay in depressive symptoms: Moderation by age, sex, and physical illness. *Psychological Medicine, 47*(10), 1836-1847.

Petrill, S. A., Lipton, P. A., Hewitt, J. K., Plomin, R., Cherny, S. S., Corley, R., & DeFries, J. C. (2004). Genetic and environmental contributions to general cognitive ability through the first 16 years of life. *Developmental Psychology, 40*, 805-812.

Petrosino, A. J., Guckenburg, S., & Turpin-Petrosino, C. (2013). *Formal system processing of juveniles: Effects on delinquency* (Vol. 9). Washington, DC: U.S. Department of Justice, Office of Community Oriented Policing Services.

Petrosino, A., Turpin-Petrosino, C., Hollis-Peel, M. E., & Lavenberg, J. G. (2013). 'Scared Straight' and other juvenile awareness programs for preventing juvenile delinquency. *The Cochrane Library*.

Pettit, G. S., & Arsiwalla, D. D. (2008). Commentary on special section on "bidirectional parent-child relationships": The continuing evolution of dynamic, transactional models of parenting and youth behavior problems. *Journal of Abnormal Child Psychology, 36*(5), 711.

Pettit, G. S., Bates, J. E., & Dodge, K. A. (1997). Supportive parenting, ecological context, and children's adjustment: A seven-year longitudinal study. *Child Development, 68*, 908-923.

Pew Research Center (2013). Views on end-of-life medical treatment: Growing minority of Americans say doctors should do everything possible to keep patients alive [report]. Retrieved from www.pewforum.org/2013/11/21/views-on-end-of-life-medical-treatments/

Pew Research Center. (2007a). *As marriage and parenthood drift apart, public is concerned about social impact.* Retrieved from http://pewsocialtrends.org/2007/07/01/as-marriage-and-parenthood-drift-apart-public-is-concerned-about-social-impact/

Pew Research Center. (2007b). *Modern marriage.* Retrieved from http://pewsocialtrends.org/2007/07/18/modern-marriage/

Pew Research Center. (2012). *More support for gun rights, gay marriage, than in 2008 or 2004.* Retrieved from www.people-press.org/2012/04/25/more-support-for-gun-rights-gay-marriage-than-in-2008-or-2004/

Pew Research Center. (2015). U.S. public becoming less religious: Modest drop in overall rates of belief, but religiously affiliated Americans are as observant as ever [report]. Retrieved from www.pewforum.org/2015/11/03/u-s-public-becoming-less-religious/

Pew Research Center. (2017). *Support for same-sex marriage grows, even among groups that had been skeptical.* Retrieved from www.people-press.org/2017/06/26/support-for-same-sex-marriage-grows-even-among-groups-that-had-been-skeptical/

Phanse, R. & Kaur, R. (2015). An exploratory study on self-renewal in mid-life voluntary career changes for managers. *Journal of Management Research and Analysis*, 2, 204-213.

Philippe, F. L., & Vallerand, R. J. (2008). Actual environments do affect motivation and psychological adjustment: A test of self-determination theory in a natural setting. *Motivation and Emotion*, 32(2), 81-89.

Phillips, J. A., & Sweeney, M. M. (2005). Premarital cohabitation and marital disruption among white, black, and Mexican American women. *Journal of Marriage and Family, 67*, 296-314.

Phinney, J. S. (1989). Stages of ethnic identity development in minority group of adolescents. *Journal of Early Adolescence, 9*, 34-49.

Phinney, J. S. (1998). Stages of ethnic identity development in minority group adolescents. In R. E. Muuss & H. D. Porton (Eds.), *Adolescent behavior and society: A book of readings* (pp. 271-280). Boston: McGraw-Hill.

Phinney, J. S. (2003). Ethnic identity and acculturation. In K. Chun, P. B. Organista, & G. Marin (Eds.), *Acculturation: Advances in theory, measurement, and applied research* (pp. 63-81). Washington DC: American Psychological Association.

Phinney, J. S. (2006). Ethnic identity exploration in emerging adulthood. In J. J. Arnett & J. L. Tanner (Eds.), *Emerging adults in America: Coming of age in the 21st century* (pp. 117-134). Washington, DC: American Psychological Association.

Phinney, J. S., Ferguson, D. L., & Tate, J. D. (1997). Intergroup attitudes among ethnic minorities. *Child Development, 68*(3), 955-969.

Phinney, J. S., Jacoby, B., & Silva, C. (2007). Positive intergroup attitudes: The role of ethnic identity. *International Journal of Behavioral Development, 31*(5), 478-490.

Piaget, J. (1929). *The child's conception of the world.* New York: Harcourt Brace.

Piaget, J. (1932). *The moral judgment of the child.* New York: Harcourt Brace.

Piaget, J. (1952). *The origins of intelligence in children.* New York: International Universities Press. (Original work published 1936)

Piaget, J. (1962). *The language and thought of the child* (M. Gabain, Trans.). Cleveland, OH: Meridian. (Original work published 1923)

Piaget, J. (1964). *Six psychological studies.* New York: Vintage Books.

Piaget, J., & Inhelder, B. (1967). *The child's conception of space.* New York: Norton.

Piaget, J., & Inhelder, B. (1969). *The psychology of the child.* New York: Basic Books.

Pike, A., Coldwell, J., & Dunn, J. F. (2005). Sibling relationships in early/middle childhood: Links with individual adjustment. *Journal of Family Psychology, 19*, 523-532.

Pillemer, K., & Suitor, J. J. (1991). "Will I ever escape my child's problems?" Effects of adult children's problems on elderly parents. *Journal of Marriage and Family, 53*, 585-594.

Pillemer, K., Connolly, M., Breckman, R., Spreng, N., & Lachs, M.S. (2015). Elder mistreatment: Priorities for consideration by the White House Conference on Aging. *The Gerontologist, 55*, 320-327.

Pillow, B. H. (2002). Children's and adult's evaluation of the certainty of deductive inferences, inductive inferences and guesses. *Child Development, 73*(3), 779-792.

Pine, D.S., Costello, J., & Masten, A. (2005). Trauma, proximity, and developmental psychopathology: The effects of war and terrorism on children. *Neuropsychopharmacology, 30*, 1781-1792.

Pino, O. (2016). Fetal memory: the effects of prenatal auditory experience on human development. *BAOJ Med Nursing, 2*, 20.

Pinquart, M. (2003). Loneliness in married, widowed, divorced, and never-married older adults. *Journal of Social and Personal Relationships, 20*(1), 31-53.

Pinquart, M. (2016). Associations of parenting styles and dimensions with academic achievement in children and adolescents: A meta-analysis. *Educational Psychology Review, 28*(3), 475-493.

Pinquart, M. (2017). Associations of parenting dimensions and styles with externalizing problems of children and adolescents: An updated meta-analysis. *Developmental psychology, 53*(5), 873.

Pinquart, M., & Forstmeier, S. (2012). Effects of reminiscence interventions on psychosocial outcomes: A meta-analysis. *Aging & Mental Health, 16*(5), 541-558.

Pinquart, M., & Sörensen, S. (2003). Associations of stressors and uplifts of caregiving with caregiver burden and depressive mood: a meta-analysis. *The Journals of Gerontology Series B: Psychological Sciences and Social Sciences, 58*(2), P112-P128.

Pinquart, M., & Sörensen, S. (2006). Gender differences in caregiver stressors, social resources, and health: An updated meta-analysis. *Journal of Gerontology: Psychological and Social Sciences, 61B*, P33-P45.

Pinquart, M., & Sörensen, S. (2007). Correlates of physical health of informal caregivers: A meta-analysis. *Journal of Gerontology: Psychological and Social Sciences, 62B*, P126-P137.

Plassman, B. L., Langa, K. M., Fisher, G. G., Heeringa, S. G., Weir, D. R., Ofstedal, M. B., . . . Wallace, R. B. (2008). Prevalence of cognitive impairment without dementia in the United States. *Annals of Internal Medicine, 14*(6), 427–434.

Pleis, J. R., & Lucas, J. W. (2009). Summary health statistics for U.S. adults: National health interview survey 2007. *Vital Health Statistics, 10*(240). Hyattsville, MD: National Center for Health Statistics.

Ploeg, J., Fear, J., Hutchison, B., MacMillan, H., & Bolan, G. (2009). A systematic review of interventions for elder abuse. *Journal of Elder Abuse & Neglect, 21*(3), 187–210.

Plomin, R. (1996). Nature and nurture. In M. R. Merrens & G. G. Brannigan (Eds.), *The developmental psychologist: Research adventures across the life span* (pp. 3–19). New York: McGraw-Hill.

Plomin, R. (2011). Commentary: Why are children in the same family so different? Non-shared environment three decades later. *International Journal of Epidemiology, 40*(3), 582–592.

Plomin, R., & Daniels, D. (1987). Why are children in the same family so different from one another? *Behavioral and Brain Sciences, 10*, 1–16.

Plomin, R., & Daniels, D. (2011). Why are children in the same family so different from one another? *International Journal of Epidemiology, 40*(3), 563–582.

Plomin, R., & Deary, I. J. (2015). Genetics and intelligence differences: five special findings. *Molecular Psychiatry, 20*(1), 98–108.

Plomin, R., & DeFries, J. C. (1999). The genetics of cognitive abilities and disabilities. In S. J. Ceci & W. M. Williams (Eds.), *The nature-nurture debate: The essential readings* (pp. 178–195). Malden, MA: Blackwell.

Plomin, R., & Kovas, Y. (2005). Generalist genes and learning disabilities. *Psychological Bulletin, 131*, 592–617.

Plomin, R., & Thompson, L. A. (1993). Genetics and high cognitive ability. *Ciba Foundation Symposium, 178*, 67–79.

Plomin, R., Owen, M. J., & McGuffin, P. (1994). The genetic bases of behavior. *Science, 264*, 1733–1739.

Pogarsky, G., Thornberry, T. P., & Lizotte, A. J. (2006). Developmental outcomes for children of young mothers. *Journal of Marriage and Family, 68*, 332–344.

Poirel, N., Borst, G., Simon, G., Rossi, S., Cassotti, M., Pineau, A., & Houdé, O. (2012). Number conservation is related to children's prefrontal inhibitory control: an fMRI study of a Piagetian task. *PloS one, 7*(7), e40802.

Polderman, T. J., Benyamin, B., De Leeuw, C. A., Sullivan, P. F., Van Bochoven, A., Visscher, P. M., & Posthuma, D. (2015). Meta-analysis of the heritability of human traits based on fifty years of twin studies. *Nature genetics, 47*(7), 702–709.

Pomerantz, E. M., & Saxon, J. L. (2001). Conceptions of ability as stable and self-evaluative processes: A longitudinal examination. *Child Development, 72*, 152–173.

Pomerantz, E. M., & Wang, Q. (2009). The role of parental control in children's development in Western and Asian countries. *Current Directions in Psychological Science, 18*(5), 285–289.

Pomery, E. A., Gibbons, F. X., Gerrard, M., Cleveland, M. J., Brody, G. H., & Wills, T. A. (2005). Families and risk: Prospective analyses of familial and social influences on adolescent substance use. *Journal of Family Psychology, 19*, 560–570.

Ponappa, S., Bartle-Haring, S., & Day, R. (2014). Connection to parents and healthy separation during adolescence: A longitudinal perspective. *Journal of Adolescence, 37*(5), 555–566.

Pope, A. (2005). Personal transformation in midlife orphanhood: An empirical phenomenological study. *OMEGA-Journal of Death and Dying, 51*(2), 107–123.

Pope, A. L., Murray, C. E., & Mobley, A. K. (2010). Personal, relational, and contextual resources and relationship satisfaction in same-sex couples. *Family Journal, 18,* 163–168.

Popenoe, D., & Whitehead, B. D. (2003). *The state of our unions 2003: The social health of marriage in America.* Piscataway, NJ: National Marriage Project.

Popenoe, D., & Whitehead, B. D. (Eds.). (2004). *The state of our unions 2004: The social health of marriage in America.* Piscataway, NJ: National Marriage Project, Rutgers University.

Pormeister, K., Finley, M., & Rohack, J.J. (2017). Physician assisted suicide as a means of mercy: A comparative analysis of possible legal implications in Europe and the United States. *Virginia Journal of Social Policy and the Law, 24,* 1–24.

Porter, P. (2008). "Westernizing" women's risks? Breast cancer in lower-income countries. *New England Journal of Medicine, 358,* 213–216.

Portes, P. R., Dunham, R., & Del Castillo, K. (2000). Identity formation and status across cultures: Exploring the cultural validity of Eriksonian Theory. In A. L. Communian & U. Geilen (Eds.), *International perspectives on human development* (pp. 449–460). Berlin: Pabst Science.

Posada, G., Gao, Y., Wu, F., Posada, R., Tascon, M., Schoelmerich, A., . . . Synnevaag, B. (1995). The secure-base phenomenon across cultures: Children's behavior, mothers' preferences, and experts' concepts. In E. Waters, B. E. Vaughn, G. Posada, & K. Kondo-Ikemura (Eds.), *Caregiving, cultural, and cognitive perspectives on secure-base behavior and working models: New growing points of attachment theory and research* (pp. 27–48). *Monographs of the Society for Research in Child Development, 60*(2–3, Serial No. 244).

Povinelli, D. J., & Giambrone, S. (2001). Reasoning about beliefs: A human specialization? *Child Development, 72,* 691–695.

Powell, L. H., Calvin, J. E., III, & Calvin, J. E., Jr. (2007). Effective obesity treatments. *American Psychologist, 62,* 234–246.

Powell, L. H., Shahabi, L., & Thoresen, C. E. (2003). Religion and spirituality: Linkages to physical health. *American Psychologist, 58,* 36–52.

Pradhan, A. D. (2014). Sex differences in the metabolic syndrome: implications for cardiovascular health in women. *Clinical Chemistry, 60*(1), 44–52.

Pratt, L. A., Dey, A. N., & Cohen, A. J. (2007). Characteristics of adults with serious psychological distress as measured by the K6 Scale: United States, 2001–04. *Advance Data from Health and Vital Statistics, No. 382.* Hyattsville, MD: National Center for Health Statistics.

Preissler, M., & Bloom, P. (2007). Two-year-olds appreciate the dual nature of pictures. *Psychological Science, 18*(1), 1–2.

Prentice, N. M., & Gordon, D. A. (1987). Santa Claus and the Tooth Fairy for the Jewish child and parent. *The Journal of Genetic Psychology, 148*(2), 139–151.

Prentice, N. M., Manosevitz, M., & Hubbs, L. (1978). Imaginary figures of early childhood: Santa Claus, Easter bunny, and the tooth fairy. *American Journal of Orthopsychiatry, 48*(4), 618.

Pressley, J. C., Barlow, B., Kendig, T., & Paneth-Pollak, R. (2007). Twenty-year trends in fatal injuries to very young children: The persistence of racial disparities. *Pediatrics, 119,* 875–884.

Preston, S. H. (2005). Deadweight? The influence of obesity on longevity. *New England Journal of Medicine, 352,* 1135–1137.

Previti, D., & Amato, P. R. (2003). Why stay married? Rewards, barriers, and marital stability. *Journal of Marriage and Family, 65,* 561–573.

Price, T. S., Grosser, T., Plomin, R., & Jaffee, S. R. (2010). Fetal genotype for the xenobiotic metabolizing enzyme NQO1 influences intrauterine growth among infants whose mothers smoked during pregnancy. *Child Development, 81*(1), 101–114.

Prince, M. J. (2015). *World Alzheimer Report 2015: The global impact of dementia: an analysis of prevalence, incidence, cost and trends.* London: Alzheimer's Disease International.

Prockop, D. J. (1998). The genetic trail of osteoporosis. *New England Journal of Medicine, 338,* 1061–1062.

Proctor, B. D., Semega, J. L., & Kollar, M. A. (2016). *US Census Bureau, Current Population Reports, P60-256 (RV): Income and Poverty in the United States: 2015.* Washington, DC: US Government Printing Office.

Profet, M. (1992). Pregnancy sickness as adaptation: A deterrent to maternal ingestion of teratogens. In L. Cosmides, J. Tooby, & J. H. Barkov (Eds.), *The adapted mind* (pp. 327–366). New York: Oxford University Press.

Pruchno, R. & Johnson, K. W. (1996). Research on grandparenting; Current studies and future needs. *Generations, 20(1),* 65–70.

Pruden, S. M., Hirsch-Pasek, K., Golinkoff, R. M., & Hennon, E. A. (2006). The birth of words: Ten-month-olds learn words through perceptual salience. *Child Development, 77,* 266–280.

Pudrovska, T., Schieman, S., & Carr, D. (2006). Strains of singlehood in later life: Do race and gender matter? *Journal of Gerontology: Social Sciences, 61B,* S315–S322.

Pulgarón, E. R. (2013). Childhood obesity: a review of increased risk for physical and psychological comorbidities. *Clinical Therapeutics, 35*(1), A18-A32.

Pulkkinen, L. (1996). Female and male personality styles: A typological and developmental analysis. *Journal of Personality and Social Psychology, 70,* 1288-1306.

Puma, M., Bell, S., Cook, R., Heid, C., Broene, P., Jenkins, F., . . . Downer, J. (2012). *Third grade follow-up to the Head Start impact study: Final report.* OPRE Report 2012-45. Washington, DC: Administration for Children & Families.

Purcell, K., Heaps, A., Buchanan, J. & Fried, L. (2013). *How teachers are using technology in the classroom.* Washington, DC: Pew Internet & American Life Project.

Pushkar, D., Chaikelson, J., Conway, M., Etezadi, J., Giannopoulus, C., Li, K., & Wrosch, C. (2009). Testing continuity and activity variables as predictors of positive and negative affect in retirement. *Journals of Gerontology, 65*(1), 42-49.

Putallaz, M., & Bierman, K. L. (Eds.). (2004). *Aggression, antisocial behavior, and violence among girls: A developmental perspective.* New York: Guilford Press.

Putney, N. M., & Bengtson, V. L. (2001). Families, intergenerational relationships, and kin-keeping in midlife. In M. E. Lachman (Ed.), *Handbook of midlife development* (pp. 528-570). New York: Wiley.

Qaseem, A., Forciea, M. A., McLean, R. M., & Denberg, T. D. (2017). Treatment of low bone density or osteoporosis to prevent fractures in men and women: A clinical practice guideline update from the American College of Physicianstreatment of low bone density or osteoporosis to prevent fractures in men and women. *Annals of Internal Medicine.*

Qaseem, A., Kansagara, D., Forciea, M. A., Cooke, M., & Denberg, T. D. (2016). Management of chronic insomnia disorder in adults: A clinical practice guideline from the American College of Physiciansmanagement of chronic insomnia disorder in adults. *Annals of Internal Medicine, 165*(2), 125-133.

Qian, J., Hu, Q., Wan, Y., Li, T., Wu, M., Ren, Z., & Yu, D. (2013). Prevalence of eating disorders in the general population: A systematic review. *Shanghai Archives of Psychiatry, 25*(4), 212.

Quamie, L. (2010, February 2). *Paid family leave funding included in budget.* Retrieved from http://www.clasp.org/issues/in_focus?type=work_life_and_job_quality&id=0009

Quattrin, T., Liu, E., Shaw, N., Shine, B., & Chiang, E. (2005). Obese children who are referred to the pediatric oncologist: Characteristics and outcome. *Pediatrics, 115,* 348-351.

Quill, T. E., Lo, B., & Brock, D. W. (1997). Palliative options of the last resort. *Journal of the American Medical Association, 278,* 2099-2104.

Quine, S., Morrell, S., & Kendig, H. (2007). *The hopes and fears of older Australians: For self, family, and society.* Retrieved from nclive.org: http://nclive.org/cgi-bin/nclsm?url=http://

search.proquest.com/docview/216243395?accountid=10939

Quinn, P. C., Westerlund, A., & Nelson, C. A. (2006). Neural markers of categorization in 6-month-old infants. *Psychological Science, 17,* 59-66.

Quirk, K., Owen, J., & Fincham, F. (2014). Perceptions of partner's deception in friends with benefits relationships. *Journal of Sex & Marital Therapy, 40*(1), 43-57.

Raabe, T., & Beelmann, A. (2011). Development of ethnic, racial, and national prejudice in childhood and adolescence: A multinational meta-analysis of age differences. *Child Development, 82*(6), 1715-1737.

Rabbitt, P., Watson, P., Donlan, C., McInnes, L., Horan, M., Pendleton, N., & Clague, J. (2002). Effects of death within 11 years on cognitive performance in old age. *Psychology and Aging, 17,* 468-481.

Racz, S. J., & McMahon, R. J. (2011). The relationship between parental knowledge and monitoring and child and adolescent conduct: A 10-year update. *Clinical Child and Family Psychology Review, 14*(4), 377-398.

Radbruch, L., Leget, C., Bahr, P., Müller-Busch, C., Ellershaw, J., de Conno, F., . . . & board members of the EAPC. (2016). Euthanasia and physician-assisted suicide: A white paper from the European Association for Palliative Care. *Palliative Medicine, 30*(2), 104-116.

Radesky, J. S., Silverstein, M., Zuckerman, B., Christakis, D. A. (2014). Infant self-regulation and early childhood media exposure. *Pediatrics, 133.* doi: 10.1542/peds.2013-2367

Rahman, R. (2011, October 25). *Who, what, why: What are the burial customs in Islam?* Retrieved from bbc.com: www.bbc.com/news/magazine-15444275

Raikes, H., Pan, B. A., Luze, G., Tamis-LeMonda, C. S., Brooks-Gunn, J., Constantine, J., . . . Rodriguez, E. T. (2006). Mother-child bookreading in low-income families: Correlates and outcomes during three years of life. *Child Development, 77,* 924-953.

Raine, A., Mellingen, K., Liu, J., Venables, P., & Mednick, S. (2003). Effects of environmental enrichment at ages 3-5 years in schizotypal personality and antisocial behavior at ages 17 and 23 years. *American Journal of Psychiatry, 160,* 1627-1635.

Raising Readers: The Tremendous Potential of Families. (1999, July). Retrieved from ed.gov: https://www2.ed.gov/pubs/startearly/ch_1.html news

Raj, M., & Kumar, K. R. (2010, November). Obesity in children & adolescents. Retrieved from *Indian Journal of Medical Research:* www.ncbi.nlm.nih.gov/pmc/articles/PMC3028965

Rakison, D. H. (2005). Infant perception and cognition. In B. J. Ellis & D. F. Bjorklund (Eds.), *Origins of the social mind* (pp. 317-353). New York: Guilford Press.

Rakison, D. H., & Krogh, L. (2012). Does causal action facilitate causal perception in infants younger than 6 months of age? *Developmental Science, 15*(1), 43-53.

Rakoczy, H., Tomasello, M., & Striano, T. (2004). Young children know that trying is not pretending: A test of the "behaving-as-if" construal of children's early concept of pretense. *Developmental Psychology, 40,* 388-399.

Rakyan, V., & Beck, S. (2006). Epigenetic inheritance and variation in mammals. *Current Opinion in Genetics and Development, 16*(6), 573-577.

Ram, A., & Ross, H. S. (2001). Problem solving, contention, and struggle: How siblings resolve a conflict of interests. *Child Development, 72,* 1710-1722.

Ramey, C. T., & Ramey, S. L. (1998a). Early intervention and early experience. *American Psychologist, 53,* 109-120.

Ramey, C. T., & Ramey, S. L. (1998b). Prevention of intellectual disabilities: Early interventions to improve cognitive development. *Preventive Medicine, 21,* 224-232.

Ramey, C. T., & Ramey, S. L. (2003, May). *Preparing America's children for success in school.* Paper prepared for an invited address at the White House Early Childhood Summit on Ready to Read, Ready to Learn, Denver, CO.

Rampey, B.D., Finnegan, R., Goodman, M., Mohadjer, L., Krenzke, T., Hogan, J., and Provasnik, S. (2016). *Skills of U.S. unemployed, young, and older adults in sharper focus: Results from the Program for the International Assessment of Adult Competencies (PIAAC) 2012/2014: First Look (NCES 2016-039rev).* U.S. Department of Education. Washington, DC: National Center for Education Statistics. Retrieved from http://nces.ed.gov/pubsearch.

Ramsey, P. G., & Lasquade, C. (1996). Preschool children's entry attempts. *Journal of Applied Developmental Psychology, 17,* 135-150.

Rapoport, J. L., Giedd, J. N., & Gogtay, N. (2012). Neurodevelopmental model of schizophrenia: update 2012. *Molecular Psychiatry, 17*(12), 1228-1238.

Rapp, S. R., Espeland, M. A., Shumaker, S. A., Henderson, V. W., Brunner, R. L., Manson, J. E., . . . Bowen, D., for the WHIMIS Investigators. (2003). Effects of estrogen plus progestin on global cognitive function in postmenopausal women: The Women's Health Initiative Memory Study: A randomized controlled trial. *Journal of the American Medical Association, 289*(20), 2663-2672.

Rathbun, A., West, J., & Germino-Hausken, E. (2004). *From kindergarten through third grade: Children's beginning school experiences* (NCES 2004-007). Washington, DC: National Center for Education Statistics.

Rauh, V. A., Whyatt, R. M., Garfinkel, R., Andrews, H., Hoepner, L., Reyes, A., . . . Perera, F. P. (2004). Developmental effects of exposure to environmental tobacco smoke and material hardship among inner-city children. *Neurotoxicology and Teratology, 26,* 373-385.

Raver, C. C. (2002). Emotions matter: Making the case for the role of young children's emotional development for early school readiness. *Social Policy Report, 16*(3).

Rawlings, D. (2012). End-of-life care considerations for gay, lesbian, bisexual, and transgender individuals. *International Journal of Palliative Nursing, 18*(1), 29–34.

Ray, B. D. (2010). Academic achievement and demographic traits of homeschool students: A nationwide study. *Academic Leadership,* Winter, 8(1).

Ray, D. C., Armstrong, S. A., Balkin, R. S., & Jayne, K. M. (2015). Child-centered play therapy in the schools: Review and meta-analysis. *Psychology in the Schools, 52*(2), 107–123.

Ray, O. (2004). How the mind hurts and heals the body. *American Psychologist, 59*, 29–40.

Raz, N., Ghisletta, P., Rodrigue, K. M., Kennedy, K. M., & Lindenberger, U. (2010). Trajectories of brain aging in middle-aged and older adults: Regional and individual differences. *Neuroimage, 51*(2), 501–511.

Raznahan, A., Shaw, P., Lalonde, F., Stockman, M., Wallace, G. L., Greenstein, D., . . . & Giedd, J. N. (2011). How does your cortex grow? *Journal of Neuroscience, 31*(19), 7174–7177.

Recchia, H. E., & Howe, N. (2009). Associations between social understanding, sibling relationship quality, and siblings' conflict strategies and outcomes. *Child Development, 80*(5), 1564–1578.

Reddy, U.M., Wapner, R.J., Rebar, R.W., & Tasca, R.J. (2007). Infertility, assisted reproductive technology, and adverse pregnancy outcomes: Executive summary of a National Institute of Child Health and Human Development Workshop. *Obstetrics and Gynecology*, 109, 967–977.

Redman, L. M., & Ravussin, E. (2009). Endocrine alterations in response to calorie restriction in humans. *Molecular and Cellular Endocrinology, 299*(1), 129–136.

Reed, A. E., Chan, L., & Mikels, J. A. (2014). Meta-analysis of the age-related positivity effect: Age differences in preferences for positive over negative information. *Psychology and Aging, 29*(1), 1–15.

Reef, S. E., Strebel, P., Dabbagh, A., Gacic-Dobo, M., & Cochi, S. (2011). Progress toward control of rubella and prevention of congenital rubella syndrome—worldwide, 2009. *Journal of Infectious Diseases, 204*(1), 24–27.

Reese, D. (1998, May). *Mixed-Age Grouping: What Does the Research Say, and How Can Parents Use This Information*. Retrieved from Kidsource. com: www.kidsource.com/mixed-age-grouping-what-does-research-say-and-how-can-parents-use-information#sthash.2Ywwka9z.7w0B5qlt.dpbs

Reese, E. (1995). Predicting children's literacy from mother-child conversations. *Cognitive Development, 10*, 381–405.

Reese, E., & Cox, A. (1999). Quality of adult book reading affects children's emergent literacy. *Developmental Psychology, 35*, 20–28.

Reese, E., & Newcombe, R. (2007). Training mothers in elaborative reminiscing enhances children's autobiographical memory and narrative. *Child Development, 78*(4), 1153–1170.

Reese, E., Sparks, A., & Leyva, D. (2010). A review of parent interventions for preschool children's language and emergent literacy. *Journal of Early Childhood Literacy, 10*(1), 97–117.

Regan, P. C., Lakhanpal, S., & Anguiano, C. (2012). Relationship outcomes in Indian-American love-based and arranged marriages. *Psychological Reports, 110*(3), 915–924.

Reichenberg, A., Gross, R., Weiser, M., Bresnahan, M., Silverman, J., Harlap, S., . . . Susser, E. (2006). Advancing paternal age and autism. *Archives of General Psychiatry, 63*(9), 1026–1032.

Reichstadt, J., Sengupta, G., Depp, C. A., Palinkas, L. A., & Jeste, D. V. (2010). Older adults' perspectives on successful aging: Qualitative interviews. *American Journal of Geriatric Psychiatry, 18*(7), 567–575.

Reid, I. R. (2014). Should we prescribe calcium supplements for osteoporosis prevention? *Journal of Bone Metabolism, 21*(1), 21–28.

Reid, J. D. (1995). Development in late life: Older lesbian and gay life. In A. R. D'Augelli & C. J. Patterson (Eds.), *Lesbian, gay, and bisexual identities over the lifespan: Psychological perspectives* (pp. 215–240). New York: Oxford University Press.

Reid, J. D., & Willis, S. K. (1999). Middle age: New thoughts, new directions. In S. L. Willis & J. D. Reid (Eds.), *Life in the middle* (pp. 272–289). San Diego: Academic Press.

Reiner, M., Niermann, C., Jekauc, D., & Woll, A. (2013). Long-term health benefits of physical activity–a systematic review of longitudinal studies. *BMC Public Health, 13*(1), 813.

Reiner, W. G. (2005). Gender identity and sex-of-rearing in children with disorders of sexual differentiation. *Journal of Pediatric Endocrinology and Metabolism, 18*(6), 549–554.

Reiner, W. G., & Gearhart, J. P. (2004). Discordant sexual identity in some genetic males with cloacal exstrophy assigned to female sex at birth. *New England Journal of Medicine, 350*(4), 333–341.

Reisberg, B., Doody, R., Stöffler, A., Schmitt, F., Ferris, S., & Möbius, H. J. (2006). A 24-week open-label extension study of memantine in moderate to severe Alzheimer disease. *Archives of Neurology, 63*, 49–54.

Reiss, A. L., Abrams, M. T., Singer, H. S., Ross, J. L., & Denckla, M. B. (1996). Brain development, gender and IQ in children: A volumetric imaging study. *Brain, 119*, 1763–1774.

Reitz, C., & Mayeux, R. (2014). Alzheimer disease: Epidemiology, diagnostic criteria, risk factors and biomarkers. *Biochemical Pharmacology, 88*(4), 640–651.

Reitz, C., Cheng, R., Rogaeva, E., Lee, J. H., Tokuhiro, S., Zou, F., . . . & Shibata, N. (2011). Meta-analysis of the association between variants in SORL1 and Alzheimer disease. *Archives of Neurology, 68*(1), 99–106.

Reitzes, D. C., & Mutran, E. J. (2004). Grandparenthood: Factors influencing frequency of grandparent-grandchildren contact and role satisfaction. *Journal of Gerontology: Social Sciences, 59*, S9–S16.

Rekker, R., Pardini, D., Keijsers, L., Branje, S., Loeber, R., & Meeus, W. (2015). Moving in and out of poverty: The within-individual association between socioeconomic status and juvenile delinquency. *PLoS one, 10*(11), e0136461.

Remez, L. (2000). Oral sex among adolescents: Is it sex or is it abstinence? *Family Planning Perspectives, 32*, 298–304.

Ren, Q., & Treiman, D. J. (2014, January). *Population Studies Center Research Reports*. Retrieved from University of Michigan : https://www.psc.isr.umich.edu/pubs/pdf/rr14-814.pdf

Rendall, M. S., Weden, M. M., Favreault, M. M., & Waldron, H. (2011). The protective effect of marriage for survival: a review and update. *Demography, 48*(2), 481.

Rende, R., Slomkowski, C., Lloyd-Richardson, E., & Niaura, R. (2005). Sibling effects on substance use in adolescence: Social contagion and genetic relatedness. *Journal of Family Psychology, 19*, 611–618.

Resing, W. C. (2013). Dynamic testing and individualized instruction: Helpful in cognitive education? *Journal of Cognitive Education and Psychology, 12*(1), 81.

Resnick, L. B. (1989). Developing mathematical knowledge. *American Psychologist, 44*, 162–169.

Reuter, M., Roth, S., Holve, K., & Hennig, J. (2006). Identification of first candidate genes for creativity: A pilot study. *Brain Research, 1069*, 190–197.

Reuter-Lorenz, P. A., Jonides, J., Smith, E. E., Hartley, A., Miller, A., Marshuetz, C., & Koeppe, R. A. (2000). Age differences in the frontal lateralization of verbal and spatial working memory revealed by PET. *Journal of Cognitive Neuroscience, 12*, 174–187.

Reuter-Lorenz, P. A., Stanczak, L., & Miller, A. (1999). Neural recruitment and cognitive aging: Two hemispheres are better than one especially as you age. *Psychological Science, 10*, 494–500.

Reyes-Ortiz, C.A., Burnett, J., Flores, D.V., Halphen, J.M., Dyer, C.B. (2014). Medical implications of elder abuse: Self-neglect. *Clinical Geriatric Medicine, 30*, 807–823.

Reynolds, A. J., Temple, J. A., Ou, S. R., Arteaga, I. A., & White, B. A. (2011). School-based early childhood education and age-28 well-being: Effects by timing, dosage, and subgroups. *Science, 333*(6040), 360–364.

Reynolds, C. F., III, Buysse, D. J., & Kupfer, D. J. (1999). Treating insomnia in older adults: Taking a long-term view. *Journal of the American Medical Association, 281*, 1034–1035.

Reynolds, G. D., Guy, M. W., & Zhang, D. (2011). Neural correlates of individual differences in infant visual attention and recognition memory. *Infancy, 16*(4), 368–391.

Rhee, S. H., & Waldman, I. D. (2002). Genetic and environmental influences on antisocial behavior: A meta-analysis of twin and adoption studies. *Psychological Bulletin, 128*, 490–529.

Ricciuti, H. N. (1999). Single parenthood and school readiness in white, black, and Hispanic 6- and 7-year-olds. *Journal of Family Psychology, 13*, 450–465.

Ricciuti, H. N. (2004). Single parenthood, achievement, and problem behavior in white, black, and Hispanic children. *Journal of Educational Research, 97*, 196–206.

Rice, K. G., & Van Arsdale, A. C. (2010). Perfectionism, perceived stress, drinking to cope, and alcohol-related problems among college students. *Journal of Counseling Psychology, 57*(4), 439–450. doi: 10.1037/a00200221

Rice, K., Prichard, I., Tiggemann, M., & Slater, A. (2016). Exposure to Barbie: Effects on thin-ideal internalization, body esteem, and body dissatisfaction among young girls. *Body Image, 19,* 142–149.

Rice, M. L. (1982). Child language: What children know and how. In T. M. Field, A. Hudson, H. C. Quay, L. Troll, & G. E. Finley (Eds.), *Review of human development research.* New York: Wiley.

Rice, M. L. (1989). Children's language acquisition. *American Psychologist, 44*(2), 149–156.

Rice, M. L., Taylor, C. L., & Zubrick, S. R. (2008). Language outcomes of 7-year-old children with or without a history of late language emergence at 24 months. *Journal of Speech, Language, and Hearing Research, 51,* 394–407.

Richards, J. B., Zheng, H. F., & Spector, T. D. (2012). Genetics of osteoporosis from genome-wide association studies: advances and challenges. *Nature Reviews Genetics, 13*(8), 576–588.

Richards, R., Merrill, R. M., & Baksh, L. (2011). Health behaviors and infant health outcomes in homeless pregnant women in the United States. *Pediatrics, 128*(3), 438–446.

Richardson, C. R., Kriska, A. M., Lantz, P. M., & Hayward, R. A. (2004). Physical activity and mortality across cardiovascular disease risk groups. *Medicine and Science in Sports and Exercise, 36,* 1923–1929.

Richardson, E. G., & Hemenway, D. (2011). Homicide, suicide, and unintentional firearm fatality: Comparing the United States with other high-income countries, 2003. *Journal of Trauma and Acute Care Surgery, 70*(1), 238–243.

Richardson, G. A., Ryan, C., Willford, J., Day, N. L., & Goldschmidt, L. (2002). Prenatal alcohol and marijuana exposure: effects on neuropsychological outcomes at 10 years. *Neurotoxicology and Teratology, 24*(3), 309–320.

Richardson, J. (1995). *Achieving gender equality in families: The role of males* (Innocenti Global Seminar, Summary Report). Florence, Italy: UNICEF International Child Development Centre, Spedale degli Innocenti.

Richman, A. L., Miller, P. M., & LeVine, P. A. (2010). Cultural and educational variations in maternal responsiveness. In R. A. LeVine (Ed.), *Psychological anthropology: A reader on self in culture* (pp. 181–192). Malden, MA: Wiley-Blackwell.

Richman, L. S., Kubzansky, L., Maselko, J., Kawachi, I., Choo, P., & Bauer, M. (2005). Positive emotion and health: Going beyond the negative. *Health Psychology, 24,* 422–429.

Rickard, I. J., Courtiol, A., Prentice, A. M., Fulford, A. J., Clutton-Brock, T. H., & Lummaa, V. (2012, August). Intergenerational effects of maternal birth season on offspring size in rural Gambia. In *Proc. R. Soc. B* (p. rspb20121363). The Royal Society.

Rideout, V. J. (2013, October 28). Zero to eight: Children's media use in America 2013. *Common Sense Media,* 101–115.

Rideout, V. J., Foehr, U. G., & Roberts, D. F. (2010). *Generation M²: Media in the lives of 8- to 18-year-olds.* Menlo Park, CA: Henry J. Kaiser Family Foundation.

Riegle-Crumb, C., Farkas, G., & Muller, C. (2006). The role of gender and friendship in advanced course taking. *Sociology of Education, 79*(3), 206–228.

Riemann, M. K., & Kanstrup Hansen, I. L. (2000). Effects on the fetus of exercise in pregnancy. *Scandinavian Journal of Medicine & Science in Sports, 10*(1), 12–19.

Riggle, E. D. B., Rotosky, S. S., & Riggle, S. G. (2010). Psychological distress, well-being and legal recognition in same-sex couple relationships. *Journal of Family Psychology, 24*(1), 82–86.

Rimm-Kaufman, S. E., Curby, T. W., Grimm, K. J., Nathanson, L., & Brock, L. L. (2009). The contribution of children's self-regulation and classroom quality to children's adaptive behaviors in the kindergarten classroom. *Developmental Psychology, 45*(4), 958–972.

Ritchie, S. J., Bates, T. C., & Deary, I. J. (2015). Is education associated with improvements in general cognitive ability, or in specific skills? *Developmental Psychology, 51*(5), 573.

Rittenour, C. E., Myers, S. A., & Brann, M. (2007). Commitment and emotional closeness in the sibling relationship. *Southern Communication Journal, 72*(2), 169–183.

Rivera, J. A., Sotres-Alvarez, D., Habicht, J.-P., Shamah, T., & Villalpando, S. (2004). Impact of the Mexican Program for Education, Health and Nutrition (Progresa) on rates of growth and anemia in infants and young children. *Journal of the American Medical Association, 291,* 2563–2570.

Roberts, B. W., Caspi, A., & Moffitt, T. E. (2003). Work experiences and personality development in young adulthood. *Journal of Personality and Social Psychology, 84,* 582–593.

Roberts, B. W., Walton, K. E., & Viechtbauer, W. (2006a). Patterns of mean-level change in personality traits across the life course: A meta-analysis of longitudinal studies. *Psychological Bulletin, 132,* 1–25.

Roberts, B. W., Walton, K. E., & Viechtbauer, W. (2006b). Personality traits change in adulthood: Reply to Costa and McCrae (2006). *Psychological Bulletin, 132,* 29–32.

Roberts, B. W., Wood, D., & Smith, J. L. (2005). Evaluating five factor theory and social investment perspectives on personality trait development. *Journal of Research in Personality, 39*(1), 166–184.

Roberts, B., & Mroczek, D. (2008). Personality trait change in adulthood. *Current Directions in Psychological Science, 17*(1), 31–35.

Robertson, D. A., Savva, G. M., & Kenny, R. A. (2013). Frailty and cognitive impairment—a review of the evidence and causal mechanisms. *Ageing Research Reviews, 12*(4), 840–851.

Robins, R. W., John, O. P., Caspi, A., Moffitt, T. E., & Stouthamer-Loeber, M. (1996). Resilient, overcontrolled, and undercontrolled boys: Three replicable personality types. *Journal of Personality and Social Psychology, 70,* 157–171.

Robinson, M., Thiel, M. M., Backus, M. M., & Meyer, E. C. (2006). Matters of spirituality at the end of life in the pediatric intensive care unit. *Pediatrics, 118,* 719–729.

Robinson, S. D., Rosenberg, H. J., & Farrell, M. P. (1999). The midlife crisis revisited. In S. L. Willis & J. D. Reid (Eds.), *Life in the middle: Psychological and social development in middle age* (pp. 47–77). San Diego: Academic Press.

Robles, T. F., Slatcher, R. B., Trombello, J. M., & McGinn, M. M. (2014). Marital quality and health: A meta-analytic review. *Psychological Bulletin, 140*(1), 140.

Rochat, P., & Striano, T. (2002). Who's in the mirror? Self-other discrimination in specular images by 4- and 9-month-old infants. *Child Development, 73,* 35–46.

Röcke, C., Li, S. C., & Smith, J. (2009). Intraindividual variability in positive and negative affect over 45 days: Do older adults fluctuate less than young adults? *Psychology and Aging, 24*(4), 863.

Röcke, C., & Lachman, M. E. (2008). Perceived trajectories of life satisfaction across past, present and future: Profiles and correlates of subjective change in young, middle-aged, and older adults. *Psychology and Aging, 23*(4), 833–847.

Rodin, J., & Ickovics, J. (1990). Women's health: Review and research agenda as we approach the 21st century. *American Psychologist, 45,* 1018–1034.

Rogers, C. H., Floyd, F. J., Seltzer, M. M., Greenberg, J., & Hong, J. (2008). Long-term effects of the death of a child on parents' adjustment in midlife. *Journal of Family Psychology, 22*(2), 203.

Rogler, L. H. (2002). Historical generations and psychology: The case of the Great Depression and World War II. *American Psychologist, 57*(12), 1013–1023.

Rogoff, B. (2003). *The cultural nature of human development.* Oxford, England: Oxford University Press.

Rogoff, B., & Morelli, G. (1989). Perspectives on children's development from cultural psychology. *American Psychologist, 44,* 343–348.

Rogoff, B., Mistry, J., Göncü, A., & Mosier, C. (1993). Guided participation in cultural activity by toddlers and caregivers. *Monographs of the Society for Research in Child Development, 58*(8, Serial No. 236).

Roisman, G. I., Clausell, E., Holland, A., Fortuna, K., & Elieff, C. (2008). Adult romantic relationships as contexts of human development: A multimethod comparison of same-sex couples with opposite-sex dating, engaged, and married dyads. *Developmental Psychology, 44,* 91–101.

Roisman, G. I., Masten, A. S., Coatsworth, J. D., & Tellegen, A. (2004). Salient and emerging developmental tasks in the transition to adulthood. *Child Development, 75,* 123–133.

Romano, E., Tremblay, R. E., Boulerice, B., & Swisher, R. (2005). Multi-level correlates of childhood physical aggression and prosocial behavior. *Journal of Abnormal Child Psychology, 33*(5), 565–578.

Romero, A. P. (2017). 1.1 Million LGBT adults are married to someone of the same sex at the two-year anniversary of Obergefell v. Hodges. *The Williams Institute.*

Roopnarine, J. L., Hooper, F. H., Ahmeduzzaman, M., & Pollack, B. (1993). Gentle play partners: Mother-child and father-child play in New Delhi, India. In K. MacDonald (Ed.), *Parent-child play* (pp. 287–304). Albany: State University of New York Press.

Roopnarine, J. L., Talokder, E., Jain, D., Josh, P., & Srivastav, P. (1992). Personal well-being, kinship ties, and mother-infant and father-infant interactions in single-wage and dual-wage families in New Delhi, India. *Journal of Marriage and Family, 54,* 293–301.

Roopnarine, J., & Honig, A. S. (1985, September). The unpopular child. *Young Children,* 59–64.

Roosa, M. W., Deng, S., Ryu, E., Burrell, G. L., Tein, J., Jones, S., Lopez, V., & Crowder, S. (2005). Family and child characteristics linking neighborhood context and child externalizing behavior. *Journal of Marriage and Family, 667,* 515–529.

Rosamond, W. D., Chambless, L. E., Folsom, A. R., Cooper, L. S., Conwill, D. E., Clegg, L., . . . Heiss, G. (1998). Trends in the incidence of myocardial infarction and in mortality due to coronary heart disease, 1987 to 1994. *New England Journal of Medicine, 339,* 861–867.

Rosamond, W., Flegal, K., Furie, K., Go, A., Greenlund, K., Haase, N., . . . Hong, Y. (2008). Heart disease and stroke statistics—2008 update: A report from the American Heart Association Statistics Committee and Stroke Statistics Subcommittee. *Circulation, 117*(4), e25–e146.

Rosario, M., Schrimshaw, E. W., & Hunter, J. (2011). Different patterns of sexual identity development over time: Implications for the psychological adjustment of lesbian, gay, and bisexual youths. *Journal of Sex Research, 48*(1), 3–15.

Roscigno, V., Mong, S., Bryon, R., & Tester, G. (2007). *Age discrimination, social closure and employment.* Retrieved from nclive.org: http://nclive.org/cgi-bin/nclsm?url=http://search.proquest.com/docview/229891354?accountid=10939

Rose, S. A., Feldman, J. F., & Jankowski, J. J. (2002). Processing speed in the 1st year of life: A longitudinal study of preterm and full-term infants. *Developmental Psychology, 38,* 895–902.

Rose, S. A., Feldman, J. F., Jankowski, J. J., & Van Rossem, R. (2012). Information processing from infancy to 11 years: Continuities and prediction of IQ. *Intelligence, 40*(5), 445–457.

Rosenbaum, J. E. (2009). Patient teenagers? A comparison of the sexual behavior of virginity pledgers and matched nonpledgers. *Pediatrics, 123,* e110–e120.

Rosenberg, S. D., Rosenberg, H. J., & Farrell, M. P. (1999). The midlife crisis revisited. In S. L. Willis & J. D. Reid (Eds.), *Life in the middle* (pp. 47–73). San Diego: Academic Press.

Rosenblatt, A., Greenberg, J., Solomon, S., Pyszczynski, T., & Lyon, D. (1989). Evidence for terror management theory: I. The effects of mortality salience on reactions to those who violate or uphold cultural values. *Journal of Personality and Social Psychology, 57*(4), 681.

Rosenbluth, S. C., & Steil, J. M. (1995). Predictors of intimacy for women in heterosexual and homosexual couples. *Journal of Social and Personal Relationships, 12*(2), 163–175.

Rosenfeld, D. (1999). Identity work among lesbian and gay elderly. *Journal of Aging Studies, 13,* 121–144.

Rosenfeld, M. J. (2014). Couple longevity in the era of same-sex marriage in the United States. *Journal of Marriage and Family, 76*(5), 905–918.

Rosenthal, B. P., & Fischer, M. (2014). Functional vision changes in the normal and aging eye. *A Comprehensive Guide to Geriatric Rehabilitation, 381.*

Rosero-Bixby, L., Dow, W. H., & Rehkopf, D. H. (2014, November 23). *The Nicoya region of Costa Rica: A high longevity island for elderly males.* Retrieved from U.S. National Library of Medicine National Institutes of Health: www.ncbi.nlm.nih.gov/pmc/articles/PMC4241350/

Roses, A. D., Saunders, A. M., Lutz, M. W., Zhang, N., Hariri, A. R., Asin, K. E., . . . & Brannan, S. K. (2014). New applications of disease genetics and pharmacogenetics to drug development. *Current Opinion in Pharmacology, 14,* 81–89.

Rosner, R., Kruse, J., & Hagl, M. (2010). A meta-analysis of interventions for bereaved children and adolescents. *Death Studies, 34*(2), 99–136.

Rossi, A. S. (2004). The menopausal transition and aging process. In O. G. Brim, C. D. Ryff, & R. C. Kessler (Eds.), *How healthy are we? A national study of well-being at midlife.* Chicago: University of Chicago Press.

Roth, G., Assor, A., Niemiec, C. P., Ryan, R. M., & Deci, E. L. (2009). The emotional and academic consequences of parental conditional regard: Comparing conditional positive regard, conditional negative regard, and autonomy supports as parenting practices. *Developmental Psychology, 45*(4), 1119–1142.

Rothbart, M. K., Ahadi, S. A., & Evans, D. E. (2000). Temperament and personality: Origins and outcomes. *Journal of Personality and Social Psychology, 78,* 122–135.

Rothbart, M. K., Ahadi, S. A., Hershey, K. L., & Fisher, P. (2001). Investigations of temperament at three to seven years: The Children's Behavior Questionnaire. *Child Development, 72*(5), 1394–1408.

Rothbart, M. K., Sheese, B. E., Rueda, M. R., & Posner, M. I. (2011). Developing mechanisms of self-regulation in early life. *Emotion Review, 3*(2), 207–213.

Rothermund, K., & Brandtstädter, J. (2003). Coping with deficits and losses in later life: From compensatory action to accommodation. *Psychology and Aging, 18,* 896–905.

Rouse, C., Brooks-Gunn, J., & McLanahan, S. (2005). Introducing the issue. *Future of Children, 15*(1), 5–14.

Roussotte, F. F., Bramen, J. E., Nunez, C., Quandt, L. C., Smith, L., O'Connor, M. J., . . .

Sowell, E. R. (2011). Abnormal brain activation during working memory in children with prenatal exposure to drugs of abuse: The effects of methamphetamine, alcohol, and polydrug exposure. *NeuroImage, 54*(4), 3067–3075.

Rovee-Collier, C. (1996). Shifting the focus from what to why. *Infant Behavior and Development, 19,* 385–400.

Rovee-Collier, C. (1999). The development of infant memory. *Current Directions in Psychological Science, 8,* 80–85.

Rowe, J.W. & Kahn, R.L. (1997). Successful aging. *Gerontologist, 37,* 433–440.

Rowe, J.W. & Kahn, R.L. (2015). Successful aging 2.0: Conceptual expansions for the 21st century. *Journals of Gerontology, Series B: Psychological Sciences and Social Sciences, 70,* 593–596.

Roy, S., Aggarwal, A., Dhangar, G., & Aneja, A. (2016). Mercury in vaccines: A review. *Global Vaccines and Immunology, 1.* doi: 10.15761/GVI.1000119

Rozman, M., Treven, S., & Cancer, V. (2016). *Stereotypes of older employees compared to younger employees in Slovenian companies.* Retrieved from nclive.org: http://nclive.org/cgi-bin/nclsm?url-http://search.proquest.com/docview/1854196758?accountid=10939

Rubin, D. C., Berntsen, D., & Hutson, M. (2009). The normative and the personal life: Individual differences in life scripts and life story events among USA and Danish undergraduates. *Memory, 17*(1), 54–68.

Rubin, D. H., Krasilnikoff, P. A., Leventhal, J. M., Weile, B., & Berget, A. (1986, August 23). Effect of passive smoking on birth weight. *Lancet,* 415–417.

Rubin, K. H., Bukowski, W., & Parker, J. G. (1998). Peer interactions, relationships, and groups. In W. Damon (Series Ed.) & N. Eisenberg (Vol. Ed.), *Handbook of child psychology: Vol. 3. Social, emotional, and personality development* (5th ed., pp. 619–700). New York: Wiley.

Rubin, K. H., Burgess, K. B., & Hastings, P. D. (2002). Stability and social-behavioral consequences of toddlers' inhibited temperament and parenting behaviors. *Child Development, 73*(2), 483–495.

Rubin, K. H., Burgess, K. B., Dwyer, K. M., & Hastings, P. D. (2003). Predicting preschoolers' externalizing behavior from toddler temperament, conflict, and maternal negativity. *Developmental Psychology, 39*(1), 164–176.

Ruble, D. N., & Dweck, C. S. (1995). Self-conceptions, person conceptions, and their development. In N. Eisenberg (Ed.), *Social development: Review of personality and social psychology* (pp. 109–139). Thousand Oaks, CA: Sage.

Ruble, D. N., & Martin, C. L. (1998). Gender development. In W. Damon (Series Ed.) & N. Eisenberg (Vol. Ed.), *Handbook of child psychology: Vol. 3. Social, emotional, and personality development* (5th ed., pp. 933–1016). New York: Wiley.

Ruble, D. N., Martin, C. L., & Berenbaum, S. A. (2006). Gender development. In W. Damon & R. M. Lerner (Series Eds.) & D. Kuhn & R. S. Seigler (Vol. Eds.), *Handbook of child psychology: Vol 2. Cognition, perception, and language* (pp. 858–932). Hoboken: NJ. Wiley.

Rudolph, K. D., Lambert, S. F., Clark, A. G., & Kurlakowsky, K. D. (2001). Negotiating the transition to middle school: The role of self-regulatory processes. *Child Development, 72*(3), 929–946.

Rudy, D., & Grusec, J. E. (2006). Authoritarian parenting in individualistic and collectivistic groups: Associations with maternal emotion and cognition and children's self-esteem. *Journal of Family Psychology, 20*, 68–78.

Rueda, M. R., & Rothbart, M. K. (2009). The influence of temperament on the development of coping: The role of maturation and experience. *New Directions for Child and Adolescent Development, 124*, 19–31.

Rueda, M. R., Posner, M. I., & Rothbart, M. K. (2005). The development of executive attention: Contributions to the emergence of self-regulation. *Developmental Neuropsychology, 28*(2), 573–594.

Rueter, M. A., & Conger, R. D. (1995). Antecedents of parent-adolescent disagreements. *Journal of Marriage and Family, 57*, 435–448.

Ruigrok, A. N., Salimi-Khorshidi, G., Lai, M. C., Baron-Cohen, S., Lombardo, M. V., Tait, R. J., & Suckling, J. (2014). A meta-analysis of sex differences in human brain structure. *Neuroscience & Biobehavioral Reviews, 39*, 34–50.

Ruitenberg, A., van Swieten, J. C., Witteman, J. C., Mehta, K. M., van Duijn, C. M., Hofman, A., & Breteler, M. M. (2002). Alcohol consumption and risk of dementia: The Rotterdam Study. *Lancet, 359*, 281–286.

Runco, M. A., Millar, G., Acar, S., & Cramond, B. (2010). Torrance tests of creative thinking as predictors of personal and public achievement: A fifty-year follow-up. *Creativity Research Journal, 22*(4), 361–368.

Runco, M. A., Noble, E. P., Reiter-Palmon, R., Acar, S., Ritchie, T., & Yurkovich, J. M. (2011). The genetic basis of creativity and ideational fluency. *Creativity Research Journal, 23*(4), 376–380.

Rushton, J. P., & Ankney, C. D. (2009). Whole brain size and general mental ability: A review. *International Journal of Neuroscience, 119*(5), 692–732.

Rushton, J. P., & Jensen, A. R. (2005). Thirty years of research on race differences in cognitive ability. *Psychology, Public Policy, and Law, 11*, 235–294.

Russ, S. W., & Wallace, C. E. (2013). Pretend play and creative processes. *American Journal of Play, 6*, 136–148.

Russel, G., & Norwich, B. (2012, April 17). Dilemmas, diagnosis and de-stigmatization: parental perspectives on the diagnosis of autism spectrum disorders. Retrieved from Pub Med: https://www.ncbi.nlm.nih.gov/pubmed/?term=22219019

Russell, J., Mauthner, N., Sharpe, S., & Tidswell, T. (1991). The 'windows task' as a measure of strategic deception in preschoolers and autistic subjects. *British Journal of Developmental Psychology, 9*(2), 331–349.

Rutledge, T., Reis, S. T., Olson, M., Owens, J., Kelsey, S. F., Pepine, C. J., . . . Matthews, K. A. (2004). Social networks are associated with lower mortality rates among women with suspected coronary disease: The National Heart, Lung, and Blood Institute-sponsored Women's Ischemia Syndrome Evaluation Study. *Psychosomatic Medicine, 66*, 882–888.

Rutter, M. (2002). Nature, nurture, and development: From evangelism through science toward policy and practice. *Child Development, 73*, 1–21.

Rutter, M. (2012). Gene–environment interdependence. *European Journal of Developmental Psychology, 9*(4), 391–412.

Rutter, M., O'Connor, T. G., & English & Romanian Adoptees (ERA) Study Team. (2004). Are there biological programming effects for psychological development? Findings from a study of Romanian adoptees. *Developmental Psychology, 40*, 81–94.

Ryan, A. S., Wenjun, Z., & Acosta, A. (2002). Breastfeeding continues to increase into the new millennium. *Pediatrics, 110*, 1103–1109.

Ryff, C. D. (1989). Happiness is everything, or is it? Explorations on the meaning of psychological well-being. *Journal of Personality and Social Psychology, 57*(6), 1069.

Ryff, C. D. (2014). Psychological well-being revisited: Advances in the science and practice of eudaimonia. *Psychotherapy and Psychosomatics, 83*(1), 10–28.

Ryff, C. D., & Keyes, C. L. M. (1995). The structure of psychological well-being revisited. *Journal of Personality and Social Psychology, 69*, 719–727.

Ryff, C. D., & Seltzer, M. M. (1995). Family relations and individual development in adulthood and aging. In R. Blieszner & V. Hilkevitch (Eds.), *Handbook of aging and the family* (pp. 95–113). Westport, CT: Greenwood Press.

Ryff, C. D., & Singer, B. (1998). Middle age and well-being. *Encyclopedia of Mental Health, 2*, 707–719.

Ryff, C. D., Keyes, C. L., & Hughes, D. L. (2004). Psychological well-being in MIDUS: Profiles of ethnic/racial diversity and life-course uniformity. In O. G. Brim, C. D. Ryff, & R. C. Kessler (Eds.), *How healthy are we? A national study of well-being at midlife* (pp. 398–424). Chicago: University of Chicago Press.

Ryff, C. D., Singer, B. H., & Palmersheim, K. A. (2004). Social inequalities in health and well-being: The role of relational and religious protective factors. In O. G. Brim, C. D. Ryff, & R. C. Kessler (Eds.), *How healthy are we? A national study of well-being at midlife.* Chicago: University of Chicago Press.

Saarni, C., Campos, J. J., Camras, A., & Witherington, D. (2006). Emotional development: Action, communication, and understanding. In N. Eisenberg, W. Damon, & R. Lerner (Eds.), *Handbook of child psychology: Vol. 3,*

Social, emotional and personality development (6th ed., pp. 226–299). Hoboken, NJ: Wiley.

Sabol, S. Z., Nelson, M. L., Fisher, C., Gunzerath, L., Brody, C. L., Hu, S., . . . Hamer, D. H. (1999). A genetic association for cigarette smoking behavior. *Health Psychology, 18*, 7–13.

Sacks, J. J., Gonzales, K. R., Bouchery, E. E., Tomedi, L. E., & Brewer, R. D. (2015). 2010 national and state costs of excessive alcohol consumption. *American Journal of Preventive Medicine, 49*(5), e73–e79.

Sadeh, A., Raviv, A., & Gruber, R. (2000). Sleep patterns and sleep disruptions in school age children. *Developmental Psychology, 36*(3), 291–301.

Saez, M. (2011). Same-sex marriage, same-sex cohabitation, and same-sex families around the world: Why 'same' is so different? *American University Journal of Gender, Social Policy & the Law, 19*, 1.

Saffran, J. R., Pollak, S. D., Seibel, R. L., & Shkolnik, A. (2007). Dog is a dog is a dog: Infant rule learning is not specific to language. *Cognition, 105*(3), 669–680.

Saffrey, R., Morley, R., Carlin, J. B., Joo, J. E., Ollikainen, M., Novakovic, B., Andronikos, R., Li, X., Loke, Y. J., Carson, N., Wallace, E. M., Umstad, M. P., Permezel, M., Galati, J. C., & Craig, J. M. (2012). Cohort profile: The peri/post-natal epigenetic twins study. *International Journal of Epidemiology, 41*, 55–61.

Sahoo, K., Sahoo, B., Choudhury, A. K., Sofi, N. Y., Kumar, R., & Bhadoria, A. S. (2015). Childhood obesity: causes and consequences. *Journal of Family Medicine and Primary Care, 4*(2), 187.

Saigal, S., Hoult, L. A., Streiner, D. L., Stoskopf, B. L., & Rosenbaum, P. L. (2000). School difficulties at adolescence in a regional cohort of children who were extremely low birth weight. *Pediatrics, 105*, 325–331.

Saigal, S., Stoskopf, B., Streiner, D., Boyle, M., Pinelli, J., Paneth, N., & Goddeeris, J. (2006). Transition of extremely-low-birth-weight infants from adolescence to young adulthood: Comparison with normal birth-weight controls. *Journal of the American Medical Association, 295*, 667–675.

Saito, E. K., Diaz, N., Chung, J., & McMurtray, A. (2017). Smoking history and Alzheimer's disease risk in a community-based clinic population. *Journal of Education and Health Promotion, 6*.

Saka, B., Kaya, O., Ozturk, G. B., Erten, N., & Karan, M. A. (2010). Malnutrition in the elderly and its relationship with other geriatric syndromes. *Clinical Nutrition, 29*(6), 745–748.

Sala-Llonch, R., Bartrés-Faz, D., & Junqué, C. (2015). Reorganization of brain networks in aging: A review of functional connectivity studies. *Frontiers in Psychology, 6*.

Salas, E., Rosen, M. A., & DiazGranados, D. (2010). Expertise-based intuition and decision making in organizations. *Journal of Management, 36*(4), 941–973.

Salkind, N. J. (Ed.). (2005). Smiling. *The encyclopedia of human development.* Thousand Oaks, CA: Sage.

Sallmen, M., Sandler, D. P., Hoppin, J. A., Blair, A., & Day, D. (2006). Reduced fertility among overweight and obese men. *Epidemiology, 17*(5), 520-523.

Salovey, P., Rothman, A. J., Detweiler, J. B., & Steward, W. T. (2000). Emotional states and physical health. *American Psychologist, 55,* 110-121.

Salthouse, T. A. (1991). *Theoretical perspectives on cognitive aging.* Hillsdale, NJ: Erlbaum.

Salthouse, T. A., & Maurer, T. J. (1996). Aging, job performance, and career development. In J. E. Birren & K. W. Schaie (Eds.), *Handbook of the psychology of aging* (pp. 353-364). San Diego: Academic Press.

Samara, M., Marlow, N., & Wolke, D., for the EPICure Study Group. (2008). Pervasive behavior problems at 6 years of age in a total-population sample of children born at 25 weeks of gestation. *Pediatrics, 122,* 562-573.

Samdal, O., & Dür, W. (2000). The school environment and the health of adolescents. In C. Currie, K. Hurrelmann, W. Settertobulte, R. Smith, & J. Todd (Eds.), *Health and health behaviour among young people: A WHO cross-national study (HBSC) international report* (pp. 49-64). (WHO Policy Series: Health Policy for Children and Adolescents, Series No. 1.) Copenhagen, Denmark: World Health Organization Regional Office for Europe.

Sampson, R. J. (1997). The embeddedness of child and adolescent development: A community-level perspective on urban violence. In J. McCord (Ed.), *Violence and childhood in the inner city* (pp. 31-77). Cambridge, UK: Cambridge University Press.

Samuelsson, M., Radestad, I., & Segesten, K. (2001). A waste of life: Fathers' experience of losing a child before birth. *Birth, 28,* 124-130.

Sandefur, G., Eggerling-Boeck, J., & Park, H. (2005). Off to a good start? Postsecondary education and early adult life. In R. A. Settersten Jr., F. F. Furstenberg Jr., & R. G. Rumbaut (Eds.), *On the frontier of adulthood: Theory, research, and public policy* (pp. 292-319). (John D. and Catherine T. MacArthur Foundation Series on Mental Health and Development, Research Network on Transitions to Adulthood and Public Policy.) Chicago: University of Chicago Press.

Sanders, A. R., Martin, E. R., Beecham, G. W., Guo, S., Dawood, K., Rieger, G., . . . & Duan, J. (2015). Genome-wide scan demonstrates significant linkage for male sexual orientation. *Psychological Medicine, 45*(7), 1379-1388.

Sanders, A., Stone, R., Meador, R., & Parker, V. (2010). Aging in place partnerships: A training program for family caregivers of residents living in affordable senior housing. *Cityscape: A Journal of Policy Development and Research, 12*(2), 85-104.

Sanders, L. D., Stevens, C., Coch, D., & Neville, H. J. (2006). Selective auditory attention in 3-to 5-year-old children: An event-related potential study. *Neuropsychologia, 44*(11), 2126-2138.

Sandin, S., Lichtenstein, P., Kuja-Halkola, R., Larsson, H., Hultman, C.M., & Reichenberg, A. (2014). The familial risk of autism. *Journal of the American Medical Association, 311,* 1770-1777.

Sandnabba, H. K., & Ahlberg, C. (1999). Parents' attitudes and expectations about children's cross-gender behavior. *Sex Roles, 40,* 249-263.

Santelli, J. S., & Melnikas, A. J. (2010). Teen fertility in transition: recent and historic trends in the United States. *Annual Review of Public Health, 31,* 371-383.

Santelli, J. S., Kantor, L. M., Grilo, S. A., Speizer, I. S., Lindberg, L. D., Heitel, J., . . . & Heck, C. J. (2017). Abstinence-only-until-marriage: An updated review of US policies and programs and their impact. *Journal of Adolescent Health, 61*(3), 273-280.

Santelli, J., Carter, M., Orr, M., & Dittus, P. (2007). Trends in sexual risk behaviors, by nonsexual risk behavior involvement. *Journal of Adolescent Health, 44*(4), 372-379.

Santos-Lozano, A., Santamarina, A., Pareja-Galeano, H., Sanchis-Gomar, F., Fiuza-Luces, C., Cristi-Montero, C., Bernal-Pino, A., Lucia, A., & Garatachea, N. (2016). The genetics of exceptional longevity: Insights from centenarians. *Maturitas, 90,* 49-57.

Sapolsky, R. M. (1992). Stress and neuroendocrine changes during aging. *Generations, 16*(4), 35-38.

Sapolsky, R. M. (2004). *Why zebras don't get ulcers: The acclaimed guide to stress, stress-related diseases, and coping-now revised and updated.* New York: Holt Paperbacks.

Sapp, F., Lee, K., & Muir, D. (2000). Three-year-olds' difficulty with the appearance-reality distinction: Is it real or is it apparent? *Developmental Psychology, 36*(5), 547.

Saraiya, A., Garakani, A., & Billick, S.B. (2013). Mental health approaches to child victims of acts of terrorism. *Psychiatric Quarterly, 84,* 115-124.

Sargent, J. D., & Dalton, M. (2001). Does parental disapproval of smoking prevent adolescents from becoming established smokers? *Pediatrics, 108*(6), 1256-1262.

Sarnecka, B. W., & Carey, S. (2007). How counting represents number: What children must learn and when they learn it. *Cognition, 108*(3), 662-674.

Sartorius, G., Spasevska, S., Idan, A., Turner, L., Forbes, E., Zamojska, A., . . . & Handelsman, D. J. (2012). Serum testosterone, dihydrotestosterone and estradiol concentrations in older men self-reporting very good health: The healthy man study. *Clinical Endocrinology, 77*(5), 755-763.

Satcher, D. (2001). *Women and smoking: A report of the surgeon general.* Washington, DC: Department of Health and Human Services.

Sattler, C., Toro, P., Schönknecht, P., & Schröder, J. (2012). Cognitive activity, education and socioeconomic status as preventive factors for mild cognitive impairment and Alzheimer's disease. *Psychiatry Research, 196*(1), 90-95.

Saudino, K. J., & Micalizzi, L. (2015). Emerging trends in behavioral genetic studies of child temperament. *Child Development Perspectives, 9*(3), 144-148.

Savage, J. S., Fisher, J. O., & Birch, L. L. (2007). Parental influence on eating behavior: Conception to adolescence. *Journal of Law, Medicine, and Ethics, 35*(1), 22-34.

Savic, I., & Lindström, P. (2008). PET and MRI show differences in cerebral asymmetry and functional connectivity between homo- and heterosexual subjects. *Proceedings of the National Academy of Sciences, USA, 105,* 9403-9408. doi: 10.1073/pnas.0801566105

Savic, I., Berglund, H., & Lindström, P. (2005). Brain response to putative pheromones in homosexual men. *Proceedings of the National Academy of Sciences, 102,* 7356-7361.

Savin-Williams, R. C. (2006). Who's gay? Does it matter? *Current Directions in Psychological Science, 15,* 40-44.

Sawicki, M. B. (2005, March 16). *Collision course: The Bush budget and Social Security* (EPI Briefing Paper No. 156). Retrieved from www.epinet.org/content.cfm/bp156

Saxe, R., Tenenbaum, J. B., & Carey, S. (2005). Secret agents: Inferences about hidden causes by 10- and 12-month old infants. *Psychological Science, 16,* 995-1001.

Sazonova, A., Kallen, K., Thurin-Kjellberg, A., Wennerholm, U., & Bergh, C. (2013). Neonatal and maternal outcomes comparing women undergoing two in vitro fertilization (IVF) singleton pregnancies and women undergoing one IVF twin pregnancy. *Fertility and Sterility, 99,* 731-737.

Scarr, S. (1992). Developmental theories for the 1990s: Development and individual differences. *Child Development, 63,* 1-19.

Scarr, S., & McCartney, K. (1983). How people make their own environments: A theory of genotype-environment effects. *Child Development, 54,* 424-435.

Schafft, K. A., Jensen, E. B., & Hinrichs, C. C. (2009). Food deserts and overweight school children: Evidence from Pennsylvania. *Rural Sociology, 74,* 153-177.

Schaie, K. W. (1977-1978). Toward a stage theory of adult cognitive development. *Journal of Aging and Human Development, 8*(2), 129-138.

Schaie, K. W. (1984). Midlife influences upon intellectual functioning in old age. *International Journal of Behavioral Development, 7,* 463-478.

Schaie, K. W. (1990). Intellectual development in adulthood. In J. E. Birren & K. W. Schaie (Eds.), *Handbook of the psychology of aging* (pp. 291-309). San Diego: Academic Press.

Schaie, K. W. (1994). The course of adult intellectual development. *American Psychologist, 49*(4), 304-313.

Schaie, K. W. (1996a). Intellectual development in adulthood. In J. E. Birren & K. W. Schaie (Eds.), *Handbook of the psychology of aging* (4th ed., pp. 266-286). San Diego: Academic Press.

Schaie, K. W. (1996b). *Intellectual development in adulthood: The Seattle Longitudinal Study.* Cambridge, UK: Cambridge University Press.

Schaie, K. W. (2005). *Developmental influences on adult intelligence: The Seattle longitudinal study.* New York: Oxford University Press.

Schaie, K. W., & Willis, S. L. (2000). A stage theory model of adult cognitive development revisited. In B. Rubinstein, M. Moss, & M. Kleban (Eds.), *The many dimensions of aging: Essays in honor of M. Powell Lawton* (pp. 173-191). New York: Springer.

Schaie, K. W., & Willis, S. L. (2010). The Seattle Longitudinal Study of adult cognitive development. *ISSBD Bulletin, 57*(1), 24.

Scharf, M., Mayseless, O., & Kivenson-Baron, I. (2004). Adolescents' attachment representations and developmental tasks in emerging adulthood. *Developmental Psychology, 40,* 430-444.

Scharf, R. J., Stroustrup, A., Conaway, M. R., & DeBoer, M. D. (2016). Growth and development in children born very low birthweight. *Archives of Disease in Childhood-Fetal and Neonatal Edition, 101*(5), F433-F438.

Scharlach, A. E., & Fredriksen, K. I. (1993). Reactions to the death of a parent during midlife. *Omega, 27,* 307-319.

Schaumberg, D. A., Mendes, F., Balaram, M., Dana, M. R., Sparrow, D., & Hu, H. (2004). Accumulated lead exposure and risk of age-related cataract in men. *Journal of the American Medical Association, 292,* 2750-2754.

Scheid, V. (2007, March). *Traditional Chinese medicine—What are we investigating?: The case of menopause.* Retrieved from U.S. National Library of Medicine National Institutes of Health: www.ncbi.nlm.nih.gov/pmc/articles/PMC2233879/

Scheidt, P., Overpeck, M. D., Whatt, W., & Aszmann, A. (2000). Adolescents' general health and wellbeing. In C. Currie, K. Hurrelmann, W. Settertobulte, R. Smith, & J. Todd (Eds.), *Health and health behaviour among young people: A WHO cross-national study (HBSC) international report* (pp. 24-38). (WHO Policy Series: Healthy Policy for Children and Adolescents, Series No. 1.) Copenhagen, Denmark: World Health Organization Regional Office for Europe.

Schemo, D. J. (2004, August 19). Charter schools lagging behind, test scores show. *The New York Times,* A1, A16.

Scher, A., Epstein, R., & Tirosh, E. (2004). Stability and changes in sleep regulation: A longitudinal study from 3 months to 3 years. *International Journal of Behavioral Development, 28*(3), 268-274.

Schetter, C. D. (2009). Stress processes in pregnancy and preterm birth. *Current Directions in Psychological Science, 18*(4), 205-209.

Scheve, T., & Venzon, C. (2017). *10 Stereotypes About Aging (That Just Aren't True).* Retrieved from howstuffworks: https://health.howstuffworks.com/wellness/aging/aging-process/5-stereotypes-about-aging.htm

Schieber, M., & Chandel, N. S. (2014). ROS function in redox signaling and oxidative stress. *Current Biology, 24*(10), R453-R462.

Schilling, O. K., & Diehl, M. (2014). Reactivity to stressor pile-up in adulthood: Effects on daily negative and positive affect. *Psychology and Aging, 29*(1), 72.

Schlenker, E. D. (2010). Healthy aging: Nutrition concepts for older adults. In T. Wilson, N. J. Temple, G. A. Bray, & M. B. Struble (Eds.), *Nutrition guide for physicians* (pp. 215-226). New York: Humana Press.

Schlotz, W., Jones, A., Phillips, D. I. W., Gale, C. R., Robinson, S. M., & Godrey, K. M. (2009). Lower maternal folate status in early pregnancy is associated with childhood hyperactivity and peer problems in offspring. *Journal of Child Psychology and Psychiatry, 51*(5), 594-602. doi: 10.1111/j.1469-7610.2009.02182.x

Schmidt, J. A., Shumow, L., & Kackar, H. (2007). Adolescents' participation in service activities and its impact on academic, behavioral, and civic outcomes. *Journal of Youth and Adolescence, 36*(2), 127-140.

Schmitt, M. T., Branscombe, N. R., Postmes, T., & Garcia, A. (2014). The consequences of perceived discrimination for psychological well-being: A meta-analytic review. *Psychological Bulletin, 140*(4), 921.

Schmitt, M., Kliegel, M., & Shapiro, A. (2007). Marital interaction in middle and old age: A predictor of marital satisfaction? *International Journal of Aging & Human Development, 65*(4), 283-300.

Schmitt, S. A., Simpson, A. M., & Friend, M. (2011). A longitudinal assessment of the home literacy environment and early language. *Infant and Child Development, 20*(6), 409-431.

Schmitz, S., Saudino, K. J., Plomin, R., Fulker, D. W., & DeFries, J. C. (1996). Genetic and environmental influences on temperament in middle childhood: Analyses of teacher and tester ratings. *Child Development, 67,* 409-422.

Schnaas, L., Rothenberg, S. J., Flores, M., Martinez, S., Hernandez, C., Osorio, E., . . . Perroni, E. (2006). Reduced intellectual development in children with prenatal lead exposure. *Environmental Health Perspectives, 114*(5), 791-797.

Schnack, H. G., Van Haren, N. E., Brouwer, R. M., Evans, A., Durston, S., Boomsma, D. I., . . . & Hulshoff Pol, H. E. (2014). Changes in thickness and surface area of the human cortex and their relationship with intelligence. *Cerebral Cortex, 25*(6), 1608-1617.

Schneider, B. H., Atkinson, L., & Tardif, C. (2001). Child-parent attachment and children's peer relations: A quantitative review. *Developmental Psychology, 37,* 86-100.

Schneider, J. P., Weiss, R., & Samenow, C. (2012). Is it really cheating? Understanding the emotional reactions and clinical treatment of spouses and partners affected by cybersex infidelity. *Sexual Addiction & Compulsivity, 19*(1-2), 123-139.

Schneider, M. (2002). *Do school facilities affect academic outcomes?* Washington, DC: National Clearinghouse for Educational Facilities.

Schneider, W. (2008). The development of metacognitive knowledge in children and adolescents: Major trends and implications for education. *Mind, Brain, and Education, 2*(3), 114-121.

Schoenborn, C. A. (2004). Marital status and health: United States, 1999-2002. *Advance Data from Vital and Health Statistics, No. 351.* Hyattsville, MD: National Center for Health Statistics.

Schoenborn, C. A., & Heyman, K. M. (2009). Health characteristics of adults aged 55 years and older: United States, 2004-2007. *National Health Statistics Reports, 16,* 1-31. Hyattsville, MD: National Center for Health Statistics.

Schoenborn, C. A., Vickerie, J. L., & Powell-Griner, E. (2006). Health characteristics of adults 55 years of age and over: United States, 2000-2003. *Advance Data from Vital and Health Statistics, No. 370.* Hyattsville, MD: National Center for Health Statistics.

Schoeni, R., & Ross, K. (2005). Maternal assistance from families during the transition to adulthood. In R. A. Settersten Jr., F. F. Furstenberg Jr., & R. G. Rumbaut (Eds.), *On the frontier of adulthood: Theory, research, and public policy* (pp. 396-416). Chicago: University of Chicago Press.

Scholten, C. M. (1985). *Childbearing in American society: 1650-1850.* New York: New York University Press.

Schomerus, G., Evans-Lacko, S., Rüsch, N., Mojtabai, R., Angermeyer, M. C., & Thornicroft, G. (2015). Collective levels of stigma and national suicide rates in 25 European countries. *Epidemiology and Psychiatric Sciences, 24*(2), 166-171.

Schondelmyer, E. (2017). Fewer married households and more living alone. *U.S. Census Bureau.* Retrieved from www.census.gov/library/stories/2017/08/more-adults-living-without-children.html

Schonert-Reichl, K. A., Smith, V., Zaidman-Zait, A., & Hertzman, C. (2012). Promoting children's prosocial behaviors in school: Impact of the "Roots of Empathy" program on the social and emotional competence of school-aged children. *School Mental Health, 4*(1), 1-21.

Schonfeld, D. J., & Quackenbush, M. (2010). *The grieving student: A teacher's guide.* Baltimore, MD: Paul H. Brookes Publishing Co.

Schonfeld, D. J., Demaria, T., & Committee on Psychosocial Aspects of Child and Family Health, Disaster Preparedness Advisory Council. (2016). Supporting the grieving child and family. *Pediatrics,* e20162147.

Schooler, C. (1990). Psychosocial factors and effective cognitive functioning in adulthood. In J. E. Burren & K. W. Schaie (Eds.), *The handbook of aging* (pp. 347-358). San Diego: Academic Press.

Schooler, C., Revell, A. J., & Caplan, L. J. (2007). Parental practices and willingness to ask for children's help later in life. *Journal of Gerontology Psychological and Social Sciences, 57B,* S3-S13.

Schore, A. N. (1994). *Affect regulation and the origin of the self: The neurobiology of emotional development.* Hillsdale, NJ: Erlbaum.

Schredl, M., Anders, A., Hellriegel, S., & Rehm, A. (2008). TV viewing, computer game playing and nightmares in school children. *Dreaming, 18*(2), 69-76. http://dx.doi.org.vwu.idm.oclc.org/10.1037/1053-0797.18.2.69

Schredl, M., Fricke-Oerkermann, L., Mitschke, A., Wiater, A., & Lehmkuhl, G. (2009). Longitudinal study of nightmares in children: stability and effect of emotional symptoms. *Child Psychiatry and Human Development, 40*(3), 439–449.

Schulenberg, J. E., & Zarrett, N. R. (2006). Mental health during emerging adulthood: Continuity and discontinuity in courses, causes, and functions. In J. J. Arnett & J. L. Tanner (Eds.), *Emerging adults in America: Coming of age in the 21st century* (pp. 135–172). Washington, DC: American Psychological Association.

Schulenberg, J. E., Johnston, L. D., O'Malley, P. M., Bachman, J. G., Miech, R. A. & Patrick, M. E. (2017). *Monitoring the Future national survey results on drug use, 1975–2016: Volume II, College students and adults ages 19–55.* Ann Arbor: Institute for Social Research, The University of Michigan. Available at http://monitoringthefuture.org/ pubs.html#monographs

Schulenberg, J., O'Malley, P., Bachman, J., & Johnston, L. (2005). Early adult transitions and their relation to well-being and substance use. In R. A. Settersten Jr., F. F. Furstenberg Jr., & R. G. Rumbaut (Eds.), *On the frontier of adulthood: Theory, research, and public policy* (pp. 417–453). Chicago: University of Chicago Press.

Schulting, A. B., Malone, P. S., & Dodge, K. A. (2005). The effect of school-based kindergarten transition policies and practices on child academic outcomes. *Developmental Psychology, 41*, 860–871.

Schulz, M. S., Cowan, C. P., & Cowan, P. A. (2006). Promoting healthy beginnings: A randomized controlled trial of a preventive intervention to preserve marital quality during the transition to parenthood. *Journal of Consulting and Clinical Psychology, 74*, 20–31.

Schulz, M. S., Cowan, P. A., Cowan, C. P., & Brennan, R. T. (2004). Coming home upset: Gender, marital satisfaction, and the daily spillover of workday experience into couple interactions. *Journal of Family Psychology, 18*, 250–263.

Schulz, R. (1978). *A psychology of death, dying, and bereavement.* Reading, MA: Addison-Wesley.

Schulz, R., & Martire, L. M. (2004). Family caregiving of persons with dementia: Prevalence, health effects, and support strategies. *American Journal of Geriatric Psychiatry, 12*, 240–249.

Schurz, M., Aichhorn, M., Martin, A., & Perner, J. (2013). Common brain areas engaged in false belief reasoning and visual perspective taking: a meta-analysis of functional brain imaging studies. *Frontiers in Human Neuroscience, 7.*

Schuur, M., Ikram, M. A., van Swieten, J. C., Isaacs, A., Vergeer-Drop, J. M., Hofman, A., . . . & Van Duijn, C. M. (2011). Cathepsin D gene and the risk of Alzheimer's disease: A population-based study and meta-analysis. *Neurobiology of Aging, 32*(9), 1607–1614.

Schwab, S. G., & Wildenauer, D. B. (2013). Genetics of psychiatric disorders in the GWAS era: an update on schizophrenia. *European Archives of Psychiatry and Clinical Neuroscience, 263*, 147.

Schwartz, B. L. (2008). Working memory load differentially affects tip-of-the-tongue states and feeling-of-knowing judgments. *Memory & Cognition, 36*(1), 9–19.

Schwartz, D., Chang, L., & Farver, J. M. (2001). Correlates of victimization in Chinese children's peer groups. *Developmental Psychology, 37*(4), 520–532.

Schwartz, D., Dodge, K. A., Pettit, G. S., Bates, J. E., & Conduct Problems Prevention Research Group. (2000). Friendship as a moderating factor in the pathway between early harsh home environment and later victimization in the peer group. *Developmental Psychology, 36*, 646–662.

Schwartz, D., McFadyen-Ketchum, S. A., Dodge, K. A., Pettit, G. S., & Bates, J. E. (1998). Peer group victimization as a predictor of children's behavior problems at home and in school. *Development and Psychopathology, 10*, 87–99.

Schweinhart, L. J. (2007). Crime prevention by the High/Scope Perry preschool program. *Victims & Offenders, 2*(2), 141–160.

Schweinhart, L. J., Barnes, H. V., & Weikart, D. P. (1993). *Significant benefits: The High/Scope Perry Preschool Study through age 27* (Monographs of the High/Scope Educational Research Foundation No. 10). Ypsilanti, MI: High/Scope.

Scott, J. (1998). Changing attitudes to sexual morality: A cross-national comparison. *Sociology, 32*, 815–845.

Scott, M. E., Booth, A., King, V., & Johnson, D. R. (2007). Postdivorce father-adolescent closeness. *Journal of Marriage and Family, 69*(5), 1194–1209.

Scott, R. M., & Baillargeon, R. (2009). Which penguin is this? Attributing false beliefs about object identity at 18 months. *Child Development, 80*(4), 1172–1196.

Scott, S., Doolan, M., Beckett, C., Harry, S., & Cartwright, S. (2012). How is parenting style related to child antisocial behaviour? Preliminary findings from the Helping Children Achieve study [research report]. Retrieved from http:// dera.ioe.ac.uk/13827/1/DFE-RR185a.pdf

Seblega, B. K., Zhang, N. J., Unruh, L. Y., Breen, G. M., Paek, S. C., & Wan, T. T. (2010). Changes in nursing home staffing levels, 1997 to 2007. *Medical Care Research and Review, 67*(2), 232–246.

Sedlak, A. J., & Broadhurst, D. D. (1996). *Executive summary of the third national incidence study of child abuse and neglect* (NIS-3). Washington, DC: U.S. Department of Health and Human Services.

Seeman, T. E., Merkin, S. S., Crimmins, E. M., & Karlamangla, A. (2009). Disability trends among older Americans: National health and nutrition examination surveys, 1988–1994 and 1999–2004. *American Journal of Public Health, 100*(1), 100–107.

Segerstrom, S. C., & Miller, G. E. (2004). Psychological stress and the human immune system: A meta-analytic study of 30 years of inquiry. *Psychological Bulletin, 130*, 601–630.

Seidler, A., Neinhaus, A., Bernhardt, T., Kauppinen, T., Elo, A. L., & Frolich, L. (2004). Psychosocial work factors and dementia. *Occupational and Environmental Medicine, 61*, 962–971.

Seifer, R., Schiller, M., Sameroff, A. J., Resnick, S., & Riordan, K. (1996). Attachment, maternal sensitivity, and infant temperament during the first year of life. *Developmental Psychology, 32*, 12–25.

Seiffge-Krenke, I. (2006). Coping with relationship stressors: The impact of different working models of attachment and links to adaptation. *Journal of Youth and Adolescence, 35*(1), 25–39.

Sellers, E. M. (1998). Pharmacogenetics and ethnoracial differences in smoking. *Journal of the American Medical Association, 280*, 179–180.

Selman, R. L. (1980). *The growth of interpersonal understanding: Developmental and clinical analyses.* New York: Academic Press.

Selman, R. L., & Selman, A. P. (1979, April). Children's ideas about friendship: A new theory. *Psychology Today*, pp. 71–80.

Salovey, P., & Mayer, J. D. (1990). Emotional intelligence. *Imagination, Cognition, and Personality, 9*, 185–211.

Seltzer, J. A. (2000). Families formed outside of marriage. *Journal of Marriage and Family, 62*, 1247–1268.

Seltzer, J. A. (2004). Cohabitation in the United States and Britain: Demography, kinship, and the future. *Journal of Marriage and Family, 66*, 921–928.

Seltzer, M. M., Floyd, F., Song, J., Greenberg, J., & Hong, J. (2011). Midlife and aging parents of adults with intellectual and developmental disabilities: impacts of lifelong parenting. *American Journal on Intellectual and Developmental Disabilities, 116*(6), 479–499.

Semega, J. L., Fontenot, K. R., and Kollar, M. A. (2017). *U.S. Census Bureau, Current Population Reports, P60-259, Income and Poverty in the United States: 2016.* Washington, DC: U.S. Government Printing Office.

Sen, A., Partelow, L., & Miller, D. C. (2005). *Comparative indicators of education in the United States and other G8 countries: 2004* (NCES 2005-021). Washington, DC: National Center for Education Statistics.

Serbin, L., Poulin-Dubois, D., Colburne, K. A., Sen, M., & Eichstedt, J. A. (2001). Gender stereotyping in infancy: Visual preferences for knowledge of gender-stereotyped toys in the second year. *International Journal of Behavioral Development, 25*, 7–15.

Sethi, A., Mischel, W., Aber, J. L., Shoda, Y., & Rodriguez, M. L. (2000). The role of strategic attention deployment in development of self-regulation: Predicting preschoolers' delay of gratification from mother-toddler interactions. *Developmental Psychology, 36*, 767–777.

Settersten Jr., R. A. (2005). Social policy and the transition to adulthood: Toward stronger institutions and individual capacities. R. A. Settersten Jr., F. F. Furstenberg Jr., & R. G. Rumbaut (Eds.), *On the frontier of adulthood: Theory, research, and public policy*, (pp. 534–560). Chicago: University of Chicago Press.

Seybold, K. S., & Hill, P. C. (2001). The role of religion and spirituality in mental and physical health. *Current Directions in Psychological Science, 10*, 21–24.

Shafto, M. A., & Tyler, L. K. (2014). Language in the aging brain: The network dynamics of cognitive decline and preservation. *Science, 346*(6209), 583-587.

Shafto, M. A., Burke, D. M., Stamatakis, E. A., Tam, P. P., & Tyler, L. K. (2007). On the tip of-the-tongue: Neural correlates of increased word-finding failures in normal aging. *Journal of Cognitive Neuroscience, 19*(2), 2060-2070.

Shah, T., Sullivan, K., & Carter, J. (2006). Sudden infant death syndrome and reported maternal smoking during pregnancy. *American Journal of Public Health, 96*(10), 1757-1759.

Shalev, I., Entringer, S., Wadhwa, P. D., Wolkowitz, O. M., Puterman, E., Lin, J., & Epel, E. S. (2013). Stress and telomere biology: A lifespan perspective. *Psychoneuroendocrinology, 38*(9), 1835-1842.

Shammas, M. A. (2011). Telomeres, lifestyle, cancer, and aging. *Current Opinion in Clinical Nutrition and Metabolic Care, 14*(1), 28.

Shankaran, S., Das, A., Bauer, C. R., Bada, H. S., Lester, B., Wright, L. L., & Smeriglio, V. (2004). Association between patterns of maternal substance use and infant birth weight, length, and head circumference. *Pediatrics, 114*, e226-e234.

Shannon, J. D., Tamis-LeMonda, C. S., London, K., & Cabrera, N. (2002). Beyond rough and tumble: Low income fathers' interactions and children's cognitive development at 24 months. *Parenting: Science & Practice, 2*(2), 77-104.

Shao, H., Breitner, J. C., Whitmer, R. A., Wang, J., Hayden, K., Wengreen, H., . . . & Welsh-Bohmer, K. (2012). Hormone therapy and Alzheimer disease dementia New findings from the Cache County Study. *Neurology, 79*(18), 1846-1852.

Shapiro, A., & Cooney, T. M. (2007). Interpersonal relations across the life course. *Advances in Life Course Research, 12*, 191-219.

Shapiro, J. R., Berkman, N. D., Brownley, K. A., Sedway, J. A., Lohr, K. N., & Bulik, C. M. (2007). Bulimia nervosa treatment: a systematic review of randomized controlled trials. *International Journal of Eating Disorders, 40*(4), 321-336.

Shapiro, P. (1994, November). My house is your house: Advance planning can ease the way when parents move in with adult kids. *AARP Bulletin*, 2.

Sharma, A. R., McGue, M. K., & Benson, P. L. (1996a). The emotional and behavioral adjustment of United States adopted adolescents, Part I: An overview. *Children and Youth Services Review, 18*, 83-100.

Sharma, A. R., McGue, M. K., & Benson, P. L. (1996b). The emotional and behavioral adjustment of United States adopted adolescents, Part II: Age at adoption. *Children and Youth Services Review, 18*, 101-114.

Sharp, E. S., & Gatz, M. (2011). The relationship between education and dementia an updated systematic review. *Alzheimer Disease and Associated Disorders, 25*(4), 289.

Sharp, E. S., Reynolds, C. A., Pedersen, N. L., & Gatz, M. (2010). Cognitive engagement and cognitive aging: Is openness protective? *Psychology and Aging, 25*(1), 60-73.

Shatz, M., & Gelman, R. (1973). The development of communication skills: Modifications in the speech of young children as a function of listener. *Monographs of the Society for Research in Child Development, 38*(5, Serial No. 152).

Shaw, B. A., Krause, N., Liang, J., & Bennett, J. (2007). Tracking changes in social relations throughout late life. *Journal of Gerontology: Social Sciences, 62B*,S90-S99.

Shaw, P., Gornick, M., Lerch, J., Addington, A., Seal, J., Greenstein, D., . . . Rapoport, J. L. (2007). Polymorphisms of the dopamine D4 receptor, clinical outcome, and cortical structure in attention-deficit/hyperactivity disorder. *Archives of General Psychiatry, 64*, 921-931.

Shaw, P., Greenstein, D., Lerch, J., Clasen, L., Lenroot, R., Gogtay, N., . . . Giedd, J. (2006). Intellectual ability and cortical development in children and adolescents. *Nature, 440*, 676-679.

Shayer, M., Ginsburg, D., & Coe, R. (2007). Thirty years on—A large anti-Flynn effect? The Piagetian Test Volume & Heaviness norms 1975-2003. *British Journal of Educational Psychology, 77*(1), 25-41.

Shaywitz, S. (2003). *Overcoming dyslexia: A new and complete science-based program for overcoming reading problems at any level.* New York: Knopf.

Shaywitz, S. E. (1998). Current concepts: Dyslexia. *New England Journal of Medicine, 338*, 307-312.

Shaywitz, S. E., Mody, M., & Shaywitz, B. A. (2006). Neural mechanisms in dyslexia. *Current Directions in Psychological Science, 15*, 278-281.

Shea, K. M., Little, R. E., & the ALSPAC Study Team. (1997). Is there an association between preconceptual paternal X-ray exposure and birth outcome? *American Journal of Epidemiology, 145*, 546-551.

Shedlock, D. J., & Cornelius, S. W. (2003). Psychological approaches to wisdom and its development. In J. Demick & C. Andreoletti (Eds.), *Handbook of adult development* (pp. 153-167). New York: Plenum Press.

Sheldon, K. M., & Kasser, T. (2001). Getting older, getting better? Personal strivings and psychological maturity across the life span. *Developmental Psychology, 37*, 491-501.

Shetgiri, R., Espelage, D. L., & Carroll, L. (2015). Bullying trends, correlates, consequences, and characteristics. In *Practical strategies for clinical management of bullying* (pp. 3-11). New York: Springer International Publishing.

Shiffman, S., Brockwell, S., Pillitteri, J., & Gitchell, J. (2008). Use of smoking-cessation treatments in the United States. *American Journal of Preventive Medicine, 34*(2), 102-111.

Shigehara, K., Konaka, H., Koh, E., Izumi, K., Kitagawa, Y., & Mizokami, A. (2015). Effects of testosterone replacement therapy on nocturia and quality of life with hypogonadism: A sub-analysis of a previous prospective randomized controlled study in Japan. *The Aging Male*, 18, 169-174.

Shimada-Sugimoto, M., Otowa, T., & Hettema, J. M. (2015). Genetics of anxiety disorders: genetic epidemiological and molecular studies in humans. *Psychiatry and Clinical Neurosciences, 69*(7), 388-401.

Shiner, R. L., Buss, K. A., McClowry, S. G., Putnam, S. P., Saudino, K. J., & Zentner, M. (2012). What is temperament now? Assessing progress in temperament research on the twenty-fifth anniversary of Goldsmith et al. *Child Development Perspectives, 6*(4), 436-444.

Shiono, P. H., & Behrman, R. E. (1995). Low birth weight: Analysis and recommendations. *Future of Children, 5*(1), 4-18.

Shoghi-Jadid, K., Small, G. W., Agdeppa, E. D., Kepe, V., Ercoli, L. M., Siddarth, P., . . . Barrio, J. R. (2002). Localization of neurofibrillary tangles and beta-amyloid plaques in the brains of living patients with Alzheimer disease. *American Journal of Geriatric Psychiatry, 10*, 24-35.

Shonkoff, J., & Phillips, D. (2000). Growing up in child care. In I. Shonkoff & D. Phillips (Eds.), *From neurons to neighborhoods* (pp. 297-327). Washington, DC: National Research Council/ Institute of Medicine.

Shor, E., Roelfs, D. J., Curreli, M., Clemow, L., Burg, M. M., & Schwartz, J. E. (2012). Widowhood and mortality: A meta-analysis and meta-regression. *Demography, 49*(2), 575-606.

Shuey, K., & Hardy, M. A. (2003). Assistance to aging parents and parents-in-law: Does lineage affect family allocation decisions? *Journal of Marriage and Family, 65*, 418-431.

Shulman, S., & Connolly, J. (2013). The challenge of romantic relationships in emerging adulthood: Reconceptualization of the field. *Emerging Adulthood, 1*(1), 27-39.

Shulman, S., Scharf, M., Lumer, D., & Maurer, O. (2001). Parental divorce and young adult children's romantic relationships: Resolution of the divorce experience. *American Journal of Orthopsychiatry, 71*, 473-478.

Shumaker, S. A., Legault, C., Kuller, L., Rapp, S. R., Thal, L., Lane, D. S., . . . Coker, L. H., for the Women's Health Initiative Memory Study Investigators. (2004). Conjugated equine estrogens and incidence of probable dementia and mild cognitive impairment in postmenopausal women: Women's Health Initiative Memory Study. *Journal of the American Medical Association, 291*, 2947-2958.

Shwe, H. I., & Markman, E. M. (1997). Young children's appreciation of the mental impact of their communicative signals. *Developmental Psychology, 33*(4), 630-636.

Shweder, R. A., Goodnow, J., Hatano, G., Levine, R. A., Markus, H., & Miller, P. (2006). The cultural psychology of development: One mind, many mentalities. In W. Damon (Ed.), *Handbook of child development* (pp. 865-937). New York: Wiley.

Siedlecki, K. L., Salthouse, T. A., Oishi, S., & Jeswani, S. (2014). The relationship between social support and subjective well-being across age. *Social Indicators Research, 117*(2), 561-576.

Siedlecki, K., Tucker-Drop, E. M., Oishi, S., & Salthouse, T. A. (2008). Life satisfaction across adulthood: Different determinants at different ages? *Journal of Positive Psychology, 3*(3), 153-164.

Siegel, M. B., Tanwar, K. L., & Wood, K. S. (2011). Electronic cigarettes as a smoking-cessation tool: Results from an online survey. *American Journal of Preventive Medicine*. doi: 10.1016/j.amepre.2010.12.006

Siegel, R. L., Miller, K. D., & Jemal, A. (2015). Cancer statistics, 2015. *CA: a Cancer Journal for Clinicians, 65*(1), 5–29.

Siegler, I. C., & Brummett, B. H. (2000). Associations among NEO personality assessments and well-being at midlife: Facet-level analyses. *Psychology and Aging, 15*, 710–714.

Siegler, R. S. (1998). *Children's thinking* (3rd ed.). Upper Saddle River, NJ: Prentice Hall.

Siegler, R. S. (2000). The rebirth of children's learning. *Child Development, 71*(1), 26–35.

Siegler, R. S. (2009). Improving the numerical understanding of children from low-income families. *Child Development Perspectives, 3*(2), 118–124.

Siegler, R. S., & Booth, J. L. (2004). Development of numerical estimation in young children. *Child Development, 75*, 428–444.

Siegler, R. S., & Opfer, J. E. (2003). The development of numerical estimation: Evidence for multiple representations of numerical quantity. *Psychological Science, 14*, 237–243.

Sierra, M., Fernández, A., & Fraga, M. (2015). Epigenetics of aging. *Current Genomics, 16*(6), 435–440.

Sieving, R. E., McNeely, C. S., & Blum, R. W. (2000). Maternal expectations, mother-child connectedness, and adolescent sexual debut. *Archives of Pediatric & Adolescent Medicine, 154*, 809–816.

Sieving, R. E., Oliphant, J. A., & Blum, R. W. (2002). Adolescent sexual behavior and sexual health. *Pediatrics in Review, 23*, 407–416.

Sijtsema, J. J., Ojanen, T., Veenstra, R., Lindenberg, S., Hawley, P. H., & Little, T. D. (2010). Forms and functions of aggression in adolescent friendship selection and influence: A longitudinal social network analysis. *Social Development, 19*(3), 515–534.

Silberg, J. L., Maes, H., & Eaves, L. J. (2012). Unraveling the effect of genes and environment in the transmission of parental antisocial behavior to children's conduct disturbance, depression and hyperactivity. *Journal of Child Psychology and Psychiatry, 53*(6), 668–677.

Silventoinen, K., Rokholm, B., Kaprio, J., & Sørensen, T. I. A. (2010). The genetic and environmental influences on childhood obesity: a systematic review of twin and adoption studies. *International Journal of Obesity, 34*(1), 29.

Silverman, W. K., La Greca, A. M., & Wasserstein, S. (1995). What do children worry about? Worries and their relation to anxiety. *Child Development, 66*, 671–686.

Silverstein, M., & Bengtson, V. L. (1997). Intergenerational solidarity and the structure of adult child-parent relationships in American families. *American Journal of Sociology, 103*, 429–460.

Simmonds, M., Llewellyn, A., Owen, C. G., & Woolacott, N. (2016). Predicting adult obesity from childhood obesity: A systematic review and meta-analysis. *Obesity Reviews, 17*, 95–107.

Simmons, R. G., Blyth, D. A., & McKinney, K. L. (1983). The social and psychological effect of puberty on white females. In J. Brooks-Gunn & A. C. Petersen (Eds.), *Girls at puberty: Biological and psychological perspectives*. New York: Plenum Press.

Simon, G. E. (2006). The antidepressant quandary—Considering suicide risk when treating adolescent depression. *New England Journal of Medicine, 355*, 2722–2723.

Simon, G. E., Savarino, J., Operskalski, B., & Wang, P. S. (2006). Suicide risk during antidepressant treatment. *American Journal of Psychiatry, 163*, 41–47.

Simons, E., To, T., Moineddin, R., Stieb, D., & Dell, S. D. (2014). Maternal second-hand smoke exposure in pregnancy is associated with childhood asthma development. *The Journal of Allergy and Clinical Immunology: In Practice, 2*(2), 201–207.

Simons, R. L., Chao, W., Conger, R. D. B., & Elder, G. H. (2001). Quality of parenting as mediator of the effect of childhood defiance on adolescent friendship choices and delinquency: A growth curve analysis. *Journal of Marriage and Family, 63*, 63–79.

Simonton, D. K. (1990). Creativity and wisdom in aging. In J. E. Birren & K. W. Schaie (Eds.), *Handbook of the psychology of aging* (pp. 320–329). New York: Academic Press.

Simonton, D. K. (2000). Creativity: Cognitive, personal, developmental, and social aspects. *American Psychologist, 55*, 151–158.

Simpson, J. A., Collins, A., Tran, S., & Haydon, K. C. (2007). Attachment and the experience and expression of emotions in romantic relationships: A developmental perspective. *Journal of Personality and Social Psychology, 92*, 355–367.

Sines, E., Syed, U., Wall, S., & Worley, H. (2007). Postnatal care: A critical opportunity to save mothers and newborns. *Policy Perspectives on Newborn Health*. Washington, DC: Save the Children and Population Reference Bureau.

Singer, D. G., & Singer, J. L. (1990). *The house of make-believe: Play and the developing imagination*. Cambridge, MA: Harvard University Press.

Singer, J. L. (2004). Narrative identity and meaning-making across the adult lifespan. *Journal of Personality, 72*, 437–459.

Singer, J. L., & Singer, D. G. (1998). Barney & Friends as entertainment and education: Evaluating the quality and effectiveness of a television series for preschool children. In J. K. Asamen & G. L. Berry (Eds.), *Research paradigms, television, and social behavior* (pp. 305–367). Thousand Oaks, CA: Sage.

Singer, L. T., Minnes, S., Short, E., Arendt, K., Farkas, K., Lewis, B., . . . Kirchner, H. L. (2004). Cognitive outcomes of preschool children with prenatal cocaine exposure. *Journal of the American Medical Association, 291*, 2448–2456.

Singer, T., Verhaeghen, P., Ghisletta, P., Lindenberger, U., & Baltes, P. B. (2003). The fate of cognition in very old age: Six-year longitudinal findings in the Berlin Aging Study (BASE). *Psychology and Aging, 18*, 318–331.

Singer-Freeman, K. E., & Goswami, U. (2001). Does half a pizza equal half a box of chocolates?: Proportional matching in an analogy task. *Cognitive Development, 16*(3), 811–829.

Singh, A. S., Mulder, C., Twisk, J. W., Van Mechelen, W., & Chinapaw, M. J. (2008). Tracking of childhood overweight into adulthood: a systematic review of the literature. *Obesity Reviews, 9*(5), 474–488.

Singh, L., Nestor, S., Parikh, C., & Yull, A. (2009). Influences of infant-directed speech on early world recognition. *Infancy, 14*, 654–666.

Singh, M. K. (2017, March 30). *At almost 106 years old Fauja Singh reveals the secret of his youthfulness*. Retrieved from SBS: http://file.scirp.org/pdf/CE_2017092615440943.pdf

Singh, T., Arrazola, R. A., Corey, C. G., et al. (2016) Tobacco use among middle and high school students—United States, 2011–2015. *Morbidity and Mortality Weekly Report, 65*(14), 361–367. Retrieved from www.cdc.gov/mmwr/volumes/65/wr/mm6514a1.htm

Singh-Manoux, A., Hillsdon, M., Brunner, E., & Marmot, M. (2005). Effects of physical activity on cognitive functioning in middle age: Evidence from the Whitehall II Prospective Cohort Study. *American Journal of Public Health, 95*, 2252–2258.

Sinnott, J. D. (2003). Postformal thought and adult development. In J. Demick & C. Andreoletti (Eds.), *Handbook of adult development*. New York: Plenum Press.

Siris, E. S., Miller, P. D., Barrett-Connor, E., Faulkner, K. G., Wehren, L. E., Abbott, T. A., Berger, M. L., . . . Sherwood, L. M. (2001). Identification and fracture outcomes of undiagnosed low bone mineral density in postmenopausal women: Results from the National Osteoporosis Risk Assessment. *Journal of the American Medical Association, 286*, 2815–2822.

Sitzer, D. I., Twamley, E. W., & Jeste, D. V. (2006). Cognitive training in Alzheimer's disease: A meta-analysis of the literature. *Acta Psychiatrica Scandinavica, 114*(2), 75–90.

Skadberg, B. T., Morild, I., & Markestad, T. (1998). Abandoning prone sleeping: Effects on the risk of sudden infant death syndrome. *Journal of Pediatrics, 132*, 234–239.

Skalicky, A., Meyers, A. F., Adams, W. G., Yang, Z., Cook, J. T., & Frank, D. A. (2006). Child food insecurity and iron deficiency anemia in low-income infants and toddlers in the United States. *Maternal and Child Health Journal, 10*. doi: 10.1007/s10995-005-0036-0

Skinner, B. F. (1957). *Verbal behavior*. New York: Appleton-Century-Crofts.

Skinner, D. (1989). The socialization of gender identity: Observations from Nepal. In J. Valsiner (Ed.), *Child development in cultural context* (pp. 181–192). Toronto, Canada: Hogrefe & Huber.

Skirbekk, V. (2008). Age and productivity capacity: Descriptions, causes and policy options. *Ageing Horizons, 8*(4), 12.

Skorska, M. N., Blanchard, R., VanderLaan, D. P., Zucker, K. J., & Bogaert, A. F. (2017). Gay male only-children: Evidence for low birth weight and high maternal miscarriage rates. *Archives of Sexual Behavior, 46*(1), 205–215.

Skulachev, V. P., Anisimov, V. N., Antonenko, Y. N., Bakeeva, L. E., Chernyak, B. V., Erichev, V. P., . . . Zorov, D. B. (2009). An attempt to prevent senescence: A mitochondrial approach. *Biochimica et Biophysica Acta, 1787*(5), 437–461.

Skultety, K. M., & Whitbourne, S. K. (2004). Gender differences in identity processes and self-esteem in middle and later adulthood. *Journal of Women & Aging, 16*(1–2), 175–188.

Slayton, S. C., D'Archer, J., & Kaplan, F. (2010). Outcome studies on the efficacy of art therapy: A review of findings. *Art Therapy, 27*(3), 108–118.

Sliwinska-Kowalska, M., & Davis, A. (2012). Noise-induced hearing loss. *Noise and Health, 14*(61), 274.

Slobin, D. (1983). Universal and particular in the acquisition of grammar. In E. Wanner & L. Gleitman (Eds.), *Language acquisition: The state of the art.* Cambridge, UK: Cambridge University Press.

Slobin, D. (1990). The development from child speaker to native speaker. In J. W. Stigler, R. A. Schweder, & G. H. Herdt (Eds.), *Cultural psychology: Essays on comparative human development* (pp. 233–258). New York: Cambridge University Press.

Slomko, H., Heo, H. J., & Einstein, F. H. (2012). Minireview: epigenetics of obesity and diabetes in humans. *Endocrinology, 153*(3), 1025–1030.

Slyper, A. H. (2006). The pubertal timing controversy in the USA, and a review of possible causative factors for the advance in timing of onset of puberty. *Clinical Endocrinology, 65*, 1–8.

Small, B. J., Fratiglioni, L., von Strauss, E., & Bäckman, L. (2003). Terminal decline and cognitive performance in very old age: Does cause of death matter? *Psychology and Aging, 18*, 193–202.

Smart, E. L., Gow, A. J., & Deary, I. J. (2014). Occupational complexity and lifetime cognitive abilities. *Neurology, 83*(24), 2285–2291.

Smedley, A., & Smedley, B. D. (2005). Race as biology is fiction, racism as a social problem is real: Anthropological and historical perspectives on the social construction of race. *American Psychologist, 60*, 16–26.

Smedley, B. D., Stith, A. Y., & Nelson, A. R. (Eds.). (2002). *Unequal treatment: Confronting racial and ethnic disparities in health care.* Washington, DC: National Academy Press.

Smetana, J. G., Metzger, A., Gettman, D. C., & Campione-Barr, N. (2006). Disclosure and secrecy in adolescent-parent relationships. *Child Development, 77*, 201–217.

Smetana, J., Crean, H., & Campione-Barr, N. (2005). Adolescents' and parents' changing conceptions of parental authority. In J. Smetana (Ed.), *Changing boundaries of parental authority during adolescence* (New Directions for Child and Adolescent Development, No. 108, pp. 31–46). San Francisco: Jossey-Bass.

Smilansky, S. (1968). *The effects of sociodramatic play on disadvantaged preschool children.* New York: Wiley.

Smith, A. R., Chein, J., & Steinberg, L. (2014). Peers increase adolescent risk taking even when the probabilities of negative outcomes are known. *Developmental Psychology, 50*(5), 1564.

Smith, A., Rissel, C. E., Richters, J., Grulich, A. E., & Visser, R. O. (2003). Sex in Australia: Reproductive experiences and reproductive health among a representative sample of women. *Australian and New Zealand Journal of Public Health, 27*(2), 204–209.

Smith, C. D., Walton, A., Loveland, A. D., Umberger, G. H., Kryscio, R. J., & Gash, D. M. (2005). Memories that last in old age: Motor skill learning and memory preservation. *Neurobiology of Aging, 26*(6), 883–890.

Smith, G. C. S., Pell, J. P., Cameron, A. D., & Dobbie, R. (2002). Risk of perinatal death associated with labor after previous cesarean delivery in uncomplicated term pregnancies. *Journal of the American Medical Association, 287*, 2684–2690.

Smith, J. R. (2012). Listening to older adult parents of adult children with mental illness. *Journal of Family Social Work, 15*(2), 126–140.

Smith, J., & Baltes, P. B. (1990). Wisdom-related knowledge: Age/cohort differences in response to life planning problems. *Developmental Psychology, 26*(3), 494–505.

Smith, L. B., & Thelen, E. (2003). Development as a dynamic system. *Trends in Cognitive Sciences, 7*, 343–348.

Smith, L. M., LaGasse, L. L., Derauf, C., Grant, P., Shah, R., Arria, A., . . . Lester, B. M. (2006). The infant development, environment, and lifestyle study: Effects of prenatal methamphetamine exposure, polydrug exposure, and poverty on intrauterine growth. *Pediatrics, 118*, 1149–1156.

Smith, P. J., Blumenthal, J. A., Hoffman, B. M., Cooper, H., Strauman, T. A., Welsh-Bohmer, K., . . . & Sherwood, A. (2010). Aerobic exercise and neurocognitive performance: a meta-analytic review of randomized controlled trials. *Psychosomatic Medicine, 72*(3), 239.

Smith, P. K. (2005a). Play: Types and functions in human development. In A. D. Pellegrini & P. K. Smith (Eds.), *The nature of play* (pp. 271–291). New York: Guilford Press.

Smith, P. K. (2005b). Social and pretend play in children. In A. D. Pellegrini & P. K. Smith (Eds.), *The nature of play* (pp. 173–209). New York: Guilford Press.

Smith, P. K., & Pellegrini, A. D. (2013). Learning through play. In R. E. Tremblay, M. Boivin, & R. Peters, R. (Eds.), *Encyclopedia on early childhood development* [online]. www.child-encyclo-pedia.com/play/according-experts/learning-through-play

Smith, R., & Chan, S. (2017, May 22). Ariana Grande Manchester concert ends in explosion, panic and death. *The New York Times.* Retrieved from www.nytimes.com/2017/05/22/world/europe/ariana-grande-manchester-police.html

Smith, S. L., Pieper, K. M., Granados, A., & Choueiti, M. (2010). Assessing gender-related portrayals in top-grossing G-rated films. *Sex Roles, 62*, 774–786. doi: 10-1007/s11199-009-9736z

Smith, T. W. (2003). *American sexual behavior: Trends, socio-demographic differences, and risk behavior* (GSS Topical Report No. 25). Chicago: National Opinion Research Center, University of Chicago.

Smith, T. W. (2005). Generation gaps in attitudes and values from the 1970s to the 1990s. In R. A. Settersten Jr., F. F. Furstenberg Jr., & R. G. Rumbaut (Eds.), *On the frontier of adulthood: Theory, research, and public policy* (pp. 177–221). Chicago: University of Chicago Press.

Smith, T. W. (2006). Personality as risk and resilience in physical health. *Current Directions in Psychological Science, 15*, 227–231.

Smithsonian. (2014, December 8). *Queen Victoria dreamed up the white wedding dress in 1840.* Retrieved from Smithsonian.com: www.smithsonianmag.com/smart-news/queen-victoria-sparked-white-wedding-dress-trend-1840-180953550/

Smits, J., & Monden, C. (2011). Twinning across the developing world. *PLoS One, 6*(9), e25239.

Smock, P. J., & Greenland, F. R. (2010). Diversity in pathways to parenthood: Patterns, implications, and emerging research directions. *Journal of Marriage and Family, 72*(3), 576–593.

Smock, P. J., Manning, W. D., & Porter, M. (2005). "Everything's there except money"; How money shapes decisions to marry among cohabitors. *Journal of Marriage and Family, 67*, 680–696.

Snow, M. E., Jacklin, C. N., & Maccoby, E. E. (1983). Sex-of-child differences in father-child interaction at one year of age. *Child Development, 54*, 227–232.

Snyder, E. E., Walts, B., Perusse, L., Chagnon, Y. C., Weisnagel, S. J., Raniken, T., & Bouchard, C. (2004). The human obesity gene map. *Obesity Research, 12*, 369–439.

Snyder, J., Bank, L., & Burraston, B. (2005). The consequences of antisocial behavior in older male siblings for younger brothers and sisters. *Journal of Family Psychology, 19*, 643–653.

Snyder, J., West, L., Stockemer, V., Gibbons, S., & Almquist-Parks, L. (1996). A social learning model of peer choice in the natural environment. *Journal of Applied Developmental Psychology, 17*, 215–237.

Snyder, T.D., de Brey, C., and Dillow, S.A. (2016). *Digest of education statistics 2015 (NCES 2016-014).* Washington, DC: National Center for Education Statistics, Institute of Education Sciences, U.S. Department of Education.

Sobolewski, J. M., & Amato, P. J. (2005). Economic hardship in the family of origin and children's psychological well-being in adulthood. *Journal of Marriage and Family, 67*, 141–156.

Sobolewski, J. M., & King, V. (2005). The importance of the coparental relationship for nonresident fathers' ties to children. *Journal of Marriage and Family, 67*, 1196–1212.

Social Security Administration. (2018). *Fact sheet.* Retrieved from www.ssa.gov/news/press/fact-sheets/basicfact-alt.pdf

Society for Neuroscience. (2008). Neural disorders: Advances and challenges. In *Brain facts: A primer on the brain and nervous system* (pp. 36–54). Washington, DC: Author.

Society for Research in Child Development (SRCD). (2007). *Ethical standards for research with children.* (Updated by SRCD Governing Council, March 2007.) Retrieved from www. srcd.org/ethicalstandards.html

Soderstrom, M. (2007). Beyond babytalk: Re-evaluating the nature and content of speech input to preverbal infants. *Developmental Review, 27*(4), 501–532.

Soderstrom-Antilla, V., Wennerholm, U., Loft, A., Pinborg, A., Aittomaki, K., Romundstad, L.B., & Bergh, C. (2016). Surrogacy: Outcomes for surrogate mothers, children, and the resulting families – a systematic review. *Human Reproduction Updates, 22*, 260–276.

Soenens, B., Vansteenkiste, M., Luyckx, K., & Goossens, L. (2006). Parenting and adolescent problem behavior: An integrated model with adolescent self-disclosure and perceived parental knowledge as intervening variables. *Developmental Psychology, 42*, 305–318.

Sokol, R. J., Delaney-Black, V., & Nordstrom, B. (2003). Fetal alcohol spectrum disorder. *Journal of the American Medical Association, 209*, 2996–2999.

Sokol, R. Z., Kraft, P., Fowler, I. M., Mamet, R., Kim, E., & Berhane, K. T. (2006). Exposure to environmental ozone alters semen quality. *Environmental Health Perspectives, 114*(3), 360–365.

Sole-Auro, A. & Crimmins, E.M. (2013). The oldest old: Health in Europe and the United States. In J. Robine, C. Jagger, & E.M. Crimmins (Eds)., *Annual Review of Gerontology and Geriatrics: Health Longevity, A Global Approach, Volume 33* (pp. 3–34). New York: Springer.

Solmeyer, A. R., McHale, S. M., & Crouter, A. C. (2014). Longitudinal associations between sibling relationship qualities and risky behavior across adolescence. *Developmental Psychology, 50*(2), 600.

Solomon, B., & Frenkel, D. (2010). Immunotherapy for Alzheimer's disease. *Neuropharmacology, 59*(4–5), 303–309.

Solomon, G. F., & Benton, D. (1994). Psychoneuroimmunologic aspects of aging. In R. Glaser & J. Kiecolt-Glaser (Eds.), *Handbook of human stress and immunity* (pp. 341–363). Cambridge, MA: Academic Press.

Solomon, J., & George, C. (2011). The disorganized attachment–caregiving system. *Disorganized Attachment & Caregiving, 25*–51.

Sommers, B. D., Gunja, M. Z., Finegold, K., & Musco, T. (2015). Changes in self-reported insurance coverage, access to care, and health under the Affordable Care Act. *JAMA, 314*(4), 366–374.

Sommerville, J. A., Schmidt, M. F., Yun, J. E., & Burns, M. (2013). The development of fairness expectations and prosocial behavior in the second year of life. *Infancy, 18*(1), 40–66.

Sood, B., Delaney-Black, V., Covington, C., Nordstrom-Klee, B., Ager, J., Templin, T., . . . Sokol, R. J. (2001). Prenatal alcohol exposure and childhood behavior at age 6 to 7 years: I. Dose-response effect. *Pediatrics, 108*(8), e461–e462.

Sophian, C., & Wood, A. (1997). Proportional reasoning in young children: The parts and the whole of it. *Journal of Educational Psychology, 89*, 309–317.

Sophian, C., Wood, A., & Vong, K. I. (1995). Making numbers count: The early development of numerical inferences. *Developmental Psychology, 31*, 263–273.

Sorof, J. M., Lai, D., Turner, J., Poffenbarger, T., & Portman, R. J. (2004). Overweight, ethnicity, and the prevalence of hypertension in school-aged children. *Pediatrics, 113*, 475–482.

Soto, C. J. (2015). Is happiness good for your personality? Concurrent and prospective relations of the big five with subjective well-being. *Journal of Personality, 83*(1), 45–55.

Soto, C. J., John, O. P., Gosling, S. D., & Potter, J. (2011). Age differences in personality traits from 10 to 65: Big Five domains and facets in a large cross-sectional sample. *Journal of Personality and Social Psychology, 100*(2), 330.

Spalding, K. L., Bergmann, O., Alkass, K., Bernard, S., Salehpour, M., Huttner, H. B., . . . & Possnert, G. (2013). Dynamics of hippocampal neurogenesis in adult humans. *Cell, 153*(6), 1219–1227.

Specht, J., Egloff, B., & Schmukle, S. C. (2011). Stability and change of personality across the life course: the impact of age and major life events on mean-level and rank-order stability of the Big Five. *Journal of Personality and Social Psychology, 101*(4), 862.

Speece, M. W., & Brent, S. B. (1984). Children's understanding of death: A review of three components of a death concept. *Child Development, 55*, 1671–1686.

Spelke, E. S. (1998). Nativism, empiricism, and the origins of knowledge. *Infant Behavior and Development, 21*(2), 181–200.

Spelke, E. S. (2005). Sex differences in intrinsic aptitude for mathematics and science? A critical review. *American Psychologist, 60*, 950–958.

Spelke, E. S. (2017). Core knowledge, language, and number. *Language Learning and Development, 13*(2), 147–170.

Spencer, J. P., Clearfield, M., Corbetta, D., Ulrich, B., Buchanan, P., & Schöner, G. (2006). Moving toward a grand theory of development: In memory of Esther Thelen. *Child Development, 77*, 1521–1538.

Sperling, M. A. (2004). Prematurity—A window of opportunity? *New England Journal of Medicine, 351*, 2229–2231.

Spiegel, C., & Halberda, J. (2011). Rapid fast-mapping abilities in 2-year-olds. *Journal of Experimental Child Psychology, 109*(1), 132–140.

Spinath, F. M., Price, T. S., Dale, P. S., & Plomin, R. (2004). The genetic and environmental origins of language disability and ability. *Child Development, 75*, 445–454.

Spinrad, T. L., Eisenberg, N., Harris, E., Hanish, L., Fabes, R. A., Kupanoff, K., . . . Holmes, J. (2004). The relation of children's everyday nonsocial peer play behavior to their emotionality, regulation, and social functioning. *Developmental Psychology, 40*, 67–80.

Spirduso, W. W., & MacRae, P. G. (1990). Motor performance and aging. In J. E. Birren & K. W. Schaie (Eds.), *Psychology of aging* (3rd ed., pp. 183–200). New York: Academic Press.

Spiro, A., III. (2001). Health in midlife: Toward a life-span view. In M. E. Lachman (Ed.), *Handbook of midlife development* (pp. 156–187). New York: Wiley.

Spitz, R. A. (1945). Hospitalism: An inquiry into the genesis of psychiatric conditioning in early childhood. In D. Fenschel et al. (Eds.), *Psychoanalytic studies of the child* (Vol. 1, pp. 53–74). New York: International Universities Press.

Spitz, R. A. (1946). Hospitalism: A follow-up report. In D. Fenschel et al. (Eds.), *Psychoanalytic studies of the child* (Vol. 1, pp. 113–117). New York: International Universities Press.

Spitze, G., & Trent, K. (2006). Gender differences in adult sibling relations in two-child families. *Journal of Marriage and Family, 68*, 977–992.

Spohr, H. L., Willms, J., & Steinhausen, H.-C. (1993). Prenatal alcohol exposure and long-term developmental consequences. *Lancet, 341*, 907–910.

Spraggins, C. E. (2003). Women and men in the United States: March 2002. *Current Population Reports* (P20-544). Washington, DC: U.S. Census Bureau.

Springer, K. W., Pudrovska, T., & Hauser, R. M. (2011). Does psychological well-being change with age? Longitudinal tests of age variations and further exploration of the multidimensionality of Ryff's model of psychological well-being. *Social Science Research, 40*(1), 392–398.

Sroufe, L. A. (1997). *Emotional development.* Cambridge, UK: Cambridge University Press.

Sroufe, L. A., Carlson, E., & Shulman, S. (1993). Individuals in relationships: Development from infancy through adolescence. In D. C. Funder, R. D. Parke, C. Tomlinson-Keasey, & K. Widaman (Eds.), *Studying lives through time: Personality and development* (pp. 315–342). Washington, DC: American Psychological Association.

Sroufe, L. A., Coffino, B., & Carlson, E. A. (2010). Conceptualizing the role of early experience: Lessons from the Minnesota Longitudinal Study. *Developmental Review, 30*(1), 36–51.

Sroufe, L. A., Egeland, B., Carlson, E. A., & Collins, W. A. (2005). *The development of the person: The Minnesota study of risk and adaptation from birth to adulthood.* New York: Guilford Press.

St. John, P. D., Mackenzie, C., & Menec, V. (2015). Does life satisfaction predict five-year mortality in community-living older adults?. *Aging &Mental Health, 19*(4), 363–370.

Staff, J., Mortimer, J. T., & Uggen, C. (2004). Work and leisure in adolescence. In R. M. Lerner & L. Steinberg (Eds.), *Handbook of adolescent development* (2nd ed., pp. 429–450). Hoboken, NJ: Wiley.

Staff. (2016, September 12). *MDG progress report of Latin America and the Caribbean in 2015.* Retrieved from mdgmonitor.org: http://www. mdgmonitor.org/mdg-progress-report-latin-america-caribbean-2015/

Stallman, H. M., & Ohan, J. L. (2016). Parenting style, parental adjustment, and co-parental conflict: differential predictors of child psychosocial adjustment following divorce. *Behaviour Change, 33*(2), 112-126.

Stanley, S. M., Amato, P. R., Johnson, C. A., & Markman, H. J. (2006). Premarital education, marital quality, and marital stability: Findings from a large, random household survey. *Journal of Family Psychology, 20*, 117-126.

Stanton, R., & Reaburn, P. (2014). Exercise and the treatment of depression: A review of the exercise program variables. *Journal of Science and Medicine in Sport, 17*(2), 177-182.

Stark, P., & Noel, A. M. (2015). Trends in High School Dropout and Completion Rates in the United States: 1972-2012. Compendium Report. NCES 2015-015. *National Center for Education Statistics.*

Stauder, J. E. A., Molenaar, P. C. M., & Van der Molen, M. W. (1993). Scalp topography of event-related brain potentials and cognitive transition during childhood. *Child Development, 64*, 769-788.

Staudinger, U. M., & Baltes, P. B. (1996). Interactive minds: A facilitative setting for wisdom-related performance? *Journal of Personality and Social Psychology, 71*, 746-762.

Staudinger, U. M., & Bluck, S. (2001). A view of midlife development from life-span theory. In M. E. Lachman (Ed.), *Handbook of midlife development* (pp. 3-39). New York: Wiley.

Staudinger, U. M., Smith, J., & Baltes, P. B. (1992). Wisdom-related knowledge in a life review task: Age differences and the role of professional specialization. *Psychology and Aging, 7*, 271-281.

Stav, W. B., Hallenen, T., Lane, J., & Arbesman, M. (2012). Systematic review of occupational engagement and health outcomes among community-dwelling older adults. *American Journal of Occupational Therapy, 66*(3), 301-310.

Steck, N., Egger, M., Maessen, M., Reisch, T., & Zwahlen, M. (2013). Euthanasia and assisted suicide in selected European countries and US states: Systematic literature review. *Medical Care, 51*(10), 938-944.

Steensma, T. D., McGuire, J. K., Kreukels, B. P., Beekman, A. J., & Cohen-Kettenis, P. T. (2013). Factors associated with desistence and persistence of childhood gender dysphoria: a quantitative follow-up study. *Journal of the American Academy of Child & Adolescent Psychiatry, 52*(6), 582-590.

Steffen, L. M., Kroenke, C. H., Yu, X., Pereira, M. A., Slattery, M. L., Van Horn, L., . . . Jacobs, D. R., Jr. (2005). Associations of plant food, dairy product, and meat intakes with 15-y incidence of elevated blood pressure in young black and white adults: The Coronary Artery Risk Development in Young Adults (CARDIA) Study. *American Journal of Clinical Nutrition, 82*, 1169-1177.

Steinbach, U. (1992). Social networks, institutionalization, and mortality among elderly people in the United States. *Journal of Gerontology: Social Sciences, 47*(4), S183-S190.

Steinberg, L. (2005). Psychological control: Style or substance? In J. Smetana (Ed.), *Changing boundaries of parental authority during adolescence* (New Directions for Child and Adolescent Development, No. 108, pp. 71-78). San Francisco: Jossey-Bass.

Steinberg, L. (2010). Commentary: A behavioral scientist looks at the science of adolescent brain development. *Brain and Cognition, 72*(1), 160.

Steinberg, L., & Darling, N. (1994). The broader context of social influence in adolescence. In R. Silberstein & E. Todt (Eds.), *Adolescence in context.* New York: Springer.

Steinberg, L., & Scott, E. S. (2003). Less guilty by reason of adolescence: Developmental immaturity, diminished responsibility, and the juvenile death penalty. *American Psychologist, 58*, 1009-1018.

Steinberg, L., Eisengard, B., & Cauffman, E. (2006). Patterns of competence and adjustment among adolescents from authoritative, authoritarian, indulgent, and neglectful homes: A replication in a sample of serious juvenile offenders. *Journal of Research on Adolescence, 16*(1), 47-58.

Steinbrook, R. (2008). Physician-assisted death—From Oregon to Washington state. *New England Journal of Medicine, 35*(24), 2513-2515.

Steinhausen, H. C. (2002). The outcome of anorexia nervosa in the 20th century. *American Journal of Psychiatry, 159*, 1284-1293.

Stelmach, A., & Nerlich, B. (2015). Metaphors in search of a target: the curious case of epigenetics. *New Genetics and Society, 34*(2), 196-218.

Stennes, L. M., Burch, M. M., Sen, M. G., & Bauer, P. J. (2005). A longitudinal study of gendered vocabulary and communicative action in young children. *Developmental Psychology, 41*, 75-88.

Stepanikova, I., Nie, N. H., & He, X. (2010). Time on the Internet at home, loneliness, and life satisfaction: Evidence from panel time-diary data. *Computers in Human Behavior, 26*(3), 329-338.

Stepler, R. (2017). Number of US adults cohabiting with a partner continues to rise, especially among those 50 and older. *Fact Tank: Pew Research Center.* Retrieved from www.pewresearch.org/fact-tank/2017/04/06/number-of-u-s-adults-cohabiting-with-a-partner-continues-to-rise-especially-among-those-50-and-older/

Stern, Y. (2012). Cognitive reserve in ageing and Alzheimer's disease. *The Lancet Neurology, 11*(11), 1006-1012.

Sternberg, R. J. (1985). *Beyond IQ: A triarchic theory of human intelligence.* New York: Cambridge University Press.

Sternberg, R. J. (1986). A triangular theory of love. *Psychological Review, 93*, 119-135.

Sternberg, R. J. (1987, September 23). The use and misuse of intelligence testing: Misunderstanding meaning, users over-rely on scores. *Education Week,* pp. 22, 28.

Sternberg, R. J. (1993). *Sternberg Triarchic Abilities Test.* Unpublished manuscript.

Sternberg, R. J. (1995). Love as a story. *Journal of Social and Personal Relationships, 12*(4), 541-546.

Sternberg, R. J. (1997). The concept of intelligence and its role in lifelong learning and success. *American Psychologist, 52*, 1030-1037.

Sternberg, R. J. (1998a). *Cupid's arrow.* New York: Cambridge University Press.

Sternberg, R. J. (2004). Culture and intelligence. *American Psychologist, 59*, 325-338.

Sternberg, R. J. (2005). There are no public policy implications: A reply to Rushton and Jensen (2005). *Psychology, Public Policy, and Law, 11*, 295-301.

Sternberg, R. J. (2006). A duplex theory of love. In R. J. Sternberg & K. Weis (Eds.), *The new psychology of love* (pp. 184-199). New Haven, CT: Yale University Press.

Sternberg, R. J., & Horvath, J. A. (1998). Cognitive conceptions of expertise and their relations to giftedness. In R. C. Friedman & K. B. Rogers (Eds.), *Talent in context: Historical and social perspectives on giftedness* (pp. 177-191). Washington, DC: American Psychological Association.

Sternberg, R. J., & Lubart, T. I. (1995). *Defying the crowd: Cultivating creativity in a culture of conformity.* New York: Free Press.

Sternberg, R. J., Castejón, J. L., Prieto, M. D., Hautamäki, J., & Grigorenko, E. L. (2001). Confirmatory factor analysis of the Sternberg Triarchic Abilities Test in three international samples: An empirical test of the triarchic theory of intelligence. *European Journal of Psychological Assessment, 17*(1), 1.

Sternberg, R. J., Grigorenko, E. L., & Kidd, K. K. (2005). Intelligence, race, and genetics. *American Psychologist, 60*, 46-59.

Sternberg, R. J., Grigorenko, E. L., & Oh, S. (2001). The development of intelligence at midlife. In M. E. Lachman (Ed.), *Handbook of midlife development* (pp. 217-247). New York: Wiley.

Sternberg, R. J., Wagner, R. K., Williams, W. M., & Horvath, J. A. (1995). Testing common sense. *American Psychologist, 50*, 912-927.

Sterns, H. L. (2010). New and old thoughts about aging and work in the present and future. *The Gerontologist, 50*(4), 568-571.

Sterns, H. L., & Huyck, M. H. (2001). The role of work in midlife. In M. E. Lachman (Ed.), *Handbook of midlife development* (pp. 447-486). New York: Wiley.

Stevens, J. C., Cain, W. S., Demarque, A., & Ruthruff, A. M. (1991). On the discrimination of missing ingredients: Aging and salt flavor. *Appetite, 16*, 129-140.

Stevens, J. H., & Bakeman, R. (1985). A factor analytic study of the HOME scale for infants. *Developmental Psychology, 21*, 1106-1203.

Stevens, W. D., Hasher, L., Chiew, K. S., & Grady, C. L. (2008). A neural mechanism underlying memory failure in older adults. *Journal of Neuroscience, 28*(48), 12820-12824.

Stevenson, D. G., & Grabowski, D. C. (2010). Sizing up the market for assisted living. *Health Affairs, 29*(1), 35-43.

Stevenson-Hinde, J., & Shouldice, A. (1996). Fearfulness: Developmental consistency. In A. J. Sameroff & M. M. Haith (Eds.), *The five- to seven-year shift: The age of reason and responsibility* (pp. 237-252). Chicago: University of Chicago Press.

Stewart, A. J., & Ostrove, J. M. (1998). Women's personality in middle age: Gender, history, and midcourse correction. *American Psychologist, 53,* 1185-1194.

Stewart, A. J., & Vandewater, E. A. (1998). The course of generativity. In D. P. McAdams & D. de St. Aubin (Eds.), *Generativity and adult development: How and why we care for the next generation.* Washington, DC: American Psychological Association.

Stewart, A. J., & Vandewater, E. A. (1999). "If I had to do it over again": Midlife review, midlife corrections, and women's well-being in midlife. *Journal of Personality and Social Psychology, 76,* 270-283.

Stewart, E. A., & Simons, R. L. (2010). Race, code of the street, and violent delinquency: A multilevel investigation of neighborhood street culture and individual norms of violence. *Criminology, 48*(2), 569-605.

Stipek, D. J., Gralinski, H., & Kopp, C. B. (1990). Self-concept development in the toddler years. *Developmental Psychology, 26,* 972-977.

Stock, H., Devries, K., Rotstein, A., Abrahams, N., Campbell, J., Watts, C., & Moreno, C.G. (2013). The global prevalence of intimate partner homicide: A systematic review. *Lancet, 382,* 859-865.

Stone, A. A., Schwartz, J. E., Broderick, J. E., & Deaton, A. (2010). A snapshot of the age distribution of psychological well-being in the United States. *Proceedings of the National Academy of Sciences of the U.S.A., 107*(22), 9985-9990.

Stothard, K. J., Tennant, P. W. G., Bell, R., & Rankin, J. (2009). Maternal overweight and obesity and the risk of congenital anomalies: A systematic review and meta-analysis. *Journal of the American Medical Association, 301,* 636-650.

Strömland, K., & Hellström, A. (1996). Fetal alcohol syndrome—An ophthalmological and socioeducational prospective study. *Pediatrics, 97,* 845-850.

Strandberg, T. E., Strandberg, A. Y., Saijonmaa, O., Tilvis, R. S., Pitkälä, K. H., & Fyhrquist, F. (2012). Association between alcohol consumption in healthy midlife and telomere length in older men. The Helsinki Businessmen Study. *European Journal of Epidemiology, 27*(10), 815-822.

Strathearn, L. (2011). Maternal neglect: oxytocin, dopamine and the neurobiology of attachment. *Journal of Neuroendocrinology, 23*(11), 1054-1065.

Straus, M. A. (1994). *Beating the devil out of them: Corporal punishment in American families.* San Francisco: Jossey-Bass.

Straus, M. A. (1999). The benefits of avoiding corporal punishment: New and more definitive evidence. Submitted for publication in K. C. Blaine (Ed.), *Raising America's children.*

Strayer, D.L., Drews, F.A., & Crouch, D.F. (2006). A comparison of the cell phone driver and the drunk driver. *Human Factors, 48,* 381-391.

Streissguth, A. P., Bookstein, F. L., Barr, H. M., Sampson, P. D., O'Malley, K., & Young, J. K. (2004). Risk factors for adverse life outcomes in fetal alcohol syndrome and fetal alcohol effects. *Journal of Developmental and Behavioral Pediatrics, 25,* 228-238.

Strenze, T. (2007). Intelligence and socioeconomic success: A meta-analytic review of longitudinal research. *Intelligence, 35*(5), 401-426.

Strickhouser, J. E., Zell, E., & Krizan, Z. (2017). Does personality predict health and well-being? A metasynthesis. *Health Psychology, 36*(8), 797.

Striegel-Moore, R. H., & Bulik, C. (2007). Risk factors for eating disorders. *American Psychologist, 62,* 181-198.

Stright, A. D., Gallagher, K. C., & Kelley, K. (2008). Infant temperament moderates relations between maternal parenting in early childhood and children's adjustment in first grade. *Child Development, 79,* 186-200.

Stringhini, S., Sabia, S., Shipley, M., Brunner, E., Nabi, H., Kivimaki, M., & Singh-Manoux, A. (2010). Association of socioeconomic position with health behaviors and mortality. *Journal of the American Medical Association, 303*(12), 1159-1166.

Stroebe, M., Gergen, M. M., Gergen, K. J., & Stroebe, W. (1992). Broken hearts or broken bonds: Love and death in historical perspective. *American Psychologist, 47*(10), 1205-1212.

Stroebe, M., Schut, H., & Stroebe, W. (2007). Health outcomes of bereavement. *Lancet, 370,* 1960-1973.

Strohschein, L. (2012). Parental divorce and child mental health: Accounting for predisruption differences. *Journal of Divorce & Remarriage, 53,* 489-502. doi:10.1080/10502556.2012.682903

Stueve, A., & O'Donnell, L. N. (2005). Early alcohol initiation and subsequent sexual and alcohol risk behaviors among urban youths. *American Journal of Public Health, 95,* 887-893.

Stutzer, A., & Frey, B. S. (2006). Does marriage make people happy, or do happy people get married? *Journal of Socioeconomics, 35*(2), 326-347.

Suanda, S. H., Tompson, W., & Brannon, E. M. (2008). Changes in the ability to detect ordinal numerical relationships between 9 and 11 months of age. *Infancy, 13*(4), 308-337.

Subrahmanyam, K. & Greenfield, P. (2008). Online communication and adolescent relationships. *The Future of Children* 18, 119-146.

Subrahmanyam, K., Reich, S. M., Waecheter, N., & Espinoza, G. (2008). Online and offline social networks: Use of social networking sites by emerging adults. *Journal of Applied Developmental Psychology, 29*(6), 420-433.

Substance Abuse and Mental Health Services Administration (SAMHSA), Office of Applied Studies. (2007b, March 30). Sexually transmitted diseases and substance use. *NSDUH Report.* Rockville, MD: Author.

Substance Abuse and Mental Health Services Administration (SAMHSA), Office of Applied Studies. (2008, April 18). State estimates of persons aged 18 or older driving under the influence of alcohol or illicit drugs. *NSDUH Report.* Rockville, MD: Author.

Substance Abuse and Mental Health Services Administration (SAMHSA). (2004a, October 22). Alcohol dependence or abuse and age at first use. *The NSDUH Report.* Retrieved from http://oas.samhsa.gov/2k4/ageDependence/ageDependence.htm

Substance Abuse and Mental Health Services Administration (SAMHSA). (2004b). *Results from the 2003 National Survey on Drug Use & Health: National findings* (Office of Applied Studies, NSDUH Series H-25, DHHS Publication No. SMA 04-3964). Rockville, MD: U.S. Department of Health and Human Services.

Substance Abuse and Mental Health Services Administration (SAMHSA). (2013a). *Results from the 2012 national survey on drug use and health: Summary of national findings.* NSDUH Series H-46, HHS Publication No. (SMA) 13-4795. Rockville, MD: Author.

Substance Abuse and Mental Health Services Administration [SAMHSA]. (2013b). *Results from the 2012 national survey on drug use and health: Mental health findings.* NSDUH Series H-47, HHS Publication No. (SMA) 13-4805. Rockville, MD. Author. Retrieved from www.samhsa.gov/data/NSDUH/2k12MH_FindingsandDetTables/2K12MHF/NSDUHmhfr2012.htm#fig3-2

Substance Abuse and Mental Health Services Administration. (2015). *National Survey on Drug Use and Health (NSDUH).* Retrieved from www.samhsa.gov/data/sites/default/files/NSDUH-DetTabs-2015/NSDUH-DetTabs-2015/NSDUH-DetTabs-2015.htm#tab6-84b.

Substance Abuse and Mental Health Services Administration. (2017). Key substance use and mental health indicators in the United States: Results from the 2016 National Survey on Drug Use and Health (HHS Publication No. SMA 17-5044, NSDUH Series H-52). Rockville, MD: Center for Behavioral Health Statistics and Quality, Substance Abuse and Mental Health Services Administration. Retrieved from https://www.samhsa.gov/data/

Substance Abuse and Mental Health Services Administration. (2013). *Results from the 2012 National Survey on Drug Use and Health: Summary of National Findings.* Rockville, MD: Substance Abuse and Mental Health Services Administration.

Suchday, S. (2015). Anger and globalization among young people in India. In E. L. Grigorenko, *The Global Context for New Directions for Child and Adolescent Development* (pp. 77-84). New York: Wiley Online Library. Retrieved from books.google.com: https://books.google.com/books?id=RgDcBgAAQBAJ&pg=PA77&dq=globalizing1adolescence&source=gbs_toc_r&cad=4#v=onepage&q=globalizing%20adolescence&f=false

Suitor, J. J., & Pillemer, K. (1993). Support and interpersonal stress in the social networks of married daughters caring for parents with dementia. *Journal of Gerontology: Social Sciences, 41*(1), S1-S8.

Suitor, J. J., Pillemer, K., Keeton, S., & Robison, J. (1995). Aged parents and aging children: Determinants of relationship quality. In R. Blieszner & V. Hilkevitch (Eds.), *Handbook of aging and the family* (pp. 223–242). Westport, CT: Greenwood Press.

Sullivan, A. R., & Fenelon, A. (2013). Patterns of widowhood mortality. *Journals of Gerontology Series B: Psychological Sciences and Social Sciences, 69*(1), 53–62.

Sullivan, K. T., Pasch, L. A., Johnson, M. D., & Bradbury, T. N. (2010). Social support, problem solving, and the longitudinal course of newlywed marriage. *Journal of Personality and Social Psychology, 98*(4), 631–644.

Sulmasy, L.S., Mueller, P.S., Ethics, Professionalism, and Human Rights Committee of the American College of Physicians. (2017). Ethics and the legalization of physician-assisted suicide: An American College of Physicians position paper. *Annals of Internal Medicine, 167*(8), 576–578.

Sumter, S. R., Valkenburg, P. M., & Peter, J. (2013). Perceptions of love across the lifespan: Differences in passion, intimacy, and commitment. *International Journal of Behavioral Development, 37*(5), 417–427.

Sun, Y. (2001). Family environment and adolescents' well-being before and after parents' marital disruption. *Journal of Marriage and Family, 63*, 697–713.

Sundet, J., Barlaug, D., & Torjussen, T. (2004). The end of the Flynn Effect? A study of secular trends in mean intelligence test scores of Norwegian conscripts during half a century. *Intelligence, 32*, 349–362.

Suomi, S., & Harlow, H. (1972). Social rehabilitation of isolate-reared monkeys. *Developmental Psychology, 6*, 487–496.

Susman, E. J., & Rogol, A. (2004). Puberty and psychological development. In R. M. Lerner & L. Steinberg (Eds.), *Handbook of adolescent psychology* (2nd ed., pp. 15–44). Hoboken, NJ: Wiley.

Sutin, A. R., Terracciano, A., Deiana, B., Naitza, S., Ferrucci, L., Uda, M., . . . & Costa, P. T. (2010). High neuroticism and low conscientiousness are associated with interleukin-6. *Psychological Medicine, 40*(9), 1485–1493.

Swain, I., Zelano, P., & Clifton, R. (1993). Newborn infants' memory for speech sounds retained over 24 hours. *Developmental Psychology, 29*, 312–323.

Swain, J. E., Tasgin, E., Mayes, L. C., Feldman, R., Constable, R. T., & Leckman, J. F. (2008). Maternal brain response to own baby cry is affected by cesarean section delivery. *Journal of Child Psychology and Psychiatry, 49*, 1042–1052.

Swallen, K. C., Reither, E. N., Haas, S. A., & Meier, A. M. (2005). Overweight, obesity, and health-related quality of life among adolescents: The National Longitudinal Study of Adolescent Health. *Pediatrics, 115*, 340–347.

Swamy, G. K., Ostbye, T., & Skjaerven, R. (2008). Association of preterm birth with long-term survival, reproduction, and next-generation preterm birth. *Journal of the American Medical Association, 299,* 1429–1436.

Swan, S. H., Kruse, R. L., Liu, F., Barr, D. B., Drobnis, E. Z., Redmon, J. B., . . . Study for Future Families Research Group. (2003). Semen quality in relation to biomarkers of pesticide exposure. *Environmental Health Perspectives, 111*, 1478–1484.

Swanston, H. Y., Tebbutt, J. S., O'Toole, B. I., & Oates, R. K. (1997). Sexually abused children 5 years after presentation: A case-control study. *Pediatrics, 100*, 600–608.

Sweeney, M. M. (2010). Remarriage and stepfamilies: Strategic sites for family scholarship in the 21st century. *Journal of Marriage and Family, 72*(3), 667–684.

Sweeney, M. M., & Phillips, J. A. (2004). Understanding racial differences in marital disruption: Recent trends and explanations. *Journal of Marriage and Family, 66*, 639–650.

Swingley, D. (2008). The roots of the early vocabulary in infants' learning from speech. *Current Directions in Psychological Science, 17*, 308–312.

Swingley, D., & Fernald, A. (2002). Recognition of words referring to present and absent objects by 24-month-olds. *Journal of Memory and Language, 46*, 39–56.

Sylaska, K.M. & Edwards, K.M. (2014). Disclosure of intimate partner violence to informal social support network members: A review of the literature. *Trauma, Violence, and Abuse, 15*, 3-21.

Tach, L., & Halpern-Meekin, S. (2009). How does premarital cohabitation affect trajectories of marital quality? *Journal of Marriage and Family, 71*, 298–317.

Tackett, J. L., Krueger, R. F., Iacono, W. G., & McGue, M. (2005). Symptom-based subfactors of DSM-defined conduct disorder: Evidence for etiologic distinctions. *Journal of Abnormal Psychology, 114*, 483–487.

Tajfel, H. (1981). *Human groups and social categories.* Cambridge, UK: Cambridge University Press.

Takachi, R., Inoue, M., Ishihara, J., Kurahashi, N., Iwasaki, M., Sasazuki, S., . . . Tsugane, S. (2007). Fruit and vegetable intake and risk of total cancer and cardiovascular disease: Japan Public Health Center-based Prospective Study. *American Journal of Epidemiology, 167*(1), 59–70.

Taliaferro, L. A., & Muehlenkamp, J. J. (2014). Risk and protective factors that distinguish adolescents who attempt suicide from those who only consider suicide in the past year. *Suicide and Life-Threatening Behavior, 44*(1), 6–22.

Tallent-Runnels, M., Thomas, J. A., Lan, W. Y., Cooper, S., Ahern, T. C., Shaw, S. M., & Liu, X. (2006). Teaching courses online: A review of the research. *Review of Educational Research, 76*(1), 93–135.

Talwar, V., & Lee, K. (2002). Development of lying to conceal a transgression: Children's control of expressive behaviour during verbal deception. *International Journal of Behavioral Development, 26*(5), 436–444.

Talwar, V., & Lee, K. (2008). Social and cognitive correlates of children's lying behavior. *Child Development, 79*(4), 866–881.

Tamborini, C. R. (2007). The never-married in old age: Projections and concerns for the near future. *Soc. Sec. Bull., 67*, 25.

Tamis-LeMonda, C. S., Bornstein, M. H., & Baumwell, L. (2001). Maternal responsiveness and children's achievement of language milestones. *Child Development, 72*(3), 748–767.

Tamis-LeMonda, C. S., Shannon, J. D., Cabrera, N. J., & Lamb, M. E. (2004). Fathers and mothers at play with their 2- and 3-year-olds: Contributions to language and cognitive development. *Child Development, 75*, 1806–1820.

Tan, Q., Heijmans, B. T., Hjelmborg, J., Soerenson, M., Christensen, K., & Christiansen, L. (2016). Epigenetic drift in the aging genome: A ten-year followup in an elderly twin cohort. *International Journal of Epidemiology, 45*, 1146–1158.

Tang, F. (2016). Retirement patterns and their relationship to volunteering. *Nonprofit and Voluntary Sector Quarterly, 45*(5), 910–930.

Tanner, J. L. (2006). Recentering during emerging adulthood: A critical turning point in life span human development. In J. J. Arnett & J. L. Tanner (Eds.), *Emerging adults in America: Coming of age in the 21st century* (pp. 21–55). Washington DC: American Psychological Association.

Tao, K.-T. (1998). An overview of only child family mental health in China. *Psychiatry and Clinical Neurosciences, 52*(Suppl.), S206–S211.

Tassell-Matamua, N. (2013). Phenomenology of near-death experiences: An analysis of a Maori case study. *Journal of Near-Death Studies, 32*, 107–117.

Tatangelo, G. L., McCabe, M., Mellor, D., & Mealey, A. (2016). A systematic review of body dissatisfaction and sociocultural messages related to the body among preschool children. *Body Image, 18*, 86–95.

Taveras, E. M., Capra, A. M., Braveman, P. A., Jensvold, N. G., Escobar, G. J., & Lieu, T. A. (2003). Clinician support and psychosocial risk factors associated with breastfeeding discontinuation. *Pediatrics, 112*, 108–115.

Taylor, J. G. (2007). Psychosocial and moral development of PTSD-diagnosed combat veterans. *Journal of Counseling and Development, 85*(3), 364–369.

Taylor, L. E., Swerdfeger, A. L., & Eslick, G. D. (2014). Vaccines are not associated with autism: an evidence-based meta-analysis of case-control and cohort studies. *Vaccine, 32*(29), 3623–3629.

Taylor, M., & Carlson, S. M. (1997). The relation between individual differences in fantasy and theory of mind. *Child Development, 68*, 436–455.

Taylor, M., Cartwright, B. S., & Carlson, S. M. (1993). A developmental investigation of children's imaginary companions. *Developmental Psychology, 28*, 276–285.

Taylor, S. E. (2006). Tend and befriend: Biobehavioral bases of affiliation under stress. *Current Directions in Psychological Science, 15*, 273–276.

Taylor, S. E., Lehman, B. J., Kiefe, C. I., & Seeman, T. E. (2006). Relationship of early life stress and psychological functioning to adult C-reactive protein in the coronary artery risk development in young adults study. *Biological Psychiatry, 60*(8), 819–824.

Teachman, J. (2003). Premarital sex, premarital cohabitation, and the risk of subsequent marital dissolution among women. *Journal of Marriage and Family, 65*, 444–455.

Teasdale, T. W., & Owen, D. R. (2008). Secular declines in cognitive test scores: A reversal of the Flynn effect. *Intelligence, 36*, 121–126.

Telzer, E. H., & Fuligni, A. J. (2009). Daily family assistance and the psychological well-being of adolescents from Latin American, Asian and European backgrounds. *Developmental Psychology, 45*(4), 1177–1189.

Temel, J. S., Greer, J. A., Muzikanskym, A., Gallagher, E. R., Admane, S., Jackson, V. A., . . . Lynch, T. J. (2010). Early palliative care for patients with metastatic non-small-cell lung cancer. *New England Journal of Medicine, 363*(8), 733–742.

Tenenbaum, H. R., Alfieri, L., Brooks, P. J., & Dunne, G. (2008). The effects of explanatory conversations on children's emotion understanding. *British Journal of Developmental Psychology, 26*(2), 249–263.

Tenenbaum, H., & Leaper, C. (2002). Are parents' gender schemas related to their children's gender-related cognitions? A meta-analysis. *Developmental Psychology, 38*(4), 615–630.

Tepper, P. G., et al. (2016). *Characterizing the trajectories of vasomotor symptoms across the menopausal transition.* Retrieved from Swanstudy.org: www.swanstudy.org/wps/wp-content/uploads/2016/08/TepperVMSMenopause2016.pdf

Terracciano, A., McCrae, R. R., & Costa, P. T. (2010). Intra-individual change in personality stability and age. *Journal of Research in Personality, 44*(1), 31–37.

Teti, D. M., & Ablard, K. E. (1989). Security of attachment and infant-sibling relationships: A laboratory study. *Child Development, 60*, 1519–1528.

Teubert, D., & Pinquart, M. (2010). The association between coparenting and child adjustment: A meta-analysis. *Parenting: Science and Practice, 10*(4), 286–307.

Tezanos-Pinto, P., Bratt, C., & Brown, R. (2010). What will the others think? In-group norms as a mediator of the effects of intergroup contact. *British Journal of Social Psychology, 49*(3), 507–523.

Thabes, V. (1997). A survey analysis of women's long-term, postdivorce adjustment. *Journal of Divorce & Remarriage, 27*, 163–175.

Tham, Y. C., Li, X., Wong, T. Y., Quigley, H. A., Aung, T., & Cheng, C. Y. (2014). Global prevalence of glaucoma and projections of glaucoma burden through 2040: A systematic review and meta-analysis. *Ophthalmology, 121*(11), 2081–2090.

Thapar, A., Fowler, T., Rice, F., Scourfield, J., van den Bree, M., Thomas, H., Harold, G., & Hay, D. (2003). Maternal smoking during pregnancy and attention deficit hyperactivity disorder symptoms in offspring. *American Journal of Psychiatry, 160*, 1985–1989.

The Conference Board, USA. (2000). *Turning skills into profit: Economic benefits of workplace education programs.* New York: Author.

The effects of immigration on the United States' Economy. (2016, June 27). Retrieved from Penn Wharton University of Pennsylvania: www.budgetmodel.wharton.upenn.edu/issues/2016/1/27/the-effects-of-immigration-on-the-united-states-economy

The Most Memorable TV Weddings of All Time. (2015). Retrieved from Bridal Guide: www.bridalguide.com/blogs/bridal-buzz/best-tv-weddings

The Week Staff. (2012, January 24). *Turning the dead into beads: South Korea's "odd" new trend.* Retrieved from The Week: theweek.com/articles/478701/turning-dead-into-beads-south-koreas-odd-new-trend

Thelen, E. (1995). Motor development: A new synthesis. *American Psychologist, 50*(2), 79–95.

Thelen, E., & Fisher, D. M. (1982). Newborn stepping: An explanation for a "disappearing" reflex. *Developmental Psychology, 18*, 760–775.

Thelen, E., & Fisher, D. M. (1983). The organization of spontaneous leg movements in newborn infants. *Journal of Motor Behavior, 15*, 353–377.

Thoits, P. A. (2010). Stress and health: Major findings and policy implications. *Journal of Health and Social Behavior, 51*(1_suppl), S41–S53.

Thomas, A. G., Dennis, A., Bandettini, P. A., & Johansen-Berg, H. (2012). The effects of aerobic activity on brain structure. *Frontiers in Psychology, 3.*

Thomas, A., & Chess, S. (1977). *Temperament and development.* New York: Brunner/Mazel.

Thomas, A., & Chess, S. (1984). Genesis and evolution of behavioral disorders: From infancy to early adult life. *American Journal of Orthopsychiatry, 141*(1), 1–9.

Thomas, A., Chess, S., & Birch, H. G. (1968). *Temperament and behavior disorders in children.* New York: New York University Press.

Thomas, J. G., Bond, D. S., Phelan, S., Hill, J. O., & Wing, R. R. (2014). Weight-loss maintenance for 10 years in the National Weight Control Registry. *American Journal of Preventive Medicine, 46*(1), 17–23.

Thomas, P. A. (2010). Is it better to give or to receive? Social support and the well-being of older adults. *Journals of Gerontology Series B: Psychological Sciences and Social Sciences, 65*(3), 351–357.

Thomas, R., Sanders, S., Doust, J., Beller, E., & Glasziou, P. (2015, February). *Prevalence of Attention-Deficit/Hyperactivity Disorder: A Systematic Review and Meta-analysis.* Retrieved from AAP News & Journals Gateway: http://pediatrics.aappublications.org/content/early/2015/02/24/peds.2014-3482

Thomas, S. P. (1997). Psychosocial correlates of women's self-rated physical health in middle adulthood. In M. E. Lachman & J. B. James (Eds.), *Multiple paths of midlife development* (pp. 257–291). Chicago: University of Chicago Press.

Thomee, S., Harenstam, A., & Hagberg, M. (2011, January 31). *Mobile phone use and stress, sleep disturbances, and symptoms of depression among young adults—prospective cohort study.* Retrieved from BMC Public Health: https://bmcpublichealth.biomedcentral.com/articles/10.1186/1471-2458-11-66

Thompson, L. A., Goodman, D. C., Chang, C-H., & Stukel, T. A. (2005). Regional variation in rates of low birth weight. *Pediatrics, 116*, 1114–1121.

Thompson, P. M., Cannon, T. D., Narr, K. L., van Erp, T., Poutanen, V., Huttunen, M., . . . Toga, A. W. (2001). Genetic influences on brain structure. *Nature Neuroscience, 4*, 1253–1258.

Thompson, P. M., Giedd, J. N., Woods, R. P., MacDonald, D., Evans, A. C., & Toga, A. W. (2000). Growth patterns in the developing brain detected by using continuum mechanical tensor maps. *Nature, 404*, 190–193.

Thompson, R. A. (1991). Emotional regulation and emotional development. *Educational Psychology Review, 3*, 269–307.

Thompson, R. A. (2011). Emotion and emotion regulation: Two sides of the developing coin. *Emotion Review, 3*(1), 53–61.

Thompson, W. R. (2016). Worldwide survey of fitness trends for 2017. *ACSM's Health & Fitness Journal, 20*(6), 8–17.

Thomsen, M. R., Nayga, Jr., R. M., Alviola, P. A., & Rouse, H. L. (2016). The effect of food deserts on the body mass index of elementary schoolchildren. *American Journal of Agricultural Economics, 98*, 1–18.

Thomson, E., & McLanahan, S. S. (2012). Reflections on "Family structure and child well-being: Economic resources vs. parental socialization." *Social Forces, 91*(1), 45–53.

Thornton, W. J. L., & Dumke, H. A. (2005). Age differences in everyday problem-solving and decision-making effectiveness: A meta-analytic review. *Psychology and Aging, 20*, 85–99.

Thorvaldsson, V., Hofer, S. M., Berg, S., Skoog, I., Sacuiu, S., & Johansson, B. (2008). Onset of terminal decline in cognitive abilities in individuals without dementia. *Neurology.* Advance online publication. doi: 10.1212/01.wnl.0000312379.02302.ba

Tilden, V. P., Tolle, S. W., Nelson, C. A., & Fields, J. (2001). Family decision-making to withdraw life-sustaining treatments from hospitalized patients. *Nursing Research, 50*(2), 105–115.

Tilvis, R. S., Kahonen-Vare, M. H., Jolkkonen, J., Valvanne, J., Pitkala, K. H., & Stradnberg, T. E. (2004). Predictors of cognitive decline and mortality of aged people over a 10-year period. *Journal of Gerontology: Medical Sciences, 59A*, 268–274.

Tilvis, R. S., Laitala, V., Routasalo, P., Strandberg, T. E., & Pitkala, K. H. (2012). Positive life orientation predicts good survival prognosis in old age. *Archives of Gerontology and Geriatrics, 55*(1), 133–137.

Tincoff, R., & Jusczyk, P. W. (1999). Some beginnings of word comprehension in 6-month-olds. *Psychological Science, 10*, 172–177.

Tindle, H. A., Chang, Y., Kuller, L. H., Manson, J. E., Robinson, J. G., Rosal, M. C., . . . Matthews, K. A. (2009). Optimism, cynical hostility and incident coronary heart disease and mortality in the women's health initiative. *Circulation, 120*(8), 656–662.

Tither, J., & Ellis, B. (2008). Impact of fathers on daughter's age at menarche: A genetically and environmentally controlled sibling study. *Developmental Psychology, 44*(5), 1409–1420.

Tiznobek, A., Mirmolaei, S. T., Momenimovahed, Z., Kazemnejad, A., & Taheri, S. (2017). Effect of counseling on sexual function and behavior in postmenopausal women and their spouses: a randomized, controlled trial (RCT) study. *Menopausal Review/Przegląd Menopauzalny, 16*(3).

Toga, A. W., Thompson, P. M., & Sowell, E. R. (2006). Mapping brain maturation. *Trends in Neurosciences, 29*(3), 148–159.

Toga, A., & Thompson, P. M. (2005). Genetics of brain structure and intelligence. *Annual Review of Neurology, 28,* 1–23.

Tokariev, A., Videman, M., Palva, J. M., & Vanhatalo, S. (2016). Functional brain connectivity develops rapidly around term age and changes between vigilance states in the human newborn. *Cerebral Cortex, 26*(12), 4540–4550.

Tolan, P. H., Gorman-Smith, D., & Henry, D. B. (2003). The developmental ecology of urban males' youth violence. *Developmental Psychology, 39,* 274–291.

Tolppanen, A. M., Solomon, A., Kulmala, J., Kåreholt, I., Ngandu, T., Rusanen, M., . . . & Kivipelto, M. (2015). Leisure-time physical activity from mid-to late life, body mass index, and risk of dementia. *Alzheimer's & Dementia, 11*(4), 434–443.

Tomashek, K. M., Hsia, J., & Iyasu, S. (2003). Trends in postneonatal mortality attributable to injury, United States, 1988–1998. *Pediatrics, 111,* 1215–1218.

Tomassini, C., Glaser, K., & Stuchbury, R. (2007). Family disruption and support in later life: A comparative study between the United Kingdom and Italy. *Journal of Social Issues, 63*(4), 845–863.

Topor, D. R., Keane, S. P., Shelton, T. L., & Calkins, S. D. (2010). Parent involvement and student academic performance: A multiple mediational analysis. *Journal of Prevention & Intervention in the Community, 38*(3), 183–197.

Torrance, E. P. (1974). *The Torrance Tests of Creative Thinking: Technical norms manual.* Bensonville, IL: Scholastic Testing Service.

Torrance, E. P. (1988). The nature of creativity as manifest in its testing. In R. J. Sternberg (Ed.), *The nature of creativity: Contemporary psychological perspectives* (pp. 43–75). Cambridge, UK: Cambridge University Press.

Torrance, E. P., & Ball, O. E. (1984). *Torrance Tests of Creative Thinking: Streamlined (revised) manual, Figural A and B.* Bensonville, IL: Scholastic Testing Service.

Totsika, V., & Sylva, K. (2004). The Home Observation for Measurement of the Environment revisited. *Child and Adolescent Mental Health, 9,* 25–35.

Towfighi, A., Zheng, L., & Ovbiagele, B. (2009). Sex-specific trends in midlife coronary heart disease risk and prevalence. *Archives of Internal Medicine, 169*(19), 1762–1766.

Townsend, N. W. (1997). Men, migration, and households in Botswana: An exploration of connections over time and space. *Journal of Southern African Studies, 23,* 405–420.

Trabulsi, J. C., & Mennella, J. A. (2012). Diet, sensitive periods in flavour learning, and growth.

International Review of Psychiatry, 24. https://doi.org/10.3109/09540261.2012.675573

Traditional Chinese Weddings. (2014). Retrieved from Cultural China: http://traditions.cultural-china.com/en/14Traditions30.html

Trautner, H. M., Ruble, D. N., Cyphers, L., Kirsten, B., Behrendt, R., & Hartmann, P. (2005). Rigidity and flexibility of gender stereotypes in childhood: Developmental or differential? *Infant and Child Development, 14*(4), 365–381.

Tremblay, R. E., Nagin, D. S., Séguin, J. R., Zoccolillo, M., Zelazo, P. D., Boivin, M., . . . Japel, C. (2004). Physical aggression during early childhood: Trajectories and predictors. *Pediatrics, 114*(1), e43–e50.

Trenholm, C., Devaney, B., Fortson, K., Quay, L., Wheeler, J., & Clark, M. (2007). *Impacts of four Title V, Section 510 abstinence education programs: Final report.* Princeton, NJ: Mathematica Policy Research.

Trimble, C. L., Genkinger, J. M., Burke, A. E., Helzlsouer, K. J., Diener-West, M., Comstock, G. W., & Alberg, A. J. (2005). Active and passive cigarette smoking and the risk of cervical neoplasia. *Obstetrics & Gynecology, 105,* 174–181.

Trionfi, G., & Reese, E. (2009). A good story: Children with imaginary companions create richer narratives. *Child Development, 80*(4), 1301–1313.

Troll, L. E., & Fingerman, K. L. (1996). Connections between parents and their adult children. In C. Magai & S. H. McFadden (Eds.), *Handbook of emotion, adult development, and aging* (pp. 185–205). San Diego: Academic Press.

Tromp, D., Dufour, A., Lithfous, S., Pebayle, T., & Després, O. (2015). Episodic memory in normal aging and Alzheimer disease: Insights from imaging and behavioral studies. *Ageing Research Reviews, 24,* 232–262.

Tronick, E. (1972). Stimulus control and the growth of the infant's visual field. *Perception and Psychophysics, 11,* 373–375.

Tronick, E. Z. (1989). Emotions and emotional communication in infants. *American Psychologist, 44*(2), 112–119.

Tronick, E. Z., Morelli, G. A., & Ivey, P. (1992). The Efe forager infant and toddler's pattern of social relationships: Multiple and simultaneous. *Developmental Psychology, 28,* 568–577.

Troseth, G. L., & DeLoache, J. S. (1998). The medium can obscure the message: Young children's understanding of video. *Child Development, 69,* 950–965.

Troseth, G. L., Saylor, M. M., & Archer, A. H. (2006). Young children's use of video as a source of socially relevant information. *Child Development, 77,* 786–799.

Trotter, R. J. (1986, August). Profile: Robert J. Sternberg: Three heads are better than one. *Psychology Today,* pp. 56–62.

Trouillet, R., Doan-Van-Hay, L. M., Launay, M., & Martin, S. (2011). Impact of age, and cognitive and coping resources on coping. *Canadian Journal on Aging/La Revue canadienne du vieillissement, 30*(4), 541–550.

Trovato, G. M. (2012, March 22). *Behavior, nutrition and lifestyle in a comprehensive health and*

disease paradigm: Skills and knowledge for a predictive, preventive and personalized medicine. Retrieved from U.S. National Library of Medicine National Institutes of Health: www.ncbi.nlm.nih.gov/pmc/articles/PMC3384462/

Trudel, G., Villeneuve, V., Anderson, A., & Pilon, G. (2008). Sexual and marital aspects of old age: An update. *Sexual and Relationship Therapy, 23*(2), 161–169.

Tsao, F. M., Liu, H. M., & Kuhl, P. K. (2004). Speech perception in infancy predicts language development in the second year of life: A longitudinal study. *Child Development, 75,* 1067–1084.

Tseng, V. L., Chlebowski, R. T., Yu, F., Cauley, J. A., Li, W., Thomas, F., . . . & Coleman, A. L. (2017). Association of cataract surgery with mortality in older women: Findings from the women's health initiative. *JAMA Ophthalmology.*

Tseng, V. L., Yu, F., Lum, F., & Coleman, A. L. (2016). Cataract surgery and mortality in the United States Medicare population. *Ophthalmology, 123*(5), 1019–1026.

Tsuchiya, K., Matsumoto, K., Miyachi, T., Tsujii, M., Nakamura, K., Takagai, S., . . . Takei, N. (2008). Paternal age at birth and high-functioning autistic-spectrum disorder in offspring. *British Journal of Psychiatry, 193,* 316–321.

Tucker, M. A., Morris, C. J., Morgan, A., Yang, J., Myers, S., Pierce, J. G., . . . & Scheer, F. A. (2017). The relative impact of sleep and circadian drive on motor skill acquisition and memory consolidation. *Sleep, 40*(4).

Tucker, M. B., Taylor, R. J., & Mitchell-Kernan, C. (1993). Marriage and romantic involvement among aged African Americans. *Journal of Gerontology: Social Sciences, 48,* S123–S132.

Tugade, M. M., Fredrickson, B. L., & Feldman Barrett, L. (2004). Psychological resilience and positive emotional granularity: Examining the benefits of positive emotions on coping and health. *Journal of Personality, 72*(6), 1161–1190.

Turati, C., Simion, F., Milani, I., & Umilta, C. (2002). Newborns' preference for faces: What is crucial? *Developmental Psychology, 38,* 875–882.

Turkheimer, E., Haley, A., Waldron, J., D'Onofrio, B., & Gottesman, I. I. (2003). Socioeconomic status modifies heritability of IQ in young children. *Psychological Science, 14,* 623–628.

Turner, P. J., & Gervai, J. (1995). A multidimensional study of gender typing in preschool children and their parents: Personality, attitudes, preferences, behavior, and cultural differences. *Developmental Psychology, 31,* 759–772.

Twenge, J. M. (2000). The age of anxiety? Birth cohort change in anxiety and neuroticism, 1952–1993. *Journal of Personality and Social Psychology, 79,* 1007–1021.

Twenge, J. M., Campbell, W. K., & Foster, C. A. (2003). Parenthood and marital satisfaction: A meta-analytic review. *Journal of Marriage and Family, 65,* 574–583.

Twenge, J. M., Sherman, R. A., & Wells, B. E. (2015). Changes in American adults' sexual behavior and attitudes, 1972–2012. *Archives of Sexual Behavior, 44*(8), 2273–2285.

U.S. Bureau of Labor Statistics. (2017). Older workers: Labor force trends and career options [news brief]. Retrieved from www.bls.gov/careeroutlook/2017/article/older-workers.htm

U.S. Census Bureau. (2014). Coresident grandparents and their grandchildren: 2012 [report]. Retrieved fromwww.census.gov/content/dam/Census/library/publications/2014/demo/p20-576.pdf

U.S. Bureau of Labor Statistics. (2017, April). *Employment characteristics of families summary* [News release]. Washington, DC: U.S. Department of Labor.

U.S. Census Bureau. (2006). Educational attainment in the United States, 2006. Data from *2006 Current Population Survey's Social and Economic Supplement.*Washington, DC: Author.

U.S. Census Bureau. (2007a, March 15). *Earnings gap highlighted by Census Bureau data on educational attainment* [Press release]. Retrieved from www.census.gov/Press-Release/www/releases/archives/education/009749.html

U.S. Census Bureau. (2007b). *The population profile of the United States: Dynamic version.* Retrieved from www.census.gov/population/www/pop-profile/profiledynamic.html

U.S. Census Bureau. (2008a). *Population profile of the United States.* Retrieved from www. census.gov/population/www/pop-profile/profiledynamic.html

U.S. Census Bureau. (2008b). *Who's minding the kids? Child care arrangements: Spring 2005.* Washington, DC: U.S. Census Bureau, Housing and Household Economic Statistics Division, Fertility & Family Statistics Branch.

U.S. Census Bureau. (2009b). School enrollment in the United States, 2007, Table 1: Enrollment status of the population 3 years old and over, by sex, age, race, Hispanic origin, foreign born, and foreign-born parentage: October 2007, Hispanic. *School enrollment–Social and economic characteristics of students: October 2007.* Washington, DC: Author.

U.S. Census Bureau. (2009c). School enrollment in the United States, 2007, Table 3. Nursery and primary school enrollment of people 3 to 6 years old, by control of school, attendance status, age, race, Hispanic origin, mother's labor force status and education, and family income. *School enrollment–Social and economic chracteristics of students: October 2007.* Washington, DC: Author.

U.S. Census Bureau. (2010). Table UC3: Opposite sex unmarried couples by presence of biological children/1 under 18, and age, earnings, education, and race and Hispanic origin/2 of both partners: 2010. Current Population Survey, 2010 Annual Social and Economic Supplement. 2010a Retrieved from **www.census.gov/population/socdemo/hh-fam/cps2010/tabUC3-all.xls**.

U.S. Census Bureau. (2010a). *America's families and living arrangements: 2010.* Retrieved from www.census.gov/population/www/socdemo/hh-fam/cps2010.html

U.S. Census Bureau. (2016). *Unmarried-partner households by sex of partner* [data sheet].

Retrieved from https://factfinder.census.gov/faces/tableservices/jsf/pages/productview.xhtml?pid=ACS_15_1YR_B11009&prodType=table

U.S. Census Bureau. (2017). U.S. Census Bureau's Current Population Survey fertility supplement [news report]. Retrieved from www.census.gov/hhes/fertility/data/cps/2016.html

U.S. Department of Agriculture (USDA). (2010). *Dietary guidelines.* Retrieved from www.cnpp.usda.gov/Publications/DietaryGuidelines/ 2010/PolicyDoc/ExecSumm.pdf

U.S. Department of Agriculture and U.S. Department of Health and Human Services. (2010, December). *Dietary guidelines for Americans, 2010* (7th ed.). Washington, DC: U.S. Government Printing Office.

U.S. Department of Education, Office of Special Education Programs, Individuals with Disabilities Education Act (IDEA) database, retrieved July 26, 2016, from *www2.ed.gov/programs/osepidea/618-data/state-level-data-files/index.html#bcc.*

U.S. Department of Health & Human Services, Administration for Children and Families, Administration on Children, Youth, and Families, Children's Bureau. (2017). *Child maltreatment 2015.* Available from www.acf.hhs.gov/programs/cb/research-data-technology/statistics-research/child-maltreatment

U.S. Department of Health and Human Services (USDHHS), Administration on Children, Youth and Families. (2008). *Child maltreatment 2006.* Washington, DC: U.S. Government Printing Office.

U.S. Department of Health and Human Services (USDHHS), Administration on Children, Youth, and Families. (2006). *Child maltreatment 2004.* Washington, DC: U.S. Government Printing Office.

U.S. Department of Health and Human Services (USDHHS). (1992). *Health, United States, 1991, and Prevention Profile* (DHHS Publication No. PHS 92-1232). Washington, DC: U.S. Government Printing Office.

U.S. Department of Health and Human Services (USDHHS). (1999b). *Mental health: A report of the surgeon general.* Rockville, MD: U.S. Department of Health and Human Services, Substance Abuse and Mental Health Services Administration, National Institutes of Health, National Institute of Mental Health.

U.S. Department of Health and Human Services (USDHHS). (2010). *How tobacco smoke causes disease: The biology and behavioral basis for smoking-attributable disease.* A Report of the Surgeon General. Atlanta, GA: U.S. Department of Health and Human Services, Centers for Disease Control and Prevention, National Center for Chronic Disease Prevention and Health Promotion, Office on Smoking and Health.

U.S. Department of Health and Human Services (USDHHS). (2012). Youth risk behavior surveillance: United States 2011. *MMWR Surveillance Summaries, 61*(4): Table 65. Retrieved from www.cdc.gov/mmwr/pdf/ss/ss6104.pdf

U.S. Department of Health and Human Services. (2014). Facts About Bullying. Retrieved from stopbullying.gov: www.stopbullying.gov/media/facts/index.html

U.S. Department of Labor, Bureau of Labor Statistics. (2013). Tabulations retrieved November 22, 2013, from www.bls.gov/cps/cpsaat07.htm.

U.S. Food and Drug Administration. (2016). FDA Communication: FDA cautions about using testosterone products for low testosterone due to aging; requires labeling change to inform of possible increased risk of heart attack and stroke with use. Retrieved from www.fda.gov/Drugs/DrugSafety/ucm436259.htm

U.S. Government Accounting Office. (2008). *Nursing homes: Federal monitoring surveys demonstrate continued understatement of serious care problems and CMS oversight weaknesses* [report]. Retrieved from www.gao.gov/assets/280/275154.pdf

U.S. Preventive Services Task Force. (2002). *Screening for breast cancer: Recommendations and rationale.* Rockville, MD: Agency for Healthcare Research and Quality. Retrieved from www.ahrq.gov/clinic/3rduspstf/breastcancer/brcanrr.htm

U.S. Preventive Services Task Force. (2006). Screening for speech and language delay in preschool children: Recommendation statement. *Pediatrics, 117,* 497–501.

U.S. Preventive Services Task Force. (2010). Screening for obesity in children and adolescents: Recommendation statement. *Pediatrics, 125*(2), 361–367. doi: 10.1542/peds.2009-2037

Uecker, J. E., & Stokes, C. E. (2008). Early marriage in the United States. *Journal of Marriage and Family, 70*(4), 835–846.

Uitterlinden, A. G., Burger, H., Huang, Q., Yue, F., McGuigan, F. E. A., Grant, S. F. A., . . . Ralston, S. H. (1998). Relation of alleles of the collagen type Iα1 gene to bone density and the risk of osteoporitic fractures in postmenopausal women. *New England Journal of Medicine, 33,* 1016–1021.

Umana-Taylor, A. J., & Updegraff, K. A. (2006). Latino adolescents' mental health: Exploring the interrelationships among discrimination, ethnic identity, cultural orientation, self-esteem and depressive symptoms. *Journal of Adolescence, 30*(4), 549–567.

Umana-Taylor, A. J., Gonzalez-Backen, M. A., & Guimond, A. B. (2009). Latino adolescents' ethnic identity: Is there a developmental progression and does growth in ethnic identity predict growth in self-esteem? *Child Development, 80*(2), 391–405.

Umberson, D. (2003). *Death of a parent.* New York: Cambridge University Press.

Umberson, D., Pudrovska, T., & Reczek, C. (2010). Parenthood, childlessness, and well-being: A life course perspective. *Journal of Marriage and Family, 72*(3), 612–629.

Umberson, D., Thomeer, M. B., Kroeger, R. A., Lodge, A. C., & Xu, M. (2015). Challenges and opportunities for research on same-sex relationships. *Journal of Marriage and Family, 77*(1), 96–111.

Umberson, D., Williams, K., Powers, D. A., Liu, H., & Needham, B. (2006). You make me sick: Marital quality and health over the life course. *Journal of Health and Social Behavior, 47*, 1–16.

UN Staff. (2007). *World Population Ageing.* Retrieved from United Nations–Department of Economic and Social Affairs: www.un.org/en/development/desa/population/publications/pdf/ageing/WorldPopulationAgeingReport2007.pdf

UNAIDS. (2013). *UNAIDS report on the global AIDS epidemic.* Retrieved from www.unaids.org/en/media/unaids/contentassets/documents/epidemiology/2013/gr2013/UNAIDS_Global_Report_2013_en.pdf

UNAIDS. (2017). *Fact sheet: Latest statistics on the status of the AIDS epidemic* [fact sheet]. Retrieved from www.unaids.org/en/resources/fact-sheet

UNAIDS/WHO Joint United Nations Programme on HIV/AIDS and World Health Organization. (2004). *AIDS epidemic update* (Publication No. UNAIDS/04.45E). Geneva: Author.

Underwood, M., Lamb, S. E., Eldridge, S., Sheehan, B., Slowther, A. M., Spencer, A., . . . & Diaz-Ordaz, K. (2013). Exercise for depression in elderly residents of care homes: a cluster-randomised controlled trial. *The Lancet, 382*(9886), 41–49.

UNESCO. (2015) EFA Global Monitoring Report: Education for All 2000–2015: Achievements and Challenges. Paris: UNESCO.

UNESCO. (2017). School Violence and Bullying: Global Status Report. Retrieved from UNESCO: http://unesdoc.unesco.org/images/0024/002469/246970e.pdf

UNICEF Millennium Development Goals. (2015). *Goal: Reduce child mortality.* Retrieved from: www.un.org/sustainabledevelopment

UNICEF. (2005, March). *Measles deaths plummet.* Retrieved from www.unicef.org/immunization/index_25339.html United States

UNICEF. (2013a). *Improving child nutrition: The achievable imperative for global progress.* Retrieved from www.unicef.org/media/files/nutrition_report_2013.pdf

UNICEF. (2013b). Undernourishment in the womb can lead to diminished potential and predispose infants to early death. *UNICEF Data: Monitoring the Situation of Children and Women.* http://data. unicef. org/nutrition/low-birthweight# sthash. BG4IvrwC. dpuf

UNICEF. (2014). Statistical tables. Retrieved from www.unicef.org/sowc2014/numbers/documents/english/EN-FINAL%20Tables%201-14.pdf

UNICEF. (2014, September). *Hidden in Plain Sight: A statistical analysis of violence against children.* Retrieved from www.unicef.org/publications/index_74865.html

UNICEF. (2015a). *Goal: Eradicate extreme poverty and hunger.* Retrieved from UNICEF: www.unicef.org/mdg/poverty.html

UNICEF. (2015b). *Goal: Reduce child mortality.* Retrieved from UNICEF Millennium Development Goals: www.un.org/sustainabledevelopment

UNICEF. (2015c). Undernutrition contributes to nearly half of all deaths in children under 5 and

is widespread in Asia and Africa. Retrieved from https://data.unicef.org/topic/nutrition/malnutrition/

UNICEF. (2015d). UNICEF data: Monitoring the situation for children and women: Maternal mortality. Retrieved from https://data.unicef.org/topic/maternal-health/maternal-mortality/#

UNICEF. (2015e). UNICEF data: Monitoring the situation for children and women: Neonatal mortality. Retrieved from https://data.unicef.org/topic/child-survival/neonatal-mortality/#

UNICEF. (2016, October). *Under-five and infant mortality rates and number of deaths.* Retrieved from UNICEF: https://data.unicef.org/topic/child-survival/under-five-mortality

UNICEF. (2017). UNICEF data: Monitoring the situation for children and women.: Immunizations. Retrieved from https://data.unicef.org/topic/child-health/immunization/#

UNICEF. (2017, May 16). *Joint child malnutrition estimates - 2017 edition.* Retrieved from UNICEF: https://data.unicef.org/topic/nutrition/malnutrition

UNICEF and World Health Organization (WHO). (2004). *Low birthweight: Country, regional and global estimates.* New York: UNICEF.

UNICEF. (2008). *State of the world's children 2009: Maternal and newborn health.* New York: Author.

United Nations Educational, Scientific, and Cultural Organization (UNESCO). (2007). *Literacy portal: United Nations Literacy Decade: Why the Literacy Decade?* Retrieved from http://portal.unesco.org/education/en/ev.php-URL_ID=53899&URL_DO=DO_TOPIC&URL_SECTION=201.htm

United Nations High Commissioner for Human Rights. (1989, November 20). *Convention on the Rights of the Child.* General Assembly Resolution 44/25.

United Nations. (2009). *Rethinking poverty: Report on the world social situation* (No. E.09.IV.10). Retrieved from www.un.org/esa/socdev/rwss/docs/2010/fullreport.pdf

United Nations. (2003). *The situation of girls & young women.* Retrieved from UN.org: www.un.org/esa/socdev/unyin/documents/ch09.pdf

U.S. Department of Education. (2017). Number and percentage of public school students enrolled in gifted/talented programs, by race/ethnicity, disability status, and English proficiency, by state, School Year, 2013-14 [data file]. Retrieved from https://ocrdata.ed.gov/StateNationalEstimations/Estimations_2013_14

U.S. Department of Health and Human Services. (2016). Costs of care [fact sheet]. Retrieved from https://longtermcare.acl.gov/costs-how-to-pay/costs-of-care.html

U.S. Department of Health and Human Services. (2017). Recommended Uniform Screening Panel. Retrieved from www.hrsa.gov/advisory-committees/mchbadvisory/heritabledisorders/recommendedpanel/index.html

U.S. Department of Health and Human Services. (2013). Managing overweight and obesity in adults [evidence report]. Retrieved from www.nhlbi.nih.gov/sites/www.nhlbi.nih.gov/files/obesity-evidence-review.pdf

U.S. Department of Labor. (2016). Working brief: Working mothers. Retrieved from www.dol.gov/wb/resources/WB_WorkingMothers_508_FinalJune13.pdf

U.S. Department of Justice Drug Intelligence Center. (2011). *The economic impact of illicit drug use on American society.* Retrieved from www.justice.gov/archive/ndic/pubs44/44731/44731p.pdf

Urry, H. L., & Gross, J. J. (2010). Emotion regulation in older age. *Current Directions in Psychological Science, 19*(6), 352–357.

U.S. Census Bureau. (2016). Historical living arrangements of children under 18 years old: 1960 to present. [Data file]. Retrieved from www.census.gov/data/tables/time-series/demo/families/children.html

Utiger, R. D. (1998). A pill for impotence. *New England Journal of Medicine, 338*, 1458–1459.

Uttal, D. H., Meadow, N. G., Tipton, E., Hand, L. L., Alden, A. R., Warren, C., & Newcombe, N. S. (2013). The malleability of spatial skills: A meta-analysis of training studies. *Psychological Bulletin, 139*, 352– 402. doi:10.1037/a0028446

Ülger, Z., Halil, M., Kalan, I., Yavuz, B. B., Cankurtaran, M., Güngör, E., & Arıoğul, S. (2010). Comprehensive assessment of malnutrition risk and related factors in a large group of community-dwelling older adults. *Clinical Nutrition, 29*(4), 507–511.

Véronneau, M. H., & Dishion, T. J. (2011). Middle school friendships and academic achievement in early adolescence: A longitudinal analysis. *The Journal of Early Adolescence, 31*(1), 99–124.

Véronneau, M. H., Vitaro, F., Brendgen, M., Dishion, T. J., & Tremblay, R. E. (2010). Transactional analysis of the reciprocal links between peer experiences and academic achievement from middle childhood to early adolescence. *Developmental Psychology, 46*(4), 773.

Vaccarino, V., Parsons, L., Peterson, E. D., Rogers, W. J., Kiefe, C. I., & Canto, J. (2009). Sex differences in mortality after acute myocardial infarction: Changes from 1994 to 2006. *Archives of Internal Medicine, 169*(19), 1767–1774.

Vagi, K. J., Olsen, E. O. M., Basile, K. C., & Vivolo-Kantor, A. M. (2015). Teen dating violence (physical and sexual) among US high school students: Findings from the 2013 National Youth Risk Behavior Survey. *JAMA Pediatrics, 169*(5), 474–482.

Vagi, K. J., Rothman, E. F., Latzman, N. E., Tharp, A. T., Hall, D. M., & Breiding, M. J. (2013). Beyond correlates: A review of risk and protective factors for adolescent dating violence perpetration. *Journal of Youth and Adolescence, 42*(4), 633–649.

Vail, K. E., Rothschild, Z. K., Weise, D. R., Solomon, S., Pyszczynski, T., & Greenberg, J. (2010). A terror management analysis of the psychological functions of religion. *Personality and Social Psychology Review, 14*(1), 84–94.

Vaillancourt, T., & Hymel, S. (2006). Aggression and social status: The moderating roles of sex and peer-valued characteristics. *Aggressive Behavior, 32*(4), 396–408.

Vaillant, G. E. (2000). Adaptive mental mechanisms: Their role in a positive psychology. *American Psychologist, 55*, 89–98.

Valero, S., Daigre, C., Rodriguez-Cintas, L., Barral, C., Gomà-i-Freixanet, M., Ferrer, M., . . . & Roncero, C. (2014). Neuroticism and impulsivity: their hierarchical organization in the personality characterization of drug-dependent patients from a decision tree learning perspective. *Comprehensive Psychiatry, 55*(5), 1227–1233.

Valladares, S., & Moore, K. A. (2009). The strengths of poor families. Research brief. Publication# 2009-26. *Child Trends.*

Van Cauwenberghe, C., Van Broeckhoven, C., & Sleegers, K. (2015). The genetic landscape of Alzheimer disease: Clinical implications and perspectives. *Genetics in Medicine, 18*(5), 421–430.

Van Cleave, J., Gortmaker, S. L., & Perrin, J. M. (2010). Dynamics of obesity and chronic health conditions among children and youth. *Journal of the American Medical Association, 303*(7), 623–630.

Van de Bongardt, D., Reitz, E., Sandfort, T., & Deković, M. (2015). A meta-analysis of the relations between three types of peer norms and adolescent sexual behavior. *Personality and Social Psychology Review, 19*(3), 203–234.

Van den Boom, D. C. (1989). Neonatal irritability and the development of attachment. In G. A. Kohnstamm, J. E. Bates, & M. K. Rothbart (Eds.), *Temperament in childhood* (pp. 299–318). Chichester, UK: Wiley.

Van den Boom, D. C. (1994). The influence of temperament and mothering on attachment and exploration: An experimental manipulation of sensitive responsiveness among lower-class mothers with irritable infants. *Child Development, 65*, 1457–1477.

Van der Graaff, J., Branje, S., De Wied, M., Hawk, S., Van Lier, P., & Meeus, W. (2014). Perspective taking and empathic concern in adolescence: Gender differences in developmental changes. *Developmental Psychology, 50*(3), 881.

van der Heide, A., Deliens, L., Faisst, K., Nilstun, T., Norup, M., Paci, E., . . . van der Maas, P. J., on behalf of the EURELD consortium. (2003). End-of-life decision making in six European countries: Descriptive study. *Lancet, 362*, 345–350.

Van Dongen, H. P. A., Maislin, G., Mullington, J. M., & Dinges, D. F. (2003). The cumulative cost of additional wakefulness: Dose-response effects on neurobehavioral functions and sleep physiology from chronic sleep restriction and total sleep deprivation. *Sleep, 26*, 117–126.

van Dyk, D. (2005, January 24). Parlez-vous twixter? *Time, 50.*

Van Geel, M., Vedder, P., & Tanilon, J. (2014). Relationship between peer victimization, cyberbullying, and suicide in children and adolescents: a meta-analysis. *JAMA Pediatrics, 168*(5), 435–442.

Van Goozen, S. H., & Fairchild, G. (2008). How can the study of biological processes help design new interventions for children with severe antisocial behavior? *Development and Psychopathology, 20*(3), 941–973.

Van Goozen, S., Fairchild, G., Snoek, H., & Harold, G. (2007). The evidence for a neurobiological model of childhood antisocial behavior. *Psychological Bulletin, 133*, 149–182.

Van Heemst, D. (2010). Insulin, IGF-1 and longevity. *Aging and Disease, 1*(2), 147.

Van Heuvelen, M. J., Kempen, G. I., Ormel, J., & Rispens, P. (1998). Physical fitness related to age and physical activity in older persons. *Medicine and Science in Sports and Exercise, 30*, 434–441.

van Hooren, S. A. H., Valentijn, S. A. M., Bosma, H., Ponds, R. W. H. M., van Boxtel, M. P. J., & Jolles, J. (2005). Relation between health status and cognitive functioning: A 6-year follow-up of the Maastricht Aging Study. *Journal of Gerontology: Psychological Sciences, 60B*, P57–P60.

Van Humbeeck, L., Piers, R. D., Van Camp, S., Dillen, L., Verhaeghe, S. T., & Van Den Noortgate, N. J. (2013). Aged parents' experiences during a critical illness trajectory and after the death of an adult child: A review of the literature. *Palliative Medicine, 27*(7), 583–595.

Van IJzendoorn, M. H., & Kroonenberg, P. M. (1988). Cross-cultural patterns of attachment: A meta-analysis of the Strange Situation. *Child Development, 59*, 147–156.

Van IJzendoorn, M. H., & Sagi, A. (1999). Cross-cultural patterns of attachment: Universal and contextual dimensions. In J. Cassidy & P. R. Shaver (Eds.), *Handbook of attachment: Theory, research, and clinical applications* (pp. 713–734). New York: Guilford Press.

Van IJzendoorn, M. H., Bakermans-Kranenburg, M. J., & Ebstein, R. P. (2011). Methylation matters in child development: Toward developmental behavioral epigenetics. *Child Development Perspectives, 5*, 305–310.

Van IJzendoorn, M. H., Schuengel, C., & Bakermans-Kranenburg, M. J. (1999). Disorganized attachment in early childhood: Meta-analysis of precursors, concomitants, and sequelae. *Development and Psychopathology, 11*, 225–250.

Van Lier, P. A., Vitaro, F., Barker, E. D., Brendgen, M., Tremblay, R. E., & Boivin, M. (2012). Peer victimization, poor academic achievement, and the link between childhood externalizing and internalizing problems. *Child Development, 83*(5), 1775–1788.

Van Lieshout, C. F. M., Haselager, G. J. T., Riksen-Walraven, J. M., & van Aken, M. A. G. (1995, April). Personality development in middle childhood. In D. Hart (Chair), *The contribution of childhood personality to adolescent competence: Insights from longitudinal studies from three societies.* Symposium conducted at the biennial meeting of the Society for Research in Child Development, Indianapolis, IN.

Van Lommel, P. (2011). Near-death experiences: the experience of the self as real and not as an illusion. *Annals of the New York Academy of Sciences, 1234*(1), 19–28.

Van Ouystel, J., Van Gool, E., Walrave, M., Ponnet, K., & Peeters, E. (2016). Exploring the role of social networking sites within adolescent romantic relationships and dating experiences. *Computers in Human Behavior, 55*, 76–86.

Van Ryzin, M. J., Stormshak, E. A., & Dishion, T. J. (2012). Engaging parents in the family check-up in middle school: Longitudinal effects on family conflict and problem behavior through the high school transition. *Journal of Adolescent Health, 50*(6), 627–633.

Van Steenbergen, E. F., Kluwer, E. S., & Karney, B. R. (2011). Workload and the trajectory of marital satisfaction in newlyweds: job satisfaction, gender, and parental status as moderators. *Journal of Family Psychology, 25*(3), 345.

Van Zalk, M. H. W., & Kerr, M. (2014). Developmental trajectories of prejudice and tolerance toward immigrants from early to late adolescence. *Journal of Youth and Adolescence, 43*(10), 1658–1671.

Van, P. (2001). Breaking the silence of African American women: Healing after pregnancy loss. *Health Care Women International, 22*, 229–243.

Vandell, D. L., & Bailey, M. D. (1992). Conflicts between siblings. In C. U. Shantz & W. W. Hartup (Eds.), *Conflict in child and adolescent development* (pp. 242–269). New York: Cambridge University Press.

Vandell, D. L., Belsky, J., Burchinal, M., Steinberg, L., & Vandergrift, N. (2010). Do effects of early child care extend to age 15 years? Results from the NICHD study of early child care and youth development. *Child Development, 81*(3), 737–756.

Vandell, D. L., Belsky, J., Burchinal, M., Steinberg, L., Vandergrift, N., & NICHD Early Child Care Research Network. (2010). Do effects of early child care extend to age 15 years? Results from the NICHD study of early child care and youth development. *Child Development, 81*, 737–756. doi: 10.1111/j.1467-8624.2010.01431.x

VanderLaan, D. P., Blanchard, R., Wood, H., Garzon, L. C., & Zucker, K. J. (2015). Birth weight and two possible types of maternal effects on male sexual orientation: A clinical study of children and adolescents referred to a Gender Identity Service. *Developmental Psychobiology, 57*(1), 25–34.

Vandewater, E. A., Ostrove, J. M., & Stewart, A. J. (1997). Predicting women's well-being in midlife: The importance of personality development and social role involvements. *Journal of Personality and Social Psychology, 72*(5), 1147.

Vandivere, S., Malm, K., & Radel, L. (2009). *Adoption USA: A chartbook based on the 2007 National Survey of Adoptive Parents.* Washington, DC: U.S. Department of Health and Human Services, Office of the Assistant Secretary for Planning and Evaluation.

Varela, R. E., Vernberg, E. M., Sanchez-Sosa, J. J., Riveros, A., Mitchell, M., & Mashunkashey, J. (2004). Parenting style of Mexican, Mexican American, and Caucasian-non-Hispanic families: social context and cultural influences. *Journal of Family Psychology, 18*(4), 651.

Varma, A. (2017, June 13). Summer reading list. Retrieved from Indian Express:

http://indianexpress.com/article/lifestyle/books/summer-reading-children-indian-authors-4701431

Vasilyeva, M., Huttenlocher, J., & Waterfall, H. (2006). Effects of language intervention on syntactic skill levels in preschoolers. *Developmental Psychology, 42,* 164–174.

Vaterlaus, J.M., Tulane, S., Porter, B.D., & Beckert, T.E. (2017). The perceived influence of media and technology on adolescent romantic relationships. *Journal of Adolescent Research.* doi: 10.1177/0743558417712611

Vauclair, C.-M., Hanke, K., Haung, L.-L., & Dominic, A. (2017). *Are Asian cultures really less ageist than Western ones?* Retrieved from https://pdfs.semanticscholar.org/5cde/9b0ed8afa73c6b00d1f8c1137777695b1a73.pdf

Vaupel, J. W. (2010). Biodemography of human ageing. *Nature, 464*(7288), 536–542.

Vaupel, J. W., Carey, J. R., Christensen, K., Johnson, T. E., Yashin, A. I., Holm, N. V., . . . Curtsinger, J. W. (1998). Biodemographic trajectories of longevity. *Science, 280,* 855–860.

Veenstra, R., Lindenberg, S., Oldehinkel, A. J., De Winter, A. F., Verhulst, F. C., & Ormel, J. (2005). Bullying and victimization in elementary schools: A comparison of bullies, victims, bully/victims, and uninvolved preadolescents. *Developmental Psychology, 41,* 672–682.

Venetsanou, F., & Kambas, A. (2010). Environmental factors affecting preschoolers' motor development. *Early Childhood Education Journal, 37*(4), 319–327.

Venkatraman, A., Garg, N., & Kumar, N. (2015). Greater freedom of speech on Web 2.0 correlates with dominance of views linking vaccines to autism. *Vaccine, 33,* 1422–1425.

Vennemann, M. M., Hummel, T., & Berger, K. (2008). The association between smoking and smell and taste impairment in the general population. *Journal of Neurology, 255*(8), 1121–1126.

Ventola, C. L. (2016). Immunization in the United States: Recommendations, barriers, and measures to improve compliance: Part 1: Childhood vaccinations. *Pharmacy and Therapeutics, 41*(7), 426.

Ventura, A. K., & Mennella, J. A. (2011). Innate and learned preferences for sweet taste during childhood. *Current Opinion in Clinical Nutrition & Metabolic Care, 14*(4), 379–384.

Ventura, A. K., & Worobey, J. (2013). Early influences on the development of food preferences. *Current Biology, 23*(9), R401–R408.

Ventura, S. J., Mathews, T. J., & Hamilton, B. E. (2001). Births to teenagers in the United States, 1940–2000. *National Vital Statistics Reports, 49*(10). Hyattsville, MD: National Center for Health Statistics.

Vereecken, C., & Maes, L. (2000). Eating habits, dental care and dieting. In C. Currie, K. Hurrelmann, W. Settertobulte, R. Smith, & J. Todd (Eds.), *Health and health behaviour among young people: A WHO cross-national study (HBSC) international report* (pp. 83–96). WHO Policy Series: Healthy Policy for Children and Adolescents, Series No. 1. Copenhagen, Denmark: World Health Organization Regional Office for Europe.

Verhulst, B., Neale, M. C., & Kendler, K. S. (2015). The heritability of alcohol use disorders: a meta-analysis of twin and adoption studies. *Psychological Medicine, 45*(5), 1061–1072.

Verschueren, K., Buyck, P., & Marcoen, A. (2001). Self-representations and socioemotional competence in young children: A 3-year longitudinal study. *Developmental Psychology, 37,* 126–134.

Verschueren, K., Marcoen, A., & Schoefs, V. (1996). The internal working model of the self, attachment, and competence in five-year-olds. *Child Development, 67,* 2493–2511.

Vespa, J. (2012). Union formation in later life: Economic determinants of cohabitation and remarriage among older adults. *Demography, 49*(3), 1103–1125.

Vespa, J., Lewis, J. M., & Kreider, R. M. (2013). *America's families and living arrangements:* 2012. *Current Population Reports,* P20-570. Washington, DC: U.S. Census Bureau.

Victor, J. L. (2015). Young people housing in Hong Kong: Why failure to launch? *Proceedings of the Korean Housing Association Conference,* 305–309.

Victora, M., Victora, C., & Barros, F. (1990). Cross-cultural differences in developmental rates: A comparison between British and Brazilian children. *Child: Care, Health and Development, 16,* 151–164

Vieno, A., Nation, M., Pastore, M., & Santinello, M. (2009). *Developmental Psychology, 45*(6), 1509–1519.

Viner, R. M., & Cole, T. J. (2005). Television viewing in early childhood predicts adult body mass index. *Journal of Pediatrics, 147,* 429–435

Vinkhuyzen, A. A., Pedersen, N. L., Yang, J., Lee, S. H., Magnusson, P. K., Iacono, W. G., . . . & Payton, A. (2012). Common SNPs explain some of the variation in the personality dimensions of neuroticism and extraversion. *Translational Psychiatry, 2*(4), e102.

Virtala, P., Huotilainen, M., Partanen, E., Fellman, V., & Tervaniemi, M. (2013). Newborn infants' auditory system is sensitive to Western music chord categories. *Frontiers in Psychology, 4.*

Vita, A. J., Terry, R. B., Hubert, H. B., & Fries, J. F. (1998). Aging, health risk, and cumulative disability. *New England Journal of Medicine, 338,* 1035–1041.

Vitaliano, P. P., Zhang, J., & Scanlan, J. M. (2003). Is caregiving hazardous to one's physical health? A meta-analysis. *Psychological Bulletin, 129,* 946–972.

Vitaro, F., Brendgen, M., Girard, A., Boivin, M., Dionne, G., & Tremblay, R. E. (2015). The expression of genetic risk for aggressive and nonaggressive antisocial behavior is moderated by peer group norms. *Journal of Youth and Adolescence, 44*(7), 1379–1395.

Vittrup, B., Snider, S., Rose, K. K., & Rippy, J. (2016). Parental perceptions of the role of media and technology in their young children's lives. *Journal of Early Childhood Research, 14,* 43–54.

Vlad, S. C., Miller, D. R., Kowall, N. W., & Felson, D. T. (2008). Protective effects of NSAIDs on the development of Alzheimer disease. *Neurology, 70,* 1672–1677.

Vliegen, N., Casalin, S., & Luyten, P. (2014). The course of postpartum depression: A review of longitudinal studies. *Harvard Review of Psychiatry, 22,* 1–22.

Voegtline, K. M., Costigan, K. A., Pater, H. A., & DiPietro, J. A. (2013). Near-term fetal response to maternal spoken voice. *Infant Behavior and Development, 36*(4), 526–533.

Voelcker-Rehage, C., Godde, B., & Staudinger, U. M. (2010). Physical and motor fitness are both related to cognition in old age. *European Journal of Neuroscience, 31*(1), 167–176.

Vogl, K., & Preckel, F. (2014). Full-time ability grouping of gifted students: Impacts on social self-concept and school-related attitudes. *Gifted Child Quarterly, 58*(1), 51-68.

Vohr, B. R., Wright, L. L., Poole, K., & McDonald, S. A., for the NICHD Neonatal Research Network Follow-up Study. (2005). Neurodevelopmental outcomes of extremely low birth weight infants<30 weeks' gestation between 1993 and 1998. *Pediatrics, 116,* 635–643.

Volkow, N. D., Baler, R. D., Compton, W. M., & Weiss, S. R. (2014). Adverse health effects of marijuana use. *New England Journal of Medicine, 370*(23), 2219–2227.

Volkow, N. D., Wang, G. J., Newcorn, J., Telang, F., Solanto, M. V., Fowler, J. S., . . . & Swanson, J. M. (2007). Depressed dopamine activity in caudate and preliminary evidence of limbic involvement in adults with attention-deficit/hyperactivity disorder. *Archives of General Psychiatry, 64*(8), 932–940.

Volling, B. L., Kennedy, D. E., & Jackey, L. M. (2010). The development of sibling jealousy. In S. L. Hart & M. Legerstee (Eds.), *Handbook of Jealousy: Theory, Research, and Multidisciplinary Approaches* (pp. 387–4317). Chicester, England: Blackwell Publishing.

Volling, B. L., Mahoney, A., & Rauer, A. J. (2009). Sanctification of parenting, moral socialization, and young children's conscience development. *Psychology of Religion and Spirituality, 1*(1), 53.

von Hippel, W. (2007). Aging, executive functioning, and social control. *Current Directions in Psychological Science, 16*(5), 240–244.

von Hofsten, C. (2004). An action perspective on motor development. *Cognitive Sciences, 8*(1), 266–272.

Von Korff, L., Grotevant, H. D., & McRoy, R. G. (2006). Openness arrangements and psychological adjustment in adolescent adoptees. *Journal of Family Psychology, 20,* 531–534.

Vondra, J. I., & Barnett, D. (1999). A typical attachment in infancy and early childhood among children at developmental risk. *Monographs of the Society for Research in Child Development, 64*(3, Serial No. 258).

Voorveld, H.A.M. & van der Goot, M. (2013). Age differences in media multitasking: A diary study. *Journal of Broadcasting & Electronic Media, 57,* 392–408.

Voss, M. W., Prakash, R. S., Erickson, K. I., Basak, C., Chaddock, L., Kim, J. S., . . . & Wójcicki, T. R. (2010). Plasticity of brain networks in a randomized intervention trial of exercise training in older adults. *Frontiers in Aging Neuroscience, 2.*

Voss, W., Jungmann, T., Wachtendorf, M., & Neubauer, A. P. (2012). Long-term cognitive outcomes of extremely low-birth-weight infants: The influence of the maternal educational background. *Acta Paediatrica, 101*(6), 569–573.

Votruba-Drzal, E., Li-Grining, C. R., & Maldonado-Carreno, C. (2008). A developmental perspective on full- versus part-day kindergarten and children's academic trajectories through fifth grade. *Child Development, 79,* 957–978.

Voydanoff, P. (2004). The effects of work demands and resources on work-to-family conflict and facilitation. *Journal of Marriage and Family, 66,* 398–412.

Voyer, D., & Voyer, S. D. (2014). Gender differences in scholastic achievement: A meta-analysis. *Psychological Bulletin, 140*(4), 1174.

Vozikaki, M., Linardakis, M., Micheli, K., & Philalithis, A. (2017). Activity participation and well-being among European adults aged 65 years and older. *Social Indicators Research, 131*(2), 769–795.

Vrijenhoek, T., Buizer-Voskamp, J. E., van der Stelt, I., Strengman, E., Sabatti, C., van Kessel, A. G., . . . Veltman, J. A. (2008). Recurrent CNVs disrupt three candidate genes in schizophrenia patients. *American Journal of Human Genetics, 83,* 504–510.

Vu, T., Liu, T., Garside, D. B., & Daviglus, M. L. (2009). Unhealthy lifestyle choices in older age and subsequent health-related quality of life: The Chicago Heart Association Detection Project. *Circulation, 120,* S482–S483.

Vuchinich, S., Angelelli, J., & Gatherum, A. (1996). Context and development in family problem solving with preadolescent children. *Child Development, 67,* 1276–1288.

Vukasović, T., & Bratko, D. (2015). Heritability of personality: A meta-analysis of behavior genetic studies. *Psychological Bulletin, 141*(4), 769.

Vuoksimaa, E., Koskenvuo, M., Rose, R. J., & Kaprio, J. (2009). Origins of handedness: A nationwide study of 30,161 adults. *Neuropsychologia, 47*(5), 1294–1301.

Vygotsky, L. S. (1962). *Thought and language.* Cambridge, MA: MIT Press. (Original work published 1934)

Vygotsky, L. S. (1978). *Mind in society: The development of higher psychological processes.* Cambridge, MA: Harvard University Press.

Wadsworth, M. E., Raviv, T., Reinhard, C., Wolff, B., Santiago, C. D., & Einhorn, L. (2008). An indirect effects model of the association between poverty and child functioning: The role of children's poverty related stress. *Journal of Loss and Trauma: International Perspectives on Stress and Coping, 13*(2–3), 156–185.

Waggoner, L. W. (2015). With marriage on the decline and cohabitation on the rise, what about marital rights for unmarried partners?

University of Michigan Public Law Research Paper No. 477.

Wahrendorf, M., & Siegrist, J. (2010). Are changes in productive activities of older people associated with changes in their well-being? Results of a longitudinal European study. *European Journal of Ageing, 7*(2), 59–68.

Wahrendorf, M., Blane, D., Matthews, K., & Siegrist, J. (2016). Linking quality of work in midlife to volunteering during retirement: A European study. *Journal of Population Ageing, 9*(1–2), 113–130.

Wainright, J. L., & Patterson, C. J. (2006). Delinquency, victimization, and substance use among adolescents with female same-sex parents. *Journal of Family Psychology, 20*(3), 526.

Wainright, J. L., Russell, S. T., & Patterson, C. J. (2004). Psychosocial adjustment, school outcomes, and romantic relationships of adolescents with same-sex parents. *Child Development, 75,* 1886–1898.

Waite, L. J., & Joyner, K. (2000). Emotional and physical satisfaction with sex in married, cohabiting, and dating sexual unions: Do men and women differ? In E. O. Laumann & R. T. Michael (Eds.), *Sex, love, and health in America: Private choices and public policies* (pp. 239–269). Chicago: University of Chicago Press.

Waite, L. J., Luo, Y., & Lewin, A. C. (2009). Marital happiness and marital stability: Consequences for psychological well-being. *Social Science Research, 38*(1), 201–212.

Waknine, Y. (2006). Highlights from MMWR: Prevalence of U.S. birth defects and more. *Medscape.* Retrieved from www.medscape.com/viewarticle/521056

Wald, N. J. (2004). Folic acid and the prevention of neural-tube defects. *New England Journal of Medicine, 350,* 101–103.

Waldfogel, J., Craigie, T. A., & Brooks-Gunn, J. (2010). Fragile families and child wellbeing. *The Future of Children/Center for the Future of Children, the David and Lucile Packard Foundation, 20*(2), 87.

Waldrop, D. P. (2011). Denying and defying death: The culture of dying in 21st century America. *The Gerontologist, 51,* 571–576.

Walk, R. D., & Gibson, E. J. (1961). A comparative and analytical study of visual depth perception. *Psychology Monographs, 75*(15).

Walker, A. J., Allen, K. R., & Connidis, I. A. (2005). Theorizing and studying sibling ties in adulthood. *Sourcebook of Family Theory and Research, 167*–190.

Walker, L. (1995). Sexism in Kohlberg's moral psychology? In W. M. Kurtines & J. L. Gewirtz (Eds.), *Moral development: An introduction* (pp. 83–107). Boston: Allyn & Bacon.

Walker, R. E., Keane, C. R., & Burke, J. G. (2010). Disparities and access to healthy food in the United States: A review of food deserts literature. *Health & Place, 16,* 876–884.

Walker, W. R., Skowronski, J. J., & Thompson, C. P. (2003). Life is pleasant—And memory helps to keep it that way! *Review of General Psychology, 7,* 203–210.

Wallace, J. M., Bachman, J. G., O'Malley, P. M., Johnson, L. D., Schulenberg, J. E., & Cooper,

S. M. (2005). Tobacco, alcohol and illicit drug use: Racial and ethnic differences among U.S. high school seniors 1976–2000. *Public Health Reports, 117,* S67–S75.

Walle, J. V., Rittig, S., Bauer, S., Eggert, P., Marschall-Kehrel, D., & Tekgul, S. (2012). Practical consensus guidelines for the management of enuresis. *European Journal of Pediatrics, 171*(6), 971–983.

Waller, M. W., Hallfors, D. D., Halpern, C. T., Iritani, B., Ford, C. A., & Guo, G. (2006). Gender differences in associations between depressive symptoms and patterns of substance use and risky sexual behavior among a nationally representative sample of U.S. adolescents. *Archives of Women's Mental Health, 9,* 139–150.

Wallhagen, M. I., Strawbridge, W. J., Shema, S. J., & Kaplan, G. A. (2004). Impact of self-assessed hearing loss on a spouse: A longitudinal analysis of couples. *Journal of Gerontology: Social Sciences, 59,* S190–S196.

Wallis, C. (2011). Performing gender: A content analysis of gender display in music videos. *Sex Roles, 64*(3–4), 160–172.

Wallis, C.J.D., Lo, K., Lee, Y., Krakowsky, Y., Garbens, A., Satkunasivam, R., Herschorn, S., Kodama, R.T., Cheung, P., Narod, S.A., & Nam, R.K. (2016). Survival and cardiovascular events in men treated with testosterone replacement therapy: An intention-to-treat observational cohort study. *The Lancet Diabetes & Endocrinology, 4,* 498–506.

Walma van der Molen, J. (2004). Violence and suffering in television news: Toward a broader conception of harmful television content for children. *Pediatrics, 113,* 1771–1775.

Walsh, T., McClellan, J. M., McCarthy, S. E., Addington, A. M., Pierce, S. B., Cooper, G. M., . . . Sebat, J. (2008). Rare structural variants disrupt multiple genes in neurodevelopmental pathways in schizophrenia. *Science, 320,* 539–543.

Wang, D. D., Leung, C. W., Li, Y., Ding, E. L., Chiuve, S. E., Hu, F. B., & Willett, W. C. (2014). Trends in dietary quality among adults in the United States, 1999 through 2010. *JAMA Internal Medicine, 174*(10), 1587–1595.

Wang, D. W., Desai, R. R., Crotti, L., Arnestad, M., Insolia, R., Pedrazzini, M., . . . George, A. L. (2007). Cardiac sodium channel dysfunction in sudden infant death syndrome. *Circulation, 115,* 368–376.

Wang, D., & MacMillan, T. (2013). The benefits of gardening for older adults: A systematic review of the literature. *Activities, Adaptation & Aging, 37*(2), 153–181.

Wang, J., Tan, L., Wang, H. F., Tan, C. C., Meng, X. F., Wang, C., . . . & Yu, J. T. (2015). Anti-inflammatory drugs and risk of Alzheimer's disease: an updated systematic review and meta-analysis. *Journal of Alzheimer's Disease, 44*(2), 385–396.

Wang, L., Wang, X., Wang, W., Chen, C., Ronnennberg, A. G., Guang, W., . . . Xu, X. (2004). Stress and dysmenorrhea: A population-based prospective study. *Occupational and Environmental Medicine, 61,* 1021–1026.

Wang, M., & Shi, J. (2014). Psychological research on retirement. *Annual Review of Psychology, 65,* 209-233.

Wang, M., Henkens, K., & van Solinge, H. (2011). Retirement adjustment: A review of theoretical and empirical advancements. *American Psychologist, 66*(3), 204.

Wang, W., & Morin, R. (2009, November 24). *Recession brings many young people back to the nest: Home for the holidays . . . and every other day.* Retrieved from http://pewresearch.org/pubs/1423/home-for-the-holidays-boomeranged-parents

Wang, W., & Parker, K. C. (2014). *Record share of Americans have never married: As values, economics and gender patterns change.* Pew Research Center, Social & Demographic Trends Project.

Wang, Y. (2002). Is obesity associated with early sexual maturation? A comparison of the association in American boys versus girls. *Pediatrics, 110*(5), 903-910.

Wang, Y., Wu, Y., Wilson, R. F., Bleich, S., Cheskin, L., Weston, C., . . . & Segal, J. (2013). *Childhood obesity prevention programs: comparative effectiveness review and meta-analysis.* Rockville, MD, USA: Agency for Healthcare Research and Quality.

Wannamethee, S. G., Shaper, A. G., Whincup, P. H., & Walker, M. (1995). Smoking cessation and the risk of stroke in middle-aged men. *Journal of the American Medical Association, 274,* 155-160.

Wardle, J., Carnell, S., Haworth, C. M., & Plomin, R. (2008). Evidence for a strong genetic influence on childhood adiposity despite the force of the obesogenic environment. *The American Journal of Clinical Nutrition, 87*(2), 398-404.

Wardle, J., Robb, K. A., Johnson, F., Griffith, J., Brunner, E., Power, C., & TovÈe, M. (2004). Socioeconomic variation in attitudes to eating and weight in female adolescents. *Health Psychology, 23,* 275-282.

Ware, J. J., & Munafò, M. R. (2015). Genetics of smoking behaviour. In *The Neurobiology and Genetics of Nicotine and Tobacco* (pp. 19-36). New York: Springer International Publishing.

Warneken, F., & Tomasello, M. (2006). Altruistic helping in human infants and young chimpanzees. *Science, 311,* 1301-1303.

Warneken, F., & Tomasello, M. (2008). Extrinsic rewards undermine altruistic tendencies in 20-month-olds. *Developmental Psychology, 44,* 1785-1788.

Warren, J. A., & Johnson, P. J. (1995). The impact of workplace support on work-family role strain. *Family Relations, 44,* 163-169.

Warren, J. R., & Lee, J. C. (2003). The impact of adolescent employment on high school dropout: Differences by individual and labor-market characteristics. *Social Science Research, 32*(1), 98-128.

Warshak, R. A. (2014). Social science and parenting plans for young children: A consensus report. *Psychology, Public Policy, and Law, 20*(1), 46.

Wartella, E., Richert, R.A., & Robb, M.B. (2010). Babies, television and videos: How did we get here? *Developmental Review, 30,* 116-127.

Wasik, B. H., Ramey, C. T., Bryant, D. M., & Sparling, J. J. (1990). A longitudinal study of two early intervention strategies: Project CARE. *Child Development, 61,* 1682-1696.

Wass, S., Porayska-Pomsta, K., & Johnson, M. (2011). Training attentional control in infancy. *Current Biology.* doi:10.1016/j.cub.2011.08.00

Wasserman, D. (2006). *Depression: The facts.* Oxford, UK: Oxford University Press.

Watamura, S. E., Donzella, B., Alwin, J., & Gunnar, M. R. (2003). Morning-to-afternoon increases in cortisol concentrations for infants and toddlers at child care: Age differences and behavioral correlates. *Child Development, 74,* 1006-1020.

Waters, E., & Deane, K. E. (1985). Defining and assessing individual differences in attachment relationships: Q-methodology and the organization of behavior in infancy and early childhood. *Monographs of the Society for Research in Child Development,* 41-65.

Waters, E., Wippman, J., & Sroufe, L. A. (1979). Attachment, positive affect, and competence in the peer group: Two studies in construct validation. *Child Development, 50,* 821-829.

Watson, A. C., Nixon, C. L., Wilson, A., & Capage, L. (1999). Social interaction skills and theory of mind in young children. *Developmental Psychology, 35*(2), 386-391.

Watson, J. B., & Rayner, R. (1920). Conditioned emotional reactions. *Journal of Experimental Psychology, 3,* 1-14.

Wayne, J., Musisca, N., & Fleeson, W. (2004). Considering the role of personality in the work-family experience: Relationships of the big five to work-family conflict and facilitation. *Journal of Vocational Behavior, 64*(1), 108-130.

Weatherbee, S. R., & Allaire, J. C. (2008). Everyday cognition and mortality: Performance differences and predictive utility of the everyday cognition battery. *Psychology and Aging, 23*(1), 216-221.

Weaver, J. M., & Schofield, T. J. (2015). Mediation and moderation of divorce effects on children's behavior problems. *Journal of Family Psychology, 29*(1), 39.

Weber, A., Fernald, A., & Diop, Y. (2017). When cultural norms discourage talking to babies: Effectiveness of a parenting program in rural Senegal. *Child Development.* doi:10.1111/cdev.12882

Webster, A. L., Yan, M. S. C., & Marsden, P. A. (2013). Epigenetics and cardiovascular disease. *Canadian Journal of Cardiology, 29*(1), 46-57.

Weg, R. B. (1989). Sensuality/sexuality of the middle years. In S. Hunter & M. Sundel (Eds.), *Midlife myths.* Newbury Park, CA: Sage.

Weinberger, J. (1999, May 18). Enlightening conversation [Letter to the editor]. *The New York Times,* F3.

Weinmayr, G., Forastiere, F., Büchele, G., Jaensch, A., Strachan, D. P., Nagel, G., & ISAAC Phase Two Study Group. (2014). Overweight/obesity and respiratory and allergic disease in children: international study of asthma and allergies in childhood (ISAAC) phase two. *PloS one, 9*(12), e113996.

Weinstein, A. R., Sesso, H. D., Lee, I. M., Cook, N. R., Manson, J. E., Buring, J. E., & Gaziano, J. M. (2004). Relationship of physical activity vs body mass index with type 2 diabetes in women. *Journal of the American Medical Association, 292,* 1188-1194.

Weinstock, H., Berman, S., & Cates, W., Jr. (2004). Sexually transmitted diseases among American youth: Incidence and prevalence estimates, 2000. *Perspectives on Sexual and Reproductive Health, 36,* 6-10.

Weisner, T. S. (1993). Ethnographic and ecocultural perspectives on sibling relationships. In Z. Stoneman & P. W. Berman (Eds.), *The effects of mental retardation, visibility, and illness on sibling relationships* (pp. 51-83). Baltimore, MD: Brooks.

Weiss, A., Bates, T. C., & Luciano, M. (2008). Happiness is a personal(ity) thing. The genetics of personality and well-being in a representative sample. *Psychological Science, 19,* 205-210.

Weiss, B., Dodge, K. A., Bates, J. E., & Pettit, G. S. (1992). Some consequences of early harsh discipline: Child aggression and a maladaptive social information processing style. *Child Development, 63,* 1321-1335.

Weissman, M. M., Warner, V., Wickramaratne, P. J., & Kandel, D. B. (1999). Maternal smoking during pregnancy and psychopathology in offspring followed to adulthood. *Journal of the American Academy of Child and Adolescent Psychiatry, 38,* 892-899.

Weisz, J. R., McCarty, C. A., & Valeri, S. M. (2006). Effects of psychotherapy for depression in children and adolescents: A meta-analysis. *Psychological Bulletin, 132,* 132-149.

Weisz, J. R., Weiss, B., Han, S. S., Granger, D. A., & Morton, T. (1995). Effects of psychotherapy with children and adolescents revisited: A meta-analysis of treatment outcome studies. *Psychological Bulletin, 117*(3), 450-468.

Welch-Ross, M. K., & Schmidt, C. R. (1996). Gender-schema development and children's story memory: Evidence for a developmental model. *Child Development, 67,* 820-835.

Wellman, H. M. (2014). *Making minds: How theory of mind develops.* Oxford: Oxford University Press.

Wellman, H. M., & Liu, D. (2004). Scaling theory-of-mind tasks. *Child Development, 75,* 523-541.

Wellman, H. M., Lopez-Duran, S., LaBounty, J., & Hamilton, B. (2008). Infant attention to intentional action predicts preschool theory of mind. *Developmental Psychology, 44,* 618-623.

Welt, C. K. (2008). Primary ovarian insufficiency: A more accurate term for premature ovarian failure. *Clinical Endocrinology, 68*(4), 499-509.

Wen, X., Wen, S. W., Fleming, N., Demissie, K., Rhoads, G. G., & Walker, M. (2007). Teenage pregnancy and adverse birth outcomes: A large population based retrospective cohort study. *International Journal of Epidemiology, 36*(2), 368-373.

Wendelken, C., Baym, C. L., Gazzaley, A., & Bunge, S. A. (2011). Neural indices of improved attentional modulation over middle childhood. *Developmental Cognitive Neuroscience, 1*(2), 175-186.

Weng, S. F., Redsell, S. A., Swift, J. A., Yang, M., & Glazebrook, C. P. (2012). Systematic review and meta-analyses of risk factors for childhood overweight identifiable during infancy. *Archives of Disease in Childhood, 97*(12), 1019-1026.

Wenger, G. C., Dykstra, P. A., Melkas, T., & Knipscheer, K. C. (2007). Social embeddedness and late life parenthood: Community activity, close ties, and support networks. *Journal of Family Issues, 28*(11), 1419-1456.

Wentworth, N., Benson, J. B., & Haith, M. M. (2000). The development of infants' reaches for stationary and moving targets. *Child Development, 71*, 576-601.

Wentzel, K. R. (2002). Are effective teachers like good parents? Teaching styles and student adjustment in early adolescence. *Child Development, 73*, 287-301.

Wentzel, K. R., & Muenks, K. (2016). Peer influence on students' motivation, academic achievement, and social behavior. In K. R. Wentzel & G. B. Ramani (Eds.). *Handbook of Social Influences in School Contexts: Social-Emotional, Motivation, and Cognitive Outcomes,* (pp. 13-30). New York: Routledge.

Werker, J. F., Yeung, H. H., & Yoshida, K. A. (2012). How do infants become experts at native-speech perception? *Current Directions in Psychological Science, 21*(4), 221-226.

Werner, E. E. (1985). Stress and protective factors in children's lives. In A. R. Nichol (Ed.), *Longitudinal studies in child psychology and psychiatry.* New York: Wiley.

Werner, E. E. (1987, July 15). *Vulnerability and resiliency: A longitudinal study of Asian Americans from birth to age 30.* Invited address at the ninth biennial meeting of the International Society for the Study of Behavioral Development, Tokyo, Japan.

Werner, E. E. (1993). Risk and resilience in individuals with learning disabilities: Lessons learned from the Kauai longitudinal study. *Learning Disabilities Research and Practice, 8*, 28-34.

Werner, E. E. (1995). Resilience in development. *Current Directions in Psychological Science, 4*(3), 81-85.

Werner, E., & Smith, R. S. (2001). *Journeys from childhood to midlife.* Ithaca, NY: Cornell University Press.

Westen, D. (1998). The scientific legacy of Sigmund Freud: Toward a psychodynamically informed psychological science. *Psychological Bulletin, 124*, 333-371.

Westerhof, G. J., & Bohlmeijer, E. T. (2014). Celebrating fifty years of research and applications in reminiscence and life review: State of the art and new directions. *Journal of Aging Studies, 29*, 107-114.

Weststrate, N. M., & Glück, J. (2017). Hard-earned wisdom: Exploratory processing of difficult life experience is positively associated with wisdom. *Developmental Psychology, 53*(4), 800.

Wethington, E. (2000). Expecting stress: Americans and the "midlife crisis." *Motivation and Emotion, 24*(2), 85-103.

Wethington, E., Kessler, R. C., & Pixley, J. E. (2004). Turning points in adulthood. In O. G. Brim, C. D. Ryff, & R. C. Kessler (Eds.), *How*

healthy are we? A national study of well-being at midlife* (pp. 586-613). Chicago: University of Chicago Press.

Wexler, I. D., Branski, D., & Kerem, E. (2006). War and children. *Journal of the American Medical Association, 296*, 579-581.

Whalley, L. J., & Deary, I. J. (2001). Longitudinal cohort study of childhood IQ and survival up to age 76. *British Medical Journal, 322*, 819.

Whalley, L. J., Starr, J. M., Athawes, R., Hunter, D., Pattie, A., & Deary, I. J. (2000). Childhood mental ability and dementia. *Neurology, 55*, 1455-1459.

Whisman, M. A., Uebelacker, L. A., Tolejko, N., Chatav, Y., & McKelvie, M. (2006). Marital discord and well-being in older adults: Is the association confounded by personality? *Psychology and Aging, 21*, 626-631.

Whitbourne, S. K. (1987). Personality development in adulthood and old age: Relationships among identity style, health, and well-being. In K. W. Schaie (Ed.), *Annual review of gerontology and geriatrics* (pp. 189-216). New York: Springer.

Whitbourne, S. K. (1996). *The aging individual: Physical and psychological perspectives.* New York: Springer.

Whitbourne, S. K. (2001). The physical aging process in midlife: Interactions with psychological and sociocultural factors. In M. E. Lachman (Ed.), *Handbook of midlife development* (pp. 109-155). New York: Wiley.

Whitbourne, S. K., & Connolly, L. A. (1999). The developing self in midlife. In S. L. Willis & J. D. Reid (Eds.), *Life in the middle: Psychological and social development in middle age* (pp. 25-45). San Diego: Academic Press.

Whitbourne, S. K., Sneed, J. R., & Sayer, S. (2009). Psychosocial development from college through midlife: A 34-year sequential study. *Developmental Psychology, 45*(5), 1328-1340.

White, H. R., McMorris, B. J., Catalano, R. F., Fleming, C. B., Haggerty, K .P., & Abbott, R. D. (2006). Increases in alcohol and marijuana use during the transition out of high school into emerging adulthood: The effects of leaving home, going to college, and high school protective factors. *Journal of Studies on Alcohol, 67*(6), 810-822.

White, J. C., & Bull, R. (2008). Number games, magnitude representation, and basic number skills in preschoolers. *Developmental Psychology, 44*(2), 588.

White, L. (2001). Sibling relationships over the life course: A panel analysis. *Journal of Marriage and Family, 63*(2), 555-568.

White, L., & Edwards, J. N. (1990). Emptying the nest and parental well-being: An analysis of national panel data. *American Sociological Review,* 235-242.

Whitebread, D., Basilio, M., Kuvalja, M., & Verma, M. (2012). *The importance of play.* Brussels, Belgium: Toy Industries of Europe (TIE).

Whitebread, D., Coltman, P., Pasternak, D. P., Sangster, C., Grau, V., Bingham, S., . . . & Demetriou, D. (2009). The development of two observational tools for assessing metacognition and self-regulated learning in young children. *Metacognition and Learning, 4*(1), 63-85.

Whitehead, B. D., & Popenoe, D. (2003). *The social health of marriage in America 2003. Essay: Marriage and children: Coming together again?* Piscataway, NJ: The National Marriage Project, Rutgers University.

Whitehurst, G. J., & Lonigan, C. J. (1998). Child development and emergent literacy. *Child Development, 69*, 848-872.

Whitehurst, G. J., & Lonigan, C. J. (2001). Emergent literacy: Development from prereaders to readers. In S. B. Neuman & D. K. Dickinson (Eds.), *Handbook of early literacy research* (pp. 11-29). New York: Guilford Press.

Whitmer, R. A., Quesenberry, C. P., Zhou, J., & Yaffe, K. (2011). Timing of hormone therapy and dementia: the critical window theory revisited. *Annals of Neurology, 69*(1), 163-169.

Whitty, M. T. (2003). Pushing the wrong buttons: Men's and women's attitudes toward online and offline infidelity. *CyberPsychology & Behavior, 6*(6), 569-579.

World Health Organization. (2014, October 29). Facts and figures on childhood obesity. Retrieved from World Health Organization: www.who.int/end-childhood-obesity/facts/en

World Health Organization. (2015, May). *MDG 4: reduce child mortality.* Retrieved from WHO: www.who.int/topics/millennium_development_goals/child_mortality/en.

World Health Organization. (2017a). *Growing up unequal. HBSC 2016 study (2013/2014 survey).* Retrieved from World Health Organization: www.euro.who.int/en/publications/abstracts/growing-up-unequal.-hbsc-2016-study-20132014-survey

World Health Organization. (2017b). *Sex differentials in Infant mortality.* Retrieved from who.int: www.searo.who.int/entity/health_situation_trends/data/chi/sex-diff-imr/en

Whyatt, R. M., Rauh, V., Barr, D. B., Camann, D. E., Andrews, H. F., Garfinkel, R., . . . Perera, F. P. (2004). Prenatal insecticide exposures and birth weight and length among an urban minority cohort. *Environmental Health Perspectives, 112*(110), 1125-1132.

Whyte, J. C., & Bull, R. (2008). Number games, magnitude representation, and basic number skills in preschoolers. *Developmental Psychology, 44*(2), 588.

Widaman, K. F. (2009). Phenylketonuria in children and mothers: Genes, environment, behavior. *Current Directions in Psychological Science, 18*(1), 48-52.

Wight, R. G., LeBlanc, A. J., & Lee Badgett, M. V. (2013). Same-sex legal marriage and psychological well-being: findings from the California Health Interview Survey. *American Journal of Public Health, 103*(2), 339-346.

Wijngaards-de Meij, L., Stroebe, M., Schut, H., Stroebe, W., van den Bout, J., van der Heijden, P., & Dijkstra, I. (2005). Couples at risk following the death of their child: Predictors of grief versus depression. *Journal of Consulting and Clinical Psychology, 73*, 617-623.

Wilcox, W. B., & Nock, S. L. (2006). What's love got to do with it? Equality, equity, commitment and women's marital quality. *Social Forces, 84,* 1321-1345.

Wilder, S. (2014). Effects of parental involvement on academic achievement: a meta-synthesis. *Educational Review, 66*(3), 377-397.

Wildsmith, E., Schelar, E., Peterson, K., & Manlove, J. (2010). *Sexually transmitted diseases among young adults: Prevalence, perceived risk and risk-taking behaviors* (2010-21). Retrieved from www.childtrends.org/Files/Child_Trends-2010_05_01_RB_STD.pdf

Willcox, B. J., Donlon, T. A., He, Q., Chen, R., Grove, J. S., Yano, K., . . . Curb, J. D. (2008). FOXO3A genotype is strongly associated with human longevity. *Proceedings of the National Academy of Sciences of the United States of America, 105*(37), 13987-13992.

Willett, W. C., Colditz, G., & Stampfer, M. (2000). Postmenopausal estrogens—Opposed, unopposed, or none of the above. *Journal of the American Medical Association, 283,* 534-535.

Williams, D. R., Priest, N., & Anderson, N. B. (2016). Understanding associations among race, socioeconomic status, and health: Patterns and prospects. *Health Psychology, 35*(4), 407.

Williams, J., Wake, M., Hesketh, K., Maher, E., & Waters, E. (2005). Health-related quality of life of overweight and obese children. *Journal of the American Medical Association, 293,* 70-76.

Williams, K. (2004). The transition to widowhood and the social regulation of health: Consequences for health and health risk behavior. *Journal of Gerontology: Social Sciences, 59B,* S343-S349.

Williams, K., & Dunne-Bryant, A. (2006). Divorce and adult psychological well-being: Clarifying the role of gender and child age. *Journal of Marriage and Family, 68,* 1178-1196.

Williams, L. R., & Steinberg, L. (2011). Reciprocal relations between parenting and adjustment in a sample of juvenile offenders. *Child Development, 82*(2), 633-645.

Willinger, M., Hoffman, H. T., & Hartford, R. B. (1994). Infant sleep position and risk for sudden infant death syndrome: Report of meeting held January 13 and 14, 1994. *Pediatrics, 93,* 814-819.

Willingham, D. T. (2004). Reframing the mind. *Education Next, 4,* 19-24.

Willis, S. L., & Schaie, K. W. (1999). Intellectual functioning in midlife. In S. L. Willis & J. D. Reid (Eds.), *Life in the middle: Psychological and social development in middle age* (pp. 233-247). San Diego: Academic Press.

Willis, S. L., & Schaie, K. W. (2005). Cognitive trajectories in midlife and cognitive functioning in old age. In S. L. Willis & M. Martin (Eds.), *Middle adulthood: A lifespan perspective* (pp. 243-276). Thousand Oaks, CA: Sage.

Willis, S. L., & Schaie, K. W. (2006). Cognitive functioning in the baby boomers: Longitudinal and cohort effects. In S. K. Whitbourne & S. L. Willis (Eds.), *The baby boomers grow up: Contemporary perspectives on midlife* (pp. 205-234). Mahwah, NJ: Erlbaum.

Willis, S. L., Martin, M., & Röcke, C. (2010). Longitudinal perspectives on midlife development: stability and change.*European Journal of Ageing, 7*(3), 131-134.

Willoughby, B. J., Farero, A. M., & Busby, D. M. (2014). Exploring the effects of sexual desire discrepancy among married couples. *Archives of Sexual Behavior, 43*(3), 551-562.

Willson, A. E., Shuey, K. M., & Elder, G. H. (2003). Ambivalence in the relationship of adult children to aging parents and in-laws. *Journal of Marriage and Family, 65,* 1055-1072.

Willyard, C. (2014). Heritability: The family roots of obesity. *Nature, 508*(7496), S58-S60.

Wilmoth, J. R. (2000). Demography of longevity: Past, present, and future trends. *Experimental Gerontology, 35,* 1111-1129.

Wilmoth, J., & Koso, G. (2002). Does marital history count? Marital status and wealth outcomes among preretirement adults. *Journal of Marriage and Family, 64,* 254-268.

Wilson, B. J. (2008). Media and children's aggression, fear, and altruism. *Future of Children, 18,* 87-118.

Wilson, D. R. (2010). Health consequences of childhood sexual abuse. *Perspectives in Psychiatric Care, 46*(1), 56-64.

Wilson, E. O. (1975). *Sociobiology: The new synthesis.* Cambridge, MA: Belknap Press of Harvard University Press.

Wilson, G. T., Grilo, C. M., & Vitousek, K. M. (2007). Psychological treatment of eating disorders. *American Psychologist, 62,* 199-216.

Wilson, R. S., & Bennett, D. A. (2003). Cognitive activity and risk of Alzheimer's disease. *Current Directions in Psychological Science, 12,* 87-91.

Wilson, R. S., Scherr, P. A., Schneider, J. A., Tang, Y., & Bennett, D. A. (2007). Relation of cognitive ability to risk of developing Alzheimer disease. *Neurology, 69,* 1911-1920.

Wilson-Costello, D., Friedman, H., Minich, N., Siner, B., Taylor, G., Schluchter, M., & Hack, M. (2007). Improved neurodevelopmental outcomes for extremely low birth weight infants in 2000-2002. *Pediatrics, 119,* 37-45.

Wingfield, A., & Stine, E. A. L. (1989). Modeling memory processes: Research and theory on memory and aging. In G. C. Gilmore, P. J. Whitehouse, & M. L. Wykle (Eds.), *Memory, aging, and dementia: Theory, assessment, and treatment* (pp. 4-40). New York: Springer.

Wink, P., & Staudinger, U. M. (2016). Wisdom and psychosocial functioning in later life. *Journal of Personality, 84*(3), 306-318.

Winner, E. (2000). The origins and ends of giftedness. *American Psychologist, 55,* 159-169.

Wisdom, N. M., Mignogna, J., & Collins, R. L. (2012). Variability in Wechsler Adult Intelligence Scale-IV subtest performance across age. *Archives of Clinical Neuropsychology, 27*(4), 389-397.

Wisner, K. L., Parry, B. L., & Piontek, C. M. (2002). Postpartum depression. *New England Journal of Medicine, 347*(3), 194-199.

Wittenborn, J., & Rein, D. (2014). The future of vision: Forecasting the prevalence and costs of vision problems. *Prevent Blindness.*

Wittstein, I. S., Thiemann, D. R., Lima, J. A. C., Baughman, K. L., Schulman, S. P., Gerstenblith, G., . . . Champion, H. C. (2005). Neurohumoral features of myocardial stunning due to sudden emotional stress. *New England Journal of Medicine, 352,* 539-548.

Woerlee, G. M. (2005). *Mortal minds: The biology of the near-death experience.* New York: Prometheus Books.

Wohlfahrt-Veje, C., Mouritsen, A., Hagen, C. P., Tinggaard, J., Mieritz, M. G., Boas, M., . . . & Main, K. M. (2016). Pubertal onset in boys and girls is influenced by pubertal timing of both parents. *The Journal of Clinical Endocrinology & Metabolism, 101*(7), 2667-2674.

Wojcik, M., Burzynska-Pedziwiatr, I., & Wozniak, L. A. (2010). A review of natural and synthetic antioxidants important for health and longevity. *Current Medicinal Chemistry, 17*(28), 3262-3288.

Wolfe, L. (2004). Should parents speak with a dying child about impending death? *New England Journal of Medicine, 351,* 1251-1253.

Wolff, P. H. (1969). The natural history of crying and other vocalizations in early infancy. In B. M. Foss (Ed.), *Determinants of infant behavior* (Vol. 4). London: Methuen.

Wolfson, A. R., Carskadon, M. A., Mindell, J. A., & Drake, C. (2006). *The National Sleep Foundation: Sleep in America poll.* Retrieved from www.sleepfoundation.org/sites/default/files/2006_summary_of_findings.pdf

Wolraich, M. L., Wibbelsman, C. J., Brown, T. E., Evans, S. W., Gotlieb, E. M., Knight, J. R., Ross, C., . . . Wilens, T. (2005). Attention-deficit/hyperactivity disorder among adolescents: A review of the diagnosis, treatment, and clinical implications. *Pediatrics, 115,* 1734-1746.

Wong, C. A., Scavone, B. M., Peaceman, A. M., McCarthy, R. J., Sullivan, J. T., Diaz, N. T., . . . Grouper, S. (2005). The risk of cesarean delivery with neuraxial analgesia given early versus late in labor. *New England Journal of Medicine, 352,* 655-665.

Wong, C. C. Y., Caspi, A., Williams, B., Craig, I. W., Houts, R., & Ambler, A. (2010). A longitudinal study of epigenetic variation in twins. *Epigenetics, 5,* 516-526.

Wong, C. C. Y., Meaburn, E. L., Ronald, A., Price, T. S., Jeffries, A. R., Schalkwyk, L. C., . . . & Mill, J. (2014). Methylomic analysis of monozygotic twins discordant for autism spectrum disorder and related behavioural traits. *Molecular Psychiatry, 19*(4), 495-503.

Wong, C. T., Wais, J., & Crawford, D. A. (2015). Prenatal exposure to common environment factors affects brain lipids and increases risk of developing autism spectrum disorders. *European Journal of Neuroscience, 42,* 2742-2760.

Wong, H., Gottesman, I., & Petronis, A. (2005). Phenotypic differences in genetically identical organisms: The epigenetic perspective. *Human Molecular Genetics, 14*(Review Issue 1), R11-R18.

Wong, K.M., Mastenbroek, S., & Repping, S. (2014). Cryopreservation of human embryos and its contribution to in vitro success rates. *Fertility and Sterility, 102,* 19-26.

Wong, M. M., Nigg, J. T., Zucker, R. A., Puttler, L. I., Fitzgerald, H. E., Jester, J. M., . . . Adams, K.

(2006). Behavioral control and resiliency in the onset of alcohol and illicit drug use: A prospective study from preschool to adolescence. *Child Development, 77*, 1016-1033.

Wong, S. S., Zhou, B., Goebert, D., & Hishinuma, E. S. (2013). The risk of adolescent suicide across patterns of drug use: a nationally representative study of high school students in the United States from 1999 to 2009. *Social Psychiatry and Psychiatric Epidemiology, 48*(10), 1611-1620.

Wood, D. (1980). Teaching the young child: Some relationships between social interaction, language, and thought. In D. Olson (Ed.), *The social foundations of language and thought* (pp. 280-296). New York: Norton.

Wood, D., Bruner, J., & Ross, G. (1976). The role of tutoring in problem solving. *Journal of Child Psychiatry and Psychology, 17*, 89-100.

Wood, R. M., & Gustafson, G. E. (2001). Infant crying and adults' anticipated caregiving responses: Acoustic and contextual influences. *Child Development, 72*, 1287-1300.

Wood, W., & Eagly, A. (2002a). A cross-cultural analysis of the behavior of women and men: Implications for the origins of sex differences. *Psychological Bulletin, 128*, 699-727.

Wood, W., & Eagly, A. H. (2012b). Biosocial construction of sex differences and similarities in behavior. *Advances in Experimental Social Psychology, 46*(1), 55-123.

Woodruff, T. J., Axelrad, D. A., Kyle, A. D., Nweke, O., Miller, G. G., & Hurley, B. J. (2004). Trends in environmentally related childhood illnesses. *Pediatrics, 113*, 1133-1140.

Woodward, A. L., Markman, E. M., & Fitzsimmons, C. M. (1994). Rapid word learning in 13- and 18-month-olds. *Development Psychology, 30*, 553-566.

Woolley, J. D., & Boerger, E. A. (2002). Development of beliefs about the origins and controllability of dreams. *Developmental Psychology, 38*(1), 24-41.

Woolley, J. D., & Cox, V. (2007). Development of beliefs about storybook reality. *Developmental Science, 10*(5), 681-693.

Woolley, J. D., Phelps, K. E., Davis, D. L., & Mandell, D. J. (1999). Where theories of mind meet magic: The development of children's beliefs about wishing. *Child Development, 70*, 571-587.

World Bank. (2016). *Poverty and shared prosperity 2016: Taking on inequality.* Washington, DC: World Bank. doi:10.1596/978-1-4648-0958-3.

World Cancer Research Fund. (2007, November). *Food, nutrition, physical activity, and the prevention of cancer: A global perspective.* London: Author.

World Health Organization & UNICEF. (2014). Trends in maternal mortality: 1990 to 2013: Estimates by WHO, UNICEF, UNFPA, The World Bank and the United Nations Population Division.

World Health Organization (WHO). (2000, June 4). *WHO issues new healthy life expectancy rankings: Japan number one in new "healthy life" system* [Press release]. Washington, DC: Author.

World Health Organization (WHO). (2003). *The world health report—Shaping the future.* Retrieved from www.who.int/wrh/2003/chapter1en/index2.html

World Health Organization (WHO). (2007b). *World health statistics 2007.* Geneva: Author.

World Health Organization (WHO). (2013). *Levels and trends in child mortality.* Retrieved from www.who.int/maternal_child_adolescent/documents/levels_trends_child_mortality_2013/en/

World Health Organization. (2012). *Global health and aging. 2011.* Geneva, Switzerland: World Health Organization Google Scholar.

World Health Organization. (2013). *Essential nutrition actions: improving maternal, newborn, infant and young child health and nutrition.* Geneva: author.

World Health Organization. (2015a). *World report on ageing and health.* Retrieved from http://apps.who.int/iris/bitstream/10665/186463/1/9789240694811_eng.pdf?ua=1

World Health Organization. (2015b). Global Health Observatory (GHO) data: Under five mortality. Retrieved from www.who.int/gho/child_health/mortality/mortality_under_five_text/en/

World Health Organization. (2015c). Healthy Life Expectancy (HALE) at birth [interactive graph]. Retrieved from www.who.int/gho/mortality_burden_disease/life_tables/hale/en/

World Health Organization. (2016a). *World Health Statistics 2016: Monitoring Health for the SDGs Sustainable Development Goals.* World Health Organization.

World Health Organization. (2016b). Adolescent health epidemiology. Retrieved from www.who.int/maternal_child_adolescent/epidemiology/adolescence/en/

World Health Organization. (2016, November 7). *New guidelines on antenatal care for a positive pregnancy experience.* Retrieved from: www.who.int/reproductivehealth/news/antenatal-care/en

World Health Organization. (2016c, November). *Maternal mortality.* Retrieved from www.who.int/mediacentre/factsheets/fs348/en

World Health Organization. (2017a). *Commission on ending childhood obesity.* Retrieved from www.who.int/end-childhood-obesity/en/

World Health Organization. (2017b). Adolescence: heath risks and solutions. [Fact sheet]. Retrieved from www.who.int/mediacentre/factsheets/fs345/en/

World Health Organization. (2017c). Autism spectrum disorders. Retrieved from www.who.int/mediacentre/factsheets/autism-spectrum-disorders/en

World Health Organization. (2017d). Deafness and hearing loss [fact sheet]. Retrieved from www.who.int/mediacentre/factsheets/fs300/en/

World Health Organization. (2017e). Elder Abuse [fact sheet]. Retrieved from www.who.int/mediacentre/factsheets/fs357/en/

World Health Organization. (2017f). Obesity and Overweight [fact sheet]. Retrieved from www.who.int/mediacentre/factsheets/fs311/en/

Worobey, J. & Worobey H.S. (2014). Body-size stigmatization by preschool girls: In a doll's world, it is good to be "Barbie." *Body Image, 11*, 171-174.

Worth, K., Gibson, J., Chambers, M. S., Nassau, D., Balvinder, K., Rakhra, A. B., & Sargent, J. (2008). Exposure of U.S. adolescents to extremely violent movies. *Pediatrics, 122*(2), 306-312.

Wortman, C. B., & Silver, R. C. (1989). The myths of coping with loss. *Journal of Consulting and Clinical Psychology, 57*(3), 349-357.

Wraw, C., Deary, I. J., Gale, C. R., & Der, G. (2015). Intelligence in youth and health at age 50. *Intelligence, 53*, 23-32.

Wright, J. D., Hirsch, R., & Wang, C. (2009). One-third of adults embraced most heart healthy behaviors in 1999-2002. *NCHS Data Brief, 17.* Hyattsville, MD: National Center for Health Statistics.

Wrosch, C., Miller, G. E., & Schulz, R. (2009). Cortisol secretion and functional disabilities in old age: importance of using adaptive control strategies. *Psychosomatic Medicine, 71*(9), 996.

Wrzus, C., Hänel, M., Wagner, J., & Neyer, F. J. (2013). Social network changes and life events across the life span: A meta-analysis. *Psychological Bulletin, 139*(1), 53.

Wrzus, C., Wagner, J., & Neyer, F. J. (2012). The interdependence of horizontal family relationships and friendships relates to higher well-being. *Personal Relationships, 19*(3), 465-482.

Wu, C., & Leinung, M. C. (2015). The biologic basis of transgender Identity: Finger length ratios in transgender individuals implicates a role for prenatal androgen activity. *Basic and Clinical Aspects of Sexual Development,* SAT-081.

Wu, T., Mendola, P., & Buck, G. M. (2002). Ethnic differences in the presence of secondary sex characteristics and menarche among U.S. girls: The Third National Health and Nutrition Survey, 1988-1994. *Pediatrics, 11*, 752-757.

Wu, Z., & Hart, R. (2002). The effects of marital and nonmarital union transition on health. *Journal of Marriage and Family, 64*, 420-432.

Wu, Z., Hou, F., & Schimmele, C. M. (2008). Family structure and children's psychosocial outcomes. *Journal of Family Issues, 29*, 1600-1624.

Wulczyn, F. (2004). Family reunification. In David and Lucile Packard Foundation, Children, families, and foster care. *Future of Children, 14*(1). Retrieved from www.futureofchildren.org

Wynn, K. (1990). Children's understanding of counting. *Cognition, 36*, 155-193.

Wynn, K. (1992a). Addition and subtraction by human infants. *Nature, 358.*

Wynn, K. (1992b). Evidence against empiricist accounts of the origins of numerical knowledge. *Mind and Language, 7*, 315-332.

Wyrobek, A. J., Eskenazi, B., Young, S., Arnheim, N., Tiemann-Boege, I., Jabs, E. W., . . . & Evenson, D. (2006). Advancing age has differential effects on DNA damage, chromatin integrity, gene mutations, and aneuploidies in sperm. *Proceedings of the National Academy of Sciences, 103*(25), 9601-9606.

Xu, F., Bao, X., Fu, G., Talwar, V., & Lee, K. (2010). Lying and truth-telling in children: From concept to action. *Child Development, 81*(2), 581–596.

Xu, J. (2016). Mortality among centenarians in the United States, 2000–2014. *NCHS Data Brief,* (233), 1–8.

Xu, J. Q., Kochanek, K. D., Murphy, S. L., & Tejada-Vera, B. (2010). Deaths: Final data for 2007. *National Vital Statistics Report, 58*(19). Hyattsville, MD: National Center for Health Statistics.

Xu, J., Kochanek, K. D., Murphy, S. L., & Tejada-Vera, B. (2016). Deaths: Final data for 2014. *National Vital Statistics Report, 65*(4). Hyattsville, MD: National Center for Health Statistics.

Xu, W., Tan, L., Wang, H. F., Tan, M. S., Tan, L., Li, J. Q., . . . & Yu, J. T. (2016). Education and risk of dementia: dose-response meta-analysis of prospective cohort studies. *Molecular Neurobiology, 53*(5), 3113–3123.

Xu, X., Hudspeth, C. D., & Bartkowski, J. P. (2006). The role of cohabitation in remarriage. *Journal of Marriage and Family, 68*, 261–274.

Yaman, A., Mesman, J., van IJzendoorn, M. H., & Bakermans-Kranenburg, M. J. (2010). Parenting and toddler aggression in second-generation immigrant families: The moderating role of child temperament. *Journal of Family Psychology, 24*(2), 208.

Yan, L. L., Daviglus, M. L., Liu, K., Stamler, J., Wang, R., Pirzada, A., . . . Greenland, P. (2006). Midlife body mass index and hospitalization and mortality in older age. *Journal of the American Medical Association, 295*, 190–198.

Yang, B., Ollendick, T. H., Dong, Q., Xia, Y., & Lin, L. (1995). Only children and children with siblings in the People's Republic of China: Levels of fear, anxiety, and depression. *Child Development, 66*, 1301–1311.

Yang, L., Neale, B. M., Liu, L., Lee, S. H., Wray, N. R., Ji, N., . . . & Faraone, S. V. (2013). Polygenic transmission and complex neuro developmental network for attention deficit hyperactivity disorder: Genome-wide association study of both common and rare variants. *American Journal of Medical Genetics Part B: Neuropsychiatric Genetics, 162*(5), 419–430.

Yang, Y. (2008). Social inequalities in happiness in the United States, 1972 to 2004: An age-period-cohort analysis. *American Sociological Review, 73*, 204–226.

Yang, Y.T., & Curlin, F.A. (2016). Why physicians should oppose assisted suicide. *Journal of the American Medical Association, 315*, 247–248.

Yau, J. P., Tausopoulos-Chan, M., & Smetana, J. G. (2009). Disclosure to parents about everyday activities among American adolescents from Mexican, Chinese and European backgrounds. *Child Development, 80*(5), 1481–1498.

Ybarra, M. L., & Mitchell, K. J. (2014). "Sexting" and its relation to sexual activity and sexual risk behavior in a national survey of adolescents. *Journal of Adolescent Health, 55*(6), 757–764.

Ybarra, M. L., Strasburger, V. C., & Mitchell, K. J. (2014). Sexual media exposure, sexual behavior, and sexual violence victimization in adolescence. *Clinical Pediatrics, 53*(13), 1239–1247.

Yeh, H., Lorenz, F. O., Wickrama, K. A. S., Conger, R. D., & Elder, G. H. (2006). Relationships among sexual satisfaction, marital quality, and marital instability at midlife. *Journal of Family Psychology, 20*, 339–343.

Yeung, W. J., Sandberg, J. F., Davis-Kean, P. E., & Hofferth, S. L. (2001). Children's time with fathers in intact families. *Journal of Marriage and Family, 63*, 136–154.

Yip, T. (2014). Ethnic identity in everyday life: The influence of identity development status. *Child Development, 85*(1), 205–219.

Yip, T., Seaton, E. K., & Sellers, R. M. (2006). African American racial identity across the lifespan: Identity status, identity content, and depressive symptoms. *Child Development, 77*, 1504–1517.

Yokota, F., & Thompson, K. M. (2000). Violence in G-rated animated films. *Journal of the American Medical Association, 283*, 2716–2720.

Yoon, V., Maalouf, N. M., & Sakhaee, K. (2012). The effects of smoking on bone metabolism. *Osteoporosis International, 23*(8), 2081–2092.

Yoshikawa, H. (1994). Prevention as cumulative protection: Effects of early family support and education on chronic delinquency and its risks. *Psychological Bulletin, 115*(1), 28–54.

Yoshikawa, H., Aber, J. L., & Beardslee, W. R. (2012). The effects of poverty on the mental, emotional, and behavioral health of children and youth: implications for prevention. *American Psychologist, 67*(4), 272.

Yoshikawa, H., Weisner, T. S., Kalil, A., & Way, N. (2008). Mixing qualitative and quantitative research in developmental science: Uses and methodological choices. *Developmental Psychology, 44*, 344–354.

You, D., Hug, L., Ejdemyr, S., & Beise, J. (2015). Levels and trends in child mortality. Report 2015. Estimates developed by the UN Inter-agency Group for Child Mortality Estimation.

Young, K. A., Holcomb, L. A., Bonkale, W. L., Hicks, P. B., Yazdani, U., & German, D. C. (2007). 5HTTLPR polymorphism and enlargement of the pulvinar: Unlocking the backdoor to the limbic system. *Biological Psychiatry, 61*(1), 813–818.

Youngblade, L. M., & Belsky, J. (1992). Parent-child antecedents of 5-year-olds' close friendships: A longitudinal analysis. *Developmental Psychology, 28*, 700–713.

Youngblade, L. M., Theokas, C., Schulenberg, J., Curry, L., Huang, I-C., & Novak, M. (2007). Risk and promotive factors in families, schools, and communities: A contextual model of positive youth development in adolescence. *Pediatrics, 119*, 47–53.

Yu, S. M., Huang, Z. J., & Singh, G. K. (2004). Health status and health services utilization among U.S. Chinese, Asian Indian, Filipino, and other Asian/Pacific Islander children. *Pediatrics, 113*(1), 101–107.

Yu, T., & Adler-Baeder, F. (2007). The intergenerational transmission of relationship quality: The effect of parental remarriage quality on young adults relationships. *Journal of Divorce and Remarriage, 3-4*, 87–102.

Yunger, J. L., Carver, P. R., & Perry, D. G. (2004). Does gender identity influence children's psychological well-being? *Developmental Psychology, 40*, 572–582.

Zadik, Y., Bechor, R., Galor, S., & Levin, L. (2010). Periodontal disease might be associated even with impaired fasting glucose. *British Dental Journal, 208*(10), E20–E20.

Zahn-Waxler, C., Friedman, R. J., Cole, P. M., Mizuta, I., & Hiruma, N. (1996). Japanese and U.S. preschool children's responses to conflict and distress. *Child Development, 67*, 2462–2477.

Zajdel, R. T., Bloom, J. M., Fireman, G., & Larsen, J. T. (2013). Children's understanding and experience of mixed emotions: The roles of age, gender, and empathy. *The Journal of Genetic Psychology, 174*(5), 582–603.

Zanardo, V., Svegliado, G., Cavallin, F., Giustardi, A., Cosmi, E., Litta, P., & Trevisanuto, D. (2010). Elective cesarean delivery: Does it have a negative effect on breastfeeding? *Birth, 37*(4), 275–279.

Zandi, P. P., Anthony, J. C., Hayden, K. M., Mehta, K., Mayer, L., & Breitner, J. C. S. (2002). Reduced incidence of AD with NSAID but no H^2 receptor antagonists. *Neurology, 59*, 880–886.

Zangl, R., & Mills, D. L. (2007). Increased brain activity to infant-directed speech in 6- and 13-month old infants. *Infancy, 11*, 31–62.

Zeitlin, M. (2011). *New information on West African traditional education and approaches to its modernization.* Dakar, Senegal: Tostan.

Zelazo, P. D., & Carlson, S. M. (2012). Hot and cool executive function in childhood and adolescence: Development and plasticity. *Child Development Perspectives, 6*(4), 354–360.

Zelazo, P. D., Müller, U., Frye, D., & Marcovitch, S. (2003). The development of executive function in early childhood. *Monographs of the Society for Research in Child Development, 68*(3, Serial No. 274).

Zelazo, P. R., Kearsley, R. B., & Stack, D. M. (1995). Mental representations for visual sequences: Increased speed of central processing from 22 to 32 months. *Intelligence, 20*, 41–63.

Zeng, Y., Gu, D., & George, L. K. (2011). Association of religious participation with mortality among Chinese old adults. *Research on Aging, 33*(1), 51–83.

Zhang, W., Johnson, T. J., Seltzer, T., & Bichard, S. L. (2010). The revolution will be networked: The influence of social networking sites on political attitudes and behavior. *Social Science Computer Review, 28*, 75–92. doi: 10.1177/0894439309335162

Zhang, Z. (2006). Marital history and the burden of cardiovascular disease in midlife. *Gerontologist, 46*, 266–270.

Zhang, Z., & Hayward, M. D. (2001). Childlessness and the psychological well-being of older persons. *The Journals of Gerontology Series B: Psychological Sciences and Social Sciences, 56*(5), S311–S320.

Zhao, Y. (2002, May 29). Cultural divide over parental discipline. *The New York Times.* Retrieved from www.nytimes.com/2002/05/29/nyregion/29DISC.html?ex

Zheng, Y., Manson, J. E., Yuan, C., Liang, M. H., Grodstein, F., Stampfer, M. J., . . . & Hu, F. B. (2017). Associations of weight gain from early to middle adulthood with major health outcomes later in life. *JAMA, 318*(3), 255-269.

Zhou, J. N., Hofman, M. A., Gooren, L. J., & Swaab, D. F. (1995). A sex difference in the human brain and its relation to transsexuality. *Nature, 378*(6552), 68.

Zigler, E., & Styfco, S. J. (2001). Extended childhood intervention prepares children for school and beyond. *Journal of the American Medical Association, 285,* 2378-2380.

Zigler, E., Taussig, C., & Black, K. (1992). Early childhood intervention: A promising preventative for juvenile delinquency. *American Psychologist, 47,* 997-1006.

Zizza, C., Siega-Riz, A. M., & Popkin, B. M. (2001). Significant increase in young adults' snacking between 1977-1978 and 1994-1996 represents a cause for concern! *Preventive Medicine, 32,* 303-310.

Zlotnick, C., Tam, T. W., & Soman, L. A. (2012). Life course outcomes on mental and physical health: the impact of foster care on adulthood. *American Journal of Public Health, 102*(3), 534-540.

Zlotnick, C., Tam, T., & Zerger, S. (2012). Common needs but divergent interventions for US homeless and foster care children: Results from a systematic review. *Health & Social Care in the Community, 20*(5), 449-476.

Zolotor, A. J., Theodore, A. D., Runyan, D. K., Chang, J. J., & Laskey, A. L. (2011). Corporal punishment and physical abuse: population-based trends for three-to-11-year-old children in the United States. *Child Abuse Review, 20*(1), 57-66.

Zosuls, K. M., Ruble, D. N., Tamis-LeMonda, C. S., Shrout, P. E., Bornstein, M. H., & Greulich, F. K. (2009). The acquisition of gender labels in infancy: Implications for gender-typed play. *Developmental Psychology, 45*(3), 688-701. doi: 10.1037/a0014053

Zucker, A. N., Ostrove, J. M., & Stewart, A. J. (2002). College-educated women's personality development in adulthood: Perceptions and age differences. *Psychology and Aging, 17,* 236-244.

Zuffianò, A., Alessandri, G., Gerbino, M., Kanacri, B. P. L., Di Giunta, L., Milioni, M., & Caprara, G. V. (2013). Academic achievement: The unique contribution of self-efficacy beliefs in self-regulated learning beyond intelligence, personality traits, and self-esteem. *Learning and Individual Differences, 23,* 158-162.

Zylke, J., & DeAngelis, C. (2007). Pediatric chronic diseases—Stealing childhood. *Journal of the American Medical Association, 297*(24), 2765-2766.

Zylstra, R.G., Prater, C.D., Walthour, A.E., & Aponte, A.F. (2014). Autism: Why the rise in rates? Our improved understanding of the disorder and increasingly sensitive diagnostic tools are playing a role—but so are some other factors. *Journal of Family Practice, 63,* 316-320.

Baker, A., 236
Baker, C. E., 182
Baker, J. L., 216
Baker, L. A., 430
Baker, S. B., 274
Bakermans-Kranenburg, M. J., 51, 141, 143, 144, 205
Bakle, I., 102
Baksh, L., 168
Balaraman, G., 175
Balayla, J., 66, 69
Baldwin, D. A., 144
Baler, R. D., 272
Balkin, R. S., 256
Ball, K., 418
Ball, O. E., 237
Ball, R. H., 60
Ballemans, J., 407
Balluz, L. S., 359
Balota, D. A., 176, 414
Balsam, K. F., 385
Balsis, S., 414
Baltes, M. M., 431
Baltes, P. B., 10, 12, 402, 421, 430, 431, 450
Bandettini, P. A., 353
Bandura, A., 22, 195, 196, 284
Bank, L., 302
Banks, A., 246
Banks, G. C., 432
Bannerjee, A., 357
Banse, R., 195
Banta, D., 74
Bao, A. M., 292
Bao, X., 175
Barbaranelli, C., 284
Barbaresco, S., 310
Barber, B., 330
Barclay, S. R., 377
Barinaga, M., 416
Barker, E. D., 232, 305
Barlaug, D., 179
Barlett, C., 254
Barlow, W., 362
Barnard, N. D., 415
Barnes, C. A., 406
Barnes, G. M., 300
Barnes, P. M., 312
Barnett, D., 140, 141
Barnett, R. C., 346, 378
Barnett, T. A., 182
Barnett, W. S., 24, 108, 184
Barnhart, M. A., 390
Baron-Cohen, S., 176
Barr, H. M., 63
Barr, R., 170, 182
Barrett, C. B., 164
Barrett-Connor, E., 360, 362
Barros, F., 102
Barroso, C. S., 164
Barry, B. K., 409
Barry, C. M., 337
Barry, R. A., 150
Bartel, K. A., 267
Barthel, M., 143
Bartick, M., 88
Bartkowski, J. P., 340

Bartle-Haring, S., 299
Bartlett, A., 338
Bartolomei, M. S., 46
Barton, J. J. S., 419
Bartrés-Faz, D., 406
Bartzokis, G., 352, 414, 415, 420
Basch, C. E., 93, 298
Basch, C. H., 93
Bascom, P. B., 462
Baser, R. E., 458
Basile, K. C., 304
Basilio, M., 197
Bassil, N., 356
Basso, G., 327
Bassuk, E. L., 168
Baste, V., 66
Basterfield, L., 213
Basu, R., 66
Bateman, D., 64
Bates, J. E., 198, 201, 202, 205, 253, 264, 306
Bates, T. C., 225, 379
Batty, G. D., 418
Batty, M., 221
Baude, A., 245
Bauer, D., 273
Bauer, J. J., 375, 378
Bauer, M. E., 405
Bauer, P. J., 110, 111, 119, 139
Bauer, S., 161
Bauer, T. N., 379
Baum, A., 364
Bauman, A., 352, 412
Baumer, E. P., 294
Baumert, J., 225
Baumgart, M., 414, 415
Baumgartner, S. E., 284
Baumrind, D., 201, 202, 204, 300
Baumwell, L., 127
Bayley, N., 107
Bayliss, D. M., 222
Baym, C. L., 212
Beach, C. A., 168
Beardslee, W. R., 8, 243
Beauchaine, T. P., 385
Beauchamp, G. K., 60, 97
Beaumont, S. L., 373
Bebenek, M., 361
Bechor, R., 413
Beck., 46
Becker, B. J., 412
Becker, G. S., 383
Becker, J. A. H., 336
Becker, K. A., 224
Becker, M., 225, 444
Becker, P. E., 346
Beckert, T. E., 304
Beckett, C., 96, 201
Beckett, N., 414
Becona, E., 242
Bedford, V. H., 444, 445
Beech, B., 216
Beekman, A. J., 193
Beelmann, A., 248, 249
Befort, C., 214
Begum, N., 437
Behne, R., 135

Behne, T., 115
Behnke, M., 62, 64
Behrman, R. E., 81, 216
Beidas, R., 257
Beidel, D. C., 255
Beise, J., 165
Bell, D. C., 300
Bell, J. F., 62
Bell, J. T., 41, 51
Bell, L., 326
Bell, L. G., 300
Bell, M. A., 112, 120
Bell, R., 61, 394
Bellander, M., 421
Beller, E., 236
Bellieni, C. V., 60, 96
Bellinger, D. C., 315
Bellizzi, D., 401
Belsky, J., 12, 136, 137, 143, 152, 153, 264, 265, 331
Bem, S. L., 195
Ben-Ari, A., 343
Benedek, M., 237, 367
Benedetti, A. M., 449
Benes, F. M., 94
Bengtson, V. L., 387–389, 391, 392, 429, 444
Benjamin, J. T., 216
Benjet, C., 201
Benkhadra, K., 362
Benner, A. D., 283, 290
Bennett, D. A., 409, 415, 419
Bennett, J., 437
Bennett, K. J., 214
Benson, E., 224
Benson, J. B., 100, 119
Benson, P. L., 247
Benton, D., 363
Benzer, S., 403
Berard, A., 62
Berenbaum, S. A., 196, 324
Berenson, A., 65
Berg, C. A., 321
Bergelson, E., 13
Bergeman, C. S., 54
Bergen, D., 198, 199
Berger, C., 251
Berger, K., 352
Berger, K. S., 252, 253
Berger, L. M., 244
Berger, R., 326
Berget, A., 66
Berglund, H., 293
Bering, J. M., 453
Berk, L. E., 181
Berkman, L. F., 316, 437
Berlin, L. J., 201
Berman, S., 296
Bernardi, F., 348
Berndt, A. E., 138, 139
Berndt, T. J., 303
Bernert, R. A., 312
Bernie, A. M., 356
Bernier, A., 141, 149
Berns, S., 335
Bernstein, A. B., 357
Bernstein, L., 312

Bernstein, N., 435
Berntsen, D., 334
Bernzweig, J., 205
Berrick, J. D., 156
Berridge, C., 428
Berteletti, I., 221
Bertenthal, B. I., 99
Berthiaume, V. G., 174
Berthier, N. E., 100
Bertone-Johnson, E. R., 319
Bessette-Symons, B., 425
Betancourt, J. R., 167
Bevans, K., 231
Bever, L., 463
Beveridge, M., 65
Bezdicek, O., 418
Bhadoria, A. S., 163, 214
Bhaskaran, K., 318
Bherer, L., 409
Bhutta, Z. A., 61, 83
Bialystok, E., 175, 220, 418
Bianchi, S., 344
Bianchini, C., 352
Biason-Lauber, A., 43
Bibbins-Domingo, K., 269
Biblarz, T. J., 246
Bichard, S. L., 337
Biederman, J., 236
Biegel, D. E., 391
Bienias, J. L., 419
Bienvenu, O. J., 335
Bierman, K. L., 205, 207, 249
Bigelow, A. E., 174
Biggs, W. S., 319
Bigler, E. D., 419
Billet, S., 366
Billick, S. B., 258
Billings, R. L., 330
Bilsen, J., 462
Bimbi, D. S., 318
Binstock, G., 340
Birch, H. G., 56, 135
Birch, L. L., 60, 262, 269
Birditt, K., 387
Birditt, K. S., 387, 444
Birmaher, B., 273, 274
Birmingham, W., 316, 384
Biro, F. M., 163, 263
Bishop, D. V. M., 182
Bissell, J., 248
Bitler, M. P., 184
Bittles, A. H., 49
Bixler, E. O., 160
Bjarnason, T., 246
Bjork, J. M., 266
Bjorklund, D. F., 115, 453
Bjorklof, G. H., 428
Bjorklund, D. F., 26, 193, 197–200, 213, 214, 223, 234, 453
Bjornstad, P., 164
Black, A. E., 202
Black, M. C., 347
Black, M. M., 155
Black, W. W., 246, 247, 301
Blackwell, D. L., 408
Blackwell, E., 363
Blaga, O. M., 115

Hansen, M., 267
Hansen, S. N., 93, 236
Hansen, T., 388
Hanson, A. R., 332
Hanson, L., 464
Hao, Y., 434
Hara, Y., 359
Harbaugh, A. G., 254
Hardy, M. A., 389, 390
Harenski, C. L., 324
Harley, V. R., 43
Harlos, M., 450
Harlow, H., 138
Harlow, H. F., 138
Harlow, M. K., 138
Harlow, S., 363
Harman, D., 402
Harold, G., 255
Harper, M. C., 377
Harris, D. G., 406
Harris, K. M., 309
Harris, M. L., 143
Harris-Kojetin, L., 436
Harrison, F., 413
Harrison, Y., 312
Harrist, A. W., 198
Harry, S., 201
Hart, C., 216
Hart, C. H., 207
Hart, C. L., 224
Hart, D., 336, 373
Hart, J. L., 197
Hart, R., 316, 348
Harter, S., 146, 188–190, 240
Hartford, R. B., 85
Hartshor, K., 106
Hartup, W. W., 199, 207, 248–250,
    303, 306, 336, 386, 443
Hasebe, Y., 299
Haselager, G. J. T., 336
Haselton, M., 145
Hasher, L., 352
Hasin, D. S., 315
Haskuka, M., 323
Haslett, S. J., 289
Hassan, N. M. M., 413
Hastings, P. D., 205
Hatzenbuehler, M. L., 316
Hatzichristou, D. G., 355
Haugaard, J. J., 247
Haukkala, A., 245
Haung, L.-L., 433
Hauser, R. M., 380
Hauser, S. T., 330
Hauser, W. A., 64
Haushofer, J., 192
Hautamaki, J., 225
Hautamäki, J., 227
Havinghurst, R., 429
Hawes, C., 436
Hawkins, J. D., 273
Hawkley, L. C., 386, 439
Haworth, C. M., 179
Haworth, C. M. A., 225
Hay, D. F., 65, 151
Haydon, K. C., 143
Hayes, S., 215

Hayflick, L., 401–403
Hayiou-Thomas, M. E., 182
Hayne, H., 170
Haynes, O. M., 13, 110, 142
Hayslip Jr, B., 393, 394
Hayward, M. D., 389
Hayward, R. A., 358, 457
He, J., 271
He, W., 397, 399, 400, 441
He, X., 36
He, Z., 174
Healy, A. J., 69
Heaps, A., 283
Heath, S. B., 226
Heatherington, E. M., 348
Heaven, T. J., 419
Hebblethwaite, S., 373
Hébert, J. R., 358
Heck, K., 315
Heckhausen, J., 375
Heckman, J. J., 185
Hedden, T., 420
Hedegaard, H., 457
Hedemark, B., 64
Hedges, L. V., 172
Heeren, T., 273, 314
Heffner, K. L., 405
Heffner, L. J., 66
Hegyl, T., 85
Heidenreich, A., 360
Heikkinen, R., 439
Heiland, F., 246
Heilbronn, L. K., 405
Heim, B. T., 368
Heiman, J. R., 382
Heinemann, K. S., 249
Heinen, B. A., 346
Heinz, W., 331
Heiss, G., 362
Heitzler, C., 214
Heller, K., 433
Hellerstedt, W. L., 247
Hellriegel, S., 161
Hellström, A., 63
Helms, H. M., 337
Helms, J. E., 9, 226
Helson, R., 375, 378, 380, 384, 387
Helvik, A. S., 428
Helwig, C. C., 278
Hemenway, D., 274, 458
Hemphill, S. A., 253
Henderson, A. K., 428
Henderson, H. A., 137, 199
Henderson, M., 294
Henderson, V. W., 415
Hendry, L. B., 387
Henkens, K., 430, 432
Hennig, J., 367
Henning-Smith, C., 436
Hennon, E. A., 124
Henry, C. S., 241
Henry, D. B., 294, 305
Henry, M., 168
Henry, P., 256
Henry, W., 429
Henshaw, S., 297
Henter, J. I., 456

Heo, H. J., 46
Hepach, R., 135
Herald-Brown, S. L., 249
Herbers, J. E., 168
Herbig, B., 322
Herbison, P., 79, 159
Herbst, J. H., 318
Herdt, G., 262
Herek, G. M., 338
Hermes, M., 425
Hernandez, D., 301
Hernandez, D. J., 269
Hernandez, S. J., 9
Hernandez-Reif, M., 81
Heron, J., 65, 66
Heron, M. P., 84
Herrnstein, R. J., 225
Herst, D. E., 376
Hertenstein, M. J., 144
Hertlein, K. M., 343
Hertsgaard, L., 143
Hertzman, C., 241
Herzog, A. R., 429
Hesketh, K., 215
Hespos, S. J., 117
Hess, S. Y., 61
Hess, T. M., 418
Hesso, N. A., 85
Heuveline, P., 340
Hewlett, B. S., 137–139
Heyman, K. M., 407, 411
Heyman, R. E., 345
Heymann, J., 346
Heywood, C., 139
Heywood, W., 410
Hickling, A. K., 171
Hickman, M., 267
Hicks, G. R., 385
Hiedemann, B., 383, 384
Higashibara, F., 240
Hildebrand, C., 438
Hill, A. L., 205
Hill, C., 332
Hill, D. A., 49
Hill, J. L., 151
Hill, J. O., 311
Hill, N. E., 231, 282
Hill, P. C., 428
Hill, P. L., 369, 373
Hill, T. D., 428
Hilli, S. D., 297
Hilliard, L. J., 200
Hillier, L., 293
Hillsdon, M., 366
Himsel, A., 83
Hinds, D. A., 359
Hines, M., 191, 194
Hingson, R., 314
Hingson, R. W., 273
Hinman, J. D., 407
Hinnant, J. B., 211
Hinrichs, C. C., 164
Hirsch, R., 358, 359
Hirschl, T. A., 343
Hirsch-Pasek, K., 124
Hirsh-Pasek, K., 13, 129
Hiruma, N., 206

Hishinuma, E. S., 275
Hitzert, M. M., 115
Ho, R. C. M., 115
Hoang, T. D., 358
Hoban, T. F., 79, 160, 161, 211, 267
Hobbs, W. R., 316
Hobson, J. A., 160
Hodes, R., 402
Hodes, R. J., 269, 397
Hodge, C., 271
Hodges, E. V. E., 252, 253
Hodnett, E. D., 76
Hofer, C., 324
Hofer, S. M., 365, 450
Hofer, T., 175
Hoff, E., 127, 128
Hoff, T., 293
Hofferth, S., 138
Hofferth, S. L., 233, 246, 344
Hoffman, C. D., 348
Hoffman, G. F., 320
Hoffman, H. T., 85
Hoffman, J. H., 300
Hoffman, M. L., 202
Hofman, M. A., 193
Hofman, S. G., 82
Hofmann, S. G., 256
Hofmann, V., 336
Hofmeyr, G. J., 76
Hogan, H., 439
Hogge, W. A., 60
Hohmann-Marriott, B. E., 340
Hohne, E. A., 122
Holcroft, C. A., 69
Holland, A., 339
Holland, C. R., 114
Hollenberg, M., 408
Holliday, R., 402, 403
Hollis-Peel, M. E., 307
Holloszy, J., 405
Holmes, R. M., 213
Holmes, T. H., 364
Holowka, S., 125
Holstein, M. B., 429
Holstrum, J., 97
Holt-Lunstad, J., 316, 384,
    385, 439
Holtzman, R. E., 439
Holve, K., 367
Holzer, H., 332
Honberg, L., 216
Honein, M. A., 61
Honeycutt, H., 53
Hong, J., 444, 456
Honig, A. S., 207
Hooper, F. H., 139
Hooper, S. R., 179
Hoorn, J., 280
Hoover, R. M., 437
Hopkins, B., 102
Hopkins, L. M., 68
Hopkins, M., 453
Hopkins, W. D., 94
Hoppin, J. A., 319
Hopwood, C. J., 424, 425
Horn, J. C., 398
Horn, J. L., 365, 366

Tach, L., 244, 348
Tackett, J. L., 176, 240, 241, 305
Tager, I. B., 408
Taheri, S., 354
Tajfel, H., 331
Takachi, R., 412
Takanishi, R., 185
Takayoshi, P., 277
Taliaferro, L. A., 275
Tallent-Runnels, M., 324
Talokder, E., 139
Talwar, V., 174, 175
Tam, T., 168
Tam, T. W., 156
Tamborini, C. R., 442
Tamis-LeMonda, C. S., 99, 127, 138, 139, 200
Tan, Q., 51
Tan, R. C., 62
Tanaka, A., 143
Tang, F., 368
Tang, Y., 415
Tangney, J., 240
Tanilon, J., 254
Tanner, J. L., 244, 245, 330
Tannock, M. T., 197
Tantleff-Dunn, S., 215
Tanwar, K. L., 314
Tarabulsy, G., 297
Tardieu, H., 366
Tardif, C., 143
Tarraf, W., 404
Tassell-Matamua, N., 450
Tatangelo, G. L., 215
Tate, B. A., 267
Tate, J. D., 331
Tausopoulos-Chan, M., 301
Taveras, E. M., 89, 211
Taylor, A., 179
Taylor, B. J., 79, 159
Taylor, C. L., 182
Taylor, E. M., 443
Taylor, J. G., 323
Taylor, J. R., 266
Taylor, L. C., 231
Taylor, L. E., 86, 93
Taylor, M., 199, 438
Taylor, M. G., 440
Taylor, M. J., 221
Taylor, R. J., 442
Taylor, S. E., 310, 363
Taylor, T., 337
Teachman, J., 340
Teasdale, T. W., 179
Tebbutt, J. S., 156
Tejada-Vera, B., 80, 81, 84, 86, 165, 359–361, 448, 457
Tekgul, S., 161
Tellegen, A., 333
Teller, T., 366
Temel, J. S., 450
Temple, J. A., 185, 306
Tenenbaum, G., 412
Tenenbaum, H., 196
Tenenbaum, H. R., 190
Tenenbaum, J. B., 117
Tennant, P. W. G., 61

Tennen, H., 312
Tepper, P. G., 355
Tepperman, L., 383
Terenzini, P. T., 327
Teresi, J. A., 438
Terplan, M., 62, 64
Terracciano, A., 373, 424
Terranova, A. M., 253
Terry, R. B., 358
Tervaniemi, M., 97, 117
Teshale, S., 351
Tester, G., 433
Teti, D. M., 150
Teubert, D., 245
Tezanos-Pinto, P., 249
Thabes, V., 348
Thacker, S. B., 74
Tham, Y., 408
Thapar, A., 66, 235
Tharp, A. T., 305
Thelen, E., 101
Theodore, A. D., 155
Thiel, M. M., 457
Thisted, R. A., 386
Thoits, P. A., 364
Thomas, A., 56, 135, 136
Thomas, A. G., 353
Thomas, J. G., 311
Thomas, K. M., 266
Thomas, P. A., 444
Thomas, R., 236
Thomas, S. P., 382, 387
Thomeer, M. B., 7
Thompson, C. P., 379
Thompson, K. M., 251
Thompson, L. A., 81
Thompson, P. M., 91, 161, 212, 224, 225, 282
Thompson, R. A., 133
Thompson, S. C., 355
Thompson, W. R., 409
Thomsen, M. R., 164
Thomson, E., 246
Thoresen, C. E., 428
Thorma, M. E., 46, 85
Thornberry, T. P., 298
Thornton, A., 340
Thornton, W. J. L., 418
Thorsen, K., 443
Thorvaldsson, V., 450
Tian, L., 415
Tidball, G., 144
Tidswell, T., 174
Tiggeman, M., 214
Tilden, V. P., 456
Tillman, T., 357
Tilvis, R. S., 414, 439
Timberlake, J. M., 340
Timonen, V., 393
Tincoff, R., 124
Tindle, H. A., 363
Tingle, L. R., 341
Tinsley, R., 139
Tipsord, J. M., 249
Tirosh, E., 78
Tither, J., 265
Tiznobek, A., 354

Tjebkes, T. L., 150
To, T., 66
Tobin, S., 429
Toga, A. W., 91, 94, 161, 212, 213, 282
Tokariev, A., 78
Tolan, P. H., 305, 306
Tolejko, N., 440
Tolle, S. W., 456, 462
Tolppanen, A. M., 358
Tomás, J. M., 427, 428
Tomasello, M., 115, 123, 134, 135, 175
Tomashek, K. M., 86
Tomassini, C., 439
Tomedi, L. E., 62
Tompson, W., 171
Tope, D., 196
Topor, D. R., 231
Torjussen, T., 179
Toro, P., 415
Torrance, E. P., 237, 367
Toth, S. L., 255
Totsika, V., 107
Touchette, E., 160
Towfighi, A., 360
Townsend, N. W., 138
Trabulsi, J. C., 97
Tran, S., 143
Tranel, D., 419
Trautner, H. M., 195
Trautwein, U., 225
Travis, C., 364
Treiman, D. J., 392
Tremblay, R. E., 160, 204, 205, 232, 282
Trenholm, C., 295
Trent, K., 391
Treven, S., 433
Trim, R. S., 273
Trimble, C. L., 314
Trionfi, G., 199
Trivedi, M. H., 413
Troll, L. E., 443, 444
Trombello, J. M., 316, 384, 440
Tromp, D., 419
Tronick, E. Z., 97, 137, 144
Troseth, G. L., 112
Trotter, R. J., 322
Trouillet, R., 427
Trovato, G. M., 313
Trudel, G., 410
Truxillo, D. M., 379
Trzaskowski, M., 179
Trzesniewski, K. H., 380
Tsai, L. H., 407
Tsao, F. M., 122
Tseng, V. L., 407, 408
Tseng, W. L., 201
Tsertsvadze, A., 168
Tsuang, H. C., 162
Tsuboi, K., 269
Tsuchiya, K., 66
Tsukayama, E., 224
Tucker, M. A., 313
Tucker, M. B., 442
Tucker, R., 13

Tucker-Drob, E. M., 56, 335
Tucker-Drop, E. M., 425
Tugade, M. M., 375, 376
Tulane, S., 304
Tune, G. B., 353
Turati, C., 114
Turiano, N. A., 335
Turkheimer, E., 225
Turner, P. J., 196
Turner, R. B., 316
Turner, R. N., 340
Turner, S. E., 324
Turner, S. M., 255
Turnley, W. H., 323
Turpin-Petrosino, C., 307
Turpin-Petrosino, C., 307
Turtle, M., 94
Twaite, J. A., 428
Twamley, E. W., 416
Twenge, J. M., 256, 338, 342, 345
Twisk, J. W., 163, 269
Tyler, J. K., 401
Tyler, L. K., 420
Tyson, D. F., 231, 282

Udry, J. R., 309
Uebelacker, L. A., 440
Uecker, J. E., 341
Uggen, C., 285
Ülger, Z., 406
Ullman, J. B., 232
Ullman, S. E., 315
Umana-Taylor, A. J., 289, 331
Umberson, D., 7, 384, 388, 440, 456
Umilta, C., 114
Underwood, L., 316
Underwood, M., 413
Updegraff, K. A., 248, 331
Urry, H. L., 425
Usher, K., 434
Usta, I., 297
Utiger, R. D., 355, 356
Uttal, D. H., 112, 218
Uzelac, P. S., 320

Vaccarino, V., 360
Vagenas, D., 437
Vagi, K. J., 304, 305
Vail, K. E., 454
Vaillancourt, T., 251
Vaillant, G. E., 426
Vaish, A., 135
Valcour, M., 346
Valdimarsdóttir, U., 456
Valeri, S. M., 274
Valero, S., 335
Valkenburg, P. M., 337
Valladares, S., 8
Vallerand, R. J., 436
Van, P., 457
van Aken, M. A. G., 336
Van Arsdale, A. C., 312
Van Bavel, J., 393
Van Braeckel, K. N., 115
Van Broeckhoven, C., 415
Van Cauwenberghe, C., 415

subject index

Page numbers in **boldface** indicate key terms. Page numbers followed by *t* indicate tables; page numbers followed by *f* indicate figures.

AAI (Adult Attachment Interview), 143–144
abandonment, 438
Abcedarian (ABC) Project, 108
abortion. *See also* spontaneous
　abortion
　during adolescence, 297*f*
absent grief pattern, 452
abstinence programs, 295
abuse
　of elders, 436–438
　environmental deprivation in
　　infants, 96
　in infancy and toddlerhood,
　　154–156
　long-term effects, 156
　sexual risk-taking in adolescence
　　and, 294
　violence in teen dating, 303–304
academic achievement
　in adolescence, 281–283
　class size and, 232
　gender and, 231, 281–282
　homeschooling and, 232–233
　influences on, 231–233, 281–283
　media use and, 233
　parenting practices and, 231, 282
　peer acceptance and, 232, 282
　quality of school and, 283
　self-efficacy beliefs and, 231, 281
　socioeconomic status and, 231–232
　technology and, 283
acceleration programs, **237**
accidental injuries. *See* injuries
accommodation, **23**
Accutane, 62
ACE inhibitors, 62
achondroplasia, 47
acquired immune deficiency
　syndrome (AIDS), **64,** 296
　breast-feeding and, 89
　prenatal development and, 64
active correlations, 54
active euthanasia, **460,** 462
activities of daily living (ADL), **399**
activity theory, **429**
acute medical conditions, **216**
AD (Alzheimer's disease), 414–416
adaptation, **23**
adaptive defenses, 426
addiction, 271
　alcoholism, 316–317
　drugs, 317
　smoking, 314
ADHD. *See* attention-deficit/
　hyperactivity disorder
ADL (activities of daily living), **399**
adolescence

academic achievement and,
　281–283
antisocial behavior in, 305–307
attitudes about death and dying,
　453–454
body image, 269
brain development, 265–266
cognitive development, 20*t,*
　275–285
cognitive maturation, 275–280
cultural constructs, 3–4
depression and, 273–274, 273*f,* 317
as developmental transition, 261
eating disorders, 270–271
education and, 281–2858
exercise and, 266–267
family and, 299–302
formal operations stage, 275–276
globalization of, 289–290
health, 266–273
identity and, 288–290
information processing and,
　276–277
language development, 277
media multitasking, 284
mental health, 271–275
moral reasoning and, 277–280
mortality, 274
obesity and, 267–269
opportunities and risks, 261
parental relationships, 299–302,
　386–387
peer relationships, 302–305
physical development, 261–275
pregnancy during, 66, 297–298,
　297*f*
psychosexual development, 19, 20*t*
psychosocial development, 20*t,*
　288–306
puberty, 261–265
rebellion during, 298–299
sexual behavior in, 293–295, 293*f*
sexuality in, 290–298
sibling relationships, 302
sleep and, 267
as social construction, 261
substance abuse and, 271–273
typical developments, 5*t*
working in, 285
adolescent growth spurt, **263**–264
adolescent rebellion, **298**–299
adoption, 247
adoption studies, 52
adoptive families, 247
adrenarche, 261–262
Adult Attachment Interview (AAI),
　143–144
adult education, 369

adulthood. *See also* aging; emerging
　and young adulthood; late
　adulthood; middle adulthood
　attitudes about death and
　　dying, 454
　death of parent in, 455–456
　parent relationships in, 331–332,
　　389–391
　paths to, 330
advance directive, **460**
Affordable Care Act, 167, 310, 368
African Americans
　academic achievement and, 281
　adolescent mortality and, 274
　age at first birth, 344
　alcohol use among, 315
　body image and, 269
　chronic conditions in late adult-
　　hood and, 411
　chronic medical conditions
　　among, 216
　cohabitation attitudes of, 340
　college education and, 325
　cross-cultural studies of, 33
　diabetes and, 217
　divorce rates among, 347
　dropping out of high school, 283
　early childhood health, 167
　end-of-life decisions, 462, 463
　ethnic group, 9
　finances in late adulthood, 434
　growth in middle childhood, 211
　health in middle age, 359
　health status in emerging and
　　young adulthood, 309, 315
　identity formation and, 290
　infant death from injuries
　　among, 86
　infant mortality among, 85, 85*f*
　IQ, 225
　life expectancy and, 401, 401*t*
　living with adult children, 435–436
　low-birth-weight babies, 81
　media use and, 233
　menopause in, 355
　miscarriages among, 60
　mutual help among family, 389
　obesity in, 163, 214, 310
　parenting styles, 204
　perceived discrimination and, 290
　psychological well-being in, 380
　puberty in, 263
　raising grandchildren, 393
　religion and spirituality, 428
　sexual behavior in adolescence,
　　293
　SIDS and, 85
　single life and, 338

single-parent homes among, 245
sleep in middle childhood, 211
smoking among, 314
spanking among, 201
stillbirths among, 83
STIs in, 319
suicide and, 275, 458
teenage pregnancy and, 297
teen dating violence and, 304
vaccinations and, 86
wedding traditions among, 342
Age Discrimination in Employment
　Act, 368, 432
ageism, **397,** 433
age-qualified active adult
　communities, 436
age-related macular degeneration,
　408
age-related vision problems, 351,
　407–408
age segregation, 208
aggression
　bullying, 252–254
　direct aggression, 205
　in early childhood, 204–206
　electronic media and, 251–252,
　　251*f*
　gender differences, 205
　influences on, 205–206
　instrumental aggression, 204
　in middle childhood, 250–254
　overt aggression, 205
　relational aggression, 205
　types of, 250–251
aging
　activity theory, 429
　ageism stereotypes, 433
　balance and, 408–409
　brain and, 406–407
　causes of, 401–403
　continuity theory, 430
　coping styles and, 427–428
　disengagement theory, 429
　endurance and, 408–409
　epigenesis and, 401
　graying population, 397–399, 398*f*
　hearing impairment, 408
　longevity and, 400–405
　memory and, 419–420
　mental and behavioral problems,
　　413–416
　nutrition and, 412–413
　optimal, 404, 428–431
　organ functioning and, 405–406,
　　405*f*
　physical activity and, 412
　physical changes, 405–410
　practical and social issues, 431–437

Subject Index | **I-27**

plasticity, 94–96
  sexual orientation and, 292–293
  theory of mind, development
    of, 176
brain stem
  in infancy and toddlerhood, 126
  prenatal development, 91, 91f, 92f
Braxton-Hicks contractions, 73
breast cancer, 361
breast-feeding, 88–89, 88t
bridged employment, 368
bulimia nervosa, **270,** 271
bullies, 252–253
bullying, **252**–253

caffeine, 63
CAH (congenital adrenal
    hyperplasia), 192
Caloric Restriction Society, 405
canalization, **53**
cancer
  breast, 361
  in middle adulthood, 357
  prenatal exposure to
    environmental hazards, 66
cardinality, 171
care, 373, 394
caregiver burnout, **390**–391
caregivers
  to aging parents, 389–391
  attachments and, 140–144
  care of the dying, 449–450
  cognitive development and, 120
  father's role, 138
  language acquisition and, 126,
    127–129
  mother's role, 138
  mutual regulation, 144
  relationships with adult
    children, 444
  sandwich generation, 390–391
  strain in, 390
case studies, **31**–32, 31t
cataracts, **407**–408
categorization, 115–117
  early childhood, understanding
    in, 171
  middle childhood, understanding
    in, 218t, 219
causality, 117
  early childhood, understanding in,
    170–171
  middle childhood, understanding
    in, 218, 218t
cell death, **93**
central executive, **177**
central nervous system, **91**
centration, **172**
cephalocaudal principle, **87**
cerebellum, 91, 91f, 92f
cerebral cortex, 92, 134
cerebrum, 91, 91f
cervix, 41
cesarean delivery, **74**–75
childbirth
  during adolescence, 297–298, 297f
  anesthesia in, 75–76

changes in, 72–73
complications, 79–83
electronic fetal monitoring, 74
home, 72
infant mortality and, 84
low birth weight, 79–82
medicalization, 72–73
medicated vs. nonmedicated,
    75–76
natural, 75
postmaturity, 82–83
prepared, 75
process of, 73–76
stages of, 73–74
stillbirth, 83
vaginal vs. cesarean delivery,
    74–75
child care
  grandparents and, 393
  infants and toddlers, 151–153,
    153t
child-directed speech, **129**
childhood. See also early childhood;
    infancy and toddlerhood; mid-
    dle childhood
  attitudes about death and dying,
    453–454
  cognitive development, 20t
  cultural constructs, 3–4
  noble savage theory of
    development, 16
  psychosexual development,
    19, 20t
  psychosocial development, 20t
  tabula rasa theory of
    development, 16
childhood depression, **255**
childhood memories, 177–178
children
  death of, 456–457
  grandparents raising, 393–394
  living with in late adulthood,
    435–436
  parenting grown, 387–388
  relationships with emerging adults,
    331–332
  relationships with maturing,
    386–389
  relationships with older parents,
    443–444
children's books, 128
  gender-typing and, 196
chlamydia, 296, 318
chlorpyrifos, 66
chorion, 58
chorionic villus sampling (CVS), 67t
chromosomal abnormalities,
    49, 49t
chromosomes, **42**
chronic grief pattern, 452
chronic medical conditions, **216**
chronosystem, 25, 25f
circular reactions, **109,** 110f
classic aging pattern, 417, 417f
classical conditioning, **21, 105**
classification. See categorization
class inclusion, **219**

class size and academic
    achievement, 232
cleft lip or palate, 46
climacteric, 354
clinical method, 22
cliques, 302
cluttered nest, 388
cocaine, 64
code-emphasis approach, **230**
code mixing, **128**
code switching, **129**
cognitive-appraisal model, **426**–428
cognitive behavioral therapy, 256
cognitive development, **3,** 20t
  in adolescence, 275–285
  approaches to study, 105
  behaviorist approach, 105–106
  cognitive neuroscience approach,
    105, 119–120
  in college, 325–326
  in early childhood, 169–185, 169t
  in emerging and young adulthood,
    321–328
  in infancy and toddlerhood,
    105–129
  information-processing approach
    (See information-processing
    approach)
  language acquisition (See language
    acquisition)
  in late adulthood, 416–421
  in middle adulthood, 364–369
  in middle childhood, 212,
    218–237, 218t
  Piagetian approach (See Piagetian
    approach)
  psychometric approach (See
    psychometric approach)
  self-concept and, 146, 188, 240
  social-contextual approach, **105,**
    120
  at work, 327
cognitive functioning
  brain cells and, 94
  intellectual disability and, 233
  in late adulthood, 404
  measurement of, 30
  physical activity and, 312, 358
  Piagetian approach and, 105
  as predictor of intelligence, 115
  resilient child and, 257
  selective optimization with com-
    pensation and, 431
cognitive neuroscience, **30**
cognitive neuroscience approach,
    105, 119–120
cognitive perspective, 20t, **22**–24
  gender and, 194–195
cognitive reserve, **415**
cognitive-stage theory, **22**–24
cohabitation
  family structure, 246, 301
  international comparisons, 339
  in late adulthood, 442
  in middle adulthood, 382–383
  in United States, 340
cohort, **11**

collective efficacy, 306
college
  cognitive growth during, 325–326
  completion, 326
  in emerging and young adulthood,
    324–326
  enrollment, 325
  work while attending, 327
color blindness, 48
commitment, **288,** 337
commitment with relativism, 326
committed compliance, **149**–150
commonly expected grief pattern,
    452
community
  abuse and neglect in, 155
  antisocial behavior and, 306
complications of childbirth, 79–83,
    80f
  ADHD and, 235
  low birth weight, 79–82, 80f
  postmaturity, 82–83
  stillbirth, 83
componential element, **227**
componential knowledge, 322
computational estimation, 221
computational models, 24
conception, **41**–42
conceptual knowledge, 119, **277**
conceptual self-awareness, 146
concordant, **51**
concrete operations stage, 20t,
    218–221
condoms, 294–295
conduct disorder, **254**
congenital adrenal hyperplasia
    (CAH), 192
congenital hypothyroidism, 78
conscientiousness
  in emerging and young adulthood,
    334–335, 335f
  in late adulthood, 425
  in middle adulthood, 372–373
consensual relationships, 382–386
consensual unions, 441
conservation
  early childhood, understanding in,
    172–173, 173t
  middle childhood, understanding
    in, 218t, 219–220
constructive play, **198**
contact with other children
  in early childhood, 206–208
  in infancy and toddlerhood,
    150–151
contextual element, **227**
contextual knowledge, 322
contextual perspective, 20t, **25**–26
contingent self-esteem, 189
continuity theory, **430**
contraceptives, 294–295, 318
control group, **33**–34
conventional morality (or morality
    of conventional role
    conformity), **278**
convergent thinking, **237**
Cooley's anemia, 47t

coping, **426**
  adaptive defenses, 426
  age differences and, 427–428
  bereavement and grief, 452*t*
  cognitive-appraisal model, 426–428
  emotion-focused, **427**
  problem-focused, 427
  religion or spirituality and, 428
  resilience and, 257
  strategies, 426–428
  with stress, 257, 312
cordocentesis, 67*t*
coregulation, **242**
core knowledge, 119
corporal punishment, **201**–202
corpus callosum, 91, 266
correlational studies, 31*t*, **32**
crawling, 99, 100–101
creativity, **237**
  age and, 368
  in middle adulthood, 367–368
crisis, 20, **288**
critical period, **11**
cross-cultural research
  baby talk, 13
  language acquisition, 124
  purpose, 33
  terrible twos, 148
  work-family balance, 346
cross-modal transfer, **115**
cross-sectional studies, 35, 36*t*
crowd, 302
crying, 122, 132–133
crystallized intelligence, **366**
cultural socialization, **289**
culture, 8–9
  abuse and neglect and, 155
  ADHD diagnosis and, 236
  ageism stereotypes and, 433
  aggression and, 205–206
  ASD diagnosis and, 236
  cognitive development and, 120
  death and, 448
  early social experiences, 137–138
  emotions and, 132
  end-of-life decisions, 462
  gender-schema theory and, 194–195
  gender-typing and, 139, 196
  grandparenting, 391–392
  identity formation and, 289
  IQ and, 226
  language acquisition and, 128–129
  language development and, 13, 33
  life-span developmental approach and, 12, 14
  marriage and, 341
  mathematics and, 220
  menopause and, 355
  middle childhood and, 221
  moral reasoning and, 323
  motor development in infants, 102
  multigenerational family and, 439
  parental relationship during adolescence, 299

  parenting styles and, 203–204, 242
  periods of life span and, 3–4
  play and, 200
  PMS and, 319
  prosocial behavior and, 204
  sexual risk-taking in adolescence and, 294
  sleep rhythms and schedules of infants, 79
  social clock and, **334**, 374–375
  terrible twos, 148
culture-fair tests, **226**
culture-free tests, **226**
custody issues, 244–245
CVS (chorionic villus sampling), 67*t*
cystic fibrosis, 47*t*

DACA (Deferred Action for Childhood Arrivals), 10
Darwinian reflex, 95*t*
data collection, 28–30
  behavioral and performance measures, 29*t*
  behavioral measures, 29–30
  laboratory observation, 29, 29*t*
  naturalistic observation, 29, 29*t*
  performance measures, 29–30
  self-reports, 28–29
dating
  in adolescence, 303–304
  in late adulthood, 442
deaf children, language acquisition in, 125
death. *See also* infant mortality rate; mortality rates; suicide
  in adolescence, 274–275
  adolescent attitudes towards, 453–454
  adulthood attitudes towards, 454
  assisted suicide, 460–461, 463
  attitudes across life span towards, 453–455
  care of the dying, 449–450
  of child, 456–457
  childhood attitudes towards, 453–454
  confronting own, 451
  cultural context of, 448
  end-of-life decisions, 462–463
  facing loss, 450–455
  finding meaning and purpose in, 464
  funeral ceremonies and rituals, 449
  hastening, 459–460
  infant death from injuries, 86
  meanings of, 448–450
  mortality revolution, 448
  mourning of miscarriage, 457
  of parent, in adulthood, 455–456
  patterns of grieving, 451–452
  physical and cognitive changes preceding, 450–451
  physician aid in dying, 461–462
  right to die, 457–463

  significant losses, 455–457
  surviving a spouse, 440–441, 455
  Terror Management Theory, 454–455
Death with Dignity Act (DWDA), 461
decenter, **172**, 220
deception, 174–175
declarative knowledge, **277**
declarative memory, 119
decoding, **229**
deductive reasoning, 218*t*, **219**
Deferred Action for Childhood Arrivals, 10
deferred imitation, **110**, 170
dehydroepiandrosterone (DHEA), 261–262
dementia, **413**–416
dendrites, 92
Denver Developmental Screening Test, **98**
deoxyribonucleic acid (DNA), **42**
dependent variable, **34**
depression
  in adolescence, 273–274, 273*f*
  childhood depression, 255
  in emerging and young adulthood, 317
  in late adulthood, 413
  postpartum, 145
  prenatal development influenced by, 65
depth perception, **100**
DES (diethylstilbestrol), 62
design stage, 162
developing self, 188–190
development
  active or reactive, 16–17
  contexts, 6–11
  continuous or discontinuous, 17
  culture and, 8–10
  description of, 2
  environment influence on, 6
  heredity influence on, 6, 50–56
  heredity mechanisms, 42–50
  influences on, 6–12
  maturation influence on, 6
  psychosexual development, 19, 20*t*
  psychosocial development, 20–21, 20*t*
  race/ethnicity and, 8–10
  theoretical issues, 16–17
  theoretical perspectives, 17–18
developmentalists, 3
developmental research designs, 35–36, 35*f*
developmental systems, 53
dextromethorphan (DXM), 271
DHEA (dehydroepiandrosterone), 261–262
diabetes, **217**, 357
  in late adulthood, 411
  low-birth-weight as risk factor, 82
  prenatal development and, 65, 66
diaries, 28, 29*t*
diazinon, 66
diethylstilbestrol (DES), 62

differentiation, **92**
difficult children, **136**
dioxin, 66
diptheria-pertusis-tetanus (DPT) vaccine, 86
direct aggression, **205**
discipline, **200**–202
discrimination
  age, 368, 397, 432–433
  foreign adoption and, 247
  identity formation and, 290
  immigrant families and, 10
  intelligence and, 225
  pay gap and, 327
  peer relations and, 248
  sexual identity and, 293, 338, 385, 442
  stress and, 364
  well-being and, 380
disengagement theory, **429**
dishabituation, **111**
disorganized-disoriented attachment, **141**
disruptive conduct disorders, 254–255
distance learning, 324
divergent thinking, **237**
diversity
  end-of-life decisions and, 462–463
  immigration and, 10
divorce, 244–245, 346–348
  grandparenting after, 393
  in middle adulthood, 383–384
  remarriage after, 348
dizygotic twins, **41**
DNA, **42**, 42*f*
dominant inheritance, **44**, 45*f*
  incomplete dominance, 48
double-blind procedures, 34
doula, **76**
Down syndrome, 46, **49**, 50*f*
  prenatal screening, 68
DPT vaccine, 86
dramatic play, 170, **198**, 199
dropping out of high school, 283
drug abuse. *See* substance abuse
drug therapy, **256**
DST (dynamic systems theory), **101**
dual-language learning, **229**
dual representation hypothesis, **113**
Duchenne muscular dystrophy, 47*t*, 48
durable power of attorney, **460**
DWDA (Death with Dignity Act), 461
DXM (dextromethorphan), 271
dyadic interactions, 302
dynamic systems theory (DST), **101**
dynamic tests, **228**
dyslexia, **234**
dysmenorrhea, 319

early child care, 151–153, 153*t*
early childhood
  accidental injuries, 165–167
  aggression, 204–206
  air pollution exposure, 168

middle childhood
  aggression and, 250-254
  anxiety disorders, 255
  brain development, 212-213, 212f
  childhood depression, 255
  cognitive development, 218-237,
    218t
  common emotional problems,
    254-255
  concrete operations stage, 218-221
  developing self, 240-241
  disruptive conduct disorders,
    254-255
  education and, 230-237
  emotional growth, 240-241
  executive function, 221-222
  family and, 241-248
  growth patterns, 211, 211t
  health and safety, 214-217
  information-processing approach,
    221-223
  language and, 228-229
  language development, 121t
  literacy and, 229-230
  literacy in, 229-230
  medical conditions, 216-217
  memory, 222-223
  mental health and, 254-258
  motor development, 213-214, 213t
  neurological development, 221
  nutritional requirements, 211
  obesity in, 214-216
  peer group and, 248-254
  physical development, 211-217
  Piagetian approach, 218-221
  play and, 213-214
  prosocial behavior, 241
  psychometric approach, 223-228
  psychosocial development,
    240-258
  selective attention, 222
  sleep requirements, 211
  typical developments, 4t
midlife. See middle adulthood
midlife crisis, **375**-376
midlife review, **375,** 379
mirror neurons, **135**
miscarriage. See spontaneous abortion
mitochondrial theory of aging, 402
mitosis, 42-43, 56
mixed age classrooms, 208
MMR vaccine, 86
mnemonic device, **223**
modeling, 22
monozygotic twins, **41**-42
Montessori method, 183
MOOCs (massive, open, online
  courses), 324
moral development
  in adolescence, 277-280
  in infancy and toddlerhood,
    148-150
  levels and stages of, 278, 279t
moral reasoning
  in adolescence, 277-280
  culture and, 323
  gender and, 324

moratorium status, 331
Moro reflex, 94, 95t
mortality rates
  adolescence, 274-275, 274f
  under age 5, 83f, 165-167
  anorexia nervosa, 271
  in emerging and young
    adulthood, 309
  infants (See infant mortality rate)
  life expectancy and, 400
  life span and, 403
mortality revolution, 448
motherese, 129
mothers
  age at first birth, 344f
  effects of employment, 151,
    301-302
  relationships with adult children,
    443-444
  role in caregiving, 138
  teenagers, 297-298
  timing of puberty and, 264
motor cortex, 127
motor development
  cultural influences, 102
  dynamic systems theory, 101
  in early childhood, 161-162
  ecological theory of perception,
    100-101
  infants, 97-102, 98t
  in middle childhood, 213-214, 213t
  milestones for infants, 98, 98t
  perception and, 99-101
MRI (magnetic resonance imaging),
  212
MSCEIT (Mayer-Salovey-Caruso
  Emotional Intelligence Test),
  322
multi-facet dementia, 413
multifactorial transmission, **45**
multigenerational households. See
  extended family
multilingual households, 128-129
multiple births, 41-42
  IVF and, 320
musical intelligence, 226, 227t
mutation, **43**
mutual help, 389
mutual regulation, **144**
myelin. See white matter
myelination, **94**
myopia, **351**

naproxen, 62
narrative psychology, 376-378
National Institute of Child Health
  and Human Development
  (NICHD), 151, 152-153
National Longitudinal Study of
  Youth (NLSY), 151
Native Americans
  academic achievement and, 281
  age at first birth, 344
  alcohol use among, 315
  diabetes and, 217
  health status in emerging and
    young adulthood, 309

infant mortality among, 85, 85f
media use and, 233
miscarriages among, 60
SIDS and, 85
suicide and, 275, 458
teenage pregnancy and, 297
nativism, **126**
natural childbirth, **75**
natural experiments, 35
naturalistic observation, 29, 29t
naturalist intelligence, 226, 227t
naturally occurring retirement
  communities (NORCs), 435
natural selection, 26
nature versus nurture debate
  canalization, 53
  genotype-environment
    correlation, 54
  genotype-environment
    interaction, 54
  heredity and environment, 50-56
  intelligence and, 55
  language acquisition, 125-126
  nonshared environmental effects,
    54-55
  obesity and, 55
  personality traits, 56
  physical and psychological traits,
    55-56
  reaction range, 53
  temperament, 56
near-death experiences (NDEs),
  450-451
negative nomination, 249
negativism, 147, 147t
neglect
  in infancy and toddlerhood,
    154-156
  long-term effects, 156
  mistreatment of elderly, 438
  sexual risk-taking in adolescence
    and, 294
neglectful parenting, 203
neonatal jaundice, **77**
neonatal period, **77**-79
neonate, **77**
neo-Piagetian approaches, 321
neurodevelopmental disorders.
  See also autism spectrum
  disorders
  vaccines and, 86
neurofibrillary tangles, **414**
neurological development
  antisocial behavior and, 305
  in middle childhood, 221
neurons, **92**
neuroticism
  in emerging and young adulthood,
    334-335, 335f
  in late adulthood, 425
  in middle adulthood, 373
neurotransmitters, 92
newborn babies
  behavioral assessment, 78
  body systems, 77
  low birth weight, 79-82
  medical assessment, 78

perception of sounds and
  structure, 122
postmaturity and, 82-83
sensory capacities, 96-97
size and appearance, 77
sleep patterns, 78-79
states of arousal, 78-79, 79t
stillborns, 83
New York Longitudinal Study,
  135-136
NICHD (National Institute of Child
  Health and Human
  Development), 151, 152-153
niche-picking, **54**
nicotine, 63, 66
nightmares, 160-161
night terrors, 160
NLSY (National Longitudinal Study
  of Youth), 151
noble savage theory of
  development, 16
nocturnal emission, 264
non-college-bound students, 285
nonnormative influences, **11**
nonorganic failure to thrive, **154**
nonshared environmental effects,
  54-55
nonsiblings, toddler contact
  with, 151
nonsocial play, 199t
nonsteroidal anti-inflammatory drugs
  (NSAIDs), 62
NORCs (naturally occurring
  retirement communities), 435
normative age-graded events, 11, 334
normative history-graded events, 11
normative influences, **11**
normative life events, **334**
normative-stage models
  in emerging and young adulthood,
    332-334, 333t
  in late adulthood, 424
  in middle adulthood, 373-374
novelty preference, 114
nuclear family, **7**
number line estimation, 221
number patterns, 171
numbers
  early childhood understanding of,
    171-172
  middle childhood understanding
    of, 220-221
  toddler understanding of, 118
number sense, 171
number transformations, 171
numerosity estimation, 221
nursing homes, 436, 438
nutrition
  in adolescence, 267-271
  adult lifestyle habits, 313
  Alzheimer's disease and, 415
  breast versus bottle, 88-89
  caloric reduction and longevity,
    405
  in infancy, 88-91
  influence on health and fitness,
    310

in late adulthood, 412–413
in middle childhood, 211
prenatal development and, 61
nutritional supplements
food insecurity and, 164
infants and toddlers, 90

obesity, **55**
in adolescence, 267–269
adverse health effects, 215–216
causes, 214–215
epidemic, 310–311, 311*f*
food insecurity and, 164
infants, 89–91
in middle childhood, 214–216
prenatal development and, 61
prevention in early childhood, 163
prevention in middle childhood, 216
treatment, 216
object permanence, **111**–112,
117–118, 118*f*
objects in space, understanding of,
170, 218
observational learning, **22**
obsessive-compulsive disorder
(OCD), **255**
occipital lobe, 91, 92*f*
OCD (obsessive-compulsive
disorder), **255**
ODD (oppositional defiant
disorder), **254**
Oedipus complex, 19
oldest old, 399, 404
old old, 399
OLSAT8 (Otis-Lennon School
Ability Test), **224**
one-parent families, 245–246, 301.
See also single-mother families
only child, 207
open adoption, 247
open-ended interviews, 29
operant conditioning, **21–22, 105**
operational definition, **30**
opiates, 62
opioid abuse, 272
oppositional defiant disorder
(ODD), **254**
optimal aging, 404, 428–431
oral stage, 19, 20*t*
ordinality, 171
organismic model, **16**–17
organization, **23, 223**
organized athletics, 214
organogenesis, 59
osteoporosis, **360**–361
Otis-Lennon School Ability Test
(OLSAT8), **224**
overextended word meanings, 125
overt aggression, **205**
ovulation, 41

pain, 96
pain cry, 132
palliative care, **449**–450
parasympathetic system, 134
parental monitoring and self-
disclosure, 300–301

parental self-reports, 28
parental *versus* adolescent authority,
300, 300*t*
parentese, 129
parents/parenting
abusive and neglectful, 155
academic achievement and,
231, 282
adolescents, relationships with,
299–302
adult children and, 387–388
aggression and, 205
antisocial behavior and, 305–306
authoritarian parenting, 202–203
authoritative parenting, 202–203
caregiver to aging parents,
389–391
cultural differences in parenting
styles, 203–204
by default, 393–394
developmental experience of,
344–345
discipline and, 200–202
early childhood and, 200–206
early media use and, 116
early social experiences and,
137–138
emerging adults, relationships
with, 331–332
emerging and young adults as,
343–346
fearfulness in early childhood, 206
influence on gender differences,
139
language acquisition and, 127–129
marital satisfaction and, 345
in middle childhood, 241–242
neglectful parenting, 203
permissive parenting, 202
poverty and, 243
prolonged parenting, 388
sandwich generation and, 392
sexual risk-taking in adolescence
and, 294
smoking, early childhood exposure
to, 168
social interaction model and, 178
stepparenthood, 348
styles of, 202–204, 203*t*, 300
substance use in adolescence, 273
terrible twos and, 147, 148
uninvolved parenting, 203
working parents, 151–153,
242–243
parietal lobe, 92, 92*f*, 127
Parkinson's disease, **413**
participant observation, **32**
Partners for Learning, 108
parturition, **73**
passion, 337
passive correlations, 54
passive euthanasia, **460**
peers
academic achievement and,
232, 282
adolescents and, 302
aggression, 250–254

antisocial behavior and, 305–306
bullying and, 250–254
effects of peer relations, 248–249
friendship, 249–250, 250*t*
gender-typing and, 196
middle childhood and, 248–254
popularity, 249
substance use in adolescence
and, 273
pelvic inflammatory disease
(PID), 296
perception
depth perception, 100
ecological theory of, 100–101
haptic perception, 100
motor development and, 99–101
perceptual awareness, 119
perceptual discrimination, 146
performance measures, 29–30, 29*t*
perimenopause, **354**
periodontal disease, 413
permissive parenting, **202,** 282
personal agency, 146
personality, 132. *See also* normative-
stage models
Alzheimer's disease and, 414
approaches to development,
332–336, 333*t*
ego-resilient, 336
heredity and environmental influences on, 56
in late adulthood, 424–425
overcontrolled, 336
predictor of emotionality, health,
and well-being, 425
psychological well-being and,
378–379
resilience and, 257–258
stability and change in late adulthood, 424–425
timing-of-events models, 333*t*, 334,
374–375
trait models, 333*t*, 334–336,
372–373
typological models, 333*t*, 336
undercontrolled, 336
pesticide exposure, 168
PET (positron emission
tomography), 30, 415
phallic stage, 19, 20*t*
phased retirement, 368
phenotype, **45**
phenylketonuria (PKU), 47*t*, 52, 78
phonemes, 122–123
phonetic approach, **230**
physical abuse, **154,** 438
physical activity
in adolescence, 266–267
adult lifestyle habits, 313, 412
influence on health, 312
in late adulthood, 408–409, 412
in middle adulthood, 379
in middle childhood, 216
during pregnancy, 61–62
physical development, **3**
adolescence, 261–275
early childhood, 159–168

emerging and young adulthood,
309–320
infants, 86–97
in late adulthood, 400–416
in middle adulthood, 351–364
middle childhood, 211–217
physical fitness
behavioral influences on, 310–315,
358
in emerging and young adulthood,
309–317
in middle adulthood, 352
in middle childhood, 214–217
physician-assisted suicide, **460**–461,
463
Piagetian approach, 20*t*, 22–24, **105**
adolescence and, 275–276
early childhood development and,
169–176
evaluation of theory, 276
formal operations stage, 275–276
imitation, 110–111
infant and toddler development
and, 108–113, 111*t*
information processing and,
115–118
middle childhood development
and, 218–221
object concept, 111–112
preoperational stage, 169–176
research evaluation, 113
sensorimotor stage substages,
109–110, 109*t*
sensory perception and processing, 114–115
symbolic development, 112–113
theory of mind, 173–176
pictorial competence, 112
pictorial stage, 162
PID (pelvic inflammatory
disease), 296
pincer grasp, 98, 99
PKU. *See* phenylketonuria
placebo, 34
placenta, 58–59
plasticity, **11**–12, 14, **94**–96
play
adaptive value of, 197
cognitive levels of, 198
constructive play, 198
culture and, 200
dramatic play, 198, 199
in early childhood, 197–200
fantasy play, 198
formal games with rules, 198
functional play, 198
gender and, 199–200
imaginative play, 198
locomotor play, 198
in middle childhood, 213–214
obesity and, 214–215
pretend play, 198
reticent play, 199
rough-and-tumble play, 213–214
social dimension of,
198–199, 199*t*
social play, 198–199, 199*t*

reality principle, 19
real self, **188**
rebellion, adolescent, 298–299
recall, **177**
recentering, **331**
receptive cooperation, **150**
recess, 213
recessive inheritance, **44**, 45*f*
reciprocal determinism, **22**
recognition, **177**
redemption, 378
reflective thinking, **321**
reflex behavior, **94**, 95*f*
reflexes, 94, 109
Reggio Emilia approach, 183–184
regional anesthesia, 76
rehearsal, **223**, 419
reinforcement, **22**, 200
relational aggression, **205**, 251
relationships. *See also* friendship; gay
    relationships; marriage
    in adolescence, 299–305
    with aging parents, 389–391
    consensual, 382–386
    with emerging adults, 331–332
    in emerging and young adulthood,
        331–337
    importance of, 438–439
    in late adulthood, 437–445
    with maturing children, 386–389
    in middle adulthood, 380–394
    with other children, 206–208
relativistic thinking, 321
religion, 428, 462
remarriage
    grandparenting after, 393
    in late adulthood, 441
    post-divorce, 348
REM sleep, 79
reorganization, 419
repetitive vocabulary, 124
representational ability, **110**
representational mappings, **188**
representational systems, 240
reproductive health. *See also* sexually
    transmitted infections (STIs)
    assisted reproductive technology,
        320
    in emerging and young adulthood,
        317–320
    in late adulthood, 410
    male sexual functioning, 354–356
    menopause, 353–354
    in middle adulthood, 353–357,
        354*t*
research designs
    attachment, study of, 142
    basic, 31–35, 31*t*
    case studies, 31–32, 31*t*
    correlational studies, 31*t*, 32
    cross-sectional studies, 35, 36*t*
    developmental, 35–36, 35*f*
    ethnographic studies, 31*t*, 32
    experiments, 31*t*, 32–35
    longitudinal studies, 35–36, 36*t*
    prenatal alcohol research, 38
    sequential studies, 36–37, 36*t*, 37*f*

research ethics, 37, 38
research methods. *See also* cross-
    cultural research
    data collection, 28–30
    groups and variables, 32–34
    quantitative and qualitative,
        27–28, 30–31
    sampling, 28
reserve capacity, **406**
resilience
    in children, 257–258
    in grieving, 452
resilient children, **257**
resistant attachment, **141**
resource allocation
    in late adulthood, 430–431
    life-span developmental approach
        and, 14
respiration, 77
respiratory distress syndrome, 82
respite care, 391
reticent play, 199
retirement
    early, 368
    in late adulthood, 431–434
retrieval, **176**, 421
reversibility, 220
revolving door syndrome, **388**
right to die, 457–463
risk factors, **8**
risk-taking, sexual behavior
    in adolescence, 294
    in emerging and young adulthood,
        318
risky drinking, **315**
RNA polymerase, 42
romantic relationships
    in adolescence, 303
    in emerging and young adulthood,
        337
rooting reflex, 94, 95*t*
rough-and-tumble play, 213–214
rubella, 64

safety
    in early childhood, 163–168
    in middle childhood, 214–217
same-sex marriage, 338–339, 385
sample, **28**
sampling, 28
sandwich generation, **390**–392
scaffolding, **24**, **179**–180
scale, understanding of, 112–113
scale error, 112
schemes, **23**, **109**
schizophrenia
    malnutrition and, 61
    maternal malnutrition and, 61
    paternal age and, 66
school phobia, **255**
schools. *See also* preschool
    education
    age segregation *versus* mixed ages,
        208
    children with disabilities and, 235
    corporal punishment in, 201–202
    first grade, 230–231

homeschooling, 232–233
    student achievement and, 283
scientific method, **27**–28
scribble stage, 162
script, **177**, 378
Seattle Longitudinal Study of Adult
    Intelligence
    cognitive abilities in late age, 417
    cognitive abilities in middle age,
        364–365, 365*f*, 365*t*
secondary aging, **398**
secondary appraisal, 426
secondary sex characteristics, **263**
second-language learning, 229
secular trend, **264**
secure attachment, **140**
selective attention, 222
selective optimization with compen-
    sation (SOC), 430–**431**
self, developing, 188–190, 240–241
    in middle adulthood, 375–380
self-awareness, **134**, 146
self-coherence, 146
self-concept, **146**, **188**, 240
self-conscious emotion, **134**
self-definition, **188**
self disclosure and parental monitor-
    ing, 300–301
self-efficacy, **22**
    academic achievement and, 231,
        281
self-esteem, **188**–189, 240, 380
self-evaluative emotions, **134**
self-locomotion, 99
self-neglect abuse, 438
self-regulation, **149**, 241
self-reports, 28–29, 29*t*
self-starvation, 270
semantic memory, **419**
senescence, **401**
sense of self, 146
sensitive periods, **11**
sensorimotor stage, 20*t*, **108**
    evaluation of, 113
    imitation, 110–111
    object concept, 111–112
    substages, 109–110, 109*t*, 110*f*
    symbolic development, 112–113
sensory capacities
    changes in middle adulthood,
        351–352
    infants, 96–97
    information-processing approach,
        114–115
    Piagetian approach, 114–115
sensory memory, **176**, **419**
separation anxiety, **142**–143
separation anxiety disorder, **255**
sequential studies, 36–37, 36*t*, 37*f*
seriation, 218*t*, **219**
SES. *See* socioeconomic status
Sesame Street, 182
severe autistic disorder, 93
sex chromosomes, **43**
    abnormalities related to, 49, 49*t*
sex determination, 43–44, 44*f*
sex-linked inheritance, 46, **48**, 48*f*

sexual abuse, **154**, 156, 438
sexual and reproductive issues
    in emerging and young adulthood,
        317–320
    in late adulthood, 410
    in middle adulthood, 353–357
sexual behavior
    in adolescence, 293–295, 293*f*
    contraceptives, use of, 294–295
    in emerging and young adulthood,
        318
    information sources, 295
    marriage and, 343
    risk-taking, 294
sexual education, 295
sexual identity
    in adolescence, 290
    in emerging and young adulthood,
        318
sexuality in adolescence, 290–298
sexually transmitted infections
    (STIs), 295–296
    in emerging and young adulthood,
        318
    risk-taking in adolescence, 294
sexual orientation, **291**–293, 318
sexual selection, theory of, **193**
shaken baby syndrome, **154**
shape stage, 162
short-term memory, 419
shyness, 136–137
siblings
    adolescents and, 302
    death of parent in adulthood, 456
    early childhood relationships with,
        206–208
    late adulthood relationships with,
        444–445
    middle adulthood relationships
        with, 391
    middle childhood relationships
        with, 247–248
    nonshared environmental effects
        and, 54–55
    toddler contact with, 150–151
sickle-cell anemia, 47*t*
SIDS, **85**
sight, 97, 351, 407–408
sign language, 125
simile, 228
single life, 338, 441–442
single-mother families
    child care and, 153
    Head Start and, 184
    homelessness and, 168
    involvement in parenthood, 344
    negative outcomes and, 246
    poverty and, 243
    views on gender roles, 139
    work and, 242–243, 301
single representations, **188**
single strain, 441
situational compliance, **149**
sleep
    adolescence and, 267
    early childhood patterns and
        problems, 159–161, 160*f*

TTCT (Torrance Tests of Creative Thinking), 237
turning points, **375,** 375*f*
two-way learning, **229**
typological approach, 333*t,* **336**

ultrasound, **60,** 67*t*
umbilical cord, 58
umbilical cord sampling, 67*t*
underextended word meanings, 125
undernutrition, 164–165. *See also* malnutrition
uninvolved parenting, 203

vaccinations
    autism spectrum disorder, 93
    childhood disease prevention, 86
    HPV, 296
    preconception care, 69
    Rubella, 64
vaginal birth after cesarean (VBAC), 75
vaginal delivery, 74–75
variable-rate theories, **402**–403
variables, 32–34
vehicle accidents, adolescent mortality, 274
vernix caseosa, 77
victims
    bullying, 252–253
    intimate partner violence, 347
violation of expectations, **117**–119
violence
    intimate partner, 347
    media and, 251–252
    in teen dating, 303–305
virtue, 21
visible imitation, **110**
vision. *See* sight
visual cliff, **100**
visual guidance, **100**
visually based retrieval, **230**
visual perception and processing, 114–115
visual preference, **114**
visual recognition memory, **114**
visual reports, 28, 29*t*
vital capacity, **353**
vitamin supplements

food insecurity and, 164
infants and toddlers, 90
vocabulary development
    in adolescence, 277
    in early childhood, 180
    in middle childhood, 228
    in toddlerhood, 127–129
voluntary childlessness, 388–389
volunteering
    in adolescence, 280
    in late adulthood, 429–430, 434
    in middle childhood, 241
    in retirement, 368

WAIS-R (Wechsler Adult Intelligence Scale), 417, 417*f*
walking, 99
walking reflex, 95*t,* 101
wear-and-tear theory, 402
Wechsler Adult Intelligence Scale (WAIS-R), **417,** 417*f*
Wechsler Intelligence Scale for Children (WISC-IV), **223**
Wechsler Preschool and Primary Scale of Intelligence, Revised (WPPSI-IV), **178**
wedding traditions, 342
weight. *See also* obesity
    in adolescence, 267–271
    in early childhood, 159, 159*t*
    low-birth-weight babies, 79–82
    in middle adulthood, 358
    in middle childhood, 211, 211*t*
    puberty and, 262, 263
weight management programs, 216
well-being
    in late adulthood, 426–431
    marital status and, 384–385
    in middle adulthood, 378–380
    personality as predictor of, 425
    relationships and, 381–382
    religion or spirituality and, 428
    voluntary childlessness and, 388–389
wet dream, 264
white Americans
    academic achievement and, 281
    adolescent mortality and, 274
    alcohol use among, 315

body image and, 269
chronic conditions and, 411
cohabitation attitudes of, 340
college graduation and, 325
dropping out of high school, 283
health status in emerging and young adulthood, 309
infant mortality among, 85, 85*f*
life expectancy and, 401, 401*t*
media use and, 233
menopause attitudes of, 355
obesity and, 310
obesity in, 214
osteoporosis in, 360
puberty in, 263
sexual behavior in adolescence, 293
smoking among, 314
spanking among, 201
suicide and, 458
teenage pregnancy and, 297
teen dating violence and, 304
white matter
    in adolescence, 265–266, 265*f*
    Alzheimer's disease and myelin breakdown, 414–415
    binge drinking and, 272
    brain development and, 212
    gender development and, 191
    in late adulthood, 407
    myelin and, 94
whole-language approach, **230**
widowhood, 440–441, 455
WISC-IV (Wechsler Intelligence Scale for Children), **223**
wisdom, 421, 424
witch's milk, 77
withdrawal of love, **202**
women. *See also* single-mother families
    generativity and, 376
    health in middle age, 359–362
    identity development in middle adulthood, 376
    life expectancy, 400
    midlife career change and, 377
    osteoporosis in, 360
    pay gap, 327
    poverty in late adulthood, 434

relationships in middle adulthood and, 381–382
word meanings, 125
work
    in adolescence, 285
    adult education and, 369
    cognitive growth during, 327, 368–369
    college attendance and, 327
    dual-income families and, 345–346
    early retirement *versus,* 368
    in emerging and young adulthood, 326–328
    in late adulthood, 431–434
    in middle age, 368–369
    midlife career change, 377
    mothers working, 151–153, 242–243, 301–302
    parents impacted by, 151–153, 242–243
    transition to, 327–328
work-family balance, 345–346
working memory
    in adolescence, 276
    in early childhood, **176**
    in infancy and toddlerhood, **120**
    in late adulthood, **419**
    in middle childhood, 222
working parents, children of, 151–153, 242–243
World Health Organization, 68
WPPSI-IV (Wechsler Preschool and Primary Scale of Intelligence, Revised), **178**
writing in middle childhood, 229–230

X chromosomes, 43–44

Y chromosomes, 43
young adulthood. *See* emerging and young adulthood
young old, 398–399

zone of proximal development (ZPD), **24, 179**
    intelligence testing and, 228
zygote, **41,** 43, 43*f*